CRIMINAL JUSTICE ADMINISTRATION

Materials and Cases

CONTEMPORARY LEGAL EDUCATION SERIES

CONTEMPORARY LEGAL EDUCATION SERIES

ADVISORY COMMITTEE

Criminal Justice Administration

MATERIALS AND CASES

Frank J. Remington

Professor of Law
University of Wisconsin

Donald J. Newman

Professor of Criminal Justice
State University of New York
at Albany

Edward L. Kimball

Professor of Law
University of Wisconsin

Marygold Melli

Professor of Law
University of Wisconsin

and

Herman Goldstein

Professor of Law
University of Wisconsin

THE BOBBS-MERRILL COMPANY, INC.
A SUBSIDIARY OF HOWARD W. SAMS & CO., INC.
PUBLISHERS • INDIANAPOLIS • KANSAS CITY • NEW YORK

Library of Congress Catalog Card Number: 68-58836
Printed in the United States of America

Preface

This book affords an opportunity to study the criminal and juvenile justice systems as methods of preventing and controlling social disorder. Primary emphasis is given to the criminal justice system.

The preparation of the book reflects the authors' belief that the prevention and control of social disorder is one of the most difficult and important problems facing this nation today and, therefore, in need of greater attention at the college and university level than it has received in the past. This includes greater attention to the criminal and juvenile justice systems because, whatever their limitations, they are the systems now relied upon to deal with the most serious kinds of crime and disorder faced by this society. The continuation of an orderly and democratic society may depend upon our ability to improve our ways of administering justice sufficiently to retain or recapture the respect and support of the vast majority of citizens: the poor as well as the rich; the black as well as the white; the young as well as the old; and, to the extent possible, the guilty as well as the not guilty.

The lack of attention to the study of criminal and juvenile justice administration has been apparent for some time. The lawyer has limited his attention too much to the formal rules and to the trial process, the social worker too much to casework techniques. The evidence of neglect is apparent. Police have been largely ignored, excluded from the attention of higher education for the most part, and the problems with which they must deal have been either overlooked or dealt with in a superficial manner. Corrections has had more adequate and respectful attention, but it too has often been looked at apart from the system in which it is one, but only one, important stage. The overall consequence is that some aspects of the criminal and juvenile justice systems may have been understood and improved but other aspects have been ignored and have remained inadequate. The important goal, the achievement of effective and fair overall systems of criminal and juvenile justice administration, has clearly not been achieved.

This book was designed particularly to be used in a second law school course on the administration of criminal justice, following a basic course on criminal law and procedure which has already acquainted the student with the broad outlines of procedure and the constitutional doctrines and rulings applicable. We hope, however, that there is here sufficient summary statement of these elementary matters to permit use of this book even by students who have not previously been exposed to criminal procedure or to constitutional restrictions upon administering criminal law. It has in fact been used in draft form by students in a school of social work and a school of criminal justice as well as by law students.

In this book, emphasis is on the problems for the criminal justice system in separating efficiently and fairly the guilty and the innocent. Some concern for the constitutional issues and technical procedural problems is reflected in the materials, but the prime interest in doing so is in the impact of constitutional standards and procedural rules on the system's operations.

Effort is made to avoid emphasis on appellate litigation. When they are used, appellate cases illustrate the system's operations, the courts' reactions to the system, and the methods of trying to effect change in the system rather than as a vehicle for communicating THE law. Illustrative fact situations, largely drawn from the field reports of the American Bar Foundation Survey of the Administration of Criminal Justice in the United States, are often used in preference to appellate cases. These help avoid to some degree the distortion which results from looking at the system only through those issues which come to the attention of the appellate court.

The form of these materials has been much influenced by the American Bar Foundation Survey of the Administration of Criminal Justice in the United States, which demonstrated the great advantage of studying the criminal justice system as a total system. Two of the authors were involved in the field research and four were involved in the analysis and writing stages of the project. Though all the authors share an interest in the overall systems for administering criminal and juvenile justice, by training and experience they have had various special concerns. Herman Goldstein is experienced in public administration, particularly in the work of police. Marygold Melli has been most concerned with the problems of the family, including the delinquent child. Donald Newman has devoted much of his academic career to a study of correctional administration. Edward Kimball and Frank Remington have been most concerned with the handling of the adult offender. Though the book is a joint product, major credit goes to Edward Kimball who worked hardest and most productively.

None of the authors would have even thought of publishing these materials were it not for the fact that we knew we could rely upon the careful and efficient help of Mrs. Lucille Hamre. We were also aided in the editing and publication by the excellent cooperation of Mr. Max Harley.

Our appreciation to the authors and publishers of the books, articles, newspapers, and magazines which we used in these materials and especially to the American Bar Foundation and Association and the American Law Institute for permission to use excerpts from their publications.

We are appreciative also of the continuing cooperation of the Wisconsin Division of Corrections and its Director, Mr. Sanger Powers, and to the Chicago Police Department and its Superintendents, O. W. Wilson and James B. Conlisk.

Our work would not have been possible without the financial support of the Ford Foundation, the Russell Sage Foundation, and the National Council on Legal Clinics (now Council on Legal Education for Professional Responsibility).

Footnotes in quoted material are generally omitted. When they are retained, the original numbers are also retained. Editorial footnotes are designated by letter rather than by number.

The court opinions used have in many cases been extensively edited to conserve space and reading time. Parallel citations for Supreme Court decisions have been deleted, and citations of authority in the opinions are generally omitted. We have not felt it necessary to indicate omissions by ellipses in every case, though we have done so where we feared confusion might otherwise result.

The Appendices are meant to supplement the main body of the material and ought to be read early in the course. The studies of the professional burglar and the streetwalking prostitute afford an opportunity to look at criminal justice administration as it deals with two difficult behavioral problems. The case of John Arthur Wilson makes it possible to acquire some familiarity with a correctional file and affords opportunity to relate some important sentencing and correctional issues to an individual offender.

Madison, Wisconsin
December 1968

Summary Table of Contents

Table of Contents

Table of Cases

Principal cases are those with page references in italics.

PART I

INTRODUCTION

Chapter 1

PERSPECTIVES OF CRIMINAL JUSTICE ADMINISTRATION

> Crime is a sore on the face of America. It is a menace on our streets. It is a drain on our cities. It is a corrupter of our youth. It is a cause of untold suffering and loss. But just saying this does not solve the problem that we have before us. We must bring it under control, and then we must root out the cause.
>
> So let the Nation know that today we have taken a pledge not only to reduce crime but to banish it.
>
> President Lyndon B. Johnson
> *Remarks to Members of the President's Commission on Law Enforcement and Administration of Justice.* September 8, 1965

> We want not only "law and order" but also justice.
>
> Resident of an inner city

All cultures experience crime and take steps to control it or, more ambitiously, to banish it. The way a society organizes to confront the crime problem, and the procedures and techniques employed in crime control not only reflect its political ideology but often come to be its hallmark. Differences between a police state and a democracy are perhaps most apparent in the way crimes are defined and in the way justice is administered. It is therefore no accident of history that the administration of criminal justice evokes intense and continual concern in the United States. Crime control is not peripheral to democracy; it is a vital part of it, putting to test basic values and challenging the ingenuity of a free people.[a]

---

[a] Mr. Chief Justice Warren of the United States Supreme Court wrote:

> When society acts to deprive one of its members of his life, liberty or property, it takes its most awesome steps. No general respect for, nor adherence to, the law as a whole can well be expected without judicial recognition of the paramount need for prompt, eminently fair and sober criminal law procedures. The methods we employ in the

It is no secret that the United States has one of the most complex crime problems of any modern society.[b] Not only is the crime rate generally high, but the types and variations of criminal conduct are perhaps unique in the world. Whether this is the inevitable result of an affluent society with a heterogeneous and mobile population, which tolerates and encourages differences and which has experienced rapid growth and change, or whether steps can be taken to discover and destroy the roots of crime without destroying the roots of democracy, remains a basic challenge to our society. The challenge is being met in two ways: (1) the implementation of programs intended to attack the causes of crime, and (2) efforts to control existing crime by apprehending and processing violators. These two approaches are related and both are necessary. They must be tested not solely by effectiveness but by the standards of propriety set up by the democratic ideology as well.

War on the Causes of Crime

There is today a major effort under way to mobilize resources to attack the root causes of crime and juvenile delinquency on a number of different levels. The domestic "wars" against poverty, ignorance, and racial discrimination are designed to ameliorate the need and discontent that underlie many of our traditional crime patterns. There is a concerted attack on problems thought to be closely related to the production of delinquency. Programs such as the Job Corps, Vista, Operation Head Start, Upward Bound, Mobilization for Youth, and the demonstration projects supported by the President's Committee on Youth Crime and by various private foundations are intended to provide incentive and opportunities for underprivileged youth, to channel their energies and direct their aspirations toward law-abiding adulthood.

Urban renewal—the clearing of vast slum areas in our major cities—is intended both to improve the health and welfare of the metropolitan poor and to overcome the depressing effects of ugliness and squalor that characterize the inner core of many

---

> enforcement of our criminal law have aptly been called the measures by which the quality of our civilization may be judged.

Coppedge v. United States, 369 U.S. 438, 449 (1962).

His reference was to Schaefer, *Federalism and State Criminal Procedure*, 70 HARV. L. REV. 1, 26 (1956).

[b] *See* the report by THE PRESIDENT'S COMMISSION ON LAW ENFORCEMENT AND ADMINISTRATION OF JUSTICE, THE CHALLENGE OF CRIME IN A FREE SOCIETY (1967) and the accompanying Task Force Reports, particularly the one entitled CRIME AND ITS IMPACT—AN ASSESSMENT (1967).

of our cities. Economically depressed rural areas are being revitalized by establishing or relocating industry and government projects, and rural people are being retrained to better compete in the modern labor market. A number of states and local communities are in the process of building more comprehensive mental health programs, designed both to treat behavioral disorders and to prevent them. Markedly increased funds from government, private foundations, and voluntary associations are currently being used to support research into the cause and cure of crime, delinquency, and related problems such as narcotics addiction, alcoholism, mental disorder, and mental retardation. The "helping" professions—including law, medicine, social work, psychology, education—are rapidly expanding their manpower and at the same time experimenting with new methods of serving more people better. Medicare, Judicare, Educare, and similar programs involve more than slogan-titles; they illustrate the expansion of the responsibility of professions to attack disease, ignorance, and inequality on the broadest possible plane.

All the programs which support this movement and the concerns from which they grow, form a concerted, fundamental attack on crime, delinquency, and related social problems. Sometimes these programs go directly, and at other times indirectly, to the roots of instability, dissatisfaction, inequality, and hostility, which in turn are linked with patterns of criminal and delinquent conduct among our people. The Great Society, in its broadest conception, implies a marked diminution of crime, and the intent of all the programs is to remove the factors giving rise to crime, whether they be economic imbalance, racial inequality, lack of education, or individual pathology.

President Johnson, in a special message to the Congress outlining his proposals for crime control and prevention, said:

> The problem runs deep and will not yield to quick and easy answers. We must identify and eliminate the causes of criminal activity whether they lie in the environment around us or deep in the nature of individual men. That is a major purpose of all we are doing in combatting poverty and improving education, health, welfare, housing and recreation. . . . We must, in short, understand that the reasons for the growth of crime are many and complicated. We must accept hard facts at every turn. But like the related problems of poverty and of education, we must face them squarely if we are to succeed. *And we must succeed.*[c]

[c] Special Message to Congress on Law Enforcement and Administration of Justice, March 8, 1965.

Eradication of the causes of crime is an enviable but distant goal. The programs advanced for achieving this are new, tentative, and in many instances, controversial. The fundamental premise that crime and delinquency arise from conditions and conditioning in the social order and that the most effective attack on crime involves the exposure and amelioration of these conditions is less controversial and more widely accepted as the proper framework for a long-lasting solution to our crime problem. All this is necessarily slow; crime and delinquency, however, are immediate and pressing. The urgency of immediate action is reflected in widespread public demand for greater safety and security.

It may be that programs directed to discovery of crime and the processing and conviction of offenders are less causatively oriented than those directed toward social conditions. But they are no less important and no less challenging, and no less controversial in concept and implementation. The means for dealing with crime which has already occurred, melded together into a complex system of criminal justice administration, is the major focus of this book.

The Organization and Purpose of Crime Control

The activities of police, prosecutors, courts, and correctional agencies and the various programs—sometimes repressive and punitive, other times therapeutic and rehabilitative—are commonly accepted as necessary to deal with the immediate problem of criminals and delinquents. These agencies are united in an intricate organizational whole, despite significant areas of federal, state, and local autonomy, and differences in perspective and purpose. This pervasive organization we refer to, for want of a more descriptive term, as the criminal justice system.[d]

---

[d] A number of terms are used by sociologists and political scientists to describe what is here called a "system." The most common, and currently the most in vogue, is "organization." This in turn is commonly modified with the terms "formal" or "complex" (*see, e.g.,* P. Blau & W. Scott, Formal Organizations (1962); A. Etzioni, Complex Organizations (1964); J. March & H. Simon, Organizations (1965)) to emphasize both the large-scale nature of the enterprises under study and the degree of structure and complexity of line-and-staff relationships which outline the organization. An older term is "bureaucracy," made theoretically and operationally important by the pioneering efforts of Max Weber (*see* T. Parsons, Max Weber: Theory of Social and Economic Organization (1947)) and still used occasionally as "bureaucratic organization" or "bureaucratic structure," to describe what sociologists call the "ideal type" of formal organization (*see, e.g.,* R. Merton, Social Theory and Social Structure (rev. ed. 1957)).

Some writers refer to "administrative decision-making" or "administrative organization" to mean much the same as these other terms (*see* H. Simon, Administrative Behavior (1957)). Finally, a term that has more limited meaning but is relevant, in part at least, to the criminal justice system is "total institutions" which refers to bureaucratic structures designed not for the common interaction of all participants but for the management and control of one stratum of participants, criminals for example, by another —those in charge of the organization who are "integrated with the outside world" such as police, judges, and wardens (*see* E. Goffman, Asylums (1961)).

None of these concepts seems precisely suitable for the analysis of crime control. It would be possible, of course, to talk about "criminal justice organization" but somehow this term implies a more closely-knit structure than is actually the case. Traditional studies of complex organizations have concentrated on industrial management, on the structure and functions of trade unions, on hospitals, on the army, and even on associational patterns in communities. The difficulty is that while all these analyses present very complicated conceptual and methodological problems, the basic structure of the organization studied is more often than not unitary, made up of many parts, but with a single, measurable perimeter. The criminal justice system, however, can at best be described as a loose federation of agencies and persons sharing in common some obligation to crime control, but in many cases distant from and independent of each other. The police officer and the probation and parole agent both have integral roles within the criminal justice system but each has an independent organizational affiliation and each a distinct professional identity and occupational destiny. In short, while they are agents of criminal justice, they are not interchangeable or even, in a line-and-staff sense, comparable. The term "organization" to cloak them both would seem to oversimplify their relationship.

"Bureaucracy" could also be used, for the nature of much decision-making in criminal justice flows from bureaucratic structures. But the term is cumbersome and has unfortunate political connotations which militate against its adoption. If the narrow use of "bureaucracy" evokes images of political structures, the broader use in the Weberian sense expands it to describe entire social institutions such as the state or a religion. In still other ways, "bureaucracy" is used in a more limited fashion to discuss the internal workings of complex agencies with little focus on the interplay of legislature and courts in operations.

"Administrative decision-making," while certainly appropriately descriptive of much activity in the criminal justice system, tends conceptually to give great weight to internal agency processes which, in a multiple agency system, is confusing. But even more importantly, it tends to play down, but not ignore, the significant role of courts in giving direction to agency policies and in intervening in agency disputes. "Court decision-making" would be equally inappropriate in describing criminal justice for here, more clearly than in most complex organizations, the courts and agencies share, not always amicably, decision-making duties. The courts are more than appeal bodies when agency policies and practices are in dispute. The trial court, at any rate, is an integral part of the day-by-day flow of the system. In this sense, the trial court acts very much as another agency, finding facts and screening those suspects who flow from the police toward post-conviction determinations. Some term is needed therefore to cross both administrative decision-making and court activities. "System," as used here, is designed to do just this.

To the sociologist of Parsonian bent the term "system" no doubt implies a set of conditions and an analytical approach of somewhat different theoretical import than intended here. *See* T. Parsons, The Social System (1951). The ambitious efforts of sociological theorists to relate the perceptive-cognitive-active "system" of the individual actor to the "system" of societal ordering, to analyze the interrelationship of "act" and "field," results

This system is elusive of definition or even of adequate description. It is made up of a loose federation of offices and agencies—police; prosecutors; prisons; probation agents; parole boards; trial and appellate courts; satellite services, such as welfare agencies; and consultative professions like psychiatry and psychology. Officials with various professional identities are part of the system: professional policemen on state, local, and federal levels; elected sheriffs; lawyers with identifiable roles in the agencies of the system as judges and prosecutors, and outside the agencies but integral to the system as defense counsel; and social workers, psychologists, prison guards, and parole authorities.

The relationship of these agencies is amorphous, partly because these segments of the system are structurally independent.

in a fortuitous use of the term, but the "system" of criminal justice is closer to "organization" than to the social-psychological use of the term.

The President's Commission on Law Enforcement and Administration of Justice uses the term "system of criminal justice" in much the same sense as it is employed here but tends to bound it by agency and trial court functions, not embracing legislatures and appellate courts as parts of the criminal justice structure as well as parts of its operational reality. In the general summarizing volume of the Commission's report, THE CHALLENGE OF CRIME IN A FREE SOCIETY 7 (1967), the criminal justice system is described:

> The system of criminal justice America uses to deal with those crimes it cannot prevent and those criminals it cannot deter is not a monolithic, or even a consistent, system. It was not designed or built in one piece at one time. Its philosophic core is that a person may be punished by the Government if, and only if, it has been proved by an impartial and deliberate process that he has violated a specific law. Around that core layer upon layer of institutions and procedures, some carefully constructed and some improvised, some inspired by principle and some by expediency, have accumulated. Parts of the system—magistrates' courts, trial by jury, bail—are of great antiquity. Other parts—juvenile courts, probation and parole, professional policemen—are relatively new. The entire system represents an adaptation of the English common law to America's peculiar structure of government, which allows each local community to construct institutions that fill its special needs. Every village, town, county, city, and State has its own criminal justice system, and there is a Federal one as well. All of them operate somewhat alike. No two of them operate precisely alike.
>
> Any criminal justice system is an apparatus society uses to enforce the standards of conduct necessary to protect individuals and the community. It operates by apprehending, prosecuting, convicting, and sentencing those members of the community who violate the basic rules of group existence.

If nothing else, the use of the concept "system" provides easy translation of criminal justice issues into the techniques of systems analysis, a research approach currently used with various complex organizational phenomena. In fact, it has been suggested that the criminal justice system lends itself very well to this type of analysis. *See, e.g.,* Blumstein, *Systems Analysis and the Criminal Justice System,* 374 ANNALS 92, 94-96 (1967).

With a bow to possible alternative titles, like "administrative process" or "complex organization," we stick with the term "criminal justice system" to encompass the complicated structures and operational functions of crime control efforts in our society.

The distinct agencies work together and function in check and balance, though often there is a lack of common agreement on specific objectives and the methods of achieving them. While dedicated to the control of crime, the translation of this broad purpose into action by the individual agency results in significant divergence in aims and efforts. The police, for example, may view their crime control function as complete when they have arrested suspects, thereby clearing their books of unsolved crimes. Whether the suspects are later convicted or whether the original arrest leads to rehabilitation are questions rarely viewed as relevant to the police function, yet they have considerable bearing on it. The problem is not unique to the police. Each agency has specialized functions and each has immediate and long-range goals, some of which may be a matter of conflict even within the agency, and many of which may not complement the purposes of other agencies.

The root of this goes far back into the history of crime control and it is an inevitable product of the complex nature of any cultural response to deviance. Separation of agencies, multiple purposes, and lack of consensus about etiology and cure are generated as societies grow and as the response to crime becomes depersonalized, routine, and massive. Private revenge is viewed as improper and the town constable is no longer effective, but retaliation and local community autonomy remain a part of the criminal justice heritage.

Attempts to deal with crime are as old as man, and over the centuries techniques as varied as can be imagined have been tried, discarded, and tried again in newer forms. The result is that the criminal justice system blends traditions and outmoded techniques with recently accentuated values and experimental enforcement and treatment techniques. At no time is the system a totally rational construct with all of its purposes clearly stated and all of its parts working smoothly and in concert. There is much disagreement in the community at large and within the criminal justice agencies about how best to control crime. All criminal justice agencies grapple with the problem of whether basic objectives are best served by dealing with the person on an individualized basis or as an example to others. This issue, deterrence or cure, is only one that must be considered. There is an historically clear mandate to punish criminals in order to control recidivism, and to deter others, as well as for revenge.[e] The

---

[e] Jerome Hall, in *Objectives of Federal Criminal Procedural Revision*, 51 Yale L.J. 723, 734 (1942), has commented:

> Finally, it is evident, also, that criminal procedure discharges non-rational functions which cannot presently be ignored. The thesis in

criminal deserves to be punished for the harm he has done or the illicit gain made. While such punishment today seldom involves physical pain or death, retribution does pervade and color even the most modern prison and the most highly professional probation service. Set against this punitive purpose is the rehabilitative ideal, which advocates professional treatment and the reintegration of the criminal into society. These values, punishment and rehabilitation, create dilemmas for all who are a part of the process.

Conflicting purposes also confound legislatures and appellate courts who are often uncertain of the long-range effects of their determinations. In brief, there is no linearity of purpose in criminal justice administration, just as there is no single, overall agency of crime control. This complicates analysis and evaluation, for it is virtually impossible to simply answer any operational question, such as whether to increase efforts to arrest, to advocate stop-and-frisk legislation, or to modify terms of sentences in a manner that will equally satisfy all the accepted objectives and purposes.

Another basis of complexity is the nature of crime itself and the range of conduct that may be considered criminal. Murder, burglary, gambling, embezzlement, and nonsupport are all crimes, yet they are distinct types of behavior and may have significantly different etiologies, requiring different means of prevention and techniques for detection and processing of suspects. Even within a single offense category, such as first degree murder, there are significant variations in personal characteristics of murderers, their motives, the conditions leading to the homicide, and their relationships with the victims.[f] Only on the broadest plane, the criminal result, is it possible to generalize about this crime.

Given the multiplicity of approaches to crime control and the range and divergence of criminal behavior, it is inevitable that the criminal justice system is complicated, with disparities and inconsistencies. But it is essential for the daily processing of

---

this regard may be stated somewhat paradoxically: it is rational to employ criminal procedure, in part, to satisfy non-rational needs. The confidence aroused by the order, publicity and rationality of criminal procedure has been noted. But there are even deeper instinctual needs that cannot soon be modified. No reform of criminal procedure may lightly ignore the public "sense of justice," the interminable conflict between conscience and animal desire, or the criminal trial as a vicarious avenue of emotional release which supports the delicate balance of adjustment to social restraint.

[f] *See, e.g.,* F. McClintock, Crimes of Violence (1963); H. von Hentig, The Criminal and His Victim (1948); M. Wolfgang, Patterns in Criminal Homicide (1958); M. Wolfgang & F. Ferracuti, The Subculture of Violence (1966).

thousands of cases, and in operation it must resolve the competing values and handle the widely differing problems posed to it. And, change is constantly induced in the system as legislatures draft new codes, as appellate courts resolve new issues and reevaluate old ones, as the behavioral sciences increasingly become involved in various aspects of the crime problem, and as the population grows and new forms of crime appear. Analysis and evaluation of criminal justice administration cannot be expected to lead to definitive, final answers to problems in crime control. However, it may lead to intelligent assessment of issues and proposals for crime control so that better choices can be made.

There is little doubt that many of the difficulties in criminal justice administration result from ignorance about the workings of the overall system. The road to crime control is littered with discarded panaceas. Many of the proposals have failed simply because they were not in harmony with administrative reality, others because they were irrelevant to the nature and causes of criminal conduct. Legislatures have attempted to cope with the problem by applying indeterminate sentences to a wide range of crimes and by enacting long, mandatory prison terms for special classes of offenders, such as narcotic users, sex deviates, and the perpetrators of whatever crime appeared epidemic at a particular time. In general, the effect of these solutions has never been systematically determined. Appellate courts, in working out elaborate controls over practices ranging from wiretapping to in-custody interrogation, have often assumed that their holdings have significantly modified police practices. But this is only one possibility, and in numerous instances the result of a sweeping decision is that there is no change in practice or an unanticipated response, such as harassment of suspects in place of arrest for prosecution.[g] Agencies support policies and follow procedures with little concern about the efficacy of the procedures or whether a practice effective for one purpose retards the achievement of others.

There is no single or magical answer to crime control. The problem, however, is important enough to deserve knowledgeable and sophisticated assessment of the effectiveness of every proposal advanced as the solution to some part of the crime problem. It

---

[g] *See generally* W. LaFave, Arrest: The Decision to Take a Suspect into Custody (1965); L. Tiffany, D. McIntyre & D. Rotenberg, Detection of Crime: Stopping and Questioning, Search and Seizure, Encouragement and Entrapment (1967); Kuh, *The Mapp Case One Year After: An Appraisal of Its Impact in New York,* 148 N.Y.L.J. 4 (1962); Remington & LaFave, *Controlling the Police: The Judge's Role in Making and Reviewing Law Enforcement Decisions,* 63 Mich. L. Rev. 987 (1965); Traynor, *Mapp v. Ohio At Large in the Fifty States,* 1962 Duke L.J. 319.

is therefore essential to confront the complexity of the criminal justice system directly, to deal with its facets and subtleties, to understand its subsystems, and to evaluate it from as many perspectives as possible.

Structural Components of the Criminal Justice System

The boundaries of the criminal justice system in our society are set in statutory law.[h] But its antecedents rest in constitutional provisions, many of its precedents are found in common law, some of its authority emanates from the executive branch, and it operates within a maze of appellate decisions and administrative rules. The system has both defining and invoking functions, involving the delineation of criminal conduct on the one hand and the processing of suspects and convicted offenders on the other. Its structure is an admixture of substantive, procedural, and administrative law, and its sources of authority range from the Supreme Court to the policeman on the beat. In short, the criminal justice system is as structurally complex as might be expected from the conflicting values of our political ideology.

Perhaps the most usual conception of the major structural components of the system—legislatures, courts, and agencies—is hierarchical, with power and responsibility ranked in that order. (Constitutional provisions, as interpreted by the courts, provide a control upon all three components; the executive, for all practical purposes, is important primarily as an initiator of legislation.) In this ranking, the legislature is most decisive, having responsibility both for defining criminal conduct and acceptable procedures and for acting as the boundary-fixer for much official

[h] Definitions of criminal conduct are generally in statutory form in our society today, although a few common-law crimes still exist in some jurisdictions. By and large the maxim, *nullum crimen sine lege*—no crime without law—is taken to mean statutory law. *See generally* J. HALL, GENERAL PRINCIPLES OF CRIMINAL LAW 35-55 (2d ed. 1960); J. SALMOND, JURISPRUDENCE (1946); Elliot, *Nulla Poena Sine Lege,* 1 JURID. REV. 22 (1956). Agency structures and budgets come from the legislatures, as do some of the objectives and procedures. Furthermore, legislatures have recently become increasingly involved with procedural matters in criminal justice as well as with recodification of substantive codes. Generally, legislation in regard to enforcement, sentencing, and other administrative procedures sets outer boundaries of delegated authority without detailed attention to operational criteria within these bounds, although increased appellate court intervention in these matters on a case-by-case basis may result in more specific, detailed legislation. *See, e.g.,* the Crime Control Act of 1968, 82 Stat. — (1968). At any rate, most of the outer dimensions of the criminal justice system can be viewed in statutory form even if its operational details remain to be filled in.

action. It also controls operational budgets, a power at least as significant as other legislative activity in crime control. The judiciary is thought to come next with responsibility for interpreting statutes in specific situations and, where necessary, devising methods of exercising supervisory control over the police and other agencies. The agencies—police, prosecutor, and corrections—would rank last, serving the ministerial functions of carrying out legislative mandate or court decree, exercising discretion and initiative only where it is delegated by higher authority. Briefly, the legislature makes the law, that is, determines which conduct is criminal and establishes enforcement procedures; courts interpret existing legislation; and the administrative agencies carry out the process of enforcement and treatment of the guilty.

This hierarchical relationship is only one way of looking at the basic structure of the system. It is also possible, and perhaps more realistic, to conceive of the three components as partners in defining the boundaries and controlling the operations of the system. Each has a peculiar competence and realm of particular responsibility but none has exclusive control over any major function of the system. All three components, in fact, perform each function at one time or another. In the determination of what conduct is criminal, for example, legislative draftsmen set the outer limits beyond which enforcement agencies and courts cannot go, but the outer limits may be grossly unrealistic, whether deliberately, inadvertently, or unavoidably, in defining which conduct will be subject to the criminal process.[i] It is there, in the enforcement of statutes which forbid such conduct as gambling, sexual misconduct, disorderly conduct, vagrancy, and the like, that the law-making function is shared by all three major components of the system, the substantive meaning of such statutes in any given community deriving from the policies and practices of the police, the prosecutor, and the trial court. And, while administrative agencies normally have wide discretion to develop operational procedures, there is currently a trend toward court intervention in these matters, sometimes in rather detailed fashion. The *Miranda*[j] decision from the United States Supreme Court, for instance, spelled out with great specificity pre-interrogation procedures which police must follow. And certain provisions in the Model Penal Code[k] suggest that legislatures may

---

[i] *See* Remington & Rosenblum, *The Criminal Law and the Legislative Process,* 1960 U. Ill. L.F. 481.

[j] Miranda v. Arizona, 384 U.S. 436 (1966).

[k] Model Penal Code (Proposed Official Draft 1962), especially Part III—Treatment and Correction.

have a role in specifying criteria for correctional decisions, a field of traditionally broadly delegated authority.

The separate yet overlapping functions of legislature, court, and agency are perhaps best illustrated by post-conviction determinations. Sentencing the criminal offender is usually a tripartite decision, with the legislature setting the extremes of minimum and maximum sentences, the judge having the discretion to fix the sentence within the statutory outer limits, and the correctional and parole authorities having further discretion to determine what portion of the sentence the offender will actually serve.[l] There are, of course, many variations to this balance, at sentencing and at other points within the system as well. In some cases legislatures attempt complete control of sentencing by fixing mandatory terms for particular crimes; in other instances completely indeterminate sentences delegate to correctional authorities full sentencing and release discretion. By and large, however, post-conviction determinations fall between these extremes, resting on a structure of fixed outer limits with interior flexibility.

The operational realities of criminal justice administration are such that any attempt by one component to completely control all decision-making is unsuccessful. For example, some legislatures in recent years have sought to curb sale of narcotics by fixing severe mandatory prison terms for conviction. This legislation precludes judicial discretion in sentencing and seriously limits or nullifies discretion of the parole authorities. When flexibility is desired, courts can obtain it by reducing charges to some lesser offense, notwithstanding evidence sufficient to support the more serious charge, thereby retaining sentencing power and returning discretion to the parole board.[m]

All this merely points up the functional intricacy of the tripartite structure and the need to view with considerable care the relationship of legislature, court, and agency at each critical point. Two extreme conceptions of the system, one that legislative mandate controls all subsequent decisions, the other that criminal processes rest fundamentally on discretionary choices of agencies, suffer in common from gross oversimplification.

The structural complications which result from overlapping functions of the three general sources of authority are increased by the profusion of statuses and roles of those responsible for decision-making. Legislatures, courts, and agencies are in reality abstractions, useful for analysis, but they are collective, composed

---

[l] *See* Note, *Statutory Structures for Sentencing Felons to Prison,* 60 Colum. L. Rev. 1134 (1960).

[m] *See generally* D. Newman, Conviction: The Determination of Guilt or Innocence Without Trial (1966).

of people with various backgrounds and skills, selected for their roles by different processes. There is no generic profession of "criminal justice administrator" nor is there any common basis of education, training, or experience which applies to the personnel in the system. Some are elected to office, others are appointed, and still others achieve their position by competitive examination. Some, like legislators and appellate judges, are involved only part time with criminal justice matters; others, particularly those in police and correctional agencies, pursue full time careers in crime control. In short, the distribution of personnel within the system is itself a structural factor of great importance. While some proposals for solving crime problems are directed to the relative balance between legislature, court, and agency (*e.g.*, creating legislative guidelines for all decisions, broadening judicial discretion, or increasing correctional autonomy) others are directed toward altering professions or changing selection patterns (*e.g.*, "professionalization" of the police, "taking judges out of politics," or providing greater citizen participation in developing and reviewing enforcement policies).

The role component of the criminal justice structure has at least three dimensions of conceptual and operational significance: (1) the extent of citizen participation in policy formulation and decision-making; (2) the extent to which criminal justice personnel are required to be professionally trained and educated for their particular function; and (3) the balance among elective, appointive, and civil service offices. It would be theoretically possible to construct systems with roles determined in various combinations of each. One extreme, for example, would be a system in which all offices from legislature to prison warden were filled by direct election; all agencies, including courts, staffed by laymen without prerequisites for office; and with major policy decisions determined by referenda or by elected councils of citizens. On the other extreme, the entire system theoretically could be staffed by highly trained professionals, with all offices (other than the legislature) filled on the basis of competitive examinations, and with policy determinations left solely to the professional administrator.

As it exists, the structure of the system approximates neither of these extremes but, with variations from one part to another, incorporates aspects of each. There is, for example, direct citizen participation in the criminal justice process in both the trial and grand jury. There is also some direct involvement by those citizens who serve on various advisory and review boards at different points in the process. Many communities have police and fire commissions and most states have some form of board of public welfare staffed by laymen, usually prominent citizens appointed by the executive, which are set up to develop broad policies in matters of program and personnel. Proposals to create civilian review boards to supervise police are currently matters of controversy in many large cities. There is also less direct citizen participation through the election of certain officials.

The question of the extent to which criminal justice offices and agencies should be staffed by trained professionals is closely linked with the degree of citizen participation in policy and decision-making. While there is variation from one jurisdiction to another, most criminal justice systems are staffed by both laymen and professionally trained career personnel, the difference between systems being the number and importance of each.[n] For example, some states have appointed citizen parole boards whereas others have boards whose members are selected by competitive examination from among professional correctional personnel. In some communities the police commissioner is a prominent layman; in others he is a career professional. Historically, probation officers were lay volunteers and only recently has the ideal of trained social workers come to dominate correctional philosophy.[o] That many probation and parole agents do not have special training is largely a result of the shortage of such personnel and not a result of disagreement with this ideal. In some jurisdictions magistrates can be laymen, not lawyers, and not long ago it was felt that juvenile judges should be ordinary citizens or welfare workers rather than lawyers.[p] While there appears to be a trend toward increasing professionalization of all criminal justice agencies, many states and communities staff their agencies with personnel who have neither special nor professional training. In part, this is a matter of economics and the scarcity of professionals; on another level, however, it is felt by some to be desirable to have citizen involvement on as wide a plane as possible in decisions of such importance to the community as releasing men from prison or determining police policies.

---

[n] See the reports of THE PRESIDENT'S COMMISSION ON LAW ENFORCEMENT AND ADMINISTRATION OF JUSTICE, particularly the Task Force Reports: THE POLICE (1967); THE COURTS (1967); CORRECTIONS (1967).

[o] *See* M. BELL & C. CHUTE, CRIME, COURTS AND PROBATION (1956); N. TIMASHEFF, ONE HUNDRED YEARS OF PROBATION (1941); THE PRESIDENT'S COMMISSION ON LAW ENFORCEMENT AND ADMINISTRATION OF JUSTICE, TASK FORCE REPORT: CORRECTIONS (1967), especially Chapter 9—Manpower and Training; Moreland, *John Agustus and His Successors,* 1941 NATIONAL PROBATION ASS'N YEARBOOK 3.

[p] See particularly A. KAHN, A COURT FOR CHILDREN (1953); H. LOU, JUVENILE COURTS IN THE UNITED STATES (1927); JUSTICE FOR THE CHILD (M. Rosenheim ed. 1962); P. TAPPAN, JUVENILE DELINQUENCY (1949); McCune & Skoler, *Juvenile Court Judges in the United States—Part I: A National Profile,* 11 CRIME & DELINQUENCY 121 (1965).

On the whole, staffing of the criminal justice system is based on a combination of elective and civil service positions. The major variations appear in the form of appointive agency heads or parole boards, or, as in the federal system, appointed judges and prosecutors. Legislators are elected. Police ranks are normally filled by career officers who win promotion by examination, although the police chief or commissioner is commonly appointed by civilian authority and may or may not be a career professional. Sheriffs are generally elected, but their staffs may be filled by career officers much like city police forces. The offices of prosecutor and attorney general are elective, except at the federal level, with a minimum requirement that incumbents be lawyers. Their staffs however, may be filled by career deputies. Judges of trial and appellate courts are commonly elected, excepting again the federal level where they are appointed by the President and confirmed by the Senate. Those elected, however, commonly run on a nonpartisan basis. Nationwide, the usual correctional structure provides a promotional system for all positions except the heads of major correctional services, such as directors of prisons, directors of probation and parole services, directors of youth programs, and parole board members. These offices are usually filled by appointment by the governor or by some state commission for specific terms.[q] Sometimes selection rests strictly on political considerations, sometimes on a desire for broad-spectrum lay involvement in correctional determinations, and sometimes on professional qualifications.

Given the variety of role-selection patterns and the complicated interplay of legislatures, courts, and agencies, it is readily apparent that the structure of criminal justice system cannot be quickly nor easily described, either as to the ranking and sources of authority or the selection of personnel. The fact that the structure is complex, multidimensional, and not uniform; the fact that many structural relationships, like those between courts and agencies, are controversial and largely unsettled; and the fact that the structure is dynamic, subject to changes and to shifts in focus, all compound the difficulty of analyzing the way the system works. Nevertheless, an awareness of this complexity and of the uncertainties about its dimensions is necessary to prevent overly facile analysis of its processes and adoption of simplistic proposals for solving its problems.

---

[q] *See* The President's Commission on Law Enforcement and Administration of Justice, Task Force Report: Corrections (1967), especially Chapter 9 and Appendix A.

The Process of Criminal Justice Administration

The criminal justice system is a process as well as a structure. While the control of crime is the major goal of the system, its focus in operation is not crime but an individual who, at first, is suspected of crime but who, in the final determination, may or may not be a criminal. The formal process has the objective of discovering those persons believed guilty of crimes, screening those who are innocent, and dealing with those found guilty. In this manner a good part of the process is devoted to detection and proof; the remainder to treating, punishing, or otherwise dealing with the lawbreaker.

The full criminal justice process flows through various stages, past more or less clear-cut decision points, in a manner somewhat analogous to that described by a production chart of an industry or flow chart of a large governmental agency.[r] There are a number of critical steps in the process, each of which involves decisions of whether to proceed to the next step or to use alternative actions. There are also various other important decisions about how suspects and defendants are to be handled or how prisoners and probationers are to be treated. Once criminal conduct has been defined and the agencies of the system created, the process in its complete form flows along this continuum: (1) the detection of crime and identification of the perpetrator by the police; (2) arrest of the suspect; (3) the charging decision, including the preliminary hearing; (4) the determination of guilt or innocence by the trial court; (5) sentencing, including the choice between probation or incarceration; (6) post-conviction treatment

---

[r] Professor Packer develops the analogy:

> The image that comes to mind is an assembly-line conveyor belt down which moves an endless stream of cases, never stopping, carrying the cases to workers who stand at fixed stations and who perform on each case as it comes by the same small but essential operation that brings it one step closer to being a finished product, or, to exchange the metaphor for the reality, a closed file. The criminal process, in this model, is seen as a screening process in which each successive stage—pre-arrest investigation, arrest, post-arrest investigation, preparation for trial, trial or entry of plea, conviction, disposition—involves a series of routinized operations whose success is gauged primarily by their tendency to pass the case along to a successful conclusion.
>
> What is a successful conclusion? One that throws off at an early stage those cases in which it appears unlikely that the person apprehended is an offender and then secures, as expeditiously as possible, the conviction of the rest, with a minimum of occasions for challenge, let alone post-audit.

This excerpt and those at 19 n.s, 29-30 are reprinted with the permission of the publisher and the author from H. PACKER, THE LIMITS OF THE CRIMINAL SANCTION (Stanford: Stanford University Press 1968). This passage appears at 159-60.

of the offender, including incarceration, release on parole, and supervision under community sentence; and (7) probation or parole revocation. Other important decisions, concurrent with many of these steps, include such matters as whether to release the suspect on bail, when and under what conditions he shall receive aid of counsel, appeals from convictions and challenges of post-conviction treatment, and various determinations on security measures and rehabilitative techniques during the correctional process.

In terms of the organizational flow of the criminal justice process there is even a "product," measurable statistically at "intake" and "output" points along the way. In this case the product is a person, theoretically presumed innocent but believed to be guilty with increased levels of confidence[8] as he moves from the intake

[8] Packer distinguishes different presumptions underlying his two Models of the criminal process. A presumption of innocence is presupposed in the Due Process Model but a presumption of guilt is the operational basis for his Crime Control Model. He comments:

> The presumption of guilt is what makes it possible for the system to deal efficiently with large numbers, as the Crime Control Model demands. The supposition is that the screening processes operated by police and prosecutors are reliable indicators of probable guilt. Once a man has been arrested and investigated without being found to be probably innocent, or, to put it differently, once a determination has been made that there is enough evidence of guilt to permit holding him for further action, then all subsequent activity directed toward him is based on the view that he is probably guilty. The precise point at which this occurs will vary from case to case; in many cases it will occur as soon as the suspect is arrested, or even before, if the evidence of probable guilt that has come to the attention of the authorities is sufficiently strong. But in any case the presumption of guilt will begin to operate well before the "suspect" becomes a "defendant."
>
> The presumption of guilt is not, of course, a thing. Nor is it even a rule of law in the usual sense. It simply is the consequence of a complex of attitudes, a mood. If there is confidence in the reliability of informal administrative fact-finding activities that take place in the early stages of the criminal process, the remaining stages of the process can be relatively perfunctory without any loss in operating efficiency. The presumption of guilt, as it operates in the Crime Control Model, is the operational expression of that confidence.
>
> It would be a mistake to think of the presumption of guilt as the opposite of the presumption of innocence that we are so used to thinking of as the polestar of the criminal process and that, as we shall see, occupies an important position in the Due Process Model. The presumption of innocence is not its opposite; it is irrelevant to the presumption of guilt; the two concepts are different rather than opposite ideas. . . .
>
> The presumption of innocence is a direction to officials about how they are to proceed, not a prediction of outcome. The presumption of guilt, however, is purely and simply a prediction of outcome. The presumption of innocence is, then, a direction to the authorities to ignore the presumption of guilt in their treatment of the suspect.

H. Packer, The Limits of the Criminal Sanction 160-61 (1968).

process of detection and arrest through charging and prosecution to conviction. His status changes from suspect to defendant, to convicted offender, to probationer or inmate, to parolee, to ex-convict. The latter is a generally negative community status that persists after the criminal justice process has finished, in spite of official disclaimers of intent.

The Basis of Force

Analogy with production systems can be carried too far. The flow of the criminal justice process is rarely as smooth, as routine, as complete, or as certain as the production of goods or services. To begin with, the "product" of the process, the suspect-defendant-inmate, is ordinarily reluctant or hostile. It is true that most defendants plead guilty rather than go to trial but this is later in the process, an accommodation to the inevitable and often combined with a bargain for leniency.[t] Except for a pathological few, most suspects do not welcome apprehension, conviction, and imprisonment. Comparison with patients seeking medical help or with clients desiring public assistance, or even with the voluntary commitment of the mentally ill, is strained and hardly relevant except in contrast. The criminal justice process rests basically on force, the authority of the state to use raw power, properly and appropriately applied, to apprehend, detain, try, and imprison. This basis of force pervades and colors the whole criminal justice system, both internally and in its entire cultural context. Within the system some difficult problems are created, particularly at the post-conviction stages where emphasis shifts from proof of guilt to treatment of the guilty. To the extent that reform and rehabilitation are objectives of the process, the authoritarian nature of the correctional setting and the involuntary client-therapist relationship of inmate and staff challenges the effectiveness of traditional rehabilitative techniques. Externally, the existence and necessity for police power evoke widespread concern with limits and controls. The police, courts, and prisons may indeed be services of the state, but, except in those moments when a citizen is a victim of a crime, they are ordinarily viewed as necessary, but potentially threatening to individual freedom. As a consequence, legislatures, courts, and in various ways the general public have traditionally focused a great deal of attention on the establishment and implementation of controls on the criminal justice process, to setting limits

[t] D. NEWMAN, CONVICTION: THE DETERMINATION OF GUILT OR INNOCENCE WITHOUT TRIAL (1966), Part III—The Negotiated Plea.

on the techniques and authority of enforcement agencies and, for that matter, on substantive definitions of conduct considered criminal. The exclusion of certain chronic forms of deviation like narcotic addiction and alcoholism from the criminal process as a sickness rather than a crime is a matter of current concern.[u]

The potential use of force colors the entire system, invading the role definitions and self-conceptions of authorities and suspects alike. A paramount concern of all agencies, and of the citizenry, is when and to what extent force should be used, and for what purposes and with what consequences. A related concern is the question of when force should be shown, displayed for all to see, rather than used directly. At the present time, these are crucial questions confronting law enforcement and the community alike in view of the civil disorders that have regularly occurred in our cities and on our campuses.

At the police level, questions of the show and use of force are particularly complex and controversial. There was a minor tempest in Chicago a few years ago when a trial judge criticized two police officers for drawing their pistols as they approached a suspect in an alley. Police are regularly criticized for shooting at fleeing automobiles and even for use of sirens and high speeds in automobile chases. In part, these criticisms relate to possible injury to the ever-present innocent bystander; in part, though, this criticism goes to what the critics feel is the unnecessary or overzealous use or display of force. The police, and other agencies as well, thus face censure both for show of force and for failure to show enough. This occurs in various circumstances, from civil rights demonstrations to routine patrol work where police agencies are sometimes caught in the dilemma of whether to exhibit a few policemen in a particular neighborhood or to saturate it with uniformed officers. Either choice is likely to bring criticism from citizens who want the police more visible or from those who are insulted by the presence of many policemen in the area. Likewise, various policing techniques, such as the use of dogs for patrolling certain areas or for crowd control, tend to raise some opposition.

The show of force is muted in courtroom stages of the process but there is an underlying question of the independent value of the dignity of the courtroom. The robed judge, the elevated bench, and the general atmosphere of the courtroom are designed not so much as a display of force as to emphasize seriousness of

[u] *See* Powell v. Texas, 392 U.S. 514 (1968); Driver v. Hinnant, 356 F.2d 761 (4th Cir. 1966); Easter v. District of Columbia, 361 F.2d 50 (D.C. Cir. 1966); *cf.* Robinson v. California, 370 U.S. 660 (1962).

purpose. It is interesting to note that a major change from criminal to juvenile court procedures was in the informality of proceedings. One of the historical purposes of a separate children's court was to escape the purportedly damaging effects of the child's being confronted by the austere, robed judicial officer. There is some evidence that the pendulum is swinging back; some observers of juvenile court hearings think that informality is ineffective in impressing upon the juvenile the seriousness with which the state views his conduct.[v]

Show of force is also a controversial issue at correctional stages of the process. The walled, barred, maximum security prison with armed tower guards on the perimeter is one of the most traditional embodiments of the full force of the state in dealing with law violators. The federal government and all the states have such institutions, easily recognized as prisons. Most of these are old, however, and some, like Alcatraz, have been closed. New prisons, even those designed to hold some dangerous prisoners, are typically unrecognizable by these standards. They are fenced, not walled, if indeed there is any perimeter security; bars have been replaced by psychiatric screening or concrete grillwork; inmates have rooms, not cells; and in general the atmosphere and appearance of these institutions are markedly different from the older penitentiaries. And it is just this change in appearance, with its absence of observable punitive symbols, that causes controversy between correctional administrators and the public, and between the correctional agency and legislative bodies. Evidence of effectiveness, relative absence of escapes, and other data in support of these newer institutions somehow does not dispel the notion that prisons should just not look this way, that inmates should not be permitted to live in this style. A radically new medium security prison was recently built in Wisconsin where, over the objections of planners but upon legislative insistence, free-standing guard towers were built outside the perimeter fence. These towers have never been manned but remain as symbols of force and as emergency control resources.

The fact that show of force is a controversial matter at various stages of the process is related in part to a conflict in objectives. The visibility of police, the formality of a court, and the bars of a prison are all assumed to have some deterrent effect on potential lawbreakers. At the same time it is thought that the particular person involved in processing will be impressed with the

---

[v] *See* THE PRESIDENT'S COMMISSION ON LAW ENFORCEMENT AND ADMINISTRATION OF JUSTICE, TASK FORCE REPORT: JUVENILE DELINQUENCY AND YOUTH CRIME (1967), especially Appendix T, Wheeler, Cottrell & Romasco, *Juvenile Delinquency—Its Prevention and Control.*

seriousness of his conduct and the futility of crime, and deterred from further brushes with the law. Offsetting this is a strong rehabilitative attitude which tends to view visible force as over-policing, courtroom pomp as excessive, and secure control as unnecessary—as building resentment and further crystallizing the criminal role and self-conception of the person dealt with by the agencies of criminal justice. Those adopting each of these positions ask a common question of the other, namely, what are the consequences of the alternatives? Do police and prisons really deter or do they increase crime? Is rehabilitation more or less effective in a system less visibly threatening? These are basic questions, largely unanswered and thereby at the root of the continuing controversy.

Beyond the deterrence-rehabilitation clash, however, questions of display of force rest on the issue of propriety of crime control methods. Even if police saturation of a neighborhood demonstrably lowers crime rates, critics might well find this technique offensive. Likewise, even if a pastel-colored, campus-like prison effects rehabilitative wonders, the question remains whether it is proper treatment of criminals in our world. It is not a budgetary issue, for most modern correctional facilities are cheaper to build than Auburn-type prisons. Many think it satisfactory to expend public money to make prisons secure but not to make them comfortable.

In many circumstances the use or display of force is momentary, as when a suspect is frisked or taken into custody, or a shot is taken at a fleeing felon. In others, it is sustained, as during long prison sentences. There is considerable variety in the visible manifestations of force, from one part of the system to others, from one time to another, and as to different persons processed through the system. Some suspects are captured at gunpoint; others appear on their own initiative in response to a summons. Some defendants are held in jail awaiting trial, others are released on bail. The exercise and extent of physical custody over those being processed by the criminal process have great impact on the individuals involved. From the perspective of forcible, sustained deprivation of liberty, there are two distinct extremes to the criminal process. One person can be retained in custody continuously from the moment of arrest through a prison term. Another, accused of the same crime, may experience a different fate. He can be summoned or surrender voluntarily, be released on bail awaiting trial and pending appeal, and serve his entire sentence on probation in the community. Except momentarily, he may never be in physical custody and the continuity of his home life and employment will not be interrupted. It is quite apparent that these two individuals have grossly different experiences with the same criminal justice system.

Routinization of the Criminal Justice Process

The criminal justice system is further complicated because it is composed of numerous subprocesses, which tend to vary with the type of criminal conduct involved and with the primacy of one or another of its several objectives. The traditional system, involving all agencies and all the steps from detection to parole, is most easily seen when it is set in motion by crimes of violence. Murder, for example, commonly evokes this full-scale response. Because murder and other serious crimes are comparatively rare they never become routine to any agency, and because the legislative and community reaction to homicide is so severe, the system is least bending, least willing merely to process the case by concessions to the defendant who cooperates. Defendants charged with crimes involving severe sentences are normally less willing to waive any steps or give up any rights, because they have little to lose by demanding full processing. It is with these serious crimes that the criminal justice system is most formal, most complete, and most visibly adversary. In its full form it is characterized by consensus as to the nature of the crime, full enforcement on the police level, the bringing of the highest provable charge, the contest of trial by jury, the likelihood of appeal, and the substantial prison sentence. Later release on parole and discharge from supervision may complete the process.

This form of the system—the full enforcement, maximum effort, trial system—is by no means the complete picture. Nor is it as common as some major variations or some distinct subsystems that have been developed to deal with particular problems. With most crimes less serious and more frequent than homicide, the process tends to become more routine and more flexible, with a wider range of alternative actions. Even in the processing of serious crimes there are at times adjustments in the system to achieve equity and individualize justice, where full, maximum implementation appears harsh and unwarranted. These tend to be highly individualized accommodations, focusing on the person, not routinized around the conduct classification. On the other hand, some patterns of lawbreaking are common; the perpetrators pretty much alike; and the conduct, while criminal, not typically viewed as particularly serious. Petty theft, minor barroom assaults, burglary, even certain robberies or forms of sexual deviation like window-peeking or exhibitionism tend to be handled in a more or less routine manner throughout the system. Individual cases receive little publicity, trials are comparatively rare, and the clear-cut steps of the process experienced in the contested homicide cases tend to merge into a relatively swift and anonymous process of apprehension, confession, guilty plea, and sentence. Many minor cases are dropped out of the process without prosecution, conviction, or sentence, if in the discretionary judgment of the police, the prosecutor, or the trial judge they are not worth pursuing. Likewise, some "good" defendants, such as those who are young or atypically respectable, or otherwise unlikely to repeat, may expect leniency in treatment in the interest of administrative efficiency if they are cooperative.

This is the routine process, a variation from the maximum system. It relies heavily on the judgment and discretion of police, prosecutor, and court to enforce the criminal law and do it efficiently, but to adjust the enforcement as equitably as possible to the persons involved and to the threat of the conduct. This is not a distinct subprocess but the routinization of the trial model, with shortcuts in the interest of administrative efficiency and with the desire to individualize justice. The objective is not to divert suspects from the criminal justice system, except where they are "sick" or otherwise atypical, but rather to reduce strain on resources while achieving a form of equity impossible in the full enforcement model. It is the full criminal justice process, but with significantly different operational characteristics, which raises its own issues and concerns. The guilty plea, for example, is a substitute for trial, yet it is a unique procedure with dimensions and controversies all its own.

Subsystems of Criminal Justice

There are a number of distinct subprocesses within the system, designed to deal with certain forms of criminal conduct by means other than conviction and sentencing. Generally these procedures involve police agencies only, or sometimes the police and the prosecutor, and they tend to be developed to deal with conduct of high frequency in which prosecution is difficult or undesirable.

In order to deal with domestic disturbances, nonsupport, and other family-centered offenses, police and prosecuting agencies sometimes develop informal "adjustment" devices ranging from counseling to "peace bonds" to "consent probation," with prosecution reserved for cases of an aggravated nature or where adjustment efforts have failed. This informal handling arises in response to a number of characteristics of typical family-dispute crimes: if fully prosecuted they would strain court and correctional facilities; complainants often fail to cooperate in prosecution because of intervening reconciliation; the adjustment devices are likely to be at least as effective as conviction and sentencing. Similar processes may develop in response to other offenses, such as bad checks or shoplifting, where the victim is satisfied with repayment and where there is little future value in conviction and sentencing.[w]

Still other subsystems grow in response to persistent but largely untreatable types of conduct that have become police matters mainly by default. Every large city has some form of skid row where the homeless, transient, borderline mentally ill, and chronic inebriates are clustered. The processing of the drunk and the vagrant is usually left to the police, who for want of better alternatives adopt a revolving door system of taking into custody those who are most visibly community nuisances or those down and out and likely to perish without care, and releasing them when they are sober or have received care.[x] Processing through conviction and sentencing is reserved for extreme cases, or for certain inebriates at their own request. In routine cases the decision not to proceed to conviction does not hinge on toleration of the conduct or difficulties of proof but rather on the futility of burdening the court and jail with persons for whom there is no effective rehabilitative therapy. Where private treatment and care are available, police, prosecutor, and court are all ordinarily more than willing to divert not only the alcoholic, but most of the homeless, the infirm, the perverted, and the mentally ill from the criminal process.

Other partial enforcement subsystems tend to develop in response to pressures to control vice. Two major factors work against full-scale processing: (1)courts, with some persistence, dismiss cases on the grounds that the police methods of enforcement, such as "encouragement" of prostitutes, are improper; and (2) even if conviction is achieved, the likelihood that a small fine will be imposed and the absence of effective correctional treatment for prostitutes, homosexuals, bookies and other small vice operators make full processing wasteful. Consequently, detection and arrest may be undertaken without intent to prosecute. This

---

[w] *See* W. LaFave, Arrest: The Decision to Take a Suspect into Custody (1965).

[x] *See* The President's Commission on Law Enforcement and Administration of Justice, Task Force Report: Drunkenness (1967); D. Pittman & C. Gordon, Revolving Door: A Study of the Chronic Police Case Inebriate (1958); Powell v. Texas, 392 U.S. 514 (1968).

forms an important subprocess of law enforcement, particularly in urban centers where vice is persistent and visible.[y]

Another variant involves a form of "overenforcement" in contrast to the "underenforcement" systems already described. This subsystem involves the use of certain statutory proscriptions ordinarily not invoked, such as those outlawing adult heterosexual misconduct, in order to convict "undeserving" defendants, *i.e.*, those who may be suspected of more serious crimes which elude detection and proof.

The proliferation of criminal laws, covering a wide range of conduct and often unavoidably ambiguous, results in giving powers and responsibilities to law enforcement agencies that are beyond their wishes or their resources. Furthermore, legislation may be enacted with no actual intention or possibility that it will be fully enforced. For example, gambling is likely to be completely outlawed so as not to afford loopholes to the professional gambler. The result is that social gambling also falls within the proscription, but the legislative purpose is certainly not a mandate to end the neighborhood poker game. Fornication and adultery are crimes in many jurisdictions but it is unlikely that the police could provide, or the community tolerate, full enforcement of these laws in cases involving consenting adults. Vague or overbroad statutes, and statutes proscribing conduct generally considered immoral but not "really criminal," turn over to enforcement agencies the task of interpreting the substantive limits of these laws and the procedures for enforcement. Gambling, disorderly conduct, adult heterosexual misconduct, and a large segment of juvenile delinquency ("endangering his morals") falls within this description since the enforcement agencies usually determine effectively what the law will be for the community and with what vigor it will be enforced. Relegation of the crime-defining tasks to the administrative agencies calls into question the traditional view that the institutions in the system have clearly distinctive functions.[z]

Major Perspectives of Criminal Justice Analysis

The criminal justice system simply has too many structural aspects, too many objectives, too many variations in procedure, to be looked at through a single window. Testing it against any

---

[y] *See* W. LaFave, Arrest: The Decision to Take a Suspect into Custody (1965).

[z] Remington & Rosenblum, *The Criminal Law and the Legislative Process,* 1960 U. Ill. L.F. 481.

one standard or evaluating one part to the exclusion of others is less than satisfactory. For example, if the system is tested against a single concern—efficiency in processing the guilty—the questions that arise are likely to be somewhat different than if another concern—the extent to which regular procedures and adversary process are employed—is the frame of inquiry. This difference in perspective is important not only theoretically but practically, because current controversies about criminal justice arise from looking at the system in different ways, as those who are participants in it do. Disputes about such things as police power, the functions of courts, and the purposes and practices of correctional agencies persist because advocates for the various positions base their arguments on different expectations and standards of evaluation.[a]

The most helpful perspectives and most important questions must relate to the system as a whole. It is possible, for example, to isolate for consideration such a matter as bail. Unless the bail process is analyzed in its context, however, concern about it tends to polarize into a strong value position—that bail is discriminatory against the poor or that bonding is an historically proper method of evaluating reliability and probable appearance at later proceedings—which could hinder rather than aid resolution of issues. Even the formal result of a bail system—the release of persons from detention—is not a discrete issue; it is a general theme that recurs throughout the process so that such matters as the choice between probation or incarceration at sentencing raise many of the same issues.

Concerns which have relevance at a number of critical decision points in the process can become pervasive themes of criminal justice administration and supply major perspectives from which to analyze the system. For example, in a contested trial the most obvious considerations are the relevancy and sufficiency of evidence necessary to establish guilt, as to which there are well-settled guidelines and strict standards. At a parole grant hearing, in contrast, standards of evidence are normally not directly in issue, and matters of proof are not prominent. The decision whether to release a prisoner does not require an adversary proceeding nor rest on a stated quantity of evidence circumscribed as to relevance. Yet the parole decision is not random nor arbitrary. Rather it is a matter of judgment, the result of weighing *some* types and *some* amounts of evidence.

---

[a] This is dramatically illustrated at a number of points in the process in H. Packer, The Limits of the Criminal Sanction ch. 8 (1968); *cf.* p. 18 n.r, *supra*.

The evidentiary questions are important at parole hearings, though muted.

There are a number of such themes running through the criminal justice process. They provide perspectives for analysis and evaluation of the system. Professor Packer, in his suggestive description of two analytical models which he calls the "Due Process Model" and the "Crime Control Model," explains the necessity and value of looking at the criminal justice system from different perspectives:

> . . . We need to detach ourselves from the welter of more or less connected details that describe the myriad ways in which the criminal process does operate or may be likely to operate in mid-twentieth-century America, so that we can begin to see how the system as a whole might be able to deal with the variety of missions we confide to it.
>
> One way to do this kind of job is to abstract from reality, to build a model. In a sense, a model is just what an examination of the constitutional and statutory provisions that govern the operation of the criminal process would produce. This in effect is the way analysis of the legal system has traditionally proceeded. It has considerable utility as an index of current value choices; but it produces a model that will not tell us very much about some important problems that the system encounters and that will only fortuitously tell us anything useful about how the system actually operates. On the other hand, the kind of model that might emerge from an attempt to cut loose from the law on the books and to describe, as accurately as possible, what actually goes on in the real-life world of the criminal process would so subordinate the inquiry to the tyranny of the actual that the existence of competing value choices would be obscured. The kind of criminal process we have depends importantly on certain value choices that are reflected, explicitly or implicitly, in its habitual functioning. The kind of model we need is one that permits us to recognize explicitly the value choices that underlie the details of the criminal process. In a word, what we need is a *normative* model or models. It will take more than one model, but it will not take more than two.
>
> Two models of the criminal process will let us perceive the normative antinomy at the heart of the criminal law. These models are not labeled Is and Ought, nor are they to be taken in that sense. Rather, they represent an attempt to abstract two separate value systems that compete for priority in the

> operation of the criminal process. Neither is presented as either corresponding to reality or representing the ideal to the exclusion of the other. The two models merely afford a convenient way to talk about the operation of a process whose day-to-day functioning involves a constant series of minute adjustments between the competing demands of two value systems and whose normative future likewise involves a series of resolutions of the tensions between competing claims.[b]

He also warns of the pitfalls of model building:

> There is a risk in an enterprise of this sort that is latent in any attempt to polarize. It is, simply, that values are too various to be pinned down to yes-or-no answers. The models are distortions of reality. . . . The attempt here is primarily to clarify the terms of discussion by isolating the assumptions that underlie competing policy claims and examining the conclusions that those claims, if fully accepted, would lead to.[c]

Subsequent chapters in this book follow the operation of the criminal justice process. Dividing the process into its principal steps is simply a way of providing a framework for analysis.

At each stage in the process there are questions of strategies and tactics, of techniques, of status and role, of personnel and budget, of interplay of legislative mandate and judicial or administrative implementation, of community norms and pressures. There is so much color and controversy in the process that it is almost too easy to get caught up in the fascination of details and to lose sight of the operation of the entire system. To avoid this, a number of pervasive themes are identified here which may be used as referents in analysis of the process as the steps are described.

1. Evidence Sufficiency. This is perhaps the most traditional, most formal, and one of the most important questions put to the system, especially in regard to decisions to investigate, to apprehend, to charge, and to convict offenders. The importance of insuring that evidence is adequate is less often recognized as an issue in the post-conviction stages or in the routine subsystems for dealing with the drunk, the juvenile, and so on. Nevertheless, the issue of standards of evidence on which decisions rest, and the translation of these standards into practice is a vital concern

---

[b] *Id.* at 152-53.
[c] *Id.* at 153-54.

where the action of a state against the wishes of an individual is being taken.

In certain instances standards of evidence have been stated in legislation in more or less standard form and have been repeatedly interpreted by appellate courts. The most stringent requirement is the trial standard of proof "beyond a reasonable doubt" for conviction at trial. While this standard may require interpretation in individual cases, it is surely the most consistently applied test in the entire system. There is less agreement about the lower standards of evidence invoked in the pretrial stages of the process. And, for that matter, there is an important question of how the reasonable doubt test relates to the vast majority of convictions based on pleas of guilty. Standard of evidence issues recur in the post-conviction stages but, in contrast to the trial situation, there is little guidance from legislatures and appellate decisions. From this perspective the presentence report is an evidentiary document and such matters as parole revocation ordinarily rest on some standard of sufficiency of evidence though not clearly articulated. The evidence sufficiency theme allows construction of a profile of the criminal justice system by ascertaining the evidence requirements of each critical stage and comparing it with the requirements at other stages of the system. But making such a profile is more difficult than it may seem. For example, the test phrased as "probable cause to believe" is often applied at each of the pretrial steps, from arrest through the preliminary hearing. But there is a serious question whether evidence sufficient for the police to arrest a suspect is always sufficient to justify the prosecutor in charging or the magistrate in binding over for trial.[d] The phrase itself gives few clues, and there is no consensus in interpretation.

The question of what kind of evidence may be considered is a recurring one. At trial and in some other formal proceedings, the issue of admissibility has been faced frequently, with the result that there are more or less clear guidelines on hearsay, credibility, and other limitations on the quality as contrasted with the quantity of evidence. There are, however, many points in the criminal process where these matters are ill-defined and subject to dispute. It is an important issue at such varied points as use of informers, release on bail, use of presentence information at sentencing, and parole revocation.

[d] *See* Goldsmith v. United States, 277 F.2d 335 (D.C. Cir. 1960); De Salvatore v. State, 52 Del. 550, 163 A.2d 244 (1960); see also, discussion of differential standards in W. LaFave, Arrest: The Decision to Take a Suspect into Custody 324-26 (1965); and in L. Tiffany, D. McIntyre & D. Rotenberg, Detection of Crime: Stopping and Questioning, Search and Seizure, Encouragement and Entrapment 9-43 (1967).

2. *Consent.* Consideration of the process from the point of view of the quantity and quality of evidence necessary to take action against a suspect involves an implicit assumption that the system is adversary. This assumption is theoretically sound, but in practice the full-scale adversary process, where a contesting defendant puts evidence to the test at each level, is comparatively infrequent. From the perspective of consent the question is the degree to which the system depends on negotiation rather than contest. The dependence on those who cooperate, who admit guilt, who "consent" to the limitations imposed by the rules of probation and parole, is characteristic of the routine criminal justice process.

The nature and conditions of waiver and consent are such that issues of evidence and proof concerning the "intelligence" of waiver and "voluntariness" of consent are raised, and in a real sense this model contains an evidence perspective. But the concerns here are different from those presented by the suspect-defendant who denies guilt and demands full, formal processing. Evidence issues here refer to the propriety of the procedures used in obtaining waivers or consent rather than to the question of guilt.

Where there is full cooperation by the suspect, the criminal process flows quickly and smoothly, the epitome of efficiency. Apprehension, search, and interrogation are unchallenged; the most demanding test of proof of guilt is bypassed; vigorous prosecution and defense are unnecessary; and the offender, having admitted his guilt, is ready for rehabilitation. Such matters as pretrial publicity, the limits of search, the affording of counsel, the dimensions of the insanity defense, the composition of jury panels, pretrial disclosure, confidentiality of presentence reports, limitations of sentencing power, and the like, which traditionally are held to be important in criminal justice administration, are foreign to consensual processing. If the defendant decides to appeal after such processing, he is at a disadvantage, for he must overcome the effect of his admissions and his waivers, which is a difficult task if the prosecution agencies have followed the relatively easy procedures of warning and have taken care to preserve a record of their deliberation and fairness.

The consent-based procedure is the bread and butter of the criminal justice system. Most criminal charges, including the entire range from the minor offense to the serious felony, are handled in this manner. It has a parallel in the system for processing juvenile delinquents, where contested cases are so rare that a committee drafting a revision of the Wisconsin Children's Code seriously proposed eliminating the right to a jury trial on the grounds that disuse had made it unnecessary. There is also a parallel in the system used to hospitalize mental patients where the paradoxical process, "voluntary commitment of the mentally ill," is by far the most frequent means of hospital admission.

There are at least two ways of describing the consent-based system. In one, consent is explicitly given by fully-informed suspects. In the other consent has been inferred from a failure to protest or make a request. The procedure based on responses by informed, duly-warned defendants is quite different from that where there is merely a failure to protest.

Courts have recently given close scrutiny to the consent-waiver issue. It has long been agreed that coercion negates apparent consent, and the third degree or physical and psychological threats are commonly viewed as leading to inaccurate, untrustworthy confessions and pleas and as improper even where not inaccurate. But the issues that are currently arising involve techniques more subtle than raw force or overt intimidation. Courts are grappling with such concepts as "freely and willingly" consented, "understandingly" or "knowingly" waived, or "voluntarily" pleaded guilty. In a system that is basically punitive, one containing few pretensions of existing for the best interests of the suspect, can a suspect freely consent to questioning by an armed, uniformed police officer? Under what conditions and with what warnings can a defendant's "consent" to be searched be relied upon? When does consent begin and end? When is there an understanding waiver of counsel? Of trial? Is a freely given plea of guilty sufficient for conviction or must other evidence of actual guilt be offered? Does inducement—*e.g.*, a promise of leniency carried out by reduction of the charge or by a light sentence—negate a confession or guilty plea in the same manner as coercion? Questioning these aspects of consent extends even to the post-conviction processes. The attitude that conditions of probation and parole and supervisory rules are binding because they have been agreed to as a type of "contract for freedom" is under attack. These and a number of variations are major issues in evaluation of the nonadversary process.

3. Fairness and Propriety of Procedures. Sufficiency of evidence, efficiency in operation, and effectiveness in producing results are not, in themselves, sufficient measures of a criminal justice system in a democratic society. Our political ideology demands that justice be viewed from the standpoint of fair dealing with suspects, defendants, and convicted criminals, and that methods of detection, apprehension, processing, and treatment be fitting for our era and cultural heritage. There are, therefore, limits on the methods and techniques used to control crime; the end does not justify every means.

While this is generally agreed to, the translation of ideals into reality is a difficult task and has been left largely to appellate courts. There are some legislative guidelines which forbid particular improper or unfair practices and in a number of jurisdictions court rules set some requirements of procedural fairness. But the basic mandate for fairness and propriety rests in constitutional guarantees—protection from unreasonable search, freedom from self-incrimination, equal protection under the law, and assurance of due process of law. The actual scope and application of constitutional guarantees of fairness are dependent on appellate court interpretation, and in recent years the courts have greatly expanded these protections.

Fairness and propriety as tests of proper criminal justice procedures are not entirely independent of the accuracy of the process in separating the guilty from the innocent, but it is not always clear in each situation which concern is paramount. For example, coerced confessions are excluded from consideration partly because such confessions may be untrustworthy but also because coercion is repugnant in a democratic society.[e] There are, however, some instances where fairness is a dominant concern almost unrelated to the issue of accuracy. For example, convictions on pleas of guilty are proper only if the trial judge has explained all the possible (not probable) consequences of sentencing to the defendant before accepting the plea.[f] This is a separate and distinct issue from the question whether the defendant is actually guilty of the criminal conduct which he admits.

Additional problems arise in determining proper and fair techniques in less clear-cut situations. Is wiretapping a proper police procedure, apart from its efficiency, in the control of organized crime? To what extent may the police encourage suspects to commit acts that will form the basis for their arrest? To what extent may pleas of guilty be negotiated by the prosecutor or judge? To what extent are correctional determinations limited by considerations of fairness?

Some fairness issues are resolved on constitutional grounds, that is, that the unfairness or impropriety is so basic as to be an infringement of the individual's constitutional rights. This test by no means exhausts consideration of the issue, however, for some practices occasionally result in allegations of unfairness or impropriety that do not rise to the level of constitutional issues.

---

[e] *See, e.g.,* Kadish, *Methodology and Criteria in Due Process Adjudication—A Survey and Criticism,* 66 YALE L.J. 319, 346-47 (1957).

[f] *See* Annot., 97 A.L.R.2d 549 (1964).

For example, the enforcement of traffic laws often takes on aspects of a game between drivers and the police. The use of radar or unmarked patrol cars is often criticized by the public, and sometimes by trial courts, as unfair, even though admittedly effective. Likewise, the nature and extent of police intervention in civil rights demonstrations is heatedly disputed and largely on the grounds of propriety. Other practices, such as charge reduction, extremely long or short sentences, early parole, unusual conditions of probation or parole, and certain correctional practices have, at one time or another, been challenged as to their propriety or fairness.

4. The Effectiveness and the Efficiency of Criminal Justice Practices. An important basis for evaluating the criminal justice system is the effectiveness of its techniques and concepts. The issue is simply the extent to which the process achieves its objectives in a manner consistent with its long-range responsibilities. The answer, however, is often unclear, partly because of a lack of consensus about objectives and responsibilities and partly because effectiveness must be considered in the light of accuracy, consent, and fairness and propriety. The system cannot employ methods to obtain confessions or provide correctional treatment that outrage standards of propriety, no matter how demonstrably effective. Assessment of the use of the "stop-and-frisk" as a proper technique depends on the balance between its contribution to enforcement and its consequences, which today include the attitudes and responses of minority groups in the community. To the extent stop-and-frisk practices are seen as a form of racial discrimination or harassment of the poor, the risk of stimulating civil disorder may far outweigh the gains in apprehending criminals or confiscating weapons. Likewise, a long sentence for the purpose of treatment is easier to tolerate if the treatment is reasonably likely to be effective. Or, the informal, even casual, juvenile court procedure may now be challenged on the basis that the promise of effectiveness has not materialized.[g] Another factor in assessment of criminal justice practices is the nature of the harm sought to be prevented. Justice Robert Jackson, in commenting on the use of police roadblocks, expressed willingness to tolerate this intervention if the life of a kidnapped child were in issue but not if the police were merely after a "few bottles of bourbon and . . . a bootlegger."[h] In the same manner, wiretapping in protection of "national security," extra enforcement precautions to prevent assassination of political leaders, and like

[g] *See In re* Gault, 387 U.S. 1 (1967); *see also* B. George, Gault and the Juvenile Court Revolution (1968).

[h] Brinegar v. United States, 338 U.S. 160, 183 (1949).

practices may be tolerated even without any certainty of effectiveness and without implying support for use of such techniques in less extreme situations.

The criminal justice system works best when it has a clear objective and the capacity to achieve it. Where incarceration of the dangerous offender is the goal, the system operates fully and formally because agencies will devote their resources to accomplish the important objective of removing this threat from society. In contrast, some subsystems develop because there is no effective way to deter or rehabilitate the types of offenders involved. Until there is some discernible way to control the recurrence of such conduct, there will likely be little interest on the part of agencies to conform to procedures for conviction. Conviction and sentencing are thought futile, and full-scale criminal processing is simply bypassed.

The effectiveness of any criminal justice procedure is difficult to measure and it may not be estimated with any assurance. There has been controversy about the consequences of various police practices, court decisions, and penal measures for a long time. Alternatives have been subjected to careful research and study so rarely that conclusions on the effect of such measures as aggressive police patrol, plea bargaining, and psychiatric therapy for offenders rarely have an objective basis and tend to be speculative.

The effectiveness of any practice may depend on complementary matters such as rules of evidence, issues of propriety, or the availability of resources and funds. Efficiency in operation is a variable in the measuring of effectiveness. The hard fact is that just so much public money will be spent on crime control. The precise amount varies with the nature and extent of the current problem, the public awareness of needs, the state of the economy, and numerous other factors. But, in general, there is a practical limit to resources that are likely to be available for crime control. Probably no metropolitan police department will ever have enough men and equipment to attend to all demands for help, to enforce all laws, and to meet all the vast and conflicting community expectations. Most prisons do not have enough psychiatrists, social workers, or other service personnel for concentrated individual therapy and probably never will. Few court systems are equipped to handle the number of jury trials that would result from all defendants suddenly demanding them.

In part, limitations on resources force agencies to be selective in processing. But these limitations create frustrations within agencies and professions in attempting to reconcile objectives with achievement. Such frustration can be used to rationalize shortcomings; thus police administrators often argue that more men and equipment would increase their effectiveness. Psychiatrists can point to high caseloads or lack of facilities for limited successes. However, agencies must get on with the job no matter how restricted their resources. Crimes are being committed, the criminal justice process continues to flow, and the various offices and agencies must continue their functions at a sufficient level to keep the processes moving. Money and staff shortages are indigenous to the system and the system has ways of accommodating. Efficiency is rarely an end in itself, for raw administrative efficiency is no measure of justice in a democratic society. But it is a very real consideration in the budgetary process and in day-to-day operations. Cost and efficiency often are employed to support arguments for changes in law or procedures and they cannot be ignored.

The need for efficiency is unlikely to be an acceptable formal argument in the courts, but it remains a factor that must be taken into account. Many police argue that no matter how high-sounding the recent Supreme Court decisions on such matters as search and in-custody interrogation, the Court is unreasonably "handcuffing" police operations. Likewise, a major argument in support of plea bargaining is that the practice must be maintained because of its obvious advantages in efficiency over the trial process. This same concern with efficiency forms part of the correctional opposition to changes that would allow inmates to have counsel at parole hearings or require probation revocation hearings to be held before trial courts. There is no consensus about how much weight, if any, should be given to efficiency of operation in these matters. Even though ofttimes not clearly articulated, it arises as a practical concern in most of the disputes relating to criminal justice administration.

Concern about efficiency arises in most agencies. A number of operational practices in law enforcement, in adjudication and sentencing, and in the correctional process are, in large part, products of accommodation of one agency to the limitations of resources or skills of another agency at a different point in the process. The activities of the police, the prosecutors, and the courts, for example, determine both the size and the characteristics of prison populations. The policies and programs of correctional institutions must adjust to any changes. And, fluctuations in prison populations are as likely to reflect changes in enforcement practices as in the level of offenses committed.

Enforcement practices also affect correctional programs. If a large police force were to decide on a rigorous arrest program for homosexual violations or narcotics offenses, and the arrests led to convictions and imprisonment, an adjustment of both the security and treatment programs in correctional institutions would be necessary. Techniques suitable for auto thieves or burglars are likely to be grossly inappropriate for drug users or homosexuals.

While there are shifts from time to time, the general staff and facility relationship among the various agencies remains remarkably in balance. Intake agencies recognize the limitations of correctional services and adjust to them, and correctional agencies let it be known in various ways what types of offender they can effectively handle and what types they wish diverted elsewhere. There are types for which prison is ineffective, others who cannot profit from probation, and those who are otherwise undesirable in correctional settings. The mentally ill, the sexually inverted, the pyromaniac, the retarded, the transvestite, the prostitute, the chronic inebriate, and assorted other deviates are very difficult to treat under the best of conditions and each creates problems of custody and care that tend to disrupt normal correctional practices. Correctional agencies may attempt to control institutional population by obtaining legislative restriction on the intake, by releasing short of maximum treatment, by informing other agencies of crowded conditions, or by presentence recommendations. Thus, the system operates in both directions to control correctional populations.[1]

A sort of homeostatic balance exists throughout the entire criminal justice system. The guilty plea and plea bargaining, the outside adjustment of family disputes, the diversion of the infirm and mentally ill, and the use of arrest power for purposes other than prosecution all serve to control the cases to be processed and to divert inappropriate and troublesome cases.

5. *Discretion.* Neither statutes nor other formal sources of law describe the way the criminal justice system actually operates in daily practice. Within the confines of substantive and procedural law and the resources available, the process operates by practices and policies that are largely discretionary, often to an extent not specifically delegated by legislation.

The contrast between the operational discretion of the system and the description obtained from legislation and decision—"law in action" versus "law in the book"—has long fascinated legal scholars and social scientists. Yet the fact that discretion is a major characteristic of the process has been treated circum-

[1] For a discussion of the nature and consequences of this type of system balance see Newman, *The Effect of Accommodations in Justice Administration on Criminal Statistics*, 46 Sociology & Social Research 144 (1962).

spectly by legislatures, by courts, by many scholars, and by the agencies of administration, as if the exercise of discretion were somehow improper.

There are, no doubt, good grounds for the general uneasiness that administrative discretion is so widespread. Most policies and practices of agencies are of low visibility compared to statutes and reported decisions. They may be discovered only by systematic and careful observation of actual operations. Discretion, implying selectivity and choices in asserting authority, inevitably generates apprehensions of misuse, discrimination, or corruption. The awesome power of the state to invoke the criminal process is of such vital concern to the democratic social order that certain ideals, like uniform and full enforcement of the law, have become slogans that seem inconsistent with discretionary authority. Although it is difficult to measure and control, discretion will in all likelihood continue to play a major part in criminal justice administration. Judge Jerome Frank once commented:

> . . . The very word "delegation," when now coupled with the words "administrative officers," strikes terror in [some] hearts. They resemble the child who was horrified when his attention was called to the facts that his tongue was wet and his shoes full of feet. For delegation is a name for something that has always been present in society and always will be. Perhaps the fright the label engenders can be reduced by observing that "discretion," which is familiar, is kin to "delegation." Almost boundless discretion has traditionally been conferred upon state and federal prosecuting officers to begin or not to begin proceedings of enforcement of some of the huge number of penal statutes (and against some rather than against other violators) and to "settle" such cases by "bargain day" methods. Wide, too, is the beneficent discretion of courts sitting in equity to relax stiff legal rules. And the power of courts in general to interpret statutes has been said by some persons to be, in practical effect, a sort of supplementary legislation which the legislature necessarily leaves to the courts.
>
> Indeed, those who today criticize the transfer of "subsidiary legislation" to administrative officers forget that, inspired by somewhat similar motives, there has been and still is much criticism of the power exercised by judges in construing statutes, that Bentham, Livingston, and their disciples (some even in our time) have insisted that all "law" must emanate solely from the legislature, and have tried, through codifica-

> tion, to destroy all "judicial legislation." Repeated attempts on the European continent to exploit that notion have invariably proved disappointing. Legal certainty to be attained by eliminating, via codification, all judicial law making is a fatuous dream.[j]

The legislature, in its discretion, states categories of crime, and defines criminal justice procedures, bound only by constitutional restrictions. It is, however, an equally important exercise of legislative discretion *not* to define certain conduct as criminal or to refrain from outlining procedures. This dual aspect of discretion, acting or refraining, applies to all agencies within the system. For example, police agencies or individual officers must decide which of the many criminal statutes require vigorous enforcement efforts, where to concentrate efforts, and the severity of steps to be taken. There is nothing automatic about law enforcement. Even the most mechanized devices, *e.g.*, parking meters, involve policy decisions, such as how often they are to be checked, by whom, and with what results. The same holds for the other participating agencies since all must work out policies and practices and develop, by drift if not otherwise, methods of operation. A grant of certiorari and revocation of a parole have common roots in the discretionary model of the criminal justice system.

Discretion in the operation of the system ordinarily takes one of two forms: (1) a decision that conduct, although criminally proscribed, should not be proceeded against, or (2) a decision that conduct should be processed with less than maximum or customary severity. Furthermore, it has at least two different levels of operation: (1) agency policy as stated by the chief officials, and (2) decisions by agency personnel, whether consistent with agency policy or independent of any policy. Thus, a prosecuting attorney may have a policy of not prosecuting bad check cases where restitution is made, a discretionary decision of the first type. An assistant in the prosecutor's office may, in the absence of office policy, decide not to prosecute a particular shoplifting case, thus invoking a discretionary decision of the second type.

Generally speaking, discretion in both forms and at both levels exists for a number of reasons. (1) It is expressly delegated by the legislature as the best way to handle a certain problem, *e.g.*, the decision to parole is delegated to correctional authorities. This may be done because a certain agency is particularly qualified to make such decisions or simply because a legislature is unable or

---

[j] Guiseppi v. Walling, 144 F.2d 608, 620 (2d Cir. 1944).

unwilling to undertake the task of spelling out specifics of operation. (2) Discretion may be required of an agency through inadvertence or deliberate vagueness of statute (as in laws forbidding gambling, disorderly conduct, and vagrancy), or by budgetary restrictions which limit agency resources. Legislation defining criminal conduct merely states a moral standard in the absence of enforcement. When the legislature fails to implement its proscription, such as by failing to make adequate appropriation for enforcement, the enforcement agencies may fairly infer that the moral proclamation satisfies legislative purposes and that full, vigorous enforcement is neither intended nor desired. (3) Agencies themselves must inevitably make discretionary decisions in allocating manpower and other resources. No police agency can fully enforce all laws, no prosecutor or court system can try all cases which might be brought, and no prison system can hold all persons who could be convicted. Each of the agencies must make decisions about where the effort is to be placed. (4) Still another reason for discretion is the desire of agency personnel to be "just." The exercise of discretion on this basis rests most commonly on a desire for equity, for individualization of treatment that often is not provided in statutes and is unrecognized in the full enforcement concept. Laws making certain behavior criminal and statutes and rules providing for enforcement are necessarily general, commonly focusing on gross categories of conduct, not on persons or their motives. There are some statutory provisions for mitigating circumstances in certain crimes and there are statutory definitions that permit defenses based on the capacity of the perpetrator, such as age and mental condition. But these too are necessarily general and sometimes abstract, usually not detailed enough to permit enforcement agencies to distinguish among the variety of persons and circumstances. The agencies of criminal justice do not deal with law in abstract, but with individuals. They must fit the law to men; they must make the general specific and the theoretical operational. Full, maximum implementation of law, uniformly and equally against all who fall into the enforcement net, would be, as Breitel says, "intolerable."[k] It would achieve a kind of paper equality, a statistical display of uniformity that ignores the greater inequality of treating unlike phenomena the same. A teenager who sells a marihuana cigarette to a friend and a professional "pusher" of heroin who sells to schoolchildren are both guilty of sale of narcotics and could receive the lengthy mandatory prison sentence provided in many

[k] Breitel, *Controls in Criminal Law Enforcement,* 27 U. CHI. L. REV. 427 (1960); *see also* T. ARNOLD, THE SYMBOLS OF GOVERNMENT (1935).

jurisdictions. Most criminal justice agencies recognize the inequity of uniform processing of like charges and commonly attempt, through the exercise of discretion, to achieve some sort of rough balance of conduct, circumstances, and consequences in making their decisions. This may be highly controversial, for the limits between distinctions based on individualized treatment and distinctions based on race or social class bias are not always clear and may be viewed differently by the one in authority and the one being subjected to the decision. (5) Still another reason for the exercise of agency discretion is the maintenance of an efficient and effective balance in the operation of the entire system. In some cases agencies bargain with offenders to achieve broader enforcement objectives. Police, for example, commonly grant at least partial immunity to informers in certain vice operations. Prosecutors and judges may do the same for certain state witnesses. In other cases an agency accommodates its activities to the desires or demands of other agencies. The police may not proceed rigorously against certain types of offenders simply because other agencies do not want to process them. Prosecutors and trial courts, for example, commonly do not want to try minor assaults caused by family disputes, because the evidence tends to "wash out" before prosecution and the great number of such cases would seriously clog court calendars. Full prosecution would produce limited results. Some types of behavior are virtually untreatable by any current correctional technique, and workers in the system would prefer to avoid dealing with them. Few social workers would welcome a caseload of chronic inebriates or street-walking prostitutes, and it would be an unusual warden who would uncomplainingly receive weekly busloads of homosexuals. Thus, discretion may be a product of an inability to achieve long-range goals because of inadequate resources or techniques.

The reality of discretionary decision-making is evident throughout, forming a major, pervasive theme of operation. It is by no means always sub-rosa, for it is delegated at points and recognized or encouraged at others.

There is ordinarily no sweeping delegation of discretion to police departments, and police are not supposed, formally, to select among laws to be enforced. Nonetheless, a denial of such discretion would be both unrealistic and undesirable. However, the expectations are such that police officials are obliged to be careful and as noncommittal as possible in explaining or justifying even the most necessary and sensible discretionary use of manpower or formulation of enforcement policies. The very next step in the process, the charging function, rests, however, on a long-standing tradition of discretion.[l] The prosecutor's discretion has been recognized over a long period even in the absence of express delegation. It has generally been considered to be a desirable, humanizing element in criminal justice. Also, the grand jury has the uncontested authority to return an indictment or not, but the magistrate or trial judge is expected to weigh the evidence and to find the facts, unconcerned with whether a particular defendant or class should or should not be the subject of special consideration. The determination of guilt at trial is presumed to rest solely on the quantity and quality of evidence. However, both the judge and jury have power to acquit the guilty even though there is no generally recognized discretionary authority to do so. At sentencing the trial judges are normally given wide discretion on whether to imprison, and on the length of the term. Judicial discretion may be denied in certain situations and for certain crimes where there are legislative controls. Generally, however, the judicial function is neatly divided in regard to discretion, with none granted in the adjudicatory functions but a great deal allowed at sentencing. Correctional decisions almost always rest on broadly delegated discretionary choices with certain legislatively imposed outer limits. Thus, the criminal justice process, in its formal structure, arrays discretionary and nondiscretionary determinations in an alternating pattern over the whole structure.

Some of the most critical current issues in criminal justice administration concern discretion. Many of these issues, interestingly enough, raise questions posed in earlier parts of this overview. Are there articulated general criteria, distinct from case-to-case decisions, upon which to base parole decisions? Should there be? Is selective nonenforcement fair under any circumstances? What are proper criteria for decisions not to arrest where evidence permits? What criteria are improper? What is the effect of plea bargaining practice on those who are ignorant of the practice or who fail to employ it properly? These are but a few of the issues currently important on the issue of discretion. There are still others which relate to the nature of controls on discretion. For example, there is the question of whether and under what conditions appellate courts can review discretionary decisions. Would such review be effective? Should discretionary practices be formalized into policy or should they be left to individual judgment? If developed into policy, who should develop the policies? The latter is particularly important in correctional

---

l *See, e.g.,* Baker, *The Prosecutor—Initiation of Prosecution,* 23 J. CRIM. L. & C. 770 (1933).

agencies since some officers think that professional expertise based on education and training is involved and that professional norms cannot be subordinated to agency restrictions. Also, there are important unresolved questions relating to the consequences of discretion and the consequences of full enforcement.

Since discretion involves inaction or the grant of a leniency there are fewer complaints from those directly involved than where full enforcement has occurred. There may be some complaints based on failure to obtain a privilege or on irregular procedure but these complaints are often ineffective. Consequently there are fewer appellate decisions and less scholarly writing on discretion and in this sense discretion is less obvious, but it is no less important as a concept because it has been discussed less.

Controls on the Criminal Justice Process

The various perspectives we have discussed act, in concert, to control and balance the system, to curb unfettered application of criminal sanctions, to contain crime control efforts within bounds set by democratic ideology, and yet to allow the process to operate. In many complex organizations—corporations, or military establishments for example—sources of authority are centralized and have channels of application even though they may have diverse functions and tolerate a large amount of autonomy at lower levels. Ultimately, however, broad objectives and policies are determined at a single source, and while they may become modified as they are put into practice, the line-staff relationship is clear. Criminal justice administration does not fit this pattern. There is no model agreed upon which applies to all locations and communities. Administration in a rural sheriff's enclave has significantly different aspects than the systems which operate in our larger metropolitan areas. Even so, there is a perennial question of the authoritative relationship among legislative bodies, courts, and enforcement agencies, unrelated to size or geography. This issue is illustrated by the difficulties encountered in trying to define the limits of decision-making authority of any agency head, such as a police chief. To whom is the chief responsible? Who determines policies in regard to such matters as the use of force? Who reviews police practices in this regard? In determining what the policy will be, the police chief has competing pressures that both urge the application and the curtailment of the use of force in such instances as fleeing criminals or widespread looting. There are, for example, legislative curbs on the use of extreme forms of force along with appellate court interpretations which further limit the conditions where it may properly be applied. On the other hand, the mayor of the city or the police or fire commission may order the police to use force under conditions incompatible with legislation or court decrees. Local courts and civilian review boards, where the latter exist, may exert different pressures or issue other commands. The police chief, therefore, may find it necessary to balance a number of conflicting sources of command and restriction or choose to ignore all of them and make his decision within his ambit of autonomy. If he follows the orders of local political authorities he may find himself censured or restricted by the courts. If he resists local demands, basing his actions on an obligation to legislative or Supreme Court directives, he may find himself removed from office. These same dimensions of guidance and control apply to all participants in the system. Legislative bodies and trial courts, for example, are subject to review by appellate courts and usually to ultimate control by the electorate.[m]

Imposing control on the criminal justice system is currently one of the most controversial issues in efforts to reduce crime. There has been an historical shift in the relative roles played by legislatures, reviewing courts, and the agencies in determining policies and practices.[n] There is today some attempt on the part of legislatures to restrict agency autonomy by spelling out criteria and procedures for making major decisions in greater detail. The Crime Control Act of 1968 is a prime example of legislative leadership in this matter.

By far the greater historical change has been the increased intervention of appellate courts, particularly the United States Supreme Court, in the operational functions of all agencies. In the past, appellate courts rarely intervened in law enforcement or correctional processes, and, then, usually by way of exclusion of physical evidence or confessions. This was essentially guidance by negation and control by indirection. By reversing a conviction the courts would inform the agencies of improper practices but there was little or no attempt to tell the agencies what they could properly do to achieve enforcement objectives. There

---

[m] For an analysis of factors involved in the conflict between community pressures and professional demands emanating from the larger society, see Gouldner, *Cosmopolitans and Locals: Toward an Analysis of Latent Social Roles,* 1 ADMIN. Q. 281-306 (Dec. 1967).

[n] In the recently enacted Crime Control Act, Congress clearly tries to play a more active role in determining law enforcement policies. Title I deals in a relatively common way with an effort to influence state and local practices by the granting of federal funds. Titles II and III try to either repeal or modify some well known United States Supreme Court cases, like *Mallory, Miranda,* and *Wade.* Whether Congress will be successful in this effort remains to be seen.

is some evidence that courts are becoming increasingly specific in spelling out proper operational procedures for agencies. The *Miranda* decision regarding preinterrogation warnings is a case in point as are other recent cases relating to procedural requirements in accepting guilty pleas and at sentencing.

On the whole, court control of agency practices is still one of indirection. Courts do not formulate or pass on total agency policies, nor are they responsible for staffing agencies or reviewing budgets. *Miranda* and other decisions aside, the technique of control is still largely one of exclusion and reversal, on a case-by-case basis, though there has been a major change in frequency and scope of intervention. The effectiveness of this control of the criminal justice process by the courts is still open to speculation and conjecture.[o]

One major effect of appellate court intervention in the process has been the expansion of the right of suspects and defendants to have assistance of counsel at other critical stages as well as at trial. The result is a form of system control of a somewhat different nature than the exclusionary rules. Requiring that counsel shall be afforded at pretrial stages, at trial, at appeal, at sentencing, during some correctional proceedings, and in the juvenile justice system has a potentially profound effect on the system, particularly in making it more adversary and its processes more visible. There is an equally significant effect on the legal profession, which is finding that it is committed on an increasingly broader basis to a long-neglected field of practice. The potential is for change in the social and economic fabric of our society as the poor, who make up the bulk of criminal defendants, find that they may now make their needs known and may challenge law enforcement and penal practices which affect a large portion of the poor.

In contrast to the situation of as recent as ten years ago, widespread interest in crime control on the part of the public, researchers, the courts, and legislatures, points to some major changes in the criminal justice system. There has been a general shift of focus from theoretical to operational concerns. What is actually taking place in the system is more clearly relevant today than it has been in the past. The operational criminal justice system is becoming more visible. There is a great deal of interest on the part of legislatures, courts, and the agencies

[o] In Terry v. Ohio, 392 U.S. 1 (1968), the Supreme Court, for the first time, expressly acknowledges the practical limitations upon the ability of judicial review (through the exclusionary rule) to control police practice, especially those practices involving police and the citizen where police do not have arrest, prosecution, and conviction as an objective.

themselves in the articulation of policies and practices and the formulation of procedures to conform with standards of due process. There is a major attempt to balance the relative tactical strengths of the state and the accused, particularly the indigent accused, at various stages in the process—by the appointment of counsel, by discovery and disclosure, and by emphasis on formal record-making and review of decisions. These changes toward visibility, balance, and control have been rapid and uneven, causing both consternation and controversy among those responsible for administering the system. Every change has had an impact on all other parts of the system.

The criminal justice system is currently confronting enforcement and control problems of scope and intensity never before experienced. The recurrence of political assassinations, widespread civil disobedience, ghetto riots, and student uprisings present dramatic challenges to legislatures, enforcement agencies, courts, and correctional institutions. The analysis of criminal justice administration can be no more static than the system itself; it is necessary to look at the system as it is being reshaped rather than as it is at any one instant.

PART II

THE SYSTEM FOR ADMINISTERING CRIMINAL JUSTICE

This part of the volume considers the normal sequence of steps in the criminal justice system, including the detection and information gathering activities, which are particularly the province of the police; the decision to prosecute and the negotiation for plea of guilty, which are particularly the responsibility of the prosecutor; the conduct of trials, the assessment of penalties, and review of convictions, which involve significantly the judiciary; and the administration of penal institutions and supervision of probationers and parolees by the correctional agency. This is done with several objectives in mind:

1. To gain an understanding of current practice (as opposed to the idealized operation embodied in statutes and frequently described in texts) and the important relationships between the stages of the criminal justice process.

2. To consider the adequacy of the criminal justice system as a means for dealing with the problem of crime.

3. To explore some of the means by which the system seeks to maintain the effectiveness of its fact-finding processes, particularly for discriminating between the innocent and the guilty through a commitment to adversary process.

4. To examine the attempts made to preserve the interests of individuals in freedom from unnecessary interference with person and property, freedom from invasions of privacy, freedom from attacks on free choice, and freedom from discrimination based on impermissible grounds such as race or wealth, without sacrificing unnecessarily the competing values of community security and morality and the instrumental value of police efficiency.

5. To understand administrative decision-making and the regulation of the administrative agencies which operate the

criminal justice system and the professions—police, lawyer, and social worker—who staff those agencies.

Stages in the Administration of Criminal Justice

A preliminary orientation to the steps in a typical system for enforcing criminal law will be offered in the next few pages, sketching briefly the sequence of events and suggesting some of the important problems currently being considered.

In response to a complaint from a victim of crime, or in fulfilling their responsibility as the community agency for suppressing criminal activity (such as gambling or prostitution) where there is no complainant, the police and other law enforcement organizations undertake to make an investigation. They often seek by the use of surveillance, informers, analysis of physical evidence left at the scene of a crime, and other detection devices to identify the perpetrator of a crime and to construct a case against the offender. Typically the first official action involving the suspect himself is his arrest, which may be lawfully made when police have "reasonable grounds" to believe he has committed a crime.

The statutes ordinarily call for the officer to take a person he has arrested promptly to a magistrate. In practice this means the next morning for most cases, though sometimes there is delay to permit a process of further investigation to be carried on. The collected evidence in the case then becomes the basis for a police decision whether to prosecute; in many jurisdictions the police will take the evidence to the prosecuting attorney who decides whether to charge the arrested person and, if so, for what offenses. The decision to charge is ordinarily evidenced by a formal complaint sworn to by the police officer or the victim and in some instances by the magistrate's issuance of an arrest warrant (even though the person is already in custody). The warrant is issued in theory after the magistrate considers the evidence but in practice it is often issued routinely by a clerk in reliance on the prosecutor's approval of the complaint and warrant.

Sometimes the victim of a crime comes directly to the prosecutor rather than to the police. This is likely to occur in the event of nonsupport, bad checks, and other nonviolent property crimes. The complainant's motive often is to force the offender to make payment or restitution, and the prosecutor serves to some degree as an arbitrator if he is willing to consider the case at all. Prosecution is likely to be viewed as a last resort. Similarly, some family disputes, like a husband's assaulting his wife, may be handled informally. The police or prosecutor may warn the husband or place him under a "peace bond"—with or without sanction in law. Prosecution follows only after efforts at pacification or compromise have failed.

If prosecution has been decided upon, the prisoner is taken before a magistrate where he is informed of the charge against him, apprised of his right to obtain an attorney (at public expense if he is indigent), notified of the conditions under which he may be released, and asked whether he wishes a preliminary examination. The purpose of the preliminary examination is to determine whether there is sufficient evidence of guilt to justify holding the accused for trial. Since the prosecution rarely fails at this stage the accused frequently waives his right to a preliminary examination unless his attorney desires to use the preliminary examination for discovery purposes. (Since the prosecutor must offer sufficient evidence to establish probable cause to believe in the prisoner's guilt, the defendant can learn a substantial amount about the case against him.)

If the suspect is held for further proceedings, the prosecutor will file a formal accusation called an information, or a grand jury will consider the evidence and return a formal accusation called an indictment. The indictment may be returned before the preliminary examination is held, making the preliminary examination unnecessary. The grand jury hearing is secret and therefore often preferred by a prosecutor who is reluctant to expose his case before trial.

The defendant is then called before the court to plead to the information or indictment. If he pleads guilty, the judge will usually inquire further to assure himself of the voluntariness and truthfulness of the plea and then enter a judgment of conviction. If the defendant pleads not guilty a time will be set for trial by a jury, or by the judge if the defendant prefers.

If the defendant is convicted either on his guilty plea or after trial, the judge will set a time for sentence. Statutes control the choices which the judge has, but he usually has freedom to impose a fine, place the offender on probation, or send him to prison. In deciding upon the appropriate sentence the judge can rely upon whatever information about the offender he has acquired during hearings and trial, upon a formal presentence report prepared for the court's use by social workers or other investigators, and upon specialized reports the judge has ordered made—particularly any psychiatric diagnosis of the offender. If the defendant has pleaded guilty and the judge has not at that time inquired about the circumstances of the crime, the presentence report may also concern itself with whether the person is in fact guilty and with the circumstances of aggravation or mitigation as well as with his personality and social history.

The choice between probation and imprisonment is the most significant, since on the one hand it exposes the community to the risk of new violations of law, but on the other hand it avoids heavy expense to the community while permitting the offender to retain his job and ties with family. Probation is often more conducive to rehabilitation than a period of imprisonment would be. If allowed to remain on probation the offender is subject to the supervision of a probation officer who can encourage the offender to comply with conditions the court has imposed and who can also recommend revocation of probation in the event the probationer fails to live up to the conditions. The revocation decision is sometimes made by the court upon recommendation of the probation officer, or may be entrusted wholly to the administrators of the probation system.

If an offender is sentenced to imprisonment, his release will come either at the end of the term set by the judge or legislature or when paroled by the parole board. Only rarely does the legislature set an exact prison term for an offense without possibility of parole. There are various combinations of maximum and minimum terms to be determined by legislature, court, or correctional agency. The parole decision, like the probation decision, requires a balancing of the risk to the community which will result from release, against the cost, hardship, and possible detriment to rehabilitation of continued incarceration. Like probation, parole subjects the parolee to compliance with conditions and to supervision by a parole agent. Violation of parole conditions may result in the revocation of parole by the correctional administration and the return of the parolee to prison.

Reference Note

A. AMSTERDAM, B. SEGAL & M. MILLER, TRIAL MANUAL FOR THE DEFENSE OF CRIMINAL CASES (1967), summarizes the system through the trial stage at pages 2-3 to 2-13.

See also Miller & Remington, *Procedures Before Trial,* 339 ANNALS 111 (1962).

The importance of interrelationships among the various stages is emphasized in Blumstein, *Systems Analysis and the Criminal Justice System,* 374 ANNALS 92 (1967).

A valuable description of the system of criminal justice and some of its major problems is found in a report by THE PRESI-

DENT'S COMMISSION ON LAW ENFORCEMENT AND ADMINISTRATION OF JUSTICE: THE CHALLENGE OF CRIME IN A FREE SOCIETY 7-12 (1967). A schematic representation of the system is found at 8-9, and reproduced on the following pages.

A general view of The Criminal Justice System

This chart seeks to present a simple yet comprehensive view of the movement of cases throug[h] criminal justice system. Procedures in individual jurisdictions may vary from the pattern shown [i] The differing weights of line indicate the relative volumes of cases disposed of at various points i[n] system, but this is only suggestive since no nationwide data of this sort exists.

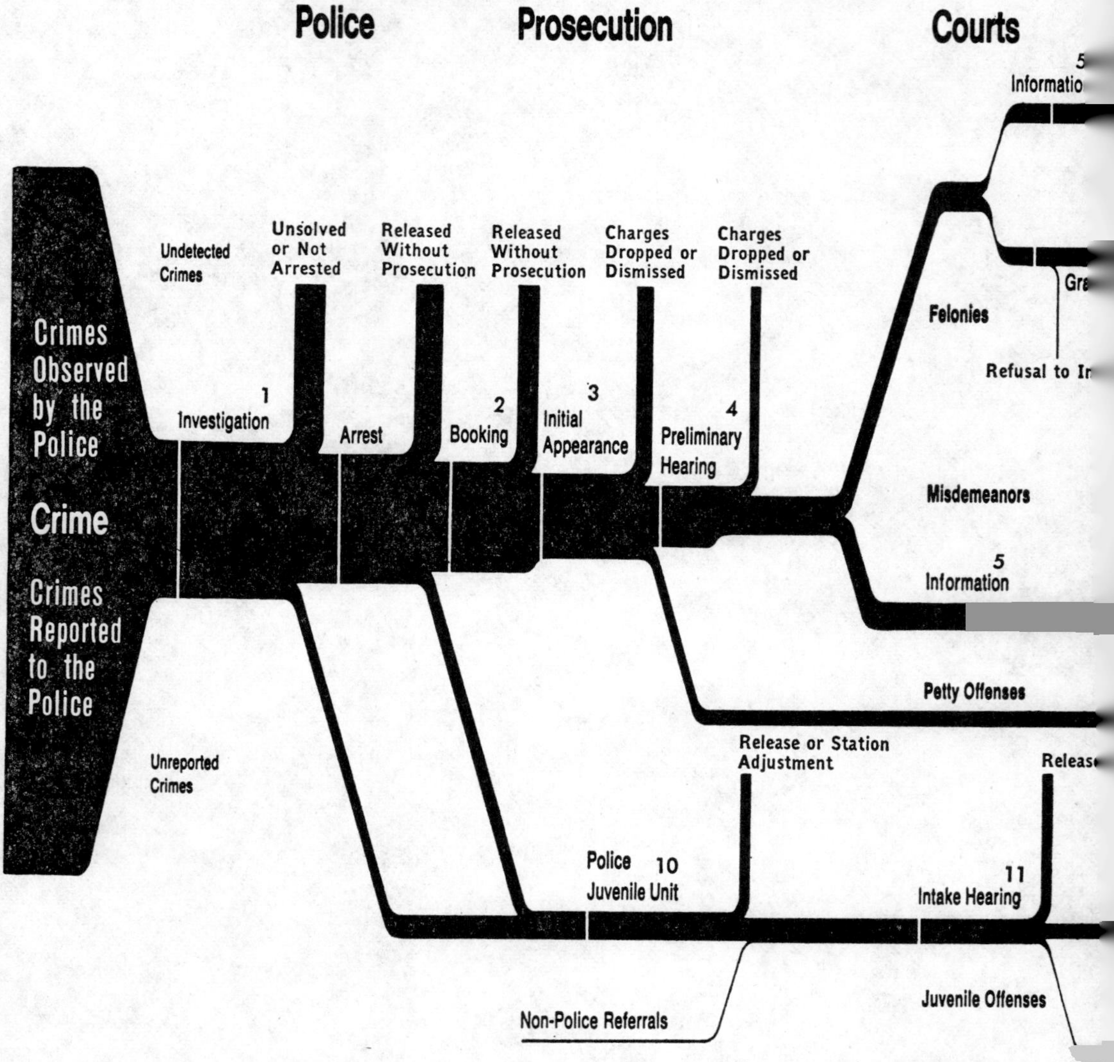

1 May continue until trial.

2 Administrative record of arrest. First step at which temporary release on bail may be available.

3 Before magistrate, commissioner, or justice of peace. Formal notice of charge, advice of rights. Bail set. Summary trials for petty offenses usually conducted here without further processing.

4 Preliminary testing of evidence against defendant. Charge may be reduced. No separate preliminary hearing for misdemeanors in some systems.

5 Charge filed by prosecutor on basis of informati[on] submitted by police or citizens. Alternative to gran[d] jury indictment; often used in felonies, almost alwa[ys] in misdemeanors.

6 Reviews whether Government evidence sufficient [to] justify trial. Some States have no grand jury system[;] others seldom use it.

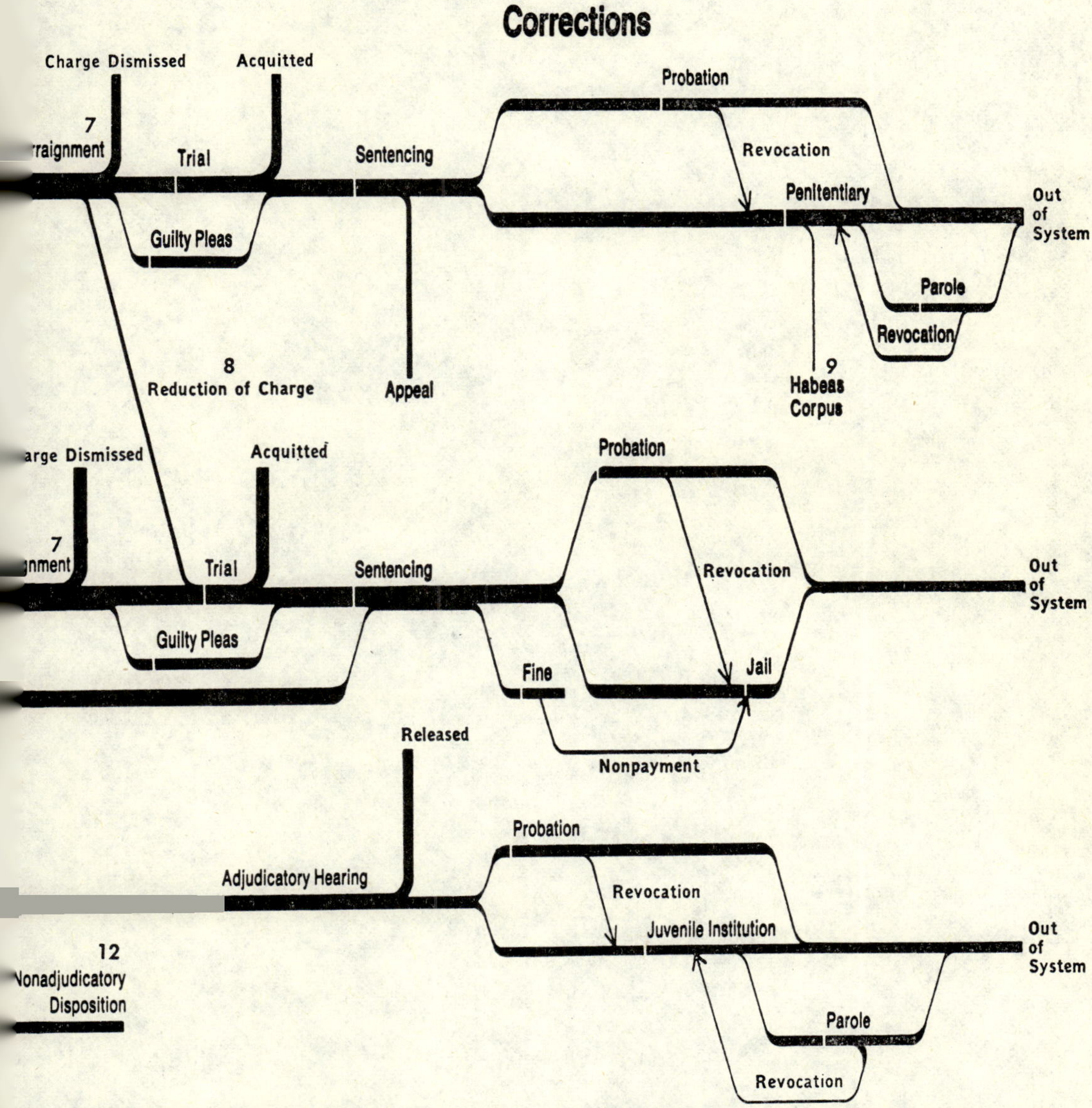

7 Appearance for plea; defendant elects trial by judge or jury (if available); counsel for indigent usually appointed here in felonies. Often not at all in other cases.

8 Charge may be reduced at any time prior to trial in return for plea of guilty or for other reasons.

9 Challenge on constitutional grounds to legality of detention. May be sought at any point in process.

10 Police often hold informal hearings, dismiss or adjust many cases without further processing.

11 Probation officer decides desirability of further court action.

12 Welfare agency, social services, counselling, medical care, etc., for cases where adjudicatory handling not needed.

Chapter 2

INSTITUTION OF INVESTIGATION

The police are the frontline agency, charged with principal responsibility for deciding whether to invoke the criminal justice process. This decision depends upon the information which police have and their judgment as to the appropriate course of action based on that information.

The information upon which police decide whether to invoke the process comes to them in various ways. Frequently police witness a crime themselves and further investigation is unnecessary before deciding whether to arrest. In other situations a complainant asserts to the police that a crime has been committed. Police must decide whether the complaint has enough merit to warrant investigating further. But for many crimes, such as the consensual offenses of narcotics sale, gambling, and prostitution, complaints are rare and police do not usually observe the offenses in their routine patrol. If these criminal laws are to be enforced the police must make affirmative efforts to ferret out the crimes.

The decision as to whether to investigate is an important exercise of discretionary power. The decision to do nothing—not to investigate at all—may be as significant as the decision to investigate intensively.

In deciding whether to investigate a reported crime or to undertake an investigation of criminal activity, like prostitution, which is often not reported, the police are influenced by a number of factors:

1. Available resources. Police do more than investigate crime. They are also called upon to render a wide variety of services ranging from ambulance services to mediating family disturbances.[a] The police administrator must, by design or default, establish priorities in the use of limited resources.

---

[a] For example, in Chicago as many as 120 police are occupied in disposing of up to 50,000 abandoned automobiles each year.

2. *Seriousness of the offense.* Especially where volume is great, police may view some offenses, like theft of hubcaps, as so minor as not to call for a serious police response.

3. *Reputation and status of the victim.* In some cases police assume that the victim will not follow through and cooperate in a prosecution. This is often true, for example, where a wife complains against her husband. In other situations, some police may conclude that the offense is not serious because the victim comes from a race or economic group which "expects" or tolerates the conduct. It is usually true that the police response to a complaint may depend upon the police assessment of the victim's status and the likelihood that the victim will cooperate with the prosecution. Typically these attitudes develop over time and constitute informal, rather than formal, departmental policy.

4. *Pressure from groups in the community.* Police, like other public officers, are responsive to pressures from individuals or groups within the community who possess "power." This is not to say that such influence is improper. But, newspaper or other expression may cause police to give more attention to the investigation of certain kinds of criminal conduct than they would otherwise do. A fundamental and difficult question is the extent to which police decisions to investigate are properly influenced by community attitude rather than professional police judgment about law enforcement priorities. Minority groups may complain that majority concern with "crime on our streets" gets reflected in inappropriate levels and methods of enforcement in their areas.

5. *Potential for solution by the criminal process.* Police are more likely to investigate if they feel that investigation will achieve a meaningful objective. For example, investigation of a seriously assaultive offense probably will, if successful, result in conviction and incarceration and thus protection of the community. On the other hand, investigation of prostitution, even if successful in producing evidence of crime, may not result in a conviction and, if there is conviction, the sentence may be only a small money fine, which can be absorbed as a "cost of doing business." It may be hard for a police administrator to justify the expenditure of resources which produce little gain for law enforcement.

6. *Concern for negative impact of enforcement.* In recent years police-community relations have been such that a police

investigation in a ghetto area, though properly conducted, may precipitate widespread disorder. This fact has affected the level of investigation in sections of a city where the risk of widespread disorder is thought to be high.

Although it has not commonly been viewed as such, it seems apparent that the decision of the police as to whether to investigate is a very important administrative decision involving the exercise of governmental power.

Particularly when the police decide to do nothing, the decision is invisible and commonly not subject to review by an agency outside the police department. Nor have police themselves traditionally reexamined departmental policies relating to investigative practices. Rather the policies have developed over time, have remained largely informal, and have been reevaluated only on occasions of crisis when public alarm or concern compels examination of the policy in question.

The exercise of discretionary power by police in deciding whether to investigate gives rise to a number of fundamental questions which are relevant also to some other decisions which take place later in the criminal justice process. Among these are: What administrative criteria should control the decision whether to investigate? Should these be made public and subject to discussion and debate? Would it be feasible and desirable for the legislature to establish priorities when it enacts a substantive criminal code? (Commonly the legislature enacts many more criminal statutes than can possibly be fully enforced but does not indicate which crimes are to have priority in enforcement.) Should there be an opportunity for judicial review of the decision to investigate or not to investigate? Is it the responsibility of the mayor or city manager to review investigation decisions or would this be unwise political influence into the affairs of police? (In New York City Mayor John Lindsay has said that he has responsibility for police policies, a position which has traditionally been viewed by members of the New York Police Department as political interference.)[b]

---

[b] For an examination of the responsibility for policymaking in criminal justice administration, see Part IV. There is increasing interest in such issues as whether responsibility ought to be vested in the mayor, or in a police commission, or in the chief of police himself. Commonly no agency acknowledges the importance of investigative policy and thus no agency assumes responsibility for such policies as exist. This has often resulted in a deep sense of frustration in ghetto communities where there may be dissatisfaction with some investigative policies but there is no governmental agency willing to discuss the practices, acknowledge their existence, or consider changing them. *See* REPORT OF THE NATIONAL ADVISORY COMMISSION ON CIVIL DISORDERS, Chapter XI—The Police and the Community, especially at 164-66.

Although attention has been given to some law enforcement practices, such as in-custody interrogation, there has been remarkably little attention given to other aspects of law enforcement like the decision as to whether to investigate, particularly when the decision is to do nothing. This kind of issue has led a leading authority on administrative law to ask, "Has fear of bureaucracy overemphasized excessive zeal and underemphasized administrative arteriosclerosis?"[c] Police administrators have commonly reacted to the problem by asserting that the answer lies in recruiting "aggressive" individuals as police officers. Their aggressiveness, which serves as a check on their doing nothing, may create other problems dealt with later in these materials.

A. INVESTIGATION IN RESPONSE TO COMPLAINTS

A large share of police investigations are instituted as a result of citizen complaints concerning crimes committed against the citizen or crimes which the citizen has witnessed. For the most part, absent reason to doubt the credibility of the informant, the police proceed in routine fashion to investigate. There may be circumstances, however, in which the police feel it undesirable even to commence an investigation.

The Practice

The following illustrate various fairly typical reactions of police to complaints:

1

The dispatcher received a call late at night from a householder in a residential neighborhood that someone had just attempted to break into the home but had been frightened off. The dispatcher sent a patrol car immediately.

2

A mentally retarded man informed the police of the existence in a particular apartment of a "blind pig" (an unlicensed bar, usually operated in a home). The officers decided to investigate.

An argument that some other agency should guide police as to which offenses should be actively sought out and which should be investigated only upon specific complaint appears in J. Goldstein, *Police Discretion Not to Invoke the Criminal Process: Low-Visibility Decisions in the Administration of Justice,* 69 YALE L.J. 543 (1960).

[c] *See* K. DAVIS, ADMINISTRATIVE LAW 50-51 (1965).

3

A woman complained to the police that her former handyman had stolen some jacks from under her house trailer. The officer recalled that on a previous occasion the woman had complained about this man stealing gas, but that the case had been nolle prossed for lack of evidence. The officer felt that the woman was fabricating these stories because she held a grudge against the man. He refused to pursue the matter.

4

A well-spoken man came to the police station to complain that his mail was being tampered with and that he had complained to postal officials without result. He stated that he was sure a large check had been mailed to him but that he had never received it. The check was for sixty-three million dollars. The policeman to whom he was speaking assured him that the matter would be investigated by the "I" (for Invisible) Squad.

5

Upon receiving a complaint that children in a slum neighborhood were violating city ordinances by climbing over the fence of a playground after it was locked for the night in order to play there, the police commander refused to assign anyone to look into the matter, commenting that, even if it were true, the children were better off there than in the street.

6

In a routine response to a call for service, a squad found a woman who complained that her boyfriend had stolen five dollars from her. They asked for information about the boyfriend but, because of the small amount involved, made no strenuous effort to locate him.

B. NONCOMPLAINT INVESTIGATIONS

Police do not simply wait for a citizen complaint. They often initiate investigations themselves. Patrol activities are designed to find and investigate suspicious circumstances in order to prevent crime or to detect crime even before the victim is aware (for example, of a burglary).

With respect to many offenses there is no complainant, either because there is no victim in the usual sense (particularly in vice crimes like gambling, prostitution, trafficking in narcotics) or because the victims are unaware of the specific harm done them (as in some business frauds or tax evasion).

Investigation may be instituted on a random basis in an effort by law enforcement agencies to deter violations of the law. Examples of this are the auditing of a certain portion of tax returns and the close inspection of some luggage at customs. Or investigation may be directed against places and individuals or classes of persons who seem especially likely to be involved in some crime, past or future, without any specific act in mind. Or investigation may be employed as a means of harassment, or as the result of bias against a person or group of persons.

Police obviously have limited resources available to them for the seeking out of unknown offenses and offenders, and the clamor for solution of notorious crimes and for responding to specific citizen complaints serves to draw attention away from other investigations. But law enforcement agencies do undertake major investigative efforts to disclose crime and amass evidence for prosecution of offenders. In doing so they respond to various pressures—local and national interest groups like a merchants' association or the American Social Health Association or political organizations, demands by mass communications media, invocation of professional standards and notions of fairness. The priorities which police establish and the intensity with which investigations are carried on result both from such pressures and from the importance which police attach to the conduct being investigated. The seriousness of the conduct is likely to be measured not only by the harm intrinsic in the conduct, but also by other activities associated with it. Prostitution, for example, is a matter of police concern because prostitutes frequently connive in the robbery of their customers (who are reluctant to complain), because prostitution is often a source of income for organized crime, because open prostitution offends public sensibilities, and because promiscuity spreads venereal disease. Police concern over liquor law violations undoubtedly reflects the fact that such violations are widely visible and that the competitive situation is such that all sellers must be made to conform to the law or none will.

To the present there is no developed body of law controlling the commencement of a criminal investigation, no recognized legal requirement that there must be some basis for suspicion before an investigation may be undertaken. There are nonetheless some stirrings in this area—some uneasiness on the part of courts, some complaint on the part of citizens who think investigations arbitrary or improperly motivated.

The Practice

The first five of the following illustrate routine investigative practices.

1

Police on patrol at night saw a car, with its motor idling and a trailer attached, pulled up beside a plumbing shop. They stopped and cautiously entered the shop. They found a man inside with tools in his hands. The man succeeded in establishing that he worked in the shop and was merely returning some equipment.

2

Three vice bureau officers, as part of their assignment to police establishments licensed to sell intoxicants, checked several bars, looking particularly for minors having liquor in their possession. Two of the officers spent some time in one of the bars while the sergeant walked from bar to bar along the avenue. At each establishment, the sergeant entered and looked around. He explained that each crew of inspectors would check at least three licensed premises in the course of an evening.

3

In the evening, traffic control officers set up a roadblock on the highway and stopped all cars going south. They asked each driver to produce his license, then waved him on. They were looking for drivers with revoked or suspended licenses.

4

The police suspected that prostitutes were operating on a certain street corner. Late at night, a police officer who was dressed in civilian clothes and driving an unmarked car stopped his automobile at the corner when he saw a woman standing alone there. She approached his car, opened the door, got in, and said, "Well?" The officer repeated her question, "Well?" She then asked, "Are you looking for a woman?" After further conversation she set a price and the officer arrested her for soliciting.

5

A newspaper editorial pointed out that the law against sale of cigarettes to minors under eighteen was not being enforced and criticized the police for failing to arrest for open violations of the law. The police chief assigned an officer to talk with school officials about the problem and learn where the cigarettes were being obtained by the schoolboys.

6

A notorious gangland figure, believed responsible for several recent gangland murders, openly expressed his contempt for the police. Feeling under considerable public pressure to take some action against him, and frustrated in their efforts to acquire adequate evidence of his role in organized crime, the police considered other possible bases for prosecution. Knowing that he had a felony record and that it was a violation of election laws for such a person to vote, the police examined election records and were able to establish that he had in fact voted in the last election. They arrested him for fraudulent voting.[d]

WHAT PRICE CONVICTION

By Malcolm Anderson, Assistant Attorney General of the United States in charge of the Criminal Division
1958 Proceedings, A.B.A. Section of Criminal Law 42

. . . [W]e are attacking the question of organized crime in a new way. . . . What we need to fight them, we feel in the Department of Justice, is a long-range, permanent plan built into the Department of Justice. We also attach to that the idea of looking at individuals, picking the top hundred, and attacking them by looking at everything they do, rather than looking to see if they violate the narcotics law, or looking to see if they violate the Hobbs Racketeering Act. We are looking at everything they do, and we are coming up with evidence of antitrust violations where they have crept into business.

We are finding Taft-Hartley violations, Securities Exchange violations, Food and Drug violations, and we are going to use this idea of looking at the individual and trying to map out everything that he is doing, concentrating on him as a means of trying to break up organized crime.

THE PRESIDENT'S COMMISSION ON LAW ENFORCEMENT AND ADMINISTRATION OF JUSTICE

TASK FORCE REPORT: ORGANIZED CRIME 11-12 (1967)

Following the Kefauver hearings [in 1950], the Department of Justice commenced a concerted drive against the leading racket figures identified in the hearings. Federal prosecutors throughout the Nation were encouraged to initiate investigations and prosecutions of such persons. As a result, a number of high level

[d] Compare the facts in United States v. Cangelose, 230 F. Supp. 544 (N.D. Iowa 1964).

organized crime participants were convicted of Federal law violations. Under authority of the immigration statutes, the Department was successful in effecting the deportation of other racketeers. In 1954, the Justice Department formed an Organized Crime and Racketeering (OCR) Section to encourage the continuation of these prosecutive efforts. Efforts to institutionalize an antiracketeering intelligence program were hindered by a lack of coordination and interest by some Federal investigative agencies. . . .

In September 1960, the Federal Bureau of Investigation began to supply the OCR Section with regular intelligence reports on 400 of the Nation's organized crime figures. But with only 17 attorneys and minimal intelligence information from other Federal agencies, the section could not adequately fulfill its functions. . . .

In 1961, the OCR Section expanded its organized crime program to unprecedented proportions. In the next 3 years, regular intelligence reports were secured from 26 separate Federal agencies, the number of attorneys was nearly quadrupled, and convictions increased. Indicative of the cooperation during this enforcement effort was the pooling of information from several Federal agencies for investigative leads in income tax cases. Over 60 percent of the convictions secured between 1961 and July 1965 resulted from tax investigations conducted by the Internal Revenue Service. Several high-level members of organized crime families in New York City were convicted through the efforts of the Federal Bureau of Narcotics. . . .

In 1965, a number of factors slowed the momentum of the organized crime drive. A Senate committee uncovered a few isolated instances of wiretapping and electronic surveillance by Treasury Department agents, and some officials began to question whether special emphasis upon organized crime in tax enforcement was appropriate or fair. The Department of Justice was accused of extensively using illegal electronic surveillance in investigations of racketeer influence in Las Vegas casinos. Federal prosecutors in some large cities demanded independence from OCR Section attorneys and prosecutive policies. Attacks appeared in the press on the intensity and tactics of the Federal investigative and prosecutive efforts. A high rate of turnover among OCR Section attorneys meant discontinuity of effort and reduced personnel by nearly 25 percent.

This combination of adverse circumstances apparently led the OCR Section to believe that it could no longer expect the high degree of cooperation it had received from some Federal investigative agencies, and the intensity of its efforts diminished.

ETHICAL CRISIS IN CRIMINAL LAW: THE PROSECUTOR'S RESPONSIBILITY[e]

By Monroe H. Freedman

Trial Magazine 34, 36 (Dec.-Jan. 1968)

There are six common practices of prosecutors that raise questions of professional responsibility and that have been given inadequate attention both in academic journals and in practice.

(1) Cases where the primary motive for the prosecution relates to matters other than commission of the particular crime for which the defendant is being prosecuted. An instance often suggested to justify this kind of conduct is the prosecution of Al Capone for tax evasion. If the government cannot successfully prosecute a notorious criminal for the numerous serious offenses he is suspected of having committed, some prosecutors consider it to be proper to subject him to prosecutions for a variety of other crimes, ranking from traffic offenses to tax evasion, for which he would not be investigated and charged were it not for his notoriety. In support of such practices, it is argued, that if the individual is, in fact, guilty of the crime with which he is charged, the motive of the prosecutor is immaterial.

This contention overlooks the fact that there are few of us who have led such unblemished lives as to prevent a determined prosecutor from finding some basis for an indictment or an information.

Thus, to say that the prosecutor's motive is immaterial is to justify making virtually every citizen the potential victim of arbitrary discretion. For a prosecutor to direct his discretionary powers of investigation and prosecution against individuals, rather than against crimes, is the very antithesis of a rule of law, and a serious violation of his professional responsibility.

ETHICAL CRISIS IN CRIMINAL LAW: DEFENSE STANDARDS QUESTIONED

By Richard L. Braun

Trial Magazine 35, 38 (Dec.-Jan. 1968)

For example, Mr. Freedman criticizes prosecutions where the primary motive relates to matters other than the particular crime for which the defendant is being prosecuted. Among others he cites the cases of Al Capone and Jimmy Hoffa.

Persecution which relies on ferreting out minor offenses for which a person would not normally be prosecuted is of course undesirable. But Mr. Freedman cites no evidence of such "common practices". The charges against Hoffa and Capone were not minor.

---

[e] This is a condensed version of Freedman, *The Professional Responsibility of the Prosecuting Attorney,* 55 GEO. L.J. 1030 (1967).

To suggest that these people should not have been prosecuted simply because they may have committed worse crimes, or incurred the wrath of the prosecutor, is unrealistic at best.

C. LIMITS ON INITIATING INVESTIGATIONS

The Practice

The following instances are not common, but illustrate situations of a borderline nature, raising questions of propriety in the police conduct. If the practices are considered improper, there remains the question whether any remedy is available.

1

"A proposed system of television surveillance by the Newport Beach, Calif., Police Dept. has been called by its detractors everything from 'Candid Camera' to 'peeping tom' to 'Big Brother,' a reference to George Orwell's novel, '1984,' in which everyone is under surveillance by secret police.

"Proponents of the network, called EPS or Electronic Protection System, point out that it would enable the town's 150-man force to give far greater protection to its 48,000 citizens at, hopefully, less cost. In addition, the Federal Government is expected to put up all but $13,500 of the estimated $478,500 cost.

"Under the pilot test program, if it is finally approved, 12 to 18 cameras would be installed at strategic spots and zeroed in to police headquarters where a few men could watch constantly a far wider area than cars or foot patrolmen could cover.

"EPS, if successful, could be the forerunner of a system of seeing-eye television cameras installed in cities throughout the nation to watch—day and night—the streets, parks, beaches, stores and highways for lawbreakers."[f]

2

As a part of the continuing police intelligence effort to establish the interrelationships of persons involved in organized crime, note is taken of gatherings where they are present. At the funeral of a prominent gangland figure, police set up a motion picture camera to take pictures of the people attending and the license numbers of the cars they came in.

3

During a political campaign the police chief ordered investigators to learn whether gambling was going on in a private club

[f] Crime Control Digest, June 5, 1968, at 12.

during a party at which the opposition candidate for mayor was expected to be present. Some gambling was discovered and the police raided the club. The mayoral candidate had left before the raid, however.

4

The police department stationed a police officer with a motion picture camera, equipped with a telephoto lens, on a balcony of the State Capitol Building to photograph a march on the Capitol by university students and faculty protesting United States military involvement in Viet-Nam. Standing next to the cameraman was a person recognized by some of the marchers as a radio commentator generally considered arch-conservative. Upon learning that the camera was operated by a policeman, various persons called upon the police chief for explanation. He stated that motion pictures were frequently taken of crowds in order to permit creation of a training film, and to serve as evidence in the event a disturbance should be created.

5

In People v. Harris, 182 Cal. App. 2d 837, 5 Cal. Rptr. 852 (1960), a new trial was ordered for failure of the trial court to admit evidence which would tend to show racially discriminatory enforcement of gambling laws. One of the offers of proof which had been rejected was: "One of the arresting officers would testify the routine city police procedure was to patrol the colored section and, on finding grouped parked cars, prowl the private premises for gambling, with no like patrol in the white section and no investigation made when cars were so parked in white areas."

6

When tax officials encountered resistance to a tax claim, they subjected the taxpayer's attorney to extensive tax examination also, combing through his returns for six years without finding error.[g]

BEAUREGARD v. WINGARD

362 F.2d 901 (9th Cir. 1966)

MERRILL, Circuit Judge. This is an appeal from judgment in favor of the police in a suit under the Civil Rights Act, Rev.Stat.

[g] Allegations as to punitive motives in this situation were made but not established in O'Donnell v. Sullivan, 364 F.2d 43 (1st Cir. 1966); *cf.* Lord v. Kelley, 240 F. Supp. 167, 169 (D. Mass. 1965).

§ 1979 (1875), 42 U.S.C. 1983 (1964). Appellant, Beauregard, was arrested, detained in jail and prosecuted for the crime of bookmaking, Calif.Penal Code 337a(1) and (3). After trial, before court without jury, appellant was acquitted. Now appellant claims that this arrest, jail detention, and prosecution violated his civil rights.

In the instant action Beauregard contends that Wingard [the police chief] instituted his investigation without reasonable grounds upon which to base a suspicion that appellant was engaged in bookmaking; that the investigation was motivated by malice because of certain political attacks by Beauregard on Wingard; that the arrest and prosecution under these circumstances violated his civil rights.

After a full trial certain issues were submitted to the jury for special verdict. The jury found that: (1) Prior to the arrest appellee Wingard did not have reasonable grounds upon which to base a suspicion that appellant was engaged in bookmaking. (2) Wingard was motivated by malice and personal bias against appellant when he directed Cowley and Michael to attempt to place a bet with appellant and did not act in the interests of law enforcement. . . . (4) In making the arrest Michael did have reasonable grounds to believe that appellant had violated the bookmaking statute.

[I]t should in any event be clear that where probable cause does exist civil rights are not violated by an arrest even though innocence may subsequently be established.

The jury's findings do not establish that appellant was arrested without probable cause. Quite to the contrary, it was expressly found that Michael had probable cause for the arrest. As for Wingard's involvement, it may simply be said that if an investigation succeeds in producing evidence of crime, probable cause for arrest is not nullified by the fact that the otherwise successful investigation was maliciously inspired.

Note on Criminal Investigation by Nonpolice Agencies

Prosecutor. The line between law enforcement agency and prosecutorial agency is not sharp. For example, the Organized Crime Division of the Justice Department, referred to previously, represents the merger between investigative and prosecutorial functions. Local prosecutors, too, sometimes have special responsibility for enforcing particular statutes and may have a corps of investigators attached to their office for this purpose. By choice, also, the police may routinely refer some kinds of complaints to the prosecutor for at least initial action. Typical of the crimes thus left to the prosecutor are embezzlement, consumer frauds, bad checks, misfeasance in office, illegal business practices, and sometimes even abortion.

Some factors which account for this referral practice are: the necessity for investigators to have legal training or accounting expertise; the complexity or obscurity of some little-used laws; the existence of strong political overtones to some charges; the social and professional status of the people involved as witnesses or suspects.

Formal Inquiries. The prosecutor, who rarely has any lawful power to compel the attendance or cooperation of witnesses,[h] has at his disposal several kinds of investigative procedures which do permit the use of compulsory process.

The coroner's inquest convenes a jury to inquire into the cause of unexplained death, using the subpoena power to examine witnesses. Its verdict is merely advisory. The inquest has such a narrow field that it is not a major investigative device.

The grand jury, though its principal function is to approve or disapprove bills of indictment submitted by the prosecutor, also has an investigative function. Its power to compel the appearance of witnesses, examine them in secret, and grant immunity from prosecution in order to remove the privilege against self-incrimination permits it to operate effectively in inquiring into such matters as official corruption and business crimes. The procedure is, however, cumbersome.

The "one-man grand jury,"[i] the "John Doe proceeding,"[j] and the "court of inquiry"[k] are examples of statutory proceedings which give the prosecutor, with the cooperation of a judge, power to make investigations—some secret, some public. The preliminary examination statutes, which empower a magistrate to hear witnesses upon the filing of a complaint, have sometimes been turned to the same end, but the appellate courts have

---

[h] KAN. STAT. ANN. § 62-301 (1963) permits the prosecutor to subpoena witnesses to investigate violations of gambling laws, liquor laws, or any law where the accused is a fugitive; *cf.* Chandler v. Garrison, 286 F. Supp. 191, 192 (E.D. La. 1968). Even without statutory authority it is not unknown for a prosecutor to issue a purported "subpoena" to persons he wishes to see.

[i] MICH. COMP. LAWS §§ 767.3, 767.4 (1948), as amended by Mich. Pub. Acts 1965, No. 251; R. SCIGLIANO, THE MICHIGAN ONE-MAN GRAND JURY (1957).

[j] WIS. STAT. § 954.025 (1965).

[k] The procedure described in *In re* McClelland, 260 F. Supp. 182 (S.D. Tex. 1966), has been modified. TEX. CODE CRIM. PROC. ANN. art. 52 (Vernon 1966).

generally characterized the use of this hearing for an open-ended investigation as an abuse of the statutory procedure.[l]

Legislative hearings such as the Kefauver and McClellan Committees held can be used to investigate and expose criminality, though prosecutions rarely flow from such investigations.

Reference Note

A discussion of the effect of noncriminal police activities on criminal law enforcement will be found in H. Goldstein, *The Police Response to the Urban Crisis,* 28 PUB. ADMIN. REV. 417 (1968). An excellent case study of this question is Parnas, *The Police Response to the Domestic Disturbance,* 1967 WIS. L. REV. 914.

---

[l] *E.g.,* State v. Brady, 18 Utah 2d 434, 425 P.2d 155 (1967).

Chapter 3

METHODS OF DETECTING CRIME AND IDENTIFYING CRIMINALS[a]

Once the objective of investigation is chosen, there is still the question of means. Each of the methods which police may use in collecting evidence of crime has its own problems—problems of effectiveness, of intrusiveness, of interference with innocent people, of susceptibility to regulation. The seriousness of the criminal conduct may affect the degree to which people will tolerate intrusive detection techniques. For example, many who condemn wiretapping generally would make exception for kidnapping or matters of national security.

A. OBSERVING AND OVERHEARING: SURVEILLANCE, INCLUDING WIRETAPPING AND ELECTRONIC EAVESDROPPING

In the preceding chapter the issue was raised as to what stimulates initiation of investigation and whether there were some circumstances in which it is inappropriate to undertake or pursue an investigation. The question here is not whether, but how, to proceed. There is an interplay among the evidence question (how certain law enforcement officials are that their surveillance will produce some proof of crime), the privacy question (how likely the surveillance is to intrude into the affairs of innocent persons, or into the innocent affairs of guilty persons), and the control question (what system exists or could be devised to supervise surveillance practices, which by their nature may be unknown if no crime is discovered thereby).

[a] Some additional significant methods by which police detect crime and identify offenders are dealt with in the next chapter. These are the complaints of victims, the identification of offenders from pictures or in a lineup, and the interrogation of suspects.

1. Surveillance Techniques

AN OUTLINE OF CRIMINAL INVESTIGATION 12-1—12-3 (1968)†

By William H. Hewitt & Philip P. Lynch

Surveillance is the process or art of keeping persons, premises, vehicles, and other material under observation for the purpose of acquiring detailed information concerning activities, operations, identities, and contacts of a Subject or Subjects. . . .

Surveillance is an *investigative tool* and an indispensable part of the training for every individual engaged in criminal investigation work. When properly conducted, surveillance produces *accurate, reliable information*. There will be occasions when only a surveillance can supply needed information. For example, we may know or suspect that an individual is involved in a crime. By the proper use of a surveillance we can learn the identity of the person, the contact point, and secure definite proof that the subject is involved. . . .

Surveillance is not to be confused with undercover. In both situations, the officer will seek to conceal his real identity. In an undercover assignment supported by a carefully planned cover story of identity, frequently based upon information obtained through surveillance, the officer seeks direct contact with the subject. Often this is accomplished by penetration into subject's organization. In surveillance, the officer *avoids direct contact* with the subject. . . .

Surveillance is an excellent means by which you can check on the *reliability of your informants*. . . .

Surveillance can be utilized to assist in the preparation and planning of an undercover operation. . . .

A surveillance can be used to obtain information for utilization during an *interrogation*. . . .

Finally, a surveillance may be used in *preparation for a raid or search.*

Because the ordinary patrolman is so much involved in performing a wide variety of social tasks, and in responding to citizen complaints of crime, he is rarely called upon to use the technique of surveillance. Specialized personnel, such as vice squad officers and detectives, however, do concentrate on the detection and solution of crimes through planned investigation. And the crimes on which they spend much of their time are

† Published by the authors, State University of New York, Farmingdale, New York.

planned crimes, frequently involving joint action, related to "vice" and carried out by criminal organizations. It is these special law enforcement agencies and these kinds of crimes which typically use and require surveillance.

LAW ENFORCEMENT IN THE METROPOLIS 24, 28 (1967)
Edited by Donald M. McIntyre, Jr.
(American Bar Foundation)

The Detroit Narcotics Bureau, the Vice Bureau, and the state police racket squad engage in undercover surveillance to gather information as a basis for future police action or to obtain a search warrant. All three units are equipped with unmarked cars with two-way radios for intercar communication. The Detroit Narcotics Bureau shares its radio facilities with the Federal Bureau of Narcotics. To build conspiracy cases against gambling rackets, surveillance must be maintained for protracted periods of time. Depending upon the size of the "numbers" operation, the conspiracy squad of the Detroit Vice Bureau may spend as long as 14 months observing the process of how bets are placed and routed through syndicate headquarters. Daily observations are made of the movements of all syndicate members, ranging in importance from those working on house-to-house collections to those suspected of being the "big boss." As the investigation progresses, the officers may conceal themselves in a truck parked close to the premises in order to better identify the individuals entering and leaving such an establishment. In all surveillance work, a daily journal of the officer's observations is maintained so that an organizational chart of the syndicate operation can be pieced together. In addition to serving as a means of obtaining warrants for the seizure of evidence and for arrest purposes, these observations serve to tie together the various individuals to prove a conspiracy charge in court.

[The officers assumed their post at 1:00 P.M. and, at 1:09, John Doe #3 and Mary Doe #1 left their residence. A brief stop was made at a residence located next to a bar, and, on leaving this residence, Patrolman *A* obtained the street number. Patrolman *B* then traced the suspects to a second address. While Mary Doe #1 sat in the car, John Doe #3 remained in what appeared to be an apartment house for some twenty minutes. He then left this house and got into a different car. The officers did not attempt to follow him but planned to do so in the future. Within ten minutes, he returned in the same car, got out and got into his own car. He was then trailed to a stop which he made in a large housing project. At this point, the officers had gotten involved in a great deal of traffic and Patrolman *A* ended up observing the progress of John Doe #3 from a considerable distance on the opposite side of the expressway. He was able to direct Patrolman *B* to a better position and, once the car was viewed by Patrolman *B*, Patrolman *A* returned to his side of the expressway. The trailing of this car was further complicated due to the fact that the driver was apparently suspicious of a scout car that had been following him—probably a mere coincidence. As a result, he followed a very roundabout route getting onto the expressway, heading north. The two officers then trailed him on the expressway—using some five or six cars for cover between the John Doe #3 car and the police vehicles. When the suspect took an exit from the expressway, one of the officers went beyond—taking the following exit, while Patrolman *B* took the same exit. Patrolman *A* then sped to the street on which the substation was located to take a position where he could observe John Doe #3 enter these premises. This position was taken in an alley two blocks away from the structure but from which position the door to the structure was plainly visible. Patrolman *A* was alerted to the fact that John Doe #3 was parking his vehicle. He was then observed entering the house. He left in a matter of minutes. Three minutes later, John Doe #1, the "money-man" in the syndicate, was observed leaving the same doorway. The officers then trailed John Doe #1 to his residence, which he uses as his office. Patrolman *B* got to the scene in advance and took up his position so that he could observe this man entering his own home. Patrolman *A* alerted Patrolman *B* to John Doe #1's arrival. Patrolman *B* observed John Doe #1 get out of his car and, with a paper-wrapped package in his possession, enter his home.[b]]

Extensive use is made of motion pictures by the vice bureau of the Detroit Police Department to document observations their undercover agents have made. This technique is most commonly used in the investigation of numbers syndicates, although it has been effectively used in developing evidence on the operation of a bawdy house.

Two officers rented a room in a flophouse and let it be known that they had just been discharged from service, had lots of money, and were going to have a good time for themselves. They selected a room which overlooked the rear of a hotel on the opposite side of the street in which the bawdy house was operated. Using a motion picture camera, and occasionally a telescopic lens, they

---

[b] This illustration is contained in the PILOT PROJECT REPORT (Vol. II, Detroit, Michigan) of the SURVEY OF THE ADMINISTRATION OF CRIMINAL JUSTICE, which is an earlier version of this same material.

photographed the activity taking place at this house. Each morning, they photographed the girls as they reported for work. The customers were photographed as they approached the house and were directed to the door by one of the girls or the madam, who would appear on a rear porch. On completion of their assignment, the officers had photographed approximately 150 men entering and leaving this establishment. On one occasion, so many men were being entertained that it was necessary for them to wait on the back porch, which was in plain view.

Other kinds of surveillance present more serious questions of propriety and legality, since they involve prying of a more intensive sort than merely following and watching.

The Practice

The following are relatively uncommon practices which are presented to raise the question of the limits of permissible surveillance techniques.

1

Tax investigators obtained from postal inspectors a report of the names and return addresses on all first-class letters received by a tax fraud suspect over a period of three months, using the correspondents as sources of information in piecing together a picture of the suspect's finances.[c]

2

Members of the narcotics squad were keeping an apartment under surveillance because of a tip that narcotics would be found there. After they saw a man knock, identify himself by name, and be admitted, one of the officers went to the door and looked through the keyhole. He saw the man empty a small box into his hand and hold the contents out to a woman. The officers kicked the door in and grabbed capsules of heroin from the man.

3

The management of a department store demanded police action when one of the store rest rooms came to be frequented by

---

[c] Cohen v. United States, 378 F.2d 751, 759-60 (9th Cir. 1967), describes the "mail cover" practice and cites the few precedents.

homosexuals, causing repeated embarrassment and annoyance to customers. The police removed a towel cabinet mounted on a closet door and substituted one which contained a one-way mirror. They could thus keep watch on persons using the rest room, having a view similar to that which anyone coming into the rest room would have, though the sound of someone's entering would have given a moment's warning. After watching for some time a policeman saw two men engage in homosexual activity. He took motion pictures of them in the act, then radioed other police waiting nearby, who made the arrest.

4

Police who suspected a man and his wife of sale of narcotics obtained permission from a neighbor 150 feet away to set up an observation post in an upstairs room. By watching through binoculars the police finally observed the suspects in their upstairs bedroom putting a white powder into capsules.

5

"Varoscanner, a new infrared night viewing device designed especially for law enforcement work, has been developed by Varo, Inc., of Garland, Texas.

"According to its developer, the Varoscanner provides the same ability to see in the dark as is available in equipment being used by American soldiers in Vietnam. The unit combines an infrared light source and a telescopic sight into a single piece which can easily be held in one hand. It enables the user to observe activities even on the darkest night while remaining invisible, the firm said."[d]

6

Narcotics officers taped one sensitive microphone over the keyhole and another at the crack between the floor and the door of an adjoining hotel room occupied by a man suspected of being a wholesale dealer in heroin. By this means they heard him arrange a meeting with a known narcotics seller.

7

When a major gangland figure purchased a home, police installed a microphone in the window casement of the den before he moved in. Police in working clothes made the installation in broad daylight while carpenters who were doing remodeling work were absent. Police listened for a year, until the man—tipped off

[d] Crime Control Digest, June 5, 1968, at 5.

by someone in the police department—discovered the microphone with the aid of a private wiretap expert.

8

Police were investigating the activities of a doctor known to serve underworld figures. A private detective working for the police department installed a tap on the doctor's telephone and established a full-time listening post. Information learned through the tap served to connect one of the callers, an attorney, with a murder.

The value to police and practical limits of usefulness of surveillance in investigating organized crime are suggested by the following excerpts:

TESTIMONY OF O. W. WILSON, SUPERINTENDENT OF POLICE OF CHICAGO, BEFORE THE ILLINOIS CRIME COMMISSION, MARCH 25, 1964

. . . Important as it is to dry up the grass-roots or seed-beds of organized crime, the fact remains that the higher-ups in the rackets continue to elude us.

. . . How can we get the necessary evidence against the top hoodlums?

There are only three ways that I know of.

First, you might persuade one of the conspirators or one of the immediate underlings to testify against his co-conspirators. This is an extremely unlikely possibility. In the underworld the penalty for talking is death. . . .

Second, you might plant an undercover operative in the upper echelon of the syndicate. This too is an extremely unlikely possibility. The syndicate is a closed corporation. Most of the principal stockholders and members of the board of directors are related by blood or marriage or bound by close ties of nationality. Access to this upper echelon is gained only after years of personal participation in felonious operations frequently involving severe beatings and even murder. Penetration of such a group by an undercover operation is virtually impossible.

The third method involves intensive surveillance and observation over an extended period of time to obtain evidence of continual association and repeated acts in concert with which to prove a conspiracy to commit crime. This kind of surveillance, to be successful, would require wire-tapping, electronic listening devices and other sophisticated audio and visual surveillance techniques. This third method is not legally possible in Illinois because of the electronic eavesdropping law.

The catalog excerpt on the opposite page is illustrative of the devices for surreptitious listening which have been advertised[e] for general usage.

ASPECTS OF THE EVIDENCE GATHERING PROCESS IN ORGANIZED CRIME CASES in THE PRESIDENT'S COMMISSION ON LAW ENFORCEMENT AND ADMINISTRATION OF JUSTICE, TASK FORCE REPORT: ORGANIZED CRIME 92 (1967)

By G. Robert Blakey

It is difficult to determine how much legal and illegal private and law enforcement electronic surveillance occurs. Federal law enforcement agencies have and are employing these techniques under varying limitations. These techniques are also being employed by law enforcement agencies on the state level. How much private use or illegal law enforcement use on the state or Federal level occurs cannot be definitely ascertained. There seems to be, however, a consensus that the use of these techniques is relatively widespread.

The widespread existence of electronic surveillance has been made possible by the tremendous scientific developments which have taken place in the last half century. Microminiaturization in electronics and the invention of the magnetic tape stand out as the two most important events. Much publicity has been given to the awesome potential of electronic devices: thumbnail-size microphones, cigarette package-size transmitters, induction coil devices for wiretapping. Methods of transforming the ordinary telephone into a microphone, which can be activated hundreds of miles away, have been demonstrated. Research has also developed a laser beam which under laboratory conditions can pick up conversations in a room from the outside window pane. Under ideal conditions, the parabolic microphone can be used to overhear conversations at distances from which they would otherwise be inaudible.

Less widespread publicity has been given to the inherent investigative limitations on the practical use of these devices. It is often difficult if not impossible to install them safely where a

---

[e] Such advertising is now prohibited. 18 U.S.C. § 2512.

Puts truth in the old chestnut...

"The walls have ears..."

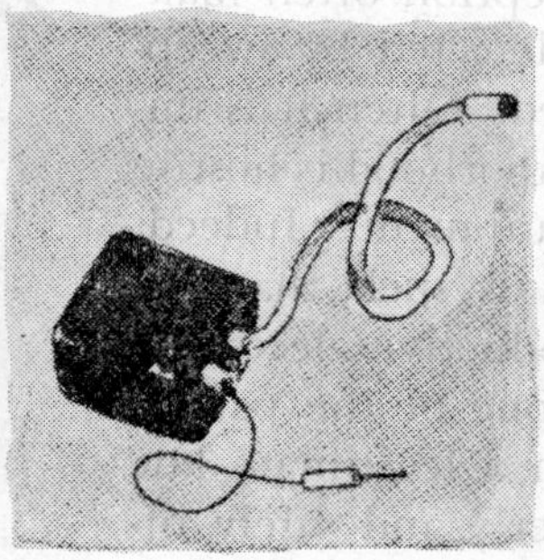

Pin hole/key hole Microphone

It's unique all right. Notice the extended acoustical tube... that's the trick. It'll fit in the smallest places and defy detection. Poke it through a door, the slightest crack, send it over a wall or get daring and unreel it like a fishing line out the window. It can get to where you couldn't go yourself. The versatility of this one makes it absolutely invaluable...

$119.50

Spike Microphone

Gives you the professional efficiency of a world-famous secret agent. This is an extremely high precision, high impedence instrument. It is, of course, extremely portable, however it is the "spike" design which makes it so efficient for "instantaneous installation." Just the thing for quiet, on-the-spot surveillance or recording. Simply insert into plaster wall (behind picture), sit back and relax.
All conversations and sounds in adjoining room will be picked up beautifully...

$79.50

Shotgun Microphone

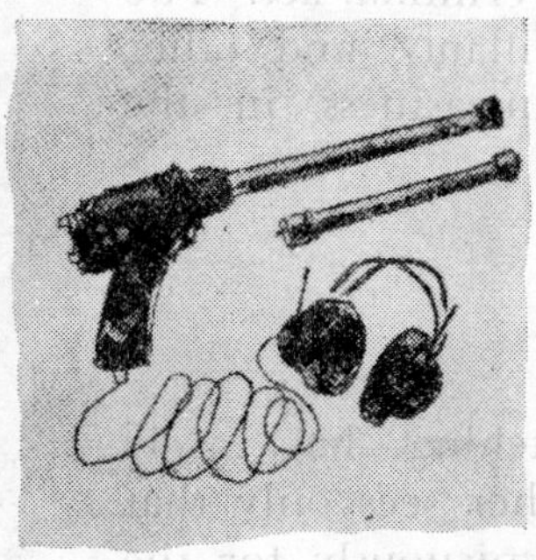

Can you hear what they're saying several hundred feet away? Of course you can! A truly unique microphone to answer an obvious need in the field of professional investigation (nothing's going to stop *you* from operating like a professional investigator). Shotgun shape lets you aim and pick out a group of voices, even in crowded areas, from several hundred feet away with fidelity and reliability. Two different size barrels, for very specific aiming, with built-in wind screen for outdoor use. Self-powered transistorized amplifier allows monitoring through cushioned aircraft type headphone while in use. Three output impedences...

$425.00

Recorder Microphone Booster

Increases clarity, sensitivity, amplification.

$50.00

surreptitious entry is required. Pairs must be located to wiretap. Often one or more additional entries are required to adjust the equipment. Power sources must be found. Monitoring them and analyzing their product consume an inordinate amount of time. Static and room noise interfere with reception often making use impractical. Wireless devices can be detected by sweeping. Wired equipment can be visually discovered. Often it is impossible to employ the devices because the neighborhood is hostile or there is insufficient time to set up the equipment. Indeed, despite the practical limitations, the potential is such that the wiretap or the wired bug remain the most productive electronic surveillance techniques where the consent of one of the parties to the conversation cannot be obtained. From a legitimate law enforcement standpoint, both require, if properly and safely installed and monitored, such an expenditure of effort, time, and manpower that normal investigative techniques are generally preferred.

The ordinary citizen in the United States enjoys relative anonymity. Unlike the citizens of many countries he is under no general obligation to carry an identification card or register his movements.[f] This freedom from supervision is highly prized. No one likes to be watched by an investigator, however innocent the activity he is engaged in. It makes him uncomfortable. Americans are not generally apprehensive, because they believe that they are not likely to come under investigation unless there is some reason to suspect them of some specific criminal act. The more widespread and intrusive secret surveillance and other investigation techniques, the greater the uneasiness in the community.

2. *Propriety of Surveillance*

Ordinary surveillance—following and watching—has rarely presented any legal problems, since the watcher sees only that which is done openly. Shadowing done conspicuously for the purpose of harassing, with no real expectation of learning any-

---

[f] The obligation to carry a draft card is the most generally applicable requirement. Former convicts may sometimes be required to register. *See* M. PAULSEN & S. KADISH, CRIMINAL LAW AND ITS ADMINISTRATION 42-44 (1962). There is a practical requirement that employment, tax returns, and many financial transactions require giving one's Social Security number, so that long-term anonymity becomes increasingly difficult.

thing, may well be impermissible,[g] but where the surveillance can be shown to be a good faith effort to prevent crime or obtain evidence of crime, simply keeping watch has seemed acceptable.

SCHERER v. BRENNAN

266 F. Supp. 758 (N.D. Ill. 1966)
Affirmed, 379 F.2d 609 (7th Cir. 1967)

Perry, District Judge. Suit was originally brought by plaintiff against defendants in the Circuit Court of Cook County, Illinois, seeking damages of $100,000 against each defendant [on the theory of trespass to property and unlawful interference with access to and occupancy of his residence]. It was removed to this Court on Petition of defendants.

Plaintiff has complained of occurrences on October 7, 1964, in and near his home at 3010 Orchard Place in Des Plaines. On that date, plaintiff was a duly licensed dealer under the National Firearms Act and the Federal Firearms Act. At and near his home, which was located within 300 yards of the O'Hare Inn, plaintiff possessed many rifles, pistols, a machine gun, a 25 m.m. cannon that could penetrate a concrete wall, and ammunition for those weapons. His home was within easy rifle shot of the O'Hare Inn. Several years before the date in question, plaintiff had been arrested by Chicago Police while in possession of a 20 m.m. cannon at O'Hare Airport.

On October 7, 1964, Michael W. Torina was Special Agent-in-Charge of the Chicago Office of the United States Secret Service, Treasury Department. On that date, the President of the United States was scheduled to arrive in the evening at the O'Hare Inn, which was the O'Hare Inn within 300 yards of plaintiff's residence. Mr. Torina therefore called Cecil M. Wolfe, to supply the assistance of his investigators to keep under surveillance the occupant or occupants of the plaintiff's home, until the President departed.

---

[g] *See* Giancana v. Johnson, 335 F.2d 366 (7th Cir. 1964), vacating for failure to allege that the amount in controversy exceeded $10,000 a district court preliminary injunction against FBI agents' constant, obvious surveillance. Agents were posted in front of Giancana's house, and followed him openly wherever he went, even playing behind him on the golf course. The district court had held that Giancana's right to be free from arbitrary intrusion into his privacy without reasonable grounds for the interference had been violated.

See Donnelly, *Judicial Control of Informants, Spies, Stool Pigeons, and Agent Provocateurs,* 60 Yale L.J. 1091, 1096 (1951), and cases cited there, all of which involve surveillance sufficiently open to drive away customers from a business.

That same day, defendants identifying themselves and their purpose to plaintiff, made repeated attempts to persuade Mr. Scherer to separate himself from his weapons until the President left. These efforts included offers to provide a room for plaintiff at a nearby motel without cost to him, and, when that was refused, the request that he willingly give up his weapons until the President left. The latter request also being refused, the defendants and other Government agents on the same assignment attempted to keep plaintiff under constant direct surveillance, accompanying him when he left and later returned to his home. At no time did defendant prevent plaintiff from entering his home or using his property freely.

A federal official, whether of high or of low rank, cannot be held personally liable in damages for an act committed within the general scope of his official authority and in pursuance of his official duties. Barr v. Matteo, 360 U.S. 564 (1959). This longstanding rule, often referred to as the "official immunity doctrine," has been consistently adhered to by the Supreme Court and by the lower federal courts.

Accordingly, it is the opinion of this court that the motion of defendants for summary judgment should be allowed and judgment should be entered against plaintiff and in favor of defendants.

STATE v. CARTWRIGHT

418 P.2d 822 (Ore. 1966)

LUSK, Justice. The defendant, Maurice Wheeler Cartwright, Jr., is an ex-convict who was convicted of the crime of possession of a pistol in violation of ORS 166.270, and has appealed.

It appears that Orville Luther swore to an affidavit reading as follows:

"I am a deputy sheriff for Multnomah County, Oregon, and in such capacity and pursuant to an undercover investigation, I have rented an apartment at 8302 S.E. Brooklyn Street, in the County of Multnomah, State of Oregon, and have been residing there since July 14, 1964; that there resides in the adjacent apartment in the same building, 8304 S.E. Brooklyn Street, one Maurice Cartwright and one Judith Hardin; that both of these subjects are known to me as narcotics users; that I have personally seen these subjects in company with other known narcotics users enter and depart from 8304 S.E. Brooklyn Street at late and unusual hours on many occasions;

"That I have personally overheard through the walls of the said apartment conversations carried on by the said Maurice Cartwright and Judith Hardin relating to their present possession of narcotics; that based upon these conversations which I have overheard I have good reason to believe that there is presently in the possession of the said Maurice Cartwright and Judith Hardin in the aforementioned premises at 8304 S.E. Brooklyn Street, the following personal property:

"26 capsules of heroin, and assorted quantities of Methedrine, Tuinal and Cocaine. That this property is possessed by them in violation of ORS 474.020 and ORS 475.100."

On the basis of this affidavit a district judge for Multnomah County issued a warrant for a search of the premises occupied by the Cartwrights. The warrant was executed by Luther, assisted by other officers, on July 25, 1964. In addition to the pistol and clip, containing six rounds of ammunition, a quantity of narcotics, hypodermic needles and other equipment used by narcotic addicts, was taken in the search.

The question here is whether the conduct of the officers in listening to the conversations between the defendant and his wife in the constitutionally protected area of their home was an unjustified intrusion upon the defendant's privacy. If so, the information thus obtained could not be the basis of a valid search warrant.

Conventional eavesdropping (if this is the proper term for it) is not, apparently, much indulged in by the police, and it is not to be compared as a menace to the privacy, whether of law-abiding persons or of criminals, with the use of modern electronic devices.

In this case the officers were in a place where they had a right to be. They committed no trespass, technical or otherwise, and the information they gained by listening at the wall could properly be made the basis for the issuance of a search warrant.

The judgment is affirmed.

SLOAN, Justice (dissenting). I cannot join in consenting to this kind of insidious police invasion of my home. If they break down my door and enter and ransack, we denounce it. But I would prefer the latter. I at least know they are there and can take means to oust them. I cannot know if they are crouching in the bushes under my window or listening through the thin wall between my apartment and the next or are tapping my telephone or using electronic eavesdropping devices a block away. By either means no doubt any citizen would condemn himself to some offense, even if it were only a minor violation that could only result in a charge that would cause embarrassment to him or his family.

I fail to see any difference in the use of a spike driven into the wall, or a sensitive microphone placed either against the wall or a block away, or the human ear pressed to the outer side of a thin wall. All should be ostracized from permissive invasion.

It would be true that if I openly shout in my house, knowing that it can be heard from without that I could not claim the protection. But that does not mean that I must take my family or guests and "whisper in the bathroom." Jerome Frank's dissent at 193 F.2d 306, 317, supra [United States v. On Lee (2d Cir. 1951)].

It is also urged that to prohibit this kind of search would limit the right of the police to keep surveillance on the outside of the house. This need not be so. It is one thing to observe who comes and goes. It is quite another to surreptitiously peep and eavesdrop to the thoughts and opinions stated inside the house.[h]

KATZ v. UNITED STATES
389 U.S. 347 (1967)

MR. JUSTICE STEWART delivered the opinion of the Court.

The petitioner was convicted in the District Court for the Southern District of California under an eight-count indictment charging him with transmitting wagering information by telephone from Los Angeles to Miami and Boston in violation of a federal statute. At trial the Government was permitted, over the petitioner's objection, to introduce evidence of the petitioner's end of telephone conversations, overheard by FBI agents who had attached an electronic listening and recording device to the outside of the public telephone booth from which he had placed his calls. In affirming his conviction, the Court of Appeals rejected the contention that the recordings had been ob-

---

[h] 2 E. MAY, CONSTITUTIONAL HISTORY OF ENGLAND 275 (1863): "Next in importance to personal freedom is immunity from suspicions and jealous observation. Men may be without restraints upon their liberty; they may pass to and fro at pleasure; but if their steps are tracked by spies and informers, their words noted down for crimination, their associates watched as conspirators—who shall say that they are free? Nothing is more revolting to Englishmen than the espionage which forms part of the administrative system of continental despotisms. It haunts men like an evil genius, chills their gayety, restrains their wit, casts a shadow over their friendships, and blights their domestic hearth. The freedom of a country may be measured by its immunity from this baleful agency. Rulers who distrust their own people must govern in a spirit of absolutism; and suspected subjects will be ever sensible of their bondage."

tained in violation of the Fourth Amendment, because "[t]here was no physical entrance into the area occupied by [the petitioner]." We granted certiorari in order to consider the constitutional questions thus presented.

The petitioner has phrased those questions as follows:

"A. Whether a public telephone booth is a constitutionally protected area so that evidence obtained by attaching an electronic listening recording device to the top of such a booth is obtained in violation of the right to privacy of the user of the booth.

"B. Whether physical penetration of a constitutionally protected area is necessary before a search and seizure can be said to be violative of the Fourth Amendment to the United States Constitution."

We decline to adopt this formulation of the issues. In the first place the correct solution of Fourth Amendment problems is not necessarily promoted by incantation of the phrase "constitutionally protected area." Secondly, the Fourth Amendment cannot be translated into a general constitutional "right to privacy." That Amendment protects individual privacy against certain kinds of governmental intrusion, but its protections go further, and often have nothing to do with privacy at all. Other provisions of the Constitution protect personal privacy from other forms of governmental invasion. But the protection of a person's *general* right to privacy—his right to be let alone by other people—is, like the protection of his property and of his very life, left largely to the law of the individual States.

Because of the misleading way the issues have been formulated, the parties have attached great significance to the characterization of the telephone booth from which the petitioner placed his calls. The petitioner has strenuously argued that the booth was a "constitutionally protected area." The Government has maintained with equal vigor that it was not. But this effort to decide whether or not a given "area," viewed in the abstract, is "constitutionally protected" deflects attention from the problem presented by this case. For the Fourth Amendment protects people, not places. What a person knowingly exposes to the public, even in his own home or office, is not a subject of Fourth Amendment protection. See Lewis v. United States, 385 U.S. 206, 210; United States v. Lee, 274 U.S. 559, 563. But what he seeks to preserve as private, even in an area accessible to the public, may be constitutionally protected. See Rios v. United States, 364 U.S. 253; Ex parte Jackson, 96 U.S. 727, 733.

The Government stresses the fact that the telephone booth from which the petitioner made his calls was constructed partly of glass, so that he was as visible after he entered it as he would have been if he had remained outside. But what he sought to exclude when he entered the booth was not the intruding eye—it was the uninvited ear. He did not shed his right to do so simply because he made his calls from a place where he might be seen. No less than an individual in a business office, in a friend's apartment, or in a taxicab, a person in a telephone booth may rely upon the protection of the Fourth Amendment. One who occupies it, shuts the door behind him, and pays the toll that permits him to place a call, is surely entitled to assume that the words he utters into the mouthpiece will not be broadcast to the world. To read the Constitution more narrowly is to ignore the vital role that the public telephone has come to play in private communication.

The Government contends, however, that the activities of its agents in this case should not be tested by Fourth Amendment requirements, for the surveillance technique they employed involved no physical penetration of the telephone booth from which the petitioner placed his calls. It is true that the absence of such penetration was at one time thought to foreclose further Fourth Amendment inquiry, Olmstead v. United States, 277 U.S. 438, 457, 464, 466; Goldman v. United States, 316 U.S. 129, 134-136, for that Amendment was thought to limit only searches and seizures of tangible property. But "[t]he premise that property interests control the right of the Government to search and seize has been discredited." Warden, Md. Penitentiary v. Hayden, 387 U.S. 294, 304. Thus, although a closely divided Court supposed in *Olmstead* that surveillance without any trespass and without the seizure of any material object fell outside the ambit of the Constitution, we have since departed from the narrow view on which that decision rested. Indeed, we have expressly held that the Fourth Amendment governs not only the seizure of tangible items, but extends as well to the recording of oral statements overheard without any "technical trespass under . . . local property law." Silverman v. United States, 365 U.S. 505, 511. Once this much is acknowledged, and once it is recognized that the Fourth Amendment protects people—and not simply "areas"—against unreasonable searches and seizures it becomes clear that the reach of that Amendment cannot turn upon the presence or absence of a physical intrusion into any given enclosure.

We conclude that the underpinnings of *Olmstead* and *Goldman* have been so eroded by our subsequent decisions that the "trespass" doctrine there enunciated can no longer be regarded as controlling. The Government's activities in electronically listening to and recording the petitioner's words violated the privacy upon which he justifiably relied while using the telephone booth and thus constituted a "search and seizure" within the meaning of the Fourth Amendment. The fact that the electronic device employed to achieve that end did not happen to penetrate the wall of the booth can have no constitutional significance.

The question remaining for decision, then, is whether the search and seizure conducted in this case complied with constitutional standards. In that regard, the Government's position is that its agents acted in an entirely defensible manner: They did not begin their electronic surveillance until investigation of the petitioner's activities had established a strong probability that he was using the telephone in question to transmit gambling information to persons in other States, in violation of federal law. Moreover, the surveillance was limited, both in scope and in duration, to the specific purpose of establishing the contents of the petitioner's unlawful telephonic communications. The agents confined their surveillance to the brief periods during which he used the telephone booth, and they took great care to overhear only the conversations of the petitioner himself.

Accepting this account of the Government's actions as accurate, it is clear that this surveillance was so narrowly circumscribed that a duly authorized magistrate, properly notified of the need for such investigation, specifically informed of the basis on which it was to proceed, and clearly apprised of the precise intrusion it would entail, could constitutionally have authorized, with appropriate safeguards, the very limited search and seizure that the Government asserts in fact took place. Only last Term we sustained the validity of such an authorization, holding that, under sufficiently "precise and discriminate circumstances," a federal court may empower government agents to employ a concealed electronic device "for the narrow and particularized purpose of ascertaining the truth of the . . . allegations" of a "detailed factual affidavit alleging the commission of a specific criminal offense." Osborn v. United States, 385 U.S. 323, 329-330. Discussing that holding, the Court in Berger v. State of New York, 388 U.S. 41, said that "the order authorizing the use of the electronic device" in *Osborn* "afforded similar protections to those . . . of conventional warrants authorizing the seizure of tangible evidence." Through those protections, "no greater invasion of privacy was permitted than was necessary under the circumstances." Id., at 57. Here, too, a similar judicial order could have accommodated "the legitimate needs of law enforcement" by authorizing the carefully limited use of electronic surveillance.

The Government urges that, because its agents relied upon the decisions in *Olmstead* and *Goldman*, and because they did no more here than they might properly have done with prior judicial sanction, we should retroactively validate their conduct. That we cannot do. It is apparent that the agents in this case acted with restraint. Yet the inescapable fact is that this restraint was imposed by the agents themselves, not by a judicial officer. They were not required, before commencing the search, to present their estimate of probable cause for detached scrutiny by a neutral magistrate. They were not compelled, during the conduct of the search itself, to observe precise limits established in advance by a specific court order. Nor were they directed, after the search had been completed, to notify the authorizing magistrate in detail of all that had been seized. In the absence of such safeguards, this Court has never sustained a search upon the sole ground that officers reasonably expected to find evidence of a particular crime and voluntarily confined their activities to the least intrusive means consistent with that end. Searches conducted without warrants have been held unlawful "notwithstanding facts unquestionably showing probable cause," Agnello v. United States, 269 U.S. 20, 33, for the Constitution requires "that the deliberate, impartial judgment of a judicial officer . . . be interposed between the citizen and the police." Wong Sun v. United States, 371 U.S. 471, 481-482. "Over and again this Court has emphasized that the mandate of the [Fourth] Amendment requires adherence to judicial processes," United States v. Jeffers, 342 U.S. 48, 51, and that searches conducted outside the judicial process, without prior approval by judge or magistrate, are *per se* unreasonable under the Fourth Amendment—subject only to a few specifically established and well-delineated exceptions.

It is difficult to imagine how any of those exceptions could ever apply to the sort of search and seizure involved in this case. Even electronic surveillance substantially contemporaneous with an individual's arrest could hardly be deemed an "incident" of that arrest. Nor could the use of electronic surveillance without prior authorization be justified on grounds of "hot pursuit." And, of course, the very nature of electronic surveillance precludes its use pursuant to the suspect's consent.

The Government does not question these basic principles. Rather, it urges the creation of a new exception to cover this case.[23] It argues that surveillance of a telephone booth should be exempted from the usual requirement of advance authorization by a magistrate upon a showing of probable cause. We cannot agree. Omission of such authorization "bypasses the safeguards provided by an objective predetermination of probable cause, and substitutes instead the far less reliable procedure of an after-the-event justification for the . . . search, too likely to be subtly influenced by the familiar shortcomings of hindsight judgment." Beck v. State of Ohio, 379 U.S. 89, 96. And bypassing a neutral predetermination of the *scope* of a search leaves individuals secure from Fourth Amendment violations "only in the discretion of the police." Id., at 97.

These considerations do not vanish when the search in question is transferred from the setting of a home, an office, or a hotel room, to that of a telephone booth. Wherever a man may be, he is entitled to know that he will remain free from unreasonable searches and seizures. The government agents here ignored "the procedure of antecedent justification . . . that is central to the Fourth Amendment," a procedure that we hold to be a constitutional precondition of the kind of electronic surveillance involved in this case. Because the surveillance here failed to meet that condition, and because it led to the petitioner's conviction, the judgment must be reversed.

It is so ordered.

Judgment reversed.

Mr. Justice MARSHALL took no part in the consideration or decision of this case.

Mr. Justice DOUGLAS, with whom Mr. Justice BRENNAN joins, concurring. While I join the opinion of the Court, I feel compelled to reply to the separate concurring opinion of my Brother WHITE, which I view as a wholly unwarranted green light for the Executive Branch to resort to electronic eavesdropping without a warrant in cases which the Executive Branch itself labels "national security" matters.

There is, so far as I understand constitutional history, no distinction under the Fourth Amendment between types of crimes.

Mr. Justice HARLAN, concurring. I join the opinion of the Court, which I read to hold only (a) that an enclosed telephone booth is an area where, like a home, Weeks v. United States, 232 U.S. 383, and unlike a field, Hester v. United States, 265 U.S. 57, a person has a constitutionally protected reasonable expectation of privacy; (b) that electronic as well as physical intru-

---

[23] Whether safeguards other than prior authorization by a magistrate would satisfy the Fourth Amendment in a situation involving the national security is a question not presented by this case.

sion into a place that is in this sense private may constitute a violation of the Fourth Amendment; and (c) that the invasion of a constitutionally protected area by federal authorities is, as the Court has long held, presumptively unreasonable in the absence of a search warrant.

As the Court's opinion states, "The Fourth Amendment protects people, not places." The question, however, is what protection it affords to those people. Generally, as here, the answer to that question requires reference to a "place." My understanding of the rule that has emerged from prior decisions is that there is a twofold requirement, first that a person have exhibited an actual (subjective) expectation of privacy and, second, that the expectation be one that society is prepared to recognize as "reasonable." Thus a man's home is, for most purposes, a place where he expects privacy, but objects, activities, or statements that he exposes to the "plain view" of outsiders are not "protected" because no intention to keep them to himself has been exhibited. On the other hand, conversations in the open would not be protected against being overheard, for the expectation of privacy under the circumstances would be unreasonable. Cf. Hester v. United States, supra.

Mr. Justice WHITE, concurring. We should not require the warrant procedure and the magistrate's judgment if the President of the United States or his chief legal officer, the Attorney General, has considered the requirements of national security and authorized electronic surveillance as reasonable.

Mr. Justice BLACK, dissenting. If I could agree with the Court that eavesdropping carried on by electronic means (equivalent to wiretapping) constitutes a "search" or "seizure," I would be happy to join the Court's opinion. For on that premise my Brother STEWART sets out methods in accord with the Fourth Amendment to guide States in the enactment and enforcement of laws passed to regulate wiretapping by government. In this respect today's opinion differs sharply from Berger v. State of New York, 388 U.S. 41, decided last Term, which held void on its face a New York statute authorizing wiretapping on warrants issued by magistrates on showings of probable cause. The *Berger* case also set up what appeared to be insuperable obstacles to the valid passage of such wiretapping laws by States. The Court's opinion in this case, however, removes the doubts about state power in this field and abates to a large extent the confusion and near paralyzing effect of the *Berger* holding.[1] Not-

[1] Berger v. New York, 388 U.S. 41 (1967): "MR. JUSTICE CLARK delivered the opinion of the Court. . . .

"We believe the statute here is equally offensive. First, as we have

withstanding these good efforts of the Court, I am still unable to agree with its interpretation of the Fourth Amendment.

A conversation overheard by eavesdropping whether by plain snooping or wiretapping, is not tangible and, under the normally accepted meanings of the words, can neither be searched nor seized. In addition the language of the second clause indicates that the Amendment refers to something not only tangible so it can be seized but to something already in existence so it can be described.

Since I see no way in which the words of the Fourth Amendment can be construed to apply to eavesdropping, that closes the matter for me. In interpreting the Bill of Rights, I willingly go as far as a liberal construction of the language takes me, but I simply cannot in good conscience give a meaning to words

---

mentioned, eavesdropping is authorized without requiring belief that any particular offense has been or is being committed; nor that the 'property' sought, the conversations, be particularly described. The purpose of the probable-cause requirement of the Fourth Amendment to keep the state out of constitutionally protected areas until it has reason to believe that a specific crime has been or is being committed is thereby wholly aborted. Likewise the statute's failure to describe with particularity the conversations sought gives the officer a roving commission to 'seize' any and all conversations. It is true that the statute requires the naming of 'the person or persons whose communications, conversations or discussions are to be overheard or recorded. . . .' But this does no more than identify the person whose constitutionally protected area is to be invaded rather than 'particularly describing' the communications, conversations, or discussions to be seized. As with general warrants this leaves too much to the discretion of the officer executing the order. Secondly, authorization of eavesdropping for a two-month period is the equivalent of a series of intrusions, searches, and seizures pursuant to a single showing of probable cause. Prompt execution is also avoided. During such a long and continuous (24 hours a day) period the conversations of any and all persons coming into the area covered by the device will be seized indiscriminately and without regard to their connection with the crime under investigation. Moreover, the statute permits, and there were authorized here, extensions of the original two-month period—presumably for two months each—on a mere showing that such extension is 'in the public interest.' Apparently the original grounds on which the eavesdrop order was initially issued also form the basis of the renewal. This we believe insufficient without a showing of present probable cause for the continuance of the eavesdrop. Third, the statute places no termination date on the eavesdrop once the conversation sought is seized. This is left entirely in the discretion of the officer. Finally, the statute's procedure, necessarily because its success depends on secrecy, has no requirement for notice as do conventional warrants, nor does it overcome this defect by requiring some showing of special facts. On the contrary, it permits unconsented entry without any showing of exigent circumstances. Such a showing of exigency, in order to avoid notice, would appear more important in eavesdropping, with its inherent dangers, than that required when conventional procedures of search and seizure are utilized. Nor does the statute provide for a return on the warrant thereby leaving full discretion in the officer as to the use of seized conversations of innocent as well as guilty parties. In short, the statute's blanket grant of permission to eavesdrop is without adequate judicial supervision or protective procedures. . . . Reversed."

which they have never before been thought to have and which they certainly do not have in common ordinary usage. I will not distort the words of the Amendment in order to "keep the Constitution up to date" or "to bring it into harmony with the times." It was never meant for this Court to have such power, which in effect would make us a continuously functioning constitutional convention.

With this decision the Court has completed, I hope, its rewriting of the Fourth Amendment, which started only recently when the Court began referring incessantly to the Fourth Amendment not so much as a law against *unreasonable* searches and seizures as one to protect an individual's privacy. By clever word juggling the Court finds it plausible to argue that language aimed specifically at searches and seizures of things that can be searched and seized may, to protect privacy, be applied to eavesdropped evidence of conversations that can neither be searched nor seized. Few things happen to an individual that do not affect his privacy in one way or another. Thus, by arbitrarily substituting the Court's language, designed to protect privacy, for the Constitution's language, designed to protect against unreasonable searches and seizures, the Court has made the Fourth Amendment its vehicle for holding all laws violative of the Constitution which offend the Court's broadest concept of privacy. As I said in Griswold v. State of Connecticut, 381 U.S. 479, "The Court talks about a constitutional 'right of privacy' as though there is some constitutional provision or provisions forbidding any law ever to be passed which might abridge the 'privacy' of individuals. But there is not." (Dissenting opinion, p. 508.) I made clear in that dissent my fear of the dangers involved when this Court uses the "broad, abstract and ambiguous concept" of "privacy" as a "comprehensive substitute for the Fourth Amendment's guarantee against 'unreasonable searches and seizures.'" (See generally dissenting opinion, pp. 507-527.)

The Fourth Amendment protects privacy only to the extent that it prohibits unreasonable searches and seizures of "persons, houses, papers and effects." No general right is created by the Amendment so as to give this Court the unlimited power to hold unconstitutional everything which affects privacy. Certainly the Framers, well acquainted as they were with the excesses of governmental power, did not intend to grant this Court such omnipotent lawmaking authority as that. The history of governments proves that it is dangerous to freedom to repose such powers in courts.

For these reasons I respectfully dissent.

Until the *Katz* decision the requirement of physical intrusion had provided a simple mechanical test for judging the ambit of the fourth amendment.[j] With that requirement now gone, there is no simple standard in its place. A series of new decisions may be required before it can be established which of the things a person considers to be private will be protected by the "search and seizure" language of the Constitution on the ground that governmental intrusion is constitutionally unreasonable.[k] Despite the Court's disclaimer that it does not find a broad "right of privacy," as such, in the fourth amendment, the decision opens up new possibilities. Investigation techniques which raise significant privacy issues, without being readily classifiable as observing or overhearing (*i.e.*, surveillance as that term is used here) or searching, are illustrated by the following:

1

Police, responsible for screening applicants for liquor licenses, suspected that an applicant was a front for a known criminal. As part of their effort to test their suspicion that the applicant did not have financial resources sufficient to permit him to open an elaborate cocktail lounge on his own, police sent a man to each of the local banks to inquire about the applicant's savings account balance and to obtain a record of his checks and deposits for the previous several months.

2

"One government agency made arrangements with Washington trash collectors to turn in all the trash picked up at some fifty addresses. When Rep. Cornelius Gallagher (D.,N.J.) learned about it, he demanded an explanation from the Sanitation Department. Commissioner C. M. Duke wrote back that the trash was segregated 'to determine from typical household units the characteristics of refuse for statistical and design purposes.' He didn't explain why the trash for this study should be collected only from people under federal investigation."[l]

---

[j] No other constitutional provisions relate so directly to surveillance, though for example surveillance of a defendant's conference with his attorney might well infringe his right to counsel.

[k] For example, the propriety of listening to conversations among jail or prison inmates or between inmates and visitors (other than counsel) may be subject to reconsideration. *See* Lanza v. New York, 370 U.S. 139, 143-44, 150 (1962).

[l] Anderson, *A New and Frightening Trend: Intimidation by Government*, PARADE, Feb. 20, 1966, at 4.

The Internal Revenue Service manual for agents reportedly suggests inspection of trash as an avenue of investigation in tax cases. *Hearings on Invasions of Privacy (Government Agencies) Before the Subcomm. on*

3

"Some 20 Federal departments or agencies currently collect and publish data, including the Internal Revenue Service, the Census Bureau, the Office of Education, the Bureau of Labor Statistics, and the Bureau of Old-Age and Survivors Insurance. Information has been supplied to these agencies by persons with the understanding that it will only be used by the receiving agency, for a specific purpose, and in most cases on a confidential basis.

"Now, it is suggested that much of this information be pooled in one central source. Presumably, current disclosure restrictions would be adhered to, but the effectiveness of these laws, in some cases, is dubious. We have even greater fear that the law in some cases is of small concern to those in law enforcement who become overeager in enforcement of that law as they view it. We do not want to see the intended good use of a data center distorted so that it simply makes confidential information more readily available to more people.

"Nor do we wish to see a composite picture of an individual recorded in a single informational warehouse, where the touch of a button would assemble all the governmental information about the person since his birth. Such a hypothetical situation could become very real, because into a data bank could be deposited records covering his birth, schooling, military service, employment history, personality traits, credit status, and practically any other aspect of his life. Although the personal data bank apparently has not been proposed as yet, many people view this proposal as a first step toward its creation. I am sure there will be pressures—both within and outside Government—to create one in the future, all, of course, in the interest of economy and efficiency.

"The presence of these records in Government files is frightening enough, but the thought of them neatly bundled together into one compact package is appalling. We cannot be certain that such dossiers would always be used by benevolent people for benevolent purposes."[m]

Administrative Practice and Procedure of the Senate Comm. on the Judiciary, 89th Cong., 1st Sess., vol. 4, pt. 4, at 1704 (1965).

See United States v. Minker, 312 F.2d 632 (3d Cir. 1962) (private trash collector turned over trash removed from apartment building where gambling suspect lived); State v. Purvis, 438 P.2d 1002 (Ore. 1968) (hotel maid turned over trash collected in cleaning narcotic suspect's room).

[m] *The Computer and Invasion of Privacy, Hearings Before a Subcomm. of the Comm. on Government Operations (Special Subcommittee on Invasion of Privacy), House of Representatives,* 89th Cong., 2d Sess. 2-3 (1966).

The *Katz* case established basic constitutional limitations upon investigative techniques by interpreting the fourth amendment to cover other intrusions into privacy than those which had theretofore been classified as "searches." The courts and legislatures have, however, imposed various other restrictions upon surveillance which overlap and sometimes go beyond the constitutional limitation. For example, if a policeman enters a suspect's yard in order to look through the window, this may be a trespass under state law and yet not a violation of the Constitution. There are also a few eavesdropping statutes (which seem directed at habitual rumormongers and gossips rather than police investigators),[n] but legislatures have not spoken to the question of ordinary police surveillance. The major legislative effort has been in the realm of regulating wiretapping or electronic eavesdropping. In 1967 the Supreme Court summarized the state law thus:[o]

> Seven States, California, Illinois, Maryland, Massachusetts, Nevada, New York, and Oregon, prohibit surreptitious eavesdropping by mechanical or electronic device. However, all save Illinois permit official court-ordered eavesdropping. Some 36 States prohibit wiretapping. But of these, 27 permit "authorized" interception of some type.

At the same time federal law made no reference to electronic eavesdropping but did outlaw wiretapping flatly, with no exceptions.[p]

In 1968, however, after a generation of debate, Congress enacted in the Federal Crime Control Act a provision which prohibits both electronic eavesdropping and wiretapping, but establishes an exception for court-authorized interception of communications in specified classes of cases.

The long-continued debate over permitting or forbidding these investigative devices to law enforcement as a weapon against crime, particularly organized crime, was often clouded by publicity about private wiretapping and eavesdropping in pursuit of business secrets, evidence of grounds for divorce, political plans, and so on. Private intrusions of this sort are strictly forbidden.

---

[n] *See* S. DASH, R. SCHWARTZ & R. KNOWLTON, THE EAVESDROPPERS 426-27 (1959).

[o] Berger v. New York, 388 U.S. 41, 47-48 (1967).

[p] Communications Act of 1934, 48 Stat. 1103.

3. Methods of Control

The problem of defining acceptable surveillance techniques is inextricably bound up with the problem of creating methods for controlling improper practices. These controls may be established by legislation, judicial decision, or administrative regulation and policymaking.

Legislation on wiretapping and electronic eavesdropping has sometimes outlawed them entirely, using criminal penalty or the exclusion of evidence as the major sanction. At other times legislation has permitted some electronic surveillance, establishing criteria and instituting a warrant procedure to make the judiciary responsible for supervising police practices.[q] Such warrant systems were given the Supreme Court's blessing in Katz v. United States, *supra,* and adopted by Congress in the Crime Control Act of 1968.

The courts in their turn have responsibility to interpret the statutes and the limiting constitutional provisions, to issue warrants where that is provided for, and to decree imposition of the sanctions which the legislature has created for violation of the statute. In addition, courts have their own powers of control. For example, some surveillance may be held to be tortious, though tort remedies are generally inadequate to control police conduct.[r] In unusual circumstances an injunction against a kind of surveillance may be obtained, with the sanction of citation for contempt upon violation of the court order.[s] Court sanctions may be against not only the offending officer personally, but also against the prosecution's case. On the ground that violations by police are motivated by a desire to obtain conviction of offenders, the courts have sought to deter police misconduct by depriving the police of the benefits they seek by their misconduct. They have refused to take the extreme step of conferring immunity from prosecution upon a criminal whose rights have been infringed,[t] and have relied instead upon creation of rules excluding from use as evidence any information or mate-

[q] Less direct legislative efforts at control include regulation of the manufacture or possession of electronic surveillance devices without registration with the State Police, MD. ANN. CODE art. 27, § 125D (1957), or except under contract with federal, state, or local government units, 18 U.S.C. §§ 2512, 2513.

[r] *See* Foote, *Tort Remedies for Police Violations of Individual Rights,* 39 MINN. L. REV. 493 (1955).

[s] *See* p. 83 n.g, *supra.*

[t] Battaglia v. United States, 383 F.2d 303, 307-08 (9th Cir. 1967), denies that a flat bar to prosecution is required as an effective deterrent against electronic eavesdropping.

rial obtained in violation of constitutional rights, statutory rights, or court-determined standards of propriety.[u]

Important as it is to consider court-imposed sanctions, it would be a mistake not to recognize that administrators (for example, police officials and prosecutorial agencies) may institute measures of self-regulation. One such device is the police disciplinary proceeding against an officer for violation of law or departmental regulation. If, however, the law violation is tacitly authorized by his superiors this device is not likely to be effective. On the other hand, if an administrative policy against use of illegal surveillance techniques is consistently followed, the individual law enforcement agents will the more readily comply.

The materials above have provided some examples of tort action against the police and of the exclusionary rule of evidence. Other methods of control are suggested by the materials which follow.

OMNIBUS CRIME CONTROL AND SAFE STREETS ACT OF 1968

Public Law 90-351, 90th Cong., June 19, 1968

18 U.S.C. § 2510. Definitions

As used in this chapter—

. . .

(2) "oral communication" means any oral communication uttered by a person exhibiting an expectation that such communication is not subject to interception under circumstances justifying such expectation;

. . .

(4) "intercept" means the aural acquisition of the contents of any wire or oral communication through the use of any electronic, mechanical, or other device.

. . .

§ 2511. Interception and disclosure of wire or oral communications prohibited

(1) Except as otherwise specifically provided in this chapter any person who—

[u] Problems raised by use of these exclusionary rules as a method of controlling police conduct are considered in more detail below, in relation to search and seizure and interrogation.

(a) willfully intercepts, endeavors to intercept, or procures any other person to intercept or endeavor to intercept, any wire or oral communication;

. . .

shall be fined not more than $10,000 or imprisoned not more than five years, or both.[v]

. . .

(c) It shall not be unlawful under this chapter for a person acting under color of law to intercept a wire or oral communication, where such person is a party to the communication or one of the parties to the communication has given prior consent to such interception.

. . .

§ 2515. Prohibition of use as evidence of intercepted wire or oral communications

Whenever any wire or oral communication has been intercepted, no part of the contents of such communication and no evidence derived therefrom may be received in evidence in any trial, hearing, or other proceeding in or before any court, grand jury, department, officer, agency, regulatory body, legislative committee, or other authority of the United States, a State, or a political subdivision thereof if the disclosure of that information would be in violation of this chapter.

§ 2516. Authorization for interception of wire or oral communications

(1) The Attorney General, or any Assistant Attorney General specially designated by the Attorney General, may authorize an application to a Federal judge of competent jurisdiction for, and such judge may grant in conformity with section 2518 of this chapter an order authorizing or approving the interception of wire or oral communications by the Federal Bureau of Investigation, or a Federal agency having responsibility for the investigation of the offense as to which the application is made, when such interception may provide or has provided evidence of—

(a) any offense punishable by death or by imprisonment for more than one year under sections 2274 through 2277 of title

---

[v] No use was ever made of the criminal provisions of the earlier wiretap statute (48 Stat. 1103) (fine of $10,000 or imprisonment of one year, or both) against law enforcement officers, though there are two reported prosecutions of private wiretappers. *See* Lee v. Florida, 392 U.S. 378, 386 n.12 (1968).

42 of the United States Code (relating to the enforcement of the Atomic Energy Act of 1954), or under the following chapters of this title: chapter 37 (relating to espionage), chapter 105 (relating to sabotage), chapter 115 (relating to treason), or chapter 102 (relating to riots);

(b) a violation of section 186 or section 501(c) of title 29, United States Code (dealing with restrictions on payments and loans to labor organizations), or any offense which involves murder, kidnapping, robbery, or extortion, and which is punishable under this title;

(c) any offense which is punishable under the following sections of this title: section 201 (bribery of public officials and witnesses), section 224 (bribery in sporting contests), section 1084 (transmission of wagering information), section 1503 (influencing or injuring an officer, juror, or witness generally), section 1510 (obstruction of criminal investigations), section 1751 (Presidential assassinations, kidnapping, and assault), section 1951 (interference with commerce by threats or violence), section 1952 (interstate and foreign travel or transportation in aid of racketeering enterprises), section 1954 (offer, acceptance, or solicitation to influence operations of employee benefit plan), section 659 (theft from interstate shipment), section 664 (embezzlement from pension and welfare funds), or sections 2314 and 2315 (interstate transportation of stolen property);

(d) any offense involving counterfeiting punishable under section 471, 472, or 473 of this title;

(e) any offense involving bankruptcy fraud or the manufacture, importation, receiving, concealment, buying, selling, or otherwise dealing in narcotic drugs, marihuana, or other dangerous drugs, punishable under any law of the United States;

(f) any offense including extortionate credit transactions under sections 892, 893, or 894 of this title; or

(g) any conspiracy to commit any of the foregoing offenses.

(2) The principal prosecuting attorney of any State, or the principal prosecuting attorney of any political subdivision thereof, if such attorney is authorized by a statute of that State to make application to a State court judge of competent jurisdiction for an order authorizing or approving the interception of wire or oral communications, may apply to such judge for, and such judge may grant in conformity with section 2518 of this chapter and with the applicable State statute an order authorizing, or approving the interception of wire or oral communications by investigative or law enforcement officers having responsibility for the investigation of the offense as to which the application is made, when such interception may provide or has provided evidence of

the commission of the offense of murder, kidnapping, gambling, robbery, bribery, extortion, or dealing in narcotic drugs, marihuana or other dangerous drugs, or other crime dangerous to life, limb, or property, and punishable by imprisonment for more than one year, designated in any applicable State statute authorizing such interception, or any conspiracy to commit any of the foregoing offenses.

. . .

§ 2518. Procedure for interception of wire or oral communications

(1) Each application for an order authorizing or approving the interception of a wire or oral communication shall be made in writing upon oath or affirmation to a judge of competent jurisdiction and shall state the applicant's authority to make such application. Each application shall include the following information:

. . .

(e) a full and complete statement of the facts concerning all previous applications known to the individual authorizing and making the application, made to any judge for authorization to intercept, or for approval of interceptions of, wire or oral communications involving any of the same persons, facilities or places specified in the application, and the action taken by the judge on each such application;

. . .

(3) Upon such application the judge may enter an ex parte order, as requested or as modified, authorizing or approving interception of wire or oral communications within the territorial jurisdiction of the court in which the judge is sitting, if the judge determines on the basis of the facts submitted by the applicant that—

(a) there is probable cause for belief that an individual is committing, has committed, or is about to commit a particular offense enumerated in section 2516 of this chapter;

(b) there is probable cause for belief that particular communications concerning that offense will be obtained through such interception;

(c) normal investigative procedures have been tried and have failed or reasonably appear to be unlikely to succeed if tried or to be too dangerous;

(d) there is probable cause for belief that the facilities from which, or the place where, the wire or oral communications are to be intercepted are being used, or are about to be used, in connection with the commission of such offense, or are leased to, listed in the name of, or commonly used by such person.

(4) Each order authorizing or approving the interception of any wire or oral communication shall specify—

(a) the identity of the person, if known, whose communications are to be intercepted;

(b) the nature and location of the communications facilities as to which, or the place where, authority to intercept is granted;

(c) a particular description of the type of communication sought to be intercepted, and a statement of the particular offense to which it relates;

(d) the identity of the agency authorized to intercept the communications, and of the person authorizing the application; and

(e) the period of time during which such interception is authorized, including a statement as to whether or not the interception shall automatically terminate when the described communication has been first obtained.

(5) No order entered under this section may authorize or approve the interception of any wire or oral communication for any period longer than is necessary to achieve the objective of the authorization, nor in any event longer than thirty days. Extensions of an order may be granted, but only upon application for an extension made in accordance with subsection (1) of this section and the court making the findings required by subsection (3) of this section. . . .

. . .

(7) Notwithstanding any other provision of this chapter, any investigative or law enforcement officer, specially designated by the Attorney General or by the principal prosecuting attorney of any State or subdivision thereof acting pursuant to a statute of that State, who reasonably determines that—

(a) an emergency situation exists with respect to conspiratorial activities threatening the national security interest or to conspiratorial activities characteristic of organized crime that requires a wire or oral communication to be intercepted before an order authorizing such interception can with due diligence be obtained, and

(b) there are grounds upon which an order could be entered under this chapter to authorize such interception,

may intercept such wire or oral communication if an application for an order approving the interception is made in accordance with this section within forty-eight hours after the interception has occurred, or begins to occur. . . .

. . .

(d) Within a reasonable time but not later than ninety days after the filing of an application for an order of approval under section 2518(7)(b) which is denied or the termination of the period of an order or extensions thereof, the issuing or denying judge shall cause to be served, on the persons named in the order or the application, and such other parties to intercepted communications as the judge may determine in his discretion that is in the interest of justice, an inventory which shall include notice of—

(1) the fact of the entry of the order or the application;

(2) the date of the entry and the period of authorized, approved or disapproved interception, or the denial of the application; and

(3) the fact that during the period wire or oral communications were or were not intercepted.

The judge, upon the filing of a motion, may in his discretion make available to such person or his counsel for inspection such portions of the intercepted communications, applications and orders as the judge determines to be in the interest of justice. On an ex parte showing of good cause to a judge of competent jurisdiction the serving of the inventory required by this subsection may be postponed.

. . .

(10) (a) Any aggrieved person in any trial, hearing, or proceeding in or before any court, department, officer, agency, regulatory body, or other authority of the United States, a State, or a political subdivision thereof, may move to suppress the contents of any intercepted wire or oral communication, or evidence derived therefrom, on the grounds that—

(i) the communication was unlawfully intercepted;

(ii) the order of authorization or approval under which it was intercepted is insufficient on its face; or

(iii) the interception was not made in conformity with the order of authorization or approval.

Such motion shall be made before the trial, hearing, or proceeding unless there was no opportunity to make such motion or the person was not aware of the grounds of the motion. . . .

. . .

§ 2520. Recovery of civil damages authorized

Any person whose wire or oral communication is intercepted, disclosed, or used in violation of this chapter shall (1) have a civil cause of action against any person who intercepts, discloses, or uses, or procures any other person to intercept, disclose, or use such communications, and (2) be entitled to recover from any such person—

(a) actual damages but not less than liquidated damages computed at the date of $100 a day for each day of violation or $1,000, whichever is higher;

(b) punitive damages; and

(c) a reasonable attorney's fee and other litigation costs reasonably incurred.

A good faith reliance on a court order or on the provisions of section 2518(7) of this chapter shall constitute a complete defense to any civil or criminal action brought under this chapter.

. . .

WISCONSIN STATUTES § 885.36 (1965)

885.36 Wire tapping.

Evidence obtained directly or indirectly as a result of the interception of a communication, by telephone or telegraph, shall be totally inadmissible in the courts of this state.

The *Katz* opinion clearly indicates that the decision to use certain surveillance techniques should be subject to prior approval of a neutral and detached magistrate rather than being left to the discretion of the police. Is there more reason to require judicial approval of surveillance methods than there is to require judicial approval of the decision to institute an investigation? A broad issue of which this is part is the proper division of responsibility between administrative decision-making and judicial decision-making.

If, as the *Katz* case says, a judge is required to decide whether certain investigative methods are reasonable under the circumstances, how much should he know about the crime problem in the community or the effectiveness or lack of effectiveness of the particular surveillance method? And how much deference should he give to the "expertise" or experience of the police?

Many police express misgivings about cases like *Katz.* They say that some judges do not take the warrant process seriously and sign anything a police officer puts in front of them, without even reading it. Obtaining a warrant under these circumstances is wasteful formality. They also say that there is wide disparity among judges as to what is an adequate basis for a warrant, with the result that police do not know what is required. Also they assert that some judges require much more than appellate courts say is required because they do not want the embarrassment of having one of their warrants held invalid. What should the judge's attitude toward the warrant process be? Should this be the function of a judge or a lower judicial officer like a justice of the peace or court commissioner? Is issuing a warrant a more or less important judicial function than presiding over a trial?

The effectiveness of a warrant system to prevent undesirable police conduct is illuminated to some degree by the experience in New York some years ago in applying its wiretap warrant requirement.

BOOK REVIEW
By Monrad Paulsen
The Eavesdroppers, by Samuel Dash, Richard F. Schwartz & Robert E. Knowlton
14 Rutgers Law Review 636 (1960)

In New York a statute (in violation of federal law) provides for wiretapping under a court order to be issued upon a showing that there is reasonable ground to believe that evidence of crime will be obtained by interception of communications on a certain telephone. *The Eavesdroppers* gives pause to anyone who is attracted by such a resolution of the wiretap problem. First of all, the author reports that law enforcement officials find no difficulty in getting such orders when they want them. The judges do not make independent inquiry into the usefulness of the order as a general matter, and those judges who do are soon avoided in favor of those more prosecution oriented. "In Manhattan," Dash reports, "two or three judges of the Court of General Sessions receive most of the district attorney's business. It is practically unheard of for a judge to fail to grant a wiretap order for the district attorney." If this is true, provision for judicial protection is an empty pretense. Secondly, law enforcement officers do not obey the law. A great deal of wiretapping goes on in New York City in spite of the federal prohibition. According to the author's estimate, between 16,000 and 29,000 wiretaps are made there every year. The overwhelming number of these intercepted communications are made without following the prescribed procedures for obtaining a warrant authorizing wiretapping. Thirdly, if the form of the request for an order set forth in the book is representative of those in general use, it would be impossible for a judge to exercise his discretion intelligently. The statement is barren of facts suggesting a reason why listening at the particular telephone might provide evidence of crime.

District Attorney Hogan's testimony to a congressional committee is surprising in the light of the New York statute. He told the committee that his office "keeps a wiretap surveillance on parolees and narcotic addicts to collect general information on their activities and contacts." It seems unlikely that this practice can be justified on the statutory standard of reasonable ground to believe that evidence of crime may be uncovered by a wiretap.

ASPECTS OF THE EVIDENCE GATHERING PROCESS IN ORGANIZED CRIME CASES in THE PRESIDENT'S COMMISSION ON LAW ENFORCEMENT AND ADMINISTRATION OF JUSTICE, TASK FORCE REPORT: ORGANIZED CRIME 95 (1967)

By G. Robert Blakey

. . . Court supervision under New York's permissive statutes at one time was often perfunctory. Today the picture has substantially changed under the impact of pre-trial adversary hearings on motions to suppress electronically seized evidence. A number of years ago there was evidence of low level police abuse. Legislative and administrative action, however, has been largely successful in curtailing its incidence. Use by New York prosecutors has been free from demonstrated abuse, and in recent years, they have shown a willingness to investigate and prosecute both private and law enforcement violation of the state electronic surveillance provisions. The techniques, moreover, have been sparingly used. Since 1959, for example, the Office of the District Attorney of New York County, where the most vigorous use of them is made, has averaged only about seventy-five wiretap orders per year—used only for leads and not court disclosure—and about nineteen bug orders per year.

There is no substantial evidence, moreover, that the commercial, political, intellectual or personal life of the New York community has measurably suffered because of the court order system. The fear that authorized electronic surveillance would seriously impair free communication therefore has proven largely unreal. Indeed, even members of the underworld, who have legitimate reason to fear that their meetings might be bugged or their phones tapped, have continued to meet and to make relatively free use of the phone.

Prior to the *Katz* case and the Crime Control Act, wiretapping which was not divulged outside the law enforcement agency—that is, which was not used in evidence—was thought not prohibited by federal law. The Attorney General and the President, however, established policies restricting use of wiretapping by federal agents even within the law's bounds.

MEMORANDUM

June 16, 1967

TO: The Heads of Executive Departments and Agencies
FROM: Office of the Attorney General, Washington, D. C.
RE: Wiretapping and Electronic Eavesdropping

It is essential that all agencies having any responsibility for law enforcement take steps to make certain that electronic and related devices designed to intercept, overhear, or record private verbal communications be subject to tight administrative control to assure that they will not be used in a manner which is illegal and that even legal use of such devices will be strictly controlled. In order further to assist you to achieve these ends, the following rules have been formulated.

I. Prohibition Against Use of Mechanical or Electronic Devices to Intercept, Overhear, or Record Conversations.

A. Prohibition Against Interception of Telephone Conversations.

1. Section 605 of the Communications Act (Title 47, U.S.C. § 605) prohibits the interception and divulgence or use of telephone communications and is applicable to federal law enforcement agents.

2. Interception by federal personnel of telephone conversations, by any mechanical or electronic device, unless with the consent of one of the parties to the conversation, is prohibited

by Presidential directive,[w] and this prohibition applies whether or not the information which may be acquired through interception is intended to be used in any way or to be subsequently divulged outside the agency involved. Any question as to whether the use of a particular device can be said to involve a prohibited interception of a telephone conversation should be referred to the Department of Justice.

3. To further assure protection of the privacy of telephone conversations, each agency shall adopt rules governing the interception by its personnel of telephone conversations under circumstances where a party to the conversation has consented. Such rules shall, where appropriate, provide for the advance approval by the agency head of such interception.

POSTAL MANUAL (5/15/67)
Subchapter 860 Mail Covers[x]
Part 861
Administration

861.1 POLICY

The Post Office Department has established rigid controls and supervision with respect to the use of mail covers as investigative or law enforcement techniques.

861.2 SCOPE

These regulations establish the sole authority and procedure for initiating, processing, placing and using mail covers. . . .

861.4 AUTHORIZATIONS—CHIEF POSTAL INSPECTOR

.41 The Chief Postal Inspector is the principal officer of the Post Office Department in the administration of all matters gov-

[w] In United States v. Desist, 384 F.2d 889 (2d Cir. 1967), defendant urged that he was the subject of electronic eavesdropping which violated a policy statement issued by President Johnson on June 30, 1965. The court noted that the policy statement was not in the record. "Therefore, we will not consider further the legal effect, if any, on the courts of an internal administrative statement."

[x] In response to the criticisms of Senator Long for the mail cover of Roy Cohen the Post Office Department issued these new regulations limiting the use of mail covers. *Hearings on Invasions of Privacy (Government Agencies) Before the Subcomm. on Administrative Practice and Procedure of the Senate Comm. on the Judiciary,* 89th Cong., 1st Sess., pt. 1, at 234-35, 320 (1965); *cf.* p. 77 n.c, *supra.*

erning mail covers. He may delegate by written order any or all authority in this regard to not more than four subordinate officials within his Bureau.

.42 The Chief Postal Inspector, or his designee, may order mail covers under the following circumstances:

a. When he has reason to believe the subject or subjects of the mail cover are engaged in any activity violative of any postal statute.

b. When written request is received from any law enforcement agency wherein the requesting authority stipulates and specifies the reasonable grounds that exist which demonstrate the mail cover is necessary to (1) protect the national security, (2) locate a fugitive, or (3) obtain information regarding the commission or attempted commission of a crime.

c. Where time is of the essence, the Chief Postal Inspector, or his designee, may act upon an oral request to be confirmed by the requesting authority in writing within 2 business days. However, no information shall be released until an appropriate written request is received.

861.5 Postal Inspectors in Charge

.51 All Postal Inspectors in Charge, and not more than three designees pursuant to delegations in writing, may order mail covers under the following circumstances:

a. Where he has reason to believe the subject or subjects are engaged in an activity violative of any postal statute.

b. Where written request is received from any law enforcement agency of the Federal, State, or local governments, wherein the requesting authority stipulates and specifies the reasonable grounds that exist which demonstrate the mail cover would aid in the location of a fugitive, or that it would assist in obtaining information concerning the commission or attempted commission of a crime. Excepting fugitive cases, any request from a Federal agency for a mail cover and the determination made shall promptly be transmitted to the Chief Postal Inspector for review. . . .

861.6 LIMITATIONS

. . .

.62 No mail covers shall include matter mailed between the mail cover subject and his known attorney-at-law. . . .

.64 Excepting mail covers ordered upon subjects engaged, or suspected to be engaged, in any activity against the national security, or activity violative of any postal law, no mail cover order shall remain in force and effect for more than 30 days. At the expiration of such period, or prior thereto, the requesting authority may be granted additional 30-day periods under the same conditions and procedures applicable to the original request. . . .

.66 Excepting fugitive cases, no mail cover shall remain in force when the subject has been indicted for any cause. If the subject is under investigation for further criminal violations, a new mail cover order must be requested consistent with these regulations.

861.7 RECORDS

. . .

.73 If the Chief Postal Inspector determines a mail cover was improperly ordered by a Postal Inspector in Charge or his designee all data acquired while the cover was in force shall be destroyed, and the requesting authority notified of the discontinuance of the mail cover and the reasons therefor. . . .

Reference Note

The best single source of current information on wiretapping and electronic surveillance is G. Blakey (reporter), *Standards Relating to Electronic Surveillance* (American Bar Association Project on Minimum Standards for Criminal Justice 1968). The proposed standards are so similar to the Crime Control Act of 1968 that the comments can serve as a gloss on the federal statute.

S. DASH, R. SCHWARTZ & R. KNOWLTON, THE EAVESDROPPERS (1959), is an extensive description of practice in the field of wiretapping and electronic eavesdropping as of its date. The book was extensively commented on in *A Symposium, The Wiretapping-Eavesdropping Problem: Reflections on The Eaves-*

droppers, 44 MINN. L. REV. 811 (1960). *See also* Book Review, at 106, *supra.*

The broad policy questions are addressed in Westin, *Science, Privacy, and Freedom: Issues and Proposals for the 1970's,* pts. 1 & 2, 66 COLUM. L. REV. 1003, 1205 (1966).

An excellent summary of practice and law immediately prior to the *Katz* decision is STATE OF NEW YORK TEMPORARY STATE COMMISSION ON THE CONSTITUTIONAL CONVENTION, INDIVIDUAL LIBERTIES: THE ADMINISTRATION OF CRIMINAL JUSTICE 72-114 (Mar. 16, 1967). *See also* Blakey, *Aspects of the Evidence Gathering Process in Organized Crime Cases* in THE PRESIDENT'S COMMISSION ON LAW ENFORCEMENT AND ADMINISTRATION OF JUSTICE, TASK FORCE REPORT: ORGANIZED CRIME 80 (1967).

The consequences of a tendency toward expanding interpretation of constitutional provisions in control of the criminal law process are discussed in Friendly, *The Bill of Rights as a Code of Criminal Procedure,* 53 CALIF. L. REV. 929 (1965).

B. UNDERCOVER OPERATIONS

In contrast to surveillance, which involves secret observation or listening, the undercover operation generally calls for a degree of involvement, participation, or other form of open contact with suspected persons by police officers or their agents. However, the true identity or allegiance of the undercover agent is not disclosed, so that this is also a kind of surreptitious detection technique.

The effort to which police go to hide their identity in working under cover depends upon the nature of the offense being investigated. In some situations nothing more is required than that a detective dressed in his ordinary civilian clothing be present at a given event or location where he believes criminal activity will take place. In other situations, however, the officer may dress and act in a way carefully designed to deceive.

Where police are themselves the undercover agents, they are faced with questions about whether they are limited as to the individuals whose activities they may investigate, whether they may properly ignore some criminal activity which comes to their attention, whether they may be justified in engaging in some criminal activity themselves in their assumed role, whether they may lie or may secretly record what they hear, whether they may put temptation in the way of a suspect to test his willingness to commit crime, whether there is any obligation to make a speedy arrest after detecting a crime, and so on.

Where police use as their "special agent" a lay person, the problems are the same as those mentioned above, essentially unchanged by the fact that the police are acting through a lay agent. Because agents drawn from the suspected offender's criminal milieu may from vindictiveness or greed have a special motive to implicate someone in crime, there is the additional problem of reliability of the information obtained from the informer.

There is no developed control mechanism in this area except the exclusion of evidence, the defense of entrapment, and some exercise of discretionary power to dismiss for police misconduct. Prosecution of the officer for his having committed a crime is a theoretical possibility.[y] There has been no effort to create a judicial authorization procedure, such as has been achieved in other areas through the warrant process. Nor is there any clear indication that police administrators have attempted to establish procedures to control the use of undercover activities. Administrative concern tends rather to be with the impact of undercover activities upon the commitment of manpower or expenditure of funds, or with the possibility of embarrassment if the undercover activity were exposed, rather than with the propriety of undercover techniques.

1. *Undercover Techniques*

The Practice

The following illustrate fairly common types of situations in vice investigations. The reasons police choose to initiate investigations into vice offenses are suggested above at 62.

1

Two investigators for a state liquor control commission suspected that a resort tavern was illegally selling liquor on a beer-wine license. Playing the role of patrons, the investigators entered the tavern one evening around 10:00 p.m. They drank beer and observed. They noticed the bartender take empty glasses into a storeroom located at the rear of the tavern and return with them containing what looked like whiskey, fill the glasses with mix, and serve them. The investigators left at 11:30 p.m., returning shortly thereafter with two women whom they

[y] The existence of privilege for police to violate one law in enforcing another is discussed in Rotenberg, *The Police Detection Practice of Encouragement,* 49 VA. L. REV. 871, 885-89 (1963).

had met outside. The investigators ordered and obtained for themselves and companions several whiskey drinks. A part of each drink was preserved for future laboratory testing.

2

The police suspected that prostitutes were operating on a certain street corner. A police officer dressed in civilian clothes and driving an unmarked car late at night stopped his automobile at the corner upon seeing a woman standing alone. She approached the car, opened the door and got in, saying, "Well?" The officer replied, "Yes." She inquired how much he had to spend. He said that he could not go over $7. She said it would cost $1.50 or $2 for a hotel room if he wanted to go to a hotel. He indicated that he did. She said, "OK." He asked what he would get. She replied, "For that price a straight lay." He placed her under arrest.[z]

3

A woman narcotics agent asked an acquaintance she had made to get some heroin for her. He did so and was later arrested for selling drugs to her. He protested that he had the impression that all he had to do to receive the woman's favors was to obtain some heroin for her. He said that it was well known in the area where heroin could be bought and he merely went to a readily available source.

4

Police were assigned to investigate a complaint that homosexuals were soliciting persons using the rest room in a department store. One of the officers assigned to the investigation loitered in the rest room, striking up conversations with men who entered. In one such contact, after both parties had used words of homosexual jargon, the other man showed the officer the key to his hotel room and offered to "take care" of him there. The officer later met him at the hotel, where the man specified what act he would perform.

THE POLICE DETECTION PRACTICE OF ENCOURAGEMENT

By Daniel L. Rotenberg

49 Virginia Law Review 871, 874-79 (1963)

"Encouragement" is descriptive of an intentional technique of police agencies used in the detection of a certain class of crimes.

---

[z] Compare the instance described at 63, *supra*.

In this article it denotes activity of the police or their agent: (1) acting in the capacity of a victim, (2) intending by his actions to suggest his willingness to be a victim, (3) actually communicating this feigned willingness to the suspect, and (4) thereby having some influence upon his commission of the crime. It is not necessarily a single act; it usually consists of a series of acts by the officer which are part of the normal interplay between victim and suspect in the specific crime. It is utilized as a device in dealing with certain crimes having the common element of vice—prostitution, homosexuality, liquor sales, narcotics, and gambling. The reason that the same technique is adapted to all these crimes is suggested by the "vice" label applicable to all of them, that these offenses are committed privately with a willing victim who will not complain, making normal detection virtually impossible. "Encouragement," to state it more succinctly, is a process of persuasion.

An example may be helpful in understanding the process: An officer of a state vice squad suspected that a tavern in a rural community was a front for prostitution in quarters at the rear of the tavern. In order to acquire sufficient evidence to support an arrest and conviction, the officer decided to encourage. He prepared a false story to explain his presence in the rural area generally and at the tavern-brothel specifically. He dressed appropriately for his assumed role. Upon arriving at the tavern he ordered a drink and engaged in small talk. He neither hurried nor lingered. At the appropriate time, he asked for a woman. After convincing the madam of his good faith, he was allowed to select a prostitute from several available. They settled the terms of the contract in private, and she examined him for venereal disease. She requested that he pay her, and he did. At that point the arrest was made.

This example fairly typifies the process and characteristics of the practice; further observations concerning encouragement may be profitably oriented to it.

It is significant to note that the officer "suspected" that the tavern was a front for prostitution. Leaving aside the corrupt and incompetent police officer and excepting narcotics sales cases, in all or almost all instances of encouragement, the police officer or unit has a reasonable suspicion that the person or institution encouraged has engaged in, is currently engaged in, or is about to engage in the crime to be detected. Further, such suspicion is held by the officer or unit before the encouragement process begins. The nature of the process demands this, for it is too complex and time-consuming a technique to be used on a hit-or-miss basis.

This raises a challenging question: If the police are able to acquire information to support a reasonable suspicion, why can they not do a little more detective work, acquire evidence of "probable cause," and then utilize the more conventional detection techniques of search, or arrest and search? This would avoid the controversial encouragement practice. A single answer has not been isolated. Perhaps it varies from locality to locality and is dependent upon local views concerning the difference between "suspicion" and the next higher "probability of guilt" standard. Two other explanations deserve consideration. First, the difference between "suspicion" and "probable cause" may be not in the *quantity* of evidence but in the *quality*, and this different kind of evidence may not be easily obtained. If this is so, then it may mean that sometimes encouragement is necessarily conducted when the officer is not *sure* of the criminal propensities of his suspect until sometime during the process, at which time the officer makes the decision to abandon the process or proceed with it until the suspect commits the crime. A second explanation is that the officer *can* acquire the evidence to bridge the gap from "suspicion" to "probable cause" and make a valid arrest or conduct a valid search, but these techniques would not produce the evidence necessary to satisfy the higher standard of guilt beyond a reasonable doubt necessary for conviction. For example, if the goal is to achieve a conviction for the illegal *sale* of narcotics, evidence that a suspect is in possession of a large quantity of narcotics and that known narcotic users are seen visiting his home may be "probable cause" for arrest, and search may reveal evidence sufficient to convict the suspect of possession, but this evidence may not be sufficient to prove a sale. Whatever the reason may be that the police cannot transcend the suspicion standard, the pervasive use of encouragement by enforcement agencies at city, state, and national levels is itself highly persuasive that alternative detection methods are simply inadequate.

As illustrated in the example, the encouraging officer seeks out the institution or individual under suspicion, not vice versa. Further, the officer actually initiates the process by hinting, suggesting, or requesting the criminal act. Precisely how he initiates it depends upon the crime and the requirements of reality. Thus if he is seeking to be solicited by a prostitute, he must not be so aggressive as to legally preclude the solicitation by her. If he is seeking a drink after hours in a tavern, he must be aggressive enough, at minimum, to order it. This does not preclude the illegal sale and is necessary to achieve the appearance of reality. Thus it is that the police role in the initiation of encouragement is not, and cannot be, passive. The confrontation of "victim" and suspect is police-planned and arranged.

The decisions which the officer must make after the process is initiated are extremely difficult. They involve questions such as: Is the suspect really innocent or just wary? What types of inducement are improper? How far may I go without legally precluding the commission of the crime by the suspect? Of course, in certain instances decision-making may be minimal. Thus if the officer is firmly convinced of the suspect's criminal propensities, he need not be on guard for indications of the suspect's innocence. He interprets reluctance and delay as signs of wariness. He does not face a decision of stopping or going on. Similarly, in the same situation, there may be no decisions concerning the propriety of inducements to be made. However, he cannot ignore the problems of simulating reality and permitting the suspect the opportunity to commit the crime. On the other hand, if the officer entertains only a suspicion that the suspect is guilty, he must reassess his evaluation of the innocence or guilt of the suspect at every turn and make decisions concerning the type of inducement he should use—one that would induce the criminal but not the innocent. The obvious danger is that the encouragement will be so realistic and persistent that a weak but innocent party may succumb and commit a crime only because of police inducement. . . .

In one large city it was observed that several of the trial judges determined the propriety of police encouragement by reference to the duration of the process. If the process took longer than the presiding judge considered proper, the case would be dismissed. Apparently it was believed that a lengthy encouragement process is consistent only with the inducement of innocent persons to commit crimes. Although this may be partially true, a lengthy process is also explicable on other grounds. As the example suggests, time is to a great extent a function of simulating reality and thus is beyond the control of the officer. Furthermore, the more criminally-sophisticated the suspect, the greater his awareness of the police use of encouragement and the greater his caution. Thus a lengthy process is as consistent with the detection of crime committed by a confirmed criminal as it is with the detection of crime committed by an "innocent" person. Finally, because at times the officer's goal is not only to establish the requisite probability of guilt for arrest but also to establish the greater probability of guilt for conviction, he must continue the process until sufficient evidence to convict is acquired. This, of course, may lengthen the process.

A REPORT ON CHICAGO CRIME FOR 1964, at 90-91 (1965)

By Virgil W. Peterson

(Chicago Crime Commission)

[T]he Nu-Way-Red-Top-Big-Five policy wheel [was] set up by the Illinois Crime Investigating Commission as an undercover device to develop evidence on the policy racket. This wheel was operated jointly with officers of the Intelligence Division of the Chicago Police Department. During its short life—from April 1964 to June 15, 1964—losses totaled $10,000.

John J. Gallagher, an undercover agent for the Illinois Crime Investigating Commission, posed as a New York ex-convict who wanted to enter the policy racket in Chicago. Gallagher stated that he approached defense attorney Robert J. McDonnell and asked him to use his influence in obtaining syndicate approval for the operation of the policy wheel. McDonnell introduced him to syndicate gambler James (Cowboy) Mirro and, according to Gallagher, McDonnell later informed him that syndicate approval for the operation of the wheel had been granted. (McDonnell admitted having introduced Gallagher to Mirro but denied that the introduction was for the purpose of obtaining syndicate clearance for the policy wheel operation.)

The Nu-Way-Red-Top-Big-Five policy wheel rented a room at 1630 South Homan Avenue in Chicago which is located in the Tenth (Marquette) Police District. A few weeks after the wheel was in operation two undercover men rented a room at 1400 North LaSalle Street in Chicago which served as one of its headquarters. Gallagher stated that a hoodlum, Robert Ferdman, was hired to help run the policy wheel. A Chicago detective, Mort Franken, who was introduced to the mob as an ex-convict from Michigan, was assigned to handle the money and keep the books.

The first drawing of the Nu-Way-Red-Top-Big-Five policy wheel was held on April 21, 1964. On the following day, according to John J. Gallagher, Robert Ferdman met Chicago policeman Robert Hopkins, a former vice control officer of the Marquette District, in a restaurant and gave him a $200 bribe to allow the policy wheel to operate. Hopkins reportedly informed Gallagher that the $200 was demanded by Chicago detective James Apostol. Hopkins allegedly promised to recruit some runners for the wheel.

The wheel employed 24 policy runners and took in $850 a day but its expenses exceeded $900 a day. It was raided 4 times. Among the employees of the wheel was a convicted burglar Ronald Krasnek, age 33 years, of 1609 North Central Avenue, Chicago. He was free on a $10,000 bond while his burglary conviction and sentence of 2 to 4 years were being appealed. Because of "leaks," Gallagher stated, it became common knowledge in the Chicago Police Department that the Illinois Crime Investigating Commission and the intelligence division of the police department were operating the policy wheel. As a result, it ceased business on June 15, 1964. During the two months of its existence, the wheel which was financed by the Chicago Police Department, lost $10,000.

The facts developed during the operation of the wheel were presented to the Cook County Grand Jury and on September 4, 1964 an indictment (number 64-2670) was returned which charged 11 defendants with conspiracy to set up and promote a policy game and to offer to sell, possess and transfer policy tickets and other similar devices. The 11 defendants named in the indictment were James Mirro, Robert J. McDonnell, Robert Hopkins, Ronald Krasnek, St. Clair Haywood, Flenoid Haywood, George Copeland, William Harris, Thomas Hendricks, William Hudson and Cornelius Haynes.[a]

Another kind of undercover technique is the "decoy." In some of the large cities police officers dressed as women, drunks, or other likely victims of personal violence roam areas in which assaults or robberies are likely to occur. The object is to offer a target for the criminal and to arrest him if he strikes. Because of the real possibility of physical harm to the officer there is in turn real possibility of injury to the offender. This detection method raises somewhat different questions of propriety than encouragement does.

2. *Propriety of Undercover Activities*

HOFFA v. UNITED STATES
385 U.S. 293 (1966)

MR. JUSTICE STEWART delivered the opinion of the Court.

The specific question before us, as framed by counsel for the petitioners, is this:

> Whether evidence obtained by the Government by means of deceptively placing a secret informer in the quarters and councils of a defendant during one criminal trial so violates

---

[a] Infiltration of organized crime beyond the lowest level is a near impossibility. *See* p. 79, *supra*.

the defendant's Fourth, Fifth and Sixth Amendment rights that suppression of such evidence is required in a subsequent trial of the same defendant on a different charge.

At the threshold the Government takes issue with the way this question is worded, refusing to concede that it " 'placed' the informer anywhere, much less that it did so 'deceptively.' " In the view we take of the matter, however, a resolution of this verbal controversy is unnecessary to a decision of the constitutional issues before us.

The controlling facts can be briefly stated. The Test Fleet trial, in which James Hoffa was the sole individual defendant, was is progress between October 22 and December 23, 1962, in Nashville, Tennessee. James Hoffa was president of the International Brotherhood of Teamsters. During the course of the trial he occupied a three-room suite in the Andrew Jackson Hotel in Nashville. One of his constant companions throughout the trial was the petitioner King, president of the Nashville local of the Teamsters Union. Edward Partin, a resident of Baton Rouge, Louisiana, and a local Teamsters Union official there, made repeated visits to Nashville during the period of the trial. On these visits he frequented the Hoffa hotel suite, and was continually in the company of Hoffa and his associates, including King, in and around the hotel suite, the hotel lobby, the courthouse, and elsewhere in Nashville. During this period Partin made frequent reports to a federal agent named Sheridan concerning conversations he said Hoffa and King had had with him and with each other, disclosing endeavors to bribe members of the Test Fleet jury. Partin's reports and his subsequent testimony at the petitioners' trial unquestionably contributed, directly or indirectly, to the convictions of all four of the petitioners.[3]

---

[3] Partin testified at the trial of this case that petitioners Hoffa and King had made the following statements during the course of the Test Fleet trial:

On October 22, the day Partin first arrived in Nashville, King told him that a meeting had been "set up on the jury that night." That evening Hoffa told Partin that he wanted Partin to stay in Nashville in order to call on some people. Hoffa explained "that they was going to get to one juror or try to get to a few scattered jurors and take their chances." The next day Partin was told by Hoffa that Hoffa might want him "to pass something for him." As Hoffa said this, he hit his rear pocket with his hand. On October 25, the day after Test Fleet juror James Tippens had reported to the trial judge that he had been approached with a bribe offer, Partin asked Hoffa about his wanting Partin to "pass something." Hoffa replied, "The dirty bastards went in and told the Judge that his neighbor had offered him $10,000," and added, "We are going to have to lay low for a few days." King told Partin on October 26 that he intended to influence a female juror, Mrs. Paschal, in Hoffa's favor, and added that

The chain of circumstances which led Partin to be in Nashville during the Test Fleet trial extended back at least to September of 1962. At that time Partin was in jail in Baton Rouge on a state criminal charge. He was also under a federal indictment for embezzling union funds, and other indictments for state offenses were pending against him. Between that time and Partin's initial visit to Nashville on October 22 he was released on bail on the state criminal charge, and proceedings under the federal indictment were postponed. On October 8, Partin telephoned Hoffa in Washington, D. C., to discuss local union matters and Partin's difficulties with the authorities. In the course of this conversation Partin asked if he could see Hoffa to confer about these problems, and Hoffa acquiesced. Partin again called Hoffa on October 18 and arranged to meet him in Nashville. During this period Partin also consulted on several occasions with federal law enforcement agents, who told him that Hoffa might attempt to tamper with the Test Fleet jury, and asked him to be on the lookout in Nashville for such attempts and to report to the federal authorities any evidence of wrongdoing that he discovered. Partin agreed to do so.

After the Test Fleet trial was completed, Partin's wife received four monthly installment payments of $300 from government funds, and the state and federal charges against Partin were either dropped or not actively pursued.

Reviewing these circumstances in detail, the Government insists the fair inference is that Partin went to Nashville on his own initiative to discuss union business and his own problems with Hoffa, that Partin ultimately cooperated closely with federal authorities only after he discovered evidence of jury tampering in the Test Fleet trial, that the payments to Partin's wife were simply in partial reimbursement of Partin's subsequent out-of-pocket expenses, and that the failure to prosecute Partin on the state and federal charges had no necessary connection with his services as an informer. The findings of the trial court support this version of the facts, and these findings were accepted by the Court of Appeals as "supported by substantial evidence." 349 F.2d, at 36. But whether or not the Government "placed" Partin with Hoffa in Nashville during the Test Fleet trial, we proceed upon the premise that Partin was

---

the juror and her husband, a highway patrolman, "loved money, and $10,000.00 [is] a lot of money." King related to Partin on November 20 a meeting that King had had with juror Paschal's husband, stating that the highway patrolman wanted a promotion rather than money. The same day Hoffa told Partin that he was disturbed because "the Highway Patrolman wouldn't take the money," adding that if he had "taken the money it would have pinned him down and he couldn't have backed up."

a government informer from the time he first arrived in Nashville on October 22, and that the Government compensated him for his services as such. It is upon that premise that we consider the constitutional issues presented.

I.

It is contended that only by violating the petitioner's rights under the Fourth Amendment was Partin able to hear the petitioner's incriminating statements in the hotel suite, and that Partin's testimony was therefore inadmissible under the exclusionary rule of Weeks v. United States, 232 U.S. 383. The argument is that Partin's failure to disclose his role as a government informer vitiated the consent that the petitioner gave to Partin's repeated entries into the suite, and that by listening to the petitioner's statements Partin conducted an illegal "search" for verbal evidence.

The preliminary steps of this argument are on solid ground. A hotel room can clearly be the object of Fourth Amendment protection as much as a home or an office. United States v. Jeffers, 342 U.S. 48. The Fourth Amendment can certainly be violated by guileful as well as by forcible intrusions into a constitutionally protected area. Gouled v. United States, 255 U.S. 298. And the protections of the Fourth Amendment are surely not limited to tangibles, but can extend as well to oral statements. Silverman v. United States, 365 U.S. 505.

Where the argument falls is in its misapprehension of the fundamental nature and scope of Fourth Amendment protection. What the Fourth Amendment protects is the security a man relies upon when he places himself or his property within a constitutionally protected area, be it his home or his office, his hotel room or his automobile. There he is protected from unwarranted governmental intrusion. And when he puts something in his filing cabinet, in his desk drawer, or in his pocket, he has the right to know it will be secure from an unreasonable search or an unreasonable seizure. So it was that the Fourth Amendment could not tolerate the warrantless search of the hotel room in *Jeffers,* the purloining of the petitioner's private papers in *Gouled,* or the surreptitious electronic surveillance in *Silverman.* Countless other cases which have come to this Court over the years have involved a myriad of differing factual contexts in which the protections of the Fourth Amendment have been appropriately invoked. No doubt the future will bring countless others. By nothing we say here do we either foresee or foreclose factual situations to which the Fourth Amendment may be applicable.

In the present case, however, it is evident that no interest legitimately protected by the Fourth Amendment is involved. It is obvious that the petitioner was not relying on the security of his hotel suite when he made the incriminating statements to Partin or in Partin's presence. Partin did not enter the suite by force or by stealth. He was not a surreptitious eavesdropper. Partin was in the suite by invitation, and every conversation which he heard was either directed to him or knowingly carried on in his presence. The petitioner, in a word, was not relying on the security of the hotel room; he was relying upon his misplaced confidence that Partin would not reveal his wrongdoing. As counsel for the petitioner himself points out, some of the communications with Partin did not take place in the suite at all, but in the "hall of the hotel," in the "Andrew Jackson Hotel lobby," and "at the courthouse."

Neither this Court nor any member of it has ever expressed the view that the Fourth Amendment protects a wrongdoer's misplaced belief that a person to whom he voluntarily confides his wrongdoing will not reveal it. Indeed, the Court unanimously rejected that very contention less than four years ago in Lopez v. United States, 373 U.S. 427.

Adhering to these views, we hold that no right protected by the Fourth Amendment was violated in the present case.

II.

The petitioner argues that his right under the Fifth Amendment not to "be compelled in any criminal case to be a witness against himself" was violated by the admission of Partin's testimony. The claim is without merit.

In the present case no claim has been or could be made that the petitioner's incriminating statements were the product of any sort of coercion, legal or factual. The petitioner's conversations with Partin and in Partin's presence were wholly voluntary. For that reason, if for no other, it is clear that no right protected by the Fifth Amendment privilege against compulsory self-incrimination was violated in this case.

III.

The petitioner makes two separate claims under the Sixth Amendment, and we give them separate consideration.

A.

During the course of the Test Fleet trial the petitioner's lawyers used his suite as a place to confer with him and with each other, to interview witnesses, and to plan the following day's trial strategy. Therefore, argues the petitioner, Partin's presence in and around the suite violated the petitioner's Sixth Amendment right to counsel, because an essential ingredient thereof is the right of a defendant and his counsel to prepare for trial without intrusion upon their confidential relationship by an agent of the Government, the defendant's trial adversary. Since Partin's presence in the suite thus violated the Sixth Amendment, the argument continues, any evidence acquired by reason of his presence there was constitutionally tainted and therefore inadmissible against the petitioner in this case. We reject this argument.

This is so because of the clinching basic fact in the present case that none of the petitioner's incriminating statements which Partin heard were made in the presence of counsel, in the hearing of counsel, or in connection in any way with the legitimate defense of the Test Fleet prosecution. The petitioner's statements related to the commission of a quite separate offense—attempted bribery of jurors—and the statements were made to Partin out of the presence of any lawyers.

B.

The petitioner's second argument under the Sixth Amendment needs no extended discussion. That argument goes as follows: Not later than October 25, 1962, the Government had sufficient ground for taking the petitioner into custody and charging him with endeavors to tamper with the Test Fleet jury. Had the Government done so, it could not have continued to question the petitioner without observance of his Sixth Amendment right to counsel. Massiah v. United States, 377 U.S. 201; Escobedo v. Illinois, 378 U.S. 478. Therefore, the argument concludes, evidence of statements made by the petitioner subsequent to October 25 was inadmissible, because the Government acquired that evidence only by flouting the petitioner's Sixth Amendment right to counsel.

Nothing in *Massiah,* in *Escobedo,* or in any other case that has come to our attention, even remotely suggests this novel and paradoxical constitutional doctrine, and we decline to adopt it now. There is no constitutional right to be arrested. The police are not required to guess at their peril the precise moment at which they have probable cause to arrest a suspect, risking a violation of the Fourth Amendment if they act too soon, and a violation of the Sixth Amendment if they wait too long. Law enforcement officers are under no constitutional duty to call a halt to a criminal investigation the moment they have the minimum evidence to establish probable cause, a quantum of evidence which may fall far short of the amount necessary to support a criminal conviction.

IV.

Finally, the petitioner claims that even if there was no violation—"as separately measured by each such Amendment"—of the Fourth Amendment, the compulsory self-incrimination clause of the Fifth Amendment, or of the Sixth Amendment in this case, the judgment of conviction must nonetheless be reversed. The argument is based upon the Due Process Clause of the Fifth Amendment. The "totality" of the Government's conduct during the Test Fleet trial operated, it is said, to " 'offend those canons of decency and fairness which express the notions of justice of English-speaking peoples even toward those charged with the most heinous offenses' (Rochin v. California, 342 U.S. 165, 169)."

The argument boils down to a general attack upon the use of a government informer as "a shabby thing in any case," and to the claim that in the circumstances of this particular case the risk that Partin's testimony might be perjurious was very high. Insofar as the general attack upon the use of informers is based upon historic "notions" of "English-speaking peoples," it is without historical foundation. In the words of Judge Learned Hand, "Courts have countenanced the use of informers from time immemorial; in cases of conspiracy, or in other cases when the crime consists of preparing for another crime, it is usually necessary to rely upon them or upon accomplices because the criminals will almost certainly proceed covertly. . . ." United States v. Dennis, 183 F.2d 201, at 224.

This is not to say that a secret government informer is to the slightest degree more free from all relevant constitutional restrictions than is any other government agent. See Massiah v. United States, 377 U.S. 201. It *is* to say that the use of secret informers is not *per se* unconstitutional.

The petitioner is quite correct in the contention that Partin, perhaps even more than most informers, may have had motives to lie. But it does not follow that his testimony was untrue, nor does it follow that his testimony was constitutionally inadmissible. The established safeguards of the Anglo-American legal system leave the veracity of a witness to be tested by cross-examination, and the credibility of his testimony to be determined by a properly instructed jury. At the trial of this case, Partin was subjected to rigorous cross-examination, and the extent and nature of his dealings with federal and state authorities were insistently explored. The trial judge instructed the jury, both specifically and generally, with regard to assessing Partin's credibility. The Constitution does not require us to upset the jury's verdict. Affirmed.

MR. JUSTICE WHITE and MR. JUSTICE FORTAS took no part in the consideration or decision of these cases.

MR. CHIEF JUSTICE WARREN, dissenting. In this case the testimony concerning the circumstances surrounding Partin's entry into Hoffa's councils was not substantially in dispute. While those circumstances are set forth in greater detail *infra,* a brief summary discloses that Partin, after discussing Hoffa with federal agents and learning of their intense and mutually beneficial interest, successfully solicited an invitation to meet with Hoffa. Partin's release from jail was assisted by the federal agents, and he was compensated in a financial sense as well; in return, he kept the federal agents fully informed of all that occurred from the outset of his contact with Hoffa.

Surely the only reasonable construction of these facts is that Partin was acting as a paid federal informer when he traveled to Nashville and attached himself to Hoffa. And the fact that Hoffa on Partin's urging agreed to a meeting in Nashville is not inconsistent with this conclusion. An invasion of basic rights made possible by prevailing upon friendship with the victim is no less proscribed than an invasion accomplished by force. See Massiah v. United States, 377 U.S. 201 (1964); Gouled v. United States, 255 U.S. 298 (1921).

At this late date in the annals of law enforcement, it seems to me that we cannot say either that every use of informers and undercover agents is proper or, on the other hand, that no uses are. There are some situations where the law could not adequately be enforced without the employment of some guile or misrepresentation of identity. A law enforcement officer performing his official duties cannot be required always to be in uniform or to wear his badge of authority on the lapel of his civilian clothing. Nor need he be required in all situations to proclaim himself an arm of the law. It blinks the realities of sophisticated, modern-day criminal activity and legitimate law enforcement practices to argue the contrary. However, one of the important duties of this Court is to give careful scrutiny to practices of government agents when they are challenged in cases before us, in order to insure that the protections of the Constitution are respected and to maintain the integrity of federal law enforcement.

Here, Edward Partin, a jailbird languishing in a Louisiana jail under indictments for such state and federal crimes as embezzlement, kidnapping, and manslaughter (and soon to be charged with perjury and assault), contacted federal authorities and told them he was willing to become, and would be useful as, an informer against Hoffa who was then about to be tried in the Test Fleet case. A motive for his doing this is immediately apparent—namely, his strong desire to work his way out of jail and out of his various legal entanglements with the State and Federal Governments. And it is interesting to note that, if this was his motive, he has been uniquely successful in satisfying it. In the four years since he first volunteered to be an informer against Hoffa he has not been prosecuted on any of the serious federal charges for which he was at that time jailed, and the state charges have apparently vanished into thin air.

Shortly after Partin made contact with the federal authorities and told them of his position in the Baton Rouge Local of the Teamsters Union and of his acquaintance with Hoffa, his bail was suddenly reduced from $50,000 to $5,000 and he was released from jail. He immediately telephoned Hoffa, who was then in New Jersey, and, by collaborating with a state law enforcement official, surreptitiously made a tape recording of the conversation. A copy of the recording was furnished to federal authorities. Again on a pretext of wanting to talk with Hoffa regarding Partin's legal difficulties, Partin telephoned Hoffa a few weeks later and succeeded in making a date to meet in Nashville where Hoffa and his attorneys were then preparing for the Test Fleet trial. Unknown to Hoffa, this call was also recorded and again federal authorities were informed as to the details.

Upon his arrival in Nashville, Partin manifested his "friendship" and made himself useful to Hoffa, thereby worming his way into Hoffa's hotel suite and becoming part and parcel of Hoffa's entourage. As the "faithful" servant and factotum of the defense camp which he became, he was in a position to overhear conversations not directed to him, many of which were between attorneys and either their client or prospective defense witnesses. Pursuant to the general instructions he received from federal authorities to report "any attempts at witness intimidation or tampering with the jury," "anything illegal," or even "anything of interest," Partin became the equivalent of a bugging device which moved with Hoffa wherever he went. Everything Partin saw or heard was reported to federal authorities and much of it was ultimately the subject matter of his testimony in this case. For his services he was well paid by the Government, both through devious and secret support payments to his wife and, it may be inferred, by executed promises not to pursue the indictments under which he was charged at the time he became an informer.

This type of informer and the uses to which he was put in this case evidence a serious potential for undermining the integrity of the truth-finding process in the federal courts. Given the incentives and background of Partin, no conviction should be allowed to stand when based heavily on his testimony. And that is exactly the quicksand upon which these convictions rest, because without Partin, who was the principal government witness, there would probably have been no convictions here. Thus, although petitioners make their main arguments on constitutional grounds and raise serious Fourth and Sixth Amendment questions, it should not even be necessary for the Court to reach those questions. For the affront to the quality and fairness of federal law enforcement which this case presents is sufficient to require an exercise of our supervisory powers. As we said in ordering a new trial in Mesarosh v. United States, 352 U.S. 1, 14 (1956), a federal case involving the testimony of an unsavory informer who, the Government admitted, had committed perjury in other cases:

> "This is a federal criminal case, and this Court has supervisory jurisdiction over the proceedings of the federal courts. If it has any duty to perform in this regard, it is to see that the waters of justice are not polluted. Pollution having taken place here, the condition should be remedied at the earliest opportunity.
>
> "The government of a strong and free nation does not need convictions based upon such testimony. It cannot afford to abide with them."

See also McNabb v. United States, 318 U.S. 332, 341 (1943).

I cannot agree that what happened in this case is in keeping with the standards of justice in our federal system and I must, therefore, dissent.

MR. JUSTICE CLARK, joined by MR. JUSTICE DOUGLAS. I would dismiss the writs of certiorari as improvidently granted.

The writs of certiorari granted by the Court in these cases are limited to the following question:

> "Whether evidence obtained by the Government by means of deceptively placing a secret informer in the quarters and councils of a defendant during one criminal trial so violates the defendant's Fourth, Fifth and Sixth Amendment rights that suppression of such evidence is required in a subsequent trial of the same defendant on a different charge."

My examination of the record reveals that at the hearing on petitioners' motion to suppress the evidence obtained by the informer, Partin, the District Judge found that "the government did not place this witness Mr. Partin in the defendants' midst . . . rather that he was knowingly and voluntarily placed in their midst by one of the defendants [Hoffa]." This specific finding was approved by the Court of Appeals as being "supported by substantial evidence and . . . not clearly erroneous." 349 F.2d, at 36. No attack is made here on the findings.

THE POLICE DETECTION PRACTICE OF ENCOURAGEMENT

By Daniel L. Rotenberg

49 Virginia Law Review 871, 890-94 (1963)

In the United States federal system, and in almost all, if not all the states, entrapment is a recognized defense. The Supreme Court has passed on the issue twice, in the well-known cases of *Sorrells v. United States* and *Sherman v. United States.* In both instances all the Justices (except Mr. Justice McReynolds, who dissented without opinion in *Sorrells*) agreed on the applicability of the doctrine, but sharply disagreed on the basis of the rule and the formulation of a test or definition. The rationale of the majority opinion in both cases was that Congress had not intended the statute to apply to cases in which the conduct was instigated by the police. The minority, on the other hand, based its opinion on policy.

The effect of the rationale of the doctrine on police practices, however, is less significant than the formulation of the rule of entrapment, and here the Court again disagreed. The rule formulated by the majority in *Sorrells* requires for the successful assertion of entrapment that the crime be planned by the police and that the defendant be otherwise innocent. In *Sherman,* Chief Justice Warren affirmed the formulation of the *Sorrells* majority, commenting that "thus the Government plays on the weaknesses of an innocent party and beguiles him into committing crimes which he otherwise would not have attempted." The minority in both cases, however, would allow entrapment to be a defense whenever the conduct of the police in a particular situation falls below certain objective standards; *i.e.,* when the encouragement by the police is *likely* to lead persons who would normally avoid crime to commit an offense. For the purposes of this test, "it is wholly irrelevant to ask if the 'intention' to commit the crime originated with the defendant or government officers, or if the criminal conduct was the product of 'the creative activity' of law-enforcement officials."

The Supreme Court, therefore, represents two essentially different views of entrapment: the majority sees it as a defense for a generally innocent offender; the minority considers it a control upon police excesses similar to the search and seizure exclusionary rule, with only indirect concern for the offender's innocence. . . .

Another formulation, by no means new, appears in some federal cases. In these the defense of entrapment requires not only the inducement of an otherwise innocent person but also the absence of a "reasonable suspicion" that the offender "is engaged in the commission of a crime or is about to do so." Thus if an otherwise innocent person is induced to commit a crime, he cannot, under this test, be exonerated by using the defense of entrapment if the police had "reasonable suspicion." This test was used by many federal courts in the pre-*Sorrells* 1920's. Although long the subject of criticism, the suspicion test did not die after either *Sorrells* or *Sherman*. It continues to be utilized by both trial and appellate courts.

The police practice described above as "encouragement" has lacked a well-established name. The abuse of the practice has the name "entrapment," and for want of an alternative writers sometimes call the whole detection technique "entrapment." This difficulty of separating the concepts is illustrated by the following newspaper report.

POLICE FORBIDDEN TO LURE DEVIATES

By Eric Pace
New York Times, May 1, 1966

LEARY SEEKS TO END USE OF ENTRAPMENT—HIS MOVE IS HAILED BY RIGHTS BODY

Police Commissioner Howard R. Leary has issued specific instructions that plainclothes men are not to entice homosexuals into making illegal overtures.

The New York Civil Liberties Union has charged that the practice, known as entrapment, has been used for arrests under a section of the State Penal Code that makes it an offense, punishable by up to six months in prison, if "any person . . . frequents or loiters about any public place soliciting men for the purpose of committing a crime against nature or other lewdness."

Police sources said plainclothes men had also been "strongly discouraged" by their superiors from making such arrests without a witness to support their word that they had been the target of homosexual advances. An example of such a witness would be a customer at a bar who had observed illegal behavior on the part of the homosexual.

Dick Leitsch, president of the Mattachine Society, Inc. of New York, an organization that helps homosexuals, hailed the new policy.

"This would make it a lot harder for the police to arrest homosexuals," he said. "It's the best thing that ever happened."

"Most homosexuals like the Mayor and Mr. Leary; they're tremendous men," he continued, adding:

"We were taken aback when the big cleanup started in Greenwich Village and Times Square, but since then they've shown good faith. If things keep on this way, we'll vote 100 per cent for Lindsay next time."

A spokesman for the Civil Liberties Union said:

"This is an extremely important victory, but I hope that the police do not revert to the practice of entrapment after the public interest in the subject dies down." . . .

Mr. Broderick's successor, Commissioner Leary, delivered his instructions about entrapment at two staff meetings, on April 28 and 29, informed sources said.

Earlier, a high police official had contended that "we don't encourage people to commit a crime that they weren't going to commit" and Chief Inspector Sanford D. Garelik had appealed to the public to report any cases of entrapment.

WILLIAMSON v. UNITED STATES
311 F.2d 441 (5th Cir. 1962)

RIVES, Circuit Judge. Williamson and Lowrey were convicted of possessing 179 gallons of whiskey in unstamped containers in violation of section 5604(a)(1), Title 26, United States Code.

The specifications of error claim (1) unlawful entrapment, (2) prejudicial argument of the United States Attorney, and (3) insufficient evidence of identity of each of the defendants.

The circumstances of the claimed unlawful entrapment were developed in the deposition of Robert Harris Moye, a Government informer, taken by agreement between the Government and the defendants on March 31, 1961, several months before the trial. Moye had been released from a federal prison on September 12, 1960 after serving three years for violating the Internal

Revenue laws relating to whiskey. Within a few weeks after his release, he contacted two investigators for the Alcohol and Tobacco Tax Division of the Treasury Department. Neither of these investigators testified as a witness in this case, and Moye's testimony as to the terms of his employment is not disputed. Because of its unusual nature, we quote at some length from Moye's deposition.

"MR. COLEMAN:

"Q. What did you agree to do with Mr. Rainer and Mr. Morris? What did they tell you they wanted you to do?

"A. They told me to give them the major violators and told me what they'd pay for them.

"Q. For you to go out and catch them, in other words?

"A. If I could catch them.

"Q. And they agreed to pay you $200.00 as to Jack Williamson?

"A. Yes, sir.

"Q. You all called him Big Boy, I believe?

"A. Yes, sir.

"Q. And $100.00 as to his half brother, the Lowrey boy?

"A. Yes, sir.

"Q. When were they to pay you the money?

"A. Wasn't nothing said about when it was to be paid.

"Q. But in the meantime they would also pay you $10.00 per day to work as an undercover agent for them and for the government?

"A. That's right.

"Q. And they did pay you the $10.00 a day?

"A. Yes, sir."

Under the law of entrapment as developed in prior decisions of the Supreme Court and of this Court, no reversible error would appear except for the evidence of employment of the informer Moye on a contingent fee basis.

The uncontradicted and unexplained testimony as to the terms of Moye's employment make it necessary that the judgments of conviction be reversed. It may possibly be that the Government investigators had such certain knowledge that Williamson and Lowrey were engaged in illicit liquor dealings that they were justified in contracting with Moye on a contingent fee basis, $200.00 for Williamson and $100.00 for Lowrey, to produce the legally admissible evidence against each of them. It may be also that the investigators carefully instructed Moye on the rules against entrapment and had it clearly understood that Moye would not induce them to commit a crime, but would simply offer them an opportunity for a sale. None of these facts or circumstances were developed in the evidence, though Moye's deposition had been taken months before the trial.

Without some such justification or explanation, we cannot sanction a contingent fee agreement to produce evidence against particular named defendants as to crimes not yet committed. Such an arrangement might tend to a "frame up," or to cause an informer to induce or persuade innocent persons to commit crimes which they had no previous intent or purpose to commit. The opportunities for abuse are too obvious to require elaboration.

No case has been cited by either of the parties involving a contingent fee agreement like that to which Moye testified, and we have found none. Under the principles settled in McNabb v. United States, 1943, 318 U.S. 332, 340, and its progeny, however, it becomes the duty of the courts in federal criminal cases to require fair and lawful conduct from federal agents in the furnishing of evidence of crimes. Moye's testimony, standing alone and unexplained, discloses a form of employment of an informer which this Court cannot approve or sanction.

Moye made the purchase from Williamson and produced the evidence against both Williamson and Lowrey. For such services the Government agents paid Moye as to Williamson $200.00, and as to Lowrey $100.00. McNabb, supra, and its progeny clearly forbid the Government to make use of the fruits of wrongdoing by its officers or agents.

John R. Brown, Circuit Judge (concurring specially). I concur in the result and in the Court's opinion. And it is evident that I agree with much that is said in the dissent.

I do not think, however, that this is an aspect of entrapment. Its kinship to entrapment is not that the act of a Government representative induced the commission of a crime. Rather, it is that the means used to "make" the case are essentially revolting to an ordered society.

Cameron, Circuit Judge (dissenting). In the majority's view, the very fact of hiring an informer on a contingency is ignoble. Such a holding would rob the Government of one of its most effective weapons in detecting crime and bringing to the bar of justice those who commit it.

For decades the use of informers has been accepted as a proper means of enforcement of the criminal law. It is recognized by all as one of the most important means. And, in practically all instances, the informer is in reality on a contingent basis.

The method chiefly used in apprehending sellers of narcotics, for instance, is the employment of addicts to make the purchases from suspects in the presence of federal officers who are secreted or in disguise. Every such informer knows that his day to day arrangement with the Government will continue only if he delivers the goods. The addict is given barely enough money to live on and supply his need for narcotics for a few days. In most cases, the Government agents are after one or more individuals to whom the informer is sent. If the addict succeeds in landing some of the criminals the Government is after, he is well paid and his services will continue. If he does not, he is dropped. As far as I know, the courts have accepted such practices as permissible. The same attitude has prevailed in connection with informers in the apprehension of liquor law violators.

Those who represent persons charged with crime have for ages made impassioned pleas—mostly to juries—that the hiring of informers, in many cases friends of the victims being sought, is dirty business. Crime itself is dirty business, and the universal experience of law enforcement officers is that the use of informers is necessary to the enforcement of law.

At a time when crime of all sorts is so definitely on the increase, I am not willing to weaken the hand of the law by interfering with a practice as well established as the one here under examination. Juries generally take into account the interest of every witness who testifies before them. What we are really dealing with here is the weight of the testimony of an interested witness employed as an informer. The juries can be counted upon to make proper discount in crediting the testimony of an informer employed on a contingent basis. It is their function to determine the extent of the discount. I do not think we ought to take such a witness off of the stand entirely. I respectfully dissent.[b]

In the following case the court takes a rather extreme view of the defense of entrapment, evidencing its real concern about police involvement in criminal activities.

UNITED STATES v. OWENS
228 F. Supp. 300 (D.D.C. 1964)

YOUNGDAHL, District Judge. Defendant in this criminal action is charged with a violation of two provisions of the United

[b] A later case observed that *Williamson* did not flatly outlaw contingent fee arrangements, but called for the government to show justification or excuse for the arrangement. Justification might be found in the relative reliability of the informer and the narrowness of his task. Sears v. United States, 343 F.2d 139 (5th Cir. 1965).

States Code, 26 U.S.C. §§ 4705(a), 4704(a), in connection with the sale of narcotic drugs on May 26, 1963. Although defendant concedes he sold the drugs to the undercover agent of the Federal Bureau of Narcotics, he contends that the evidence in the Government's case shows as a matter of law that he was entrapped by said agent into securing the illicit drugs. Defendant has moved for judgment of acquittal at the close of the Government's case.

In January, 1963, William H. Turnbou, an undercover agent of the Federal Bureau of Narcotics, came to Washington to undertake an undercover investigation. Turnbou was put in touch with one Gladys Irby, a known user of cocaine who was under indictment for violation of the narcotics laws. About the middle of January, 1963, while in a bar at Seventh and T Streets, N. W., in the District of Columbia, said Irby introduced Turnbou to the defendant, stating that Turnbou "was a friend of her nephew's," that he "was all right," and that she "would appreciate" his showing Turnbou around.

Irby introduced Turnbou into a group of cocaine users, and Turnbou began frequenting certain bars, restaurants, and other places where members of the narcotics group would be present. In furtherance of his plan to become accepted by the group, Turnbou for five months—from January until late in May, 1963—attended fifty or sixty "after-hour parties" at which cocaine was freely used, contrary to law, liquor was sold illegally, and illegal gambling—including a craps table, with a "take" for the "house"—took place.

Turnbou himself participated actively in these parties. On several occasions, he feigned the use of cocaine, by taking cocaine powder into the bathroom, exchanging it with a form of sugar with which his superiors at the Narcotics Bureau had provided him, and then—in the presence of others—taking what appeared to be narcotics. He also bought liquor where it was illegally sold at the parties, both for himself and sometimes also for the informer Irby; he was reimbursed for the cost of this liquor from funds provided by the Narcotics Bureau. He also participated in the gambling activities, but had to pay for this out of his own pocket, in accord with an established policy of the Narcotics Bureau. The Narcotics agents were unable to explain to the Court why they were reimbursed for liquor illegally purchased but were not so reimbursed for the agent's illegal gambling activities authorized by the policy of the Bureau. Although the stakes were sometimes as high as one hundred dollars or more, he generally would gamble only up to about ten dollars' worth in an evening. He undertook these activities in order to establish rapport with the group.

The defendant was present at about twenty or twenty-five of the "after-hours parties" attended by agent Turnbou; Turnbou and the defendant went to the "parties" together on a number of occasions.

On March 7, 1963, agent Turnbou called the defendant on the telephone and told him that he wanted some cocaine. Defendant replied that Turnbou should come to a certain address. The agent went, where he found the defendant and another individual named Murphy (who in fact was already known to the agent). The defendant introduced Turnbou to Murphy, saying, "This is Henry, a friend of mine." A conversation then followed between Murphy and the defendant which the agent did not hear. Defendant then told Turnbou to go to 810 Randolph Street, N. W., and to wait there. Turnbou and Murphy then went to that address and waited. After waiting for some time, Murphy called the defendant on the telephone to find out if the defendant was coming or not. The defendant never came, but the agent made a "buy" from Murphy that day.

After midnight, in the early morning hours of May 26, the agent called the defendant on the telephone at a "carry-out" shop frequented by the group of cocaine users. Turnbou told the defendant that he wanted to get a "bag" of cocaine. The defendant asked where he was and then said he would come by. At about 4:00 a. m., the defendant arrived by car with the informer Irby and two other people. Turnbou came out and entered the car, which then was driven to 1810 Lawrence Street, N. E. Turnbou then gave the defendant fifty dollars of funds advanced by the Narcotics Bureau, and the defendant went inside the premises at 1810 Lawrence Street, N. E. He thereafter emerged, and handed Turnbou something that looked like narcotics wrapped in a cellophane wrapper from a pack of cigarettes. The contents turned out to be cocaine, which agent Turnbou turned over to his superiors at the Narcotics Bureau.

Defendant had merely been seen in the company of other users and some sellers—but such association is not sufficient to indicate a *predisposition to sell* narcotics, as distinct from a predisposition to use narcotics. The fact that defendant was observed talking to sellers is reasonably explained as an expression of the defendant's need to obtain narcotics for his own use. There is no evidence that defendant made any profit from the sale to the agent. Rather, the evidence indicates that the agent had posed as a fellow user; that he gradually gained defendant's confidence over a five-month period; that he asked defendant for narcotics for his own use; that he used funds advanced from the Narcotics Bureau; and that his action was clearly calculated to persuade an otherwise unwilling defendant to do something he had not done in the past—namely to sell narcotics.

Aside from the above considerations, which alone would lead this Court to hold that no reasonable juror could return a verdict of guilty, thereby requiring this Court to set aside the jury's verdict in the event of a conviction, there is an added factor in this case which deserves comment, and which places the above discussion in a larger context. It is shocking to this Court that in order to obtain evidence of a sale of narcotics, the undercover agent, with the approval of his superior officers, participated with others at the "after-hours parties" in open and conceded violation of the local laws against gambling, the illegal sale of liquor, and the illegal possession and use of cocaine. It seems unnecessary to state that we have arrived at a low level of appropriate law enforcement when in order to secure evidence of narcotics violations Federal Narcotics agents themselves have to violate the law and thus be *in particeps criminis* with the very criminals they are trying to detect. True it is that the narcotics traffic is vicious and degrading and brings the downfall of many of our citizens to a pitiful state of existence. Likewise do we agree with the contention that every effort should be made by law enforcement officials to bring to the bar of justice those who are participating in this illegal traffic. Moreover, the Court realizes that informers, who are not the highest type of citizens, must be used in securing evidence in narcotics cases. But the main thrust of enforcement should be to get at the source of supply and those who are engaged in the traffic for a profit. This is not always easy to accomplish. Nevertheless, it does not alter the fact that the addict who is so weak as to be unable to resist the temptation to use drugs and who secures funds in other illegal ways to finance his own habit should not be encouraged and tempted by law enforcement officials to intensify his habit by methods of inducement and persuasion such as occurred in the present case. Such inducement merely compounds the serious implications of drug addiction.

It is in relation to this kind of individual—the user—that we must evaluate the appropriateness of the methods used by the undercover agent. For five months, three kinds of illicit activity were carried on with the knowledge of Federal Narcotics officials—the illegal sale of liquor, illegal gambling, and the illegal use of narcotics. There are evils implicit in any governmental official knowing of such activities without taking speedy action—evils which can erode the very law enforcement agencies themselves.

In the present case, the undercover agent has been completely candid with this Court; his honesty, integrity, and frankness are a credit to himself and to the Narcotics Bureau. Nevertheless, the risks inherent in any law enforcement techniques which condone illegal activities must always be a foremost concern of the courts, and when a law enforcement agency has exceeded the bounds of propriety, it is the duty of the courts to say so.

In view of the undisputed evidence presented by the prosecution, this Court would be remiss in its duty if it did not grant judgment of acquittal on the ground that as a matter of law the defendant was entrapped.

It is so ordered.

The conflict between the needs of effective law enforcement and the desire to give an accused ample opportunity to prepare his defense is shown by the following decision.

ROSS v. UNITED STATES
349 F.2d 210 (D.C. Cir. 1965)

Before WASHINGTON, DANAHER, and MCGOWAN, Circuit Judges.

PER CURIAM. Although we have no reason to reject such facts as were found by the District Court, we do not think that its conclusions of law are compelled by them. Speaking only to what this record discloses, we think there was an undue subordination of appellant's interests which should not, at least in a record as barren of reassuring corroboration as this one, result in a sustainable conviction. Accordingly, we reverse.

I

There is, of course, a substantial public interest in effective police work to detect violations of the narcotics laws. To this end the Metropolitan Police have employed their own members as undercover agents to make purchases of narcotics. It is elemental that the effectiveness of such an agent does not survive the time when it becomes known that he is a policeman. That time is ordinarily the moment when he appears before a magistrate to swear out complaints against those from whom he has made purchases. Thus, it is the practice for such an agent to postpone all swearing out of complaints until he has completed his underground service. At that point, and armed with his notebook of notations, he swears out all the complaints at once.

Officer Bush, the policeman involved in this case, first joined the force on March 5, 1962. His undercover work began very shortly thereafter on March 18. It terminated on December 5, 1962, at which time Bush swore out complaints against 51 persons, including appellant, from whom he asserted that he had purchased narcotics at one time or another during the preceding seven months. During the seven months, Bush made a total of 125 purchases, an appreciable number of which were so-called "burns" or "dupes," *i.e.,* the articles represented to be narcotics were not so in fact. During the last three months of his undercover service, there were 66 transactions in all, 15 of which were with persons from whom he had already made purchases prior to September 5, and 23 of which were second or third purchases from persons first dealt with after September 5. There is some conflict in the record as to exactly how many new contacts there were in the last three months, but it is clear that a substantial part of Bush's work during this period duplicated his earlier contacts.

The record suggests that the principal limitation on the number of men assigned to undercover work is budgetary. With more funds for more personnel, more undercover agents could be used and qualified persons would be available. The Captain of the Narcotics Squad decides when an undercover investigation is to end, but he acts to do so only when the matter is brought to his attention by two particular detectives serving on the Narcotics Squad. These latter have never received any instructions from higher authority as to the criteria to be applied in weighing whether to terminate an undercover assignment. A number of factors were identified which they have thought to be relevant, but none of these in any way takes account of the interest of an accused in knowing as soon as possible of the charge against him in order that he may prepare most effectively to rebut it.

We do not conclude from all this that the delay in moving against appellant was, in the trial court's words, "necessitated by the requirements of effective law-enforcement." It seems to us, contrarily, that the latter part of Bush's service was marked by declining effectiveness, at least of such proportions as to fail to balance the scale against appellant's accelerating need to know that, unless Officer Bush mislaid his notebook, he was ultimately going to be charged with having committed a crime at a certain time and place on May 10. It is always to be remembered that the withholding of this information is a conscious act on the part of the police. That alone does not condemn it, because the Department is motivated solely by a purpose to enhance its effectiveness in the public interest. But the Constitution contemplates a separate interest in fair procedures for the citizen faced with the loss of his liberty by reason of criminal charges. When interests of this nature impinge upon each other, as they have a way of doing, they must be accommodated. A balance must be struck, if one or the other is not to be sacrificed completely. We see no inevitable necessity for such a sacrifice here. Certainly there need be none if the Police Department in pursuing the one interest is not wholly oblivious of the other. Of course the Department must have some considerable latitude for the planning and organization of its undercover program, but this record suggests strongly that that latitude, if it were informed by any awareness whatsoever of the due process interest, could and would result in a program reasonably adequate to the demands made upon it by differing aspects of the public interest.[2]

It may be urged that, the human memory being what it is, the difference between, say, four months and seven months would be of little consequence to appellant. But no one can say this for certain; and, in any event, mutual dissatisfaction is a well-nigh inevitable phenomenon of balancing. What we can say is that, where there appear to be other means for achieving the desired result, there is no justification for overlooking this fact on the speculation that appellant's mnemonic capacities might not have been enlarged by earlier notice. The building of a framework of procedural fair play, like other constructions, rests to some degree upon probabilities. And the probabilities here are in favor of the shorter period.

The record before us is, thus, one which shows (1) a purposeful delay of seven months between offense and arrest, (2) a plausible claim of inability to recall or reconstruct the events of the day of the offense, and (3) a trial in which the case against appellant consists of the recollection of one witness refreshed by a notebook. We are not convinced that successful police operations against narcotics in this jurisdiction depend upon proceedings of such slender dimensions. The Government's case should, at the least, have more substance than the one before us if it is to override the appellant's interest in earlier notification. Without attempting to define the precise reach of the Fifth Amendment in this context, a due regard for our supervisory responsibility for

[2] Whatever the outer limits of such a period may be, the point is that, being purposeful, the delay should result only from arrangements which reflect a conscious effort to accommodate fairness and efficiency. [In Jackson v. United States, 351 F.2d 821, 822 (D.C. Cir. 1965), the government stipulated: "There are no instructions, suggestions, directives or related documents issued by the Federal Bureau of Narcotics to or for its agents specifying the length of time to be spent by an agent in an undercover narcotics investigation. It is the policy of the Bureau that such undercover investigations continue as long as they are effective."]

criminal proceedings in this jurisdiction requires, in our view, the reversal of this conviction.

It is so ordered.

DANAHER, Circuit Judge (dissenting). I dissent from the position announced by my colleagues.

It seems to me that the law is clear, and is definitely contrary to the position the majority now asserts. I have no doubt that many judges like many lawyers, in their approach to these narcotics cases, are moved consciously or not by the heavy penalties which follow convictions for narcotics violations. But policy considerations in such matters are for Congress, not for the courts. Mr. Justice Frankfurter said as much in Gore v. United States. He had pointed out that the penalties prescribed by Congress reveal a legislative determination "to turn the screw of the criminal machinery—detention, prosecution, and punishment—tighter and tighter." Other judges seem to think that a narcotics violator, if an addict, may be entitled to acquittal by reason of insanity.

So, without the citation of a single authority contrary to our well-established law, my colleagues renew the assault upon the pre-arrest delay. They would have us in terms of an undefined standard of "fairness" make an ad hoc determination despite an error-free trial.

My colleagues assume that Ross suffered from a loss of memory as to the events of May 10th. He testified flatly, however, that he never sold any narcotics whatever to Bush. He testified fully with respect to the raid of May 18, even to full details as to his discussion with Officers Didone and Paul.

Perhaps greater importance should be accorded to the present issue, since experience has shown a delayed arrest may be deemed essential in yet other areas of law enforcement. The passing of counterfeit money by one of many confederates is a ready instance of where the utterance of a single counterfeit note may seem of far less significance at the time than that the plates be located and the actual printers of the illicit currency be apprehended. Another example occurs in cases of use of the mails in furtherance of a scheme to defraud. In United States v. Graham, 102 F.2d 436, 440 (2 Cir.), cert. denied, 307 U.S. 643 (1939), an immediate arrest might have frustrated the entire enforcement effort. Other instances will come to mind where continued surveillance may be essential to proper law enforcement. How far and in what circumstances the rule announced by my colleagues might have impact in such situations, we can not know.

Subsequent to the *Ross* case, another panel of the same court upheld a conviction because the accused failed to meet the burden of establishing prejudice resulting from prearrest delay.[c] The opinion said:

> Use of undercover agents is a necessary and accepted police practice, and the interest of the Government in keeping an agent's identity secret for a reasonable period is a legitimate basis for delaying the arrest of an individual wrongdoer while the agent is continuing his covert investigations. . . . Extensive, time-consuming investigations by undercover operatives, who daily risk their lives, are required to get to the retail and wholesale sources of illicit narcotics.

In dissent, Judge Wright argued:

> At the appointed time, months after the purchases of narcotics, using his diary as his prop, the undercover policeman files charges against all of the persons from whom he has made buys, in this instance 102. He then goes out on the street with other officers to find the people accused. In this search the undercover officer's primary prop is his own mental picture of the sellers. I suggest that it defies human experience for any man, particularly a new policeman, to remember and to identify with absolute conviction the particular 102 faces, as distinguished from hundreds of others, that passed through his mind, many on just one occasion, during the kaleidoscope of his months-long undercover investigation. Indulging the unlikely assumption that he can remember the 102 particular faces, to suggest that he can allocate each face to the appropriate time and place shown in his diary offends credulity. . . . This spectre apparently does not disturb the majority of this panel. I find it frightening.[d]

3. *Methods of Control*

The previous materials have illustrated methods used to control undercover operations—suppression of evidence obtained by improper undercover investigation, the defense of entrap-

[c] Powell v. United States, 352 F.2d 705 (D.C. Cir. 1965).

[d] The panel in Woody v. United States, 370 F.2d 214 (D.C. Cir. 1966), reversed even though there was only a four-month delay, pointing out as another variable the low quality of the identification testimony, much as Judge Wright did.

ment (either on the ground that the accused is not guilty of the crime or on the ground that the supervisory power of the courts should be used to prevent prosecution of one who has been drawn into crime by improper police methods), police self-restraint in establishing policies or practices narrower than the law might permit, and dismissal in the interest of controlling the police and increasing fairness to the accused, relying on judicial responsibility to oversee law enforcement.[e]

There is in legislation neither approval, condemnation, nor regulation of these police practices. The courts have with rare exceptions been concerned only with whether the police practice constituted entrapment, and police conduct can rarely be so characterized. In the absence of substantial external controls the police have not felt impelled to articulate their policies with respect to undercover activities.

DANCY v. UNITED STATES
395 F.2d 636 (D.C. Cir. 1968)

Before BAZELON, Chief Judge, and EDGERTON, Senior Circuit Judge, and McGOWAN, Circuit Judge.

McGOWAN, Circuit Judge. This court has recognized that some balance must be struck between the narcotics defendant's right to be convicted only upon a reasonably reliable identification, and the public interest in effective police control of the trafficking in illegal drugs. We have indicated that a delay of the order of four months or less might customarily be regarded within the latitudes where the public interest is dominant, although we have had to recognize that, even within these limits, there may be special circumstances of prejudice which place the defendant's interests in the ascendant. Woody v. United States, 125 U.S.App.D.C. 192, 195, 196, 370 F.2d 214, 217, 218 (1966). Because the police action here predated *Ross*, we weigh this case narrowly by reference to the factual considerations deemed important in *Ross*.

By that standard we find no necessity to reverse. The delay here was less than four months; and appellant has advanced no peculiarly prejudicial consequences of that delay other than his

---

[e] Comment, *Judicial Control of Secret Agents,* 76 YALE L.J. 994 (1967), urges creation of a system of judicial authorization before the state could use secret agents (1) to penetrate a constitutionally protected place (such as Hoffa's hotel room), (2) to betray friendship (such as Hoffa's friendship with Partin), or (3) to solicit the commission of crime. The use of secret agents over an extended period (such as the two months in Hoffa's case) would be controlled by the terms of the judicial authorization.

general inability to reconstruct the events of the day of the alleged sale. Moreover, unlike *Ross,* Moore testified that he had seen appellant before December 7, recognized him that day, and recognized him again shortly after filing the complaint against him.

Appellant, through his appointed counsel, has ably pressed upon us what is essentially the argument that security against faulty identification can not be made to reside in arbitrary definitions of allowable time span. That argument, on the facts of this record and in the present state of our decisions, does not lead to nullification of this conviction. It does remind that we recognized its force in *Ross* when we noted that, the human memory being what it is, the difference between four and seven months, for example, may not be a universally meaningful one. We regarded *Ross* more as a challenge to the police than as a license—a challenge to exhibit some awareness of the very real dangers of misidentification lurking in the narcotics undercover agent practice, and to endeavor consciously to devise methods and procedures which would reduce those dangers as much as possible consistent with effective law enforcement.

One of the less impressive aspects of the evidentiary inquiry on our remand in *Ross* was the low level of authority within the Police Department at which the formulation of undercover agent policies was carried on, and the complete absence from the criteria employed "of the interest of an accused in knowing as soon as possible of the charge against him in order that he may prepare most effectively to rebut it." We said in *Ross* that we had no reason to think that the public and private interests could not be reasonably accommodated without sacrifice of the one or the other. Of the inevitability of such a sacrifice we said:

> Certainly there need be none if the Police Department in pursuing the one interest is not wholly oblivious of the other. Of course the Department must have some considerable latitude for the planning and organization of its undercover program, but this record suggests strongly that that latitude, if it were informed by any awareness whatsoever of the due process interest, could and would result in a program reasonably adequate to the demands made upon it by differing aspects of the public interest.

349 F.2d at 213.

With respect to arrests made subsequent to *Ross,* there will hopefully be some indication of a conscious response to this admonition not to leave the interests of the arrestee wholly out of account in planning the procedures to be followed by undercover agents. There is no reason why legal planning to achieve legitimate ends by appropriate means needs to be confined to minimizing estate taxes or facilitating corporate mergers. The police are carrying increasingly heavy responsibilities for the protection of the public interest, and they deserve and require greater resources of all kinds. One of them is certainly the bringing to bear on a problem such as this the wide-ranging and informed inventiveness which lawyers are called upon to supply every day to private and public clients.[3]

The judgment of conviction is affirmed.

4. The Special Problem of Secret Recording

The following situations illustrate a special problem of undercover operations:

1

A "special agent" equipped with a wireless transmitter entered the place of business of a suspect, who was a longtime acquaintance, and engaged him in conversation. During the discussion the suspect made some incriminating statements about narcotics which were heard by police stationed outside, listening to a radio receiver.

2

In order to obtain evidence against a traffic patrolman suspected of accepting bribes, the police internal investigation unit equipped a plainclothesman with a recording device. The investigator then drove 65 m.p.h. in a zone posted for 45 and was stopped by the suspect. The investigator stated that he would like very much to avoid a traffic ticket. The suspect was wary, however, and searched the investigator, finding the hidden recording device.

---

[3] A conscious effort to engineer the undercover system in order to strengthen its reliability would undoubtedly turn up a number of useful devices not necessarily involving a shortening of the period of underground service. Multiple transactions can, for example, be very helpful in corroborating identification even if less than all become the basis of punishment. The documentary record on identification could apparently be improved, since it appears to consist at the moment of random and unsystematic note-taking by individual officers. A standard form, with a check-list of identification features and other details, and designed to serve as a continuing file on the defendant in which all observations are to be entered, would appear to be worth consideration.

Now you see it...now you don't!

A Lilliputian World of Miniature Microphones (for use with transmitters or tape recorders)

Button Hole Microphone

Don't let the size fool you...this is a highly sensitive instrument designed to be concealed behind a tie, in a cuff...

$29.95

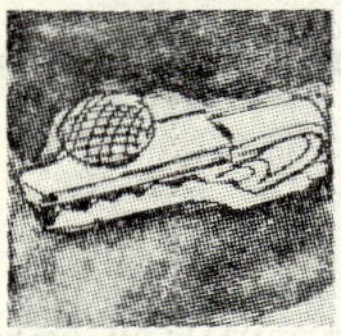

Tie Microphone

People will admire its handsome jewelry look without ever realizing it's a microphone...and you can record or transmit without arousing the slightest suspicion...

$29.95

Fountain Pen Microphone

This one stares them right in the face...only they're seeing a fountain pen (dummy case, of course contains an ultra-sensitive miniature microphone)...

$29.95

Flat sub-miniature Microphone

Don't mistake it for a contact lens...it's only $^3/_4$"x$^1/_2$"x$^1/_4$"...just think, there's practically no place you can't conceal it...and powerful!

$24.95

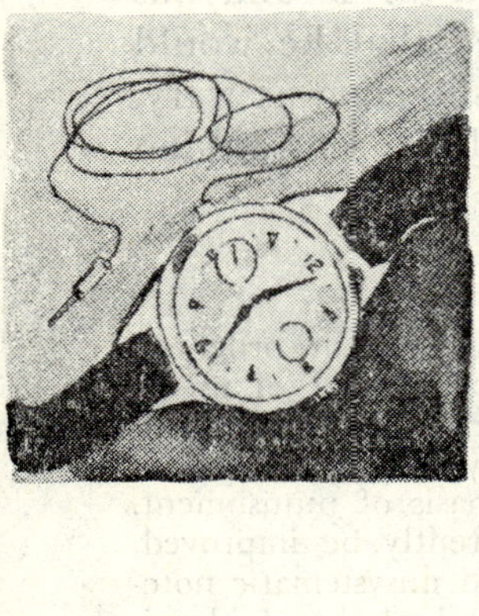

Wristwatch Microphone

While it won't keep you on time...it keeps you on the beam. Picks up vital conversations and information in the guise of a watch. The fantastically sensitive microphone is embedded in the handsome, realistic watch case, as if you didn't know.

$79.50

When an undercover agent reports what he learned in a conversation with a suspect, there is little doubt that the suspect has no valid ground for objection. In all communication there is a risk of divulgence by the other party, except in those circumstances where the communication is protected by special rules of privilege (usually limited to communications to doctors, lawyers, and clergymen in their professional capacity). But when the undercover agent secretly records or transmits the conversation, the similarity to eavesdropping and wiretapping has made for uneasiness. In a case similar to those above, Justice Brennan wrote, in dissent:[f]

> I believe that there is a grave danger of chilling all private, free, and unconstrained communication if secret recordings, turned over to law enforcement officers by one party to a conversation, are competent evidence of any self-incriminating statements the speaker may have made. In a free society, people ought not to have to watch their every word so carefully.[g]

Nonetheless, in the absence of contrary statute, secret recording by undercover agents is presently lawful.[h]

ILLINOIS CRIMINAL CODE
ILLINOIS REVISED STATUTES (1967)
Chapter 38—Criminal Law and Procedure

§ 14-1. Definition.]

(a) Eavesdropping device.

An eavesdropping device is any device capable of being used to hear or record oral conversation whether such conversation is conducted in person, by telephone, or by any other means; Provided, however, that this definition shall not include devices used for the restoration of the deaf or hard-of-hearing to normal or partial hearing.

---

[f] Lopez v. United States, 373 U.S. 427, 452 (1963).

[g] The same concern is evidenced by the telephone regulation requiring a warning beep every fifteen seconds when a telephone conversation is being recorded.

[h] Hajdu v. State, 189 So. 2d 230 (Fla. App. 1966), applies a more stringent rule, excluding testimony by one who listened to a covertly broadcast conversation, though allowing the undercover agent herself to testify to what she had been told. United States v. White, — F.2d — (7th Cir. 1968) and Doty v. United States, — F.2d — (10th Cir. 1968) (telephone conversation) concluded that the *Katz* case forbids such practice.

(b) Eavesdropper.

An eavesdropper is any person, including law enforcement officers, who operates or participates in the operation of any eavesdropping device contrary to the provisions of this Article. . . .

§ 14-2. Elements of the Offense.] A person commits eavesdropping when he:

(a) Uses an eavesdropping device to hear or record all or any part of any oral conversation without the consent of any party thereto; or

(b) Uses or divulges any information which he knows or reasonably should know was obtained through the illegal use of an eavesdropping device.

§ 14-4. Penalty.] Any person convicted of eavesdropping shall be fined not to exceed $1,000 or imprisoned in a penal institution other than the penitentiary not to exceed one year, or both, or imprisoned in the state penitentiary from one to two years.

§ 14-5. Evidence Inadmissible.] Any evidence obtained in violation of this Article is not admissible in any civil or criminal trial, or any administrative or legislative inquiry or proceeding, nor in any grand jury proceedings. . . .

§ 14-6. Civil Remedies to Injured Parties.] Any or all parties to any conversation upon which eavesdropping is practiced contrary to this Article shall be entitled to the following remedies:

(a) To an injunction by any court of competent jurisdiction prohibiting further eavesdropping by the eavesdropper and by or on behalf of his principal, or either;

(b) To all actual damages against the eavesdropper or his principal or both;

(c) To any punitive damages which may be awarded by the court or by a jury. . . .

The statutes of several states have attempted to regulate the recording of conversations by one of the participants. The Illinois statute set out above was interpreted to forbid recording unless every party had given consent. Similar, but more clearly stated provisions were adopted in Oregon ("no person shall . . . [o]btain or attempt to obtain the whole or any part of a conversation by means of any device, contrivance, machine or apparatus, whether electrical, mechanical, manual or otherwise, if all participants in the conversation are not specifically informed that their conversation is being obtained")[i] and Maryland ("It is unlawful for any person in this State to use any electronic device or other device or equipment of any type whatsoever in such manner as to overhear or record any part of the conversation or words spoken to or by any person in private conversation without the knowledge or consent, expressed or implied, of that other person.").[j] In both the latter states a warrant procedure was established which would permit law enforcement officers to record conversations with court approval. In Illinois no warrant procedure was established, perhaps because the court interpretation given to the statute was not foreseen.[k]

Though there is no statutory authority for issuance of such a "recording warrant" in the federal system, the federal court in Tennessee gave its approval to such recording during investigation of alleged jury tampering by one of James Hoffa's attorneys. The United States Supreme Court held that if there were any objection to secret recording by undercover agents it was satisfied in this case by the warrant-type procedures followed.[l]

MEMORANDUM

June 16, 1967

TO: The Heads of Executive Departments and Agencies
FROM: Office of the Attorney General, Washington, D. C.
RE: Wiretapping and Electronic Eavesdropping
[Another portion of this memorandum appears at 108, *supra.*]

3. Under presently controlling court decisions, however, certain uses of electronic devices are legal. See, for example, the decisions in Lopez v. United States, 373 U.S. 427 (1963), and in Osborn v. United States, 385 U.S. 323 (1966), where the use of recording devices was held to be legitimate if the consent of a party to the conversation had been obtained. Moreover, the use of mechanical or electronic equipment to record statements intended to be disseminated to the public generally, public

[i] ORE. REV. STAT. § 165.540 (1965).

[j] MD. ANN. CODE art. 27, § 125A (Supp. 1965).

[k] This is suggested by the fact that an amendment to § 14-2 to change "any party" to "all parties" was vetoed by the governor in 1963 on the ground that it would prevent undercover police recording as well as recording by private individuals.

[l] Osborn v. United States, 385 U.S. 323 (1966).

speeches for example, is clearly not illegal and is not subject to the rules formulated in this memorandum.

4. In the light of the immediately foregoing discussion in paragraphs 1-3, any use of mechanical or electronic devices by federal personnel to overhear or record nontelephone conversations involving a violation of the constitution or a statute is prohibited.

5. In order further to assure protection of the right to privacy, to resolve questions which may arise under paragraph 4 and strictly to limit legal electronic surveillance, agencies shall, except [in emergency situations] . . . obtain advance written approval from the Attorney General for any use of mechanical or electronic devices to overhear or record nontelephone conversations without the consent of all of the parties to such conversations.

Reference Note

The most helpful treatment of encouragement is L. Tiffany, D. McIntyre & D. Rotenberg, Detection of Crime, pt. III (1967), in the American Bar Foundation series on the Administration of Criminal Justice. It describes current practice and the limited control mechanisms available. Rotenberg has elaborated his work by discussing the legal controls over encouragement in *The Police Detection Practice of Encouragement,* 49 Va. L. Rev. 871 (1963), and *The Police Detection Practice of Encouragement: Lewis v. United States and Beyond,* 4 Houston L. Rev. 609 (1967).

An interesting description of current practice in Chicago narcotics enforcement and the legal controls in Illinois is Bancroft, *Administration of the Affirmative Trap and the Doctrine of Entrapment: Device and Defense,* 31 U. Chi. L. Rev. 137 (1963).

Mikell, *The Doctrine of Entrapment in the Federal Courts,* 90 U. Pa. L. Rev. 245 (1942), provides a good doctrinal history of the defense of entrapment up to that time. Analysis of the legal issues is supplemented by the comments to the entrapment provision in the Model Penal Code 14 (Tent. Draft No. 9, 1959). *See also* Donnelly, *Judicial Control of Informants, Spies, Stool Pigeons, and Agent Provocateurs,* 60 Yale L.J. 1091 (1951).

Informers in Federal Narcotics Prosecution, 2 Colum. J.L. & Soc. Prob. 47 (1967), is a good descriptive study. M. Harney & J. Cross, The Informer in Law Enforcement (1960), is more general but tends to be anecdotal. Both encouragement and use of informers in a California city are discussed in J. Skolnick, Justice Without Trial chs. 5-7 (1966).

C. STOPPING AND QUESTIONING

Most surveillance and undercover operations are the assignments of specialists in the police department. The ordinary patrolman rather, as his title designates, patrols the streets. His concern is to prevent crime by his presence and to apprehend offenders—confronting suspicious persons, watching for anything unusual, being close at hand in the event a citizen calls for help. He is a generalist, responding to varied demands as they come.

1. *The Investigative Technique of Stopping and Questioning*

Stopping and questioning, or field interrogation as it is often called, is one of the most common kinds of police-citizen contacts. The stopping itself is usually intended only to provide opportunity for brief questioning on the street. The questioning permits the officer to ascertain quickly whether a person observed in suspicious circumstances can provide a satisfactory explanation for his actions or not. Sometimes the person questioned may be able to satisfy the officer of his innocence, or the process of questioning and observation may provide sufficient incriminating information to justify taking the person into custody. Sometimes suspicion will persist and cannot be resolved on the street.

A common concomitant of stopping and questioning is frisking, a "patting down" for weapons in order to assure the officer that he is not in danger of attack while he pursues his questioning.

By its nature stopping and questioning is an important point of contact between the ordinary police officer and the ordinary citizen. Reactions of citizens vary from approval on the part of the law-abiding citizen who finds reassurance in this sort of police action, if politely conducted, to violent antagonism on the part of some residents of a ghetto community who see in the practice discrimination against them because of their race or poverty.

MODEL CODE OF PRE-ARRAIGNMENT PROCEDURE
§ 2.02, Comment at 95-97 (Tent. Draft No. 1, 1966)†

A law enforcement officer in the performance of his duties will be confronted with innumerable situations in which it seems necessary to make some inquiry of a person whose name he does

† This and other excerpts from the Model Code are reprinted with the kind consent of the American Law Institute, the copyright holder.

not know and whom, if further action is not taken, he is most unlikely ever to find again. An inquiry may appear appropriate because such a person is behaving in a suspicious or unusual manner which suggests possible involvement in crime. Thus, he may be a person running with a heavy package at 2 A.M. in a business neighborhood. Or he may correspond to a description of the perpetrator of a recent crime, but because he is traveling in an automobile it is impossible to be sure. Or he may be walking slowly down a street at night, looking into the windows of parked cars.

The person to whom the officer would like to direct an inquiry may clearly not be involved himself in criminality. He may be a person who was near the scene of a crime, and thus a potential source of information. Or it may be impossible to tell in advance whether the person to be stopped is a suspect or a source of information. Justice Jackson, in his dissenting opinion in Brinegar v. United States, 338 U.S. 160, at 183 (1949), puts a most compelling case, the roadblock involving all cars departing the area of a kidnapping. There will be other situations of this sort. It would be disingenuous to recognize this need in terms of an authority to detain suspects, since the officer will often simply not know and should not be required to decide whether some or all of the persons at the scene of a crime are suspects.

It has been argued by some that in all such cases, where reasonable cause for an arrest does not exist, the police must rely on voluntary cooperation to achieve their purposes, and if they cannot, it is only because society is reluctant to go to the trouble and expense of hiring more and better police. But this argument disposes too easily of the case for a power to stop. No police force can be large enough to allow officers to follow and observe every suspicious person they encounter. If an authority such as we propose here is not granted, the real choice for the police in such situations is between an attempt to secure voluntary cooperation and an arrest. If cooperation cannot be secured and an arrest is unjustified, the person must be allowed to disappear, and with him must disappear any information he might have provided. . . .

. . . If, as some have argued, the only power to restrain a person, even briefly, is by arresting him on reasonable grounds to believe him guilty of a crime, the police will be foreclosed from responding to confused, emergency situations in the way that seems most natural and rational. For in such circumstances, where a crime may have been committed and a suspect or important witness is about to disappear, it seems irrational to deprive the officer of the opportunity to "freeze" the situation for a short time, so that he may make inquiry and arrive at a considered judgment about further action to be taken. To deny the police such a power would be to pay too high a price in effective policing and in the police's respect for the good sense of the rules that govern them, in order to avoid brief inconveniences that most innocent persons would be prepared to undergo.

. . . [I]t is unrealistic to expect a police officer in the field to exercise a responsible judgment as to whether or not to make an arrest the very moment that he is first aware that he is in the presence of a critical situation. Further, without a limited "stop" power there will be tremendous pressure to relax the "reasonable cause" standard for arrest to enable the police to exercise some authority in suspicious circumstances, circumstances which should not give rise to full-scale stationhouse custody but which will do so in the absence of a more limited available alternative. Without an authority to stop, there are likely to be more arrests on a lesser basis, and what is more important more arrests of innocent persons.

CHICAGO POLICE DEPARTMENT TRAINING BULLETINS

Vol. VII No. 23, 6 June 1966

There are two basic tactics that should be employed by an officer on patrol.

1. Check the physical security of a business premises. . . .

2. Stop suspicious persons and question them. Use the field interrogation to get information as to the identity of strangers and people that are obviously "out of character" with the surroundings or are up to no good.

The man loitering on the corner near a currency exchange or supermarket may be a look-out for criminals inside robbing or burglarizing the location. Question him and make him produce identification.

Vol. II No. 7, 13 Feb. 1961

Officers enroute to a recently completed robbery, burglary, larceny, or any other crime should be aware of persons leaving the general area of the crime in haste. Anyone found in the vicinity of a prowl should be interrogated. Persons loitering at the scene of a disturbance, juveniles and known gang members should be the subject of interrogation. . . .

Actions, dress, or location of a person often classify him as suspicious in the mind of the police officer. Men loitering near schools, public toilets, playgrounds, and swimming pools may be sex perverts. Men loitering near bars at closing time, or any other business at closing time, may be robbery suspects. Men or youths walking along looking into cars may be car thieves or looking for something to steal. Persons showing evidence of recent injury, or whose clothing is disheveled, may be victims or participants in an assault or strong-arm robbery. Any person who shows excess emotion at the scene of a fire may be a pyromaniac.

Servicemen in uniform who are driving automobiles may be auto theft suspects. They often steal cars to return to their stations after running out of money. Young boys who drive expensive cars, clean cars with dirty plates, or dirty cars with clean plates should arouse the police officer's suspicion. Cars with the front vent window knocked out, or illegally parked cars with doors open and engines running may have been stolen.[m]

Vol. II No. 28, 17 July 1961

There is no rigid rule to govern when a person should be stopped for a field interrogation. The decision to stop a person must be based upon the circumstance of each case. Generally, the circumstances will involve the elements of time, location, appearance, and activity of a person. When one or more of these elements appears to be out of the ordinary, it indicates that the person involved should be the subject of a field interrogation.

The Practice

The following illustrate typical situations in which police on patrol are likely to stop and question. There is often no clear line between the unquestionably consensual response of a person who desires to be helpful to police or who thinks he can successfully bluff,[n] and the response which results from fear or unquestioning acquiescence.

---

[m] The Denver police manual lists additional "suspicion arousers": persons who show undue interest in the activities of the police; persons who make an apparent effort to avoid meeting an officer or who, at the sight of an officer, attempt to conceal or dispose of some article; persons who carry bundles at unusual times or places; persons who seem unfamiliar with the vehicle they are operating; and persons who engage children in prolonged conversation.

[n] United States v. Vita, 294 F.2d 524, 528-31 (2d Cir. 1961): ". . . Vita was told that he was not under arrest, that he was free to leave at any time, that anything he said could be used against him, and that he had the right to

(a) General suspicious circumstances

1

The officers saw a person seated behind the steering wheel of a parked car. The car was facing the street. It had been backed into the space between two houses. The driver was wide awake and seemed to be making motions with his hands in front of his face. The two officers approached the car and asked him what he was doing there. He showed them that he was eating chicken.

2

Coming to a street intersection, the officers observed a man crossing the intersection who did not appear to know where he was going. The officers alighted from the car, questioned this man, and searched him. He provided the police with full credentials and indicated that this was the first occasion on which he had ever been questioned by a police officer. His answers satisfied the officers that this man was quite "legitimate." They thanked him for his cooperation and sent him on his way.

3

In an area where a number of burglaries and thefts from autos had been reported, the officers saw three young men standing by a car in which two others were seated. When the men saw the squad car they turned and rapidly walked away. The police stopped and asked the two in the car to step out. As they did, one of them dropped two cigarettes on the ground. The officer examined them and found they contained marihuana.

---

counsel. For the next two and one-half hours Vita was continuously questioned about the bank robbery. . . . Vita was apparently confident of his ability to talk himself clear of whatever suspicions the F.B.I. had of his possible complicity. Surprising as it may seem, the guilty are often as eager as the innocent to explain what they can to law enforcement officials. The very same naive optimism which spurs the criminal on to commit his illegal act in the belief that it will not be detected often leads him to feel that in a face-to-face encounter with the authorities he will be able to beguile them into exculpating him. Having chosen to talk with the F.B.I. agents, Vita cannot now be heard to complain because his calculated risk worked to his disadvantage. . . . Most persons, even hardened criminals, will not refuse to cooperate altogether;[3] they are far more likely to talk and make a pretense of cooperation.

"[3] See, for example, United States v. Bufalino, 2 Cir., 1960, 285 F.2d 408 where, of 58 persons who were stopped for questioning about their meeting at Joseph Barbara's estate in Appalachin, New York, in 1957, only one refused to answer any questions at all. Of the 58, about 25 had police records. United States v. Bonanno, supra, 180 F. Supp. at page 76."

(b) Police record of suspect or his associates

4

Officers on patrol observed a man who had previously been investigated in connection with strong-arm robberies. Because he was in company with an unknown man, the police stopped him and questioned him about his intentions. They warned the other man that they believed the suspect to be responsible for the robberies of persons the suspect "picked up" and that he might be in danger.

5

Officers observed an individual whom they knew to be a parolee walking along the street. He was dressed in a new and expensive coat. The officers stopped the man, frisked him, and asked him when he got out of prison. He indicated he was released three months previously. When they asked him where he got the coat he replied that he paid $160 for it at a store and had obtained the money in "social gambling" (a clear violation of parole). The officers told him to get on his way.

6

The cruiser car officers observed a known narcotic user standing in the doorway of a store. The officers had found fifty capsules of heroin on this man in September and he was turned over to the narcotics bureau at that time. The officers searched this man in the doorway, but found no narcotics on him. They asked if his case had gotten into court. He indicated that he had been released by the narcotics bureau and had not been prosecuted.

(c) Suspicious activities with respect to property

7

Scout car 8-4 observed a man alight from a vehicle and enter a drugstore with a small suitcase. The officer indicated that he was curious as to what the man was carrying in his suitcase and decided that he was going to find out. He followed the man into the drugstore and, on approaching him, asked, "Can I see what you have in your suitcase?" The man indicated that he would be most happy to show the officer what he had and opened it for the officer's inspection. The man then displayed his credentials which identified him as a Fuller Brush salesman. He expressed his disappointment that the officer was unwilling to make a purchase.

8

Officers on patrol at night observed two men who had a trailer attached to their car in the parking lot of a closed service station. Upon inquiry about the ownership of the trailer, the men stated that they were returning it and produced papers showing that it had been rented to them for that date.

9

A young Puerto Rican boy carrying expensive-looking luggage in a suburb was stopped and questioned about ownership of the suitcase. The boy claimed the luggage belonged to a "friend," but was unable to locate him. After being taken into custody, the boy confessed to stealing the luggage from a parked car.

(d) Suspicious loitering

10

Police had received several reports of child molestations occurring at the same approximate location. No description was available, but officers on a subsequent occasion approached a man found parked in the area at the time school let out, and asked him to get out of his car. When asked an explanation for his presence he was able to satisfy the officers.

11

Officers at night observed a car parked near a beach in a no-parking area. Several persons were in the car and as the patrol car approached, the headlights of the parked car were flashed on and off several times. The officers stopped and observed the car and during that time a teenager walked to the car from the beach area. He was stopped and the occupants were asked to get out of the car. The teenagers, three boys and three girls, were questioned as to their identity and reason for being there, and the driver was required to establish ownership of the car. The car was searched, including the trunk, but nothing of significance to the officers was found.

(e) Citizen complaints

12

A patrol officer received a radio call that a citizen had complained of some drunks parked in a car near her home. He observed two college couples in a parked car who were acting in an orderly manner and showed no signs of drinking. He nonetheless required them to identify themselves. He later complained at having to respond this way to citizen calls about neighborhood annoyances.

13

Police received a telephone complaint at 1:00 a.m. from a woman who was home alone and unable to sleep because she was worried about a car with one man in it which had been parked in front of her house for an hour. It was a residential neighborhood and she said the car did not belong to any of the neighbors. A patrol car was dispatched. The patrolman asked for identification and asked what the man was doing there. He said he had had a fight with his wife and was sitting there cooling off. The officer suggested it was time he went home and the man drove off.

14

A patrolman received a radio assignment to investigate a "suspicious man" in a gangway. When he arrived at the location he observed a man leaving and stopped him. Upon questioning, the man admitted that he did not live there and that he had been peeping in the basement window. He said he had peeped in several hundred windows and that he was under psychiatric treatment by a state psychiatrist but could not overcome his problem. (Thirty-seven complaints were cleared by his admissions.)

(f) Identifying perpetrators of reported crime

15

Officers in a large city received a radio call that a yellow Falcon had been used in a robbery. The suspected robbers were described only as two white men. The officers observed a yellow Falcon approaching that had two white men in it and stopped it, despite the fact that the robbery had occurred some distance away. When the men identified themselves as local businessmen the officers apologized for the inconvenience and let them go on their way.

2. The Propriety of Stopping and Questioning

The police training materials and the descriptions of police practice above point out that the officer on patrol responds primarily to the unusual. He does not expect that each inquiry will produce evidence of crime; he knows from experience that most unusual situations have innocent explanations. But he also knows that the unusual circumstances he observes are often associated with criminal activity. He feels justified in making stops on the basis of possible crime, relying upon his experience as providing special competence in spotting the suspicious situation.

The President's Commission Task Force on the Police stated:[o]

> Many actions which the police officer takes are based upon the knowledge and experience which he has accumulated in his years of service. For example, an officer may, in deciding whether a situation is a suspicious one, reach a judgment quite different from that which would be reached by an inexperienced layman or even an experienced trial judge. An officer may have the ability to recognize the smell of narcotics or the sound of a press used in printing illegal numbers or policy tickets. Yet there has been little effort made to capitalize upon police experience or to attempt to assess its reliability: to distinguish accurate inferences from inaccurate ones; or to systematize experience so that it can be effectively communicated through police training to new police officers and to others, like judges, when the propriety of police action is challenged.

That police do have expertise is acknowledged occasionally by the courts in finding that action taken by police is reasonable even though a layman would not recognize the need for action.[p] A substantial question is presented, however, whether police may properly rely on some indicators of guilt. A Negro in a white neighborhood late at night may seem to the officer so unusual and suspicious a situation as to call for stopping and questioning

[o] THE PRESIDENT'S COMMISSION ON LAW ENFORCEMENT AND ADMINISTRATION OF JUSTICE, TASK FORCE REPORT: THE POLICE 20 (1967).

[p] Police expertise was acknowledged in United States v. Kuntz, 265 F. Supp. 543 (N.D.N.Y. 1967) (officers at roadblock recognizing overcooperative behavior as suspicious); United States v. Bostic, 251 F. Supp. 306 (E.D. Pa. 1966) (bank guard recognizing suspicious conduct of men intending to rob bank); Louisiana *ex rel.* Johnson v. Middlebrooks, 260 F. Supp. 517 (E.D. La. 1966) (narcotics officers' experience leading them to know that fleeing addict possessed narcotics or had committed crime). *See also Terry v. Ohio,* at 163, 166-67, *infra.* A seeming unwillingness to rely on police expertise is illustrated by United States v. Margeson, 259 F. Supp. 256 (E.D. Pa. 1966). On the question of expertise, see Remington, *Social Change, the Law and the Common Good,* in PAPERS PRESENTED AT THE TENTH ANNUAL NATIONAL INSTITUTE ON POLICE AND COMMUNITY RELATIONS (Michigan State University 1964); and Schwartz, *Stop and Frisk,* 58 J. CRIM. L.C. & P.S. 433, 445-47 (1967).

the man, but if the Negro is innocent the stopping is likely to appear an act of racial discrimination. The fact that Negroes as a class are involved in more street crimes than whites as a class in a particular community may make race a relevant factor in an officer's assessment of suspiciousness, but race is merely an obvious and convenient characteristic which is meaningful only because it is correlated with poverty, cultural deprivation, and oppressive environment which—rather than race—are likely to be the causal factors.

Stopping and questioning for purposes of investigating possible crimes is often discussed as though it were interchangeable with stopping and frisking which is intended to find and confiscate weapons or which is intended to deter crime by frequent, aggressive spot checking and by fostering the impression of police omnipresence.

THE PRESIDENT'S COMMISSION ON LAW ENFORCEMENT AND ADMINISTRATION OF JUSTICE TASK FORCE REPORT: THE POLICE 183-85 (1967)

Field Interrogation

In many communities, field interrogations are a major source of friction between the police and minority groups. Many minority group leaders strongly contend that field interrogations are predominantly conducted in slum communities, that they are used indiscriminately, and that they are conducted in an abusive and unfriendly manner.

The police consider field interrogations to be an important method of preventing and investigating crime, since they rarely encounter a crime in progress. Normally, by the time a police officer has arrived at a crime scene, the perpetrator has fled, people have gathered, and confusion has ensued. Further, the police believe that they can prevent much crime if they are permitted to stop and question persons whose behavior strongly suggests that a criminal act is being contemplated:

> A law enforcement officer in the performance of his duties will be confronted with innumerable situations in which it seems necessary to make some inquiry of a person whose name he does not know, and whom, if further action is not taken, he is most unlikely ever to find again. An inquiry may appear appropriate because such a person is behaving in a suspicious or unusual manner which suggests a possible involvement in crime. Thus, he may be a person

running with a heavy package at 2:00 a.m. in a business neighborhood. Or he may correspond to a description of the perpetrator of a recent crime, but because he is traveling in an automobile it is impossible to be sure. Or he may be walking slowly down a street at night, looking into the windows of parked cars.

The person to whom the officer would like to direct an inquiry may clearly not be involved in criminality. He may be a person who was near the scene of a crime, and thus a potential source of information. Or it may be impossible to tell in advance whether the person to be stopped is a suspect or a source of information.

The limits of police authority to stop persons briefly for purposes of criminal investigation are unclear in most jurisdictions. In some States, there is specific statutory authority for officers to stop suspicious persons. For example, a recently enacted statute in New York gives an officer authority to stop for questioning a person whom "he reasonably suspects is committing, has committed, or is about to commit" a felony or other specified crimes and authorizes the officer to use whatever force is necessary to effectuate such stops.

In most States, however, there is no specific statute which defines this authority. As a result, police departments are given little guidance as to when a person may be stopped, whether or how long he may be detained, whether force may be used to detain him, what degree of force may be used, whether a person may be searched, whether he may be compelled to answer certain questions, and under what circumstances he must be advised of his legal rights.

A few police departments have policies governing the conduct of field interrogations. Training materials of the Oakland, Calif. Police Dept., for example, carefully describe the types of persons who should be stopped; the San Diego, Calif. Police Dept. specifically forbids officers to restrain persons being questioned against their will; and the Tampa, Fla. Police Dept. defines conditions under which a person may be searched.

The Commission believes that there is a definite need to authorize the police to stop suspects and possible witnesses of major crimes, to detain them for brief questioning if they will not voluntarily cooperate, and to search such suspects for dangerous weapons when such a precaution is necessary. This need was also recognized by the reporters for the American Law Institute Model Pre-Arraignment Code Project:

> If, as some have argued, the only power to restrain a person, even briefly, is by arresting him on reasonable grounds to believe him guilty of a crime, the police will be foreclosed from responding to confused, emergency situations in the way that seems most natural and rational. For in such circumstances, where a crime may have been committed and a suspect or important witness is about to disappear, it seems irrational to deprive the officer of the opportunity to "freeze" the situation for a short time, so that he may make inquiry and arrive at a considered judgment about further action to be taken. To deny the police such a power would be too high a price in effective policing and in the police's respect for the good sense of the rules that govern them, in order to avoid brief inconveniences that most innocent persons would be prepared to undergo.

Misuse of field interrogations, however, is causing serious friction with minority groups in many localities. This is becoming particularly true as more police departments adopt "aggressive patrol" in which officers are encouraged routinely to stop and question persons on the street who are unknown to them, who are suspicious, or whose purpose for being abroad is not readily evident. The Michigan State survey found that both minority group leaders and persons sympathetic to minority groups throughout the country were almost unanimous in labelling field interrogation as a principal problem in police-community relations:

> . . . race has an undue influence on who is stopped.
>
> . . . practice is o.k., but the way it was carried out was unfriendly, abusive, etc. Not against method, but how it is used.
>
> Personally, I found it offensive and was affronted on occasions of its use in New York.
>
> Spanish-Americans are picked up sooner.
>
> Many Negroes stopped in other neighborhoods and questioned. Happens more to Negroes than to others.

The Commission has found that field interrogations, used sometimes in conjunction with aggressive, preventive patrol, are often conducted on a broad-scale basis by many police departments. First, field interrogations are often conducted with little or no basis for suspicion. In San Diego, written reports were made of over 200,000 stops in 1965 and there were probably about as many stops which were not recorded. The effect on attitudes which can result is revealed by the following comment of a lower income Negro:

> When they stop everybody, they say, well, they haven't seen you around, you know, they want to get to know your name, and all this. I can see them stopping you one time, but the same police stopping you every other day, and asking you the same old question.

A study of juvenile offenses in a western city with high police standards found that Negroes were stopped more frequently than other juveniles "often even in the absence of evidence that an offense had been committed."

Second, field interrogations are sometimes used in a way which discriminates against minority groups, the poor, and the juvenile. For example, the Michigan State survey found, on the basis of riding with patrol units in two cities, that members of minority groups were often stopped, particularly if found in groups, in the company of white people, or at night in white neighborhoods, and that this caused serious problems. Similarly, in a midwestern city, using aggressive patrol and field interrogations seems to cause, as in San Diego, the major problem in police-community relations. In contrast, in Philadelphia the field interrogation is used less and is not a major item of criticism by minority groups or others.

Finally, field interrogations are frequently conducted in a discourteous or otherwise offensive manner which is particularly irritating to the citizen. For example, even in San Diego, where officers are instructed specifically and at length to give the citizen an explanation and to act courteously, the University of California study found that an explanation is frequently not given. In some cities, searches are made in a high proportion of instances not for the purpose of protecting the officer but to obtain drugs or other incriminating evidence. In New York, for example, where searches are permitted only when the officer reasonably believes he is in bodily danger, searches were made in 81.6 percent of stops reported. However, a Commission survey of police practices in several large cities, found that one out of every five persons frisked was carrying a dangerous weapon—10 percent were carrying guns and another 10 percent knives.

TERRY v. OHIO
392 U.S. 1 (1968)

[Plainclothes detective McFadden, who had been a policeman for thirty-nine years, was patrolling a downtown Cleveland street at 2:30 on an October afternoon. He observed two men standing at a corner. One would walk past some stores, look in a store window, walk on a short distance, return to the store window for another look, and return to the corner and confer with the other man. Then the other would follow the same pattern. This continued for about ten minutes, with about a dozen trips in all, when the men walked off together. Officer McFadden strongly suspected the men were "casing a job, a stickup." He followed them and saw them stop to talk with a third man they had earlier conferred with on the corner. The officer approached and asked their names. When they mumbled something in response he turned one of the men around so he was between the officer and the others and patted down his clothing, discovering a .38 caliber revolver in his overcoat pocket. In frisking the other two men Officer McFadden found another gun. The two men with guns were taken to the police station and charged with carrying concealed weapons.]

MR. CHIEF JUSTICE WARREN delivered the opinion of the Court.

On the motion to suppress the guns the prosecution took the position that they had been seized following a search incident to a lawful arrest. The trial court rejected this theory, stating that it "would be stretching the facts beyond reasonable comprehension" to find that Officer McFadden had had probable cause to arrest the men before he patted them down for weapons. However, the court denied the defendant's motion on the ground that Officer McFadden, on the basis of his experience, "had reasonable cause to believe . . . that the defendants were conducting themselves suspiciously, and some interrogation should be made of their action." Purely for his own protection, the court held, the officer had the right to pat down the outer clothing of these men, whom he had reasonable cause to believe might be armed. The court distinguished between an investigatory "stop" and an arrest, and between a "frisk" of the outer clothing for weapons and a full-blown search for evidence of crime. The frisk, it held, was essential to the proper performance of the officer's investigatory duties, for without it "the answer to the police officer may be a bullet, and a loaded pistol discovered during the frisk is admissible."

After the court denied their motion to suppress, Chilton and Terry waived jury trial and pleaded not guilty. The court adjudged them guilty, and the Court of Appeals for the Eighth Judicial District, Cuyahoga County, affirmed. The Supreme Court of Ohio dismissed petitioner's appeal on the ground that no "substantial constitutional question" was involved. We granted certiorari, to determine whether the admission of the revolvers in evidence violated petitioner's rights under the Fourth Amendment, made applicable to the States by the Fourteenth. We affirm the conviction.

Unquestionably petitioner was entitled to the protection of the Fourth Amendment as he walked down the street in Cleveland. . . . The question is whether in all the circumstances of this on-the-street encounter, his right to personal security was violated by an unreasonable search and seizure.

Our first task is to establish at what point in this encounter the Fourth Amendment becomes relevant. That is, we must decide whether and when Officer McFadden "seized" Terry and whether and when he conducted a "search." There is some suggestion in the use of such terms as "stop" and "frisk" that such police conduct is outside the purview of the Fourth Amendment because neither action rises to the level of a "search" or "seizure" within the meaning of the Constitution. We emphatically reject this notion. It is quite plain that the Fourth Amendment governs "seizures" of the person which do not eventuate in a trip to the station house and prosecution for crime—"arrests" in traditional terminology. It must be recognized that whenever a police officer accosts an individual and restrains his freedom to walk away, he has "seized" that person. And it is nothing less than sheer torture of the English language to suggest that a careful exploration of the outer surfaces of a person's clothing all over his or her body in an attempt to find weapons is not a "search." Moreover, it is simply fantastic to urge that such a procedure performed in public by a policeman while the citizen stands helpless, perhaps facing a wall with his hands raised, is a "petty indignity." It is a serious intrusion upon the sanctity of the person, which may inflict great indignity and arouse strong resentment, and it is not to be undertaken lightly.

In this case there can be no question, then, that Officer McFadden "seized" petitioner and subjected him to a "search" when he took hold of him and patted down the outer surfaces of his clothing. We must decide whether at that point it was reasonable for Officer McFadden to have interfered with petitioner's personal security as he did.[16] And in determining

---

[16] We thus decide nothing today concerning the constitutional propriety of an investigative "seizure" upon less than probable cause for purposes of "detention" and/or interrogation. Obviously, not all personal intercourse between policemen and citizens involves "seizures" of persons. Only when the officer, by means of physical force or show of authority, has in some way restrained the liberty of a citizen may we conclude that a "seizure" has occurred. We cannot tell with any certainty upon this record whether any such "seizure" took place here prior to Officer McFadden's initiation

whether the seizure and search were "unreasonable" our inquiry is a dual one—whether the officer's action was justified at its inception, and whether it was reasonably related in scope to the circumstances which justified the interference in the first place.

The scheme of the Fourth Amendment becomes meaningful only when it is assured that at some point the conduct of those charged with enforcing the laws can be subjected to the more detached, neutral scrutiny of a judge who must evaluate the reasonableness of a particular search or seizure in light of the particular circumstances. And in making that assessment it is imperative that the facts be judged against an objective standard: would the facts available to the officer at the moment of the seizure or the search "warrant a man of reasonable caution in the belief" that the action taken was appropriate?

Applying these principles to this case, we consider first the nature and extent of the governmental interests involved. One general interest is of course that of effective crime prevention and detection; it is this interest which underlies the recognition that a police officer may in appropriate circumstances and in an appropriate manner approach a person for purposes of investigating possibly criminal behavior even though there is no probable cause to make an arrest. It was this legitimate investigative function Officer McFadden was discharging when he decided to approach petitioner and his companions. He had observed Terry, Chilton, and Katz go through a series of acts, each of them perhaps innocent in itself, but which taken together warranted further investigation. There is nothing unusual in two men standing together on a street corner, perhaps waiting for someone. Nor is there anything suspicious about people in such circumstances strolling up and down the street, singly or in pairs. Store windows, moreover, are made to be looked in. But the story is quite different where, as here, two men hover about a street corner for an extended period of time, at the end of which it becomes apparent that they are not waiting for anyone or anything; where these men pace alternately along an identical route, pausing to stare in the same store window roughly 24 times; where each completion of this route is followed immediately by a conference between the two men on the corner; where they are joined in one of these conferences by a third man who leaves swiftly; and where the two men finally follow the third and rejoin him a couple of blocks away. It would have been poor police work indeed for an officer of 30 years' experience in

---

of physical contact for purposes of searching Terry for weapons, and we thus may assume that up to that point no intrusion upon constitutionally protected rights had occurred.

the detection of thievery from stores in this same neighborhood to have failed to investigate this behavior further.

The crux of this case, however, is not the propriety of Officer McFadden's taking steps to investigate petitioner's suspicious behavior, but rather, whether there was justification for McFadden's invasion of Terry's personal security by searching him for weapons in the course of that investigation. We are now concerned with more than the governmental interest in investigating crime; in addition, there is the more immediate interest of the police officer in taking steps to assure himself that the person with whom he is dealing is not armed with a weapon that could unexpectedly and fatally be used against him. Certainly it would be unreasonable to require that police officers take unnecessary risks in the performance of their duties. American criminals have a long tradition of armed violence, and every year in this country many law enforcement officers are killed in the line of duty, and thousands more are wounded. Virtually all of these deaths and a substantial portion of the injuries are inflicted with guns and knives.

Petitioner does not argue that a police officer should refrain from making any investigation of suspicious circumstances until such time as he has probable cause to make an arrest; nor does he deny that police officers in properly discharging their investigative function may find themselves confronting persons who might well be armed and dangerous. Moreover, he does not say that an officer is always unjustified in searching a suspect to discover weapons. Rather, he says it is unreasonable for the policeman to take that step until such time as the situation evolves to a point where there is probable cause to make an arrest. When that point has been reached, petitioner would concede the officer's right to conduct a search of the suspect for weapons, fruits or instrumentalities of the crime, or "mere" evidence, incident to the arrest.

There are two weaknesses in this line of reasoning, however. First, it fails to take account of traditional limitations upon the scope of searches, and thus recognizes no distinction in purpose, character, and extent between a search incident to an arrest and a limited search for weapons. The former, although justified in part by the acknowledged necessity to protect the arresting officer from assault with a concealed weapon, Preston v. United States, 376 U.S. 364, 367 (1964), is also justified on other grounds, *ibid.*, and can therefore involve a relatively extensive exploration of the person. A search for weapons in the absence of probable cause to arrest, however, must, like any other search, be strictly circumscribed by the exigencies which justify its initiation.

Warden v. Hayden, 387 U.S. 294, 310 (1967) (MR. JUSTICE FORTAS, concurring). Thus it must be limited to that which is necessary for the discovery of weapons which might be used to harm the officer or others nearby, and may realistically be characterized as something less than a "full" search, even though it remains a serious intrusion.

A second, and related, objection to petitioner's argument is that it assumes that the law of arrest has already worked out the balance between the particular interests involved here—the neutralization of danger to the policeman in the investigative circumstance and the sanctity of the individual. But this is not so. An arrest is a wholly different kind of intrusion upon individual freedom from a limited search for weapons, and the interests each is designed to serve are likewise quite different. An arrest is the initial stage of a criminal prosecution. It is intended to vindicate society's interest in having its laws obeyed, and it is inevitably accompanied by future interference with the individual's freedom of movement, whether or not trial or conviction ultimately follows. The protective search for weapons, on the other hand, constitutes a brief, though far from inconsiderable, intrusion upon the sanctity of the person. It does not follow that because an officer may lawfully arrest a person only when he is apprised of facts sufficient to warrant a belief that the person has committed or is committing a crime, the officer is equally unjustified, absent that kind of evidence, in making any intrusions short of an arrest. Moreover, a perfectly reasonable apprehension of danger may arise long before the officer is possessed of adequate information to justify taking a person into custody for the purpose of prosecuting him for a crime. Petitioner's reliance on cases which have worked out standards of reasonableness with regard to "seizures" constituting arrests and searches incident thereto is thus misplaced. It assumes that the interests sought to be vindicated and the invasions of personal security may be equated in the two cases, and thereby ignores a vital aspect of the analysis of the reasonableness of particular types of conduct under the Fourth Amendment.[q]

---

[q] Goldsmith v. United States, 277 F.2d 335, 344, 345 (D.C. Cir. 1960):

"At the risk of stating the obvious, we take note that the processes of law enforcement must, of necessity, proceed step by step. They begin in a typical case with notice to police that a crime has been committed. This compels police inquiry. The process of inquiry may involve some restraint on the individual liberty of some people of whom police make inquiries without arrest. It would be absurd to suggest that police must arrest a person before they can ask him questions, just as it would be absurd to require that all questioning be deferred until after arraignment. Many people to whom questions are addressed are *not* thought to be suspects—

Our evaluation of the proper balance that has to be struck in this type of case leads us to conclude that there must be a narrowly drawn authority to permit a reasonable search for weapons for the protection of the police officer, where he has reason to believe that he is dealing with an armed and dangerous individual, regardless of whether he has probable cause to arrest the individual for a crime. The officer need not be absolutely certain that the individual is armed; the issue is whether a reasonably prudent man in the circumstances would be warranted in the belief that his safety or that of others was in danger. And in determining whether the officer acted reasonably in such circumstances, due weight must be given, not to his inchoate and unparticularized suspicion or "hunch," but to the specific reasonable inferences which he is entitled to draw from the facts in light of his experience. . . . The sole justification of the search in the present situation is the protection of the police officer and others nearby, and it must therefore be confined in scope to an intrusion reasonably designed to discover guns, knives, clubs, or other hidden instruments for the assault of the police officer.

The scope of the search in this case presents no serious problem in light of these standards. Officer McFadden patted down the outer clothing of petitioner and his two companions. He did not place his hands in their pockets or under the outer surface of their garments until he had felt weapons, and then he merely reached for and removed the guns.

The policeman carefully restricted his search to what was appropriate to the discovery of the particular items which he sought. Each case of this sort will, of course, have to be decided on its own facts. We merely hold today that where a police officer observes unusual conduct which leads him reasonably to conclude in light of his experience that criminal activity may be afoot and that the persons with whom he is dealing may be armed and presently dangerous; where in the course of investigating this behavior he identifies himself as a policeman and makes

---

even though in some cases persons interrogated but not suspected may later turn out to be guilty. . . .

A vital factor to bear in mind is that as these steps progress the burden of the law enforcement agency increases. What may constitute probable cause for arrest does not necessarily constitute probable cause for a charge on arraignment. In turn, what may satisfy a reasonable magistrate on probable cause to believe the suspect committed the crime, may not satisfy a Grand Jury. And the evidence which persuades a Grand Jury to indict may not, and often does not, satisfy a Petit Jury to convict. Hence at each stage, and especially at the early stage, when little is known that is sure, police must not be compelled prematurely to make the hard choices, such as arraigning or releasing, on incomplete information. . . ."

reasonable inquiries; and where nothing in the initial stages of the encounter serves to dispel his reasonable fear for his own or others' safety, he is entitled for the protection of himself and others in the area to conduct a carefully limited search of the outer clothing of such persons in an attempt to discover weapons which might be used to assault him. Such a search is a reasonable search under the Fourth Amendment, and any weapons seized may properly be introduced in evidence against the person from whom they were taken. Affirmed.

MR. JUSTICE BLACK concurs in the judgment and the opinion except where the opinion quotes from and relies upon this Court's opinion in *Katz v. United States* and the concurring opinion in *Warden v. Hayden.*

MR. JUSTICE HARLAN, concurring. The facts of this case are illustrative of a proper stop and an incident frisk. Officer McFadden had no probable cause to arrest Terry for anything, but he had observed circumstances that would reasonably lead an experienced, prudent policeman to suspect that Terry was about to engage in burglary or robbery. His justifiable suspicion afforded a proper constitutional basis for accosting Terry, restraining his liberty of movement briefly, and addressing questions to him, and Officer McFadden did so.

I would affirm this conviction for what I believe to be the same reasons the Court relies on. I would, however, make explicit what I think is implicit in affirmance on the present facts.

MR. JUSTICE WHITE, concurring.

MR. JUSTICE DOUGLAS, dissenting. We hold today that the police have greater authority to make a "seizure" and conduct a "search" than a judge has to authorize such action. We have said precisely the opposite over and over again.

To give the police greater power than a magistrate is to take a long step down the totalitarian path. Perhaps such a step is desirable to cope with modern forms of lawlessness. But if it is taken, it should be the deliberate choice of the people through a constitutional amendment. Until the Fourth Amendment, which is closely allied with the Fifth, is rewritten, the person and the effects of the individual are beyond the reach of all government agencies until there are reasonable grounds to believe (probable cause) that a criminal venture has been launched or is about to be launched.

a. The Evidentiary Standard

UNITED STATES v. THOMAS
250 F. Supp. 771 (S.D.N.Y. 1966)

[Two officers of the New York Central Railroad Police Department, who were assigned to patrol the railroad marshalling yards, encountered the defendants on one of the streets adjacent to the yards. Each of the defendants was carrying a large carton. Since it was unusual to see any pedestrian traffic at that hour and since cartons were not customarily transported in that fashion, the officers decided to investigate. The officers stopped the defendants and questioned them about the cartons. The defendants claimed that they had found the cartons at a certain location and were intending to sell them. The explanation appeared to be evasive, and certain of the statements of the defendants were patently false. The officers asked the defendants to accompany them to the railroad police office where the ownership of the cartons could be cleared up. While the defendants remained at the office, the officers checked the defendants' story and within two hours discovered the owner of the cartons and the fact that the cartons had been stolen from an interstate shipment. Shortly thereafter, the defendants were formally arrested by a federal agent. At trial the defendants moved to suppress the evidence as seized during an illegal search.]

TENNEY, District Judge. Under the law of New York a police officer may stop "any person abroad in a public place whom [the police officer] reasonably suspects is committing, has committed or is about to commit a felony or any of the crimes specified in section five hundred fifty-two of this chapter, and may demand . . . an explanation of his actions." (New York Code of Criminal Procedure, Section 180-a(1)).

Since the consequences of a stop and detention are less serious than those of arrest, and a stop and detention a lesser form of seizure, the requisite showing to justify its imposition is accordingly lesser as well.

While it is thus clear that a lesser quantum of proof is necessary, how is the standard of "reasonably suspects" to be defined?

"In order for a detention to be valid the officer must reasonably and in good faith suspect the individual detained of being involved in some form of criminality. A mere good faith suspicion will not suffice; it must be such that a reasonable man would also entertain it. However, it is not necessary for an officer to have a specific crime in mind or if he does to believe that the person detained probably committed it. Suspicion in this context means that it must be reasonably possible that the individual has committed some crime." Leagre, The Fourth Amendment & The Law of Arrest, 54 J.Crim.L., C. & P.S., 395, 413 (1963).

What is thus envisioned is a step profile, to wit, that the probability of guilt required to subject a person to official action is directly correlated to the degree of interference with individual freedom contemplated by the action. LaFave, Detention for Investigation By the Police: An Analysis of Current Practices, 1962 Wash.U.L.Q. 331, 358-60. Indeed, the Uniform Arrest Act contemplates only a stop and question based on reasonable suspicion but permits stationhouse detention when the added element of unsatisfactory explanation of actions is present.

There is no doubt that formulating a workable standard will be difficult, but the difficulty of the task should not dissuade the Court from undertaking it.

While practicalities should not dictate what decision a court of law should reach, they surely should play some part in a decision which affects in a very practical sense both the citizen and law enforcement authorities.

As a practical matter, the activity described herein is a necessary police technique and one universally engaged in. Rather than shut one's eyes to the obvious the Court considers it more expeditious to recognize the right and set down the circumstances under which it should be utilized.

SIBRON v. NEW YORK

392 U.S. 40 (1968)

MR. CHIEF JUSTICE WARREN delivered the opinion of the Court.

These are companion cases to No. 67, Terry v. Ohio, *ante*, p. 1, decided today. They present related questions under the Fourth and Fourteenth Amendments, but the cases arise in the context of New York's "stop-and-frisk" law, N. Y. Code Crim. Proc. § 180-a. This statute provides:

"1. A police officer may stop any person abroad in a public place whom he reasonably suspects is committing, has committed or is about to commit a felony or any of the crimes specified in section five hundred fifty-two of this chapter, and may demand of him his name, address and an explanation of his actions.

"2. When a police officer has stopped a person for questioning pursuant to this section and reasonably suspects that he is in danger of life or limb, he may search such person for a dangerous weapon. If the police officer finds such a weapon or any other thing the possession of which may constitute a crime, he may take and keep it until the completion of the questioning, at which time he shall either return it, if lawfully possessed, or arrest such person."

The appellants, Sibron and Peters, were both convicted of crimes in New York state courts on the basis of evidence seized from their persons by police officers. The Court of Appeals of New York held that the evidence was properly admitted, on the ground that the searches which uncovered it were authorized by the statute. Sibron and Peters have appealed their convictions to this Court, claiming that § 180-a is unconstitutional on its face and as construed and applied, because the searches and seizures which it was held to have authorized violated their rights under the Fourth Amendment, made applicable to the States by the Fourteenth.

The facts in these cases may be stated briefly. Sibron, the appellant in No. 63, was convicted of the unlawful possession of heroin. . . .

At the hearing on the motion to suppress, Officer Martin testified that while he was patrolling his beat in uniform on March 9, 1965, he observed Sibron "continually from the hours of 4:00 P. M. to 12:00, midnight . . . in the vicinity of 742 Broadway." He stated that during this period of time he saw Sibron in conversation with six or eight persons whom he (Patrolman Martin) knew from past experience to be narcotics addicts. The officer testified that he did not overhear any of these conversations, and that he did not see anything pass between Sibron and any of the others. Late in the evening Sibron entered a restaurant. Patrolman Martin saw Sibron speak with three more known addicts inside the restaurant. Once again, nothing was overheard and nothing was seen to pass between Sibron and the addicts. Sibron sat down and ordered pie and coffee, and as he was eating, Patrolman Martin approached him and told him to come outside. Once outside, the officer said to Sibron, "You know what I am after." According to the officer, Sibron "mumbled something and reached into his pocket." Simultaneously, Patrolman Martin thrust his hand into the same pocket, discovering several glassine envelopes, which, it turned out, contained heroin.

Peters, the appellant in No. 74, was convicted of possessing burglary tools under circumstances evincing an intent to employ them in the commission of a crime. The tools were seized from his person at the time of his arrest, and like Sibron he made a pretrial motion to suppress them. When the trial court denied the motion, he too pleaded guilty, preserving his right to appeal. Officer Samuel Lasky of the New York City Police Department testified at the hearing on the motion that he was at home in his apartment in Mount Vernon, New York, at about 1 p. m. on July 10, 1964. He had just finished taking a shower and was drying himself when he heard a noise at his door. His attempt to investigate was interrupted by a telephone call, but when he returned and looked through the peephole into the hall, Officer Lasky saw "two men tiptoeing out of the alcove toward the stairway." He immediately called the police, put on some civilian clothes and armed himself with his service revolver. Returning to the peephole, he saw "a tall man tiptoeing away from the alcove and followed by this shorter man, Mr. Peters, toward the stairway." Officer Lasky testified that he had lived in the 120-unit building for 12 years and that he did not recognize either of the men as tenants. Believing that he had happened upon the two men in the course of an attempted burglary, Officer Lasky opened his door, entered the hallway and slammed the door loudly behind him. This precipitated a flight down the stairs on the part of the two men, and Officer Lasky gave chase. His apartment was located on the sixth floor, and he apprehended Peters between the fourth and fifth floors. Grabbing Peters by the collar, he continued down another flight in unsuccessful pursuit of the other man. Peters explained his presence in the building to Officer Lasky by saying that he was visiting a girl friend. However, he declined to reveal the girl friend's name, on the ground that she was a married woman. Officer Lasky patted Peters down for weapons, and discovered a hard object in his pocket. He stated at the hearing that the object did not feel like a gun, but that it might have been a knife. He removed the object from Peters' pocket. It was an opaque plastic envelope, containing burglar's tools.

The parties on both sides of these two cases have urged that the principal issue before us is the constitutionality of § 180-a "on its face." We decline, however, to be drawn into what we view as the abstract and unproductive exercise of laying the extraordinarily elastic categories of § 180-a next to the categories of the Fourth Amendment in an effort to determine whether the two are in some sense compatible. The constitutional validity of a warrantless search is pre-eminently the sort of question which can only be decided in the concrete factual context of the individual case.

The operative categories of § 180-a are not the categories of the Fourth Amendment, and they are susceptible of a wide variety of interpretations.[20] New York is, of course, free to develop its own law of search and seizure to meet the needs of local law enforcement, see Ker v. California, 374 U.S. 23, 34 (1963), and in the process it may call the standards it employs by any names it may choose. It may not, however, authorize police conduct which trenches upon Fourth Amendment rights, regardless of the labels which it attaches to such conduct. The question in this Court upon review of a state-approved search or seizure "is not whether the search [or seizure] was authorized by state law. The question is rather whether the search was reasonable under the Fourth Amendment. Just as a search authorized by state law may be an unreasonable one under that amendment, so may a search not expressly authorized by state law be justified as a constitutionally reasonable one." Cooper v. California, 386 U.S. 58, 61 (1967).

Turning to the facts of Sibron's case, it is clear that the heroin was inadmissible in evidence against him. The inference that persons who talk to narcotics addicts are engaged in the criminal traffic in narcotics is simply not the sort of reasonable inference required to support an intrusion by the police upon an individual's personal security. Nothing resembling probable cause

---

20 It is not apparent, for example, whether the power to "stop" granted by the statute entails a power to "detain" for investigation or interrogation upon less than probable cause, or if so what sort of durational limitations upon such detention are contemplated. And while the statute's apparent grant of a power of compulsion indicates that many "stops" will constitute "seizures," it is not clear that all conduct analyzed under the rubric of the statute will either rise to the level of a "seizure" or be based upon less than probable cause. . . . There are, moreover, substantial indications that the statutory category of a "search for a dangerous weapon" may encompass conduct considerably broader in scope than that which we approved in *Terry v. Ohio.* At least some of the activity apparently permitted under the rubric of searching for dangerous weapons may thus be permissible under the Constitution only if the "reasonable suspicion" of criminal activity rises to the level of probable cause. Finally, it is impossible to tell whether the standard of "reasonable suspicion" connotes the same sort of specificity, reliability, and objectivity which is the touchstone of permissible governmental action under the Fourth Amendment. Compare Terry v. Ohio, *supra,* with People v. Taggart, *supra.* In this connection we note that the searches and seizures in both *Sibron* and *Peters* were upheld by the Court of Appeals of New York as predicated upon "reasonable suspicion," whereas we have concluded that the officer in *Peters* had probable cause for an arrest, while the policeman in *Sibron* was not possessed of any information which would justify an intrusion upon rights protected by the Fourth Amendment.

existed until after the search had turned up the envelopes of heroin.

If Patrolman Martin lacked probable cause for an arrest, however, his seizure and search of Sibron might still have been justified at the outset if he had reasonable grounds to believe that Sibron was armed and dangerous. *Terry v. Ohio.* The suspect's mere act of talking with a number of known narcotics addicts over an eight-hour period no more gives rise to reasonable fear of life or limb on the part of the police officer than it justifies an arrest for committing a crime. Nor did Patrolman Martin urge that when Sibron put his hand in his pocket, he feared that he was going for a weapon and acted in self-defense. His opening statement to Sibron—"You know what I am after"—made it abundantly clear that he sought narcotics, and his testimony at the hearing left no doubt that he thought there were narcotics in Sibron's pocket.

Even assuming *arguendo* that there were adequate grounds to search Sibron for weapons, the nature and scope of the search conducted by Patrolman Martin were so clearly unrelated to that justification as to render the heroin inadmissible. The search for weapons approved in *Terry* consisted solely of a limited patting of the outer clothing of the suspect for concealed objects which might be used as instruments of assault. Only when he discovered such objects did the officer in *Terry* place his hands in the pockets of the men he searched. In this case, with no attempt at an initial limited exploration for arms, Patrolman Martin thrust his hand into Sibron's pocket and took from him envelopes of heroin.

We think it is equally clear that the search in Peters' case was wholly reasonable under the Constitution. . . . By the time Officer Lasky caught up with Peters on the stairway between the fourth and fifth floors of the apartment building, he had probable cause to arrest him for attempted burglary.

As we noted in Sibron's case, a search incident to a lawful arrest, may not precede the arrest and serve as part of its justification. It is a question of fact precisely when, in each case, the arrest took place. Rios v. United States, 364 U.S. 253, 261-262 (1960). And while there was some inconclusive discussion in the trial court concerning when Officer Lasky "arrested" Peters, it is clear that the arrest had for purposes of constitutional justification already taken place before the search commenced. When the policeman grabbed Peters by the collar, he abruptly "seized" him and curtailed his freedom of movement on the basis of probable cause to believe that he was engaged in criminal activity. See Henry v. United States, *supra,* at 103. At that point he had the authority to search Peters, and the incident search was obviously justified "by the need to seize weapons and other things which might be used to assault an officer or effect an escape, as well as by the need to prevent the destruction of evidence of the crime." Preston v. United States, 376 U.S. 364, 367 (1964). Moreover, it was reasonably limited in scope by these purposes. Officer Lasky did not engage in an unrestrained and thorough-going examination of Peters and his personal effects. He seized him to cut short his flight, and he searched him primarily for weapons. While patting down his outer clothing, Officer Lasky discovered an object in his pocket which might have been used as a weapon. He seized it and discovered it to be a potential instrument of the crime of burglary.

We have concluded that Peters' conviction fully comports with the commands of the Fourth and Fourteenth Amendments, and must be affirmed. The conviction in No. 63, however, must be reversed, on the ground that the heroin was unconstitutionally admitted in evidence against the appellant.

MR. JUSTICE HARLAN, concurring in the results. I fully agree with the results the Court has reached in these cases. They are, I think, consonant with and dictated by the decision in *Terry v. Ohio*.

The forcible encounter between Officer Martin and Sibron did not meet the *Terry* reasonableness standard.

Turning now to No. 74, *Peters,* I again agree that the conviction should be upheld, but here I would differ strongly and fundamentally with the Court's approach. The Court holds that the burglar's tools were recovered from Peters in a search incident to a lawful arrest. I do not think that Officer Lasky had anything close to probable cause to arrest Peters before he recovered the burglar's tools.

I find it hard to believe that if Peters had made good his escape and there were no report of a burglary in the neighborhood, this Court would hold it proper for a prudent neutral magistrate to issue a warrant for his arrest.

Although the articulable circumstances are somewhat less suspicious here than they were in *Terry,* I would affirm on the *Terry* ground that Officer Lasky had reasonable cause to make a forced stop. Unlike probable cause to arrest, reasonable grounds to stop do not depend on any degree of likelihood that a crime *has* been committed. An officer may forcibly intrude upon an incipient crime even where he could not make an arrest for the simple reason that there is nothing to arrest anyone for. Hence although Officer Lasky had small reason to believe that a crime had been committed, his right to stop Peters can be justified if he had a reasonable suspicion that he was about to attempt burglary.

It was clear that the officer had to act quickly if he was going to act at all, and, as stated above, it seems to me that where immediate action is obviously required, a police officer is justified in acting on rather less objectively articulable evidence than when there is more time for consideration of alternative courses of action. Perhaps more important, the Court's opinion in *Terry* emphasized the special qualifications of an experienced police officer. While "probable cause" to arrest or search has always depended on the existence of hard evidence that would persuade a "reasonable man," in judging on-the-street encounters it seems to me proper to take into account a police officer's trained instinctive judgment operating on a multitude of small gestures and actions impossible to reconstruct. Thus the statement by an officer that "he looked like a burglar to me" adds little to an affidavit filed with a magistrate in an effort to obtain a warrant. When the question is whether it was reasonable to take limited but forcible steps in a situation requiring immediate action, however, such a statement looms larger.

DETECTION OF CRIME 18-19 (1967)

By Lawrence P. Tiffany, Donald M. McIntyre, Jr. & Daniel L. Rotenberg
(Little, Brown & Company)

Police do stop and question suspects on the street when there is insufficient evidence to justify arrest. The typical situation, however, involves some evidence of guilt, not just the subjective "hunch" of an officer.

The task of formulating a meaningful, generalized statement of the evidentiary requirements for conducting a field interrogation is difficult for a number of reasons. Deciding when it is appropriate to conduct a field interrogation involves the identification of reliable symptoms from which one can infer that certain kinds of antisocial behavior have been engaged in, a matter about which it is obviously difficult to be categorical. Generalized formulas such as "suspicious circumstances" do not give a very specific indication of the content of current practice, and generalized statements about reasonableness fail to distinguish the requirements of field interrogation from the requirements for arrest. It is not easy to find the words for a meaningful formulation which describes less than "reasonable grounds" but more than mere "hunch." The isolation of such factors as age and sex of the suspect, location, and time of day, which may be relied upon by police as signs of criminality, tends to oversimplify the situations encountered in practice, which involve a number of factors in combination. Some kinds of evidence, such as a call for help, may establish the commission of crime; others, such as presence in the vicinity of a recent crime, may tend to identify the offender. In other situations a single factor—flight, for example—may seem to indicate both the existence of a crime and participation in it by the person who flees.

b. Legislative Formulation

CALIFORNIA PENAL CODE § 647
(West Supp. 1966)

Every person who commits any of the following acts shall be guilty of disorderly conduct, a misdemeanor: . . .

(e) Who loiters or wanders upon the streets or from place to place without apparent reason or business and who refuses to identify himself and to account for his presence when requested by any peace officer so to do, if the surrounding circumstances are such as to indicate to a reasonable man that the public safety demands such identification.[r]

PEOPLE v. HARR
235 N.E.2d 1 (Ill. 1968)

SEIDENFELD, Justice. The defendant, Frederick J. Harr, after a bench trial, was found guilty of driving a motor vehicle while his operator's license was suspended. The Magistrate imposed a sentence of seven days in the county jail and a fine of one hundred dollars and costs, from which defendant appeals.

Defendant contends that the court erred in denying his motion to suppress evidence without a hearing; and in denying the same motion after evidence adduced by the State. The evidence sought to be suppressed was defendant's driver's license which showed an expired date on its face, and the certificate of the Secretary of State showing the suspension.

The testimony of the police officer as stipulated was: at about 1:30 A.M. on April 15, 1967, he observed the defendant's motor vehicle coming out of a gas station which was closed for business for the night; that the vehicle proceeded westbound on Warren Street; that the vehicle and its driver appeared suspicious and

---

[r] This statute was held unconstitutional by a trial court as inconsistent with the privilege against self-incrimination, but upheld by an intermediate appellate court. People v. Weger, 251 Cal. App. 2d 584, 59 Cal. Rptr. 661 (1967), *cert. denied,* 19 U.S. 840 (1968), 43 WASH. L. REV. 844 (1968) (criticizing the statute).

since he had not seen this vehicle in this vicinity before, he made a routine stop of the defendant's vehicle to determine who the defendant was, where he was going and where he had been; that he asked the defendant for his driver's license and the defendant produced an expired license.

The State claims the right to stop the motorist initially under the provisions of Chap. 95½, Sec. 6-118, Illinois Revised Statutes 1965, which provides:

"*License and permits to be carried and exhibited on demand.* Every licensee or permittee shall have his operator's or chauffeur's license or permit in his immediate possession at all times when operating a motor vehicle and, for the purpose of indicating compliance with this requirement, shall display such license or permit if it is in his possession upon demand made, when in uniform or displaying a badge or other sign of authority, by a member of the Illinois State Highway Police, a sheriff or other peace officer or designated agent of the Secretary of State. However, no person charged with violating this Section shall be convicted if he produces in court or the office of the arresting officer satisfactory evidence that an operator's or chauffeur's license was theretofore issued to him and was valid at the time of his arrest."

The facts in this case indicate that the police officer here did not stop the defendant's car for the purpose of enforcing this statute. He stopped it, on the admitted facts, for the purpose of finding out who the defendant was, where he had been and where he was going. The statute cannot, in any event, be made applicable as authority to inspect the license as a mere subterfuge to obtain information or evidence not related to the licensing requirement. Cox v. State, 181 Tenn. 344.

The conviction is reversed.

UNIFORM ARREST ACT

Section 2. Questioning and Detaining Suspects

I. A peace officer may stop any person abroad whom he has reasonable ground to suspect is committing, has committed or is about to commit a crime, and may demand of him his name, address, business abroad and whither he is going.

II. Any person so questioned who fails to identify himself or explain his actions to the satisfaction of the officer stopping him may be detained and further questioned and investigated.

III. The total period of detention provided for by this section shall not exceed two hours. Such detention is not an arrest and shall not be recorded as an arrest in any official record. At the end of the detention period the person so detained shall be released unless arrested and charged with a crime.

Section 3. Searching for Weapons

A peace officer may search for a dangerous weapon any person whom he is questioning or about to question as provided in section 2, whenever he has reasonable ground to believe that he is in danger if such person possesses a dangerous weapon. If the officer finds a weapon, he may take and keep it until the completion of the questioning, when he shall either return it or arrest the person. The arrest may be for the illegal possession of the weapon.

Note

The Uniform Arrest Act was proposed by the Interstate Commission on Crime in 1941. *See* Warner, *The Uniform Arrest Act,* 28 VA. L. REV. 315 (1942). It has been adopted with little change in New Hampshire, Delaware, and Rhode Island. Other states, *e.g.,* Nebraska, have statutes patterned after the Uniform Act. The Delaware court in De Salvatore v. State, 52 Del. 550, 163 A.2d 244 (1960), upheld the statute as constitutional because, as interpreted by the court, it permitted detention only upon reasonable grounds to believe the detained person was guilty. The court thereby nullified the distinction which the statute had attempted to establish between "suspect" and "believe." The Rhode Island Supreme Court, in Kavanagh v. Stenhouse, 93 R.I. 252, 174 A.2d 560 (1961), upheld the constitutional power of the legislature to permit the lesser personal interference of limited detention upon the lesser ground of reason to suspect, but it did so in the context of a civil action for false imprisonment against the police officer. The court emphasized that an officer acting reasonably ought not to have to fear false arrest actions.

The New York statute is set out above in *Sibron v. New York (see also* p. 183, *infra).* Most states have no statute dealing with stopping and questioning.

A proposal was made by the drafting committee of the 1963 Illinois Code of Criminal Procedure to include provision that "[a] peace officer may under reasonable circumstances inquire of any person his name, address, and the circumstances of his presence." And also, "[a] peace officer may under reasonable circumstances detain for investigation for a reasonable period of time any person whom he believes has committed, is committing, or is about to commit any offense, even though the nature of the offense may be unknown. A period of detention in excess of four hours shall be prima facie unreasonable." The provisions were deleted because of opposition by both civil liberties groups and the Chicago Police Department. The concern of civil liberties groups was largely with possible reading of the provisions to permit detention for four hours of anyone who did not satisfy the police with their answers, with practically unlimited discretion in the police to determine cause for the detention. The police, on the other hand, objected that the mild right of inquiry section might imply that police did not have the power to stop and question, that police were not informed whether they might consider refusal to answer in determining whether to detain, that police power to frisk during interrogation was not spelled out, and that the four-hour detention would become a rule-of-thumb even though it was too long for some circumstances and too short for others.

The A.L.I. MODEL CODE OF PRE-ARRAIGNMENT PROCEDURE (Tent. Draft No. 1, 1966) proposed a somewhat similar, but much more complex, statute justifying stopping and questioning.

3. Controls

The major sanction against improper stopping and questioning and frisking is the exclusion from evidence of incriminating statements made and of physical evidence seized incident to the wrongful action.[s]

In addition to the exclusionary rule, other judicial controls upon stopping and questioning which are theoretically available are tort actions for false imprisonment and battery and even criminal penalties, but tort actions and criminal penalties are for obvious reasons not very effective controls in this area.[t]

Still another kind of control is the internal regulation of the law enforcement agency. Upon the enactment of the New York

[s] The exclusionary rule is discussed in some detail at 249, *infra*.

[t] Compare the curious case of Clark v. Bird, 354 F.2d 977 (1st Cir. 1966). A man, inappropriately dressed and acting suspiciously, abandoned a car in the park within sight of police and ran when they approached. Police stopped him and questioned him, but he refused to answer. They took him to the police station where he was identified and released without being booked. He sued for false imprisonment—his ninth pending suit—but dismissal was affirmed on the principle volenti non fit injuria.

statute, New York police administrators undertook in a statement of policy to inform officers of the provisions of the law, to communicate an attitude toward the statute, and to warn against some possible distortions or abuses of the powers it conferred. Such clear, self-restraining statements by police of enforcement policies are uncommon.[u]

INSTRUCTIONS TO MEMBERS OF THE FORCE CONCERNING THE "STOP AND FRISK" (CHAPTER 86) AND "NO KNOCK" (CHAPTER 85) LAWS

Police Department, City of New York, Office of the Police Commissioner Circular No. 25, New York, June 26, 1964

Two new statutes, with major impact on police authority, become effective in New York State on July 1, 1964.

These laws, if properly utilized, can be of considerable aid in safeguarding our communities. Their passage resulted in part from the combined strenuous efforts expended by New York State's various law enforcement agencies. As is the case with all other law enforcement powers, whether or not these sorely-needed enactments will withstand the attacks that will be made upon their constitutionality, and will stand as laws upon the books of this State, will depend in large measure upon the fashion in which they are carried out. They should be enforced with full recognition that their purposes are to protect the community, while simultaneously protecting and treating fairly all persons in it.

Every member of the force has the responsibility of seeing to it that the powers conferred by these new statutes are used to further those purposes for which they were enacted. Some guidelines for proper conduct pursuant to these statutes are set forth herein:

I. THE "STOP-AND-FRISK" LAW (Chapter 86, Laws of 1964)

The new statute, which becomes § 180-a of the Code of Criminal Procedure, provides as follows:

§ 180-a. Temporary questioning of persons in public places; search for weapons.

1. A police officer may stop any person abroad in a public place whom he reasonably suspects is committing, has com-

[u] Greater use of such policymaking was urged in THE PRESIDENT'S COMMISSION ON LAW ENFORCEMENT AND ADMINISTRATION OF JUSTICE, TASK FORCE REPORT: THE POLICE 13-38 (1967).

mitted or is about to commit a felony or any of the crimes specified in section five hundred fifty-two of this chapter, and may demand of him his name, address and an explanation of his actions.

2. When a police officer has stopped a person for questioning pursuant to this section and reasonably suspects that he is in danger of life or limb, he may search such person for a dangerous weapon. If the police officer finds such a weapon or any other thing the possession of which may constitute a crime, he may take and keep it until the completion of the questioning, at which time he shall either return it, if lawfully possessed, or arrest such person.

A. General principles:

1. The new law does not permit an officer to stop just any passer-by and search him, nor does it allow the search of any person merely because he has a criminal record.

2. The new law does not permit the stopping and searching of any person found in the vicinity of a crime scene, merely because he happens to be there.

3. The new law does not dispense with the need for adequate observation and investigation, depending upon all the circumstances, before a stop is made.

4. No officer should stop anyone, under the new law, unless he is prepared to explain, with particularity, his reasons for stopping such person.

5. No officer should stop anyone, under the new law, unless the crime he reasonably suspects is a felony or one of those misdemeanors listed in § 552 of the Code of Criminal Procedure.

6. When a person is stopped under the new law, the officer—if not in uniform—must properly and promptly identify himself to the person stopped.

7. Not everyone stopped may be searched; searches are only permitted when the officer reasonably suspects that he is in danger.

8. The right to stop provided in the new law in no way changes the previously existing authority of an officer to make an arrest without an arrest warrant, as provided by § 177 of the

Code of Criminal Procedure. The new rights to stop and to search, as defined in the new statute, are separate and distinct from the established right to arrest, as provided by existing law, and to make a complete search incident to such arrest.

9. Whether or not an arrest follows a stopping under the new law, whenever any force is used in stopping the suspect, or whenever any frisk or search is made, a written report shall be made to the officer's superior officer. Form for such reports, together with instructions for their use, will be distributed with separate orders.

B. The right to "stop".

1. "stop":

The new statute gives the officer the right to stop a person under the indicated circumstances. If the suspect refuses to stop, the officer may use reasonable force, but only by use of his body, arms and legs. He may not make use of a weapon or nightstick in any fashion. (Of course, if there is an assault on the officer or other circumstances sufficient to justify an arrest, the officer may use necessary force to effect that arrest.)

2. "abroad in a public place":

a. For the purposes of practical enforcement procedures, this phrase is viewed as being restricted to public highways and streets, beaches and parks (to include outdoor facilities open to the public even though privately owned), depots, stations, and public transportation facilities.

b. For the purpose of practical enforcement procedures, this phrase is viewed as not including the public portions of private buildings such as hotel lobbies, moving picture theatres, licensed premises, etc.

c. Definitions of the words "public place" as found in other laws, such as those dealing with disorderly conduct, are not to be substituted for the strict definition of "abroad in a public place" as outlined above.

3. "whom he reasonably suspects":

a. The words "reasonably suspects" are not to be lightly regarded; they are not just an incidental phrase; they have real meaning. "Reasonable suspicion" is clearly more than "mere suspicion." At the same time it is something less than "reasonable ground for believing" that a crime is being committed, as is necessary for an arrest.

b. No precise definition of "reasonably suspects" can be provided, other than that it is such a combination of factors as would merit the sound and objective suspicions of a properly alert law enforcement officer, performing his sworn duties. Among the factors to be considered in determining whether or not there is "reasonable suspicion" are:

i. The demeanor of the suspect.

ii. The gait and manner of the suspect.

iii. Any knowledge the officer may have of the suspect's background or character.

iv. Whether the suspect is carrying anything, and what he is carrying.

v. The manner in which the suspect is dressed, including bulges in clothing—when considered in light of all of the other factors.

vi. The time of the day or night the suspect is observed.

vii. Any overheard conversation of the suspect.

viii. The particular streets and areas involved.

ix. Any information received from third persons, whether they are known or unknown.

x. Whether the suspect is consorting with others whose conduct is "reasonably suspect."

xi. The suspect's proximity to known criminal conduct. (This listing is not meant to be all inclusive.)

c. "Reasonable suspicion" of any crime at all does not afford a basis for stopping under the new law; there must be reasonable suspicion that the suspect is committing, has committed, or is about to commit either any felony or one of those misdemeanors enumerated in § 552 of the Code of Criminal Procedure. (These misdemeanors are weapons crimes, burglar's tools, receiving stolen property, unlawful entry, escape, impairing, carnal abuse, indecent exposure, obscenity and other indecency provisions, sodomy, rape, narcotics, amphetamines, and hypodermic needles.) Suspicion of disorderly conduct, an offense, is not for the purpose of practical enforcement procedures a basis for stopping.

C. The right to "question".

1. No questions are to be asked until the officer has, either by being in uniform or by showing his shield and stating he is a police officer, identified himself.

2. Promptly thereafter, the suspect should be questioned (and frisked, when appropriate) in the immediate area in which he was stopped.

3. Should the suspect refuse to answer the officer's questions, the officer cannot compel an answer and should not attempt to do so. The suspect's refusal to answer shall not be considered as an element by the officer in determining whether or not there is a basis for an arrest.

4. In ascertaining "his name" from the suspect, the officer may request to see verification of his identity, but a person shall not be compelled to produce such verification.

5. If the suspect does answer, and his answers appear to be false or unsatisfactory, the officer may question further. Answers of this nature may serve as an element in determining whether a basis for arrest exists. (But if an officer determines that an answer is "unsatisfactory" and relies upon this in part to sustain his arrest, he should be able to explain with particularity the manner in which it is "unsatisfactory".)

6. If, after he has been stopped and the officer has identified himself, the suspect attempts to flee from the officer, this fact may be an element in determining whether a basis for arrest exists. However, the officer should not resort to the use of a weapon or other extraordinary means to stop the flight unless he has information which now leads him to reasonably believe that the suspect has committed a felony.

D. The right to "search".

1. Clearly no right to search exists unless there is a right to stop.

2. Nor is a search lawful in every case in which a right to stop exists. A search is only justified under the new law when the officer reasonably suspects that he is in danger. This claim is not to be used as a pretext for obtaining evidence. In instances in which evidence is produced as a result of a search, the superior officers, the prosecutors, and—it is anticipated—the courts, will scrutinize particularly closely all the circumstances relied upon for justifying the stopping and searching.

3. No search is appropriate unless the officer "reasonably suspects that he is in danger." Among the factors that may be considered in determining whether to search are:

a. Nature of the suspected crime, and whether it involved the use of a weapon or violence.
b. The presence or absence of assistance to the officer, and the number of suspects being stopped.
c. The time of the day or night.
d. Prior knowledge of the suspect's record and reputation.
e. The sex of the suspect.
f. The demeanor and seeming agility of the suspect, and whether his clothes so bulge as to be indicative of concealed weapons.
(This listing is not meant to be all inclusive.)

4. Initially, once the determination has been made that the officer may be in danger, all that is necessary is a frisk—an external feeling of clothing—such as would reveal a weapon of immediate danger to the officer.

5. A search of the suspect's clothing and pockets should not be made unless something is felt by this frisk—such as a hard object that feels as if it may be a weapon. In such event, the officer may search that portion of the suspect's clothing to uncover the article that was felt.

6. If the suspect is carrying an object such as a handbag, suitcase, sack, etc. which may conceal a weapon, the officer should not open that item, but should see that it is placed out of reach of the suspect so that its presence will not represent any immediate danger to the officer.

E. An example.

An example may help to illustrate. Assume that a mugging has just occurred. The officer questions the victim. She says that her pocketbook was taken and she gives a description of the suspect stating, among other things, that he is about six feet tall and was wearing a brown leather windbreaker. While the victim is receiving medical treatment, the officer starts a search of the area. He sees a man hurrying down a dark street. The man's hand is clutching at a bulge under his brown windbreaker, and he glances back at the officer repeatedly. The suspect meets the description of the perpetrator except for one discrepancy: he is only five feet tall.

The officer does not have reasonable grounds to arrest the suspect for his description is clearly inconsistent with the victim's estimate of the perpetrator's height. However, from the officer's experience he realizes that victims of crime, in an excited condition, often give descriptions which are not correct in every detail. Although he lacks reasonable grounds to make an arrest, from all of the circumstances the officer "reasonably suspects" that the man he has spotted has committed the crime. Under the new law, the officer may stop this person, and may ask for his identification and an explanation of his actions. And because the crime involved violence and the suspect's windbreaker seems to conceal unnatural bulges, a frisk may be in order.

DETECTION OF CRIME 92-94 (1967)

By Lawrence P. Tiffany, Donald M. McIntyre, Jr. & Daniel L. Rotenberg
(Little, Brown & Company)

There are two basic approaches to the problem of defining and enforcing proper field interrogation practices. One is to assume that the basic responsibility lies with the law enforcement agencies themselves, subject to review and perhaps change by courts or legislatures where this is necessary. The other alternative is to assume that the basic responsibility lies outside of law enforcement, in which case the legislatures and courts would initiate and implement the needed standards and procedures.

In the past, neither police nor legislatures and courts have assumed the responsibility for control of field interrogations. Recently, some legislatures, appellate courts, and police departments have made some efforts to do so, but these efforts are sporadic, and it is too early to tell which agency will finally assume responsibility. If the experience with other issues, such as search and seizure, is repeated with field interrogation, the trend will be in the direction of greater and greater judicial involvement with very little meaningful police participation.

There are disadvantages in putting primary reliance upon judicial rules as a method of controlling field interrogation practices: (a) Appellate judicial review of policy issues is often limited to constitutional issues, which may or may not deal with many of the significant questions involved in field interrogation programs. (b) As judicial rules become more elaborate, they become more difficult to change, and an undesirable reduction in administrative flexibility may result. (c) Because the appellate court may lack adequate means to keep fully informed of the factual context out of which the issues arise, judicial rules may not be entirely responsive to the realities of the practice. (d) If law enforcement agencies do not have the responsibility for developing rules, they may come to feel that they are regarded as incapable of doing this, and, in turn, this feeling may lessen their incentive to provide adequate enforcement of the rules. The consequences may be ineffective judicial control of field interrogation, due partly to police administrators' resistance to judicial power and partly to the lack of effective means of communication between the courts and police.

The task is easy to state. Obviously, ways must be devised to involve law enforcement agencies in the development and enforcement of appropriate policies on field interrogation, and effective methods of review of these policies must be found which will not unduly restrict the flexibility needed by the enforcement agency. The government faces a similar task in any area where there is a need for creative administrative action. The difficulty in the law enforcement field is that there has been no tradition of responsible administrative participation in policy development. As a consequence, the alternative has been either no standards at all or the development of specific legislative or judicial rules and procedures for insuring compliance with these rules.

Although field interrogation is receiving increasing attention from legislatures and courts, it is too early to tell what the future holds. Absent a substantial and sustained effort by police to develop standards and adequate means of administrative control for field interrogation, it seems likely that legislatures and courts will step in, as they have with search and in-custody interrogation, and prescribe detailed rules implemented by the exclusion of any evidence obtained in violation of those rules.

From the police viewpoint, however, it would be advantageous for police to develop their own administrative policies and procedures to control field interrogation practices, for this would improve the status of law enforcement agencies in the criminal justice process and would contribute to their becoming more "professional." Only, however, when police demonstrate a willingness and ability to confront the major social issues with which law enforcement agencies are called upon to deal, will they truly achieve this objective.

ADMINISTRATIVE PROBLEMS IN CONTROLLING THE EXERCISE OF POLICE AUTHORITY

By Herman Goldstein

58 Journal of Criminal Law, Criminology and Police Science 160, 168-70 (1967)†

Inadequacies in Existing and Proposed Methods of External Control

. . .

1. *Civil Action.* The instituting of a civil action against a police officer is perhaps least satisfactory, both as a means of seeking redress and as a means for positively influencing police conduct. Because it is a complex process requiring the assistance of counsel, the cost involved makes it unavailable to the vast majority of persons who have a basis for complaint. Juries are not likely to have compassion for a plaintiff, however abused, if he is guilty of a crime or is disreputable.

Most police officers and police administrators view a civil action as an attack from "outside" that must be defended at any cost. Counsel is usually assigned to officers named in a suit, however indefensible the action of the officers may have been. Attorneys on a city's legal staff who are regularly assigned to defending such actions, or who are retained for the purpose, generally view their function as being limited to providing the best defense for the individual officer. They do not conceive it to be their role, even when it is established that the officer was at fault, to suggest a reevaluation of the departmental practices that appear to have given rise to the officer's actions in the particular case. If such an effort were made, the time required for processing a civil action would most likely divorce the impact of the finding from the practices to which it relates.

A civil action may interfere with administrative efforts to control police conduct. The filing of a suit in some jurisdictions results in the suspension of any form of internal disciplinary action because it is feared that such action may prejudice the pending litigation.

2. *Judicial Review.* The enforcement of the various exclusionary rules required by constitutional interpretation or court policy places all trial judges very explicitly in the role of controlling police practices. Judicial control is, however, limited to

the review of only those aspects of police functioning that relate to acquiring evidence in cases in which there is an intention to initiate a prosecution. Such cases represent but a very small segment of the total number of actions in which the police are typically engaged. For every incident in which a police officer exerts his authority as the first step in a process leading to a prosecution, he handles a multitude of other incidents in which he checks out suspicious circumstances, separates combatants, orders people to disperse, or in some other manner uses his powers without effecting an arrest. And even if an arrest is made, it is not always indicative of a desire to prosecute. In many cases it is intended only to serve some other more short-lived objective, such as the harassment of prostitutes or the safeguarding of drunks.

In those cases in which the legality of police performance is questioned by introduction of a motion to suppress evidence, rulings are made in a manner which serves neither to influence the future behavior of the officer nor to influence the policies and practices of the police agency. Judges seem content to consider each motion to suppress as a review of the conduct of individual officers, even when the officer's conduct appears to be consistent with departmental practices. Not only are the broader problems not addressed, but the suppression of evidence has no effect upon the behavior of the individual officer. Given the choice, the officer is likely to conform to the expectations of his most immediate superiors rather than of the courts.

Should the individual officer desire to adhere to judicial requirements, he would often find it difficult to do so. Motions to suppress are frequently granted without an adequate explanation to the officer as to the reasons why his actions in acquiring evidence were considered illegal. Secondly, the absence of uniformity among the views of judges sitting in the multiple courts of large cities results in subjecting the individual officer to conflicting instructions.

It is possible and certainly desirable to modify the current system of judicial review so as to increase its effectiveness and to make it a constructive instrument for the improvement of police functioning. To accomplish this will require a number of basic changes in judicial practice and an ability and willingness of a police administrator to devise means for assuring the conformity of his personnel.[20]

---

[20] Specific proposals for strengthening the existing system of judicial control are made in LaFave and Remington, *Controlling the Police: The Judge's Role in Making and Reviewing Law Enforcement Decisions,* 63 MICH. L. REV. 987 (1965); LaFave, [*Improving Police Performance Through*

3. *Civilian Review Boards.* Most of the recent efforts to establish civilian review boards have been intended primarily to provide citizens—and especially those members of minority groups residing within ghetto areas—an opportunity to air their grievances regarding the exercise of police authority. The several boards that have actually been established are without power to control police behavior. They are authorized to receive complaints, to hold hearings, and, as their concluding action, to advise police authorities on the form of disciplinary action, if any, that ought to be taken.[21] The boards are no better equipped than are police chiefs to initiate action against what appears to be improper—but legally authorized—police actions. Nor are they expected to initiate inquiries into the policies and practices of a police agency. Their primary orientation is toward the review of individual wrongdoing, and their influence upon police behavior not specifically subject to their review appears limited to the deterrent effect which their existence creates.

Grievance procedures, in themselves, are of major importance. It is essential that citizens be provided with easily accessible means for expressing their concern over an alleged abuse of governmental power. It is especially important, in the interests of fairness and equality of treatment, that such means be made available to the least articulate segment of the community whose members are most often subject to police action. The essential nature of this need is underlined by recognizing that the frustrations resulting from unaired complaints and grievances against the police and other agencies of government are among the factors generally viewed as contributing to the kind of violence that has recently erupted in several of the country's largest urban areas.

Important as they are, however, it must be recognized that grievance procedures that air complaints against individual police officers serve a limited function. The broader objective must remain that of correcting or eliminating the situations that give rise to such complaints. Progress toward this goal, in the long run, is dependent upon the development of more effective

---

the Exclusionary Rule], 30 Mo. L. Rev. 391, 566 (1966); and *A Report by the Police Task Force, President's Commission on Law Enforcement and Administration of Justice,* Chapter 2, (April, 1967).

[21] For a succinct description of the development and experience of existing civilian review boards, see Gellhorn, When Americans Complain 170-195 (1966). See also Beral and Sisk, *The Administration of Complaints by Civilians Against the Police,* 77 Harv. L. Rev. 499, 511-519 (1964).

For a discussion of some of the arguments for and against such boards, see Inbau, *Democratic Restraints Upon the Police,* 57 J. Crim. L., C. & P. S. 265, 269 (1966) and Packer, *The Courts, the Police, and the Rest of Us,* 57 J. Crim. L., C. & P. S. 238, 241 (1966).

means for controlling police conduct. This suggests, as a very minimum, that grievance machinery be constructed with an appropriate concern for the manner in which it affects control mechanisms. The complaint process ought to support and reinforce the system of internal discipline upon which primary dependence is placed for the control of police conduct.

While the point has not been made explicitly, it has been argued that civilian review boards would have the opposite effect. Because of the adversary relationship between the complainant and the accused police officer to which the existence of such a board would give emphasis, it is claimed that whatever force or commitment may have developed within a police agency for self-discipline would be abandoned in the face of a more compelling desire on the part of police personnel to support a brother officer who stands accused before such a board.

4. *The Ombudsman Concept.* Stimulated by the current wave of interest in the control of police conduct, increased support appears to be developing for adopting the ombudsman concept—so well established in the Scandinavian countries and in New Zealand—as a form of control over the full range of governmental functions in the United States.[23]

The concept has much to be said in its favor as a means for airing grievances, for controlling official conduct, and, at the same time, for improving the effectiveness and fairness of administrative operations. Among its features is the fact that the ombudsman achieves his control through the support and reinforcement of internal systems of discipline. When he has a basis for criticism, the criticism is typically directed at the head of an agency, who is held responsible for the performance of his subordinates, rather than against individual employees. Agency heads are expected to investigate allegations of wrongdoing and to take appropriate action. The ombudsman becomes involved only when he has reason to believe that a complaint alleging wrongdoing has been inadequately dealt with by administrative officials or when he believes that the policies and practices to which a complaint relates ought to be subject to review and possibly to modification.

There are a number of other features in the ombudsman concept that have special value when related to the problems encountered in the control of police conduct. The mere presence of a detached, independent critic would serve, in a very

---

[23] For the most comprehensive treatment of the ombudsman concept, see GELLHORN, OMBUDSMEN AND OTHERS: CITIZENS' PROTECTORS IN NINE COUNTRIES (1966).

important way, to support a police administrator desirous of making the right choice when confronted with strong pressures that move him in the other direction. Application of this form of control to all agencies of government would lessen the defensive posture which police assume when singled out from among other agencies for special scrutiny. And the transfer in emphasis from exclusively negative criticism—in the form of recommendations for disciplinary action or in the form of dismissal of criminal charges because of the way in which evidence was acquired—to constructive suggestions for change and improvement would afford the opportunity for making the complaint process serve as an effective method for strengthening administration.

Reference Note

The best discussions of stopping and questioning are L. TIFFANY, D. MCINTYRE & D. ROTENBERG, DETECTION OF CRIME, pt. I (1967), and Schwartz, *Stop and Frisk,* 58 J. CRIM. L.C. & P.S. 433 (1967).

Other descriptive studies are LAW ENFORCEMENT IN THE METROPOLIS [Detroit] 18-22 (D. McIntyre ed. 1967); Pilcher, *The Law and Practice of Field Interrogation,* 58 J. CRIM. L.C. & P.S. 465, 487-91 (1967); Note, *Philadelphia Police Practices and the Law of Arrest,* 100 U. PA. L. REV. 1182 (1952); and Note, *Detention, Arrest, and Salt Lake City Police Practices,* 9 UTAH L. REV. 593, 610-16 (1965).

A rationale for a limited right to stop and question is given, along with a draft statute, in A.L.I., A MODEL CODE OF PRE-ARRAIGNMENT PROCEDURE, § 2.02 with Note and Comment (Tent. Draft No. 1, 1966).

D. ENTERING PREMISES OR SEARCHING THE PERSON

In a great many cases the detection devices discussed above will be ill-suited to expose the existence of crime or to identify the perpetrator of known crime. As an alternative, law enforcement personnel may make a search of persons or private premises thought to conceal ongoing criminal conduct, evidence of past crime, or weapons which are accessible to a suspect being detained and which are thus dangerous to the police.

In many kinds of crime, entering premises or searching the person is of no particular significance as a detection device. In other kinds of crime the technique is vital. Whenever the crime involves possession of material which itself is the best evidence of the commission of the crime—narcotics, gambling paraphernalia, counterfeit money, smuggled goods, or the like—the power to locate and take control of such objects is critically important. Persons guilty of these crimes will commonly have the physical objects in their possession but usually will make elaborate efforts to hide them where they cannot easily be found. Because a prosecutor will generally feel he needs physical evidence in these cases, the task for law enforcement is to obtain the evidence by methods which will allow it to be introduced at the trial.

Physical interference with a person or his property is obviously a matter of great sensitivity. The fourth amendment, applicable to state as well as federal officers through interpretation of the due process clause of the fourteenth amendment, says:

> The right of the people to be secure in their persons, houses, papers, and effects against unreasonable searches and seizures, shall not be violated, and no Warrants shall issue, but upon probable cause, supported by Oath or affirmation, and particularly describing the place to be searched, and the persons or things to be seized.

Traditionally, entry upon private premises, searching a person, and opening up personal property such as a suitcase or an automobile have been at the heart of the constitutional conceptual category of "search and seizure," but are not necessarily its whole scope. Great concern for individual privacy has exerted continual pressure for expansion of the protection so that "search and seizure" has come to include more than physical invasion or taking complete control. This pressure can be seen in the previous discussions of wiretapping, electronic eavesdropping, use of peepholes, stopping and questioning, and frisking.

1. The Concept of "Search and Seizure"

The root notions of "search" as an opening up of something closed (a house, an automobile, a box, a pocket), and of "seizure" as an assumption of complete control over a person or a thing, have traditionally dominated these concepts. For a long time heavy reliance was placed upon tort and property doctrines in determining whether there was a search or seizure, and they were often applied rather mechanically, but the 1967 decision in *Katz v. United States* explicitly rejected these limitations and shifted the emphasis to concern for safeguarding the individual's reasonable expectations of privacy. Consequently, conduct can now be a violation of the fourth amendment (and characterized as a "search") without trespass. At the same time courts are sometimes willing to take the position that not every trespass on property is such an intrusion as to be governed by the fourth amendment. As with any doctrinal concept, there are real difficulties in defining the limits of "search and seizure."

BROWNE v. STATE
24 Wis. 2d 491, 129 N.W.2d 175 (1964)

[A detective of the Milwaukee police department vice squad received an anonymous phone call informing him that Arthur Browne and a woman were, at that moment, using narcotic drugs in Browne's room.

Having previous knowledge that Browne was a narcotics user, the officers went to the location to investigate the claim. They were admitted into the building by a woman who was a roomer living on the second level. They identified themselves as police officers, and told her that they wanted to speak with Arthur Browne. She led them to the second-floor level into a kitchen area. A number of rooms adjoined the kitchen. Roomers, including the woman and Browne, lived in these rooms and jointly shared the kitchen facilities.

Browne's door was open. The officers, while standing in the kitchen area, observed a person lying on a bed in the adjoining room. When he saw them, he picked up an eyedropper with an attached hypodermic needle and threw it on the floor between the head of the bed and the wall. At this point, the officers entered the room and arrested Browne for the illegal use of drugs.]

WILKIE, J. [It is] necessary to determine whether there was any violation of constitutional rights on the part of the police in entering the building and proceeding to the upstairs kitchen.

At the moment the officers entered the kitchen they lacked probable cause to arrest.

But because the officers lacked probable cause to arrest, it does not follow that they were not legally permitted to be in the kitchen.

Certainly the police may investigate claims of crime on evidence not sufficient to justify an arrest. The anonymous tip, coupled with their previous knowledge of Browne's narcotics offenses, justified their trip to his house to investigate for the purpose of gathering evidence sufficient to arrest. When they followed Browne's fellow roomer who conducted them from the front door to the kitchen they were continuing to make a reasonable investigation of the crime concerning which they still had a reasonably aroused suspicion. Although both the Fourth amendment and sec. 11, art. I, protect against police invasion of personal privacy, police officers should be permitted to conduct a reasonable investigation when their suspicion has been reasonably aroused. Whether an inquiry is considered reasonable must depend upon the facts in each case and must turn on the application of what is essentially an indeterminate and flexible test.

We do not think it is helpful in making a determination as to the validity of the investigation to consider whether or not the defendant "consented" (actual or implied) to his landlord or fellow roomer to let the police in and to guide them to the threshold of his second-floor room. Since criminal convictions require substantial evidence, the police must be given reasonable power to gather probative evidence. These two values conflict (personal privacy and the need for probative evidence), and in our system of government the difficult task of striking a satisfactory balance falls upon courts. Do trips through the technicalities of the law of trespass aid in the balancing task?

Thus, whether or not a search or investigation is reasonable is not a matter for the application of the comparatively rigid rules of tort and property law, but is rather a matter of an inquiry as to whether the search or investigation is constitutionally reasonable under the circumstances. If police conduct is not considered unreasonable in the circumstances, it is not made unreasonable if it is deemed to have involved a civil trespass.

In the case at bar, and considering the nature of the crime involved, the police conduct in presenting themselves at the rooming house after receiving the phone call, in identifying themselves as police officers, in being ushered by the fellow roomer to the kitchen, in asking as to the whereabouts of Browne, and in viewing him through the open door, constituted a reasonable investigation on the part of the police officers that warranted any invasion of privacy Browne suffered from having the officers brought to the threshold of his room without his affirmative consent.

2. *Justifications for Entering Premises or Searching the Person*

In entering premises or searching persons, law enforcement officers may rely on search warrants issued by judicial officers, the need to preserve evidence which may be in the possession of a person at the time of his arrest, consent by a person otherwise entitled to object to the search, and the authority to make inspections essential to enforcement of laws relating to specially regulated activities such as crossing international borders or selling intoxicants. The law recognizes such police action as proper. There are also some exceptional circumstances in which the lawfulness of search has been recognized.

a. *Search Warrants*

DETECTION OF CRIME 99-100 (1967)
By Lawrence P. Tiffany, Donald M. McIntyre, Jr. & Daniel L. Rotenberg
(Little, Brown & Company)

Appellate courts commonly assert that searches ought, whenever possible, to be conducted with a search warrant. Insistence upon the preferred status of a warrant is motivated by the view that the decision to search should be made by a neutral and detached judicial officer rather than by a law enforcement officer who is engaged in the "competitive enterprise of ferreting out crime,"[2] or by the "hurried action of [police] officers . . . who may happen to make arrests."[3]

But in practice the search warrant is rarely used. For example, during the years 1956-1957, 29 search warrants were issued in Detroit; approximately 30 in Milwaukee; and 17 in Wichita. The number of search warrants issued has remained fairly constant during the years since 1956-1957.[4]

There is some evidence that *Mapp v. Ohio*[5] has resulted in an increased use of search warrants in some states that did not previously follow the exclusionary rule. Certainly this is true in New York City, where, prior to *Mapp,* search warrant usage was negligible; in 1963, after *Mapp,* 5132 search warrants were used in that city.[6] There is, however, adequate evidence that the presence or absence of an exclusionary rule is only one factor in determining whether search warrants will be widely used. In

---

[2] Johnson v. United States, 333 U.S. 10, 14 (1948).

[3] Aguilar v. Texas, 378 U.S 108, 110-111 (1964).

[4] . . . It is interesting to note from earlier literature that the frequency of search warrant usage appears to be much the same in other cities. Seventeen search warrants, for example, were used in Los Angeles County in 1954. Barrett, Exclusion of Evidence Obtained by Illegal Searches—A Comment on People v. Cahan, 43 Calif. L. Rev. 565, 570 (1955). In Philadelphia a sample of 770 arrests occurring in 1952 showed that only about 3 per cent were authorized by arrest warrants and, despite the fact that searches were involved, "the use of search warrants in the cases examined was virtually non-existent." Note, 100 U. Pa. L. Rev. 1182, 1192 (1952).

[5] 367 U.S. 643 (1961).

[6] Letter from Leonard E. Reisman, Deputy Commissioner of Police for Legal Matters, New York City Police Department, to author, June 8, 1964. Interestingly, 4282 of these warrants were issued for gambling offenses and 682 for narcotic offenses.

fact, reliance upon search warrants in Wichita, where the exclusionary rule did not apply, was greater than in Detroit, where the exclusionary rule applied to all offenses except those involving narcotics and dangerous weapons, and was as great in proportion to the population as in Milwaukee, where the exclusionary rule applied to all offenses.

In the three states studied by the American Bar Foundation survey, the small number of cases in which warrants were used tended to be situations where some special advantage was seen to their use. For example, in Detroit search warrants were used almost exclusively against gambling offenses. Cases against the higher echelon of the syndicates could be built only with great patience, and the climax of the detection program was the simultaneous raiding of various headquarters of the gambling operation at a moment when the top men and the evidence were believed to be present. Use of warrants permitted a judicial preview of the case to see if probable cause had been made out, allowed precise timing of the raid, and legitimated more extensive search than might otherwise have been legal. In Wichita search warrants were used particularly for simultaneous raids on premises where liquor was being sold illegally, so as to avoid the first raid putting other offenders on guard. Police there also indicated they believed use of warrants made a favorable impression on judges and juries. The pattern in Milwaukee was similar, with warrants being used also in narcotics and pornography cases.

The traditional reluctance to use warrants, except where they offer some special advantages, exists for several reasons: (1) The justification that a search is made with consent or is incident to an arrest can almost always be as easily relied on and avoids the inconvenience of having to obtain a warrant. Even when a warrant is sought, it is likely to be an arrest warrant, since the prosecutors and magistrates who pass on requests for warrants are more liberal in approving arrest warrants and require less paper work of the officers. In sum, if alternatives are less burdensome and equally effective, police see no reason to seek search warrants. (2) If the police have no intention of prosecuting and are therefore unconcerned with the legality of the search, they will not seek a warrant. (3) The evidentiary standard in obtaining a search warrant may be higher, practically speaking, than in justifying a search incident to an arrest.[v]

[v] This is to be contrasted with the formal law, which prefers warrant searches over those made without warrants. Aguilar v. Texas, 378 U.S. 108, 110-11 (1964).

Psychologically, the courts are likely to be more favorably inclined toward upholding a search which has already produced proof of serious misconduct than toward issuing a warrant to intrude on the citizen's privacy on uncertain evidence. Though the abstract phrasing of the standard is the same "probable cause" in both warrant and nonwarrant searches, there is a vague common understanding that something more substantial is needed in obtaining a warrant. In addition, the probable cause for arrest relates to the guilt of the suspect, whereas in obtaining a search warrant it must point toward the occurrence of a crime, toward connection of particular items with the crime, and toward their location in a particular place. In contrast to the federal system and many states, where hearsay stating facts constituting probable cause will support issuance of both search and arrest warrants (and arrest without warrant as well), many other states require personal knowledge of the facts on the part of the person swearing to the affidavit for a search warrant. When the informant wishes to remain anonymous or refuses to become further involved, police in these states have no practical way of obtaining a warrant and are pushed toward using alternative bases for justifying search. (4) Search warrants are governed by statute and frequently the statutory listing of objects which may be searched for is far from complete. The things used as the means for committing the crime, stolen goods, and objects produced by criminal activity are usually listed as proper objectives of a search warrant, but other objects which are only evidentiary of crime may not be listed in the statute as authorized targets of a warrant search. Until recently there was substantial doubt that the Constitution would permit a search warrant to issue for "mere evidence," but this doubt was banished by a 1967 Supreme Court decision.[w] (5) The practical necessity for quick action may mean that obtaining a warrant would greatly reduce the likelihood of successful police effort. (6) Police may fear an information leak through court clerks which would doom the search to failure.

JONES v. UNITED STATES

362 U.S. 257 (1960)

MR. JUSTICE FRANKFURTER delivered the opinion of the Court.

This is a prosecution for violation of federal narcotics laws. Prior to trial petitioner duly moved to suppress the evidence

[w] Warden, Maryland Penitentiary v. Hayden, 387 U.S. 294 (1967), a portion of which case appears at 224, *infra*. The decision is now codified in 18 U.S.C. § 3103a.

obtained through the execution of the search warrant on the ground that the warrant had been issued without a showing of probable cause.

The question raised is whether sufficient evidence to establish probable cause to search was put before the Commissioner by the officer, Didone, who applied for the warrant. The sole evidence upon which the warrant was issued was an affidavit signed by Didone.

Didone was a member of the Narcotic Squad in the District of Columbia. His affidavit claimed no direct knowledge of the presence of narcotics in the apartment. He swore that on the day before making the affidavit he had been given information, by one unnamed, that petitioner and another "were involved in the illicit narcotic traffic" and "kept a ready supply of heroin on hand" in the apartment. He swore that his informant claimed to have purchased narcotics at the apartment from petitioner and another "on many occasions," the last of which had been the day before the warrant was applied for. Didone swore that his informant "has given information to the undersigned on previous occasion and which was correct," that "[t]his same information" regarding petitioner had been given the narcotic squad by "other sources of information" and that the petitioner and the other implicated by the informant had admitted being users of narcotics. On this basis Didone founded his oath that he believed "that there is now illicit narcotic drugs being secreated [*sic*] in the above apartment by Cecil Jones."

This affidavit was, it is claimed, insufficient to establish probable cause because it did not set forth the affiant's personal observations regarding the presence of narcotics in the apartment, but rested wholly on hearsay. We held in Nathanson v. United States, 290 U.S. 41, that an affidavit does not establish probable cause which merely states the affiant's belief that there is cause to search, without stating facts upon which that belief is based. *A fortiori* this is true of an affidavit which states only the belief of one not the affiant. That is not, however, this case. The question here is whether an affidavit which sets out personal observations relating to the existence of cause to search is to be deemed insufficient by virtue of the fact that it sets out not the affiant's observations but those of another. An affidavit is not to be deemed insufficient on that score, so long as a substantial basis for crediting the hearsay is presented.

What we have ruled in the case of an officer who acts without a warrant governs our decision here. If an officer may act upon probable cause without a warrant when the only incriminating evidence in his possession is hearsay, it would be incongruous to hold that such evidence presented in an affidavit is insufficient basis for a warrant. If evidence of a more judicially competent or persuasive character than would have justified an officer in acting on his own without a warrant must be presented when a warrant is sought, warrants could seldom legitimatize police conduct, and resort to them would ultimately be discouraged. Due regard for the safeguards governing arrests and searches counsels the contrary. In a doubtful case, when the officer does not have clearly convincing evidence of the immediate need to search, it is most important that resort be had to a warrant, so that the evidence in the possession of the police may be weighed by an independent judicial officer, whose decision, not that of the police, may govern whether liberty or privacy is to be invaded.

We conclude therefore that hearsay may be the basis for a warrant. We cannot say that there was so little basis for accepting the hearsay here that the Commissioner acted improperly. The Commissioner need not have been convinced of the presence of narcotics in the apartment. He might have found the affidavit insufficient and withheld his warrant. But there was substantial basis for him to conclude that narcotics were probably present in the apartment, and that is sufficient. It is not suggested that the Commissioner doubted Didone's word. Thus we may assume that Didone had the day before been told, by one who claimed to have bought narcotics there, that petitioner was selling narcotics in the apartment. Had that been all, it might not have been enough; but Didone swore to a basis for accepting the informant's story. The informant had previously given accurate information. His story was corroborated by other sources of information. And petitioner was known by the police to be a user of narcotics. Corroboration through other sources of information reduced the chances of a reckless or prevaricating tale; that petitioner was a known user of narcotics made the charge against him much less subject to scepticism than would be such a charge against one without such a history. Vacated and remanded.[x]

---

[x] The decision also deals with the problem of standing, which is a major doctrinal issue in application of the exclusionary rule. The Court held that "anyone legitimately on premises [here a guest] where a search occurs may challenge its legality by way of a motion to suppress, when its fruits [here the claiming of which would constitute admission of crime] are proposed to be used against him." *Compare* People v. Kelley, 23 Ill. 2d 193, 177 N.E.2d 830 (1961) (reading the *Jones* case restrictively), *with* People v. Martin, 45 Cal. 2d 755, 290 P.2d 855 (1955) (rejecting for California any standing requirement).

Courts express their preference for police use of warrants by establishing lenient criteria for review. The Supreme Court has said:

> Thus, when a search is based upon a magistrate's, rather than a police officer's, determination of probable cause, the reviewing courts will accept evidence of a less "judicially competent or persuasive character than would have justified an officer in acting on his own without a warrant," and will sustain the judicial determination so long as "there was substantial basis for [the magistrate] to conclude that narcotics were probably present. . . ."[y]

> [W]hen a magistrate has found probable cause, the courts should not invalidate the warrant by interpreting the affidavit in a hypertechnical, rather than a commonsense, manner. Although in a particular case it may not be easy to determine when an affidavit demonstrates the existence of probable cause, the resolution of doubtful or marginal cases in this area should be largely determined by the preference to be accorded to warrants. . . .[z]

The search warrant procedure has been adapted to new areas of law enforcement, raising a whole new set of problems in making the procedure meaningful.

CAMARA v. MUNICIPAL COURT OF THE CITY AND COUNTY OF SAN FRANCISCO

387 U.S. 523 (1967)

MR. JUSTICE WHITE delivered the opinion of the Court.

In Frank v. Maryland, 359 U.S. 360, this Court upheld, by a five-to-four vote, a state court conviction of a home-owner who refused to permit a municipal health inspector to enter and inspect his premises without a search warrant.

On November 6, 1963, an inspector of the Division of Housing Inspection of the San Francisco Department of Public Health entered an apartment building to make a routine annual inspection for possible violations of the city's Housing Code. The building's manager informed the inspector that appellant, lessee of the ground floor, was using the rear of the leasehold

---

[y] Aguilar v. Texas, 378 U.S. 108, 111 (1964).

[z] United States v. Ventresca, 380 U.S. 102, 109 (1965). *Cf.* People v. Sesslin, 439 P.2d 321 (Cal. 1968) (dissenting judges would have upheld an arrest warrant by assuming magistrate had followed his normal practice of informally interrogating the complainant at length to establish probable cause before issuing a warrant).

as a personal residence. Claiming that the building's occupancy permit did not allow residential use of the ground floor, the inspector confronted appellant and demanded that he permit an inspection of the premises. Appellant refused to allow the inspection because the inspector lacked a search warrant.

The inspector returned on November 8, again without a warrant, and appellant again refused to allow an inspection. A citation was then mailed ordering appellant to appear at the district attorney's office. When appellant failed to appear, two inspectors returned to his apartment on November 22. They informed appellant that he was required by law to permit an inspection under § 503 of the Housing Code:

"Sec. 503 Right to Enter Building. Authorized employees of the City departments or City agencies, so far as may be necessary for the performance of their duties, shall, upon presentation of proper credentials, have the right to enter, at reasonable times, any building, structure, or premises in the City to perform any duty imposed upon them by the Municipal Code."

Appellant nevertheless refused the inspectors access to his apartment without a search warrant. Thereafter, a complaint was filed charging him with refusing to permit a lawful inspection in violation of § 507 of the Code. Appellant was arrested on December 2 and released on bail. When his demurrer to the criminal complaint was denied, appellant filed this petition for a writ of prohibition.

Having concluded that *Frank v. Maryland*, to the extent that it sanctioned such warrantless inspections, must be overruled, we reverse.

To the *Frank* majority, municipal fire, health, and housing inspection programs "touch at most upon the periphery of the important interests safeguarded by the Fourteenth Amendment's protection against official intrusion," 359 U.S., at 367, because the inspections are merely to determine whether physical conditions exist which do not comply with minimum standards prescribed in local regulatory ordinances. Since the inspector does not ask that the property owner open his doors to a search for "evidence of criminal action" which may be used to secure the owner's criminal conviction, historic interests of "self-protection" jointly protected by the Fourth and Fifth Amendments are said not to be involved, but only the less intense "right to be secure from intrusion into personal privacy." *Id.*, at 365.

We may agree that a routine inspection of the physical condition of private property is a less hostile intrusion than the typical policeman's search for the fruits and instrumentalities of crime. For this reason alone, *Frank* differed from the great bulk of Fourth Amendment cases which have been considered by this Court. But we cannot agree that the Fourth Amendment interests at stake in these inspection cases are merely "peripheral." It is surely anomalous to say that the individual and his private property are fully protected by the Fourth Amendment only when the individual is suspected of criminal behavior. For instance, even the most law-abiding citizen has a very tangible interest in limiting the circumstances under which the sanctity of his home may be broken by official authority, for the possibility of criminal entry under the guise of official sanction is a serious threat to personal and family security. And even accepting *Frank*'s rather remarkable premise, inspections of the kind we are here considering do in fact jeopardize "self-protection" interests of the property owner. Like most regulatory laws, fire, health, and housing codes are enforced by criminal processes. In some cities, discovery of a violation by the inspector leads to a criminal complaint. Even in cities where discovery of a violation produces only an administrative compliance order, refusal to comply is a criminal offense, and the fact of compliance is verified by a second inspection, again without a warrant. Finally, as this case demonstrates, refusal to permit an inspection is itself a crime, punishable by fine or even by jail sentence.

The *Frank* majority suggested, and appellee reasserts, two other justifications for permitting administrative health and safety inspections without a warrant. First, it is argued that these inspections are "designed to make the least possible demand on the individual occupant." 359 U.S., at 367. The ordinances authorizing inspections are hedged with safeguards, and at any rate the inspector's particular decision to enter must comply with the constitutional standard of reasonableness even if he may enter without a warrant. In addition, the argument proceeds, the warrant process could not function effectively in this field. The decision to inspect an entire municipal area is based upon legislative or administrative assessment of broad factors such as the area's age and condition. Unless the magistrate is to review such policy matters, he must issue a "rubber stamp" warrant which provides no protection at all to the property owner.

In our opinion, these arguments unduly discount the purposes behind the warrant machinery contemplated by the Fourth Amendment. Under the present system, when the inspector demands entry, the occupant has no way of knowing whether enforcement of the municipal code involved requires inspection of his premises, no way of knowing the lawful limits of the inspector's power to search, and no way of knowing whether the inspector himself is acting under proper authorization. These are questions which may be reviewed by a neutral magistrate without any reassessment of the basic agency decision to canvass an area. Yet, only by refusing entry and risking a criminal conviction can the occupant at present challenge the inspector's decision to search. And even if the occupant possesses sufficient fortitude to take this risk, as appellant did here, he may never learn any more about the reason for the inspection than that the law generally allows housing inspectors to gain entry. The practical effect of this system is to leave the occupant subject to the discretion of the official in the field. This is precisely the discretion to invade private property which we have consistently circumscribed by a requirement that a disinterested party warrant the need to search.

The question is not, at this stage at least, whether these inspections may be made, but whether they may be made without a warrant. For example, to say that gambling raids may not be made at the discretion of the police without a warrant is not necessarily to say that gambling raids may never be made. In assessing whether the public interest demands creation of a general exception to the Fourth Amendment's warrant requirement, the question is not whether the public interest justifies the type of search in question, but whether the authority to search should be evidenced by a warrant, which in turn depends in part upon whether the burden of obtaining a warrant is likely to frustrate the governmental purpose behind the search.

The Fourth Amendment provides that, "no Warrants shall issue, but upon probable cause." Borrowing from more typical Fourth Amendment cases, appellant argues not only that code enforcement inspection programs must be circumscribed by a warrant procedure, but also that warrants should issue only when the inspector possesses probable cause to believe that a particular dwelling contains violations of the minimum standards prescribed by the code being enforced. We disagree.

In cases in which the Fourth Amendment requires that a warrant to search be obtained, "probable cause" is the standard by which a particular decision to search is tested against the constitutional mandate of reasonableness. To apply this standard, it is obviously necessary first to focus upon the governmental interest which allegedly justifies official intrusion upon the constitutionally protected interests of the private citizen. For example, in a criminal investigation, the police may undertake to recover specific stolen or contraband goods. But that public interest would hardly justify a sweeping search of an entire city conducted in the hope that these goods might be found. Consequently, a search for these goods, even with a warrant, is "reasonable" only when there is "probable cause" to believe that they will be uncovered in a particular dwelling.

Unlike the search pursuant to a criminal investigation, the inspection programs at issue here are aimed at securing city-wide compliance with minimum physical standards for private property.

There is unanimous agreement among those most familiar with this field that the only effective way to seek universal compliance with the minimum standards required by municipal codes is through routine periodic inspections of all structures. It is here that the probable-cause debate is focused, for the agency's decision to conduct an area inspection is unavoidably based on its appraisal of conditions in the area as a whole, not on its knowledge of conditions in each particular building.

Unfortunately, there can be no ready test for determining reasonableness other than by balancing the need to search against the invasion which the search entails. But we think that a number of persuasive factors combine to support the reasonableness of code-enforcement area inspections. First, such programs have a long history of judicial and public acceptance. See Frank v. Maryland, 359 U.S., at 367-371. Second, the public interest demands that all dangerous conditions be prevented or abated, yet it is doubtful that any other canvassing technique would achieve acceptable results. Many such conditions—faulty wiring is an obvious example—are not observable from outside the building and indeed may not be apparent to the inexpert occupant himself. Finally, because the inspections are neither personal in nature nor aimed at the discovery of evidence of crime, they involve a relatively limited invasion of the urban citizen's privacy.

Having concluded that the area inspection is a "reasonable" search of private property within the meaning of the Fourth Amendment, it is obvious that "probable cause" to issue a warrant to inspect must exist if reasonable legislative or administrative standards for conducting an area inspection are satisfied with respect to a particular dwelling. Such standards, which will vary with the municipal program being enforced, may be based upon the passage of time, the nature of the building (*e.g.*, a multi-family apartment house), or the condition of the entire area, but they will not necessarily depend upon specific knowledge of the condition of the particular dwelling. It has been suggested that so to vary the probable-cause test from the standard applied in criminal cases would be to authorize a "synthetic search warrant" and thereby to lessen the overall protections of the Fourth Amendment. Frank v. Maryland, 359 U.S., at 373. But we do not agree. The warrant procedure is designed to guarantee that a decision to search private property is justified by a reasonable governmental interest. But reasonableness is still the ultimate standard. If a valid public interest justifies the intrusion contemplated, then there is probable cause to issue a suitably restricted search warrant.

Since our holding emphasizes the controlling standard of reasonableness, nothing we say today is intended to foreclose prompt inspections, even without a warrant, that the law has traditionally upheld in emergency situations. On the other hand, in the case of most routine area inspections, there is no compelling urgency to inspect at a particular time or on a particular day. Moreover, most citizens allow inspections of their property without a warrant. Thus, as a practical matter and in light of the Fourth Amendment's requirement that a warrant specify the property to be searched, it seems likely that warrants should normally be sought only after entry is refused unless there has been a citizen complaint or there is other satisfactory reason for securing immediate entry.

The judgment is vacated and the case is remanded for further proceedings not inconsistent with this opinion.

MR. JUSTICE CLARK, with whom MR. JUSTICE HARLAN and MR. JUSTICE STEWART join, dissenting. There is nothing here that suggests that the inspection was unauthorized, unreasonable, for any improper purpose, or designed as a basis for a criminal prosecution; nor is there any indication of any discriminatory, arbitrary, or capricious action affecting the appellant in either case. Indeed, Camara was admittedly violating the Code by living in quarters prohibited thereby; and See [387 U.S. 541 (1967)] was operating a locked warehouse—a business establishment subject to inspection.

The majority say, however, that under the present system the occupant has no way of knowing the necessity for the inspection, the limits of the inspector's power, or whether the inspector is himself authorized to perform the search. Each of the ordinances here is supported by findings as to the necessity for inspections of this type and San Francisco specifically bans the conduct in which appellant Camara is admittedly engaged. Furthermore, all of these doubts raised by the Court could be resolved very quickly. Indeed, the inspectors all have identification cards which they show the occupant and the latter could easily resolve the remaining questions by a call to the inspector's superior or, upon demand, receive a written answer thereto. The record here shows these challenges could have been easily interposed.

The basis of "probable cause" for area inspection warrants, the Court says, begins with the Fourth Amendment's reasonableness requirement; in determining whether an inspection is reasonable "the need for the inspection must be weighed in terms of these reasonable goals of code enforcement." It adds that there are "a number of persuasive factors" supporting "the reasonableness of code enforcement area inspections." It is interesting to note that the factors the Court relies upon are the identical ones my Brother Frankfurter gave for excusing warrants in Frank v. Maryland, *supra.* They are: long acceptance historically; the great public interest in health and safety; and the impersonal nature of the inspections—not for evidence of crime—but for the public welfare. Upon this reasoning, the Court concludes that probable cause exists "if reasonable legislative or administrative standards for conducting an area inspection are satisfied with respect to a particular dwelling." These standards will vary, it says, according to the code program and the condition of the area with reference thereto rather than the condition of a particular dwelling. The majority seem to hold that warrants may be obtained after a refusal of initial entry; I can find no such constitutional distinction or command. These boxcar warrants will be identical as to every dwelling in the area, save the street number itself. I daresay they will be printed up in pads of a thousand or more—with space for the street number to be inserted—and issued by magistrates in broadcast fashion as a matter of course.[a]

---

[a] Note that though the *Camara* case created a new warrant procedure its requirements for evidentiary basis seem to be different from those used in ordinary search warrant situations. Is this because the motive is not to punish but to abate a hazardous or socially undesirable condition? Is it because persons other than regular police officers can be expected to obtain and execute the warrants? Is it because the penalties likely to be imposed for violations detected are low and financial rather than personal?

The extension of the warrant procedure in the *Katz* and *Camara* cases raises anew the question whether such procedure is an effective control on arbitrary police action and how effectiveness might be enhanced. Is this review of police practice by an outside agency enough, or should we concentrate on educating and professionalizing police so they can be better expected to exercise self-restraint? If the lower courts supervise the police, who supervises these courts?

MEMORANDUM
Department of Health, Education, and Welfare;
Food and Drug Administration

July 26, 1967

To: District Directors
From: Bureau of Regulatory Compliance
Subject: Warrants for Inspections

In Camara v. Municipal Court, No. 92, and See v. Seattle, No. 180, decided June 5, 1967, the Supreme Court held that the Fourth Amendment to the Constitution allows both a homeowner and a business proprietor to refuse inspection unless the Inspector presents a "search warrant". The Court said that most persons would voluntarily consent to inspection, making routine use of warrants unnecessary, but that if consent was not given, the agent should have a simplified procedure for obtaining a warrant; and the Court eased the procedure for obtaining this sort of warrant. The decisions also recognized certain emergency situations, where there is an immediate health hazard, in which inspections could be conducted without first obtaining a warrant.

In view of these decisions, the following procedures should be adopted immediately:

Approach:

1. In general, inspections of establishments will be scheduled and conducted as they are at present. The Inspector will present his credentials and a written Notice of Inspection in the usual manner to the owner, operator, or agent in charge, and he will proceed with the inspection when permission or acquiescence is obtained.

2. In the event of an outright refusal of entry, the Inspector should withdraw for the purpose of obtaining a warrant. He should not refer management to section 301(f) at this point.

3. In a case where refusal is to be expected from past performance, and where an uninterrupted inspection is needed, or where surprise is essential, a warrant should be obtained before inspection is attempted.

4. *All inspections of parts of premises used for living quarters* should be conducted with a warrant. . . .

Obtaining the Warrant for Inspection:

In order to obtain an inspection warrant, we are required to show that the proposed inspection is a reasonable one. The Supreme Court stated that this may be done by showing that an inspection is required by legislative direction, and by reasonable administrative standards for the effective enforcement of the regulatory law. In the case of registered establishments, the law itself specifies the maximum time between inspections. In the case of other establishments, it is sufficient to show that the establishment has not been inspected for a period of time, or that there is a reason in addition to the mere passage of time since the last inspection. The General Counsel would like to make the justification for the warrant as simple as possible—a justification for a routine inspection—and to use special justifications such as complaints, violative samples, etc., in exceptional cases.

Refusal or Partial Refusal to Permit Inspection Pursuant to Warrant:

Despite the fact that the Supreme Court said that force may be used to complete inspections of commercial establishments pursuant to search warrants, our General Counsel advises that Inspectors should definitely *not* use force during such inspections. Should the Inspector encounter *outright refusal to permit entry,* he should return to the U.S. Attorney and ask that he obtain from the Judge an order to show cause why the person should not be punished for resisting a lawful writ.

Should the Inspector encounter *partial refusal or resistance* (following service of the warrant) in obtaining access to anything FDA is authorized to inspect, he should briefly inform the management of the inspection authority under section 704 and the provisions of section 301(f). If management maintains an attitude of refusal, the Inspector should leave the premises. . . .

It will be necessary that you prepare your own documents for both the Applications and the Warrants. We expect to order pads of the finished forms in due course, but we anticipate that early experience with the procedure may dictate important changes, and we want the benefit of that experience before we order a large quantity of the forms.

The *Camara* decision is codified in Wisconsin legislation.

WISCONSIN STATUTES §§ 963.10–963.11 (1967)

963.10 SPECIAL INSPECTION WARRANTS.

. . .

(2) Except in cases of emergency where no special inspection warrant shall be required, special inspection warrants shall be issued for inspection of personal or real properties which are not public buildings or for inspection of portions of public buildings which are not open to the public only upon showing that consent to entry for inspection purposes has been refused. The definition of "public building" under s. 101.01(12) applies to this section.

963.11 SPECIAL INSPECTION WARRANT FORMS. The following forms for use under s. 963.10 are illustrative and not mandatory:

AFFIDAVIT

STATE OF WISCONSIN ________ County. In the ________ court of the ________ of ________.

A. F., being duly sworn, says that on the ________ day of ________, A. D., 19__, in said county, in and upon certain premises in the (city, town or village) of ________ and more particularly described as follows: (describe the premises) there now exists a necessity to determine if said premises comply with (section ________ of the Wisconsin statutes) and/or (section ________ of ordinances of said municipality). The facts tending to establish the grounds for issuing a special inspection warrant are as follows: (set forth brief statement of reasons for inspection, frequency and approximate date of last inspection, if any, which shall be deemed probable cause for issuance of warrant).

Wherefore, the said A. F. prays that a special inspection warrant be issued to search such premises for said purpose ________ (Signed) A. F.

Subscribed and sworn to before me this ________ day of ________, 19__ ________________ Judge of the ________ Court.

Execution of Warrant

Even when a search warrant is properly issued upon a showing of probable cause, the concern for minimizing the degree of intrusion persists in restrictions upon the method of executing the search warrant. Principal among the restrictions is the general requirement that the householder be given an opportunity to submit to the search peacefully before force can properly be used to break in. This obviously presents a problem to the police when successful prosecution depends upon seizure of evidence which can be readily destroyed.

UNITED STATES *ex rel.* MANDUCHI v. TRACY

233 F. Supp. 423 (E.D. Pa. 1964)
Affirmed, 350 F.2d 658 (3d Cir. 1965)

LUONGO, District Judge. Richard Joseph Manduchi, petitioner in this habeas corpus proceeding, was tried in the Court of Quarter Sessions of Lancaster County, and convicted of the misdemeanor of bookmaking.

On March 1, 1961, Detective S. Kenneth Cliff of the Lancaster City Police obtained a search warrant for the apartment of Richard Manduchi as a result of information obtained by other police officers. When Detective Williams arrived, he tried the door, found it to be locked, knocked, heard a "scuffling noise" inside the apartment (the noise was never more precisely described), and without giving anyone inside the apartment the opportunity to open the door, and without announcing his authority and purpose, proceeded to hit the door with a sledge hammer. On the second blow the door flew open and Detective Williams entered the apartment. Simultaneously, two other detectives broke open another door to the apartment with a section of wooden telephone pole.

Detective Williams testified at the trial that upon entering the apartment he saw Manduchi put a piece of paper in his mouth and swallow it. Other papers found in the apartment were seized and admitted into evidence over defense counsel's objection. In addition, the detectives remained in the apartment for about an hour answering telephone calls made by persons asking for "Red." One such caller made numerous bets. Testimony concerning these calls was also given at the trial.

The issue raised by this petition is whether the evidence so obtained should have been excluded from the trial as the product of an unreasonable search and seizure prohibited by the Constitution of the United States. More narrowly stated, the issue is whether, under the circumstances, the entry by state officers armed with a search warrant without first announcing their authority and purpose violated constitutional safeguards against unreasonable search and seizure.

The Fourth Amendment's prohibition against unreasonable searches and seizures, with its accompanying sanction that evidence so obtained must be excluded from trial, is applicable to the states through the Fourteenth Amendment. Mapp v. Ohio, 367 U.S. 643 (1961). Mapp did not furnish a definitive answer to the question whether a federal or state standard was to be applied in determining the reasonableness of a search, but the more recent case of Ker v. California, 374 U.S. 23 (1963) did. The standard to be applied is federal. It was stated in the following language in the opinion of Mr. Justice Clark for the Court in Ker:

> . . . the standard of reasonableness is the same under the Fourth and Fourteenth Amendments . . . the reasonableness of a search is in the first instance a substantive determination to be made by the trial court from the facts and circumstances of the case and in the light of the "fundamental criteria" laid down by the Fourteenth Amendment and in the opinions of this Court applying that Amendment. Findings of reasonableness, of course, are respected only insofar as consistent with federal constitutional guarantees. Id. at 33.

One of the requirements of a reasonable search and seizure, under federal standards, is that the police officers must, prior to entry, make an announcement of their authority and their purpose for seeking entry unless there are circumstances excusing failure to do so. This requirement is an outgrowth of the traditional common law concept that a man's home is his castle. As early as 1603 an English court noted that ". . . in all cases when the King is a party, the sheriff (if the door be not open) may break the party's house, either to arrest him, or to do other execution of the King's process, if otherwise he cannot enter. But before he breaks it, he ought to signify the cause of his coming, and to make request to open doors. . . ." Semayne's Case, 77 Eng.Repr. 194, 195 (1603).

In holding that the evidence seized in Ker's apartment as the result of the unannounced entry was admissible, the Court stressed circumstances which excused compliance with the requirement to announce authority and purpose.

> Here justification for the officers' failure to give notice is uniquely present. In addition to the officers' belief that Ker was in possession of narcotics, which could be quickly and easily destroyed, Ker's furtive conduct in eluding them shortly before the arrest was ground for the belief that he might well have been expecting the police. Id. at 40.

The search in Ker was incident to an arrest without a warrant for a felony, whereas in the instant case the search was pursuant to a validly issued search warrant. This is not a ground for distinction. The search warrant serves no greater function, in the one case, than does reasonable cause to believe that a felony has been committed, in the other; each makes lawful the presence of the officers *at the door*. If that door is not open, under the ruling of Ker, it may not be broken to apprehend a felon without prior announcement, except under exigent circumstances. If constitutional safeguards must be observed before the door may be broken for the purpose of apprehending a felon, *a fortiori* they must be observed before the door may be broken for the purpose of seeking *evidence* of a *misdemeanor*. The fact that a valid search warrant had issued is immaterial when that which is in issue is the *means of entry* as opposed to the *right of entry*.

The petition for writ of habeas corpus will be granted.[b]

As part of the same policy statement above (at 183), guidance was given also to police in relation to execution of search warrants.

INSTRUCTIONS TO MEMBERS OF THE FORCE CONCERNING THE "STOP AND FRISK" (CHAPTER 86) AND "NO KNOCK" (CHAPTER 85) LAWS

Police Department, City of New York, Office of the Police Commissioner Circular No. 25, New York, June 26, 1964

II. THE "KNOCK, KNOCK" LAW

The new statute amends section 799 of the code of criminal procedure, which will read as follows:

> § 799. Officer may break open door or window to execute warrant. The officer may break open an outer or inner door or window of a building, or any part of the building, or any

[b] *Cf.* Sabbath v. United States, 391 U.S. 585 (1968), which applied the federal statute requiring a demand before entry to execute a search warrant to a situation involving entry to make arrest without a warrant.

thing therein, to execute the warrant, (a) if, after notice of his authority and purpose, he be refused admittance, or (b) without notice of his authority and purpose, if the judge, justice or magistrate issuing the warrant has inserted a direction therein that the officer executing it shall not be required to give such notice. The judge, justice and magistrate may so direct only upon proof under oath, to his satisfaction that the property sought may be easily and quickly destroyed or disposed of, or that danger to the life or limb of the officer or another may result, if such notice were to be given.

A. General principles:

1. Seeking to dispense with the usual notice requirements when executing search warrants should be the exception, not the rule. Stereotyped forms should not be prepared that might encourage too ready use of this extraordinary procedure. When it is to be used, it should be upon carefully drafted papers.

2. The facts relied upon as indicating that "the property sought may be easily and quickly destroyed or disposed of, or that danger to the life or limb of the officer or another may result if such notice were to be given" should be spelled out in detail in the affidavits.

3. Every application for this type of search warrant should have the endorsement or approval of a superior officer, who must be satisfied that the case is of sufficient significance to justify this procedure, and that the danger or risk of destruction is soundly anticipated.

4. When it is permitted, unannounced entry should be made with the least disruption possible. Often a passkey or the help of a superintendent may assist an officer to enter the premises with a minimum of disturbance. Every action possible should be taken to allay the fears of the occupants of the premises, or others, which may be occasioned by an unannounced entering.

5. Copies of all affidavits and court orders should be filed in the office or command of the executing officer. A proposed form will be provided for reporting the execution of all search warrants.

b. Search Authorized by Arrest

The common law recognized the power of an officer to search anyone whom he had lawfully arrested. The rationale given was that otherwise the person arrested might have hidden on his person a weapon or other means of escape and also evidence of the crime, which he would destroy upon first opportunity. Justice Frankfurter, dissenting in United States v. Rabinowitz, 339 U.S. 56, 68 (1950), took the position that this historical justification for searching an arrested person must be taken as limiting the meaning of "reasonableness" when used in the fourth amendment. He urged that search was permissible only when necessary to protect the officer and to prevent destruction of evidence by the offender. The majority of the Supreme Court justices took the position that "reasonableness" is not so limited, though they did not give any definition. Subsequent decisions still have not defined the legal limits for search except in their case-by-case plotting of the limits of reasonableness. Among the factors which the courts frequently consider are the time between arrest and search, the area over which the search extends, the characteristics of the objects sought, the motive of the arrest, the relationship of the things sought to the offense, and the intensity with which the search is made, as well as the need to protect the officer and prevent destruction of evidence. Still another factor, the existence of opportunity to obtain a search warrant, has thus far been considered as having no proper bearing on the reasonableness of searching without a warrant, though there is continuing pressure to consider that factor.[c] The existence of ample opportunity to obtain a warrant has not invalidated a nonwarrant search, and the absence of opportunity to get a warrant will not validate a nonwarrant search (in the absence of an arrest, consent, or exceptional circumstances), however reasonable the belief that contraband or evidence of crime would be found.

The Practice

The search as an incident to arrest is a very common police method of searching. Persons who are arrested are normally

---

[c] *E.g.,* Niro v. United States, 388 F.2d 535 (1st Cir. 1968) (despite United States v. Rabinowitz, 339 U.S. 56 (1950), police must obtain a warrant when they have ample time). *Compare* the dictum in Terry v. Ohio, 392 U.S. 1, 20 (1968):

> We do not retreat from our holdings that the police must, whenever practicable, obtain advance judicial approval of searches and seizures through the warrant procedure, see, e.g., Katz v. United States, 389 U.S. 347 (1967) [electronic eavesdropping]; Beck v. Ohio, 379 U.S. 89, 96 (1964) [dictum stating preference for warrant]; Chapman v. United States, 365 U.S. 610 (1961) [search of house on probable cause but not incident to arrest], or that in most instances failure to comply with the warrant requirement can only be excused by exigent circumstances, see, e.g., Warden v. Hayden, 387 U.S. 294 (1967) (hot pursuit); cf. Preston v. United States, 376 U.S. 364, 367-368 (1964) [dictum that search incident to lawful arrest is proper].

searched for weapons, and their clothing, car, and immediate surroundings are searched if police have any reason to think they might find something incriminating. The case law—interpreting the constitutional command that searches must not be unreasonable—is consistent in approving such searches when they come in the routine course of police operations. The assumption is that arrest, being a necessary step in processing offenders, is the prime motivation.

Though arrest is usually for purposes of prosecution, in practice arrest is frequently also used to legitimize the search for evidence or weapons where special circumstances suggest to the officer that evidence or weapons may be found. As a matter of normal practice, police do not arrest every person they see committing a minor offense. In large cities, for example, vagrants and drunks are not arrested when they are creating no disturbance and seem able to care for themselves, and a large portion of technical traffic offenses are overlooked. Even when arrests for these offenses are made, search will ordinarily be superficial if made at all. However, police who have some suspicion about such person's involvement in more serious crime freely stop, question, and search the suspect, having in mind that the drunkenness, vagrancy, or traffic offense will serve as justification for the search in the event evidence of other criminality turns up. Both the fact of arrest (which is often only tentative, with the suspect being released if the search proves fruitless) and the intensity and scope of the search are motivated by the suspicion of other criminality, not by the minor offense itself. The reliance on some minor offense to justify arrest and search stems partly from a desire for good public relations—it makes the search more acceptable if the search which produces no incriminating evidence results in the offender's being released without any charge on the minor offense. Police also assume that existence of a basis for the arrest will permit them to avoid personal liability or loss of the evidence if either should be brought into issue later. The particular problem of search incident to a traffic arrest has been litigated repeatedly in recent years, with many of the cases resulting in exclusion of the evidence on the ground that the search was not merely incidental to the arrest but was the prime police objective, while the arrest was mere excuse. The principal police motivation to search is all the clearer when vice squad officers arrest for traffic offenses and discover narcotics in their search, or when the arrest is timed to permit the broadest possible chance of finding incriminating evidence.

1

Members of a police "gambling detail" observed a suspect park his automobile too close to a crosswalk and go into a building, where they assumed he was picking up policy slips. They waited twenty minutes until he emerged. As they approached he hastily reentered the building. The police arrested him on the parking violation and searched him, finding policy slips on him.

2

An arrest warrant was obtained, charging the suspect with sale of narcotics. Members of the narcotics squad carried the warrant with them on their tour of duty that night. They saw the suspect driving his car along one of the main streets and followed him. After about twenty blocks of surveillance, he pulled up in front of his residence and went in. The officers knocked at the door and arrested the suspect when he answered it. A thorough search of his small flat produced no evidence of narcotics. Although the suspect was taken to headquarters and booked, no charges were filed against him. He was released the next morning.

Police may act without clear intent to arrest or not to arrest. They search suspicious persons, releasing them if nothing incriminating is found, holding them if evidence of crime is discovered. When the police are called on after the fact to justify their action they describe it in terms of (1) arrest, (2) search incident to the arrest. In fact the sequence is not nearly so clear.

3

The officers in the patrol car noticed a shabbily dressed man standing in the entryway to a store. They pulled up and one alighted from the car. After frisking the suspect for weapons, the officer asked for identification and for an account of why the subject was at that particular place at 12:30 a.m. No incriminating evidence was found, so the subject was sent on his way.

4

On a Sunday evening police stopped a man in a downtown area, carrying a suitcase and wearing a coat despite hot weather, who looked unfamiliar and out of place. In response to questioning he stated he had little money and had been out of work for three months and was just passing through. In response to questions whether he had a weapon he pointed to his suitcase. One officer opened the suitcase and took out an unloaded pistol.

He was taken to the station and booked for "vagrancy" and "investigation as a fugitive from justice."

5

Before leaving headquarters for his tour of duty the officer showed me his notebook containing the descriptions of cars stolen over the past month and physical descriptions of about twenty men for whom arrest warrants had been issued. He keeps this notebook with him in the patrol car and constantly refreshes his memory on the information in it. He indicated that he "checks out" several persons each tour of duty because they resemble the descriptions. He also pointed out that the descriptions are handy for justifying stopping any suspicious person. A sergeant instructor in the training school had advised this, saying that "an officer is a poor policeman if he cannot find a description to fit any suspect from the bulletins for thirty days."

6

Narcotic agents obtained a warrant to search a man's hotel room on the basis of reliable information from two sources that he was selling heroin, corroborated by their observing numerous visits to his room by known peddlers of narcotics. As they approached his room they met the man in the hall. The agents pushed him back into the room and told him they were looking for heroin. They found ten capsules of white powder in his pocket and seventy-five more in a drawer next to his bed.[d]

Problems of extent and intensity of search may also often arise.

7

After stopping a car for excessive speed the officer approached the driver. He recognized the driver as an individual with a criminal record who, on occasion, had been picked up for carry-

[d] The fact that police did not make a clear arrest, though they had grounds which would have authorized arrest, is thought by some courts to prevent reliance on the rule that search may be made incident to an arrest. *E.g.*, United States v. Haywood, 284 F. Supp. 245 (E.D. La. 1968). Justice Harlan, concurring in Sibron v. New York, 392 U.S. 40, 77 (1968), urged the opposite: "There is *no* case in which a defendant may validly say, 'Although the officer had a right to arrest me at the moment when he seized me and searched my person, the search is invalid because he did not in fact arrest me until afterwards.' "

The police may have grounds to arrest, yet know that no prosecution can succeed unless additional evidence is discovered by search. They see no point in making a formal arrest until the discovery is made.

ing concealed weapons. The driver was ordered out and frisked. The glove compartment and a box on the floor of the car were searched, and the trunk was opened and inspected. No weapons were found.

8

Arriving at the scene of a one-car accident, police first took the injured driver and his passenger to the hospital for emergency treatment. They then told the driver, who smelled of liquor, that he was under arrest and that they would have to take a blood sample for evidence. He objected, but at the policemen's direction a doctor drew the blood sample with a hypodermic needle.

9

United States v. James, 378 F.2d 88, 89, 90-91 (6th Cir. 1967), Weick, Chief Judge:

"Appellant James' sole complaint is that the trial court erred in denying her motion to suppress the evidence of narcotics seized by federal narcotics agents in a search made without a search warrant, of the apartment in which she was living.

"In the evening of September 26, 1963, approximately ten agents and police officers assembled at the Highland Park Police Station for the avowed purpose of planning the arrest of James and Mallory. They intended to search the apartment if an arrest was made. After making their plans, they descended en masse upon the apartment at 9:35 P.M., and one or two officers were assigned by Agent Miller to search each of the five rooms of the apartment. Mallory was not present but was arrested later. James was arrested in the dining room of the apartment, and the search was commenced in each of the five rooms and continued for one hour. The officers remained in the apartment for two and one-half hours. In a bedroom closet was found a vacuum cleaner which contained the narcotics.

"Taking into account all of the admitted facts and circumstances of the case, including the large aggregation of agents and police officers, it seems to us that the agents and officers were interested in something more than merely making an arrest. It is clear that their primary purpose was to make a general exploratory search of the apartment, with the hope of finding narcotics. This search, in our judgment, was unreasonable and violated the rights of Appellant James under the Fourth Amendment to the Constitution. United States v. Harris, 321 F.2d 739 (6th Cir. 1963). . . .

"It follows that the District Court erred in denying the motion to suppress. The judgment of conviction is reversed and the cause is remanded with instructions to grant the motion to suppress."

c. *Searches of Conveyances for Contraband; Searches of Premises to Find a Suspect*

Law enforcement officers sometimes are confronted with the special problem of a vehicle in which they have reasonable grounds to believe contraband (bootleg liquor, narcotics, counterfeit money, smuggled goods, and so on) is hidden. Obtaining a search warrant may be wholly impractical, because the vehicle is likely to be gone when they return. Under these circumstances the United States Supreme Court in Carroll v. United States, 267 U.S. 132 (1925), held that the search was reasonable. The fact that an arrest and incidental search could have been made was not considered; the issue was not whether there was another way to make a reasonable search but whether the way chosen was itself reasonable.

The reasoning of the *Carroll* case would apply as well to any situation in which contraband may likely disappear while a warrant is being sought—for example, when narcotics are believed to be in a suspect's pocket—but the rule has been used almost exclusively in the search of vehicles. In the other cases in which it might apply, the decision is much more likely to be based on the alternative justification of arrest and search incident to that arrest. It is usually only when the search is conducted prior to the arrest (and the court feels that sequence is vital) or when for some other reason the arrest is invalid that the *Carroll* rule is brought into play.[e]

In a situation somewhat similar to the *Carroll* case, the police may have reason to believe that a person whom they wish to arrest—either with or without a warrant—is hiding in a particular place. If they are denied consent to enter and are forced to leave to obtain a search warrant, their quarry may be gone when they return. The questions of whether they may use force to enter, and whether they must make announcement of their purpose and authority before they may use force to enter (*see*

[e] Two other doctrines are similarly used to justify a seizure which does not fit in any of the major categories. These doctrines are that police may seize instrumentalities of crime (*e.g.*, State v. McCoy, 437 P.2d 734 (Ore. 1968) (car in which rape occurred); State v. Bean, 157 N.W.2d 736 (Minn. 1968) (car used to escape from burglary scene)) and property subject to forfeiture (*e.g.*, Cooper v. California, 386 U.S. 58 (1967)).

United States ex rel. Manduchi v. Tracy, at 214, *supra*), are not susceptible of clear answer in all cases, but the Supreme Court has approved immediate entry at least in hot pursuit of an armed robber.

WARDEN, MARYLAND PENITENTIARY v. HAYDEN

387 U.S. 294 (1967)

MR. JUSTICE BRENNAN delivered the opinion of the Court.

About 8 a. m. on March 17, 1962, an armed robber entered the business premises of the Diamond Cab Company in Baltimore, Maryland. He took some $363 and ran. Two cab drivers in the vicinity, attracted by shouts of "Holdup" followed the man to 2111 Cocoa Lane. One driver notified the company dispatcher by radio that the man was a Negro about 5′8″ tall, wearing a light cap and dark jacket, and that he had entered the house on Cocoa Lane. The dispatcher relayed the information to police who were proceeding to the scene of the robbery. Within minutes, police arrived at the house in a number of patrol cars. An officer knocked and announced their presence. Mrs. Hayden answered, and the officers told her they believed that a robber had entered the house, and asked to search the house. She offered no objection.[4]

The officers spread out through the first and second floors and the cellar in search of the robber. Hayden was found in an upstairs bedroom feigning sleep. He was arrested when the officers on the first floor and in the cellar reported that no other man was in the house. Meanwhile an officer was attracted to an adjoining bathroom by the noise of running water, and discovered a shotgun and a pistol in a flush tank; another officer who, according to the District Court, "was searching the cellar for a man or the money" found in a washing machine a jacket and trousers of the type the fleeing man was said to have worn. A clip of ammunition for the pistol and a cap were found under the mattress of Hayden's bed, and ammunition for the shotgun was found in a bureau drawer in Hayden's room. All these items of evidence were introduced against respondent at his trial.

We agree with the Court of Appeals that neither the entry without warrant to search for the robber, nor the search for him without warrant was invalid. Under the circumstances of this

4 The state postconviction court found that Mrs. Hayden "gave the policeman permission to enter the home." The federal habeas corpus court stated it "would be justified in accepting the findings of historical fact made by Judge Sodaro on that issue . . . ," but concluded that resolution of the issue would be unnecessary, because the officers were "justified in entering and searching the house for the felon, for his weapons and for the fruits of the robbery."

case, "the exigencies of the situation made that course imperative." McDonald v. United States, 335 U.S. 451, 456. The police were informed that an armed robbery had taken place, and that the suspect had entered 2111 Cocoa Lane less than five minutes before they reached it. They acted reasonably when they entered the house and began to search for a man of the description they had been given and for weapons which he had used in the robbery or might use against them. The Fourth Amendment does not require police officers to delay in the course of an investigation if to do so would gravely endanger their lives or the lives of others. Speed here was essential, and only a thorough search of the house for persons and weapons could have insured that Hayden was the only man present and that the police had control of all weapons which could be used against them or to effect an escape.

We do not rely upon Harris v. United States, *supra,* in sustaining the validity of the search. The principal issue in *Harris* was whether the search there could properly be regarded as incident to the lawful arrest, since Harris was in custody before the search was made and the evidence seized. Here, the seizures occurred prior to or immediately contemporaneous with Hayden's arrest, as part of an effort to find a suspected felon, armed, within the house into which he had run only minutes before the police arrived. The permissible scope of search must, therefore, at the least, be as broad as may reasonably be necessary to prevent the dangers that the suspect at large in the house may resist or escape.

LANKFORD v. GELSTON

364 F.2d 197 (4th Cir. 1966)

SOBELOFF, Circuit Judge: There is no dispute over the facts. On the evening of December 24, 1964, several persons committed an armed robbery of a liquor store in Baltimore City, in the course of which Police Lieutenant James Maskell was shot and seriously wounded. A suspect was soon apprehended near the scene of the crime and after questioning him, several police officers visited homes in the area in search of other suspects. At about 4:50 a. m., on December 25, Police Sergeant Jack Cooper, a uniformed officer in a cruising car and a member of the search party, was found fatally shot near his cruiser.

Early in the morning of December 25, warrants were issued for the arrest of Samuel Veney and his brother Earl, charging them with the robbery of the liquor store and with assaulting and shooting Lieutenant Maskell. The Veney brothers were justifiably believed by the police to be armed and extremely dangerous. Later that day, the then Police Commissioner, Bernard Schmidt, authorized a special squad to be formed under the command of Captain Joseph Mahrer to search for the Veneys. About 50 or 60 police officers were members of the squad at one time or another.

Between December 25 and January 12, the Baltimore police made more than 300 "turn-ups" in an unsuccessful effort to locate and arrest the Veneys. In police parlance a turn-up is an investigation of a location and usually includes a search of the premises. Most of the searches here were of private residences. The Veneys are Negroes, and most of the dwellings searched were occupied by Negroes.

Few specific instances need be detailed to illustrate the consequences of police reliance on anonymous tips and the terrifying experiences to which occupants of the searched homes were subjected.

Mr. and Mrs. Wallace have made their home at 2408 Huron Street for 21 years. They live with a three-year-old son, three daughters, Lucinda (a Baltimore public school teacher), Harrietta (a college student), and Sharon (a high school student), and two other relatives. At 8:30 p. m. on December 30, 1964, Lieutenant Coll of the Southwest District was told by a clerk at another police station that she had received an anonymous call from a man who said that the Veneys were being sheltered at this address. Lieutenant Coll testified that since this was the first time that the Veneys had been placed in this neighborhood, he felt that an investigation was in order. A little after 9:00 p. m. Lieutenant Coll had about 14 officers to the house. When the police arrived, Lucinda Wallace was showing slides to a group of her family and guests. Mr. and Mrs. Wallace were both out, Mrs. Wallace at a beauty shop she operated four doors away. Six officers armed with shotguns and rifles entered and searched the home; others who were stationed outside would not allow Mrs. Wallace to enter and refused to explain what was happening. Reduced to tears, she was finally admitted to her home, where she was joined by her children, all crying hysterically. As the policemen were departing, they told Lucinda and her mother that they had received an anonymous call that the Veneys were in the house.

At the trial several police officers, each with long experience on the Baltimore police force, testified that in serious cases it was routine practice to make searches of homes on the basis of anonymous calls. They recognized the difficulty in authenticating such tips, and testified that they attempted to do so by evaluating the tone of voice used by the caller. The officers further stated that not infrequently they would also conduct searches based on tips received from the outside and transmitted to them by police telephone clerks.

On January 8, 1966, plaintiffs' attorneys brought the complaint to the chambers of the District Judge and asked for a temporary restraining order. At a hearing held that afternoon, the Deputy Attorney General represented to the court that the Police Commissioner would promptly issue a general order dealing with the problems raised in the complaint. Based on that representation, the District Court denied the request for a temporary restraining order, and set the case for trial on January 14.

On January 11 the Police Commissioner did issue General Order No. 10388.[4] In essence the Order forbids police officers from searching "any premises for the purpose of arresting a person for whom an arrest warrant has been issued" unless "the officer has probable cause to believe the accused person to be on the premises to be searched." The determination of what constitutes probable cause is still left to the policeman, and there is nothing in the Order which specifically prohibits officers from conducting searches grounded only on anonymous tips,

---

[4] *"General Order:* January 11, 1965. *No. 10388 "Subject: Service of Arrest Warrants*

"The question has recently arisen as to the precise scope of the authority conferred upon police officers by arrest warrants, and specifically whether such warrants authorize entry upon private property for the purpose of locating and arresting the defendant named in the warrant.

"A police officer may make a peaceable or a forcible entry to search any premises for the purpose of arresting a person for whom an arrest warrant has been issued, if, but only if, the officer has probable cause to believe the accused person to be on the premises to be searched.

"In this context, 'probable cause' is said to exist where the facts and circumstances within the officer's knowledge and of which he has reasonably trustworthy information are sufficient in themselves to warrant a man of reasonable caution to believe that the accused person is on the premises to be searched.

"The officer should, where practicable, seek admission to the suspected premises by announcing his identity, the existence of the arrest warrant, and his desire to search for and arrest the accused person. If the officer has any doubt as to the existence of 'probable cause', he should immediately either seek the issuance of a search warrant, or consult with the office of the State's Attorney for Baltimore City or of the Attorney General of the State of Maryland before attempting entry upon private premises in search of the accused person.

"In all instances, consideration should be given to the convenience of the persons whose premises are to be searched and the other residents of the neighborhood. In this connection, it may at times be necessary, and in the public interest, to make such searches in the nighttime when most of the residents would not be on the street, when the possibility of warning and escape would be less, and when greater safety would be afforded the arresting officer.

"Copies: Inspectors, All Districts, Divisions, Units."

which is precisely the evil to which the Complaint was addressed. We therefore find nothing in General Order No. 10388 which would make the issuance of an injunction unnecessary.

In refusing injunctive relief, the District Court emphasized the reluctance of the federal judiciary to employ its equity power to control police practices and noted that "this Court has now stated the basic principles which must be observed by the police in determining whether there are reasonable grounds for a contemplated entry. The Court is satisfied that the Police Commissioner and other police officers will make a bona fide effort to observe those rules. They did observe them during the remainder of the search for the Veneys after the Commissioner issued General Order No. 10388 on January 11." 240 F. Supp. at 561.

We conclude, however, that in striking the balance between the role of the federal court in the preservation of the constitutional rights of the appellants and the independence of state officials, the District Court erred when it refused to issue an injunction prohibiting the police from conducting searches based only on uncorroborated anonymous tips and hence without probable cause.

This case reveals a series of the most flagrant invasions of privacy ever to come under the scrutiny of a federal court. The undisputed testimony indicates that the police in conducting the wholesale Veney raids were engaging in a practice which on a smaller scale has routinely attended efforts to apprehend persons accused of serious crime. If denying relief in these circumstances should be held a proper exercise of judicial restraint, it would be difficult to envision any case justifying judicial intervention. The parties seeking redress have committed no acts warranting violation of the privacy of their homes; there has never been any suspicion concerning them or their associations. It was not contended by the Attorney General, nor could it have been contended, that information from an anonymous and unverifiable source is probable cause for the search of a home.

Instances have often come to the attention of courts in which persons accused of crime have sought to prevent the use against them of illegally seized incriminating evidence. But it is only in the rare instance that a person not accused or even suspected of any crime petitions the court for redress of police invasion of his home. The reason is not that such invasions do not occur but, as Mr. Justice Jackson eloquently put it:

"Only occasional and more flagrant abuses come to the attention of the courts, and then only those where the search and seizure yields incriminating evidence and the defendant is at least sufficiently compromised to be indicted. If the officers raid a home, an office, or stop and search an automobile but find nothing incriminating, this invasion of the personal liberty of the innocent too often finds no practical redress. There may be, and I am convinced that there are, many unlawful searches of homes and automobiles of innocent people which turn up nothing incriminating, in which no arrest is made, about which courts do nothing, and about which we never hear.

". . . There is no opportunity for injunction or appeal to disinterested intervention. The citizen's choice is quietly to submit to whatever the officers undertake or to resist at risk of arrest or immediate violence." Brinegar v. United States, 338 U.S. 160, 181-182 (1949) (Mr. Justice Jackson dissenting).

There can be little doubt that actions for money damages would not suffice to repair the injury suffered by the victims of the police searches. Neither the personal assets of policemen nor the nominal bonds they furnish afford genuine hope of redress. Nor is there any provision for compensation from public funds. In any event the wrongs inflicted are not readily measurable in terms of dollars and cents. Indeed, the Supreme Court itself has already declared that the prospect of pecuniary redress for the harm suffered is "worthless and futile." Moreover, the lesson of experience is that the remote possibility of money damages serves as no deterrent to future police invasions.

We are persuaded that the injunction should issue even though the Veney raids have ceased and notwithstanding the Police Commissioner's General Order No. 10388. These raids were not isolated instances undertaken by individual police officers. They were rather the effectuation of a plan conceived by high ranking officials.

The General Order, in reciting no more than that probable cause is required to conduct a search, is in no sense a recognition that the conduct complained of fell short of established legal standards; it adds nothing to the general rule with which the rank-and-file policeman should already have been familiar. It is too vague to provide even a faint warning that searches based only on anonymous tips do not constitute proper police tactics. It would not have been too much to expect in these circumstances a forthright statement that officers conducting such illegal searches in the future will subject themselves to disciplinary action.

The plaintiffs, in their argument in the District Court maintained that the police behavior was racially discriminatory since most of the homes searched were occupied by Negroes. This contention the District Court rejected, reasoning that the police concentrated on Negro residences because the Veneys are Negroes and most of the information received related to their supposed presence in Negro neighborhoods. While this ruling of the District Court is not contested on appeal, we think that it has a substantial bearing on the question of whether injunctive relief is appropriate. The District Judge himself noted that "[t]he evidence does show what has become common knowledge in Baltimore—that the relations between the Negro community and the police have deteriorated seriously." 240 F. Supp. at 556 n. 4.

Baltimore City has escaped thus far the agony and brutality of the riots experienced in New York City, Los Angeles, Chicago, and other urban centers. Courts cannot shut their eyes to events that have been widely publicized throughout the nation and the world. Lack of respect for the police is conceded to be one of the factors generating violent outbursts in Negro communities. The invasions so graphically depicted in this case "could" happen in prosperous suburban neighborhoods, but the innocent victims know only that wholesale raids do not happen elsewhere and did happen to them. Understandably they feel that such illegal treatment is reserved for those elements who the police believe cannot or will not challenge them. It is of the highest importance to community morale that the courts shall give firm and effective reassurance, especially to those who feel that they have been harassed by reason of their color or their poverty.

In ordering the issuance of an injunction we have not blotted from our consideration the serious problems faced by the law enforcement officer in his daily work. His training stresses the techniques of the prevention of crime and the apprehension of criminals, and what seems to him to be the logical and practical means to solve a crime or to arrest a suspect may turn out to be a deprivation of another's constitutional rights. And where one policeman is killed and another wounded, the police, and the public, too, are understandably outraged and impatient with any obstacle in the search for the murderer. While fully appreciating the exceedingly difficult task of the policeman, a court must not be deterred from protecting rights secured to all by the Constitution.

The appellants, however, would have us go further. They urge this court to order an injunction much broader in scope than one limited to prohibiting searches based only on anonymous tips and without probable cause. They contend that the determination of the existence of probable cause should not be left to policemen but should be vested in a judicial officer, and that absent exceptional circumstances the police should be required to obtain a search warrant from a magistrate before entering the private home of a stranger in search of an offender, even when the police have in their possession a warrant for the arrest of the person they are seeking. Appellants point out that the existence of an arrest warrant establishes only that there is probable cause for the arrest of the person named therein, but that it reflects no judgment at all as to where the suspect may be found.

It is settled law, of course, that subject to established exceptions, a search warrant is constitutionally required to enable the police to conduct a search for "things." Agnello v. United States, 269 U.S. 20 (1925). The gravity of the invasion is precisely the same whether the policeman's objective is to search for a person or for an inanimate object, and the resulting injury is not mitigated by the fact that the officer may have a warrant to arrest some person but has not bothered to obtain a warrant from a judicial officer to search specified premises—not the premises of the person named in the arrest warrant. The contention is that the determination of probable cause for searching a particular home for a suspect who does not live there is the function of the magistrate, not the policeman.

Appellants frankly concede that no case explicitly upholds their contention, but they refer us to a few cases which may be construed as supporting their reasoning. See Morrison v. United States, 262 F.2d 449 (1958); District of Columbia v. Little, 178 F.2d 13, 17 (1949), aff'd, 339 U.S. 1 (1950). They criticize as inadequately and incorrectly reasoned the contrary statements in Love v. United States, 170 F.2d 32 (4th Cir. 1948), cert. denied, 336 U.S. 912 (1949).

We have no occasion now to accept or reject the legal theory thus advanced by the appellants or to canvass countervailing arguments. The injunction which we order fully protects them and all similarly circumstanced from future violations of the character described in this record, and we find it unnecessary to consider the advisability of a broader decree.

The case will be remanded for the entry of a decree enjoining the Police Department from conducting a search of any private house to effect the arrest of any person not known to reside therein, whether with or without an arrest warrant, where the belief that the person is on the premises is based only on an anonymous tip and hence without probable cause.

Reversed and remanded.

d. Consent Searches

Obviously where there is free consent to a search by someone with authority to give consent, the search can hardly be called unreasonable. Police frequently rely on consent of the suspect to justify their search, even in some cases where they could obtain a search warrant or make a search incident to arrest. Consent is seen as the cleanest way of making a search, avoiding both the administrative inconvenience of obtaining a search warrant and the commitment to action which is implicit in making an arrest to justify a search incident thereto.

The principal problems in this area are (1) the ascertainment of the facts as to what was said and done by police and what was perceived by the allegedly consenting person, (2) establishing who, other than the offender himself, may consent to a search, and (3) determining as a matter of law and policy how "free" the consent must have been.

One person may admit police and allow the search of another's property. The question then is whether there is in law capacity to give such purported consent.

1

Police went to the apartment house where the suspect resided and asked the landlady to take them to his room. She admitted them to the room with her passkey. The detectives went through the drawers and closet and looked under the bed for a knife which had been used in a homicide.

2

After taking a bank robbery suspect to the station, police returned to his home and asked his wife whether they might look in the suspect's basement workroom for money taken from the bank. She said, "It's all right with me." They searched the basement.

The most difficult question, whether consent of the suspect himself or of another is at issue, is whether the consent was sufficiently free to justify the search in the eyes of the law.

The implication or direct statement by police that they are suspicious of the subject's behavior will frequently bring a spontaneous invitation to make an inspection. Allaying the officers' suspicions prevents further annoyance of continued police investigation.

3

Two officers entered a bar which had in the past been involved in selling numbers. The proprietor was asked if he was "keeping his nose clean." He invited the police to examine the area inside and behind the bar for evidence of gambling.

4

Officers went to an apartment where a person suspected of gambling activity lived. When he answered the door and saw the officers, whom he knew, he said he was "clean." The officers asked to be invited in and they were; they looked around the room and especially at papers around the telephone for indications of gambling.

5

An officer was stationed in a neighborhood which had recently experienced a series of pocketbook snatchings by offenders in their late teens. The officer asked boys who resembled the very general description to show identification, which they did. Two teenagers carrying large paper bags were asked "if they minded" showing the contents. They did not hesitate to do so.

The state of mind of the suspect who has something to hide is often unclear.

6

Two policemen knocked at an apartment door to question the man about a complaint from a former roommate that he had stolen a suit and some bedding. When he answered the door and the police told him why they had come, he denied knowledge of the suit or bedding but seemed very nervous. The police said that if he had nothing to hide he would let them in to look for the stolen goods. He said they could come in and look. They did not find the suit or bedding, but in picking up a pair of pants one officer uncovered a pan of solution containing a negative of a $10 bill.

7

After a suspect in a burglary case had been arrested he was questioned for some time at the police station concerning general criminal activity and possession of burglar tools and clothing that might have been worn during the burglary. Police asked him whether he minded their going to his room to look for a pair of shoes. He said that he had nothing to hide and that they could go there and see for themselves. They did go and seized the shoes, which matched footprints at the scene of the burglary.

8

At 2:30 in the morning two investigators from the district attorney's office accompanied a social worker to the home of a woman receiving welfare assistance for herself and her children. When she answered the door they asked for permission to come in and talk with her. She opened the door wider and they entered. They asked if it was all right if they looked around and she nodded. Looking in the bedroom they found a man sleeping in her bed. The man admitted that he lived there some of the time and helped out with rent and food sometimes.[f]

The problem of consent is sometimes clouded by the officer's entry in plain clothes or upon misrepresenting his identity.

9

Police had heard that a gambling party was to be held in a private home. It had been widely advertised by word of mouth. After the party had been going for a while an ordinary, neatly-dressed police officer in plain clothes knocked on the door, stated that he would like to join the party, and was admitted. After observing gambling going on he signaled to other officers outside, who raided the house.

10

Customs agents suspected that a man was engaged in smuggling Swiss watches into the country. They learned that a mechanic was going to repair the air conditioner in the house and arranged for one of the agents to pose as his helper. The agent entered with the mechanic, carrying a geiger counter to try to detect radiations emitted from the watch dials.

---

[f] *See* Reich, *Midnight Welfare Searches and the Social Security Act*, 72 YALE L.J. 1347 (1963). *Compare* Parrish v. Civil Service Comm'n, 66 Cal. 2d 253, 425 P.2d 223, 228 (1967): "[T]he authorities instructed the searchers to refrain from forcing their way into any home. . . . The record also establishes that welfare recipients must depend to a remarkably high degree upon the continued favor of their social workers, who are vested with wide discretion to authorize or prohibit specific expenditures."

MAXWELL v. STEPHENS

348 F.2d 325 (8th Cir. 1965)

Before MATTHES, BLACKMUN, and RIDGE, Circuit Judges.

BLACKMUN, Circuit Judge. The offense took place at approximately three o'clock in the morning of November 3, 1961. It was raining and wet. The victim was promptly taken by the police to a hospital. At the hospital she described her assailant to Captain Crain of the Hot Springs Police Department and to Officer O. D. Pettus, a Negro. Pettus thereupon suggested that it might have been Maxwell. Officer Childress, who was on car patrol duty and in uniform at the time, was directed by radio to pick up Maxwell. He went to the Maxwell home. The defendant's mother, then age 38, answered his knock. He told her he wanted to talk to William. She let him enter, checked to see if her son was in, and led Childress to the bedroom occupied by Maxwell and two younger sons. Childress told Maxwell he wanted to talk to him down town and asked him to dress.

Maxwell was taken to the hospital and before the victim. She at first did not identify him as her attacker but witnesses described her as visibly disturbed and shaking when he stood before her. She later said she had recognized him but feared for her life if she identified him. Maxwell was taken from the hospital to the police station.

Captain Crain, with Officer Timms, went to the Maxwell home about five a. m. to get, as he testified at the habeas corpus hearing, "some more clothes that we thought might help us in our investigation of this case" or, as he testified at the trial, "I was looking for a particular object . . . I wanted what he was wearing that night". They had no search warrant. Mrs. Maxwell permitted them to enter. They were in uniform. The testimony is in conflict as to whether Mrs. Maxwell was then informed of any charge against her son; Crain said he so advised her but she stated, "He didn't say nothing about no rape case". (The district court found she had been so advised). She directed the officers to the clothes closet. The blue coat in question was obtained from that closet. It was eventually sent to the FBI laboratory. At the trial there was expert testimony that fibers in the coat matched others found on the victim's pajamas and on part of a nylon stocking picked up near the scene of the crime, and that fibers in the pajamas matched those found on the coat.

Mrs. Maxwell was understandably upset at the times the officers called at her home. In the margin we quote her testimony as to both the first call[12] and the second call.[13] Maxwell's father worked at night and was not home when the officers called.

[T]he defense argues that there is a presumption that a consent is coerced unless proved otherwise by the government and that the facts here—the early morning calls at the Maxwell home, the presence of men clothed with the uniform of authority, the confrontation of a Negro mother by white police, and her obvious concern and confusion—"militate against finding voluntary consent".

We recognize that it has been said that the government has the burden to establish the legal sufficiency of a consent. Judd v. United States, 89 U.S.App.D.C. 64, 66, 190 F.2d 649, 651 (D.C.Cir. 1951); United States v. Page, 302 F.2d 81, 83-84 (9 Cir. 1962). Nevertheless, the existence and voluntariness of a consent is a question of fact. And Judge Young specifically found that there was a consent here and that it was voluntary. We cannot say that his finding was either erroneous or unsupported by substantial evidence. The record clearly discloses no concealment of identity, no discourtesy, no abuse or threat, and no ruse or force exerted by the officers. It contains testimony that Mrs. Maxwell showed and directed them to the closet where her son's clothes were. On cross-examination she herself conceded that she permitted the officers to enter and to obtain the coat. She fully cooperated.

RIDGE, Circuit Judge (dissenting). One or two hours thereafter, Capt. Crain and Officer Timms went to the Maxwell home, without a search warrant, and took possession of appellant's "blue coat" under circumstances as related in the majority opinion. The conversation those two police officers then had with appellant's mother does not raise a question of credibility. The only issue presented thereby is whether "consent" as claimed by the State was freely given to those officers to search the Maxwell home, and whether appellant's mother had power

---

12 ". . . [I]t was late and I was asleep and someone knocked on the door and I woke up and I asked who was it and he said the policeman and I went to the door to let him in. He asked me did I have a son here by the name of William and I told him yes and he just come on in, he didn't have a search warrant or anything and I let him. I didn't know any better myself but I—I didn't know that he—you know, everything was all right, my children were at home and all and I just let him in."

13 "I opened the door and I was afraid to not let them in because—you know—when they said they were police officers—well, you just—I've just always—I just let the police officers in because I just feel like he is for peace and all, and I just—I don't know, I didn't know anything—I never been in anything like this and I just let them in and I still didn't think anything, didn't any of those officers have any search warrant or anything, didn't show me anything like that."

of possession to release appellant's personal belongings to the custody of such officers.

I do not consider the conversation appellant's mother had with Capt. Crain and Officer Timms to have any probative value in making a determination of the validity of the search and seizure made by those officers. Mere acquiescence in the apparent authority of a police officer is not usually considered consent. What was then said by appellant's mother "was but showing her respect for and obedience to the law and she was not consenting to the search regardless (of lack of a) search warrant." Stroud v. Commonwealth, 295 Ky. 694, 175 S.W.2d 368, 370, citing Amos v. United States, 255 U.S. 313 (1921). As the majority opinion notes, the validity of arrest and search and seizure here must be determined by reasonableness in light of the particular circumstances revealed. I consider the factual circumstances in the case at bar reveal "implied coercion."

UNITED STATES v. BLALOCK

255 F. Supp. 268 (E.D. Pa. 1966)

Joseph S. Lord, III, District Judge. This is a motion to suppress twenty-one twenty dollar bills seized by the F.B.I. in a search of defendant's hotel room in Miami, Florida.

Defendant was suspected of robbing the Parke Towne Branch of the Broad Street Trust Company. The bank had kept in its cash drawers "bait money", the serial numbers of which had previously been recorded. On the night of July 24, 1965, three agents of the F.B.I. encountered defendant as he entered his hotel lobby. They had no search warrant. After identifying themselves and after some preliminary questioning, defendant, accompanied by an agent, went to the men's room where he was frisked. The defendant and the agents then proceeded to his room. Defendant opened the door of the room and the party entered. One of the agents questioned defendant about the Philadelphia robbery, but defendant denied any knowledge of the crime. One of the agents then asked defendant whether, since he was not involved in the robbery, he would mind if they searched his room. Defendant replied that he had no objection. It was during the search which then ensued that the money was found.

Generally speaking, a warrantless search and seizure is regarded as unreasonable and violative of the Fourth Amendment. In order to overcome the prima facie unconstitutionality of the search here involved, the Government relies solely on the asserted consent of the defendant to the search, in other words, a waiver by defendant of his Fourth Amendment right. However, rights given by the Constitution are too fundamental and too precious for waiver lightly to be found. It is apparent that where consent is relied upon to validate a warrantless search, the Government must prove that the consent was (a) intelligent and (b) voluntary.

First, the consent must have been "intelligent." Obviously, the requirement of an "intelligent" consent implies that the subject of the search must have been aware of his rights, for an intelligent consent can only embrace the waiver of a "known right." Johnson v. Zerbst, 304 U.S. 458 (1938); United States ex rel. Mancini v. Rundle, 337 F.2d 268 (C.A.3, 1964). Certainly, one cannot *intelligently* surrender that which he does not know he has. The agents here properly warned defendant of his right to counsel and his right to remain silent, but they did not warn him of his right to refuse a warrantless search. The Fourth Amendment requires no less knowing a waiver than do the Fifth and Sixth. The requirement of knowledge in each serves the same purpose, i.e., to prevent the possibility that the ignorant may surrender their rights more readily than the shrewd. Conceivably, the assent of the defendant may have been "the false bravado of the small-time criminal"; or it may have been an untutored submission to authority. Which it was could have been resolved by the officers at the scene. To require law enforcement agents to advise the subjects of investigation of their right to insist on a search warrant would impose no great burden, nor would it unduly or unnecessarily impede criminal investigation. Here, the evidence shows no such warning, nor is there any other evidence that Blalock was aware of his Fourth Amendment right. It cannot be said, then, that the Government has sustained its burden of showing that there was an intelligent waiver of a known right. This being so, we need not consider whether the consent was voluntary.[g]

Defendant's motion to suppress will be granted. It is so ordered.

PEOPLE v. GAGLIANO

Crim. No. 63-3670, Cir. Ct. Cook County, Ill. (1963)

Ruling on Motion to Suppress Evidence.

At noon on December 9, 1963, OFFICER BRANDT together with several other police officers, including SERGEANT DOJUTREK,

[g] Authority on the need for warning of a right not to allow search is divided. *Compare* United States v. Nikrasch, 367 F.2d 740 (7th Cir. 1966), *with* Gorman v. United States, 380 F.2d 158 (1st Cir. 1967).

The FBI's use of a written consent to search is illustrated in United States v. Wallace, 272 F. Supp. 841, 845 (S.D.N.Y. 1967).

arrested CARDI at MOON'S Restaurant. . . . Officer BRANDT took CARDI into the back room of the restaurant, told him he was under arrest; told him to take off his coat and asked him to empty his pockets. CARDI took out a wallet and keys. Officer BRANDT asked CARDI where his car was parked. CARDI told him and Officer BRANDT gave the keys to Officer KING who approached the dark blue Chevrolet parked behind a place across the street . . . entered it with Officer OHANION and drove to . . . the CARDI residence. Officer OHANION wore old green pants and a jacket and a cap. Officer OHANION rang CARDI'S bell on the first floor and a woman came down a few steps and opened the door and identified herself as Mrs. RENE CARDI. Officer OHANION said, "Willie and Dick were just picked up and I was sent here to pick up the books." She asked him, "Do you want all the books?" He said, "Yes." He told her he was to get the books out of the house, that maybe the State's Attorney would come with a search warrant. She testified further that she put her head out the door because she wanted to make sure that, ". . . that was our car. So I checked the license plate number."

No evidence was adduced that, at the time of his arrest without a warrant, CARDI was engaged in the commission of a crime or had committed a crime, or that the arresting officers had reasonable grounds to believe that a warrant for CARDI'S arrest had been issued in this State or in another jurisdiction.

The Issue.

Can police, however, obtain by deceit or trickery, that which they cannot obtain by a lawful arrest, by a search warrant or by the subpoena process?

Perhaps their ingenuity and guile are to be commended. Their purpose was a high one. Their alacrity in carrying out their assignment is certainly to be respected. But are the methods employed here, regardless of the objective, to be permitted? If so, we point the way to circumvent the Fourth and Fifth Amendments and we supplant all warrants and subpoenas with cunning, deceit and trickery. True, these are the recognized tools of the policeman who acts as an undercover agent. The undercover agent first wins the confidence of the defendant or prospective defendant and then learns from the unsuspecting defendant the evidence, or leads to evidence, which will convict him. The undercover agent does not first arrest the defendant—take his property without a shred of lawful authority and then by deceit and guile lead the defendant's wife to give demonstrative evidence against him! Was CARDI's wife beguiled or deluded by Officer OHANION—or, as he put it, "tricked," or was she *coerced* by his statement that Willie and Dick had just been picked up and that the State's Attorney's police were on their way with a search warrant?

Clearly if OHANION had crossed the threshold of CARDI'S residence—there is some dispute as to whether OHANION waited in the private hallway just outside CARDI'S living room or whether he stepped into the living room—his "invasion" of the CARDI home would bring into play the condemnation of an unlawful "search" enunciated in Catalanotte v. United States, 208 F.2d 264, 268, and Nelson v. United States, 208 F.2d 505, where tacit consent to entry was claimed by the prosecution.

The State as well as the petitioner seem immersed in the concept that what is in issue is a "search" or "seizure" or both. . . . What took place, however, was a combination of coercion and fraud. The arrest of RENE CARDI's husband and the use of the CARDI automobile coupled with the threat of the imminent search by State's Attorney's police had the effect of causing Mrs. CARDI to give evidence against her husband without permitting her to "use her rational intellect and a free will." (See Lynumn v. State of Illinois, 372 U.S. 528 (1963).)

It seems to this Court that the Fourteenth Amendment fundamental concept of fairness has been violated.

All items specified in CARDI's motion are hereby suppressed and, except the blackjack, shall be returned to him.

LEWIS v. UNITED STATES
385 U.S. 206 (1966)

MR. CHIEF JUSTICE WARREN delivered the opinion of the Court.

On December 3, 1964, Edward Cass, an undercover federal narcotics agent, telephoned petitioner's home to inquire about the possibility of purchasing marihuana. Cass, who previously had not met or dealt with petitioner, falsely identified himself as one "Jimmy the Pollack [*sic*]" and stated that a mutual friend had told him petitioner might be able to supply marihuana. In response, petitioner said, "Yes. I believe, Jimmy, I can take care of you," and then directed Cass to his home where, it was indicated, a sale of marihuana would occur. Cass drove to petitioner's home, knocked on the door, identified himself as "Jim," and was admitted. After discussing the possibility of regular future dealings at a discounted price, petitioner led Cass to a package located on the front porch of his home. Cass gave petitioner $50, took the package, and left the premises. The package contained five bags of marihuana. On December 17, 1964, a similar transaction took place, beginning with a phone conversation in which Cass identified himself as "Jimmy the Pollack" and ending with an invited visit by Cass to petitioner's home where a second sale of marihuana occurred. Once again, Cass paid petitioner $50, but this time he received in return a package containing six bags of marihuana.

Petitioner was arrested on April 27, 1965, and charged by a two-count indictment with violations of the narcotics laws relating to transfers of marihuana.

Petitioner does not argue that he was entrapped, as he could not on the facts of this case; nor does he contend that a search of his home was made or that anything other than the purchased narcotics was taken away. His only contentions are that, in the absence of a warrant, any official intrusion upon the privacy of a home constitutes a Fourth Amendment violation and that the fact the suspect invited the intrusion cannot be held a waiver when the invitation was induced by fraud and deception.

Both petitioner and the Government recognize the necessity for some undercover police activity and both concede that the particular circumstances of each case govern the admissibility of evidence obtained by stratagem or deception. Indeed, it has long been acknowledged by the decisions of this Court, that, in the detection of many types of crime, the Government is entitled to use decoys and to conceal the identity of its agents. The various protections of the Bill of Rights, of course, provide checks upon such official deception for the protection of the individual. See, *e.g.*, Massiah v. United States, 377 U.S. 201 (1964); Trupiano v. United States, 334 U.S. 699 (1948).

Petitioner argues that the Government overstepped the constitutional bounds in this case and places principal reliance on Gouled v. United States, 255 U.S. 298 (1921). But a short statement of that case will demonstrate how misplaced his reliance is. There, a business acquaintance of the petitioner, acting under orders of federal officers, obtained entry into the petitioner's office by falsely representing that he intended only to pay a social visit. In the petitioner's absence, however, the intruder secretly ransacked the office and seized certain private papers of an incriminating nature. This Court had no difficulty concluding that the Fourth Amendment had been violated by the secret and general ransacking, notwithstanding that the initial intrusion was occasioned by a fraudulently obtained invitation rather than by force or stealth.

In the instant case, on the other hand, the petitioner invited the undercover agent to his home for the specific purpose of executing a felonious sale of narcotics. Petitioner's only concern was whether the agent was a willing purchaser who could pay the agreed price. Indeed, in order to convince the agent that his patronage at petitioner's home was desired, petitioner told him that, if he became a regular customer there, he would in the future receive an extra bag of marihuana at no additional cost; and in fact petitioner did hand over an extra bag at a second sale which was consummated at the same place and in precisely the same manner. During neither of his visits to petitioner's home did the agent see, hear, or take anything that was not contemplated, and in fact intended, by petitioner as a necessary part of his illegal business. Were we to hold the deceptions of the agent in this case constitutionally prohibited, we would come near to a rule that the use of undercover agents in any manner is virtually unconstitutional *per se.* Such a rule would, for example, severely hamper the Government in ferreting out those organized criminal activities that are characterized by covert dealings with victims who either cannot or do not protest. A prime example is provided by the narcotics traffic.

The fact that the undercover agent entered petitioner's home does not compel a different conclusion. Without question, the home is accorded the full range of Fourth Amendment protections. But when, as here, the home is converted into a commercial center to which outsiders are invited for purposes of transacting unlawful business, that business is entitled to no greater sanctity than if it were carried on in a store, a garage, a car, or on the street. A government agent, in the same manner as a private person, may accept an invitation to do business and may enter upon the premises for the very purposes contemplated by the occupant. Affirmed.

[JUSTICES BRENNAN and FORTAS concurred; JUSTICE DOUGLAS dissented.]

e. Regulatory Searches or Inspections

Persons who choose to engage in certain activities thereby open themselves to search upon grounds short of probable cause. Common carriers, automobile dealers, and premises licensed for the sale of liquor are examples of places subject to routine inspection without further cause because of special governmental concern with regulating their businesses. In order to prevent smuggling, persons entering the country are subject to "border search," with the intensity varying with the grounds for suspicion. Parolees may be subjected to greater limitations than ordinary citizens. Premises where there has been a fire may be entered and examined by fire marshals.

Area inspections under zoning or fire regulations were held "searches" requiring consent or warrants in *Camara v. Municipal Court* (*see* p. 204, *supra*). It is uncertain whether inspection of licensed premises will be treated differently; the Supreme Court expressly reserved judgment on this issue.

The Practice

Some of the kinds of regulatory searches or inspections are suggested by the following:

1

Police assigned the duty of inspecting bars entered a tavern which had earlier been involved in writing numbers. After identifying themselves the plainclothesmen made a complete search of the premises. They found, in a compartment behind the bar, a blank pad with suspicious impressions on the top sheets. On the floor in front of the bar a numbers slip was found. The owner and bartender denied any knowledge of gambling. The police made no arrests but warned that they would be back often.[h]

2

Upon receiving a tip that one of his probationers had a gun, a probation officer set out to look for him. When he saw the probationer sitting in his car, the probation officer told him to step out, frisked him, and then searched the car. No gun was found.

RIVAS v. UNITED STATES
368 F.2d 703 (9th Cir. 1966)

BARNES, Circuit Judge. This was a border search. Border searches are unique.

Mere suspicion is enough—probable cause is not required.[3]

---

[h] United States v. Duffy, 282 F. Supp. 777 (S.D.N.Y. 1968) (adopting the view that the *Camara* case does not require a warrant where inspection of licensed premises is authorized by law).

[3] "In conferring upon Customs officers such broad authority, circumscribed only by Constitutional limitations of the Fourth Amendment, the

While it may well shock the average citizen to learn of the common use today of body cavities to smuggle narcotic drugs into the United States, those facing the task of policing our borders are fully familiar with the practical consequence of the failure to make searches of such cavities.

Appellant urges "there must be a clear indication of the possession of narcotics" before a search at a border may be made, using the language of the Supreme Court in Schmerber v. State of California, 384 U.S. 757 (1966). We agree. While we know of no accepted meaning of that term in law or as a word of art, it can be readily defined.

"Indication" is defined as "an indicating; suggestion." "Clear" is defined as "free from doubt"; "free from limitation"; "plain." An honest "plain indication" that a search involving an intrusion beyond the body's surface is justified cannot rest on the *mere chance* that desired evidence may be obtained. Thus we need not hold the search of any body cavity is justified merely because it is a border search, and nothing more. There must exist facts creating a clear indication or plain suggestion, of the smuggling. Nor need those facts reach the dignity of nor be the equivalent of "probable cause" necessary for an arrest and search at a place other than a border.

Thus, drawing the line between the two poles of proof raises a present problem. The uncertainty of what constitutes a "clear indication" over and beyond a "mere suspicion" is difficult, but not impossible to resolve.

We believe a previously convicted and registered user of narcotics (18 U.S.C. § 1407), coming across the border under the influence of narcotics, as readily shown by his eyes, disclosing thirty "recent" needle marks on one arm, and "recent" needle marks on the other, who acts "in an extremely nervous manner," may be searched, as one reasonably portraying a "clear indication" he may be smuggling contraband.

We then reach the question: How much of a search is permissible?

In determining this, we are required as a fact of life to recognize that many people crossing the border, desiring to smuggle

---

Congress has in effect declared that a search which would be 'unreasonable' within the meaning of the Fourth Amendment, if conducted by police officers in the ordinary case, would be a reasonable search if conducted by Customs officials in lawful pursuit of unlawful imports. Judicial recognition of this distinction has given rise to the term 'border search', in order to distinguish official searches which are reasonable because made solely in the enforcement of Customs laws from other official searches made in connection with general law enforcement. . . ." Alexander v. United States, 362 F.2d 379, 381-82 (9th Cir. 1966).

goods, and more particularly narcotics, do, and unless stopped, will continue to utilize body cavities, including any of an adequate size that will make such smuggling economically profitable.

Must the United States stand idly by, and permit this? Or should the extent of border searches be governed by the practical knowledge of the extent to which smugglers are willing to degrade their bodies in order to obtain the drugs they crave or the money they desire?

Certainly *Schmerber* suggested in determining what constitutes a "clear indication" that will justify a border search of body cavities that the decision had better be left to "a neutral and detached magistrate instead of being judged by an officer engaged in the often competitive enterprise of ferreting out crime." *Schmerber,* supra at 770, citing Johnson v. United States, 333 U.S. 10, 13-14 (1948).

But as in *Schmerber,* supra, (where the condition of drunkenness was fast fading away) some action had to be taken. Appellant could not be unnecessarily detained without arrest. He was committing no federal crime in being under the influence of narcotics; he had made his required report as a returning addict. With this in mind, were the border officers required to let him pass, and thus allow the possible entry of contraband into the United States? We think not.

The judgment of conviction on each count is affirmed.[1]

f. Exceptional Circumstances

Police are sometimes confronted with a situation in which it appears to them that to aid someone in distress or preserve property against loss or damage they must make an entry. When there is no explicit consent, police may assume that consent would be given if there were opportunity to communicate with the appropriate person, or they may—quite understandably—fail in an urgent rescue situation to consider the question of technical propriety at all. When the danger to a person in distress has come from criminal conduct, the motivation of the officer is likely to be a mixture of giving help and obtaining evidence of criminality.

---

[1] *Compare* Henderson v. United States, 390 F.2d 805 (9th Cir. 1967), holding unconstitutional a border search based on "mere suspicion." Comment, *Border Searches and the Fourth Amendment,* 77 YALE L.J. 1007 (1968); Comment, *At the Border of Reasonableness: Searches by Customs Officials,* 53 CORNELL L. REV. 871 (1968).

1

A man had reported his car stolen. When police located it they opened the unlocked car door and examined the interior. They found a gun under the floor mat and some stolen property. Further investigation established that the owner of the car was himself also a thief, that he owned the gun and had stolen the property found in the car.

2

Two patrolmen heard screams coming from a rooming house at 2:00 a.m. There was only one lighted window and they went to that room and knocked. A man asked who was knocking and they answered, "The police." After some minutes a woman opened the door and the officers entered. She responded to their questions by saying she knew of no screams, but that she might have been having a nightmare. The officers then heard a toilet flush, and a man came out of the bathroom. The officers then went into the bathroom and saw currency floating in the toilet. They retrieved the bills and found them to be counterfeit.

3

Police received an anonymous telephone call that there was "trouble" at a particular address. When officers arrived they knocked but received no answer. They looked through the window and, though it was dark, could see someone lying on the floor. They forced entrance and found a dead woman. In looking through the house they found a bloodstained knife with fingerprints on it.

4

Police saw a truck parked near an intersection without lights and with its left wheels over on the paved road. It appeared in danger of being run into. They stopped to investigate. Opening the door and looking under the seat, they found money and lottery slips.

PEOPLE v. GALLMON

19 N.Y.2d 389, 227 N.E.2d 284 (1967)

BREITEL, Judge. The issue is whether the arrest of the defendant was unlawful because in violation of section 178 of the Code of Criminal Procedure.

The statute in question (Code Crim. Proc., § 178) provides: "To make an arrest, as provided in the last section, the officer may break open an outer or inner door or window of a building, if, after notice of his office and purpose, he be refused admittance."

The undisputed evidence establishes that the police officer on radio patrol duty received a "radio run" to the effect that there was a "disorderly man at 404 West 115th Street." He proceeded to a rooming (converted apartment) house at this address where he was met by the night manager. The officer heard "shouting, screaming, clapping of hands" and the manager stated "that that had been going on for several evenings."

The manager then directed the police officer and a fellow officer to a fifth floor "apartment," evidently a division of the converted apartment house. The noise was coming from this apartment. As the officer knocked on the door, the shouting stopped, and a male voice inside said three times: "Wait a minute. Wait a minute, I'm not dressed." After a minute's wait, the officer directed the manager to open the door with his passkey. Upon opening the door they saw defendant standing in the middle of the room, stripped to the waist, and wet with perspiration. He was holding "a syringe, an eye dropper, with a needle on the end of it, in his right hand." When defendant saw the three men, he threw the contraband under a bed and the officer placed him under arrest.

Defendant contends that there was no probable cause to make an arrest and that the evidence was seized as a result of an entrance in violation of the quoted statute and, therefore, should have been suppressed.

The statute is not applicable. The officer did not come to the premises or to the apartment to make an arrest. He had responded to a call from the manager of a rooming house to investigate an unusual, noisy disturbance. What was the cause of the disturbance and what action would be required upon ascertaining the cause was not determinable in advance by the police or the manager. The inquiry might result in no action, in succor for a person or persons in distress with or without criminal causation, in a direction to quiet down, or in a criminal arrest (2 Alexander, Law of Arrest, § 637). The presence of the police and the entrance into the apartment was investigatory and not for the purpose of making an arrest to which the application of section 178 is limited. Apart from the statute, a peace officer was under no duty, by statute or under the common law, to give notice of his office or purpose prior to making an entry into private premises unless the purpose was to make an arrest or to execute other process. (Miller v. United States, 357 U.S. 301, 305-310).

Of course, no person may forcibly enter private premises without a privilege to do so. And it is reasonable that the privilege requires a stronger basis where the purpose of the entry is not to make an arrest or execute process. This is the difficult part of the case, although the issue was tendered only on the theory that the entrance violated the arrest statute.

It is critically significant that a rooming house is involved rather than demised premises to which the tenant is entitled to exclusive and undisturbed possession. Rooming houses and inns are equivalent for purposes of determining the legality of entry by the landlord or his agents. In the leading case of de Wolf v. Ford (193 N.Y. 397, 86 N.E. 527, 21 L.R.A.,N.S., 864) the general rule was expressed as follows: "If the guest is assigned to a room upon the express or implied understanding that he is to be the sole occupant thereof during the time that it is set apart for his use, the innkeeper retains a right of access thereto only at such proper times and for such reasonable purposes as may be necessary in the general conduct of the inn or in attending to the needs of the particular guest. If, for instance, there should be an outbreak of fire, a leakage of water or gas, or any other emergency calling for immediate action in a room assigned to a guest, the innkeeper and his servants must necessarily have the right to enter without regard to the time of day or night, and without consulting the wish or convenience of the guest." (193 N.Y., p. 403, 86 N.E., p. 530.)

This license to the landlord, of course, does not afford the police an unqualified privilege to engage in otherwise unlawful practices merely on the consent of the hotel proprietor. (Stoner v. State of California, 376 U.S. 483). Here, however, the manager was not acting as the cat's paw of the police; rather, he had made a call for assistance to which the officers had responded. As such, they were acting in aid of the manager in performance of his duty to the occupants of the building including defendant. There is no evidence that he or they knew what was occurring in the room. Indeed, the officers were called to find out.

Perhaps it is of the greatest significance to this case that the police officer's entry was pursuant to his general obligation to assist people in distress—a purpose often independent of considerations affecting the criminal law. Police are expected and often required to investigate the unquelled crying of babies, sounds and blows in what turn out to be matrimonial disputes, to assist in child deliveries, and to resolve the causes of unusual sounds suggesting harm to persons, animals and property. Their functions are just not confined to criminal law enforcement, a matter frequently of great concern to those seeking to make limited police resources more effective. In this context it has been suggested that an officer's entry is based neither on consent nor license and that even the refusal of consent may be of no avail (cf. Meiers v. Fred Koch Brewery, 229 N.Y. 10, 12, 15, 127 N.E. 491, 492, 13 A.L.R. 633; Beedenbender v. Midtown Props., 4 A.D.2d 276, 281, 164 N.Y.S.2d 276, 280; 2 Alexander, Law of Arrest, § 634).

Accordingly, the judgment of the Appellate Term should be affirmed.

FULD, Chief Judge (dissenting). It is both realistic and proper to regard policemen, who are duty bound to respond to such a call, as having received the implied consent of the occupant to enter the premises in order to render aid. If, in the course of such humanitarian work, undertaken for good reason and in good faith, evidence of crime should be uncovered, it would undoubtedly be admissible in a subsequent prosecution. However, in the case before us, the record does not disclose any basis for a claim—and the People have never made any such claim—that the police entered the defendant's room in the belief that he was ill or otherwise in need of assistance. On the contrary, the fact that the defendant responded to the knock on the door with his "Wait a minute. I'm not dressed" thoroughly negates the idea that he was in distress.

I would sum up my views in this way. If the police had probable cause to arrest the defendant for disorderly conduct, their entry into the defendant's room was illegal because it was not preceded by "notice of [their] office and purpose." (Code Crim. Proc., § 178; see Miller v. United States, 357 U.S. 301, supra.) If, on the other hand, the police did not go into the defendant's room for the purpose of arresting him, their entry was unauthorized and contravened the Fourth Amendment.

3. *Control of Search Practices by the Exclusionary Rule*

One cannot adequately discuss the problem of search and seizure without including reference to the consequences which flow from concluding that the search or seizure was unconstitutional. The most obvious is that the police officer who has acted illegally may be liable for damages in tort or under statutory provision.[j] But the inadequacy of the existing tort and statutory

---

[j] "The common law provides actions for damages against the searching officer; against one who procures the issuance of a warrant maliciously and without probable cause; against a magistrate who has acted without jurisdiction in issuing a warrant; and against persons assisting in the execution

remedies is obvious. Other remedies, such as criminal prosecution, departmental discipline, and injunction, are likewise inadequate. As a consequence the courts have felt compelled to use another sanction which is within their power—the exclusion from use at trial of evidence obtained through the improper search and seizure.

The exclusionary rule is the vehicle through which the issue of illegal search[k] is nearly always raised, and, since a search incident to an unreasonable arrest is in turn unreasonable, the exclusionary rule serves also to raise the issue of illegal arrest. It is not unfair to say that so far as appellate case law is concerned, arrest law has come to be a subheading of search law,

---

of an illegal search. One may also without liability use force to resist an unlawful search.

"Statutory sanctions in the main provide for the punishment of one maliciously procuring a search warrant or willfully exceeding his authority in exercising it. Some statutes more broadly penalize unlawful searches. Virginia also makes punishable one who issues a general search warrant or a warrant unsupported by affidavit. A few States have provided statutory civil remedies. And in one State, misuse of a search warrant may be an abuse of process punishable as contempt of court." Wolf v. Colorado, 338 U.S. 25, 30 n.1, 31 n.2 (1949).

[k] The phrase "illegal search" is the one ordinarily used, but more precisely we ought to speak of "unconstitutional search" or "unreasonable search." A search may be illegal, yet reasonable and constitutional, if it violates some technical rule of law. For example, in United States v. Scolnick, 392 F.2d 320 (3d Cir. 1968), police searched a safe deposit box with a warrant issued upon a showing of probable cause without complying with a state law that required 48-hour notice to the holder of the box (to permit him to show cause why the box ought not be opened). The court held the evidence found in the box admissible. On the other hand, in dissenting, Judge Freedman urged:

> This is a federal trial, subject to our supervisory power over the administration of criminal justice and in my view a federal court should not permit the receipt in evidence of the fruits of a search of a safe deposit box effected by Philadelphia police officers in violation of the Pennsylvania statute.
>
> The decisions in Elkins v. United States, 364 U.S. 206 (1960) and Rios v. United States, 364 U.S. 253 (1960) could readily form the basis of elaborate discussion. I think it is enough simply to record my view that they are not decisive of the present question but leave it open for decision whether as a matter of policy the evidence should be excluded. I read them as dealing with state determinations whether the searches there involved were constitutionally invalid and not as decisive of the question of policy which we have before us.
>
> I see no reason why the policy of the state that there should be a special procedure for the protection of the privacy of safe deposit boxes should not be respected, especially by state officers, sworn to uphold the state's laws. To allow them to violate the statute and produce to a federal prosecutor the information thus obtained for use in a federal trial is to lend federal encouragement to the violation by state officers of the laws which control their conduct. It constitutes the unspoken expression by federal agencies of approval of the illegal acts of state officers, and its only foundation can be an acceptance of the view that the end justifies the means.

which is in turn essentially a matter of constitutional evidence rules. This means that arrest issues are raised almost exclusively when a search has been made, and that both arrest and search issues are raised almost exclusively when police and prosecutor seek to use seized evidence at trial.[l] As a consequence, reading appellate cases alone gives one a distorted view of the law enforcement practices.[m]

---

[l] The rule excludes not only things obtained in an unconstitutional search, but also the "fruit of the poisonous tree"—evidence discovered through exploitation of the illegally seized objects. The use which has been made of this "derivative evidence rule" is summarized in Pitler, *"The Fruit of the Poisonous Tree" Revisited and Shepardized,* 56 CALIF. L. REV. 579 (1968).

[m] Appellate cases suggest that there was little problem with police search practices until the Prohibition era. What seems more likely, however, is that anxiety about police encroachment upon the rights of citizens merely became acute during that time. Many people who had not previously broken the law suddenly began to fear a search, and this new-found concern rather quickly came to be reflected in court opinions. Though police practices may not have changed substantially, public attitude toward them did. To illustrate the pattern, in Wisconsin in 1903 and 1905 cases unsuccessfully urged that clothing seized from a rape suspect should be excluded from evidence. There were no other search and seizure cases until the early 1920's, when the flood of liquor cases began. Over one hundred appeals since that time have involved search issues.

The Supreme Court first clearly set out the exclusionary rule as binding on federal courts in Weeks v. United States, 232 U.S. 383 (1914). In Wolf v. Colorado, 338 U.S. 25 (1949), the Court first had to decide whether the exclusionary rule was obligatory upon the states through the fourteenth amendment. It held that state as well as federal officers were forbidden to make unreasonable searches and seizures, but that the particular sanction used in the federal system was not constitutionally required of the states. The states were divided—some voluntarily following the federal pattern, others adhering to the view stated by Justice Cardozo in People v. Defore, 242 N.Y. 13, 150 N.E. 585, 587, 588, 589 (1926):

> [In adoption by the Supreme Court of the exclusionary rule] there has been no blinking the consequences. The criminal is to go free because the constable blundered. . . . The privacy of the home has been infringed, and the murderer goes free. Another search, once more against the law, discloses counterfeit money or the implements of forgery. The absence of a warrant means the freedom of the forger. Like instances can be multiplied. We may not subject society to these dangers until the Legislature has spoken with a clearer voice. . . . No doubt the protection of the statute would be greater from the point of view of the individual whose privacy had been invaded if the government were required to ignore what it had learned through the invasion. The question is whether protection for the individual would not be gained at a disproportionate loss of protection for society. On the one side is the social need that crime shall be repressed. On the other, the social need that law shall not be flouted by the insolence of office. There are dangers in any choice.

In People v. Cahan, 44 Cal. 2d 434, 282 P.2d 905 (1955), the California Supreme Court shifted its position in a significant decision. Justice Traynor, writing for the majority, concluded:

> Finally it has been pointed out that there is no convincing evidence that the exclusionary rule actually tends to prevent unreason-

For the exclusionary rule to be effective in achieving its objective it would have to deter police arrests and searches forbidden by the Constitution. It was obviously adopted on the assumption that it would achieve that objective, since otherwise the Court would have been unwilling to accept the inevitable cost to the system of freeing some guilty persons.[n] But the

---

able searches and seizures (see Comment, 47 Nw.L.Rev. 493, 497; *cf.* Allen, *The Wolf Case,* 45 Ill.L.Rev. 1, 20; 42 Cal.L.Rev. 120) and that the "disciplinary or educational effect of the court's releasing the defendant for police misbehavior is so indirect as to be no more than a mild deterrent at best." (Jackson, J., in Irvine v. California, 347 U.S. 128, at pp. 136-137.)

Despite the persuasive force of the foregoing arguments, we have concluded, as Justice Carter and Justice Schauer have consistently maintained, that evidence obtained in violation of the constitutional guarantees is inadmissible. We have been compelled to reach that conclusion because other remedies have completely failed to secure compliance with the constitutional provisions on the part of police officers with the attendant result that the courts under the old rule have been constantly required to participate in, and in effect condone, the lawless activities of law enforcement officers.

Justice Spence, dissenting, stated:

In my opinion, the cost of the adoption of the exclusionary rule is manifestly too great. It would be far better for this state to adhere to the nonexclusionary rule, and to reexamine its laws concerning the sanctions to be placed upon illegal searches and seizures. If the present laws are deemed inadequate to discourage illegal practices by enforcement officers, the Legislature might well consider the imposition of civil liability for such conduct upon the governmental unit employing the offending officer, in addition to the liability now imposed upon the officer himself. It might also consider fixing a minimum amount to be recovered as damages in the same manner that a minimum has been fixed for the invasion of other civil rights. (Civ. Code, § 52.) These methods would be far more effective in discouraging illegal activities on the part of enforcement officers and such methods would not be subject to the objection, inherent in the adoption of the exclusionary rule, that "It deprives society of its remedy against one lawbreaker because he has been pursued by another." (Irvine v. California, *supra,* 347 U.S. 128, 136.)

In 1961 the United States Supreme Court, referring specially to the conclusion of California that other remedies were in practice simply inadequate to protect basic constitutional rights, ruled that "all evidence obtained by searches and seizures in violation of the Constitution is, by that same authority, inadmissible in a state court." Mapp v. Ohio, 367 U.S. 643 (1961). Four of the justices reasoned that the constitutionally guaranteed right of privacy, which the Court had earlier found in the fourteenth as well as the fourth amendment, carried with it a demand for an effective sanction. In the absence of alternatives, they found the exclusionary rule "an essential part of the right to privacy." Another justice concluded that the fifth amendment, when read together with the fourth, required the exclusionary rule. Though they disagreed as to the rationale, a majority of the Court agreed that the fourteenth amendment forbade the states' using unconstitutionally seized evidence in criminal trials.

[n] A succinct statement favorable to the various exclusionary rules is Schwartz, *Excluding Evidence Illegally Obtained: American Idiosyncrasy and Rational Response to Social Conditions,* 29 Modern L. Rev. 635 (1966).

degree to which police are induced to conform by the exclusionary rule is uncertain. E. PUTTKAMMER, ADMINISTRATION OF CRIMINAL LAW 85-86 (1953), said, before the *Mapp* case:

> One concluding point needs to be made as to the choice between the federal and the state rules. The arguments made are all abstract, in the sense that they do not ask the most important question of all: How do the two rules work? Does the federal rule, tying officers' hands as it certainly does, constitute an absolutely necessary restraint on the police? In states following the state rule is there far more unreasonable searching? The adoption of the federal rule certainly has meant that we have sacrificed a very definite and provable social advantage in regard to law enforcement. Is there in fact a corresponding gain? Perhaps, and perhaps not. But this is the kind of evaluation that must be made before we can jump to any conclusion one way or the other.

Mr. Justice Stewart in Elkins v. United States, 364 U.S. 206, 218-19 (1960), said:

> Empirical statistics are not available to show that the inhabitants of states which follow the exclusionary rule suffer less from lawless searches and seizures than do those of states which admit evidence unlawfully obtained. Since as a practical matter it is never easy to prove a negative, it is hardly likely that conclusive factual data could ever be assembled. For much the same reason, it cannot positively be demonstrated that enforcement of the criminal law is either more or less effective under either rule.
>
> But pragmatic evidence of a sort is not wanting. The federal courts themselves have operated under the exclusionary rule of *Weeks* for almost half a century; yet it has not been suggested either that the Federal Bureau of Investigation has thereby been rendered ineffective, or that the administration of criminal justice in the federal courts has thereby been disrupted.[8]

---

[8] The Director of the Federal Bureau of Investigation has written as follows: "Civil rights violations are all the more regrettable because they are so unnecessary. Professional standards in law enforcement provide for fighting crime with intelligence rather than force. . . . In matters of scientific crime detection, the services of our FBI Laboratory are available to every duly constituted law enforcement officer in the nation. Full use of these and other facilities should make it entirely unnecessary for any officer to feel the need to use dishonorable methods. . . ." FBI Law Enforcement Bulletin, September, 1952, pp. 1-2.

THE FBI STORY 339-40, note 2 (1956)†
By Don Whitehead

The FBI conducts two types of security investigations—one to uncover admissible evidence to be used in the prosecution of an individual or group in federal court, the other for intelligence purposes only. The intelligence investigation is intended to identify and determine the activities of individuals who are potentially dangerous to the nation's security, thereby supplying information on which to base preventive or counterespionage action. Often clandestine methods are necessary to uncover clandestine operations, as for example, obtaining an espionage agent's diary or secret papers. The evidence in the diary may be inadmissible in federal court, but it may contain information which would enable the United States to protect itself at a later date. This is in contrast to a case where legal evidence, admissible in court, has to be obtained to convict the espionage agent of violating the laws of the United States.

TERRY v. OHIO
392 U.S. 1 (1968)

[Another portion of the opinion appears at 163, *supra*.]

MR. CHIEF JUSTICE WARREN delivered the opinion of the Court.

The State has characterized the issue here as "the right of a police officer . . . to make an on-the-street stop, interrogate and pat down for weapons (known in the street vernacular as 'stop and frisk')." But this is only partly accurate. For the issue is not the abstract propriety of the police conduct, but the admissibility against petitioner of the evidence uncovered by the search and seizure. Ever since its inception, the rule excluding evidence seized in violation of the Fourth Amendment has been recognized as a principal mode of discouraging lawless police conduct. Thus its major thrust is a deterrent one, and experience has taught that it is the only effective deterrent to police misconduct in the criminal context, and that without it the constitutional guarantee against unreasonable searches and seizures would be a mere 'form of words." Mapp v. Ohio, 367 U.S. 643, 655 (1961). The rule also serves another vital function—"the imperative of judicial integrity." Elkins v. United States, 364 U.S. 206, 222 (1960). Courts which sit under our Constitution cannot and will not be made party to lawless invasions of the constitutional rights of citizens by permitting unhindered govern-

† Reprinted with consent of Random House, Inc.

mental use of the fruits of such invasions. Thus in our system evidentiary rulings provide the context in which the judicial process of inclusion and exclusion approves some conduct as comporting with constitutional guarantees and disapproves other actions by state agents. A ruling admitting evidence in a criminal trial, we recognize, has the necessary effect of legitimizing the conduct which produced the evidence, while an application of the exclusionary rule withholds the constitutional imprimatur.

The exclusionary rule has its limitations, however, as a tool of judicial control. It cannot properly be invoked to exclude the products of legitimate police investigative techniques on the ground that much conduct which is closely similar involves unwarranted intrusions upon constitutional protections. Moreover, in some contexts the rule is ineffective as a deterrent. Street encounters between citizens and police officers are incredibly rich in diversity. They range from wholly friendly exchanges of pleasantries or mutually useful information to hostile confrontations of armed men involving arrests, or injuries, or loss of life. Moreover, hostile confrontations are not all of a piece. Some of them begin in a friendly enough manner, only to take a different turn upon the injection of some unexpected element into the conversation. Encounters are initiated by the police for a wide variety of purposes, some of which are wholly unrelated to a desire to prosecute for crime.[9] Doubtless some police "field interrogation" conduct violates the Fourth Amendment. But a stern refusal by this Court to condone such activity does not necessarily render it responsive to the exclusionary rule. Regardless of how effective the rule may be where obtaining convictions is an important objective of the police, it is powerless to deter invasions of constitutionally guaranteed rights where the police either have no interest in prosecuting or are willing to forego successful prosecution in the interest of serving some other goal.

Proper adjudication of cases in which the exclusionary rule is invoked demands a constant awareness of these limitations. The wholesale harassment by certain elements of the police

---

[9] See Tiffany, McIntyre & Rotenberg, Detection of Crime: Stopping and Questioning, Search and Seizure, Encouragement and Entrapment 18-56 (1967). This sort of police conduct may, for example, be designed simply to help an intoxicated person find his way home, with no intention of arresting him unless he becomes obstreperous. Or the police may be seeking to mediate a domestic quarrel which threatens to erupt into violence. They may accost a woman in an area known for prostitution as part of a harassment campaign designed to drive prostitutes away without the considerable difficulty involved in prosecuting them. Or they may be conducting a dragnet search of all teenagers in a particular section of the city for weapons because they have heard rumors of an impending gang fight.

community, of which minority groups, particularly Negroes, frequently complain, will not be stopped by the exclusion of any evidence from any criminal trial. Yet a rigid and unthinking application of the exclusionary rule, in futile protest against practices which it can never be used effectively to control, may exact a high toll in human injury and frustration of efforts to prevent crime. No judicial opinion can comprehend the protean variety of the street encounter, and we can only judge the facts of the case before us. Nothing we say today is to be taken as indicating approval of police conduct outside the legitimate investigative sphere. Under our decision, courts still retain their traditional responsibility to guard against police conduct which is overbearing or harassing, or which trenches upon personal security without the objective evidentiary justification which the Constitution requires. When such conduct is identified, it must be condemned by the judiciary and its fruits must be excluded from evidence in criminal trials. And, of course, our approval of legitimate and restrained investigative conduct undertaken on the basis of ample factual justification should in no way discourage the employment of other remedies than the exclusionary rule to curtail abuses for which that sanction may prove inappropriate.

SEARCH AND SEIZURE IN ILLINOIS: ENFORCEMENT OF THE CONSTITUTIONAL RIGHT OF PRIVACY

Comment, 47 Northwestern University Law Review 493, 497-99 (1952)†

A study of the records of Branch 27 of the Chicago Municipal Court—popularly known as the "Racket Court"—for the year 1950 indicates that the rule has failed to deter any substantial number of illegal searches. In 4,673 out of 6,649 cases, the legality of the method of obtaining evidence was put in issue by the defendant. In 4,593 of these cases, the court determined that the search had in fact been illegal and granted the motion to suppress the evidence. No cases were found in which a conviction was secured despite the suppression of the evidence. . . .

Careful consideration must be given to the type of offense included in this study, since this court does not deal with any of the more serious crimes. It is interesting to note the difference in the percentage of illegal searches in the two most serious offenses studied—carrying concealed weapons and narcotics violations—and those in the gambling offenses. These figures, coupled with the fact that with the passage of time the number of cases involving illegal searches which have reached the Illinois Supreme Court has decreased, may indicate that the exclusionary rule is most effective in discouraging illegal searches in cases involving serious offenses, where conviction is important. Conversely, where the police believe that a policy of harassment is an effective means of law enforcement, the exclusionary rule will not deter their use of unlawful methods. From observations made in the court, it is obvious that the police are aware of the requirements of the rule. Indeed, in gambling cases, their testimony seems calculated to insure the exclusion of the seized evidence, or at least to save time in disposing of a case in which the search is obviously illegal. Rarely is any attempt made by either the officer or the prosecutor to secure a denial of the motion to suppress, unless the seizure was legal beyond any possible doubt. Judicial practice has also contributed to the wide scope of the rule in gambling cases. If, in the prosecution of several defendants arrested in a gambling raid, the evidence must be excluded as to the principal offender (such as the keeper), the court excludes it as to all defendants. In effect, the judges of Branch 27 have extended the exclusionary rule to the limits advocated by those denying the dependence of the rule on the privilege against self-incrimination.

A finding, however, that the rule has no substantial effect on police conduct in minor offenses does not mean that the exclusionary rule should be abolished. Unless some other device can be suggested which will reach all cases, the problem facing the lawmakers and courts is that of finding some supplement to the rule which will deter violations of the right of privacy in conjunction with minor offenses.

. . . Five reasons are generally assigned for the predilection of the police to invade the privacy of individuals notwithstanding enforcement of the exclusionary rule: (1) ignorance; (2) corruption; (3) fear of a "tip-off"; (4) over-technical search warrant requirements; (5) harassment.

TWO VIEWS OF CHICAGO, I. HOW THE POLICE CHIEF SEES IT

By O. W. Wilson

Harper's Magazine 140, 143-44 (April 1964)†

In gambling cases defense attorneys resort to a variety of technicalities. Sometimes they make a preliminary motion to suppress the evidence, arguing that the search was illegal because it was made without a search warrant. If it was made with a warrant, they may claim that the warrant was defective. They take full advantage of the fact that individual trial judges differ widely in their interpretations of the law of search and seizure. One may issue a search warrant based upon evidence which he believes constitutes probable cause. However, after the raid has been made and the case comes before him for trial he may reverse himself and hold that the grounds upon which he himself issued the search warrant were insufficient. Thereupon he quashes the search warrant and "suppresses" the evidence. The gamblers go free even though the raid disclosed a large gambling operation.

Sometimes the judge denies the motion to "suppress" the evidence. Defense counsel will then demand a jury trial. This automatically results in a continuance and reassignment of the case to another judge. When he hears the case, the defense attorney renews the motion to "suppress" the evidence hoping that this judge will accede. The jury trial is not really wanted, of course. It is immediately waived when defense counsel has achieved his real objective, which is simply another hearing from another judge on his motion to quash the search warrant or suppress the evidence. The defense attorney has every expectation that eventually a judge will rule in his favor. So he applies for continuances, or for a change of venue, or for a jury trial until he gets the case before the right judge. Such maneuvers are usual, not exceptional.

The inconsistent views of different judges facilitate such defense tactics and, of course, thwart the police. Some judges, for example, feel strongly that gambling raids should not be made without search warrants even in public places where gambling is openly observed. In an effort to comply with this view, the police obtain search warrants based upon observations made by plainclothes police who gain admission to gambling rooms as patrons. Often, however, other judges will quash such search warrants on the ground that the plainclothesmen should have announced the fact that they were policemen before entering the gambling room. Because they failed to do this—in the view of these judges—the police were "trespassers." Other judges may concede that the plainclothesmen were not trespassers. But they hold that observations of gambling made on one date do not establish that gambling will be going on the following day when the raid is made. Still other judges will hold that the grounds for the search warrant are insufficient because the observations by plainclothesmen are not corroborated and substantiated by "disinterested third persons."

All of these judges may be acting from the best of motives. But their decisions result in a "what's the use?" attitude among policemen detailed to gambling and vice assignments. Finding them futile, the police, unfortunately, tend to abandon efforts to suppress gambling and vice by *legal* means. However, the continuing pressure of their superiors and the fear of newspaper exposés force them to make some attempt to suppress gambling and vice. So they resort to harassing raids and arrests without warrants, with little hope of successful prosecution in our courts. Thus a vicious circle of contempt for law enforcement and the administration of criminal justice is set up. The courts lose respect for the police; the police lose respect for the courts; and the public loses respect for both.

DETECTION OF CRIME 187-89 (1967)

By Lawrence P. Tiffany, Donald M. McIntyre, Jr. & Daniel L. Rotenberg
(Little, Brown & Company)

In police parlance an entry into premises for the purpose of confiscating property is a "tip-over," "kick in," or "bust in." Sometimes the practice is referred to as a "raid," but this term is also used to describe an entry sanctioned by the execution of a search warrant or when the police have grounds to arrest the persons inside the premises. . . .

Sometimes a tip-over will occur when officers have sufficient evidence to obtain a search warrant, but obtaining one is thought not worth the effort. On the other hand, a tip-over of a place suspected of selling liquor unlawfully (sometimes referred to as a "blind pig," and often a place where prostitution, narcotics traffic, and gambling are carried on) will sometimes be made simply because a large number of persons are seen entering or leaving a building at a late hour, an inadequate reason for obtaining a search warrant. . . .

Tip-overs generally are used with respect to relatively small-time gambling and liquor violations, which may or may not be tied in with a large syndicate operation. A tip-over or confiscation of gambling paraphernalia, illegal liquor, and other property is apt to be a greater economic deterrent to the small operation not under the aegis of the syndicate than to the larger, syndicate-backed operation.[o]

---

[o] *See also* W. LAFAVE, ARREST: THE DECISION TO TAKE A SUSPECT INTO CUSTODY 472-77 (1965).

ARREST: THE DECISION TO TAKE A SUSPECT INTO CUSTODY
428-29 (1965)
By Wayne R. LaFave
(Little, Brown & Company)

It is difficult to assess the effectiveness of the exclusionary rule in practice. It is clear that the rule does have a significant impact upon police practice in some situations. It is equally clear that it does not produce police conformity with the requirements of law in all cases. The extent to which the exclusionary rule does achieve its objective depends upon a number of factors, which may vary from case to case:

(1) Whether the police know the legal requirements well enough to conform to them. It is clear, at least in the jurisdictions studied, that the police often are not aware of the norms laid down by the appellate courts of their states. Although, generally speaking, there is greater awareness of the attitudes of the local judiciary with respect to specific arrest and detention practices, these attitudes come to the direct attention of only those officers appearing in court. Communication to the rest of the department, if it occurs, is usually only by word of mouth.

(2) Whether police desire a conviction sufficiently to take the steps necessary to conform to the requirements of the law. It is sometimes said that police are not concerned with conviction once a case is solved. However, in the jurisdictions studied officers frequently indicated a strong interest not only in solving a case but in ultimately bringing about the conviction of the offender. In situations involving serious offenses, the police are highly critical of instances of acquittal on any ground if it appears certain that the defendant is guilty. In certain other cases, such as minor gambling violations, the desire for conviction may not be strong enough to induce compliance with existing norms. This is particularly likely to be true when the consequences of conviction are slight and the means of obtaining a conviction place great demands upon available police resources.

(3) Whether there are short cuts to conviction. It is possible to create the impression that legal requirements have been complied with. This can be done, for example, in situations where arrests and searches are made upon inadequate grounds but the officer testifies later that the person arrested fitted a general description given in a police bulletin of a person wanted by the police. This process of making the law fit what was done, rather than conforming the practice to the requirements of law, pro-

duces an appearance of conformity and thus may make it possible to achieve conviction without having, at the same time, to change the practice.[p]

THE MAPP CASE ONE YEAR AFTER: AN APPRAISAL OF ITS IMPACT IN NEW YORK

By Richard H. Kuh

148 New York Law Journal 4, note 2 (Sept. 19, 1962)†

Skeptics, including in their rank some very able and very wise trial judges—as well as prosecutors and police—suggest that with the Mapp decision came an increase, significant in its proportions, in "accommodation" by police officers of *their stories,* not always of *their actions,* to the law. Increasingly since June 19, 1961, there have been cases involving items of contraband concealable upon the person—narcotics, for instance—in which police testimony indicates that as the arresting officer approached, the defendant removed an object from his pocket and threw it to the ground; the object turned out to be a glassine envelope containing a white powder; that powder, upon analysis, was found to contain heroin. This simplifies everything: the heroin having been thus "abandoned" no search and seizure problem exists! Increasingly, defendants profusely "invite" police officers

---

[p] Consider the applicability of the available legal sanctions, including the exclusionary rule, in the situations described previously, if police do not seek to prosecute.

The usual assumption is that the exclusionary rule represents a policy of deterring improper searches and seizures. Police sometimes feel that if they have no intention of using the evidence they may properly search. There is some authority suggesting that the exclusionary rule is intended merely to deprive police of one incentive to improper search. In United States v. Tate, 209 F. Supp. 762, 765-66 (D. Del. 1962), police arrested defendant for speeding and, after putting him in the police car, searched his car and found a sawed-off shotgun. The court said:

> I hold that the facts of this case render the search unreasonable and unconstitutional, since the reasons supporting this exemption from obtaining a warrant seem to have been totally lacking. This is not to say, however, that the officer in question, not trained in the law, should necessarily be criticized for doing his duty as he saw it. In a close case such as this, it is perhaps better that the arresting officer be overzealous and, in finding a deadly weapon, thus prevent some brutal intended crime such as murder, leaving it to trained prosecuting authorities to determine at leisure whether the facts warrant prosecution for the offense thus uncovered.

Similarly in a case of kidnapping or a major robbery police may see recovery of the victim or of the stolen property as more important than successful prosecution. It has been suggested that if stopping and frisking be permitted, abuse of the practice might be minimized by excluding from evidence anything other than a weapon which may be found through the frisk.

† Reprinted by permission from New York Law Journal.

to inspect their persons or to search their homes. Here, too, if the "invitation" is truly voluntary, there is no search or seizure problem! . . . Certainly, the overwhelming portion of police are honest. But the seeming increase of *improbable* testimony along these lines by police officers since the Mapp decision, and the illogic of believing that oft-arrested and hence "professionalized" defendants are not fully cognizant of the protections Mapp provides them, creates some question as to the degree that Mapp has affected police testimony and the degree to which it has affected police actions.

DETECTION OF CRIME 200-05 (1967)

By Lawrence P. Tiffany, Donald M. McIntyre, Jr. & Daniel L. Rotenberg
(Little, Brown & Company)

There are three basic methods of resolving important policy issues that arise with respect to search and seizure practices. The first is close legislative and judicial supervision. Specific rules could be formulated to control search practices and provision could be made for sanctions to insure adherence to those rules. The advantage of this alternative is that policy-making would be done by agencies of government that have traditionally assumed a policy-making responsibility. The disadvantage is that, as search and seizure rules proliferated and became more specific, the system might develop a rigidity that would prevent it from responding adequately to the changing problems that confront law enforcement. A second alternative would limit legislative and judicial attention to the prescription of general policy requirements, such as the rule that a search must be reasonable, so that the police could develop, with a fair degree of flexibility, search policies and practices in conformity within the broad limits set for them. The advantage of this alternative lies in its flexibility and in involving the agency with the greatest knowledge of the problems in the policy-making functions. The disadvantage is that police agencies have not conceived themselves to be, nor have they been looked upon by others as, an administrative agency with important policy-making responsibility. As a consequence, such latitude as they have is unacknowledged; policies are seldom articulated or reevaluated, and thus the process tends to be neither visible nor responsive to orderly review.

Finally, trial judges and magistrates could make the decision as to whether to search in individual cases, thus making it a judicial rather than a police decision. In theory, this alternative has the advantage of interposing an impartial magistrate between the police and the place or person to be searched. In practice, many law enforcement decisions, including the decision to search, must be made quickly and without sufficient time to consult a judicial officer. Even when there is time, judicial officers tend not to take the prior review of a decision to search as seriously as they do when a motion to suppress is made during subsequent litigation. There also tends to be wide judicial disparity in some multi-judge courts as to when there is sufficient evidence to justify the issuance of a search warrant.

The traditional commitment in this country has been in the direction of a maximum legislative and judicial control over criminal law policy issues, leaving to police the task of carrying out the prescribed policies. There is, nonetheless, variation in the degree of legislative and judicial control over police practice. Whereas legislatures, and to a much larger extent the courts, have enunciated numerous specific rules about what police may and may not do in searching for physical evidence of crime, no such legislative and judicial involvement has occurred in connection with such other important police investigative practices as encouragement of the suspect to commit a crime, which is discussed in detail in Part III of this volume. The greater concern with search and seizure can be partially explained on an historical basis. Widespread searches of the houses of our colonial ancestors by English officers resulted in the constitutional prohibition, embodied in the Fourth Amendment, against unreasonable searches, and this provision serves as a constant reminder to the courts that physical intrusion on the privacy of citizens is a police activity to be carefully scrutinized. Another explanation for frequent judicial attention to search and seizure practice is the presence of the exclusionary rule of evidence as a sanction against unreasonable searches. Probably for these reasons, the question of the legality of a search arises more often than the issue of entrapment, a defense that does not have a specific constitutional or legislative basis and is grounded on the innocence of the accused rather than on the impropriety of the police practice.

In arriving at a judgment about the relative advantage of close legislative and judicial control, on the one hand, and the maintenance of a system of substantial police-administrative flexibility on the other, it is obviously important to know how each alternative would work in practice. An examination of search and seizure affords a basis for identifying the successes and failures of close legislative and judicial control.

In the area of search and seizure it appears that close legislative and judicial control works best when compliance with those controls serves a meaningful law enforcement objective and works least well when compliance, especially if costly in time and money, contributes little to any basic enforcement objective. Thus search rules are conformed to by police in important gambling cases, where they increase the likelihood of conviction and the conviction itself actually results in the imposition of a substantial penalty. Conformity is less common when conviction, even if obtained, results only in a small money fine. For example, there is little incentive to comply with search and seizure rules in minor gambling cases where the "runner," if convicted, will be given a small fine that does not operate as a significant deterrent against the large gambling syndicate.

If appellate courts and legislatures wish to induce police compliance with specific, often complex, search and seizure rules, then they must give attention to ways of better achieving that objective. Some alternatives are apparent. First, convictions can be made more meaningful in the troublesome vice cases by providing for, and imposing, sanctions which have significance either in terms of rehabilitation of the offender or as a deterrent to vice activity generally. A second alternative would be to relieve the police of tasks that cannot meaningfully be dealt with by arrest, prosecution, and conviction. One way of achieving this would be to legalize conduct that is now criminal, like gambling, but such a proposal may not receive popular support. Alternatively, enforcement responsibility could be assigned to nonpolice agencies that would not be bound by rules designed specifically against the police. This is the situation where health inspectors are allowed to search, where police cannot, because their objective is preservation of public health and not the prosecution of offenders. To treat minor criminality, vice particularly, as social illness with agencies specially equipped for preventive effort is perhaps possible but obviously difficult. Whatever else is done, the chance of compliance is increased if the rules are responsive to the legitimate needs of law enforcement. It is apparent that these needs are not always made sufficiently clear in law briefs and arguments submitted to appellate courts.[2]

At least one reason for the trend toward great specificity in court rules relating to search and seizure is the failure of law enforcement to accept the responsibility for controlling its own policies and practices. Often police have assumed that they can properly search whenever there is no court rule preventing a

---

2 See LaFave, Arrest: The Decision to Take a Suspect into Custody 505 (1965); Remington and LaFave, Controlling the Police: The Judge's Role in Making and Reviewing Law Enforcement Decisions, 63 Mich. L. Rev. 987 (1965).

search, and as a consequence, courts have commonly assumed that police will make a practice of improper searches unless there is a specific prohibition. It seems apparent, in retrospect at least, that for the police to have had a significant role in the development of search and seizure law, they should have assumed a major responsibility for insuring the propriety of their own methods. Such a responsibility means that the self-imposed standards of the law enforcement agency probably should be higher than those imposed from without by judicial decision, if flexibility is to be maintained.[3] To equate propriety with what courts have said is necessary is to force courts to set the standards for law enforcement, and this is what has occurred with respect to search and seizure.

Whether the close judicial and legislative control over search and seizure rules should be relaxed is an important question and one that is not easily resolved. In a sense the advantage of flexibility for the development of administrative policies and practices would seem to be as important for law enforcement as for other governmental agencies, where it has long been thought desirable. But for the police to assume this kind of responsibility would require fundamental and costly changes in the level of police education and training, in the achievement of greater centralization of responsibility among numerous, independent local police agencies, and in a different attitude by police concerning their responsibility for their own policies and practices.

There is no rigid requirement in the law that a decision to search, even of premises, be made by a judicial officer rather than the police. Such a requirement may be forthcoming, however. Much will depend on whether the courts conclude that the police can be trusted with administrative discretion. It is clear that in the absence of a requirement that a search warrant be used when feasible, police usually will not obtain a warrant except when it is administratively advantageous to do so. Theoretically, a search warrant is desirable because it insures that the subsequent search will be held lawful if challenged. In practice, however, the warrant does not always give this insur-

[3] An example of when the police could take the lead is in advising suspects of their rights when seeking consent to a search. In contrast to the requirement that admonitions be given when a suspect is to be interrogated, no such requirement has been imposed when a waiver of Fourth Amendment rights is sought. Both trial and appellate courts, however, have expressed great incredulity over an alleged consent, especially if the suspect's guilt is primarily, if not solely, dependent upon the seizure of incriminating evidence in a suspect's home or pockets. A police policy and practice indicating their willingness to give admonitions may encourage the courts to accept consent searches, or to permit the police, without revealing their identity, to be admitted to a vice den to observe the activities therein.

ance. The reason is that, when issuing search warrants prior to a search, some judicial officers do not give the matter as careful consideration as they do subsequently, when the warrant is challenged by a motion to suppress. This may be due to the fact that the subsequent challenge is by an adversary process with the defendant's position argued. Whatever the reason, warrants are sometimes issued and suppressed by the same judge, or by a judge of the same court as the one who issued the warrant.

There is also substantial disparity between magistrates as to how much evidence is required to obtain a search warrant. Often this disparity reflects a difference of opinion about the seriousness of the conduct. The judge who considers gambling a minor problem may grant a motion to suppress in a borderline case in which another judge, sitting as a magistrate and viewing gambling as a serious, syndicate-type vice crime, may have felt that there was sufficient probable cause to issue the warrant.

The situation is further complicated by the fact that often an arrest warrant will serve as effectively as a search warrant in making it possible to conduct an "incidental" search of a person or premises when the arrest is made. The fact that a judicial officer participated in the decision to arrest (and, by implication, to search) may be influential in establishing the legality of the search. Despite this fact, many judicial officers take a radically different view of their responsibility when issuing an arrest warrant on the one hand and a search warrant on the other. In deciding whether to issue a search warrant, the judicial officer may carefully review the evidence, and strict adherence to legal formalism may be required. The arrest warrant, by contrast, is often issued by the clerk without the judicial officer even seeing the complaint on which it is issued.

All in all, there is uncertainty about the standards to be used by magistrates in determining whether a search should be conducted, and by the trial judge in ruling on the reasonableness of a search once it is made. This uncertainty may be a contributing factor to police decisions to harass vice operations by confiscating property without judicial approval either before or after the search is conducted. Very little has been done to resolve the conflict by a dialogue between the police and the courts.

There are no data available to measure the over-all effect of searches designed to harass vice operations and to confiscate weapons. Whether searches designed to harass vice operations and to confiscate weapons are successful in reducing the crime rate is questionable, but in any case the problems provoking the police to use these techniques are not apt to be fully exposed to courts and legislatures, and these agencies are not apt to share responsibility for solving the problems.

SEARCH AND SEIZURE: "THE COURSE OF TRUE LAW . . . HAS NOT . . . RUN SMOOTH"

By Wayne R. LaFave

1966 University of Illinois Law Forum 255, 387-89

The prevailing view in this country is that only the defendant can take an appeal from a lower court ruling on a motion to suppress. The prohibition on government appeal, said to rest upon "historic principle" and "practicalities in the administration of criminal justice,"[788] has been removed by only a few legislatures notwithstanding continuing criticism of the restriction.[789] This means that in most jurisdictions "the decisions of trial judges are substantially immune from effective appellate supervision."[790] It also means that appellate courts are not in the best position to undertake an orderly development of search and seizure law. The fortuitous circumstances under which defendant-supplied fact situations reach a court will limit the opportunity of that court to "build" upon existing law.[791] In contrast, if the state can also select some of these fact situations, then a more systematic growth of significant legal principles will result from this "managed series of educational cases, judiciously selected. . . ."[792] As Llewellyn pointed out, "a bit of management in bringing on a related group of cases in a series looks to be much more of a value than an ill."[793]

In 1961 the Illinois Legislature passed a bill providing that "the People may sue out interlocutory writs of error to review any order or judgment quashing an arrest or search warrant or suppressing evidence entered preliminary to trial."[794] The ex-

788 DiBella v. United States, 369 U.S. 121 (1962).

789 See, *e.g.*, SENATE COMM. ON THE JUDICIARY, SUMMARY OF FINDINGS AND RECOMMENDATIONS OF THE SUBCOMMITTEE ON IMPROVEMENTS IN THE FEDERAL CRIMINAL CODE, S. REP. NO. 1478, 85th Cong., 2d Sess. 15 (1958).

790 Allen, [*The Exclusionary Rule in the American Law of Search and Seizure,* 52 J. CRIM. L.C. & P.S. 246] at 249.

791 For example, defendants may bring factual situations to the court notwithstanding the fact that the court has recently upheld without question the identical practice. *E.g., compare* People v. Perroni, 14 Ill. 2d 581, 153 N.E.2d 578 (1958), *with* People v. Shambley, 4 Ill. 2d 38, 122 N.E.2d 172 (1954).

792 LLEWELLYN, THE COMMON LAW TRADITION: DECIDING APPEALS 262 (1960).

793 *Id.* at 263.

794 ILL. REV. STAT. ch. 38, § 747 (1961) is the statute as amended by the bill. The substance of this provision was carried over into the new Code of Criminal Procedure, ILL. REV. STAT. ch. 38, § 120-1 (1965), now [superseded] by Ill. Sup. Ct. Rule 27(4), which makes no change.

perience under this statute clearly supports the view that appellate courts can make a more significant contribution in defining norms for police conduct when state appeal is possible. A recent survey of the Illinois cases disclosed that prosecutors have taken five cases to the Illinois Supreme Court and eight cases to the Illinois appellate court and have obtained a reversal of the suppression order *in every case*.[798] Included in this small group of cases are some situations of real importance which would not likely have reached the appellate level absent a right of prosecution appeal. For example, in one of the five cases reaching the Illinois Supreme Court it was held that reliable hearsay could be used to obtain a search warrant, thereby overruling two prior cases by that court which probably would otherwise have been followed in future cases by trial judges. Similarly, in another of these cases the court held that a police officer need not disclose his identity when he enters private premises posing as a customer of the illegal activity occurring within. Suppression of evidence in such circumstances was theretofore common, and found some support in a prior Illinois Supreme Court case. Some of the cases brought to the Illinois appellate court by prosecutors are equally significant.

Of course, the extent to which the right of prosecution appeal from suppression of evidence broadens the opportunity of the appellate courts to clarify arrest and search norms on matters of importance will depend considerably upon the criteria employed in selecting the cases to be appealed. The tendency is for some prosecutors to choose the "big" cases, those involving serious crimes and the subject of greatest publicity. From the police standpoint, however, the need for clarification may be much greater as to enforcement practices used against relatively minor offenses, such as misdemeanor gambling.

The Crime Control Act of 1968 granted to federal prosecutors the right to appeal from any pretrial order suppressing evidence, so long as the evidence in question is "a substantial proof of the charge."[q]

---

[798] The fact that only 13 cases were appealed during the period studied certainly shows that appellate courts are not unduly burdened by granting the prosecution the right to appeal in such cases. Of course, this does not mean that prosecutors in the state have viewed only 13 instances of suppression as improper. Because of the limited resources of his office, the prosecutor obviously cannot appeal in every case in which there is some basis for questioning the trial judge's decision that the police conduct was improper.

[q] 18 U.S.C. § 3731.

Reference Note

The major effort to describe the practical questions involved in search and seizure is L. TIFFANY, D. MCINTYRE & D. ROTENBERG, DETECTION OF CRIME, pt. II (1967).

A discussion of problems in making the exclusionary rule an effective control upon police practices is LaFave, *Improving Police Performance Through the Exclusionary Rule—Part I: Current Police and Local Court Practices,* 30 MO. L. REV. 391 (1965).

A recent summary of the rules governing search and seizure is LaFave, *Search and Seizure: "The Course of True Law . . . Has Not . . . Run Smooth,"* 1966 U. ILL. L.F. 255 (an excerpt from which appears at 267, *supra*). The particular rules are those in Illinois, but the problems discussed are universal. The major change subsequent to the article is the abolition of the "mere evidence rule" in Warden v. Hayden, 387 U.S. 294 (1967).

E. EXPLOITING FEELINGS OF GUILT

A not uncommon police tactic is to approach a person who is in some way suspect with the hope that his fear of being found out will cause him to panic and thus betray himself. It is particularly exemplified in the case of narcotics offenders who, upon finding themselves the object of police attention, make an effort to dispose of narcotics in their possession. Though prior to that time the police may have had no more than vague suspicions, this reaction on the part of the offender to an apparent attempt to question or arrest him may give the police a basis for arresting him which they did not have before. Or a car thief who believes himself about to be stopped by police may try to outrace them or may abandon the car and run.

The Practice

1

An informer, whose reliability was not established, told officers that a woman was selling narcotics. They found the woman and followed her and observed her engage in conversation with a known user. When they approached her, she tried to evade them and tried to swallow a white powder in a rubber balloon. They knocked it from her hand and arrested her.

2

Officers observed several men talking on the street at midnight, one of whom was known to them as a safecracker. Two cars were parked near them, both with the trunk standing open. As the officers approached them, one of the men threw an object to the ground which was found to be a woman's garment with the price tag still on it.

3

Officers saw a man talking to another on the street and as he walked past their car they observed that he had his hand cupped as if he were concealing something in it. They called to him to stop, but he kept walking. He then dropped a yellow-brown cigarette and ran. The cigarette was marihuana and he was apprehended.

4

Late in the evening a welfare investigator called at the home of a woman welfare recipient suspected of living with a man who could support her. As the investigator was admitted, a man left through the rear entrance. Two other investigators waiting there stopped him.

MASSACHUSETTS v. PAINTEN

368 F.2d 142 (1st Cir. 1966)

Before ALDRICH, Chief Judge, MCENTEE and COFFIN, Circuit Judges.

ALDRICH, Chief Judge. Petitioner was convicted in the state court of armed robbery and various connected offenses, and was given extensive sentences. His conviction was affirmed *sub nom.* Commonwealth v. Binkiewicz, 1961, 342 Mass. 740, 175 N.E.2d 473. Thereafter he sought a writ of error in the state court, raising, for the first time, the matters now before us. The writ was dismissed. Having thus exhausted his state remedies, he filed a petition for habeas corpus in the district court. The writ was granted, Painten v. Commonwealth, D. Mass., 1966, 252 F. Supp. 851, and the Commonwealth appeals.

Very briefly, two policemen, knowing of a holdup but having no substantial clues, came across petitioner and one Ash, and followed them to petitioner's apartment. Their grounds for suspicion did not, even remotely, amount to probable cause for arresting either Ash or petitioner, either for the holdup or for any other crime. After arranging for plainclothesmen to station themselves at the back of the building one of the uniformed officers then knocked on the door. He testified as follows:

"I rapped on the door, and a voice said, 'Who is it?' I said, 'Police officers.' The door opened about three inches, and Mr. Painten looked out at me. He saw us. I had my badge in my hand. He said, 'Will you wait a minute?' I said, 'Sure.' He closed the door. As he closed the door, maybe ten seconds later I heard what to me sounded like a window opening and closing. He then, a few seconds after the door was opened, we were allowed to enter. . . . I asked who lived there. Painten volunteered it was his apartment."

After entering the apartment, the police noticed a bulge in Ash's pocket, and removed some $200 in crumpled bills. They then called to the plainclothesmen to come up, and received the response that "someone" had thrown "something" out the window. This information led to the discovery on the fire escape on a floor below of a paper bag containing two pistols and some cartridges. Petitioner was thereupon arrested; the apartment was searched, and a large amount of currency was found under a mattress. At petitioner's trial the guns and bills were introduced in evidence.

This case falls over the permissible line that we recently sought to delineate in Robbins v. MacKenzie, 1966, 1 Cir., 364 F.2d 45, cert. den. 10/17/66. In that case the district court found, on adequate evidence, that no search was intended. We held that where the police, having reasonable suspicion but not probable cause, knocked on a door and asked to talk, and had no other purpose, they were entitled to treat an invitation to enter as voluntary consent. Our discussion need not be repeated, but we distinguished cases where the purpose of the police was not merely to talk, but to make a search.

In the case at bar the police sought entry without stating their purpose. If this was a request to make a search, acquiescence when police knock and exhibit a badge is not true consent to a search, as the cases cited in Judge Coffin's dissenting opinion in *MacKenzie* make clear. The Commonwealth's own evidence indicates that a search was in fact intended.

It follows that, as the court said in Hobson v. United States, 8 Cir., 1955, 226 F.2d 890, at 894, "The defendant's action in throwing the package was not voluntary but was forced by the actions of the police," and since their actions were improper, the police were not entitled to the fruits. The state could not use the guns, even as probable cause, if they were such, to justify their subsequent conduct in making an arrest, or the search in which they discovered the money. Wong Sun v. United States, 1963, 371 U.S. 471, 482-484.

Affirmed.

COFFIN, Circuit Judge (concurring). What troubles me about the opinion of my brothers is their reasoning that, since the officers harbored an improper purpose, their knocking on the door and identifying themselves was also "improper" and immunized from use any objects jettisoned into public view and beyond petitioner's premises.[r]

CONSTITUTIONAL PROTECTION ON SEARCH AND SEIZURE DEAD?

By Irving Younger

Trial Magazine 41 (Aug.-Sept. 1967)

When the Supreme Court lays down a rule to govern the conduct of the police, the rule does not enforce itself. A hearing is almost always necessary in each particular case to determine the facts. Such hearings usually follow a standard pattern.

In a hearing on a motion to suppress evidence under *Mapp*, for example, the policeman testifies to his version of the circumstances of the search and seizure, invariably reflecting perfect legality. The defendant testifies to his version, invariably reflecting egregious illegality. The judge must choose between the two versions, and, not surprisingly, he habitually accepts the policeman's word.

The difficulty arises when one stands back from the particular case and looks at a series of cases. It then becomes apparent that policemen are committing perjury at least in some of them, and perhaps in many of them.

Take narcotics prosecutions in New York City. Before *Mapp*, the policeman typically testified that he stopped the defendant for little or no reason, searched him, and found narcotics on his person. This had the ring of truth. It was an illegal search (not based upon probable cause), but the evidence was admissible because New York had not adopted the exclusionary rule. Since it made no difference, the policeman testified truthfully.

After *Mapp*, it made a great deal of difference. For the first few months, New York policemen continued to tell the truth, with the result that in a large number of cases the evidence was suppressed. Then the police made the great discovery that if the defendant drops the narcotics on the ground, after which the policeman arrests him, the search is reasonable and the evidence is admissible.

[r] In Massachusetts v. Painten, 389 U.S. 560 (1968), the Supreme Court dismissed its writ of certiorari as improvidently granted, but four of the justices indicated that the officer's intent to make an illegal search if the suspect did not consent to entry would not invalidate such consent.

Spend a few hours in the New York City Criminal Court these days, and you will hear case after case in which a policeman testifies that the defendant dropped the narcotics on the ground, whereupon the policeman arrested him.

The judge has no reason to disbelieve this "dropsy" testimony in any particular case. Naturally, he must decide each case on its own evidence, without regard to the testimony in other cases. Surely, though, not in *every* case was the defendant rash enough or unlucky enough to drop his narcotics at the feet of a policeman. It follows that at least in some of these cases the police are lying.

Why? Policemen believe themselves to be fighting a two-front war—against criminals in the street and against "liberal" rules of law in the court. All's fair in this war, including perjury, to subvert those "liberal" rules that might free defendants who "ought" to be jailed.

F. ANALYSIS OF PHYSICAL TRACES

Many police investigative practices do not raise significant problems for the law. They are effective and not considered unreasonably intrusive by anyone. The essential problem for the law then is not fairness in the obtaining of the evidence, but accuracy in assessing the persuasive power of such evidence.

Some sources of information, such as eyewitness identification, are notoriously fallible. On the other hand, scientific detection methods are less subject to error, and as a consequence there is a widespread impression that the fight against crime calls for investment in more refined scientific techniques.

It is quite possible, however, that the value of scientific techniques for police is overplayed. Every large police department employs technicians who can compare fingerprints, match glass and paint fragments, conduct ballistics experiments, and so on. These activities receive substantial publicity but represent only a tiny part of the total police effort. In many offenses—like armed robbery—there is rarely any physical evidence on which the police technician can even begin to work. In others—like professional burglary—physical traces can be examined, but they are useful only for identifying as the offender a suspect who is already in hand to be examined for correspondence of material on his clothing with debris from the burglary, or correspondence of tools in his possession with marks left at the scene. The burglary is likely to be solved initially by prosaic police work, for which the scientific tests serve merely as corroboration. Fingerprints are clearly the most useful kind of evidence, since they are kept on file and can identify one man out of a crowd, but the proportion of cases in which classifiable prints are obtained is very small.

Despite its limited use to them, the police have fostered the impression that scientific detection is an important part of their operation. Perhaps this claim to scientific detection is thought to add to professional stature. Or it may be thought that an aura of omniscience about the police will serve to deter potential criminals. On the other hand, a common impression that the police can solve crimes by use of scientific tests has the disadvantage of building up unrealistic expectations and weakening police claims that they need broader investigative powers. For example, editorial reaction to the arrest of mass-murderer Richard Speck emphasized that the case was built without questioning him at all, and that "too many police departments have grown dependent on confessions at the expense of more scientific—and more difficult—methods of detection."[s] A prominent defense lawyer was quoted as saying, "This is a perfect example of how the police, when making a concentrated effort and using scientific devices, were able to build a sufficient case without infringing on rights."

---

[s] Editorial, LIFE, July 29, 1966.

Chapter 4

TAKING INTO CUSTODY

The decision of the police to take a person into custody is an important stage in the criminal justice system for two reasons: (a) The invocation of the arrest power usually constitutes the initial step in the prosecutorial system; it starts the wheels turning toward conviction. (b) Deprivation of freedom constitutes a very substantial interference with the rights otherwise enjoyed by the individual affected.

The term "arrest" has various definitions, and discussion of police practices is often confused by failure to agree on the meaning of arrest.[a] In these materials the term "arrest" will refer to placing a suspect in custody in order to take him to the station house for some purpose, whether or not prosecution is contemplated. This definition, which excludes stopping and questioning or on-the-street detention, is reflected in administrative practice. Police see stopping and questioning as a matter which does not require record keeping (except in a few departments which require field interrogation reports) and which has less significant consequences for the individual involved. When a suspect is taken to the station in custody, the police view the interference as a more serious one which results in a booking and creation of an arrest record.

Although there are some arrests for purposes other than prosecution, such as arrests of intoxicated persons for their own safety or of prostitutes as a method of control, the main stream of the criminal justice system flows toward prosecution. In this chapter we shall concentrate on the decision whether to arrest, the evidentiary standards for a lawful arrest, the various views

[a] At one extreme "arrest" means any circumscription of one's movement against his will, whether by force, threat, or assertion of authority. "[T]he imprisonment need not be for more than an appreciable length of time, and . . . it is not necessary that any damage result from it . . ., since the tort is complete with even a brief restraint of the plaintiff's freedom." W. PROSSER, TORTS 55 (3d ed. 1964). At the other extreme "arrest" takes place only when a person is taken into custody for the purpose of prosecution. *E.g.,* N.Y. CODE CRIM. PROC. § 167 (1958). The distinction between "arrest" and "detention" is discussed in Terry v. Ohio, 392 U.S. 1 (1968).

of the function which arrest serves in the system, and the methods of controlling the arrest decision.[b]

A. THE DECISION WHETHER TO ENFORCE THE LAW

One of the ideals to which the community subscribes is that the criminal law should be fully enforced, that it is not for the law enforcement agency to pick and choose which known offenders shall be arrested and which shall be left free. To deny universal enforcement of laws enacted by democratic process is conceived as attacking the underpinnings of government and order.

With respect to most of the serious crimes, such as murder, robbery, and kidnapping, there is in fact full enforcement of the law. The police, having sufficient evidence to justify their action, will take into custody every person believed to have committed such a crime. In many other circumstances, however, the police consciously refrain from making arrests which they are empowered by the law to make. The obvious fact is that full enforcement of all the laws is neither possible nor desirable, yet it continues to be retained as an ideal. Acknowledgment of the propriety as well as the necessity of police exercising discretion in this way has been slow in coming.

1. *The Problems of Nonenforcement*

SHALL POLICE CHIEF DECIDE WHICH LAWS TO ENFORCE?
The [Madison, Wisconsin] Capital Times Editorial, Sept. 9, 1961

A strange philosophy of law enforcement has been expounded by Madison Police Chief Wilbur H. Emery. The Chief says his officers cannot enforce the letter of the law setting a curfew of 10 p.m. on city streets for children under 17 who are not accompanied by a parent.

Chief Emery says he does not think the public would stand for strict enforcement of the letter of the law. The courts, too, he feels, would take a dim view of overly strict enforcement.

Since when, we feel compelled to inquire, is it the function of the police chief to decide which laws can or cannot be enforced? By what authority does he claim the right to interpret what the "public" will or will not stand for in law enforcement?

[b] A matter of substantial concern not dealt with herein is the use of force —particularly deadly force—in effecting arrests. *See* Chapter 20.

In a representative government the will of the people is expressed through their elected public bodies. The curfew law is an official city ordinance, duly passed by the city council, and as such is open to no other interpretation but that it is the will of the people. The essence of our system of government is that we are governed by law, not by whim or decree. It is the function of the police to enforce these laws. If the law needs revision or repeal that is for the people to decide through the city council. Meantime, the Chief is legally and morally obliged to carry out the letter of the law.

As far as we can see the curfew law poses no insuperable problems of enforcement. It specifically provides for exemptions of students returning from "functions authorized by the governing body of any public or parochial school in the city of Madison" provided that such young people carry identification cards approved by the police and the school.

This would make it possible for boys and girls to attend school dances, football games, basketball games, school plays and other events.

The police and the school officials have not provided these identification forms for students. They are in effect violating the law, not helping to make it work the way it was intended.

This, we repeat, is a strange philosophy of law enforcement. If the curfew law may be violated with impunity why should not other citizens violate other laws which they might find irksome? This is the road to anarchy.

The Practice

The following illustrations suggest some of the wide variety of situations in which police, having power to arrest, choose not to arrest.

1

A police officer received a complaint that an itinerant salesman was selling obscene magazines. The officer examined the material objected to but was unable to determine whether such matter was covered by the rather ambiguous obscenity statute of the state. The officer refrained from making an arrest even though the salesman was about to leave the jurisdiction.

2

A police officer came upon a "bum," a man wandering the streets clearly without any means of support. Though such conduct is explicitly proscribed by the vagrancy statute of the state, no arrest was made.

3

A game warden came upon a hunter carrying a rifle in a closed hunting area. Under the fish and game laws, the presence of a person with a gun in such an area in itself constitutes a violation. However, it was decided not to arrest when the warden learned the hunter was not familiar with the country and apparently had made a mistake as to his location.

4

A Negro informed a police officer that he had just been refused service in a nearby restaurant. The officer accompanied the complainant to the establishment, where the proprietor admitted the charge. The officer then advised the proprietor of the state civil rights law, which makes it a misdemeanor to refuse public accommodations on the basis of race, creed, or color. When the proprietor then agreed to serve the Negro, the officer took no further action.

5

A local welfare director presented positive proof to the police that a local welfare recipient was engaging in an adulterous relationship. Notwithstanding a repetition of the complaint on another occasion, the police refrained from taking any action against the violator.

6

A police officer came upon a merchant who was operating his business on Sunday. Such conduct was prohibited by a Sunday blue law, passed in 1860, covering all gainful employment. The officer knew that for years merchants had operated on Sundays without complaint and without enforcement of this law. No action was taken.

7

A police officer saw a motorist make an illegal left turn. The officer stopped the driver, brought the violation to his attention, but did not make an arrest and did not write a ticket.

8

A report that a stabbing had taken place came in to the station of a precinct predominantly Negro in population. An officer reported to the address and learned that a Negro woman had seriously stabbed her husband with a pair of scissors. The husband commented that there had been a little argument and requested transportation to the hospital. The officer, who had served in the precinct for some time, had reported to such calls in the past and had received similar responses. Although the conduct constituted a felonious assault, no official action was taken.

9

A merchant called the police after having apprehended a shoplifter in his store. When the merchant was asked by the officer whether he was willing to appear in court to testify, he replied that he could not take time out from his work for this. The officer declined to arrest the shoplifter.

10

An officer responding to a call learned that the complainant wanted his neighbor arrested for tearing down a part of his fence. The officer's investigation disclosed that this was merely the latest chapter in a continued neighborhood dispute between the complainant and offender. Although the property destruction was a criminal violation, the officer declined to take any official action.

11

A man entered a precinct station and complained that he had just been cheated of $20. Asked to explain, he said that he had given the money to a prostitute who had agreed to meet him at a certain time and place, but that she had failed to appear. The police, although familiar with this kind of racket, subjected the complainant to some ridicule, suggested that he had learned his lesson, and sent him on his way.

12

In a routine frisk of a group of persons found under suspicious circumstances, a small quantity of narcotics was found on one of them. The officers recognized this man as one who from time to time informed the police on narcotics peddlers. No arrest was made.

13

A woman returned home from work in a disheveled condition and told her husband that she had been kidnapped and raped. The husband called the police, and they began an investigation. Upon questioning the woman the following day, the police discerned some discrepancies in her story, and she finally admitted that she and a man had engaged in love-making by mutual consent, and that she had fabricated the story in order to explain her absence to her husband. Since proceeding against the woman for a false felony report would have endangered her marriage, the police decided to take no action.[c]

POLICE DISCRETION: THE IDEAL VERSUS THE REAL

By Herman Goldstein

23 Public Administration Review 140 (1963)

A policy of "full enforcement" implies that the police are required and expected to enforce all criminal statutes and city ordinances at all times against all offenders. It suggests that the police are without authority to ignore violations, to warn offenders when a violation has in fact occurred, or to do anything short of arresting the offender and placing a charge against him for the specific crime committed. It views the police function to be that of relating the provisions of the law to a fine measurement of the quantum of evidence. Out of this cold and somewhat mechanical calculation evolves an answer which provides the basis for police action.

The exercise of discretion, on the other hand, suggests that the police are required, because of a variety of factors, to decide overtly how much of an effort is to be made to enforce specific laws. It recognizes that actions short of arrest may achieve the desired goal. It implies that a police officer may decide not to make an arrest even in those situations in which an offense has been committed and both the offender and the evidence are at hand. It tends to portray police officers as something other than automatons—as reasonable men whose judgment is essential in determining whether or not to invoke the criminal process. . . .

The bibliography of thinking on this subject is rapidly increasing. This body of thought and analysis is of more than academic interest to the police. It has some very practical implications.

What is the position of the average police administrator in these deliberations? He is most likely to support the view—somewhat hesitatingly—that he is committed to a policy of full enforcement. It is, after all, the policy most commonly enun-

[c] Arrests mean paper work and court appearances, often without full compensation and at substantial inconvenience. Police are therefore commonly reluctant to arrest for petty misconduct for this reason as well as for others suggested above. Chapter 8 of the book by John Gardiner on traffic law enforcement (to be published in 1969 by Harvard Press) points to a difference in level of traffic enforcement between cities in which the officer must be present when the case is first called and those in which he must appear only when trial has been set on a plea of not guilty.

ciated by police agencies. In contrast, the mere suggestion that a police administrator exercises discretion in fulfilling his job may be taken as an affront—an attack upon the objective and sacrosanct nature of his job—that of enforcing the law without fear or favor. Here too, there is a little hesitation—an awareness that discretion must be and is exercised. . . .

Do we have full enforcement, as the term is defined here? Obviously, we do not. How often have law enforcement personnel released a drunk and disorderly person without charging him? released a juvenile offender to his parents? warned a driver who had clearly committed a violation? ignored the enforcement of some city ordinances? not arrested an individual known to have committed fornication or adultery? arranged for the release of a narcotic addict in exchange for information? dropped charges against an assailant when the victim failed to cooperate in the prosecution? ignored Sunday blue laws or simply been instructed not to enforce a specific law?

And yet, in acknowledging that some or all of these practices exist, police officials feel a sense of guilt; that these actions were not quite proper; and that they had no basis in law. Why, then, do police officials do these things? Because they are, consciously or unconsciously, acknowledging what they do not wish to proclaim—that the police must exercise discretion.

THE EXERCISE OF DISCRETION

Why must discretion be exercised? . . .

. . . By its action, the legislature has attempted to establish those forms of conduct which its members desire to be declared criminal. But this action, as reflected in the statement of the criminal law, is often expressed in such broad terms as to render a clear interpretation of the legislature's intentions most difficult. Ambiguity may be intentional so as to provide greater flexibility in enforcement; it may result from a failure to envisage the day-to-day problems encountered by the police; or it may simply be a result of language limitations. Whatever the basis for the broad statement of the law, the need for resolving these ambiguities frequently places the police in the position of having to determine the forms of conduct which are to be subject to the criminal process. . . .

Both state statutes and city ordinances may be explicit in defining conduct to be considered criminal, but there may be little expectation on the part of those who enacted the laws that they be enforced to the letter. The statute or ordinance may be stating the ideals of the community; that adulterous activity, for example, will not be tolerated. Through this action, the community is placed on record as opposing a form of conduct considered morally wrong. Lawmakers and citizens alike derive a certain degree of comfort from having legislated against such activity. . . . [It] falls to the police agency to live with the law without enforcing it.

The problem does not always stem from a double standard in matters of morality. Often it stems from mere obsolescence. . . .

Another major factor which forces the exercise of discretion is the limitation on manpower and other resources—a factor to which previous reference was made. Few police agencies have the number of personnel that would be required to detect the total amount of criminality which exists in a community and to prosecute all offenders. Rarely is consideration given to the relationship between the volume of what can be termed criminal acts and the resources available to deal with them. New legislation declaring a form of conduct to be criminal is rarely accompanied by an appropriation to support the resources for its enforcement. . . .

In establishing priorities of enforcement, greater attention is ordinarily given to more serious crimes. A determination not to arrest is most common at the level of the petty offender—and especially if the offender is an otherwise law-abiding citizen. Policies—albeit unwritten—begin to evolve. Just as social gamblers may be arrested only if their activities become organized and move into public places, so drunkards may be arrested only if they are belligerent and homeless as distinct from those who are cooperative and long-established residents.

Discretion may be exercised on the basis of a police officer's particular assignment. Many police agencies have officers assigned to specific types of investigations, such as those relating to homicide, burglaries, or narcotics. Officers so assigned understandably consider their respective specialized function as being of greatest importance to the department. The generalization can be made that police officers frequently refrain from invoking the criminal process for conduct which is considered of less seriousness than that which they are primarily responsible for investigating. A group of officers, intent on solving a homicide, for example, will complain bitterly of the lack of prostitutes on the streets from whom they may obtain information. Narcotic detectives will likewise make frequent use of gamblers and may even tolerate petty larcenies and minor drug violations on the part of their informants. Whatever the merits of the practice, the goal is an acceptable one: that of solving the more serious crime.

Where the volume of criminal activity is high, it is common to observe police policies which result in the dropping of charges against minor assailants when the victim is unwilling to testify. Without a complainant, the case cannot usually be prosecuted successfully. . . .

Discretion is often exercised by the police in a sincere effort to accomplish a social good. This is a sort of humanitarian gesture in which the police achieve the desired objective without full imposition of the coldness and harshness of the criminal process. The drunk may be ushered home; the juveniles turned over to their parents; the new woman driver warned of being found headed in the wrong direction on a one-way street. It is the exercise of discretion such as this to accomplish a desired goal to which others refer when they exhort the police to enforce the "spirit" rather than the "letter" of the law. . . .

Reasons for Not Acknowledging the Exercise of Discretion

To acknowledge that law enforcement officials do exercise discretion requires an overt act—the articulation of a position—an action which is rare among those in the police field. Most law enforcement officials long ago resigned themselves to the role of the underdog upon whom the unsolved problems of society were piled high. Having developed what might best be termed a defensive posture, the police have, for example, widely accepted responsibility for all that is criminal despite the fact that crimes are not committed by the police, but rather by the citizens of the community they serve. How often do we hear a police official admonish a community for a rise in crime? How often does a police official point an accusing finger at conditions which produce crime and criminals? Instead, whenever the publication of crime statistics indicates a rise in crime, he feels that he has in some way failed and that his department has failed. In carrying such a burden, the average police official sees nothing especially strange about having to carry responsibility for a type of enforcement he is unable to fulfill. He has learned two characteristics of his job: he must bear this burden well and he must refrain from discussing it lest it be a source of embarrassment to him and the community.

If he should have the urge to discuss his problem of achieving full enforcement, the average police official would not wish to do so in public. To acknowledge the exercise of discretion belies the very image in which he takes such pride and which he strives so hard to achieve. This is the image of total objectivity—of impartiality—and of enforcement without fear nor favor. A cursory examination of the typical oath of office administered to police officers, the rules and regulations of police departments, and the several codes governing police conduct give the general impression that strict adherence to the "letter of the law" has come to be the ideal toward which all well-intentioned police officers should strive. There is great difficulty in recognizing that discretion can be exercised without being partial. It is, of course, extremely important that police officers be impartial in their enforcement policies, but it is possible for them to be so and still exercise discretion.

Impartiality requires the establishment of criteria for uniform action—a difficult task and one which perhaps constitutes the most valid objection to acknowledging discretionary powers. It is easy, from an administrative standpoint, to support a program of full enforcement. Instructions and training are simple. One need only teach the difference between black and white. If discretion is to be exercised, criteria become essential. And here the problems begin: (1) there is a general reluctance to spell out criteria as to those conditions under which an arrest is to take place lest this written modification of existing laws be attacked as presumptuous on the part of an administrative agency and contemptuous of the legislative body; (2) in the absence of written instructions, it is extremely difficult to communicate to large numbers of policemen the bounds of the discretion to be exercised; (3) an officer cannot be forced to exercise discretion, since the broad oath which he takes places him under obligation to enforce all laws and he can maintain that he is adhering to this higher authority; and (4) if a written document is desired, the preparation of criteria for the exercise of discretion requires an expert draftsman—one more skilled than the legislative draftsman who may have tried and failed. Is it any wonder that the typical reaction of the police administrator to the mere suggestion that discretion be acknowledged is likely to be: "It isn't worth the trouble!"?

Broadly-stated laws are, after all, one of the lesser concerns of the police. Most attention of law enforcement officers in recent years has focused upon legal provisions which are too narrow. The average police official is not very concerned about having the authority to enforce adultery statutes and not having the manpower or the community support necessary to do so. He is much more concerned because of his inability to attack organized crime effectively. And there may be an occasion upon which he can use an obscure or otherwise unenforced law to launch an oblique attack against a situation or activity which he feels warrants action on his part. His attitude is often that the law should be left on the books; it may come in handy sometime. Why impose self-limitations on police authority beyond those established by the legislature?

Another contention is that discretion breeds corruption and for this reason should be denied. This constitutes another strong administrative argument against acknowledging its existence. The average police administrator spends a considerable portion of his time worrying about the integrity of his force. Corruption, when it does exist, usually stems from the misuse of authority in order to attain selfish ends or from restraint from exerting authority in exchange for personal gain. It is always difficult to investigate. But, it is easier to do so, if policemen are expected to function on a black or white basis. . . .

There is, among police officers, a healthy respect for "the law" in its generic form whatever the attitude may be toward specific provisions of either the substantive or procedural codes. It is one thing to ignore a law; it is much more serious to acknowledge publicly that it is being ignored.

One of the factors that results in a healthy respect for the law is the knowledge on the part of every police officer that he may personally be held accountable in a legal suit for actions which he takes as a police officer. Should he be subject to legal action, he knows that a literal interpretation of his authority and his actions will determine the outcome; and that any exercise of discretion on his part is, in the eyes of the court, clearly outside the law. Concern for legal actions fosters support for a concept of full enforcement.

There is some basis to share the concern expressed for the legal obligation to enforce all laws without the exercise of discretion. In 1960, the then Police Commissioner of Philadelphia asserted that for lack of funds and personnel, he would limit initial enforcement of the Sunday closing law to large retail establishments. When a Pennsylvania court reviewed this action, they ruled in favor of one of the large retail merchants and stated that "The admitted discrimination in enforcement is a calculated result of a definite policy on the part of a public official and thus results in a denial to the plaintiff of the equal protection of the law to which it is entitled by virtue of the fourteenth amendment of the United States Constitution."[2] . . .

. . . The whole thought of trying to defend a policy of selective enforcement is a bit frightening. It is asking for trouble. So, he often concludes that it is, in his opinion, much safer to maintain he has no discretion in these matters.

2 Bargain City U.S.A. Inc. v. Dilworth [29 U.S. Law Week 2002 (Pa.C.P. June 10, 1960)].

The Advantages Inherent in a Policy of Recognizing the Exercise of Discretion

. . . Once and for all, acknowledging discretion would enable the police to climb out from underneath the impossible burden which has been placed upon them and which has placed them on the defensive in dealing with the public. And they would be doing so, not by abdicating their legal responsibilities, but by simply acknowledging the true magnitude of their responsibilities. It is the function of the police to demonstrate the impossibility of full enforcement to the community—making citizens aware that the enactment of laws does not cure a problem unless consideration is given to the means for enforcement. An appeal must be made to the public to accept the best judgment and efforts of the police in their approach to the total problem of criminal law enforcement. The community can be given the alternatives of providing additional funds for a level of enforcement closer to full enforcement, of relieving the police of non-police functions which deplete the effort devoted to criminal law enforcement, or of providing the police with more realistic legal guidance in how to fulfill their broad responsibilities. Citizens will choose a level of enforcement, if it is put to them in terms of cost. Somewhere between the extremes of having a police officer for each citizen and having none, a determination must be made as to the number of officers to be employed. Placed in these terms, the degree to which full enforcement can be achieved is a matter known not only to the police agency, but to the community as a whole.

In the administration of governmental affairs, respect for the law takes a second place only to the need for honesty in dealing with the public. Because police officials have been placed in so awkward a position for so long and have felt compelled to deny the obvious, the public typically reacts with initial shock and subsequent pleasure when a police official is refreshingly forthright in his public pronouncements. Keeping the public well informed on police problems, including police shortcomings, clearly develops support for good law enforcement—and public support is the key to the solution of most police problems. . . .

The police have sought professional status. But, professional status does not normally accrue to individuals performing ministerial functions. One of the marks of a true profession is the inherent need for making value judgments and for exercising discretion based upon professional competence. To deny that discretion is exercised gives support to those citizens who maintain that the job of a police officer is a simple one, that it requires little judgment, and that it is not worthy of professional status. By acknowledging the discretionary role the police do fulfill, the drive toward a higher degree of respect and recognition for law enforcement personnel is given impetus. . . .

STREET CORNER SOCIETY xvii, 136-38 (1943)
By William Foote Whyte
(The University of Chicago Press)

In the heart of "Eastern City" there is a slum district known as Cornerville, which is inhabited almost exclusively by Italian immigrants and their children. . . .

There are prevalent in society two general conceptions of the duties of the police officer. Middle-class people feel that he should enforce the law without fear or favor. Cornerville people and many of the officers themselves believe that the policeman should have the confidence of the people in his area so that he can settle many difficulties in a personal manner without making arrests. These two conceptions are in a large measure contradictory. The policeman who takes a strictly legalistic view of his duties cuts himself off from the personal relations necessary to enable him to serve as a mediator of disputes in his area. The policeman who develops close ties with local people is unable to act against them with the vigor prescribed by the law. . . .

. . . A police captain who was well known for his incorruptability once said to me:

> We don't judge the efficiency of an officer by the number of arrests he makes. There are so many arrestable offenses committed even by the law-abiding citizen that if the officer made all the arrests that he could, he would be a very, very busy man. If a man makes too many arrests, he isn't doing his job right. Of course, if he doesn't make any arrests at all, we know something is wrong. We rate the efficiency of the man as a variable considering the character of his route and how quiet he keeps it. If a man has a difficult section and he keeps it quiet so that there isn't much violence, places aren't being robbed, and the women aren't being bothered, then we know he is doing a good job.

. . . Observation of the situation in Cornerville indicates that the primary function of the police department is not the enforcement of the law but the regulation of illegal activities.

The policeman is subject to sharply conflicting social pressures. On one side are the "good people" of Eastern City, who have written their moral judgments into the law and demand through their newspapers that the law be enforced. On the other side are the people of Cornerville, who have different standards. . . .

. . . Under these circumstances the smoothest course for the officer is to conform to the social organization with which he is in direct contact and at the same time to try to give the impression to the outside world that he is enforcing the law. He must play an elaborate role of make-believe, and, in so doing, he serves as a buffer between divergent social organizations with their conflicting standards of conduct.

THE PRESIDENT'S COMMISSION ON LAW ENFORCEMENT AND ADMINISTRATION OF JUSTICE THE CHALLENGE OF CRIME IN A FREE SOCIETY 103, 104, 106 (1967)

The Development of Guidelines for Police Action

In view of the importance, complexity, and delicacy of police work, it is curious that police administrators have seldom attempted to develop and articulate clear policies aimed at guiding or governing the way policemen exercise their discretion on the street. Many police departments have published "general order" or "duty" or "rules, regulations, and procedures" manuals running to several hundred pages. They deal extensively, and quite properly, with the personal conduct of officers on and off duty, with uniform and firearms regulations, with the use of departmental property, with court appearances by officers, with the correct techniques of approaching a building in which a burglary may be in progress. They instruct an officer about taking a suspect into custody and transporting him to the station, or about dealing with sick or injured persons, or about handling stray dogs, or about cooperating with the fire department, or about towing away abandoned automobiles—with, in short, dozens of situations in which policemen commonly, or uncommonly, find themselves. What such manuals almost never discuss are the hard choices policemen must make every day: whether or not to break up a sidewalk gathering, whether or not to intervene in a domestic dispute, whether or not to silence a street-corner speaker, whether or not to stop and frisk, whether or not to arrest. Yet these decisions are the heart of police work. How they are made determines to a large degree the safety of the community, the attitude of the public toward the police and the substance of court rulings on police procedures.

No doubt there are several reasons for the failure of the police to set forth consistent law enforcement policies. One is that it is an extremely hard thing to do. . . .

Another reason that law enforcement policies are seldom stated is that many of them would turn out to be, if clearly set forth, highly controversial. For example, if the police announced publicly that nondisorderly drunks would be arrested only if they had no home to go to, they might be accused of discriminatory treatment.

Probably the most pervasive reason that the police do not articulate policy formally is that they usually do not realize that they make policy informally every day. The police are not accustomed to thinking of themselves as employees of an agency that much more often enforces laws administratively than by invoking the formal criminal process through arrest. Yet a decision by a policeman to order a sidewalk gathering to "break it up," or to take a delinquent youth home rather than arrest him, or to "cool off" a drunk in a precinct lockup rather than formally charge him, is an administrative decision. Not only should policemen be guided by departmental policy in the making of such delicate decisions, but the people who will be affected by these decisions—the public—have a right to be apprised in advance, rather than ex post facto, what police policy is. . . .

Finally, the police should openly acknowledge that, quite properly, they do not arrest all, or even most, offenders they know of. Among the factors accounting for this exercise of discretion are the volume of offenses and the limited resources of the police, the ambiguity of and the public desire for nonenforcement of many statutes and ordinances, the reluctance of many victims to complain and, most important, an entirely proper conviction by policemen that the invocation of criminal sanctions is too drastic a response to many offenses.

But while the Commission believes strongly that it is not only appropriate, but necessary, for policemen to exercise discretion about arrests, it also believes that it is both inappropriate and unnecessary for the entire burden of exercising this discretion to be placed on individual policemen in tumultuous situations. It is incumbent on police departments to define as precisely as possible when arrest is a proper action and when it is not.[d]

[d] Though their existence may be publicly denied, many police agencies have express policy on enforcement of traffic offenses and particularly speed limits. "Tolerance manuals" issued to traffic officers are closely guarded, for fear that the public will feel entitled to rely on the tolerance limits if they are widely known.

POLICE DISCRETION NOT TO INVOKE THE CRIMINAL PROCESS: LOW-VISIBILITY DECISIONS IN THE ADMINISTRATION OF JUSTICE

By Joseph Goldstein

69 Yale Law Journal 543, 557, 560-61, 586-88 (1960)

Within the area of *full enforcement,* the police have not been delegated discretion not to invoke the criminal process. On the contrary, those state statutes providing for municipal police departments which define the responsibility of police provide:

> It shall be the duty of the police . . . under the direction of the mayor and chief of police and in conformity with the ordinances of the city, and the laws of the state, . . . to pursue and arrest any persons fleeing from justice . . . to apprehend any and all persons in the act of committing any offense against the laws of the state . . . and to take the offender forthwith before the proper court or magistrate, to be dealt with for the offense; to make complaints to the proper officers and magistrates of any person known or believed by them to be guilty of the violation of the ordinances of the city or the penal laws of the state; and at all times diligently and faithfully to enforce all such laws. . . .[e]

. . . *Full enforcement,* however, is not a realistic expectation. In addition to ambiguities in the definitions of both substantive offenses and due-process boundaries, countless limitations and pressures preclude the possibility of the police seeking or achieving *full enforcement.* Limitations of time, personnel, and investigative devices—all in part but not entirely functions of budget—force the development, by plan or default, of priorities of enforcement. Even if there were "enough police" adequately equipped and trained, pressures from within and without the department, which is after all a human institution, may force the police to invoke the criminal process selectively. . . .

The mandate of *full enforcement,* under circumstances which compel selective enforcement, has placed the municipal police in an intolerable position. As a result, nonenforcement programs have developed undercover, in a hit-or-miss fashion, and without regard to impact on the overall administration of justice or the

---

[e] MICH. STAT. ANN. § 5.1752 (1949). In contrast to the tenor of this statute Goldstein does not mean by "full enforcement" that police arrest for every crime known to them. He means that they must investigate every crime coming to their attention (whether by complaint or by observation) and present evidence amounting to probable cause to the prosecutor for *his* decision if they do not themselves undertake to arrest. At 559-60, 568 n.94.

basic objectives of the criminal law. Legislatures, therefore, ought to reconsider what discretion, if any, the police must or should have in invoking the criminal process, and what devices, if any, should be designed to increase visibility and hence reviewability of these police decisions.

The ultimate answer is that the police should not be delegated discretion not to invoke the criminal law. It is recognized, of course, that the exercise of discretion cannot be completely eliminated where human beings are involved. The frailties of human language and human perception will always admit of borderline cases (although none of the situations analyzed in this Article are "borderline"). But nonetheless, outside this margin of ambiguity, the police should operate in an atmosphere which exhorts and commands them to invoke impartially all criminal laws within the bounds of *full enforcement.* If a criminal law is ill-advised, poorly defined, or too costly to enforce, efforts by the police to achieve *full enforcement* should generate pressures for legislative action. Responsibility for the enactment, amendment, and repeal of the criminal laws will not, then, be abandoned to the whim of each police officer or department, but retained where it belongs in a democracy—with elected representatives.

Equating *actual enforcement* with *full enforcement,* however, would be neither workable nor humane nor humanly possible under present conditions in most, if not all, jurisdictions. Even if there were "enough police" (and there are not) to enforce all of the criminal laws, too many people have come to rely on the nonenforcement of too many "obsolete" laws to justify the embarrassment, discomfort, and misery which would follow implementation of *full enforcement* programs for every crime. *Full enforcement* is a program for the future, a program which could be initiated with the least hardship when the states, perhaps stimulated by the work of the American Law Institute, enact new criminal codes clearing the books of obsolete offenses.

In the interim, legislatures should establish Policy Appraisal and Review Boards not only to facilitate coordination of municipal police policies with those of other key criminal law administrators, but also to assist commissions drafting new codes in reappraising basic objectives of the criminal law and in identifying laws which have become obsolete.

a. An Example: The Social Gambler

THE GAMBLING BUSINESS: AN AMERICAN PARADOX

By Herbert A. Bloch

8 Crime and Delinquency 355-57, 363 (1962)

A long-standing embarrassment of the American social and economic scene is the incapacity of the public and its officialdom to make up their minds.

Our Contradictory Attitudes

Much of this dilemma arises from the peculiarly American ambivalent penchant for moral disapproval of a variety of publicly enjoyed practices. The Volstead experiment was agony because it outlawed what people wanted—America is a drinking nation. . . . This peculiar inner dialogue of the American public conscience is expressed as well in American sexual patterns, as the Kinsey reports of recent memory so amply testify, and in the subject of this discussion—the gambling business. . . .

Confused Views toward Gambling

Within our historic culture there has never been a clearcut conception of the immorality or the so-called evils of gambling. Indeed, in the early history of the Republic, some of our most worthy educational institutions were financed through public lotteries. Further, certain compulsive factors that lead to pervasive gambling are deeply imbedded within the American social structure itself. It is important to recognize also that in a country as socially and culturally heterogeneous as our own, stemming from national and ethnic backgrounds which have frequently been congenial to public forms of gambling, it becomes extremely difficult to lay down a basis for a universal proscription against it.

The rationales which have frequently been advanced against gambling in any form, ordinarily by religious denominations of fundamentalist persuasion, are based upon quasi-theological views, themselves open to serious question and limited in their conception of practices which satisfy utilitarian objectives. Virgil Peterson notes that "even when fraud and manipulation are absent," the gambling business "operates on a one-sided percentage basis that makes it impossible for the patrons as a class to derive any benefit." That the "sucker" hardly ever gets a fair break in most forms of organized gambling today cannot be denied, but whether or not the individual gambler derives any benefit from the activity as seen from his own standpoint is a different matter. How can we assess the kinds of recreational satisfaction, for example, that large masses of the public derive from gambling? . . .

Social Control of Gambling

The history of the attempt to control gambling in the United States is a record of contiguous cycles. In the initial stage of the cycle, the more flagrant abuses of public tolerance lead to imposition of controls on the more egregious aspects of public gambling enterprise. This, in turn, frequently leads to further efforts to extend control, occasionally ranging from rigid prohibition of off-track betting to the curbing of bingo games. Attempts at such broad control have invariably led in the past to widespread public tolerance of syndicated underworld control, to syndicate absorption or domination of legitimate enterprises, and, more disastrously, to deals with and pay-offs to corrupt law enforcement officials. Usually the next stage is indignant public recoil and an attempt at new approaches and appraisals, leading to greater relaxation of existent standards or more feasible legal control. This, in turn, often leads to further relaxation until excesses and abuse of public tolerance once again give birth to efforts to impose rigid restrictions, and thus the cycle is reintroduced.

ILLINOIS REVISED STATUTES (1967)
Chapter 38, § 28-1

§ 28-1. Gambling. (a) A person commits gambling when he:

(1) Plays a game of chance or skill [excluding bona fide professional contests] for money or other thing of value; or

(2) Makes a wager upon the result of any game, contest, or any political nomination, appointment or election. . . .

(c) Penalty.
A person convicted of gambling under subsection (a)(1) or (a)(2) of this Section shall be fined not to exceed $500 or imprisoned in a penal institution other than the penitentiary not to exceed one year, or both. . . .

THE CRIMINAL LAW AND THE LEGISLATIVE PROCESS

By Frank J. Remington & Victor G. Rosenblum

1960 University of Illinois Law Forum 481, 490-91

Ambiguity by Design—Eliminating Possible Loopholes

One who sets out to eliminate ambiguity in the substantive law very soon is confronted with the argument that he thus creates loopholes through which the guilty can escape.

The effort to be explicit as to the precise mental state required is often resisted by law enforcement agencies, not on the grounds that persons ought to be convicted who lack the prescribed mental state, but rather on the ground that the explicit requirement will create a loophole through which some of the guilty can escape.

If the legislative contribution is to be a major one, clarity as an objective ought to prevail even at the cost of creating opportunity of escape for some who ought to be convicted. There are, however, some situations in which the line is not easily drawn in a way that will exempt conduct which it is not desired to proscribe without seriously hindering enforcement against conduct which it is desirable to proscribe. In this case the temptation is strong to overgeneralize, leaving it to enforcement agencies not to invoke the process against conduct which is not serious. The consequence is, of course, the delegation of broad discretion. For example, this problem confronted the draftsmen of the Model Anti-Gambling Act:

> The Commission has also had great difficulty with this problem of finding a formula which would exclude the social or casual gambler from prosecution and punishment, yet which would not result in opening a large breach in the statute for the benefit of professional gamblers and their patrons. The Commission recognizes that it is unrealistic to promulgate a law literally aimed at making a criminal offense of the friendly election bet, the private, social card game among friends, etc. Nevertheless, it is imperative to confront the professional gambler with a statutory facade that is wholly devoid of loopholes.

The combination of the attitude that loopholes might result and that overgeneralization has not been abused in practice tends to support a continuation of the ambiguity created by criminal statutes which are intended to proscribe a much narrower range of conduct than that defined by the terms of the statute.

MICHIGAN REVISED CRIMINAL CODE—FINAL DRAFT, COMMENT TO §§ 6105–6106 (Sept. 1967)

The Draft is intended to preserve the present coverage of Michigan law, though in a considerably more simplified form. In only two respects does the new language limit existing law: (1) THE CITIZEN WHO PLACES THE BET IS NOT CRIMINAL. This recognizes the fact that gambling is widespread and that there is in actuality no widespread condemnation of the conduct as such. It is only those who exploit the popular urge to gamble who are within the coverage of Chapter 61. . . .

(2) FRIENDLY SOCIAL GAMES ARE NOT CRIMINAL, AND A PERSON DOES NOT PROMOTE OR ADVANCE GAMBLING IF HE MERELY INVITES FRIENDS IN FOR A GAME AND PROVIDES CARDS OR OTHER GAMBLING PARAPHERNALIA. This results from the qualification of the term "player" in § 6101(h) exempting one who "gambles at a social game of chance on equal terms with other participants" as long as he does nothing more than to provide without fee or remuneration the use of premises or the necessary equipment. Private consensual games are generally accepted as socially if not legally proper, and there is no point in preserving the fiction that they are undesirable. However, to control evasion by professional gamblers, the burden of injecting the issue that he is a player is on the defendant.

All exploitive gambling and lottery schemes, however, are made criminal. There are two basic kinds of activity which are penalized. One is "advancing" unlawful gambling activity. This is defined in § 6101(a) to include any activity that goes beyond being a "player" under § 6101(h), including setting up the game, acquisition of the necessary equipment, providing the place, bringing in the players and financing the operation. . . .

The other activity is "profiting" from unlawful gambling activity, the receipt of money or other property, other than as a player as defined in § 6101(h) as proceeds from gambling activity based on a prior agreement or understanding to that effect. . . .

The basic activities of advancing and profiting from gambling are punished as Class A misdemeanors under § 6106. However, this is not a sufficient penalty in the case of large-scale gambling enterprises that are the domain of organized crime. Section 6105, therefore, makes available Class C felony penalties against a person who either (1) engages in bookmaking in which in any one day he takes more than five bets totaling more than $500.00, or (2) in a lottery or mutuel operation receives money or records from someone who is not a player or receives more than $500 in any one day of operation. . . .

POLICE ADMINISTRATION 301-04, 312-13 (2d ed. 1963)
By O. W. Wilson
(McGraw-Hill)†

[P]olice control of vice is made difficult by the diversity of opinion among citizens about the nature and extent of regulation that should be applied. . . . Customer participants may also exert pressure so that their vices may be indulged. Some business groups, such as retail merchants, restaurant owners, and hotel proprietors, may consider laxity in vice control essential for prosperity and business development. Others who have no personal or monetary interest may oppose regulation on the ground that it is an infringement of personal liberty contrary to the best interests of society. . . .

. . . Persons who oppose strict enforcement of vice laws frequently make no determined effort to repeal the legislation but attempt to gain their objective by putting pressure on the police or on the local governing board to relax police control. . . .

. . . In opposition to these groups is the so-called reform element that thinks that the police can and should completely eradicate all forms of vice, even though they cannot eliminate stealing, traffic violations, and other offenses. . . .

. . . There is no simple rule to guide the chief in formulating a vice-control policy, and consequently a high order of administrative judgment is required. He should not join either of the two opposing forces because the interests of one are contrary to the public good and clearly illegal (to the extent that the acts are prohibited by law) and the goal of the other is impossible to attain. Aided by facts derived from analysis of the current problem, the police chief must map a course of action predicated on what can be done, on what is legal, on what is best for the community, and on what the public desires.

A sound stand for the police is to treat vice offenses as they would any law violation and do their best to eliminate them, just as they attempt to eliminate burglary, robbery, and speeding. So long as the police are charged with the enforcement of vice laws, they have no alternative but to impose such regulation or prohibition as may be required by law. Public attitude, however, influences in a subtle way the degree of enforcement. . . .

The proportion of police effort to be directed into the several fields of police control is a matter of administrative judgment,

---

based in part on the interpretation of public opinion. . . . A community that is extremely traffic-conscious justifies greater police attention to traffic control, and likewise a community that is intolerant of commercialized vice justifies a greater proportion of police effort in that field.

However, there can be no compromise with vice any more than there can be compromise with other crime. Variations in enforcement pressure to meet variations in public opinion are made by increasing or decreasing the manpower devoted to vice control, not by countenancing violations. Officers assigned to vice control must make no compromise, and their best efforts must be directed toward carrying out the policy of strict enforcement, even though the number applying the enforcement is cut in half. . . .

Charity gambling, conducted by churches, fraternal, social, and other organizations, is a form that proves especially annoying to the police. Various types of lotteries, pools, punchboards, and bingo are the most popular; and it is interesting and ironic to note that even where these games have been legalized, organized criminals frequently manage to gain control over their earnings, not only to the financial detriment of the groups which play, but to the detriment of their integrity as well. One such group testified before a committee investigating New York's experiment in legalized bingo that before two years had elapsed following legalization, church and fraternal-society members were falsifying reports of their gains from this source in order to meet the demands of the organized criminals who had succeeded in taking over the operation of the games.

The police chief in a city which does not have legalized forms of gambling for charitable or nonprofit purposes must not condone the activity so long as it is a violation of the law. He has no authority to suspend a law, and when permission for such games is requested, he must state his policy clearly to avoid possible misunderstanding.

The police should not dissipate their limited force in ferreting out private gambling; action must be taken, however, when it is carried on flagrantly in public. Examples of private noncommercial gambling include bets of every variety between friends, pools made up among a group of friends on athletic and other events, and card games played within the home. Gambling in a private home for profit, however, should be impartially dealt with by the police.

POLICE DISCRETION: THE IDEAL VERSUS THE REAL

By Herman Goldstein

23 Public Administration Review 140, 142 (1963)

The State of Illinois has a typically broad statute defining gambling. Under its provisions, the flip of a coin to determine who shall purchase coffee or the playing of penny-ante poker must be considered a violation. As a general policy, the Chicago Police Department devotes its efforts to seeking out gambling activities which are part of an organized operation. We do not devote manpower to ferreting out social card games conducted in the privacy of a home. But, upon complaint, we have an obligation to conduct an investigation of any alleged gambling activity.

In March of this year, the department received a complaint of gambling in the basement of an American Legion Post. Three police officers were sent to investigate. They quickly established that the affair was being run by the post auxiliary as a benefit and that a variation of bingo was to be played with the proceeds going to the men at a veterans' hospital. The officers politely warned against any activity which would be considered gambling and left. The patrons of the social, however, got panicky, grabbed their hats and coats and fled. The expected flurry of letters and newspaper articles followed. . . .

DEAR SUPT. WILSON—LEAVE THE GOOD PEOPLE ALONE

By John Justin Smith

Chicago Daily News, Mar. 2, 1963†

It was a very fine party . . . for a while. People laughed and had a good time.

But, wait, let's start at the beginning.

The party, called a Heart Social, was held last Sunday afternoon in the basement of the Central Park American Legion Post at 3356 W. 83th St.

Sponsors were the good women of the post auxiliary. Mrs. Bridget Musacco, head of the auxiliary, explained the purpose of the party thus:

"We needed money for our hospital program. We keep the boys in the West Side and Hines (Veterans Administration) hospitals supplied with stuff like socks, razor blades, combs, cigarets and what-not.

---

† Reprinted with permission.

"In the past we've raised money with things like bake sales, dances and rummage sales. Frankly, we didn't do so hot. Once we cleared about $6 and that's not enough."

So somebody dreamed up the Heart Social. It sounded like a sure-fire way to get more money and it was.

The ladies of the Auxiliary, Robin Hood fashion, ranged Archer Ave. in their Brighton Park neighborhood, putting the sleeve on merchants for gifts . . . towels, dishes, pans, gift certificates for a dollar or two, costume jewelry.

The good women augmented the list of gifts with homemade items, mostly baked goods.

The idea proved to be a good money raiser. About 160 persons, mostly women, paid $1 each to attend the Heart Social.

The party began at 3 p.m. and consisted of a game similar to, ahem, Bingo.

At about 5 p.m., the Heart Social came to a crashing halt.

Let Mrs. Musacco tell you what happened:

"The post commander came down to the basement and told me three guys wanted to see me upstairs and I said, 'What for . . . for heaven's sake?'

"And the commander said the cops were up there. The place was raided."

The three policemen were polite but firm. They said they had received a complaint that there was gambling in the place.

They went downstairs and, as they say in Brighton Park and elsewhere, cased the joint. Mrs. Musacco said:

"They said they wouldn't arrest me because they couldn't see any money, but one of them told me: 'You better close down before the dicks from downtown get here or they will pinch you.' "

Having done this brave thing, the policemen galloped away over the horizon.

Meanwhile, down in the basement, the patrons of the Heart Social got panicky, grabbed their hats and coats and fled the scene.

"We didn't even get a chance to serve coffee and cake to most of them," Mrs. Musacco lamented.

An Answer for Supt. Wilson

Many months ago, in a conversation with Police Supt. O. W. Wilson, the old professor parried a question by asking one:

"Do you worry that Chicago will ever be too clean?"

I laughed and never bothered to answer. I'll take the chance now.

Yes, Prof. Wilson, I do think Chicago can be what you called "too clean." It is right now . . . in some respects.

Most of the people of Chicago don't want you or your men to raid Heart Socials.

They want you to go chase some crooks and leave the good people alone.

OUR KEYSTONE COPS

Chicago Sun-Times, Dec. 23, 1964†

It is difficult to believe any Chicago policeman is as stupid as indicated by Dr. Max Linn's version of the raid on his Near North Side apartment. However, police reports were fragmentary. Even the comment made by Police Supt. O. W. Wilson was enigmatic.

Dr. Linn's version is that five women, all friends of Mrs. Linn, meet in his home almost every Sunday evening and play poker for small stakes. We can understand this, Sunday evening TV being what it is. They were doing so last Sunday evening when, according to Linn, police raided his apartment without a warrant, seized a card table, a deck of cards, two chip racks and $3.60 in a pot and then carted Dr. Linn and the players, all past 60, off to the police station where each had to give $200 bond. These bonds cost $140 for the seven; a cost which is not recoverable.

This isn't the kind of law enforcement needed in Chicago.

In the first place, it is about time Chicago police get warrants before invading private premises. They know raids conducted without warrants are illegal and that cases built upon them are as worthless as two pair against a royal flush. In the second place, raiding private homes to break up a social game of cards isn't, under most circumstances, going to reduce the city's crime rate. We don't need Keystone cops in Chicago. We need real crime smashers; not penny-ante raiders.

Policemen who waste their time in the manner alleged by Dr. Linn should be put to patrolling those Chicago streets upon which one cannot walk at night without being mugged.

As noted, the public has nothing other than Dr. Linn's version of the affair. If that version stands up, and it does to date,

† Chicago Sun-Times editorial, Dec. 23, 1964. Reprinted with permission.

the Police Board should inform itself as to what is going on in the Town Hall district. It doesn't smell good. Until it does, we suggest that respectable residents of that district quit trying to fill an inside straight at Sunday evening home games.

Those gallant vice squad raiders may not be able to make a case against the Syndicate but they can sure raise hell with little old ladies.

HOW NOT TO FIGHT CRIME
Chicago Tribune, Dec. 23, 1964†

When an anonymous telephone caller told the police that there was big time gambling in an apartment on Surf street Sunday evening, three vice detectives sped to the address given. This was the last intelligent thing they did that evening.

Common sense should have told the detectives to shake hands with the "big time gamblers," explain that even anonymous reports must be investigated, and depart. The Chicago police department has more important things to do than become a party to what was obviously somebody's idea of a practical joke.

CHICAGO POLICE APOLOGIZE FOR RAID ON POKER GAME
Wisconsin State Journal, Dec. 26, 1964

CHICAGO (UPI)—Police Supt. O. W. Wilson apologized Thursday for a police raid on a penny ante poker game and said gambling charges would be dropped against six elderly women and one man arrested during the raid.

Nine policemen, including three vice squad detectives, raided the apartment of Dr. Max Linn, 69, Sunday in response to an anonymous telephone call that a large-scale gambling operation was in progress.

They confiscated $3.60, a deck of cards, a poker table, and some poker chips. They also arrested Linn, an optometrist, along with his wife and five other women, ages 58 to 66, and had Linn fingerprinted and photographed.

Linn said the penny-ante game was a regular Sunday night get-together. The ladies would have dinner and talk, then play cards for stakes of 15 cents or a quarter, he said.

Wilson's statement apologized "for our actions in this case" and said that the officers did not have a search warrant and "should not have invaded the privacy of Dr. Linn's home."

---

† Reprinted, courtesy of the Chicago Tribune.

Wilson said gambling even for minor stakes is contrary to law but added, "Our primary emphasis must always be against commercialized gambling rather than friendly poker games."[f]

ARREST: THE DECISION TO TAKE A SUSPECT INTO CUSTODY 89, 90-91, 148-49, 155-56, note 16 (1965)

By Wayne R. LaFave

(Little, Brown & Company)

A police officer was led by a complainant to a private residence where, through a window, the occupants could be observed playing poker for money. The officer refused to take any action against the card players, although the state statute expressly covered all forms of gambling. . . .

The police do experience some difficulty, however, in drawing a line between social gambling and professional gambling. Generally, gambling occurring in private homes is exempted from enforcement, as was the case in the illustration, but the police must assure themselves that a professional game has not been moved into a private home in order to give the appearance of a social gathering. One tactic used by Detroit police when they are called to such a gathering is to take a number of the persons in the group aside and ask them to identify all other members of the group. This device, to some extent, allows the police to distinguish the gathering of a group of friends from the professional operations at which customers come and go at intervals and are not socially acquainted.

Gambling outside private homes is generally proceeded against unless it is clearly social in nature. Professional gambling in so-called private clubs is a subject of strict enforcement, although detection is difficult. Some uncertainty has been expressed, however, as to whether minor gambling in such places as pool halls ought to be looked upon as social or commercial. It is not professional in the sense of any substantial income to the proprietor of the establishment. He will collect a small sum from the players for the use of the table, but may receive no portion of the gambling money directly. While this situation comes to the

---

[f] When a gambling complaint is received by the Chicago Vice Control Division and gambling is found, arrest will almost surely follow: (1)A report must be filed and the officer cannot acceptably report that he discovered gambling and did nothing. (2)The officer may believe much more money was involved in the game than the small amount on the table when he was admitted. (3)And failure to arrest would expose him to the imputation of corruption.

As a result of this incident there was an orally communicated policy not to raid games in homes.

attention of the police fairly frequently during routine inspection of such licensed premises, arrest is not likely so long as the social aspects outweigh the professional aspects. It is usually recognized that such activity is the equivalent of social gambling engaged in at home by persons higher in the community class structure.

(155-56 n.16)

[16] Official recognition by a police agency that the police may exercise discretion seldom occurs, and when it does it is usually prompted by a serious challenge to certain instances of nonenforcement. Following a recent John Doe investigation in Milwaukee, the head of the vice squad was charged with misconduct in office for alleged improper handling of tavern gambling device investigations, including failure to arrest or report certain known violations. This officer's counsel was reported as saying: "It does seem entirely clear, however, that it has been the practice in the Milwaukee police department for many years to do precisely what Capt. Kuszewski is alleged to have done under these counts, that is, make a determination of whether arrests should be made for violations on a case by case basis. . . .

"Capt. Kuszewski's vice squad made about 7,500 arrests during the time alleged violations occurred. Only six nonarrest situations are involved in the charges. He has been making these determinations openly for 16 years, and he has never been told by anyone that it is not within his authority to do so." Milwaukee Journal, March 3, 1963, p. 1, col. 2.

The chief of police in Milwaukee, who asked for a legal opinion from the city attorney on whether the police could exercise discretion, was quoted as saying: "Use of good judgment is a primary function of a good policeman in every case involving possible violation of a city ordinance or state law.

"We must secure a legal opinion determining to what extent policemen may exercise judgment in possible law violations to safeguard the officers themselves from possible prosecutions. Police judgment in the enforcement of the law has been required since the first patrolman walked a beat anywhere in the world." Milwaukee Journal, March 4, 1963, p. 1, col. 6.

When police do arrest in cases of nonprofessional gambling, . . . this is prompted by a desire to avoid the impression of nonenforcement. Generally, however, it is possible to maintain a reasonably good image of full enforcement while following a policy of nonenforcement in regard to many offenses since most instances of a failure to arrest are less visible than those concerned with open gambling. Sometimes, current public concern about a particular, widely-publicized incident also prompts a higher level of enforcement against certain conduct than otherwise would be undertaken.

Basically the question is whether it is desirable for the public to be aware of a policy of less than full enforcement. Widespread recognition of the exercise of discretion by the police makes the appearance of impartiality more difficult to achieve. Public pressure on the police for nonenforcement in individual cases is greatest when it is known that the conduct is not usually subject to full enforcement. Perhaps this is the implication of the assertion that "the worst evil of disregard for some laws is that it destroys respect for all law."

b. The Propriety of Current Administrative Practice

The practice of refraining from arresting in circumstances justifying an arrest is rarely the subject of litigation, except when it is part of a pattern of corruption. When failure of police to arrest is raised, the typical response of the courts is to disapprove strongly, whether it is failure in an individual case or failure as a result of general police policy.

GOWAN v. SMITH

157 Mich. 443, 122 N.W. 286 (1909)

The purpose of this proceeding is to review by the writ of certiorari the action of the respondent in refusing an order to show cause upon a petition by the relator for a peremptory mandamus to compel Frederick W. Smith, police commissioner of the city of Detroit, to enforce, generally and in a specific instance a statute and an ordinance of the city controlling and regulating the liquor saloons in that city, which, according to the brief in behalf of the respondent, number 1,780, and to set aside his order or instruction permitting saloons to keep open on Sundays from 12 o'clock noon to 8 o'clock p. m. So far as material to the questions involved, the statement of the petition is as follows:

The relator is a physician and a citizen of Detroit; in 1902 he established a sanitarium and residence for himself and family at No. 75-77 East High street; he has since conducted his business, which has become successful and profitable; at the time he established said sanitarium no saloons existed in the vicinity; two years ago one Snook opened a saloon adjacent to this sanitarium; said saloon has been conducted in constant and open violation of the statute and ordinance; such open violations have greatly injured the relator's business, and threaten its ruin; he applied to said police commissioner, both orally and in writing, to enforce the statute and ordinance, and to vacate the order which said commissioner had made permitting saloons to remain open on Sundays between 12 noon and 8 o'clock p. m., in violation both of the law of the State and the ordinance of the city; said commissioner not only refused to take any action in the matter, but promptly ordered the relator from his office.

GRANT, J. We now come to the meritorious question in the case, namely, Does the petition present a state of facts which, if admitted or proven, justify the issuance of the writ to compel the respondent: *First,* to set aside an order or instruction (the name is immaterial) directing the police officers under his control to permit saloons to keep open in direct violation of the law of the State and of the ordinance; *second,* to compel the respondent to enforce the law in the particular case? The use of the writ to compel the performance of official duty and to restrain illegal official action is old and too well established to require the citation of authorities.

In State v. Police Board of Columbus, 19 Wkly. Law Bul. (Ohio) 347, the police board was compelled by mandamus to enforce the law in a case precisely like the one here involved. While that case was in a *nisi prius* court, a portion of the opinion is worthy here to be quoted:

"Three defenses were made in this case. The first is one of law, challenging the jurisdiction of this court. The other two cannot be classified. They are remarkable. They are reprehensible. One is that the execution of the law was not practicable, and that was one of the reasons why nothing had been done; and to sustain that view it was said that a number of cases involving violations of the Sunday law, and sent to court by a former mayor, have been nollied. This court takes judicial notice of the fact that those cases are still on its docket, and have not been tried for want of time, since the present incumbent has been on the bench. Neither the board nor the mayor had the right to decide that the execution of the law is not feasible. They should do their duty, and let the failure to execute the balance of the law, if any should occur, rest where it shall belong. Besides, in certain contingencies and certain cases, the mayor has the power to try the cases under this law, and, with or without the aid of a jury, determine them finally. The other defense mentioned is that the law had not been enforced because there was a diversity of sentiment touching the wisdom and rightfulness of the law. But whence does the board or the mayor derive the power to decide that the laws may be repealed, as it were, because they think that some people, even a large number of people, are opposed to their execution? Nowhere does such power exist. Upon a parity of reasoning, nearly every law might be nullified by executive and judicial officers. It would be a suspension, a repeal of law, by those who have not the power to do such a public act, by those whose duty it is to enforce the law. I know of only two cases where even judicial officers have a right to confine, to limit, the laws in the enforcement of them. That is where, as Lord Bacon said, penal laws are 'sleepers of long,' or where they have 'grown unfit for the time.' But the law sought to be enforced here is not of either class. It was enacted in nearly its present form a few years ago, and only a few weeks ago re-enacted by the supreme lawmaking authority of this State. The logic of these two last-named defenses is the logic of nullification, though I do not use this term in a political sense at all. The personal or private opinions of the judge of this court, or of the mayor, or of the members of the board touching the expediency of the Sunday law under consideration ought to have no influence upon their official action. Where their duty is clear, they forswear themselves if they do not perform it. They have taken an oath to faithfully discharge their duty; one of these duties is to carry into effect the laws of the State and enforce their solemn mandates."

Something is said about a discretion lodged in the respondent. The only discretion lodged in him is to refuse to make complaints when, after proper and honest investigation, he has become satisfied that no offense has been committed. He has no discretion to refuse to enforce the law. To hold that he has, would be subversive of government by law, and place in the hands of officials the power to set any law of the State aside, as, according to the allegations of the petition, the respondent has done in this case. No case cited in behalf of respondent intimates that there is any discretion in this particular lodged in the officer.

BROOKE, J. I am unable to agree with the conclusions reached by my Brother GRANT in this matter. . . .

While it is true that a writ of mandamus will issue commanding a public official to perform a specific ministerial act, it does not lie against officials to compel the enforcement of the criminal law by obtaining complaint for its violation and by arrest. This is a discretionary executive power, and should not be subjected to the control of the courts except in cases of gross and manifest abuse.

Should this court issue the writ, it could only command the police commissioner to proceed to enforce the law as to Snook's saloon, in which event the commissioner would gather evidence of Snook's infraction of the law, make complaint before the proper officer, and proceed to prosecute through the prosecuting attorney. In obeying the mandate of this court in this respect, the commissioner is bound to use the discretion with which he is clothed. He is charged not alone with the execution of the liquor laws of the State within the city of Detroit, but he is likewise charged with the suppression of all crime and the conservation of the peace. To enable him to perform the duties imposed upon him by law, he is supplied with certain limited means. It is entirely obvious that he must exercise a sound discretion as to how those means shall be applied for the good of the community. He cannot withdraw the entire force at his command from their ordinary duties and detail them to collect evidence against lawbreaking saloon keepers, lest other crimes should multiply. That a certain portion of his force was so employed is apparent from the averments of the petition. The writ should not issue unless this court is prepared to exercise a constant or recurring supervision over the daily acts of the police commissioner, and a definite control of the discretion with which he is clothed by law. This cannot be done.

STATE ex *rel.* PARKER v. McKNAUGHT

152 Kan. 689, 107 P.2d 693 (1940)

SMITH, J. This is an action in quo warranto brought by the state on the relation of the attorney general whereby the state seeks to oust the defendant from the office of chief of police of the city of Topeka.

The commissioner, in connection with his findings as to the Cooney liquor, found as follows:

> (p) The Kansas Peace Officers' Convention was held in Topeka during the month of October, 1939. . . .
>
> (q) One of the hotels in Topeka was named as convention headquarters. In consideration for this designation the

hotel furnished some rooms for the use of those attending the convention. The defendant had to do with the making of arrangements with the hotel, and from time to time, during the three-day session of the convention, the defendant was in these rooms together with others who were there attending the convention. During this time some liquor was served in these rooms. There is no evidence whatever that any of what is called the "Cooney liquor" was brought to those rooms or that the defendant had anything whatever to do with the furnishing of any liquor. He was, however, in the rooms at various times and saw others there drinking liquor. There is no evidence that the defendant himself drank any liquor there or had any part in connection with the rooms except as stated herein.

Did the conduct of the defendant set out in the above findings constitute grounds for ouster? The commissioner thought not. We must start our consideration of the question by remembering that this incident occurred in the city of which defendant was the head of the police force. He was charged with the duty of directing the enforcement of all the laws of the state and ordinances of the city. When he saw drinks containing intoxicating liquors being served there in the hotel room he knew that someone had violated the law by bringing the liquor there and someone was violating the law by having it in his possession. There is no way intoxicating liquor may be served in Kansas without the law being violated in two or three particulars. The duty of the defendant was clear under the circumstances. He should have taken steps immediately to arrest and cause the prosecution of those persons guilty of these violations. This may seem like a harsh rule, but defendant assumed this duty when he took the oath and qualified as chief of police. The legislature of the state and governing body of the city have passed on that situation. There is a discretion to be exercised, but that discretion is reposed in these bodies. They have left no room for the exercise of discretion on the part of officials charged especially with the duty of seeing that the laws are enforced.

Defendant presses upon our attention the rule laid down by this court in State v. Trinkle, 70 Kan. 396, 78 Pac. 854; State, *ex rel.*, v. Foley, 107 Kan. 608, 193 Pac. 361; and State, *ex rel.*, v. Wilson, 108 Kan. 641, 196 Pac. 758. In those cases this court laid down the general rule that an officer must be accorded a reasonable discretion in directing the business of his office, and some scope must be conceded to him for the exercise of his best judgment in respect to any matters committed to his charge. He argues that this is a case where that rule should be invoked and that in the absence of any showing of corrupt motive on the part of defendant this incident is not grounds for ouster. Defendant states in his brief that "the people do not want 100 percent law enforcement of the law. . . ." "Many different and double standards prevail." The trouble with that argument on the part of defendant is that it would allow each law-enforcement officer to decide when the law should be enforced and when it should not be enforced. Neither the governing body of the city nor the state legislature have conferred any such discretion on defendant. Such discretion has not been conferred on this court. There is more to the incident than the mere fact that someone consumed a drink containing intoxicating liquor while defendant was in the room. Some significance must be given the fact that the other people in the room who were drinking went right ahead with their drinking and mixing drinks while he was there. This establishes at least a tacit consent on the part of defendant that the liquor should be there in the possession of somebody.

This conduct our commissioner found to be wrong and a violation of defendant's duty. It was passed over, however, with the statement that there was no wrongful motive on the part of defendant, but merely a mistaken idea of hospitality. We are unable to treat the matter so lightly. We have concluded that it was misconduct on the part of defendant, which requires a judgment of ouster.

STATE v. LOMBARDI
8 Wis. 2d 421, 99 N.W.2d 829 (1959)

At the time in question defendant-appellant Lombardi was the sheriff of Waukesha county. The verdict found him guilty of wilful dereliction of duty in connection with numerous events occurring in his county. The events and the derelictions were specified in the informations in which appellant was charged and specified also in the verdicts.

BROWN, J. Count 3, Information "B," pertains to an assault by Dominic Picciurro against Peter Picciurro.

The alleged assault took place at Dominic's tavern, Club 166. Eyewitnesses were at all times available for a prompt and thorough investigation. They testified at the trial that Dominic severely and brutally beat his son Peter about the head and face while Peter made no resistance. While this was going on the sheriff's office was notified by phone and deputies were sent to the scene. When they arrived the assault had ended. Peter's jaw was broken on both sides of his face. Sheriff's deputies took Peter to the hospital where he was hospitalized for several days. On the trip there Peter told the deputies that he was injured by falling down the tavern steps. He also told them that his father must have hit him 40 times. One of the deputies, Nordseth, who came to the scene, made a report with a complaint of assault attached to it. At the trial Nordseth testified that in his report to the sheriff he listed the names of the witnesses. The report cannot now be found.

When the sheriff received the report on the following day he said he would take care of it personally. Lombardi then interviewed Peter Picciurro at the hospital. Peter said he would not file a complaint against his father; that Dominic had not injured him but Peter had hurt himself. Lombardi made no further investigation or at least he testified to none. He made no report to the district attorney of his own volition, but the next day the district attorney heard rumors about the trouble at the tavern and inquired about it from the sheriff. Lombardi told him that he had investigated the matter and it turned out to be merely family trouble, the son did not want to sign a complaint against his father, and the matter required no further attention. No further attention was given it either by the sheriff or the district attorney. But the sheriff did not tell the district attorney that the deputy sheriff had attached an assault complaint to his report, with names of witnesses, the sheriff did not interview the witnesses, nor did the sheriff inform the district attorney of the serious injuries which Peter had received. The record fully substantiates the conclusion that the sheriff found no facts to incriminate Dominic Picciurro because he preferred not to find them and he withheld from the district attorney the few important facts which the sheriff did know. The record sustains the verdict in Count 3, Information "B," finding Michael Lombardi guilty of failing to arrest Dominic Picciurro and of withholding material facts from the district attorney. The judgment and sentence on this count must be affirmed.

The remaining information and verdict is that of Count 5, Information "A." In brief, the state accuses and convicts the defendant of wilful neglect of his duty in the period between January 1, 1955, and June 30, 1956, in that he, the sheriff, knowingly permitted a tavern and night club known as Club 166 to operate in violation of the laws regarding prostitution, gambling, and sale of liquor; and the sheriff not only did not, himself, enforce the laws in those respects but prevented his deputies from interfering with the illegal operations of the club.

The club was operated by Mr. and Mrs. Dominic Picciurro. The record shows that the sheriff was a frequenter of the club and was a long-time, close friend to Dominic. An employee at the club testified that between January 1, 1955, and June 30, 1956, liquor was served there later than at legal hours and gambling was conducted there. During that time detectives from the state treasurer's office found evidence of such liquor sales and gambling and the district attorney prosecuted and convicted Mrs. Picciurro of those offenses. Defendant's familiarity with the premises, his intimacy with the proprietors, and the testimony of the sheriff's deputies that Lombardi directed them to cease their surveillance of the club sustain the verdict that the sheriff knew of the violations of the liquor and gambling laws but wilfully failed to take any action to suppress them.

The contrasting attitude of the President's Commission on Law Enforcement and Administration of Justice toward the propriety of nonenforcement, particularly when resulting from well-considered police policy, was noted above at 288.

2. *The Problem of Selective Enforcement*

Even in circumstances which persuade police that preferable policy is not to try arresting each offender against the law, there is a question of fairness in picking out some one person or some one group of offenders to proceed against. The issues are several: (a) whether selective enforcement is ever permissible (the issue dealt with in § 1 above), (b) what criteria for selection are appropriate, if any are, and (c) the legal devices for enforcing compliance with criteria.

The Practice

The following cannot be called typical police practices, though neither are they highly unusual. They represent a range of circumstances in which police may be moved to arrest even though their usual practice would be to avoid arresting.

1

Police reporting to the scene of a disturbance found a family squabble, involving a minor assault on a spouse. Although the usual procedure was merely to restore order and leave, the officers recalled that they had received repeated calls to this particular address in the past. Therefore the offender was arrested.

2

A police patrol stopped a car that had been traveling at 39 m.p.h. in a 30 m.p.h. zone. They decided prior to leaving the squad car that they would only issue a warning. When the deputies approached, the driver said in a sarcastic tone, "What in hell have I done now?" Because of his belligerent attitude the driver was placed under arrest.

3

The police were aware of the operation of a private card game in which there was no house "cut." Since this operation therefore qualified as mere social gambling, no action was taken against the offenders. However, the operators of the game made no attempt to conceal the operation, and it was soon apparent to the general public that the police must be aware of it. Realizing this, the police arrested the gamblers.

4

The police learned of a minor property theft. As the victim was not interested in prosecution, the police, in accord with their usual policy, decided not to arrest. However, when they learned that the offender was known to the police department as a "bad actor," and that the police had been unsuccessful in obtaining his conviction for other, more serious offenses, they arrested him.

5

Officers saw a man leave an out-of-state car in the vicinity of a pawnshop with a jacket on his arm. The suspect, when questioned, said that he had no employment but had come to the city to find work. He could provide no identification, but explained this by saying that his wallet had recently been stolen. He was somewhat evasive in answering other questions. The police suspected him of burglary, but lacking evidence for this charge, they arrested him for vagrancy.

PEOPLE v. UTICA DAW'S DRUG CO.

16 App. Div. 2d 12, 225 N.Y.S.2d 128 (1962)

HALPERN, J. This case presents the question of the proper way in which to deal with a claim by a defendant in a criminal case that the law has been enforced in a discriminatory manner against him in violation of the equal protection clauses of the State and Federal Constitutions.

The defendant maintains a drugstore in the City of Utica, New York, which operates under a policy of selling at reduced prices, generally characteristic of stores known as "cut-rate" stores or discount houses. The drugstore is open on Sunday as all drugstores are permitted to be under the Sunday statute (Penal Law, § 2147). However, the items which drugstores are permitted to sell on Sunday are limited by the statute. The defendant was indicted for violation of the Sunday statute, it being charged that defendant on Sunday, December 18, 1960, "unlawfully did publicly sell and expose for sale certain property, to wit, a pair of gloves, a doll, a brown belt and a drinking cup" in violation of section 2147 of the Penal Law.

The defendant did not contest the charge that the enumerated items had been sold and offered for sale in its store but contended that similar items had been sold and offered for sale on Sunday throughout the City of Utica and County of Oneida by all other drugstores and that other items, the sale of which on Sunday was prohibited by section 2147 of the Penal Law, had been regularly offered for sale and sold in other types of stores, without any attempt on the part of the public authorities to interfere with the sale or to prosecute the vendors. Only the defendant and one other company (not a drugstore) also engaged in a discount operation were prosecuted. The defendant maintained that the prosecution was part of a discriminatory design aimed at the defendant and others engaged in the same type of "cut-rate" operation. It maintained that the public authorities intentionally discriminated against that class and allowed others outside the class to continue to sell the forbidden items in violation of the Sunday law without molestation.

The trial court, with the acquiescence of the District Attorney, held that the defendant's contention, if established, would constitute a good defense to the criminal charge and it submitted the case to the jury accordingly. It left it to the jury to decide as a question of fact whether the defendant's proof established "a clear and intentional discrimination against this defendant and against those in the same class." At the request of the defendant, the court charged in language taken from Yick Wo v. Hopkins (118 U.S. 356, 373-374): "Though the law itself be fair on its face and impartial in appearance, yet, if it is applied and administered by public authority with an evil eye and an unequal hand, so as practically to make unjust and illegal discriminations between persons in similar circumstances, material to their rights, the denial of equal justice is still within the prohibition of the Constitution." The jury found the defendant guilty and this appeal followed.

Under the theory upon which the case was tried and submitted, the judgment of conviction cannot be permitted to stand. While the court accurately stated the principle of *Yick Wo v. Hopkins* and the cases which have followed it, it did not consistently apply the principle during the course of the trial. The defendant attempted to prove that 21 other drugstores in the City of Utica had engaged in offering for sale and in selling forbidden items on Sunday, December 18, 1960, and on other Sundays but the court sustained objections to most of the questions designed to elicit this proof. While the court allowed the defendant to prove that the stores had been open on Sunday, it sustained objections to questions as to the items which they had offered for sale on Sunday. The court also sustained objection to a question designed to show that a witness who was in the business of selling flags and decorations, advertised that his business was open on Sunday and that in fact he had sold flags and decorations on Sunday. Similar objections were sustained with regard to proof of sales on Sunday by various other types of stores.

It also appeared upon the trial that, after the defendant's arrest on December 18, the defendant engaged a private detective, formerly a member of the police department, to make an investigation on its behalf. On the following Sunday, December 25, he found that throughout the City of Utica in various drugstores which he listed by name and address, he was able to purchase and did purchase items forbidden for sale on Sunday under the statute. He also made purchases of forbidden items at smoke shops, news stores and grocery stores. The private detective then, at the request of the defendant's counsel, went to the Clerk of the City Court and offered to sign and swear to depositions with respect to each of the purchases made by him but the secretary of the City Court Judge who handled the matter declined to accept the depositions. Proof of these facts was admitted upon the trial. However, the court refused to allow the defendant's counsel to prove that he had subsequently written a letter to the Chief of Police of the city, a copy of which was marked for identification, advising of the purchases made by the investigator and offering to have the investigator sign and swear to depositions with respect thereto and requesting the Chief of Police to have officers in his department execute the necessary informations and obtain warrants of arrest. Objection to the admission of the letter into evidence was sustained and the Chief of Police was not allowed to testify with respect to its receipt and his failure to take action thereon.

It is thus apparent that while the court recognized the validity of the defense put forward by the defendant, it prevented the defendant from introducing material evidence which would have tended to support the defense. The court held that the evidence was irrelevant, upon the authority of People v. Friedman (302 N.Y. 75, appeal dismissed 341 U.S. 907); Snowden v. Hughes (321 U.S. 1) and other cases holding that nonenforcement of itself is not sufficient to establish discrimination. In so ruling, the court misconstrued the cases upon which it relied. While it is true that they held that mere nonenforcement is insufficient of itself to establish discrimination, they did not hold that proof of nonenforcement is not admissible in evidence, in a case in which the defendant asserts that there had been intentional discrimination. It is true that in order to find a violation of the constitutional guarantee, the trier of the facts must be satisfied that there was intentional discrimination, and not mere laxity in enforcement, but in the effort to persuade the trier of the facts of the truth of its ultimate contention, the defendant is entitled to introduce evidence of nonenforcement as relevant evidence bearing upon that contention. (People v. Harris, 182 Cal. App. 2d 837; 5 Cal. Rep. 852.)

We have therefore concluded that, upon the basis upon which the case was tried and submitted, the judgment of conviction must be reversed because of errors in the exclusion of evidence.

However, we believe that the entire approach to the problem, adopted by the trial court with the approval or acquiescence of the counsel on both sides, was erroneous and that a different approach should be followed, upon the remand of the case. The claim of discriminatory enforcement should not be treated as a defense to the criminal charge, to be tried before the jury and submitted to it for decision, but should be treated as an application to the court for a dismissal or quashing of the prosecution upon constitutional grounds. Insofar as a question of fact may be involved, the court should take the evidence in the absence of the jury and should decide the question itself. If the court finds that there was an intentional and purposeful discrimination, the court should quash the prosecution, not because the defendant is not guilty of the crime charged, but because the court, as an agency of government, should not lend itself to a prosecution the maintenance of which would violate the constitutional rights of the defendant.

As was said in a concurring opinion by Mr. Justice ROBERTS speaking for himself and for Mr. Justice BRANDEIS and Mr. Justice STONE in a different context: "It is the province of the court and of the court alone to protect itself and the government from such prostitution of the criminal law . . . [It] should be dealt with by the court no matter by whom or at what stage of the proceedings the facts are brought to its attention" and further: "Recognition of the defense . . . as belonging to the defendant and as raising an issue for decision by the jury called to try him upon plea of the general issue, results in the trial of a false issue wholly outside the true rule which should be applied by the courts." (Sorrells v. United States, 287 U.S. 435, 457, 458.)

These statements were made in a case involving the defense of entrapment. They are applicable a fortiori to the problem here presented. The approach for which Mr. Justice ROBERTS argued in his concurring opinion is much more appropriate to the type of problem with which we are here concerned than it is to a claim of entrapment. An argument can be that entrapment is a true defense establishing that the defendant was not in fact guilty of the crime charged within the contemplation of the statute defining the crime; that was the position taken by the majority in the *Sorrells* case. No such argument can be made as to the claim of discriminatory enforcement. All the elements of the crime are present; the only question is whether the prosecution for the crime should be barred because it would violate the constitutional guarantee of equal protection of the laws to allow it to proceed. In the recent case of Sherman v. United States (356 U.S. 369) the majority found it unnecessary to decide whether the approach advocated by Mr. Justice ROBERTS as to the claim of entrapment should be adopted but in a strong concurring opinion by Mr. Justice FRANKFURTER, in which Mr. Justice DOUGLAS, Mr. Justice HARLAN and Mr. Justice BRENNAN joined, the court was urged to adopt the ROBERTS' approach. "[S]uch a judgment, aimed at blocking off areas of impermissible police conduct, is appropriate for the court and not the jury" (p. 385).

The equal protection clause of the Constitution applies to all agencies of government, including the courts (Shelley v. Kraemer, 334 U.S. 1). "[T]he prohibitions of the [Fourteenth] Amendment refer to all the instrumentalities of the State, to its legislative, executive, and judicial authorities, and, therefore, whoever by virtue of public position under a state government deprives another of any right protected by that amendment . . . 'violates the constitutional inhibition; and . . . his act is that of the State.'" (Chicago, Burlington & Quincy R. R. Co. v. Chicago, 166 U.S. 226, 233-234; and, see, comment in 59 Yale L.J., p. 358.)

Treating the claim of discriminatory enforcement as a motion to quash the prosecution, addressed to the court, puts it in the same category as a motion to suppress illegally seized evidence under the Federal criminal procedure (Fed. Rules Crim. Pro., rule 41, subd. [e]) or the similar procedure now mandated in the State courts under Mapp v. Ohio (367 U.S. 643).

While there is no statutory provision for the motion here suggested, there is ample precedent for the entertaining of a motion to quash a prosecution based upon constitutional grounds, for which no statutory provision has been made. Thus it was held in People v. Glen (173 N.Y. 395) that a motion to dismiss an indictment because it had been found without sufficient evidence, in violation of the State Constitution, would be entertained notwithstanding the fact that the statutory provision for motions to dismiss did not include this ground among the enumerated grounds. See, in this connection, the opinion of Judge ABRAHAM GELLER of the Court of General Sessions, entertaining a motion to suppress illegally seized evidence under *Mapp v. Ohio,* prior to the adoption of any implementing statute providing therefor (People v. Gonzales, 31 Misc 2d 486).

As the concurring opinions in the entrapment cases cited above strongly argue, matters of this kind should be dealt with by the court rather than the jury. This places the power and the responsibility where it belongs,—in the court. The claim of discriminatory enforcement does not go to the question of the guilt or innocence of the defendant, which is within the province of the jury. The question is rather whether in a community in which there is general disregard of a particular law with the acquiescence of the public authorities, the authorities should be allowed sporadically to select a single defendant or a single class of defendants for prosecution because of personal animosity or for some other illegitimate reason. The wrong sought to be prevented is a wrong by the public authorities. To allow such arbitrary and discriminatory enforcement of a generally disregarded law is to place in the hands of the police and the prosecutor a power of the type frequently invoked in countries ruled by a dictator but wholly out of harmony with the principle of equal justice under law prevailing in democratic societies. The court is asked to stop the prosecution at the threshold, not because the defendant is innocent but because the public authorities are guilty of a wrong in engaging in a course of conduct designed to discriminate unconstitutionally against the defendant. Clearly, a contention of this kind is addressed to the court and should be passed upon by the court and not left to the jury.

In most cases in other jurisdictions, the claim of discriminatory enforcement has been raised in the past by actions in equity to enjoin the criminal prosecution (Wade v. City and County of San Francisco, 82 Cal. App. 2d 337; City of Covington v. Gausepohl, 250 Ky. 323; Boynton v. Fox, 60 F.2d 851; cf. Two Guys v.

McGinley, 366 U.S. 582). We see no reason why it may not be raised in the criminal proceeding itself by an appropriate motion, and we see many advantages in having it dealt with in that way by the court which has jurisdiction over the criminal charge.

The courts in some States have indicated a reluctance to enjoin a criminal prosecution on the ground of unconstitutional discrimination, for fear that guilty persons would thereby escape prosecution and the flouting of the law would be encouraged (e.g., Society of Good Neighbors v. Detroit Mayor, 324 Mich. 22). This fear, in our opinion, is an unfounded one. As has been pointed out, the burden resting upon the defendant is a heavy one and, even if the defendant succeeds in sustaining it, he will not be immune from a new prosecution, when and if the public authorities undertake a generalized enforcement of the law. Furthermore, even if the enforcement of a particular law is selective, it does not necessarily follow that it is unconstitutionally discriminatory. Selective enforcement may be justified when the meaning or constitutionality of the law is in doubt and a test case is needed to clarify the law or to establish its validity. Selective enforcement may also be justified when a striking example or a few examples are sought in order to deter other violators, as part of a bona fide rational pattern of general enforcement, in the expectation that general compliance will follow and that further prosecutions will be unnecessary. It is only when the selective enforcement is designed to discriminate against the persons prosecuted, without any intention to follow it up by general enforcement against others, that a constitutional violation may be found. (See generally, two excellent and comprehensive notes on this subject, one entitled "Discriminatory Law Enforcement and Equal Protection *from* the Law" in 59 Yale L.J. 354 and the other, "The Right to Nondiscriminatory Enforcement of State Penal Laws", 61 Col. L. Rev. 1103.)[g]

For these reasons, the judgment of conviction should be reversed and new trial granted but the court below should, prior to the commencement of the new trial, entertain an application by the defendant to dismiss or quash the prosecution upon the grounds set forth by it in its offers of proof upon the first trial.

WILLIAMS, P. J., BASTOW, GOLDMAN and HENRY, J.J., concur.

Judgment of conviction unanimously reversed on the law and facts and a new trial granted.

---

[g] To these should now be added Comment, *Equal Protection as a Defense to Selective Enforcement by Police Officers,* 14 J. PUB. L. 223 (1965).

GROPPI CHARGES HARASSMENT
Milwaukee Journal, Sept. 6, 1966

Father James E. Groppi, adviser of the local youth council of the National Association for the Advancement of Colored People, Tuesday accused the Milwaukee police department of harassment after seven youths were arrested at the group headquarters Monday. . . .

Inspector Hans Kremsreiter refused to comment on Father Groppi's accusations. Police Chief Harold A. Breier was not available for comment.

Four youths were arrested for allegedly shooting dice behind a home at 2024 N. 5th st., next door to the Freedom House; the other three were fighting outside, police said.

Police said about eight youths had taken part in the game, which they said neighbors had complained of all summer, but that only four were caught.

A total of 96¢ was confiscated after the game.

The four were arrested about 2:30 p.m., Father Groppi said, but were not released until about 10 p.m. after Court Commissioner Jack L. Goodsitt granted a writ of habeas corpus requested by attorneys for the youth council. Goodsitt released three of the four without bail and ordered $100 bail on the fourth. The $100 was posted. . . .

Of the alleged dice game, Father Groppi said: "The thing that disturbed us is that the thing could have been settled very easily if somebody would have just contacted us. I would have broken the game up. Now they took them downtown, fingerprinted them, mugged (photographed) them all for a $1.35 crap game.

"When they were arrested one fellow had 10¢ in his pockets; one had 4¢; the banker had 82¢, and one fellow had nothing. I guess there was $1.35 in the pot."

Police said, however, that there was no pot.

"The policemen making the arrest," Father Groppi said, "chased them around the block, caught a 16 year old, ripped his shirt off, twisted his arm behind his back, and handcuffed him. . . ."

HARASSMENT
Milwaukee Journal, Sept. 30, 1966

Early Thursday morning a young woman was arrested and charged with littering by a policeman who said she discarded a cigaret on the ground outside Freedom House, headquarters of the youth council of the National Association for the Advancement of Colored People. She was held in jail the rest of the night. Later Thursday the city attorney's office refused to prosecute her.

Littering is against the law and presumably a discarded cigaret butt is "litter." But if the officer was only doing his job, which is enforcing the law, why isn't the law enforced with equal zeal everywhere else? Anybody with half an eye can see a shower of cigaret butts flicked onto any given block of Wisconsin Ave. in the pedestrian rush. How many of the offenders get arrested?

Unless the law is enforced uniformly, outside the Freedom House and everywhere else in town, this sort of thing can be regarded only as deliberate harassment, a shocking misapplication of the police power.

Note

Consider the "super enforcement" described at 1207 n.g, *infra*.

In People v. Harris, 182 Cal. App. 2d Supp. 837, 5 Cal. Rptr. 852 (1960), the convictions of Negro gamblers were reversed because the trial court had erroneously rejected the following offers of proof:

> "1. Racial population figures and percentages in Pasadena.
>
> "2. Record of Pasadena gambling arrests showing for the year 1957, 16 white persons arrested, 276 Negroes; 1958, 9 white, 82 Negroes; 1959, all persons arrested, Negroes.
>
> "3. Existence of gambling for years in three men's clubs, all members of which were white, and no arrests made. That the chief of police was a member of one of the clubs and aware of the gambling.
>
> "4. One of the arresting officers would testify the routine city police procedure was to patrol the colored section and, on finding grouped parked cars, prowl the private premises for gambling, with no like patrol in the white section and no investigation made when cars were so parked in white areas. That no arrests were made when, shortly before the instant arrests, police found white men gambling, some of them city police officers."

The court commented that discriminatory enforcement could be raised by suit for injunction, by habeas corpus, or as a defense in a criminal prosecution.

In People v. Winters, 171 Cal. App. 2d Supp. 876, 342 P.2d 538 (1959), the trial court dismissed complaints against Negro gamblers after taking judicial notice of discriminatory enforcement in the following language:

"Some three weeks or a month ago, this Court had the occasion to write a letter to the Chief of Police calling attention to the fact that, in this Court's opinion, the gambling laws of this city are enforced mainly against members of the Negro race.

"The Chief took exception to that statement and pointed out, by his statistics, that in the last two years 12,000 Negroes were arrested for gambling and 1,200 Caucasians. Of course, I know that the figures are deceptive because of the fact that the 1,200 Caucasians mentioned were arrested in areas other than the Central Los Angeles area: In Van Nuys and San Pedro and other areas.

"But, I also take great exception to what I term a discriminatory pattern of enforcement of the gambling laws of this city. It is my opinion they are enforced mostly against members of the Negro race. If I were to take the Chief's figures as they speak of this, it would lead me to believe that Negroes, who constitute 10% of the population of this city, are responsible for 90% of the gambling in this city. I refuse to believe that as the truth. I refuse to believe that the people who make their money off of gambling in this city are making it from the penny-ante gambling that goes on in Negro homes and Negro districts.

"The Chief has also invited me to point out to him instances where gambling is going on unraided. Of course, I don't have to do that because that isn't my job. That is his job to ferret out gambling.

"But, I only have to say that gambling is going on in all sections of our city: All private clubs; it is going on in fraternal organizations; it is going on in every fight stadium on fight night in the first few rows of the ringside. Where men wave dollar bills at each other openly and notoriously, and under the view of the very officers that are present. And the exchange of money at the end of the bout—I strongly suspect it must be gambling."

The appellate court reversed his action and reinstated the complaints because purposeful discrimination in law enforcement is not an appropriate subject for judicial notice. It might still be proved as a defense.

UNITED STATES v. McLEOD

385 F.2d 734 (5th Cir. 1967)

Wisdom, Circuit Judge. These cases are the product of the racial unrest in 1963 in Dallas County, Alabama, of which Selma is the county seat.

The complaint alleges that the mass arrests of September and October, together with the action of the Grand Jury in subpoenaeing Justice Department lawyers and Negroes active in the voter registration drive, intimidated Negroes with respect to their right to vote in violation of 42 U.S.C. § 1971(b). The United States asked for an injunction to prevent county officials from continuing their coercive actions.

The district court denied relief in both cases.

The arrests for improper license-plate lights do raise the *Leflore* question. In *Leflore,* the Court said:

> Clearly, the state and its subdivisions may reasonably enforce their criminal laws. Often such valid enforcement may incidentally have an inhibiting or intimidating effect upon the exercise of a protected right. Yet, the unfortunate incidental effect may not be grounds for setting aside or enjoining the otherwise justifiable enforcement of the valid criminal law. 371 F.2d at 371.

This broad language could be taken to mean that no arrest of a guilty person could violate section 1971(b). The case, however, does not stand for that proposition. The Act does not exempt from its prohibition acts directed against persons guilty of crime. It does exempt acts done for purposes other than interfering with the right to vote. It is here that the probable guilt or innocence of the person arrested becomes relevant. If the person is clearly guilty, the probability that the police have acted for a legitimate reason is much greater than it is if the arrest is clearly baseless. But the fact that the person is guilty does not end the inquiry. Police may arrest guilty people for reasons other than their guilt—for example for the reason that they are Negroes who want to register and vote.

In the *Leflore* sort of case, then, the focus of inquiry is on the real purpose of the arrests, and the inference to be drawn depends on all of the surrounding facts. Factually we think *Leflore* is distinguishable from this case. In *Leflore* Negroes staged a mass demonstration near midnight in a residential section. The participants caused at least some disorder. The state's interest in enforcing the law was urgent—to preserve order in the community at night. The strength of this state interest alone points to the conclusion that the police acted for legitimate reasons. But in *Leflore* there were other indicia of justifiable enforcement. There was no history of official interference with the registration drive. There had been many previous meetings without disturbance. Local authorities affirmatively cooperated with these meetings by maintaining parking areas near the church. There was no evidence that any of the defendants had interfered with the actual registration process.

Here, on the other hand, every indication is that the police made arrests not to redress violations of the law, but simply to harass voting workers. It is common knowledge that the police often overlook violations of relatively trivial traffic laws. Rarely if ever do police mount massive law enforcement drives to eradicate the sinful practice of driving with burned out license-plate lights. When they do so on the evening of a voter registration meeting and, fortuitously of course, catch twenty-nine Negroes on their way home from that meeting and no one else, the inference of justifiable enforcement so compelling in *Leflore* loses much of its force. What little force is left is dissipated by the history of official obstruction of the voting registration process so clearly established in this record. The only purpose was to harass voting workers—a purpose proscribed by the Act.

A federal court is always reluctant to interfere with state criminal proceedings, because of statutory restraints and because of respect for the doctrine of comity. "But the sharp edge of the Supremacy Clause cuts across all such generalizations. When a State, under the pretext of preserving law and order uses local laws, valid on their face, to harass and punish citizens for the exercise of their . . . federally protected statutory rights, the general principle must yield to the exception: the federal system is imperiled." Cox v. State of Louisiana, 5 Cir. 1965, 348 F.2d 750, 752.

We therefore hold that the district court should enter an order requiring the appropriate officials of Dallas County to return all fines, and to expunge from the record all arrests and convictions resulting from the prosecutions which form the basis for these suits.

The district court should take whatever additional action is necessary to return individuals to their status quo ante.[h]

---

[h] Civil liability under section 1983 of the Civil Rights Act of 1871 offers one possibility of redress against discriminatory selection of persons for arrest. In Pierson v. Ray, 386 U.S. 547 (1967), 1968 Wis. L. Rev. 275, the Court held that officers would be liable unless their arrests were made on "good faith and probable cause." If good faith means anything more than probable cause, it would seem to mean an absence of ulterior motive. It may be that arresting a protest leader on a charge of littering for discarding a gum wrapper in the steet would be a violation of the Civil Rights Act.

SOCIETY OF GOOD NEIGHBORS v. VAN ANTWERP

324 Mich. 22, 36 N.W.2d 308 (1949)

BUSHNELL, J. Plaintiff Society of Good Neighbors, a nonprofit corporation, has appealed from an order dismissing its bill of complaint, in which it sought injunctive relief, restraining the mayor, commissioner of police, superintendent of police, and deputy superintendent of police of the city of Detroit "from in any way interfering with the plaintiff in its conduct of any bingo parties or any of its other activities."

It is the claim of plaintiff that for some years it has been operating a charitable organization which renders assistance in emergency cases to all persons regardless of race, color or religion. It has financed itself by voluntary contributions and operated with the aid of volunteer workers, in addition to about 30 individuals on its pay roll. According to plaintiff, in 1944, due to increased costs of living and operating expenses, it undertook to augment its income by conducting bingo parties.

It is stated that several years later an instance arose which brought about a prejudiced attitude on the part of the police department towards plaintiff's operations, which developed into an "animus" on the part of defendants, resulting in "a campaign of inquisition" and repeated visits of the police, which plaintiff claims were merely for the purpose of frightening patrons at its bingo games and thereby suppressing its activities. Later, a grand-jury investigation was instigated and representations were made by defendants to the revenue officers of the Federal government and certain State officers respecting plaintiff's operations. Plaintiff asserts that many religious, charitable, service, patriotic and other nonprofit organizations are operating bingo, raffles, and lotteries in the city of Detroit, without being molested by the police, but that plaintiff has been singled out as the sole object of police interference.

The trial judge accepted the allegations of the bill of complaint as true and stated in a filed opinion that the court believed itself to be without jurisdiction to restrain defendants in that plaintiff's operations constituted "a game of lottery, a game of chance. It is gambling." The court was also of the opinion that plaintiff had an adequate remedy at law and entered an order dismissing the bill of complaint.

Well-pleaded allegations in a bill of complaint, and inferences drawn therefrom, must be taken as true and construed in a light most favorable to the plaintiff. Gilmer v. Miller, 319 Mich. 136. Nevertheless, a right to violate the law can never be conferred by laxity in its enforcement as to others. The very foundation of a court of equity is good conscience, and it will not lend its aid by way of the extraordinary writ of injunction to assist law violators. He who hath committed iniquity shall not have equity, McCredie v. Buxton, 31 Mich. 383, 388, and he who comes into equity must come with clean hands, Hoff v. Hoff, 48 Mich. 281.

We are not here concerned with other law violators. If peace officers are derelict in their duties as herein charged, we cannot adjudge that complaint within the confines of the instant case. It is enough now to say that the law draws no distinction between commercial and charitable lotteries, each being *malum prohibitum*.

THE ROLE OF POLICE IN A DEMOCRATIC SOCIETY

By Frank J. Remington

56 Journal of Criminal Law, Criminology and Police Science 361, 362-63 (1965)†

A few years ago the Pennsylvania legislature enacted an amendment to its "Sunday Blue laws" to make it clear that selling goods on Sunday is a crime in Pennsylvania. Apparently the legislature was concerned with the tremendous growth of so-called "bargain city centers" operating at the outskirts of large cities which do a large volume of business, particularly on Sunday. Their growth has seriously affected the downtown stores. The police commissioner in Philadelphia announced that he did not have resources enough to enable him to proceed against all violators. Because of this he indicated that he would proceed against the large violators. This seems to be an obviously realistic and sensible position for the commissioner to take. When prosecution was brought against a large violator, the violator raised, as a defense, the issue of denial of equal protection.[3] His ground was that it was a violation of the constitutional guarantee of equal protection to differentiate in the law enforcement policy between the large violator and the small violator. The Philadelphia court sustained the defendant's claim and dismissed the prosecution, apparently on the assumption that police can proceed against all violators simultaneously, an obviously impossible course to follow.

It is interesting to contrast a case decided by the United States Supreme Court which involved a similar issue, but instead of the

[3] Bargain City v. Dilworth, 29 U.S.L.Week 2002 (Pa. Ct. Com. Pls. June 10, 1960).

Philadelphia Police Department the Federal Trade Commission was involved. The Court upheld the Federal Trade Commission's decision to proceed against certain violators rather than others stating:

> . . . the Commission alone is empowered to develop that enforcement policy best calculated to achieve the ends contemplated by Congress and to allocate its available funds and personnel in such a way as to execute its policy efficiently and economically.[4]

If the Federal Trade Commission is to have responsibility "to develop that enforcement policy best calculated to achieve the ends contemplated" by the legislature, why not recognize that the Philadelphia police have a similar responsibility? Both the Federal Trade Commission and the police department are enforcement agencies. But it is apparent that the one is thought of as having an important policy making role in government; the other is thought of as an agency with a mission to do what it is told to do. This reflects a prevalent and unfortunate misconception of the function of police, a misconception for which police themselves are partly responsible.

B. THE EVIDENTIARY STANDARD REQUIRED FOR LAWFUL ARREST

If police determine that under the circumstances as they see them arrest is desirable, they are confronted with the law's insistence that they may do so only if the likelihood of arresting an innocent person is small.

The fourth amendment forbids "unreasonable . . . seizures" of persons as well as property. The same prohibition applies to

[4] Moog Industries v. Federal Trade Commission, 355 U.S. 411 (1958). [In Federal Trade Comm'n v. Universal-Rundle Corp., 387 U.S. 244 (1967), the Supreme Court reaffirmed its view that the FTC could not arbitrarily pick out one of many law violators in an industry for enforcement of law, when this would operate to destroy that violator economically, but held that the FTC had not acted unreasonably. The court of appeals had held that for the FTC to proceed only against a minor manufacturer, which was one of the less serious offenders, was an abuse of discretion.

A related question is whether official action or inaction can be said to raise an estoppel. Cox v. Louisiana, 379 U.S. 559 (1965), indicated that conviction under an antipicketing statute was precluded by defendants' reliance on the advice of local police officials. The general proposition that the government should not be estopped from prosecution by inaction is supported by United States v. Socony-Vacuum Oil Co., 310 U.S. 150, 225-28 (1940). To the contrary is United States v. New Orleans Chapter, 238 F. Supp. 273 (E.D. La. 1965), 1965 DUKE L.J. 649. The defense of entrapment is akin to estoppel.]

the states under the Supreme Court's interpretation of the fourteenth amendment. The power of police to take a person into custody is thus clearly subject to this broad constitutional limitation. As was noted in Chapter 3, there was for a long time uncertainty whether stopping and questioning was a "seizure" within the meaning of the Constitution, but there was never any dispute that the more serious interference of taking into custody and removal to the police station was a "seizure." Arrest, or taking into custody, thus constitutes infringement of constitutional rights unless it is reasonable. As a matter of fact, however, discussions of arrest are rarely cast in constitutional terms. Concern is rather with whether the arrest is "lawful."[i] And the standard of lawfulness is one worked out through common law and sometimes in legislation. The common-law arrest standards have always been assumed to satisfy the constitutional requirement of reasonableness, even though there has been some slight development of expanded common-law arrest powers in the period since the adoption of the constitutional provisions. Even statutory expansions of police arrest powers have rarely been attacked as unconstitutional.[j]

The common law governing arrests by police officers at the time the Constitution was adopted was only slightly different from that applicable to arrests by private persons, since at that time professional police services were only beginning to emerge. With respect to felony, the officer could arrest without a warrant if he had reasonable belief that a felony had been committed by the person arrested. For misdemeanors, an officer could arrest without first obtaining a warrant only when a misdemeanor amounting to a breach of the peace was committed in his presence.

The standards for felony arrest have remained essentially the same, but the standards for misdemeanor arrest have been substantially liberalized.[k] Statutory changes have tended to permit

---

[i] The phrase "illegal arrest" and the constitutional phrase "unreasonable seizure" are often used interchangeably. Nonetheless it is quite possible to have an arrest which is "illegal" because it violates a statute but is not "unreasonable," within the meaning of the Constitution. United States *ex rel.* Eidenmuller v. Fay, 240 F. Supp. 591 (S.D.N.Y. 1965); *cf.* p. 250 n.k, *supra.*

[j] The fairly common provision that an officer may arrest one who is in fact guilty of a felony has been widely assumed to be unconstitutional. *See* Badillo v. Superior Ct., 46 Cal. 2d 269, 294 P.2d 23 (1956).

[k] The difference may become important when law enforcement officers act while off duty or outside their own jurisdiction. Some federal enforcement agencies have no statutory arrest powers and are governed by the limitations on private citizens. *See, e.g.,* Alexander v. United States, 390 F.2d 101 (5th Cir. 1968) (postal inspectors).

arrest for all misdemeanors committed in the officer's presence, whether or not they constitute breach of the peace. Some courts have arrived at this conclusion without legislative action. A few statutes, *e.g.*, California, extend the misdemeanor arrest power to situations in which there is reasonable ground to believe that a misdemeanor is being committed in the officer's presence; these provisions are designed to protect the officer in the event that what reasonably appears to be a crime turns out to be no crime at all. Some court decisions arrived at this conclusion without aid of statute. There are even some statutes which abandon the in-presence requirement for misdemeanor arrests. For example, the Wisconsin statute permits misdemeanor arrests based on probable cause (that is, even if no crime has in fact occurred), provided there is reason to believe that the offender will cause further harm or cannot be arrested later. The Illinois statute goes further yet and permits arrest upon reasonable grounds to believe that a misdemeanor or a violation of a penal ordinance has been committed by the person arrested. This puts arrest for misdemeanors and ordinance violations on precisely the same footing as arrest for felonies.

The commonly used misdemeanor arrest standard, that a misdemeanor must in fact have occurred in the presence of the officer, presents some difficult problems of application—hearing the card game for money through a hotel room door,[l] the glimpse of a pistol which turns out to be lawfully carried under a permit, the smelling of marihuana smoke coming through a transom, the complaint from a wife that her husband has been beating her and threatens to continue to do so, the disturbance created by one of several persons when none will admit it and there is no immediate way of telling which is guilty. In each of these situations there is some question whether a traditional, narrow interpretation of the common-law standard requiring guilt in fact and commission in-presence is satisfied; yet in all of them one can expect that police will make an arrest.[m] There is no express administrative policy to encourage such arrests if they are illegal in that state. Indeed, the police training literature is wholly orthodox in its definition of arrest powers. But

[l] Extremes are suggested by observation of a misdemeanor through a telescope, Roynon v. Battin, 55 Cal. App. 2d 861, 132 P.2d 266 (1942) (illegal hunting of burros), and over the telephone, People v. Bradley, 152 Cal. App. 2d 527, 314 P.2d 108 (1957) (bookmaking).

[m] Officers can sometimes achieve their objective indirectly, by suggesting that a person who was present at the time of the misdemeanor, *e.g.*, a wife whose husband has beaten her, make a citizen's arrest. The officer then feels safe in taking over the prisoner for transportation to jail.

in another sense the rather uniform practice of a police force is its real policy.

The nearly universal standard for felony arrests—"reasonable grounds to believe" that the person to be arrested is guilty of a felony—is more liberal than the common misdemeanor standard. Greater danger to the community from felonies is thought to warrant interference with the freedom of citizens upon less certain evidence. This "reasonable grounds" standard leaves a number of difficult questions unanswered: whether the standard varies with the seriousness of the suspected offense,[n] whether the officer has a duty before arresting to investigate beyond initial appearances when there is opportunity to do so, whether evidence inadmissible in court may be relied on, whether police expertise may properly be considered,[o] whether the officer must be able to conclude that the suspect has committed a particular crime, or whether the officer may arrest more than one suspect when there is clearly only one offender. Court decisions have not sought in a systematic way to answer these kinds of questions. They have passed only on the concrete disputes brought to them. And even with the cumulation of thousands of appellate cases dealing with arrest problems, many of the uncertainties left by the statutes remain. The principal reason for this is that arrest questions are nearly always raised through defendant's attempt to prevent use of tangible evidence which has been seized pursuant to an arrest.[p] Many arrest situations are rarely

---

[n] Consider the statement of Justice Jackson in Brinegar v. United States, 338 U.S. 160, 183 (1949):

> If we assume, for example, that a child is kidnaped and the officers throw a roadblock about the neighborhood and search every outgoing car, it would be a drastic and undiscriminating use of the search. The officers might be unable to show probable cause for searching any particular car. However, I should candidly strive hard to sustain such an action, executed fairly and in good faith, because it might be reasonable to subject travelers to that indignity if it was the only way to save a threatened life and detect a vicious crime. But I should not strain to sustain such a roadblock and universal search to salvage a few bottles of bourbon and catch a bootlegger.

It is arguable that the term "unreasonable" in the fourth amendment makes gravity of the crime a proper consideration. In any event the varying seriousness of offenses will undoubtedly have a practical effect upon judges' rulings. This was explicitly acknowledged by Judge Friendly in United States v. Soyka, 394 F.2d 443, 452 (2d Cir. 1968).

[o] *See* p. 159 n.p, *supra.*

[p] The defendant may take the position that he was arrested too soon (before probable cause existed), too late (with unreasonable delay after probable cause appeared, Godfrey v. United States, 358 F.2d 850 (D.C. Cir. 1966); *cf.* p. 124, *supra),* that minor detention constituted arrest made without sufficient grounds, that major detention did not constitute arrest, and so on —whatever position would make the case that the search was not incident to a valid arrest.

called into question because they have arisen in kinds of crimes where seized evidence is not significant to prosecution.

Despite the inadequacies of court-made arrest doctrine, the police are acutely conscious of arrest law, and court decisions play a large role in determining the circumstances in which arrests will be made. In spite of this, there is frequent discrepancy between what the courts say is permissible and common police practice. Sometimes this results from the inevitable vagueness of the "reasonable grounds" standard, sometimes from failure of communication between courts and police, and sometimes from police belief that proper execution of their job requires them to make arrests which are at the borderline of legality.

1. *Application of the "Reasonable Grounds" Standard*

Police obtain much help from citizens who have knowledge about crime. The angry victim of crime, the public spirited citizen who has witnessed an offense or who learns something about a past or planned crime, the person close to the offender or from his milieu who for spite or reward betrays him—these are major sources of information. The principal problem arising from dealings with complainants and ordinary citizens is knowing whether the information is reliable.

There is no legal requirement of preliminary screening before information is relied on. The formal legal controls are all after the fact, the principal ones being the power of the judge to dismiss a case and his authority to suppress evidence acquired as a consequence of reliance on untrustworthy information.

The Practice

The following illustrate problems of the reliability of complainants.

1

The police were called to a burglary at a gasoline station. The owner and his wife said that they had observed the entry from the window of their home across the street. When the owner left his house to investigate, the three culprits fled. The wife said she recognized one of them as a youth who lived nearby, although she had observed him only from across the street and it was a dark night. The boy was arrested, but it later developed that he was not responsible.

2

A woman complained to the police that her former handyman had stolen some jacks from under her house trailer. The officer recalled that on a previous occasion the woman had complained about this man stealing gas, but that the case had been nolle prossed for lack of evidence. The officer felt that the woman was fabricating these stories because she held a grudge against the man. He refused to make an arrest.

3

A woman complained to police that she had been sexually attacked by a certain man. The police asked both the suspect and the complainant to take a lie detector test. The suspect took the test which showed no deception. The complainant refused to take the test. The police decided to drop the matter.

4

Two patrolmen were approached by a woman who said that her seven-year-old daughter claimed two boys had stolen her purse while she was on her way to the movies. The girl described the boys, saying that one boy wore a black jacket with orange seams, blue jeans, and sneakers, while the other wore a tan coat. She thought that they, too, were going to the same movie theater. The patrolmen went to the nearby theater, where the cashier told them the boy in the black jacket might be the youth who had just entered. The officers found the boy and two companions and brought them to the lobby. The girl did not recognize any of them and noted that none had on a black jacket. One of the officers noticed that one had on a reversible jacket and had him reverse it. It was black with red seams. The child still insisted this was not the boy. Nevertheless, the officers decided to arrest. On the way to the station one of the three boys spontaneously admitted he was involved and the purse was recovered where he said he had thrown it.

ARREST: THE DECISION TO TAKE A SUSPECT INTO CUSTODY 265-73 (1965)

By Wayne R. LaFave
(Little, Brown & Company)

A. Arrest on the Basis of Information from an Informant

Illustration No. 1: The police were told by an informant that a particular worker in an automobile plant would bring marijuana into the plant on a given date in an automobile of a particular description and license number. This informant had provided tips on previous occasions, and his information had been found reliable. Officers set up a stakeout and arrested the suspect when he appeared at the time predicted in the described vehicle. [He was not carrying narcotics, but some were found at his home.] . . .

Illustration No. 3: The police received a telephone call from a man who refused to identify himself. He said that a man of a given description could be found on a certain street carrying a large black suitcase which contained narcotics. Officers were dispatched to the scene and arrested a man fitting the description. [No narcotics were found.] . . .

1. *Completeness of the information.* Assuming the reliability of the informant, the police must consider whether the information is sufficiently complete to provide reasonable cause to believe that a felony has been, is being, or will be committed by a particular person. In a Michigan informant case the court said that the officer could not have made an arrest had the information been "in the nature of a mere rumor," as opposed to "when he is informed in positive terms that a crime has been committed by an individual, naming him."[4]

Information provided by informants is usually adequate in this respect because the informant usually makes a flat statement that a named person has committed or will commit a crime. Most often the informant gives information about a crime which will be committed in the future, as in the illustrations above. The assertion that a certain event will happen is usually made without any reasons being given as to why the informant thinks it will happen.[5] If the offender cannot be named, the informant is usually able to give a good description. Only occasionally is the information not specific enough for the police to focus upon one suspect. For example, one informant merely stated that a Mexican man, staying at a certain hotel, possessed marijuana, without further identifying the suspect.

---

[4] People v. Ward, 226 Mich. 45, 52, 196 N.W. 971, 972 (1924).

[5] If the informant identifies the person and indicates he is or will be engaged in certain criminal conduct, the information is complete enough if reliability is otherwise established. That disclosure of the underlying facts or basis for the informant's assertions relates to the matter of reliability rather than to completeness of the information is supported by Draper v. United States, 358 U.S. 307 (1959), where the court upheld an arrest based upon the word of an informer, although he did not disclose his grounds, only when they found the informer's reliability to be established by police confirmation of some predicted events.

A lack of complete and specific information is most likely in cases involving anonymous letters and telephone calls, as they usually consist of reports of rumors or general reputation rather than a direct assertion that a crime has been or will be committed. This may in part explain the reluctance of the police to act in these cases, although the anonymity of the informant also casts doubt on his reliability. But where an anonymous letter does give detailed information the police do not hesitate to make an arrest.

In the relatively infrequent case where the informant names the perpetrator of a past reported crime, more information is usually required by the police than when the informant tells them that a crime will be committed. Because it is unusual for the informer to have been an actual witness to the offense, the police usually ask these informants to give some indication of the basis for their suspicion. However, the police may arrest upon less than a direct accusation without any further explanation when a serious crime is involved.

The appellate courts of the jurisdictions studied have not indicated how indirect the informer's knowledge may be and still meet the reasonable cause test.[9]

2. *Reliability of the informant.* By far the more serious problem with regard to the use of informants is that of determining when they can be considered sufficiently reliable to justify arrest of the person named. Except for the public-spirited citizen, persons who furnish police with information are generally not the most reliable members of the community and are often engaged in some criminal activity themselves. In addition to the great number of narcotics users acting as informants, police receive information from such sources as mentally retarded persons and pimps acting with the ulterior motive of getting their competition off the streets. The police are also accustomed to getting a great deal of information, mostly false, from persons who have

[9] People v. Ward, 226 Mich. 45, 196 N.W. 971 (1924), says "mere rumor" is not enough, but there is no indication there or elsewhere as to how far removed the informant may be, that is, how many persons the story may have passed through. The nature of the problem is illustrated by a recent federal case. The informant told the police that he had been told by a friend that the friend's brother and another had committed a certain robbery. The police, without first checking with the informant's friend, arrested the suspects, since they fitted the very general description of the offenders. Goldsmith v. United States, 277 F.2d 335 (D.C. Cir. 1960). The court upheld the arrest. However, one writer, citing cases from other jurisdictions, has asserted that when an informant gives information on a past crime, the officer must inquire whether his information is firsthand, and can arrest only if the answer is affirmative. See Note, 32 Ind. L. Rev. 332, 338-341 (1957).

been arrested and who hope, by giving information, to obtain favorable treatment. Paid informants have also proved unreliable, since they sometimes fabricate stories in order to receive compensation. Nevertheless, since informers are a very important source of knowledge, the police must attempt in each case to ascertain whether the informer is sufficiently reliable to justify use of the information that he supplies. . . .[13]

[T]he Michigan court has indicated that an arrest may be valid even though the source of the information is unknown, if there are other factors which establish the reliability of the information. Some of the important, recurring factors are separately considered.

a. *Observation of predicted events.* The most frequently noted and apparently the most important factor in considering the propriety of an arrest based on information from an informant is the confirmation by direct police observation of some of the information given. Thus, where an informant states that a suspect will be at a certain place at an approximate time, it is of considerable significance that the officer later observes the suspect at the time and place given. The more detailed the information given by the informant, that is, the more individual facts which can be verified by the officer's observation, the better the case. . . .

b. *Failure of suspect to exculpate self.* A second factor which the Michigan court has recognized as contributing to the inform-

[13] In the recent federal case of Draper v. United States, 358 U.S. 307 (1959), the court upheld an arrest upon an informant's accusation without requiring that the information in support be passed on to the officer, but other evidence of the informant's reliability was required. Justice Douglas, in dissent, agreed that hearsay information might be used as a basis for arrest, but took the position that the arrest was invalid because the officers, with their own information, could not have obtained a warrant. "They could swear only to the fact that the informer had made the accusation. They could swear to no evidence that lay in their own knowledge. "They could swear only to the fact that the informer had made the accusadisclosed." 358 U.S. at 324.

The view of the majority in Draper may have lost some of its vitality in the recent case of Aguilar v. Texas, 378 U.S. 108 (1964). There the court said that the probable cause needed for a search warrant may be based upon hearsay and need not reflect direct personal knowledge of the affiant, but the magistrate must be informed of some of the underlying circumstances on which the informant based his conclusions and of some of the underlying circumstances from which the officer concluded that the informant was reliable. [The view of the *Aguilar* case has been applied also to arrests without warrant in McCray v. Illinois, 386 U.S. 300 (1967). Since the identity of the informer need not be disclosed if his reliability is otherwise attested to by the officer's testimony, critics have urged that this is simply an invitation to police perjury which cannot be exposed by the defense. Younger, *The Perjury Routine*, 3 CRIM. L. BULL. 551 (1967).]

ant's reliability is the failure of the suspect to explain what he is doing or to submit to a search. The court has taken note of one suspect's failure to give a reasonable account of himself, another's refusal to state his business, and another's refusal to open his suitcase.

. . . Whether a refusal or an inability to explain may properly be considered a factor requires a judgment as to the propriety of the questioning. Giving consideration to a refusal to submit to search is more questionable. The suspect in many cases would be left with the unpleasant choice of either submitting to a search or being arrested because of his refusal to cooperate and then searched as an incident to the arrest.

c. *Prior reliability of the informant.* A third factor contributing to the reliability of information is the proved reliability of the informant on previous occasions. Prior reliability is of importance in practice because of the frequent use of professional, or at least habitual, informants. Persons who, in the past, were paid for information which proved reliable are likely to continue to be reliable. This is particularly true where the informant receives a greater payment for information which leads to conviction. Persons who receive immunity from prosecution in exchange for accurate information are also likely to continue to be reliable, since the giving of false information would probably terminate their immunity status. However, the mere fact that a person has given reliable information on a previous occasion does not insure his reliability. Information from informers whose past tips have frequently proved inaccurate is likely to be ignored.

d. *Opportunity to judge the informer.* The Michigan court has also stressed the opportunity for the officer to judge the reliability of the informant. A distinction is drawn between an informant who supplies information by telephone or letter and one who reports it directly to the officer. . . .

e. *Prior suspicion of person informed against.* A fifth factor considered in practice is the prior suspicion of the named person by the police. If police have suspected that the person is engaging in the kind of conduct alleged by the informant, they then have some corroboration of the informant's story. . . .

There are two situations involving informants which are not dealt with in detail in this chapter. In some cases, especially where the reliability of the informant is in doubt, the information received is used not as a basis for arrest but only as a basis for further investigation of a person or place. If an arrest is later made, it is upon the basis of information developed during the investigation. The reliability of the evidence in such a situation depends upon the adequacy of the investigation. In other cases the informant is an undercover agent and the arrest is based upon police observation of a transaction between the informant and another person.[3]

2. *Differing Interpretations by Police and Courts*

CONTROLLING THE POLICE: THE JUDGE'S ROLE IN MAKING AND REVIEWING LAW ENFORCEMENT DECISIONS

By Wayne R. LaFave & Frank J. Remington

63 Michigan Law Review 987, 1005-08 (1965)

. . . The trial judge seldom explains his decision in a way likely to be understood by the police officer, and the prosecutor assigned to the case rarely assumes it to be his duty to inform the police department of the meaning of the decision or of its intended impact upon current police practice. The individual officer whose case has been lost is not expected to report the reason for the decision to his superiors. Some decisions, usually those the officer believes to be particularly outrageous, may be passed on to other officers by word of mouth, but they often become distorted in the retelling. If a "court officer" is assigned to the court by the police department, his responsibilities do not include reporting the judge's rulings on police conduct. Obviously, police can not be affirmatively influenced to change their methods of law enforcement by the exclusion of evidence when there is no communication to them of why the decision was made.

Inconsistency in trial court rulings further complicates the situation. For one thing, there is often a substantial disparity in the standards applied by the various judges of a multi-judge

---

[3] For example, narcotics officers often have their informant arrange for a "buy." The informant is thoroughly searched to make certain he does not possess narcotics, is given marked bills, and then is observed meeting the suspect. The arrest is based on the fact that the informant is searched again after the meeting and found to possess narcotics. This elaborate procedure is resorted to not because the police demand a high probability of guilt in these cases, but rather because in this manner they are allowed to present the case in court without bringing in or disclosing the identity of their informant. Disclosure of the identity of the informant is not usually required where the probable cause for the search may be established independently. See Annot., Accused's Right to, and Prosecution's Privilege Against, Disclosure of Identity of Informer, 76 A.L.R.2d 262 (1961). While an accused is entitled to disclosure of the identity of an informer who participated in the offense, id. at 313, the usual practice is to charge with possession rather than sale, which apparently obviates this difficulty.

court. Once an officer learns of the conflicting attitudes of these judges, his acceptance of the court's role as supervisor of police practices is lessened; he is likely to conclude that whether evidence will be excluded in a given case depends in large part upon the ability of defense counsel to maneuver the case before a judge who will rule in his favor. The decisions of a single judge also may vary, depending upon the nature of the crime involved. "What is 'reasonable' to a judge in a narcotics case is not 'reasonable' to the *same* judge in a gambling case." . . .

Communication between police and appellate courts is also less than adequate and occurs on a haphazard basis. . . .

. . . Training materials become outdated, and officers who have completed their training often are not kept up to date on legal developments relevant to their work; some departments make no effort to disseminate such information to personnel at the operational level. Even when appellate opinions are made available to the police, it is evident that they are not written in a way which makes it easy for the police to understand what they are expected to do. . . .

The translation of appellate cases into operating police practice is handicapped by the fact that most police agencies do not have effective legal counsel available to them. Prosecuting attorneys seldom make a systematic effort to act as legal advisers to police departments within their jurisdiction. Most of them, for example, would not think it their responsibility to translate *Escobedo* into a specific statement of appropriate interrogation policy. Even the largest police departments are usually without competent legally-trained personnel on their staff, and, when a request for such personnel is made, it will likely be denied on the ground that the corporation counsel furnish the needed service. In point of fact, however, the corporation counsel typically respond only when a specific question is asked, is generally removed from the problems of criminal justice, and do not conceive of their responsibility as including participation in the development of proper law enforcement policies for police.

Police may be deterred from making doubtful arrests by their own notion of proper police conduct in areas where the law is unclear, by fear of personal legal liability for false arrest, by concern for bad publicity resulting from charges of police lawlessness, or by expectation that an illegal arrest may cause exclusion of crucial evidence and consequent failure of prosecution. Despite all these, arrests which the courts would label unlawful are common.

Police often see themselves as frontline soldiers in a war against crime and have difficulty taking a dispassionate view of the rules. The natural tendency of police training officers is to define arrest powers for their men in terms of the most favorable interpretations of statute or case law.[q]

This common inclination of police to take the broadest view of their powers is offset somewhat by occasional admonitions to officers that they need not use the full powers they have. To illustrate, see the New York Police Department circular on stopping and questioning in Chapter 3. Also, Chicago Police Department Training Bulletin, vol. V, no. 5 (1964), which states:

> In the case of certain minor violations, an officer might appropriately decide not to arrest the offender and subject him to prosecution if the matter can be adequately dealt with in some other way. For example, arrest and prosecution may not appear necessary in the case of a minor property crime not involving violence, if the offender has indicated a willingness to restore the property to its rightful owner.

And New York Police Commissioner Michael J. Murphy in remarks before the annual convention of the National Association of Municipal Judges, Dec. 2, 1964, said:

> Finally, the idea of on-the-street summons . . . is being explored. The presently contemplated centralization of background information on criminals from throughout New York State into a computer system offers the promise of quick verification of an arrestee's prior criminal record as well as his residence, family and employment. It is conceivable that this request for verification might be initiated by a police car on the street with a prompt response that would enable the officer to decide whether or not an arrested person should be summonsed or processed to court by the arrest procedure.

C. THE FUNCTION OF ARREST IN THE SYSTEM

The disparity one finds among views as to what constitutes arrest and what are appropriate standards of arrest may be

[q] Justice Jackson, dissenting in Brinegar v. United States, 338 U.S. 160, 182 (1949), said, "We must remember that the extent of any privilege of search and seizure without warrant which we sustain, the officers interpret and apply themselves and will push to the limit."

explained, at least in part, by differences in view as to the function arrest is to serve.

1. Arrest for Purposes Other than Prosecution

Arrest serves various purposes even when prosecution is impossible or thought undesirable. It is used not as a matter of choice, but because no meaningful alternatives are available to police who are faced with a situation which seems to demand some action. A person may be placed under arrest and taken to the police station as a means of cooling off an explosive situation—the husband who has been violently quarrelling with his wife, or boys engaged in a street fight. The intention is to release the persons arrested after they have calmed sufficiently to make resumption of the dispute unlikely.[r] Or one may be taken into custody for his own safety—the drunk who is held only until he sobers up. Or arrest may serve as a minor penalty—the prostitute who is locked up overnight, or the known criminal repeatedly picked up obstensibly "for investigation." There is not likely to be any challenge to these arrests even if they are not based on probable cause.[s]

ARREST: THE DECISION TO TAKE A SUSPECT INTO CUSTODY 440-41, 451-53, 456, 466-67 (1965)

By Wayne R. LaFave

(Little, Brown & Company)

THE PRACTICE OF ARRESTING DRUNKS FOR PURPOSES OTHER THAN PROSECUTION

In Detroit, intoxicated persons who are arrested but released without charge after they become sober are called "golden rule

[r] Because of some old cases holding that release of a prisoner without having presented him before a magistrate constituted proof that the arrest was illegal, police have been wary of assuming responsibility for releasing prisoners. Though the old cases would not likely be followed today (*but cf.* Alexander v. United States, 390 F.2d 101 (5th Cir. 1968)) they have greatly affected practice. In Chicago, even though the statute permits release, police practice requires approval of the watch commander before release of a person brought into the station house.

[s] There may also be arrests of civil rights demonstrators or political protestors that are intended to deter the demonstrations even though there is no expectation that convictions will flow from the arrests. If "the statute was enforced against them with no expectation of convictions but only to discourage exercise of protected rights" it appears that the federal courts will enjoin enforcement of an invalid state law, Dombrowski v. Pfister, 380 U.S. 479 (1965), and even of a valid state law, Cameron v. Johnson, 390 U.S. 611 (1968) (*semble*).

drunks." Although this procedure finds explicit recognition in the Detroit Police Manual, no criteria for deciding whom to treat as a "golden rule drunk" are set forth. The number of golden rule drunks is substantial:

	1951	*1952*	*1953*	*1954*	*1955*	*1956*
Golden rule drunks	9,303	8,064	8,592	7,249	6,626	5,865
Drunks prosecuted	8,443	7,840	10,181	10,124	10,513	8,665[11]

The decision to subject a drunk to the golden rule procedure may be made by the arresting officer at the time of arrest, or it may be made by the supervisory officer at the desk in precinct headquarters when the drunk is brought before him.[12] Indeed, in the first situation the arresting officer sometimes obtains the cooperation of the drunk by assuring him that he will be released the next morning.[13] In either event, golden rule drunks are held in the precinct detention quarters until the supervisory officer decides they are sober, usually the following morning. No attempt is made to require them, as a condition of release, to sign a waiver relieving the police department of liability for their detention.

The golden rule procedure is normally confined to nonhabitual drunks and is regularly applied to this class unless they are belligerent or "down and out," or request a more extended period of incarceration.[14] Because the procedure is thus limited, it is more commonly applied to those found outside the "skid row" area. Nevertheless, skid row drunks who are known not to have substantial arrest records are also likely to be "golden ruled." The "down-and-out" drunk is not processed under the

[11] Detroit Police Dept., 91st Stat. Ann. Rep., Table III-B (1956).

[12] Thus on one occasion a woman in a highly intoxicated condition was brought before the lieutenant. Upon inquiry, she stated that she had a family and that she was ashamed of herself for being in her present state. The lieutenant quickly decided to book this woman as a golden rule drunk to be released after she had sobered up.

[13] A special detail of two officers, referred to as the "bum squad," is assigned to the "skid row" area of Detroit in an effort to keep the streets clear of drunks. On one occasion, they caught up with a drunk staggering down the street and poured the contents of his bottle in the street. "Aw, hell, boys, give me a break," the drunk pleaded, but the officers responded that he was too drunk. They added, "We will G.R.D. you if you don't have a traffic warrant, how's that?" The drunk thought this was fine.

[14] Because the golden rule decision is often made after arrest, a more detailed discussion of these criteria will be found in the volume on Prosecution. Of more immediate interest in this chapter is the effect which this policy has upon the legality of these arrests.

golden rule, because he needs a lengthy period of incarceration for medical treatment. Other skid row drunks may request jail terms in the winter simply to secure protection from the cold weather. . . .

Arrest to Control the Prostitute

Even if the legislature makes other forms of prostitution criminal, the streetwalker remains the major problem for the policeman. Public knowledge of the existence of streetwalkers results in pressures on the department for action. These are in turn translated into pressures on precinct supervisors and on individual patrolmen to keep their areas "clean." The concern in this chapter is with police attempts to control the streetwalker by resorting to arrest without thought of prosecution.

The Practice of Arresting Prostitutes for Purposes Other than Prosecution

Suspected prostitutes are clearly the largest category of offenders arrested in Detroit for purposes other than prosecution. Practically all of these arrests are made in one city precinct, in a relatively small area where streetwalking by individual prostitutes flourishes. There are no houses of prostitution; rather, patrons are solicited on the streets and in taverns and other public places, and then escorted to nearby rooms.

The arrest of suspected prostitutes without intent of prosecution is almost exclusively a practice of the precinct officer. While some of these arrests are made by regular patrol car officers, a great majority of them are brought about by officers assigned to the precinct "whore squads." These officers operate with unmarked cars, and although they are uniformed, they remove their caps to prevent easy identification. Members of these squads do not conceal their identity to the extent of plainclothes officers attempting to make accosting and soliciting cases. They are interested only in preventing the girls from seeing them approach in time to take shelter in some nearby residence. Each night these squads arrest from forty to fifty women believed or known to be prostitutes. Most of these women are arrested as they are standing in doorways or on street corners, or while they are slowly walking down the street. On occasion, they are pursued into residences in the area or are arrested while sitting in a restaurant or other public place. Occasionally the officers see and arrest a girl as she is in the process of making a contact with a man.

A booking of D.P.I. (Disorderly Persons Investigation) is always used in this precinct for prostitutes who are not to be prosecuted. In other precincts, where prostitution is far less of a problem, the bookings are either D.P.I. or "investigation of larceny from the person." The latter booking is based upon the fact that many of these girls participate in the "Murphy game."[10] The procedure is the same whichever entry is made. The women are not searched at the time of booking at the precinct, but are immediately placed in a large detention area reserved for women prisoners. When the number of D.P.I.'s reaches ten, the patrol wagon transports them to the women's detention quarters located at police headquarters. There the women are searched and fingerprinted.

On the morning after arrest (except Sundays), a registered nurse reports to the women's detention quarters at 6:30. She immediately takes a smear and culture on each girl with a D.P.I. booking, and if the girl is not a "regular customer" a treatment record is prepared. By 8:00 A.M. the girls are ready for a brief examination by a doctor, also an employee of the city health department. The results are obtained from the laboratory before 11:00 A.M. At this time the girls are called out one at a time for a brief interview with a patrolman from the vice bureau. This officer observed that most of them "would not tell me the right time of day." However, he does manage to build some pandering cases on information obtained from those few, usually inexperienced, prostitutes who will identify their pimps. The infected prisoners are given medication and are asked to report back the next day, which most of them do. In fact, they are not released if they refuse to take medication or refuse to promise to return the following day. Ordinarily, most of these women are back on the street by 11:00 A.M.

The magnitude of this program is indicated by the fact that arrests of the above type often comprise nearly half of this precinct's total arrests. For example, an analysis of all of the bookings in this precinct for a typical two-day period disclosed a total of 75 arrests, 34 of which were D.P.I.'s. The "cleanup squad," charged with vice enforcement at the precinct level, reported 2942 D.P.I. arrests in a six-month period, in which time arrests for accosting and soliciting totaled only 53. There are no departmental statistics which accurately portray how many D.P.I. arrests are made in comparison with the number of prostitutes arrested for purposes of prosecution. . . .

---

[10] The "Murphy game" is a racket in which the prostitutes and their male employers or friends endeavor through trickery to relieve the men who frequent this area of whatever funds they may have.

Reasons for the Practice

While part of the process involves a health examination, it is clear that the police view this as merely a side benefit, and that the practice of arresting suspected prostitutes without intent of prosecution is thought necessary by the police as the only effective means available to deal with prostitution. Said one key official in the department, "Disorderly persons investigation arrests, as practiced primarily in one of the precincts, is a harassment program. The police department has no other means of dealing with prostitution." Similarly, another department official emphasized that an officer makes a D.P.I. arrest to accomplish several purposes:

> First, to get them off the street; second, as a means of harassment. It's a deterrent. They know when certain officers are on the job they are very likely to be picked up and they won't go over on that corner. These particular women I referred to are not only prostitutes but they are decoys for the so-called Murphy game. There have been persons murdered who came into contact with them. As a general rule, in fact almost invariably, these women are out there at two o'clock when the saloons close, when the prospective customers have a lot of liquor in them. They don't want to go home; they are looking for strange experiences. And we've had murders. We had one fellow that was found in an ashcan. Now what should we do under those circumstances? There's our problem—we have no crimes committed in the presence of the police officer, nothing that legally warrants the arrest. Shall we say, "Well, now because our hands are tied, we are going to let these women alone"? . . .

Police are also concerned with the transvestite, the person appearing in public dressed in the clothing of the opposite sex. This conduct is obviously offensive to a large segment of the community. Moreover, some transvestites and persons appearing to be transvestites use this as a method of committing other crimes, such as robbery. Detection and identification of the perpetrator after the robbery takes place is difficult.

In practice, police sometimes attempt to control the problem created by the transvestite by a program of arrest and release without prosecution. This program is the subject of this chapter.

The Practice of Arresting Transvestites for Purposes Other than Prosecution

In Detroit, the police frequently arrest male homosexuals who are found on the street dressed in female attire. These persons, referred to by the police as "fags," are brought in whenever they are spotted on the street by an officer. When the homosexual is brought to the station, he is booked for investigation of larceny from a person. This booking is explained on the basis that a large number of these transvestites "roll" their customers when engaged in their perverted sexual activities, and many participate in the "Murphy game," in which "johns" (men looking for girls) are tricked out of their money. The homosexual is held in jail overnight, and the next morning he is questioned by a detective before release. This procedure is used principally with male homosexuals found on the streets dressed as females. Occasionally a female dressed as a male is accorded similar treatment. Associates of these transvestites may also be arrested on the assumption that they are homosexuals.

This arrest practice is limited to transvestites and their associates and is not used with respect to other persons known to have homosexual tendencies.

2. *Arrest in Anticipation of Possible Prosecution*

Most arrests do look forward to prosecution as the probable consequence. There is some difference of opinion whether the arrest decision should constitute a commitment to prosecution or should really represent only a commitment to investigate the evidence to see whether prosecution is appropriate.

One view of the function of arrest is exemplified by the conclusion to Justice Frankfurter's opinion for the Court in Mallory v. United States, 354 U.S. 449, 456 (1957):

> Presumably, whomever the police arrest they must arrest on "probable cause." It is not the function of the police to arrest, as it were, at large and to use an interrogating process at police headquarters in order to determine whom they should charge before a committing magistrate on "probable cause."

The implication of this statement is that the evidentiary standard for arrest is the same as the evidentiary standard for charging and that therefore police should only arrest when they are prepared to charge. It may be that this is not the present position of the Supreme Court; if the *Mallory* statement suggests that interrogation is improper investigative practice, later case law seems to approve interrogation under specified safeguards.

Much more often, arrest is recognized as occurring properly during the investigative phase, to prevent the escape of a suspect or to make him available for interrogation or physical observation. The doctrinal issue is whether arrest is justified when there is a substantial possibility of guilt or only when there is reasonable belief that guilt is probable. A test case is provided by the facts of *Mallory v. United States,* though the issue litigated was not the propriety of the arrest. A rape occurred in the basement of an apartment house. The rapist was masked, and the victim could only report that the offender was a Negro of a certain build. Living in a basement apartment in the building were a Negro janitor, his wife, two grown sons, a younger son, and his half brother. The two grown sons and the half brother all fitted the general description. It appeared unlikely that any other persons would have had access to the basement at the time of the crime. The police arrested all three.

The *Goldsmith* case states, "The quantum of evidence necessary to sustain an arrest is not, in all circumstances, the same quantum necessary to make out probable cause for charging a person with the crime."[t] The court there took the position that the arrest was justified upon thirdhand information that the defendant had committed a robbery (*A* told the police that *B* had said that defendant did it), but that it would be indefensible for police to charge the defendant formally without more evidence of guilt.

Police often label their arrests "for investigation" or "on suspicion," with or without specifying a particular crime. This can mean that there is only suspicion and not probable cause; it can also mean that there is probable cause but the police are not persuaded as to guilt and wish to avoid the additional stigma which may come from having been arrested for a crime (as

---

[t] Goldsmith v. United States, 277 F.2d 335, 343 (D.C. Cir. 1960). On the problem of quantity of proof see also W. LAFAVE, ARREST: THE DECISION TO TAKE A SUSPECT INTO CUSTODY 259-63 (1965).

Compare Phillips v. State, 29 Wis. 2d 521, 534-35, 139 N.W.2d 41, 47 (1966): "But the right to interrogate after arrest is limited and must be for the purpose of determining whether to release the suspect or if he has been arrested without a warrant to make a formal complaint. . . . [T]he police cannot continue to detain an arrested person to 'sew up' the case by obtaining or extracting a confession or culpable statements to support the arrest or the guilt."

opposed to having been arrested for investigation of possible complicity in a crime).

Because arrests "for investigation" are thought of by police as merely tentative, and therefore not so harmful to the person in custody, there may be laxity concerning the evidentiary standards applied and failure to distinguish between lawful and unlawful arrests. "Arrests for investigation" which slip below the level of probable cause are, of course, unlawful. "Arrests for investigation" based on probable cause are often undiscriminatingly criticized along with those not based on probable cause.[u]

REPORT AND RECOMMENDATIONS OF THE COMMISSIONERS' COMMITTEE ON POLICE ARRESTS FOR INVESTIGATION, DISTRICT OF COLUMBIA 2-3, 112, 113, 117, 126 (July 1962)

Police officers in the District of Columbia—as elsewhere in the United States—may arrest with or without a warrant of arrest. This Report is not concerned with the former. The arrests for "investigation" with which we have been concerned are necessarily made without a warrant. . . .

"The District of Columbia follows the common law rule that a law officer may arrest without a warrant if (1) there is probable cause to believe that a felony has been committed and that the arrested person committed it, . . . or (2) if a misdemeanor has been committed in the presence of an arresting officer." Stephens v. United States, 271 F.2d 832, 833, n. 1 (D.C. Cir. 1959).

This Report is not concerned with arrests for specific felonies or misdemeanors, made without warrants but pursuant to this common-law rule. As will appear below, these are the overwhelming proportion of all arrests—where the officer arrests because he is present when a misdemeanor is committed, or where he arrests for a specific felony because he has "probable cause" to believe that the person arrested has committed that particular crime.

We have been concerned, rather, with arrests in connection with felonies made by the police officers of the District of Columbia in which the requirement of "probable cause"—even though it may exist—is not the standard, and some lesser stand-

[u] Staples v. United States, 320 F.2d 817 (5th Cir. 1963), and Collins v. United States, 289 F.2d 129 (5th Cir. 1961), held that bookings for "investigation" and "on suspicion" invalidated arrests which were in fact based on probable cause.

ard is used—"suspicion," "reasonable suspicion," "reasonable ground to suspect." As will appear below, the standard is not susceptible of specific statement. When such an arrest is made, the prisoner is booked not for a specific crime (although there may be probable cause to do so) but "for investigation of" a felony which he may have committed—murder, rape, housebreaking, or whatever.

The difference between an arrest for "investigation" of the sort with which we are concerned, and the usual arrest without a warrant on probable cause is much more, however, than the difference in the standard used by the police. Where the person arrested is charged with a specific felony (or misdemeanor), Section 140, quoted above, requires that the arresting officer "shall immediately, and without delay, upon such arrest, convey in person such offender before the proper court, that he may be dealt with according to law." Where the arrest is for "investigation," the practice of the police is to assume that the statutory mandate does not apply. The prisoner is arrested by the police, held in police custody, and—unless he is later charged with a crime—released by the police, with no intervention by any judicial officer whatever. Indeed, this is an essential characteristic. A United States Commissioner or a judge, were a person arrested for "investigation" brought before him, would necessarily and automatically order his immediate discharge from custody, since he has not been charged with a crime, but only with "investigation," which is not an offense for which a person may be committed by a magistrate. . . .

Disposition	*Time Held*	*Reasons for Arrest*
Charged	17 mins.	"Responded for a cutting there. Inv was made and the defendant was found in his room with blood on his clothing, that was fresh. He was the only one on the floor at this time, and was placed under arrest for Inv at that time."
. . .		
Released	8 hrs., 15 mins.	"The above defendant was arrested driving a 1956 ________ the owner of which is wanted by this precinct for A.D.W. This man fit the description of the man wanted. If the witness identifies him as the defendant in the case he will be

		charged. If he is not identified he will be released."
. . .		
Released	16 hrs., 21 mins.	"Defendant was seen on the southeast corner of _____ talking to another known shoplifter and narcotic drug addict by name of _____. Other defendant had a large paper bag which contained 7 pairs of childrens overalls. Above defendant is also a known shoplifter and narcotic drug peddler, etc."
. . .		
Released	5 hrs., 8 mins.	"_____, reported 1-11-60 by breaking vent window and [stealing] a mink coat and other items valued at $1000.00 while parked in front of _____. Def. is known for other offenses of this type and when arrested he had a screw driver and pliers in his pocket. Also a ladies make up kit with flower design on same."

CAPITAL CIVIL LIBERTIES UNION NEWS
Vol. II, no. 1, at 1 (Jan. 1963)

D.C. Bans Illegal Arrest

On January 10, only weeks after continued arrests for investigation by the Metropolitan Police came under fire from NCACLU and other community groups, the District Commissioners ordered a halt to the illegal practice. The ban will become effective March 15. After that date, no arrests can be made unless police have probable cause to believe an individual has committed a particular crime. . . .

Coupled with the Commissioners' ban on arrests for investigation, however, was an endorsement of proposed legislation to permit questioning without arrest of persons believed to have knowledge of a crime. The proposal would provide for issuance of subpoenas to such persons; they would then be taken before a judge or U.S. Commissioner, advised of their right against self-incrimination, and could then be questioned by police for up to six hours.

3. *Arrest Used Because of Inadequate Development of Alternatives*

The suggestion is made, though not often embodied as a legal rule, that police ought to use the citation and judicial officers the summons wherever possible and not make an arrest unless there is some special need for immediately taking the person into custody.

ARREST: THE DECISION TO TAKE A SUSPECT INTO CUSTODY 202-05 (1965)
By Wayne R. LaFave
(Little, Brown & Company)

The question of whether a suspect should be taken into custody or, if already in custody, whether he should be released, arises at each stage in the criminal justice process. It is first involved when a decision is made as to whether to make an immediate arrest. If an arrest is made, the question of release from custody arises in the police station during the period prior to the initial appearance of the suspect before the magistrate. At the appearance before the magistrate the bail question is traditionally decided.

By viewing this series of custody decisions in relation to each other it is possible to construct a sort of "custody profile" of the criminal justice system. The most striking characteristic of the profile, reflected in both law and practice, is the almost complete lack of concern over whether custody is necessary at the arrest and police detention stages in contrast with the great concern about the need for custody at the initial appearance.

1. *Custody and the arrest decision.* Only about a third of the states have enacted statutes authorizing the use of a summons instead of a warrant of arrest. To the extent that the general practice conforms to that in the three jurisdictions studied, in that most arrests are made without warrant, such statutes can have only limited effect. Statutes giving the officer the right to issue a summons on the street instead of making an arrest without a warrant are rare.[v]

The summons and notice to appear have not become routine police methods in crimes other than traffic violations partly because legislation authorizing such alternatives is seldom to be found. But, even if legislation were passed, there are reasons in

[v] Congress enacted such a provision for the District of Columbia. D.C. CODE § 23-610 (1967).

practice to continue to make arrests even in situations where it appears that the suspect will appear voluntarily in court. An immediate arrest may make it possible to conduct a search, an in-custody interrogation, or an in-custody health inspection. An immediate arrest may also minimize the risk of future crimes by the suspect pending his appearance in court.[w]

D. METHODS OF PROMOTING COMPLIANCE WITH LEGAL STANDARDS FOR ARREST

The arrest decision is a particularly sensitive one, and no other stage of the criminal justice system, except perhaps the contested trial, has received as much attention. A number of methods of fostering proper use of the arrest power have been used or suggested.

Some methods are positive. They include upgrading police personnel and improving police training so that the men making arrest decisions have powers of sound judgment, understanding what the law requires of them, and knowledge of the complex factors which must be considered in deciding whether it is appropriate to make an arrest which the law permits. Another positive method is the consideration by police departments of their frequently unarticulated or informal arrest policies and the promulgation of explicit guidelines for individual officers. If the guidelines are merely a restatement of the department's understanding of the outer limits of the law, this contributes little, but if the policies attempt to suggest proper concrete actions consistent with the spirit and objectives of constitutional rules, this is a constructive contribution to desirable channeling of police conduct. Such explicit attention to arrest policy is rare.

Other major methods of promoting compliance are essentially negative. One such method is to expose the police officer who oversteps the bounds of legality to personal loss through tort liability, statutory damage actions (particularly the Civil Rights Acts), criminal prosecution, or departmental discipline. Penalizing the individual officer has had only limited success in inducing compliance.[x]

---

[w] *See* A.B.A. Project on Minimum Standards for Criminal Justice, Standards Relating to Pretrial Release §§ 1.4—3.4 and Commentary (1968).

[x] The threat of injunction and the departmental response of reforming its practice are illustrated in Hughes v. Rizzo, 282 F. Supp. 881 (E.D. Pa. 1968):

> FULLAM, District Judge. On June 17, 1967, at about 9:15 p.m., members of the Philadelphia police department conducted a raid in

A second negative method is to remove the incentive for deviation from legal standards by requiring the courts to exclude from use as evidence physical objects seized or oral admissions made at the time of an illegal arrest.[y] As indicated previously, these exclusionary rules can only operate when the police action is oriented toward prosecution and crucial evidence is in fact obtained through the arrest. To meet this objection it has been urged that illegal arrest should result in nullification of criminal charges, but this has seemed too drastic a sanction.[z] A prisoner illegally detained may obtain his freedom by writ of habeas

---

the public park known as Rittenhouse Square in the City of Philadelphia, and arrested approximately 27 young persons, including the plaintiffs, Hughes and Frederick. Those arrested were either "hippies", persons conversing with "hippies", or persons who sought to protest, or make inquiries concerning the arrests. All of the persons arrested were transported in police vehicles to the police station-house at 13th and Thompson Streets, about eight or ten blocks away from the scene of the arrests. All were photographed. All were questioned, individually, by police officers; the questions included inquiries concerning "sexual orientation" and "political affiliation." There were no questions concerning any alleged criminal conduct, but some of those arrested were asked general questions about possession and use of narcotics and dangerous drugs. Those arrested were detained at the police station for about an hour, and then released.

At various other times during June and July, 1967, "hippies" and other young persons associating with "hippies" were taken into temporary custody by Fairmount Park guards in Rittenhouse Square. They were taken to the guardhouse located at one end of Rittenhouse Square, where they were searched and interrogated, and warned to stop frequenting Rittenhouse Square.

There is no evidence that the defendants, or anyone else exercising top-level supervision over the police or park guards, authorized or directed the police activities outlined above. It would indeed be surprising if that were the case. On the other hand, it is not especially reassuring to suppose that under existing administrative regulations, individual police officers and park guards, or their immediate superiors, are at liberty to ignore the constitutional rights of individuals at their pleasure. . . . [A]ny attempt at broad-spectrum injunctive relief should be avoided. Courts are simply not equipped to supervise the day-to-day operations of police officers by injunction. Moreover, the entry of an injunction might tend to encourage the plaintiffs and their associates further to disregard the rights and sensibilities of other users of Rittenhouse Square.

But I am satisfied that the defendants, as responsible officials, do not need to be compelled to prevent a recurrence of such violations. Indeed, the course of events since these matters were brought to the attention of the defendants by reason of the hearings in this case, is proof that the plaintiffs' constitutional rights are no longer threatened.

As a precautionary measure, jurisdiction will be retained so that appropriate relief can be granted should the need arise.

[y] Wong Sun v. United States, 371 U.S. 471 (1963); Mapp v. Ohio, 367 U.S. 643 (1961).

[z] *See* United States v. Blue, 384 U.S. 251 (1966); Frisbie v. Collins, 342 U.S. 519 (1952).

corpus, but the illegality of the original detention does not bar rearrest for the same offense when proper grounds exist and does not bar conviction. However, there is some indication that prosecution may be barred in the event the arrest was discriminatory, particularly if motivated by a desire to suppress activities protected by the Constitution as free speech or free assembly.[a]

A third method is to shift responsibility for making the decision from the police to the judiciary by requiring or rewarding the use of arrest warrants. Although the warrant system is formally conceived as the rule, and the nonwarrant arrest as the exception,[b] the use of warrants was an unusual event until recently. Since *Mapp v. Ohio* the use of warrants has increased somewhat.

1. *The Arrest Warrant System*[c]

FORD v. UNITED STATES
352 F.2d 927 (D.C. Cir. 1965)

FAHY, Circuit Judge, *with whom* Chief Judge BAZELON and Circuit Judges WASHINGTON, DANAHER, BURGER, WRIGHT, McGOWAN, TAMM, and LEVENTHAL *join*. We have reheard the cases *en banc,* with appellants represented by counsel we appointed. They and the United States Attorney at the request of the court have addressed themselves particularly to the questions whether under the Fourth Amendment to the Constitution or under our supervisory jurisdiction an arrest warrant is or can be required where it is practicable to obtain one, and whether it was practicable in this case to obtain a warrant before making the arrests.

The facts as developed on the motion to suppress and at the hearing on the remand are that the robbery occurred at about 4:30 a. m. August 10, 1962, at a tourist home located in this city. Two men participated, one of whom used a pistol in aid of the robbery. A Miss Williams was required to open the money locker, from which one of the men took about $85. About ten

---

[a] *Cf.* the discussion of selective enforcement at 311, *supra,* and Cameron v. Johnson, 390 U.S. 611 (1968).

[b] "The rule which permits arrest for felonies, as distinguished from misdemeanors, if there are reasonable grounds for believing a crime has been or is being committed . . . grew out of the need to protect the public safety by making prompt arrests. . . . Yet, apart from those cases where the crime is committed in the presence of the officer, arrests without warrants, like searches without warrants, are the exception, not the rule, in our society." Justice Douglas, dissenting in Draper v. United States, 358 U.S. 307, 315-16 (1959).

[c] For related materials, see the discussion of search warrants at 199, *supra.*

minutes after it occurred Detective Harris and Officer Caldwell, of the Robbery Squad, responded to a report of the robbery. They were advised by one Winston, "a good informant of the police department," and by a person named Dodson, that appellants had been in Winston's "place" shortly before the robbery and had asked Winston to accompany them on a "hustle." Winston and Dodson also told the police that they saw both appellants running past Winston's place and through an alleyway at about the time of the robbery. The officers brought Miss Williams to Police Headquarters where she identified Kimble's picture from among a number of others shown to her. His photograph was also identified by Winston and Dodson. Early the next morning, August 11, the officers received a telephone call from Winston to the effect that appellants were then sitting in a Buick parked in front of Winston's house. The officers immediately went to the scene. When they arrived the Buick, with four occupants, was nearby but had been moved a block before arrival of the officers. They then arrested its occupants. Ford was in the driver's seat with Kimble sitting next to him. One of the officers removed a pistol, the questioned evidence, from the floorboard of the automobile where it rested on a white towel at Kimble's feet. The arrests occurred at about 7:55 a. m. At a lineup at about 9 a. m. Miss Williams identified both appellants as the robbers.

The protection of the Amendment, however, whatever may be thought to have been its primary thrust, is to be broadly applied. It embraces arrests, and the test it prescribes is reasonableness. We think this test, considered in light of history, decisional law and statutes, may not appropriately be held by us to depend upon a further test turning upon a decision as to the practicability of obtaining a warrant in case of an arrest in a public place for a felony on probable cause. Such an ingredient of reasonableness has never been adopted by the Supreme Court, and has been implicitly if not explicitly rejected there, by the courts in general throughout our history, and by Congress through enactment of statutes which, as we have seen, have been relied upon by the Supreme Court as though constitutional.

However, the practice of arresting without a warrant when it is practicable to obtain one is not to be encouraged. On the contrary. In a doubtful or marginal case of probable cause an arrest may be sustainable on a warrant where without one it would fall.[d] And in any event the intervention whenever prac-

---

[d] "While an arrest pursuant to a warrant is prima facie evidence of probable cause, . . . the prosecutor should be forced to come forward with evidence of probable cause in the absence of a warrant. . . . Without such

ticable of the independent judgment of a magistrate should be sought. We hold, however, that the Constitution did not require the securing of warrants for the arrests of appellants.

We come now to consider whether in the exercise of our supervisory jurisdiction we should adopt a rule, not required by the Fourth Amendment, that a felony arrest on probable cause, without a warrant, will not be deemed valid if it were practicable to obtain a warrant. We think the existing situation does not call for the adoption of such a rule. In so deciding we consider several factors. The conduct of the officers here, as Judge Pine stated on the remand, was not unreasonable or oppressive. Probable cause for the arrests was strong, and when appellants' whereabouts was learned it was sensible for the officers to proceed immediately with the arrests. Moreover, Congressional enactments to which we have referred authorize warrantless arrests on probable cause. These are at least some deterrence to the adoption by us of an inconsistent rule. Additionally, we have Rule 5, FED.R.CRIM.P. It requires a person arrested to be taken before a magistrate without unnecessary delay for determination of the issue of probable cause. The Supreme Court has given life to this Rule by excluding at the trial evidence obtained by its violation. Compliance with Rule 5(a), with the accompanying exclusionary rule, tends to lessen any untoward consequences in this jurisdiction of warrantless arrests. This argues against the exercise now of our supervisory authority to invalidate the arrests in this case. That authority, of course, continues to remain available if we ever become persuaded that a practice of not getting warrants, even though practicable to do so, was resulting in a significant number of unreasonable arrests, inflicting an injustice upon the immediate victims as well as a strain upon the judicial machinery.

We have considered other contentions advanced and find no reversible error.

Affirmed.

J. SKELLY WRIGHT, Circuit Judge (concurring). The Fourth Amendment, of course, protects the person against illegal arrest as well as property against unlawful search. Unfortunately, however, a different set of principles has evolved with respect to the protection of each. As to the search of property, with certain well defined exceptions, it is clearly the law that a search warrant must be obtained. When a police officer has evidence which he deems to be probable cause for the search, he must

---

a rule there would be little reason for law enforcement agencies to bother with the formality of a warrant." Rogers v. United States, 330 F.2d 535, 542-43 (5th Cir. 1964).

place that evidence before a judicial officer who will make that judgment. The security of property is not left to the judgment of a police officer "engaged in the often competitive enterprise of ferreting out crime." Johnson v. United States, 333 U.S. at 14.

With reference to the protection of persons from illegal arrest and subsequent search pursuant thereto, not only of their persons but of their immediate surroundings, it has been held that state law determines the validity of arrests without warrant. Johnson v. United States, *supra* Note 1, 333 U.S. at 15 n. 5; United States v. Di Re, 332 U.S. 581 (1948). Most states follow the old common law principle that a police officer may make a valid arrest without a warrant for a misdemeanor or a felony committed in his presence and for a felony not committed in his presence where he has probable cause to believe that a felony has been committed and that the person arrested committed it.

Currently there appears to be a certain amount of uneasiness with this dichotomy between search and arrest. The Supreme Court, in Giordenello v. United States, 357 U.S. 480, 486 (1958), held that the issuance of an arrest warrant under Rules 3 and 4, FED.R.CRIM.P., must be based on the judgment of "a neutral and detached magistrate" who, in determining probable cause, "should not accept without question the complainant's mere conclusion that the person whose arrest is sought has committed a crime." In Jones v. United States, 357 U.S. at 499-500, where the Government sought to justify the entry of a home to arrest without an arrest warrant, the Supreme Court stated:

> "These contentions, if open to the Government here, would confront us with a grave constitutional question, namely, whether the forceful nighttime entry into a dwelling to arrest a person reasonably believed within, upon probable cause that he had committed a felony, under circumstances where no reason appears why an arrest warrant could not have been sought, is consistent with the Fourth Amendment. . . ."

This court has several times ruled on the *Jones* situation and has held that such arrests are illegal in the District of Columbia. And in Gatlin v. United States, 117 U.S.App.D.C. 123, 128 n. 10, 326 F.2d 666, 671 n. 10 (1963), we said: "The police here, as in Wong Sun [v. United States, 371 U.S. 471 (1963)], acted without an arrest warrant. Thus they failed to place their information before a 'neutral and detached magistrate' who obviously is in a better position to determine probable cause than an 'officer engaged in the often competitive enterprise of ferreting out crime.' Johnson v. United States, 333 U.S. 10, 14 (1948). This failure alone, absent exceptional circumstances, may be sufficient to invalidate this arrest. [Citing cases.]"

Thus we see, as the dissents in *Giordenello,* 357 U.S. at 489-492, and *Jones,* 357 U.S. at 500-503, clearly indicate, the law with reference to the necessity of arrest warrants is in a state of flux with change possibly impending. This change would, of course, eliminate some of the problems which now arise from warrantless arrests followed by interrogation of the accused. For example, if probable cause for arrest were just established before a judicial officer, there would be no occasion for attempting to have the arrestee provide additional evidence of probable cause prior to being brought before the Commissioner. See Rule 5(c), FED.R. CRIM.P. Thus the disreputable and unconstitutional practice of arresting for investigation and interrogation would be discouraged.

The trial court here held that, after obtaining information amounting to what they considered probable cause for the arrest of appellants, it would have been practicable for the police to obtain arrest warrants. The trial court held further, however, that the arrests were legal without them.

In the present state of the law this ruling was undoubtedly correct. Nevertheless, I have no doubt that before too long personal liberty will be accorded the same protection under the Fourth Amendment as the ownership and possession of property now enjoy. See Barrett, Personal Rights, Property Rights, and the Fourth Amendment, in 1960 SUPREME COURT REVIEW 46.

JACKSON v. UNITED STATES

353 F.2d 862 (D.C. Cir. 1965)

Before BAZELON, Chief Judge, and WRIGHT and MCGOWAN, Circuit Judges.

WRIGHT, Circuit Judge: Officer Bello testified that on November 15, 1962, he and another officer were approached by one Ethel Gaskins who informed them that "a Negro male, five foot nine, 25 to 27 years, wearing a brown cap, a tan zipper waist-length jacket, green corduroy trousers, dark complexion," was in the Franklin Delicatessen and had heroin in his possession. On this information alone—the officers had never heard of appellant—the policemen entered the store, found appellant and another Negro male, and asked both of them to step outside. Once outside, a search first of the person arrested with appellant was unproductive. A subsequent search of appellant disclosed he was carrying contraband narcotics.

The District Court concluded that the quality of the information the officer allegedly received was clearly such as would normally lead directly to the suspect, and that the informant was reliable as she had previously given accurate information to Officer Bello. We agree that the information was sufficiently detailed so that the officers should have been led directly to the suspect. But we reject as clearly erroneous the District Court's assumption or implied finding that the officers in fact received this detailed information. It follows that the conclusion of probable cause is unacceptable. We have "the definite and firm conviction" that if the officers had the detailed description of the suspect they claimed to have, they would have arrested but one man. Their action, in the circumstances of this case, in arresting two men, and searching the wrong one first, makes their testimony as to the description of the suspect allegedly received from the informant inherently incredible.[15]

Reversed.

McGOWAN, Circuit Judge (dissenting). With all respect for the views of the majority as to the disposition to be made of this admittedly close case, my own feeling is that reversal is not required.[1]

---

[15] Of course, if an officer obtained a warrant before making a legal along with an illegal arrest, the detailed information he allegedly received would have been presented to a neutral judicial body and recorded in an affidavit. We might then be compelled to accept the argument that he acted lawfully as to one person and unlawfully as to the other. But where he has not obtained a warrant, has not secured judicial confirmation of his possession of the description and thereby obviated the necessity of any speculation as to the true facts, this failure on his part should operate against acceptance of his testimony. The Supreme Court has stated that the warrantless arrest will be more closely scrutinized than one based upon a warrant. One reason for this may well be the possibility that officers will fabricate evidence after the arrest to justify their acts, and the difficulty of proving such fabrication. It is true that we do not guard against after-the-fact fabrication in all cases by requiring that a warrant be obtained whenever practicable. But this does not preclude us from attaching significance to the failure to obtain a warrant in appropriate cases. If anything, our decision not to impose a blanket rule requires us to scrutinize more closely the testimony in cases involving warrantless arrests.

[1] The alleged informant, Gaskins, testified flatly that she never talked to Officers Bello and Ralls at all. The majority accepts the trial court's finding to the contrary, and states that "it is possible that Gaskins had given information in the past, and did tell Bello that there was a Negro man in Franklin's Delicatessen who had heroin in his possession." It rejects "only the implied finding that the officers received the detailed description they claimed." It founds this rejection upon the belief that, had the detailed description in fact been given, the officers would never have taken two men from the store into the street and searched the appellant second. This does not seem to me so improbable as it does to my brethren, however illegal it may have been in respect of the second man. The officers said that they were approached abruptly by Gaskins and told that one man, possessing heroin and dressed in a certain way, was in a neighboring store. When

ARREST: THE DECISION TO TAKE A SUSPECT INTO CUSTODY 31-33 (1965)

By Wayne R. LaFave

(Little, Brown & Company)

NATURE OF THE WARRANT-ISSUANCE PROCESS

1. *The practice in Kansas.* In Kansas the law requires that an arrest warrant for a state offense be issued by a magistrate, that is, a judge of a district court, a justice of the peace, or a similar officer. No mention is made of concurrence or participation by the prosecutor. However, in practice it is the prosecutor or his assistant who is actually consulted by the police officer or private person desiring to initiate a prosecution. The complainant appears at the county attorney's office, where the county attorney or his assistant listens to the facts and, if he decides a warrant should be issued, dictates a complaint (the carbon copy of which is the warrant) to his stenographer. The papers are prepared in his office and then sent to the office of the deputy clerk of court. There the deputy clerk swears the party who is to sign the complaint, the complaint is signed, and the deputy clerk then issues the warrant. A judicial officer does not enter the picture at any point.

. . . Police control is even more striking when a warrant is obtained after regular business hours, as then the city ordinance warrants are issued by a supervisory officer of the police department who has been designated as a clerk pro tem. If the clerk or clerk pro tem does not desire to issue a warrant demanded by an insistent complainant, the matter is referred to the city attorney.

2. *The practice in Michigan.* In Michigan the law provides that an arrest warrant shall be issued by a magistrate, that is, a judge of a circuit court, a justice of the peace, or a similar officer. But these judicial officers cannot issue a warrant without the concurrence of the prosecuting attorney, except in certain specified

---

they entered the store they found two men together. Even though the description fitted only one, it strikes me as not unlikely that, having found two in company when they expected only one, they requested the two to come outside, with a purpose to search both. One does not have to condone this in respect of the second man in order to think that a finding of probable cause could rationally be made as to the arrest and search of appellant. The varying explanations given by Bello of why the second man was seized may reflect his consciousness of vulnerability to criticism in respect of that arrest, but they do not seriously undermine his position *vis-a-vis* Gaskins as to who was telling the truth about their talk, or explain away the fact that the officers were able to go directly to appellant even though they unforewarnedly found him in the company of another man.

minor cases. Generally, the practice is for the prosecutor to approve the issuance of the warrant, and no meaningful review of his decision is made by the magistrate at the time of warrant issuance.

In Detroit an officer requesting a warrant takes a typed report of the case to the prosecuting attorney's office and selects one of the five or six assistant prosecutors from whom to request warrant approval. The assistant looks at the case report and may also question the officer. If approval is granted, he signs the back of the report, which constitutes authorization for the officer to have one of the typists prepare a request for warrant form. He then goes to one of the two senior assistant prosecutors, who must review the case. If the senior assistant prosecutor also approves, he will sign the request form, which is the authorization for the warrant clerk to prepare the complaint and warrant. The officer then takes these documents to the court, where the clerk takes them and either asks the officer to swear to the matter in the complaint or merely asks him if the information is correct and if the signature is his. The clerk or officer then passes the documents on to the judge, who signs the warrant without any independent inquiry. . . .

3. *The practice in Wisconsin.* Warrants for arrest may be issued in Wisconsin by a magistrate, that is, a judge of a court of record, a court commissioner, or a justice of the peace, and also by a district attorney. There is no requirement that either the district attorney or the magistrate obtain the concurrence of the other party. Yet, as in Kansas and Michigan, the prevailing practice is for the matter to be brought first to the prosecutor, who makes the actual decision of whether an arrest should be made.

Thus in Milwaukee County a policeman or private complainant who desires an arrest warrant goes first to the office of the district attorney. Investigators in the office have the task of assigning these persons to one of the assistant district attorneys on duty. . . .

If the assistant decides that a warrant should be issued, the police officer or complainant goes to the complaint stenographic pool in the office of the district attorney, where a stenographer prepares a complaint. . . . The complaint is then taken to the office of the clerk of criminal court, where the warrant is prepared. The warrant is signed by the chief clerk or deputy clerk of the criminal court, notwithstanding the statutory requirement that the warrant be signed by a magistrate or district attorney.

. . . In some counties it is signed by either the clerk or the judge, in some always by the judge, and in others ordinarily by the district attorney. But, regardless of who actually signed the warrant, nowhere did it appear that any discretion was exercised at this point. Rather, it was in all cases treated as a mere ministerial duty, with the real decision having been made in the office of the prosecutor.[e]

CONTROLLING THE POLICE: THE JUDGE'S ROLE IN MAKING AND REVIEWING LAW ENFORCEMENT DECISIONS

By Wayne R. LaFave & Frank J. Remington

63 Michigan Law Review 987, 992-93 (1965)

Arrest warrants are seldom obtained prior to arrest. Even when a warrant is obtained, . . . in large urban areas particularly, arrest warrants are commonly issued without any meaningful participation by a judicial officer. If the judge actually signs the warrant, as is almost always required by law, he is likely to do so without a careful reading of the complaint and without any direct examination of the complainant. This task is often performed by the judge while he is engaged in the trial of cases or the holding of preliminary examinations. Illustrative is the following report:

"All during the preliminary examinations this morning the judge was signing arrest warrants. It was difficult for me to judge the number of warrants signed, since this was going on while witnesses in the preliminary examinations were being questioned. I noticed that the clerk would sometimes go to the opposite side of the courtroom, administer the oath to the officer or complainant wishing to have the warrant signed, and then, very quietly, take the warrant to the bench for the judge's signature. This judge was not appreciably bothered by this duty, since he merely signed his name to the warrant while listening to the testimony of the witnesses in other matters. The clerk, incidentally, administered the oath as quietly as he could so that the proceedings would not be disturbed. I would say that, between the hours of 9:30 and 11:00 a.m., the judge signed ten or fifteen warrants."

---

[e] In 1965 the Wisconsin Supreme Court held that a district attorney could not properly be authorized to issue a warrant, since by virtue of his partisan interest he could not be the "neutral and detached magistrate" which constitutional principles were held to require. State *ex rel.* White v. Simpson, 28 Wis. 2d 590, 137 N.W.2d 391 (1965). The Minnesota Supreme Court held similarly that even court clerks could not be authorized to issue warrants. State v. Paulick, 277 Minn. 140, 151 N.W.2d 591 (1967).

When court is not in session, judges seldom make any greater inquiry into the basis for issuing the process.[38] In some jurisdictions the judge has his clerk sign the warrant and thus does not even see the complaint upon which the arrest is to be based.

The failure of police to use warrants more frequently is understandable, since obtaining action by a magistrate may be very difficult and seem purposeless. In one large city, for example, the courts are in session from 9:30 a.m. to about 3:00 p.m. At all other times judges are practically unavailable. The need for an available judicial officer is, of course, greatest at night and on weekends. Further, the time it takes to obtain a judge's signature can be substantial and the police may feel that they need to take expeditious action. When the judge does act he may give little attention to the task, and when the warrant is challenged at a later time other judges (and on occasion even the same judge) may conclude that the warrant was improperly issued.

a. *Obtaining an Arrest Warrant Before Arrest*

It is most often true in the case of felonies that a police officer who has sufficient evidence of a suspect's guilt to permit him to obtain an arrest warrant also has sufficient evidence to justify making an arrest without a warrant.[f] Generally police proceed without obtaining a warrant. When police *do* seek a warrant in a felony case it is likely to be for some administrative or tactical advantage or because they wish to obtain the prosecutor's or judge's evaluation of the evidence.

---

38 For example, this incident was reported by a field researcher for the American Bar Foundation: "After arriving in court, the police officer went directly to the court room of the examining magistrate. The court was not in session, so the officer went to a back room adjacent to the judge's chambers where a group of men were playing cards. One of them said that the judge was on his way out of the building. The officer returned to the hallway and found the judge about to board an elevator. They exchanged a brief greeting with the officer extending the warrant toward the judge. Without completely unfolding the document, and certainly without reading it, the judge signed and returned it without any question. The officer thanked him as the latter disappeared into the elevator. It appeared to me that the only possible information which the judge could have learned about the case from this transaction would be an inference that the defendant was involved in a burglary, since the officer was assigned to the holdup and breaking and entering bureau."

f In fact, if a warrant is defective the arrest may still be upheld if the officer had grounds to make an arrest without a warrant. *E.g.*, Dearinger v. United States, 378 F.2d 346 (9th Cir. 1967); People v. Chimel, 439 P.2d 333 (Cal. 1968).

The Practice

Some illustrations follow of common circumstances in which police chose to obtain a warrant.

1

A particular person was wanted in connection with a recent murder. Officers sent to the man's residence did not find him, and he failed to appear there during a brief stakeout. Members of his family reported that they thought he had fled to a neighboring state. The police obtained an arrest warrant through the prosecutor's office, and the man's name was thereupon added to the list of persons wanted.

2

Agents of the state Beverage and Tax Division, Department of Taxation, charged with enforcement of liquor, gambling, and prostitution laws, had just entered a county to conduct an undercover investigation. Finding youths drinking in a bar, they did not make an arrest but followed the youths from the tavern, stopped them to insure they were under age, and obtained brief statements from them. A week later, after having uncovered a number of other violations in the county, the agents sought a warrant from the local prosecutor.

3

Officers of the narcotics bureau had observed a number of "buys" from a particular narcotics seller. Desiring to build the best case possible against him, they thought it best to acquire, by means which could not be challenged successfully, narcotics thought to be in the offender's apartment. The officers obtained an arrest warrant and then went to the apartment, placed the offender under arrest, and searched the apartment for narcotics.

4

Officers suspected a man of a recent burglary. Available circumstantial evidence made him an extremely likely suspect and constituted sufficient grounds for arrest. It was the police view that conviction would be impossible without additional evidence and that no other evidence would become available unless a confession by the suspect were obtained. The police decided to obtain an arrest warrant prior to arrest in the hope that the arrestee's awareness of its existence would prompt a confession.

5

A conservation agent came upon a man in a boat running a set line in violation of the law. The man apparently had been drinking and was quite belligerent. At first he refused to identify himself, and then he refused to accept a summons from the officer, saying he would not appear in court. The officer did not then arrest the violator, though he had authority to do so, but rather left for the prosecuting attorney's office in order to obtain a warrant. He returned with the warrant shortly thereafter and placed the offender under arrest. The offender did not resist upon being shown the warrant.

6

A plainclothes officer purchased a number of magazines at a newsstand. Upon examining the magazines, he reached the conclusion that they contained obscene matter. However, rather than make an immediate arrest, the officer took the magazines to the prosecutor's office, where an assistant prosecutor examined them with great care, concluded they were obscene, and approved the issuance of a warrant for the arrest of the newsstand operator.

7

A merchant presented to the police evidence indicating an insufficient funds check violation and demanded arrest and prosecution of the offender. The police refused to take any action, instructing the complainant to take the matter up with the district attorney. He did so; the district attorney made some attempts at accomplishing restitution, and, when these failed, he authorized the issuance of a warrant for the offender's arrest.

8

The police investigated a burglary committed in a barbershop. They learned that the property had been taken by a man who until recently had been employed in the shop as a barber. The owner of the shop, upon learning this, indicated his reluctance at pursuing prosecution, especially if it would mean spending time in court which could otherwise be spent operating the shop. The police, having devoted considerable time and effort to investigation of the case, persuaded the owner of the shop that he should cooperate. Having done so, they immediately went to the prosecutor with the owner and had him sign a complaint. One of the officers commented that the owner was now "committed" to cooperate in the prosecution.

b. *Nonuse of the Warrant, Though Required by Law*

When an officer has probable cause to believe a suspect has committed a felony, he may usually choose between obtaining a warrant and arresting without one; but the officer who has probable cause to believe his man guilty of a misdemeanor not committed in his presence is nearly everywhere forbidden to make an arrest without first obtaining a warrant. When the officer can give this as a ground for refusing to make an arrest in a domestic quarrel, he finds the rule convenient. On the other hand, it often interferes with his duty as he perceives it. The officer may arrest for the misdemeanor even without the required warrant when he thinks it important, or he may occasionally try to make the warrant unnecessary.

The Practice

The following are some fairly uncommon situations illustrating the kinds of situations in which unauthorized arrests may be deliberately made.

1

Traffic officers responded to an accident call and found that a car had left the roadway, resulting in some front-end damage to the car. The driver had been drinking and was quarrelsome, but clearly was not drunk. The officers, after questioning the driver, concluded that the accident had been brought about by a misdemeanor driving violation. Because the driver was not a resident of the state, and was presently on his way back to his home, he was placed under arrest.

2

Officers were called to a domestic disturbance. Upon their arrival at the apartment in question, they found the husband and wife in a vigorous argument, although it was not loud enough to warrant a breach of the peace arrest. The wife, who had called the police, related to them what had happened and said she was willing to sign a complaint. The officers concluded that a misdemeanor assault and battery had occurred. Also, the circumstances suggested that recurrence after the officers left the premises was not at all unlikely. Consequently, they decided to arrest the husband.

3

Officers responded to a wife's complaint of an assault by her husband. The disturbance had subsided by the time they arrived at the home of the couple. The wife showed her bruises to the police, but the husband, who appeared to be intoxicated, had little to say. One of the officers suggested to the husband that because it was a warm night the matter could be discussed further outside the house. The husband followed the officer out to the sidewalk, where he was promptly arrested for public intoxication.

4

An officer reporting to the scene of a traffic accident concluded that the accident was caused by a misdemeanor violation by one of the drivers, a nonresident. The officer told the offending driver that a complaint would have to be made against him for the violation, and that the driver should accompany him to the station while this was done. After a warrant was obtained a formal arrest was made, and the driver then posted bail.

Reference Note

Among the writings on arrest most useful from the viewpoint stressed in these materials, the preeminent one, worth reading in its entirety, is W. LaFave, Arrest: The Decision to Take a Suspect into Custody (1965).

On the exercise of discretion whether to enforce the law by arrest, J. Goldstein, *Police Discretion Not to Invoke the Criminal Process: Low Visibility Decisions in the Administration of Justice,* 69 Yale L.J. 543 (1960), best puts the case for severe limitation. The President's Commission on Law Enforcement and Administration of Justice, Task Force Report: The Police ch. 2 (1967), urges the desirability and inevitability of police exercise of discretion and proposes the articulation of police policies as a method of exerting some control over that exercise. Chapters 3-8 of LaFave's book are pertinent to this issue. A good general discussion of police discretion and policymaking and of the interrelationships among the various agencies of the criminal justice system is Ruth, *Promoting Consistent Policy in the Criminal Justice Process,* 53 Va. L. Rev. 1489 (1967).

Arrest practices in several jurisdictions are interestingly described in Note, *Detention, Arrest, and Salt Lake City Police Practice,* 9 Utah L. Rev. 593 (1965); Note, *Philadelphia Police Practices and the Law of Arrest,* 100 U. Pa. L. Rev. 1182 (1952); Barrett, *Police Practices and the Law—From Arrest to Release or Charge,* 50 Calif. L. Rev. 11 (1962) (California); and LaFave's book (principally describing Detroit). Chapter 9 of a book by John Gardiner on traffic law enforcement (to be published in 1969 by Harvard Press) discusses the factors which affect variation in enforcement levels of laws governing moving traffic.

A helpful discussion of the warrant system is LaFave & Remington, *Controlling the Police: The Judge's Role in Making and Reviewing Law Enforcement Decisions,* 63 MICH. L. REV. 987 (1965).

Chapter 5

DEALING WITH THE PRISONER IN CUSTODY

A. OBJECTIVES

After a suspected criminal offender has been taken into custody he is likely to be "frisked," taken to the police station, fingerprinted, photographed, searched, questioned, exhibited in lineups, and locked in a cell.[a] These acts of the police are motivated by several principal concerns: identifying the prisoner, keeping him securely, and accumulating evidence.

1. Keeping the Prisoner Securely

Since the arrested person must be kept for further processing, the police wish to make sure that he cannot escape, that he cannot harm anyone, and that he does not introduce into the jail anything which unnecessarily complicates the custodial task. The prisoner will ordinarily be frisked at the scene of the arrest for any weapons which would endanger the officer who transports him to the station. At the jail his pockets will be emptied and his possessions inventoried and filed to avoid allegations that something was stolen by police or other prisoners, as well as to prevent bringing into the jail weapons, money, narcotics, or anything else which might interfere with smooth, safe operation of the jail. In some cases a "strip" search is also made for the same purposes. If the prisoner was operating an automobile at the time of his arrest, the automobile may also be impounded and the contents inventoried, since the officers who arrest a person stand responsible for safeguarding property thus left unattended.[b]

---

[a] *See* Comment, *The Role of "Booking" in the Administration of Criminal Justice,* 1963 U. ILL. L.F. 685.

[b] If the motivation is safeguarding contents of the car against loss or safeguarding police against false claim of loss, the examination of the car may be permissible. Heffley v. State, 423 P.2d 666 (Nev. 1967). Evidence uncovered when a policeman opened the door of an impounded car to roll up the windows against rain was held properly discovered in Harris v. United States, 390 U.S. 234 (1968).

Some questioning is necessary for proper administration of a jail. It is important to establish the prisoner's identity, the names of relatives who should be notified or should be permitted to visit, whether the prisoner is addicted to narcotics, and so on. There is no doubt that these security measures will sometimes produce evidence of crime on the part of the prisoner and that they may be carried out with mixed motives, but the law enforcement position has been that they are justified on the grounds of administrative needs and not as evidence-seeking efforts. One such instance is as follows:

The police, having substantial evidence that a man had murdered his wife, arrested him. He was warned of his rights and lodged in the jail. Next day he was brought to a classification officer who asked questions listed on an interview form which elicited information such as names of relatives, employment, military service, prior convictions, and the prisoner's version of the offense for which he had been arrested. The information was routinely used to determine who might visit, what level of security was needed, and so on. In response to the question about his offense the prisoner made a statement which showed he had guilty knowledge of his wife's death.

2. *Accumulating Evidence by Observation*

As noted, the various kinds of search and inventorying incident to arrest and imprisonment serve not only to identify the prisoner, but also to collect evidence against him. Furthermore, the arrested person can be physically examined with a minimum of cooperation in the pursuit of evidence through fingerprinting,[c] photographing, lineup for identification by witnesses to the crime, and subjection to chemical tests. Still other evidence can be obtained only through the prisoner's cooperation—he may speak for voice identification, give handwriting samples for analysis, submit to a lie detector examination, or give his consent to a search of premises that could not otherwise be lawfully searched.[d]

---

[c] The propriety of fingerprinting a person arrested for a misdemeanor regulatory offense is upheld after exhaustive discussion in United States v. Laub Baking Co., 283 F. Supp. 217 (N.D. Ohio 1968).

[d] It is now settled that the taking of nontestimonial evidence from an accused in lawful custody is not violative of his privilege against self-incrimination (Schmerber v. California, 384 U.S. 757 (1966); but compare United States v. Green, 282 F. Supp. 373 (S.D. Ind. 1968)), but the constitutionality of taking such evidence from one illegally arrested is uncertain. Search of such a person is clearly impermissible; the taking of fingerprints was rejected in Bynum v. United States, 262 F.2d 465 (D.C. Cir. 1958), cited

The Practice

The following illustrate some common police practices with respect to a person in custody.

1

Immediately after making the arrest for being party to a robbery, the officers opened the woman's handbag and searched it for narcotics or weapons. Finding none, they put her in the police car with handcuffs holding her hands behind her back (because they had not searched her person for weapons) and took her to the detention center. Two matrons took the woman into a separate room where she was asked to remove her clothing so it could be searched and so that the matrons could examine her body to see whether narcotics were secreted in her vagina.[e]

2

In a hearing on motion to suppress evidence, police testified as follows: After a burglary suspect had been arrested, he was questioned for some time concerning his involvement in various burglaries, possession of burglar tools, and possession of clothing that might have been worn during the burglary. Police then asked him whether he minded their going to his room to look for a pair of shoes. He said that he had nothing to hide and that they could go there and see for themselves. They did go and seized the shoes, which matched footprints at the scene of the burglary.

3

FBI agents arrested a man for a bank robbery in which the robber had used a handwritten note demanding money. The agents required the man to write the words of the note several times. A handwriting expert examining the note and the examples of the prisoner's handwriting concluded that he had written the note.

4

A rape victim was called to the police station to see if she could identify a suspect as the offender. She picked him out of

approvingly in Wong Sun v. United States, 371 U.S. 471 (1963). Identification in a lineup may be permitted. State v. Hodgson, 44 N.J. 151, 207 A.2d 542 (1965). Taking handwriting exemplars is of doubtful propriety, even after warning the prisoner that he need not create them and could consult his attorney first. People v. Sesslin, 439 P.2d 321 (Cal. 1968).

[e] McIntyre & Charaja, *The Intensive Search of a Suspect's Body and Clothing,* 58 J. Crim. L.C. & P.S. 18 (1967); *cf.* Lucero v. Donovan, 258 F. Supp. 979 (C.D. Cal. 1966) (upholding a strip search after three civil trials).

a group of six men in the lineup and identified him as the rapist.

UNITED STATES v. WADE
388 U.S. 218 (1967)

MR. JUSTICE BRENNAN delivered the opinion of the Court.

The question here is whether courtroom identifications of an accused at trial are to be excluded from evidence because the accused was exhibited to the witnesses before trial at a post-indictment lineup conducted for identification purposes without notice to and in the absence of the accused's appointed counsel.

The federally insured bank in Eustace, Texas, was robbed on September 21, 1964. A man with a small strip of tape on each side of his face entered the bank, pointed a pistol at the female cashier and the vice president, the only persons in the bank at the time, and forced them to fill a pillowcase with the bank's money. The man then drove away with an accomplice waiting in a stolen car outside the bank. On March 23, 1965, an indictment was returned against respondent, Wade, and two others for conspiring to rob the bank, and against Wade and the accomplice for the robbery itself. Wade was arrested on April 2, and counsel was appointed to represent him on April 26. Fifteen days later an FBI agent, without notice to Wade's lawyer, arranged to have the two bank employees observe a lineup made up of Wade and five or six other prisoners and conducted in a courtroom of the local county courthouse. Each person in the line wore strips of tape such as allegedly worn by the robber and upon direction each said something like "put the money in the bag," the words allegedly uttered by the robber. Both bank employees identified Wade in the lineup as the bank robber.

At trial, the two employees, when asked on direct examination if the robber was in the courtroom, pointed to Wade. The prior lineup identification was then elicited from both employees on cross-examination. At the close of testimony, Wade's counsel moved for a judgment of acquittal or, alternatively, to strike the bank officials' courtroom identifications on the ground that conduct of the lineup, without notice to and in the absence of his appointed counsel, violated his Fifth Amendment privilege against self-incrimination and his Sixth Amendment right to the assistance of counsel. The motion was denied, and Wade was convicted. The Court of Appeals for the Fifth Circuit reversed the conviction and ordered a new trial at which the in-court identification evidence was to be excluded, holding that, though the lineup did not violate Wade's Fifth Amendment rights, "the lineup, held as it was, in the absence of counsel, already chosen to represent appellant, was a violation of his Sixth Amendment rights. . . ." 358 F.2d 557, 560. We granted certiorari, 385 U.S. 811, and set the case for oral argument with No. 223, Gilbert v. California, *post,* p. 263, and No. 254, Stovall v. Denno, *post,* p. 293, which present similar questions. We reverse the judgment of the Court of Appeals and remand to that court with direction to enter a new judgment vacating the conviction and remanding the case to the District Court for further proceedings consistent with this opinion.

I.

Neither the lineup itself nor anything shown by this record that Wade was required to do in the lineup violated his privilege against self-incrimination. We have only recently reaffirmed that the privilege "protects an accused only from being compelled to testify against himself, or otherwise provide the State with evidence of a testimonial or communicative nature. . . ." Schmerber v. California, 384 U.S. 757, 761. We there held that compelling a suspect to submit to a withdrawal of a sample of his blood for analysis for alcohol content and the admission in evidence of the analysis report was not compulsion to those ends. We have no doubt that compelling the accused merely to exhibit his person for observation by a prosecution witness prior to trial involves no compulsion of the accused to give evidence having testimonial significance. It is compulsion of the accused to exhibit his physical characteristics, not compulsion to disclose any knowledge he might have. It is no different from compelling Schmerber to provide a blood sample or Holt to wear the blouse, and, as in those instances, is not within the cover of the privilege. Similarly, compelling Wade to speak within hearing distance of the witnesses, even to utter words purportedly uttered by the robber, was not compulsion to utter statements of a "testimonial" nature; he was required to use his voice as an identifying physical characteristic, not to speak his guilt. We held in Schmerber, *supra,* at 761, that the distinction to be drawn under the Fifth Amendment privilege against self-incrimination is one between an accused's "communications" in whatever form, vocal or physical, and "compulsion which makes a suspect or accused the source of 'real or physical evidence,'" Schmerber, *supra,* at 764. We recognized that "both federal and state courts have usually held that . . . [the privilege] offers no protection against compulsion to submit to fingerprinting, photography, or measurements, to write or speak for identification, to appear in court, to stand, to assume a stance, to walk, or to make a particular gesture." *Id.,* at 764. None of these activities becomes testimonial within the scope of the privilege because required of the accused in a pretrial lineup.

II.

The fact that the lineup involved no violation of Wade's privilege against self-incrimination does not, however, dispose of his contention that the courtroom identifications should have been excluded because the lineup was conducted without notice to and in the absence of his counsel. Our rejection of the right to counsel claim in *Schmerber* rested on our conclusion in that case that "[n]o issue of counsel's ability to assist petitioner in respect of any rights he did possess is presented." 384 U.S., at 766. In contrast, in this case it is urged that the assistance of counsel at the lineup was indispensable to protect Wade's most basic right as a criminal defendant—his right to a fair trial at which the witnesses against him might be meaningfully cross-examined.

When the Bill of Rights was adopted, there were no organized police forces as we know them today. The accused confronted the prosecutor and the witnesses against him, and the evidence was marshalled, largely at the trial itself. In contrast, today's law enforcement machinery involves critical confrontations of the accused by the prosecution at pretrial proceedings where the results might well settle the accused's fate and reduce the trial itself to a mere formality. In recognition of these realities of modern criminal prosecution, our cases have construed the Sixth Amendment guarantee to apply to "critical" stages of the proceedings. The guarantee reads: "In all criminal prosecutions, the accused shall enjoy the right . . . to have the Assistance of Counsel *for his defence.*" (Emphasis supplied.) The plain wording of this guarantee thus encompasses counsel's assistance whenever necessary to assume a meaningful "defence."

As early as Powell v. Alabama [287 U.S. 45 (1932)], we recognized that the period from arraignment to trial was "perhaps the most critical period of the proceedings . . . ," *id.,* at 57, during which the accused "requires the guiding hand of counsel . . . ," *id.,* at 69, if the guarantee is not to prove an empty right.

It is central to that principle that in addition to counsel's presence at trial, the accused is guaranteed that he need not stand alone against the State at any stage of the prosecution, formal or informal, in court or out, where counsel's absence might derogate from the accused's right to a fair trial. The security of that right is as much the aim of the right to counsel as it is of the other guarantees of the Sixth Amendment—the right of the accused to a speedy and public trial by an impartial jury, his right to be informed of the nature and cause of the accusation, and his right to be confronted with the witnesses against him and to have compulsory process for obtaining witnesses in his favor. The presence of counsel at such critical confrontations, as at the trial itself, operates to assure that the accused's interests will be protected consistently with our adversary theory of criminal prosecution.

III.

The Government characterizes the lineup as a mere preparatory step in the gathering of the prosecution's evidence, not different—for Sixth Amendment purposes—from various other preparatory steps, such as systematized or scientific analyzing of the accused's fingerprints, blood sample, clothing, hair, and the like. We think there are differences which preclude such stages being characterized as critical stages at which the accused has the right to the presence of his counsel. Knowledge of the techniques of science and technology is sufficiently available, and the variables in techniques few enough, that the accused has the opportunity for a meaningful confrontation of the Government's case at trial through the ordinary processes of cross-examination of the Government's expert witnesses and the presentation of the evidence of his own experts. The denial of a right to have his counsel present at such analyses does not therefore violate the Sixth Amendment; they are not critical stages since there is minimal risk that his counsel's absence at such stages might derogate from his right to a fair trial.

IV.

But the confrontation compelled by the State between the accused and the victim or witnesses to a crime to elicit identification evidence is peculiarly riddled with innumerable dangers and variable factors which might seriously, even crucially, derogate from a fair trial. The vagaries of eyewitness identification are well-known; the annals of criminal law are rife with instances of mistaken identification. A commentator has observed that "[t]he influence of improper suggestion upon identifying witnesses probably accounts for more miscarriages of justice than any other single factor—perhaps it is responsible for more such errors than all other factors combined." Wall, Eye-Witness Identification in Criminal Cases 26. Suggestion can be created intentionally or unintentionally in many subtle ways. And the dangers for the suspect are particularly grave when the witness' opportunity for observation was insubstantial, and thus his susceptibility to suggestion the greatest.

Moreover, "[i]t is a matter of common experience that, once a witness has picked out the accused at the line-up, he is not likely to go back on his word later on, so that in practice the issue of identity may (in the absence of other relevant evidence) for all practical purposes be determined there and then, before the trial."[8]

But as is the case with secret interrogations, there is serious difficulty in depicting what transpires at lineups and other forms of identification confrontations. Improper influences may go undetected by a suspect, guilty or not, who experiences the emotional tension which we might expect in one being confronted with potential accusers. Even when he does observe abuse, if he has a criminal record he may be reluctant to take the stand and open up the admission of prior convictions. Moreover, any protestations by the suspect of the fairness of the lineup made at trial are likely to be in vain; the jury's choice is between the accused's unsupported version and that of the police officers present. In short, the accused's inability effectively to reconstruct at trial any unfairness that occurred at the lineup may deprive him of his only opportunity meaningfully to attack the credibility of the witness' courtroom identification.

The potential for improper influence is illustrated by the circumstances, insofar as they appear, surrounding the prior identifications in the three cases we decide today. In the present case, the testimony of the identifying witnesses elicited on cross-examination revealed that those witnesses were taken to the courthouse and seated in the courtroom to await assembly of the lineup. The courtroom faced on a hallway observable to the witnesses through an open door. The cashier testified that she saw Wade "standing in the hall" within sight of an FBI agent. Five or six other prisoners later appeared in the hall. The vice president testified that he saw a person in the hall in the custody of the agent who "resembled the person that we identified as the one that had entered the bank."

The lineup in Gilbert, *supra,* was conducted in an auditorium in which some 100 witnesses to several alleged state and federal robberies charged to Gilbert made wholesale identifications of Gilbert as the robber in each other's presence, a procedure said to be fraught with dangers of suggestion. And the vice of suggestion created by the identification in Stovall, *supra,* was the presentation to the witness of the suspect alone handcuffed to police officers. It is hard to imagine a situation more clearly

---

[8] Williams & Hammelmann, Identification Parades, Part I, [1963] Crim. L. Rev. 479, 482.

conveying the suggestion to the witness that the one presented is believed guilty by the police.

Insofar as the accused's conviction may rest on a courtroom identification in fact the fruit of a suspect pretrial identification which the accused is helpless to subject to effective scrutiny at trial, the accused is deprived of that right of cross-examination which is an essential safeguard to his right to confront the witnesses against him. Pointer v. Texas, 380 U.S. 400.

Since it appears that there is grave potential for prejudice, intentional or not, in the pretrial lineup, which may not be capable of reconstruction at trial, and since presence of counsel itself can often avert prejudice and assure a meaningful confrontation at trial, there can be little doubt that for Wade the post-indictment lineup was a critical stage of the prosecution at which he was "as much entitled to such aid [of counsel] . . . as at the trial itself." Powell v. Alabama, 287 U.S. 45, 57. Thus both Wade and his counsel should have been notified of the impending lineup, and counsel's presence should have been a requisite to conduct of the lineup, absent an "intelligent waiver." See Carnley v. Cochran, 369 U.S. 506. Moreover, we leave open the question whether the presence of substitute counsel might not suffice where notification and presence of the suspect's own counsel would result in prejudicial delay.[27]

Legislative or other regulations, such as those of local police departments, which eliminate the risks of abuse and unintentional suggestion at lineup proceedings and the impediments to meaningful confrontation at trial may also remove the basis for regarding the stage as "critical."

V.

We think it follows that the proper test to be applied in these situations is that quoted in Wong Sun v. United States, 371 U.S. 471, 488, "'[W]hether, granting establishment of the primary illegality, the evidence to which instant objection is made has been come at by exploitation of that illegality or instead by means sufficiently distinguishable to be purged of the primary taint.' Maguire, Evidence of Guilt 221 (1959)." . . .

On the record now before us we cannot make the determination whether the in-court identifications had an independent origin. This was not an issue at trial, although there is some evidence relevant to a determination. That inquiry is most prop-

[27] Although the right to counsel usually means a right to the suspect's own counsel, provision for substitute counsel may be justified on the ground that the substitute counsel's presence may eliminate the hazards which render the lineup a critical stage for the presence of the suspect's *own* counsel.

erly made in the District Court. We therefore think the appropriate procedure to be followed is to vacate the conviction pending a hearing to determine whether [there is clear and convincing evidence that] the in-court identifications had an independent source, or whether, in any event, the introduction of the evidence was harmless error, Chapman v. California, 386 U.S. 18, and for the District Court to reinstate the conviction or order a new trial, as may be proper. . . .

MR. JUSTICE WHITE, whom MR. JUSTICE HARLAN and MR. JUSTICE STEWART join, dissenting in part and concurring in part. But if the rule is premised on the defendant's right to have his counsel know [the circumstances of the confrontation], there seems little basis for not accepting other means to inform. A disinterested observer, recordings, photographs—any one of them would seem adequate to furnish the basis for a meaningful cross-examination of the eyewitness who identifies the defendant in the courtroom.

I would not extend this system [in which defense counsel may properly protect his client's interest even at the cost of disrupting the search for truth], at least as it presently operates, to police investigations and would not require counsel's presence at pretrial identification procedures. Counsel's interest is in not having his client placed at the scene of the crime, regardless of his whereabouts. Some counsel may advise their clients to refuse to make any movements or to speak any words in a lineup or even to appear in one. To that extent the impact on truthful fact-finding is quite obvious. Others will not only observe what occurs and develop possibilities for later cross-examination but will hover over witnesses and begin their cross-examination then, menacing truthful fact-finding as thoroughly as the Court fears the police now do. Certainly there is an implicit invitation to counsel to suggest rules for the lineup and to manage and produce it as best he can. I therefore doubt that the Court's new rule, at least absent some clearly defined limits on counsel's role, will measurably contribute to more reliable pretrial identifications.

[Other opinions are omitted.][f]

---

[f] Though the Supreme Court avoided the issue, there is some precedent that use of evidence obtained through "a pretrial identification procedure, even though not violative of the defendant's right to counsel or of his privilege against self incrimination, may be so unfair as to amount to a denial of due process of law" because the identification procedure was unnecessarily suggestive and conducive to irreparable mistaken identification. People v. Ballott, 20 N.Y.2d 600, 233 N.E.2d 103, 106 (1967). The situations which have been held to deny due process have involved witnesses with limited opportunity to observe the offender closely at the time of the crime, who were usually presented with a single suspect for identifica-

The Crime Control Act of 1968 sought to lift the burden imposed by the *Wade* case upon the federal government to establish that eyewitness testimony was not tainted by an improper lineup procedure:

> § 3502. Admissibility in evidence of eye witness testimony
>
> The testimony of a witness that he saw the accused commit or participate in the commission of the crime for which the accused is being tried shall be admissible in evidence in a criminal prosecution in any trial court ordained and established under article III of the Constitution of the United States.[g]

3. Accumulating Evidence by Interrogation

Traditionally one of the major sources of information tending to establish guilt of crime has been the suspect's own answers to questions. Occasionally an offender is so driven by guilt feelings that he will appear spontaneously at the police station and disclose his crime. More often he is too fearful to volunteer a confession, but can be induced through careful questioning to relieve his conscience by admitting guilt. Even an offender who is initially resistant to confessing may finally see denial as futile after he has been drawn into the trap of making explanations which can be shown to be lies.[h]

There are, of course, a significant number of cases in which solution of the crime seems to require interrogation of suspects and persons under arrest, but it is easy to exaggerate the importance of interrogation as an evidence-gathering technique. Confessions are often used for the sake of convenience even when other evidence is available to be used in its stead. And interrogation is particularly useful in clearing the books of unsolved crimes when no prosecution is intended, since an offender faced with one charge will often readily admit his guilt of others upon the understanding that he will not be charged with them;

tion. *See* Palmer v. Peyton, 359 F.2d 199 (4th Cir. 1966), 19 STAN. L. REV. 479 (voice identification); People v. Caruso, 65 Cal. Rptr. 336, 436 P.2d 336 (1968) (in the lineup only defendant fit the offender's reported general description).

[g] 18 U.S.C. § 3502. The question whether this provision is constitutional will probably be put to the Supreme Court very soon. A brief in support of the constitutionality of such legislation is set out in S. REP. No. 1097, 90th Cong., 2d Sess. 53-63 (1968).

[h] Much interrogation takes place without custody. The principal reason a suspect will come to the police station and respond to questions without being in custody is his desire to avoid guilty-seeming behavior. *See* REPORT AND RECOMMENDATIONS OF THE COMMISSIONERS' COMMITTEE ON POLICE ARREST FOR INVESTIGATION [D.C.] 62 (July 1962).

the function of interrogation then is essentially the housekeeping task of tying up loose ends.

Interrogation has been subjected to substantial restrictions growing out of two principal ideas. The first is the concern that out of a desire for information police may succumb to the temptation to use coercive and on rare occasions even brutal interrogation methods—methods which might induce an innocent man to confess.[i] The second idea is that self determination and individual integrity have high social value, and that a man should not be made the instrument of his own undoing. This is reflected in an expanding interpretation of the constitutional privilege against self-incrimination to include situations outside the courtroom where the privilege had traditionally belonged.

Despite the acknowledged dangers of granting the police the right to interrogate, there continues a strong tradition that the police have such right, subject to substantial restrictions. It is interesting to note, however, that in our system of criminal justice there is no provision for interrogation of the prisoner at all. In formal law the arrest is often defined as a taking into custody in order that the person answer for a crime, implying that arrest is only for the purpose of securing the presence of the offender before the courts, not for the purpose of permitting in-custody interrogation. In addition, the statutes requiring that an arrested person be promptly brought before a magistrate suggest that no time is to be reserved for interrogation. And after the prisoner has been brought before the magistrate he will generally be admitted to bail immediately.[j] At the preliminary examination, arraignment, and trial the accused is never asked to respond in any fashion except to plead, and even there he may stand mute and have a plea of not guilty entered automatically.[k]

---

[i] Sterling, *Police Interrogation and the Psychology of Confession,* 14 J. Pub. L. 25 (1965). Reasons a man may confess, other than coercion, are suggested in State v. Bower, 440 P.2d 167 (Wash. 1968).

[j] If the prisoner is remanded to custody, responsibility for him typically shifts from the police to the jailer or warden. Jail regulations frequently make it difficult, if not impossible, for police to interrogate the prisoner thereafter. The prisoner is subject to judicial, not police, control. Cooperative jailers may give the police relatively free access and the judge may permit police questioning (*see* United States *ex rel.* Dickerson v. Rundle, 238 F. Supp. 218 (E.D. Pa. 1965), 363 F.2d 126 (3d Cir. 1966)), yet the change in custody can be a serious limitation upon questioning the suspect. Compare the dissent in United States *ex rel.* Stovall v. Denno, 355 F.2d 731, 742, 743-44 (2d Cir. 1966).

[k] In contrast to the modern situation, it is true that until the nineteenth century there was in the common-law system judicial interrogation of the prisoner when he was brought before the magistrate. L. Orfield, Criminal Procedure from Arrest to Appeal 53-58 (1947). Resurrection of this older practice was the Wickersham Commission's solution to problems of the "third degree."

B. THE VALUE OF INTERROGATION

There are strongly divergent views about the significance of interrogation to successful police work.

WATTS v. INDIANA
338 U.S. 49, 57-58 (1949)

Mr. Justice Jackson, concurring in the result. These three cases, from widely separated states, present essentially the same problem. Its recurrence suggests that it has roots in some condition fundamental and general to our criminal system.

In each case police were confronted with one or more brutal murders which the authorities were under the highest duty to solve. Each of these murders was unwitnessed, and the only positive knowledge on which a solution could be based was possessed by the killer. In each there was reasonable ground to *suspect* an individual but not enough legal evidence to *charge* him with guilt. In each the police attempted to meet the situation by taking the suspect into custody and interrogating him. This extended over varying periods. In each, confessions were made and received in evidence at the trial. Checked with external evidence, they are inherently believable, and were not shaken as to truth by anything that occurred at the trial. Each confessor was convicted by a jury and state courts affirmed. This Court sets all three convictions aside.

The seriousness of the Court's judgment is that no one suggests that any course held promise of solution of these murders other than to take the suspect into custody for questioning. The alternative was to close the books on the crime and forget it, with the suspect at large. This is a grave choice for a society in which two-thirds of the murders already are closed out as insoluble.

"FAIR PLAY" IN CRIMINAL INVESTIGATIONS AND PROSECUTIONS
By Fred E. Inbau
Northwestern University "Tri-Quarterly," vol. 3, no. 2, at 3, 5-9 (Winter 1961)

Criminal Interrogation:

1. Many criminal cases, even when investigated by the best qualified police departments, are capable of solution only by means of an admission or confession from the guilty individual or upon the basis of information obtained from the questioning of other criminal suspects.

One completely false assumption accounts in large measure for the technical and practical restrictions on police interrogations. It is this, and the fallacy is certainly perpetuated to a very considerable extent by mystery writers, the movies, and TV: Whenever a crime is committed, if the police will only look carefully at the crime scene they will almost always find some clue that will lead them to the offender and at the same time establish his guilt; and once the offender is located, he will readily confess or disclose his guilt by trying to shoot his way out of the trap. But this is pure fiction; in actuality the situation is quite different. As a matter of fact, the art of criminal investigation has not developed to a point where the search for and the examination of physical evidence will always reveal a clue to the identity of the perpetrator or provide the necessary proof of his guilt. In criminal investigations, even of the most efficient type, there are many, many instances where physical clues are entirely absent, and the only approach to a possible solution of the crime is the interrogation of the criminal suspect himself, and of others who may possess significant information. . . .

2. Criminal offenders, except, of course, those caught in the commission of their crimes, ordinarily will not admit their guilt unless questioned under conditions of privacy, and for a period of perhaps several hours.

This point is one which should be readily apparent not only to any person with the least amount of criminal investigative experience, but also to anyone who will reflect momentarily upon the behavior of ordinary law-abiding persons when suspected or accused of nothing more than simple social indiscretions. Self-condemnation and self-destruction not being normal behavioral characteristics, human beings ordinarily do not utter unsolicited, spontaneous confessions. They must first be questioned regarding the offense. . . . It is also impractical to expect admissions or confessions to be obtained under circumstances other than privacy. Here again recourse to our everyday experience will support the basic validity of this requirement. For instance, in asking a personal friend to divulge a secret we carefully avoid making the request in the presence of other persons, and seek a time and place when the matter can be discussed in private. The very same psychological factors are involved in a criminal interrogation, and even to a greater extent. For related psychological considerations, if an interrogation is to be had at all, it must be one based upon an unhurried interview, the necessary length of which will in many instances extend to several hours, depending upon various factors such as the nature of the case situation and the personality of the suspect.

3. In dealing with criminal offenders, and consequently also with criminal suspects who may actually be innocent, the interrogator must of necessity employ less refined methods than are considered appropriate for the transaction of ordinary, everyday affairs by and between law-abiding citizens.

To illustrate this point, permit me to revert to the previously discussed case of the woman who was murdered by her brother-in-law. His confession was obtained largely as a result of the interrogator adopting a friendly attitude in questioning the suspect, when concededly no such genuine feeling existed; by pretending to sympathize with the suspect because of his difficult financial situation; by suggesting that perhaps the victim had done or said something which aroused his anger and which would have aroused the anger of anyone else similarly situated to such an extent as to provoke a violent reaction; and by resorting to other similar expressions, or even overtures of friendliness and sympathy such as a pat on the suspect's shoulder or knee. In all of this, of course, the interrogation was "unethical" according to the standards usually set for professional, business and social conduct. But the pertinent issue in this case was no ordinary, lawful, professional, business or social matter.

MEMORANDUM

[Excerpt from a memorandum by a law student police intern, August, 1967, reporting on the importance of interrogation in a metropolitan police force:]

The police officers make most of their arrests only upon observing a misdemeanor being committed, *i.e.*, a disorderly man, a simple assault, a drunk, and so forth. Thus, because they have observed the offender committing the offense, there is no need to ask any questions (save for the basic identification questions) either in the scout car or at the station house. The detectives, on the other hand, make most of their arrests upon serving a warrant.

In both of these situations—the police officer observing a misdemeanor and a detective arresting upon a warrant—no questioning is essential and is therefore most often not even attempted. In addition, in those instances where the police officer on the beat does make an arrest for a felony, he almost invariably brings the suspect to the detectives' office for questioning by the detectives about this offense as well as about other offenses possibly committed by this defendant. . . .

[T]here were at least a dozen instances where the detectives went to a home, served a warrant for arrest upon a defendant, and took him to the station house without asking a single question. The booking of the defendant in these cases was accomplished in a matter of minutes. No questions in any of these instances were asked of the defendant; and, therefore, no warnings were given. The police officers in charge (detectives) made the point, however, that, prior to Miranda, questions would have been asked of these defendants, mostly about possible past unsolved crimes similar to the one for which the arrest was made. In other words, they said that limiting interrogation did not, nine times out of ten, affect the arrest or the suspect as regards the particular offense for which the arrest was made, but it did limit their ability to close out past cases. To those officers who express a concern with the crime statistics, it is in this way that Miranda is considered a hindrance to police work.

INTERROGATIONS IN NEW HAVEN: THE IMPACT OF *MIRANDA*

Comment, 78 Yale Law Journal 1519, 1578-80, 1593-96 (1967)†

THE ROLE OF INTERROGATIONS AND CONFESSIONS IN CRIMINAL LAW ENFORCEMENT

Miranda provoked an immediate rash of comment from prosecutors, police officials and commentators about the role of interrogations in crime prevention. The overwhelming majority warned that interrogations are essential to effective law enforcement. This assumption, coupled with the assumption about the impact of warnings on suspect behavior, led them to conclude that law enforcement would be substantially hampered by the *Miranda* rules.

In the year since the decision, however, a small but growing number of officials and commentators have come to the conclusion that "the value of confessions in law enforcement has been grossly exaggerated." They argue that most cases can be solved by other investigative techniques.

Several empirical studies have considered this issue, but a number of questions remain unanswered.[158] By focusing only on

† Reprinted by permission of the Yale Law Journal and Fred B. Rothman & Company.

158 *E.g.:* Detroit Police Dep't, Confessions in Felony Prosecutions for the Year of 1961 as Compared to January 20, 1965 through December 31, 1965 (July 27, 1966) (unpublished report); E. Younger, Dorado-Miranda Survey,

confessions and admissions, these studies neglect cases in which other evidence is already available or where interrogation provides new leads which eventually bring a conviction. There is, moreover, little information about the role of interrogations in achieving other law enforcement objectives, such as convicting accomplices or retrieving stolen goods.[160] No study has considered whether the police could use other methods of investigation to obtain conclusive evidence without reliance on confessions.[161] Finally, there is no evidence about the effect on *Miranda* on the success of interrogations in the crucial cases where there are no investigative alternatives to police questioning. . . .

Aug. 4, 1966 (available from the Office of the District Attorney for the County of Los Angeles); N. SOBEL, [THE NEW CONFESSION STANDARDS: MIRANDA V. ARIZONA 136-50 (1966)]. For a discussion of these studies, *see* App. I.

[160] The role of interrogations and confessions in the early stages of the criminal process is considered in Barrett, *Police Practices and the Law—From Arrest to Release or Charge,* 50 CALIF. L. REV. 11, 35-45 (1962). This study provides some interesting statistics about the screening function of questioning. The data was obtained in two surveys conducted by the chiefs of police in two unidentified California cities during two three-month periods in 1960. The members of the detective division in each city were required to complete a form for each adult arrested on felony charges and processed by them during the particular three-month period.

In "City A" detectives interrogated 391 of the 399 suspects comprising the sample (98%); in "City B" all 59 suspects studied were interrogated by either the detectives or the arresting officers. Confessions or admissions (undefined) were reported to have been obtained from 58.1% of the 399 suspects arrested in City A and 88.1% of the 59 suspects arrested in City B. When consideration was limited to suspects arrested and subsequently charged, excluding those subsequently released, these figures rose to 75.6% (198 of 262) and 89.6% (43 of 48) respectively. A surprisingly high number of the suspects released in each of these cities also gave confessions or admissions. In City A, 34 of 137 did so (24.8%); in City B, 9 of 11 did (82%). Barrett suggests that the suspects were released in these cases because of insufficient evidence, a refusal to prosecute by the complaining witnesses, or a refusal to issue a complaint by the prosecuting attorney "in the interests of justice." *Id.* 39.

[161] Several comparative studies of clearance rates imply that investigative alternatives to interrogation are not only available but are successfully resorted to by law enforcement agencies when judicial rulings restrict or inhibit the use of interrogations and confessions. Thus the percentage of solutions of major crimes in the District of Columbia increased after 1957, despite the restrictive rule laid down that year in Mallory v. United States, 354 U.S. 449 (1957). *See Hearings on District of Columbia Appropriations, 1960, Before a Subcomm. of the House Comm. on Appropriations,* 86th Cong., 1st Sess. 440-41 (1959) (testimony of Deputy Chief Executive Officer Covell of the Metropolitan Police Department); *Hearings on District of Columbia Appropriations, 1961, Before a Subcomm. of the House Comm. on Appropriations,* 86th Cong., 2d Sess. 619 (1960) (testimony of Chief Murray); Rogge, *Proof by Confession,* 12 VILL. L. REV. 1, 101 (1966). *But cf. Hearings on District of Columbia Appropriations, 1961, Before a Subcomm. of the House Comm. on Appropriations,* 86th Cong., 2d Sess. 621-23 (1960). The results of these studies are far from conclusive, however, because clearance rates are affected by many factors, not the least of which is statistical manipulation.

Taking all assumptions and reservations into account, it appears that interrogations may be even less necessary than our figures indicate. In almost every case last summer the police had adequate evidence to convict the suspect without any interrogation. Interrogation usually just cemented a cold case or served to identify accomplices.

This finding is probably explained by the fact that the police were rarely able to arrest even a single person for crimes where no witnesses were available. Significantly, the evidence obtained by the President's Commission indicates that this is true of other cities as well. In a study of 1,905 crimes reported in Los Angeles the Commission research showed that 86 per cent of the crimes where a suspect was named were solved while only 15 per cent for which no suspect was named were solved. In most of these later cases no arrests were ever made. Thus, even in a force as scientifically advanced as Los Angeles', there is strong evidence that confessions are of small importance, since arrests can be made only where the crime is for the most part already solved because such substantial evidence is available before interrogation.

C. *Other Purposes of Interrogation*

1. *Identification and Implication of Accomplices*

Interrogation is often used to obtain information about accomplices: the suspect can be asked to identify accomplices when the police know that he did not commit the offense alone, or to implicate an accomplice already identified. Occasionally, the suspect unexpectedly reveals an accomplice whose existence was previously unknown to the police.

Multiple suspects were involved in at least 36 of the 90 cases observed this summer. They were apprehended together in 21 cases; in at least 13 other cases the police knew that accomplices were involved and questioned the suspect about them. Finally, in two instances interrogation uncovered the previously unknown involvement of other persons. . . .

2. *Clearance of Other Crimes*

One of the most persistent claims of *Miranda's* critics is that interrogations are needed to clear other crimes committed by a suspect, regardless of whether questioning is necessary to solve the immediate crime being investigated. The "clearance" rate is generally used as an index of the effectiveness of a law enforcement agency. Since an overwhelming majority of crimes reported and on file in any given police department are unsolved, an interrogator will frequently question a confessed suspect about other crimes he may have committed. This information may be sought for use in prosecution, either for the newly disclosed crimes or for the original crime. But clearance is also desired, rightly or wrongly, as a goal in itself. The police may want simply to close their books on as many cases as they can and improve the "record" of the department; or particular officers may seek the satisfaction of solving a crime. . . .

While interrogations may be important for clearance, the importance of clearance to law enforcement seems debatable. Police officials claim that clearance gives policemen a sense of achievement, and our interviewers agreed. Clearance of crimes was the standard by which detectives measured their own accomplishments. Clearance is also supposed to be important for sentencing, and for convicting defendants of the additional crimes. But suspects generally do not receive higher sentences because more counts are brought against them. Actually, the suspect may benefit, since his cooperation in clearing other crimes may earn a recommendation of leniency from the prosecutor. . . .

3. *Miscellaneous*

These categories do not exhaust the uses of interrogations. In the interviews conducted six months after the summer field study, the detectives mentioned several other objectives sought through questioning.

Recovery of stolen goods and the weapons used to commit the crime is facilitated by interrogation. The detectives are particularly anxious to remove weapons from the community. The discovery of stolen goods and illegal instruments also increases the likelihood of conviction by corroborating the evidence already available.

Interrogations are used to discover crimes and improve crime prevention. The detectives frequently mentioned that they can discover general patterns of criminal activity through questioning. They mentioned one case, for example, where a suspect said that he committed a burglary in a particular area because it was poorly policed. Interrogation is also used to discover "victimless crimes" such as gambling and narcotics violations. . . .

C. LIMITATIONS PLACED UPON INTERROGATION

Much as in the area of search, the principal sanction which the courts have utilized to control police interrogation practices is the exclusion from trial of statements obtained through improper practices and of any evidence derived from such statements.[l] Legislatures have rarely spoken to this issue explicitly, but Congress recently responded to Supreme Court rulings by establishing a federal standard for admissibility of confessions. The statute did not attempt to alter the requirements which the Federal Rules of Criminal Procedure and Supreme Court decisions have imposed upon police, but countermands the Court's rulings that confessions obtained in disregard of those requirements must be excluded from use in evidence. The statute makes "voluntariness" of the confession the major test of admissibility. The Supreme Court will be required to answer directly whether the exclusionary rules are subject to legislative control.

1. *Exclusion of Statements Induced by "Coercion"*

Historically the admissibility of confessions has been discussed in terms of "voluntariness" of the confession or statement. The emphasis was upon exclusion of confessions obtained by means which cast doubt upon their trustworthiness. The major concern was for protecting innocent persons who might have been coerced to give a false confession.

In recent years the judicial limitations upon use of confessions in evidence have expanded in two ways. One way is the creation of formal prerequisites, such as are discussed in the following sections. Another way is the disapproving of an increasing number of interrogation methods. The Supreme Court continues to use the language of "voluntariness" and "coercion" even though the emphasis is no longer simply on trustworthiness of the confession but also on the propriety of police conduct. The concern is no longer only with protecting the innocent against the pos-

[l] It is unsettled if, and when, such evidence may be used solely to impeach the defendant as a witness. Comment, *The Collateral Use Doctrine: From Walder to Miranda,* 62 Nw. U.L. Rev. 912 (1968).

As a result of the 1968 legislation, 18 U.S.C. § 3731 provides for appeal by the government from a pretrial order suppressing evidence. Though there is no requirement of a pretrial motion to suppress an improperly obtained confession, some states follow such practice. It is unclear whether this appeal statute would apply to rulings on confessions as well as rulings on seized evidence. With *Katz v. United States,* the line between words and things has become of less significance.

sibility of false confession, but also with protecting even the guilty against inappropriate methods of obtaining statements from them.

The Supreme Court has, over the years, drawn a more and more stringent standard of admissibility, finding even fairly subtle psychological pressures enough to make confessions inadmissible even though the confessions were true. The Court has considered a number of different factors as bearing on the question of admissibility: denial of rights (such as holding incommunicado, delaying presentation before a magistrate, denial of access to counsel, and failure to warn of rights to counsel and to remain silent); questioning techniques (relay interrogation for long periods, pretense of friendship); threats or acts tending to reduce resistance (pain, fear, indignity, fatigue, promises, possible loss of child custody, involvement of others); status (age, education, intelligence, language, sanity, health, experience with police); loss of self control (truth serum); and the psychological effect from having made a prior confession even though it is known to be inadmissible. The first Supreme Court case forbidding use of a confession in state courts (in 1936) involved sadistic torture of a prisoner; recent cases have moved so far as to exclude confessions obtained principally by deception.[m]

The Crime Control Act of 1968 made "voluntariness" of any self-incriminating statement the criterion of admissibility in federal prosecutions. In addition to the factors relevant to determination of "voluntariness" developed by case law the statute specified that

> (b) The trial judge in determining the issue of voluntariness shall take into consideration all the circumstances surrounding the giving of the confession, including (1) the time

[m] *E.g.,* Leyra v. Denno, 347 U.S. 556 (1954) (state psychiatrist implied he wanted to help the accused); Spano v. New York, 360 U.S. 315 (1959) (accused's friend asserted he would be in trouble if accused did not confess). In addition to the deception there were also other factors making the finding of inadmissibility easier.

The use of an undercover agent before a man has been arrested was approved in *Hoffa v. United States,* at 119, *supra.* The use of an undercover agent to get further information from a man after he has been indicted and is represented by counsel was forbidden by Massiah v. United States, 377 U.S. 201 (1964). In McLeod v. Ohio, 381 U.S. 356 (1965), the Court summarily reversed on the authority of *Massiah* a conviction based upon an admission volunteered by a prisoner after his indictment when he had not been specifically warned of his right of counsel; no deception was involved. *See* Hancock v. White, 378 F.2d 479 (1st Cir. 1967), interpreting the *McLeod* case. It seems probable that the principle of *Massiah* is not limited to post-indictment information gathering. See the dissenting opinion in Miller v. California, 392 U.S. 616 (1968).

elapsing between arrest and arraignment of the defendant making the confession, if it was made after arrest and before arraignment, (2) whether such defendant knew the nature of the offense with which he was charged or of which he was suspected at the time of making the confession, (3) whether or not such defendant was advised or knew that he was not required to make any statement and that any such statement could be used against him, (4) whether or not such defendant had been advised prior to questioning of his right to the assistance of counsel; and (5) whether or not such defendant was without the assistance of counsel when questioned and when giving such confession.

The presence or absence of any of the above-mentioned factors to be taken into consideration by the judge need not be conclusive on the issue of voluntariness of the confession.[n]

One method which has been suggested for avoiding coercion is to entrust someone other than the police with the responsibility for conducting the interrogation. Sometimes, particularly when the offense is serious, the prosecutor is called in to take statement, but generally interrogation has been left to the police. We have no tradition for formal interrogation of suspects except in grand jury investigations.

Since the determination of the facts on which admissibility depends is so difficult, the Court has in recent times sought a technique for preventing police coercion or at least for providing better evidence of what happened during the interrogation than simply the conflicting testimony of police officer and prisoner. This is reflected in the Court's suggestion in Miranda v. Arizona, *infra,* that defense counsel is properly allowed to be present when his client is interrogated, and in the suggestion that the burden of showing counsel was present or that the prisoner affirmatively and intelligently waived his right to an attorney rests upon the prosecution. The proposal that police should be required to record their interrogation sessions is espoused by the draft of the American Law Institute Model Code of Pre-Arraignment Procedure.

MODEL CODE OF PRE-ARRAIGNMENT PROCEDURE
§ 4.09(3), at 38-40 (Tent. Draft No. 1, 1966)

(3) Sound Recordings. The regulations relating to sound recordings shall establish procedures to provide a sound recording of

[n] 18 U.S.C. § 3501(b).

(a) the warning to arrested persons pursuant to Section 4.01(2); and

(b) any questioning involving more than a few brief questions.

Such recording shall include an indication of the time of the beginning and ending thereof. The arrested person shall be informed that the sound recording required hereby is being made and the statement so informing him shall be included in the sound recording. The station officer shall be responsible for insuring that such a sound recording is made.

Note on Section 4.09

. . . Subsection (3) is designed to help eliminate factual disputes concerning what was said to the arrested person and what prompted any incriminating statements, by requiring a sound recording of critical parts of the investigation. It is of course true that means can be devised to keep the recording in a particular case from being complete and accurate, and that making such recordings may be an impediment to productive questioning. But these problems do not seem significant enough to deprive such a provision of its value in helping to meet one of the great problems involved in permitting any period of police questioning.

The requirement of making sound recordings of questioning will pose administrative problems and require the expenditure of funds. Concerns about these matters led a narrow majority of the Advisors to recommend that the requirement be imposed only for serious crimes. It is, however, the Reporters' view that in a model code the keeping of such records should be made mandatory with respect to all crimes.

It was also suggested that the Code should permit, in lieu of sound recording, the keeping of a written transcript of interrogations, to be made by a stenographer independent of police control. This would provide a third person who could testify to what took place and would meet some concerns raised as to the technical feasibility of obtaining an accurate sound recording. The Reporters are doubtful whether testimony by a stenographer would be of assistance in many of those cases where there may be close questions as to the coerciveness of police conduct, and believe that a sound recording is a more effective and economical method of monitoring warnings and interrogation.

The requirement in subsection (3) of this section that there be disclosure that a sound recording is being made will make it more difficult to obtain information in those cases where the arrested person finds the knowledge that his words are being recorded distracting or specially threatening. Nonetheless, such disclosure is consistent with the Code's recognition of the importance of an arrested person's being made aware of the significance of his position. Thus, although a majority of the Advisors favored eliminating this requirement, the Reporters recommend that it be retained.

2. *Exclusion of Statements Obtained Under the Excitement of an Illegal Arrest or Search*

Another limitation imposed by the law upon interrogation is that statements may not be used in evidence which are taken from a person in custody while he is still under the influence of excitement flowing from an unconstitutional arrest or search.

WONG SUN v. UNITED STATES
371 U.S. 471, 484-86 (1963)

[Police unlawfully entered Toy's home and confronted him with the statement that they had evidence Toy furnished narcotics to others. Toy responded, "No · I haven't been selling narcotics at all. However, I do know somebody who has." He then identified the person and admitted having smoked heroin with that person the night before. These statements proved self-incriminating on the charge of transportation and concealment of heroin.]

MR. JUSTICE BRENNAN delivered the opinion of the Court.

It is conceded that Toy's declarations in his bedroom are to be excluded if they are held to be "fruits" of the agents' unlawful action.

The exclusionary rule has traditionally barred from trial physical, tangible materials obtained either during or as a direct result of an unlawful invasion. It follows from our holding in Silverman v. United States, 365 U.S. 505, that the Fourth Amendment may protect against the overhearing of verbal statements as well as against the more traditional seizure of "papers and effects." Similarly, testimony as to matters observed during an unlawful invasion has been excluded in order to enforce the basic constitutional policies. McGinnis v. United States, 227 F.2d 598. Thus, verbal evidence which derives so immediately from an unlawful entry and an unauthorized arrest as the officers' action in the present case is no less the "fruit" of official illegality than the more common tangible fruits of the unwarranted intrusion. See Nueslein v. District of Columbia, 115 F.2d 690. Nor do the policies underlying the exclusionary rule invite any logical distinction between physical and verbal evidence.

The *Wong Sun* case has been largely ignored by the courts. Many have taken it as merely suggesting a factor to be taken into account in assessing the voluntariness of the confession or statement. Others have seen it as raising a kind of presumption of involuntariness. Some have treated it as creating a rule of exclusion which can be avoided by finding the taint of illegality purged by time, advice of counsel, or some other event seen as sufficiently intervening. It may be that any illegality would be purged by warnings in compliance with the *Miranda* case, discussed below; the Supreme Court has not yet made this clear.[o]

3. Exclusion of Statements Made in Ignorance of Constitutional Rights

Another limitation that has been placed upon interrogation by the Supreme Court, but which was already being followed in part by some police agencies, is that before any in-custody interrogation may take place that hopes to produce admissible evidence the prisoner has to be warned of his rights to remain silent and to have the advice of counsel prior to answering questions, should he choose to speak.

The Crime Control Act of 1968 did not attack directly the Supreme Court requirement that police warn prisoners of their rights, but sought to nullify the Court ruling that failure to give such warning would result in exclusion of the confession. The legislation made the prisoner's awareness of his rights merely one of the factors which must be considered in determining the "voluntariness" of the incriminating statement.[p]

MIRANDA v. ARIZONA
384 U.S. 436 (1966)

MR. CHIEF JUSTICE WARREN delivered the opinion of the Court.

We encourage Congress and the States to continue their laudable search for increasingly effective ways of protecting the rights of the individual while promoting efficient enforcement of our

---

[o] The Crime Control Act of 1968 seems not to have addressed itself to this problem.

[p] 18 U.S.C. § 3501. *See* p. 397, *infra*.

criminal laws. However, unless we are shown other procedures which are at least as effective in apprising accused persons of their right of silence and in assuring a continuous opportunity to exercise it, the following safeguards must be observed.

At the outset, if a person in custody is to be subjected to interrogation, he must first be informed in clear and unequivocal terms that he has the right to remain silent. For those unaware of the privilege, the warning is needed simply to make them aware of it—the threshold requirement for an intelligent decision as to its exercise. More important, such a warning is an absolute prerequisite in overcoming the inherent pressures of the interrogation atmosphere. It is not just the subnormal or woefully ignorant who succumb to an interrogator's imprecations, whether implied or expressly stated, that the interrogation will continue until a confession is obtained or that silence in the face of accusation is itself damning and will bode ill when presented to a jury. Further, the warning will show the individual that his interrogators are prepared to recognize his privilege should he choose to exercise it.

The Fifth Amendment privilege is so fundamental to our system of constitutional rule and the expedient of giving an adequate warning as to the availability of the privilege so simple, we will not pause to inquire in individual cases whether the defendant was aware of his rights without a warning being given. Assessments of the knowledge the defendant possessed, based on information as to his age, education, intelligence, or prior contact with authorities, can never be more than speculation; a warning is a clearcut fact. More important, whatever the background of the person interrogated, a warning at the time of the interrogation is indispensable to overcome its pressures and to insure that the individual knows he is free to exercise the privilege at that point in time.

The warning of the right to remain silent must be accompanied by the explanation that anything said can and will be used against the individual in court. This warning is needed in order to make him aware not only of the privilege, but also of the consequences of foregoing it. It is only through an awareness of these consequences that there can be any assurance of real understanding and intelligent exercise of the privilege. Moreover, this warning may serve to make the individual more acutely aware that he is faced with a phase of the adversary system—that he is not in the presence of persons acting solely in his interest.

The circumstances surrounding in-custody interrogation can operate very quickly to overbear the will of one merely made aware of his privilege by his interrogators. Therefore, the right to have counsel present at the interrogation is indispensable to the protection of the Fifth Amendment privilege under the system we delineate today. Our aim is to assure that the individual's right to choose between silence and speech remains unfettered throughout the interrogation process. A once-stated warning, delivered by those who will conduct the interrogation, cannot itself suffice to that end among those who most require knowledge of their rights. A mere warning given by the interrogators is not alone sufficient to accomplish that end. Prosecutors themselves claim that the admonishment of the right to remain silent without more "will benefit only the recidivist and the professional." Brief for the National District Attorneys Association as *amicus curiae,* p. 14. Even preliminary advice given to the accused by his own attorney can be swiftly overcome by the secret interrogation process. Cf. Escobedo v. Illinois, 378 U.S. 478, 485, n. 5. Thus, the need for counsel to protect the Fifth Amendment privilege comprehends not merely a right to consult with counsel prior to questioning, but also to have counsel present during any questioning if the defendant so desires.

The presence of counsel at the interrogation may serve several significant subsidiary functions as well. If the accused decides to talk to his interrogators, the assistance of counsel can mitigate the dangers of untrustworthiness. With a lawyer present the likelihood that the police will practice coercion is reduced, and if coercion is nevertheless exercised the lawyer can testify to it in court. The presence of a lawyer can also help to guarantee that the accused gives a fully accurate statement to the police and that the statement is rightly reported by the prosecution at trial. See Crooker v. California, 357 U.S. 433, 443-448 (1958) (DOUGLAS, J., dissenting).

An individual need not make a pre-interrogation request for a lawyer. While such request affirmatively secures his right to have one, his failure to ask for a lawyer does not constitute a waiver. No effective waiver of the right to counsel during interrogation can be recognized unless specifically made after the warnings we here delineate have been given. The accused who does not know his rights and therefore does not make a request may be the person who most needs counsel.

Accordingly we hold that an individual held for interrogation must be clearly informed that he has the right to consult with a lawyer and to have the lawyer with him during interrogation under the system for protecting the privilege we delineate today. As with the warnings of the right to remain silent and that anything stated can be used in evidence against him, this warning is an absolute prerequisite to interrogation. No amount of circumstantial evidence that the person may have been aware of this right will suffice to stand in its stead. Only through such a warning is there ascertainable assurance that the accused was aware of this right.

If an individual indicates that he wishes the assistance of counsel before any interrogation occurs, the authorities cannot rationally ignore or deny his request on the basis that the individual does not have or cannot afford a retained attorney. The financial ability of the individual has no relationship to the scope of the rights involved here. The privilege against self-incrimination secured by the Constitution applies to all individuals. The need for counsel in order to protect the privilege exists for the indigent as well as the affluent. In fact, were we to limit these constitutional rights to those who can retain an attorney, our decisions today would be of little significance. The cases before us as well as the vast majority of confession cases with which we have dealt in the past involve those unable to retain counsel. While authorities are not required to relieve the accused of his poverty, they have the obligation not to take advantage of indigence in the administration of justice. Denial of counsel to the indigent at the time of interrogation while allowing an attorney to those who can afford one would be no more supportable by reason or logic than the similar situation at trial and on appeal struck down in Gideon v. Wainwright, 372 U.S. 335 (1963), and Douglas v. California, 372 U.S. 353 (1963).

In order fully to apprise a person interrogated of the extent of his rights under this system then, it is necessary to warn him not only that he has the right to consult with an attorney, but also that if he is indigent a lawyer will be appointed to represent him. Without this additional warning, the admonition of the right to consult with counsel would often be understood as meaning only that he can consult with a lawyer if he has one or has the funds to obtain one. The warning of a right to counsel would be hollow if not couched in terms that would convey to the indigent—the person most often subjected to interrogation—the knowledge that he too has a right to have counsel present. As with the warnings of the right to remain silent and of the general right to counsel, only by effective and express explanation to the indigent of this right can there be assurance that he was truly in a position to exercise it.

Once warnings have been given, the subsequent procedure is clear. If the individual indicates in any manner, at any time prior to or during questioning, that he wishes to remain silent, the interrogation must cease. At this point he has shown that he intends to exercise his Fifth Amendment privilege; any statement taken after the person invokes his privilege cannot be other than the product of compulsion, subtle or otherwise. Without the right to cut off questioning, the setting of in-custody interrogation operates on the individual to overcome free choice in producing a statement after the privilege has been once invoked. If the individual states that he wants an attorney, the interrogation must cease until an attorney is present. At that time, the individual must have an opportunity to confer with the attorney and to have him present during any subsequent questioning. If the individual cannot obtain an attorney and he indicates that he wants one before speaking to police, they must respect his decision to remain silent.

This does not mean, as some have suggested, that each police station must have a "station house lawyer" present at all times to advise prisoners. It does mean, however, that if police propose to interrogate a person they must make known to him that he is entitled to a lawyer and that if he cannot afford one, a lawyer will be provided for him prior to any interrogation. If authorities conclude that they will not provide counsel during a reasonable period of time in which investigation in the field is carried out, they may refrain from doing so without violating the person's Fifth Amendment privilege so long as they do not question him during that time.

If the interrogation continues without the presence of an attorney and a statement is taken, a heavy burden rests on the government to demonstrate that the defendant knowingly and intelligently waived his privilege against self-incrimination and his right to retained or appointed counsel. Escobedo v. Illinois, 378 U.S. 478, 490, n. 14.

Our decision is not intended to hamper the traditional function of police officers in investigating crime. See Escobedo v. Illinois, 378 U.S. 478, 492. When an individual is in custody on probable cause, the police may, of course, seek out evidence in the field to be used at trial against him. Such investigation may include inquiry of persons not under restraint. General on-the-scene questioning as to facts surrounding a crime or other general questioning of citizens in the fact-finding process is not affected by our holding. It is an act of responsible citizenship for individuals to give whatever information they may have to aid in law enforcement. In such situations the compelling atmosphere inherent in the process of in-custody interrogation is not necessarily present.

In dealing with statements obtained through interrogation, we do not purport to find all confessions inadmissible. Confessions remain a proper element in law enforcement. Any statement given freely and voluntarily without any compelling influences is, of course, admissible in evidence. The fundamental import of the privilege while an individual is in custody is not whether he is allowed to talk to the police without the benefit of warnings and counsel, but whether he can be interrogated. There is no requirement that police stop a person who enters a police station and states that he wishes to confess to a crime, or a person who calls the police to offer a confession or any other statement he desires to make. Volunteered statements of any kind are not barred by the Fifth Amendment and their admissibility is not affected by our holding today.

What underlying value does the *Miranda* rule attempt to achieve? There are several alternatives: (a) The rule may be intended merely to protect a person from incriminating himself under a mistaken belief that he is obligated to do so. If the rule has this limited objective it would apply only when police intend to use the information against the person interrogated. Therefore, if the police already have ample evidence to convict and intend to use answers only to "clear the books" of unsolved crimes, to identify accomplices, or to recover stolen property, the warnings would not have to be given.[q] (b) A second possibility is that the rule is intended to prevent any questioning of a person in custody, without the warning, regardless of the purpose of the interrogation. The value, in other words, would be privacy—freedom from any in-custody interrogation without being informed of a right to silence, even though answers given would not be used against the prisoner. If this is the purpose, police should always give the warning before questioning. (c) A third possibility is that the *Miranda* rule is designed to prevent only coercive or otherwise improper interrogations, particularly by conferring the right to have the advice of counsel before the interrogation takes place. If this is its objective the requirement of warning would seem applicable to any interrogation since the possibility of coercion or other impropriety exists whether or not the statement is to be used in evidence against the person interrogated.

Ascertaining the purpose of a rule is important because it has significant implications for practice. For example, in the fourth amendment area some police who arrest or search without ade-

---

[q] This view seems consistent with the common statutory provision for requiring a person to testify in court after having been formally granted immunity against prosecution.

quate grounds explain that they know the law but do not, in the particular case, intend to prosecute the prisoner or to try to use the physical evidence in court. This is clearly improper since the constitutional protection is basically against illegal arrest or search, not against the institution of prosecution or against the use of the evidence.[r] In the fifth amendment area, if interrogation without warning is the evil, lack of intent to use the evidence against the prisoner does not affect the wrongfulness of the interrogation. But if self-incrimination is the evil, the police might properly say, "I need not give the *Miranda* warning because I do not intend to use the prisoner's answers against him."

The concern in *Miranda* that persons should be made aware of their rights may relate to reinforcing them against coercion, or to attempting to equalize the standing before the law of all prisoners, whatever their intelligence, education, or cultural background.[s] Of course, this effort cannot wholly succeed so long as waiver of the rights is permitted, since willingness to waive rights may also be related to intelligence, education, or cultural pattern. The step which would most nearly result in equal treatment would therefore be the actual provision of a lawyer to give advice on the question of waiver of the right to a lawyer.[t]

In the Crime Control Act of 1968 Congress sought directly to overturn the *Miranda* decision, despite outcry that the legislation itself would be held unconstitutional by the Supreme Court.[u]

§ 3501. Admissibility of confessions

(a) In any criminal prosecution brought by the United States or by the District of Columbia, a confession, as defined in subsection (e) hereof, shall be admissible in evidence if it is voluntarily given. Before such confession is received in evidence, the trial judge shall, out of the presence of the jury, determine any issue as to voluntariness. If the trial judge determines that the confession was voluntarily made

[r] *Cf.* p. 261 n.p, *supra.*

[s] This interpretation is weakened by the Court's approval of use of spontaneous statements by an accused, which may be ill advised and in ignorance of rights.

[t] In Commonwealth v. Taper (3 Cr. L. 2143, Pa. 1968), the court required police to inform a prisoner that an attorney can advise him more fully of the meaning of the charges, possible defenses, and desirable strategy.

[u] The arguments on both sides are stated in S. Rep. No. 1097, 90th Cong., 2d Sess. (1968); see particularly 53-63.

it shall be admitted in evidence and the trial judge shall permit the jury to hear relevant evidence on the issue of voluntariness and shall instruct the jury to give such weight to the confession as the jury feels it deserves under all the circumstances.[v]

(b) The trial judge in determining the issue of voluntariness shall take into consideration all the circumstances surrounding the giving of the confession, including (1) the time elapsing between arrest and arraignment of the defendant making the confession, if it was made after arrest and before arraignment, (2) whether such defendant knew the nature of the offense with which he was charged or of which he was suspected at the time of making the confession, (3) whether or not such defendant was advised or knew that he was not required to make any statement and that any such statement could be used against him, (4) whether or not such defendant had been advised prior to questioning of his right to the assistance of counsel; and (5) whether or not such defendant was without the assistance of counsel when questioned and when giving such confession.

The presence or absence of any of the above-mentioned factors to be taken into consideration by the judge need not be conclusive on the issue of voluntariness of the confession.

. . .

(d) Nothing contained in this section shall bar the admission in evidence of any confession made or given voluntarily by any person to any other person without interrogation by anyone, or at any time at which the person who made or gave such confession was not under arrest or other detention.

(e) As used in this section, the term "confession" means any confession of guilt of any criminal offense or any self-incriminating statement made or given orally or in writing.[w]

4. Exclusion of Statements Obtained During Delay in Presentation Before a Magistrate

The statutory or procedural rule requiring police to bring their prisoner promptly before a magistrate sets a time limit upon interrogation. In *Mallory v. United States*,[x] the Supreme Court held that any confession obtained by federal officers after they should have presented the arrested person before a magis-

[v] This prior screening of confessions by the court, out of the jury's presence, is required by Jackson v. Denno, 378 U.S. 368 (1964).

[w] 18 U.S.C. § 3501.

[x] 354 U.S. 449 (1957).

trate must be excluded from evidence. Delay for processing the prisoner was said to be permissible, but not delay for interrogation. Though this standard of proper police conduct still stands, by the Crime Control Act of 1968 Congress has nullified the exclusionary sanction that the Court had attached to it.

> (c) In any criminal prosecution by the United States or by the District of Columbia, a confession made or given by a person who is a defendant therein, while such person was under arrest or other detention in the custody of any law-enforcement officer or law-enforcement agency, shall not be inadmissible solely because of delay in bringing such person before a commissioner or other officer empowered to commit persons charged with offenses against the laws of the United States or of the District of Columbia if such confession is found by the trial judge to have been made voluntarily and if the weight to be given the confession is left to the jury and if such confession was made or given by such person within six hours immediately following his arrest or other detention: *Provided,* That the time limitation contained in this subsection shall not apply in any case in which the delay in bringing such person before such commissioner or other officer beyond such six-hour period is found by the trial judge to be reasonable considering the means of transportation and the distance to be traveled to the nearest available such commissioner or other officer.
>
> (d) Nothing contained in this section shall bar the admission in evidence of any confession made or given voluntarily by any person to any other person without interrogation by anyone, or at any time at which the person who made or gave such confession was not under arrest or other detention.[y]

The *Mallory* decision proceeded on a nonconstitutional ground, applying the Court's power to exercise supervision over the lower federal courts (and thereby indirectly over federal law enforcement), but the Court has since said that it was based "principally" on non-constitutional grounds.[z] This suggests the possibility that this provision of the Crime Control Act might be held inconsistent with the fourth amendment or some other constitutional principle.[a]

[y] 18 U.S.C. § 3501.

[z] Wong Sun v. United States, 371 U.S. 471, 486 n.12 (1963).

[a] The *Mallory* rule has been followed by almost none of the states because they saw it as a federal policy decision, not as a constitutional mandate. Wisconsin, however, adopted the *Mallory* rule as a matter of

D. THE EFFECT OF LIMITS PLACED ON INTERROGATION

The *Miranda* decision provided a major test of the assumption that the Supreme Court could reshape police practices through the exclusion of evidence. The law enforcement response to *Miranda* was sometimes grudging and at other times generous in following the guidelines.[b]

The Practice

Some of the varying practices existing after the *Miranda* decision may be seen in the following illustrations.

1

After arresting a burglary suspect the detective took him to the station and placed him in one of the interrogation rooms. The detective read to him the *Miranda* warning and asked him if he wanted a lawyer or would answer questions. The man responded, "I don't have no lawyer. I don't have no money for a lawyer so I guess I'll answer your question." The detective then reread the part of the warning which states that the suspect is entitled to a lawyer even though he cannot afford one and explained that since there was no provision for appointing counsel while the suspect was in the police station he would get counsel when he appeared in court. The man then said, "I would rather have a lawyer than say anything." No attempt was made to interrogate him.

2

A woman of thirty-five called police to her home and complained of an assault by her ex-boyfriend. Inadvertently she disclosed that she had helped the boyfriend steal a number of tires from his place of employment. The police then interrupted

---

state constitutional law. Phillips v. State, 29 Wis. 2d 521, 139 N.W.2d 41 (1966). In Reimers v. State, 31 Wis. 2d 457, 143 N.W.2d 525 (1966), the court said that detention over the weekend and a Monday holiday (after arrest Saturday night) might be unreasonable even though judges do not usually work on Sundays or holidays. If a defendant is to be held, ways must be developed for making a judge available.

[b] The guidelines are by no means free from ambiguity, and lower court decisions interpreting the case have varied greatly. This has left substantial excuse for police to read *Miranda* narrowly. On the other hand, despite cases holding *Miranda* inapplicable to noncustodial interviews by tax investigators, the IRS required its special agents to read to the taxpayer a *Miranda*-type warning. *See* United States v. Turzynski, 268 F. Supp. 847, 854 (N.D. Ill. 1967). Some of the subsequent cases have held *Miranda* governs these cases, too. *Cf.* Mathis v. United States, 391 U.S. 1 (1968).

to give her the *Miranda* warning. She hesitated to say anything further, but upon urging by a friend who was present she finished the story and showed the police where three of the tires were stored. She was not arrested, and the policemen left. The police later explained that they didn't know whether the warnings were required, but that they were not sure that no prosecution would follow from their report and that they did not want it said they had not followed the law's requirements.

3

The day after a murder by stabbing, a man who lived next door informed police that his brother carried a knife and had told him he had done something awful the previous night. Police arrested the brother, took his knife, and brought him to the precinct station. He was warned that he was entitled to counsel before being questioned and that he did not have to say anything, but was told also that he would feel better if he told the truth. Within ten minutes the suspect had admitted the killing.

4

A young man was identified by a girl as the ex-boyfriend who had been refused entrance into her apartment and had shot through the door, hitting a man in the room. When police arrested him they found no gun. After taking him to the station and after some preliminary discussion, the detective said, "Now, you know you don't have to answer any questions if you don't want to, but you'll only be making things worse for yourself." After some denials there was a phone call from the hospital stating that the victim had suffered only a superficial wound. The detective returned and announced, "You know, you even have a right to a lawyer, but no lawyer will want your case now because unless you come clean I'm going to have to book you for murder." The suspect then gave a full confession to having fired the shot, denying only that he had tried to hurt anyone.

5

A young man of twenty-one was picked up by two officers and identified by a fifteen-year-old girl complainant as the man who had exposed himself to her and made an indecent proposal. When the man was in the car the officers said only, "You're not under arrest now, but we've got to take you to the station to answer some questions." At the station no warnings were given. The young man denied having done as the girl charged. Other police left the room and one detective stayed to talk longer. After ten minutes the detective came out and said that the boy now admitted it all and was terribly ashamed.

6

Officers noted an automobile with an out-of-state license plate. The occupants were acting in a suspicious manner and apparently trying to avoid the police patrol car. The officers stopped the car and questioned the occupants about ownership of the car, without giving any warning. None of them could establish ownership of the car. The three men were placed under arrest and taken to police headquarters, where they were kept apart until they could be questioned in more detail by detectives. No warnings were given. When each of the three gave substantially the same account of the circumstances they were released.

7

A woman reported to police that she had been drinking with a man in a bar and had left with him in a car, that she had passed out and had later awakened on the ground to find her clothing torn off and evidence that someone had had intercourse with her. The next day she saw, in a restaurant, the man she had been with and she notified the police. The policeman who arrested the suspect knew him slightly and told the suspect that he was accused of rape, that things looked bad for him, and that he should get a lawyer. The suspect then responded that the woman had consented, thus providing the police with their only significant evidence that the suspect was the one who had intercourse with the woman.

INTERROGATIONS IN NEW HAVEN: THE IMPACT OF *MIRANDA*

Comment, 78 Yale Law Journal 1519, 1551-52, 1555, 1562-63, 1571-73, 1600 (1967)†

Despite increasing adherence to the letter of *Miranda,* however, both groups of detectives complied less readily with its spirit. By and large the detectives regarded giving the suspect this advice an artificial imposition on the natural flow of the interrogation—an imposition for which they could see little reason. Most incorporated into their tactical repertoire some sort of hedging on the warnings, when they were given. Some changed the warning slightly: "Whatever you say may be used *for* or against you in a court of law." Often, the detectives advised the suspect with some inconsistent qualifying remark, such as "You don't have to say a word, but you ought to get everything cleared up," or "You don't have to say anything, of course, *but* can you explain how. . . ."

Even when the detective advised the suspect of his rights without these undercutting devices, he commonly de-fused the advice

† Reprinted by permission of the Yale Law Journal and Fred B. Rothman & Company.

by implying that the suspect had better not exercise his rights, or by delivering his statement in a formalized, bureaucratic tone to indicate that his remarks were simply a routine, meaningless legalism. Instinctively, perhaps, the detectives heightened the unreality of the *Miranda* advice by emphasizing the formality of their statement. Often they would bring the flow of conversation to a halt and preface their remarks with, "Now I am going to warn you of your rights." After they had finished the advice they would solemnly intone, "Now you have been warned of your rights," then immediately shift to a conversational tone to ask, "Now, would you like to tell me what happened?"

In the few cases where a suspect showed an interest in finding a lawyer and did not already know one, the police usually managed to head him off simply by not helping him to locate one. Sometimes they refused to advise the suspect whether he should have a lawyer with him during questioning; more often they merely offered him a telephone book without further comment, and that was enough to deter him from calling a lawyer. . . .

. . . In a very few cases the suspect made it plain, either at the beginning or during the interrogation, that he was determined not to answer questions, and the police quickly gave up questioning.

But many of the suspects who tried more half-heartedly to end the questioning were coaxed into talking.[93] Forty-three suspects expressed some wish to terminate their interrogations. The detectives continued to question 17. The detectives' compliance with this aspect of the *Miranda* decision was strongly related to the seriousness of the crime and the amount of evidence available prior to questioning. Whenever the detectives were dealing with a less serious crime, or had sufficient evidence to ensure the suspect's conviction, they were very likely to allow him to end the interrogation at his own will. But they were unlikely to let him terminate it when they needed information to ensure his conviction for a serious crime. . . .

V. The Effects of Warnings

The *Miranda* majority stated that warnings are necessary to protect individuals "who in other circumstances might have exer-

[93] This group provided an important test of the detectives' desire to comply with the *Miranda* rules, and the Court's realism in formulating them. That the police should not beat a statement out of an unwilling man, they could understand; that they should not nudge an almost-willing man into telling them about the crime he had almost surely committed, because to do so would be "coercion," they could not understand.

cised their constitutional rights." Critics of the decision maintain that whatever protection is provided by the warnings is purchased at too great a price: a crippling of the interrogation process and a consequent reduction in ability of the police to solve crimes, convict criminals, and recover stolen property. Their position rests on the assumption that a number of suspects who would have cooperated with the police will no longer do so after receiving the warnings, either because they will remain silent or because they will request a lawyer who will advise silence. In this section we examine the impact of the warnings[114] on the behavior of suspects, and consequently on the success of interrogations.[c]

We conclude that warnings had little impact on suspects' behavior. No support was found for the claim that warnings reduce the amount of "talking." Other factors such as the seriousness of crime involved, the amount of evidence available, and whether or not the suspect had a record seemed much more determinative of interrogation outcome. We have also concluded that warnings failed to protect some of the suspects they apparently were particularly designed to help. . . .

The conclusion that warnings had little impact is not surprising in view of our impressions of the process. In the first place,

---

114 This section examines the impact of the warnings actually given. As indicated elsewhere, these frequently fell short of the legal norm. Better warnings might have had different effects.

c Seeburger & Wettick, *Miranda in Pittsburgh: A Statistical Study,* 29 U. PITT. L. REV. 1 (1967), concludes that though confessions decreased somewhat after *Miranda* there was no significant decrease in convictions.

An extreme view of the consequences of the *Mallory* and *Miranda* decisions is presented by Munn, *Citizens at Bay,* Life Line Freedom Talk No. 38 (Aug. 26, 1966): "Back in June of this year the Supreme Court of the United States, by a five to four margin, set down some new regulations that make it difficult, if not impossible, for police to win a confession in any major crime. Top police authorities in this country estimate that as many as 85% of all major crimes, in the past, have been solved largely on the type of confessions that will now be held inadmissible in court.

"The Supreme Court decision is merely the latest in a long series of decisions dating back to 1957 when it handed down the so-called Mallory rule. Wherever you go in this country you will find law enforcement officers quoting Supreme Court decisions as the number one reason for the current soaring crime rate. Major crime has been on the increase for the past nine years, but its rate of acceleration has increased sharply since the June 1966 decision of the Supreme Court.

". . . A check of the District of Columbia police records is very revealing. Between June 1957, the date of the Mallory ruling, through December 31, 1965, the number of homicides in Washington doubled, the number of robberies quadrupled, and the number of house-breakings tripled. . . .

". . . During fiscal year 1957, before the Mallory rule, 58% of all major crimes committed in Washington were eventually solved by the police. Last year, 1965, that percentage had dropped to only 34% of the major crimes having been solved."

although most interrogations were not intimidating, they were designed to discourage any initiative on the part of the suspect. We have indicated previously that the warnings, when given, were often intoned in a manner designed to minimize or negate their importance and effectiveness. Since most suspects had little education—many could not even read—and appeared both ill-at-ease and dazed by the process, the warning so given seemed to have little impact. This was even true for many previous offenders who, despite their previous brushes with the law, often seemed to have little appreciation of the legal consequences of their action. Many seemed to operate under the misconception that talking to the police could not hurt them as long as they did not put anything in writing. Several said, when advised of their right to counsel, that they would get a lawyer at arraignment or trial. Thus, unless the detectives made it absolutely clear what the warnings meant—which they rarely did—most suspects appeared unable to grasp their significance.

Perhaps equally important, almost every person arrested this summer had committed the crime for which he was arrested and knew that the police had evidence of this. When he remained silent, the police would confront him with the evidence. Most suspects apparently felt compelled to give some alibi. Usually they lied and in so doing were caught in their lie. From then on the process was all downhill—from the suspect's point of view. Once a suspect said anything he usually had taken the first step towards incriminating himself.

In addition to these two factors, the warnings did not have an impact on a number of suspects who, knowing they were guilty, apparently saw no point in denying their guilt. Perhaps previous exposure to the process made them believe silence was futile—several of the defendants we interviewed expressed this belief.

Finally, the warnings had no apparent impact on the behavior of the 26 suspects who seemingly believed they were giving exculpatory statements. Such statements were particularly common in assault cases, where a suspect would admit his participation but blame the fight on someone else. Most of those who began by attempting to justify their actions ended by incriminating themselves to some degree.

It is even possible that our seemingly paradoxical finding in the statistical analysis—i.e., that warnings tend to correlate with success—makes sense for reasons other than the detectives' practice of giving warnings when they would have no effect. On several occasions we noted that a suspect seemed to be thrown off guard by the warnings. He apparently thought that if the police could give these warnings they must have him. In such cases—albeit a small number—warnings may actually have aided in obtaining a statement. . . .

VII. Lawyers.

Our findings suggest *Miranda* will rarely bring lawyers to the stationhouse. Defendants, told of their right to counsel, usually neglect the offer and let interrogation proceed.[222]

The function of a lawyer, once he is brought into a case as a result of the *Miranda* warning, is still unclear. At the very least an attorney present at the interrogation of his client would serve as an outside observer of police conduct. He can also insure that the client fully understands his rights and may urge him to remain silent. Justice Jackson, concurring in Watts v. Indiana, 338 U.S. 49, 59 (1949), made this often-quoted statement:

> The suspect neither had nor was advised of his right to get counsel. This presents a real dilemma in a free society. To subject one without counsel to questioning which may and is intended to convict him, is a real peril to individual freedom. To bring in a lawyer means a real peril to solution of the crime, because, under our adversary system, he deems that his sole duty is to protect his client—guilty or innocent—and that in such a capacity he owes no duty whatever to help society solve its crime problem. Under this conception of criminal procedure, any lawyer worth his salt will tell the suspect in no uncertain terms to make no statement to police under any circumstances.

A variation on this theme appears in Lee v. United States, 322 F.2d 770, 776-77 (5th Cir. 1963):

---

[222] This also appears true of other cities. A recent press release by the Georgetown Institute of Criminal Law and Procedure indicated that only 7.2% of the first 800 felony suspects arrested [in the District of Columbia] after *Miranda* called a lawyer, although all were advised of their right to do so, [and free legal services were made available on a twenty-four hour basis to indigents who called a central switchboard number. *Impact of Miranda Decision in Nation's Capital,* Georgetown University News Service, July 9, 1967. The Philadelphia Defender Association also arranged to make counsel available day or night to represent persons being interrogated. It was called upon only in "a small number of occasions" at the beginning, but more often as time went on. DEFENDER ASSOCIATION OF PHILADELPHIA, 33rd Annual Report 8 (1967)].

> Had an attorney been present it is likely that if he were "worth his salt," as Justice Jackson put it, he would have told the defendant "in no uncertain terms to make no statement to [the] police." Even if not fully worth his salt, we may be sure that he would have insisted that any admission would have to be in the form of a written statement, signed or approved by the accused or a record of some kind made and attested to by a court reporter. There would have been some assurance of the accuracy of the agent's recital of what Lee reputedly admitted. Here we have a narrative of oral conclusory statements, the accuracy of which is dependent upon the memory and conscience of the inquisitor. . . .

The lawyer even at this early stage might be able to bargain with the police or prosecutor for the benefit of his client, trading cooperation for some consideration. And if he did recommend that his client cooperate by responding to questions, counsel might protect his client against falling into the trap of admitting more than he meant to or of answering a trick question, as occurred in the following instances:

1

"Petitioner, a layman, was undoubtedly unaware that under Illinois law an admission of 'mere' complicity in the murder plot was legally as damaging as an admission of firing of the fatal shots. The 'guiding hand of counsel' was essential to advise petitioner of his rights in this delicate situation."[d]

2

"Federal agents arrested defendant on a warrant at his place of employment. Before removing him from the premises, after warning him of his right to remain silent but not of his right to counsel, an agent asked him a series of questions from a prepared form. Defendant answered all the questions, giving miscellaneous personal information, but insisting that he was not in the wagering business. Instead of asking directly whether he knew of the federal revenue requirements (to serve as a basis for charging a willful violation), the form question was phrased hypothetically, whether, if defendant were in the wagering business, he would have registered and purchased a federal stamp (i.e., paid the special occupational tax). The defendant replied, 'I suppose so. I would if I were in the business.' At the trial, over objection, the government introduced defendant's state-

[d] Escobedo v. Illinois, 378 U.S. 478, 486 (1964).

ments of his name, address, and occupation, which it used as a foundation for its evidence that he had not registered or purchased a stamp, and introduced his response to the hypothetical question as an admission of his knowledge that he should have done so."[e]

3

"The defendant [age sixteen] claims that the confession was obtained by subterfuge, objecting specifically to being asked at the interrogation what he would say if told his fingerprints were found on the ax [used to kill during a burglary]. His reply to this question, according to the State, was that they couldn't be because he had wiped them off."[f]

INTERROGATIONS IN NEW HAVEN: THE IMPACT OF *MIRANDA*

Comment, 78 Yale Law Journal 1519, 1601-04 (1967)†

B. *The Lawyer's Interviews*

We asked the defense attorneys what advice they would give to a client before interrogation. For most of the attorneys, the question was hypothetical: only 11 had ever entered a case at such an early stage. Most of the respondents who had met with clients at the stationhouse disliked doing so—not because the police denied them access to their clients or adequate time for consultation, but simply because there is no suitable conference room at headquarters. Lawyers who were called after arrest usually preferred to advise their clients over the telephone.

We expected the interviews to confirm Justice Jackson's dictum "Any lawyer worth his salt will tell the suspect in no uncertain terms to make no statement to police under any circumstances." Almost all lawyers did say that, on arrival at the stationhouse, they would counsel the client to "say nothing while I size up the situation." And even after discovering the facts, 51 of 55 lawyers said they would normally advise a client against making any statement at the time of arrest. Only four said they would frequently recommend cooperation—though one of these, the public defender, handles over 40 per cent of New Haven's criminal cases. The four felt that cooperation would generally improve the defendant's bargaining position.

---

[e] Flaherty v. United States, 355 F.2d 924, 925 (1st Cir. 1966).

[f] State v. White, 146 Mont. 226, 405 P.2d 761, 765 (1965).

† Reprinted by permission of the Yale Law Journal and Fred B. Rothman & Company.

But in further discussion, 40 of the lawyers admitted they would, under certain circumstances, advise a client to answer questions. Cooperation might be prudent, they said, given specified facts about the suspect's age, the nature and circumstances of the offense, and the strength of the evidence in the hands of the police. In appropriate situations the attorneys said they would tell their client that cooperation might help him, and then let the suspect decide whether to cooperate.

Many lawyers think that suspects picked up for narcotics and morals offenses, misdemeanors, and domestic disputes would be wise to answer police questions. In narcotics cases, the prosecutor might be willing to recommend leniency in return for information about sources of supply. Several attorneys thought that the detectives would reward cooperation in sex cases, misdemeanors, and family squabbles by recommending leniency to the prosecutor because the detectives feel their time should be spent investigating more major crimes. The harshness of possible penalties for some of these offenses also induced the attorneys to consider cooperation.

The lawyers also said they might advise a minor to confess, hoping that the prosecutor would save a repentant youngster from a felony charge. Also, they would advise cooperation where the police have substantial evidence or the suspect has a long record. Mercy, the only available plea, would most easily grace a defendant who had confessed, especially if he had identified accomplices or helped recover stolen goods.

Some experts have claimed that *Miranda* will delay the release of innocent suspects who could clear themselves if their lawyer had not told them to remain silent. We found that almost all lawyers would advise a client to cooperate with the police if he could clear himself by doing so. A lawyer's presence may even help a client to tell his story coherently.[236]

Many attorneys will advise the type of cooperation most needed by the police—identifying accomplices, fences and suppliers, or aiding recovery of stolen goods—especially when their client was caught in the act and is obviously guilty. Moreover,

---

236 We were told of several instances in which innocent suspects were tripped up or confused during interrogation and failed to establish their innocence because they did not fully understand the detectives' questions. In one bigamy case the police had records of two marriages for a man legally divorced from his first wife. The divorce had not been recorded. The suspect gave contradictory answers to police questions, and was especially confused by the question "Are you married to two women?" He repeatedly answered "Yes," because he *had* been twice married. So the police took his response as a confession to bigamy. In 9 of the 17 cases where the prosecutor entered a nolle prosequi, innocent suspects were booked because they failed to give consistent answers to police questions.

they will advise co-operating immediately rather than waiting until plea bargaining, since in many cases only immediate cooperation will enable the police to apprehend accomplices.

Despite these majority views, 11 of the 55 attorneys told us they would never advise cooperation. Some thought that cooperation was useless to the defendant because the police had no power over sentencing. Others said that the police do have influence, but never use it in favor of a defendant merely because he confesses. Also, cooperation may backfire. Invariably, the lawyers who would always counsel silence dislike the police and prefer not to deal with them.

We found no simple explanation for this sharp diversity of opinion. None of our background data such as age or experience distinguished lawyers who would advise cooperation from those who would not.[239] The diversity probably reflects the varying experiences each lawyer has with the police, the prosecutors, and his own clients.

We found some evidence to support the view that cooperation can be helpful. In misdemeanor cases, for example, defendants who confessed generally received suspended sentences, while others got short jail terms. Minors charged with breaking-and-entering or theft, another large category, also did better if they confessed.[240]

Our interviews with prosecutors also suggest the value of cooperation. According to the prosecutors, the police do influence sentencing. Often the prosecutor will consult with the police officer involved in a case before making a sentence recommendation to the court. Judges, they say, respond favorably to a presentence-report notation that the defendant cooperated fully with the police. However, many of these benefits may also accrue to the suspect who is silent in the station but who cooperates with the prosecutor. A suspect who remains silent until this later part of the process may often be even better off. Only with the advice of a lawyer, however, can he make this decision.

---

239 Even the 75% of the lawyers who said that cooperation with the police might help in certain cases disagreed widely on what cases they thought most suitable for cooperation. For example, some lawyers asserted that helping the police in narcotics cases might result in a suspended sentence, but others said that they would not cooperate in narcotics cases because of the severe penalties possible.

240 In each case the attorney must make a difficult judgment whether cooperation will help. For example, defendants in the sample who implicated accomplices were not automatically treated more leniently. According to counsel, implicating accomplices benefited only five of the eleven suspects who did so; for the rest, a confession plus implication only made matters worse.

Reference Note

The single major inquiry into interrogation practice is Comment, *Interrogations in New Haven: The Impact of Miranda,* 76 YALE L.J. 1519 (1967); Faculty Note, *A Postscript to the Miranda Project: Interrogation of Draft Protesters,* 77 YALE L.J. 300 (1967). A.L.I., A MODEL CODE OF PRE-ARRAIGNMENT PROCEDURE (Study Draft No. 1, 1968), summarizes the existing factual studies of interrogation and confessions; it also proposes alternatives for regulating in-custody questioning consistent with the *Miranda* decision. *See also* Medalie, Zeitz & Alexander, *Custodial Police Interrogation in Our Nation's Capital: The Attempt to Implement Miranda,* 66 MICH. L. REV. 1347 (1968).

An excellent broad consideration of the applicable doctrines is *Developments in the Law—Confessions,* 79 HARV. L. REV. 935 (1966), supplemented by discussion of the *Miranda* decision in *The Supreme Court, 1965 Term,* 80 HARV. L. REV. 91, 201-07 (1966).

English practice is described in St. Johnston, *The Judges' Rules and Police Interrogation in England Today,* 57 J. CRIM. L.C. & P.S. 85 (1966).

Chapter 6

CHARGING—THE DECISION TO PROSECUTE

In the typical criminal case the suspect is arrested without a warrant, then questioned and booked at the police station. The decision must then be made what further to do with the prisoner. Sometimes that decision is made by the police, with the prosecutor's involvement coming only later; but ordinarily the prosecutor makes the decision what to do with the prisoner at a very early stage. This decision is one of the prosecutor's major functions in the criminal justice system, along with negotiating guilty pleas and trying the contested cases.

Unlike the traditional image of the policeman as one responsible for full enforcement of the law, the public prosecutor has always been accorded discretionary power to choose between prosecuting and not prosecuting. Quite recently, the prosecutor has been recognized as having the even broader responsibility of choosing among various alternative ways of disposing of an offender. Where community resources exist the prosecutor may choose referral to social agencies, informal probation, compulsory treatment for alcoholism or drug addiction or mental disturbance, or invocation of yet other programs. He is not restricted simply to the choice of criminal prosecution or nothing. This new characterization suggests more clearly the complex role of the prosecutor. It remains true, however, that the decision whether to institute criminal prosecution is the critical one.

There is no single pattern for making the charging decision. At one extreme the prosecutor takes whatever comes into his hands and prosecutes without exercise of independent judgment on the merits of the prosecution. The charging decision is therefore essentially a police decision.[a] At the other extreme all cases, except the most petty, must be screened by the prosecutor.[b] There the police have power to prevent prosecution by not

[a] The President's Commission on Law Enforcement and Administration of Justice, Task Force Report: The Courts 121-28 (1967) (Baltimore).

[b] American Bar Foundation, Law Enforcement in the Metropolis 97-99 (D. McIntyre ed. 1967) (Detroit).

arresting or not bringing the matter to the attention of the prosecutor, but the prosecutor also exercises power to refuse prosecution.

In some cases, usually involving routine minor offenses—ordinance violations, traffic offenses, fish and game violations—the prosecutor will ordinarily not even appear in court to handle trial of the matter, and the whole responsibility for prosecution is left to the police.[c] Where the press of business is great, the police may be left to make initial charging decisions in felony cases also. The prosecutor's power to control the case is then exercised by dismissal or amending the charges. This is the situation in Chicago.

In other situations, involving such matters as business frauds and negligent homicide, the decision whether to prosecute is normally made before the suspect is arrested. In these instances there is no need for immediate police action and it is practical to permit the prosecutor to consider the matter before taking the person into custody. This is also characteristic of the federal system (other than the District of Columbia), where federal law enforcement officers commonly consult with the United States Attorney before taking a suspect into custody.[d]

The variation in charging practice is not dictated by statute, since the typical statutory scheme does not involve the prosecutor at all.[e] For example, the Illinois Code of Criminal Procedure says:[f]

---

[c] Cases in which the prosecutor ordinarily does not appear are described in W. LaFave, Arrest: The Decision to Take a Suspect into Custody 53-59 (1965).

[d] Greilsheimer, *The U.S. Commissioner System, Hearings on the Federal Magistrates Act before the Subcommittee on Improvements in Judicial Machinery of the Senate Committee on the Judiciary,* 89th Cong., 2d Sess., and 90th Cong., 1st Sess. 371, 379 (1967).

[e] The absence of the prosecutor from the statutory scheme is presumably the result of the common-law tradition. In England private citizens have had the power to prosecute offenders for crimes. With the development of police forces the police have assumed the major responsibility for prosecution, employing lawyers to represent them in handling the cases. Today in England the Director of Public Prosecutions still handles less than 1% of the indictments, and even fewer nonindictable offenses. R. Jackson, Enforcing the Law 49 (1967).

It is possible in the United States for a private citizen to initiate the criminal process by complaint to the police or the prosecutor, but not by private prosecution except under special statutes allowing it, *e.g.,* assault and battery or nuisance statutes, which sometimes provide for private prosecution. A manual for United States Commissioners advised them to encourage citizen complainants to obtain the approval of the United States Attorney before filing their complaint.

The noncommon law origins of the public prosecutor are described in Comment, *The District Attorney—A Historical Puzzle,* 1952 Wis. L. Rev. 125.

[f] Ill. Rev. Stat. ch. 38, § 109-1(a) (1967).

A person arrested without a warrant shall be taken without unnecessary delay before the nearest and most accessible judge in that county, and a charge shall be filed.

The decision to charge is not an adversary one. The suspect is almost never present.[g] If the prosecutor is to be involved, the police will take their evidence to the prosecutor while the arrested person remains in jail. In many jurisdictions the police use a filled-in complaint form as their request to the prosecutor for his authorization to proceed with the case. If he agrees that there should be prosecution he approves the complaint, or has his staff draft the complaint if it has not already been prepared.[h] The police then take the complaint, along with their prisoner, to the magistrate.[i]

For minor offenses, drafting of the complaint and filing it with the judge is the whole charging process, since the complaint serves as the formal accusatory document upon which trial will proceed at the first appearance of the prisoner before a judge. But for more serious crimes the complaint, which serves to bring the case before the magistrate for initial appearance and for preliminary examination (if the accused requests it), will be replaced by another charging document—either an information filed by the prosecutor, or an indictment returned by the grand jury. As the charging process thus continues through several procedural stages the initial decision to prosecute may be modified by changing the offense charged against the accused, or by dropping the case—sometimes even after the trial has begun.

---

[g] Counsel for defendant is occasionally in contact with the prosecutor at the charging stage. For example, in a situation where a death had resulted from a traffic accident, counsel presented a brief to the district attorney giving arguments against the filing of negligent homicide charges.

[h] In some jurisdictions an arrest warrant as well as a complaint is drafted and issued, even though the offender is already in custody. For the history of this anomalous use of the arrest warrant *after* arrest, see W. LaFave, Arrest: The Decision to Take a Suspect into Custody 35 (1965). The warrant does serve the function of naming the magistrate before whom the prisoner is to be brought.

[i] After arrest a prisoner is commonly "booked," which includes entering on the arrest book some ground for arrest—either a crime or "suspicion" of a crime or occasionally "for investigation." This procedure is sometimes called "charging," but we reserve the term for the decision by the prosecutor (or other agency responsible for that decision) to proceed to formal prosecution. The booking procedure is a matter of internal accounting and is significant as giving the person an arrest record, yet it has few other implications for the system. *See* Comment, *The Role of "Booking" in the Administration of Criminal Justice,* 1963 U. Ill. L.F. 685.

A. ALTERNATIVES TO PROSECUTION

To prosecute or to do nothing are the principal alternatives which the prosecutor has, but there are still other possibilities for disposing of at least some offenders. The crime surveys of a generation ago fostered the idea that maximum prosecution is desirable. There is a movement now toward the position that ideally the fewest possible people should be prosecuted and that prosecution represents a kind of failure. Several avenues to avoid prosecution exist. Some are recognized legal procedures; others are informal practices.

1. *Legal Procedures Providing Alternatives to Prosecution*

The Practice

1

A man who was arrested for burglary admitted participation in twelve burglaries and larcenies. He had previously been sentenced to prison for ten years on a second degree burglary conviction and placed on probation. Because it was clear that the court would revoke probation the prosecutor decided not to proceed with charging the offender.

2

Two seventeen-year-old boys exploded firecrackers in a restaurant, injuring two people. The prosecutor referred them to the juvenile court (which for boys that age had concurrent jurisdiction with the criminal courts) saying, "As far as you boys are concerned, it will keep you from getting a record so that when you grow up and have more sense and try to get a job you will not be dogged by this foolish prank. On the other hand, the juvenile judge is no softy."

3

Wisconsin Statutes § 51.09 (1965):

Inebriates and drug addicts. (1) Hearing. If it appears to any court of record, by an application of 3 reputable adult residents of the county, that a resident of the county or person temporarily residing therein is an inebriate or addicted to the use of narcotic drugs or barbiturates and in need of confinement or treatment, the court shall fix a time and place for hearing the application. . . . At such hearing if the court finds that such person is an inebriate or a drug addict, and requires confinement or treatment, or that it is necessary for the protection of himself or the public or his relatives that he be committed, he may be committed to the county hospital or to the county reforestation camp or to the rehabilitation facilities [established as an extension of the county jail]. . . .[j]

4

Iowa Code §§ 225A.2, 225A.11 (1966):

When any person is charged with a public offense and it shall appear to the county attorney . . . that such person is a criminal sexual psychopath . . . he shall prepare a petition. . . .

If the person is found to be a criminal sexual psychopath the court may commit him to a state hospital for the mentally ill, where he shall be detained and treated until released in accordance with the provisions of this chapter. . . .[k]

5

Police responded to a call from one of the neighbors that someone was screaming hysterically in a house. They found a woman who told them that she had beaten her baby to death because it had refused to drink its milk. They found that the baby was not dead, but severely bruised. A psychiatrist was asked to examine the woman in jail and reported to the prosecutor that a preliminary examination of her disclosed a hyperthyroid condition which would produce a feeling of acute anxiety, and that her mental condition would probably continue to deteriorate. The prosecutor decided to file a petition to have her committed as insane.

Additional legal procedures which offer substitutes for prosecution are paternity proceedings in cases of bastardy, applications for support orders in cases of nonsupport or abandonment, padlocking of premises in abatement of nuisances where premises are used for prostitution or other vice crimes, revocation of liquor licenses, suits for civil penalties, forfeiture proceedings for property (particularly automobiles) used in gambling and other crimes, release to the authorities of another jurisdiction desiring to extradite and prosecute, or proceeding under city ordinances rather than criminal statutes.

---

[j] *See* Driver v. Hinnant, 356 F.2d 761 (4th Cir. 1966); The President's Commission on Law Enforcement and Administration of Justice, Task Force Report: Drunkenness (1967); and Powell v. Texas, 392 U.S. 514 (1968).

[k] For a helpful discussion of the prosecutor's role in initiating proceedings under the Michigan sexual psychopath law, see American Bar Foundation, Law Enforcement in the Metropolis 99-101 (D. McIntyre ed. 1967).

2. *Informal Alternatives to Prosecution*

Under threat of prosecution persons may be induced to do various things without any formal procedure—make restitution, agree to give support, undertake outpatient psychiatric treatment for sexual deviancy, close down an activity (such as a social club where gambling has been going on) which may result in law violations, delete allegedly obscene portions of a film, take treatment for venereal disease, submit to informal probation supervision, consult with a family service counselor or other social agency.

In Detroit, settlement of disputes by mediation and the unique practice of imposition of "peace bonds" is another alternative to prosecution.[l] It has no legal basis but proves effective.

> A complainant, fifty-three, stated to the prosecutor that a former boyfriend of hers had come to see her while drunk and had caused trouble, breaking several windows. She wanted him prosecuted to be sure that he stayed away. The prosecutor requested her to report back in a week's time. He explained that the man would be notified to appear at the same time and that "Judge Smith" would hear the case. "Judge Smith" is a police detective who sits in a room in the prosecutor's office and deals with cases of this sort. After hearing both sides of the dispute, the "judge" said, "I'm going to put you on a peace bond for one year." The defendant asked, "What does that mean?" The "judge" explained, "That means that you have got to leave her alone." He lectured the man on his problem with drinking, and then addressed the woman, "If you have any trouble with him, call the police and tell them that you want the case to come back to this office. If we get the case again, we will then request that a warrant be issued and the case will be taken to court."

The seriousness with which the people involved take the procedure is illustrated by the following incident:

---

[l] AMERICAN BAR FOUNDATION, LAW ENFORCEMENT IN THE METROPOLIS 103-06 (D. McIntyre ed. 1967). There is a legal procedure for imposition of a peace bond, which will be forfeit upon violation of the condition that the person refrain from threatened illegal action. The Detroit practice is a parody. In Folsom v. Fisco, 62 Mont. 194, 204 P. 367 (1922), a man was detained twenty-three months because unable to provide a $500 peace bond as guarantee against carrying out threatened violence against another. *See* Comment, *Peace and Behavior Bonds*, 52 VA. L. REV. 914 (1966).

A lady came into the prosecutor's office one evening at about closing time and stated she had been placed under a peace bond by the "judge" about six months earlier and wanted to know if her time ran out today as she thought it did. The office girl of whom she inquired was not familiar with the status of the "bond" and could not find it in the filing system (since the only record is a pencil notation on the police offense report). The woman was asked why it was so important that she find out that very evening. She replied that if the time was up, the next day she was going to go out and get even with the other party to the dispute.[m]

THE PRESIDENT'S COMMISSION ON LAW ENFORCEMENT AND ADMINISTRATION OF JUSTICE TASK FORCE REPORT: THE COURTS 8-9 (1967)

Noncriminal Alternatives. When the prosecutor decides that a case should not be prosecuted criminally, a simple dismissal will often be appropriate: Investigation may reveal that the accused is not guilty of the offense for which he was arrested, or that although he is guilty, the offense is minor and there is no reason to believe he will commit such an offense again. But there are many cases where some followup should be provided: The offender may be an alcoholic or a narcotics addict; he may be mentally ill; he may have been led to crime by his family situation or by his inability to get a job. If he is not helped, he may well return to crime.

There are many cases in which minimal intrusions on the defendant's liberty would be all that seem necessary. Often it will be enough simply to refer the offender to the appropriate agency in the community, and hope that he will take advantage of the help offered. The prosecutor might, for example, be willing to drop charges if the defendant goes to an employment agency and makes a bona fide effort to get a job, or if he consults a family service agency, or if he resumes his education. The prosecutor retains legal power to file a charge until the period of limitations has run, but as a practical matter, unless the offense is repeated, it would be unusual for the initial charge to be revived.

While ideally there should be no intrusion on the defendant's liberty without a judicial finding of guilt and imposition of sanc-

[m] Though arrest and release of prostitute, transvestite, and drunk (*see* p. 339, *supra*) is a police practice, not a prosecutor policy as such, it is nevertheless done with the tacit approval of the prosecutor in most instances. The police practice results from the prosecutor's inability or unwillingness to take such cases through trial. The prosecutor may in turn reflect judicial attitudes.

tion, it may not be feasible to insist on this protection when the intrusion is so minimal. As noted above, there is a great deal of informal adjustment of cases now. A prosecutor might develop statements of policy with the approval of the court, defining with some precision the kinds of dispositions he proposes to make without seeking court approval. It might be advisable to limit the time during which the prosecutor would be authorized to reinstitute charges, as the Commission recommends in the juvenile area when youths are referred to a Youth Services Bureau. Such a disposition would not require elaborate procedural steps. A simple notation in the prosecutor's files would show that the charges were dismissed and the accused referred to a particular agency. Offenders would know that if they were arrested for the same offense again, full prosecution would be very likely.

But there are some cases where a simple referral may be inadequate: The offender may present too great a danger to the community; he may require longer supervision, or referral may have been tried before unsuccessfully. Yet subjecting the offender to the stigma of a criminal conviction may be undesirable. If the disposition involves significant restrictions on the accused or is of sustained duration, approval by the court should be required to assure that there is a factual basis for the charge, that no undue pressure has been put on the defendant to accept the disposition, and that the disposition is appropriate. Such an agreement might entail the kinds of conditions that would be appropriate for probation following conviction. The agreement might, for example, require supervision of the defendant's activities by a probation officer; it might require that the defendant give up certain associates; it might require that he cooperate with a program of treatment for alcoholism, narcotics addiction, or mental illness; it might require that he reside in a halfway house, or enter a mental institution for some definite period of time.

In such cases a written agreement, executed by the prosecutor, defense counsel, and the accused, should be submitted to the court and become effective only upon court approval. Depending upon local procedure, this agreement could take the form of a consent decree, and the prosecutor would be authorized to initiate prosecution only if the accused violated its terms. A substantial modification of the terms of the disposition should be presented to the court for review as part of an amended decree. Normal time limitations governing the filing of the charges might be suspended. If the prosecutor fears that it might not be feasible to try the charge at a later date, the decree could include an admission by the defendant, a stipulation of facts, or the depositions of witnesses.

There are of course dangers in granting such discretionary power to prosecutors and judges. Ordinarily the state can apply compulsory sanctions, inside prison or out, only after an offense has been proved or a guilty plea has been entered. And the permissible sanctions are limited by a maximum fixed by the legislature. There is a danger that the prosecutor's agreement to dismiss charges may induce the defendant to accept an alternate disposition consisting of onerous, unreasonable, or even illegal conditions. There is an additional danger that an alternate disposition could become a justification for indeterminate commitment. Recently reported instances of judicial attempts to obtain consent to sterilization and of prosecutorial intervention in the family life of the accused illustrate the possibilities of abuse. One safeguard is that the offender must, at any point in the process, have the right to insist on trial and criminal disposition. But there is nevertheless a danger that the prospect of criminal prosecution would be so dire as to force the offender to accept an unreasonable, although less onerous, alternative. The proposal here that the agreement be recorded and submitted to court for approval would tend to minimize this danger.

An accused might be induced to accept a burdensome, although noncriminal, program of treatment on the basis of a flimsy charge of which he clearly would be found not guilty if he insisted on his right to trial. Obviously the accused is under strong pressure to accept any disposition which does not carry the stigma of a criminal conviction. The problem is very similar to that which arises in the negotiation of a guilty plea. Similar protections, discussed in more detail in the following section, should be provided. The reviewing judge should, in the first place, determine that there is a factual basis for the charge. If the judge determines that there is no basis for the charge, he should inform the accused, who then would be free to pursue or reject the recommended program without the threat of a criminal charge. The judge should also consider the amount of pressure that was put on the accused to agree to a noncriminal alternative and determine whether it constituted an overwhelming inducement to surrender the right to trial. If he is not satisfied, the case should be set for trial. When the agreement includes any factual admissions or depositions prejudicial to the defendant, he should be allowed to withdraw them. When feasible, trial should take place before a different judge, who would not be influenced by involvement in the consent decree decision.

The final safeguard would be the presence of counsel, which should be required wherever an intrusive disposition is under consideration. Counsel would ensure that the other safeguards provided are meaningful. And counsel is necessary for the accused to make an informed decision whether to agree to a noncriminal disposition requiring burdensome performance on his part.[n]

B. THE DECISION AS TO CHARGE

The prosecutor's decision to charge is one of great significance. At the very least it requires the person to provide bail or remain in custody while further steps are taken, and unless the case is later dismissed it means that he will incur the costs and face the hazards of defending himself in the criminal prosecution. The decision to charge also constitutes an implicit rejection of the alternative methods of dealing with the offender.

The prosecutor has historically been acknowledged to have almost unlimited power to decide whether to charge at all and also to decide the particular charge when, as is usually true, various statutes may be invoked. Exercise of this broad power not only affects individuals involved, but also has important impact on the development of law enforcement policy in the community, since police see the prosecutor's policies as a practical definition of how the law should and can effectively be enforced.

---

[n] Further discussion of alternatives to prosecution appears at 6-7 of this same report.

The recommendation that criminal conduct should increasingly be handled by methods other than prosecution and conviction raises fundamental issues for other parts of the criminal justice process also. For example, if consent probation were made the responsibility of the same correctional agencies which now supervise persons placed on probation after conviction, this would give corrections a whole new clientele and would require corrections to deal with the prosecutor as well as with the judge. Carried far enough, this trend could result in corrections no longer dealing primarily with the convicted offender but, instead, devoting substantial correctional resources to the implementation of programs designed to serve as alternatives to criminal prosecution and conviction. Sensible carrying out of this kind of program would obviously require that the prosecutor be knowledgeable about treatment alternatives to prosecution. Perhaps, for example, a "pre-prosecution" report would have to be prepared by a correctional officer to serve as a basis for the decision to prosecute or to use an alternative to prosecution. *Compare* Chapter 12, § B4.

The tendency toward diverting as many cases as possible away from formal adjudication of guilt which is illustrated in the recommendation constitutes a pattern familiar in the juvenile justice system. Thus, the trend of the adult system may, in this regard, be toward greater conformity with the juvenile systems. *See* Chapter 15.

THE PROSECUTOR—INITIATION OF PROSECUTION

By Newman F. Baker

23 Journal of Criminal Law and Criminology 770-71 (1933)†

"To prosecute or not to prosecute?" is a question which comes to the mind of this official scores of times each day. A law has been contravened and the statute says he is bound to commence proceedings. His legal duty is clear. But, what will be the result? Will it be a waste of time? Will it be expensive to the state? Will it be unfair to the defendant (the prosecutor applying his own ideas of justice)? Will it serve any good purpose to society in general? Will it have good publicity value? Will it cause a political squabble? Will it prevent the prosecutor from carrying the offender's home precinct when he, the prosecutor, runs for Congress after his term as prosecutor? Was the law violated a foolish piece of legislation? If the offender is a friend, is it the square thing to do to reward friendship by initiating criminal proceedings? These and many similar considerations are bound to come to the mind of the man responsible for setting the wheels of criminal justice in motion. The prosecutor who holds an exaggerated notion of duty can easily arouse such a storm of protest as a result of strict attention to his responsibilities that he will gain the reputation of being a "persecutor" thus alienating the police, the sheriff's force and the judges, and creating, by the loss of their cooperation, an insurmountable obstacle to the successful conduct of really important cases. Moreover, his days as a state official are numbered for he cannot continue long without public support. On the other hand, a prosecutor who takes his duties lightly probably will last longer but, in failing to give a reasonable amount of protection to his community, inevitably he will create in the minds of the public the belief that he is easy or dishonest and should be replaced. The average prosecutor must steer a middle course, statutes or no statutes, trying to serve and protect his community as best he can, but aware of the ultimate futility of combatting public opinion.

THE PROSECUTING ATTORNEY'S OFFICE AND THE CONTROL OF ORGANIZED CRIME

By Morris Ploscowe & Milton H. Spiero

Organized Crime and Law Enforcement 216, 219 (M. Ploscowe ed. 1952)

The prosecutor is not necessarily inefficient or corrupt when he refuses to prosecute, although information is brought to his

† Reprinted by special permission of the Journal of Criminal Law and Criminology (Northwestern University School of Law).

attention that a crime has been committed. Every prosecutor's office, even the most honest and efficient, must be selective in choosing the cases in which the machinery of the criminal law will be set in motion to punish offenders. The prosecutor does not swing into action as soon as he has a complaint. There may be many legitimate reasons for a prosecutor's failure to prosecute. . . . The expense to the County in carrying on the prosecution may far outweigh the advantages to be gained in obtaining a conviction. The prospective defendant may only have committed a technical violation of the law, and a warning may suffice to prevent future repetition. The prosecutor may feel that while a crime may have been committed, the chances of obtaining a conviction against the prospective defendant are remote. These are some of the considerations which a prosecutor takes into account before going ahead in any particular case.

1. *The Practice of Refusing to Charge or Charging Less Than Is Permissible*

D.A. 'CALLS' BAR POKER PLAYERS

By June Dieckmann
Wisconsin State Journal, Aug. 6, 1963

Next Time, They'll Be Charged

Dist. Atty. William D. Byrne scolded and warned fellow lawyers Monday that they will be charged "next time" if there is a repeat of a high-stakes poker game in which some of them played at the Dane County Bar Assn. summer outing at Nakoma Country club last Tuesday night.

Byrne said he did not learn until Monday—from "reliable sources" whom he declined to name—that there was "at least one $1,600 pot" in a poker game across the club's card room from where he and "probably 40 other attorneys" were engaged in "quarter-limit" games at the time.

No Arrests

"I'm not ordering any arrests. This is a once-a-year gathering of lawyers in which one table got out of hand—not a commercial gambling type of game that occurs frequently.

"I'm certain the Bar Assn. will not let this happen again and if there is a repeat, there will be charges filed against the players," Byrne declared.

Byrne said his "reliable sources" did not give him the names of the participants in the high-stakes game. However, he said there were seven players in the game, at least one of whom was a Madison businessman guest at the attorneys' outing.

Loser Reimbursed

He said his sources informed him that one attorney, who had been drinking heavily, was the "big loser" and that several of the personal checks the attorney put into the poker pots and lost were returned to him after the game.

Byrne said he had unconfirmed reports that the inebriated attorney's losses were as much as $3,000 before his checks were returned to him.

The unnamed businessman was reported to be the "big winner" and "kicked back" some of the checks to the losing attorney, Byrne said his sources told him.

"I can't arbitrarily say that a 25-cent limit poker game is legal, or even a penny game. Technically they're not under strict interpretation of the law, but if we arrested all the poker players having sociable games in their homes and clubs, we'd have to arrest at least half and maybe 75 per cent of the adult population of Dane county," Byrne said.

Warning on Big Bets

As for the high-stakes games, Byrne said the players found in those will be prosecuted "on the basis of investigation of the individual games."

"Even just once a year is too often for that kind of a game," Byrne said with emphasis to the Dane County Bar Assn. committee planning its next outing.

"Primarily, the law enforcement officials and courts seek to wipe out high-stakes poker games that involve commercial gambling, such as the Segoe Rd. gambling house raid last year where the houseman was taking as much as $100 from every pot for his cut," Byrne said.

Byrne said he was "surprised and amazed" when he learned a "big game" was going on without his knowledge at the Bar meeting. "I'll tell you honestly, I was concentrating on my nickel and dime bets at our table and had no idea there were stakes that high on another table," he said.

"In fact, I think it's asinine for any attorney to participate in a game like that. Any attorney I know doesn't have that kind of money," Byrne said.

'NEXT TIME' JUSTICE MIGHT BE YOU

Wisconsin State Journal Editorial, Aug. 14, 1963

HIGH POLITICAL STAKES

The law forbids gambling in Wisconsin, but it looks like Dist. Atty. William Byrne is sticking to his promise to prosecute his fellow attorneys "next time." We waited a reasonable time for another statement.

If the district attorney of Dane county really wanted to take action "this time," there's plenty of evidence available. And he shouldn't have any trouble finding witnesses, because he was there playing cards himself with about 40 other lawyers present at the Dane County Bar Assn.'s summer outing.

As Byrne pointed out, he would be a pretty busy man if he attempted to put a halt to penny ante poker, nickle-and-dime golf bets, and living room bingo. But obviously he would be a pretty embarrassed man if he decided to press charges against any of the 40 lawyers in the cardplaying room in as much as he first indicated to the public that he didn't even know about the gambling party.

What would the district attorney do if he heard about a high stakes card game going on involving just people, not lawyers, and not himself? Would the district attorney raid any private game on the East side or the West side involving dozens of players and thousands of dollars? Or would he tell them that "next time" there would be arrests?

Without trying to be penny ante ourselves, we'd like to point out that the district attorney is picking and choosing his cases with extreme self-interest. Not only is there a need for equal protection under law, but equal prosecution, too. By ducking the issue, Byrne has damaged his ability to indiscriminately handle the legal affairs of the county.

LAWBREAKING IS MAIN ISSUE IN GAMBLING ROW

Wisconsin State Journal, Aug. 14, 1963

MORNING MAIL

Sirs—in your headlines editorial Aug. 7 you deride the editor of the Capital Times for his proclamation regarding the gambling at Nakoma Country club by a group of attorneys, including elected and defeated legal officials. Your attack appears to revolve around his manner of reporting and lack of editorial comment, yet both of you have failed to discuss the major issue.

And that is, gambling laws were broken—by the citizenry and by an elected official who is charged with upholding the laws—

not amending them. The major question remaining is, "what is going to be done about an admitted gambling violation?" Are you, as a responsible editor, going to condone this violation and in effect say that the boys really didn't break the law just because they could afford to lose?

A point of comparison: Several months ago, a group of Negro citizens were arrested and paraded before the court and Madison newspapers for breaking the gambling laws. The reported stakes were much lower than those involved at the legal Bar social.

Does the law distinguish between groups who can "ill-afford" to gamble and groups who can "afford" to win or lose much larger amounts, and who by professional training can twist these laws to their favor? This could well serve as an example of race discrimination in Madison.

I join many citizens in Madison in asking, "What is the price tag for justice in Madison?"—J. C. Trautman, 5125 Door Dr.

FOOTBALL POOLS BRING CHARGES
Milwaukee Journal, Oct. 22, 1963

Madison, Wis.—UPI—Eight persons were to appear Tuesday in Dane county criminal court on charges of conducting illegal lotteries. A crackdown by authorities Monday night brought the charges.

Asst. Dist. Atty. Glenn Henry said state beverage tax agents signed the complaints, charging the eight with selling $1 to $4 chances on $100 football pools.

The arrests included owners and employes of bars, a bowling alley and coffee shop. Named in complaints were William Grab, Robert Ridenour, Alma Baltes, Robert Faren, Margaret Simon, Shirley Pruitt, Clarence Walrath and Larry O'Kroley.

Dist. Atty. William Byrne said the "friendly office type" football pools, on which chances cost $1 or less and where no profit is made by the pool seller, would not be prosecuted as commercial gambling.

PRIEST IS CHARGED
Wisconsin State Journal, July 9, 1967

Bethlehem, Pa. UPI—A Roman Catholic priest has been released on $500 bail after being charged with operating an illegal bingo game in his church parish.

Although bingo games are illegal in Pennsylvania, some local officials permit churches and nonprofit clubs and organizations to hold bingo games.

In Lehigh County, where Dist. Atty. George A. Joseph has set an unofficial limit on prizes of $200 in merchandise, Msgr. Thomas J. Doyle, rector of the Notre Dame Catholic Church, was charged Friday with conducting a lottery.

The warrant was sworn out by a man who was arrested on a lottery charge last February and later fined $300. It charged that Msgr. Doyle's bingo game of July 3 offered prizes of up to $255.

The material above has focused on the issue whether the conduct was of a sort to deserve prosecution. There are also other factors in the determination whether to prosecute—the special personal circumstances of the accused, the willingness of the victim to cooperate in the prosecution, the difficulty or cost of prosecution, the willingness of the offender to become an informer.

BAIR REPAYS HALF OF STOLEN COURT FUNDS
Wisconsin State Journal, Aug. 20, 1960

Robert M. Bair, 50, the discharged Dane County Court register in probate who dipped in the court till for $444.44 the past 2½ months, repaid half of the shortage Friday, Dist. Atty. William D. Byrne reported.

Byrne said Bair is obtaining a loan on an insurance policy and promised to repay the rest of the missing funds next Wednesday.

Meanwhile, it was evident that no criminal charges will be filed against Bair, with County Judge Carl Flom, County Board Chairman George Harb, and Byrne declaring that none of them will sign a complaint.

Flom said he felt the responsibility of signing a complaint rests with the DA's office since county funds are involved. Byrne said the policy of his office is to prosecute complaints signed by anyone, not sign them.

In Bair's case, Byrne said he would not start criminal action on his own complaint because Bair is making restitution; he is a first offender with no previous record; he has lost his near-$600 a month position and faces possible disbarment as a lawyer, and that he and his ailing wife and three children, who live at 2921 Baskerville Rd., have been "affected enough by publicity and loss of his job which he brought upon himself."

Harb said he feels Bair has been "punished enough," but added that he will inform the County Board audit committee at its meeting next Friday about details of the case "and obtain their opinion about whether they want to press criminal charges to deter other county employes from doing the same thing."

Bair admitted taking cash from the filing fee fund in County Court and substituting his personal checks written on an overdrawn bank account. He claims he did not know the account was overdrawn.

The Practice

1

After a separation a common-law husband came to the woman's house and argued with her over money. In a fight which he started the man twisted her foot and broke her knee. When police investigated she stated she was willing to sign a complaint. Later, when she accompanied the officer to the prosecutor's office she said she had to drop her complaint. There was no effort to dissuade her and she was merely asked to sign a statement that she did not wish to prosecute.

2

In a particular community the local attitude toward state liquor laws was such that the prosecutor would charge offenders for liquor violations only when they became extensive or notorious or were combined with other vice crimes. He said that though the state legislation was strict the laws were unpopular in his county and it was almost impossible to get a jury that would convict.

3

A warrant had been issued for passing bad checks and the offender arrested in a distant state. The prosecutor, noting that it would cost about $500 to extradite him and that the checks amounted only to $60, decided against requesting extradition. The prosecutor stated that if the checks had totaled $100 or more he would probably have gone ahead with extradition.

4

In a case of burglary where the evidence was somewhat weak, the prosecutor agreed with the one of two offenders whom he considered only a follower not to charge him with burglary if he would agree to testify against the other. The fellow said he would, and the prosecutor pointed out that the charge could always be filed later on if he backed down.

The considerations which move a prosecutor not to charge at all can also motivate him to choose to charge a lesser offense, or fewer offenses, than the evidence would justify. He frequently has wide range of choice as to the charge, since most offenders are guilty of more than one offense. For many, criminal activity is a livelihood and numerous separate incidents are involved. And even when only a single criminal episode is in question a fairly simple course of conduct may be so analyzed as to bring it under various related or overlapping statutes.

The Practice

The following are common occurrences.

1

Two young men entered a liquor store and stole some beer. As they were carrying the cases out of the store a policeman spotted them and chased them. In attempting to hide, they jumped into a parked automobile. They noticed that the keys had been left in the ignition and they drove off. They were later arrested and charged with burglary and auto theft. The deputy county attorney discovered, however, that neither had a prior record and said, "I hate very much giving felony records to these boys. I think they have learned a lesson and there's no point in putting a blight on their whole future." He reduced the charges to misdemeanors. Both pleaded guilty and received probation.

2

A seventeen-year-old defendant in Michigan was charged with sale of narcotics based upon the sale of some marihuana cigarettes to a friend. While the state's evidence was clearly sufficient to establish the crime of "sale," the prosecutor's office reduced the charge to "possession," a lesser offense. A prosecutor explained, "We can't take these kinds of cases to trial. In the first place the law isn't intended to cover this type of situation. In the second place, when juries find out that the mandatory penalty is twenty years to life they just won't convict. Who is going to send a seventeen-year-old to prison for twenty years? And the judges don't like the law either, because they are caught in the same bind." The defendant pleaded guilty to the "possession" charge.

3

Police pursuing a traffic violator saw her throw out slips of paper, which they recovered after they had stopped her. The papers were mutuel bet slips and the evidence would have supported a charge of possession of gambling paraphernalia. The police recommendation that a warrant issue charging her with engaging in an illegal occupation was accepted by the prosecutor. The police chose the lesser offense because it was triable summarily, whereas the other, a high misdemeanor, might involve separate appearances for initial appearance, preliminary examination, and trial, yet their experience was that the judge would probably impose a sentence of ninety days in either case.

4

A suspect was apprehended in the act of breaking into and entering a clothing store in the nighttime. During in-custody interrogation he was urged to "clean himself up" and admit other offenses in which he had been involved. He was told that these were "free" and that he would not be prosecuted for them, but that if he did not admit other offenses and his involvement were later discovered he would be prosecuted for them separately. He admitted to thirty-seven separate burglaries. An assistant prosecutor approved a warrant charging him with the single offense of breaking into and entering the clothing store. The cleanup sheet was circulated to the precincts to permit them to note that the thirty-seven burglaries were "cleared." Judges ordinarily impose concurrent sentences even when multiple offenses are charged, and the information that the offender had admitted other crimes would come to the judge through the presentence report.

5

The deputy county attorney was attempting to persuade the defense attorney to plead his client guilty to the offense charged, in return for a promise not to invoke the habitual criminal statute, saying that once the defendant saw the evidence the state would produce at the preliminary examination he would surely go for such a deal. He described the expected testimony of one of the police officers and counsel looked quite discouraged when he heard it.

6

During the several months since he had been released from prison, the suspect had committed six major burglaries. In exchange for being charged with only one of the six offenses, he agreed to plead guilty and to testify against one of his accomplices and their fence. After being charged, the suspect refused to perform his part of the bargain. Two more burglary charges were brought against him.

a. *The Evidence Needed for Charging*

Prosecutors frequently refuse to prosecute, or choose to prosecute for some lesser offense than they believe the offender committed, because of the weakness of the evidence against him. There is no agreement, however, about the evidentiary standard which is appropriate in making the decision whether to charge a particular offense. The lack of definition is partially attributable to the absence of a practicable way to challenge the charging decision on evidentiary grounds. It is sometimes asserted that the charging standard is "probable cause," just as the arrest standard. But we are left with the question whether "probable cause" must mean the same thing in both contexts. If it does, one can say that police may arrest only those who can be charged, and that charging may follow arrest without concern for obtaining any new information. But equating of arrest and charging standards is questionable. Though others have rarely addressed themselves to this problem,[o] Judge Burger in the *Goldsmith* case (*see* p. 345 n.t, *supra*) asserted that the two evidentiary standards are different.

The ascertainment of the minimum evidentiary standard for charging has implications for the question whether there can properly be some delay for investigation between arrest and presentation before a magistrate, as discussed in the previous chapter. But a different question is whether prosecutors should and do apply such a standard. There is indication that they often use a higher standard than "probable cause" in deciding whether or not to charge. They are concerned with the likely outcome of a trial. In making their evaluation of the evidence, prosecutors try to anticipate rulings by the court on admissibility of evidence, particularly under the various exclusionary rules, even though it is possible that in a given case the accused would plead guilty or that, for whatever reason, his counsel might not raise the issue.

---

[o] In the ordinary case police do develop additional information subsequent to the arrest—by search, interrogation, victim's identification, physical evidence, questioning of witnesses, and so on. As a consequence, the problem does not often exist in pure form. It is most likely to arise in case law as a challenge by habeas corpus to the bindover order on the ground that it was based on inadequate proper evidence, *see, e.g.,* State *ex rel.* Donovan v. District Ct., 26 Mont. 275, 67 P. 943 (1902); or it might arise as a challenge to the information on the ground that the information may be lawfully filed only pursuant to a valid preliminary examination decision to bind over.

The Practice

1

A man and woman had lived together for several years, then had broken off. One night he forced his way into her apartment, beat her with his fists and forced her to have intercourse with him and committed an act of sexual perversion. The prosecutor approved a charge of assault and battery, commenting, "If we had taken that on anything but assault and battery, we would never have got a conviction and no good would have come from the case. Right away I knew what the attitude of any given judge over there would be to such a case, considering the people who were involved and their obvious lack of morality."

2

Two prostitutes complained that several times a pair of men had forced them at knife point to have intercourse and that the last time one of the girls had sustained a slight cut on her throat. She said, "It is not a question that we want our money, but we don't want to be found dead in a gutter some day." The prosecutor refused the warrant, saying, "There is no doubt in my mind that these girls have been subjected to fear for their lives, but if we get these men in here, and they get counsel which they are certain to do, he could easily get the case thrown out."

3

Police were called to the hospital where a man had been brought in for treatment for narcotics poisoning. He was arrested and, when questioned, told police he had taken two capsules of heroin and then passed out. The doctor said he could not state that the man was addicted but could state that he had suffered from an overdose of narcotics. The prosecutor said, "Even though this man admitted to taking narcotics, because he was under the influence of some drug at the time the officers talked to him, this could be disproved in court. So there is no use in taking it to court."

4

A service station attendant reported to police that while he was fixing a tire he heard the bell on the cash register ring. He went inside and saw a man with his hand in the cash drawer. When the man saw him he closed the drawer. No money was missing and the man denied to police that he had opened the cash register. They arrested him for attempted larceny from a building, but the prosecutor refused a warrant.

PROSECUTOR DOMINANCE OF THE WARRANT DECISION: A STUDY OF CURRENT PRACTICES

By Frank W. Miller & Lawrence P. Tiffany

1964 Washington University Law Quarterly 1, 12-23

III. Self-Imposed Evidence Sufficiency Controls

With the decline of judicial participation in, and the prosecutor's parallel rise to power over, the issuance of arrest warrants, that process may now be described accurately as one of self-limitation. Reasons are obvious why a prosecutor would find intolerable a situation in which warrants were issued charging a substantial number of persons who later proved unconvictable. Not only would the ends of justice be disserved, limited resources would be dissipated to the detriment of the protection of society. If, as folklore has it, prosecutors tend to believe that the public judges them in terms of their conviction records, another barrier to charging unconvictables is present.

These factors alone would provide an adequate incentive for establishing administrative controls to insure that his assistants—to whom are entrusted the daily routine decisions of the office—would charge only when the evidence of guilt nearly precluded acquittals. When this consideration is coupled with a desire to treat suspects uniformly—both to further widely-held values of fairness and equality and to escape criticism for doing otherwise—a search for devices to insure that suspects are not charged on inadequate evidence is nearly inevitable.

Three principal methods might be utilized to accomplish these ends. The most obvious one would be complete examination and evaluation of evidence available at the time the charging decision must be made. A second would be the establishment of intra-office review procedures, and a third the development of specialization within the office, or reliance on specialists in other departments. A consideration of the extent to which these methods are utilized constitutes the bulk of this section.

A. *Investigation of Available Evidence*

As a general proposition, a detailed consideration of the available evidence itself would be more likely to result in an accurate evaluation of its adequacy than would reliance on a police officer's oral or written summary of it. Perhaps in the interest of saving time, a detailed consideration is not customary in any of the jurisdictions studied.

In each of them, the source of information most often relied on is the police officer and his report or summary of the case which he brings with him when he requests a warrant. Occasionally witnesses, the suspect, or the victim are also interviewed, but there is no readily discernible pattern. Indeed, it depends to some extent on whether the requesting police officer brings them with him, and to some extent on whether the request is made by a private complainant rather than the police. In some cases, but by no means routinely, reports of medical examiners, results of polygraph tests, and physical evidence either of the crime or the condition of the victim are examined. And occasionally, defense attorneys are permitted to present arguments about the sufficiency of the evidence and even to call the attention of the prosecutor to additional evidence. It remains true, however, that in the usual case, maximum efforts to scrutinize each piece of evidence carefully are not made. Inevitably this must mean that screening on evidence sufficiency grounds is not so complete as it might be.

B. *Intra-office Review Procedures*

A quite highly regularized system of intra-office review was established in the prosecutor's office in Detroit largely because of dissatisfaction over practices which had developed in the absence of such a system. Police officers, considering themselves familiar with the individual characteristics and reaction patterns of various assistants in that office, "shopped around" for the particular assistant who, they believed, would regard their requests for warrants most sympathetically. To insure uniformity in charging, both in its evidence sufficiency and policy aspects, as well as to alert more experienced personnel to problems sensitive because of unusual community interest or political connotations, the prosecutor requires that the initial decisions of junior assistants be reviewed by one of two experienced senior assistants. Although recommendations of warrants for felonies are thus normally reviewed, review of recommendation for misdemeanor warrants is far from uniform. This is partly the result of misunderstanding among the assistants, and partly it reflects the fact that some misdemeanors are regarded as more important than others. Whether denials of recommendations are similarly subject to review is also a matter of some disagreement in the office. The result is that some assistants send the denials for review and others do not. Despite the fact that other goals are served as well, in actual operation the most significant effect of the system is to provide a review of the sufficiency of the evidence for the purpose of assuring conviction.

In Detroit, the police officer seeking a warrant may still select his initial review assistant on any basis he wishes, and he conceivably would do so on the assumption that an initially favorable reaction would carry some weight with the final review assistant. Indeed, to the extent that negative decisions are not reviewed, it would be surprising if police officers did not continue to place importance on selection of the initial review assistant. A similar result would be anticipated in the case of misdemeanors when they are not subject to review.

The same shopping around practices existed in Milwaukee, but the response there differed from the Detroit response. In Milwaukee, an investigator has been given the task of assigning police officers who come in with warrant requests to one of the assistant prosecutors. Since reference is made to whichever assistant happens to be free at that time, shopping around is effectively precluded. But there is no regularized review procedure as in Detroit. In Wichita, neither of the above techniques has been used. Police officers are free to select the assistant to whom they make their warrant requests, and the action of the assistant is not subject to any systematic review. Perhaps the much smaller size of the office in Wichita is a reason why the problem has not created difficulties there. Of course, nothing precludes informal non-systematic consultation among prosecutors in any of the offices.

C. *Specialization*

Another obvious way to insure that only suspects against whom the evidence is adequate are charged, is to leave the determination to those with special knowledge of the proof requirements in particular classes of cases. Specialization among the assistant prosecutors at the charging level is uncommon. Apparently the office in Wichita is completely unspecialized. There are some areas of specialization in Detroit. A single assistant handles all requests for warrants in traffic cases not handled as ordinance violations, and another all cases in which a proceeding under the Sex Psychopath statute is indicated. In addition, the Felony Bureau of the prosecutor's office, a group of detectives assigned to the office, conducts investigations in areas of white collar crime, and makes recommendations directly to one of the senior review assistants, thus by-passing the initial review stage. Similarly, there are some areas of specialization within the prosecutor's office in Milwaukee. For example, all cases of obscene literature are referred to a specific assistant, as are cases dealing with narcotics and automobile financing problems. Nevertheless, the percentage of cases which fall within any of these categories is relatively small, and for the most part the warrant decision is not made by specialized assistants.

IV. Critique

It is difficult to analyze comparatively the formal law and current administrative practices in the area of control over warrant issuance without concluding that an aura of unreality surrounds the problem. Nowhere does the declared law seem so at odds with the facts of the law in action. Yet the formal law statements—as well as expressed concern over the situation—seem, on the surface at least, to be aimed at shadows. The substance is not at all what the commentators seem to assume it is.

Several systems for controlling charging to make it conform to widely held community ideals of fairness and efficiency can be posited. A simple one might leave the decision to the private citizen, with the risk of bearing the cost of unsuccessful prosecution as a deterrent to the spiteful and the frustrated. Arguably such a system would most accurately and directly reflect community mores. Another might leave the decision to the police, and such a choice could find its principal justification in the notion that, because of their greater familiarity with all of the problems of administering a complex system of criminal justice with limited means, society might come closer to getting maximum benefit from its tax dollars. Still another system might place a heavy obligation—with strict sanctions for violation—on private citizens and police alike to bring to the attention of the prosecutor all instances in which anyone is suspected of crime, leaving the decision whether to prosecute entirely to that official. In another system, the prosecutor could be placed under the same obligation as the private citizens and the police, with the charging decision residing solely with a judicial official. Each of the latter two choices might be regarded as insuring equality of treatment and impartiality more certainly than the others. Aspects of all four of those systems can be found—or have existed—in parts of the United States.

In fact, however, the dominant system in the United States today purports to be a combination of the third and fourth alternatives described above. In form, it more closely resembles the fourth than the third; in practice, however, a distinction must be drawn between the system as it operates for minor offenses and serious crimes. For serious crimes, the possibility of the preliminary examination means that the decision may be shared by the prosecutor and magistrate, but for minor offenses, unlike the formal law model, the power to charge resides exclusively with the prosecutor.

Against this background, some analysis of criticism of the present system is in order, partly to determine the merits of the criticism, and partly to point out that the criticism does not relate to situations which its language is broad enough to encompass.

Most commentators who insist that the impartial judgment of a third person is vital to a satisfactory warrant issuing process, seldom make clear whether such impartial judgment—judicial or not—is designed to protect the citizen from improper arrest, or the suspect already in custody from improper prosecution. This lack of clarity results in part from the fact that arrest warrants are commonly used to serve both purposes. But another factor may be more significant. It is best illustrated by a consideration of the assumption underlying *Giordenello v. United States.* There the Court emphasized the need for an impartial judicial inquiry to serve as a curb on the consequences of *police* self-interest. The assumption seems to be that the confrontation is between the police and the magistrate. If federal police officers regularly sought pre-arrest warrants from federal commissioners without the prior approval of the United States Attorney, the assumption would be validated, and the concern of the Court that a Federal Commissioner make an independent judgment—and have the facts before him in sufficient detail to make it intelligently—would be understandable. It is clear, in any event, that the Supreme Court of the United States, when it requires a complaint replete with facts from which the inference of probable cause may be drawn instead of a bald assertion of probable cause, is concerned not with the requirements for charging but those for arrest.

Even if the assumption is correct that a high percentage of arrests in the federal system are made on warrants, the further assumption that those warrants are issued without the concurrence of the prosecutor is not correct. More important, neither assumption is valid when the state systems under scrutiny here are considered. Police officers do not seek warrants from magistrates—either before or after arrest—without the prior approval of the prosecutor. At least in the three states under intensive investigation here, the warrant is rarely an arrest document: it is issued after arrest and serves as the charging document in the overwhelming majority of cases.

It is just this step which seems to be overlooked, or, at least, discounted completely, in discussions of the need for inquiry about the presence of probable cause. It may be that the proponents of a system of judicial inquiry are so obviously dissatisfied with a system of screening by prosecutors that they deem it unworthy of mention, and prefer that both at the initial and final charging stages—the warrant and the preliminary examination—the decision be made by a judicial official. If so, they are dissatisfied with the present system, for there is no evidence that any but the most trivial cases are prosecuted without the prior approval of the prosecuting attorney. Effective judicial review of the charging decision occurs not at all in minor offenses, and only at the preliminary examination level in serious ones. When one considers that preliminary examinations are waived in as many as ninety per cent of the cases in some jurisdictions, the extent of judicial participation in charging is even less. It is more likely that proponents of judicial screening have in mind only pre-arrest warrants—probably based on the fallacious assumption that most arrests are accomplished with a warrant, or a conviction that they should be. But that assumption is wholly unrealistic in metropolitan communities certainly, and is probably seldom realistic in rural areas as well. There can, of course, be no real basis for believing that what critics have in mind is judicial control of arrests and prosecutor control of charging, since they have apparently not considered the problem in those terms.

Finally, it is possible that the prosecutor is viewed as somehow less able—or more biased—than a magistrate, and that the approval of both should be obtained, not only for pre-arrest warrants, but for post-arrest warrants as well. At least to the extent that prosecutors are lawyers and magistrates laymen, the conclusion about relative ability is not tenable. And a potent factor in making the charge of greater bias invalid as well is the notorious interest of elected prosecutors in maintaining a good conviction record. In summary, meshing this oft-stated need for independent judicial determination of probable cause at the warrant stage with the facts of current criminal justice administration is a difficult task. In that light, it is also hard to agree with the reasons stated for the need. To the extent that the formal law still vests in magistrates the power to determine whether warrants should be issued, it is well founded in English common law, but anomalous under a public prosecutor system as it now exists in the United States.

2. *The Practice of Charging Where Refusal to Charge Is Normal, Upgrading Charges Beyond Those Normally Filed, and Filing Repeated Charges*

The previous section related to the prosecutor's choice to charge less than the law would have permitted. As we have seen, in many situations such a choice becomes the normal practice. It then is significant to ask under what circumstances the prosecutor deviates from this norm—what factors seem to him to call for fuller use of his prosecutorial power.

The Practice

Except for the first one, the following illustrations represent reasonably common prosecutor reactions.

1

A 78-year-old man was arrested for indecent exposure upon complaint of the father of a young girl who had seen him. The old man had no record and explained that he was merely urinating in the alley and offered to get a statement from his doctor to the effect that he had a kidney ailment. The prosecutor asked the father what he wanted done and the father said, "I think the man should be punished for what he did." The prosecutor said, "Well, he's pretty old, and has never committed any offense before. Don't you think jail is the wrong place for him?" The father replied, "He committed a crime and I think he ought to be punished." The prosecutor eventually shrugged his shoulders and approved the warrant recommendation.

2

Police stopped a known criminal for a traffic offense and searched his car, finding a loaded pistol in the glove compartment. The police arrested him for carrying a concealed weapon and the prosecutor approved the charge even though he knew the case would be lost as soon as a motion was made to suppress the only evidence of guilt.

3

Several inmates of the House of Corrections had escaped and were apprehended. In recent months there had been a large number of escapes. Though escapees from the House of Corrections (in contrast to the prison) were usually charged under a misdemeanor statute, an assistant prosecutor approved warrants charging each of this latest group with a felony.

4

The suspect had committed several armed robberies in Milwaukee. Newspapers gave the case more than the usual amount of publicity. An assistant prosecutor approved the police recommendation for three warrants, each charging one of the robberies, even though he did not expect this to have any effect on sentence.

5

A 66-year-old man had been plaguing the prosecutor's office and courts with his frequent misconduct as a beggar. He was arrested for begging and $199 in cash was found on him. He also had in his possession two bank books showing deposits of $5,700. He had been arrested some thirty-five times and convicted twenty times of begging or some related offense. It was felt by the prosecuting attorney's office that it was time to teach the old man a lesson. The charge was that of being a third offender, with substantially higher maximum penalty.

6

A young lady complained to the police that a dentist slapped her across the face when she told him he was hurting her while extracting a tooth. He failed to respond to the letter routinely sent to professional men about complaints of that nature. In a phone conversation as a follow-up to the letter, he told the police sergeant to go to hell. He failed to appear at the police felony detail at the requested time for a discussion of the matter. His firm had been repeatedly complained against for fraud but there was never enough evidence to support charges. Despite the practice not to charge doctors and dentists with minor offenses alleged by their patients, a warrant was issued charging this dentist with assault and battery.

7

A young, innocent-looking man was apprehended for breaking and entering. During cleanup he admitted thirteen other breaking and entering offenses. He was charged with one of the offenses, tried and acquitted by the jury. Another charge was lodged and again he was acquitted. There was a third charge and a third acquittal. Finally, on the fourth trial, he was convicted of breaking and entering.

8

An offender had shot his wife and three children and burned their bodies. He was charged with first degree murder of his wife and convicted, the jury fixing the penalty at twenty years.

He was tried and convicted for the death of one of the children and sentenced to forty-five years imprisonment. The prosecutor tried him again for the death of a second child and this time succeeded in obtaining the death penalty from the jury.[p]

9

Charles "Lucky" Luciano and others were charged with ninety counts of placing women in houses of prostitution, receiving money for so placing them, and receiving part of their earnings without consideration. Upon conviction on sixty-two counts the court imposed cumulative sentences.

10

The defendant had been negligently operating his motor boat on Lake St. Claire when he rammed it into another craft, killing one of its occupants. He was charged with and tried for manslaughter, but the jury found him guilty only of simple assault. The state prosecutor and an assistant United States Attorney then decided that the defendant should be tried for his violation of federal law. He was charged with the same crime for which he had been prosecuted in the state court. This time the defendant was convicted of manslaughter.

HENDERSON v. UNITED STATES

349 F.2d 712 (D.C. Cir. 1965)

BAZELON, Chief Judge (dissenting). There is a further matter which deserves comment, although it does not affect the result. In Hutcherson v. United States, 120 U.S.App.D.C.[274], 345 F.2d 964, decided March 18, 1965, I discussed the question of prosecutorial standards for choice among the various criminal statutes applying to narcotics traffic in the District of Columbia. I noted that the United States Attorney appeared to have elected an indiscriminatingly harsh approach to these choices. In *Hutcherson,* as in the earlier case of Lloyd v. United States, 119 U.S.App. D.C. 373, 343 F.2d 242 (1964), an addict defendant found more or less by accident to be in possession of a few days' supply of narcotics was prosecuted as severely as possible under the applicable statutes. In a substantial number of narcotics cases recently before us, involving the sale of small quantities of narcotics by narcotic addicts, similar harshness has been shown.

---

[p] In addition to dissatisfaction as to verdict or sentence, the severe limitations upon the right of the prosecution to appeal from trial error resulting in full or partial acquittal account for part of the prosecutor's use of serial prosecutions.

Here, violations of much larger proportions seem to have been involved. The record suggests that appellant made a sale of narcotics to an undercover policeman or informant. Marked money was used. Although in our experience the police frequently are willing to wait six to eight months to make arrests after such transactions when dealing with local peddlers, here an arrest was made almost immediately. Two hundred eighty-two capsules, assayed at more than fifteen per cent heroin content, were found. This is fifty to one hundred times the amount of narcotics found on Hutcherson, with a value in the thousands of dollars. Appellant had no previous narcotic convictions.

Although he is not an addict, appellant was prosecuted *solely* under 26 U.S.C. § 4704(a)—the most lenient federal prosecution possible. Of course, appellant does not complain of his good fortune. Although requested, Government counsel before this court could not explain why the five-year mandatory minimum sentence, 21 U.S.C. § 174, which is regularly imposed in cases of apparently lesser consequence, was not invoked here. Since no more need be proved under § 174 than § 4704(a), protection of an informer could not have been the motive. And although this lenient treatment may have been given in exchange for information, appellant's substantial efforts on defense, particularly his attempts to uncover the informer, would indicate otherwise. So does the unusual dispatch with which the police acted to apprehend appellant once they knew they had their man.

At oral argument I asked Government counsel why this appellant, a non-addict found with large quantities of narcotics, was treated so much better than addicts accidentally found in possession of $40 worth of drugs, or persuaded into making a $10 sale to a police undercover agent or informer. Government counsel offered this explanation: the United States Attorney may have reason to think that such addicts are substantial operators, but may have no way to prove it. Such reasoning is at the heart of the tyranny in the invisible prosecutorial choice he is permitted to make. I am dismayed at the proposition that a prosecutor may sentence offenders to jail terms longer than appears to be warranted by the transactions with which they are charged, because he *thinks* they are involved in bigger stuff—and that this choice may never be reviewed. In any event, the stricter treatment of apparently small operators is not explained by the contention that they are appellant's equals.[q]

---

[q] *In re* Losasso, 15 Colo. 163, 170-71, 24 P. 1080, 1082 (1890): "It is a fact that prosecuting officers, actuated by motives of policy, generally endeavor to procure indictments for the higher rather than for either of the lesser grades of homicide. An indictment for murder is not, without reason, supposed to render a conviction of manslaughter more certain. On the other hand, under

C. LIMITATIONS UPON THE PROSECUTOR'S CHARGING DECISION

1. Legal Restraints

a. Refusal to Prosecute

The prosecutor's discretion to refuse prosecution is very broad, though the limits of that discretion are reached upon a showing of bad faith or corruption.[r] Various devices have been used to attack the prosecutor's refusal to prosecute—contempt, mandamus, quo warranto, and so forth.

UNITED STATES v. COX

342 F.2d 167 (5th Cir. 1965)

[In a civil rights dispute in Mississippi the federal judge concluded that two Negro witnesses had perjured themselves in

the charge of manslaughter, a conviction for murder would be impossible; yet the evidence adduced at the trial may greatly exceed in strength that upon which the indictment was found, and fully warrant such conviction. In theory, these considerations should have no weight either with the prosecutor or grand jury; but in practice, we know that they often turn the scales in favor of the graver accusation."

T. Arnold, The Symbols of Government 153-54 (1935): "[T]he problem of the police and prosecutor is the suppression of the occasional dangerous individual. For this purpose the ideal that all laws should be enforced without a discretionary selection is impossible to carry out. It is like directing a general to attack the enemy on all fronts at once. It conveys no idea whatever as to what the prosecution should do. The prosecutor therefore must look at the criminal law, not as something to be enforced because it governs society, but as an arsenal of weapons with which to incarcerate certain dangerous individuals who are bothering society. . . . The fact that there are more laws than he can ever enforce is not a handicap but an aid to the prosecutor because it gives him so many offensive weapons against any particular individual. Obsolete laws may be revived and used for purposes that their authors never dreamed of, to sink into obscurity again when the particular individual has been put behind the bars."

[r] In Nagelberg v. United States, 377 U.S. 266 (1964), the Supreme Court recognized the propriety of reducing charges against a defendant as compensation for cooperation. Before sentence on a guilty plea the defendant moved to withdraw his plea and plead not guilty so that the government could move to dismiss and substitute a lesser charge as a reward for the defendant's cooperation. The trial judge ruled that he had no power to permit withdrawal of the guilty plea on such grounds, though he did impose the minimum sentence permitted by the statute on the original narcotics charge. The Supreme Court held that the trial judge was mistaken and that he did have discretion to permit withdrawal of a guilty plea for the reason existing in this case.

In Dixon v. District of Columbia, 394 F.2d 966 (D.C. Cir. 1968), the prosecutor agreed not to charge traffic violations upon tacit agreement of the defendant to drop his complaint against conduct of the arresting officer. When the defendant did pursue the complaint the traffic charges were pressed. Even though the original agreement not to charge defendant was improper, charging him in retaliation for his complaining against the officer was also improper. The court ordered the charges dismissed, but could not agree on the precise ground.

testifying that the voting registrar had refused to give them application forms. The judge referred the matter to a grand jury, which sought to return indictments. On orders from the attorney general, the United States Attorney refused to sign the indictments—leaving them without force—and the federal district court cited him for contempt. The United States Attorney appealed.]

JONES, Circuit Judge. The role of the grand jury is restricted to a finding as to whether or not there is probable cause to believe that an offense has been committed. The discretionary power of the attorney for the United States in determining whether a prosecution shall be commenced or maintained may well depend upon matters of policy wholly apart from any question of probable cause. Although as a member of the bar, the attorney for the United States is an officer of the court, he is nevertheless an executive official of the Government, and it is as an officer of the executive department that he exercises a discretion as to whether or not there shall be a prosecution in a particular case. It follows, as an incident of the constitutional separation of powers, that the courts are not to interfere with the free exercise of the discretionary powers of the attorneys of the United States in their control over criminal prosecutions.

[T]he contempt order must be reversed.

JOHN R. BROWN, Circuit Judge (concurring specially). All must be aware now that there are times when the interests of the nation require that a prosecution be foregone. These instances will most often be in the area of state secrets and national security.

And even in less sensitive areas, the practical operation of the prosecutorial function makes imperative the need for executive determination. The familiar example is the deliberate choice between those to be prosecuted and those who, often equally guilty, are named as co-conspirators but not as defendants, or others not named who are used as star government witnesses. And in other situations, of which the instant case may well be typical, the executive's purpose to effectuate specific policies thought to be of major importance would be frustrated or encumbered were a Grand Jury given the sole prerogative of determining when a prosecution is to be effectively commenced.[8]

---

[8] There may be some situations in which a person wishes to be prosecuted as a method of publicizing what he deems to be an undesirable law (civil disobedience), as a way of challenging a law believed unconstitutional (*see* Freedman, *The Professional Responsibility of the Prosecuting Attorney*, 55 GEO. L.J. 1030 (1967)), or to clear his name of suspicion (*see* Vogt v. Internal Revenue Service, 278 F. Supp. 821 (E.D. Pa. 1967)). There is, however, apparently no right to be prosecuted.

POWELL v. KATZENBACH

359 F.2d 234 (D.C. Cir. 1965)

Before BAZELON, Chief Judge, WASHINGTON, Senior Circuit Judge, and WRIGHT, Circuit Judge.

PER CURIAM. Appellant brought an action in the nature of mandamus against the Attorney General of the United States in order to force prosecution of a national bank and certain persons who appellant alleges were parties to a conspiracy in violation of various sections of Title 18 of the United States Code. Upon motion of appellee, the District Court struck two paragraphs of the complaint under Rule 12(f) of the Federal Rules of Civil Procedure, and dismissed with prejudice the remainder of the complaint for failure to state a cause of action. This appeal followed.

It is well settled that the question of whether and when prosecution is to be instituted is within the discretion of the Attorney General. Mandamus will not lie to control the exercise of this discretion. We will assume, without deciding, that where Congress has withdrawn all discretion from the prosecutor by special legislation, a court might be empowered to force prosecutions in some circumstances. Appellant cites 68 Stat. 998 (1954), 5 U.S.C. § 311a (1958), as such a statute. However, the language of that provision and its legislative history fail to disclose a congressional intent to alter the traditional scope of the prosecutor's discretion. The complaint in its entirety fails to state a cause of action, and we thus need not reach the issue as to whether the striking of two of its paragraphs was warranted. Accordingly, the judgment of the District Court is

Affirmed.[t]

STATE ex *inf.* McKITTRICK v. GRAVES

346 Mo. 990, 144 S.W.2d 91 (1940)

HAYS, J. Original action in *quo warranto* commenced by the attorney general filing an information on May 10, 1939, by which

[t] An attempt to control prosecutor discretion in obscenity cases was made in an initiative defeated in the 1966 California election. A portion of the proposal read: "Whenever there is reason to believe that any person knowingly has committed or is committing any of the acts proscribed by this chapter, and the responsible prosecuting attorney neglects and refuses to perform the duties imposed upon him, a civil action may be instituted, to require such performance. If such prosecuting attorney shall, after demand in writing, refuse to undertake the performance of said duties within 10 days and thereafter prosecute the same to conclusion within a reasonable time, any citizen may maintain a civil action against such prosecutor to compel him to perform all of the duties imposed by this chapter, failing which he shall be subject to removal from office according to law."

he seeks to oust the respondent from the office of Prosecuting Attorney of Jackson County.

There was considerable evidence adduced by the relator to show that during the period from January 1, 1939, to the date of the filing of the information the operation of public gambling houses was widespread throughout Kansas City.

There was similar evidence to the effect that in a large number of establishments in the downtown metropolitan area of Kansas City and elsewhere the laws in regard to the sale of intoxicating liquor were openly and flagrantly violated, and that houses of prostitution were maintained whose inmates often frequented the streets openly soliciting men who were passing by.

In addition to proof of the open and flagrant character of the law violations here involved, from which the inference of general public knowledge thereof is irresistible, relator over the objection of respondent introduced a series of over fifty newspaper articles appearing in the Metropolitan Press of Kansas City concerning the widespread character of gambling and similar law violation in that community. Several of these articles listed specific places where violations were occurring, and others were illustrated by the photographs of the places involved. Respondent admitted that he subscribed to two of the newspapers during the entire period.

Yet the record clearly shows that respondent made no *bona fide* effort to investigate these conditions or to institute proceedings to combat the evils described. His attitude seems to have been one of waiting for some other officer or private citizen to file a formal complaint upon which he could base criminal informations.

The commissioner has found no facts tending to sustain the charge in the information that respondent was guilty of corrupt practice in dismissing criminal proceedings pending in the courts of his county.

The third charge made against respondent has to do with his failure to prosecute persons alleged to have been guilty of fraud in connection with the general election in 1936.

The record discloses that a grand jury of the District Court of the United States for the Western District of Missouri returned a large number of indictments in which over two hundred individuals were charged with fraudulent and otherwise illegal conduct in connection with the 1936 election. It is also shown that many of the defendants so charged pleaded guilty, thus admitting the truth of the charges against them.

They [the pleas of guilty] clearly show that frauds and irregularities on a wide scale existed in connection with the 1936 election, and the existence of these facts which were well known to the respondent certainly required an investigation on his behalf. Yet, by his own admission, respondent made no such investigation. He did not even choose to discuss the matter with the Federal prosecutor. We take judicial notice of the fact that at the election of 1936, in addition to the election of numerous Federal officers, State officers were also elected. While violations in regard to the election of Federal officers lay within the jurisdiction of the courts of the United States, those which affected the election of State officers were within the jurisdiction of the State.

We conclude therefore that our commissioner properly found that respondent, by failing to perform the duties of his office, has forfeited the same.[u]

b. *Improper Motive for Prosecution*

Even though under generally accepted doctrine the prosecutor may charge any and all possible offenses which he has sufficient evidence to prove the offender has committed against the laws of the jurisdiction, there is some possibility of objection in the event his decision is motivated by racial or religious bias, personal vengeance, corruption, or other clearly improper factor.[v] Even then the remedy is uncertain and difficult.

BAILLEAUX v. GLADDEN
230 Ore. 606, 370 P.2d 722 (1962)

WARNER, J. Petitioner first asserts that the Habitual Criminal Act was applied in a discriminatory manner as to him. Paragraph VI(1) of his petition reflecting this position reads as follows:

---

[u] In rare instances a prosecutor may be subject to criminal charges. *See* State v. Langley, 323 P.2d 301 (Ore. 1958), affirming a conviction under ORE. REV. STAT. § 167.515, which made willful failure to prosecute gamblers an offense punishable by fine of $50 to $500 and by forfeiture of office. The case involved corrupt motive.

[v] Compare the material at 311-26, *supra*.

When a statute has not been used for generations, one who is prosecuted under it may raise the argument that the statute is invalid for nonuse. This civil law concept of desuetude had no established place in American law. There is a related concept of obsoleteness, where the reason for the statute's enactment no longer exists. Both concepts are helpfully discussed in United States v. Elliott, 266 F. Supp. 318, 325-26 (S.D.N.Y. 1967).

Consider in this context p. 326 n.4, *supra*.

"That notwithstanding the fact that Oregon's habitual criminal act (ORS 168.010 et seq.) provides no basis for distinguishing one offender from another, the prosecuting attorneys for the State of Oregon possess and follow a fixed, continuous and concerted plan not to enforce the habitual criminal laws against any offender of Negro, Chinese, Mexican or Indian race; that, on the contrary, the prosecuting attorneys for the State of Oregon knowingly, willfully, and by design enforce the habitual criminal laws exclusively against white offenders, which constitutes an illegal and unjust discrimination against petitioner, a white Caucasian, imprisoned in the Oregon State Penitentiary pursuant to action brought under the Oregon habitual criminal act; and that the said arbitrary, intentional, collusive, wrongful, and deliberate discriminatory intent on the part of the prosecuting attorneys for the State of Oregon and the law enforcement officials of the State of Oregon and the defendant herein, now existing in the administration of the habitual criminal act, deprive petitioner of the equal protection of the laws and equal justice, in violation of Article I, Section 20 of the Oregon Constitution and the Fourteenth Amendment of the United States Constitution."

For the reasons which follow, we find no merit in petitioner's appeal.

The gravamen of petitioner's assertion of discrimination is, as we have observed, the failure of the various district attorneys of this state to file informations against previously-convicted felons who are Negroes, Chinese, Mexicans or Indians.

1. On the authority of State v. Hicks, 213 Or 619, 325 P2d 794, cert den 359 US 917, we hold that discrimination of the kind and character the petitioner attempts to plead does not fall within the purview of the Equal Protection Clause. See, also, the recent case of Oyler v. Boles, 368 US 448. It is not a denial of equal protection that one person amenable to an enhanced penalty under the Habitual Criminal Act has his penalty increased and the act is not applied to other previously-convicted felons. . . .

2. We are impressed with the analysis of the Yick Wo doctrine (Yick Wo v. Hopkins, 118 US 356) made in People v. Montgomery, 47 Cal App 2d 1, 117 P2d 437, 446, and cited with approval at page 640 in *State v. Hicks,* supra. We note again its statement that the remedy for unequal enforcement of the law "does not lie in the exoneration of the guilty at the expense of society." . . .

MOSS v. HORNIG

314 F.2d 89 (2d Cir. 1963)

Before LUMBARD, Chief Judge, and WATERMAN and MARSHALL, Circuit Judges.

LUMBARD, Chief Judge. Joseph Moss, whose prosecution for violation of the Connecticut Sunday Closing Law, Conn.Gen.Stat. § 53-300, is pending in the Connecticut courts, seeks a federal injunction against that prosecution.

Moss operates a shoe store on Route 7 in Brookfield, Connecticut. He keeps the store open on Sundays and realizes one-third of his $276,000 annual gross receipts from sales on that day. On February 23, 1962, Hornig, as prosecuting attorney for the third judicial circuit in Connecticut, filed an information against Moss for violation of the state Sunday Closing Law.

Federal courts of equity have always been loathe to restrain criminal prosecutions by states, even on constitutional grounds, where all constitutional issues can be decided in the first instance as a matter of course by the state courts.

But it has been held, see People v. Montgomery, 117 P.2d 437 (Calif. Ct. App. 1941), that "discriminatory enforcement" is not available as a defense in a criminal proceeding. It is therefore incumbent upon the federal courts, where sufficiently specific allegations are made, to make a preliminary inquiry such as was made here.

Mere failure to prosecute other offenders is no basis for a finding of denial of equal protection. See United States v. Rickenbacker, 309 F.2d 462 (2d Cir. 1962) [sole prosecution for refusal to fill out census form]. To show that unequal administration of a state statute offends the equal protection clause one must show an intentional or purposeful discrimination. Snowden v. Hughes, 321 U.S. 1, 8 (1944).

In Oyler v. Boles, 368 U.S. 448, 456 (1962), the Supreme Court rejecting petitioner's contention that the [highly] selective enforcement of the West Virginia [mandatory] habitual offenders penalty statute was a denial of his right to equal protection said:

> "[T]he conscious exercise of some selectivity in enforcement is not in itself a federal constitutional violation. Even though the statistics in this case might imply a policy of selective enforcement, it was not stated that the selection was deliberately based upon an unjustifiable standard such as race, religion, or other arbitrary classification. Therefore grounds supporting a finding of a denial of equal protection were not alleged."

The Oyler case seems to indicate that the relief for denial to equal protection is limited to cases where class discrimination is proved.[w]

In the instant case, Moss alleged an intentional or purposeful discrimination against him as an individual. We are not convinced that the Oyler case precludes our granting relief if a plaintiff can show that a state official purposefully discriminated against him. However, Moss has made no such showing. He evoked testimony that only two persons, including himself, had been prosecuted in the Third Circuit since [1951,] that Hornig knew other stores were open, and that Hornig failed to bring other prosecutions. These facts do not prove purposeful discrimination.

It is likely that proof that others have violated the law and have not been prosecuted could be offered with respect to almost every lesser offense proscribed by the laws of Connecticut or of any other state. If such facts alone were sufficient to make out a case under the Civil Rights Act almost every state prosecution would be subject to interference on the claim of discrimination and the offer of such proof. Clearly the Civil Rights Act was not intended to provide such a means for frustrating the administration of criminal justice by state authorities.[x]

PEOPLE v. UTICA DAW'S DRUG CO.

16 App. Div. 2d 12, 225 N.Y.S.2d 128 (1962)

[This case also appears at 312, *supra*.

Defendant was convicted of selling goods on Sunday. He contended that the public authorities responsible for his prosecution

---

[w] *Compare* Evans v. Cunningham, 335 F.2d 491, 495, 496 (4th Cir. 1964), in which the Virginia repeater statute was used only against persons who had prior Virginia convictions:

> Considered abstractly, there is superficial appeal in the contention that "geographical" classification of prior convictions as the basis for imposition of additional punishment under the recidivist statute is arbitrary. There are practical reasons for it, however. Indeed, it is probable that Virginia's Director of the Department of Welfare and Institutions does not ordinarily have "knowledge" of out of state prior convictions within the meaning of the statute.
>
> It thus appears that the real basis of classification is not geographic, as Evans contends, but practical utility. The Director reports all knowledge which comes to him in the form of competent evidence to establish the facts [*i.e.*, Virginia convictions]. He does not report information [*i.e.*, out-of-state convictions] which, without further investigation and collection of materials, he has no means of proving.

[x] In a curious variation on this problem a defendant vainly complained that he had been unfairly denied opportunity to escape prosecution by becoming an informer, while other defendants had been granted immunity in return for turning informer. State v. Jourdain, 225 La. 1030, 74 So. 2d 203 (1954).

had singled out only businesses engaged in discount selling. The trial court and the district attorney agreed that this contention, if proved, constituted a defense to the criminal charge and the jury was instructed accordingly that they should acquit if they found "a clear and intentional discrimination against this defendant and against those in the same class." The jury convicted. On review, the Appellate Division reversed.]

HALPERN, J. The claim of discriminatory enforcement should not be treated as a defense to the criminal charge, to be tried before the jury and submitted to it for decision, but should be treated as an application to the court for a dismissal or quashing of the prosecution upon constitutional grounds. Insofar as a question of fact may be involved, the court should take the evidence in the absence of the jury and should decide the question itself. If the court finds that there was an intentional and purposeful discrimination, the court should quash the prosecution, not because the defendant is not guilty of the crime charged, but because the court, as an agency of government, should not lend itself to a prosecution the maintenance of which would violate the constitutional rights of the defendant.

The claim of discriminatory enforcement does not go to the question of the guilt or innocence of the defendant, which is within the province of the jury. The question is rather whether in a community in which there is general disregard of a particular law with the acquiescence of the public authorities, the authorities should be allowed sporadically to select a single defendant or a single class of defendants for prosecution because of personal animosity or for some other illegitimate reason. The wrong sought to be prevented is a wrong by the public authorities. To allow such arbitrary and discriminatory enforcement of a generally disregarded law is to place in the hands of the police and the prosecutor a power of the type frequently invoked in countries ruled by a dictator but wholly out of harmony with the principle of equal justice under law prevailing in democratic societies. The court is asked to stop the prosecution at the threshold, not because the defendant is innocent but because the public authorities are guilty of a wrong in engaging in a course of conduct designed to discriminate unconstitutionally against the defendant.

As has been pointed out, the burden resting upon the defendant is a heavy one and, even if the defendant succeeds in sustaining it, he will not be immune from a new prosecution, when and if the public authorities undertake a generalized enforcement of the law. Furthermore, even if the enforcement of a particular law is selective, it does not necessarily follow that it is unconstitutionally discriminatory. Selective enforcement may be justified when the meaning or constitutionality of the law is in doubt and a test case is needed to clarify the law or to establish its validity. Selective enforcement may also be justified when a striking example or a few examples are sought in order to deter other violators, as part of a bona fide rational pattern of general enforcement, in the expectation that general compliance will follow and that further prosecutions will be unnecessary. It is only when the selective enforcement is designed to discriminate against the persons prosecuted, without any intention to follow it up by general enforcement against others, that a constitutional violation may be found.[y]

GANGER v. PEYTON
379 F.2d 709 (4th Cir. 1967)

CRAVEN, Circuit Judge. Ganger received a six-month sentence in Stafford County for assaulting his wife.

The Stafford County conviction is constitutionally invalid. The district court found that the state prosecuting attorney represented Ganger's wife in the prosecution of a divorce action which was pending at the time of the criminal trial and was based upon the same alleged assault on Mrs. Ganger. Ganger testified that the prosecuting attorney offered to drop the assault charge if Ganger would make a favorable property settlement in the divorce action.

[T]he district judge concluded that there had been such an offer. His finding is supported by substantial evidence and is not clearly erroneous.

The Assistant Attorney General of Virginia concedes that the Commonwealth's Attorney should not have prosecuted the criminal case at the same time he was representing Ganger's wife in the divorce proceeding. We agree. Such a conflict of interest clearly denied Ganger the possibility of fair minded exercise of the prosecutor's discretion. Not every criminal case goes to trial. Prosecuting attorneys frequently decline to charge, or nol pros, criminal cases—especially ones arising out of domestic relations. Aside from the possibility of a favorable charge decision, including nol pros, there is always the prospect of plea bargaining.

Because of the prosecuting attorney's own self-interest in the civil litigation (including the possibility that the size of his fee would be determined by what could be exacted from defendant),

---

[y] *See Recent Decision,* 51 VA. L. REV. 499 (1965), commenting on People v. Walker, 14 N.Y.2d 901, 200 N.E.2d 779, 252 N.Y.S.2d 96 (1964) (permitting defendant to offer proof of a revenge motive behind aggressive prosecution of her for violation of a frequently enforced statute).

he was not in a position to exercise fair-minded judgment with respect to (1) whether to decline to prosecute, (2) whether to reduce the charge to a lesser degree of assault, or (3) whether to recommend a suspended sentence or other clemency.

Although conceding that the prosecuting attorney should not have represented Ganger's wife in private litigation at a time when he was charged with the duty to fairly prosecute or otherwise fairly dispose of the criminal charge against Ganger, the State contends that the improper conduct resulted in no harm to Ganger. We cannot so assume. It is true that although charged with a serious assault that could have resulted in imprisonment to the extent of twenty years, Ganger was convicted of a lesser assault and sentenced to only six months. But we do not know and cannot now ascertain what would have happened if the prosecuting attorney had been free to exercise the fair discretion which he owed to all persons charged with crime in his court. "[B]efore a federal constitutional error can be held harmless, the court must be able to declare a belief that it was harmless beyond a reasonable doubt." Chapman v. California, 386 U.S. 18 (1967).

The judgment of the district court granting the writ of habeas corpus and vacating the sentence in the Stafford County case is affirmed.

GREENWALD v. STATE

35 Wis. 2d 146, 150 N.W.2d 507 (1967)

CURRIE, C. J. Defendant in his written confession not only admitted the two burglaries and one attempted burglary for which he was prosecuted and convicted, but also a third burglary. On January 21, 1965, the day following his arrest, a complaint was filed which charged defendant with having committed only the third burglary. The charge was contested in a trial to the court presided over by Judge JOHN L. COFFEY, which trial took place June 3, 1965. After testimony was taken the case was continued for decision and on July 23, 1965, the day after the instant charges were instituted, the court dismissed the charge. A notation in the docket makes it clear that the dismissal was not announced until the instant charges had been instituted. Defendant contends that the three charges of June 22d, were brought primarily to punish him for contesting the earlier burglary case. The trial court found:

"I do not think that the mere filing of charges later is necessarily an implication that it is being done out of revenge or undue harsh punishment. It can just as conversely logically apply that if a prosecution had been successful in the one case, which is entirely separate and distinct from the others, that the District Attorney might, out of practical realism or maybe humane consideration, decide—well, that's enough to encompass everything so far as potential punishment is concerned."

[W]e find no merit to defendant's contention that due process requires a holding that the state was estopped from prosecuting the instant charges.

By the Court.—Judgment affirmed.

c. *Excessive Charging*

Another kind of objection may be to unwarranted severity of the charge, for example overcharging in order to gain leverage in negotiating a guilty plea, or multiplying counts to expand the penalty. If the harshness is wrongly motivated, by bias, personal antipathy, or corruption as suggested previously, there is a possibility of challenging the prosecutor's decision, but otherwise the principal judicial solution is the more devious one of statutory construction, *e.g.*, holding invalid a felony prosecution where the statutes also contained a misdemeanor penalty for the same conduct[z] or finding a legislative intent that conduct such as transporting two prostitutes on a single interstate trip constitutes a single offense.

STATE v. STEVENS

93 Ariz. 375, 381 P.2d 100 (1963)

JENNINGS, Justice. On December 15, 1961 the respondent Paul Raymond LaCross surrendered himself to the Scottsdale police and admitted that he had held up a 7-11 Market in Scottsdale on December 8, 1961. He then made full restitution of the money taken.

At the time of the holdup LaCross was 20 years of age and had a clean record. He was without funds, behind in his rent, and in a state of disheveled personal appearance so that he could not find employment. LaCross claimed that the holdup was a spur-of-the-moment act and that he had not had a gun or other weapon, but only an empty pop bottle in his pocket. With the money LaCross squared his debts, improved his personal appearance, secured a job and saved his earnings so that he could make restitution.

[z] *E.g.*, State v. Chavez, 77 N.M. 79, 419 P.2d 456 (1966).

Respondent LaCross pleaded "not guilty" to a criminal information charging him with robbery—punishable by imprisonment for not less than five years. Thereafter, LaCross withdrew his former plea and entered a plea of "guilty" which was accepted by Judge D. H. Hays. The record does not indicate whether judgment of conviction was entered on the plea. On February 6, 1962, the day set for sentencing, LaCross appeared before Judge Henry S. Stevens, who continued the time for sentencing until February 13, 1962 with the recommendation that the information be amended to charge LaCross with grand theft—punishable by imprisonment for not less than one year. The County Attorney of Maricopa County refused this suggestion and time for sentencing was again continued until December 18, 1962. During the intervening months LaCross' conduct was exemplary.

On December 18, 1962 the County Attorney again refused to amend the information. Judge Stevens, noting that the County Attorney had reduced the charge from robbery to grand theft in several less meritorious instances, and feeling that LaCross had not earned a robbery conviction and that it was more just that he go forth into life with no conviction than to go forth as a convicted robber, set aside the plea of guilty and dismissed the cause with prejudice. The County Attorney seeks a writ of certiorari to review the lower court's proceedings.

A court has no power, in the absence of statute or rule, to dismiss a good information or indictment over the protests or objection of the prosecuting attorney.

The County Attorney has formulated a policy against reducing charges for violent crimes. In arriving at his decision to prosecute respondent LaCross for robbery rather than for grand theft, the County Attorney considered the nature of the offense (a crime against the person); the prevalence of that crime in the county at that time; the fact that a crime had been committed; and the fact that respondent LaCross had pleaded guilty to robbery and such plea had been accepted. In view of these considerations we cannot say that the petitioner abused his discretion in prosecuting this respondent pursuant to the law and the policy of his office.

The order dismissing the information against Paul Raymond LaCross is annulled and set aside.

A closely-related objection is to repeated prosecution. For example, the prosecutor may choose to withhold some charges so that he will have a basis for later prosecution if the result in the first is disappointing to him, *e.g.*, separate prosecutions of a man for shooting his wife and two of his children, or separate prosecutions of a man for robbing several victims in the same tavern holdup. This serial prosecution is permitted by present constitutional interpretation but is frequently controlled by statute. A substantial number of jurisdictions require that all offenses growing out of a single course of conduct be joined in one prosecution; others merely permit such joinder; a few take the opposite position of forbidding prosecution for more than one offense at a time. (In these the technical objection is that the charge is "duplicitous.")

Within this category one also finds the circumstances which are challenged as double jeopardy, including those involving successive prosecutions by state and federal governments for conduct which violates the laws of both governments. Present constitutional interpretation leaves technically open the question whether protection against double jeopardy by repeated state prosecutions is to be found in the due process clause of the fourteenth amendment; almost surely due process will be so interpreted.[a] Instead, the live issue is whether the fourteenth amendment protection against state action is the same as the fifth amendment protection against the federal government. As to successive federal and state prosecutions the Supreme Court rulings thus far permit them, though the question continues to be a close one.

UNITED STATES v. SUTTON
245 F. Supp. 357 (D. Md. 1965)

NORTHROP, District Judge. Sutton is charged with having transported falsely-made money orders across state lines, with unlawful and fraudulent intent, knowing them to have been falsely made. The basis of Sutton's motion to dismiss is a directed verdict of acquittal rendered him by Judge Prendergast in the Criminal Court of Baltimore City. The indictment which brought him to that court included charges of larceny and receiving the same money orders now described in the federal indictment.

II. DOUBLE JEOPARDY

In United States v. Lanza,[6] prosecution in the federal courts was allowed to follow prosecution and conviction in the state

---

[a] *See* State v. Fletcher, 3 CR. L. RPTR. 2153 (Ohio Ct. Common Pleas, Cuyahoga County 1968).

[6] 260 U.S. 377 (1922).

courts for the same acts. Relying on Lanza, a majority of six justices again allowed a federal prosecution to follow a state conviction in Abbate v. United States.[7] A majority of five justices allowed a state prosecution to follow a federal acquittal in Bartkus v. Illinois.[8] Admittedly, these cases do not cover precisely the present sequence of state acquittal followed by federal prosecution. Prior consideration of the present factual pattern is not, however, totally absent.

I now turn to the recent case of Ferina v. United States,[13] which is relied upon strongly by the United States.

"The plea of double jeopardy is not only inappropriately raised where, as in the instant case, there is a lack of identity between the two offenses due to the dissimilarity in the elements of proof, . . . but also is improvidently asserted even if given identical offenses, [for] their proscription emanates from different sovereigns. . . . [citing Abbate, Bartkus, and Lanza]

"Counsel for petitioner urges that we take the initiative and hold contrary to the majority opinions in these decisions because subsequent changes in personnel on the bench of the Supreme Court have resulted in a realignment of majority opinion now favoring the dissenter's argument that the Fifth Amendment prohibition against double jeopardy was 'intended to establish a broad national policy against federal courts trying or punishing a man a second time after acquittal or conviction in any court.' Dissenting opinion of Mr. Justice Black, Abbate v. United States, supra, 359 U.S. at 203.

> "This Court does not forecast the law of the Supreme Court when and if it should decide to reverse itself on the issues raised here. We are obliged to rigorously apply the prevailing, majority precedent."[15]

This court has studied with care the six separate opinions in Abbate and Bartkus. Further, it recognizes that Barnhart[16] involved elements of frontier justice and Indian wars, that the lengthy quotation from Ferina is dictum, that there is no Fourth Circuit case on point, that Bartkus involved the Fourteenth Amendment while the present case involves the Fifth Amendment, and that situations such as the one now presented are rare (perhaps indicating a certain understandable distaste for prosecutions following acquittals). While one can appreciate Mr. Justice

---

7 359 U.S. 187 (1959).

8 359 U.S. 121 (1959).

13 340 F.2d 837 (8 Cir. [1965]).

15 Id. at 839.

16 22 Fed. 285 (C.C.D. Ore. 1884).

Black's lament in Abbate that "the legal logic used to prove one thing to be two is too subtle . . . to grasp,"[17] this court reads the majority opinions in Abbate and Bartkus as permitting a subsequent federal prosecution where, as here, the charges are of different offenses against different sovereigns, where the interests sought to be protected by each sovereign are different, and where the defendant has not yet been placed in jeopardy in a federal court for a federal offense which differs materially from any prior offense, arising out of the same or related conduct, for which he has been tried.

It is, therefore, this first day of September, 1965,

Ordered that the motion to dismiss the indictment be, and hereby is, denied.

Though not available as a remedy in any individual case, one of the possibilities for limiting prosecutor discretion is the enactment of more precise substantive laws. Legislative commands to the prosecutor to act are likely to be ineffectual except as a general admonition.

THE CHALLENGE OF A MODEL PENAL CODE
By Herbert Wechsler
65 Harvard Law Review 1097, 1102 (1952)†

. . . A society that holds, as we do, to belief in law cannot regard with unconcern the fact that prosecuting agencies can exercise so large an influence on dispositions that involve the penal sanction, without reference to any norms but those that they may create for themselves. Whatever one would hold as to the need for discretion of this order in a proper system or the wisdom of attempting regulation of its exercise, it is quite clear that its existence cannot be accepted as a substitute for a sufficient law. Indeed, one of the major consequences of the state of penal law today is that administration has so largely come to dominate the field without effective guidance from the law. This is to say that to a large extent we have, in this important sense, abandoned law—and this within an area where our fundamental teaching calls most strongly for its vigorous supremacy.

2. *Self-imposed Policies as to Prosecution*

As was noted at 432-39, the prosecutor (or the police when they bear prime responsibility for decision on prosecution questions) sometimes establishes for himself and his subordinates

---

17 359 U.S. at 202.

guidelines as to when not to charge. Similarly he may articulate policies regarding when to charge with the more severe of alternatives and when to charge a second time one who has been previously prosecuted for the same course of conduct. Though informal guidelines in the sense of routine practice in an office are common enough, articulated policy standards are unusual.

The Justice Department has adopted a policy in tax cases to prosecute only where there is both subjective belief in the offender's guilt and near certainty of conviction. Kaplan, *The Prosecutorial Discretion—A Comment,* 60 Nw. U.L. Rev. 174, 191 (1965), cites as Department of Justice policies that Mann Act prosecutions are to be avoided in noncommercial cases where no aggravating circumstances exist, and that petty violations of the Taft-Hartley Act (such as exchanges of small Christmas gifts between labor leaders and employers) should not be prosecuted. For some time there was a rigid policy of prosecuting all persons guilty of airplane bomb hoaxes (by joking about a bomb in their luggage). When one of the jokesters turned out to be a Roman Catholic priest the rule of automatic prosecution was replaced by a more flexible policy. A prosecution of a husband and wife for mailing obscene matter (by having mailed undeveloped films of one another posing in the nude to an out-of-state firm for developing) was inconsistent with written Department of Justice policy that obscene private correspondence should be prosecuted only in cases of repeated violations or other aggravating circumstances. Though conviction was obtained and affirmed on appeal, the Solicitor General moved in the Supreme Court to have the judgment vacated and the information dismissed. The motion was granted.[b]

---

[b] Redmond v. United States, 384 U.S. 264 (1966). In the similar case of Cox v. United States, 370 F.2d 563 (9th Cir. 1967), the court of appeals asked the Solicitor General to express his views on the case before it. In response the Justice Department moved that the case be ordered dismissed. But in Heath v. United States, 375 F.2d 521 (8th Cir. 1967), the court of appeals refused to vacate the judgment on the motion of defendant where the Solicitor General had made no such request. The *Redmond* policy was approved also in a state case, State v. Haas, 159 N.W.2d 118 (Minn. 1968). *Compare* Note, *The Confession of Error,* 1968 Utah L. Rev. 286, 303-05.

In Orlando v. United States, 387 F.2d 348 (9th Cir. 1967), the court of appeals ordered the conviction vacated upon motion of the Justice Department because conviction was obtained in violation of a policy against multiple prosecutions for offenses growing out of a single transaction. In dissent Justice Pope said, "I think it is no part of our function to take orders from the Department of Justice in respect to the latter's policies. As stated in *Coronet v. United States,* . . . 'There comes a time in the processes of the enforcement of the law when a case belongs to the court. No error of the trial court is suggested by the government, but only a change in its prosecution policies.' The Government's motion to vacate the judgment of conviction was denied and properly, I think."

LAW TRAINING BULLETIN SERIES
Chicago Police Department, vol. 1, no. 1, Aug. 15, 1966

SYNDICATED GAMBLING

A new section prohibiting syndicated gambling (§ 28-1.1) was added to the Criminal Code. . . .

. . . Thus with regard to policy, neither the bettor himself nor the person he places the bet with such as the "policy station" operator or "walking writer" can be charged with syndicated gambling, but each person in the chain after that, such as the "pickup men" or "runners," the "turn-in spot" operators, and the wheel headquarters personnel can be charged with syndicated gambling. . . .

There is no minimum number or amount of bets which must be proven in order to get a conviction for syndicated gambling when operation of a policy game is charged.

Under 28-1.1(b) a person also commits syndicated gambling when he engages in the business of bookmaking. . . .

In order for such bookmaking to constitute syndicated gambling, however, the accused must have accepted *more* than *five* bets or wagers totaling *more* than $2,000. The subsection does not tell us whether the required number and amount of bets must be taken in one hour, day, week, or lifetime, but it is clear that bets on more than one race or other event may be added together to reach the required number and amount. This will be a matter for the courts to decide. . . .

Great care should be taken in charging syndicated gambling for several reasons.[c] First, as can be seen from subsection (a) of this section, it is aimed specifically at professional gambling and the purpose of a law should always be borne in mind in determining whether a violation has been committed. Second, syndicated gambling is a serious offense. It is a felony and carries a mandatory one year and up to a possible five-year maximum penalty. It is a new law enforcement tool designed to combat organized crime. If it is used indiscriminately we will in effect lose it. The courts will be reluctant to find a defendant guilty and sentence him to one year (minimum) in the penitentiary for what the judge believes to be unimportant or minor violation of the law. The courts will find or make loopholes in the law in order to free the accused. These decisions will become precedent and then even the serious offender will go unconvicted. Finally, the law is unclear in several respects and requires judicial interpretation. If only the best cases go before

[c] In Chicago the initial charging responsibility is left to the police in most cases.

the courts, they will be inclined to interpret the section favorably to the police.

For these reasons, *no charges should be brought under § 28-1.1 without the prior approval of the Director of the Vice Control Division, Bureau of Inspectional Services.* If it is determined that Syndicated Gambling should not be charged the defendant should of course be charged with gambling under § 28-1.

MEMORANDUM

February 17, 1956

TO THE STAFF:
FROM: W.J. [District Attorney]
RE: Abandonment and Nonsupport Cases; Use of URESA

Recently several cases have come to my attention which left me with the impression that some of you may be a little "pencil happy" when it comes to issuing warrants for abandonment and nonsupport.

In two of the instances referred to, although the arrearage was only a couple of hundred dollars over a short period of time and a complete address was available for the husband, no attempt was made to contact him by letter nor was it referred to Mrs. Kent for action under the URESA. In the one case it was learned after extradition proceedings had progressed to the point where the man was picked up on the warrant, that he had been unemployed for several months and thus had been unable to keep up his payments. Naturally our extradition proceedings were dropped, but think of the unnecessary work involved.

In the future in handling complaints of nonsupport and abandonment where the URESA has not been attempted and where the case is not flagrant or aggravated, and where you have the husband's complete address, I suggest that you:

(1) Contact the husband by letter, and if that fails to bring satisfactory results, then
(2) Refer the case to Mrs. Kent for action under URESA.

MEMORANDUM

April 11, 1955

TO THE STAFF:
FROM: W.J.

On complaints for sale of mortgaged property or conditional sales or failure to inform of encumbrance, where there is a sale, be sure the complainant has exhausted all remedies.

If alleged wrongdoer is in state try to handle it by correspondence or getting party into office.

Do not be so hasty in making criminals out of people who may just have run into some tough luck.[d]

'TACTICS' CAUSED DALTON'S OUSTER
Wisconsin State Journal, June 27, 1968

MARINETTE (AP)—Atty. Gen. Bronson C. La Follette said Wednesday he ousted his criminal investigation chief because he feared "totalitarian tactics" might be used to combat organized crime.

"I do not believe the awesome powers of criminal investigation should ever be used to harass anyone," . . .

"If we accept Mr. Dalton's philosophy concerning criminal process, then the prosecutor becomes the sole judge of who poses a threat," . . .

When Dalton's ouster was disclosed a week ago, La Follette explained that Dalton had undertaken without his knowledge an investigation of a Milwaukee tavern in which banker Howard J. Meister had a financial interest. [Meister had been acquitted of allegedly improper conduct with respect to branch banking legislation.]

La Follette cited "main differences" he had with Dalton concerning the philosophy of criminal investigation and prosecution.

"He believes," La Follette said, "that whenever possible, even though the state may not have a good case, one should be brought anyway to focus public attention on corruption . . . and to expose the accused because information garnered from the intelligence files indicates that the person is already guilty of being a part of an overall criminal conspiracy."

"That is why many of the most important cases he brought were lost in court," the attorney general added.[e]

---

[d] "On June 23, the New Jersey County Prosecutors, in a meeting in Trenton, proposed a liberalized interpretation of the state's 118-year-old abortion law:

"Physicians should be allowed to perform abortions in cases other than when a mother's life is endangered.

"There was one dissent—Middlesex County Prosecutor Edward J. Dolan—and two others did not vote. It was not clear whether the proposal would be binding on all." Trial Magazine, June-July 1967, at 40.

Police and prosecutor policies are frequently considered highly confidential, to prevent criticism for "rewriting the law." *See, e.g.*, United States v. Edwards, 368 F.2d 722, 724 (4th Cir. 1966) (referring to confidential policy manual in forfeiture matters).

[e] *Compare with* pp. 64-67 and pp. 311-26.

MEMORANDUM
United States Government, Department of Justice

December 23, 1963

To: Members of the Advisory Committee on the Federal Rules of Criminal Procedure
From: Herbert J. Miller, Jr., Assistant Attorney General Criminal Division
Subject: Proposed Amendments to Rule 8

The Department of Justice is opposed to the adoption of the proposed amendment to Rule 8, which would require the compulsory joinder of "all offenses based on the same act or transactions" known to the Government attorney at the time an indictment or information is filed. The comments attached to the Committee's proposal indicate that the purpose of the amendment is to prevent repeated prosecution of substantially the same conduct. The type cited is that found in Hoag v. New Jersey, 356 U.S. 464 (1958) (multiple prosecutions to obtain a robbery conviction) and that typified by Ciucci v. Illinois, 356 U.S. 571 (1958) (multiple prosecutions to obtain the death penalty). However, in the Federal system there is a Governmental policy against such prosecutions, so that a Rule for this purpose is unnecessary. Moreover, the proposed amendment would both create substantial problems to the effective enforcement of the criminal laws, and could well work to the prejudice of criminal defendants. In the absence of some present abuse, there is no justification for approving a Rule certain to give rise to new difficulties.

1. The Federal policy against multiple prosecutions stems from that announced following the Supreme Court's decision in Abbate v. United States, 359 U.S. 187 (1959), which held that the Federal Government may, consistent with the double jeopardy clause of the Constitution, try a defendant for conduct previously the subject of state prosecution. One week after *Abbate* had been decided, the Attorney General issued a memorandum to all United States Attorneys, declaring that the power to bring a second prosecution would, as in the past, be "used sparingly by the Department of Justice. . . . After a state prosecution, there should be no Federal trial for the same act or acts unless the reasons are compelling" and unless approval is obtained from an Assistant Attorney General, with the consent of the Attorney General. . . .

"In such event I doubt that it is wise or practical to attempt to formulate detailed rules to deal with the complex situation which might develop, particularly because a series of related acts are often involved. However, no Federal case should be tried when there has already been a state prosecution for substantially the same act or acts without the United States Attorney first submitting a recommendation to the appropriate Assistant Attorney General in the Department. No such recommendation should be approved by the Assistant Attorney General in charge of the Division without having it first brought to my attention."[f] . . .

Shortly thereafter, in December 1959, this policy was expressly declared to apply to successive Federal prosecutions. In Petite v. United States, 361 U.S. 529 (1960), certiorari was granted to consider a double jeopardy claim raised by a conviction for the subornation of perjury with regard to two false statements made in Baltimore. The defendant in that case had previously been convicted of conspiracy in another district on his plea of *nolo contendere,* two of the overt acts charged in the earlier indictment having been the making of the false statements in Baltimore. The case was disposed of when the Court granted the Solicitor General's motion to vacate the judgment below and to remand for dismissal of the indictment, the Court noting the following expression of policy set forth in the Government's brief:

> It has generally been the policy of the Federal Government that several offenses arising out of a single transaction should be alleged and tried together and should not be made the basis of multiple prosecutions, a policy dictated by considerations both of fairness to defendants and of efficient and orderly law enforcement. Govt. Br. No. 45, 1959 Term, pp. 3-4; 361 U.S. at 530.

The policy of self-restraint recognized in *Petite* has thus far been faithfully observed by Federal authorities. In Marakar v. United States, 370 U.S. 723 (1962), the defendants were convicted of violating 21 U.S.C. 174 after previously having been acquitted by the court on a conspiracy charge relating to the same conduct. On petition for certiorari, the Solicitor General again moved the Supreme Court for an order vacating the affirmance of the conviction because the second prosecution was

---

[f] At the outset the policy was not applied to wagering tax, liquor tax, and narcotics tax cases, but in 1965 the policy was extended to these cases also.

"not in accord with the policy of the Federal Government as stated in the Government's memorandum filed in the *Petite* case," Govt. Br., Nos. 1191 Misc., 1234 Misc., 1961 Term, p. 2, and the motion was granted. In United States v. Bundy (M.D. Tenn., 1960), the Department of Justice directed the United States Attorney to move for the vacation of a conviction under 18 U.S.C. 472 and 473, where the defendant had previously been convicted of conspiring to violate the same statutes. . . .

In the *Petite* brief, however, it was also recognized by the Government that exceptional circumstances might arise in which a second prosecution would be justified. Govt. Br. pp. 4-5. Such circumstances may arise because of the constitutionally imposed restrictions on the Government's right to amend an indictment, *Ex Parte* Bain, 121 U.S. 1 (1886); Stirone v. United States, 361 U.S. 212 (1960), and to appeal from a judgment of acquittal despite clear trial court error, Fong Foo v. United States, 369 U.S. 141 (1962). . . .

Thus, the Department has authorized a second prosecution in rare cases in which prior indictments have been dismissed as defective. . . .

Though given consideration by the Department, the *Petite* policy has also been deemed inapplicable in some instances involving related but separate transactions, ordinarily where evidence of the other offense was not available at the time of the original indictment. In United States v. Sanchez, (S.D. Calif., 1963), the defendant was tried and convicted for transporting heroin in February, 1963, after he had been acquitted, upon a finding of entrapment, for a similar offense committed in July, 1963. The two offenses were not charged in the same indictment because no evidence to corroborate the testimony of the Government informer was available as to the February offense at the time the first indictment was returned. In United States v. Flanagan, (N.D. Tex., 1963), the defendant was indicted separately for two Mann Act offenses, the first based on the transportation of a woman from Dallas, Texas, to Hot Springs, Arkansas, and the second based on her transportation back to Big Spring, Texas, five days later. Separate trial and conviction on the second indictment were deemed appropriate because the Government lacked evidence corroborating the victim's testimony when the indictments were returned, and because the indictments could not have been tried together without the defendant's consent, the two Texas towns being located in different judicial districts. (See Brief in Opposition to Petition for Certiorari, No. 1083 Misc., 1962 Term, at 7 n. 4). In United States v. McCue, (D. Conn., 1959), after the culmination of criminal proceedings for the wilful evasion of income taxes for the years 1950 and 1951, the Department authorized a prosecution under 18 U.S.C. 1001 for the making of false statements in 1954 to IRS agents who were investigating the defendant's 1950 and 1951 tax liabilities.[10] And on occasion the Department has also authorized perjury prosecutions based on the false testimony made by a defendant during the course of prior proceedings against him.[11]

A final instance of a second indictment justified by the earlier unavailability of critical evidence is the case of United States v. Slaughter, (E.D. N.C., 1963), where the defendant has been indicted for first degree murder under 18 U.S.C. 1111, after having previously been acquitted of a Dyer Act charge relating to the transportation of the car the defendant allegedly had stolen from the murder victim. When indicted for the Dyer Act charge, the United States Attorney considered that he did not at the time have sufficient evidence for a murder indictment.[12]

3. *External Pressures upon the Prosecutor*

The prosecutor is a political official, a member of a profession, and an individual. In each capacity he feels pressures. He would hope to avoid the ire of powerful interest groups in the

[10] In this case the Department was of the view that substantial justice had not been done in tax evasion prosecution because a United States Attorney, contrary to Department policy and to clear and repeated instructions, had allowed one defendant to plead *nolo contendere* to the violation of Sec. 145(a) of the 1939 Code, a misdemeanor section, although he had been indicted under Sec. 145(b), a felony provision. The Department sought to vacate the first judgment on the ground that Sec. 145(a) is not a lesser included offense included in Sec. 145(b), but the motion was denied. The United States Attorney had consented to the dismissal of the indictment against the second defendant. See Brief in Opposition to Petition for Certiorari, No. 981, 1961 Term, at 10-14.

[11] In United States v. VanLiew (N.D. Tex., 1961), the defendants were first charged with mislabeling in violation of the Food, Drug, and Cosmetic Act, 21 U.S.C. 301-92. They were subsequently indicted for perjury committed in a civil action to enjoin the same mislabeling. The Department was of the view that each prosecution was based on a separate and different act.

[12] Other considerations which prompted the Department to proceed with the murder charge were that the crime was a heinous one, a calculated and brutal murder, the murder was of a soldier, it occurred on an Army base where 40,000 troops were stationed, it was surrounded by much publicity, and the prosecution was strongly favored by the Department of Defense. The acquittal of the Dyer Act charge was granted by the Court on the ground that there was no evidence that the victim owned the car or that the defendant lacked permission to drive it. Moreover, the defendant is considered a person dangerous to society, who should be confined; the Government has moved in the second case for an examination pursuant to 18 U.S.C. 4244, to determine whether Slaughter is presently competent to stand trial.

community, the criticism of the newspapers, criticism from the bench and bar, withdrawal of cooperation by other agencies on whom he must rely, ridicule or rejection by friends. These concerns constantly operate to help shape his choices as prosecutor.

JUDGE CRITICIZES 'INCONSISTENCY' IN D.A.'S OFFICE

Wisconsin State Journal, May 20, 1965

Judge William L. Buenzli Wednesday criticized the district attorney's office for "inconsistency" in its handling of petty theft cases.

Buenzli, sitting in Criminal Court, noted that in the past two days defendants with nearly identical records were prosecuted for nearly identical crimes but charged with different offenses.

Buenzli leveled the criticism after Asst. Dist. Atty. Earl H. Munson Jr. charged one defendant with disorderly conduct for shoplifting less than $5 worth of merchandise and immediately thereafter Asst. Dist. Atty. James C. Boll charged another defendant with petty theft for shoplifting merchandise worth a similar amount.

The judge noted that Tuesday three other persons were charged with petty theft for stealing similar amounts of merchandise and all had similar records.

"I think it would be much better for law enforcement if people were charged with a proper charge rather than a fictitious charge," Buenzli said, referring to the disorderly conduct charge.

The judge said that different charges for the same offenses at the discretion of the assistant district attorney who is handling the case are unfair and inconsistent.

CURBS ON SHOPLIFTING URGED

By Richard W. Jaeger

Wisconsin State Journal, June 30, 1968

Reduction of Charges Is Criticized

Dane County courts are not helping to curb the $1.5 million problem of shoplifting that faces the Madison metropolitan area, Richard Johnston, assistant director of the Madison Chamber of Commerce, charges.

Johnston's criticism comes in light of recent court actions reducing petty theft charges against shoplifters to charges of disorderly conduct.

Most of the charge reductions have been granted to first-time offenders. The contention has been that petty theft charges on their records would blemish their futures.

Petty theft charges are for violations of state law. The disorderly conduct charge is an ordinance violation and a lesser charge. . . .

"The district attorney has used a get-tough policy by asking for strong penalties in the prosecution of offenders," Johnston added.

Dist. Atty. James Boll has recently criticized the courts for reducing the petty theft charges. He charges that this has hindered his department in prosecuting offenders. . . .

Circuit Judge Richard W. Bardwell offered a suggestion of enacting a city shoplifting ordinance in an effort to curb the reduced charges trend.

Bardwell himself had reduced petty theft charges in two cases against University of Wisconsin students when sitting as a County Judge.

He said that the thefts involved items valued under $2 and felt that the petty theft law which governs thefts up to $100 was too strict in the cases involved.

D. THE RELATION OF THE CHARGING DECISION TO THE PRACTICES OF OTHER AGENCIES

The prosecutor does not act in isolation. His decisions are affected by what others do, and in turn his decisions help create the context in which others act.

To whatever extent the prosecutor fails to exercise careful discretion in operation of his office, he thrusts greater responsibility upon the police or the courts to exercise discretion in their handling of cases. If he prosecuted fully every case in which the evidence would support a conviction, clearly someone else would have to screen out unwise or overly severe charges. For example, the police might feel compelled to refuse to arrest or to bring the matter to the prosecutor's attention; or the court might feel obliged to dismiss charges or exercise its wide power over sentence. On the other hand, if the prosecutor is thought to be undercharging, either out of a different evaluation of the conduct or out of a desire to express his disapproval of police conduct, he prevents the case getting to the courts and has substantial impact on police practices. With respect to many crimes where police are motivated by a desire to see offenders prosecuted, the refusal to prosecute has some sanctioning power and conformity may follow. But if police find conformity impractical the prosecutor forces them to alternative actions. Of course, in many circumstances prosecution is not the prime police concern (*see* pp. 252-59, *supra*). In these situations the prosecutor's position is essentially irrelevant.[g]

ARREST: THE DECISION TO TAKE A SUSPECT INTO CUSTODY 514-17 (1965)

By Wayne R. LaFave

(Little, Brown & Company)

The role of the prosecutor. Although the prosecuting attorney is an important participant in the criminal justice system, he does not ordinarily play a major role in the arrest decision. However, by the manner in which he makes decisions on whether to charge arrested suspects, he may have an important indirect effect upon police practice. This is particularly so in cases in which the police view conviction as the primary objective of the arrest.

The rural prosecutor is more likely to play a significant role in the development and carrying out of a law enforcement policy than is the urban prosecutor. He is accessible to the police and in some situations may be regularly consulted prior to arrest. The contribution of the rural prosecutor is limited primarily by the fact that he is commonly inexperienced. In contrast, the urban prosecutor seldom becomes involved in a case prior to arrest. Nor does he ordinarily have occasion to review or evaluate existing law enforcement policies and practices. His attention is usually focused upon individual cases of assumed major importance, while his often overworked and inexperienced assistants find that all of their time is needed in determining charges,

---

[g] The interrelationship of objectives is complex. For example, there can be charging which is not expected to result in full prosecution but is dictated by administrative considerations. Chicago police who stop and frisk a person without adequate cause and find a gun know that prosecution for illegal possession of the weapon is futile because there is no admissible evidence of guilt, yet they routinely file charges against him. They are not motivated principally by a desire to inconvenience the offender as much as they can, or by the hope that the issue may not be raised by him, but by the necessity to justify confiscation of the gun. The gun must be accounted for in police department channels, and it would be unacceptable to identify it as taken from a person who had not been arrested and charged. Knives seized in similar situations may simply be discarded or dumped in a basket without identification, but guns (which can be identified, may have been licensed, or might have been used in a crime which could be solved through ballistic examination) require special treatment.

preparing for and appearing at trials, and conducting the routine business of the office.

Appraisal of the role of the prosecutor is made difficult because that role is inevitably more ambiguous than that of the police or the trial court. It is clear that the police are concerned with the detection of crime and the identification and apprehension of offenders; it is likewise apparent that courts must decide the issue of guilt or innocence. A prosecutor, however, may conceive of his principal responsibility in a number of different ways. He may serve primarily as trial counsel for the police department, reflecting the views of the department in his court representation. Or he may serve as a sort of "house counsel" for the police, giving legal advice to the department on how to develop enforcement practices which will withstand challenge in court. On the other hand, the prosecutor may consider himself primarily a representative of the court, with the responsibility of enforcing rules designed to control police practices and perhaps otherwise acting for the benefit of persons who are being proceeded against. Another possibility is that the prosecutor, as an elected official (while the police are increasingly appointive and the judiciary is increasingly insulated from political pressures), will try primarily to reflect community opinion in the making of decisions as to whether to prosecute. The uncertainty as to whether the prosecutor is responsible for all these tasks and as to which is his primary responsibility creates difficult problems in current administration.[h]

Prosecutors do serve as trial counsel, at least in cases involving relatively serious crimes. The difficulty is that when certain police practices are brought into question in court the prosecutor is not likely to be in a position to articulate the relevant problems as they appear to the police. This is because he is relatively detached from the day-to-day problems of the police and from the enforcement practice which gives rise to the legal issue. While private counsel representing a business client would believe it to be of utmost importance to consult fully with his client, prosecutors commonly proceed on the assumption that the police need not be consulted. A prosecutor who understood the problems of the police would not only be in a better position to focus the attention of the trial courts on the true nature of the issues before them, but also could better decide what issues are in greatest need of clarification from the appellate courts.

---

[h] There has been little concern for insuring high quality of the prosecutor in the past; *but see* THE PRESIDENT'S COMMISSION ON LAW ENFORCEMENT AND ADMINISTRATION OF JUSTICE, TASK FORCE REPORT: THE COURTS 72-75 (1967).

There is uncertainty as to which agency has responsibility for serving as "house counsel" for the police. The prosecutor has seldom assumed this function; indeed, in many locales communication between the prosecutor and the police chief is almost nonexistent. The police, if in need of a "legal advisor," are expected to deal with the city attorney or the municipal corporation counsel, although these officers do not have responsibility for the trial of criminal cases or for arguing the propriety of police practices on appeal. However, the city attorney and the corporation counsel seldom view consultation with police as a major responsibility, and typically the relationship is limited to occasional consultation on the propriety of certain practices which might cause an action against the officer or the city. Efforts of police departments to add competent counsel to their staffs have been resisted on the ground that legal advice is adequately provided by the city attorney, corporation counsel, or prosecuting attorney.

There are occasions when the prosecutor does act, in effect, as a representative of the court in controlling police practices and in insuring maximum protection of those subjected to arrest, search, and detention. Involvement of the prosecutor in certain minor cases seems explainable only on the ground that there is a need to minimize the effect of unfair police action. Yet prosecutors are sometimes criticized for not utilizing their most direct means of control: refusal to charge when the fact of prosecution would constitute tacit approval of clearly improper police conduct. It is unclear, however, whether the prosecution agency should assume other tasks directly related to the protection of persons being subjected to the process. This is sometimes done, as illustrated by the existence of the Detroit Release Bureau, operated by the prosecutor's office to afford a means of prompt release without bail in minor cases. If additional safeguards are added, they may conceivably be made the responsibility of the prosecutor.

Response to public opinion by the prosecutor may take many forms but is most likely to involve an exercise of what traditionally has been referred to as "the prosecutor's discretion." However, this fashioning of enforcement policy by the prosecutor is essentially negative in character; the prosecutor does not directly determine arrest policies but can only eliminate certain of the cases which reach him. There would be greater impact if the prosecutor were to articulate his policies and communicate them to the police. With some exceptions, the police would arrest in conformance with these policies if they knew what they were. While this feedback of the prosecutor's discretion would not eliminate the need for police discretion, it would aid in accomplishing discretionary enforcement at the police level on a much more consistent basis than is presently the case.

Reference Note

Baker, *The Prosecutor—Initiation of Prosecution,* 23 J. CRIM. L. & C. 770 (1933), is an old but still useful discussion of the prosecutor's responsibilities. A number of more recent articles and books give helpful glimpses of the prosecutor's exercise of discretion: Note, *Prosecutor's Discretion,* 103 U. PA. L. REV. 1057 (1955) (Philadelphia); Brezner, *How the Prosecuting Attorney's Office Processes Complaints,* 27 DETROIT LAWYER 3 (1959) (Detroit); Kaplan, *The Prosecutorial Discretion—A Comment,* 60 NW. U.L. REV. 174 (1965) (federal); Mills, *The Prosecutor: Charging and "Bargaining,"* 1966 U. ILL. L.F. 511; Note, *Discretion Exercised by Montana County Attorneys in Criminal Prosecutions,* 28 MONT. L. REV. 41 (1966); E. SUBIN, CRIMINAL JUSTICE IN A METROPOLITAN COURT 29-39, 52-57 (1966) (District of Columbia).[1]

Chapters 7 and 8 of D. NEWMAN, CONVICTION: THE DETERMINATION OF GUILT OR INNOCENCE WITHOUT TRIAL (1966), deal with charge reduction and consider factors equally applicable to the initial decision to charge.

A major study of the charging decision by Frank W. Miller, entitled Prosecution, based upon the American Bar Foundation survey, will be published soon.

---

[1] Gillespie, *The Securities and Exchange Commission and Criminal Violations of the Federal Securities Laws,* 1 IND. L.F. 152, 184-88 (1967), describes policy and practice of investigation and prosecution of securities offenses by the SEC.

Hurried in-court charging decisions are illustrated by M. MAYER, THE LAWYERS 149-55 (1967) (New York felony "arraignment" court).

Chapter 7

INITIAL APPEARANCE

Almost universally, police are commanded by statute to take arrested persons promptly before a magistrate. One of the principal objectives of this initial appearance[a] before the magistrate is to establish bail on which the prisoner may be released. Consequently the police are reluctant to take the prisoner for his initial appearance until the investigation is complete. Sometimes the investigation has been completed before arrest, or it may be completed within a short time after the arrest, so that loss of control by the police over the person arrested does not interfere with the investigation. But in other instances police consider it important to retain control.

In the federal system the command to take the prisoner before a magistrate without unnecessary delay was reinforced, under the *McNabb* and *Mallory* cases, by a rule excluding any confession obtained during an improper delay. The Supreme Court has not yet identified this exclusionary rule as a matter of constitutional requirement, so the states almost universally refused to follow suit.[b] As a consequence, delay for the purpose

---

[a] This procedure is often called "arraignment," but that term is more generally reserved for the proceeding at which an accused formally pleads to the indictment or information filed against him. Distinction may be made between "arraignment on the warrant" and "arraignment on the indictment." This procedure is also sometimes called the "preliminary examination" or "preliminary hearing," which confuses it with the subsequent proceeding in which the magistrate reviews the evidence to see whether a prisoner can properly be held in jail, or under bail, to await trial. The term "presentation before a magistrate" is not so much confusing as cumbersome. "Initial appearance" seems the least confusing and most convenient term.

[b] Wisconsin has adopted the *McNabb-Mallory* rule as a matter of state and federal constitutional law, with one qualification: "[T]he due process clause does not foreclose completely the police from interrogating the person after arrest and before taking him before a magistrate. But the right to interrogate after arrest is limited and must be for the purpose of determining whether to release the suspect or if he has been arrested without a warrant to make a formal complaint. . . . While one may be detained by the police and interrogated to secure sufficient evidence to either charge him with a crime or to release him, the police cannot continue to detain an arrested person to 'sew up' the case by obtaining or extracting a confession or culpable statements to support the arrest or the guilt." Phillips v. State, 29 Wis. 2d 521,

of completing the investigation sometimes occurs in the states. And since the Crime Control Act of 1968 undertook to overturn the *McNabb-Mallory* rule, the exclusion of confessions is no longer available in the federal system either.[c] But in any event, if no confession is sought or obtained, there is no established alternative sanction in either state or federal courts.[d]

Because prompt presentation for initial appearance before a magistrate is important for release on bail, for contacting counsel, and for expeditious handling of criminal cases, it is worth inquiring into the reasons for and mechanisms of delay.

ARREST: THE DECISION TO TAKE A SUSPECT INTO CUSTODY 303-08 (1965)

By Wayne R. LaFave

(Little, Brown & Company)

In a great many cases no investigation is needed and appearance before the magistrate occurs on the day of arrest or the next morning. Those held for investigation are processed to the detective bureau for interrogation or other checking. Thus the availability of detectives is a significant factor in the length of time a particular suspect is held, and this is dependent on the working hours of the detectives. For example, in Detroit the bulk of the detective force goes on duty at 8:00 A.M. Though cases involving a suspect in custody take precedence over others, each detective team has a number of cases assigned to it, often more than can be disposed of in one day. Most judges in Recorder's Court will not handle initial appearances after 11:00 A.M. and this means that the detectives must have satisfied themselves that there is sufficient evidence for a warrant and must be at the prosecutor's office not later than 10:00 A.M. so that the complaint and warrant can be prepared and approved. Thus, unless the investigation can be completed in two hours, the suspect who is to be charged will probably be held over to the following day.

534-35, 139 N.W.2d 41, 47 (1966). Apparently an effort must be made to obtain a magistrate rather than wait until the next court day. Reimers v. State, 31 Wis. 2d 457, 143 N.W.2d 525 (1966) (excessive delay when weekend was followed by holiday).

[c] 18 U.S.C. § 3501(c); *see* p. 399, *supra.*

[d] Mallory v. United States, 354 U.S. 449 (1957), and United States v. Hall, 348 F.2d 837 (2d Cir. 1965), suggest that while delay for the purpose of interrogation is improper there may be some delay to permit the mechanical steps of booking, to give opportunity for recovery of stolen property or location of a kidnapped person, to allow checking out exculpatory statements, or to avoid warning to a confederate who is still being sought.

Investigation of persons in custody usually involves questioning but may also include holding a lineup, checking records on recent offenses, or checking physical evidence. Some of these investigative devices take considerable time, and additional time is required when the suspected offense is of a kind investigated by a specialized bureau in the department. If the suspect is still at the precinct, he must be transported to headquarters and then back to the precinct. This transfer to specialized bureaus occurs most frequently for robbery, breaking and entering, car theft, and narcotics offenses. . . .

In most cases the investigation is concluded by the time the prosecutor's office becomes involved. If the police are uncertain as to the need for any further investigation they will sometimes confer with the prosecutor without taking the suspect to his office. Occasionally a statement may be taken by the prosecutor, but it is primarily intended as a review of the evidence and verification of the facts provided by the police.

In-custody interrogation is also employed in rural areas, but here the need for such investigation is not so great as in urban centers. The police in urban areas often justify in-custody investigation by referring to the unique problems of a large city, particularly the mobility of the population and the greater number of professional criminals, a point which has received some judicial recognition. Personnel of rural law enforcement agencies are less likely to be aware of the legal limitations on detention and often are not adept at conducting investigations. A local municipal force may depend upon the sheriff to aid in a serious case and the sheriff in turn usually relies upon the district attorney when the case calls for obtaining a statement from the suspect.

When the police have made a formal arrest but feel that further investigation is needed, the practice is to detain the suspect for up to seventy-two hours. At the end of this period the police ordinarily either release the suspect or have him charged and brought before a magistrate for his initial appearance, at which time bail is set. Because this appearance marks the point at which police may lose custody of the suspect, they usually assume that it is necessary to complete their investigation by this time. In many localities even the suspect who cannot make bail will be insulated from the police to some extent by being remanded to other authorities.

As noted earlier, the opportunities for release prior to initial appearance before the magistrate are few. Even if some special procedures have been established for release, they are generally not made available to those whom the police want to retain in custody for further investigation. The suspect may challenge his detention by way of writ of habeas corpus. Even when this procedure is used, particularly in Detroit, and to a lesser extent elsewhere in Michigan and in Wisconsin, judges at habeas corpus hearings will continue the hearing for twenty-four or forty-eight hours and return the suspect to police custody when the police make some showing that they are presently engaged in an in-custody investigation.

Special steps are sometimes taken by the police to insure that they will be able to complete an in-custody investigation without successful challenge. Such measures may be employed because it is doubtful whether there are adequate grounds for arrest for the offense suspected; because of uncertainty about the validity of any in-custody investigation (which is the case in Kansas); or because the police desire a period of time for investigation longer than that ordinarily allowed by the courts. One technique is to arrest for a minor offense, often vagrancy. Either the suspect is convicted of vagrancy or the case is continued for a time. In either event the police will have about ten days to complete their investigation. A similar device, used when the suspect is a probationer or parolee, is to employ a "hold" booking, signifying that he is being held for the probation-parole authorities because his suspicious conduct may constitute possible grounds for revocation. This may or may not be with the concurrence of the probation and parole officials. The probation or parole "hold" is assumed to justify a detention for about ten days.

In those cases in which the investigation is made on the street or at the station prior to arrest, the objective of the officer is to decide whether to make an arrest. In the more frequent case in which an in-custody investigation is made after an arrest, the objective is to obtain additional information sufficient to meet the requirements for the next step in the process, charging the suspect with a crime. The charging decision is ordinarily made by a member of the prosecutor's staff and involves a judgment as to whether there is sufficient evidence to justify prosecution and whether the case is one which ought to be prosecuted under the policy of the prosecutor. In current practice the charging decision is made prior to the first regular appearance of the defendant before a judicial officer and is manifested by the prosecutor's approval of an arrest warrant.

In some cases the police conduct an in-custody investigation even though there is evidence already at hand sufficient to satisfy the prosecutor. Sometimes the objective is to gather more evidence to increase the probability of conviction. In other instances the investigation is directed toward discovering the identity of other offenders or of clearing up other outstanding offenses.

The magistrate has several responsibilities at the initial appearance of an arrested person. At a minimum, the magistrate notifies him of the complaint against him, sets bail, and apprises the defendant of his right to a preliminary examination at which the sufficiency of the evidence to justify prosecution may be tested. Although practice varies, with increasing frequency the magistrate also warns the defendant of his rights to an indictment (in jurisdictions requiring indictment), to remain silent, and to retain counsel or have counsel assigned to assist him if he is indigent.[e]

A. NOTIFYING OF THE CHARGES IN THE COMPLAINT

At the initial appearance the defendant will be notified of the charges against him either by oral statement of the offense or by reading the complaint which contains the charge.

As noted, the period between arrest and initial appearance is used sometimes not only for investigation but also to give the prosecutor an opportunity to approve the charge. In such jurisdictions the prosecutor's office drafts a complaint—and sometimes also an arrest warrant even for a person already under arrest. In other jurisdictions, drafting the complaint is the responsibility of the police department.

This complaint is the formal document essential to the proceedings before the magistrate. When the complaint has been submitted to the magistrate prior to arrest as a basis for obtaining a warrant, its purpose is to set forth the evidentiary facts which justify arrest. When issued following arrest, its function is less clear. At the least, it notifies the defendant of the charge against him by citing the statute allegedly violated. Sometimes it will also set forth evidentiary allegations. The complaint therefore constitutes essential information for the magistrate in setting bail by identifying the charges which the defendant faces,

---

[e] Where there are multiple courts the initial appearance may serve as an occasion for assignment to a particular court. For example, one arrested Friday night in Chicago for an offense involving a gun will appear on Saturday morning in "holiday court" to be ordered held for another initial appearance Monday morning in "gun and rackets court." There bail will be set and an automatic ten-day continuance will be ordered to permit ballistic examination of the gun for possible connection with some other crime.

and sometimes by setting forth additional information concerning the offense.

At the initial appearance the magistrate presumably has power to make substantial inquiry into the facts of the case, but he rarely does so beyond reading the complaint. The congestion in his court is likely to be so great that he has no time for close scrutiny of individual cases.

The Supreme Court said in Mallory v. United States, 354 U.S. 449, 454 (1957):

> The scheme for initiating a federal prosecution is plainly defined. The police may not arrest upon mere suspicion but only on "probable cause." The next step in the proceeding is to arraign the arrested person before a judicial officer as quickly as possible so that he may be advised of his rights and so that the issue of probable cause may be promptly determined.

This language suggests that the magistrate properly reviews the question of probable cause, but this is not commonly the practice. A proposal has been made to amend the Federal Rules of Criminal Procedure so that the magistrate will have a duty at initial appearance to ascertain whether an arrest made without a warrant was valid and thus whether adequate grounds exist to keep the person in custody. At present, the only way a prisoner can demand an establishment of probable cause at this early stage is by petitioning for a writ of habeas corpus, but this device is clumsy for testing probable cause.

1. *Summary Trial for Petty Offenses*

The complaint and initial appearance are the early procedural steps in serious cases, but for a great mass of petty offenses the complaint is the formal charging document upon which the case will be tried and the initial appearance is also the time for trial. The magistrate has the power and duty to try the case and dispose of it on the spot.[f] Numerically these cases constitute the vast majority of all criminal cases, and probably in

[f] In the context of right to jury trial the Supreme Court explored the bounds of summary jurisdiction in Duncan v. Louisiana, 392 U.S. 947 (1968) (two-year possible penalty is beyond petty offense); Bloom v. Illinois, 391 U.S. 194 (1968) (two-year contempt commitment requires jury trial); and Dyke v. Taylor Implement Co., 391 U.S. 216 (1968) (ten-day contempt commitment requires no jury trial). *Cf.* Cheff v. Schnackenberg, 384 U.S. 373 (1966) (six-month contempt commitment requires no jury trial).

terms of impact upon citizens as participants disposition of these petty offenses is more significant than the disposition of serious offenses. The quality of justice in these summary trials is often shabby, as has been repeatedly described.[g] The judge feels free to dispose of cases in a casual manner, for example dismissing the case because he feels conviction is undeserved in spite of technical guilt, or because the offender is willing to recompense his victim for damage caused, or because the arresting officer is not present to testify. The trial may consist of informal conversation among the judge, defendant, and complainant, which gets at the facts. Formally the defendant nearly always pleads guilty; the discussion relates to sentence or other disposition, including dismissal. Occasionally the defendant makes a serious contest, even having counsel present, and in that event the case will probably be set over for trial at another time. All kinds of people stream through these magistrate's courts—*e.g.*, the drunk, the streetwalker, the vagrant, the businessman who has violated some regulation, the drunken driver—and the typical handling of their cases may vary greatly among these categories. Despite the significance of the summary trial, it remains largely neglected by the various people interested in the criminal justice system.

JUDGING THE JUDGES—CRITICS SAY LOWER COURT IN NEW YORK EXEMPLIFIES FAULTS IN U.S. JUSTICE

By Felix Kessler

Wall Street Journal, Dec. 7, 1967†

POLITICS CALLED KEY IN NAMING MEN TO BENCH; CASE GLUT NECESSITATES HASTY TRIALS— BUT SOME JUDGES RATED GOOD

New York—Criminal Court Judge Manuel A. Gomez balefully surveys a tardy defendant scurrying to present himself before the bench. "Is this the idiot that's supposed to be in this case?" the magistrate inquires. There is nervous laughter in the courtroom.

---

[g] THE PRESIDENT'S COMMISSION ON LAW ENFORCEMENT AND ADMINISTRATION OF JUSTICE, TASK FORCE REPORT: THE COURTS ch. 3 (1967), and the studies cited therein.

The summary jurisdiction of the United States Commissioner system is discussed in *Hearings on S. 3475* (89th Cong., 2d Sess. (1966)) *and S. 945* (90th Cong., 1st Sess. (1967)) *Before the Subcomm. on Improvements in Judicial Machinery of the Senate Comm. on the Judiciary,* at 246-56, 494-97 (1967).

† Reprinted with permission of The Wall Street Journal.

Judge Walter J. Bayer dismisses a prostitute with an admonition: "Stay away from Broadway—all of it." A moment later he discovers that another woman arrested at the same time has inadvertently left the courtroom. "OK—the same thing goes for her," the judge calls out.

Judge Howard B. Gliedman ponders a man charged with disorderly conduct who insists on defending himself. But judges are loath to have defendants appear without counsel. So Judge Gliedman takes over the burden of the defense.

He questions the defendant and the policeman who made the arrest. Then Judge Gliedman addresses the bench—himself. "At this time the defense makes a motion that the charge be dismissed on grounds of insufficient evidence," he intones.

"Motion granted, charge dismissed," Judge Gliedman replies in practically the same breath. The bewildered defendant, still primed to argue his case, is directed away by a court attendant, unaware that the judge actually has done him a favor.

Biggest and Busiest

All this hardly sounds like orthodox courtroom procedure. But this is no textbook court. It is New York City's Criminal Court, the biggest and busiest of the nation's lower court systems, with 78 judges appointed to sit in all five boroughs of the city. A judge here may routinely handle more than 100 cases before lunch.

There is a brusqueness in the manner of Judges Gomez, Bayer and Gliedman—characteristic of much of New York life—that doesn't necessarily affect the quality of justice. But critics cite Criminal Court as an illustration of what the President's National Crime Commission recently called the "inequity, indignity and ineffectiveness" found in lower courts around the nation.

Enormous case loads and inadequate manpower are the chief ingredients of the problem across the country, and the burden of work on judges is almost impossibly large. However, many legal experts who deplore the state of the lower courts wonder if the judges are helping to solve the problem—or if they are part of it.

Politics and Boredom

The quality of the judges on New York's Criminal Court varies widely, according to those familiar with its workings. There is consensus that many of the judges are intelligent, hardworking and compassionate. But there are frequent charges that many aren't qualified for the job, primarily because appointments are politically controlled.

Lawyers and others who observe Criminal Court say that many judges become cynical, bored or weary after years on the bench, that some of them demean rather than uplift the dignity of the proceedings, that many use bail as a punitive weapon and that a decision may depend less on the merits of the case than on the judge's mood, his opinion of the lawyers involved or the idiosyncrasies of his personality. . . .

"We all become so emotionally involved in our clients," says one lawyer, "that the judges know they're hitting at you through your clients." In such a case, the judge's dislike of a lawyer can be unfortunate for the defendant.

There is a litany of other complaints. Judges read newspapers while court is in progress. Judges lean back to "rest their eyes" so that the lawyers can't tell if they are listening. Judges have unjustified tantrums. Judges are prejudiced against certain minority groups. Judges advise an attorney privately to "plead him (a client) guilty." Judges allow their health or morale to determine their severity on a given day. . . .

Shoplifters and Fighters

Criminal Court handles many felony cases, but the bulk of its work is the lesser crimes, or misdemeanors, such as petty shoplifting, disorderly conduct and assault. The court also considers complaints such as those made by feuding neighbors ("The women in the Bronx are the fightingest I've ever seen," recalls one former judge) and, with its 1,000 personnel, disposes of several million parking and traffic violations each year.

The setting for the drama of justice isn't ideal. Except for a modern courthouse in the borough of Queens, the buildings are gloomy, dilapidated and ancient. In the Manhattan courts, the American flag is covered with a plastic sheet to keep soot from settling on it.

Working conditions are chaotic. A constant buzz fills the courtroom as defendants, complainants, policemen and lawyers move to and from the bench. The "bridgeman"—the court aide who monitors the calendar—calls the docket number of the next case while the judge disposes of the current one. Occasionally a Spanish interpreter's voice adds to the din.

Judges react to the tumult in various ways. At a recent session, Judge Bayer kept the calendar moving with the cry, "Let's go, let's go, I've got to leave here at 12:30 to get to a funeral." As the judge finished one case and turned to a second, he made certain that the parties involved in a third were handy. "Stay right where you are, you're next," he told a waiting policeman. "We've got seven minutes. Let's go."

The brisk pace produces serio-comic episodes. One afternoon not long ago a Legal Aid lawyer made an impassioned plea before Judge Bayer in behalf of a youth arrested on a morals charge. "I cry for mercy, your honor," the lawyer said.

"I heed your cry," the judge returned. "Fifteen days." This was the maximum sentence. Reminded of this, the judge reduced the sentence to 10 days. And the next case was hurried before the bench.

Legal authorities agree that the job of Criminal Court judge is formidable, if not impossible. Rapid decisions must be made constantly, without benefit of detailed study. These experts note that petty criminals are in theory more susceptible to rehabilitation than hardened offenders, and they emphasize the importance of the judge in the apprehension-trial-punishment-rehabilitation process.

The major attention of those concerned with criminal justice administration has been with the more elaborate system for dealing with serious offenders, who are thought to constitute substantial threat to the community and who are faced with severe penalties upon conviction. Concern for accuracy and fairness is more acute there, since more is at stake on both sides.

B. NOTIFYING OF THE RIGHT TO A PRELIMINARY EXAMINATION

At the initial appearance the prisoner is notified of his right to a preliminary examination at which the prosecutor will be required to establish a prima facie case to justify proceeding further with prosecution.

Even though the defendant may derive substantial benefits from the preliminary examination as a discovery device, as discussed in Chapter 8, the observations of the American Bar Foundation survey make clear that a large majority of offenders waive the preliminary.[h] In the federal system about 70% waive.[i]

[h] Miller & Dawson, *Non-use of the Preliminary Examination: A Study of Current Practices,* 1964 Wis. L. Rev. 252.

[i] *Hearings on the U.S. Commissioner System Before the Subcomm. on Improvements in Judicial Machinery of the Senate Comm. on the Judiciary,* 89th Cong., 1st Sess. 9 (1965). When there is substantial voluntary disclosure of evidence by the prosecutor, waiver is nearly universal. *Id.* at 163-64.

This may be the result of carefully balancing the advantages and disadvantages, particularly when the defendant is represented by counsel. More often waiver seems to result from ignorance that anything is to be gained from the hearing when there is no doubt that a prima facie case can be established. The prospect that demanding the hearing may delay the case for two or three weeks may or may not favor waiver, depending upon the tactical advantages of delay and upon whether the defendant can obtain release on bail.

For the bulk of defendants who are unrepresented at the initial appearance the significance of the choice they are asked to make between demanding or waiving the preliminary examination is unclear. They may not even be aware that there is a choice. It has been quite common for the magistrate at the initial appearance simply to ask the prisoner "how he pleads" to the charge against him and to take a "guilty plea" as a waiver of the preliminary examination, since it can be taken as an admission that there is at least sufficient evidence of guilt to justify holding for trial.[j] If the accused is not asked to "plead" or if he "pleads" not guilty, he will be asked directly whether he wishes a preliminary, but there may be no more explanation than, "Do you wish a preliminary examination, or would you rather go directly to trial?" If there is an expression of confusion by the defendant, some further explanation may be given, such as, "An examination is simply a hearing to see if there is enough evidence to hold you for trial."

There is rarely any effort to encourage defendant to request a hearing. But, on the other hand, even though holding the preliminary examination delays trial and imposes some burdens on the prosecutor and the court, there is apparently little effort to induce the accused to waive the preliminary examination.[k] The following, therefore, represent only occasional occurrences.

1

After the judge had given two women charged with embezzling $2,500 from a department store a few minutes in which to decide about preliminary examination, they looked puzzled and said, "Gee, we don't know what to do." A police detective said to them, "Look, there is nothing to this procedure. Take my word for it, just waive. When the judge gets back tell him you waive." When the judge returned, the women waived the preliminary.

---

[j] With respect to use of the "plea" as evidence at trial, consider White v. Maryland, 373 U.S. 59 (1963), at 545, *infra*.

[k] Compare *Whitty v. State*, at 494, *infra*.

2

Addressing a woman before the bench on initial appearance, the clerk of the examining magistrate stated, "Mary Jones, you are charged with murder in the first degree. How do you plead?" The defendant replied, "Yes, I is guilty." At this point, the judge interrupted the sobbing defendant and stated, "I refuse to accept this plea [which would have the effect of waiving the preliminary]. Let her stand mute and get an attorney before deciding whether or not she wishes a preliminary examination."

Because most persons are unaware of the possible value of preliminary examination, some courts refuse to permit waiver by an unrepresented defendant. If counsel is appointed or employed prior to the date set for the hearing, he may still waive the hearing. For tactical reasons attorneys frequently do prefer to waive the preliminary examination. On the other hand, the court may accept waiver by an unrepresented defendant, but out of concern for the possibility that the waiver was improvident the court may give counsel, when he is appointed later in the process, the right to demand remand of the case for the purpose of a belated preliminary examination. This latter is the practice, for example, under the statutes of Michigan and Wisconsin and without statute in Utah.[l] In these states such remand procedures are frequently invoked.

C. NOTIFYING OF THE RIGHT TO COUNSEL

The defendant at the initial appearance should be apprised by the magistrate of his right to be represented by counsel of his choice at every stage of the proceedings against him, or to have counsel appointed for him by the court if he is indigent.[m] It is unclear, however, precisely at what point the right to assigned counsel accrues. Constitutional doctrine at present is that an indigent is entitled to be provided counsel at every "critical stage" of the proceedings. Thus far the preliminary examination itself has not always been considered a critical stage. It is even less clear that a defendant has a constitutional right to counsel to advise him whether to demand or waive the pre-

---

[l] MICH. STAT. ANN. § 28.982 (1954); WIS. STAT. § 955.18(2)(a) (1965); Seibold v. Turner, 20 Utah 2d 165, 435 P.2d 289 (1967).

[m] See the statement of A. Kenneth Pye at 552, *infra*.

liminary examination.[n] Whatever the constitutional right, it is clear that increasingly the practice is to provide counsel at the initial appearance stage.[o] However, unless a public defender is present at the outset there is no practicable way of providing counsel immediately and the initial appearance may have to be continued to permit counsel to be appointed. In some jurisdictions when counsel is requested there is an automatic continuance of the initial appearance, without admitting defendant to bail, until a lawyer is appointed—sometimes a period of several days.

D. NOTIFYING OF THE RIGHT TO REMAIN SILENT

The Federal Rules of Criminal Procedure require the magistrate to inform the prisoner at initial appearance that he need make no statement and that whatever he says may be used against him. Before *Miranda v. Arizona,* prompt presentation before a magistrate had as a major function the communication to the prisoner of this constitutional right. The magistrate's giving the warning now has less significance, because police are obligated to give the same warning before asking the prisoner questions about his criminal conduct. Some urge that it is important for such warning to be given by an impartial party rather than by the police, who may give the warning in a deprecating manner.[p]

---

[n] *E.g.*, Pearce v. Cox, 354 F.2d 884 (10th Cir. 1965), concluded (in dictum) that the initial appearance, at which the defendant must decide whether to request or waive a preliminary examination, is a critical stage and that counsel must be provided for the indigent defendant at that point.

[o] *E.g.*, Rule 44 of the Federal Rules of Criminal Procedure, as amended in 1966, provides for assigned counsel for the indigent "from his initial appearance before the commissioner or the court." Public defender offices often assume responsibility to provide representation at this early stage; and, where there is no public defender system, specialized lawyer staffs have sometimes been created to provide interim representation before the magistrate prior to assignment of permanent counsel by the court.

Jones v. State, 37 Wis. 2d 56, 154 N.W.2d 278, 285 (1967): "[W]e adopt a rule, for prospective application only, that at an indigent defendant's initial appearance before a court or magistrate he be advised of his right to counsel and that counsel be appointed at that time unless intelligently waived." The court emphasized the value of counsel in the setting of bail, decision whether to request a preliminary examination, and early preservation of evidence and preparation of defense.

[p] *See* Model B in A.L.I., A Model Code of Pre-Arraignment Procedure (Study Draft No. 1, 1968).

E. SETTING BAIL

At the initial appearance the magistrate will determine on what conditions the prisoner may obtain his release pending further proceedings. Further custody is the responsibility of the court rather than the police. With the exception of very few offenses and limited circumstances, all accused persons are entitled to "reasonable bail," by either constitution or statute.

For minor offenses the bail may be set mechanically by a court-established bail schedule of offenses charged, so that a man can be released at the police station upon posting the scheduled amount, without appearance before a magistrate at all. Where this would result in releasing a drunken driver to drive off again, the danger is sometimes avoided by delaying the release or impounding the arrested person's car. The procedure involved in recovering the vehicle usually takes long enough so that the driver is sober by the time it can be completed.

A somewhat related procedure for permitting release of a prisoner without appearance before the magistrate is the "station house release" coupled with use of a "summons" to notify the prisoner of his obligation to return at a specified time.

EXPERIMENTS IN THE CRIMINAL JUSTICE SYSTEM

By Herbert Sturz

25 Legal Aid Briefcase 111, 112 (1967)

We [The Vera Institute of Justice] found that the police already had statutory power to substitute a summons for an arrest in misdemeanor cases but were using it primarily for traffic or ordinance violations. Beginning in the spring of 1964, we worked out with the New York City Police Department and the courts an experimental program in three Manhattan precincts for extending the use of police summonses into cases of simple assault, petit larceny, and disorderly conduct. Vera provided the fact-finding investigators to interview defendants at the station house. The same kind of criteria used to free defendants on their own recognizance in court was used to allow release from the precinct within an hour or so after arrest.

The Manhattan Summons Project has worked well: 1,396 persons have been released; only 3.5 per cent have failed to appear in court at arraignment. In December, 1966, the police extended the program to all twenty-three precincts in Manhattan and are now doing their own interviewing and verifying; the list of crimes for which station-house release on a summons is permissible has been expanded to all but the most serious misdemeanors.

In fact, in May, 1966, Commissioner Leary, addressing the Judicial Conference of the District of Columbia Circuit, raised the possibility of issuing police summonses in selected felony cases.

1. *Bail to Prevent Flight*

Under present interpretations of the Constitution, only one question should be involved in releasing a prisoner pending trial: What will insure the appearance of the defendant at the next stage of the proceedings which requires his presence?[q] Under our system of law the defendant is entitled to be present at the proceedings against him, and this has been interpreted to mean that his presence is more than a right—it is a requirement which he cannot waive. Trials in absentia are not possible.[r]

Though in theory bail has been accorded the single objective of guaranteeing appearance, in fact bail may be set mechanically, without real regard for its being enough but not too much to achieve its objective. Bail may also be set so high, in response to community outrage or to the likelihood of the prisoner's committing further antisocial acts while free on bail, as to be unattainable by the prisoner. Historically, a bail was a person who undertook to guarantee personally the appearance of the prisoner. In modern times bail has been transmuted to property which will be forfeited if the bailed person does not appear. Growing dissatisfaction with the money bail system has produced recent experiments with other methods of insuring the defendant's return to court.

THE PRESIDENT'S COMMISSION ON LAW ENFORCEMENT AND ADMINISTRATION OF JUSTICE
THE CHALLENGE OF CRIME IN A FREE SOCIETY 131-33 (1967)

Pretrial Release

One-half or more of the defendants who are brought into a police or magistrate's court are released or convicted and sentenced within 24 hours of their arrest. The cases of the remainder, including all those against whom the accusation of a serious crime can be maintained, await final disposition for days or

[q] The major consideration by the Supreme Court of bail problems was in Stack v. Boyle, 342 U.S. 1 (1951), and Yates v. United States, 356 U.S. 363 (1958) (involving the same litigation).

[r] People v. Davis, 235 N.E.2d 634 (Ill. 1968). Distinction is made between this and the situation where defendant absents himself after trial has begun.

weeks or sometimes months, depending on the prosecutor's case-load, the gravity and complexity of the case, and the condition of the calendar in the court that will hear it.

The magistrate is empowered to decide whether or not such defendants will be released pending trial. The importance of this decision to any defendant is obvious. A released defendant is one who can live with and support his family, maintain his ties to his community, and busy himself with his own defense by searching for witnesses and evidence and by keeping in close touch with his lawyer. An imprisoned defendant is subjected to the squalor, idleness, and possibly criminalizing effects of jail. He may be confined for something he did not do; some jailed defendants are ultimately acquitted. He may be confined while presumed innocent only to be freed when found guilty; many jailed defendants, after they have been convicted, are placed on probation rather than imprisoned. The community also relies on the magistrate for protection when he makes his decision about releasing a defendant. If a released defendant fails to appear for trial, the law is flouted. If a released defendant commits crimes, the community is endangered.

The device that is used in most magistrates' courts to resolve these complicated issues is money bail in an amount fixed by the magistrate; a defendant without access to that amount of money is remanded to jail. The ordinary method defendants use to furnish bail is to pay a fee, commonly from 5 to 10 percent of the full amount of the bail, to a bail bondsman, who posts a bond for the full amount with the court. By and large, money bail is an unfair and ineffective device. Its glaring weakness is that it discriminates against poor defendants, thus running directly counter to the law's avowed purpose of treating all defendants equally.[8] A study in New York, where the bondsman's fee is 5 percent, showed that 25 percent of arrested persons were unable to furnish bail of $500—i.e., raise $25; 45 percent failed at $1,500; 63 percent failed at $2,500. A massive side effect of money bail is that it costs taxpayers millions of dollars a year. A community spends from $3 to $9 a day to house, feed, and guard a jailed defendant.

Beyond this, evaluating a defendant's reliability in terms of dollars is so difficult that, perhaps inevitably, most jurisdictions

---

[8] A problem that relates not to fairness, but to equal treatment, is the exposure of imprisoned persons to the greater likelihood of identification in a lineup while persons who have been released on bail can avoid this identification procedure. The majority in Rigney v. Hendrick, 355 F.2d 710 (3d Cir. 1965), did not find this an invidious discrimination against the poor; the dissent strongly urged the contrary.

have come to use what might be called a standard crime-pricing system. On the theory that the likelihood of a defendant's appearance depends on the size of the penalty he faces and therefore on the seriousness of a charge against him, bail rates are often preordained by stationhouse or judicial schedules: so and so many dollars for such and such a crime. The effect of standard rates and their disparity from place to place is to leave out of consideration not only the important question of a defendant's financial means but also the equally important ones of his background, character, and ties to the community.

Although bail is recognized in the law solely as a method of insuring the defendant's appearance at trial, judges often use it as a way of keeping in jail persons they fear will commit crimes if released before trial. In addition to its being of dubious legality, this procedure is ineffective in many instances. Professional criminals or members of organized criminal syndicates have little difficulty in posting bail, although, since crime is their way of life, they are clearly dangerous.

If a satisfactory solution could be found to the problem of the relatively small percentage of defendants who present a significant risk of flight or criminal conduct before trial, the Commission would be prepared to recommend that money bail be totally discarded. Finding that solution is not easy. Empowering magistrates to jail defendants they believe to be dangerous might well create more of a problem than the imposition of money bail, in the light of the difficulty of predicting dangerousness. Such a system also might raise issues under State and Federal constitutional grants of a right to bail, issues that have not been determined by the Supreme Court.

A partial solution for the problem would be to provide an accelerated trial process for presumably high-risk defendants. In Philadelphia, for example, a special calendar for defendants charged with crimes of violence has recently been set up; such defendants are to come to trial no more than 30 days after indictment. It is still too early to know whether and how much this lessens the likelihood that released defendants will commit dangerous acts, but other studies have shown that the risks are closely related to the length of time that elapses before trial. The use of conditions and restrictions short of detention to control potentially dangerous persons may provide an adequate and more clearly permissible approach and should be tried.

In any case, money bail should be imposed only when reasonable alternatives are not available. This presupposes an information-gathering technique that can promptly provide a magistrate with an array of facts about a defendant's history, circumstances, problems, and way of life. The Vera Institute of Justice in New York has been a pioneer in devising such a technique. The Institute prepared a short standard form on which pertinent facts about a defendant were entered. Employees of the criminal court's probation department now question defendants as they await their appearance before the judge, and fill out the form. Often they check by telephone the facts they are given with the defendant's family or neighbors or employer. The entire procedure can take as little as 20 minutes, and by the time the defendant makes his court appearance, the judge knows enough about him to make an informed decision about whether bail is appropriate or whether the defendant can be released on his own recognizance, that of a member of his family, or his lawyer's. Since the Vera Institute established this approach, more than a hundred other jurisdictions have adopted the same or similar techniques.

TRIAL JUDGES AND THE POLICE—THEIR RELATIONSHIPS IN THE ADMINISTRATION OF CRIMINAL JUSTICE

By Herman Goldstein

14 Crime and Delinquency 14, 16 (1968)

"STATION HOUSE" BAIL

Some formal arrangement between police and courts is required so that the police can act on behalf of a judge in releasing persons pending their initial appearance in court. Usually, judges have chosen to deal with this by providing the police with a "bail schedule" which, in effect, authorizes them to release designated categories of offenders who are capable of posting a specified amount of bail. The alternative would be to require contact between a defendant and a judge whenever an arrest is made, a procedure not feasible in any jurisdiction where more than a few arrests are made each day.

Such a one-shot effort, by which the court discharges its bail-setting responsibilities before initial appearance, has obvious inadequacies. In many situations the single criterion for justifiable release—the likelihood of later appearance before the magistrate—is met, but the rigidity of the bail schedule compels the police to retain the arrested person in custody. For example, when an out-of-state student enrolled at a local college is arrested for a traffic offense, he usually has neither the credentials—a local driver's license or a bail card—nor the funds called for by the judicially established bail schedule. Similarly, the police usually have no alternative to retaining a person in custody when presented with bail in the form of a personal check. Most jurisdictions prohibit acceptance of a check even though the person offering it enjoys an excellent reputation in the community and cannot provide cash because the banks are closed at the time bail must be posted. Such problems reflect the lack of flexibility in most "bail schedules" and illustrate the defects of the court's attempt to meet the need for contact with the police simply through the issuance, without prior consultation, of a set of written instructions.

The Practice

Where a bail schedule has not been used, the magistrate regularly considers how much bail is needed to guarantee appearance. The seriousness of the crime is only one of the factors he considers.

1

Police officers arrested an eighteen-year-old boy for theft of a $120 radio. Rather than keep him in custody until he could be brought before a judicial officer the following morning, the police took him home and turned him over to his parents upon their promise to appear with him in court on the next day. When they did appear in court the next day, the judge released the boy again to his parents' custody pending further proceedings.

2

A Negro defendant was brought before the magistrate, charged with felonious assault. The magistrate examined the case report and noted that the assault was on another Negro and that there were no other witnesses. He released the defendant on his own recognizance. "There'll probably be no conviction here," he noted. "In these cases the victim usually 'forgets' what happened. I don't think the defendant will run."

3

A numbers writer was brought before the magistrate for the setting of bail. Without inquiry into any of the specific facts of this case, the magistrate immediately set an extremely low bail. "These people would not leave town if an atomic bomb were dropped on it," he remarked.

4

A defendant charged with sale of narcotics, which carries a minimum sentence of twenty years in the event of conviction, was brought before the magistrate. Without inquiry into the defendant's background the magistrate set bail at $10,000.

5

After the seizure of over two hundred pounds of heroin—one of the largest seizures ever made in the United States—the defendant was indicted for conspiring to import narcotics. The United States Commissioner set bail at $100,000. After failing to obtain a reduction in bail, defendant's attorney soon produced in court a cashier's check for $100,000. The court then released him, making special stipulation that his bail was conditioned upon his not entering any transportation terminal, not leaving the city, and not being away from home at night without prior notice to the prosecutor's office as to where he would be.

WHITTY v. STATE

34 Wis. 2d 278, 149 N.W.2d 557 (1967)

HALLOWS, J. According to the evidence, which the jury apparently believed, Whitty on May 22, 1965, approached a group of children playing in an alley near North Thirty-sixth and West Brown streets in the city of Milwaukee. He asked the complaining witness, a girl of ten years, if she would help him find a black and white rabbit which he had lost—a nonexistent little rabbit which reappears in the case to raise one of the important questions to be decided. The little girl removed her roller skates and followed Whitty down the alley, through a yard and into the basement of a house in search of the rabbit. While in the basement Whitty took indecent liberties with the child. The owner of the house, Robert Lutz, became aware of a noise in his basement, investigated and found the little girl who warned him of Whitty's presence and asked for his help. Lutz discovered Whitty behind a furnace, scuffled with him and knocked him down several times, but Whitty escaped up the stairs by swinging a ball-peen hammer at Lutz. Lutz' brother-in-law arrived as Whitty emerged from the rear door and gave chase with Lutz but Whitty escaped. Meantime the little girl ran to the nearby home of her aunt where her mother was visiting and reported the incident. A search was made and two days later Whitty was arrested.

A new trial is sought on the ground Whitty's constitutional right to reasonable bail and to due process was violated. Sec. 6, art. I of the Wisconsin constitution and the Eighth amendment to the United States constitution provide "Excessive bail shall not be required." Whether the Eighth amendment is directly applicable to this state criminal prosecution or is a specific provision of the Bill of Rights which is "incorporated" or "absorbed" as such by the Fourteenth amendment and applicable under the doctrine of due process, the result is the same. While the record is not entirely clear, it sufficiently appears that at Whitty's first appearance before Milwaukee County Judge F. RYAN DUFFY, JR., bail was set at $10,000 and a preliminary examination scheduled for a later date. Whitty appeared with counsel on the appointed day and bail was reduced to $1,500 in return for his waiver of the preliminary examination. Whitty now contends he was forced to purchase his right to reasonable bail and was prejudiced by the loss of the advantages of a preliminary hearing.

Whether $10,000 or $1,500 was a reasonable bail, we need not decide. An accused has a constitutional right to reasonable bail and the amount thereof should be determined solely in reference to the purpose of bail, namely, to assure the appearance of the accused when it is his duty to appear to answer the criminal prosecution. Secs. 954.36, 954.39, Stats. The fixing of bail should not be a matter of bartering or negotiating, or be conditioned upon the waiver of other rights. Nor should the denial of reasonable bail be used as a punishment or retaliation prior to conviction. Proper considerations in fixing a reasonable amount of bail which will assure the defendant's appearance for trial include the ability of the accused to give bail, the nature and gravity of the offense and the potential penalty the accused faces, the character and reputation of the accused, his health, the character and strength of the evidence, whether the accused is already under bond in other pending cases, and whether the accused has in the past forfeited bond or was a fugitive from justice at the time of arrest. Anno. Bail—Factors Fixing Amount, 72 A.L.R. 801; Stack v. Boyle (1951), 342 U.S. 1.

While we must condemn what was done in this case, it does not automatically follow that Whitty is entitled to a new trial. It is true Whitty was given the choice of reduced bail or preliminary examination and he waived his preliminary examination, but he argues this choice was inevitable because bailed defendants tend to fare better at trial than those who cannot make bail. In support of this proposition he cites Rankin, The Effect of Pretrial Detention, 39 New York University Law Review (1964), 641; Ares, Rankin & Sturz, The Manhattan Bail Project: An Interim Report on the Use of Pre-Trial Parole, 38 New York University Law Review (1963), 67, 90; Foote, The Coming Constitutional Crisis in Bail: II, 113 University of Pennsylvania Law Review (1965), 1125, 1148. While these studies are most interesting and it may be true the greater percentage of convictions is of those defendants who cannot make bail before trial, we are not prepared to accept the thesis that prejudice to a defendant on the issue of guilt or innocence flows from pretrial incarceration. . . .

While the denial of a preliminary hearing is not *per se* a breach of a constitutional right, State v. Strickland (1965), 27 Wis. 2d 623, 135 N.W.2d 295, nevertheless in the context of this case Whitty's constitutional right to reasonable bail was violated. Such constitutional violation is subject to the harmless-error rule because it did not occur during trial of the issue of guilt or innocence and did not directly affect that issue. We believe the error was harmless beyond a reasonable doubt on the issue of Whitty's guilt or innocence.

ALTERNATIVES TO THE PRESENT BAIL SYSTEM

By Wayne R. LaFave

1965 University of Illinois Law Forum 8, 10-12, 14-17

Focusing now on bail-setting by the magistrate in current practice, the following observations from the report of the Allen committee [Poverty and the Administration of Federal Criminal Justice, Report of the Attorney General's Committee on Poverty and the Administration of Criminal Justice (1963)] are relevant:

"It is disturbing to discover . . . that American bail administration largely fails to provide the bail-setting authority with relevant factual data indispensable to sound bail decisions. This failure in the fact-finding process transforms what must, at best, be a difficult task into one impossible of satisfactory performance. In many instances, both in state and federal courts, virtually the only pertinent facts supporting the initial bail decision are the charge upon which the defendant was arrested and such other circumstances surrounding commission of the alleged offense as may be communicated by the prosecuting attorney. The consequence is that many highly relevant considerations are not adverted to or, at most, are given insufficient weight. The result may be dangerous, not only to the liberty of the accused, but, on occasion, to the security of the criminal process. The absence of a proper factual basis for decision may also encourage consideration of irrelevant factors, thereby leading to improper and sub rosa uses of the bail-setting power."

Another complaint, highlighted in Beeley's 1927 study and still made today, concerns the dominant role of the professional bondsman. One federal judge puts it this way:

"The professional bondsmen hold the keys to the jail in their pockets. They determine for whom they will act as surety—who in their judgment is a good risk. The bad risks in the bondsmen's judgment, and the ones who are unable to pay the bondsmen's fees remain in jail. The court and the commissioner are relegated to the relatively unimportant chore of fixing the amount of bail."

The result, of course, is that a substantial number of criminal defendants must remain in jail to await trial, which may come weeks or months later. The number of defendants unable to make bail varies from place to place; some illustrative figures from recent years are: St. Louis, 79%; Baltimore, 75%; Miami, 71%; San Francisco, 57%; Boston, 54%.

The impact of pretrial detention is substantial. Some of the more significant consequences are as follows:

(1) The punitive aspects of detention. The conditions in most American detention facilities are deplorable. Many are overcrowded, lack proper sanitation equipment, lack recreational facilities, and indiscriminately mix together offenders of all kinds. Persons awaiting trial ordinarily are not confined separately from or treated differently than those who have been convicted. Conditions in these local jails are far inferior to those in state penitentiaries. Professor Foote, commenting on a study in New York a few years ago, observed: "Indeed, the most ironic finding in the whole study is the revelation that accused persons, whom our law presumes to be innocent and who are not to be punished, are confined pending trial under conditions which are more oppressive and restrictive than those applied to convicted and sentenced felons."

(2) The human costs of detention. There is of course the economic burden on the defendant and his family. The defendant in custody may lose his job, or at least will lose pay during his absence from work, all during a time when his need for financial resources is greatest. His family may be humiliated, and his relations with his wife and children may be severely damaged.

(3) Impact on the defense against the criminal charge. For one thing, the defendant in custody and not working will likely lack the resources necessary to finance an adequate pretrial investigation of his case. The defendant is not free to locate and induce reluctant witnesses to come forward, a task which often only he can perform effectively. Detention may impede the lawyer's

contacts with his client. It is often difficult for defense counsel to travel to the detention quarters, and the facilities available there for interviewing often are inadequate. Studies in a number of locales have established that the probability of conviction for one detained before trial is much higher than for one at liberty.

(4) Impact on the defendant's sentence. It is clear, I believe, that one who has been released prior to trial and has been able to retain his job and continue his family relationships is a much more likely candidate for probation. Moreover, a defendant who has been subjected to the debilitating experience of pretrial detention somehow seems less amenable to rehabilitation via probation than the defendant who has not been subjected to undesirable contacts and influences. Again, statistical studies of current practices support this sentencing distinction; a prison term is much more likely in the case of a defendant unable to make bail than with a defendant who was not incarcerated before trial.

(5) The cost to the government. The costs of maintaining detention facilities vary from community to community, but most of the figures I have examined range between $4 and $8 per day per person. In New York in 1962, over 58 thousand persons spent an average of 30 days apiece in pretrial detention; this is nearly two million jail days, which, at a cost of $6.25 per day, required an expenditure of over ten million dollars. Most important, perhaps, as Police Commissioner Murphy of New York City pointed out, is that this is extremely costly "in terms of the manpower removed from the primary function of patrol and detection of crime." Another cost which should not be overlooked is that of providing public assistance to the families of defendants who are not at liberty and cannot provide for their dependents. . . .

In many locales, it is not feasible to take every arrestee immediately before a magistrate for release on bail. Thus, persons arrested are held in custody briefly, usually until the following morning, when they then are brought into court. Legislation allowing a station officer to release an arrested person outright or on his own recognizance is the exception rather than the rule, and consequently few police agencies attempt to review the need for custody once the arrestee reaches the station. Some communities do have a station house bail system, whereby a person can obtain his immediate release by posting a fixed amount of cash. However, the amount to be posted is determined by a fixed schedule geared to the nature of the offense, and thus it bypasses any effort to determine the accused's likelihood to return and discriminates most forcefully against defendants without money.

In the case of many minor offenses, it would appear that a brief inquiry at the station would establish that the arrestee has sufficient roots in the community to justify immediate release. Thus, the need here is for explicit authority for release by the police after arrest. Of course, it is also important to establish some modest fact-finding machinery at the police station level so that some brief background investigation of defendants can be undertaken. The Manhattan Summons Project, sponsored by the Vera Foundation, illustrates what can be done here. Law students are serving at various precinct stations, where they interview persons arrested for minor offenses. If the interview establishes that the defendant has sufficient roots in the community, Vera recommends his release on a written notice to appear. In most cases the desk officer will concur in the recommendation, and the defendant is released after having spent approximately an hour at the station.

Moving now to the traditional bail decision made by a judicial officer, one great need is to improve the fact-finding machinery. To set bail consistent with existing law, the magistrate needs to have verified information about the defendant's family, employment, residence, finances, character and background. In most jurisdictions today, the judge does not have this information available; indeed, he has no resources for gathering such data. The impressive record of the Manhattan Bail Project, where law students were used to conduct the necessary investigations, shows what can be accomplished when adequate fact-finding machinery is made available. I will not take time to describe that project to you; most of you, I am sure, are already familiar with it, and you will be hearing more about it later during this conference.

I would merely add that though law students can be successfully utilized to get similar programs going elsewhere, the long-range need is for the fact-finding process to be carried out by public officials regularly assigned this responsibility. As you may know, the City of New York has now allocated funds to enable their Office of Probation to take over from the Vera Foundation the work of the Manhattan Bail Project. Similarly, a key proposal of the Allen committee on federal criminal justice was that the Federal Probation Service be supplied adequate staff and budget for performance of such services.

Certainly a reform which goes hand in hand with that just described is a move to greater use of the so-called "r.o.r."—release of the defendant on his own recognizance. The traditional administration of bail in the United States relies primarily on a system of financial inducements to insure the presence of the accused at the trial. Liberty pending trial is conditioned upon the accused's supplying financial securities which are subject to forfeiture in the event of nonappearance. It is highly questionable whether this system provides the most effective deterrence of nonappearance, and it is clear that it results in the denial of freedom to many persons who are unable to supply even modest financial securities.

As suitable alternative in a great many criminal cases would be the following: The magistrate should allow the accused to sign a solemn undertaking in circumstances of some formality whereby he obligates himself to appear at the subsequent proceedings. No additional assurances in the form of a surety bond or other acceptable securities would be required. Great care should be taken at the bail hearing to insure that the defendant understands the nature of the obligation to appear for trial, and this understanding should be reinforced by the sending of letters to him restating the accused's obligation to present himself for trial. The experience with this procedure in New York and other locales has been highly successful.

A measure of deterrence which probably is equally or more successful than using financial inducements is possible within the r.o.r. procedure, although this would require legislation in many states. Illustrative of what can be done is the new Illinois code, which makes failure to appear on such a recognizance a criminal offense, subject to a maximum penalty of 5 years and $5,000 in felony cases, and 1 year and $1,000 in misdemeanor cases. As recommended by the Allen committee, the defendant released on recognizance should be informed of the criminal penalties attaching to failure to appear at trial as directed.

Of course, there is much more which can be done by way of deterring nonappearance by those who have been released without financial obligations. The supervision of persons at liberty to insure against violation of the conditions upon which that liberty was granted is not a problem at all new to American law; for years we have faced this problem with some measure of success as to those already convicted of crime. It is unfortunate but true that current bail administration has not taken advantage of this experience. As the Allen committee pointed out, "The rich fund of experience derived from decades of administration of parole and probation laws is highly relevant to the formulation of a sound policy of pre-trial release. . . ."

What can be done? One possibility is a form of supervised release, with certain conditions imposed upon the accused while he is at liberty. Most important, perhaps, would be a requirement that he periodically check in with the police, probation office, or court. Or, perhaps some defendants can be paroled to the custody of a willing private third party, such as their attorney, minister, or employer. This practice would be similar to that now commonly employed in disposing of juvenile cases. A third possibility for those who cannot safely be granted full-time release would be daytime release, which would allow the defendant to continue his employment. The experience in Wisconsin under the Huber Law, authorizing daytime release of certain convicted misdemeanants, would seem relevant here.

Now, we have been talking about release on conditions other than money. For the defendant who can raise bail and whose risk of nonappearance requires attaching some conditions to pretrial release, the use of money to induce return may still be appropriate. Some improvements on existing practices, however, are still needed. For one thing, the amount of bail presently required in most cases is excessive. A downward revision to more realistic levels is urgently needed. Beyond this, it may be desirable to provide alternatives to dealing with the bail bondsmen, such as by allowing the defendant to post a small cash deposit with the court. For example, here in Illinois a defendant may post 10% of his bail with the court and thereby obtain his release; if he appears as required, he receives 90% of the amount posted back. Thus, if bail is $1,000, the cash deposit is $100, and $90 of that will be returned when the case is over. Professor Bowman will report in more detail tomorrow on our experience under these provisions.

THE FEDERAL BAIL REFORM ACT OF 1966
18 U.S.C. §§ 3146, 3150

§ 3146. Release in noncapital cases prior to trial

(a) Any person charged with an offense, other than an offense punishable by death, shall, at his appearance before a judicial officer, be ordered released pending trial on his personal recognizance or upon the execution of an unsecured appearance bond in an amount specified by the judicial officer, unless the officer determines, in the exercise of his discretion, that such a release will not reasonably assure the appearance of the person as required. When such a determination is made, the judicial officer shall, either in lieu of or in addition to the above methods of release, impose the first of the following conditions of release which will reasonably assure the appearance of the person for trial or, if no single condition gives that assurance, any combination of the following conditions:

(1) place the person in the custody of a designated person or organization agreeing to supervise him;
(2) place restrictions on the travel, association, or place of abode of the person during the period of release;
(3) require the execution of an appearance bond in a specified amount and the deposit in the registry of the court, in cash or other security as directed, of a sum not to exceed 10 per centum of the amount of the bond, such deposit to be returned upon the performance of the conditions of release;
(4) require the execution of a bail bond with sufficient solvent sureties, or the deposit of cash in lieu thereof; or
(5) impose any other condition deemed reasonably necessary to assure appearance as required, including a condition requiring that the person return to custody after specified hours.

(b) In determining which conditions of release will reasonably assure appearance, the judicial officer shall, on the basis of available information, take into account the nature and circumstances of the offense charged, the weight of the evidence against the accused, the accused's family ties, employment, financial resources, character and mental condition, the length of his residence in the community, his record of convictions, and his record of appearance at court proceedings or of flight to avoid prosecution or failure to appear at court proceedings. . . .

§ 3150. Penalties for failure to appear

Whoever, having been released pursuant to this chapter, willfully fails to appear before any court or judicial officer as required, shall, subject to the provisions of the Federal Rules of Criminal Procedure, incur a forfeiture of any security which was given or pledged for his release, and, in addition, shall, (1) if he was released in connection with a charge of felony, or while awaiting sentence or pending appeal or certiorari after conviction of any offense, be fined not more than $5,000 or imprisoned not more than five years, or both, or (2) if he was released in connection with a charge of misdemeanor, be fined not more than the maximum provided for such misdemeanor or imprisoned for not more than one year, or both, or (3) if he was released for appearance as a material witness, shall be fined not more than $1,000 or imprisoned for not more than one year, or both.

2. *To Prevent Further Misconduct by the Offender*

The Practice

Though "preventive detention" is not a formally recognized function of bail, the following instances illustrate the widespread willingness of magistrates to consider the possibility of further misconduct in setting bail:

1

The defendant, who was charged with trafficking in narcotics, had threatened to kill the two narcotics agents who had effected his arrest. The judge set bail at $50,000, later explaining that he felt the defendant would not be able to furnish bail of that magnitude.

2

The defendant was charged with deriving support from a prostitute. He had a record of twelve prior felony charges, each of which had been dismissed for want of prosecution. The chief witness against him was a young woman who had lost several teeth, had been scarred with acid, and had suffered a broken shoulder at the hands of an unknown assailant whom she suspected acted at the instance of the defendant. She told the police she would testify only if the defendant were kept in jail. The magistrate, at police request, set high bail.

3

A man arrested for burglary was brought before the magistrate for the setting of bail. The magistrate set high bail, explaining that he was concerned that persons arrested for such offenses might commit others while on bail in order to pay for the expenses of their defense.

The attitude of courts toward preventive detention is illustrated by the following case. The decision relates to bail pending appeal, which is discretionary, so that the language would apply the more strongly to bail pending trial, which is a matter of right.

WILLIAMSON v. UNITED STATES

184 F.2d 280 (2d Cir. 1950)

Mr. Justice JACKSON, as Circuit Justice for the Second Circuit. These Communist Party leaders were convicted for conspiring to advocate and teach the violent overthrow of the United States Government and to organize the Communist Party for that purpose.

After the Court of Appeals affirmed the convictions, defendants expressed an intention to petition the Supreme Court to review their cases. The prosecution asked that bail be revoked and defendants remanded to jail. Two grounds were advanced: first, that no substantial question as to the validity of the conviction survived the affirmance, and second, that defendants, while at large, *have pursued* and *will continue to pursue* a course of conduct and activity dangerous to the public welfare, safety and national security of the United States.

I regard the case as one in which substantial questions are open to review by the Supreme Court, and in which I am therefore empowered to grant bail, as ordinarily would be done.

The Government's alternative contention is that defendants, by misbehavior after conviction, have forfeited their claim to bail. Grave public danger is said to result from what they may be expected to do, in addition to what they have done since their conviction. If I assume that defendants are disposed to commit every opportune disloyal act helpful to Communist countries, it is still difficult to reconcile with traditional American law the jailing of persons by the courts because of anticipated but as yet uncommitted crimes.[7] Imprisonment to protect society from predicted but unconsummated offenses is so unprecedented in this country and so fraught with danger of excesses and injustice that I am loath to resort to it, even as a discretionary judicial technique to supplement conviction of such offenses as those of which defendants stand convicted.

---

[7] There are ways of dealing with certain threats to commit crime. In these cases the law only imprisons in default of furnishing an undertaking, but the person held is released if he furnishes the required undertaking to abide the court's order and "keep the peace." New York Code of Criminal Procedure, §§ 84-99; assimilated into Federal Law, 36 Stat. 1163, 18 U.S.C. § 3043, 18 U.S.C.A. § 3043. [It should be noted that "peace bond" procedures exist widely. For example, Chapter 962 of the Wisconsin Statutes (1965) provides for setting of bail bond upon a person who "has threatened to commit a crime against the person or property of another." Until the bail bond is provided, the person is committed to jail, with a maximum time of six months at a time. Because of the requirement of a threat these statutes do not meet the needs of broad preventive detention, but they suggest legislative acknowledgment of the problem of preventing crime by bail bond or incarceration of a probable offender.]

Their bail as fixed by the Court of Appeals is therefore continued until the Supreme Court of the United States shall deny their petition for certiorari or, if it be granted, shall render judgment upon their cause.[t]

CARBO v. UNITED STATES
288 F.2d 282 (9th Cir. 1961)

Before HAMLEY, HAMLIN and MERRILL, Circuit Judges.

HAMLEY, Circuit Judge. These appeals, consolidated for purposes of hearing and disposition, are from district court orders exonerating appellants' bail bonds and remanding appellants to the custody of the United States Marshal, denying motions to vacate that order, denying motions to reset bail pending trial, and denying an application for a writ of habeas corpus.

The appellants are Paul John Carbo, Frank Palermo, Joseph Sica and Louis Tom Dragna. They are four of the five defendants now on trial in a criminal action in the United States District Court for the Southern District of California, Central Division. Appellants are on trial under a ten-count indictment charging conspiracy, extortion through use of interstate communications, and conspiracy to violate the anti-racketeering act, in violation of 18 U.S.C.A. §§ 371, 875(b) and 1951.

The bail bonds set and posted by the court on the return of the indictment were as follows: Carbo, $100,000; Palermo, $100,000; Sica and Dragna, $25,000 each; and the remaining defendant, Truman Gibson, Jr., not an appellant here, $5,000. The bail of all appellants except Carbo was thereafter reduced to $2,500.

When the trial opened on February 21, 1961, counsel for the Government without prior notice orally moved to exonerate the bail bonds and remand appellants and defendant Gibson to the custody of the United States Marshal. Counsel for the Government stated that the motion was addressed to the court's discretion "in maintaining orderly proceedings and assuring the presence of the defendants during the course of a long trial." It was estimated that the trial would in all probability require six to eight weeks.

In arguing that maintenance of "orderly proceedings" required that appellants be held in custody, counsel for the Government stated that over a two-year period the Government's principal

[t] Setting bail on an alleged burglar in the amount of $1,500,000 was characterized as judicial misconduct in Sarisohn v. Appellate Div., 21 N.Y.2d 36, 233 N.E.2d 276 (1967), but as insufficient cause for removal.

witness had received over a hundred threatening telephone calls. It was represented that the witness had for this reason been forced to have his home telephone removed. Calls then began coming to his place of business, making it necessary for the witness to leave his job. All of these telephone conversations related to the testimony the witness was expected to give at the trial.

The motion was orally granted at the end of the morning session of the first day of trial. In explanation of this action the court stated:

"I have on only one occasion in my career on the bench sequestered defendants during a trial. I have the impression it should be done in this case."

During the afternoon session of the court on the same day counsel for appellants Sica and Dragna and defendant Gibson filed written motions to reset bail. Oral motions to the same effect were made on behalf of Carbo and Palermo. The court granted the motion as to Gibson, resetting his bail at $5,000. As to the four appellants the motion was denied, the court indicating that he believed they were in the throes of an "intangible hysteria which made these defendants not the best possible bail risks during the actual progress of the trial."[2]

Appellants argue first that the district court did not have constitutional, statutory or inherent power to deny bail before conviction in this non-capital case.

When a criminal trial is in actual progress there must be an accommodation between the right of a defendant to be free on bail and the inherent power of the court to provide for the orderly progress of the trial. Where release on bail poses no substantial threat to the orderly progress of the trial, the imperatives of the Constitution and the rule require that the right to preconviction bail be honored.

If, however, there is reason to believe that a trial actually in progress may be disrupted or impeded by the flight of the defendant, or by his activities in or out of the courtroom during the

---

2 After stating these two additional considerations which were given weight with respect to Carbo, the court said:

". . . I just don't have any faith in the defendant Carbo being here unless he is restrained during the trial.

"Now, I don't think the giving of a bond is adequate assurance. I decline to fix bond for the defendant Carbo, and I do it regretfully, because I realize he is not a well man and that he has suffered a term of imprisonment which has ended as of about two hours ago.

"But while this is, in a practical way, depriving him of liberty, it is done to assure his presence here and protect him against the impulses and the hysteria which sometimes come upon defendants during the presentation of a case which has complicated emotional elements which are present in this case."

trial, the fair administration of justice is itself jeopardized. In that event the court may give precedence to its inherent power and revoke bail if necessary for the duration of the trial.

What appellee states concerning threats to a Government witness may be set to one side because there is nothing to indicate that the trial judge took that into consideration. Where the exercise of discretion is under review, we must pass judgment on what the trial judge said were his reasons, whatever support the record might afford for other reasons.

[A]ccording to the judge's own remarks, he seemed to have been partly motivated by some subconsciously-induced reaction to appellants as individuals and as a group. Then there was the court's view that appellants were under the influence of incipient hysteria, presumably based upon the judge's limited opportunity to observe appellants in the courtroom.

Under the indicated circumstances neither of these factors appeals to us as a sufficient base upon which to predicate a sound exercise of discretion. Nor do records of prior arrests and convictions in our view add substantial support for the court's conclusion. Moreover, the court seemed not to rest its action to any extent upon those records.

As to Carbo, the court had additional reasons. But however weighty these reasons might have been in fixing the amount of bail, they are not of a kind which warrants revocation of bail. Carbo's avoidance of arrest elsewhere on other charges seems hardly relevant when the fact is undisputed that he has always responded to bail when posted.

We desire nothing which is said above to tie the hands of the trial court as of this time, or at any time during the trial, in responding quickly and effectively to any real threat to the orderly progress of the trial, including, if deemed necessary, revocation of bail. The trial court has wide discretion in the matter and may exercise such discretion without a record based on Wigmore evidence. If, for example, testimony already received or which may be received during the course of the trial indicates to the trial judge that appellants are likely to abscond, or that appellants' freedom on bail constitutes a personal danger to trial witnesses or others, bail may be immediately revoked and appellants remanded to custody of the United States Marshal. We hold only that, taking at face value the trial court's statement of supporting reasons, they do not provide a substantial foundation for the action which the trial judge took at the outset of this trial in revoking the bail of these appellants.

HAMLIN, Circuit Judge (dissenting). To me, the representations made to the court, together with his personal observations, were such that I am unable to say that the action of the district judge should be reversed.[u]

SETTING HIGH BAIL TO PREVENT PRE-TRIAL RELEASE

By Herman Goldstein

Address Before National Conference on Bail and Criminal Justice, May 27-29, 1964

National Conference on Bail and Criminal Justice, Proceedings 151-60 (1964)

The use of the bail system to serve a purpose quite different from that which it was designed to serve has frustrated the efforts of those concerned with introducing some logic into our bail policies. Obviously, their problems would be greatly simplified if the use of bail were restricted to assuring the reappearance of the defendant for trial. But employing a procedure designed for one purpose to serve quite a different purpose is not unusual in our criminal justice system. Rather, there is a pattern of adaptations, modifications and accommodations in the administration of the system which, in a somewhat awkward manner, often fulfill socially acceptable goals which are not provided for by the legal system. The purposes which bail has come to serve may be without foundation in law, but they cannot be rejected for this reason without at last examining the needs which they fulfill.

Chief among these expressed needs is the desire to protect the community from the defendant who it is felt will commit additional crimes if allowed to go free. The problem centers most specifically around the professional burglar, the narcotic offender, and the armed robber—individuals who are often characterized as hardened criminals committed to a life of crime and who give the impression that they have "nothing to lose" in the pursuit of their criminal activities. When the activities of such criminals

[u] Upon renewed application for release the district court again refused, this time basing its action explicitly upon its concern for safety of the witnesses. The court of appeals affirmed. Carbo was convicted and sentenced to twenty-five years' imprisonment and $10,000 fine. Pending appeal he was again denied release on bail out of fear he might flee, Carbo v. United States, 300 F.2d 889 (9th Cir. 1962), and Justice Douglas, sitting as Circuit Justice, refused bail pending appeal also out of concern for the principal government witness who had received over two hundred threats and had been beaten by an unknown assailant. Justice Douglas referred to the fact that Carbo had previously been tried for murder, with the trial resulting in a hung jury. He was not retried because one witness was killed and another disappeared. Carbo v. United States, 82 S. Ct. 662 (1962). Dictum in a per curiam Supreme Court opinion approved preventive detention during trial to protect the trial process—for example, to protect witnesses. Bitter v. United States, 389 U.S. 15 (1967).

become a subject of public discussion or when a specific crime committed by one of them enrages the community, the community tends to label the alleged offender as dangerous and the judge often reflects this view in his use of bail to maintain the alleged offender in custody. But in our large cities, where the problem of crime is most aggravated, the professional criminal may enjoy a degree of anonymity not unlike that of the majority of city dwellers. Public pressure does not develop in many aggravated cases in which the police feel that the public interest would be better served were the alleged offender detained. . . .

The pattern in the *Massari* case [*see* p. 1324, *infra*] is often repeated. The offender launches himself on a cycle. He commits more crimes in order to acquire more money in order to meet larger amounts of bail and the accumulation of attorney's fees. He often becomes more daring in the types of crimes he commits and is more likely to use force as his concern for the eventual consequences of his actions decreases.

The possibility that an offender will do harm to a witness or a victim is the second most common source of concern for the police. Another case, drawn from Chicago, illustrates this need as expressed by the police.

Frank Wallace was, at the age of 19, convicted of rape and sentenced to the Illinois State Penitentiary for three years. Approximately one year after his release, Wallace was suspected as being the individual responsible for a wave of robberies of pensioners. Bits of information came to the attention of the police that a number of old men had been attacked and threatened with bodily harm if they complained to the police. Detectives identified one of the victims and from him obtained sufficient information to identify Wallace as the perpetrator of these crimes. A warrant was signed and Wallace was arrested and charged with robbery. Shortly after being arraigned and released on bail, Wallace broke into the apartment of a 71 year old man, beat the victim about his head, kicked him numerous times and left him in an unconscious state. He then ransacked the apartment, taking approximately $3,000 in currency and a 38 caliber revolver. The victim required seven stitches in his head and suffered a possible concussion. Wallace was identified by the victim and quickly apprehended. He was arrogant toward the arresting officers; threatened to shoot them on sight after his release; and boasted that he would be on the street immediately after his appearance in court. Most of the currency and the revolver were found on his person. While in custody, he was identified by another pensioner as having robbed him and threatened him with bodily harm if he complained to the police. He was indicted on two counts of robbery and released on bail of $1,500.

Upon his release, Wallace returned to the home of the victim and again assaulted the old man in an overt effort to dissuade him from testifying. He was again apprehended and charged with aggravated battery. Bail was, at the initial arraignment, set at $50,000 and the case scheduled for the grand jury within twelve days. On the scheduled date, a request for continuance was granted and the amount of bail was reduced to $5,000—enabling Wallace to be released.

If the defendant is released on bail, it is not uncommon in such situations to arrange for the detention of the victim. This occurs most frequently when a man stands accused of incest with his daughter. With the release of the father on bail, the daughter may be placed in custody for her own safety and to insure that she will testify free of threats. The release of the suspect is accomplished, in other words, at the expense of incarcerating the victim.

. . . When the needs as expressed by the police are recognized as well by the judge, the situation may be dealt with by the denial of bail or the setting of bail in an especially high amount. High bail may be tantamount to denial if the action of the judge is interpreted by the bail bondsmen as intended to assure that the defendant remains in custody. Bail bondsmen, who require the cooperation of the court in their work, may refuse to write a bond which would have the effect of offending a judge. . . .

Committed as we are to the concept that an individual is presumed to be innocent until proved guilty, the use of bail for preventive detention is considered by some to be totally repugnant, in conflict with our basic system of justice and an outright perversion of the legally established provisions. It is argued that sacrificing community security to individual rights is basic under our system of government, that it is preferable to allow a crime to be committed than to chip away in any measure at the presumption of innocence concept; that it is foreign to our system to speculate as to guilt prior to trial; and that it is equally foreign to take official action against an individual to protect society from those crimes which are unconsummated.

On the other hand, it is argued that the presumption of innocence is a rule of evidence to secure a fair trial and implies that the guilt of an accused must be proved at his trial beyond all reasonable doubt. It is contended that this concept does not mean that those who discharge administrative functions prior to trial should be bound to act as though the suspect had behaved as a law-abiding citizen or that he would behave as such pending trial.

These considerations place this problem within the same context as so many of the other critical issues in the criminal justice system: the need for striking a delicate balance between the concern for the protection of society and the desire to guarantee maximum freedom for the individual; the desire to prevent future crimes versus the desire to allow the suspect to be free prior to trial. . . .

Like so many issues in criminal justice administration, the issue of preventive detention is complicated by the fact that we do not really know, in quantitative terms, what the social costs are of the several alternatives. We have only fragments of information on how many crimes are committed by individuals while on bail. And where such figures are available, we have no indication of the extent to which these figures are influenced by the prevalent practice of detaining those who would be the most serious risks. We do not know whether those crimes which are committed are similar to those with which the individual has already been charged. We do not know how many of these crimes could have been prevented. And we have little quantitative knowledge of the inconvenience or damage which prevalent practice in the use of bail causes the individual.

The legal issues which are involved have not been squarely raised and resolved. With little dissent, the courts have held that, under existing legislative provisions, the only legitimate purpose of bail is to secure the presence of the accused at trial. The constitutional prohibition against excessive bail has meaning only insofar as it can be related to a criterion for establishing excessiveness. This, in turn, must be measured on the basis of the purposes being served. Since the only purpose of bail which is set forth in existing federal or state law is that of assuring the reappearance of the defendant for trial, it would appear that the question of whether bail is excessive must be determined on the basis of the criteria which predict the likelihood of reappearance.

It is not at all clear how the constitutional issue might be resolved if a law were enacted specifically authorizing the use of bail for preventive detention. To date, the constitutional question has been raised in the abstract about a policy judgment which has never been made. There has not been an effort on the part of a legislature in this country to consider the question and make a careful judgment as to the merits of the issue. Appellate courts have ruled on the actions of individual judges in specific cases, functioning under existing laws. We have not had the reaction of an appellate court to a preventive detention provision specifically authorized by a legislative body.

. . . The questions to which we might profitably direct our attention are four in number: (1) Is preventive detention justifiable under any conditions? (2) If not, what measures should be taken to prevent current administrative distortion of our bail system? (3) If preventive detention is a justifiable social policy, should a more formal legal procedure be substituted for the current administrative manipulation of bail to serve this purpose? (4) And finally, are there alternatives to bail which will serve as effective means by which the need for preventive detention might better be fulfilled?[v]

3. *To Achieve Other Ends*

The Practice

Bail may be set on the basis of considerations other than guaranteeing appearance and preventing further misconduct by the prisoner, as illustrated by the following examples:

1

A defendant of very limited means was charged with sexually molesting a child. The father of the child had threatened to kill the defendant. Bail was set at $15,000.

2

Officers arrested a man for homosexual conduct. He was a local resident, not likely to flee. Bail was set very high because of an incident some months previously in which a schoolteacher who had been released on such a charge had committed suicide.

3

Officers brought a woman before the magistrate on a charge of obtaining money by false pretenses. The magistrate set bail at $3,000. A detective then spoke to the judge, informing him

---

[v] The problem of preventive detention is helpfully discussed in American Bar Association Project on Minimum Standards for Criminal Justice, Standards Relating to Pretrial Release, §§ 5.5—5.8 and Commentary, and Appendix C (1968). The law issues are analyzed in Comment, *Preventive Detention Before Trial,* 79 HARV. L. REV. 1489 (1966); Comment, *Preventive Detention,* 36 GEO. WASH. L. REV. 178 (1967).

that the defendant had been extremely cooperative in identifying and leading police to her accomplice. After further discussion, the magistrate said he would release the defendant on her signature to a personal bond providing that she would be responsible for appearance or forfeit $500.

4

A man was arrested after social workers interviewing his stepdaughter heard her allege that he had engaged in sexual intercourse with her. The magistrate set extremely high bail, remarking that he wanted to insure that he was not released and in a position to induce his stepdaughter to change her story.

5

A young man was arrested after he recklessly discharged a shotgun on the street, wounding four persons. The magistrate set bail at $100,000—$25,000 on each of four charges of assault with a deadly weapon.

6

A man who allegedly paid a blind newsdealer with stage money was charged with petty larceny. The magistrate set bail at $10,000, explaining that this was the meanest case that had come before him in eight years on the bench.

Reference Note

The relationship between the initial appearance and the preliminary examination is explored in Miller & Dawson, *Non-use of the Preliminary Examination: A Study of Current Practices,* 1964 Wis. L. Rev. 252.

Bail has been much discussed in recent years. Among the most helpful treatments, with citations to the extensive literature, are American Bar Association Project on Minimum Standards for Criminal Justice, Standards Relating to Pretrial Release (1968), and The President's Commission on Law Enforcement and Administration of Justice, Task Force Report: The Courts 37-41 (1967). The relationship between bail and the rest of the criminal justice system is treated in R. Goldfarb, Ransom: A Critique of the American Bail System (1965).

The several earlier field studies of bail practices are summarized and commented on in D. Freed & P. Wald, Bail in the United States: 1964, at 9-21 (Report to the National Conference on Bail and Criminal Justice 1964). A later major program is described in R. MOLLEUR, BAIL REFORM IN THE NATION'S CAPITAL (1966). The wide variations in bail practices are demonstrated by Silverstein, *Bail in State Courts—A Field Study and Report,* 50 MINN. L. REV. 621 (1966). Foote, *The Coming Constitutional Crisis in Bail II,* 113 U. PA. L. REV. 1125 (1965), is helpful in the understanding of constitutional principles as they apply to bail.

Chapter 8

THE DECISION TO HOLD FOR TRIAL—THE PRELIMINARY EXAMINATION AND THE GRAND JURY

At the prisoner's initial appearance before a judicial officer one of the questions he is asked is whether he wants a preliminary examination or is willing to waive it. If preliminary examination is not waived a date is set for this evidentiary hearing, since witnesses are not usually all available at the initial appearance. In jurisdictions which give the defendant the additional right to be prosecuted only after a grand jury has returned an indictment, he may also be informed of this right and given opportunity to waive grand jury consideration of his case. Most defendants waive both preliminary examination and grand jury.

A. FUNCTIONS OF THE PRELIMINARY EXAMINATION OR GRAND JURY

There are several different functions served by the preliminary examination and the grand jury hearing: to test the sufficiency of the evidence; to pass on the propriety of proceeding even where the evidence is sufficient; to allow the defendant limited discovery of the case against him; to preserve testimony which might otherwise be unavailable at trial. Only the first of these is expressly acknowledged in most jurisdictions.

1. *Testing the Sufficiency of the Evidence*

The formal function of the preliminary examination or the grand jury is to ascertain whether there is sufficient evidence of guilt to justify carrying the case to the trial stage. In reality, however, this function of evaluating the prosecution's evidence to see if it will support the charges in the complaint is of relatively little importance because the prosecutor has screened the cases before deciding to charge and has satisfied himself of the sufficiency of the evidence.[a] If the defendant asks for a prelimi-

[a] Of the minority of defendants who ask for a preliminary examination, the percentage discharged in the federal system is in the range of five to ten

nary examination, therefore, it is likely to be for its value to him as a discovery device, or as a dilatory tactic, rather than in hope of dismissal. Waiver of the preliminary examination, which is considered a concession that the evidence is sufficiently strong to justify holding the defendant for further proceedings, is very common.

On the other hand, in some jurisdictions the prosecutor does not effectively screen cases prior to their coming before a judge. In this event the preliminary examination or the grand jury hearing will serve as the stage at which effective screening of the police-instituted charges is done. There are also cases in which a prosecutor is reluctant to refuse to charge because he fears his decision will be looked upon as motivated by political or other favoritism. He may bring the case before the judicial officer at the preliminary examination in the view that public confidence will be greater if the judicial officer decides that there is insufficient evidence.

Because the grand jury system is cumbersome and can easily be overloaded, there is substantial pressure upon the judge at the preliminary examination in high volume jurisdictions to dismiss unpromising cases. The judge may dismiss cases either because the defendant is thought deserving of leniency, because the evidence does not rise to the required standard of probable cause, or because the grand jury system needs to be protected against overload. In Chicago, for example, this situation exists.[b] There the initial appearance becomes itself a kind of quick preliminary examination, and the case will be dismissed unless police are present and able to make some ex parte showing of probable cause. Even when probable cause is shown, the judge frequently downgrades felony charges to misdemeanors, which need not go before the grand jury.

JUDICIAL DOMINANCE OF THE CHARGING PROCESS: THE PRELIMINARY HEARING IN CHICAGO 15-16 (1967)

By Donald M. McIntyre

(American Bar Foundation manuscript)

As earlier indicated, there is relatively little screening of felony cases by the police and state's attorney's office prior to

percent. *See Hearings on the United States Commissioner System Before the Subcomm. on Improvements in Judicial Machinery of the Senate Comm. on the Judiciary,* 89th Cong., 2d Sess., pt. 1, at 9 (1966); *Hearings on S. 3475* (89th Cong., 2d Sess. (1966)) *and S. 945* (90th Cong., 1st Sess. (1967)) *Before the Subcomm. on Improvements in Judicial Machinery of the Senate Comm. on the Judiciary* 477-79 (1967).

[b] Oakes & Lehman, *The Criminal Process of Cook County and the Indigent Defendant,* 1966 U. Ill. L.F. 584, 607-10, 618-23.

the preliminary hearing [which takes place in Chicago at the time of the initial appearance]. It is the police, in fact, who have responsibility for formally initiating the criminal charge by completing their arrest report and complaint, which is filed in the preliminary hearing court. In deciding to invoke the formal criminal process the police are guided by the strong belief that analysis of the evidence, in regard to both its admissibility and its weight, are matters to be decided by higher authority. As a consequence, when there is sufficient evidence to arrest, the implied assumption is that there is enough to charge and possibly to convict. Procedural and substantive law technicalities, rules of evidence and legal presumptions which dictate the outcome of the case, are regarded by the police in many instances to be beyond their competence. Under these circumstances, many cases that are in fact too weak to prosecute or are only misdemeanors, but about which doubt exists as to the precise crime committed, are initiated as felonies.

The police are also under a certain amount of pressure to establish an impressive "crime clearance rate," which may add insight into their "charging" practices. [The number of persons charged is used as a statistical measure of efficiency.]

Although the formal standards for issuance of an arrest warrant and binding over at the preliminary examination are presumably the same—evidence sufficient to convince the judicial officer that there is probable cause to believe the suspect is guilty of a crime—there are important theoretical and practical differences which make the standard at the preliminary examination a great deal higher than that for an arrest warrant. In some jurisdictions hearsay is properly used as a basis for an arrest warrant, but is not admissible at the preliminary. Other jurisdictions, including many federal courts, allow hearsay in both, but the likelihood is that in fact, because there has been time to prepare before the preliminary, a higher level of proof may be expected. Thus, it does not follow that everyone for whom an arrest warrant has issued will be bound over. The evidence standard before the grand jury is presumably also the same (though it remains surprisingly vague, because there is little litigation on the issue) and its purpose is conceptually the same—to ascertain probable cause.[c] The duplication of procedures in

---

[c] The use by the grand jury of illegally seized evidence is discussed in United States v. Margeson, 259 F. Supp. 256, 273-74 (E.D. Pa. 1966), and in A. Goldstein, *The State and the Accused: Balance of Advantage in Criminal Procedure,* 69 Yale L.J. 1149 nn. 52, 53, 62 (1960). It is generally assumed

jurisdictions which have both the preliminary examination and the grand jury is a recent phenomenon. Until the nineteenth century, the preliminary examination was for the purpose of interrogating the prisoner. In the 1800's it came to be a device to protect the prisoner against unjust detention. This change reflected partly a concern for the fact that a prisoner who could not satisfy bail requirements might wait a long time before a grand jury was convened, particularly in rural communities, without opportunity to obtain his freedom if the evidence against him failed to warrant detention.

THE STATE AND THE ACCUSED: BALANCE OF ADVANTAGE IN CRIMINAL PROCEDURE

By Abraham S. Goldstein

69 Yale Law Journal 1149, 1166-72 (1960)†

The Preliminary Hearing

Pressure on the arresting officer to act responsibly in screening the charges of crime would ordinarily come in the preliminary hearing before the magistrate. It is the magistrate who must determine whether the policeman's "reasonable belief," when made visible, constitutes "probable cause" to believe a crime has been committed; or a "prima facie" case; or sufficient evidence to warrant a jury's finding the accused guilty. Almost everywhere, however, the showing is held to be sufficient if the prosecution presents a skeletal outline of evidence admissible in court to support each element of the offense. This skeletal quality is virtually assured by certain grim facts. In most jurisdictions, no provision is made for appointment of counsel at this stage. Neither the due process clause of the fourteenth amendment nor state constitutional provisions have been held to require it. And most states make no statutory provision for appointment of counsel, though a considerable number require that he be advised of his right to retain counsel. Since, therefore, defense counsel is usually either not present, or insufficiently informed to play his role properly, it ordinarily falls to the magistrate, almost alone, to test the sufficiency of the evidence to warrant holding the accused for the grand jury, or for trial where there is no grand jury. Yet, most magistrates are either unskilled, or too busy, or too closely linked with police

---

that objections of this sort are not appropriate at the preliminary examination, and should be raised by pretrial motion to suppress the evidence.

† Reprinted by permission of the Yale Law Journal and Fred B. Rothman & Company.

or prosecutor, or insufficiently mindful of the "judicial" nature of their role to perform this function adequately. And the sole review of the sufficiency of the evidence before them is the limited one afforded by habeas corpus, which looks only for some "legally competent evidence" to support the order committing the accused for trial. But even that is a limited safeguard because the unrepresented, or poorly represented, defendant may not learn until after his trial that there was insufficient evidence at the preliminary hearing to warrant passing the case on to trial. If the case has proceeded to trial, no remedy is available to the accused for the defect in the preliminary hearing. He must then look, on appeal, solely to the inadequacy of the evidence at trial.

In practical effect, therefore, the preliminary hearing in the United States does not add significantly to the police evidentiary screen which has preceded it. As in the case of arrest, the point is not to suggest that the screening function of the preliminary hearing should be made more rigorous; or that every "error" requires a remedy. It is merely to indicate first, that the institutions empowered to do the screening job do it in quite limited fashion and, second, that the cumulation of noninterventionist attitudes serves to make very slight indeed the external pressures on policeman, prosecutor and magistrate to act as responsible screens. Entirely too much is left to self-discipline and tradition, which have been notoriously slow in developing in most American police forces and magistracies.

It would be misleading to leave the inference that there are not a substantial number of drop-outs at the arrest and preliminary hearing stages. What is not at all clear, however, is whether they are the result of the formal evidentiary screen, thereby reinforcing the probability of guilt, or whether they derive from something else—for example, the virtually undefined and unreviewable exercise of discretion by police and prosecutor not to proceed further, in accordance with criteria so subjective as to afford no assurance that the rule of law is being applied equally to all.

The Grand Jury

In perhaps half the states, mostly in the West, the preliminary hearing is the last formal screening device before trial. But in the remaining states and in the federal system, the grand jury stands as yet another screen. Though it may serve as an initiator of investigation and accusation, by far the greatest proportion of matters coming before it has already passed through arrest and preliminary hearing.

The grand jury is unquestionably the most celebrated of the pre-trial screening devices. Originally conceived as an extension of the royal authority over the citizen, it reached its greatest glory as a barrier against the state, refusing to indict for crime where the evidence was inadequate or the law creating the crime unpopular. During the nineteenth century, a great many jurisdictions set about to "judicialize" the grand jury proceeding, principally because the return of an indictment, without more, was recognized as bringing serious extra-legal sanctions with it. Beginning with a hearing restricted to the prosecution's case alone, with a firm ban on calling the defendant or his witnesses, most states soon authorized the grand jury to hear them if it chose. A considerable number enacted statutes providing that the grand jury was to hear only "legal evidence," or that it "ought" to indict only on the basis of such evidence. And those requirements were frequently enforced through the granting of motions to quash indictments based on no evidence at all, or no evidence as to an element of the crime, or "utterly insufficient" evidence. The nature of the judicial inquiry tended to resemble the manner in which courts now review the action of administrative agencies—to ascertain whether they are acting within the limits of their authority. The net effect of this development was to impose upon the prosecution the obligation to proceed more cautiously and circumspectly with the business of prosecuting crime than it might otherwise have done.

In the late '20's and early '30's, a complete change in judicial attitude toward the grand jury took place. There came to be increasing feeling, manifested most clearly in the report of the Wickersham Commission, that the grand jury was an inefficient "rubber stamp" for the prosecutor who conceived its investigations, directed its secret proceedings, and drafted its indictment. Apart from its subpoena authority, which could conceivably be better lodged with the prosecutor who exercised the power de facto, the grand jury hearing seemed to serve no useful purpose. The adjudication of probable guilt would have to be made again by a petit jury after a fuller and fairer hearing than the grand jury could possibly provide. And besides, there was the preliminary hearing, which could be used to do the screening job hitherto done by the grand jury. There came to be increasing reluctance on the part of the courts to examine the sufficiency of the evidence before the grand jury. That body became its own judge of the kind of evidence it would hear and the amount and quality of evidence it would require for indictment.

United States v. Costello [350 U.S. 359 (1956)] placed the imprimatur of the Supreme Court upon this conception of the grand jury. The Court held that an indictment based completely upon hearsay evidence is neither defective, dismissible on motion, nor ground for reversal of a conviction. The attempt by Justice Burton to place his concurrence on a narrower ground—that the hearsay was clearly reliable—and the failure of the Court to incorporate that ground into its opinion, indicated strongly that, henceforth, the federal grand jury was to police itself.[d] Except for their very limited relationship to it before and during the proceedings, courts were no longer to interfere if the grand jury was "legally constituted and unbiased." The reason for this approach, fairly clearly stated in *Costello,* is that the accused will get his fair, "judicial," hearing at his trial. Due process, and the Supreme Court, require no more. Stated in somewhat more rhetorical fashion, why protect the defendant at the grand jury stage against an indictment based on little or no evidence when the exacting standards of the trial process will make such indictments meaningless?

The Relationships Among the Screens

In sum, the evidentiary standards of the pretrial screening process, implicitly relied upon by trial and appellate courts as a basis for relaxing trial standards, have themselves been relaxed in reliance upon the assumed vigor of the trial process. It by no means follows, however, that the pretrial process should be "judicialized" to assure that only the "really guilty" come to trial. Though a tightening of the screens might well decrease the danger that innocent men would be convicted, it might also distort other functions, such as investigation, which are perhaps equally important.

The point, simply stated, is this: the looseness of the pretrial screens makes questionable the move toward abandonment of the traditionally strict trial standards called for in *Isbell* and *Curley*. Only if the criminal sanction were to lose the special stigma associated with it in our society, or if the threat of imprisonment did not loom ominously in the background, or if there had been fewer instances in our history of conviction

[d] Hearsay has been commonly accepted at the preliminary examination, though the question is still an open one. *See Washington v. Clemmer,* at 558, *infra,* and text following. The Department of Justice (Memo No. 511, April 10, 1967) takes the position that hearsay may be used, pointing out the impracticality of avoiding hearsay in preliminary examinations held hundreds of miles from the scene of the crime, as in Dyer Act cases.

of innocent persons, would it be appropriate to treat the question of sufficiency of evidence in criminal trials in the same manner as in civil trials.

When cases do drop out at the preliminary examination stage for insufficiency of evidence, it is usually not because the police or prosecutor acted hastily, but because witnesses have turned uncooperative after the decision to charge was made. There may also sometimes be doubt that the evidence will persuade the jury even though perhaps technically probable cause could be found.

The Practice

1

In a lineup a witness had identified the accused as the robber. At the preliminary examination the witness expressed doubt concerning his previous identification. The magistrate discharged the prisoner.

2

In a preliminary examination on a charge of statutory rape against her boyfriend, the complainant proved to be an unwilling witness, apparently because she had made up with the defendant. The complaint was dismissed by the magistrate.

3

In a preliminary examination on a charge of breaking and entering during the nighttime, it had definitely been established that somebody stole cigarettes and money from a vending machine in a service station. There were no eyewitnesses and no confession. The defendant was linked to the crime only through finding his fingerprints on the outside of the machine. The case was dismissed.

4

A man and his wife returned home from a movie one night and found a stranger in their living room. They lived in a neighborhood that was predominantly white and the stranger was a Negro. He simply pushed past the couple, explaining that he was in the wrong house. An investigation of the contents of the house revealed nothing stolen or disturbed. The stranger was apprehended and charged with breaking and entering. He was dismissed at preliminary examination.

5

At the preliminary examination, the complaining witness testified he saw the defendants removing a window fan from a tavern at four a.m. Long and heated cross-examination on the accuracy of his vision in the early morning light failed to weaken this witness' testimony. The defendant was bound over.

It is possible, too, that the defendant will himself put in some evidence of innocence or justification to affect the magistrate's decision.

6

In a preliminary examination on a charge of first degree murder, the prosecution produced seven witnesses to a tavern brawl in which the defendant-bartender shot and killed a customer. The defendant did not testify, but three defense witnesses testified that the defendant had tried to break up a fight involving the customer, that the customer had lunged toward him with a knife, and that defendant had only then shot the customer. The magistrate dismissed the case.

7

At the preliminary hearing on a charge of taking indecent liberties with a child, the boy and his mother testified. The defendant's attorney objected strongly to the judge's making any decision until he could present witnesses he claimed would contradict the boy's testimony. The judge refused to hear the defense witnesses and bound the defendant over for trial.

2. *Passing on the Desirability of Prosecution*

Just as the police and prosecutor exercise discretion, so also the judge who holds a preliminary examination or the grand jury considering whether to return an indictment may dismiss a case or may reduce the charge on other grounds than the insufficiency of the evidence. The right of the grand jury to refuse to indict on policy grounds is acknowledged but there is considerable doubt in theory whether this right is possessed by the magistrate who presides at a preliminary examination. In many jurisdictions the magistrate at preliminary examination is extremely reluctant to alter the charge and conceives his function as limited to considering the sufficiency of the evidence. This is particularly likely to be true where the prosecutor has carefully screened the cases before they get to the magistrate. Yet even in these jurisdictions the magistrate will occasionally dismiss or alter the charge in expression of his views as to desirable prosecution policy. In jurisdictions where cases come directly to the magistrate without review by the prosecutor, it is common for the magistrate to exercise the same kind of discretion to charge or reduce charges which would be normally exercised by the prosecutor were he involved.

The decision of the magistrate to dismiss or to downgrade the charges is not res judicata and the prosecutor may, if he pleases, try again with the same magistrate or another.[e] The same is true of the grand jury's refusal to indict. The discovery of new evidence, or the failure at the first preliminary to put in sufficient evidence even though it was available, or occasionally a conclusion that the magistrate or grand jury acted unreasonably can motivate the prosecutor to try again. However, the prosecutor must bear in mind the continuing nature of his relationship with the magistrate. In fact, the prosecutor almost universally accepts the dismissal as a final disposition of the case.

The Practice

These instances are suggestive of the varying degrees to which the judge feels free to exercise discretion in dismissing at the preliminary examination stage charges he feels inappropriate.

1

In a preliminary examination on a charge of concealing mortgaged property, the evidence was that the defendant, an illiterate fellow, had driven a car across the state line not knowing he was violating a statute. After the last witness testified, the judge called the attorneys into his office and suggested that the case be dismissed on the ground that a jury conviction was virtually impossible. The assistant prosecutor urged a bindover because for some time he had been harassed by the complainant, a used car company, to prosecute. The defendant was bound over.

2

Eight tavern owners were prosecuted for operating gambling devices in violation of a statute. It was testified that they paid nickels for games won on their pinball machines. At preliminary

[e] *See, e.g.*, Patterson v. Conlan, 123 Cal. 453, 56 P. 105 (1899) (four successive preliminary examinations). Tell v. Wolke, 21 Wis. 2d 613, 124 N.W.2d 655 (1963), held that the Wisconsin statute which provides for a second preliminary examination only upon the discovery of new evidence is directory only and does not bar a second examination on the same evidence.

examination the judge dismissed the cases, commenting that he did not think pinball machines were nearly as bad as slot machines.

JUDICIAL DOMINANCE OF THE CHARGING PROCESS: THE PRELIMINARY HEARING IN CHICAGO 38-41, 46, 54-55 (1967)

By Donald M. McIntyre
(American Bar Foundation manuscript)

[T]here are two aspects of the preliminary hearing that should be understood. . . .

The first concerns limitations on criminal justice resources in Cook County. All the functionaries of the system are acutely aware that the single grand jury sitting in Cook County, and the eleven circuit court judges assigned to the trial of felony cases, cannot handle more than their present caseload, which is about 4500 cases per annum. Penal institutions and probation services are also taxed to their limit. Even if these facilities could handle greater numbers it seems clear that only a fraction of the felony charges filed by the police merit further prosecution. Hence the court's primary task is to bind over only the most serious cases involving defendants who pose a genuine threat to the community and against whom the state can be reasonably assured of a conviction should the case go to trial. . . .

The second important aspect of the preliminary hearing is its preoccupation with the criminal behavior of minority groups. . . . [A] large number—perhaps 90%—of persons waiting to be heard either as defendants or as witnesses are from economically depressed areas of the city. A majority of these are Negroes, with white "hillbillies" and Spanish speaking persons making up most of the remainder. . . .

A question the court faces many times a day is whether these persons should be held accountable for their conduct to the same extent as persons living under better conditions. In making this decision the court considers, along with many other things, the motives of the complainant-victim, the mores of the neighborhood or groups of which the defendant and complainant are members, and whether full, strict enforcement of the law would serve any useful purpose, or would indeed make matters worse. The question, to take some examples frequently appearing in court, is whether a robbery involving a small sum of money between skid row bums, or a felonious assault between neighbors in a slum tenement whose uninhibited show of violence is common, should go any further than the preliminary hearing stage. . . .

> The complainant, a middle-aged Negro woman, testified that the defendant, a middle-aged Negro man, twisted her arm, grabbed her purse and took $8.00 from it. The judge interrupted the testimony to ask if she knew the defendant: "Is he your boyfriend?" She acknowledged that he "used to be." On further questioning she admitted having lived with him for over a year, and they were on a date on the night in question. The case was dismissed with an admonition to the defendant that any further misconduct would not be treated leniently. . . .

Charge Reductions and Misdemeanor Convictions. Felony Court has jurisdiction to accept pleas of guilty to misdemeanors or to determine guilt or innocence of a misdemeanor pursuant to a hearing. Upon hearing the evidence on a felony charge the judge frequently rules that an offense has been committed but it is a misdemeanor or that at least it should be disposed of as a misdemeanor. The defendant is then asked to enter a plea to it. Five out of six times when this occurs a guilty plea is entered followed by an immediate imposition of sentence or probation. In most instances the court itself will decide whether a misdemeanor disposition is appropriate; on those rare occasions when the state's attorney objects to a reduction and pushes hard for a bindover the court is inclined to acquiesce if the facts support such a decision.

3. *Discovery of the Prosecution's Case*

A very important function of the preliminary examination for the defendant who seriously considers pleading not guilty and contesting the case is the opportunity it affords the defense to learn something of the case against him. Thus experienced defense counsel will request a preliminary even though he is certain the prosecution will establish probable cause to hold the defendant for trial. However, the prosecutor ordinarily is not required to put on all his evidence (some judges interrupt whenever they are satisfied) and he tends to call as few witnesses as he thinks will suffice, so it will be only partial discovery. Defense counsel customarily will cross-examine the prosecution witnesses. He is usually permitted to put on witnesses in behalf of the defense, but rarely does so, since to do that would disclose his hand to the prosecutor.

Just as the defendant cannot always avoid a preliminary examination over the prosecutor's objection, so also he cannot as a practical matter always obtain a preliminary examination if he wants one. The prosecutor has the alternative of putting the case before the grand jury, and in those states where the grand jury is commonly used he may be able to obtain an indictment before the date set for the preliminary, making the examination unnecessary. In fact, the court may postpone the preliminary examination to permit just such practice. The advantage to the prosecutor lies in the secrecy with which the grand jury hears evidence, since disclosure of the prosecution's case can thus be prevented. The grand jury is sometimes criticized as being a rubber stamp for the prosecutor, thus not serving as an effective evidence screen, but the prosecutor's self interest in not going to trial with a weak case ordinarily serves as a strong guarantee that the available evidence rises at least to the level of probable cause.

FEDERAL MAGISTRATES ACT HEARINGS

Hearings on S. 3475 (89th Cong., 2d Sess. (1966)) and S. 945 (90th Cong., 1st Sess. (1967)) Before the Subcommittee on Improvements in Judicial Machinery of the Senate Committee on the Judiciary at 240-41a (1967)

[Remarks of Senator Tydings]

Let me briefly review the present confused and inconsistent status of the preliminary hearing: Rule 5(c) of the Federal Rules of Criminal Procedure requires that a preliminary examination—to determine whether there is probable cause to believe that a crime has been committed and that the accused has committed it—be held within "a reasonable time" after initial presentment of the accused, unless this right is waived by the accused. In practice, in some districts, this actually occurs, and preliminary hearings are routinely held within a week or so after presentment. In other districts, grand juries are in continuous session and are able to return indictments, mooting the preliminary hearings—in most cases within several days of the presentment. In still other districts, however, preliminary hearings are not held even though the grand jury backlog is such that the delay between presentment and indictment is a month or more. This is done in at least one important district by routinely granting continuances to the prosecution, often ex parte, without any opportunity for the defendant to object. In addition, in many districts the majority of defendants waive preliminary hearing, but they do so before they have an opportunity to consult retained or appointed counsel. Some commissioners have told us that it is virtually impossible to explain to an uncounseled defendant the nature and purpose of the preliminary hearing so that he may make an intelligent choice.

We think that this situation is highly unsatisfactory, and that congressional action is needed to clarify the purpose of the rule and establish a uniform procedure throughout the country. We feel that an individual's liberty should not be restrained for more than a minimum period of time in the absence of a judicial determination that his continued restraint is justified. This is particularly true when the individual is in actual custody without bail or for failure to make bail. But it is also true if the individual's liberty is restricted by bail or other conditions of release.

Our bill therefore sets outer limits within which a determination of probable cause must be made—either by a magistrate at a preliminary hearing or by a grand jury through the indictment process. These outer limits are 10 days after presentment for anyone in actual custody and 20 days after presentment for those released under bail or other conditions. Let me emphasize that these are only outer limits, and that the bill reaffirms the requirement that the preliminary hearing be held within a reasonable time. In most cases a reasonable time may be well within the outer limits. No continuance beyond these limits may be granted without the defendants' consent, except upon the order of a judge of the United States after his finding that extraordinary circumstances exist, and that the delay of the preliminary hearing is indispensable to the interests of justice.

The bill further provides that if at the end of the 10-day or 20-day period there has been neither a preliminary hearing nor a grand jury indictment or information, the accused must be discharged from custody or from bail or any other condition of release. Finally, the bill requires that any waiver of preliminary hearing and any consent to a continuance of the hearing must be made after opportunity to consult counsel.

We anticipate that the effect of the preliminary hearing provision of our bill will be to increase the use of preliminary hearings in those districts in which the grand jury meets infrequently and in those districts in which the grand jury backlog is such that no action can be expected within a short time after arrest and presentment. It will also provide something of an incentive for prompt grand jury action, in that a prosecutor who wishes to avoid a preliminary hearing can do so only by getting his case to the grand jury quickly, knowing that he cannot obtain a continuance of the preliminary hearing beyond the 10- or 20-day limit. The ultimate result in our busy urban districts may be the virtual elimination of preliminary hearings, but only if the present grand jury delays are eliminated first.

At our hearings, there was a considerable amount of discussion of the preliminary hearing as a discovery device. Most witnesses concluded, however, that they would prefer that adequate discovery be provided by other means, and that the discovery question be treated separately from that of the preliminary hearing. We agree. The preliminary hearing is not well suited for discovery for a number of reasons. First, under current doctrines it will always be possible to bypass the preliminary hearing—and therefore discovery—by proceeding rapidly to indictment after arrest, or by arresting the defendant only after an indictment has been returned, in which case the rule 5 preliminary hearing process is not involved at all. Second, it is possible to hold a preliminary hearing on only one of several charges, and later to indict and try the defendant on other charges. Third, the amount of discovery that a defendant receives in a preliminary hearing depends on the amount of proof the commissioner requires the Government to bring forward to establish probable cause; this may be quite a bit, or it may be very little, but in either event it need not be all the evidence within the possession of the Government that should be subject to discovery. Moreover, the preliminary hearing should be conducted promptly after arrest, but a discovery proceeding is probably more efficiently conducted at a later stage, closer to trial, after counsel has had an opportunity to reflect at leisure about the defense, and when the evidence against the accused is likely to be more complete.

We believe that discovery in criminal cases should stand on its own feet. It should not be inextricably entwined in the process of establishing probable cause, but should be designed to facilitate an exchange of information making the trial a more rational method of determining the truth. As such, discovery should be available to all defendants, including those whose arrest following indictment takes them out of the rule 5 preliminary hearing process, and including those who for one reason or another do not get a preliminary hearing.

Therefore, we feel that discovery, apart from the preliminary hearing, should be handled in the Federal Rules of Criminal Procedure.

BURKE v. SUPERIOR COURT IN AND FOR COUNTY OF PIMA

3 Ariz. App. 576, 416 P.2d 997 (1966)

HATHAWAY, Judge. Michael Burke has petitioned this court for a writ of prohibition, praying that the respondent court and the Honorable Porter Murry, a judge thereof, be prohibited from proceeding with the arraignment, trial setting and trial on an indictment returned by the grand jury, since he was denied a preliminary hearing.

On January 20, 1966 the grand jury of Pima County indicted Burke for aggravated assault.

The petitioner contends that the refusal to grant him a preliminary hearing denied him equal protection of the laws as guaranteed by the Fourteenth Amendment to the Constitution of the United States. He argues that despite statutory silence with regard to a preliminary hearing when one is accused by indictment, the existence of optional procedures of prosecution requires that a preliminary hearing be granted when timely requested, otherwise he would be denied equal protection of the laws.

Article 2, Section 30 Arizona Constitution, A.R.S. provides:

"No person shall be prosecuted criminally in any court of record for felony or misdemeanor, otherwise than by information or indictment; no person shall be prosecuted for felony by information without having had a preliminary examination before a magistrate or having waived such preliminary examination."

He argues that to have equal protection of the laws, he is entitled to a preliminary hearing, since a preliminary hearing is a substantial protection of the law for persons in like circumstances—those charged with the commission of a felony by information. The following statements in State v. Essman, supra, are relied on by petitioner as denotive of the significance of a preliminary hearing:

"'Although the formal purpose of the preliminary examination is to establish probable cause to hold the defendant for trial, its principal purpose in practice is to afford defense counsel an opportunity to learn the nature of the prosecutor's case.'"

From the petitioner's reliance on the reference in *Essman* to the purpose of a preliminary hearing from a defense standpoint, he appears to stake his claim of denial of equal protection of the laws on the deprivation of "discovery" afforded by a preliminary hearing. Though frequently a useful source of information to a defendant, disclosure of the prosecution's case is not the purpose of a preliminary hearing. Its legal purpose, as unequivocally reiterated by the Supreme Court of this state, is to determine whether the evidence is sufficient to find probable cause to hold a person to answer for the offense charged.

We believe that the reasoning of the court was sound and hold that the petitioner was not denied equal protection of the laws by the refusal to grant him a preliminary hearing.

MOLLOY, Judge (specially concurring). I concur in the result reached and in general with the reasoning of the foregoing opinion. I am not, however, able to reconcile the result reached with the decision of State v. Essman, 98 Ariz. 228, 403 P.2d 540 (1965). *Essman* holds that a conviction in a criminal action, after a regularly and properly conducted jury trial, must be reversed because of the refusal of the magistrate conducting the preliminary hearing to permit the defendant to call witnesses, ". . . including police officers who saw appellant on the night of his wife's death and whose testimony on cross examination might support the defense theory that the charge should be one other than murder." (98 Ariz. at 231, 403 P.2d at 542.) If there were any other witnesses offered at the preliminary hearing, the *Essman* opinion does not indicate who they might have been nor the nature of their testimony. Presumably, the reversal is predicated upon the refusal of the justice of the peace to listen to the testimony of police officers called by the accused, without any offer of proof being made as to the nature of their testimony.

In supporting its conclusion that reversible error had been committed, the court quotes from Miller and Remington, Procedures Before Trial, 339 Annals of the American Academy of Political and Social Science 111, 122:

> "'Although the formal purpose of the preliminary examination is to establish probable cause to hold the defendant for trial, its principal purpose in practice is to afford defense counsel an opportunity to learn the nature of the prosecutor's case. Experienced defense counsel will, therefore, typically request a preliminary examination even though they are certain the prosecution will establish probable cause to hold the defendant for trial.'"

The holding and reasoning of *Essman,* considered together with our constitutional admonition against reversal for non-prejudicial error, Ariz. Const. Art. 6, § 27, indicate that there is a substantial right of pretrial discovery guaranteed in this state to a defendant charged with a felony by information.

If this is so, then the writer would believe it to be a violation of the equal protection clauses of both the state and the federal constitutions to deny a preliminary hearing to a person selected for prosecution by indictment. Years of trial practice have indicated to the writer that discovery is of the essence of successful advocacy. In civil actions, the outcome of trial is often determined by the thoroughness of pretrial discovery procedures. The writer has no reason to believe that a similar effect would not prevail in a criminal action.

There is no rule or statute which sets any standard for the county attorney to follow in determining which cases should be prosecuted by information and those which he may choose to lay before a grand jury. There is no showing in the subject action why this particular defendant was singled out for grand jury indictment. Our Supreme Court has said that the purpose of the constitutional protection under consideration is to secure equality to all persons similarly situated and that legislative power is proscribed from making distinctions in rights between individuals unless there is a reasonable ground for classification.

As to so substantial a right as that of full discovery at a preliminary hearing, the writer would conceive it to be beyond the power of the legislature, and of our Supreme Court by rules of criminal procedure, to vest the absolute discretion in the county attorney to determine whether an accused will or will not have such a right. I concur in the opinion of the majority only because I am convinced that the *Essman* decision is not in accord with subsequent pronouncements of our Supreme Court, such as those contained in State v. Smith, 99 Ariz. 106, 407 P.2d 74 (1965), and State v. Chambers, 100 Ariz. 368, 414 P.2d 742 (1966). These decisions hold that a defendant is not prejudiced by failure to assign counsel to represent an indigent accused at a preliminary hearing. These later decisions are premised upon the recognition that a preliminary hearing has a very limited function. If there is a right of discovery at a preliminary hearing, such holdings are, in my view, indefensible under equal protection provisions and due process clauses. The Supreme Court of the United States has expressed itself as being most adamant that the outcome of criminal trials should not depend to any substantial degree upon the financial status of the accused.

The use of a preliminary hearing for discovery purposes, if this be a right of the accused, can only be exploited properly by professional counsel, with rare exceptions. And if we are to grant this right only to defendants able to employ their own counsel, certainly the spirit of the above cited decisions of the Supreme Court of the United States is being violated in our state.

However, if *Essman* correctly reflects the state of our law, and subsequent decisions have not expressly overruled it, then the result reached here runs too much counter to fundamentals of equal protection to long survive. Without *Essman,* the result reached today remains in great jeopardy because of the current trends in our criminal law.

UNITED STATES v. MOTTE
251 F. Supp. 601 (S.D.N.Y. 1966)

TENNEY, District Judge. It appears that the defendants were arrested without a warrant on or about October 22, 1965, and a preliminary hearing before the Commissioner was set for December 3, 1965. On that date, the Government applied for and was granted, over the objection of the defendants, a one-week adjournment and the hearing was rescheduled for December 10, 1965. On December 10, 1965, prior to the time scheduled for the hearing, an indictment was returned against these defendants charging them with violations of the Narcotics law. The Commissioner, in view of the return of the indictment, then closed the hearing.

It has been consistently held that an accused has no constitutional right to a preliminary hearing.

The only purpose served by a preliminary examination is to determine whether there is sufficient evidence to warrant a defendant being held in custody or, as here, on bail to await action of a grand jury. The grand jury, by returning an indictment, resolved that issue, the indictment conclusively establishing the probable cause and thereby eliminated the necessity for the preliminary hearing before the Commissioner.

Accordingly, it would not appear that defendants' rights were violated by reason of the failure to hold a preliminary hearing[3],

---

[3] The decision in Blue v. United States, 119 U.S.App.D.C. 315, 342 F.2d 894 (D.C. Cir. 1964), cert. denied, 380 U.S. 944 (1965)—which apparently motivated the within motion—is not a decision of the Court of Appeals of this circuit and therefore not binding on this Court. This is especially so in view of the decisions of the Court of Appeals for this circuit subsequent to *Blue* which have reiterated the almost universally followed rule that the return of an indictment constitutes the finding of probable cause which obviates the necessity of thereafter holding a preliminary hearing. See United States v. Heap, 345 F.2d 170 (2d Cir. 1965); United States v. Gilchrist, 347 F.2d 715 (2d Cir. 1965) (Per curiam).

Moreover, I believe the premise upon which the *Blue* decision is based, namely, that a defendant has a right to a preliminary hearing for discovery purposes, to be an incorrect one.

It has often been stated that "[t]he only purpose of a preliminary hearing is to determine whether there is sufficient evidence against an accused to warrant his being held for action by a grand jury. . . ." Barber v. United States, 142 F.2d 805, 807 (4th Cir.), cert. denied, 322 U.S. 741 (1944). However, as is obvious, an incidental result of the hearing is discovery by the and the motion is in all respects denied for the reasons set forth above.

So ordered.

BLUE v. UNITED STATES

342 F.2d 894 (D.C. Cir. 1964)

Before BAZELON, Chief Judge, and BASTIAN and MCGOWAN, Circuit Judges.

MCGOWAN, Circuit Judge. The principal question presented by this appeal relates to the adequacy of the pre-trial proceedings held before the United States Commissioner. Because of an asserted defect in this regard, we are asked to direct the dismissal of the indictment. There is nothing in this record which remotely suggests that he was apprised of these benefits [the right to appointment of counsel at the initial appearance if he is indigent], and, indeed, the shorthand formalism of the papers recording the appearance before the Commissioner raises a strong inference to the contrary. These pre-trial proceedings, thus, do not seem to us to have measured up to the standard fixed by the Congress in the 1960 statute; and we regard the uncounselled status of this appellant when he waived preliminary hearing as infecting that waiver.

The Government suggests to us that, even if the pre-trial proceedings before the Commissioner in this case were inadequate, the subsequent return of an indictment cured any inadequacy.

We think, on the contrary, that the express preoccupation of Congress with preliminary hearings in the Legal Aid Act denotes a legislative recognition and acceptance of the view that criminal

---

defendant of some of the Government's evidence. But what the *Blue* decision in effect accomplishes is to accord to the incidental result of discovery a status equal to that of the primary purpose of the hearing and rights protected by reason of its being conducted, so that even absent the necessity and purpose for a hearing, it nonetheless must be held in order to accomplish the incidental result.

The sum total of the decision, if viewed in this light, is to accord to a defendant indicted after apprehension a right of discovery not available to defendants apprehended after indictment, namely, the right of a preliminary hearing to discover the Government's evidence. Such is not the law either in this circuit or in any other jurisdiction, other than the District of Columbia.

In addition, the *Blue* decision can be very narrowly read so as to be applicable only where the defendant, without the assistance of counsel, waives a preliminary hearing by reason of the failure of the Commissioner to properly advise him of his right to assigned counsel.

In any event, for the reasons hereinbefore noted I choose not to follow the rationale of the *Blue* decision.

prosecution is a continuous and unitary process, and that each stage along the way has its own intrinsic importance as well as a frequently significant relationship to the final result. Preliminary inquiries can on occasion have great value for one charged with crime. Where a defendant is denied out of hand the opportunity to consider utilizing that value, we do not think that that denial is to be swept under the rug of a grand jury indictment. Neither do we think that the availability of a remedy should depend upon the outcome of a race between counsel seeking habeas corpus or mandamus and the grand jury acting upon the charge. We, therefore, conclude that relief in such a situation is not to be foreclosed solely by reason of an intervening indictment.

There are, it appears to us, three possible avenues of remedial action open for the redress of infirmities in preliminary proceedings. One, of course, is the dismissal of the indictment, which, as noted above, is the alternative pressed upon us in this case. The argument is that only in this way can a prosecution be assured which is free of defects in all its stages. Wiping the slate clean is always a tidily appealing solution, but we are not convinced that it is necessary to go so far, either generally or in this case.

A second remedy would be to reverse the conviction and remand for a new trial. As a sanction providing a potent deterrent to disregard of pre-trial requirements, there can be little question of the efficacy of this approach, although the weight of the blow would fall, in the first instance at any rate, upon those not responsible for the error. On the remedial level as well there is something to be said for it, inasmuch as it would inevitably operate to convert the first trial into a rough equivalent of the defective or omitted preliminary hearing. However, it would provide no incentive to defendants to seek pre-trial resolution and cure of claims of defects in pre-trial proceedings. It would be most wasteful indeed if a visible flaw in the early stages of the criminal process were not asserted, adjudicated, and, if necessary, corrected before a full-scale trial takes place. Justice to an accused does not require that he be permitted to visit this consequence of his own dilatoriness upon the offending system.

It is, therefore, the third alternative of intervention by habeas corpus or mandamus prior to trial that we conceive to be the remedy best calculated to combine adequate relief to accused persons with the least burden to the Government and the courts. Thus, an accused who is permitted to waive hearing without proper advice or who is wrongfully denied an opportunity to present witnesses in his own behalf will be entitled to an order of release unless a hearing is held, or to an order reopening the hearing for presentation of further evidence.[7] With such opportunities available for relief before trial despite intervening indictment, there will, of course, be a corresponding obligation to make a timely assertion of the alleged defects or, in default thereof, be thereafter foreclosed from reliance upon them as invalidating the conviction. Every counsel who enters a criminal case will presumably review the preliminary proceedings and determine whether or not a defect of substance has occurred. With counsel appearing either at the preliminary hearing stage itself, or, at the latest, before arraignment upon the indictment, there is normally adequate time before trial to file the necessary petitions if they are called for. Naturally, an attorney will be entitled, upon consultation with his client, to decide that a minor flaw is not worth challenging, or that, as a tactical matter, it is to the defendant's advantage to forego the point. Thus, unless some reason is shown why counsel could not have discovered and challenged the defect before trial, it will generally be assumed that any objections to the preliminary proceedings were considered and waived, and no post-conviction remedies will be available.

ROSS v. SIRICA
380 F.2d 557 (D.C. Cir. 1967)

Before BAZELON, Chief Judge, and FAHY and WRIGHT, Circuit Judges.

PER CURIAM. We are asked to issue a writ in the nature of mandamus directing the District Judge to remand this case for a proper preliminary hearing.

Petitioner was arrested on a charge of first degree murder and brought before a United States Commissioner. A continuance was granted to permit counsel assigned by the Legal Aid Agency to represent petitioner at the preliminary hearing. Prior to the hearing, counsel sought issuance of subpoenas to compel the

---

[7] These remedies should, of course, be asserted at the earliest possible moment. Where, however, indictment occurs before it is feasible for assertion or resolution of the claim to have been made, relief is not to be denied for that reason alone. In a preliminary hearing held or reopened after indictment, the Commissioner would continue under the necessity of making his own independent determination of probable cause. If he were persuaded that no such cause existed, that finding would result in his release of the defendant. It would not affect the indictment, although the Commissioner's action would presumably cause the prosecutor to review the indictment again with care. The defendant could be made to respond to the indictment by summons, or a resumption of custody could be sought by application for a bench warrant. In the latter case, such a singular circumstance as a finding of no probable cause by the Commissioner would presumably be a factor for consideration by the court.

attendance of three witnesses. He supported this request with an allegation that these witnesses were "material and necessary to the defense, and that they were alleged eye-witnesses to the so-called occurrence." The Commissioner refused to issue subpoenas. The Commissioner found probable cause and ordered petitioner held to answer in the District Court.

An indictment was subsequently returned and present counsel was appointed to represent petitioner in the District Court. A number of motions were filed, including a motion to dismiss the indictment or, alternatively, to remand for a proper preliminary hearing. When that motion was denied, petitioner instituted this proceeding.

[A]n accused who demands the preliminary hearing as is his right is entitled to such a hearing and if the point is properly and timely pressed, a denial of that hearing cannot be excused by pointing to an intervening grand jury indictment.

Where an accused is adequately represented by counsel in the interim between the hearing and arraignment following the return of an indictment, and where no adequate excuse for failure to raise the preliminary hearing defect earlier is tendered, a serious question of timeliness would be presented. However, since neither the District Judge nor the Government raised this point, and since this is a capital case, we are not inclined to decide the issue *sua sponte.*

We think the District Judge should have granted petitioner's motion and remanded for a proper preliminary hearing where he could subpoena and examine the three witnesses whose attendance he timely and adequately sought.

ORDER

PER CURIAM. On consideration of respondent's petition for rehearing *en banc* and of petitioner's memorandum in opposition thereto, it is

Ordered by the court, *en banc,* that respondent's aforesaid petition is denied.

STATEMENT OF CIRCUIT JUDGE FAHY

FAHY, Circuit Judge. Moreover, the several opinions and statements now filed by members of the court demonstrate that a majority of the nine judges authorized to participate are of the opinion that the issuance of an indictment does not necessarily bar a supplementary hearing in case of serious defect in the preliminary hearing. The purpose of the Government's petition for rehearing en banc was to establish the contrary principle. Its contention has been before us a number of times and consideration has been given to the petition for rehearing en banc. So while the position has not formally been presented in a brief styled a brief on the merits, or orally argued at this time, it is one that has been pondered long and hard.

STATEMENT OF CIRCUIT JUDGES McGOWAN AND LEVENTHAL AS TO WHY THEY VOTE TO DENY REHEARING *En Banc*

The Government would also immunize from judicial scrutiny a practice whereby preliminary hearings are avoided through continuances granted routinely until mooted by an indictment. If such a practice were attempted in the District, we would find no insuperable barrier in meeting the problem through the sanction of requiring a hearing after indictment. Similarly, we see no jurisdictional barrier to a like sanction for coping with the withholding of critical witnesses whose testimony is the key to the issue of the reasonableness of continued detention. The compelling reason justifying that sanction is to avoid the threat to personal liberty—the risk of unlawful detention without probable cause—inherent in such practices, and not their denial of the limited degree of discovery which a preliminary hearing incidentally, though inescapably, provides. Whether and how that sanction is to be used should await delineation in cases involving the claim that indictments caused the frustration of timely efforts to cure defective proceedings.

It is our belief that discovery in criminal cases should be substantially enlarged, and we regret that those who had the drafting of the Federal Rules in charge did not go beyond the amendments effective July 1, 1966. But the preliminary hearing is neither a proper nor an adequate substitute for the more comprehensive discovery which we think those Rules should be enlarged to provide. We see no reason why the scope of the discovery available to a defendant should turn on whether he has been proceeded against in the first instance by complaint before a magistrate or by grand jury indictment.

STATEMENT OF CIRCUIT JUDGES BURGER AND TAMM ON VOTES TO GRANT REHEARING *En Banc*

Despite the fact that a Grand Jury has returned an indictment, the opinion of the sitting division which four judges voted to review directs the District Court to order another preliminary hearing before the accused is tried.[1] The opinion of the sitting division does not tell us what can be accomplished by such a remand or whether a United States Commissioner can conduct some sort of "appellate" review of the action of a Grand Jury. The sitting division's opinion, therefore, presents a very important and recurring question as to the relationship between a preliminary hearing and an indictment; it intensifies the confusion surrounding the role of the preliminary hearing which began with a misconception of what the *Blue* opinion really meant. For these reasons we voted to grant the government's petition for rehearing *en banc*.[2]

UNITED STATES *ex rel.* WHEELER v. FLOOD

269 F. Supp. 194 (E.D.N.Y. 1967)

WEINSTEIN, District Judge. Petitioners—as yet unindicted though in federal custody—seek a writ of habeas corpus in order to compel a United States Commissioner to hold a preliminary examination pursuant to subdivision (c) of Rule 5 of the Rules of Criminal Procedure. For the reasons set out below, if such a hearing is not granted forthwith, petitioners are entitled to be released.

---

2 Judges McGowan and Leventhal express a desire for a reserved power of "sanction" against prosecutors and United States Commissioners but it is interesting to note that the sitting division did not order the hearing as a sanction. Judges McGowan and Leventhal pose, in their "sanction" point, a very important question which has not been briefed or argued and we are not in a position to pass on it. We note, however, that they reserve this "sanction" power on the basis of a statement attributed to a Senator that "in at least one important district" (unnamed) the Government is receiving continuances of preliminary hearings until the Grand Jury acts and mootness can be claimed.

In this case, of course, Appellant had a preliminary hearing long before he was indicted. Thus Judges McGowan and Leventhal are talking about "sanctions" simply on the basis of a statement in Congress about the Government's practice in *one* of the 90 United States Districts and without regard to the facts of this case or inquiry into whether there is any such practice in *this* district. If, on evidence, we should ever find that a United States Commissioner is acting improperly this Court and the District Court can summarily direct him to alter his practices. We have no evidence whatever on this score.

If we assume the extraordinarily remote possibility that the United States Commissioner after hearing the alleged "critical witnesses" concludes no probable cause is shown, would anyone suggest he could *reverse* the Grand Jury! The heart of the "sanction" therefore is that the Commissioner and the United States Attorney will have been made to "stand in the corner" because subpoenas were not issued. We ought not suggest the use of judicial power so casually and with so little purpose.

[This case is disapproved in Sciortino v. Zampano, 385 F.2d 132 (2d Cir. 1967). *See* Note, *The Preliminary Hearing in the District of Columbia: An Emerging Discovery Device,* 56 GEO. L.J. 191-212 (1967).]

Petitioner Susan Wheeler has been in custody since her arrest on May 12, 1967, pursuant to a warrant issued upon a detailed sworn complaint. She was charged with conspiring to illegally import narcotic drugs. 21 U.S.C. § 174 (illegal importation of narcotic drug into United States); 26 U.S.C. § 4704(a) (sale of untaxed narcotic). She was brought before a Commissioner that day. Represented by counsel she demanded an immediate preliminary examination. Charged with the same conspiracy, petitioner Robert Wyler has been in custody since May 17, 1967; he appeared before a Commissioner on May 18, 1967 when his counsel also sought such an examination.

At the request of the United States, the Commissioner set June 5, 1967 in both cases for preliminary examination—some three and one-half weeks after Wheeler's arrest and two and one-half weeks from Wyler's arrest. The adjournment was sought, in the words of the Assistant United States Attorney prosecuting the two cases, "to allow me sufficient time to gather up my evidence in a presentable form." Bail was set for $25,000 for each petitioner but they have remained in custody.

On May 22, 1967, petitioners obtained an order to show cause, returnable May 24th, why a writ of habeas corpus should not issue in view of the failure to provide a preliminary examination. The next day, May 23rd, the United States Attorney began presenting evidence in the matter to the Grand Jury.

The Assistant United States Attorney argues that in good faith he sought an adjournment of the preliminary examination until June 5 and that subsequent events permitted him to proceed earlier before the Grand Jury. He declares that inasmuch as the "hearing date had been fixed by the United States Commissioners," he had "not the right to advance the date" nor did he have an obligation to let the defendant know that the United States was in fact prepared to present evidence to the Commissioner.

While the argument was not made on behalf of the United States, it might have been added that in this case the government was following a widespread practice "of delaying preliminary hearing until an indictment can be obtained." 8 Moore's Federal Practice, ¶ 5.04[3]. Most courts have felt compelled to deny relief on the ground that the issue of delay was mooted by indictment.

Part of the prosecution's attitude undoubtedly stems from its view that both preliminary examinations and Grand Jury indictments serve equally to assure that an accused is being held on probable cause—a main purpose of our criminal pretrial machinery. But from the defendant's vantage point—looking forward to a possible trial at which he will have to defend himself—these devices operate quite differently.

Rule 5 preliminary hearings require the government to produce evidence—although it is not clear whether it must be admissible at a trial—before a Commissioner, who in this district is an experienced lawyer. The defendant is entitled to have counsel present even if he cannot afford to pay an attorney; the government's witnesses are subject to cross-examination; the defendant has the right to present evidence and to subpoena witnesses. He may obtain a transcript whether or not he has funds to pay for it.

At least since the opinion in United States v. Costello, 350 U.S. 359, 363 (1956), evidence introduced before the Grand Jury need not be admissible at a trial. The defendant cannot be present while evidence against him is received. If he appears, he is not permitted to have counsel with him. He has no opportunity to cross-examine witnesses and the Grand Jury minutes are generally not available to him.

Under the Federal Rules the choice of waiver is the defendant's, not the government's. Upon a defendant's demand, a hearing is required within a "reasonable time." While some delay is envisaged (see, e.g., United States v. Gray, 87 F.Supp. 436, 438 (D.D.C.1949)), the hearing cannot, as in this case, be put off for weeks. It is significant that the Task Force on Administration of Justice of the President's Commission on Law Enforcement and Administration of Justice recently declared: "If the defendant is jailed, the preliminary hearing should be held within 72 hours." p. 85 (1967). The Task Force suggested a maximum of seven days delay where the defendant is not in custody. Ibid. The New York system—which, in many respects seems more protective of defendant's rights prior to trial than does the federal system—limits adjournments of the preliminary examination to 48 hours. N. Y. Code of Criminal Procedure, § 191.

It was unreasonable in this case to delay a preliminary hearing for incarcerated accuseds beyond the time the United States was prepared to present the matter to the Grand Jury. Should the United States Attorney ask for an adjournment of the preliminary examination on the ground that he is not prepared to proceed with the hearing, he should assume the obligation to inform defense counsel when he is ready. He should then cooperate in arranging for the examination as promptly as possible.

At the insistence of the defendant, the preliminary hearing of a defendant brought before a Commissioner prior to indictment should take place before, or simultaneously with, presentment to the Grand Jury unless, of course, the Grand Jury is operating independently of the United States Attorney—a circumstance most rare. Cf. Orfield, Criminal Procedure under the Federal Rules, 256 (1966) ("court may proceed with a preliminary examination even though a grand jury is in session"). Inconvenience to the prosecutor is never an excuse for denying the preliminary examination. Inconvenience to witnesses can be minimized. "Where the preliminary hearing serves as a discovery device, presentment of the case to the grand jury on the same day as the preliminary hearing would avoid bringing the witnesses to the courthouse twice." Task Force on Administration of Justice, The President's Commission on Law Enforcement and Administration of Justice, 85 (1967).

Accordingly, Susan Wheeler and Robert Wyler are ordered released from custody unless a hearing is held today, May 24, 1967, pursuant to subdivision (c) of Rule 5 of the Rules of Criminal Procedure for the United States District Court.

It is so ordered.

4. *Firming Up the Prosecutor's Case*

A CONVERSATION WITH DEFENSE COUNSEL ON PROBLEMS OF A CRIMINAL DEFENSE

By Harris B. Steinberg & Monrad G. Paulsen

7 The Practical Lawyer (No. 5) 25, 30 (1961)†

In certain cases, it may be well to make the prosecution show what they have, in a preliminary hearing, and even to cross-examine, to some extent, to pin a witness down. In many other cases, however, the advantages are illusory, while the disadvantages may be real. Consider the following: (1) The publicity may be vastly increased, by getting morbid details in the hands of the press, so that it is harder to get a jury. (2) A witness may be important to the prosecution, yet if he does not testify in a hearing, subject to cross-examination, his testimony is not perpetuated. Thus if he dies or disappears before trial, his testimony may not be read and the case may fall. (3) A witness may have a change of heart after the lapse of time. A victim of an assault may mellow when his scars heal; the victim of a bad check may relent when the check is later made good. If he has not committed himself in sworn testimony at the hearing, his testimony at the trial may be somewhat more favorable than might otherwise be the case. (4) Once you have cross-examined a witness in court, he is more likely to identify himself with the prosecutor's side

† Reproduced with the permission of The Practical Lawyer, 101 N. 33rd St., Philadelphia, Pa. Subscription rates: $10 a year, $2 single issue.

and resist any interviews. He is more likely to throw himself enthusiastically into the opposition's camp.[f]

Though the preliminary hearing is usually thought of as for the accused's protection the prosecutor may himself desire that it be held and may by statute be given the right to insist. For example:

Three defendants were charged with "conspiracy to sell narcotics." At their initial appearance their attorneys announced that the preliminary examination would be waived. However, the assistant prosecutor was present in the courtroom for the express purpose of moving that a preliminary examination be held. As explained by the prosecutor the purpose was to perpetuate the testimony of the three state's witnesses in case they would not be available at the time of trial. The three defendants were rather notorious narcotics sellers in Detroit, who had extensive contacts in New York. The witnesses had also been involved in the handling and sale of narcotics and had received numerous threats.

B. INSURING PROPER FUNCTIONING OF THE PRELIMINARY EXAMINATION

1. *Providing Counsel*

Obviously the defendant would be benefited by the assistance of counsel to raise objections to improper conduct of the preliminary examination, to cross-examine witnesses, to present favorable witnesses where that is permitted and desirable, and in general to see that the defendant's interests are protected. The traditional position has been, however, that while a person who has an attorney may consult with him and be represented by him, an indigent cannot insist that one be appointed at public expense at this early stage in the proceedings. Some jurisdictions give the defendant a statutory right to counsel at the preliminary examination;[g] most do not:

The prosecutor asked the accused at his initial appearance if he wanted an examination, or "Do you want to go right to trial?" "I want an attorney," stated the accused. The prosecutor replied,

---

[f] Concerning the perpetuation of testimony, see Note, *Preliminary Hearing—An Interest Analysis*, 51 IOWA L. REV. 164, 171-73 (1965).

[g] This has been true in federal courts since the revision of Rule 44 in 1966, and in the District of Columbia since 1960, though the right in the District only became settled by the decision in Blue v. United States, 342 F.2d 894 (D.C. Cir. 1964).

"We do not appoint attorneys for you at this time. If you want an attorney, you'll get one appointed before you go to trial." The defendant stated, "I want an examination." "Very well," said the court, and set a date.

The prosecuting attorney called as his only witness at the preliminary examination the victim, who had been cut several times in a barroom fight. The witness described the fight and pointed out the defendant as the man who cut him. The prosecutor stated to the accused, "Is there anything you want to ask this witness?" The accused stated, "Man, I want an attorney." The prosecutor said, "No attorneys at this stage." The court then bound the accused over for trial.

The constitutionality of failing to provide counsel at this hearing is brought into question by *White v. Maryland,* reproduced below, establishing that in at least some circumstances, due process requires the provision of counsel for indigents who desire them at the initial appearance and presumably under similar circumstances at the preliminary examination. The *White* case relies in turn on *Hamilton v. Alabama,* in which the Supreme Court found the defendant had been denied due process when, at the arraignment on the indictment for a capital offense, he pleaded not guilty without the aid of counsel and without having waived his right to counsel. The Court said in the *Hamilton* case:[h]

> [T]he . . . pitfalls [that face the unrepresented defendant at trial] face an accused in Alabama who is arraigned without having counsel at his side. When one pleads to a capital charge without benefit of counsel, we do not stop to determine whether prejudice resulted. . . . [T]he degree of prejudice can never be known. Only the presence of counsel could have enabled this accused to know all the defenses available to him and to plead intelligently.

The *White* case involves the common practice of asking an accused at the initial appearance, "How do you plead, guilty or not guilty?" This is not a formal plea, since a response of "guilty" is not binding on the accused (as such a plea would be if made at trial) except as a waiver of the preliminary examination, since it is taken as acknowledgment that there is sufficient basis

---

[h] 368 U.S. 52, 55 (1961).

to hold the accused for trial. There is disagreement among courts whether answering "guilty" at the initial appearance could be proved against the accused at trial if he were represented by counsel at the time he made the admission.

WHITE v. MARYLAND
373 U.S. 59 (1963)

Per Curiam. Petitioner, who was sentenced to death while his co-defendant was given life, appealed to the Maryland Court of Appeals which affirmed his conviction.

Petitioner was arrested on May 27, 1960, and brought before a magistrate on May 31, 1960, for a preliminary hearing. But that hearing was postponed and not actually held until August 9, 1960. At that time petitioner was not yet represented by a lawyer. When arraigned at that preliminary hearing he pleaded guilty. What Maryland calls the "arraignment" was first held September 8, 1960; but since petitioner was not represented by counsel, his arraignment was postponed and counsel appointed for him on September 9, 1960. He was finally arraigned on November 25, 1960, and entered pleas of "not guilty" and "not guilty by reason of insanity." At his trial the plea of guilty made at the preliminary hearing on August 9, 1960, was introduced in evidence. Since he did not have counsel at the time of the preliminary hearing, he argued that Hamilton v. Alabama, *supra,* applied. The Court of Appeals disagreed, saying that arraignment in Alabama is "a critical stage in a criminal proceeding" where rights are preserved or lost (368 U.S. 53-54), while under Maryland law there was "no requirement (nor any practical possibility under our present criminal procedure) to appoint counsel" for petitioner at the "preliminary hearing . . . nor was it necessary for appellant to enter a plea at that time." 227 Md., at 625, 177 A.2d, at 882.

Whatever may be the normal function of the "preliminary hearing" under Maryland law, it was in this case as "critical" a stage as arraignment under Alabama law. For petitioner entered a plea before the magistrate and that plea was taken at a time when he had no counsel.

We repeat what we said in Hamilton v. Alabama, *supra,* at 55, that we do not stop to determine whether prejudice resulted: "Only the presence of counsel could have enabled this accused to know all the defenses available to him and to plead intelligently." We therefore hold that *Hamilton v. Alabama* governs and that the judgment below must be and is reversed.

The lower federal courts and the state courts have almost uniformly refused to reverse in similar circumstances where there was no prejudice, for example, in that a "plea of guilty" at the initial appearance was not used at trial.

The subsequent case of *Pointer v. Texas*[i] held that the admission into evidence at trial of testimony taken at a preliminary hearing at which the defendant had not been represented by counsel and hence was unable to cross-examine effectively constituted a denial of the accused's right to confront the witnesses against him. The Court refused to decide whether the denial of counsel was itself a deprivation of due process because

> the State informs us that at a Texas preliminary hearing, such as is involved here, pleas of guilty or not guilty are not accepted and that the judge decides only whether the accused should be bound over to the grand jury and if so whether he should be admitted to bail. Because of these significant differences in the procedures of the respective States, we cannot say that the *White* case is necessarily controlling as to the right to counsel. Whether there might be other circumstances making this Texas preliminary hearing so critical to the defendant as to call for appointment of counsel at that stage we need not decide on this record, and that question we reserve.[j]

Even though the Supreme Court has dealt with formal aspects of the preliminary hearing—pleading and confrontation—in finding that stage of the proceedings so critical as to require representation by counsel, one might ask whether the trial preparation and discovery aspects of the preliminary examination are not of equal practical importance.

HARRIS v. WILSON

239 F. Supp. 204 (N.D. Cal. 1965)

WEIGEL, District Judge. In April, 1954, Fred Russell Harris was convicted of armed robbery by a California Superior Court. He had pled guilty, but did not have the assistance of counsel at any stage of the proceedings against him. He now seeks a writ of habeas corpus, claiming that his constitutional rights have been violated (1) by the failure of the magistrate at his Preliminary Examination to assign counsel and (2) by the similar failure

---

[i] 380 U.S. 400 (1965).

[j] *Id.* at 402-03.

of the presiding judge at arraignment in Superior Court. It appears that petitioner has exhausted his available state remedies.

II. *The Preliminary Examination*

The most recent Supreme Court decisions on the general matter of the stage of criminal proceedings at which counsel must be appointed are Hamilton v. Alabama, 368 U.S. 52 (1961) and White v. Maryland, 373 U.S. 59 (1963).

The combined meaning of these two cases is partly summarized by the court in United States ex rel. Cooper v. Reincke, 333 F.2d 608 (2d Cir., 1964):

"From Hamilton v. Alabama and White v. Maryland, it is plain that there is no arbitrary point in time at which the right to counsel attaches in pre-trial proceedings. Even in White, decided after Gideon, the Court did not refer to counsel 'at every stage.' Rather, the 'critical' point is to be determined both from the nature of the proceedings and from that which actually occurs in each case." Id. at 611.

Considering the emphasis in both White and Hamilton on the irrelevance of a showing of *prejudice* from the failure to appoint counsel in any particular case, it seems that the controlling principle is this: Any stage of the judicial proceedings which is not purely "formal," any stage where the advice of counsel could "affect the whole trial," is a "critical point" at which, absent valid waiver, counsel must be appointed if the defendant is unable to obtain his own.

The White, Hamilton and Powell decisions are all distinguishable on their facts from this case. In each of them, defendants were denied counsel either at the time they entered pleas or during the period thereafter. In the California Preliminary Examination, on the other hand, it is true that no plea can be made when the defendant is not represented by counsel. Furthermore, as the Attorney General has pointed out, no "incriminating statement taken from . . . [petitioner] at that time when he was not represented by counsel [could] have been used in evidence against him [in California]." Also, "[u]nlike Hamilton v. Alabama, supra, under California law petitioner could not have waived any defense, procedural or substantive, by anything that occurred at the time of the preliminary examination."

Even so and despite these differences between the circumstances pertaining in California judicial proceedings and the situations in White, Hamilton and Powell, the rationale of the latter cases dictates a holding that the Examination *is* a "critical" stage at which the right to counsel attaches.

Perhaps the most convincing reason that presence of defense counsel at Preliminary Examination might "affect the whole trial" is the fact that the Examination is an initial adversary confrontation. The rest of the judicial proceedings can be completely avoided if the defendant achieves a victory at this stage. Moreover, it is the type of adversary hearing where counsel is most helpful. As Witkin points out, "[a]lthough the quantum of proof is less than that required on a trial of guilt . . ., the same rules of admissibility [of evidence] govern. Consequently no valid commitment can be based entirely on incompetent evidence. . . . However, incompetent evidence received without objection may be given its full probative effect." Id. at 133, 134. Furthermore, prosecution witnesses may be cross-examined and the defense may proffer its own witnesses. In all of these matters, the absence of defense counsel could have a crucial effect on the accused's opportunity to obtain a complete termination of the criminal proceedings at this early stage.

The fact that the Preliminary Examination is a species of criminal pre-trial discovery is another reason for requiring appointment of counsel at this point. On cross-examination, counsel could elicit information helpful for the defense. What is discovered at this point could affect the defense strategy for the rest of the criminal proceedings. If the prosecution's case seems irrefutable, it might be wise for counsel to advise a plea of guilty at arraignment in Superior Court, shifting the defense efforts to the pursuit of a more favorable sentence. On the other hand, if some major weakness in the prosecution's case should be exposed in cross-examination, this would bolster the defendant's determination to win acquittal.

The fact that the Examination serves the purpose of preserving testimony would be an important consideration in some cases, even though no facts have been adduced in this case to show whether this function of the Examination might have been significant here.

Very frequently in California, the Preliminary Examination is all the "trial" a defendant is accorded.

"It is a not uncommon practice for the defendant, on trial in the superior court after being held to answer, to stipulate that a transcript of the evidence taken at the preliminary examination may be introduced at the trial in lieu of the testimony covered therein. . . .

"This procedure may go to the extent of a stipulation for waiver of a jury and submission of the entire case to the trial judge on the reporter's transcript of testimony at the preliminary examination. (See People v. Wallin, supra [Cal., 208 P.2d 400]; People v. Romero (1950) 100 C.A.2d 352, 223 P.2d 511; . . .)" Witkin, supra, § 355, pp. 346-47.

In many cases, if there has been defense counsel at the Preliminary Examination, it may be good strategy for the defendant to plead innocent and submit the case on the transcript. The prosecution's burden of proof in the Preliminary Examination is much less than the burden of proof required for conviction; since the prosecution usually holds back some of its evidence until trial, the defendant may have a better chance on the prosecution's lesser showing.

Finally, the State of California itself has decided that an indigent defendant is entitled to assigned counsel at the Preliminary Examination. California Penal Code § 859, referring to the Preliminary Examination, now provides that "If the defendant desires and is unable to employ counsel, the court must assign counsel to defend him." This is manifest recognition of the critical importance of the presence of counsel at the Examination under California law and procedure.[3]

For these reasons, it must be concluded that the federal constitutional right to counsel attaches at the California Preliminary Examination.[4]

Hence, for the failure of the state to provide the petitioner with counsel at the Preliminary Examination, the writ of habeas corpus must be issued.[k]

---

[3] The discussion in text is limited to the requirements of the right to counsel insofar as they are imposed on the states by the Due Process Clause of the Fourteenth Amendment. But Supreme Court decisions based on the Equal Protection Clause could well compel the same result. See Douglas v. California, 372 U.S. 353 (1963).

[4] It should be pointed out that my brother, Judge E. Avery Crary, reached the opposite conclusion on this question for reasons set out in Wells v. State of California, 234 F. Supp. 467 (S.D. Calif. 1964).

[k] The court of appeals reversed, Wilson v. Harris, 351 F.2d 840 (9th Cir. 1965), stating in explanation (at 845):

> This reasoning, however, overlooks the fact that the right reserved to appellant at the hearing was merely not to be held in custody without probable cause. Consequently, the possible denial of that right is the only thing of which he can now complain. Whatever collateral benefit that might have accrued, just as the prejudice he may have suffered, is altogether conjectural and certainly cannot amount to the deprivation of a constitutional right. Appellant has the burden of showing his trial to have been fundamentally unfair, a burden that is not met by speculations as to what could have happened had any number of events occurred differently.

SPARKMAN v. STATE

27 Wis. 2d 92, 133 N.W.2d 776 (1965)

Error to review a judgment of the municipal court of Racine county.

The plaintiff in error Milton Sparkman, hereinafter called "defendant," was found guilty by a jury on a plea of not guilty of violating sec. 943.10(1)(a), Stats. (burglary), and sentenced to an indeterminate term of ten years. The defendant being indigent counsel was appointed by this court to prosecute this writ of error.

Defendant was arrested in Chicago, Illinois, for disorderly conduct on April 22, 1959. At that time he had in his possession items of personal property which had been burglarized from the Photo Craft Shop in Racine, Wisconsin, the night before. He was later extradited to Wisconsin. At the preliminary hearing his request for counsel was refused. The defendant did not waive the preliminary hearing and proceeded to represent himself, cross-examining witnesses and taking the stand as a witness. He was cross-examined by the district attorney. After the hearing he was bound over for trial and later an information was filed against him. Counsel was appointed who represented the defendant on arraignment and at the trial.

HALLOWS, J. The defendant contends the due-process and the equal-protection clauses of the Fourteenth amendment of the federal constitution and sec. 7, art. I of the state constitution providing "in all criminal prosecutions" the accused has the right to the assistance of counsel entitle him as an indigent to appointed counsel at his preliminary hearing.

We do not reach the question whether an indigent has a constitutional right to appointed counsel at a preliminary hearing on this record. Although extradition papers are not in the record, it is stated in several places the defendant was extradited from Illinois. A fugitive from justice within the meaning of the constitution and the laws of the United States is not entitled to a preliminary hearing before an information is filed against him. This is one of the exceptions to the requirement of a preliminary hearing in sec. 955.18(1), Stats. Johns v. State (1961), 14 Wis. (2d) 119, 109 N.W.(2d) 490.

However, on grounds of public policy we adopt a rule for prospective application only that an indigent is entitled to appointed counsel at or prior to a preliminary hearing unless intelligently waived. Wisconsin from early statehood has been concerned with its duty to provide counsel in criminal cases for indigents and has not depended upon or awaited the increasing scope of the commands of the Fourteenth amendment.

There are many statutory provisions recognizing an accused needs counsel before trial if such representation is to be effective and the accused is to be afforded the opportunity to be fairly tried.

Other compelling reasons for requiring the defendant to be represented by counsel at least as early as the preliminary hearing include the avoidance of the adverse psychological factors affecting an unrepresented defendant, the furnishing of opportunity for effectively preparing the defense of cross-examining government witnesses at the preliminary, and the preservation of testimony of other witnesses which might be lost.

But we think a most compelling ground of public policy is the prevention of the possibility of the violation of constitutional right of a fair trial occurring at the trial itself.

The concept of the critical stage when the appointment of counsel should have been made as developed in Hamilton v. Alabama (1961), 368 U.S. 52, and in White v. Maryland (1963), 373 U.S. 59, appears to depend not *per se* on the absence of counsel prior to trial but on whether there was some occurrence or omission which subsequently affected the fairness of the trial and which occurrence or omission presumably would have been avoided if the accused had been represented by counsel. In *Hamilton* the arraignment was held to be a critical stage because under Alabama state law certain pleas were required to be made at that time or they were waived. In *White* the indigent entered a plea of guilty at a preliminary hearing although not required to do so and such plea was later admitted in evidence against him.

The cases since *Hamilton* and *White* have continued to find a violation of due process only in situations where actual prejudice resulted.

However, it must be recognized that the appointment of counsel at the preliminary hearing examination would tend to insure fairness at the trial stage and to avoid the type of situation which led to a reversal in White v. Maryland, *supra.*

This holding that the indigent accused is entitled to representation at public expense at a preliminary hearing is made prospective only and any violation thereof is subject to the harmless-error rule. Pulaski v. State (1964), 24 Wis. (2d) 450, 129 N.W.(2d) 204. In the instant case no claim of prejudice is made; reversal is urged solely because the denial of counsel was *per se* a violation of a claimed constitutional right to counsel. But the question of a constitutional right to counsel we expressly reserve for future consideration. In addition Mr. Justice WILKIE and the writer would reach the constitutional question on this record and hold that the indigent accused has a constitutional right to appointed counsel at a preliminary hearing on the grounds: (1) Such hearing is a necessary part of "in all criminal prosecutions" under sec. 7, art. I of the Wisconsin constitution, (2) to insure a fair trial under the due-process clause of the Fourteenth amendment of the United States constitution, and (3) because an accused has a statutory right to retained counsel at a preliminary hearing, an accused who is indigent is entitled to appointed counsel under the equal-protection clause of the Fourteenth amendment.

By the Court.—Judgment affirmed.*

UNITED STATES COMMISSIONER SYSTEM

Hearings on the United States Commissioner System Before the Subcommittee on Improvements in Judicial Machinery of the Senate Committee on the Judiciary, 89th Cong., 2d Sess., pt. 3, at 266-72 (1966)

Statement of A. Kenneth Pye, Professor of Law and Associate Dean, Georgetown University Law Center

. . . As I understand Mr. Olney's testimony, the new proposal would provide that an arrested person should be taken before the commissioner without unnecessary delay. Counsel would be appointed for him, bail would be fixed and a deadline would be set within which an indictment should be returned. If not indicted by that date, the defendant would be entitled to discharge unless "good cause to the contrary was shown."

Mr. Olney argues that this change is desirable because the commissioner's hearing has become obsolete. The claim of obsolescence rests upon the assumption that because the commissioner's hearing originated at a time when a lengthy delay was required before a grand jury could meet and because grand juries can now meet more frequently; necessarily, the preliminary hearing must have outlived its usefulness. The utility of hearings as conducted in States such as California is viewed as irrelevant because of the sixth amendment requirement that Federal felony prosecutions be initiated by indictment and the conclusion that "there is no good reason why a defendant should waive indictment."

It must be conceded that in the past the provision giving the defendant a right to a hearing before the commissioner has not played a significant role in criminal procedure. Mr. Olney has indicated that last year 70 percent of the defendants waived their

*Compare *Jones v. State,* at 487 n.o, *supra,* extending the Sparkman rule to the initial appearance.

hearings and of those who had hearings, only 8 percent were discharged. From these statistics, Mr. Olney concluded, "Few defendants believe a hearing will be of benefit to them."

I do not think that this conclusion is justified. In the first place, during the period in which the statistics were compiled, a defendant was informed only of "his right to retain counsel." He was not informed of his "right to request the assignment of counsel if he is unable to obtain counsel." Furthermore, prior to the Criminal Justice Act, the commissioner had no authority to appoint counsel if a defendant requested him to do so. We know that approximately 60 percent of the defendants brought before the Federal courts are unable to afford counsel. Knowledge of the right to retain counsel was not of much use to these defendants. I do not think it is fair to conclude that defendants in the future will conclude that a hearing will be of no benefit to them because they waived hearings in the past when they did not have the benefit of counsel.

The point can be illustrated by the experience in the District of Columbia. Judges of the District of Columbia Court of General Sessions exercise the functions of a U.S. commissioner under rule 5. They also appoint counsel for defendants brought before them. Last year almost 50 percent of the approximately 1,200 defendants brought before these judges asserted their right to a preliminary hearing.

Prior to October of 1964, the U.S. commissioner did not inform indigent defendants of the availability of Legal Aid Agency staff attorneys, although Congress had specifically authorized these lawyers to provide representation for defendants before the commissioner, and the agency offices were in the same building with the commissioner. As a result of the *Blue* decision, the commissioner began to inform defendants not only of their right to retain counsel, but that lawyers were available to represent those who could not afford counsel. The result was a dramatic increase in the number of cases in which lawyers were requested. I have asked the agency to provide the committee with the exact statistics. . . .

The main thesis of the proposal is that grand juries can consider any case where a defendant has been arrested without substantial delay, and hence, we can avoid hardships to defendants who might have to wait a long time after being arrested without the necessity of a commissioner's hearing.

Mr. Olney has indicated that it is practical to have a grand jury available to hear cases promptly in any district. Substantial changes in existing procedure would be necessary to accomplish that result. In the District of Columbia the time period between a commissioner's hearing and indictment is at least 6 weeks. It is my understanding that the U.S. attorney and the grand jury are processing the cases as quickly as possible. The subcommittee should collect data from throughout the country to determine the delay period between arrest and preliminary hearing and between preliminary hearing and grand jury action before any final conclusions are reached.

In any case, the mere decision that a grand jury can meet promptly does not mean that a preliminary hearing before a commissioner has no social utility. The purposes of the hearing have evolved through history. It is quite fallacious to assume that the reason for its initiation constitutes the only basis justifying its continuance.

One of the most important purposes is to provide protection against arrests for investigation. It is not only a determination of probable cause but a determination of probable cause shortly after the arrest which is significant. The requirement that the defendant be brought before the commissioner without unnecessary delay and the right of the defendant to have a hearing to determine whether there is probable cause combine to discourage law enforcement officers from arresting on suspicion and then investigating the case at their leisure to determine whether there is probable cause. The elimination of the commissioner's hearing is an open invitation to arrests for investigation. If a subsequent investigation develops no probable cause, or establishes the defendant's innocence, the grand jury can be requested to return an ignoramus. During the interval, the defendant will have been deprived of his liberty in violation of the Constitution, but will be without redress. The present hearing provision is one of the best devices which we have found to implement the fourth amendment's requirement to arrest on probable cause. A motion to suppress at a later time provides protection only if real evidence or a statement has been obtained from the defendant. It provides no protection for either the innocent defendant or the guilty defendant who remained silent and from whom no evidence was seized.

Furthermore, the purpose of a commissioner's hearing is not only to have another determination of whether there is probable cause, but to do so in an adversary proceeding. This is why a defendant is given the right to cross-examine, to call witnesses and to testify in his own behalf. He does not have these rights before a grand jury. Indeed, it is a crime for him to communicate with the grand jury without authority. Probable cause has already been determined ex parte by either an officer arresting without a warrant or by a commissioner or judge in issuing a warrant. One reason for the commissioner's hearing is to test the assertion of probable cause by the best truth-seeking device which we have been able to develop—cross-examination by counsel.

It was partly for this reason that Congress made provision for the appointment of counsel for those who are unable to afford a lawyer in the Criminal Justice Act of 1964. There is no reason to assume that the adversary system is less suitable for finding the truth before trial when the standard of proof is probable cause than it is at trial when the standard is beyond a reasonable doubt. I question whether an ex parte grand jury proceeding is a more effective device to determine the existence of probable cause than a preliminary hearing.

We should not forget that we are dealing with people and public institutions. I think that fundamental fairness requires that a citizen who has been deprived of his liberty have an opportunity to determine the charge against him from a judicial officer and to confront either his accuser or the police in a judicial setting as soon as it is feasible to provide the opportunity. One of the defects in using the grand jury is the secrecy which surrounds it. A defendant does not confront his accuser. Society has no means of evaluating the manner in which it functions. The public hearing, rather than the secret inquest, has many advantages in a free society.

A third important function which can and should be performed by the preliminary hearing is to provide the mechanism for encouraging waiver of indictments, the breaking down of charges and the entry of pleas of guilty to lesser included offenses. A great deal of unnecessary time and effort is wasted in Federal criminal procedure in processing cases before grand juries when pleas to the principal offense will be entered in approximately 78 percent of the cases. In the past, the decision whether to plead and the negotiations conducted in order to obtain a favorable disposition of the case have usually taken place after indictment, because the defendant usually did not have a lawyer before indictment. Under the Criminal Justice Act, lawyers will now be appointed at the initial presentment before the commissioner. We are provided with an excellent opportunity to eliminate unnecessary steps in the process and limit the delay between arrest and sentencing by using the commissioner's hearing as the catalyst for disposing of cases by agreement without the necessity of waiting until the grand jury indicts before negotiations can begin.

The defendant can, of course, insist on a grand jury consideration of the charges against him. However, I do not agree with Mr. Olney's conclusion that there is no real advantage to a defendant to waive indictment. There is a real advantage in avoiding the delay between the date of his arrest and the action of the grand jury. A defendant may receive no credit for time spent in jail if he is unable to make bail. Over 87 percent of defendants charged in the Federal courts are convicted. Over 78 percent plead guilty. Over 73 percent of those who try their cases to juries are convicted. Outside of the District of Columbia, 80 percent of those who plead guilty do so at arraignment. Counsel who understands the strength of the government's case from the preliminary hearing may readily reach the conclusion that there is no reasonable chance of the grand jury returning an ignoramus and, consequently, that it is to the interest of his client to waive indictment, particularly if the government is prepared to reduce the charge and permit him to plead to a lesser included offense.

Furthermore, the likelihood that his client will receive a lenient sentence may be enhanced by a prompt plea of guilty in some districts. In 1964, in the District of Columbia, approximately 56 percent of the defendants who pleaded guilty at arraignment received probation while only 13.1 percent of these individuals were sentenced to a term of imprisonment in excess of 3 years. However, 28.9 percent of the defendants who pleaded not guilty originally but changed their plea to guilty received probation, while 37.9 percent of these defendants received a sentence of over 3 years' imprisonment. Only 13.8 percent of the defendants who were convicted as a result of a jury trial received probation, and 68.8 percent of these defendants received a sentence of imprisonment of over 3 years.

In other districts defendants who were tried and convicted by jury also received the heaviest sentences, although sentence disparity between defendants who pleaded guilty at arraignments, and those who pleaded not guilty initially, but changed their pleas to guilty later, was not as great as in the District of Columbia. In many districts a defense counsel might consider that the advantages of negotiating a plea promptly more than compensate for the unlikely possibility that a grand jury might refuse to indict.

We have some experience in the District of Columbia. For many years, judges of the District of Columbia Court of General Sessions have exercised the functions of U.S. commissioners. They have also appointed counsel for defendants brought before them. A practice has developed by which defense counsel negotiate with the Government, felonies are broken to misdemeanors, and pleas are entered to misdemeanors. Likewise, during the 14 months in which the Legal Aid Agency has been providing counsel to a substantial number of defendants before the U.S. commissioner, a process has begun to evolve in which counsel initiate conferences with the Office of the U.S. Attorney with regard to possible disposition of cases before indictment. We may find that, with the advent of appointed counsel under the Criminal Justice Act, a practice may develop in other districts in which the necessity of grand jury action will be eliminated in many cases.

A fourth possible purpose of the preliminary hearing is discovery. Whether discovery is an appropriate purpose of a preliminary hearing is a matter of considerable dispute among the authorities. Even within the District of Columbia circuit, there are different views expressed in the *Blue*,[7] *Crump*,[8] and *Dancy*[9] opinions.

Most courts would probably deny that discovery is an appropriate purpose. However, the handwriting is on the wall. In *Brady v. Maryland*,[10] the Supreme Court indicated that due process requires that the defendant have an opportunity to obtain the information he needs to present his case and to meet the Government case at some stage of a criminal proceeding. The days of the fox hunt and the suppression of evidence are on their way out. The question in criminal procedure in the future will be how to regulate the exercise of discovery, not whether it should be permitted. In the District of Columbia it has been suggested that the preliminary hearing provides such a device. The Advisory Committee on the Federal Criminal Rules has suggested modifications of rules 16 and 17 and the use of pretrial conferences. Judge Levin achieves the same results through judicial encouragement of "voluntary" disclosure. I am not sure which device is best.

Fortunately, we are not required to solve this problem at this time. We may agree that discovery is not a primary function and still recognize the utility of the preliminary hearing as a protection against unlawful arrests, a mechanism to test probable cause in an adversary proceeding, and a process which may result in encouraging waiver of indictments and pleas of guilty.

2. *Casting the Proceeding in an Adversary Mold*

Though the typical preliminary examination is routine and perfunctory, consisting essentially of calling one or two witnesses

[7] Blue v. United States, 342 F.2d 894 (D.C. Cir. 1964).
[8] Crump v. Anderson [352 F.2d 649 (D.C. Cir. 1965)].
[9] Dancy v. United States [361 F.2d 75 (D.C. Cir. 1966)].
[10] Brady v. Maryland, 373 U.S. 83 (1963).

to state a prima facie case, it is possible for the preliminary examination to be a trial in miniature. After such witnesses as the prosecutor calls have testified, they are subject quite generally to cross-examination, objections may be made to admissibility of evidence, defense witnesses may be called and cross-examined, and argument may be made on whether the defendant should be bound over for trial or for grand jury action.[l] Obviously little of this will take place if the defendant is unrepresented. The unaided defendant may make some efforts (occasionally self-defeating) at cross-examination, but rarely does more. Even when defense counsel is present he ordinarily contents himself with cross-examination. Effective cross-examination is the defendant's principal discovery device at this stage. Only in a rare case will the defense present witnesses (*see* illustrations 6 and 7, at 523, *supra*) or serious argument on the merits, since this involves disclosure by the defense of its theory.

The adversary nature of the preliminary examination provides motivation for the prosecutor's going directly to the grand jury if he is allowed to. It is also the basis for argument that preliminary examination should be mandatory unless waived by the accused, since only in this way can he secure an opportunity to persuade a judicial officer that he ought not be held for trial.

WASHINGTON v. CLEMMER

339 F.2d 715 (D.C. Cir. 1964)

Before BAZELON, Chief Judge, and WASHINGTON and WRIGHT, Circuit Judges.

PER CURIAM. This is a *habeas corpus* case challenging the lawfulness of the procedures used in a preliminary hearing. Appellant, an indigent juvenile, was charged with the capital offense of abetting a rape. After the juvenile court waived jurisdiction, he was brought before the United States Commissioner on May 7, 1964, for a preliminary hearing to determine whether there was probable cause to believe that an offense had been committed and that the appellant had committed it. Rule 5(c), FED.R.CRIM.P.

I.

The appellant requested the Commissioner to obtain a stenographic reporter for the preliminary hearing. As the Government concedes in its petition, the Commissioner has the authority to secure a reporter for his hearings. The Commissioner's failure to grant the request here was error.

---

[l] Geis, *Preliminary Hearings and the Press,* 8 U.C.L.A.L. REV. 397 (1961), discusses the problem of newspaper coverage of the preliminary examination.

Generally it would be desirable to record the testimony given at every stage of the criminal process. The preliminary hearing is an adversary judicial proceeding necessary to authorize continued constraint of the accused. Absence of a transcript makes it difficult, if not impossible, to review the Commissioner's finding of probable cause. And verbatim recording of testimony at an early stage of the process perpetuates the fresh memory of witnesses, making it available in case of subsequent death, disability, or flight, and allowing impeachment or refreshing of recollection at trial. Accordingly, early recording also serves to discourage threats against witnesses and suborning of perjury.

And even if the absence of a transcript might ultimately be found not prejudicial, obviously it is not possible to predict such an eventuality, and the Commissioner should therefore ordinarily grant a request for a reporter.

We think these reasons justify the exercise of our supervisory power over the administration of criminal justice in the District of Columbia to require stenographic recording of testimony at the preliminary hearing.

We also think this course is required by minimal standards of fair and equal justice. Defendants who have funds are entitled to employ their own reporters. To deny this opportunity to an indigent defendant would be to permit invidious discrimination based on wealth. Furthermore, since the Government may have a reporter at the hearing, the accused must be afforded the same right in order to meet the requirements of fundamental fairness.

II.

The defendant requested that subpoenas issue; the Commissioner denied the request without explanation. The United States Attorney concedes in his petition that the Commissioner has authority to secure subpoenas at the request of the defendant. Rule 5(c), FED.R.CRIM.P., guarantees to the accused before the Commissioner the right to "introduce evidence in his own behalf." Rule 17(a), FED.R.CRIM.P., provides that "A subpoena shall be issued by a commissioner in a proceeding before him, but it need not be under the seal of the court." We read Rules 5(c) and 17(a) to require the Commissioner to subpoena material witnesses reasonably requested by the accused. The Commissioner's failure to do so here was error.

The said writ is to be made absolute at that time unless the return shows that prior thereto a preliminary hearing before any committing magistrate, under Rule 5 of the Federal Rules of Criminal Procedure, has been held in compliance with the following:

(1) That probable cause be established by competent evidence.

(2) That there be present at the preliminary hearing a stenographic reporter furnished by the United States District Court or the United States Attorney or the committing magistrate.

(3) That reasonable requests for subpoenas be granted in compliance with Rule 5(c) and Rule 17 of the Federal Rules of Criminal Procedure. (See Greenwell v. United States, 115 U.S.App.D.C. 44, 317 F.2d 108 (1963).)

DANAHER, Circuit Judge, with whom WILBUR K. MILLER and BASTIAN, Circuit Judges, join, filed the following statement.

At No. 2 Precinct a line-up was created by Detective Holden. The complaining witness positively identified Washington and Burton. Thereupon, in confrontation, she stated in the presence of Washington that he was the man driving the cab, he had not had intercourse with her but the other man did. She said that Washington was the one who had punched her in the mouth and put a knife against her. At first, both Burton and Washington denied knowledge of the episode. When separated, Washington stated to Detective Holden: "You heard what the woman said. Everything she said was true." He added that he had not raped the complaining witness. Thereafter Detective Holden searched the taxicab. On the back seat he found a woman's shoe. The complaining witness identified the shoe as hers.

The Commissioner on such evidence ruled that probable cause had been established. If his finding were open to review, I would affirm without the slightest question.

Even were we free in this proceeding to review the Commissioner's judicial decision, it has not been shown that he erred. In Holt v. United States, 218 U.S. 245, 247 (1910), Mr. Justice Holmes pointed out that an officer had testified before a grand jury as to admissions by the prisoner, obtained under circumstances which made them incompetent. Speaking for a unanimous Court, he concluded that there was no basis for reviewing the discretion of the trier. Again, in Costello v. United States, 350 U.S. 359, 363 (1956), Mr. Justice Black discussed the subject of inadequate or incompetent evidence before the grand jury. Were an indictment to be subject to challenge on such grounds, he wrote, "the resulting delay would be great indeed. The result of such a rule would be that before trial on the merits a defendant could always insist on a kind of preliminary trial to determine the competency and adequacy of the evidence before the grand jury. This is not required by the Fifth Amendment. An indictment returned by a legally constituted and unbiased grand jury, *like an information drawn by the prosecutor,* if valid on its face, is enough to call for trial of the charge on the merits. The Fifth Amendment requires nothing more." (Emphasis added.)

BURGER, Circuit Judge (statement as to reasons for vote on Motion for hearing en banc). If, in fact, a Motions Panel of the Court was undertaking to lay down a rule to require transcripts in all preliminary hearings, or require government witnesses to be subpoenaed in all cases, or altering the long standing law as to what constitutes competent evidence to warrant holding an accused for the Grand Jury, I would surely vote for en banc consideration. However, I am not willing to assume that a Motions Panel would undertake to amend, in such a fundamental and far reaching manner, the Federal Rules of Criminal Procedure, which Congress approved for the administration of justice; such an action would be reckless and irresponsible.

As I see it, the Motions Panel now explicitly negates any intention of deciding probable cause cannot be established by hearsay evidence before the United States Commissioner or other magistrate in order to hold an accused for the Grand Jury. Few legal concepts have been more universally accepted than the proposition that "competent" evidence before a magistrate to establish probable cause at that stage is very different from "competent" evidence in the context of a criminal trial. The standard of proof before the committing magistrate or for issuance of a warrant is "accordingly correlative to what must be proved." Brinegar v. United States, 338 U.S. 160, 175 (1949). An arrest can be made, a warrant can issue and a Grand Jury can indict on hearsay and other forms of evidence not competent for admission at trial. See Costello v. United States, 350 U.S. 359 (1956). A fortiori the intermediate step of deciding to hold an accused until a Grand Jury can consider evidence against him may be taken on such evidence.

WASHINGTON v. CLEMMER
339 F.2d 725 (D.C. Cir. 1964)

Before BAZELON, Chief Judge, and WASHINGTON and WRIGHT, Circuit Judges.

PER CURIAM. This case, concerning the procedures required by law for a preliminary hearing, returns to us again.

The Commissioner's examination was reopened on May 13; there was present a stenographic reporter assigned by the District Court without cost to the indigent accused, in compliance with our order. The accused requested the Commissioner to subpoena the complaining witness, averring that she would not positively identify him as the aider and abetter of the person who raped her and that, therefore, her testimony was material to his defense. The Commissioner refused, stating that the accused's averment was false. This finding was based on the testimony, given at the prior unrecorded hearing by the arresting officer, that four weeks earlier, following the arrest, the complainant had told the officer that the accused was one of her assailants.

The preliminary hearing is an adversary judicial proceeding. Wood v. United States, 75 U.S.App.D.C. 274, 128 F.2d 265, 141 A.L.R. 1318 (1942). Rule 5(c), F.R.Cr.P., specifically provides that at the preliminary hearing "[t]he defendant may cross-examine witnesses against him and may introduce evidence in his own behalf." The accused and the police having offered conflicting sworn statements as to whether or not the victim could positively identify the accused, it was improper to refuse to allow the victim to be called to testify for herself. Certainly the Commissioner was not justified in closing his mind to the possibility of a significant discrepancy between the police officer's hearsay and the complaining witness' own sworn testimony. If the complaining witness were in fact unable, under oath and after cross-examination, to identify the accused, it may well be that the Commissioner would find probable cause for holding the accused had not been made out.

Where, as here, the accused is not able to make bond, a commitment by the Commissioner to await grand jury action is in effect a sentence of imprisonment. Consequently, a *pro forma* compliance with the requirements of Rule 5, in addition to defeating the purpose of the preliminary hearing, may result in real injustice. The presumption of innocence our law affords defendants has meaning at the preliminary hearing; the accused is entitled to his liberty unless the Government can establish probable cause for his detention through procedures which accord with our concept of fair process.

3. *Judicial Review*

By habeas corpus[m] or by a motion to quash the information[n] (and perhaps also by other devices),[o] a defendant can raise the

[m] *E.g.*, United States *ex rel.* Waldron v. Lennox, 244 F. Supp. 239 (E.D. Pa. 1965).

[n] *E.g.*, People v. Kennedy, 9 Mich. App. 346, 155 N.W.2d 855 (1968).

[o] *See* pp. 529-42, *supra*.

question of the propriety of the decision to hold him for trial or grand jury action. Under the usual view, however, such question is mooted by the grand jury's returning an indictment. In its turn, the grand jury action can be tested by habeas corpus or motion to quash the indictment.

The challenge may go to the sufficiency of the evidence in terms of quantity, it may question the propriety of considering evidence which would be inadmissible at trial, or it may challenge the validity of the proceedings on such grounds as lack of jurisdiction over the subject matter, absence of counsel, denial of defendant's right to cross-examine witnesses against him, and so on.

There seems rather widespread agreement that the evidence justifying holding for trial must establish probable cause, but a question so basic as whether the examining magistrate should pass on witness credibility or resolve all disputes as to credibility in favor of the prosecution has never been explored. Such an issue would normally be raised at the instance of the prosecution, but since the prosecutor cannot usually appeal he will either abandon prosecution or simply seek a new hearing before another magistrate or present the matter to the grand jury. A related question is whether only the state's case is to be considered or whether proof offered in defense should be weighed also.

Whether the rules of evidence applicable to jury trials must also be applied in the preliminary examination is unclear. For example, statements that hearsay evidence is properly received can be found,[p] as can contrary views: "In view of the nature and purpose of the proceeding, the fact that the crime charged had been committed could not be established by hearsay testimony."[q] The American Bar Foundation survey[r] concludes that, whatever the formal law position, jury trial rules of evidence are in fact generally applied. If critical evidence of guilt would be inadmissible at trial there seems little reason to hold the prisoner for trial. Argument on the other side emphasizes that the magistrate who conducts the preliminary examination may be without legal training and is, therefore, an inappropriate person to rule on questions of admissibility of evidence. In addition, the argument against excluding hearsay uniformly is that some inadmissible hearsay may be highly reliable and can

---

[p] *E.g.,* the opinion of Judge Burger in *Washington v. Clemmer,* at 558, *supra.*

[q] People v. Asta, 337 Mich. 590, 612, 60 N.W.2d 472 (1953) (involving statutory right to have witnesses examined in the defendant's presence).

[r] F. Miller, Prosecution ch. 5 (manuscript).

be replaced by direct evidence at the trial. For example, the hearsay might be an affidavit from a distant witness who can be produced at trial, or the hearsay might be a summary from numerous witnesses who can be required to appear at the trial itself.[8]

The same question—what evidence is properly considered—is similarly open to dispute with respect to grand jury proceedings. The absence of a judicial officer to pass on evidentiary matters makes application of evidentiary rules all the more awkward in the grand jury context.

Reference Note

The classic arguments for and against the use of the grand jury will be found in Antell, *The Modern Grand Jury: Benighted Supergovernment,* 51 A.B.A.J. 153 (1965), and Wickersham, *The Grand Jury: Weapon Against Crime and Corruption,* 51 A.B.A.J. 1157 (1965). Operation of a particular grand jury system is described in Comment, *The California Grand Jury—Two Current Problems,* 52 CALIF. L. REV. 116 (1964).

The records of the congressional hearings looking toward revision of the United States Commissioner system (excerpts from which appear at 527 and 552) are major documentary resources. Of particular interest in understanding the preliminary examination in the federal system is the survey at 477-93 of the Federal Magistrates Act hearings.

The various functions served by the preliminary examination are analyzed in Note, *The Preliminary Hearing—An Interest Analysis,* 51 IOWA L. REV. 164 (1965).

An excellent brief discussion of the evidentiary standards used at preliminary examination and of the right to counsel at that stage is contained in Comment, *Preliminary Examination—Evidence and Due Process,* 15 KAN. L. REV. 374 (1967).

The practitioner's view of these proceedings may be found in I. MENDELSON, DEFENDING CRIMINAL CASES 23-36 (rev. ed. 1967), and A. AMSTERDAM, B. SEGAL & M. MILLER, TRIAL MANUAL FOR THE DEFENSE OF CRIMINAL CASES ch. IX (1967).

A major study of the preliminary examination by Frank W. Miller, entitled Prosecution, based upon the American Bar Foundation survey, is to be published soon.

---

[8] United States v. Costello, 350 U.S. 359 (1956).

Chapter 9

ARRAIGNMENT AND THE GUILTY PLEA PROCESS

If a defendant is bound over by the magistrate at preliminary examination, a formal charging document must be filed. In some jurisdictions this must be an indictment returned by a grand jury. In other jurisdictions it may be an information filed by the prosecutor without necessity for grand jury action. In either event the information or indictment is the formal pleading to which he must respond. It will be more or less complex, depending upon the practice in the jurisdiction, but in order to comply with constitutional standards of fair notice the written document must specify the offense with which he is charged with reasonable particularity. The occasion for defendant's response to the charge is the arraignment.

At the arraignment on the indictment or information the principal items of business are: (1) to provide an attorney for the indigent who lacks one, unless he makes an understanding waiver of that right; (2) to read the charging document to the prisoner and consider any challenges his attorney might make to it—such as alleging a defect in form or substance, or urging some bar to prosecution like former jeopardy or grant of immunity; and (3) to take a plea. The usual pleas are "guilty" or "not guilty."[a] If defendant pleads guilty the judge is empowered to enter a judgment of conviction, though in exceptional cases he may refuse to accept the guilty plea and may order a plea of not guilty entered on behalf of the prisoner. If the judge thinks the prosecution ill-advised he may even dismiss the case

---

[a] The plea of nolo contendere, non vult, or no contest means that the defendant does not dispute the charge. It is not an admission of guilt and cannot be used in civil proceedings which may grow out of the same acts, but it authorizes conviction without more. *See* American Bar Association Project on Minimum Standards for Criminal Justice, Standards Relating to Pleas of Guilty 14-16 (1967).

Other special pleas such as the statute of limitations, double jeopardy, or lack of mental capacity to stand trial must be made at arraignment. In addition some jurisdictions require that notice of intention to use the defense of insanity or alibi be given at arraignment.

On the arraignment, see A. Amsterdam, B. Segal & M. Miller, Trial Manual for the Defense of Criminal Cases ch. XII (1967).

outright despite the offered plea. If the defendant pleads not guilty the case will normally be set for trial.

Motions for discovery and to suppress evidence are usually thought of as post-arraignment matters, in preparation for trial. In fact such motions can also be made prior to arraignment as a method of preparing for negotiating a plea of guilty agreement. The accused needs to learn as much as he can about the evidence which will be marshaled against him at trial in order to decide intelligently whether he is wiser to plead guilty or not guilty. The motion for discovery may give him such information directly; the motion to suppress evidence serves as an additional discovery device and may succeed in limiting the evidence which can be used against him. Of course, the defendant can plead not guilty, pursue his motions, and later change his plea if he concludes it is to his advantage. But his control over the alternatives is greater if he makes his motions before arraignment.[b]

A. THE GUILTY PLEA PROCESS AND ITS ADMINISTRATIVE IMPORTANCE

Most discussions of criminal procedure in the past have simply referred to the guilty plea as one of the ways of terminating a prosecution. They then pass on to consider the trial process. Sometimes they have cited statistics indicating that eighty-five percent or more of all criminal prosecutions are disposed of upon plea of guilty, but few have recognized that there is a distinct guilty plea process which constitutes the main stream of the criminal justice system.[c] The process is informal and relies heavily upon discretion of the prosecutor in framing the charges and of the judge in sentencing. As a result it is neither very visible nor is it recognized in the formal law. Despite this, there is a growing awareness of the importance of the process.

Maintenance of the plea of guilty system is of obvious practical importance to the community, for if substantial numbers of persons who now plead guilty were to insist upon jury trials, the burden upon the existing court system would soon become intolerable. The system of justice we now have therefore de-

---

[b] *See* A. Amsterdam, B. Segal & M. Miller, Trial Manual for the Defense of Criminal Cases, § 184 (1967).

[c] It would, of course, be theoretically possible to require that every case be tried. The Supreme Court has strongly endorsed the ancient practice of allowing a defendant to plead guilty and avoid trial. United States v. Jackson, 390 U.S. 570, 581-85 (1968).

pends upon most defendants' pleading guilty.[d] It is obviously important to know why most do plead guilty and why those who insist on trial do so, but one cannot readily learn this from what goes on in the courtroom, as the following arraignments illustrate:

1

MR. CORDES [the prosecutor]: To plead. Mr. Lester, you were previously arraigned in this case on January 14, 1952, at which time you entered a plea of not guilty. I wish to advise you before we proceed any further that you have a right to have counsel, that is, a lawyer, now or any other stage of this proceeding. Do you wish to have a lawyer now or at any stage?

DEFENDANT: No, sir.

MR. CORDES: Counsel waived. Will the record show that Mr. Lester has already received a copy of the indictment and will you state for the record that you have received a copy of the indictment?

DEFENDANT: Yes.

MR. CORDES: The Grand Jury charges in three counts—inasmuch as the United States is going to move to dismiss the first and third counts I will simply read the second count to which the defendant states he wishes to plead. (Indictment read.) Mr. Lester, do you understand that charge?

DEFENDANT: Yes.

MR. CORDES: How do you plead?

DEFENDANT: Guilty.

MR. CORDES: Plea of guilty entered to the second count of the indictment and the United States moves to dismiss the first and third counts.

THE COURT: August 9th.

MR. CORDES: It is satisfactory that bail be continued.

2

COURT: You are charged in the information filed against you in this court with the crime of breaking and entering in the daytime, two counts. Do you understand what this means?

DEFENDANT: Yes.

COURT: And how do you plead to this charge?

DEFENDANT: Guilty.

COURT: Are you pleading guilty because you actually are guilty?

---

[d] Though the emphasis in this chapter is on more serious offenses, what is said is relevant also to guilty pleas before a judge who may try petty cases summarily. *See* pp. 480-84, *supra*.

DEFENDANT: Yes.

COURT: Has the prosecuting attorney, any of the officers of this court, or any other person threatened you or made you any promises or inducements to influence you to plead guilty?

DEFENDANT: No.

COURT: You are pleading guilty freely and voluntarily?

DEFENDANT: Yes.

COURT: Prior to your plea did you understand that you had a constitutional right to a trial by jury and that if you were financially unable to employ counsel that the court would appoint a lawyer for you?

DEFENDANT: Yes.

COURT: You do not want a trial or a lawyer?

DEFENDANT: No, Sir.

COURT: You understand that upon accepting your plea of guilty it is my duty to impose sentence on you?

DEFENDANT: I understand.

COURT: And that the penalty for daytime breaking and entering might involve a prison term up to five years?

DEFENDANT: Yes.

COURT: Very well, I will accept your plea of guilty and set the date for sentencing three weeks from today, that is, on December 10.[e]

A plea of guilty is binding upon the defendant only if it is "voluntary." The term, however, has uncertain meaning here, just as it does when used with respect to a nonjudicial confession.

1. *Concern for Defendant's Motivation in Pleading Guilty*

There is no doubt that threats of physical violence or of prosecution of family members will invalidate a plea of guilty made in response to those threats. It appears also that a plea of guilty which flows from an improperly obtained confession (which would not be admissible at trial) is tainted and invalid.[f]

---

[e] A much more detailed arraignment is reproduced in Nelson v. State, 144 Mont. 439, 397 P.2d 700 (1964).

[f] If the defendant believes the confession can be used against him and therefore pleads guilty the plea is invalid. The leading case is Pennsylvania *ex rel.* Herman v. Claudy, 350 U.S. 116 (1956). *See also* Norris v. Wilson, 378 F.2d 324 (9th Cir. 1967); Smiley v. Wilson, 378 F.2d 144 (9th Cir. 1967). In Chambers v. Florida, 309 U.S. 227 (1940), coercion which resulted in confession continued to operate at the time of the guilty plea. The presence of

But the major concern of the courts is less with the sort of coercion which may be feared in police interrogation of a prisoner, and more with the propriety of the inducements offered the defendant to motivate his pleading guilty.

Difficult questions are raised when the prosecutor merely points out to the defendant that he is considering bringing yet other charges or dropping some of the charges which have already been filed against the defendant.[g] The prosecutor likewise has the power in many jurisdictions to make a sentencing recommendation to the judge; it does not bind the judge, but can be expected to carry substantial influence. Threat to do what the prosecutor legitimately may do, and promise to be more lenient than he need be, are two sides of the same coin.[h] In fact, as discussed below, a substantial portion of guilty pleas are the result of the defendant's bartering a willingness to plead guilty for a reduction in the seriousness of the charge or for a promise of recommendation of leniency by the prosecutor. The summary questioning by the court about threat or promise is not likely to disclose the real circumstances of such a bargain, since it is understood as part of the bargain that the defendant should deny that his plea is the result of either threat or promise. The question whether the plea bargain is improper has not been clearly answered, though there seems to be growing support for viewing plea bargaining as proper in many circumstances.[i] If so, the process will become more visible. In the future the distinction is more likely to be drawn between proper and improper plea bargaining and between promises kept and promises dishonored.

---

counsel makes the causal connection less likely, since competent counsel will have pointed out to defendant that the confession cannot be used against him, but the presence of counsel is not itself a guarantee that the plea is "voluntary." United States *ex rel.* Cuevas v. Rundle, 258 F. Supp. 647 (E.D. Pa. 1966).

[g] *See, e.g.*, Austin v. State, 91 Idaho 404, 422 P.2d 71 (1966); *cf.* Machibroda v. United States, 368 U.S. 487 (1962) (threat to file additional charges).

[h] Reference is made to threats and promises, implying that inducements are offered by a person—whether police, prosecutor, judge, or social worker—whereas the inducements may be built into the system. Whenever there is discretion in someone to deal with the prisoner in alternative ways, there is inducement to the prisoner to do whatever he believes will please that person. Similarly, if pleading guilty will limit discretion to impose harsh penalty, this constitutes an inducement to plead guilty.

[i] But even if plea bargaining were improper, it would not follow that every plea of guilty motivated in part by some such inducement would be "involuntary" or "coerced." Even the fact that one can avoid the possibility of the death penalty by pleading guilty is not necessarily sufficiently strong motivation in every case to make the guilty plea "coerced" in that situation. United States v. Jackson, 390 U.S. 570 (1968). The question remains the defendant's whole motivation.

2. *Concern for Accuracy of the Plea*

Of course one aspect of the coerced plea is that it may be untrue, but even a plea of guilty which is not the result of coercion can be untrue. The defendant may be emotionally disturbed; he may be motivated by desire to protect someone else or to cover up more serious conduct; he may think it preferable to take a known lesser penalty rather than risk the possibility of conviction for a major crime even though he is not guilty. Or he may misconceive the elements of the crime with which he is charged and plead guilty even when under the law's definition his conduct does not constitute the offense he thinks it does, or even though he may have some valid defense.

There is increasing concern with the accuracy of guilty pleas in terms of their factual basis as well as in their character as consent to conviction. This is reflected in the 1966 revision of Rule 11 of the Federal Rules of Criminal Procedure (new matter in italics):

RULE 11. PLEAS

A defendant may plead not guilty, guilty or, with the consent of the court, nolo contendere. The court may refuse to accept a plea of guilty, and shall not accept *such* plea *or a plea of nolo contendere* without first *addressing the defendant personally and* determining that the plea is made voluntarily with understanding of the nature of the charge. *Notwithstanding the acceptance of a plea of guilty the court shall not enter a judgment upon such plea without making such inquiry as may satisfy it that there is a factual basis for the plea.* If a defendant refuses to plead or if the court refuses to accept a plea of guilty or if a defendant corporation fails to appear, the court shall enter a plea of not guilty.[j]

---

[j] Questioning of the defendant prior to accepting a plea is ordinarily leading in the sense that "Yes" or "No" is sufficient answer and the proper answer is readily apparent. More meaningful questioning would require the defendant to respond more fully. *See, e.g.*, State v. Starratt, 153 N.W.2d 311, 317-18 (N.D. 1967) ("What is burglary?" "Is this a felony or is it a misdemeanor?" "What is a felony?").

The sanction in the federal system for violation of Rule 11 is not yet settled. The Fifth (by dictum), Ninth, and Tenth Circuits hold that failure to make the factual determination as to voluntariness requires reversal of the conviction, while decisions of the First, Third, Seventh, and Eighth Circuits are to the effect that the determination of voluntariness may be made at the time the prisoner raises the matter. *See* Stephens v. United States, 376 F.2d 23 (10th Cir. 1967); United States v. Boyance, 258 F. Supp. 935 (E.D. Pa. 1966). Michigan, with a statute similar to Rule 11, reverses for failure to comply. *E.g.*, People v. Smith, 5 Mich. App. 139, 145 N.W.2d 798 (1966). *See also* Mich. Gen. Ct. Rules 785.3.

HENDRICK v. BETO
253 F. Supp. 994 (S.D. Tex. 1965)

INGRAHAM, District Judge. Petitioner alleges that he is being held unconstitutionally under the five convictions to which he pled guilty because the state failed to introduce any evidence into the record showing the guilt of the defendant. It is pointed out that Article 12, Vernon's Ann. Texas Code of Criminal Procedure, makes it mandatory to a conviction on a guilty plea that there be sufficient evidence to support the plea. The failure of the state to comply with this statute, it is urged, deprived petitioner of his constitutional rights under the Fourteenth Amendment to the Constitution of the United States. Respondent urges, on the other hand, that the failure of the state to comply with that statute is not grounds for federal habeas corpus relief—but is only a misapplication of state law.

This court agrees with respondent that the alleged right to have evidence submitted to corroborate a plea of guilty is solely a creature of Texas statute and does not rise to Constitutional stature. That this right of corroboration of a guilty plea is not essential to a fair trial is clearly demonstrated by the fact that such corroboration is not even required in criminal cases in the federal courts.

The Practice

There are several ways in which the judge who is concerned with the voluntariness and accuracy of a guilty plea can protect himself against the possibility that a defendant offering to plead guilty is not in fact guilty of the offense charged or of something more serious.[k]

1

A woman charged with murder in the second degree admitted guilt at arraignment and, in response to inquiry by the judge, said she did not want an attorney even at state expense. She said, "I am guilty but I didn't plan or intend to kill anybody." After some discussion with her, the judge refused the plea,

[k] Inquiry as to the factual basis of a plea may be not whether defendant is guilty of the precise charge he pleads to, but of some crime of equal or greater seriousness, though the A.B.A. Standards Relating to Pleas of Guilty 3.1(b)(ii) would add that the crime should be reasonably related. A plea of guilty to an impossible crime may be permitted as part of a bargain. *See* People v. Foster, 19 N.Y.2d 150, 225 N.E.2d 200 (1967) (attempted manslaughter); D. NEWMAN, CONVICTION: THE DETERMINATION OF GUILT OR INNOCENCE WITHOUT TRIAL 101 (1967) (driving the wrong way on a one-way street, when there are no such streets in the city).

assigned counsel, and rescheduled arraignment. At the second arraignment the judge asked the defense attorney if he had conferred with his client and discussed the case with her. The attorney replied in the affirmative, stating that the defendant's recollection of what happened was vague, and in fact she could not remember any significant details. The judge then asked the defendant, "Do you wish to continue your plea of guilty?" The defendant answered, "Yes, I will plead guilty to get this over with. The suspense of not knowing what I have done is driving me crazy." The judge then asked the defense counsel, "Do you as counsel agree that defendant should continue in her plea of guilty?" The attorney answered, "Yes, I do," whereupon the court accepted the plea and sentenced the defendant to from fourteen to eighteen years in prison.

2

In some instances the judge does not accept a guilty plea when there is doubt as to its accuracy, but "takes it under advisement" until he receives a presentence report. In such cases the report tends to take an investigative rather than diagnostic approach and devotes much attention to the question of guilt in fact, noting that the defendant "admits the crime" or describing the statements of others relating to the circumstances of the crime.

3

After receiving and accepting a guilty plea from the defendant the court required the defendant to take the stand, under oath, and state that he did commit the crime and exactly how he committed it. The judge himself did the questioning. Witnesses for the state were also sworn and required to testify in detail regarding their knowledge of the circumstances of the case. The defendant was asked if he wished to cross-examine or to call witnesses in his own behalf. The judge reported afterward that occasionally he found the state's evidence insufficient or the charge an inaccurate reflection of the real crime, in which cases he would dismiss or order rearraignment. Occasionally, too, he would become convinced that the defendant should be committed for psychiatric evaluation.

4

PROSECUTOR: You want to enter a plea, Counsel?

COUNSEL: Yes, enter a plea, withdraw original plea of not guilty to first degree murder, and enter a plea for second degree or manslaughter depending upon the determination of the court.

COURT: You have counsel and have gone over it with your lawyer? You know you can have trial if you want it?

DEFENDANT: I leave it up to him. Whatever he says will be all right with me.

COURT: You are pleading to either offense of murder or manslaughter as the court finds, understand that?

DEFENDANT: I understand it.

COURT: And have you been offered any promises or had any threats to get you to make a plea?

DEFENDANT: No.

COURT: All right, I will accept your plea and set a hearing for such proof as you want to bring in.

McCOY v. UNITED STATES
363 F.2d 306 (D.C. Cir. 1966)

Before BAZELON, Chief Judge, FAHY and DANAHER, Circuit Judges.

FAHY, Circuit Judge. Appellant had pled not guilty to a charge of violating D.C. Code § 22-2204, unauthorized use of a motor vehicle, punishable by a fine not exceeding $1,000 or imprisonment not exceeding five years, or both. At the conclusion of the Government's case in chief a plea to the lesser offense of taking property without right, carrying a maximum sentence of six months or a fine of $100.00, or both, D.C. Code § 22-1211, was discussed. Defendant was advised by the court of this maximum sentence and that the time he had spent in jail would be considered; but he was also advised by the court that he must clearly understand the court was not making any promise whatever. The defendant stated, "I will plead to taking property without right." In response to inquiries by the court he stated that he had been advised of his right to a speedy trial, that he could not withdraw his plea, that he could have the assistance of counsel if he went to trial, and that he understood the nature of the charge against him, which was explained in some detail. The following then transpired:

> The Court: Did you in fact do that?
>
> The Defendant: Did I take somebody's property?
>
> The Court: Did you take their property without right—in this case an automobile?
>
> The Defendant: No, sir.

At this point the court advised him that if he did not take the property the court could not let him plead guilty. Defendant then stated, "Your Honor, if I am willing to plead to this lesser charge, could I plead?" The court replied: "You can't plead before me to a charge to which you say you are not guilty. No sir, you cannot do that."

The trial was resumed, resulting in a jury verdict of guilty of unauthorized use of a motor vehicle. Appellant was sentenced to eight months to three years.

Appellant's position is that the court erred in refusing to accept the plea to the less serious offense, for which reason, it is contended, the judgment should be reversed and the case remanded to allow such a plea to be entered. We think appellant is not entitled to this relief.

The cases relied upon by appellant to the effect that in a criminal prosecution a defendant has a right to plead guilty do not hold acceptance of such a plea is mandatory in all cases, certainly not by a federal court governed by Rule 11.

While it would be improper for a court to accept such a plea unless satisfied there was significant evidence that the accused was involved or implicated in the offense, the court is not required to insist that the accused concede the inevitability or correctness of a verdict of guilty were the case tried. Such a verdict would depend upon a jury being satisfied of guilt beyond a reasonable doubt. An accused, though believing in or entertaining doubts respecting his innocence, might reasonably conclude a jury would be convinced of his guilt and that he would fare better in the sentence by pleading guilty; or for other reasons he might wish to avoid further contest: "Reasons other than the fact that he is guilty may induce a defendant to so plead . . . and the right of the defendant to so plead has never been doubted. He must be permitted to judge for himself in this respect." State v. Kaufman, 51 Iowa 578, 2 N.W. 275, 276. This may very properly be deemed dictum in the opinion, but it has much soundness; for guilt, or the degree of guilt, is at times uncertain and elusive. The result of trial of a particular case rests with a jury of twelve, or with a trial judge where there is no jury. An inflexible standard for accepting a guilty plea, in order to serve the desirable purpose of avoiding a subsequent motion to withdraw the plea, leads to an undesirable consequence, namely, a requirement that in order to be able to plead guilty and accept sentence without trial an accused must not only enter the plea voluntarily and with full knowledge of the nature of the charge as required by Rule 11, but must publicly resolve all doubts as to guilt against himself. Since Rule 11 does not require this the District Court need not.

In this case, considering the whole exchange between the court and appellant, partly reproduced above, we find no basis for holding that the court abused its discretion in refusing to accept the plea to the less serious offense, though tendered in compliance with Rule 11.

Affirmed.

BAZELON, Chief Judge (dissenting). Three factors must clearly and affirmatively appear in the record before the trial court in exercising its discretion to accept a plea of guilty. First, that the defendant, advised by counsel, fully understands the significance of his action. Second, that he is acting intelligently and voluntarily and not as a result of any threats, promises or incapacity. Third, that there is at least prima facie evidence tending to establish that the defendant committed the crime to which he is pleading guilty. This can be supplied not only by an admission of guilt, but also from the government's evidence, or from other information before the court.

Here, the third requirement was satisfied by the government's evidence at trial, presented before the question of pleading guilty arose. The trial judge, however, rejected the defendant's guilty plea. The judge was apparently of the view that only an unequivocal confession of guilt would suffice. Since the judge acted on an incorrect premise, I would remand the case for a proper consideration of the offer to plead guilty.

ARRAIGNMENT OF CHESTER JENSEN

September 16, 1963

COURT: All right, sir, do you fully realize what you are charged with?

DEFENDANT: Yes.

COURT: What are you charged with, what is the offense before this Court?

DEFENDANT: Indecent behavior is the way that I understood it.

COURT: With a child under 16?

DEFENDANT: Yes.

COURT: All right, what is your plea to this charge?

DEFENDANT: I plead guilty.

[Three days later, at the post-plea-of-guilty hearing:][l]

DOUGLAS ZELLMER, being first duly sworn on oath, testified as follows:

DIRECT EXAMINATION BY MR. STEINMETZ:

Q. Your name is Douglas Zellmer?

A. Yes, sir.

---

l *See* illustration 3, at 572, *supra*.

Q. You are a police officer with the Milwaukee Police Department, is that right?

A. Yes, sir, I am.

Q. Would you at this time inform the Court as to the information you have learned?

A. Sir, on Sunday, September 1st at 12:15 a.m. I was sent to a disturbance. When I arrived I found a young girl, aged fifteen, laying in bed crying. When I asked her mother what had happened, she claimed her daughter was screaming her father had been molesting her. She stated she found her daughter with her brassiere around her neck and with her slacks and underclothing pulled over her shoes. I had the girl taken to the hospital at which time she told me her father had been molesting her for the past four years. We had her ordered down to the vice squad and when she came down to the vice squad, two of her sisters came down also and they claim this had happened to them also when they were her age. The sisters, one is twenty-five years of age. The other daughter is twenty-eight right now. According to my investigation, Beverly was home alone with her father while the mother was at the show with the other children in the house. Her father forced her to drink the wine, some wine. She drank the wine and went to bed and she woke up with her father—her clothes pulled over or off of her and her father playing with her. At which time she started to scream and she swung at him and he left her alone at which time the mother came home.

Q. Were you told at that time whether there had been an exposure of his privates at all?

A. Not this time.

Q. Did the girl describe how frequently in the past before that time this sort of thing happened?

A. She stated as far as she can remember the time before this was three months ago when they lived in Idaho.

Q. This is the only one in the City of Milwaukee, County of Milwaukee?

A. Yes, sir.

Q. Now you have had the opportunity to question this defendant about these allegations?

A. Yes, sir, I have.

Q. What does he tell you?

A. He states, he denied the acts, both at the scene and at the hospital and at the vice squad room. Then in the district attorney's office he changed his plea, he said he was guilty.

Q. He did say then he had done these things?

A. No, he didn't come right out and say he committed these acts. He said he was guilty and he felt he wanted some help.

Q. Has he ever admitted in your presence he touched the privates of his daughter, Beverly, on the evening of August 31st, 1963?

A. No, sir, he denied that all the way through.

Q. The first you know in the district attorney's office he said he would plead guilty because he was guilty?

A. No, sir, he wanted to plead guilty because he felt he wanted some medical help. Mental help.

MR. STEINMETZ: I have no further question.

COURT: Chester Jensen, let me advise you at this time it is not necessary for you to testify in this case. On the other hand, should you wish to testify, this is your opportunity. Do you wish to testify in this case?

DEFENDANT: I don't quite understand what testimony means.

COURT: Do you want to get up where the officer is to explain anything to this Court concerning the said testimony that the officer has given?

A. No, sir.

COURT: Is everything that the officer said here in open Court true and correct?

A. Yes.

COURT: Did you hear everything that he said?

A. Yes.

COURT: All right, now do you wish to explain anything to this Court?

A. Nothing any more than I am sorry for everything that happened, that is all I can say.

COURT: All right sir, would you please walk forward. Chester Jensen, at this time the Court does find you guilty pursuant to the information on file with this Court.

[During the next three years in prison the defendant continued to deny having committed the act with which he was charged.][m]

In such situations correctional treatment is complicated by the practical necessity of assuming inmates are in fact guilty of the crimes for which they are imprisoned.

---

[m] An analogous case is United States *ex rel.* Elksnis v. Gilligan, 256 F. Supp. 244 (S.D.N.Y. 1966), in which the judge accepted a guilty plea to manslaughter even though questioning of the defendant prior to acceptance of the plea produced explanations which would have supported defenses of self-defense and insanity.

3. Concern for Other Aspects of Fairness

In addition to concern for absence of coercion and for guilt in fact, the court at the time of reception of a guilty plea must concern itself with other aspects of fairness. There is the court's concern that the defendant be aware of the possible consequences of his plea, that he have sufficient time to consider seriously the alternatives open to him, that promises of leniency made to the defendant be kept (or he be permitted to withdraw his plea), that he have access to counsel if he wishes, and sometimes that he have equal access to the prosecutor concessions which may be had for the asking.

a. Awareness of Rights

There is an overall problem of effective communication. It is particularly true of arraignment for minor offenses in crowded courts that the pressures for speed in handling cases results in some of the formal warning of rights becoming gibberish. In setting aside a conviction for disorderly conduct, a New York judge cited the following description of what happens in criminal court: "After rushing through the reading of the charge in a 'blur of language' the court officer advised the defendant: On-these-charges-rightta-counsel-evvy-stage-ada-proceedings-rightta-telephone-call-warden's-office-free-a-charge-rightta-hearing-this-court-rightta-trial-by-one-judge-a-panel-three-judge-howdya-plead-guiltya-not-guilty."[n] This problem is not likely to be nearly so common or acute in arraignment on more serious charges, but there is often substantial question whether the accused really understands what is happening to him.

b. Awareness of Possible Consequences

Judges routinely tell defendants of the maximum penalties for their particular crimes and whether the sentences are mandatory, but rarely go beyond this to indicate what their practice is with respect to sentence under the circumstances of this case. He may well assume that the prosecutor in discussing the plea with defendant has made a shrewd estimate what the judge will do, knowing particularly whether the judge will rely heavily on the prosecutor's recommendation. Obviously the mere statement of maximum prison term does not realistically apprise the defend-

[n] N.Y. Times, Nov. 4, 1965, at 43.

ant what to expect. For example, penalties may be higher if defendant has been convicted previously. The conditions of imprisonment and all the ancillary consequences of conviction are never explained, perhaps because they are not readily explainable.[o] Eligibility for probation or parole and the practices of the parole board are never explained, even though they may substantially qualify the real meaning of the sentence.[p] Full explanation of the possible sentence can be a difficult matter.[q]

PEOPLE v. CAIRNS

4 Mich. App. 633, 145 N.W.2d 345 (1966)

HOLBROOK, Presiding Judge. *"The Court:* You understand that by entering a plea of guilty, you submit yourself to the judgment and discretion of this court as to whether you may be sentenced to prison for a maximum term of four and one-half years, this being charged as a second offense, you understand that?

"The Defendant: Yes, sir.

"The Court: Under such circumstances your plea of guilty will be accepted and you will be returned to the custody of the warden until Thursday afternoon when your case will be finally disposed of. That's all." (Emphasis supplied)

The proceeding at the sentencing of the defendant dated November 6, 1958, appears in the record as follows:

"The Court: You have entered a plea of guilty of breaking prison. Is there anything that you care to say before sentence is imposed upon you, or any reason why sentence should not now be imposed?

"The Defendant: Yes, Your Honor, I would like to know if this sentence of escape will run concurrently with my old sentence?

"The Court: No, under the statute last passed dealing with this subject, it provided that such sentence should be com-

---

[o] For a list of ancillary consequences of conviction, see A. AMSTERDAM, B. SEGAL & M. MILLER, TRIAL MANUAL FOR THE DEFENSE OF CRIMINAL CASES, § 205 (1967).

[p] Trujillo v. United States, 377 F.2d 266 (5th Cir. 1967), concluded that Rule 11 does not require that a defendant be apprised that if he pleaded guilty to the narcotics charge he would be ineligible for parole, noting that the two prior decisions in point had disagreed. The court cited cases holding it unnecessary to point out that one pleading guilty may lose his passport, may be deported, may be barred from voting, or may be discharged from the armed forces.

[q] *Compare Calvert v. Burke,* at 790, *infra.*

menced at the end of the sentence which you are now currently serving.

"The Defendant: Would you be lenient on me?

"The Court: Well, we've got to discourage these people making these escapes."

However, in informing defendant of the consequences of a plea of guilty the court failed to state that the sentence would be one that would be served consecutively rather than concurrently with the sentence that he was then serving. The sentence being one that would be served at a later time or served consecutively was a vital factor in the consequences or maximum penalty that could be exacted under the law. Defendant not being properly informed of the penalty at any time before the court accepted his plea, we conclude, that the plea of guilty was made at a time when defendant was not fully informed of the maximum penalty or consequences and therefore not understandingly made. Under the circumstances we rule that defendant has not been afforded due process.

To the degree that courts are aware that the prosecutor has made representations to the defendant about probable sentence, they will usually make clear that they are not bound by any such recommendations and that the defendant may not rely on them. A few judges go to the opposite extreme and indicate to the defendant what the sentence will be if he pleads guilty. Many go through the ritual of asking the accused whether he is pleading because of any threats or promises, receiving a negative answer, then imposing a sentence responsive to the prosecutor's recommendation with tacit assurance that this reflects a bargain struck by the defendant and the prosecutor. If the real difference in consequences of pleading guilty or not guilty is substantial, and the consequences are explained to the defendant as they should be, the explanation may itself seem coercive.

c. Opportunity to Consider

The quick-justice cases cast reflections upon the propriety of processing an accused from arrest through guilty plea to sentence within a few hours.[r] The concern of the courts seems to be principally that the plea under these circumstances may not be a free decision, particularly when the offender is young,

---

[r] D. NEWMAN, CONVICTION: THE DETERMINATION OF GUILT OR INNOCENCE WITHOUT TRIAL 33-35 (1967).

unrepresented, and faced with serious, complicated charge, but there is also an underlying concern for more general notions of fairness in giving an accused adequate time to evaluate his position and make a fully considered decision as to his course of action. Most such cases have upheld the convictions, yet there has been sufficient criticism of the practice to induce courts ordinarily to proceed more deliberately.

d. Advice of Counsel

The right of indigents to appointment of counsel at the arraignment is well established, but most defendants who are guilty of criminal conduct and willing to plead guilty are also likely to waive counsel, consistent with a popular conception that the function of counsel is limited to litigation. Counsel is seen as involving unnecessary expense if privately retained or as possibly antagonizing the prosecutor or court if counsel must be furnished at public expense. Judges occasionally appoint lawyers even when defendants are willing to waive their right to counsel.[8] This may be because the judge has doubts about the actual guilt of the accused, about his competency to plead guilty or to waive counsel, or about his understanding of the unfamiliar court process. In other instances an attorney may be appointed for young or inexperienced defendants who are apparently willing to plead guilty to serious crimes, particularly when they involve mandatory sentences which seem inappropriate under all the circumstances.

STROETZ v. BURKE
268 F. Supp. 912 (E.D. Wis. 1967)

TEHAN, Chief Judge. In determining the fairness of allowing a purported waiver of counsel to stand, however, it is our opinion that at the very minimum a defendant must understand not only the nature of the charge but the seriousness of the penal-

[8] ". . . The fact that an accused may tell him that he is informed of his right to counsel and desires to waive this right does not automatically end the judge's responsibility. To be valid such waiver must be made with an apprehension of the nature of the charges, the statutory offenses included within them, the range of allowable punishments thereunder, possible defenses to the charges and circumstances in mitigation thereof, and all other facts essential to a broad understanding of the whole matter. A judge can make certain that an accused's professed waiver of counsel is understandingly and wisely made only from a penetrating and comprehensive examination of all the circumstances under which such a plea is tendered." Von Moltke v. Gillies, 332 U.S. 708, 724 (1948).

ties the law prescribes for the violation. In the instant case, petitioner had no way of knowing whether the infraction carried a penalty of imprisonment for one month or five years, much less that the conviction could lead to confinement for an indeterminate period which could conceivably last the rest of his life. It is noted that based upon the jurisdiction obtained over the person of the defendant, he has already had his liberty curtailed by the State of Wisconsin for thirteen years.

In recognition of these principles the Supreme Court of Wisconsin has prescribed the duties of a trial court before accepting a plea of guilty and waiver of counsel. See Burnett v. Burke (1964), 22 Wis. 2d 486, 126 N.W.2d 91, in which the Supreme Court stated that it was the duty of trial courts to (1) determine the extent of defendant's education and general comprehension; (2) establish his understanding of the crime and range of punishment; (3) ascertain whether any promises or threats had been made in connection with his appearance, his refusal of counsel and his proposed plea of guilty; (4) alert the petitioner to the possibility that a lawyer may discover defenses or mitigating circumstances; (5) make sure that the defendant understood that if indigent, counsel would be provided at no expense to him.

Although in State ex rel. Kline v. Burke (1965), 27 Wis. 2d 40, 133 N.W.2d 405, the Wisconsin Supreme Court held that the failure of the trial court to follow its recommendations in *Burnett* did not invalidate the convictions if in fact the defendant's waiver was freely, voluntarily and understandingly made—in this case, the State has failed to establish that the defendant did have such understanding.

LORRAINE v. GLADDEN

261 F. Supp. 909 (D. Ore. 1966)

Solomon, Chief Judge. While petitioner was without counsel the prosecutor came to petitioner's cell and bargained for a guilty plea. The prosecutor threatened petitioner and his codefendant with a life sentence under the mandatory provisions of Oregon law if they were found guilty.

The critical stage in these proceedings occurred during the bargaining with the prosecutor while petitioner was without counsel and when petitioner made his decision to plead guilty. The appointment of counsel after the successful negotiation of the guilty plea and minutes before its entry was ineffective, and did not give petitioner the representation required by the Constitution. Appointed counsel could not have reviewed the facts of the crime, the possible defenses or the hazards of a trial, nor could he have evaluated the bargain offered by the prosecutor. For all practical purposes, the petitioner entered his plea of guilty without advice of counsel.

e. *Equal Access to Concessions*

Where plea negotiation is common, there is a question whether there should be fair and consistent opportunity for all defendants to participate in the bargaining process. The benefits of bargaining must usually be actively sought by the defendant, whether it be downgrading charges or sentence promises. However, practices develop so that if he knows enough to make the demand, certain charges are nearly always reduced. For example, the American Bar Foundation researchers found that in Michigan armed robbery was reduced to unarmed robbery if the defendant agreed to plead guilty; sale of narcotics was almost invariably reduced to possession, nighttime burglary to daytime burglary, and felonious assault to simple assault. The frequency of these practices raises the issue whether the defendant should be informed of them so that he does not from ignorance plead guilty to a charge and receive a mandatory sentence inconsistent with that given others who engaged in the same conduct. In some cases the judges actively arrange for the reduction of the charge, in others they appoint counsel especially for that purpose—usually in the case of the young or inexperienced offenders. The disparate sentences resulting from failure to take advantage of the available concessions can present major problems for correctional authorities, both in terms of attempting rehabilitation of a person who feels he has been treated unfairly and in terms of administration of parole policies when the crime for which the prisoner was committed does not consistently reflect his criminal conduct.

DORROUGH v. UNITED STATES
385 F.2d 887 (5th Cir. 1967)

GEWIN, Circuit Judge. [T]he appellant strenuously contends that he was not adequately informed of the nature of the charges against him and that his plea was not voluntarily made with understanding of the nature of the charge and the consequences of the plea. He also contends that the offense with which he was charged contained a lesser included offense which provided for only a ten-year mandatory penalty and that it was incumbent upon the trial court to fully advise him of this fact. We reject all of the contentions of the appellant and conclude that the requirements of the decisions and Rule 11 F.R.Crim.P. were fully complied with. When the charge against the defendant completely, adequately and accurately describes the conduct of the defendant and when the evidence and circumstances clearly demonstrate that the defendant was fully aware and consciously participated in such conduct, we believe it is unnecessary to require the court to go into detailed and fine spun explanations and definitions of other crimes with which the defendant might have been charged. In this case the offense as described in the information exactly coincides with the conscious conduct of the appellant.

GOLDBERG, Circuit Judge (dissenting). The statute under which the defendant was charged here is akin to a double-edged sword. Unlike those statutes which enumerate a specific crime with a range of punishments therefor, § 2114 sets out a range of crimes, each with separate penalties. It provides for the greater crime of robbing a postal employee and wounding him or putting his life in jeopardy, with a mandatory 25-year penalty. The defendant was charged and convicted of this offense. However, § 2114 also provides for a lesser included offense.

Nothing appears in the record here to indicate that the trial judge either affirmatively advised the defendant, or conducted an inquiry which yielded the information that the defendant knew, that under this statute he might be guilty of robbing the vehicle while merely assaulting rather than endangering the life of the postal employee. Because Dorrough could have been convicted of this lesser offense upon the same information which charged him of the greater, I believe that Dorrough was not advised of the charge against him within the meaning of Rule 11.

[It] depends on a good deal more than whether he thinks he is guilty or not guilty. He must be apprised of more than a mere description of the charge because he must weigh the risks of trial against the length of punishment and the kind of punishment. Crucial to such an evaluation is knowledge of the complete range of crimes charged by the indictment or information, so that the defendant may be aware of the range of possibilities in a jury verdict when he considers whether he wishes to stand trial. He may decide that he has a chance that the jury will disregard or disbelieve a weak portion of the government's case, but only if the jury knows that there is a lesser crime of which it might still convict him. A defendant cannot weigh his chance with a jury if he does not know that there is a lesser ground for conviction upon which it might resolve its doubts. Knowledge of the existence of such a lesser crime might just convince a defendant to risk his case with a jury where he otherwise would not.

It would be uncandid also to fail to mention that upon learning of a lesser included offense, the defendant might announce to the prosecution that he would consent to plead guilty only to the lesser offense, in the hope that the prosecution would allow him so to plead rather than go through the risk and bother of a trial. Plea-bargaining, at present, must be recognized as part of our system.

NEWMAN v. UNITED STATES
382 F.2d 479 (D.C. Cir. 1967)

Before BAZELON, Chief Judge, and DANAHER and BURGER, Circuit Judges.

BURGER, Circuit Judge. The sole issue presented on appeal raises for the first time whether it was a denial of Appellant's constitutional rights for the United States Attorney to consent to a guilty plea tendered by Appellant's co-defendant for a lesser included offense under the indictment, while refusing to consent to the same plea for Appellant.

Appellant and one Anderson were indicted for housebreaking and petty larceny. Negotiations between Anderson's counsel and an Assistant United States Attorney led to Anderson's being allowed to plead guilty to misdemeanors of petty larceny and attempted housebreaking. The United States Attorney declined to consent to the same plea for Appellant. The essence of Appellant's claim on appeal is that the United States Attorney's conduct denied him due process, "equal standing," and equal protection. He argues that both Appellant and Anderson "were equally guilty . . . and to permit one party an avenue of escape with relatively minor punishment while refusing the same procedure to Appellant violates the standard of fairness demanded of the law by the Constitution. . . ."

To say that the United States Attorney must literally treat every offense and every offender alike is to delegate him an impossible task; of course this concept would negate discretion. Myriad factors can enter into the prosecutor's decision. Two persons may have committed what is precisely the same legal offense but the prosecutor is not compelled by law, duty or tradition to treat them the same as to charges. On the contrary, he is expected to exercise discretion and common sense to the end that if, for example, one is a young first offender and the other older, with a criminal record, or one played a lesser and the other a dominant role, one the instigator and the other a follower, the prosecutor can and should take such factors into account; no court has any jurisdiction to inquire into or review his decision.

It is assumed that the United States Attorney will perform his duties and exercise his powers consistent with his oaths; and while this discretion is subject to abuse or misuse just as is judicial discretion, deviations from his duty as an agent of the Executive are to be dealt with by his superiors.[t]

B. BARGAINING FOR PLEA OF GUILTY

The guilty plea is sometimes the result of an offender's conscience pangs or of his despair in the face of overwhelming evidence of his guilt. At other times it is a strategic choice, made in exchange for advantage. The exchange may not be overt, but may flow from routine practice of extending leniency in some manner when a defendant pleads guilty. The bargain may also be openly agreed upon. Such actual negotiations for guilty pleas are common but not universal. Apparently there is little explicit bargaining in Baltimore, for example.[u] One suspects that the pressures which elsewhere are alleviated by plea bargaining are accommodated in Baltimore some other way.[v]

The frequency of guilty pleas may be affected by several factors, among them the fear by attorneys that their failure to contest vigorously their client's case may be characterized later as ineffective representation[w] and the hope by clients that if they fight their cases all the way something—such as a new Supreme Court ruling—may occur to save them.

1. The "Implicit Bargain"—Leniency upon Pleading Guilty Without Overt Negotiation

UNITED STATES v. WILEY

184 F. Supp. 679 (N.D. Ill. 1960)

CAMPBELL, Chief Judge. As Justice Lummus of the Supreme Judicial Court of Massachusetts has pointed out in his book, "The Trial Judge" at pages 46-47:

"If all the defendants should combine to refuse to plead guilty, and should dare to hold out, they could break down the adminis-

[t] Dissenting in Henderson v. United States, 349 F.2d 712 (D.C. Cir. 1965), Judge Bazelon urged as a relevant consideration in granting a new trial that the pretrial error had interfered with the defendant's ability to consider, and calculate the advantages of, a guilty plea.

[u] THE PRESIDENT'S COMMISSION ON LAW ENFORCEMENT AND ADMINISTRATION OF JUSTICE, TASK FORCE REPORT: THE COURTS 126 (1967).

[v] *Cf.* Myhre, *Conviction Without Trial in the United States and Norway: A Comparison*, 5 HOUSTON L. REV. 647 (1968).

[w] *See* p. 614, *infra.*

tration of criminal justice in any state in the Union. But they dare not hold out, for such as were tried and convicted could hope for no leniency. The prosecutor is like a man armed with a revolver who is cornered by a mob. A concerted rush would overwhelm him, but each individual in the mob fears that he might be one of those shot during the rush. When defendants plead guilty, they expect more leniency than when convicted by a jury, and must receive it, or there will be no such pleas. The truth is, that a criminal court can operate only by inducing the great mass of actually guilty defendants to plead guilty, paying in leniency the price for the plea.

"This, I agree, is a stark reality, not the ideal. In an ideal judicial system, leniency would be a free gift from the sovereign people to an erring citizen. The criminal would have no voice in the decision, much less barter for it with his sovereign. But courts are not free, and never have been free, from the pressure in favor of criminals that the very volume of criminal business exerts. The defenders of criminals know this perfectly. It is their principal asset. The actual trial of criminal cases is only a small part of the work of a criminal lawyer. Since his clients are usually guilty, and a good part of them would be found guilty by a jury, he seeks to turn to their advantage some defect in the machinery of public justice."

Besides the need for exchanging some degree of leniency in return for a plea of guilty because, as Justice Lummus indicates, of our overwhelming volume of criminal cases, I should also like to point out as an additional reason, the great saving of expense and time to the government that is possible and that is achieved by properly inducing defendants to plead guilty. For example, in the cause before me, the official total cost to the government for the complete investigation up to the time of sentencing was $11,250. The Assistant United States Attorney, upon representation spent three days in preparation for Wiley's trial and one day on trial. Several investigators likewise spent three days in preparation for trial and one day at the trial. I myself spent one half day in preparation for trial and then one day on trial and accordingly the Court was totally occupied for a day and a half. Though the expense and time that would have been saved the government if Wiley had pled guilty is fairly obvious, I suggest that, if this had been a criminal trial lasting weeks or months as many of our trials actually do, then the saving of time and expense to the government would have been far more striking.

Finally, there is one more reason for affording some degree of leniency in exchange for a plea of guilty. One of the principal considerations in the imposition of a criminal sentence is reformation. Where, as here, the defendant first pleads guilty and then, with the permission of the Court, withdraws his plea of guilty, enters a plea of not guilty and exercises his constitutional right to trial despite the fact that the evidence of his guilt is overwhelming, I find it difficult to believe that the defendant is actually repentant and seriously concerned with rehabilitation which is generally true when a defendant pleads guilty.

For these reasons, I believe, and it is generally accepted by trial judges throughout the United States, that it is entirely proper and logical to grant some defendants some degree of leniency in exchange for pleas of guilty. If then, a trial judge grants leniency in exchange for a plea of guilty, it follows, as the reverse side of the same coin, that he must necessarily forego leniency, generally speaking, where the defendant stands trial and is found guilty.

In addition to these reasons, I should also like to point out that throughout the United States there were a total of 35,517 defendants in criminal proceedings commenced during the fiscal year 1959. Since each of these defendants must be dealt with by one of the 248 district judges in the United States with the great majority of defendants falling within the jurisdiction of the greater metropolitan districts such as the Northern District of Illinois, it is perhaps easier to understand why, in accord with the thinking of Justice Lummus, I might make general reference to a "standing policy" not to consider probation where a defendant stands trial even though I do not in fact strictly adhere to such a policy.

2. *Active Negotiation*

A typical negotiation conference between the assistant prosecutor and a defendant's attorney proceeded as follows:

A defendant was charged with possession of heroin, namely nineteen caps, an offense carrying a ten-year maximum. Present in the hallway were defendant (in the bullpen, behind a screened, barred door), his counsel, the police officer in charge of the case, and the assistant prosecutor. The assistant prosecutor offered defendant a reduced charge of addiction which would carry a one-year maximum. Defense counsel thought this was a good deal and talked with his client, but the client, faced with the year sentence, backed off and said he wanted a jury trial on the possession charge. Defense counsel thought the evidence sufficient to convict him (he had had the heroin in a violin case and when approached by the police, threw the case away) and asked if the prosecutor would recommend probation on the one-year user maximum if defendant pleaded guilty. The prosecutor snorted at this, stating that anyone having nineteen caps of heroin had some to sell, that no user would have this much for his own use alone. He said defendant in spite of no prior convictions was too old (twenty-eight) to consider for probation and had too much heroin. After some haranguing back and forth, the prosecutor said he wouldn't favor or oppose probation and that he would go along if the court saw fit to grant it. He refused to change from this position and eventually defendant pleaded guilty to being an addict and was sentenced to one year in prison.

Overcharging is not customarily used to induce pleas, but on the other hand no charging leniency is shown at the outset in the kinds of cases where pleas are commonly negotiated. An assistant prosecutor explained:

> The other day the bargaining prosecutor came in and told us, "For God's sake, give me something to work with over there. Don't reduce these cases over here; let me do it over there or many of these guys will be tried on a misdemeanor." What he was referring to is, that if we had graded a case at the lowest charge in the class of offenses in which it logically belongs, a defense attorney could conceivably get his man to plead to even a lower crime, a misdemeanor for example. We will limit to the highest possible charge because we expect a reduction in court for a plea.[x]

3. *The Propriety of Bargaining*

The granting of leniency to persons who plead guilty without overt negotiations will be raised in practice only by objection of codefendants who received a greater sentence after a contested conviction. In the *Wiley* case, as dealt with in the Court of Appeals,[y] Judge Duffy commented, in concurring:

---

[x] A defendant who wants to plead not guilty, yet obtain favorable consideration from having obviated trial, can do so by stipulating that the case may be determined by the court upon the basis of the evidence received at the preliminary examination. *See, e.g,* Poole v. Fitzharris, 396 F.2d 544 (9th Cir. 1968); Butler v. Wilson, 365 F.2d 308 (9th Cir. 1966).

[y] United States v. Wiley, 278 F.2d 500 (7th Cir. 1960); see the lower court opinion at 586, *supra*.

The trial judge announced from the bench that it was the standard policy in his court that once a defendant stands trial, probation for such a defendant would not be considered. This policy or rule is self-imposed. It is contrary to the statute and the rule of criminal procedure authorizing probation. Such a rule should not be followed. A defendant in a criminal case should not be punished by a heavy sentence merely because he exercises his constitutional right to be tried before an impartial judge or jury.

In the case at bar, McGhee, the four-time convicted felon, and the ringleader, received a two-year term. The three defendants other than Wiley, all of whom had criminal records, received sentences of one year and a day. Yet, Wiley, who had a good previous record except for one juvenile matter when he was thirteen years old, received a three-year term. A realistic appraisal of the situation compels the conclusion that Wiley's comparatively severe sentence was due to the fact that he stood trial. No other possible basis is suggested for the disparity. Consciously or not, the learned trial judge again applied the standard of his rule when he reimposed the three-year sentence. I agree this sentence should not be permitted to stand.

SHELTON v. UNITED STATES

246 F.2d 571 (5th Cir. 1957)

[Defendant pleaded guilty to violation of the Dyer Act in reliance on the promise of the Assistant United States Attorney that he would receive a one-year sentence. The sentence was for one year. Defendant subsequently moved to vacate the sentence on the ground that his plea was not voluntary and that he was in fact innocent. A panel of the court of appeals held, 2-1, that the defendant's plea was involuntary. A motion by the United States for rehearing was granted.]

Before HUTCHESON, Chief Judge, and RIVES, TUTTLE, JONES and BROWN, Circuit Judges, en banc.

TUTTLE, Circuit Judge. Upon a motion for rehearing this Court determined to consider such motion en banc.

It is Shelton's contention that if a motivating cause which impelled him to enter the plea was a promise by the Government to seek the dismissal of an additional count in the pending indictment and the dismissal of an indictment pending in another district and to recommend a sentence of a year the plea could not, as a matter of law, be voluntary.

In light of the full record, showing that the accused was not only willing but anxious to have his plea accepted by the court, the present claim of involuntariness after he has fully enjoyed the benefit of the dismissal of an additional count in the Atlanta indictment and the nolle prossing of the "more serious federal indictment" (as characterized by Shelton) in Miami—the reinstatement of which is now barred by statutes of limitations—and the imposition of the sentence *requested by him* in the principal case, cannot deprive the plea thus given of its character of voluntariness.

Moreover, in considering the bona fides of this belated claim it is relevant to note that a month after the entry of the plea now asserted to have been involuntary, Shelton wrote to the assistant district attorney who had handled the prosecution a letter relative to the lifting of the detainers in Atlanta and Miami to which the Government had agreed; he concluded: "Thanking you for your efforts in my behalf, and trusting that the entire transaction can be wound up soon, I am respectfully yours, J. Paul Shelton." It was only after the entire "transaction" was "wound up" thereafter and Shelton had reaped the full benefit of his agreement that he claimed for the first time that he had been coerced or overreached.

There is not a line of evidence to sustain a finding that he was in any way misled or imposed on. There was evidence that as a result of his plea he expected to receive favorable treatment. It was for the trial court to decide whether this expectation was so induced as to make the plea of guilty involuntary as a matter of law.

The motion for rehearing is granted; the previous judgment of this Court is set aside and the judgment of the trial court is affirmed.

HUTCHESON, Chief Judge (concurring specially). [T]he dissenters fall into the fatal basic error of declaring, in the teeth of the authorities cited and quoted from above, that *a plea of guilty is the same as an extra judicial confession of guilt and is to be regarded and dealt with in accordance with the rules governing confession.* As pointed out above, the exact contrary of this is true. *A plea of guilty is not a confession; it is a conviction.* Proceeding upon and from this error, which in my opinion is the head and front of their whole misapprehension, they further compound it with the error of declaring, in the face of the authorities above cited holding that this is not so, that it is the duty of a judge when a plea of guilty is entered to determine "that the plea is so voluntarily made as to furnish reliable and trustworthy testimony that the accused is in fact guilty. For if, on judicial inquiry, the conclusion is that it was that promise, whether subsequently made good or not, that really brought about the guilty plea, then the plea was congenitally defective because it was the product of a decisive, potent, but extraneous force," [246 F.2d 579] and this in the teeth of the authorities that *the question of guilt or innocence is not to be examined on a motion to vacate a sentence or on the entry of the plea itself.* [Amendment of Rule 11 has altered this.]

Upon the basis of these views above set out, the dissenters come up with this final view, that *it is a fundamental requirement of our system that if a promise or representation entered into the matter at all, a plea of guilty is not good.*

RIVES and BROWN, Circuit Judges (dissenting). With deference, we submit that a plea of guilty, a confession in open court, is subject to no less rigorous tests than those applicable to simple confessions. In either case, voluntariness requires that the confession be not induced by a promise or a threat, and more, that it be in fact voluntarily made. The reason of the requirement in each instance is to make certain that the confession is *trustworthy* testimony of guilt and to avoid accepting a plea of guilty from an accused who may be innocent.

We recognize the existence of the practice stated by our Brother Tuttle in his dissent from the former opinion:

"It is generally known that the great bulk of criminal cases are disposed of by pleas of guilty made after some discussion between the defendant and/or his counsel and the prosecuting attorney in which the latter frequently makes some commitment as to the sentence he will recommend or as to other charges or prosecutions he will drop; if this were not so, or if this Court holds that it may not be so, there would be few inducements for any person to plead guilty." 242 F.2d 101, 115.

The very statement of that practice, however, concedes that such promises or commitments *are inducements* for the accused to plead guilty. Such inducements in any particular case may be sufficient to elicit an untrue plea of guilty. The prevalence of that practice demonstrates the importance, indeed the imperative necessity, for the court itself to determine that the plea is so voluntarily made as to furnish reliable and trustworthy testimony that the accused is in fact guilty. For if, on judicial inquiry, the conclusion is that it was that promise, whether subsequently made good or not, that really brought about the guilty plea, then the plea was congenitally defective because it was the product of a decisive, potent, but extraneous force.

We err grievously when we allow ourselves to be diverted by other inquiries, such as whether the accused made a good bargain and whether the bargain was kept; the sole inquiry should remain, was the plea of guilty made under such circumstances as to constitute it reliable and trustworthy evidence of the accused's guilt of the offense with which he was charged.

With deference, we submit that the only answer that can be reached on the present record is "No." The accused had from the beginning contended that he was innocent; on a plea of not guilty, he had undergone one trial until a mistrial was declared through no fault of his; he had then offered to waive a jury and be tried before the court, and the Government had declined; on the hearing of the present motion, he offered to prove his innocence and his offer was declined by the Court; not once has he in any way confessed his guilt, except by the plea of guilty under attack; and it is conceded that he entered that plea in reliance upon not one, but several, material promises on the part of the Government. To this good day the record, as supplemented upon the last hearing, discloses no reliable and trustworthy reason to believe that the accused was guilty of the offense for which he was convicted.

The entry of a judgment of conviction upon such a plea of guilty was, we think, beyond the pale of due process. We therefore, respectfully dissent.[z]

Negotiating is usually done by the prosecutor. He has practical if not theoretical control over dropping of charges but can only recommend leniency in sentence. Because sentence is often involved in the bargaining, the judge sometimes takes a hand directly.

PEOPLE v. FENTON
141 Cal. App. 2d 357, 296 P.2d 829 (1956)

SHINN, P. J. On the day preceding sentence another conference was had in chambers which was reported. This consisted of a discussion between Mr. Poster and the judge as to what had been said at the first conference. Mr. Poster repeatedly asserted that at the first conference he gained the impression from the

[z] In a per curiam decision the Supreme Court reversed, "upon consideration of the entire record and confession of error by the Solicitor General that the plea of guilty may have been improperly obtained." 356 U.S. 26 (1958). The Fifth Circuit considers the Court's action neither approval nor disapproval of plea bargaining. Brown v. Beto, 377 F.2d 950, 954 (5th Cir. 1967).

judge's remarks that the court would be lenient in its sentence, he reported that fact to his client, who was induced thereby to submit the case under the grand theft charge upon stipulated facts. The judge consistently denied having intimated what the sentence might be and insisted that he had said nothing whatever to encourage a belief that leniency would be shown.

The grounds upon which a new trial may be granted do not include the ground that in the course of the trial the defendant was led into a stipulation from which he should justly have been released.

We believe we should avoid any misunderstanding of our opinion by making clear our belief that a conference of all counsel and the court, duly reported, respecting the court's attitude toward accepting a plea of guilty, or its equivalent, is of every day occurrence and often a necessary step in the disposition of criminal cases. But when inexperienced attorneys overstep the bounds of professional ethics and accepted court procedure by endeavoring to make a "deal" with the court as to punishment, we can only refer to the remarks of the patient but harassed judge when he found himself confronted with that situation and expressed himself as follows: "This type of business only leads me to a conclusion that I formed one time, and deviated from, that a judge should never have any conferences with attorneys at all, because this is just what you are faced with when you do, see. Somebody is always willing at some time along the line to put another interpretation on the conference." We may add that there were experienced and competent attorneys in the case who realize the futility as well as the impropriety of endeavoring to obtain leniency for a client by prearrangement with the court. The above remark was not addressed to them.

UNITED STATES *ex rel.* McGRATH v. LaVALLEE

348 F.2d 373 (2d Cir. 1965)

Before LUMBARD, Chief Judge, and SMITH and KAUFMAN, Circuit Judges.

KAUFMAN, Circuit Judge. The appellant John McGrath, presently serving a state court recidivist sentence of 29 to 30 years' imprisonment based upon a plea of guilty to second degree robbery, challenges the constitutionality of his detention, contending that the plea was induced by improper mental or psychological coercion and entered without fair knowledge of the alternatives.

Both at arraignment and after his indictment, appellant pleaded not guilty to the robbery charge. Before the trial, however, the Queens County District Attorney expressed a willingness to recommend that the court accept a plea to a reduced charge of second degree robbery, to cover all counts of the indictment. McGrath's counsel, through whom this information was transmitted, advised his client that acceptance would reduce the multiple-offender sentencing range from 15 to 60 years (for a first degree conviction) to 7½ to 30 years.

But following a side-bar conference, in which the experienced trial judge, Hon. William B. Groat, was advised of McGrath's refusal to follow his counsel's advice and accept the prosecution's offer to recommend a plea to a lesser offense, the parties adjourned to the latter's chambers to recanvass the alternatives open to the defendant.

[The stenographic transcript of the conference in chambers reads as follows:

The Court: Let the record show there is no jury here. It is in chambers.

They tell me that this boy was caught by an off-duty policeman. He has a long record.

Mr. George: That's right.

The Court: Do you realize what is happening? Do you realize the sentence you might have to face as a second offender in a first-degree robbery? That is one of the reasons I am talking to you now. I do not like to give long, long sentences.

Mr. George: I have advised him, Judge.

The Defendant: Yes, sir.

Mr. George: 15 and 16 years as a first—

The Court: I advise you to think it over. If you are convicted, I might have to send you away for the rest of your life.

As I see it, the likelihood of your being acquitted is not too good. Of course, if you want a trial, you will certainly get a fair trial. But you must remember this: If you are convicted as a second offender of robbery in the first degree, you will be entitled to no consideration of any kind from me.

The Defendant: Yes, sir.

The Court: On the other hand, a very, very fair plea is being offered by the District Attorney. He is willing to give you that plea if you go downstairs and tell the whole truth.

I make you no promises as to your sentence, but I will give you every consideration if you are truthful and there is an indication that you want to start a new life for yourself. Do you understand me?

The Defendant: Yes, sir.

The Court: You have to make up your mind, son, now. Once you are before the jury, you will be tried as indicted.

You have a very able counsel here, one of the best. I am not telling you what you should do or what you should not do. I am merely pointing out to you what you face.

The Defendant: Could you give me a chance to make up my mind?

The Court: I certainly will give you a chance to make up your mind, but this case is ready today, son. Both the District Attorney and your own lawyer have answered ready, and we are ready to proceed to trial today.

First of all, you have to make up your mind, asking yourself, "Did I do what is alleged in the indictment?" You and God know the answer to that question. The District Attorney has told me that, in his opinion, he has many witnesses who can prove his case. You, yourself, know whether you did it or not.

We are in chambers. There is no jury here. I repeat that you will receive a fair trial.

The decision is yours. You know whether or not you did what is claimed you did do. Considering your record and the case, only you can decide whether you wish to go to trial on the indictment of robbery in the first degree before a jury.

As I said, if the District Attorney proves the case as he has outlined, the likelihood of your being acquitted is not good. Or do you want to take a plea to robbery in the second degree and have some opportunity of receiving a shorter sentence? If I sentence you after a conviction of robbery in the first degree, you are going to be away until you are an old man. But I emphasize that I am not telling you what to do, son.

Are you married?

The Defendant: No.

The Court: After considering your case very carefully, I find this is your chance to serve a shorter term. If you choose the other course and are convicted, you are going to be away for a long time. You know you are a second offender. But I reiterate that I am not telling you what to do.

Mr. George, I do not like to see a boy who is offered a plea such as this—

Mr. George: Judge, I have worked before your Honor on many occasions. I have been out here and I know the fairness of the Court.

The Court: This boy has been a bad boy. There is no question about that. From what I have heard about this case, this is a very serious crime. The defendant must consider that in relation to his chances which are—

Mr. George: I know he hasn't any, Judge.

The Court: If he is convicted, I am faced with a mandatory first-degree robbery as a second offender.

Mr. George: Your hands are tied. Your hands are tied at 15.

The Court: If there is a conviction of robbery in the first degree, then there can be no consideration.

What do you want to do, son?

The Defendant: I will take it.

Mr. George: We will accept the plea.

The Court: Son, if this is what you want to do, when we return to the courtroom and I question you concerning your plea, you must answer categorically. That means, when I ask you if you plead guilty, you must say yes.

The Defendant: Yes.]

[T]he parties returned to the courtroom.

There, the defendant formally withdrew his not guilty plea, but not until after he was advised by the judge, on four occasions, that as a consequence of the changed plea he would face "a long prison term." The change was also preceded by McGrath's affirmative response to the judge's inquiry as to whether he realized "that no promise has been made to you, your attorney, or anyone else in your behalf concerning any sentence or punishment that might be meted out to you should such plea be accepted." Defense counsel then commended the judge for his fairness in considering the reduced plea and expressed his gratitude after the plea was entered and accepted.

All of the problems presented on this appeal were triggered some two and one-half months later, in February 1954, when McGrath was sentenced to 29-30 years' imprisonment. Before imposing this punishment, the judge indicated he was influenced by the accused's unsavory criminal record, see 319 F.2d at 311 n.1, specifically detailed in a probation report very recently made available to him, but not completed and transmitted to him before he accepted the guilty plea. Indeed, the judge expressed regret, at the time of sentencing, that he had accepted the plea to the lesser offense and indicated that appellant's exceptionally bad record called for a prison term not materially below the statutory maximum.

The testimony adduced at the hearing—from McGrath, his close relatives, the prosecuting attorney, and the trial judge—reinforces our reading of the judge's remarks, on the initial appeal, "not as an enticement or threat by means of a prior commitment by the judge to the prisoner's sentence, but as merely a fair description of the consequences attendant upon the prisoner's choice of plea, a description which was manifestly essential to an informed decision on [his] part." 319 F.2d at 314. All the evidence supports the District Court's conclusion that appellant's claims are based on afterthoughts rooted in frustrated, unjustified expectations of leniency.

Since, as McGrath perforce concedes, the mere fact that the judge conversed with him was not *per se* antithetical to the dictates of due process, the question is whether, judging from the general tenor of the discussion, the defendant's freedom of will was impermissibly affected. See United States v. Tateo, 214 F. Supp. 560 (S.D. N.Y. 1963). Considering McGrath's entire background and all the circumstances before, during and after acceptance of the plea, the finding that it was not so affected is fully supported by the evidence.

Prior to appellant's plea in the instant case, he had pleaded guilty on two other occasions to felony offenses, both on the advice of retained counsel. His entire course of conduct in this case was typical of the shrewd, intelligent and experienced bargainer. As revealed by the record before us, he admitted that he would have been willing to plead to third degree robbery, knowing that it carried a maximum 20-year sentence, and his only hesitancy in accepting the original offer by the prosecutor to recommend that the judge permit a second degree plea resulted from the absence of a written commitment as to the length of sentence—a condition precedent he told his lawyer he would insist upon. Moreover, the testimony indicates that the defendant told his sisters that "he didn't think that he had much of a chance" and he admittedly never discussed with his retained counsel any possible defenses to be raised at trial nor any possible witnesses who might testify in his behalf.

In addition, as we remarked in our first opinion, 319 F.2d at 313, the lack of any protest at the time of sentencing, or soon thereafter, that an implied promise had been broken, and the failure to raise the issue of coercion on direct appeal combine to cast doubt upon the veracity of the present allegations, first advanced many years after sentencing. Furthermore, defense counsel's continued presence throughout the conference in the judge's chambers is of considerable significance and justified the District Court's reluctance to "presume that counsel sat silent and in effect abandoned his client to judicial coercion." Under the circumstances, there was more than ample justification for the District Court's finding that the trial judge's statements did not overawe this sophisticated defendant.

GARNICK v. MILLER
81 Nev. 372, 403 P.2d 850 (1965)

ZENOFF, D. J., concurring. My concern is for the future, that trial judges will refuse to consider change of pleas in chambers because of a natural apprehension of later accusations that negligent or false conduct misled the person accused and caused him to change his plea, or that he did not get what he was promised, or that he was threatened or coerced in the judge's chambers, and ad infinitum. The only safe course would be a formal proceeding in open court, hardly conducive to a pre-trial conference.

The trial courts of Nevada are already overburdened with criminal matters that by reason of a statutory priority, are depriving civil litigants of their day in court. If the trial court cannot safely accept change of plea opportunities the number of costly time consuming trials will be multiplied immeasurably.

My concern is directed at the crass audacity of the defendant who took advantage of a situation created by her own conduct and that of her husband, and now points an accusing finger at the judge who gave her the probation which she obviously sought and bargained for.

UNITED STATES *ex rel.* ELKSNIS v. GILLIGAN
256 F. Supp. 244 (S.D.N.Y. 1966)

[Another portion of this opinion appears at 606, *infra.*]

WEINFELD, District Judge. Petitioner first considered surrendering his right to trial and his defenses when his counsel informed him of the proposed reduction in the charge from murder to manslaughter, and that if he pleaded thereto the judge was agreeable to a sentence not to exceed ten years. As against the proffered sentence his lawyer stressed a possible term of from forty years to life in the event of conviction on the second degree murder charge. Then followed the chambers conference at which the judge made the express promise to the defendant. That it induced the plea cannot be gainsaid. To deny the compelling force of the promise is to deny the reality of experience.

The unequal positions of the judge and the accused, one with the power to commit to prison and the other deeply concerned to avoid prison, at once raise a question of fundamental fairness. When a judge becomes a participant in plea bargaining he brings to bear the full force and majesty of his office. His awesome power to impose a substantially longer or even maximum sentence in excess of that proposed is present whether referred to or not. A defendant needs no reminder that if he rejects the proposal, stands upon his right to trial and is convicted, he faces a significantly longer sentence. One facing a prison term, whether of longer or shorter duration, is easily influenced to accept what appears the more preferable choice. Intentionally or otherwise, and no matter how well motivated the judge may be, the accused is subjected to a subtle but powerful influence. A guilty plea predicated upon a judge's promise of a definite sentence by its very nature does not qualify as a free and voluntary act. The plea is so interlaced with the promise that the one cannot be separated from the other; remove the promise and the basis for the plea falls.

It may well be, as has been suggested, that voluntary, as distinguished from coercive, bargaining between the prosecutor and the defendant has been sanctioned by propriety and practice—in some measure they deal at arm's length. But this is quite different from approbation of plea bargaining between the judge and the accused, where the disparity of positions is extremely marked. As has been urged:

> "Our concept of due process must draw a distinct line between, on the one hand, advice from and 'bargaining' between defense and prosecuting attorneys and, on the other hand, discussions by judges who are ultimately to determine the length of sentence to be imposed."

Finally, a bargain agreement between a judge and a defendant, however free from any calculated purpose to induce a plea, has no place in a system of justice. It impairs the judge's objectivity in passing upon the voluntariness of the plea when offered. As a party to the arrangement upon which the plea is based, he is hardly in a position to discharge his function of deciding the validity of the plea—a function not satisfied by routine inquiry, but only, as the Supreme Court has stressed, by "a penetrating and comprehensive examination of all the circumstances under which such a plea is tendered."[a]

---

[a] A system which sought consistently to foster bargaining would not perpetuate the dilemma which is put to an accused who cannot appeal from adverse ruling on a pretrial motion to suppress evidence unless he pleads not guilty and goes through trial. For example, United States v. Moretti, 353 F.2d 672 (2d Cir. 1965), held:

> There is no force in Moretti's contention that since he could not have appealed from the denial of his motion to suppress the evidence obtained by the search, DiBella v. United States, 369 U.S. 121 (1962), refusal to hear him now [after pleading guilty] would frustrate assertion of a constitutional right; he could have preserved all his rights by standing trial and raising a proper objection to introduction of the fruits of the search if the Government chose to offer them.

A new provision of the N.Y. CODE CRIM. PROC., § 813-c, solves this problem by permitting review on appeal despite the guilty plea.

STATE v. JOHNSON
156 N.W.2d 218 (Minn. 1968)

PETERSON, Justice. Defendant was indicted in Ramsey County on June 1, 1966, for the crime of murder in the first degree. An information charging defendant with murder in the third degree was filed on June 30, 1966, whereupon defendant pleaded guilty to that crime and the indictment was dismissed.

Defendant asserts that the charge of third-degree murder was a "settlement" arranged between counsel for the prosecution and the defense, and he concedes that it "may very likely [have been] a provident one from [defendant's] point of view." Nevertheless, defendant contends that the court, in view of the apparent "possibility of a successful defense based on intoxication," should have ascertained whether the reduction to manslaughter in the first degree rather than murder in the third degree would have been a more justly appropriate bargain under the circumstances.

Plea bargaining between competent counsel and with the intelligent acquiescence of the defendant, it may be observed at the outset, is not in conflict with public policy. Both the Advisory Committee on Criminal Trial of the American Bar Association Project on Minimum Standards for Criminal Justice and the President's Commission on Law Enforcement and Administration of Justice have endorsed the propriety of plea discussions and plea agreements as in the interest of the public in the effective administration of criminal justice.

Public policy, however, requires that this prevalent practice be controlled by the observance of certain essential conditions. One obvious condition is that the prosecuting attorney may engage in such discussion with the defendant only through counsel, except where defendant does not have counsel because he either is not eligible for counsel or does not desire counsel. A plea of guilty must, of course, be made by the individual defendant himself and in open court.[5] Another important condition, addressed to both court and counsel, is that the criminal charge for which the plea of guilty is bargained in lieu of the more serious charge shall be reasonably related to defendant's conduct in the sense that "the reduction be to a charge which bears some categoric similarity to the original charge."[7] Yet another condition, addressed even more specifically to the trial court and as a standard for the acceptance of *any* plea of guilty is that "the court should not enter a judgment upon such plea without making such

5 Minn. St. 630.29.

7 A.B.A. Project on Minimum Standards for Criminal Justice, Standards Relating to Pleas of Guilty (tentative draft), p. 68.

inquiry as may satisfy it that there is a factual basis for the plea."[8]

The ultimate judicial responsibility must be to make reasonably certain that a person innocent of *any* crime has not been improperly induced to plead guilty to a crime. It is likewise a judicial responsibility to protect society against a defendant's being permitted to bargain for a plea excessively lenient for the gravity of the crime apparently in fact committed. Although the court should neither usurp the responsibility of counsel nor participate in the plea bargaining negotiation itself, its proper role of discreet inquiry into the propriety of the settlement submitted for judicial acceptance cannot seriously be doubted.

We are unable to hold, on this record, that the trial court accepted defendant's plea of guilty without factual foundation. The defendant, it is conceded, is guilty of some degree of criminal homicide and is not an innocent person. The crime of third-degree murder bears a categoric similarity to the original charge of first-degree murder and is reasonably related to defendant's conduct as it appears on this record. There is indication in the record, moreover, that the state's amenability to a plea to this lesser offense was not prompted simply by doubt as to the provability of the originally indicted crime but was prompted as well by a sympathetic concern for a young man who had no prior criminal record.

Affirmed.

4. Reasons for Bargaining

The defendant who bargains may have any of various objectives and motivations. By pleading to a lesser offense he may be seeking to limit the maximum sentence which could be imposed on him; he may be avoiding mandatory sentence, often set by statute for murder, sex offenses, narcotics crimes, and traffic offenses; or he may want to avoid the label of "sex deviate" or "felon." He may insist upon the prosecutor's promise to recommend probation or leniency. Or he may ask for an indication from the judge what sentence is likely to be given.

1

A defendant in Wisconsin entered a small store and at knife point ordered the lone female proprietor into the basement, where he forcibly disrobed her and attempted sexual assault. Failing to complete the crime of rape, he left the store taking

[8] Id. p. 30.

some money and goods. He was originally charged with attempted rape but, unwilling to be branded with this label, he bargained to plead guilty to the crime of armed robbery, which carried a longer maximum sentence.

2

A defendant in Kansas was originally charged with drunk and disorderly conduct. He explained to the court that conviction as a drunk would "ruin his career." He was allowed to plead guilty to disorderly conduct.

There are several motivations on the part of the prosecutor and the courts in compromising with the defendant. A major one, mentioned previously, is avoiding the cost in time and effort of trying cases unnecessarily. Another reason is the uncertainty of conviction. No matter how strong the case, conviction is only probable, and there are frequently substantial uncertainties about obtaining a verdict even when guilt is clear.

3

A defendant had stabbed and seriously wounded his girl friend with whom he was living. He was charged with assault with intent to do great bodily harm less than murder, and at arraignment pleaded not guilty. On the date set for trial, the victim-complainant approached the prosecutor and said she did not want to testify against the defendant. The defendant, however, had a poor criminal record and the prosecutor's office, in consultation, decided to proceed with the trial. Just as the trial was about to begin, the prosecutor, realizing that he "would probably get nowhere without the cooperation of the complainant," offered to let the defendant plead guilty to felonious assault, a lesser included offense. The defendant's attorney agreed that "under the circumstances this would probably be the best move" because there was a possibility of the state introducing another eyewitness to the fracas (who, only the prosecutor knew, was also reluctant to testify) and defendant pleaded guilty to felonious assault.[b]

The reluctance to testify on the part of the victim is common in family or lover assault cases, when the offender is involved in organized crime, when testimony might be embarrassing (as in

[b] If defendant is aware that pleading guilty will serve as a bar to testing unfavorable pretrial rulings, this can serve to dampen his interest.

many sex offenses), or when restitution has been made. The prosecutor may be influenced by the judge's evaluation of the evidence.

4

A prosecutor and the defendant's counsel met in conference with a trial judge to review the appropriateness of a charge of indecent liberties in a particular case. The prosecutor, while certain that indecent liberties best described the offense, revealed his own doubts about securing a conviction because both the victim and her mother were of low intelligence and would make poor witnesses. The judge agreed that the case was doubtful, that the testimony would likely be confusing, and that perhaps "some evidence was lacking." However, he insisted that the court wanted "control" of the defendant because he was "dangerous" and suggested a reduced charge of assault. Both prosecutor and defense counsel agreed to the lesser charge.

Sometimes the evidence may be ample, yet the likelihood of conviction is slight.[c]

5

In Wisconsin an otherwise respectable couple was arrested in a parked automobile and charged with adultery. The prosecutor reduced the charge to disorderly conduct, explaining, "Adultery cases are probably the toughest to get convictions on. Where adults are involved and it's clearly a consensual situation, juries just won't convict." The couple pleaded guilty.

6

A defendant was arrested for "accosting and soliciting" because of homosexual overtures made to an officer of the vice squad. The charge was reduced to "disorderly person." A prosecutor commented, "In these kinds of cases, it is the officer who is on trial rather than the defendant. Judges claim that the vice squad entices these people into their criminal actions and they not only acquit them but bawl out the officer." The defendant pleaded guilty.

The prosecutor and the court may use the downgrading of charges as a way of individualizing justice.[d]

[c] *See also* illustration 2, at 433, *supra*.

[d] *See also* illustration 1, at 430, *supra*.

7

A 45-year-old defendant in Milwaukee was charged with larceny when he was apprehended shoplifting some sports equipment in a department store. He had no prior record, was a reputable businessman, and could only explain his action on the basis of "a sudden impulse." The judge reduced the charge to disorderly conduct because it "carried less onus" and avoided a "period of unnecessary probation supervision."

8

A married defendant had picked up a juvenile and had sexual relations with her. He was originally charged with statutory rape but allowed to plead guilty to contributing to the delinquency of a minor when the prosecutor informed the court that "the girl is a little tramp. She has knocked around a great deal, has been with carnivals and circuses. She's more to blame than he is."

9

A Michigan defendant with a reported I.Q. of fifty-two was allowed to plead guilty to simple larceny, a charge reduced from larceny from a building (which was already less than the breaking and entering charge which the facts and the defendant's own admissions would have supported) simply because of his limited intelligence. He was unemployed and on probation but seemed unable to comprehend the rules and was a constant, if inadvertent, violator. The probation agent said, "The judges won't revoke probation when he violates because of his low intelligence. There's not much I can accomplish except hope he makes it—that is, stays out of serious trouble until his expiration date."

10

A defendant was arrested for felonious assault, having beaten his victim seriously about the head and face with a beer bottle in a tavern. The charge was reduced to simple assault and battery when various witnesses told investigating officers that the victim, a much larger man than the defendant, had started the fight and had "pushed and slugged" the defendant as well as having called him obscene names.

5. *Failure to Keep the Bargain*

"Voluntariness" often means to the courts only that the bargain has been kept. See, for example, Bailey v. MacDougall, 247 S.C.

1, 145 S.E.2d 425 (1965), where defendant pleaded guilty to murder with a life sentence in reliance on the promise of the prosecutor and chief of police to recommend pardon or parole at the end of ten years. The prosecutor and chief of police kept their word, but defendant was not paroled. He filed a petition for habeas corpus which the trial judge granted, ordering him to be granted a new trial. The state supreme court reversed:

> A study of the entire record in this case leads us to the conclusion that the respondent has failed to prove by a preponderance of the evidence that he was misled, deceived or overreached in any way. There is nothing to show that the plea was induced by coercion, false promises or misrepresentations. The respondent's plea of guilty was freely, voluntarily and understandingly made after full consultation with his brother and his employed counsel [and] after full disclosure to him by his counsel of its nature and possible consequences.

On the other hand, failure to keep the bargain presents the double problem of "voluntariness" and fair treatment.

UNITED STATES *ex rel.* ELKSNIS v. GILLIGAN

256 F. Supp. 244 (S.D.N.Y. 1966)

[Another portion of this opinion appears at 599, *supra.*]

WEINFELD, District Judge. Petitioner, now serving a sentence of from seventeen and one-half to thirty-five years under a judgment of conviction entered in the County Court, Westchester County, on his plea of guilty to manslaughter in the first degree, seeks his release under a writ of habeas corpus.

The court finds that the defendant's withdrawal of his original plea of not guilty and the entry of a plea of guilty was based upon the judge's promise that the sentence to be imposed would not exceed ten years. The defendant, in return for the judicial promise, gave up his right to have the state establish his guilt beyond a reasonable doubt on a jury trial. Deferring at this point consideration of whether the guilty plea was voluntary, nevertheless the imposition by the judge of a sentence contrary to his express promise is wholly irreconcilable with constitutional safeguards and due process of law.

Fundamental fairness, as a concept of due process of law, requires when an accused has entered a plea of guilty based upon a promise by a judge who thereafter, whatever the reason, fails to adhere to his promise, that the judge, on his own motion, reinstate the not guilty plea and reinvest the defendant with the fundamental rights accorded him under our accusatory system of justice. Of course, an accused so restored to his original position may well decide to plead guilty again, but this must be a matter of his own free will and reasoned choice.

The state, however, urges that the judge was released from his promise because it was made upon an assumption that the defendant was a first felony offender.

Knowing whether there has in fact been a bargain, and what its terms are, may sometimes be a real problem. For example, the existence of an explicit bargain may be hotly disputed,[e] and there is difficulty in knowing whether an "implicit bargain" is to be found in the court's consistent but unexpressed practice of being lenient with all those who plead guilty.[f]

C. THE LAWYER'S ROLE AT ARRAIGNMENT

Gideon v. Wainwright, 372 U.S. 335 (1963), established that the fourteenth amendment imposed upon the states a duty in all serious cases to provide counsel for indigent criminal defendants who do not intelligently waive that right. It did not determine whether that right to appointment of counsel extends to minor offenses or whether one who pleads guilty may complain at not having had the assistance of counsel.[g]

UNITED STATES *ex rel.* DUROCHER v. LaVALLEE
330 F.2d 303 (2d Cir. 1964)

KAUFMAN, Circuit Judge, with whom WATERMAN, SMITH, HAYS and MARSHALL, Circuit Judges, concur. Claiming that they were not advised of their right to counsel when pleading guilty, four New York prisoners serving increased sentences as second offenders seek to invalidate their first convictions under the due process clause of the Fourteenth Amendment.

In his application for a writ of habeas corpus, Durocher alleged that he had been unaware of his right to counsel at the time of his guilty plea, that he had not been offered an attorney,

---

[e] *See, e.g.*, the *McGrath* case at 594, *supra*.

[f] *See, e.g.*, the *Wiley* case at 586, *supra*.

[g] The right existed, of course, in the federal courts. Von Moltke v. Gillies, 332 U.S. 708, 721 (1948).

although indigent, and that he had not understood the "legal interpretation" of the charges against him.

At a hearing granted upon his application, it was revealed that Durocher had been seventeen years of age at the time of his Massachusetts conviction, and that he had received a "partial seventh grade education." Testifying below in his own behalf, Durocher asserted that he could "read average," but admitted to considerable difficulty with "big words." The hearing further established that the Massachusetts offense had been Durocher's first, and that he had run away from home a year prior to his arrest.

Although finding no indication that Durocher had been advised of his right to counsel, the District Judge denied the petition on the basis of his conclusion that Durocher's conviction was not lacking in fundamental fairness. In so holding, the Judge emphasized that Durocher had understood the nature of the charges against him, and had not requested the assistance of an attorney. He relied heavily, moreover, upon Durocher's admission, at the time of his arrest, to entering a home and stealing several wrist watches; he abruptly dismissed Durocher's contentions that an attorney might have been able to prove that he had not "broken" into the home, as charged in the complaint, but rather had entered through an open door.

Simply stated, we are convinced that Gideon's requirement of court-appointed counsel cannot be limited to cases in which a "not guilty" plea has been entered—the context in which Gideon itself was decided. Indeed, we would be less than candid were we even to consider the question as an original matter; even if Gideon may be said to have left the issue open, our conclusion seems plainly required by the Supreme Court's recent disposition of Doughty v. Maxwell, 376 U.S. 202.

Doughty had been indicted for rape in 1958. Although "discussing" the possibility of securing counsel with his wife, he entered a plea of guilty in January of 1959, without ever requesting the assistance of an attorney. Sentenced to prison, he sought habeas corpus in the state courts of Ohio, alleging, *inter alia,* that his right to counsel had been infringed. In an opinion filed before Gideon was decided, the Supreme Court of Ohio rejected his petition, on the ground that Doughty had waived his right to counsel by pleading guilty. Doughty v. Sacks, 173 Ohio St. 407, 183 N.E.2d 368 (1962).

Doughty's petition for certiorari reached the Supreme Court after the decision in Gideon. In a brief *per curiam* opinion, the Court reversed and remanded the Ohio judgment for "further consideration in light of Gideon v. Wainwright." 372 U.S. 781

(1963). On remand, however, the Ohio Court adhered to its previous decision after concluding that Gideon was not dispositive because Doughty had failed to request the assistance of counsel. 175 Ohio St. 46, 191 N.E.2d 727 (1963). It was this second Ohio decision, refusing to apply Gideon to a case in which the defendant pleaded guilty and did not request counsel, which the Supreme Court summarily reversed in a brief *per curiam* order, on the authority of Gideon and Carnley v. Cochran, 369 U.S. 506 (1961).

It is well established in federal prosecutions that the failure to advise a defendant of his right to counsel will invalidate a plea of guilty even in the absence of a showing of prejudice. United States v. Lavelle, 306 F.2d 216 (2d Cir. 1962); cf. United States v. Tribote, 297 F.2d 598 (2d Cir. 1961) (counsel must be afforded not only at time of plea but at sentence as well). In light of the Gideon rationale and the precise ruling in Doughty, we feel constrained to hold that state convictions, when founded on a plea of guilty by a defendant unaware of his right to counsel, similarly cannot stand.

Bewildered by the mystifying language in which legal documents are cast, he will generally be incapable "of determining for himself whether the indictment is good or bad." Overwhelmed by the seemingly overpowering resources of the state, he may elect to plead guilty because he feels woefully ill-equipped to prepare his defense, "even though he have a perfect one." Unlike the defendant financially able to retain an attorney, he may be unaware of legal defects and complexities in the charges against him, and plead guilty to an offense which he has not committed. Indeed, the appeals now before us furnish striking proof that this possibility is more than theoretical. Thus, for example, had Durocher been aided by counsel, he might have been advised that he had not technically "broken" into a private dwelling as charged in the complaint, or lacked the intent required by the relevant state statute, and hence had a good defense to the serious offense charged.

In the words of Mr. Justice Brennan, writing for the Court in Carnley v. Cochran, 369 U.S. 506, 513 (1962), "it is settled that where the assistance of counsel is a constitutional requisite, the right to be furnished counsel does not depend on a request." Indeed, as early as 1945, the Supreme Court held in Rice v. Olson, 324 U.S. 786 (1945), that a plea of guilty cannot operate as a waiver of court-appointed counsel, and that the absence of a request therefor was totally irrelevant to a determination of whether counsel should have been appointed.

Especially as applied to Gideon, this doctrine clearly seems correct. If we were to hold that Gideon might not be invoked by those who did not request the assistance of counsel, we would be penalizing precisely those defendants whom Gideon was most intended to protect—those so ignorant of or unfamiliar with criminal procedures that they were not even sufficiently sophisticated to request court-appointed counsel.

HULETT v. SIGLER

242 F. Supp. 705 (D. Neb. 1965)

VAN PELT, District Judge. Petitioner was convicted of burglary on his own plea, the voluntary nature of which forms the controverted issue which must now be decided. During all critical stages of his prosecution Hulett was represented by counsel of his own choosing.

Under what circumstances is a plea of guilty deemed constitutionally involuntary where the defendant is represented by counsel and where his attorney and the prosecuting attorney deal or bargain to exchange a plea of guilty for dismissal of charges under a recidivist statute?

Subsequent to preliminary hearing where Hulett entered a plea of not guilty the information was amended to include an habitual criminal count. That the statute itself was applicable to petitioner is without dispute. Learning of this change petitioner's attorney conferred with the prosecuting attorney about the possibility of dropping the recidivist charge if a guilty plea were entered to the burglary count.

The proposition of withdrawing the habitual criminal charge in exchange for the guilty plea was presented to the judge, and he at least tacitly assented. After an additional conference between the presiding judge and the probation officer Hulett's counsel was informed by the probation officer that the sentence would probably run in the neighborhood of five years. This information was conveyed to petitioner, although he was specifically admonished that no promises or assurances could be made, and that neither his attorney, nor the deputy county attorney nor the probation officer could speak for the judge. Petitioner apparently agreed to the proposal, for a guilty plea was entered and accepted by the court. Also accepted by the court was the prosecuting attorney's recommendation that the habitual criminal charge be dropped.

Petitioner attempts to find his solace in this court's determination in Shupe v. Sigler, 230 F. Supp. 601 (1964), and to that extent relies considerably on that decision. Though certainly not inapposite, the ultimate ruling therein is not determinative in the instant situation. In Shupe the court concluded "that for a prosecuting attorney to talk with the defendant in the absence of his counsel and attempt to have him change a plea of not guilty to a plea of guilty and in the absence of counsel to reach an agreement as to the length of his sentence, whether made with or without authority of the court, is to deprive the defendant of the effective assistance of counsel at a time when it was needed." Hulett, however, was at all times represented by counsel, and all bargaining was done at the behest and with the concurrence of his attorney.

Rather than Shupe, the court feels the present determination is more properly guided by a recent decision of the Ninth Circuit. In Cortez v. United States, 337 F.2d 699 (9 Cir. 1964), which was a motion for vacation of sentence pursuant to 28 U.S.C. § 2255, the movant's contention was that his plea of guilty was coerced because of a "deal" between the United States Attorney and his counsel to exchange his plea for reduced charges against his wife. Cortez's position was rejected with the observation that such rationale would vitiate all guilty pleas entered as a result of a bargain. Instead, the more proper inquiry is whether the inducement for the guilty plea was one which necessarily overcame the defendant's ability to make a voluntary decision. Cortez v. United States, supra, at 701. The court went on to observe:

"We take judicial notice of the fact that the vast majority of those who are indicted for federal crimes plead guilty. We know, too, that in many of the cases where this occurs the plea will be to one count, or less than all counts, of a multicount indictment, or to a lesser offense than that originally charged. In a sense, it can be said that most guilty pleas are the result of a 'bargain' with the prosecutor. But this, standing alone, does not vitiate such pleas. A guilty defendant must always weigh the possibility of his conviction on all counts, and the possibility of his getting the maximum sentence, against the possibility that he can plead to fewer, or lesser, offenses, and perhaps receive a lighter sentence. The latter possibility exists if he pleads guilty, as Cortez did, to the whole charge against him."

And after emphasizing that a lawyer who did not explore the possibility of a reduced charge in exchange for a plea of guilty, so long as he fully advises his client of his rights, would be derelict in his duty, the court concluded:

"The important thing is not that there shall be no 'deal' or 'bargain,' but that the plea shall be a genuine one, by a defendant who is guilty; one who understands his situation, his rights, and the consequences of the plea, and is neither deceived nor coerced."

MARTIN v. COMMONWEALTH OF VIRGINIA

365 F.2d 549 (4th Cir. 1966)

Before HAYNSWORTH, Chief Judge, and SOBELOFF and BOREMAN, Circuit Judges.

SOBELOFF, Circuit Judge. The Commonwealth of Virginia here appeals from the District Court's order vacating a state court's judgment of conviction and directing a new trial. For reasons to be stated we affirm.

On August 9, 1960, James Edward Martin and two other Negro prisoners escaped from a road gang in Montgomery County, Virginia. Sometime the next evening they came upon the house of Mr. Joseph E. "Ted" Willard, whose automobile was parked in his driveway. As they were pushing the car down the drive into the highway and trying to get it started, the three escapees were chased away by Mr. Willard. Soon afterward they were recaptured and returned to the road camp. While they were at large, the radio broadcast news bulletins every few minutes, and feeling ran high in the community.

On October 3, 1960, Martin and his two fellow prisoners were indicted, tried and convicted for escape and grand larceny. The indictments were handed up by the grand jury between eleven and eleven thirty that morning, and the trial judge appointed an experienced member of the local bar to represent Martin. After discussing the case with Sergeant Reynolds, the officer in charge of the road camp, the attorney spoke briefly with Martin. It is noteworthy that Sergeant Reynolds was present during this conference, at which Martin simply stated that he wanted to plead guilty and "get it over with."

Court was recessed for lunch at twelve o'clock. The appointed counsel sought to negotiate a guilty plea to some lesser charge, but he found the Commonwealth's Attorney "rather bitter because of the situation which created quite a disturbance in our community." At this stage in his representation, the court-appointed attorney had spent less than 30 minutes investigating the case. No change of venue was sought.

After lunch, the attorney talked with several others and conferred again with Martin. Sergeant Reynolds was present at this conference also, and Martin simply repeated his desire to plead guilty. Because of his inability to strike a bargain with the Commonwealth's Attorney, and because in his view—based on his brief acquaintance with the case—there were no possible defenses, the attorney concluded that such a plea would be advisable.

The court reconvened at two o'clock, and Martin and his codefendants were called for trial about three, less than four hours after the indictment. Martin's attorney entered a guilty plea, and several witnesses for the State testified without cross-examination as to the general background of the offenses. Martin was found guilty, and the attorney made a short statement asking for leniency. Although no aggravating circumstances appeared, the court imposed consecutive sentences of five years for the escape (the maximum) and three years for the alleged grand larceny (of a five year maximum). No appeal was taken from these judgments.

These and other cases, while differing in their particular facts, establish the principle that a lawyer's duty in representing a person charged with crime may not be discharged perfunctorily or mechanically. Representation is not adequate and a trial does not meet the standard of fundamental fairness if a court-appointed attorney is not afforded an adequate opportunity to investigate and reflect upon his client's case.[4]

In this case the District Court found that the likelihood of prejudice arising from an interval of only three and one-half hours from indictment to trial was so substantial that in the interest of fairness a new trial was required.

We were informed at the oral argument that pursuant to a recommendation of the Attorney General against indicting and trying on the same day, the practice is being abandoned in the courts of Virginia. This recognition of the dangers lurking in hasty trials reinforces the appropriateness of the District Court's order under review.

Affirmed.[h]

---

[4] See Braxton v. Peyton, 365 F.2d 563 (4th Cir. decided this day). Some indication of the range of questions a court-appointed lawyer must consider in the preparation of a case is provided by a checklist prepared for the use of counsel appointed to represent indigent defendants in federal criminal trials in the District Court of Maryland. See report on the Criminal Justice Act of the Judicial Conference of the United States, 36 F.R.D. 277, 338-341 (1965). In addition to conferences with the accused, the arresting officers, and witnesses, this form suggests some 32 different possible defenses and tactical motions that should be considered. While many of these may not apply in a given case, they emphasize the variety of factors that must be evaluated, and make plain the danger of overlooking a significant feature when the attorney has only a few hours to prepare.

[h] *Cf.* Evans v. Kropp, 254 F. Supp. 218 (E.D. Mich. 1966), holding the defendant was denied due process when his attorney permitted him to plead guilty without bringing to the court's attention psychiatric diagnosis which suggested he might be insane.

The presence of counsel in guilty plea cases is reassuring to the trial judge, who can assume that counsel has inquired into the facts to be sure that the plea is accurate and truly consensual, and that the accused is competent to plead, knows his rights to trial, and has been apprised of the probable consequences of pleading guilty. The judge's reliance may not always be justified, yet he rests easier in accepting a plea of guilty when the defendant has a lawyer. Nonetheless, the judge may still interrogate the defendant for the record—to protect both the court and the lawyer—and may conduct a post-plea hearing into the circumstances of the case and defendant's satisfaction with his lawyer's representation. Thus the guilty plea process is becoming more formalized and surrounded with safeguards.[1]

One of the prerequisites for the smooth working of the criminal law system as presently constituted is that most defendants plead guilty. Today the rules are changing so that more and more defendants are represented by counsel. So long as counsel can see that his client's advantage lies in pleading guilty this will have little consequence. But as counsel comes to feel that failure to raise all possible defenses and objections may be later labeled incompetency in representation he is likely to raise all possible arguments on behalf of his client—both because the court says that his client is entitled to such defense and because he wishes to protect himself. There is a clear judicial trend in recent years toward willingness to find representation by counsel constitutionally inadequate, whether counsel is appointed by the court or privately employed by the defendant. This trend seems to discourage negotiating for plea.

REPORT OF THE STATE'S ATTORNEY'S OFFICE OF BALTIMORE CITY 3-4 (1965)

Crime Trend Reflected Here

The year did not break stride with the trend of metropolitan crime in recent years. There was a quantitative increase as the number of new cases continued to rise. There was a qualitative increase of even greater significance as several factors converged to make for far greater complexity in the trial of the average criminal case.

One was the growing estrangement between the defendant and the defense attorney. Time was when that relationship was an "entente cordial" with respect and trust flowing reciprocally

---

[1] People v. Taylor, 9 Mich. App. 333, 155 N.W.2d 723 (1968), sets out elaborate procedure to be used by trial courts in determining whether to accept guilty pleas.

between the two. That once firm professional alliance is now little more than an uneasy coexistence—and even that of rather brief duration.

Defense Attorneys New Targets

The law quite properly extends to every convicted prisoner an opportunity for a post-conviction hearing to test the propriety of his original conviction. Almost every prisoner, not nearly so properly, seizes that opportunity whether he has any meritorious claim to advance or not. A stock claim in all such petitions today is that the original defense attorney was "professionally incompetent." Thus almost every prisoner in the dock is looking at the champion who is resolutely defending his liberty as a potential "professional incompetent" for post-conviction petition purposes. Conversely, the beleaguered defense attorney must keep one eye to his front to do combat with the prosecutor and another "weather eye" to his flanks for the client who will be attacking him the moment an adverse verdict is returned.

The major result of this deteriorated attorney-client relationship in the criminal courts has been the almost total disappearance of the guilty plea. A sound professional tactic in days of not-too-distant yore for a defense attorney faced with a hopeless case was to enter a guilty plea and to submit the case on a statement of fact. This calculated underplaying of the case frequently minimized the gravity of the offense in the mind of the sentencing judge and often resulted in a lesser sentence for the defendant. This was no mean service to the defendant who was certain to be found guilty whether he so pleaded or not.

Today most defense attorneys are fearful of entering or even suggesting a guilty plea even where the tactical situation clearly calls for it. As a result, hundreds of cases a year that would have been disposed of in ten or fifteen minutes are now consuming hours and even days of futile effort, save the protection of the attorney from his client.

This professional cold-war manifests itself in other ways as well. Many defense attorneys now file pre-trial motions that have little merit save to build a record on paper of services rendered. Historically, defense attorneys have been able informally to confer with the prosecutor and to learn everything about the case. When asked why today they are delaying the trials and complicating the issues with formal "Motions for Discovery and Inspection" and "Bills of Particulars" where a casual visit or phone call would accomplish the same end, defense counsel admit with undisguised exasperation that they are simply "protecting the record."

When counsel does undertake to bargain on behalf of his client there is some doubt what limits should be imposed on his tactics. The adversary system of justice assumes it proper in a contested case to give even the guilty defendant the "best possible defense." There is no such well-established tradition whether in pleading his client guilty the attorney has a responsibility to get his client the "best possible deal." Is it proper to maneuver cases to judges who are likely to impose light sentence by adjournment, by informing the assignment clerk that jury trial will be waived if the case is assigned to a particular judge, or by demanding a jury trial so that the trial will be set at a later time before another judge—with intention to plead guilty before the desired judge? Is the process of negotiating charge reduction or prosecutor's recommendation for leniency in return for a guilty plea to be viewed as gaining something to which the client is not entitled, or is it to be seen as obtaining for him treatment consistent with that available to others and consistent with what individualized justice calls for? The lawyer has not been taught what he should do in preparation for attempting to negotiate with the prosecutor, what information he needs, or what standards govern the negotiation.[j]

Reference Note

The principal source for understanding the guilty plea process is D. NEWMAN, CONVICTION: THE DETERMINATION OF GUILT OR INNOCENCE WITHOUT TRIAL (1966), in the American Bar Foundation Series on the Administration of Criminal Justice in the United States. This is heavily relied on and reflected in shorter form in the American Bar Association Project on Minimum Standards for Criminal Justice, Standards Relating to Pleas of Guilty (1967), and in Enker, *Perspectives on Plea Bargaining,* in THE PRESIDENT'S COMMISSION ON LAW ENFORCEMENT AND ADMINISTRATION OF JUSTICE, TASK FORCE REPORT: THE COURTS 108-19 (1967).[k] A comparison of the recommendations of the A.B.A. and the President's Commission is made in Rosett, *The Negotiated Guilty Plea,* 374 ANNALS 70 (1967).

---

[j] On possible new functions of counsel, see Medalie, *The Offender Rehabilitation Project: A New Role for Defense Counsel at Pretrial and Sentencing,* 56 GEO. L.J. 2 (1967).

[k] *See also* THE PRESIDENT'S COMMISSION ON LAW ENFORCEMENT AND ADMINISTRATION OF JUSTICE, TASK FORCE REPORT: THE COURTS 9-13 (1967).

A. BLUMBERG, CRIMINAL JUSTICE (1967), offers useful hypotheses about the operation of the guilty plea system, but is of limited value as a descriptive study. *See* Kimball, Book Review, 14 CRIME & DELINQUENCY 274 (1968).

Excellent discussion of the practical considerations in preparing for arraignment, in advising a client whether to plead guilty, and in negotiating with the prosecutor, is to be found in A. AMSTERDAM, B. SEGAL & M. MILLER, TRIAL MANUAL FOR THE DEFENSE OF CRIMINAL CASES chs. XII, XIII (1967).

Chapter 10

PREPARATIONS FOR TRIAL

When an accused pleads not guilty at arraignment a time will be set for his trial, and his bail will be continued. Almost always, one who pleads not guilty will be represented by counsel. The plea may be made either with the intention of proceeding to trial or for some tactical advantage. The defendant may plan eventually to plead guilty but may be delaying the plea in order to await assignment of the case to a different judge. The defendant may also wish to await the outcome of various pretrial motions before finally deciding whether to plead guilty. It will be possible up to, and even during, the trial to change his plea to guilty if that seems the preferable thing to do.

In advance of trial the defendant may make any of numerous motions—*e.g.*, he may move that his trial be severed from that of codefendants, he may ask for postponement or a change of venue, he may raise a question whether he is mentally fit to stand trial and cooperate with his attorney, he may request discovery of evidence in the hands of the prosecutor, he may move to suppress evidence (seized objects, confessions, observations, overheard conversations) obtained in violation of constitutional or statutory rights of the defendant. He may also give notice, when required by statute to do so, of certain matters he will wish to establish at trial—alibi, insanity, entrapment.

Of the pretrial motions which the defendant might make, the ones raising the most acute issues for the criminal justice system are the demand for disclosure of evidence and the demand for suppression of evidence.

In the area of discovery the criminal prosecution is undergoing basic revision. The adversary system traditionally permitted each party to disclose his case only at trial, but for the past generation discovery has been steadily enlarged in civil cases. More recently discovery has also begun to be extended in criminal cases.

The demand for suppression of evidence is another focus of activity. The use of judicial control over admissibility of evidence as a device to regulate police action, and the procedures by which such control should be exercised, are central issues for the system.

A. DISCOVERY

The adversary system is based on the premise that a neutral tribunal will be able to determine the true facts of a dispute and reach a just resolution if it hears the evidence and arguments most favorable to each side, presented through vigorous advocacy. Traditionally partisan advocacy meant that each party was to develop its evidence and arguments independent of the other side. Any assistance to the opposing side was considered as out of place in litigation as in a prize fight. In the 1930's a radical change in the adversary system was heralded by the adoption of the Federal Rules of Civil Procedure, which fostered extensive disclosure by both sides. The framers of the rules thought that this change would actually strengthen the adversary system by eliminating surprise and permitting the real persuasive power of the evidence to be tested. In subsequent years many states have adopted similar discovery procedures in civil matters. Thus far, however, discovery in criminal cases has been narrowly limited in most jurisdictions. The Federal Rules of Criminal Procedure provide for substantial pretrial discovery, and California has led the way in development of common-law rights to discovery on the part of both prosecution and defense, but in most states discovery as a matter of right is still very limited.[a]

THE STATE AND THE ACCUSED: BALANCE OF ADVANTAGE IN CRIMINAL PROCEDURE

By Abraham S. Goldstein

69 Yale Law Journal 1149, 1180-94 (1960)†

DISCOVERY BY THE DEFENDANT

The elimination of precise pleading, the general unavailability of particulars, and the increasing elasticity given to indictments all leave a good deal of room for "surprise" at trial. And not all such "surprise" is readily curable by granting a continuance. Civil procedure seeks to minimize this problem by permitting each party to inform himself to the utmost about the other's case —to sift legal issues and evidence in detail before trial through depositions, requests for admissions, and discovery of documents.

[a] But compare the changing view reflected in People v. Tribbett, 90 Ill. App. 2d, 232 N.E.2d 523 (1967).

This process has as its object the harnessing of the full creative potential of the adversary process, bringing each party to trial as aware of what he must meet as his finances and his lawyer's energy and intelligence permit.

Yet virtually no such machinery exists for the defendant accused of a crime. No deposition or admissions procedure is ordinarily available to him. Though a motion for discovery of documents before trial is technically available, attempts to invoke it are rarely successful. When they are, they usually enable the defendant to get only materials which are not central to his task of preparing a defense. For example, motions for leave to subpoena before trial commercial records of various sorts—in short, materials in the hands of nongovernmental persons involved in the prosecution—are often granted. Confessions, guns, bullets, chemical analyses and autopsy reports are also beginning to be made available, albeit reluctantly and in only a few jurisdictions. But the statement of a government witness—at best, a poor substitute for a deposition, since defense counsel was not there to cross-examine when it was made—is virtually unobtainable. The few federal cases making such statements available before trial, such as *Fryer v. United States,*[105] have probably been overruled by the legislation which followed in the wake of *United States v. Jencks.*[106] Even before that legislation was enacted, *Jencks* had done little to open the government's files. It said no more than that defense counsel, *at trial,* must be given access to prior statements of a witness *on the stand* regarding the subject matter of that witness's testimony. The case did not address itself either to the pretrial stage or to the statements, in government files at time of trial, of witnesses not testifying but potentially helpful to the defense. Only a handful of fairly limited due process cases deal with the latter problem—and none of them explicitly with the right to obtain such materials before trial.

If the defendant should wish to use his own resources in searching out those witnesses who have spoken to police, prosecutor, or grand jury, he will, more often than not, find that they have been advised not to discuss their testimony with him. Without the subpoena, he can do nothing effective to break the wall of silence. If he should try, he runs the risk of being charged with tampering with witnesses. Even his search for evidence at large is inevitably restricted because he has neither a crime laboratory nor vast identification and fingerprint files available to him. Most often, he has no investigative assistance whatever.

---

[105] 207 F.2d 134 (D.C. Cir.), *cert. denied,* 346 U.S. 885 (1953).

[106] 353 U.S. 657 (1957).

The one institution on the scene which might be used to afford the accused effective pretrial discovery of the prosecution's case is the preliminary hearing. But American courts have consistently refused to shape it in the mold of its British counterpart, in which the prosecution is obligated to make complete disclosure of the evidence it will use at trial. In its present form, the American preliminary hearing provides a minimal opportunity to discover the government's case and to confront and cross-examine witnesses. It requires only so much disclosure as is necessary to make out "probable cause" to believe that defendant committed the crime, or a "prima facie" case, or some other formulation of a minimal evidentiary burden.

Even this obligation can be evaded through subtle pressures designed to maximize waiver—for example, through failure to provide for appointment of counsel at this stage, thereby making it less likely that a hearing will be requested by the defendant. Where indictment by grand jury remains the general rule, continuance of the preliminary hearing until the grand jury has returned an indictment withdraws the limited opportunity for discovery at the preliminary hearing. For he who has already been indicted by a grand jury is not "entitled" to a preliminary hearing.

Once the case is placed in the grand jury's hands, it is shrouded with secrecy. Only under the most extraordinary circumstances may the defendant obtain the minutes of that body, though the government may use them for many purposes. And neither defendant nor his counsel sees, nor is given the opportunity to examine, the witnesses against him. True, in many states the names of witnesses before the grand jury are required by statute to be endorsed on the ensuing indictment. But, in most of them, witnesses whose names are not endorsed will be permitted to testify. And in the others, there is nothing the defendant can do to make the named witnesses talk to him or to get copies of their statements to the prosecutor.

In sum, if police or prosecution choose to withhold from the defendant their evidence or legal theories, or if they continue the preliminary hearing until indictment, the defendant has only the notice given him by the indictment, the occasional bill of particulars, and the even more occasional pretrial discovery. Is the prosecution similarly handicapped?

Discovery by the Government

Denial of pretrial discovery to the defendant is justified most often as a necessary counterweight to the alleged fact that the accused "need not disclose the barest outline of his defense [and] . . . is immune from question or comment on his silence." The justification is unsatifactory for two entirely separate reasons. First, by assigning a central tenet of our accusatorial procedure to the bargain-counter, the defendant is made to pay dearly for his privilege of silence, whether or not he makes use of it. Second, and more immediately relevant, the Hand view grossly exaggerates the protection which this "immunity" affords.

Though the defendant still need not file a detailed responsive pleading in most states, more and more require that the defenses of alibi and insanity be pleaded specially before trial. Even at the trial, where the accused is most clearly immune from being called by the prosecution as its witness (or, in most jurisdictions, from having his failure to testify made the subject of comment by the prosecution), the protection means less to the defendant than appears: first, the accused will testify in his own behalf in most cases and thus subject himself to cross-examination; second, the prosecutor will rarely wish to make the accused his witness; third, the failure of the accused to testify is so conspicuous, particularly in this day of frequent invocation of the fifth amendment, that he is under the utmost pressure to take the stand to rebut the inference of guilt which will likely be drawn by the jury, whether or not his silence is explicitly called to their attention; finally, admissions made by the accused to the police before trial are freely and regularly used at the trial [subject to the requirements of *Miranda v. Arizona*], placing defendants under pressure to take the stand to explain the admissions away. . . . And, virtually everywhere, the body of the accused may be used fairly freely to incriminate him. Although, on a theoretical level, such use of the body is not within the concept of self-incrimination, it remains a significant factor in assessing the total balance, or lack of it, between prosecution and accused. The accused's fingerprints and footprints may be taken; his blood and urine may be removed, provided the job is done scientifically; his handwriting and his voice may be used in most jurisdictions; he may be required to exhibit himself, in a line-up or otherwise, wearing particular kinds of clothing, though such exhibition may well increase the likelihood that he will be identified as the culprit.

When the grand jury investigation begins, most jurisdictions recognize the immunity of the accused from interrogation only if he has already been named a defendant by arrest, by information, or by earlier indictment. If the prosecutor chooses to defer arrest or formal charge and hales the target of his investigation before the grand jury as a "witness," that target need not, except in a few jurisdictions, be advised that it is he whose conduct is under scrutiny. As a result, he may testify where otherwise he might refrain from doing so. If he should assert complete immunity (for example, a privilege not to appear, or not to be sworn) on the ground that he is the accused *de facto,* most jurisdictions would deny the claim, thereby compelling him to testify or to virtually concede his indictment by invoking his privilege against self-incrimination.

Not only is the accused himself subject to considerable use by police and prosecution before trial, but every witness, his as well as the prosecution's, may be subjected to similar interrogation before trial. This may be done formally before a grand jury, which affords a full-fledged deposition procedure for the prosecution without the embarrassing presence of defendant or his counsel. Or it may be done informally at the police station, where the specter of being held as a material witness—or of being charged with one of many vaguely defined crimes as a means of detaining for questioning—offers a considerable inducement for cooperation. As if all this were not enough, extensive legislative and administrative subpoena power exists to assist the government in investigating virtually every major field of regulatory activity. These too may serve as discovery and trial preparation devices available to the government and unavailable to the defense.

Fairly clearly, pretrial discovery by the prosecution is far-reaching. And it cannot in any sense be said to be matched by what is available to the defendant or by what he can keep from the prosecution—even when his "immunity" from self-incrimination is thrown into the scales. While the possibility that the defendant may produce a hitherto undisclosed witness or theory of defense is always present, the opportunity for surprise is rendered practically illusory by the government's broad investigatory powers and by the requirement in many states that the defenses of alibi and insanity must be specially pleaded. The sum of the matter is that the defendant is not an effective participant in the pretrial criminal process. It is to the trial alone that he must look for justice. Yet the imbalance of the pretrial period may prevent him from making the utmost of the critical trial date. And the trial, in turn, has been refashioned so that it is increasingly unlikely that it will compensate for the imbalance before trial.

Implications for Reform

If a procedural system is to be fair and just, it must give each of the participants to a dispute the opportunity to sustain his position. It must not create conditions which add to any essential inequality of position between the parties but rather must assure that such inequality will be minimized as much as human ingenuity can do so. In the case of enforcement of the criminal law, it seems quite clear that our existing institutional arrangements, as construed by the courts, aggravate the tendencies toward inequality between state and accused. How can a halt be called to these tendencies?

Several tiers of solutions are necessary—some within the scope of this article and some without. Among the latter are the various measures now being taken to make the indigent accused "equal before the law"—such as providing him with counsel and trial transcripts—and those which should be taken, such as making public investigative resources available to the accused. Most immediately relevant, however, is the creation of a free deposition and discovery procedure. For this would afford the accused the ability to draw upon all that the prosecution has gathered, compensating in part for all that the prosecution has learned from the accused and his witnesses. Every one of the many excellent arguments which carried the day for pretrial discovery in civil cases is equally applicable on the criminal side. If the trial is to be the occasion at which well prepared adversaries test each other's evidence and legal contentions in the best tradition of the adversary system, there can be no substitute for a deposition, discovery, and pretrial procedure. Whether this is accomplished through an expansion of the preliminary hearing, following the English model, or through incorporation of the discovery provisions of the Federal Rules of Civil Procedure, as in Professor Donnelly's proposed Puerto Rican Penal Code, is less important than that the job be done. If a choice is to be made, however, it should probably be for the Donnelly proposal since it draws upon a body of rules with which our courts are thoroughly familiar.

The argument customarily advanced in opposition to such a reform is that advice to the accused as to the details of the case against him will be an invitation to him to fabricate evidence, to suborn others to do so, or to intimidate the witnesses against him. Such a view implies that the presumption of innocence is inapplicable before trial. Indeed, its operational assumption is that all persons are guilty; since they expect to be convicted "for what they did," they can be expected to take any measures necessary to prevent conviction. This view builds a procedural system upon the assumption that virtually all are guilty when some twenty-three per cent to thirty-six per cent of persons who actually stand trial are acquitted. Moreover, it treats existing laws against lying, bribing, and intimidating witnesses as ineffective to deter persons charged with crime. In place of such assumedly ineffective criminal sanctions, it attaches a crippling procedural handicap to all defendants. . . .

But perhaps the most significant reason of all is the fact that the range of civil and criminal substantive law is too broad to permit the generalization that one involved in civil litigation is far less likely to suborn perjury or intimidate witnesses. It is difficult to believe that the defendant to charges of income tax evasion, false advertising, mail fraud, et cetera, will regularly tamper with justice on the criminal side of the court but that he will not do so when defending against the same or comparable charges on the civil side. . . . [T]he only approach to disclosure consonant with equality of opportunity and with the presumption of innocence is that used on the civil side of the court. It places its faith in the freest possible discovery as an aid to truth and as a means of searching out falsehood. But most important, it leaves to a more selective process than a blanket distinction between civil and criminal cases the development of techniques for coping with the special problems which may arise in some criminal cases.

1. *Voluntary Disclosure by the Prosecutor*

The formal law permitting a defendant to require disclosure by the prosecutor has been only occasionally of assistance to counsel in preparing his defense. In practice great reliance has had to be placed upon the prosecutor's willingness to divulge the information in his possession without compulsion. That willingness may grow out of various motivations.

UNITED STATES COMMISSIONER SYSTEM

Hearings on the United States Commissioner System Before the Subcommittee on Improvements in Judicial Machinery of the Senate Committee on the Judiciary, 89th Cong., 1st Sess., pt. 2, at 162, 164 (1965)

STATEMENT BY THEODORE LEVIN, CHIEF JUDGE, U.S. DISTRICT COURT, EASTERN DISTRICT OF MICHIGAN

The practical purpose of a [preliminary] hearing is to provide a means for defense counsel to ascertain the Government's evidence. We [in Detroit] accomplish the same result through a policy of disclosure of evidence by the U.S. attorney to defense counsel informally, except in cases of organized crime. Defense attorneys learn more in this manner than they could at a preliminary hearing. The only information withheld is a certification of witnesses' names where the Government feels that premature disclosure will result in physical or economic hardship.

This procedure of informal disclosure in lieu of hearings accounts for the large number of waivers of indictment and actually decreases the court's burden in many instances by encouraging guilty pleas. Many times a disclosure of the documentary evidence has brought about a guilty plea, especially in cases involving income tax evasion and fraudulent use of the mails. Frequently, defense counsel, after Government disclosure, realizes his client has not been entirely candid with him. This recently occurred in a serious bank robbery case. On the other hand, disclosure can also result in discontinuance of prosecution in cases where defense counsel can informally advise the U.S. attorney of exculpating circumstances that further investigation may confirm.[b]

UNITED STATES COMMISSIONER SYSTEM

Hearings on the United States Commissioner System Before the Subcommittee on Improvements in Judicial Machinery of the Senate Committee on the Judiciary, 89th Cong., 2d Sess., pt. 3, at 223-24, 227 (1966)

Statement of Irving Younger, Associate Professor, New York University School of Law

Legal Aid attorneys will never press for a preliminary hearing, and never even make a discovery motion of any kind. But because of the relationship of trust and confidence that exists between the particular men who are there representing the defendants through the Legal Aid Society and the assistants [to the federal prosecutor], there is a great deal of informal discovery, and I do mean informal. It is a matter of sitting in a lunchroom and the Legal Aid attorney saying, what do you have on so and so, and the assistant U.S. attorney will tell him. Then it will be a question of the Legal Aid attorney being able to form a reasonable determination of whether his client should plead guilty or not.

. . .

[b] In order to foster voluntary disclosure, federal Judge Marovitz of the Northern District of Illinois requires that a defendant moving for discovery recite his personal efforts to obtain information from the prosecutor. In practical effect a burden is imposed upon the prosecutor to explain why he has not provided the requested information. Defender Newsletter, Vol. 6, No. 6, Nov. 1967, at 72.

Discovery is possible only where attorneys have this relationship of mutual trust and confidence. Some non-Legal Aid attorneys have it with the U.S. attorney, primarily alumni of the office. But outside counsel who are unknown do not have it, and so with them this practice cannot be followed.

Senator TYDINGS. Do the judges in the U.S. District Court for the Southern District of New York take any active interest in the informal criminal discovery meetings between the Government and defense?

Mr. YOUNGER. No; quite the contrary. They take an affirmatively disinterested position. They refuse to involve themselves, and I believe properly, in any informal conversations between prosecutor and defense counsel.

Senator TYDINGS. They do not call the U.S. attorney in and say let us try to narrow the issues, what do you intend to offer and prove, and so on?

Mr. YOUNGER. No. It may occasionally happen in a protracted or complex criminal case that the judge will call counsel in prior to trial simply to premark documents and agree upon authenticity of documents, but that is not really narrowing the issues. Beyond that, no judge that I know of presently active in the southern district will make any attempt to foster this informal discovery proceeding. Rather, they will limit themselves simply to deciding the formal discovery motions that are brought on in the usual course, and they will usually deny those motions.

Senator TYDINGS. Are there any areas in which you feel, based on your experience as assistant U.S. attorney, that criminal discovery should not be given, for instance, in the areas of national security or witness security in organized crime cases, racketeer cases?

Mr. YOUNGER. Well, in the southern district, while I was in the U.S. attorney's office, we had experience with both of those situations. We had cases in which witnesses were killed, and we also had cases in which witnesses were simply put under 24-hour guard. It is the latter that I would recommend. If you are dealing with the kind of people whom you think might endanger the lives or welfare of witnesses, you give them whatever are their rights, and you make sure that nothing happens to those witnesses. The Government has enough manpower for the job.

DISCOVERY IN FEDERAL CRIMINAL CASES

Junior Bar Section of the Bar Association of the District of Columbia
33 F.R.D. 101, 113, 116, 120-22 (1963)

Empirical Data: Current District of Columbia Discovery Practice

A. Factual Data

Interviews were held with fourteen assistant United States Attorneys and seventeen defense counsel practicing in the United States District Court for the District of Columbia. . . .

Assistant United States Attorneys and defense counsel were asked to check the factors which they thought substantially affect the prosecutor's decision on whether to grant discovery informally. The factors checked most often as *favoring* discovery, and the proportion of each group checking them, are set out below:

	Prosecutors	Defense Counsel
1. U. S. Attorney's personal acquaintance with defense counsel	86%	88%
2. Likelihood of a guilty plea	79%	94%
3. Material available by formal motion	79%	52%
4. Defendant's willingness to disclose his defenses	57%	53%
5. Preponderance of evidence against the defendant	57%	82%
6. Defendant's ability to get the same information elsewhere	36%	35%
7. U. S. Attorney's opinion of defendant's guilt	29%	24%
8. Availability of material under the Jencks Act	21%	24%
9. Indigency of defendant	7%	53%

Some respondents listed these same factors as militating *against* discovery. . . .

B. Tentative Conclusions

1. Pretrial Discovery. a. More extensive pretrial discovery is afforded to defendants through the informal practice of prosecutors than by formal motion to the court. The discretion of

the individual assistant, rather than any policy of the United States Attorney's office, appears controlling. There are extremely wide variations among assistants.

b. Even among experienced criminal defense practitioners, there appears to be a lack of familiarity with the full range of available formal and informal discovery. A great many lawyers simply do not ask for information which prosecutors will frequently make available on request.

c. The extent of disclosure by individual assistant United States Attorneys appears to hinge on their favorable relationship with defense counsel, and the likelihood of securing a guilty plea.

d. Defendants who do not plead guilty, but elect to go to trial instead, constitute the group most hampered by restrictive discovery. This view was expressed particularly by attorneys whose practice is largely confined to indigents. Lack of access to the names and statements of government witnesses is reported to constitute the most serious obstacle to effective trial preparation by defense counsel.

e. Contrary to many preconceptions, indigency is rarely a factor which influences prosecutors to disclose information to the defense.

f. Oral summarization of written material or divulgence of selected portions, rather than full disclosure and inspection, appears to be the typical informal procedure employed by prosecutors. Material favorable to the government is more likely to be disclosed than data favorable to the defense.

g. Defense fact-finding is frequently hampered by prosecutors who discourage government witnesses from talking to defense counsel.

h. There is substantial disagreement between prosecutors and defense lawyers as to whether perjury, fabrication and intimidation of witnesses would increase if pretrial discovery were broadened. But in light of the central importance of these traditional fears to prosecutors and judges, consideration should be given to broadening judicial control over discovery by, for example, conditioning disclosure of sensitive information to defense counsel (similar to the handling of trade secrets in civil cases) on the requirement that he not impart it to the defendant.

i. Although the possibilities of perjury, fabrication and intimidation of witnesses are considerably less applicable to disclosure of scientific reports and tangible objects than to revealing witness names and statements, substantial reluctance to permit inspection of such materials is reported.

j. Most prosecutors do not consider defendants to be significantly hampered by existing discovery practice. Most defense lawyers, particularly those defending indigents, feel seriously hampered.

k. Neither prosecutors nor defense lawyers are entirely satisfied with the amount of discovery they obtain under present rules. In light of the large number of defense counsel willing to disclose defenses in return for increased discovery, particularly in cases involving indigents, the possibilities for reciprocal or two-way street discovery merit exploration.

2. Trial Discovery. a. Court rulings on trial production of Jencks statements* are considered by defense counsel to be less restrictive than pretrial discovery decisions. Defense lawyers frequently make Jencks motions and appear generally satisfied with the extent of production of witnesses' statements at trial by assistant United States Attorneys.

b. There is widespread dissatisfaction with the amount of time afforded to defense counsel to inspect and reflect on the contents of Jencks statements in the midst of trial.

c. Adequate time to inspect and utilize Jencks statements entails delay in trial proceedings. Serious consideration is warranted for the practice suggested by the Court of Appeals for the Ninth Circuit in Ogden v. United States, 303 F.2d 724 (1962), that Jencks statements be produced at the beginning of, or before, trial.

3. Role of the Court. a. A high correlation exists between rules or local court decisions expressly allowing discovery of particular items, and the informal practice of prosecutors to grant those items on request.

b. Because defense counsel rarely seek discovery by motion, the discretion of prosecutors rather than of judges is the major determinant of discovery in the District of Columbia.

THE DEFENDANT'S CASE FOR MORE LIBERAL DISCOVERY

By A. Kenneth Pye

33 F.R.D. 82, 84-85, 96 (1963)

The law enforcement agencies are available to assist the prosecutor. Personal interviews with police officers, or at a minimum the reports of police officers, are available to any United States Attorney who desires to utilize them. In some cases grand jury minutes may be available; in others, summaries of these minutes will be available. The United States Attorney can always look to the indigent's motion for the issuance of a subpoena *in forma*

* Jencks v. United States, 353 U.S. 657 (1957) permitted the defense to obtain federal witnesses' statements in the prosecutor's possession after they have testified. The rule is codified in 18 U.S.C. § 3500.

pauperis to find what witnesses defense counsel plans to call and what testimony he plans to elicit from them. If everything else fails, he may issue one of those extraordinary documents which we have come to know as an "informal subpoena," requesting the unsophisticated witness to appear for interrogation prior to trial. None of these devices is available to the defendant.

The defendant may rely upon the willingness on the part of some United States Attorneys in some cases to give some information. The survey recently conducted by the Junior Bar Section indicates a wide difference in the attitudes of the United States Attorneys concerning what information should be given, to whom it should be given, and in what form it should be given. I think that it is fair to say that most United States Attorneys provide broad discovery to a defense counsel when the evidence is so overwhelming that the counsel will be required to recommend a plea of guilty to his client. Most United States Attorneys will be open and candid with an inexperienced defense counsel who knows so little about the trial of a criminal case that a successful defense is improbable. Liberal access to the Government's case might also be permitted in the unlikely eventuality that the United States Attorney thought that there was a reasonable possibility that the defendant might be innocent. Some United States Attorneys permit the defendant access to more information than others. Many "summarize" documents which they will not permit to be inspected. Some, as a practical matter, permit no discovery in those cases where it is most important.

I have heard the view expressed that a prosecutor always opens his files to any counsel whom he trusts. Implicit in this view is the attitude that a defense counsel who "won't spin you" can be trusted, while counsel who has "spun" an assistant in the past is in a different category. In fairness, it must be admitted that any attorney relies upon his judgment of the ethics of an adversary in determining how to deal with him. Too often, however, what the United States Attorney regards as "spinning" may only be the legitimate use of cross-examination by an intelligent, experienced, well-informed adversary. . . .

I would be the last to deny that the court should exercise a responsible role in supervising the discovery process. I think, however, that we ought to approach it from a slightly different viewpoint. Let us provide by rule that the defendant has the right to witness names and addresses, to confessions of a codefendant, and to records of prior convictions, subject to a protective order. If the United States has any reason to believe that this counsel or this defendant is going to intimidate or bribe anyone, let the United States appear before the trial judge and get an order protecting it from the ordinary obligation of disclosure.

I think it ought to be the basic approach of the rules that a defendant is entitled to discovery unless there is reason why he should not receive it in a particular case.

Experience under 7(f), the bill of particulars, has indicated that it has not been administered with a viewpoint of providing a great deal of information to the defendant. I think the same thing should be true if we entrusted the entire matter to the discretion of the individual judges.

I think another undesirable result would occur also, and this would be lack of uniformity and "shopping for judges."

2. The Changing Law on the Right to Discovery

a. Discovery by the Defendant

The law has always provided for some disclosure by the prosecution. The information or indictment must state the charge, with some scant information about the crime, the victim, the time and place. Sometimes a bill of particulars may be demanded to provide additional facts. Frequently the indictment must be endorsed with the names of witnesses examined by the grand jury or the information must list witnesses whom the state intends to call at trial. Generally the defendant cannot compel these witnesses to talk to him (though it is improper for the prosecutor to urge the witnesses to refuse). Under some circumstances it may be possible to take depositions of the witnesses. At the preliminary examination, if one is held, the defendant can learn something of the state's case and cross-examine the state's witnesses under oath. In fact, however, the prosecutor frequently avoids the preliminary examination by seeking an indictment. Pretrial motions to suppress evidence likewise may force disclosure of some prosecution evidence in order to justify admissibility of the challenged evidence.

Beyond these devices, the principal discovery technique is a petition for mandamus or a motion for discovery addressed to the court. The defendant may desire any of various kinds of information—for example, statements made by defendant, by codefendants, or by prosecution witnesses; grand jury transcripts; medical, scientific, or police investigation reports; physical objects or documents connected with the offense; lists of witnesses to be used by the prosecution.

Each of these has its own body of precedent. The courts have been most willing to allow pretrial discovery of the defendant's own statements and of physical evidence seized from him for use at trial. The defense claim to personal connection with these is obviously strongest. There is otherwise marked judicial reluctance to venture very far into discovery. This is illustrated by the cases below. Discovery during the trial, when opportunity for tampering is less, is correspondingly more liberal.

STATE v. FOSTER

242 Ore. 101, 407 P.2d 901 (1965)

SLOAN, J. Defendant was convicted of manslaughter. His appeal from the conviction poses a question not previously considered by this court. To put the problem in perspective it will be better to relate the basic facts.

Defendant was charged with shooting and killing a woman during the course of a spree at a rural residence in Klamath county. It was claimed, in his defense, that defendant was not present when the shooting occurred. Some of the state's evidence was that the shooting may have occurred at about 10 p.m. of the day of the event. One of the alleged eye-witnesses, Thompson, testified that it had happened at about 3 p.m. Defendant was present at the scene in the afternoon but was not there after about 5 p.m. The difference in time was, therefore, very material to the defense. There was some evidence that in a pre-trial written statement of the eye-witness, Thompson, he had stated that the shooting was later in the evening. During the cross-examination of Thompson defendant asked to have the pre-trial statement made available to him so that he could use it on cross-examination to impeach the witness' direct testimony. The court refused. The question presented is: Did the court err in denying defendant access to the pre-trial written statement of the state's witness for the purpose of cross-examination?

1. Although there are cases to the contrary, the rule now generally accepted is that a previous written statement of a witness should be made available to defendant for possible impeachment on cross-examination of the witness. State v. Hunt, 1958, 25 NJ 514, 138 A2d 1, is a treatise on the subject. The opinion, by Mr. Justice Jacobs, examines all of the contending authorities and concludes that ". . . where it appears that a state's witness had made prior notes or statements relating to the subject matter of the direct testimony which he has given, the defense is entitled to inspect and use on cross-examination the prior notes or statements if they are or can be made available. . . . And the principle is generally applicable without any preliminary showing of inconsistency . . . or any resulting right in the State to introduce the notes or statements as corroborative evidence on its behalf." 138 A2d 10. The *Hunt* opinion is so exhaustive that it would

be fruitless repetition to again discuss the authorities and reasons which justified the quoted conclusion. A similar opinion is found in People v. Riser, 1956, 47 Cal 2d 566, 305 P2d 1.

2. It is contended that the statements or documents should not be produced unless it can be shown that they would be admissible into evidence if they are made available. The fallacy of the argument is obvious. Neither counsel or court can determine the admissibility of a writing until it is examined. It is more than likely that statements by witnesses could contain matter that would provide usable impeaching statements but also contain prejudicial irrelevances that could not go to the jury. Gordon v. United States, 1953, 344 US 414, 416. People v. Riser, supra, 305 P2d 14. If the statement were to be admitted, the screening out of irrelevant matter would present no more difficulty than the courts frequently consider in admitting written material. The fact that the statement might not be admissible does not justify a refusal to permit the use of the statement for proper impeachment purposes.

It has been urged that the rule we approve is of recent origin and comes as an aftermath of Jencks v. United States, 1957, 353 US 657, and the subsequently enacted Jencks Act (18 USCA 3500, (1957)), and is, therefore, limited to practice in the Federal courts. In essence the Jencks Act only codifies the rule that had been of long standing in both federal and many state courts. Orfield, Discovery and Inspection in Federal Criminal Procedure, 1957, 59 W Va L Rev 221. See Gordon v. United States, supra, 344 US 419, where the court, in adopting this rule, made this mention of its prior existence: "Despite some contrary holdings on which the courts below may have relied, we think their reasoning is outweighed by that of highly respectable authority in state and lower federal courts in support of the view that an accused is entitled to the production of such documents." The *Gordon* opinion utilized a statement, also found in other cases, by Judge Cooley in People v. Davis, 1884, 52 Mich. 569, 573, 18 NW 362: "The State has no interest in interposing an obstacle to the disclosure of facts, unless it is interested in convicting accused parties on the testimony of untrustworthy persons."

3. In the instant case the error requires reversal. The contradictory statement, if it were made, would have been crucial to defendant's ability to fully cross-examine the witness.

4. Before the trial defendant filed a motion which requested a pre-trial examination of the alleged written statements of several witnesses and the right to examine an autopsy report. The trial

court allowed access to the autopsy report but denied the right to examine the statements of the witnesses. This pre-trial refusal is also assigned as error. We think the court was right.

All of the courts have recognized a distinction between a pre-trial examination of the statements of the state's witnesses and the right to examine a statement during trial for purposes of cross-examination. It is generally held that pre-trial discovery of the state's evidence is not permissible. 6 Wigmore, Evidence (3d ed 1940), § 1859, pages 475, 476.

It is said that pre-trial discovery permits an accused to fabricate evidence for his defense. More important, however, "it was felt, furthermore, that to allow the defendant to compel production when the prosecution could not in its turn compel production from the defendant because of the privilege against self incrimination would unduly shift to the defendant's side a balance of advantages already heavily weighted in his favor." People v. Riser, supra, 47 Cal 2d 585, 305 P2d 13. We recognize that the rule restraining pre-trial discovery is the subject of debate and criticism. See, for example, Krantz, Pretrial Discovery in Criminal Cases, 1962, 42 Neb L Rev 127. We are not convinced that the rule is unsound. There was no error in the court's refusal to permit the pre-trial discovery.

The other assignments do not warrant discussion. Reversed and remanded for a new trial.

PEOPLE v. HALL

83 Ill. App. 2d 402, 227 N.E.2d 773 (1967)

ALLOY, J. In the cause now before us, defendants James Hall and Raymond Gathright were indicted for the crime of Indecent Liberties with a Child. Following arraignment of the defendants, their attorney filed a motion to require the State to furnish "any written statements or memoranda containing statements made by witnesses for the People given to a law enforcement officer and containing a substantially verbatim account of a conversation between a witness for the People and a law enforcement officer." The motion was made prior to the trial. The trial court entered an order requiring the State's Attorney to furnish the defendant's attorney with such statements. Thereupon, the Assistant State's Attorney refused, contending the order was improper. A rule to show cause was thereafter issued. Upon the continued refusal of the Assistant State's Attorney he was found to be in contempt of court and fined $50. He appeals to this court from such finding of contempt of court and the fine.

The prosecution argues that the present rules in view of the Miranda case and similar cases have weighted the rules against the prosecution and that to add a further limitation requiring delivery of statements made by prosecution witnesses prior to trial (and who in fact may not even be called as witnesses) would severely hamper the prosecution of similar cases and put such witnesses under great pressure and duress from defendants or their representatives. Defendant, on the other hand, asserts that the prosecution has a staff of investigators and is well equipped to proceed with whatever is required in investigating a case whereas a defendant is not in position financially to afford such investigators. Under the laws of the State of Illinois, a defendant in a criminal case has certain rights relative to discovery which are granted by the State. These include serving him with a copy of the charge, a bill of particulars, a list of witnesses for the prosecution, a copy of any written or oral confessions made by defendant, and a sample of handwriting to be used at the trial if this becomes relevant. No statute of the State of Illinois nor any precedent which has been discovered by us or cited by the litigants requires the production of prosecution witnesses' statements to the defendant prior to the trial.

To impose upon the trial judge the discretionary right to order production of documents, it appears to us, would create a standard which would be very difficult to follow and which would impose an unreasonable burden upon the trial judge. Defendant asserts in this court that the trial judge would know all the attorneys and would be able to exercise a discretion which would prevent the prosecution witness from being harassed or threatened prior to trial. How this could possibly apply in a community the size of Chicago or some of the larger communities in the State is not clear to us. The probability of an objection to such a standard on the ground that it does not give each defendant equal protection of the laws in permitting any defendant to have the same rights to access to prosecution witnesses' statements appears to us to be a very cogent reason for having a rule which applies equally to all parties and does not put the trial judge in the unenviable position of exercising such a difficult discretion in criminal cases.

We feel that no precedent authorizes the production of prosecution witnesses' statements prior to trial, but that such statements can only be required to be produced during the trial when the party in fact becomes a witness and then can be used for impeachment purposes only. We, therefore, conclude that the trial court improperly ordered the production of prosecution witnesses' statements and that the contempt order which followed in an attempt to enforce such invalid order was improper.

In contrast, California cases have required: production of confessions and statements made by defendant, by codefendant, and by prospective witnesses; specimens taken by the autopsy surgeon; report of scientific analysis of material taken from defendant's shoes; a victim's statement which was used in interrogating defendant; the transcript of the preliminary examination; results of a lie detector test given the prosecutrix; identification photographs which had been shown the victim.

The pressure to expand the rights of discovery is persistent, resulting in large part from the openness now routine in civil cases and the expanding view of the Supreme Court as to what fairness in criminal procedure demands. Significant variables in the development of the law are the phrasing of the issue (whether we deal with a defendant's right to discovery or a court's discretionary power to allow discovery) and the likelihood that the defendant could and would abuse the information (which is affected by the nature of the evidence, the character of the defendant and his associates, and whether discovery is requested before trial or during trial).

The development proceeds not only through individual court decisions, but also by rules and statutes.

FEDERAL RULES OF CRIMINAL PROCEDURE
Effective March 21, 1946

Rule 16. Discovery and Inspection

Upon motion of a defendant at any time after the filing of the indictment or information, the court may order the attorney for the government to permit the defendant to inspect and copy or photograph designated books, papers, documents or tangible objects, obtained from or belonging to the defendant or obtained from others by seizure or by process, upon a showing that the items sought may be material to the preparation of his defense and that the request is reasonable. The order shall specify the time, place and manner of making the inspection and of taking the copies or photographs and may prescribe such terms and conditions as are just.

FEDERAL RULES OF CRIMINAL PROCEDURE
Effective July 1, 1966

Rule 16. Discovery and Inspection

(a) Defendant's Statements; Reports of Examinations and Tests; Defendant's Grand Jury Testimony. Upon motion of a defendant, the court may order the attorney for the government to permit the defendant to inspect and copy or photograph any relevant (1) written or recorded statements or confessions made by the defendant, or copies thereof, within the possession, custody or control of the government, the existence of which is known, or by the exercise of due diligence may become known, to the attorney for the government, (2) results or reports of physical or mental examinations, and of scientific tests or experiments made in connection with the particular case, or copies thereof, within the possession, custody or control of the government, the existence of which is known, or by the exercise of due diligence may become known, to the attorney for the government, and (3) recorded testimony of the defendant before a grand jury.

(b) Other Books, Papers, Documents, Tangible Objects or Places. Upon motion of a defendant the court may order the attorney for the government to permit the defendant to inspect and copy or photograph books, papers, documents, tangible objects, buildings or places, or copies or portions thereof, which are within the possession, custody or control of the government, upon a showing of materiality to the preparation of his defense and that the request is reasonable. Except as provided in subdivision (a)(2), this rule does not authorize the discovery or inspection of reports, memoranda, or other internal government documents made by government agents in connection with the investigation or prosecution of the case, or of statements made by government witnesses or prospective government witnesses (other than the defendant) to agents of the government except as provided in 18 U.S.C. § 3500.

(c) Discovery by the Government. If the court grants relief sought by the defendant under subdivision (a)(2) or subdivision (b) of this rule, it may, upon motion of the government, condition its order by requiring that the defendant permit the government to inspect and copy or photograph scientific or medical reports, books, papers, documents, tangible objects, or copies or portions thereof, which the defendant intends to produce at the trial and which are within his possession, custody or control, upon a showing of materiality to the preparation of the government's case and that the request is reasonable. Except as to scientific or medical reports, this subdivision does not authorize the discovery or inspection of reports, memoranda, or other internal defense documents made by the defendant, or his attorneys or agents in connection with the investigation or defense of the case, or of statements made by the defendant, or by government or defense witnesses, or by prospective government or defense witnesses, to the defendant, his agents or attorneys.

(d) Time, Place and Manner of Discovery and Inspection. An order of the court granting relief under this rule shall specify the time, place and manner of making the discovery and inspection permitted and may prescribe such terms and conditions as are just.

(e) Protective Orders. Upon a sufficient showing the court may at any time order that the discovery or inspection be denied, restricted or deferred, or make such other order as is appropriate. Upon motion by the government the court may permit the government to make such showing, in whole or in part, in the form of a written statement to be inspected by the court *in camera.* If the court enters an order granting relief following a showing *in camera,* the entire text of the government's statement shall be sealed and preserved in the records of the court to be made available to the appellate court in the event of an appeal by the defendant.

(f) Time of Motions. A motion under this rule may be made only within 10 days after arraignment or at such reasonable later time as the court may permit. The motion shall include all relief sought under this rule. A subsequent motion may be made only upon a showing of cause why such motion would be in the interest of justice.

(g) Continuing Duty to Disclose; Failure to Comply. If, subsequent to compliance with an order issued pursuant to this rule, and prior to or during trial, a party discovers additional material previously requested or ordered which is subject to discovery or inspection under the rule, he shall promptly notify the other party or his attorney or the court of the existence of the additional material. If at any time during the course of the proceedings it is brought to the attention of the court that a party has failed to comply with this rule or with an order issued pursuant to this rule, the court may order such party to permit the discovery or inspection of materials not previously disclosed, grant a continuance, or prohibit the party from introducing in evidence the material not disclosed, or it may enter such other order as it deems just under the circumstances.[c]

In opposition to a proposal that Rule 16 should require advance disclosure of material witnesses known to the govern-

[c] *See* Wright, *Recent Changes in the Federal Rules of Procedure,* 42 F.R.D. 552, 567-71 (1967).

ment, the Justice Department has cited numerous instances in which witnesses known to the defense were murdered or threatened or bribed.[d] In *United States v. Estep*,[e] the judge names twenty-two persons who were murdered in the Dallas area who were known or suspected to be informers. And in the more polite area of business crimes there is real danger of economic reprisals, even sufficient to destroy a business, with the result of unwillingness of witnesses to give testimony.[f] It has been suggested that to meet this objection the court be granted discretion to withhold the names of witnesses when the government can make a sufficient showing of threatened abuse. The Justice Department has also taken the position that this requirement would impose an impossible burden in cases where there is only strong suspicion that the defendant or his associates would approach the witnesses, would call for voicing unproved suspicions about the character of defense counsel, would make it impossible to assure informers that their names would not be disclosed before trial, and would give the defendant very little additional protection in view of the prosecutor's obligation at trial to disclose witnesses who would be helpful to defendant's case.[g]

BARNES v. UNITED STATES
347 F.2d 925 (8th Cir. 1965)

Before VAN OOSTERHOUT, BLACKMUN, and MEHAFFY, Circuit Judges.

VAN OOSTERHOUT, Circuit Judge. Defendants do not contend that any statute or rule gives them a right to the disclosure of

[d] Compare the materials at 503, *supra* (illustration 1); 508 n.u, *supra;* and 509, *supra* (Wallace illustration).

[e] 151 F. Supp. 668, 673 (N.D. Tex. 1957).

[f] *Cf.* Bergen Drug Co. v. Parke, Davis & Co., 307 F.2d 725 (3d Cir. 1962); House of Materials, Inc. v. Simplicity Pattern Co., 298 F.2d 867 (2d Cir. 1962).

[g] The identity and whereabouts of informers are often sought by defendants. If the defendant has been mistakenly identified or has been entrapped, he is seeking the information earnestly, in the hope that the informer will prove valuable as a defense witness. In other instances the request is tactical, either as a discovery technique to prepare to meet the prosecution's case or hoping that the prosecutor will choose to drop the charges rather than disclose the informer's identity. If, under the circumstances, it appears that the informer is a significant witness to the crime, the defense is entitled to learn his identity. *E.g.*, Roviaro v. United States, 353 U.S. 53 (1957); United States v. Russ, 362 F.2d 843 (2d Cir. 1966). If, on the other hand, the informer is only involved as the source of information which provided the police probable cause to make an arrest, and there is other evidence of the informer's reliability, his identity need not be disclosed. McCray v. Illinois, 386 U.S. 300 (1967). The informer system on which police rely for help in solving many serious crimes is of obvious importance.

the names of witnesses but urge that the right is one guaranteed by the Constitution. Defendants do not point to the constitutional provision upon which they rely. We find nothing in the Constitution expressly or impliedly granting defendants the absolute right to the names of Government witnesses under all circumstances.

It is quite possible that cases may arise where a court in the proper exercise of its discretion should order the Government to disclose the names of its witnesses. Here the Government, in response to defendants' request, advised the court that when defendant Childress came to Minneapolis in response to the arrest warrant and while free on bond he was accompanied by three or four others each of whom had guns and that the lives of the Government witnesses would be in jeopardy if the identities of the witnesses were disclosed. Such statement was not challenged. The court stated, "Well, under those circumstances I will sustain the Government's objection."

Moreover, if a defendant is unfairly surprised by any Government testimony, the right exists to move for a continuance upon proper showing of need for time to meet the testimony.[h]

b. *Discovery by the Prosecution*

In addition to the formal and informal discovery devices available to the prosecution which are mentioned above, there has recently been renewed interest in the question whether the government may properly demand that the defendant disclose his theory of defense and the evidence on which he will rely.[i] Special pleading of the defenses of alibi and insanity is common and there is some insistence that entrapment be specially pleaded also.[j]

[h] Rule 16 does not necessarily exclude the possibility of discovery outside its terms under inherent judicial power. United States v. Nolte, 39 F.R.D. 359 (N.D. Cal. 1965) (holding); United States v. Williams, 37 F.R.D. 24 (S.D.N.Y. 1965) (holding); Shores v. United States, 174 F.2d 838 (8th Cir. 1949) (dictum); Note, *Scope of Discovery Against the Prosecution of Criminal Cases—How Far Should It Be Widened?*, 67 HARV. L. REV. 492 (1954). It may be possible, therefore, for the court to order disclosure if the defendant can show that he needs the information and that he is not likely to abuse the disclosure.

[i] Doubts about the constitutionality of Rule 16(c) in conditioning defense discovery upon willingness to permit prosecution discovery, as an impermissible penalty upon the defendant who relies on his privilege against self-incrimination, are voiced by Wright, *Recent Changes in the Federal Rules of Procedure*, 42 F.R.D. 552, 570 (1967).

[j] A new Federal Rule 12A was proposed in 1962, which would have required the defendant to give advance notice of his intention to raise the defense of alibi otherwise than through his own testimony. Preliminary

JONES v. SUPERIOR COURT
58 Cal. 2d 56, 22 Cal. Rptr. 879, 372 P.2d 919 (1962)

TRAYNOR, J. On October 30, 1961, the day set for his trial on the charge of rape, petitioner filed a motion for continuance and an affidavit in which he alleged that he was and for a long time had been impotent and that he needed time to gather medical evidence including medical reports in connection with injuries he suffered in 1953 and 1954. The motion was granted. On November 3 the district attorney filed a motion for discovery, requesting petitioner and his attorney to make available to the prosecution: (1) the names and addresses of any and all physicians and surgeons subpoenaed to testify on behalf of petitioner with respect to certain injuries suffered by him in 1953 and 1954 and bearing on the question of whether or not petitioner is impotent; (2) the names and addresses of all physicians who have treated petitioner prior to the trial; (3) all reports of doctors or other reports pertaining to the physical condition of petitioner relating to said injuries and bearing on the question whether petitioner is impotent; and (4) all X-rays of petitioner taken immediately following the 1953 and 1954 injuries. The court granted the motion over petitioner's objection. Petitioner seeks a writ of prohibition to restrain enforcement of the trial court's order.

In People v. Riser, 47 Cal. 2d 566, 585-586, [305 P.2d 1 (1956)], we noted that ". . . Absent some governmental requirement that information be kept confidential for the purposes of effective law enforcement, the state has no interest in denying the accused access to all evidence that can throw light on issues in the case, and in particular it has no interest in convicting on the testimony of witnesses who have not been as rigorously cross-examined and as thoroughly impeached as the evidence permits. To deny flatly any right of production on the ground that an imbalance would be created between the advantages of prosecution and defense would be to lose sight of the true purpose of a criminal trial, the ascertainment of the facts. [Citations.]" Similarly, absent the privilege against self-incrimination or other privileges provided by law, the defendant in a criminal case has no

---

Draft of Proposed Amendments to Rules of Criminal Procedure for the United States District Courts (Dec. 1962). The proposal was dropped because of doubts as to its constitutionality, even though the few state cases in point had uniformly upheld the constitutionality of alibi statutes, except insofar as they would limit the defendant's own testimony. About one-fourth of the states have such statutes.

With respect to statutes requiring that other affirmative defenses be pleaded in advance, see Note, *Pre-Trial Disclosure of Criminal Cases,* 60 YALE L.J. 626 (1951).

valid interest in denying the prosecution access to evidence that can throw light on issues in the case.

Pretrial discovery in favor of defendants is not required by due process. Accordingly, when this court permitted discovery in advance of as well as at the trial, it was not acting under constitutional compulsion but to promote the orderly ascertainment of the truth. That procedure should not be a one-way street.

When the prosecution has ample evidence of the existence, identity, and authenticity of documents in the defendant's possession and thus does not need to rely on his knowledge to locate and to identify them or on his testimony to authenticate them, it may be that his implied admission alone that the documents produced were those he was ordered to produce would involve too trivial a degree of incrimination to justify invoking the privilege. We are not confronted with such a case, however, for the prosecution has no independent evidence of the existence of the reports and X-rays it seeks or the names of the witnesses who have treated or will examine petitioner and who could authenticate any reports or X-rays they have made or will make. The prosecution seeks more than to require petitioner tacitly to admit that the materials are those requested; it seeks the benefit of his knowledge of the existence of possible witnesses and the existence of possible reports and X-rays for the purpose of preparing its case against him. Moreover, insofar as the prosecution seeks reports made or to be made by physicians to whom petitioner "was sent by his attorney for examination, as distinguished from advice and treatment," it would violate the attorney-client privilege, for such reports are communications from petitioner to his attorneys through such physicians.

The prosecution, however, is entitled to discover the names of the witnesses petitioner intends to call and any reports and X-rays he intends to introduce in evidence in support of his particular affirmative defense of impotence. A number of states have statutes permitting or requiring discovery in criminal cases of the identity of witnesses who are to be called to testify for a defendant in connection with a particular defense, such as an alibi. Although such discovery may require a defendant to disclose information that would lead to effective rebuttal of his defense, these statutes have uniformly been upheld against the claim that they violate the privilege against self-incrimination. The identity of the defense witnesses and the existence of any reports or X-rays the defense offers in evidence will necessarily be revealed at the trial. The witnesses will be subject to cross-examination, and the reports and X-rays subject to study and challenge. Learning the identity of the defense witnesses and of such reports and X-rays in advance merely enables the prosecution to perform its function at the trial more effectively.

Such information is discoverable. The order, however, is not limited to the discovery of such information, and therefore cannot be enforced in its present form.

STATE v. REED

71 Wash. 2d 537, 429 P.2d 870 (1967)

PER CURIAM. By information filed in October, 1964, the prosecuting attorney for Pierce County charged defendant Reed with robbery of an employee of the Western Union Telegraph Company on September 16, 1964. Defendant, a soldier stationed at Fort Lewis, obtained release on surety bail and returned to duty. While thus at liberty on bail, but under military jurisdiction, he was hospitalized and received medical treatment for mental illness at military hospitals from military doctors.

November 26, 1965, defendant entered a plea of not guilty, and a special plea of not guilty by reason of insanity at the time the offense was alleged to have been committed, but asserting a restoration of mental competency at the time of the plea.

Then occurred the events giving rise to this petition. Defendant's counsel informed the superintendent of Western State Hospital and his staff that defendant considered all of his medical records privileged and confidential; that these records should not be delivered to any other persons under pain of civil liability; and that the hospital authorities could not divulge to anyone, except with defendant's consent, their observations and findings. The superintendent and staff, yielding to this admonition and advice, thereupon refused to turn over to the prosecuting attorney any medical records pertaining to defendant or give the prosecuting attorney their findings, observations and conclusions.

The prosecuting attorney then filed a pleading denominated "Motion by the State for Discovery of Evidence," directed not to the superintendent of Western State Hospital but to the defendant, asking the defendant to produce for the prosecutor's inspection all records reflecting psychiatric tests administered to defendant, all X rays taken after September 16, 1964, used as a basis for evidence of organic brain damage, and the names of all doctors, psychologists and psychiatrists "who have examined the defendant for the purpose of establishing his defense of insanity."

The trial court, after argument, granted the state's motion by written order allowing the prosecution access to all such evidence before trial and directed defendant's counsel to make all such evidence in his possession or control available for inspection by the prosecuting attorney. It is this order which is now before us for review. We are of the opinion that the order must be vacated, not because the state has no right to inspect the medical records, but because the order seems to have been improvidently granted.

The state, in presenting its motion, apparently made no showing that it had employed any of the ordinary means available to it for an inspection and production of the very evidence it sought by its motion. Instead of proceeding along the lines available to the state for obtaining the evidence by other means, it demanded that the defendant supply it. We think an order to produce evidence does not lie where the evidence sought is as readily available to the movant as it was to the party from whom it is sought.

Finally, as to the names of medical witnesses defendant intends to call concerning the issue of insanity, we refer the parties to RCW 10.37.030 which imposes a duty on the defendant to timely submit a list of defense witnesses. This obligation is as binding upon the defendant as it is upon the state to endorse its witnesses upon the information. State v. Hein, 32 Wash. 2d 315, 201 P.2d 691 (1949). The record does not disclose that the state ever demanded a list of defendant's witnesses before moving as it did in this case.

3. *The Prosecutor's Duty to Volunteer Information Helpful to the Defense*

The prosecutor's duty with respect to evidence which might be helpful to the defendant is manifold. He must, of course, respond to a valid court order granting discovery. In addition he must refrain from interfering with defense efforts to obtain evidence by independent efforts. For instance, the prosecutor may not properly discourage prospective witnesses from talking to defense counsel[k] or obstruct efforts to have tests made of defendant.[l] It has long been established that the prosecutor may not knowingly put forth perjured testimony in support of his case, and there is a related obligation to disclose perjury even though he learns of it only afterwards. Much more recently the Supreme Court has held that the prosecutor has a duty to respond to a request for any evidence in his possession which is favorable to the accused on the issue of either guilt or punishment.[m] The

[k] State v. Chaney, 5 Ariz. App. 530, 428 P.2d 1004 (1967).

[l] *Cf. In re* Martin, 58 Cal. 2d 509, 24 Cal. Rptr. 833, 374 P.2d 801 (1962) (police prevented defense blood test after drunk driving arrest).

[m] Brady v. Maryland, 373 U.S. 83 (1963) (the evidence, that codefendant had done the actual shooting, would have been important on the penalty

Supreme Court has not gone further, though invited to do so,[n] but there is growing authority in the state and lower federal courts that the prosecutor has affirmative duty to provide defendant not only with exculpatory evidence but with impeachment evidence, even in the absence of request by him.[o] This trend may result in a new character for the system of criminal justice.

DANGER AHEAD FOR ADVERSARY SYSTEM

By Edward L. Barrett, Jr.

Trial Magazine 19, 21 (Dec. 66-Jan. 67)

PRE-TRIAL DISCOVERY

Pre-trial discovery in criminal cases is rapidly coming into its own in this country. While the recent expansion of such discovery for the federal courts in revised Rule 16 of the Rules of Criminal Procedure for the United States District Courts is a conspicuous example, it merely follows the lead by courts and rule-makers in many of the states. See *e.g.*, Traynor, "Ground Lost and Found in Criminal Discovery," 39 N.Y.U. L. Rev. 228 (1964).

Furthermore, constitutional considerations have recently come to the fore, which may compel even more dramatic increases in discovery accorded defendants—at least of information which may be regarded as favorable to them. See, Brady v. Maryland, 373 U.S. 83 (1963); also note, "The Prosecutor's Constitutional Duty to Reveal Evidence to the Defendant," 74 Yale L.J. 136 (1964).

---

issue). If disclosure is required only upon request, failure of defense counsel to make the request may produce a new ground of reversal—inadequacy of representation; *cf.* State v. Cathey, 32 Wis. 2d 79, 145 N.W.2d 100 (1966) (trial counsel had been ignorant of his right to obtain a copy of defendant's statement to the police, but defendant failed to establish prejudice).

[n] *See* Giles v. Maryland, 386 U.S. 66 (1967).

[o] *E.g.*, United States v. Poole, 379 F.2d 645 (7th Cir. 1967) (prosecutor failed to produce report of physical examination which would have tended to impeach the alleged victim of kidnapping; the court reversed in the exercise of its supervisory power, not on due process grounds); Barbee v. Warden, 331 F.2d 842 (4th Cir. 1964) (prosecutor was unaware of police lab report that the bullet did not come from defendant's gun); State v. Fowler, 101 Ariz. 561, 422 P.2d 125 (1967) (prosecutor probably was unaware of police finding a knife at the scene, tending to support defendant's assertion of self defense); Levin v. Katzenbach, 363 F.2d 287 (D.C. Cir. 1966) (negligent nondisclosure of bank employee's inability to remember changing $1,000 bills, tending to support defendant's contentions).

The problem is acutely discussed in United States v. Keogh, 391 F.2d 138, 146-48 (2d Cir. 1968).

Long Overdue

This movement towards discovery by defendants, a long overdue corrective of a previous imbalance, raises a number of serious problems which must be faced in the process of determining the form and content of the rules to govern such discovery. I allude here to only two of such problems:

1. Determining the prosecutor's obligation;
2. Analyzing the impact of the new rules on the adversary system.

As we move towards more complete discovery, an increasing burden is placed upon the prosecutor to determine what should be shown to the defendant. To the extent that the defendant can specify the items he seeks, the problem is relatively simple. Even a general request to see evidence which is to be produced at the trial can be complied with relative ease and failure to do so becomes visible at the trial.

But general requests for information which may be helpful to the defense in its preparation for trial create more difficult problems. The prosecutor must decide what information is relevant to the defense since only he can know what is in his files. This decision may not be an easy one—especially if the prosecutor is unable to anticipate the nature of the defendant's case.

In fact on this issue of relevance, it may be, as was said by the Supreme Court in a different context, that in our adversary system: "The determination of what may be useful to the defense can properly and effectively be made only by an advocate." See Dennis v. United States, 384 U.S. 855, 875 (1966).

Yet it is quite clear that there is no alternative but to rely on the prosecutor to make the decision. Defense lawyers do not have the time to examine at large prosecutor and police files, nor is it in the public interest to permit them to do so.

The problem is made even more complex by the fact that, in most instances, there will be no way in the trial process to check the adequacy of the disclosure insofar as it relates to information not used at the trial.

Hence, enforcement of the prosecutor's obligation may come, if at all, only in the context of post-conviction proceedings initiated at some later stage when the existence of information becomes known.

It is not surprising then to find the California Supreme Court recently refusing to require a prosecutor to comply with a very general request for information, stating: "A defendant's motion for discovery must nevertheless describe the requested information with at least some degree of specificity and must be sustained by plausible justification." See Ballard v. Superior Court, 64 A. C. 165, 173, 410 P.2d 838, 843 (1966).

Difficult Problem

An even more difficult problem is posed by suggestions that the prosecutor has an obligation to go beyond items known to him, and to ascertain evidence existing in government files which may not have become part of the "prosecutor's file."

Obviously, the prosecutor should not be able to defeat discovery by avoiding knowledge of relevant information. Equally obvious, the prosecutor cannot know everything which reposes in government files.

Federal Rule 16, for example, attempts to deal with this problem in certain areas by requiring the attorney for the government to disclose items in the possession of the government "the existence of which is known, or by the exercise of due diligence may become known" to him.

In a case now pending before the United States Supreme Court, it is being argued that the prosecutor has a constitutional duty to use due diligence to become aware of evidence favorable to an accused which exists in the files of another law enforcement agency—in this case, an adjoining county. See Giles v. Maryland, 238 Md. 458, 212 A.2d 101, (1965) cert. granted 383 U.S. 941 (1966).[p]

Here again the problem is made difficult by the inability in most cases to judge the adequacy of the prosecutor's compliance at the trial stage and the consequent danger of expanding the already large scope of post-conviction review.

Lying behind the problems just discussed is another which will increasingly come to the fore as the boundaries of discovery are expanded: the extent of the government's privilege to resist discovery in the public interest.

In civil litigation this problem has proved extremely troublesome. See *e.g.*, Hardin, "Executive Privilege in the Federal Courts," 71 Yale L.J. 879 (1962). Predictably it will be even more difficult in criminal cases as defense lawyers seek to probe into the investigative files of law enforcement agencies.

Adversary System Effect

A second major problem which needs to be faced and examined is the potential effect of the new discovery doctrines on the

[p] In Giles v. Maryland, 386 U.S. 66 (1967), the Court avoided the constitutional issue and remanded for further consideration.

adversary system. The law is moving rapidly in the direction of reducing the adversariness of the prosecutor. He is expected to screen out weak cases and proceed to trial only in those cases where the likelihood of guilt is high. He is now expected upon demand to provide the defendant with any information which may tend to exculpate him or reduce the penalty. See Brady v. Maryland, 373 U.S. 83 (1963).

He may soon be expected to go further, seek out, and perhaps offer such evidence to the defendant.

He is reminded by the Supreme Court:

> Society wins not only when the guilty are convicted but when criminal trials are fair; our system of the administration of justice suffers when any accused is treated unfairly. 373 U.S. at 87.

The defense lawyer, on the other hand, is free to be adversary almost to the point of abuse. The privilege against self-incrimination limits the extent of the defendant's obligation of pre-trial disclosure. The fact that the government may not appeal a judgment of acquittal enables the defense lawyer to use trial tactics not open to a prosecutor whose case, if successful, must satisfy scrutiny on appeal.

A law professor has seriously advanced the proposition, disputed to be sure by others, that a defense lawyer's duty to his client extends to requiring him, on occasion, to engage in purposeful deception, not only of the prosecutor but also of the court. See Freedman, "Professional Responsibility of the Criminal Defense Lawyer: The Three Hardest Questions," 64 Mich. L. Rev. 1469 (1966).

The question must be faced squarely whether such adversary imbalance can be expected to continue in the long run. It is true that often the adversary advantage accorded the defense lawyer at trial hardly compensates for the investigative advantages which the government has. But at the trial stage the imbalance often becomes acute.

The danger is that the more "responsible" and less adversary we make the prosecutor, the greater will be the pressure to push the defense lawyer in the same direction.

If the prosecutor is transformed into a "good" man seeking "justice," can the defense lawyer continue to play his present role which may then appear to be that of a "bad" man seeking "injustice"?

Will not the pressures against "adversariness" and toward "responsibility" be greater as the burden of criminal defense is assumed by a wider segment of the bar with the costs of such defense borne by the government?

These questions have no easy answers but they need to be discussed and thought about as we redesign our system of the administration of criminal justice.[q]

B. PRETRIAL MOTIONS AND THE "OMNIBUS HEARING"

Among the numerous possible pretrial motions, probably the most significant has been the motion to suppress illegally seized evidence under the "exclusionary rule." The merits of the motion to suppress depends usually on the constitutional law of search and seizure; the effectiveness of suppression of evidence as a sanction to control police conduct depends upon the extent of police desire to achieve successful prosecution through the use of seized evidence. These have both been dealt with previously. Our concern here is with the procedures by which the suppression issue is raised and resolved.

Traditionally, various motions relating to evidentiary matters have been made at trial, at the time when the evidence is offered. It was thought inappropriate to attempt to anticipate the evidence which might be offered, since if the evidence is not offered at all the consideration of its admissibility will have been unnecessary. The one major exception to that tradition has been the motion to suppress unconstitutionally seized evidence. The United States Supreme Court in *Weeks v. United States* established the exclusionary rule and permitted the pretrial raising of the issue. It subsequently has required that the motion be made in advance of trial if the seizure (and perhaps some indication of its illegality) was known to the defense at that time, unless the government's proof at the trial itself establishes the grounds for exclusion. The judge may have discretion to treat an untimely motion, but need not. The special procedure seems to have resulted (1) from the reluctance of the Court to permit interruption of the trial for consideration of a collateral issue relating to logically relevant evidence, and (2) from the fact that the device used by counsel in the *Weeks* case to raise the constitutional issue was a motion made prior to trial for the return of property wrongfully in the possession of an officer of the

[q] State *ex rel.* Sowers v. Olwell, 64 Wash. 2d 828, 394 P.2d 681 (1964), presents the contrasting problem—defense counsel's duty to disclose. Defense counsel apparently came into possession of a knife belonging to defendant and used in the homicide with which he was charged. The Washington Supreme Court held that the attorney could not be required to disclose how the knife came into his possession, since the attorney-client privilege applied, but did have an obligation to turn the knife itself over to the prosecution.

court (the prosecutor). The requirement that the motion be made in advance of trial was imposed as a special burden upon the use of the exclusionary rule. In fact, however, it may also work to the advantage of the defendant to obtain an early adjudication of the search and seizure issue. To some extent the hearing on his motion serves a discovery function.[r] And getting the trial judge's ruling on a critical issue of the case permits the defendant to make a better informed decision whether to plead guilty.[s] The prosecutor, too, obtains some advantage in the pretrial determination of the admissibility of what is often key evidence. If the evidence is suppressed he will know that other evidence must be produced at trial to take its place, so that the prosecution does not founder after jeopardy has already attached. If the motion to suppress fails, the prosecutor is reassured about the strength of his case; failure of the motion may also precipitate an offer to plead guilty in a case which would otherwise have gone to trial.

On the other hand, if the defendant thinks the ruling is erroneous, he may still be reluctant to plead guilty, since the plea of guilty will constitute a waiver of any error in the ruling. In order to avoid putting defendant in this dilemma, and in order to encourage guilty pleas, a recently enacted New York statute provides: "If the motion is denied, the order denying such may be reviewed on appeal from a judgment of conviction notwithstanding the fact that such judgment of conviction is predicated upon a plea of guilty."[t]

Because the pretrial motion to suppress is so often critical to the success of a prosecution, there has also been pressure for pretrial appeal of the judge's ruling on the motion. In Montana,

---

[r] In Henderson v. United States, 349 F.2d 712, 713 (D.C. Cir. 1965), Justice Bazelon, dissenting, urged, "In my view, also, the discovery function of these pre-trial hearings [on motion to suppress seized evidence] is important, although auxiliary, and should be protected by reversal of conviction [rather than by a hearing nunc pro tunc] in cases where, as here, such a hearing is improperly denied."

[s] The same issues as are raised by a pretrial motion to suppress may be raised even before indictment by an injunction to prevent the government from using evidence obtained from the petitioner. Bohrod v. United States, 248 F. Supp. 559 (W.D. Wis. 1965), citing Perlman v. United States, 247 U.S. 7 (1918); Burdeau v. McDowell, 256 U.S. 465 (1921); Cogen v. United States, 278 U.S. 221 (1929); and *In re* Fried, 161 F.2d 453 (2d Cir. 1947). In *Bohrod,* at 564, the court said, "[T]he matter of pre-indictment remedies requires extensive study. . . . The reported decisions thus far have dealt most inadequately with the contradictions inherent in a civil proceeding whose very purpose is to inhibit or prevent a criminal prosecution. It is troublesome, for example, that in seeking protection against unjust indictment, a petitioner appears to carry a heavy burden of proof from which he may be excused when he invokes similar protections after indictment."

[t] N.Y. CODE CRIM. PROC. § 813-c (McKinney Supp. 1967).

for example, the writ of prohibition has been used for the purpose of obtaining review.[u] In the federal system there is a special statute permitting appeal from rulings on pretrial motions to suppress in narcotics cases,[v] but otherwise the appealability of an order refusing to suppress evidence depends upon its finality. "Finality" of the order is found by some courts if the motion was filed prior to the filing of the information or indictment, since the motion can then be characterized as an independent rather than ancillary proceeding. Other courts see any motion to suppress as part of an incipient criminal proceeding so that the ruling will always be interlocutory rather than final.[w] Appeal by the state as well as by defendant is allowed in some jurisdictions,[x] and interlocutory appeal is allowed in others.[y]

The same reasons which call for pretrial disposition of the search and seizure issue would seem to call for pretrial disposition of other evidence issues. Conversations intercepted by illegal wiretapping or confessions obtained without adequate warning of the right to remain silent or to have counsel present, for example, are closely analogous to papers which have been illegally seized, except that they are intangible. The evidence is clearly relevant, but a privilege exists in the defendant to have it suppressed. The trend of recent times has been, first, to permit these other motions to be made before trial, and then to urge that they be required to come before trial. For example, in Wisconsin the statute reads, "the use of illegal means to secure evidence (except confessions) must be raised before trial by motion or be deemed waived. But the court may, in its discretion, entertain such motion at a later stage. . . ."[z] In Illinois the rule is that "prior to the trial of any criminal case a defendant may move to suppress as evidence any confession or admission given by him on the ground that it was not voluntary."[a] The Pennsylvania rule is mandatory: "Such application shall be made . . . before . . . trial" unless justice requires an exception be made.[b]

---

[u] Note, *Procedures for Suppressing Illegally Seized Evidence—The Exclusionary Rule,* 20 MONT. L. REV. 225 (1959).

[v] 18 U.S.C. § 1404.

[w] This problem is well discussed in United States v. Koenig, 290 F.2d 166 (5th Cir. 1961).

[x] *E.g.,* WIS. STAT. § 958.12 (1965); 18 U.S.C. § 3731, as amended by the Crime Control Act of 1968.

[y] ILL. SUP. CT. RULE 27(4), discussed in LaFave, *Search and Seizure: "The Course of True Law . . . Has Not . . . Run Smooth,"* 1966 U. ILL. L.F. 255, 387-89.

[z] WIS. STAT. § 955.09(3) (1965).

[a] ILL. REV. STAT. ch. 38, § 114-11 (1967).

[b] PA. CRIM. PROC. RULES 323, 324 (417 Pa. (1965)).

Even though there is continued resistance to what is seen as piecemeal adjudication, the trend is toward pretrial disposition of many evidentiary questions,[c] and toward consolidation of all the pretrial motions in a single hearing to minimize the fragmentation of the procedure.

A substantial procedural innovation is the "omnibus hearing" prior to trial at which mutual discovery is had and various pretrial motions are made. A checklist of possible defense actions is provided to avoid counsel's overlooking something important.

As the "omnibus hearing" has been used in the United States District Court for the Southern District of California, it serves both as preparation for guilty plea and as preparation for trial in the event of a not guilty plea. At arraignment the defendant routinely pleads not guilty and an "omnibus hearing" is set.[d] Prior to that hearing the expectation is that there will be extensive voluntary, mutual discovery, including specification by the defendant of some defenses he will use. Second, the period before the hearing is a time for plea bargaining, which is encouraged. Third, when the hearing is held the defense is expected to present all his pretrial motions, including specifically motions to suppress physical evidence and confessions, so that they may be disposed of. After discovery of the evidence against him, negotiating for a plea, or seeing his motions fail, the defendant may decide to plead guilty. If he does not, the "omnibus hearing" can serve the traditional function of a pretrial conference, with effort to arrive at stipulations with respect to evidence so as to simplify the trial, particularly if the trial might be protracted or involve much documentary proof.

If there is a guilty plea, the "omnibus hearing" will have given the judge reason to believe that the plea is well considered. The checklist used by counsel in the hearing is some guarantee that possible defenses and procedural steps have been weighed.

UNITED STATES DISTRICT COURT
SOUTHERN DISTRICT OF CALIFORNIA

UNITED STATES OF AMERICA,
Plaintiff,
v.
____
____________________,
Defendant(s).

Case No. __________

---

[c] *See* Note, *Pretrial Exclusionary Evidence Rulings,* 1967 WIS. L. REV. 738.

[d] Miller, *The Omnibus Hearing—An Experiment in Federal Criminal Discovery,* 5 SAN DIEGO L. REV. 293-328 (1968).

Omnibus Application by Defendant.

Prosecution Application.

For Rulings prior to trial and for further Discovery.

Exposure and Disposition of latent procedural and constitutional issues.

Check List for Defense Counsel and Prosecution.

Come now the parties, through their attorneys and make the applications or motions checked off below. It is stipulated that the Omnibus hearing and the reporter's record made thereof will bind the parties in all further proceedings in the case, unless request is made for continued hearing for the purpose of preparing formal affidavits, documents, memoranda, or the calling of witnesses and taking of testimony, hearing argument making written findings or orders.

A.

The *defendant* makes the following applications:
(Defendant's counsel will check those the defendant desires to press. The court may consider others as well as those checked by the defendant.)

1. To *dismiss* for failure of the indictment (or information) to state an offense.
2. To *dismiss* on the ground of duplicity.
3. To *sever* defendant's case and for a separate trial.
3.(a) To *sever* counts and for a separate trial.
4. For a *Bill of Particulars.*
5. For *discovery* of all oral, written or recorded statements made by defendant to investigating officers or to third parties and in the possession of the plaintiff.
6. For *discovery* of the names of plaintiff's witnesses and their statements.
7. To *inspect* physical or documentary evidence in plaintiff's possession.
8. To *suppress* physical evidence in plaintiff's possession because of (1) illegal search, (2) illegal arrest.

9. To *suppress* admissions or confessions made by defendant because of—

(a) Delay in arraignment;
(b) Coercion or unlawful inducement;
(c) Violation of the *Miranda* Rule;
(d) Unlawful arrest.

10. To take the *deposition* of a witness to perpetuate testimony under Rule 15, FRCrP (but not for discovery).

11. To *secure the appearance* of a witness at trial or hearing.

12. To inquire into the reasonableness of *bail.*

To Require the Prosecution

13. To state—(a) if there was an *informer* involved; (b) whether he will be called as a witness at the trial and (c) to state the name and address of the informer or claim the privilege.

14. To disclose evidence in plaintiff's possession, favorable to defendant on the issue of guilt.

15. To disclose whether it will rely on prior *acts or convictions* of a similar nature for proof of knowledge or intent.

15.a. Advise whether any expert witness will be called, and if so, supply—

1. Name of witness, qualification and subject of testimony;
2. Report.

16. (a) to state whether any *proceedings before the grand jury* was recorded; (b) if so, to supply transcriptions of the grand jury testimony of the accused, and of all persons whom the prosecution intends to call as witnesses at a hearing or trial.

17. To supply any *reports or tests of physical or mental examinations* in the control of the prosecution.

18. To supply any *reports of scientific tests, experiments or comparisons* and *other reports of experts* in the control of the prosecution, pertaining to this case.

19. To permit *inspection and/or copying of any books, papers, documents, photographs* or tangible objects which the prosecution (a) obtained from or belonging to the defendant, or (b) which will be used at the hearing or trial.

20. To supply any information concerning a *prior conviction* of persons whom the prosecution intends to call as witnesses at the hearing or trial.

21. To inform the defendant of any information he has indicating *entrapment* of the defendant.

22. To inform the defendant whether there has been any (a) electronic surveillance of the defendant or his premises; (b) leads obtained by electronic surveillance or third persons or premises.

Date: (Sign)

____

Attorney for Defendant(s)

(1)________________________

(2)________________________

B.

The *prosecution* applies for discovery in the following matters:

1. Defendant to state whether or not he will rely on an *alibi* and if so, will furnish a list of his alibi witnesses;

2.(a) Defendant to state whether or not he will rely on a defense of *insanity* at time of offense, and if so supply the name of his witnesses on the issue, both lay and professional, and to permit the prosecution to inspect and copy all medical reports under his control or the control of his attorney;

2.(b) Defendant will also state whether or not he will submit to a psychiatrist examination by a court-appointed doctor;

3. Defendant to furnish results of *scientific* tests, experiments or comparisons and the names of persons who conducted the tests;

4. Defendant to state the *general nature of his defense;*

5. Defendant to appear in a *lineup;*

6. Defendant to speak for *voice identification* by witnesses;

7. Defendant to be *finger printed;*

8. Defendant to pose for photographs (not involving a reenactment of the crime);

9. Defendant to *try on articles of clothing;*

10. Defendant to permit taking of specimens of material *under fingernails;*

11. Defendant to permit taking *samples of blood, hair and other materials of his body* which involve no unreasonable intrusion;

12. Defendant to provide samples of his *handwriting;*

13. Defendant to submit to a physical *external inspection of his body;*

14. Defendant shall state whether there is any claim of incompetency to stand trial.

Date: (Sign)

____
Attorney for the United States

Defendant hereby consents to disclose or submit to examination for purpose of the items checked above.

Date:

____
Defendant

____
Attorney for Defendant

The form used in the "omnibus hearing" does not exhaust the possibilities of pretrial motions. The range of possible motions is great, and new ones are created to meet newly perceived needs. A more complete list, but still obviously not exhaustive, follows:

Motions in preparation of defendant's case—Discovery

- Motion for a bill of particulars
- Motion for identification of informer (who was a participant in or material witness to the crime, or whose information provided the basis for arrest or search)
- Motion for discovery of particular evidence in the hands of the prosecutor (*e.g.*, statements by defendant, results of scientific tests, grand jury minutes, names of witnesses, seized objects, criminal record of prosecution witnesses)
- Motion for production of any evidence favorable to the accused
- Motion for remand for holding of a preliminary examination
- Motion for notice of prosecutor's intent to prove prior crimes by defendant

Motions in preparation of defendant's case—Securing evidence

- Motion for issuance of subpoena (for witnesses or objects or papers) or to perpetuate testimony by deposition
- Motion for appointment of defense investigator or expert witness
- Motion for mental examination of defendant

Motions to limit the prosecutor's case

- Motion to suppress illegally obtained evidence (seized evidence, wiretap evidence, results of electronic surveillance, confessions obtained without warning of rights, confessions obtained during a period of unreasonable delay in taking the defendant before a magistrate; the fruits of any of the foregoing)

Motions to prevent trial

- Motion to dismiss (based on such grounds as defects in the institution of the prosecution or in return of the indictment, former jeopardy, res judicata, statute of limitations, failure of the charge to state an offense, lack of jurisdiction over the subject matter, unconstitutionality of the substantive statute, delay before arrest or before trial prejudicial to defendant's defense, "the interests of justice")

Motions affecting trial arrangements

- Motion for a pretrial conference
- Motion for severance or consolidation of parties or charges
- Motion to compel election between duplicitous charges
- Motion for appointment of additional counsel (because of conflict of interest among defendants)
- Motion to allow proceeding in forma pauperis
- Motion for public or closed trial
- Motion for change of venue
- Motion for removal to federal court from state court
- Motion for speedy trial
- Motion for continuance (to permit preparation for trial or to await dissipation of prejudicial publicity)
- Motion for disqualification of judge
- Motion for judicial determination of defendant's fitness to stand trial
- Motion for separate trial on the issues of guilt and penalty
- Motion to vacate the jury panel

Miscellaneous motions

- Motion for reduction of bail or release on defendant's own recognizance
- Motion to withdraw plea of guilty

In addition to these motions, the defendant may sometimes be required by statute to give notice of affirmative defenses he wishes to raise at trial. The ones frequently required are notice of alibi and of insanity, though it has been urged that defendant should give similar notice that he will raise entrapment or self defense.

Pretrial motions on the part of the prosecutor are much less common than such motions by the defense, but there are some. The trend toward mutuality of discovery represented by the requirement that defendant give notice of defenses is also reflected in the prosecutor's motion for reciprocal discovery under Federal Rule 16 and under cases like *Jones v. Superior Court*[e] or in his motion for a pretrial conference under Rule 17.1.[f] The prosecution will move for issuance of subpoenas, for mental examination of defendant, for amendment of the charges, and for trial arrangements desired (severance or consolidation, public or closed trial, postponement or advancement of trial date). It is also proper for the prosecutor in the interest of justice to raise some matters on behalf of defendant in the event his counsel does not or in the event defendant is unrepresented. For example, the prosecutor may move to dismiss, or for an adjudication of fitness to stand trial, or for the reduction of bail.

Reference Note

The writing on the discovery question is voluminous. Among the most useful treatments are Junior Bar Section of the Bar Association of the District of Columbia, *Discovery in Federal Criminal Cases,* 33 F.R.D. 101 (1963), excerpted at 629, *supra;* Rezneck, *The New Federal Rules of Criminal Procedure,* 54 GEORGETOWN L.J. 1276-309 (1966); and A. AMSTERDAM, B. SEGAL & M. MILLER, TRIAL MANUAL FOR THE DEFENSE OF CRIMINAL CASES, §§ 116, 179, 183, 265-76 (1967).

On other pretrial preparations and motions see the last-cited book, chs. XIV–XXIII.

---

[e] *See* p. 643, *supra.*

[f] *See Report on Recommended Procedures in Criminal Pretrials,* 37 F.R.D. 95 (1965); and Kaufman, *Pre-Trial in Criminal Cases,* 42 J. AM. JUD. SOC'Y 150 (1959).

Chapter 11

THE ADJUDICATION OF GUILT OR INNOCENCE

The trial of a criminal case, in classic form, is relatively uncommon. By far the greatest majority of criminal offenders charged—as many as ninety percent in some jurisdictions—plead guilty. Of the remainder, some are dismissed by the judge upon learning something of the facts. Others are fully tried, but to the court, a jury having been waived. Only a small group will actually be tried by a jury.

A. DISMISSAL OF CASES AT THE TRIAL STAGE: ACQUITTAL OF THE GUILTY

The cases which come to the trial stage will not necessarily be tried fully, or at all. In a large city court the mass of misdemeanors are tried to the court and are disposed of quite informally, usually at the offender's first appearance.[a] But if the pressure of business is great, even felony cases may be quickly and informally disposed of if the judge is willing to be lenient. The police often exercise their discretion not to arrest and process an offender; the prosecutor also often exercises his discretion not to charge. But if there is unwillingness to exercise that discretion liberally or if the caseload is so great that inadequate attention is given the cases at earlier stages and they are simply passed on, the judge may be frequently faced with situations in which he thinks conviction is undesirable even though guilt may be clear. In some such instances the court "finds" the defendant not guilty. In others he "dismisses" the action. In still others he orders the defendant "released from custody" or "continues" the case indefinitely. Even though some of these dispositions might permit reopening of the case at a later time, the cases in fact rarely are reopened. They are allowed instead to disappear from the records unless repeated misconduct renews concern with the same offender. Even after a guilty plea the

[a] *See* p. 480, *supra*.

court may inquire into the circumstances of the case and determine that the defendant should be released.[b] In some instances the court feels that the violations are trivial, or otherwise inappropriate for use of the criminal process; more often the court feels that conviction would work an excessive hardship on the particular defendant in view of his individual circumstances. Sometimes acquittal is used to express disapproval of police practices.

The continuance is commonly used in preference to outright acquittal or dismissal when there is a desire to indicate to the defendant that the matter is merely suspended. He may then be induced to act in a particular way to avoid reopening of the case. There is, however, no systematic follow-up by the court to find out if the defendant in fact does what is ordered.

1. *Acquittal for Conduct Resulting from Emotional Disturbance*

There are some instances of criminal conduct which are apparently symptoms of mental disorder, but where the defense of insanity is inappropriate (or would be unacceptable to the defendant). Homosexual offenders are often viewed by courts as sick rather than criminal and may be acquitted, particularly where there was police encouragement. One judge explained his feelings:

> These poor souls who should be pitied and medically treated rather than abused and taken advantage of are deliberately, surreptitiously and unethically enticed into committing acts that they may not have committed for years and years and which they may never commit again were it not for these appalling maneuvers by the vice squad.

Homosexuals, transvestites, window peepers, and similar "mild" sex offenders are not thought to benefit from imprisonment and, indeed, they present institutional problems. Courts typically will acquit if the offender agrees to obtain psychiatric care. Attempted suicides are similarly dealt with.

1

A nineteen-year-old college student was charged with burglary committed in order to steal women's underwear. He pleaded guilty. His attorney stated that his client had committed a whole series of such burglaries, that he wanted to stop, and that he had

---

[b] *See, e.g.,* illustration 3, at 572, *supra.*

begun private psychiatric treatment. The judge dismissed the action.

2. *Acquittal Because the Conduct Is Thought of as a Matter of Private Morality or De Minimis*

2

A husband and wife, neither having a previous criminal record, were charged with public intoxication after being arrested on the way home from a party. The judge dismissed, commenting, "This type of case should be handled at the precinct level."

3

A Michigan judge, in acquitting two defendants of petty gambling charges, stated, "Upstairs in the Detroit Athletic Club more than likely there are members sitting around playing cards for money. In a great many of the houses in the city there are people gambling for money. Many other fraternal and civic organizations are gambling right now also. Why then should I send these petty gamblers to jail when so many of my own friends and associates are committing the same crimes without being charged? The operators who make a racket out of gambling are the ones who should be jailed."

3. *Acquittal Because the Conduct Is Considered Normal to the Subculture*

4

A judge in dismissing an assault charge against the male partner in a white, "hillbilly" common-law relationship, explained, "These people couldn't care less about marriage, divorce or other relationships. They are ignorant and their moral standards are not like ours. They come from the backwoods in the South where even incest is the accepted thing. There is no point in this court acting as a referee in these relationships."

4. *Acquittal Because Alternatives Better than Conviction Exist*

Over the years certain alternatives to invoking the criminal process have been developed to handle recurrent problems. Nonsupport cases are often handled by special adjustment techniques, including "consent probation," in which charges are dismissed if the offender agrees to return to his family and support them and report regularly to a probation officer. The Misdemeanor Complaint Bureau of the Detroit Police Department attempts to settle family and neighborhood quarrels and assaults by imposing fictitious "peace bonds" and otherwise persuading persons to make peace.

5

A defendant charged with a series of sexual offenses involving window peeping and exhibitionism had all charges dismissed when his family agreed to commit him to a state mental hospital.

The continuance, or acquittal, upon condition the defendant enlist in the military service is a particularly common practice. Judges see the service as removing the troublesome young man from the community, but more significantly as removing him from his criminal environment, imposing some healthy discipline, and offering vocational training. Until higher military authorities put a stop to it, a recruiting office was opened in a Michigan courthouse so that enlistment could be completed without leaving the building. Another Michigan judge developed a "court of no record" in which defendants of enlistment age appeared before him in a room other than the courtroom and were given the choice between enlistment and conviction.

6

A defendant who had written a number of bad checks had criminal charges dropped when he agreed to make full restitution. This was his only bad check offense and the judge commented, "If there is a next time, you will not get off so lightly even if you return double what you have stolen."

7

A young man was charged with statutory rape when the father of the underage girl, upon discovering that his daughter was pregnant, complained to the prosecuting attorney. The trial judge dismissed the charge when the young man agreed to marry the girl, on the ground that this was "the proper solution to this kind of problem."

8

Defendant, on parole from a burglary sentence, had two charges of bad checks dismissed when the parole agent told the court that defendant's burglary parole would be revoked and he would be returned to prison.

5. Acquittal to Avoid the Stigma of Criminal Record

9

A defendant who was vice-president of a large bank was arrested on a charge of soliciting and accosting on the basis of conduct involving his homosexual overtures to a member of the police vice squad. At his court appearance he admitted both the particular act and his homosexual proclivities. However, he explained that he was presently receiving private psychiatric counseling and pleaded for "mercy" on the grounds that conviction would destroy his family life and would probably cost him his position at the bank. The judge dismissed the charge and admonished the defendant to continue counseling and to control his impulses.

10

Two codefendants were charged with gross indecency growing out of their sexual misconduct with young girls. The older of the defendants, who had a previous criminal record, was convicted and sentenced to from two to five years in prison. The charge against the other defendant, who was a college student, was dismissed by the judge because the defendant was "otherwise a respectable boy" who came from "a good family" and had merely "fallen under the influence" of the older man.

6. Acquittal Where Circumstances Mitigate the Conduct

11

A defendant was charged with felonious assault growing out of a fight with his landlord in which he had shot and wounded the landlord. The judge learned that the landlord in attempting to evict the defendant had struck the first blow and that the entire neighborhood had somehow become involved in the melee. At the time of the shooting, the victim was flailing at one and all with a tire chain. The trial judge dismissed the assault charge but ordered the defendant to pay the victim's medical costs.

12

A defendant was charged with larceny based on his taking money from the victim on a promise to "get him a girl" and absconding. The judge turned to the complainant and asked, "Did you give this man money to get you a girl?" The defendant replied that he did. The judge continued, "And you did this on Hastings Street?" The defendant replied in the affirmative and the judge said, "Case dismissed."

7. Acquittal to Control or Aid Other Parts of the Criminal Justice Process

Judges sometimes use acquittal, just as they may use reduction in charges, as a means of avoiding what seems to them undesirable limitations in the system. For example, where the judge feels that no probation supervision is necessary for a particular offender he may decide to acquit rather than to convict and suspend sentence, if supervision is mandatory under the statute.

13

The court in acquitting a female defendant of charges of accosting and soliciting for immoral purposes commented, "The vice officer purchased dance hall tickets with state funds and deliberately set out to arrest one of the girls. This is going too far; this is deliberate enticement and it will not be tolerated."

14

A judge in dismissing drunk and disorderly charges against some defendants arrested in a tavern commented that it is "not a proper police function to go into bars to see who is drunk or not. I don't believe this is your duty. The police have plenty of other things to do rather than making the rounds and bothering tavern patrons."

There may be acquittal to support police efforts, as well as to control them. Judges often acquit informers and defendants willing to turn state's witness.

B. THE TRIAL OF CONTESTED CASES

Despite the relative infrequency of the full-dress trial, it looms large in public imagination. The open combat between champions for the defendant and the state, with the life or liberty of the accused at stake, is one of the most intensely dramatic aspects of the criminal justice process. The trial has also been a focus of attention for the lawyer, and has probably been given a disproportionate amount of time in his training. Nonetheless, the cases which are actually tried are often notorious or important ones, where the jury's expression of community values plays as great a part as the jury's ascertainment of facts. The trial process stands as a symbol of our ideals of justice, with elaborate safeguards for the accused, reliance on the judgment of lay representatives of the community, and the notion that out of fair competition between advocates the truth will prevail.

The fact that this ultimate recourse is available, at the defendant's option, substantially affects the operation of the whole system, and particularly the process of negotiation. The chance of defendant's acquittal by the jury and the burden he can impose on the state by demanding a jury trial give him some leverage in bargaining.

Because the trial itself has been given so much attention elsewhere, no effort is made here to do more than indicate the nature of the trial process and its place in the total system.

1. *Concern for the Accuracy of Adjudication*

The contested trial is preeminently an inquiry into the fact of guilt or innocence, and most of the procedural rules applicable at trial are designed to foster the truth-finding capacity of the procedure.

a. *Evidentiary Standard*

The evidentiary standard for conviction is proof beyond a reasonable doubt, or proof that satisfies each member of the jury[c] to a moral certainty that the defendant is guilty. The standard is deliberately set at the highest level in the view that even a high probability of guilt is an inadequate basis for imposition of the criminal law's severe sanctions. Formally the standard in the trial of minor offenses is the same, though in fact the jury seems to be satisfied with less when the penalty is less. In many jurisdictions some facts tending to establish the prosecutor's case are presumed—for example, sanity is presumed,[d] as is that one present at an illegal still is engaged in operating it[e]—so that either practically or formally the defendant in such instances bears some burden of disproving the government's case.[f]

b. *Availability of Proof*

The ability of the state to establish the truth of its case depends upon the success of its detection and evidence-gathering activities,

[c] De Stephano v. Woods, 392 U.S. 631 (1968), leaves open whether jury unanimity is constitutionally required.

[d] Leland v. Oregon, 343 U.S. 790 (1952); *cf.* People *ex rel.* Juhan v. District Court, 439 P.2d 741 (Colo. 1968).

[e] United States v. Gainey, 380 U.S. 63 (1965).

[f] It is not clear, for example, that the reasonable doubt standard is constitutionally required. United States *ex rel.* Morton v. Mancusi, 393 F.2d 482 (2d Cir. 1968).

which were discussed previously, but even if the evidence exists it has little value unless it can be produced in court. Unlike durable physical evidence, oral testimony, which is the evidence most often relied on, can easily disappear. Witnesses who might otherwise have been willing to testify can be worn out and deterred by the repeated delays which the defense uses as a major tactical weapon.[g]

> A boy and girl, age seventeen, had sexual intercourse. The girl's father became enraged when he learned of this and demanded that the boy be prosecuted. The defense was able to obtain a series of delays by requesting continuances "for professional reasons," by filing a writ of prejudice against the judge, by moving for a change of venue. When the case came to trial after a year the prosecutor learned that the father had taken a different job and the family had moved to a distant state. The charges were dropped.

The defense faces similar problems of witnesses becoming unavailable or unwilling to testify in some cases, but prosecutor delay for this purpose is rare. Indeed, if such motivation for delay were established the defendant might object that he had been denied his constitutional right to speedy trial.

c. *Reliability of Evidence*

Even though miscarriages of justice may be uncommon, the possibility of convicting an innocent person is ever present.[h] One possible source of error is the coincidence of circumstantial evidence.[i] Another is perjury on the part of a state's witness.[j] Still a third is mistaken eyewitness identification.[k] These are problems with which the system is faced despite the high standard of proof required. The major reliance of the system is upon cross-examination and diligent preparation of defense counsel. These possibilities of error have been in some measure responsible for the practical disappearance of the death penalty.

---

[g] *See* The Professional Burglar, at 1305, *infra;* Banfield & Anderson, *Continuances in the Cook County Criminal Courts,* 35 U. CHI. L. REV. 259 (1968).

[h] E. BORCHARD, CONVICTING THE INNOCENT (1932); J. FRANK & B. FRANK, NOT GUILTY (1957).

[i] *E.g.,* State v. Doyle, 441 P.2d 846 (Kan. 1968) (coincidence plus slipshod expert testimony).

[j] The landmark decision is Mooney v. Holohan, 249 U.S. 103 (1935). A matter of concern is the state's unintentionally giving motivation to perjury. *See, e.g., Williamson v. United States,* at 131, *supra,* and illustration 4, at 429, *supra.*

[k] See the discussion in *United States v. Wade,* p. 370, *supra,* at 373.

d. *Integrity of the Fact-Finding Machinery*

Many of the other rules governing conduct of the trial are wholly or primarily intended to promote accuracy: The trial must be held in the area where the crime was committed, where the witnesses should be available.[l] The jury panel must not be selected in a way which will deliberately exclude the class of people to which defendant belongs.[m] Both sides are entitled to exclude individuals from the jury for cause or peremptorily.[n] The jury is to be protected from being influenced by any pressure or information not properly part of the trial.[o] The trial must be open to public scrutiny.[p] Rules of evidence attempt to discriminate between reliable and unreliable or inflammatory evidence.[q] Neither the lawyers nor the judge may inject matter into the trial which is inadmissible or argue unfairly to the jury.[r] The accused must be present, to confront the witnesses and assist

---

[l] However, in defining the substantive crime the legislature can establish extended venue. *See, e.g.*, United States v. Johnson, 323 U.S. 273 (1944); United States v. Luros, 243 F. Supp. 160, 173 (N.D. Iowa 1965) (mail order obscenity case held triable where received as well as where mailed).

[m] Most commonly the allegation is that Negroes have been systematically excluded from the jury panel. *See* Swain v. Alabama, 380 U.S. 202 (1965); *cf.* Witherspoon v. Illinois, 391 U.S. 510 (1968) (exclusion of persons expressing objection to capital punishment is improper).

[n] *See* Swain v. Alabama, 380 U.S. 202 (1965); Aldridge v. United States, 283 U.S. 308 (1931).

[o] American Bar Association Project on Minimum Standards for Criminal Justice, Standards Relating to Fair Trial and Free Press (1966), discusses one of the major pressures which can influence prospective jurors. If the local community is hostile to a defendant so that he may not be able to obtain a fair trial in the local courts on a charge related to civil rights, he may be able to remove the prosecution to the federal courts. Georgia v. Rachel, 384 U.S. 780 (1966). On the use of the contempt power to limit prejudicial publicity, see Worcester Telegram & Gazette, Inc. v. Commonwealth, 238 N.E.2d 861 (Mass. 1968), and Shaw v. Commonwealth, 238 N.E.2d 876 (Mass. 1968).

On individual influences, see Parker v. Gladden, 385 U.S. 363 (1966).

[p] *See* United States *ex rel.* Bruno v. Herold, 246 F. Supp. 363 (N.D.N.Y. 1965).

[q] *E.g.*, the hearsay rule has acquired sanctity through the right of confrontation. *See* Pointer v. Texas, 380 U.S. 400 (1965). Reliance on instructions that the jury should not consider a codefendant's confession which mentions him in deciding the defendant's case is recognized as futile in Bruton v. United States, 391 U.S. 123 (1968). Impeachment of defendant when he takes the witness stand may be so prejudicial as to distort the jury's perception of the evidence. *See* Luck v. United States, 348 F.2d 763 (D.C. Cir. 1965); *cf.* Comment, *Collateral Use Doctrine: From Walder to Miranda*, 62 Nw. U.L. Rev. 912 (1968) (impeachment by use of inadmissible confession).

[r] A much debated issue is whether the jury can be expected to follow instructions to consider incriminating evidence for only one purpose. *See* Bruton v. United States, 391 U.S. 123 (1968); Spencer v. Texas, 385 U.S. 554 (1967); Jackson v. Denno, 378 U.S. 368 (1964).

his counsel.[s] The accused is entitled to counsel[t] and to evidence[u] needed to help him test the evidence and present his defense.

Each of these propositions, and others, is the subject of a substantial jurisprudence. We make no effort to develop them here, since they are commonly dealt with in other courses. They have in common their purpose to protect the defendant, and to lesser extent the state, against the possibility of error in the ascertainment of guilt or innocence.

2. *Other Defense Interests to Be Protected*

Though accuracy of the verdict is the prime consideration in any contested case, there are other rights of the defendant which must be protected in the course of trial.

Defendant is entitled to a speedy trial.[v] Though delay may make his defense more difficult and thus have some effect on the accuracy of the verdict, his right is equally grounded in his interest in an early clearing of his name and obtaining of his release if he has been unable to make bail. If he is already serving a prison term for some other offense the fact that a detainer has been placed against him often serves to prejudice his chances at parole; even a conviction, if he were to receive a concurrent sentence, might serve the defendant's interest better than delay in such a case.

Defendant is entitled to a jury trial except for petty offenses.[w] Though the jury can serve as a last recourse against high-handed

---

[s] *See In re* Hunt, 276 F. Supp. 112 (E.D. Mich. 1967); People v. Davis, 39 Ill. 2d 325, 235 N.E.2d 634 (1968).

[t] *See* American Bar Association Project on Minimum Standards for Criminal Justice, Standards Relating to Providing Defense Services (1967).

[u] *E.g.*, Jencks v. United States, 353 U.S. 657 (1957) (largely codified in 18 U.S.C. § 3500, relating to discovery of prior statements of government witnesses); United States v. Youngblood, 379 F.2d 365 (2d Cir. 1967) (adopting as policy in normal cases full disclosure of grand jury minutes); Washington v. Texas, 388 U.S. 14 (1967) (defense right to call any witness); Earl v. United States, 361 F.2d 531 (D.C. Cir. 1966) (defense cannot demand that his reluctant witnesses be granted immunity); Ward v. United States, 346 F.2d 423 (D.C. Cir. 1965) (government failed to make diligent effort to arrest codefendant, whom defendant wanted as witness).

[v] *See* American Bar Association Project on Minimum Standards for Criminal Justice, Standards Relating to Speedy Trial (1967); Barker v. Municipal Ct., 64 Cal. 2d 806, 51 Cal. Rptr. 921, 415 P.2d 809 (1966) (attempted murder prosecution delayed eighteen years while defendant was imprisoned on another conviction).

Related is the provision against double jeopardy. *See, e.g.*, United States v. Burdick, 284 F. Supp. 685 (E.D. Pa. 1968).

[w] *See* American Bar Association Project on Minimum Standards for Criminal Justice, Standards Relating to Trial by Jury (1968); Duncan v. Louisiana, 392 U.S. 947 (1968).

law enforcement, and this is essentially the ground on which the constitutional right was created, it is clear that trial by the court is as likely to be accurate.

The full jury trial is used when the defendant has nothing to lose—when he is unable to work out a deal with the prosecutor and when the penalty is mandatory or is unlikely to be affected by his demanding the jury trial.[x] The defendant may also call for a jury in hope that some emotional element which would not affect the judge will produce an acquittal or disagreement.[y] Sometimes he asks for a jury trial with intention of later waiving the jury, after he has had the advantage of the delay attendant on getting the case on the jury calendar or the advantage of getting a different judge assigned to handle the case.[z] Trial to the court is much more expeditious and less costly than jury trials and thus often preferred by both defense and prosecution.[a] Sometimes trial to the court is used when the defendant does not seriously contest his guilt, but wishes to present extenuating circumstances in hope of obtaining a dismissal or leniency in sentencing.[b] When the facts are not significantly in dispute, but the defendant wishes to preserve his objections to pretrial rulings by the judge on various exclusionary rules, he may stipulate to "trial" on the basis of the transcript of evidence heard at the preliminary examination.[c] Such a nominal trial might also be used when the defendant feels he cannot improve his position by trial and when the defendant hopes for leniency as a result of his practical waiver of trial.

Defendant may not be called as a witness by the state. Accuracy would be fostered by the defendant's taking the stand and

---

[x] *See United States v. Wiley,* at 586, *supra.*

[y] If the jury disagrees the defendant can be retried, but delay usually works in his favor. The judge may not so strongly urge the jury to come to an agreement. The "dynamite" or "Allen" instruction approved in Allen v. United States, 164 U.S. 492 (1896), is clearly the maximum pressure the judge may exert, and that instruction is sometimes held coercive. *See* People v. Carter, 69 Cal. Rptr. 297, 442 P.2d 353 (1968); State v. Randall, 137 Mont. 534, 353 P.2d 1054 (1960).

[z] In minor cases the threat of imposition of costs for jury fees sometimes serves as a deterrent; this sanction obviously cannot operate at all against the indigent.

[a] But under federal law both the defendant and the government must agree to a jury waiver. Singer v. United States, 380 U.S. 24 (1965).

[b] Waiver of jury trial must be made voluntarily and understandingly. Hatcher v. United States, 352 F.2d 364 (D.C. Cir. 1965). Waiver may not be coerced by fear of the death penalty, under statutes which require a jury recommendation for imposition of capital punishment. United States v. Jackson, 390 U.S. 570 (1968).

[c] Compare the procedure used in Brookhart v. Janis, 384 U.S. 1 (1966); A. Amsterdam, B. Segal & M. Miller, Trial Manual for the Defense of Criminal Cases 2-273 (1967).

testifying, but the constitutional privilege against self-incrimination is interpreted as leaving the option of testifying solely to the defendant. The right is deeply rooted in the notion that personal integrity, even of a guilty man, is too much infringed in forcing a man to be "the instrument of his own downfall."[d] Related to this are various other privileges which the defendant may invoke —to prevent his wife's testifying against him; to prevent his attorney or doctor disclosing information he has confided in them; to prevent the state's using evidence obtained in violation of his constitutional or statutory rights. These privileges operate to suppress the truth in the interest of some other social policy.

3. Controls upon the Trial Process

The proper conduct of the trial is left largely in the hands of the trial judge. He has broad discretion in the procedures to be followed and the evidence to be admitted and the instructions to be given the jury. His integrity and wisdom are of central importance. His power to hold either prosecutor or defense counsel in contempt for misconduct, his power to declare a mistrial, and his power to dismiss the case all represent sanctions he can use to shape the trial by more than persuasion.

The representation of defendant by counsel is another method of controlling the trial process. The Constitution has been interpreted so as to require that counsel be provided by the government for indigents in every serious case,[e] and in some jurisdictions the right to counsel has been extended even to petty offense prosecutions.[f] A question of major importance today is whether counsel, once provided, has acted competently and is provided with essential assistance in preparing his case.[g]

In the contested trial the adversary system operates in its purest form. The defense counsel has a responsibility to present his client's position as strongly as it can be put without use of perjurious testimony, irrespective of the attorney's private views as to his client's guilt. Unless the attorney accepts the role of champion, limited only by his ethical obligation to avoid chicanery, he cannot fully serve the function assigned to him.[h]

---

[d] Values reflected in the privilege are catalogued in Murphy v. Waterfront Comm'n, 378 U.S. 52, 56 n.5 (1964).

[e] Gideon v. Wainwright, 372 U.S. 335 (1963).

[f] Harvey v. Mississippi, 340 F.2d 263 (5th Cir. 1965); *In re* Turrieta, 54 Cal. 2d 816, 8 Cal. Rptr. 737, 356 P.2d 681 (1960); but compare People v. Letterio, 16 N.Y.2d 307, 266 N.Y.S.2d 368, 213 N.E.2d 670 (1965).

[g] Bailey, *Defense Counsel Incompetence in Criminal Trials,* 10 S. TEX. L. REV. 121 (1968).

[h] *See* Freedman, *Professional Responsibility of the Criminal Defense Lawyer: The Three Hardest Questions,* 64 MICH. L. REV. 1469 (1966); Noonan,

The jury is to be controlled by limiting the evidence they hear and sequestering them to insulate them from unwanted influences, but the jury also serves as a control upon the court and prosecution. Because a directed verdict of conviction is not permitted,[i] the jury has the power to acquit even the clearly guilty defendant if they feel the prosecution is unwarranted. Though the jury will be told of their responsibility to convict if they find the evidence supports the charge beyond a reasonable doubt, the defendant sometimes appeals to the jury to acquit nonetheless. The acquittal of a husband who has killed his wife's paramour may rely on "the unwritten law," and the acquittal of a man for committing acts against a Negro or civil rights worker may rely on this jury power. The same power which permits the technical offender to escape a harassing prosecution can permit the serious, but popular, offender to escape a wholly legitimate prosecution.

A final, major method of control is appellate court review.[j] The review may be by appeal or by extraordinary writ—most often habeas corpus or its statutory equivalent—and the issues the court will consider may be any prejudicial error of law or may be only prejudicial constitutional errors. It is clear, however, that the review process cannot cure all errors and operates only to catch the more serious errors and to deter a careless approach to the trial on the part of trial level participants. Only those cases which are brought to the court will be considered; and only those errors which can be fully established on the record[k] (or, for constitutional errors not of record, established by proof) will be ground for relief.

Reference Note

The court decision to dismiss cases despite adequate evidence of guilt is best described in D. NEWMAN, CONVICTION: THE DETERMINATION OF GUILT OR INNOCENCE WITHOUT TRIAL (1966).

The Purposes of Advocacy and the Limits of Confidentiality, 64 MICH. L. REV. 1485 (1966); Bress, *Professional Ethics in Criminal Trials: A View of Defense Counsel's Responsibility,* 64 MICH. L. REV. 1493 (1966).

People v. Wilder, 160 N.W.2d 749 (Mich. App. 1968) applied an extreme notion of adversary trial in reversing a conviction in a nonjury trial because the judge asked too many questions of the witnesses.

[i] *See* Horning v. District of Columbia, 254 U.S. 135 (1920).

[j] *See* American Bar Association Project on Minimum Standards for Criminal Justice, Standards Relating to Post-Conviction Remedies (1967).

Special problems for the system are preventing frivolous appeals without unduly penalizing one who wishes to appeal.

[k] Jones, *Translating Recent Supreme Court Decisions into Courtroom Reality,* 19 BAYLOR L. REV. 371 (1967), describes how to create an adequate record to preserve possible errors for review.

On the tactics and procedures of trial a major resource is A. AMSTERDAM, B. SEGAL & M. MILLER, TRIAL MANUAL FOR THE DEFENSE OF CRIMINAL CASES (1967). A much shorter work is I. MENDELSON, DEFENDING CRIMINAL CASES (rev. ed. 1967).

The various proposals by the American Bar Association Project on Minimum Standards for Criminal Justice are excellent references, also. Draft standards have been published relating to Joinder and Severance (1967), Providing Defense Services (1967), Speedy Trial (1967), Fair Trial and Free Press (1966), Trial by Jury (1968), Sentencing Alternatives and Procedures (1967), Appellate Review of Sentences (1967), and Post-Conviction Remedies (1967).

Chapter 12

SENTENCING

> It is perhaps ironic that trends in modern corrections toward more humane treatment and greater emphasis on rehabilitation and community supervision have increasingly raised issues of fair process and the rights of offenders. At one time an offender's correctional course was largely determined at trial. If he was sentenced to prison, he went and served the term appointed for him by the judge or statute, and by and large he was treated in prison just like everybody else. But today correctional decisions are far more numerous and complex, and many of them are made administratively by correctional staff rather than by a judge or statute.
>
> *The President's Commission on Law Enforcement and Administration of Justice, Task Force Report: Corrections* 12 (1967)

Sentencing, probation, institutional treatment of offenders, release on parole, and probation and parole revocation are stages of the criminal justice process perhaps most unfamiliar to lawyers and most clearly the province of professional social workers. For years it was generally assumed that a defense lawyer's function ended once his client was acquitted or convicted. However, this has changed and it is now widely recognized that there are important functions for lawyers to serve in the process of the correctional treatment of the convicted offender.

It also had been long assumed that convicted offenders have only "privileges" not "rights" and therefore that the correctional administrator did not have to concern himself with legal limitations upon his authority to develop and implement correctional programs. This too has changed, and correctional practices are increasingly being subjected to judicial review, and as a consequence the administrative law aspects of corrections have become of increasing significance.

Understanding the criminal justice system requires knowledge about correctional processes. The criminal justice system is not neatly divided into two parts: one leading to the court, where a determination of guilt or innocence is made; and the other leading away from it to a separate and distinct process for dealing with persons who have been convicted of crimes. Instead, the various stages of the criminal process, from arrest to parole revocation, are related to one another so that activity or inactivity at one point has consequences elsewhere. Furthermore, anticipation of these consequences affects early decisions, and the entire system becomes one of accommodation and response. For example, the guilty plea process, particularly the negotiated plea, has a major effect on the sentencing decision, while at the same time sentencing structure strongly influences the type and frequency of guilty pleas and of plea bargaining. Experienced probation officers know that while a suspended sentence with community supervision is indeed a good treatment device, it is also a sentencing alternative of administrative significance to both the prosecutor and the trial court. Some clients in the probation agent's caseload are there not so much because they are good supervision risks but because they have exchanged a guilty plea for a sentencing break. On the other side of the coin, experienced defense counsel, prosecutors, and trial judges realize that knowledge about actual sentencing conditions and release procedures as well as knowledge about the powers and duties of probation officers and correctional administrators is crucial both to their clients and to the operations of the defense, of the prosecutor's office, and of the court calendar.

Analysis of sentencing and of other post-conviction stages of the criminal justice process reintroduces many of the important public policy issues in criminal justice administration but set against a new background. No longer is the major concern the separation of the guilty from the innocent. Now the issue is what to do with those who have been determined to be guilty of criminal conduct. In asking this question, the post-conviction processes can be looked at from many of the same perspectives that were applied at the police, prosecutor, and court stages of the process. For example, in selecting among alternative sentences some degree and type of evidence sufficiency are involved even though the standards have not been as formally articulated as the "probable cause" of the prosecutor or the "beyond a reasonable doubt" of the court. Yet the judge must decide whom to incarcerate and whom to place on probation, and, in making this decision, he must have information and he must apply some criteria in evaluating these facts if he is to avoid arbitrary and capricious selection. Discretion and controls on discretion are obviously of major importance in the post-conviction stages. The fairness and propriety of methods of dealing with the guilty are important here just as they are in dealing with suspects and defendants. The necessity for and desirability of adversary proceedings are also in issue. For example, one matter of current controversy in the adversary process leading to trial is pretrial discovery, the question being the extent to which the prosecution must or should reveal its evidence to the defense prior to trial in order to prevent surprise and to give the defendant a chance to prepare his defense. A similar question is whether the defendant ought to have access to the report of the presentence social investigation which is submitted to the court by probation officers to aid in the sentencing decision or whether, as has been traditional, this presentence report should be read only by the judge and not shared with the defendant or his counsel. Another issue is whether the sentencing decisions should be subjected to review by the appellate courts.

Such issues as evidence sufficiency, discretion, propriety and fairness, discovery, and judicial review, while parallel in the early and late stages of the process, are not exactly the same. Checks and controls on procedures to separate the guilty from the innocent are traditional and have received a good deal of study and attention. Following conviction, the defendant stands as a labeled criminal and, excepting appeal, his guilt or innocence is no longer in issue. Decisions about him after conviction have traditionally been made by procedures that have not been adversary but have operated largely on broad discretion delegated by legislatures to the sentencing judge and to correctional agencies. The question today is whether the mere fact of conviction and the nonadversary nature of correctional processes make such a significant difference as to require tests of evidence and fairness and procedures for determining facts different from those used in the preconviction stages. To say no more than "parole is a privilege and not a right" is less than satisfactory, and to argue that the issue of pretrial discovery is significantly different from confidentiality of the presentence report simply because conviction has intervened tends to ignore the basically similar philosophical question and common administrative concerns.

Not only has it been customary to deal with parts of the criminal justice system in relative isolation from other stages, but it has been equally common to treat separately those various professions—police, lawyers, and social workers—chiefly responsible for administering the criminal justice process. These professions have had little sense of common purpose. Each is devoted to the control of crime, of course, and each offers allegiance to democratic ideology; but operationally the three professions often are in disagreement and sometimes in open antagonism over methods, over the primacy of objectives, over budget, and over recognition and reward. These all have their effect upon sentencing law and practice.[a]

A. RESPONSIBILITY FOR THE INITIAL DETERMINATION OF SENTENCE

1. *Legislative Allocation of Responsibility*

a. Sentencing Agencies

It is natural to think of sentencing as the responsibility of the judge. This is true in the sense that the judge formally pronounces the sentence, but it is not always true that he determines what the sentence will be. The allocation of sentencing responsibility is first of all made by the legislature. Occasionally the legislature retains for itself sole determination of the sentence, by setting a flat, mandatory sentence. Most often, however, the legislature assumes responsibility only for setting the outer limits and entrusts discretion to the judge, jury, or administrative board to determine the sentence for a particular offense within limits established by statute.

The jury is used particularly in capital cases, to choose between the death penalty and life imprisonment. In a decision of this sort it has seemed to the legislature that the sentiment of the community, as reflected by the jury, should be given expression.[b]

In other states, notably California, the responsibility for sentencing is given to an administrative board, which is typically composed of lawyers, psychiatrists, social workers, and others recognized as legal or behavioral experts.

Most commonly sentencing responsibility is entrusted to the trial judge.

b. Types of Sentence

The trial judge may have a wide range of sentence possibilities. For petty offenses sometimes only a money fine is provided for in the statutes, and for the most serious offenses sometimes only imprisonment is available, but for the great bulk of offenses the

---

[a] Compare the discussion of professional roles at 14-17, *supra.*

[b] Though in most states the death penalty is nominally available for a few crimes, its imposition is infrequent and its execution has nearly ceased. The death penalty has shaped legal procedures and its influence persists even though use of the penalty has practically disappeared.

judge has as alternatives the money fine, probation, imprisonment, or some combination of these.

The money fine is the characteristic penalty for many minor crimes, but it is not often utilized for more serious criminal behavior, either instead of or in addition to imprisonment. The majority of offenders have no financial resources from which to pay a fine.

Probation involves releasing the offender in the community under supervision. It is widely used. In Wisconsin, for example, at any given time approximately two-thirds of all felony offenders are serving their sentences in the community on probation.

Incarceration may be in a jail or prison, and conditions vary widely among institutions. The judge in some jurisdictions may use the "Huber Law," under which the offender must spend nights and weekends in jail but is released from his cell during the day in order to work, keep house, or attend school. Income is handled by the jailer, who uses it for the purpose of paying the expenses incurred by the county and also to support the family of the offender.

Finally, in some states, such as New York, the judge has the lawful power to suspend sentence altogether. This has the effect of avoiding all direct penalty except the fact of conviction. Other jurisdictions deny the judge this power. In Wisconsin, for example, a judge cannot suspend sentence unless he places the offender on probation.

c. *The Length of Imprisonment*

Whereas the decision as to the type of sentence, that is, fine, probation, or incarceration, is typically left to the trial judge, the decision as to length of sentence if incarceration is imposed is a somewhat more complex matter. For certain offenses, such as sale of narcotics, some legislatures have provided for mandatory sentences. The judge is left no discretion in either type or length of sentence. For most offenses, however, responsibility for fixing the length of incarceration is shared by the legislature, the trial judge, and the administrative agency, typically a parole board, which decides what proportion of the sentence a particular offender actually will serve in prison. There are a number of variations in this process. Some states require the imposition of legislatively prescribed maxima for all offenses, with low legislatively fixed minimum terms, thus conferring on the parole board extensive power either to retain the offender to the maximum or to release him at any time after his minimum term. Other states give the trial judge the power to fix the maximum sentence (within a legislatively set upper limit) but not the minimum, thus allowing parole authorities to release him earlier but not later than the judge thinks proper. Depending on the degree to which the legislature trusts the parole board's judgment, it may set a higher or lower minimum sentence, or it may allow the trial judge to vary the minimum as a way of controlling the scope of discretion granted the parole board. Some states grant the trial judge wide discretion to increase the minimum, in some cases nearly up to the maximum (so that it would be possible for a judge to impose a sentence of from nine to ten years for a particular offense) but others give the judge discretion only to set the minimum as high as some fraction (usually one-half or one-third) of the maximum. This type of sentencing structure precludes early parole in those cases where the trial judge believes it undesirable.[c]

2. Constitutional Limits on Allocating Responsibilities in Sentencing

From time to time it has been suggested that the trial judge's function be limited to the determination of guilt or innocence of defendants and that the sentencing of those found guilty be delegated to administrative boards composed of persons with special expertise in behavioral sciences. This type of sentencing arrangement has been established in California where the Adult Authority fixes the length and conditions of sentences within the limits prescribed by statute. Even in states where the judge sets the initial sentence, parole boards commonly decide the actual length of time an inmate will serve in prison. The constitutionality of such arrangements has been generally upheld. However, the question continues to be controversial, particularly in special programs of correctional treatment.

HUEBNER v. STATE

33 Wis. 2d 505, 147 N.W.2d 646 (1967)

The plaintiff in error John J. Huebner was convicted of the crime of attempting to persuade or entice a child under eighteen years of age into his motor vehicle with intent to commit a crime against sexual morality.

---

[c] For a description of alternative sentencing structures in the United States, see Note, *Statutory Structures for Sentencing Felons to Prison*, 60 COLUM. L. REV. 1134 (1960).

HALLOWS, J. The Sex Crimes Act was enacted by ch. 542, sec. 2, Laws of 1951 and presently provides in sec. 959.15(1), Stats., that upon conviction of rape, sexual intercourse without consent, indecent behavior with a child, or for attempted rape or sexual intercourse without consent, a temporary commitment of a defendant to the state department of public welfare for a presentence social, physical and mental examination is mandatory. Upon conviction for other sex crimes, such presentence examination is discretionary with the trial court.

Huebner was committed for a presentence examination under this permissive section and the commitment for this purpose has not been questioned.

Upon a completion of the examination but not later than sixty days after commitment, a report of the examination with the recommendations of the department is sent to the court. If it appears from such report that the department does not recommend specialized treatment for the defendant's mental and physical aberrations, the defendant is sentenced for the crime on a punitive basis as any other criminal, sec. 959.15(5), Stats. However, if the department recommends specialized treatment, it is mandatory for the court under sec. 959.15(6), to either place the defendant on probation under the control and supervision of the department with the requirement he receive such inpatient or outpatient treatment as the court shall prescribe, or to commit the defendant to the department for care as an inpatient at the sex deviate facility. Under the authority conferred by this section, Huebner was committed to the state department of public welfare. Significantly too, this finding automatically determines the initial maximum period of incarceration for mandatory treatment and in addition subjects the defendant to potential continuing incarceration and treatment under the Sex Crimes Act.

We consider this commitment procedure so essentially different from penal sentencing as to amount to an independent proceeding which determines such important rights of the defendant unrelated to the determination of guilt that due process requires a hearing thereon as much as it does for subsequent hearings on the same issue.

We think due process does not end with conviction any more than it begins only with the commencement of the trial of the issue of guilt.

While we do not rest our decision on a denial of equal protection of the laws, we are aware that initial commitments under the Mental Health Act, ch. 51, for mental illness, infirmity or deficiency are upon a hearing to the court, and if requested to a jury of six persons, with the right to examine medical witnesses appointed by the court and to offer evidence. While equal protection does not require all persons to be treated in the same manner, the distinction must have some relevance to the purpose of the classification. The conviction of a sex crime as a basis for the denial of a hearing on the issue of mental aberrations and the need for specialized treatment does not seem to be a relevant distinction for the purpose of treatment. The commission of a sex crime may be sufficient grounds to require an examination, but is not sufficient to deny the right in court to contest the agency's findings and recommendations. Nor does the law determine who falls within what classifications, but membership rests upon the unreasonable basis of an uncontestable and unreviewable determination by the department of public welfare.

We think the language in State *ex rel.* Volden v. Haas [264 Wis. 127, 58 N.W.2d 577 (1953)], that due process does not require a hearing on the administrative report and recommendation for specialized treatment can no longer be approved and is hereby withdrawn. We hold that when a person is convicted of a sex crime and subject to a presentence social, physical and mental examination and the report of the department recommends specialized treatment, that before a court can place such person on probation in the department with treatment or commit him to the department for treatment under sec. 959.15(6), Stats. he shall be afforded a hearing on the issue of the need for specialized treatment for his mental or physical aberrations unless such hearing is expressly waived by him. The defendant shall be afforded such hearing with counsel, process to compel attendance of witnesses, production of evidence, an examination by a doctor or psychiatrist of his own choosing, and if he is unable to provide counsel, he shall have counsel appointed for him at public expense, all as provided in sec. 959.15(14), for hearings after commitment to the department. After such hearing the court shall make its finding and either sentence the defendant under criminal law as provided in sec. 959.15(5) or commit him to the department under the alternatives of sec. 959.15(6). In short, the department's recommendation is not mandatory on the court, which shall hold a hearing thereon and make its determination upon the evidence.

CURRIE, C. J. (*dissenting*). The majority opinion rests on the fallacious assumption that the determination of whether a convicted sex offender shall be committed to the department for such specialized treatment must be made by the judiciary and that it is a denial of due process for the legislature to entrust it to an administrative agency such as the department of public welfare. This issue was laid to rest long ago when the courts upheld the constitutionality of indeterminate sentence laws. It is not a valid ground of constitutional attack that such laws vest the power to determine the length of sentence in an administrative agency instead of the courts. This is because the legislature "has [the] power to define crimes and fix punishments, . . . limited only by the provision that they shall not be cruel or unusual or disproportionate to the character of the offense."

If the legislature can vest in an administrative agency the power to fix the length of a sentence it can also vest in an administrative agency the power to determine whether a person convicted of a sex crime should receive the specialized treatment provided by our Sex Crimes Act and bind the sentencing court to sentence in accordance with such determination.

The fact that a convicted sex offender, whom the department determines is in need of specialized treatment, has such specialized treatment imposed on him as well as imprisonment while another sex offender whom the department finds is not in need of such treatment receives only imprisonment, does not violate the equal protection of the laws clause of the Fourteenth amendment. The classification made by the legislature rests on a reasonable basis, *i.e.,* the determination by the department of the convicted offender's need for treatment.

3. *Operational Accommodation to Sentencing Structures*

The formal allocation of responsibility for determining length of incarceration among the legislature, trial judge, and the parole board has important consequences not only for defendants who are sentenced but for effective administration of the correctional system and, depending upon the number of restrictions on sentencing discretion, for earlier stages in the process, such as charging and adjudication, as well. In assessing the relative merits of different types of sentencing structure, it is necessary to balance the advantages of each system against the likely accommodations that take place if the structure precludes discretion to those who must administer it. For example, a system of legislatively fixed sentences supposedly has the advantage of creating uniformity by requiring all judges in the state to impose the same sentence upon defendants convicted of the same offense. At the same time, the mandatory aspect of fixed sentencing systems can be avoided by reducing the charge to one which carries a lower sentence when this is felt to be appropriate to fit the penalty to the conduct in particular cases, or by accepting a plea to a lesser charge as part of plea bargaining. Conversely, sentencing structures which give the judiciary wide flexibility in setting maximum sentences have been alternately praised for permitting "individualization" of justice and damned for causing sentence disparity. In either situation, parole authorities are confronted with numbers of prisoners convicted of similar crimes but with a wide range of sentences. The parole authorities find themselves in the position of reevaluating the judicial individualization decision or of "equalizing" disparate sentences by releasing like inmates at about the same time to the extent that is in the parole board's power, whatever the differences in the sentences.

B. DEVICES FOR ENSURING PROPER SENTENCING

The sentencing decision can reasonably be called one of the most important decisions ever made by a governmental agency about the fate of an individual. It is usually entrusted to the wisdom of one man, who lacks special training for the task and who often must act on the basis of partial information. There are some controls upon the sentencing process, but surprisingly few.

1. *Sentencing Councils*

THE PRESIDENT'S COMMISSION ON LAW ENFORCEMENT AND ADMINISTRATION OF JUSTICE TASK FORCE REPORT: THE COURTS 24-25 (1967)

The sentencing council is a procedure by which several judges of a multijudge court meet periodically to consider what sentences should be imposed in pending cases. Sentencing councils have been instituted on a regular basis in three U.S. district courts; no evidence of their systematic use in State courts has been found. The basic operation of a sentencing council as it is employed in the Eastern District of Michigan, the first district court to develop the procedure, is described in the following comments:

> Under the practice of our district, these meetings are held at an hour in the morning, before the commencement of the day's routine, when the judges may give the matters their undivided attention. The judges meet in panels of three, each judge having the presentence investigation report from the probation department and having prepared

> a study sheet, not only for the offenders he must sentence, but also for those who are the primary responsibility of the other two judges. Customarily, the one judge will call his first case, merely stating the name of the offender and giving a brief statement of the offense. He will then state to his brother judges the factors, in his judgment, believed to be controlling as to disposition, and will recommend a disposition to be made. Each of the other two judges will then give, in turn, the factors believed by him to be controlling, together with his recommended sentence. The sentences will normally vary, although I have observed with a great deal of interest that the sentences of judges working together in this manner tend, as time goes on, to approach a common ground. It is in the discussion following the recommendation as to sentencing that the Council performs its most useful function. . . . The weights assigned the various factors thought to be controlling as to disposition of the case are sometimes modified by the sentencing judge in the light of the experience of his brother judges with their own previous sentences.

Under the practice followed in the Northern District of Illinois the 10 district court judges are equally divided into two panels. The first panel meets each week to consider the cases in which the judges of the panel must impose sentence during the following week. The second panel of judges devotes its full attention to reviewing cases certified to it by the other panel.

Although the ultimate responsibility for determining sentence in both jurisdictions rests with the judge to whom the case is assigned, the interplay among judges has tended to repress the imposition of excessively severe or lenient sentences. The Michigan council produced changes from the sentencing judge's initial recommendation in slightly over 40 percent of the cases considered during its first five months of operation. Among the cases in which the judges altered their original disposition, the number in which sentence was made more severe was approximately equal to the number in which it was reduced.

Foremost among the advantages of the sentencing council is that it reveals to the participating judges their differences in sentencing philosophies, and it provides a forum in which these differences may be debated in the context of particular cases and from which a consensus on sentencing standards may emerge. It also promotes fuller consideration of the sentencing alternatives available to the court. Finally, where the sentencing council procedure is accompanied by the collection of data on the initial recommendations and final sentencing decisions, as in Michigan and Illinois, it provides a mechanism for periodic evaluation of the sentencing practices of the court.

One troublesome aspect of existing sentencing council procedures is that the judges meet prior to the sentencing hearing. The sentencing judge thus presides over the hearing after having heard the views of his colleagues about the case and after having taken a position himself within the sentencing council. This may impair the judge's ability to give openminded consideration to the arguments and information presented at the sentencing hearing. At the same time the judges participating in the council do not have the benefit of the facts and insights presented by the prosecutor, defense counsel, or the defendant himself. Particularly where there is disclosure of the presentence report, the hearing may reveal that the deliberations in the sentencing council were based on inaccurate or incomplete information.

Some of these difficulties might be avoided by permitting defense counsel and the prosecutor to make a presentation at the sentencing council. However, this would greatly encumber the procedure and perhaps make it impractical for busy urban courts. A preferable solution would be to hold the sentencing council after the hearing, at which time the sentencing judge could inform his colleagues of the arguments and information presented at the hearing and of his resolution of disputed factual questions. Although this would require a separate proceeding for the imposition of sentence, it is likely that the additional burden on the courts could be minimized by careful scheduling.

2. *Appellate Review of Sentences*

THE PRESIDENT'S COMMISSION ON LAW ENFORCEMENT AND ADMINISTRATION OF JUSTICE TASK FORCE REPORT: THE COURTS 25-26 (1967)

One of the most serious aspects of the disparity problem is the imposition of sentences which are grossly excessive in relation to the seriousness of the crime or the character of the offender. As James V. Bennett, former Director of the Federal Bureau of Prisons, observed:

> In one of our institutions a middle-aged credit union treasurer is serving 117 days for embezzling $24,000 in order to cover his gambling debts. On the other hand, another middle-aged embezzler with a fine past record and a fine family is serving 20 years, with 5 years probation to follow. At the

> same institution is a war veteran, a 39-year-old attorney who has never been in trouble before, serving 11 years for illegally importing parrots into this country. Another who is destined for the same institution is a middle-aged tax accountant who on tax fraud charges received 31 years and 31 days in consecutive sentences. In stark contrast, at the same institution last year an unstable young man served out his 98-day sentence for armed bank robbery.

In all Western countries except the United States, grossly excessive sentences are subject to routine review and correction by appellate tribunals. The great majority of jurisdictions in the United States, however, vest sentencing power solely within the discretion of the trial judge, with appellate review available only to correct sentences which do not conform to the statutory limits. Authority for appellate review of the merits of sentences has been expressly granted by the legislatures of about one-quarter of the States and by Congress for military courts. In addition the appellate courts of a few States have construed general review statutes as including such authority.

Among the States which have adopted appellate review of sentences there are two major variations in procedure. In most of these States sentences are reviewed by the regular appellate courts, and the appellate court has the power to review the merits of the sentences in any case over which it otherwise has jurisdiction. In four States, however, a specially created court staffed by experienced trial judges is convened solely for the purpose of reviewing the merits of sentences; only sentences of imprisonment in the penitentiary may be appealed, and the review division is empowered to increase as well as to reduce sentences.

In recent years adoption of appellate review of sentences has substantially increased. . . .

The most important contribution of appellate review is the opportunity it provides for the correction of grossly excessive sentences. Although appellate review will not totally eliminate the problem of disparity of sentences, by reducing the peaks of disparity, it would narrow the range in which individual differences among judges can affect the length and type of sentences.

Moreover, appellate review aids the development of a uniform sentencing policy within a jurisdiction. It tends to cause both trial and appellate courts to give sustained consideration to the justification for particular sentences. And the opinions of appellate courts in modifying excessive sentences can provide a body of law to guide trial courts in all cases.

Finally, appellate review would tend to reduce the number of anomalous decisions on procedural and substantive law which appellate courts have made in order to reverse cases involving unusually harsh sentences. As former Chief Judge Simon E. Sobeloff of the Fourth Circuit Court of Appeals has stated:

> Many appeals are docketed today only because of the severity of the sentence pronounced in the district court and since the appellate tribunal cannot tackle the real issue in a forthright manner, it may, and often does, in its endeavor to strike down a harsh penalty, give the law a strained construction liable to work havoc in future cases.

The primary objection to appellate review is that it might greatly increase litigation because review would become available for all those defendants who plead guilty—between 70 and 90 percent of all convicted offenders—and who are generally unable to obtain direct review of their convictions. And it is possible that the expanded availability of counsel would encourage many of these defendants to appeal their sentences. Jurisdictions permitting appellate review, however, have not experienced an unreasonable burden on the reviewing court. From 1960 through 1965 in Massachusetts, for example, there was an average of about 300 sentence appeals per year, and the review division sat for an average of 15 days a year. Judge Charles D. Breitel of the New York State Court of Appeals has estimated that although excessiveness of sentence is mentioned in about three-fourths of the criminal appeals heard in the Appellate Division of the Supreme Court, "this issue is seriously argued in very few, and . . . even then, little additional work is involved."

A second objection to appellate review is that sentencing is a discretionary matter involving questions of judgment and not of law such as appellate courts are used to handling. In view of the importance of sentencing to the defendant and to the effectiveness of the criminal processes it is unreasonable to consider sentencing as a matter of such exceptional discretion that it should be immune from appellate review. Appellate courts routinely are called upon to review discretionary rulings by trial judges in both civil and criminal cases. Appellate review is not an occasion for the appellate court to resentence the defendant to a punishment which it would have imposed had it been the trial court. The policy of the English Court of Criminal Appeal is that a sentence will be altered only when it represents such a substantial departure from the norm that the court is satisfied that the trial judge failed to apply the correct principles. Experience with appellate review of sentences indicates that appellate judges in this country have not substituted their discretion for that of the trial court.

A third objection is that appellate judges are less able to assess an appropriate sentence because of their inability to observe the defendant. But inability to observe the defendant, although relevant in determining the latitude of appellate review, does not place the reviewing court at a great disadvantage. In the majority of cases the trial court's confrontation of the defendant is extremely brief because no trial is held. And even when conviction follows a trial, the unusual and difficult circumstances facing a criminal defendant are not the most favorable for a fair assessment of his character.

3. *Counsel*

There is no longer any doubt that the right to counsel applies to the sentencing stage.[d] Counsel has traditionally concerned himself with trial, but there is much he can do at sentencing also.

MARTIN v. UNITED STATES
182 F.2d 225 (5th Cir. 1950)

[Martin was convicted of bank robbery and sentenced to fifteen years imprisonment. He was represented by counsel at trial, but counsel was not present at the time of sentencing.]

RUSSELL, Circuit Judge. The very nature of the proceeding at the time of imposition of sentence makes the presence of defendant's counsel at that time necessary if the constitutional requirement is to be met. There is then a real need for counsel. The advisability of an appeal must then, or shortly, be determined. Then is the opportunity afforded for presentation to the Court of facts in extenuation of the offense, or in explanation of the defendant's conduct; to correct any errors or mistakes in reports of the defendants' past record; and, in short, to appeal to the equity of the Court in its administration and enforcement of penal laws. Any Judge with trial Court experience must acknowledge that such disclosures frequently result in mitigation, or even suspension, of penalty. That it is also true that such discussion sometimes has a contrary result, does not detract from the fact that the nature and possibilities of this important stage of the proceedings are such as make the absence of counsel at this time presumably prejudicial.

---

[d] Mempa v. Rhay, 389 U.S. 128 (1967), reproduced at 942, *infra*.

The trial Court properly refused to order a new trial, but erred in failing to vacate the sentence. That judgment is reversed, and the cause remanded for imposition of the sentence of the Court upon the defendant in proceedings had with his counsel present.

4. Presentence Investigation

Where conviction follows a full trial or where a post-plea of guilty hearing is held, the judge may learn a substantial amount about the crime and the defendant, but neither may necessarily produce such significant sentencing information as the defendant's prior record, his social background, or his psychological makeup. Today the trial judge usually defers sentencing until he has received a presentence investigation report. In some jurisdictions use of the presentence investigation is mandatory, in others it is discretionary with the judge.[e] The nature and contents of presentence reports, the skill and training of the investigators, and the use made of these reports obviously have important bearing on the sentencing decision.

PRESENTENCE REPORT
Willow County Court
Johnstown, Wisconsin
Confidential Presentence Investigation

October 11, 1968

Defendant: Thomas Bales Rogers — Born: June 4, 1945 Age: 23
Court: Willow County, Branch #1 — Race: White Sex: Male
Prosecution: John R. Day — Judge: Hon. Ralph Tibbetts
Defense: Patrick H. Durmer
Offense: Injury By Conduct Regardless of Life — Plea: Not Guilty
Received for Investigation: Sept. 17, 1968 — Report Due: October 15, 1968

Present Offense: I, John R. Day, District Attorney, Willow County, hereby inform the court that on the 10th day of July

[e] The MODEL PENAL CODE § 7.07 (1962) would require a presentence investigation in all but minor cases.

in the year of 1968 at the said County of Willow, Wisconsin, the said defendant, Thomas B. Rogers, being then and there armed with a dangerous weapon, to wit: a loaded automatic pistol, did then and there maliciously and feloniously make an assault in and upon one Frank Jameson in a manner evincing a depraved mind regardless of human life, without any premeditated design to effect the death of said Frank Jameson, and under such circumstances that if death had resulted to him, the said Frank Jameson, he, the said Thomas Bales Rogers, would then and there have been guilty of murder in the second degree, contrary to section 940.23 and against the peace and dignity of the State of Wisconsin.

Rogers was stopped by police officer Jameson and arrested for a traffic violation. The police officer frisked the defendant and searched the automobile. The defendant had two guns. He shot the arresting police officer. The defense was based upon the contention that Jameson had attempted to shoot first, that his gun had jammed, and that the defendant had in fact been defending himself.

The defendant was found guilty by a jury and on September 14, 1968, the matter was referred to the Willow County Welfare Department for a presentence investigation.

Prior Record: The defendant has the following record of arrests on file in the Police Department of Johnstown in Willow County:

April 4, 1963	Assault Regardless of Life Age: 18	1-4 years (Wisconsin State Reformatory)
May 12, 1967	Disorderly Conduct (State) Age: 22	Placed on day-to-day calendar in the Willow County Court on June 16, 1967

The prior assault resulting in injury regardless of life took place on or about March 3, 1963. The defendant had become involved in an argument with a neighbor, Steven Richards, who lived in the vicinity of Rt. 1, Johnstown, where the defendant and his brother had a shack on property owned by the defendant's mother. Steven Richards claimed that the defendant had shot one of his ducks, and it appears that during the argument about this there was some assaulting of the defendant by Richards. The defendant, who had in his possession a .22 caliber rifle, aimed it at Richards. The defendant's brother, Donald Rogers, aged 14, knocked the gun down but the defendant raised it again and fired a shot. Steven Richards dropped to the ground, and the bullet struck Sidney Rolltree, who was also at the scene of the affair but apparently had not entered into the argument. The defendant pleaded not guilty, had a jury trial, and was found guilty.

On May 12, 1967, the defendant was in the County Court of Willow on a charge of Disorderly Conduct. This offense took place on or about May 8, 1967, when the defendant had a gun and threatened to shoot himself. Police were dispatched to the home at the request of his mother. He was examined at the Willow County Hospital and found not psychotic; appeared in the County Court on May 12 and the case was referred to probation authorities for a presentence investigation. Two weeks later the presentence investigator reported to the Court and recommended that probation be denied and that the defendant be committed to a mental hospital for more extensive mental examination and observation. Court records indicate that he was again examined by the psychiatrist attached to the court, Dr. Blackwell, and a week later the case was continued for cause for seven months. At the end of this time the case was placed on the day-to-day calendar of the Willow County Court.

Wisconsin State Reformatory Report: Records and files of the State Department of Public Welfare, Division of Corrections, indicate that on April 16, 1963, shortly after the defendant had been admitted to the Reformatory, the Guidance Department made an admission summary and progress report. A part of that report is as follows:

(a.) Ass't Sup't: Impressions and Disciplinary Prognosis:

"A very frail subject and very stubborn and resistive character who maintains innocence. He is bitter toward his younger brother and went so far as to write in a letter to his mother to get rid of his brother . . . and the gun that was used in the crime he now serves.

General Recommendations: Custody: Maximum. He will require full-time guidance and counseling."

(b.) Psychologist's Impressions:

Total I.Q.: 106. Indicates average intelligence. Verbal I.Q. 110, performance I.Q. 99. "This man is very naive, gullible and highly suggestive. At present he is anxious, depressed, and confused regarding his incarceration."

The WSR files and records further indicate that while at the WSR the defendant was very well adjusted and earned two additional months good time by working as a trustee outside the walls.

Parole Applications from WSR: The State Department records indicate that the defendant applied for parole after 13 months, but it was denied and was also denied after 19 months. After 24 months he again appeared before the Parole Board, at which time he was deferred four months. After 28 months the Parole Board denied his parole. However, the records indicate that following his deferment (after 24 months) the defendant informed his parole officer that he was no longer interested in parole and that he would serve his entire sentence. The defendant said his reason for refusing the parole was that "I'm afraid I couldn't keep it." The defendant further contended that parolees were generally harassed by the police.

Defendant's Background: The defendant's father, Samuel B. Rogers, now about 55 years of age, was born in Wisconsin, is a laborer by occupation, and has been employed for a number of years at the Wharton Milling Company. When he was about 40 years old, he was under observation at the Wisconsin General Hospital—"paranoid delusions." At one time he was addicted to the use of alcohol, but at age 35 he suffered a "nervous collapse" and as far as is known he has not overindulged in liquor since that time.

The defendant's mother, Laura (Thomas) Rogers, age 47, has been employed for a number of years at various dry cleaners in Johnstown.

The defendant's parents were married about 28 years ago in Mankato, Minnesota, one year after the first child was born. The family lived on a 10 acre piece of sandy land located about eight miles northwest of Rhinelander, from their marriage until 14 years later. This farm was not productive enough to support the family and consequently they were on the relief rolls of the County. Fourteen years ago, not long after the father's release from the mental hospital, the family moved to Johnstown in Willow County and has resided here continuously since that time. Seven years later the defendant's mother filed for divorce, which decree became final in 1962.

Family life was poorly organized and it appears that the children were subjected to the acrimony and abuse which accompanied the poor marital adjustment of the parents. The father is known to have often cursed at the children but at no time was he cruel to them. Most of his cruelty was directed to the wife. Following the divorce, the defendant's mother, Laura Rogers, has kept the family intact.

Siblings are as follows:

Mary, age 29, divorced, lives with the mother near Johnstown.
Frederick, age 25, married, two children.
Thomas (the defendant), age 23, single.
John, age 19, U.S. Navy.
Donald, age 17, single, lives at home.
Claudia, age 16, lives at home.
Phyllis, age 13, lives at home.
Kathleen, age 11, lives at home.
Ruth, age 9, lives at home.

Education and Religion: The defendant started school at the age of seven in a rural school in Glacier, Wisconsin and attended until he was nine, when the family moved to Johnstown. He then attended various public schools and completed the tenth grade at the Memorial High School. His school grades were below normal and he was considered an attendance and behavior problem.

The defendant's parents are Catholic but he was not baptized. He claims that he occasionally attends Protestant services.

Military: The defendant has been classified 4F by his draft board because of his record of felony convictions.

Marital: The defendant is single and lives at home.

Employment Record: The defendant's employment record is very poor and shows a lack of vocational objectives. Prior to his being committed to the Wisconsin State Reformatory in 1963 he worked as a newspaper carrier, at the Western Union, and the Olson Manufacturing Company. The defendant admits that since he has been released from the Reformatory he has not worked longer than two months for any one employer. He worked four weeks at the Flamo Furnace Company, about one month for a landscaper, and about one month for the Vista Sign Company.

Psychological Studies: After his first conviction for Assault Regardless of Life and prior to his commitment to the WSR, the defendant was studied for two weeks at a mental hospital. Dr. Pitt, who examined him at that time, reported as follows:

> Not psychotic; he is somewhat schizoid, somewhat anxious; some neurotic features.
>
> Total mental age of 14.9. Minnesota Multiphasic: High scores in area of psychopathic personality, closely followed by ratings on the depression scale and the hysteria scale indicating the presence of considerable anxiety and possible hysteria-conversion symptomology. Also scores high on the paranoid scale indicating a tendency toward paranoid ideation. All other findings within normal, including measures of validity and reliability. (A Rorschach Inventory at the same time confirmed previous findings of the Minnesota Multiphasic.)

After serving 18 months at the Wisconsin State Reformatory the defendant was examined by a private psychiatrist in the City of Green Bay, who reported as follows:

> He cannot get along with his age group nor can he get along with those in authority over him. He is more apt to increase in his attitudes of suspicion, resentment, and paranoia. There is no question about his showing the symptoms of an early paranoiac state.
>
> Diagnosis: Early paranoia with the recommendation that he be transferred to a mental hospital for psychotherapy treatment.

Thirteen months ago, following his conviction in the Willow County Court on a charge of Disorderly Conduct, the defendant was examined by Dr. Brown and Dr. Chickering. Dr. Brown reported as follows:

> I find this man is definitely psychotic, deficient in judgment, refused to accept the jurisdiction of the Court as being of any value, stating that he is held contrary to law, that no one has authority to require him to be on probation or to be placed in an institution. This he asserts positively and vehemently. I am now satisfied that he is definitely mentally ill.

Dr. Chickering reported as follows:

> I was unable to find any evidence of mental illness. There seemed to be much maladjustment and social conflict but

no evidence of disturbance of reality functioning. Impression: Sociopathic personality, without psychosis.

Summary and Recommendation: The defendant appears in this Court with one previous felony conviction. Records of the State Department of Public Welfare indicate that he has no interest in parole. Reports of various psychiatrists indicate that the defendant's mental condition is not normal. It is the impression of the Investigating Officer that he lacks insight, does not accept his guilt, possesses impaired judgment, does not realize the potential consequences of his conduct. He appears to be a poor probation risk because of his attitude toward probation and parole and general background, and law enforcement. I recommend incarceration for the maximum period (10 years) provided by law.

Richard L. Turgent, M.S.W.
Probation Officer

The presentence report has been customarily treated by probation workers as a confidential document to be shown to the judge alone and not revealed to the defendant or his counsel. The presentence investigation is designed as a diagnostic and prognostic evaluation of the offender in terms of his criminal behavior, his background, and his personality. In theory it is a neutral document, its purpose being neither adverse nor favorable to the sentencing fate of the defendant. It is intended accurately to reflect his educational, employment, and previous criminal records; a professional evaluation of such things as his relationship with his family, with peers and associates, and with authority; and a professional judgment of the type of community adjustment that he likely will make should he be released on probation. In theory the presentence report is prepared by persons of professional competence, typically trained social workers, who are as interested in information favorable to the defendant as they are in information unfavorable to him. It is felt by many social workers that this professional document should not be subject to the adversary process, for the investigating social worker is a professional and has to rely on information obtained from other persons to whom he has promised confidentiality.

There can be no doubt that the presentence report is a great aid to the judge in making an informal sentencing decision. It is possible, however, that the report may contain misinformation. Suggestions have been made that the offender ought to be apprised of at least the factual content of the presentence report—information such as previous record or employment history—and afforded an opportunity to challenge its accuracy. Social workers, as well as lawyers, are aware that inadvertent error can find its way into the most carefully prepared presentence report.

Illustrations from Presentence Investigation Reports

The following statements have been taken from various presentence social investigations. Some illustrate certain common practices, such as the use of hearsay and the reporting of rumors which, in carefully done reports, are clearly so labeled. Some illustrate a commitment of social investigators to do more than list factual data—to diagnose clients and to give professional assessment of their probable future behavior.

1

"While [the defendant] apparently never engaged in any serious criminal conduct before, and while he has never shown any tendency to use violence, it is rumored in the factory, and evidently widely believed, that about two years ago he murdered his boss's wife."

2

"Although it was never brought out in court, the little girl's mother told me that her daughter said [he] had a knife when he made the indecent overtures."

3

"His wife reports that he is given to murderous rages."

4

"In my opinion [as an experienced, graduate-trained probation and parole agent], he is the type of person who, if not checked soon, will kill somebody someday."

5

"There is a broad, deep base of sexual psychopathy in this boy. His offense may technically be burglary but he is basically a sex deviate."

6

"He is a loser, plain and simple. He is sexually inadequate, vocationally inadequate, and mentally inadequate. He has failed in everything—school, jobs, military service, with his family, and with his wife. He has even failed as a crook. There is absolutely no reason to think he can make it on probation and probably prison won't help him much. The only thing I can recommend is incarceration for as long as possible and then hope for the best."

7

"He is a nice looking, clean cut, all-American appearing young man. Beneath this, however, he is as cold as ice. He is an expert manipulator, playing one person against another, with an amazing ability to say just what he thinks you want to hear."

8

"He is pre-schizophrenic, paranoid type, who, at present, exhibits a high level of psychopathic behavior. He is potentially very dangerous."

9

"He is a follower, not a leader. He is passive, emotionally shallow, with characteristic hesitancy in his speech, a quiet voice, and flatness to everything he says. 'I want a hamburger' and 'I want to kill you' would, I am sure, be delivered with the same pitch and intensity. The chances are that if he is left alone or put with law-abiding people he will conform. If sufficiently provoked, or if influenced by stronger-willed troublemakers, he will violate."

STATE v. LECKIS

79 N.J. Super. 479, 192 A.2d 161 (1963)

Per Curiam. The report which was before the sentencing judge on June 30 falls far short of what a presentence report should be. It does not even qualify as a complete and definitive "Social Investigation" (so captioned). It first gives defendant's name, address, age (48) and birthday. The offense is then described as "Assault and Battery." Under "Previous Offenses" there is an entry of a nonsupport charge in another county in 1948, although there is nothing to show that defendant has ever been married or fathered a child. Completely uninformative is a notation that defendant was committed to the New Jersey State Hospital in 1948. The reason for the commitment is not stated, nor does the report indicate when defendant was discharged or his mental condition then or now. Under "Previous Offenses" there are also notations of disorderly conduct charges brought on October 8 and December 11, 1960, respectively resulting in 10-day and 30-day county jail sentences.

The major part of the report is devoted to the "Details of Offense." It is fairly obvious that these "details" were obtained from the prosecutor's file. There would be nothing essentially wrong with this were the source of the information given and, at the same time, defendant's version of what occurred laid before the judge. Preparation of a good presentence report requires that the probation department interview the accused as well as the accusers, summarizing their respective versions of the affair. The statement of witnesses is equally important, as is that of the official investigation. We find strong indications in the record suggesting that if defendant had been fairly interviewed by a probation department representative in whom he had some confidence, and the entire background of the occurrence disclosed, the degree of his offense might well have been tempered and his punishment proportionately lightened.

The rest of the report consists of a repetition of defendant's previous record, a very brief family history limited to the names, ages, religion and residence of his father, mother and sister, his claim that he was never married, the fact that defendant attended school only through eighth grade, his employment record, army service record, religion and a notation that in his leisure time he admits to drinking too much. There is little in the report that would give a judge an accurate idea of defendant's personal background—his mentality, personality, habits and the like—or of the family background which would give the case a meaningful setting.

So much depends upon the completeness and balanced presentation of a presentence report that anything less would fall short of providing the sentencing judge with the information he must have in order to impose a just sentence.

The concluding remarks of the trial judge before he imposed sentence go beyond the information contained in the presentence report and reflect what appears to be a personal familiarity with the incident and those who figured in it. The judge said, "You have been a nuisance for years. You drink too much. You fight too much." In passing sentence a judge should limit himself to what he has learned in the course of the trial or hearing before him, and the information officially and reliably recorded in the presentence report.

Reversed and remanded.

The presentence investigation report has traditionally been defined by those investigators who prepare it as a confidential document for the eyes of the judge alone to assist him in his sentencing task and not to be shown to the defendant or his counsel. In practice some judges allow some defendants to review all or part of the report prior to sentencing but in other cases, and with some judges in all cases, the report is withheld from the defendant. The trend toward at least partial disclosure seems to be growing.

There have been a number of recent attempts to modify strict presentence report confidentiality practices through proposals for new legislation or changes in court rules.

MODEL PENAL CODE § 7.07
American Law Institute
(Proposed Official Draft 1962)

(5) Before imposing sentence, the Court shall advise the defendant or his counsel of the factual contents and the conclusions of any pre-sentence investigation or psychiatric examination and afford fair opportunity, if the defendant so requests, to controvert them. The sources of confidential information need not, however, be disclosed.

MODEL SENTENCING ACT (1963)*
(National Council on Crime and Delinquency)

ARTICLE II. PRESENTENCE INVESTIGATIONS

§ 4. AVAILABILITY OF REPORT TO DEFENDANTS AND OTHERS

As to defendants sentenced under section 9 of this Act [relating to ordinary offenders], the judge may, in his discretion, make the investigation report or parts of it available to the defendant or others, or he may make the report or parts of it available while concealing the identity of persons who provided confidential information. As to defendants sentenced under section 5 or section 7 of this Act [relating to extended terms for dangerous offenders], the judge shall make the presentence report, the report of the diagnostic center, and other diagnostic reports available to the attorney for the state and to the defendant or his counsel or other representative upon request. Subject to the control of the court, the defendant shall be entitled to cross-examine those who have rendered reports to the court. Such reports shall be part of the record but shall be sealed and opened only on order of the court.

---

* The Model Sentencing Act is reproduced in 9 CRIME & DELINQUENCY 337 (1963). It is discussed in Flood, *The Model Sentencing Act,* 9 CRIME & DELINQUENCY 370 (1963).

PROPOSED REVISIONS AND ADOPTED DRAFT OF RULE 32(c) PRESENTENCE INVESTIGATION
Federal Rules of Criminal Procedure

(Proposed 1962)

(2) Report. The report of the presentence investigation shall contain any prior criminal record of the defendant and such information about his characteristics, his financial condition and the circumstances affecting his behavior as may be helpful in imposing sentence or in granting probation or in the correctional treatment of the defendant, and such other information as may be required by the court. *Upon request of the defendant the court before imposing sentence shall disclose to the defendant or his counsel a summary of the material contained in the report of the presentence investigation and afford an opportunity to the defendant or his counsel to comment thereon. The sources of confidential information need not, however, be disclosed.*

(Revised Proposal 1964)

(2) Report. The report of the presentence investigation shall contain any prior criminal record of the defendant and such information about his characteristics, his financial condition and the circumstances affecting his behavior as may be helpful in imposing sentence or in granting probation or in the correctional treatment of the defendant, and such other information as may be required by the court. *If the defendant is represented by counsel and so requests, the court before imposing sentence shall permit counsel for the defendant to read the report of the presentence investigation (from which the sources of confidential information may be excluded) and shall afford such counsel an opportunity to comment thereon. If the defendant is not represented by counsel and so requests, the court shall communicate, or have communicated, to the defendant the essential facts in the report of the presentence investigation (from which communication the sources of confidential information may be excluded) and shall afford the defendant an opportunity to comment thereon. Any material disclosed to the defendant or his counsel shall also be disclosed to the attorney for the government.*

(Adopted 1966)

(2) Report. The report of the presentence investigation shall contain any prior criminal record of the defendant and such information about his characteristics, his financial condition and the circumstances affecting his behavior as may be helpful in

imposing sentence or in granting probation or in the correctional treatment of the defendant, and such other information as may be required by the court. The court before imposing sentence may disclose to the defendant or his counsel all or part of the material contained in the report of the presentence investigation and afford an opportunity to the defendant or his counsel to comment thereon. Any material disclosed to the defendant or his counsel shall also be disclosed to the attorney for the government.

There is considerable opposition to disclosure.

A CORRECTIONAL ADMINISTRATOR'S VIEW OF THE MODEL SENTENCING ACT

By Sanger B. Powers

9 Crime and Delinquency 398, 401 (1963)

Presentence Disclosure Objectionable

The Model Act would require great reliance on the presentence investigation and on reports of the diagnostic facility. Few correctional or probation administrators (and few judges for that matter) will applaud Section 4 of the Act, which provides that, as to nondangerous defendants, "the judge may, in his discretion, make the investigation report or parts of it available to the defendant or others, or he may make the report or parts of it available while concealing the identity of persons who provided confidential information." The section further requires, with respect to defendants sentenced as dangerous offenders or after conviction of murder, that "the judge shall make the presentence report, the report of the diagnostic center, and other diagnostic reports available to the attorney for the state and to the defendant or his counsel or other representative upon request." Such provisions can only serve to dry up many sources of information and to reduce such reports to a mere recital of prior criminal involvement. Information contained in the confidential records of other social agencies and information which might be obtained from relatives or friends will not usually find its way into a presentence report that is not held confidential. Since at the time the information is solicited there is no assurance that the defendant will or will not qualify as a "dangerous" offender, all potential informants would have to be informed that the source of the information might be revealed to the defendant himself.

The resources used by the probation officer conducting the presentence investigation run a wide gamut—immediate family, relatives, friends, employers, clergy, schools, police, and other social agencies. If the information obtained from any of these resources will be revealed to the defendant or his attorney, the investigator is morally bound to so inform the person or agency from whom information is sought. Some will argue that this insures that the information will be factual, pertinent, and verifiable. On the other hand, the resource person may not be willing to supply the information sought if he feels it might be damaging to his personal relationship with the defendant. If the defendant were, in fact, "dangerous," fear of reprisal might well silence the informant if the information were not held confidential. In the case of the nondangerous offender, holding the source of information confidential would be of little help in those situations where information could have come from only one source. Further, the defendant's condition or situation at the time of sentencing may be such that he cannot properly understand, and in fact might be damaged by, certain information relating to his physical or mental condition or that of his family.

COMMENTS IN OPPOSITION TO THE PROPOSED AMENDMENT TO RULE 32 (1963)

(Memorandum to Advisory Committee on Federal Rules of Criminal Procedure)

By Ben S. Meeker, Chief U.S. Probation Officer
Northern District of Illinois

1. I do not believe there is any significant ground swell on the part of federal judges or defense attorneys in Federal Courts for a change of the Rules. In my opinion, the Rule as now stated which gives the Court adequate discretion to disclose information in the presentence report, when the court feels it is necessary or desirable, has proven to be a very adequate Rule. By way of documentation in more than fifteen years of association with this District Court, I can think of only two or three instances when there was any strong pressure exerted by defense counsel to review the findings of the presentence report. On the contrary, most defense lawyers in this district encourage their clients to cooperate fully with the probation office and are anxious to assist in providing information to the probation office which might be relevant to an understanding of the behavior and character of their clients.

By way of documentation, this year on April 24, at a meeting of the Illinois Probation-Parole Association which convened at the Aurora Hilton Hotel, attended by approximately two hundred probation and parole officers from all over the State of Illinois, four very prominent defense lawyers, all of whom have heavy practices in the Federal Court here, conducted a very stimulating seminar on probation and presentence practices.

All of these lawyers have had very extensive experience in working with probation officers, not only in this district but with other courts in this community, and although they touched on almost every aspect of the probation officer's work and the relationship of defense counsel to probation departments, the issue of disclosure was not once raised. Inasmuch as I am sure that these four defense lawyers are representative of their calling, it seemed to me quite significant that there was no anxiety or concern shown at all in their evaluation of probation and its current practices relative to disclosure. Since there were many controversial issues brought up at that session, I am certain that if there had been any real feeling about this particular issue, it would also have been thoroughly aired at this meeting.

2. Limitations on the discretion of federal judges should be avoided. I am opposed to mandatory sentences or any other encroachment upon the traditional discretion and the powers of the courts. I see this as a further effort to administratively limit what I believe to be an inherent value which should be given full discretion in all such matters. Appellate review seems to me to be adequate to regulate or handle any abuses of discretion.

3. Any influence which tends to limit the sources of information which may be of value to the sentencing, control and treatment of an offender should be avoided. A mandatory requirement that upon request a summary of information from the presentence investigation must be disclosed will, in my estimation, lead eventually to embarrassing situations with reference to sources and content of information contained in the report.

I do not believe the implications of this Rule in relation to sources of information have been adequately studied. For example, the federal probation office in Chicago has been for twenty years a member of the Welfare Council. As a member of the Welfare Council, our agency agrees to abide by certain professional standards in relation to the protection and use of information given it by other social agencies, medical clinics, psychiatrists, etc. Our membership also entitles us to join the Social Service Exchange. When we joined the Exchange, which as you know makes available information from other members of the Exchange, we signed an agreement that professional information secured from other social agencies will not be disclosed and will be used only to guide the probation office, the court, and the correctional institution in its treatment and control of the individuals.

If it becomes known that the federal courts are required to disclose confidential information which may relate to family conflict, infidelity, illegitimacy, insanity, and all other intimate and yet often pertinent information needed for the evaluation of the individual, I fear that we may lose our status in this community as a highly respected professional agency.

Although this is perhaps an extreme illustration, one of our reports was recently made available to a defense counsel and subsequently it was made a matter of record and filed with the Clerk of the Court. I am sure quite inadvertently, as far as the court was concerned, an enterprising newspaperman had access to the report and without our knowledge a rather lurid story later appeared in the press in which certain intimate details of the family composition, makeup, and some of the problems which had existed between that family and the Welfare Department were written up in the press. The information we had secured from the Welfare Department about this family was highly relevant to the disposition in this case, but the story was embarrassing, both to the probation office and to the Welfare Department. This is a prime example of the problem as we had to subsequently re-build our bridges with the caseworker of the agency who provided us with this information.

At present, we have free access to much of the information from mental hygiene clinics, from psychiatric facilities, family social agencies, and other valuable sources because there has never been any question of disclosure or unauthorized use of information which we provide the court or the institution. The problem of retaining certain confidence here is not merely that of protecting sources, but it is also protecting certain kinds of information which may be upsetting and embarrassing to the defendant.

For example, I recall a case in which the court handed the presentence investigation to defense counsel because the court felt there were certain kinds of information that the defense counsel should know about his client and I am sure the court did not contemplate that defense counsel would then call the defendant, his wife and son together during a recess of the hearing and read completely the presentence report to the family. In this report was detailed intimate material about marital and family relationships which proved extremely embarrassing to defense counsel as he read the report and he realized himself that this report had not been written in such a fashion that such disclosure could be made without upsetting his client and family.

4. Will not this Rule change result in a whole new set of procedures? It is my impression that insufficient research and thought have been given to the implications of the Rule change in terms of operational and procedural problems. Is the court prepared to set up rules and regulations to govern the controversies which inevitably develop if defense counsel begins to evaluate the presentence investigation material in terms of quasi rules of evidence? Will defense counsel be permitted to file briefs in answer to certain professional evaluations of the conduct, behavior, and character of the defendant? How can the sources of information be protected when the content of a statement is attacked? Once the foot is in the door will not there be a tendency for presentence reports to become semi-formal documents largely concerned with innocuous types of public data which provide very little interpretation, evaluation, or color to the personality and basic character of the individual?

5. Is the purpose of the Rule change to police the probation office? If so, I believe this ignores the logical approach to review and evaluation of presentence reports which is an administrative matter to be handled by the courts and the administrative office. If there is concern about the quality or content of presentence reports, they should strengthen their directives to the probation office concerning such matters rather than permitting open court disclosure to correct or regulate presentence practices. Disclosure will tend to strain relationships between probation officer and defendant.

6. It is one thing to disclose in a formal fashion an individual's social history and quite another to discuss such information informally with the defendant.

Rehabilitation usually commences with the onset of the presentence investigation. The probation officer is obligated throughout the period of visiting to acquaint the defendant with the general findings both positive and negative. The officer's interpretation of these findings is in the context of the total investigation during which the probation officer can exercise his professional skill and judgment in discussing the implications of marital discord, family problems, character defects, etc., without the hazard of open disclosure. Positive relationships often develop during the period of the presentence investigation which may be nullified by disclosure of information beyond the court or correctional setting.

THE PROBATION OFFICER INVESTIGATES 14 (1960)
By Paul W. Keve
(University of Minnesota Press)

The Long-Range View

If all probation officers were highly skilled professionals with time to do the job right on each investigation, it might be easier to say that it would be safe and perhaps even desirable to make reports regularly available to the defendants. At the same time, we are faced with the suggestion that the presence of an untrained, unskilled probation officer would argue all the more for a practice of disclosure, for in that case the defendant especially deserves the right to see and protect himself from what may be an inept report. This is a negative argument, however, and the more worthy course seems to be a continuing devotion to the principle of training highly competent probation officers whose work will not jeopardize but will seek the best interests of each defendant.

After considering all sides of the question, it must be my position here that privacy of the report, meaning denial of access to the defense, is still the best rule. One powerful support of this stand is the simple fact that the great majority of thoughtful persons on the bench and in social work hold this view. Undeniably there are many times when a skilled probation officer can disclose his report to the defendant with good effect, and it would certainly be desirable to permit this as an exceptional procedure when the probation officer and his judge see it as appropriate in the individual case. Meanwhile, until there is reason to think otherwise, it seems safest to let disclosure be the exceptional practice while the general rule should be that reports are private in the more conservative sense.

Whatever the merits of disclosure for accuracy and in the interest of fairness, opponents of disclosure point to the administrative problems which would be created if the presentence report could be challenged. They argue that in effect sentencing would become a second trial. This would not only delay proceedings but it would be a type of trial about issues which are not particularly clarified by the adversary process. While such factual material as employment history or previous criminal record could be improved in accuracy by challenge of any errors, diagnostic and evaluative material is not particularly amenable to cross-examination if it is to be truly frank and meaningful. There is fear that the social workers who prepare the reports would become unwilling to express their clinical judgments if these were to be subjected to what is perceived as insulting attack by defense counsel. The result, it is claimed, would be a sterile report containing merely a listing of easily verifiable facts such as work history and educational achievement, while evaluation and diagnosis—the most valuable contributions of the trained social worker and perhaps the most significant part of the report for the sentencing judge—would be missing.

In taking the position that confidentiality of the presentence report is properly a question of administrative policy, great reliance has been placed on the Supreme Court decision in *Williams v. New York.*[f] In that case the Court upheld imposition of the death penalty based on information in the presentence report concerning thirty burglaries other than the one which resulted in homicide and defendant's "morbid sexuality."

The decision was widely interpreted to mean that all presentence investigation information might properly be held confidential. There are, however, other views on the meaning of the case.

THE LAW OF CRIMINAL CORRECTION 98-101 (1963)
By Sol Rubin, Henry Weihofen, George Edwards & Simon Rosenzweig

§ 17. Williams v. New York

A United States Supreme Court case, Williams v. New York, is sometimes cited as standing for the proposition that the presentence report need not be disclosed to a defendant or his counsel, an erroneous interpretation to which those who believe this should be the rule are prone. The case actually stands for a quite different rule—that under the particular statute existing at the time, a defendant is not entitled to confront and cross-examine persons who provided information for the presentence investigation report.

At the time of sentence the question of availability of the report to the defendant was not at issue. The defendant had been told by the bench some of the content of the report and had not made a demand for any other information in it. The question of access was not raised on the appeal. Throughout the Supreme Court's opinion the issue is confrontation and cross-examination, not access to the report itself. . . .

---

[f] 337 U.S. 241 (1949). Fourteen years later Williams obtained his release by habeas corpus on the ground that his confession, the principal evidence at his trial, was coerced. United States *ex rel.* Williams v. Fay, 323 F.2d 65 (2d Cir. 1963).

[The issue is clearly defined:] confrontation and cross-examination, not access by defendant to the report. Furthermore, other comments in the opinion suggest that the Court would regard denial of access to the report as a violation of due process: "The accuracy of the statements made by the judge as to appellant's background and past practices were not challenged by appellant or his counsel, nor was the judge asked to disregard any of them or to afford appellant a chance to refuse or discredit any of them by cross-examination or otherwise." This not only makes it clear that defendant's access to the report was never an issue, but also suggests that perhaps a substantial question would have been raised *if* the defendant had asked the trial judge to disregard some of the findings or afford him a chance to refute or discredit any of the statements.

. . .

The Supreme Court has not dealt with the question of due process involved in a defendant's request to inspect the presentence report and denial of the request by the judge who then passed sentence on the basis of the report. In the light of some of the comments it made in the Williams case ("The accuracy of the statements made by the judge as to appellant's background and past practices were not challenged by appellant or his counsel," and so forth) and in view of the Court's record on due process and the right to access of information in criminal cases, as well as the general test of fairness, the Court—should the question be raised squarely—might well be expected to decide that the defendant has a right to see the report and that denial, . . . is a cause of reversal.[g]

The decision was widely hailed as a major milepost in the effort of the social work profession to obtain recognition of their expertise.[h] The Court said:[i]

> Under the practice of individualizing punishments, investigational techniques have been given an important role. Probation workers making reports of their investigations have not been trained to prosecute but to aid offenders.

---

[g] In Specht v. Patterson, 386 U.S. 605 (1967), the Court distinguished *Williams v. New York,* holding that one committed for an indefinite term under a Sex Offenders Act in a proceeding characterized as "the making of a new charge" was entitled to confront witnesses against him, to cross-examine, and to offer evidence of his own. Failure of the Sex Offenders Act to provide such safeguards made it deficient in due process.

[h] The similar strivings of the police profession, and the acknowledgment of police expertise in *Terry v. Ohio,* have already been referred to.

[i] Williams v. New York, 337 U.S. 241, 249-50 (1949).

Their reports have been given a high value by conscientious judges who want to sentence persons on the best available information rather than on guess-work and inadequate information. To deprive sentencing judges of this kind of information would undermine modern penological procedural policies that have been cautiously adopted throughout the nation after careful consideration and experimentation.

Reference Note

Opposition to disclosure of the presentence report is well stated in Hincks, *In Opposition to Rule 32(c)(2), Proposed Federal Rules of Criminal Procedure,* 8 FED. PROB. 3 (Oct.-Dec. 1944). *See also* Note, *Employment of Social Investigation Reports in Criminal and Juvenile Proceedings,* 58 COLUM. L. REV. 702 (1958); Roche, *The Position for Confidentiality of the Presentence Investigation Report,* 29 ALBANY L. REV. 206 (1965); P. KEVE, THE PROBATION OFFICER INVESTIGATES chs. 1, 2 (1960). The Keve book presents in addition a very thorough analysis of how to prepare a professional report.

For views favoring disclosure of the presentence report, see P. TAPPAN, CRIME, JUSTICE AND CORRECTION 558 (1960); Note, *Right of Criminal Offenders to Challenge Reports Used in Determining Sentence,* 49 COLUM. L. REV. 567 (1949); Note, *Criminal Law—Presentence Investigation—Right of Confrontation,* 41 N.C.L. REV. 260 (1963). In S. RUBIN, H. WEIHOFEN, G. EDWARDS & S. ROSENZWEIG, THE LAW OF CRIMINAL CORRECTION ch. 3 (1963), the authors argue that prisoners will be more likely to understand and accept their sentences if they have had an opportunity to read their presentence reports.

Wyzanski, *A Trial Judge's Freedom and Responsibility,* 65 HARV. L. REV. 1281, 1291 (1952), urges that, as a matter of fair play, the sentencing judge should never take into account any evidence, fact, or report that is not brought to the attention of the defendant. This is a much quoted article.

Thomsen, *Confidentiality of the Presentence Report: A Middle Position,* 28 FED. PROB. 8 (Mar. 1964), suggests that a two-part report be used—a factual part which is disclosed and a confidential part which evaluates the defendant and makes recommendations.

Sharp, *The Confidential Nature of Presentence Reports,* 4 CATHOLIC U.L. REV. 127 (1955), presents an analysis of the legal and professional issues in the confidentiality controversy by the former chief of the Federal Probation Service.

C. CHOICE OF SENTENCE—OBJECTIVES AND PRESSURES

PRELIMINARY REPORT OF THE GOVERNOR'S SPECIAL COMMITTEE ON CRIMINAL OFFENDERS 29-30 (1968) (New York)

The objectives of the criminal treatment system are to prevent crime and to prevent public unrest that stems from failure of government to demonstrate a determination to uphold certain standards of conduct (*i.e.,* prevention of anomie). The system comprises all functions from and including sentencing through parole; and it carries out its objectives as follows:

1. By administering sanctions that have a sufficient degree of unpleasantness to (a) demonstrate to the public at large that the threats annexed to prohibitions cannot be ignored without consequences (*i.e.,* general deterrence), and
(b) reinforce the confidence of the public in the fact that the state is determined to uphold norms, through a demonstration of action taken against wrongdoers (*i.e.,* prevention of anomie); and

2. By preventing recidivism through the use of sanctions as a vehicle for administering (a) rehabilitative techniques to bring offenders to the point where they will voluntarily observe the prohibitions set forth in the criminal law, and
(b) preventive force through incarceration or close community supervision of the offender so as to limit his opportunity to offend again, and
(c) punishment to make the threats a reality to the individual offender so that he will be more responsive to them in the future (*i.e.,* individual deterrence).

Variations in the type of sentencing structure may serve some purposes to the exclusion of others. For example, sentencing provisions which require all offenders to be incarcerated up to a statutory maximum may serve the purpose of providing for the maximization of in-prison treatment and therapy. At the same time, of course, the fixed sentencing system does not enable the judge to distinguish between offenders by their degree of criminal involvement or by the intensity of community reaction to their offenses. Judicial discretion to fix sentences allows the trial judge to do this but may result in an increase in sentence disparity which militates against rehabilitation by its seeming unfairness. Authorities have a hard time explaining to one offender why he received a ten-year sentence whereas another inmate convicted of the same offense is serving only a two-year term.

It is often assumed that long minimum sentences for certain offenses have a deterrent effect. This is a debatable proposition in itself, and long minimum sentences prevent correctional authorities from releasing an offender at the point where he is most ready to return to the community. The resolution of these and of other competing objectives in sentencing remains a major problem of current concern.

In their sentencing, judges give expression to a wide range of objectives and respond to various pressures.

The Practice

1

In sentencing a narcotics addict the judge explained, "For your own protection I am forced to send you into a period of confinement, so that you will be able to lose the habit of taking narcotics. You may then become a worthwhile citizen. I sentence you to from one to five years in the state prison."

2

Two elderly, shabbily dressed women were brought before the court, charged with drunkenness. The probation officer indicated to the judge that these two women had no place to go and were not well. The judge sentenced them to thirty days in the house of corrections, saying that they would be better off there than on the street.

3

A man was charged with being drunk and entered a plea of guilty. The defendant said that this was his first offense. The arresting officer described the man's belligerency and his resistance to arrest. The judge said that he would ordinarily suspend sentence in a case like this were it not for the difficulties with the officer. The judge asked how much money the defendant had, and he replied, "$30." The judge said, "All right, $30 or 30 days."

4

A twenty-year-old man was in court for the first time on a charge of possessing narcotics. Ordinarily the judge would have put a first offender on probation. During the trial the judge noticed that a group of young men were in the courtroom.

During a recess he asked one of the detectives who the men were. The detectives told him they were members of a gang and the defendant was their leader. This decided the judge to impose a jail sentence.

5

A 25-year-old woman was charged with vandalism in breaking a window of a house bought by a Negro family in a white neighborhood. This was one of a series of acts by whites against the family. The judge imposed a ten-day jail sentence, saying "This sort of thing is going to stop. I want you to tell all your friends what happens here."

6

A man with a long narcotics record was arrested for sale of narcotics to a police undercover agent. He immediately expressed a desire to "do himself some good." He helped the police set up a case against his supplier. As a result he was charged with possession rather than sale, and the judge, having been informed privately that the informer had been responsible for making an important case, imposed a very light sentence.

IMPROPER PENALTY
Milwaukee Journal Editorial, Apr. 20, 1964

Since when should a defendant be penalized for insisting upon his constitutional right to a trial by jury?

County Judge F. Ryan Duffy, Jr., indicated that was what he was doing, in part, when he passed sentence Friday on the 16 persons arrested last fall for their civil rights sit-in demonstration at city hall. A jury found them guilty of disorderly conduct. Their leader, John H. Givens, Jr., had demanded the jury procedure.

In fining Givens twice as much as the others and levying costs against him, too, the judge remarked upon his being the leader and also upon his demand for the jury. The leadership role was a fair distinction; the jury demand was irrelevant.

Of course, jury trials are more time consuming for the courts and more expensive for the taxpayers. But the right to trial by jury exists. Defendants must not be either intimidated out of exercising it or penalized for doing so.[j]

---

[j] *Cf.* United States v. Jackson, 390 U.S. 570 (1968), holding the federal kidnapping statute invalid insofar as it allowed the death penalty only upon recommendation of the jury, thus inducing defendants to waive jury trial.

SENTENCING STRUCTURE: ITS EFFECT UPON SYSTEMS FOR THE ADMINISTRATION OF CRIMINAL JUSTICE

By Lloyd E. Ohlin & Frank J. Remington

23 Law and Contemporary Problems 495, 500-03 (1958)

[T]he agencies of criminal justice administration . . . may evaluate sentencing structures not primarily in terms of their suitability with regard to the objectives of rehabilitation, deterrence, and community reassurance, but rather in terms of whether they facilitate the principal task of maintaining a relatively expedient, economical system. There is sufficient variation among the way the police, the prosecutor, and the trial court view their primary function to warrant a brief description of each.

Function of the Police and Its Relation to Sentencing

The average police officer is under terrific administrative pressure to clear known offenses by arrest and conviction. This pressure can be met short of influencing the sentence which may be imposed upon offenders following conviction, for police efficiency is measured largely in terms of offenses cleared by arrest and percentage of convictions. Accordingly, arrest and conviction have long since come to be considered the primary police objectives in handling offenders, and no systematic effort has been made to correlate successful police work with the type and length of sentence imposed, or even to keep information concerning sentences. The policeman, therefore, is not likely to think of a sentence in relation to its appropriateness for the particular offender or to think explicitly about the effect of sentencing upon general deterrence or community reassurance.

Reinforcing this attitude is the fact, too, that in the large department, the number of offenders processed is so great that an individual police officer does not develop a continuing interest in specific offenders. The single exception is the highly-specialized unit which deals with specific kinds of offenses, such as those associated with narcotics, which are very serious in nature, where the investigation task is difficult, and where offenders are likely to be recidivists. Here, there may, indeed, be a specific police objective of lengthy incarceration, since the specialized unit may consider premature release of the offender back into the community as making more difficult their job.

. . .

Function of the Prosecutor and Its Relation to Sentencing

Although the prosecutor is more likely to assess the adequacy of a sentence in relation to the particular offender, it is, nonetheless, true that most urban prosecutors' offices assume that only a small minority of cases will have to be tried. If all cases had to be formally adjudicated, the size of the prosecutor's staff would have to be greatly increased. There is, consequently, strong pressure to operate the system in such a way as to induce most offenders to plead guilty, thus obviating the need for full preparation and presentation of most cases.

To induce pleas of guilty typically requires real or apparent sentencing concessions. If the judge has discretion and offenders believe that he is willing to give lighter sentences to those who plead guilty, there may be such pleas to "on-the-nose-charges" filed by the prosecutor. If, however, the judge does not have discretion—as is the case where there is a fixed maximum term, for example—pressure may be exerted upon the prosecutor to make concessions by accepting a plea of guilty to a reduced charge carrying a lesser penalty.

Since this practice, to some extent, relieves court congestion, the prosecutor may be expected to have the sympathetic understanding and support of the trial judge, who is not likely to be dissatisfied so long as he considers the sentence for the lesser offense to be adequate punishment for the conduct involved. In this assessment, he is likely to rely upon his understanding of the prevailing parole practice relating to time of release. For example, suppose the mandatory maximum term for armed robbery is ten years, the mandatory maximum term for unarmed robbery is five years, and armed robbers are usually paroled after having served four years. The trial judge in this situation will probably be quite satisfied with the reduction practice, since the offender will get out in four years whether convicted of armed or unarmed robbery, and he can be convicted of unarmed robbery without the time and expense of a trial. This assumes, of course, that the parole board will treat the case on its facts rather than according to the offense of which the person was convicted, although there is reason to believe that this may not necessarily be so.

Function of the Trial Court and Its Relation to Sentencing

It is obvious that a trial court must consider adjudication its central responsibility. It is not so obvious, however, that it ought to consider sentencing less important. But if sentencing can be handled in such a way as to facilitate adjudication, this would be undesirable only if the concessions necessary to induce a high percentage of pleas of guilty were to result in a sentencing practice which did not meet the objectives of rehabilitation, deterrence, and community reassurance, as those objectives are conceived by the particular system. It is important for a trial judge to avoid court congestion, particularly of the criminal docket, for congestion may require long-term incarceration of some persons awaiting trial, an evil to be avoided even at the risk of other social hazards.

The inducements offered by the trial court to plead guilty may vary. In some systems, an offender may be told the sentence he will receive if he pleads guilty, thus allowing him to decide in full possession of all of the facts. It seems likely that this can induce pleas of guilty, however, only if it is assumed that the consequence of a plea of not guilty will be a heavier sentence. A less obvious way is the maintenance of a system where the common assumption of offenders is that a plea of guilty will result in sentencing concessions. And in this connection, many, if not most, judges make explicit their view that it is appropriate to reduce a sentence in return for a plea of guilty, because of the resultant contribution to the efficient and economical administration of the law.

DISCUSSION AT PILOT INSTITUTE ON SENTENCING
26 F.R.D. 231, 285
(Boulder, Colorado 1959)

The Effect of a Plea of Guilty upon Sentence

The first issue raised was whether a defendant who is willing to plead guilty ought to receive a lighter sentence than he would receive if he pleads not guilty and puts the government to the expense of trial. There were at least three different views expressed: (1) The willingness to plead guilty ought not to have any independent significance in sentencing; (2) The willingness to plead guilty may have sentencing significance depending upon the total circumstances of the case; (3) Giving a shorter sentence to those who plead guilty is both appropriate and practically necessary in order to achieve the proper administration of criminal justice particularly in congested urban districts.

Judge Alfred A. Arraj expressed the view that it is not proper for the courts to suggest to defendants in any way that they will do better if they plead guilty. He said:

"I think it is almost dishonest to suggest to a man that he can bargain with the court and that he can come in and plead guilty and be treated better. In my district we believe positively that a man has a constitutional right to a trial by jury. Statistics show that we try more cases percentage-wise than most other districts.

This is because we do not get as high a percentage of pleas of guilty. I do not want to participate in any program where a court uses a big club over persons accused of a crime and in effect says to them if you come in and plead guilty I will treat you well. Rather we emphasize to each defendant his right to a trial by jury asking him whether he understands his right and whether counsel has instructed him on his right to trial by jury. It may be that it is proper for enforcement agencies to urge defendants to plead guilty, but in my judgment it is not proper for the court to become a party to such a proceeding."

. . .

Judge George H. Boldt expressed an intermediate view, to the effect that the willingness to plead guilty may or may not have sentencing significance depending upon the facts of the individual case. He said:

"I do not consider whether a man pleads guilty or not guilty in fixing sentence, since I am of the opinion that he has a right under the constitution of the United States to plead not guilty. The only concern I have in this respect is that after hearing the evidence in a 5-day trial I may feel less leniently disposed toward the defendant than if he were before me for less than a half hour at the time of sentencing. . . .

"I do not think any judge here would hold it against the defendant if he demanded a trial and presented a reasonable defense, either on the government's failure of proof or otherwise. On the other hand, if the defendant presents a fraudulent defense, or adds perjury to his other crimes, I think it ought to be considered in determining his sentence."

A number of judges took the position that it was proper to reflect the willingness to plead guilty in a less severe sentence than would otherwise be imposed. . . .

Judge William J. Campbell expressed a similar view:

"In a large metropolitan court it would be impossible to keep abreast of the large number of criminal cases if it were not generally known among the practicing bar that consideration is given to those who are willing to plead guilty."

. . .

A similar view was expressed by Judge Robert L. Taylor:

"I favor the view that some consideration should be given the defendant in an income tax case who pleads guilty. I do not mean to say that a person who pleads not guilty should be penalized for demanding a trial, provided that he does not engage in perjury. This view is strengthened by experience in my court where I have had only seven income tax cases. According to my memory I have tried five cases involving considerable money. Two of them resulted in acquittal and three in mistrials. In other words, juries in Eastern Tennessee do not readily convict for this offense. Two other cases involved pleas of guilty. Certainly this willingness, under the circumstances, ought to be reflected in sentencing those who do plead guilty."

Finally Judge Randolph H. Weber's position is that sentencing consideration can be given to those who plead guilty without the court engaging in bargaining with criminal defendants:

"I think we are using inappropriate phraseology when we talk of an 'implied threat' by the Court. A Court can justifiably take the manner of disposition of the case into account in passing sentence. Take the example of two defendants charged with the same offense and one pleads guilty and the other stands trial. One, in effect, says: 'I admit my crime, I stand repentant and place myself upon the mercy of the Court.' The other, in effect, says: 'I invoked every right the law afforded, took my chance, was found guilty and I now stand before you, unrepentant, yet asking the leniency of the Court.' If the sentencing judge believes both to be guilty, hasn't he discriminated against the confessing defendant if both receive the same sentence? Therefore, I believe it is a logical and fair conclusion for a Court to reach when the judge shows more leniency to one who confesses his crime and disposes of his case without cost or consumption of the time of the Court. However, I do not think the Court should ever bargain with defendants or counsel, nor should the United States Attorney be informed that any concession will be made to those who plead guilty. The Court's practice will soon be found out without the Court making a statement of policy. The policy of stiffer sentences to those who stand trial, in the more congested districts at least, will help to solve some of the problems of that congestion. Yet, it is not a 'threat' but is merely one of the factors which should be taken into consideration in reaching a proper sentence and the Court still retains the authority to withhold or grant leniency."

STANDARDS RELATING TO PLEAS OF GUILTY 36-37, 51-52 (1967)
A.B.A. Project on Minimum Standards for Criminal Justice

1.8 Consideration of plea in final disposition.

(a) It is proper for the court to grant charge and sentence concessions to defendants who enter a plea of guilty or nolo contendere when the interest of the public in the effective administration of criminal justice would thereby be served. Among the considerations which are appropriate in determining this question are:

(i) that the defendant by his plea has aided in ensuring the prompt and certain application of correctional measures to him;

(ii) that the defendant has acknowledged his guilt and shown a willingness to assume responsibility for his conduct;

(iii) that the concessions will make possible alternative correctional measures which are better adapted to achieving rehabilitative, protective, deterrent or other purposes of correctional treatment, or will prevent undue harm to the defendant from the form of conviction;

(iv) that the defendant has made public trial unnecessary when there are good reasons for not having the case dealt with in a public trial;

(v) that the defendant has given or offered cooperation when such cooperation has resulted or may result in the successful prosecution of other offenders engaged in equally serious or more serious criminal conduct;

(vi) that the defendant by his plea has aided in avoiding delay (including delay due to crowded dockets) in the disposition of other cases and thereby has increased the probability of prompt and certain application of correctional measures to other offenders.

(b) The court should not impose upon a defendant any sentence in excess of that which would be justified by any of the rehabilitative, protective, deterrent or other purposes of the criminal law because the defendant has chosen to require the prosecution to prove his guilt at trial rather than to enter a plea of guilty or nolo contendere.

COMMENTARY

Section 1.8(b)

. . .

It has been contended, of course, that if any disparity exists between the defendant who stands trial and other defendants, the former has received excessive punishment. Comment, 66 YALE L.J. 204, 220 (1956). That view is rejected here. The Advisory Committee believes that there is an essential difference between sytem *A,* in which defendants who go to trial receive the greatest punishment justifiable under accepted principles of penology and some defendants who plead guilty or *nolo contendere* receive something less because of the circumstances surrounding their plea, and system *B,* in which disparity results from giving defendants who stand trial greater punishment than can be justified.

D. CHOICE OF SENTENCE—IMPRISONMENT OR RELEASE IN THE COMMUNITY

1. Probation

Probation (*i.e.,* suspension with supervision) is the most common form of sentence. It is widely used, and increasingly so, in most states for both major and minor criminal offenses. In some jurisdictions certain serious offenses like murder, armed robbery, and sale of narcotics are defined as nonprobationable by the legislature. In other jurisdictions all offenders are eligible for probation at the discretion of the sentencing judge although, in practice, conviction of homicide or of other serious crime almost inevitably means imprisonment.

In making the probation determination, the judge often relies heavily on the presentence report and, in some cases, upon the recommendation of the social worker who makes this report. In addition, he may request a recommendation as to probation or incarceration from the prosecuting attorney or even from the police. Recommendations of these latter agencies are often the basis of plea bargaining. Ultimately, however, the judge is responsible for the sentencing decision within whatever bounds are set by legislation.

Probation implies more than merely a suspended sentence; it requires supervision of the defendant by a probation officer who, along with the court and sometimes along with the legislature, has authority to set conditions and rules for the probationer where he is serving sentence.

In some states, supervision may be minimal where probation agents are untrained or have such large caseloads that any effective attempt at individualization of treatment is lacking. In other jurisdictions, probation agents are trained professional social workers and have small enough caseloads to make supervision more than merely a record keeping device. Even in the most highly professional correctional agencies, however, the shortage of professional personnel has resulted in the employment of agents with less educational background than the master's degree in social work which is considered ideal.

Probation is often confused with parole but as the terms are used here they are distinct. A person on parole has served some of his sentence in a correctional institution and has been released for community supervision prior to expiration of the maximum term. In contrast, the probationer is immediately placed under community supervision at sentencing and does not serve any time in a correctional institution. There are some minor variations. In the federal sentencing system, for example, trial judges are authorized to impose "split sentences," under which the defendant may spend up to six months in jail (not prison) followed by a period of probation. And some states allow "daytime parole" under provisions similar to Wisconsin's Huber Law whereby the prison inmate is allowed to work at his regular job during the day and is locked up only at night.

Probation is widely used in jurisdictions with competent, professional correctional services. There are a number of reasons for this. Probation has proved to be a more desirable and effective method of rehabilitating many offenders than incarcerating them in the artificial society of the prison. It allows the offender to maintain family and employment ties and to learn to meet his problems in the real world of the community rather than in the confined society of the prison. Recidivism is much lower for probation populations than for parolees, although the initial selective factor accounts for much of this. To some extent, although admittedly less so than incarceration, probation serves whatever punitive or deterrent objectives the court may have in sentencing. Conditions of probation can be as stringent as required by the personality and risk probability of the particular person. It is not merely judicial leniency; it is a very real sentence. Furthermore, probation is a far less expensive method of treatment than incarceration. Basic state costs, not counting such things as loss of tax revenue from prisoners, welfare expenses to support their families during imprisonment, and the like, are only about a tenth as much for a probationer as for an inmate. It is becoming apparent that most states are unable and unwilling to build correctional facilities to hold all persons convicted of serious crimes in the growing population. It is likely that the use of probation will continue to increase markedly and that present correctional structures will be used increasingly to care for only the most serious and chronic criminal violators.

PRESENTENCE REPORT[k]
United States District Court
Northern District of Illinois
Office of the Probation Officer

Honorable Raymond Pinder — Docket No. 60 CR 83
Disposition 6-19-60

Name: James Ciccio
Address: 36 Rosita Road, Metro, Ill.
Age: 50, born 5-18-10
Sex: Male
Race: White

Citizenship: U.S. Native Born
Marital Status: Married
Number of Dependents: Two
Offense: Income Tax Evasion, In violation of Section 7201, Title 26, U.S. Code. (1 count)

Offense: On January 26, 1960, the defendant, James Ciccio, was named in a four-count indictment by the January 1960 Grand Jury, charging that the subject had evaded over $15,000 in Federal Income Tax for the years 1953 through 1956.

Mr. Ciccio was arrested in Chicago on January 27, 1960, and released on $1,000 bond that same date.

On March 6, 1960, subject appeared before Your Honor and entered a plea of guilty to Count II of the Indictment (Evasion of $4,945.49 in taxes for 1954). Counts I, III, and IV relating to 1953, 1955, and 1956 were dismissed. The cause was referred to the Probation Office for a presentence investigation and disposition was set for June 19, 1960.

Details of the Offense: During the years in question (1953-1956), the defendant owned and operated a gravel pit, excavating business and farm in the Metro, Illinois area. He also engaged in real estate development and sale, purchasing land and subdividing. Mr. Ciccio operated and managed his own business affairs and made the entries in all his records. He personally figured his bids and operated most of his own equipment which consisted of heavy equipment. His tax returns were prepared by a Township Official from information furnished by the defendant

---

[k] This presentence report is of an actual federal case, with names and places changed. It has been used in federal sentencing institutes as a basis for discussing when probation is appropriate—a chronically difficult issue for judges in income tax cases. Relevant federal sentencing provisions are found in Appendix C. For an analysis of the way federal judges determined sentence in this case, see Remington & Newman, *The Highland Park Institute on Sentence Disparity,* 26 Fed. Prob. 3 (Mar. 1962).

on looseleaf sheets on which he listed total income by months. He listed all receipts personally and said he computed monthly income by adding deposits listed in his bank account deposit book. Expenses were allegedly computed by summarizing his checks. However, not all receipts were deposited and not all deposits were, in fact, recorded or the records submitted to the individual preparing the defendant's tax returns. Because of the incomplete records, investigating Internal Revenue Agents found it necessary to repeatedly resort to third party records.

The defendant reported only part of his total income from every one of many moneymaking enterprises. It became obvious that the defendant wilfully and consistently understated his income. The magnitude of the falsity is shown in the tables below:

AMOUNTS INVOLVED

Year	*Reported Income*	*Net Income Corrected*
1953	$ 2,023.60*	$27,579.00
1954	5,779.87	22,045.56
1955	2,690.49*	15,515.53
1956	7,518.86	13,179.36
Totals	$18,012.82	$78,319.45

*Adjusted Gross Income.

TAX

Year	*Reported*	*Corrected*	*Additional*
1953	$ 60.71*	$ 6,937.68	$ 6,876.97
1954	686.38**	4,945.49	4,243.41
1955	84.71*	2,835.37	2,750.66
1956	930.52	2,238.88	1,308.36
Totals	$1,778.08	$16,957.42	$15,179.40

* Self-employment tax only.

** $702.08 was reported due to mathematical error, and this amount was reduced to $686.38 and the difference refunded.

Other evidence which may infer that Mr. Ciccio knew the figures he submitted were inaccurate include the fact that he did not report any deposits to his farm bank account in two of the years—1953 and 1954. Such deposits included approximately $8,000 in receipts from sales. From the large amount of the sales deposits it is inferable that subject knew of the fact of their deposit and knew that they were not reflected in the figures submitted to the accountant. During the entire period in question certain deposits to the general account were not recorded by the taxpayer in the monthly records which he submitted to the accountant. Defendant also failed to inform his accountant of rental income and stated to him that the figures he submitted represented all his receipts. This also indicates wilfulness.

In another instance, Mr. Ciccio cashed checks at a bank other than the Metro Bank, where he had an account, and did not report these. He stated that these checks were cashed for the benefit of John Taber, then Mayor of Metro, and the proceeds rebated to Taber by subject.

Mr. Ciccio claimed that 10% of the receipts for work he performed for the city were also rebated to Taber. Taber denied receipt of any rebates. There were, however, some questionable items which indicate that subject may have been telling the truth, although this is not entirely substantiated.

In another instance, Mr. Ciccio deposited money to the general account, but did not report this to his accountant. His defense was that he probably did not have his passbook with him at the time the deposits were made and since he took his receipts from the deposit book, these receipts were inadvertently omitted. Unreported deposits total approximately $36,000. Needless to say, it is most incredible that subject would be inadvertent with respect to $36,000.

Mr. Ciccio cooperated with investigating Internal Revenue Agents to the extent of admitting, upon receipt, such records as he said were available. He has sent a check dated 6-10-60 in the amount of $20,255.55 to the Internal Revenue Department to cover the amount of principal and interest in the indictment.

Defendant's Statement to the Probation Officer: Although admitting the tax evasion as charged, Mr. Ciccio seeks to create the impression that the evasion was not wilful. He represents himself as a hard working and honest, albeit administratively ignorant, laborer. For instance, relating to the farm he bought and subdivided, Mr. Ciccio says he failed to report the income as he regarded this as re-investing in the farm. He also feels he was forced to kick back money to the ex-mayor of Metro in order to obtain city business. The defendant feels that he is being made "the goat." He says that he was "picked on" by the Government as an example. On the other hand, Mr. Ciccio also appeared deeply shamed by the effect of this prosecution on his family and his reputation.

Prior Arrest Record: None, either as an adult or juvenile.

Family History:

Father: Mario Ciccio was born in Italy and died at the age of 59 of cancer in Metro, Illinois. He was a farmer with a fourth grade education.

Mother: Mary Ciccio, age 70, was born in Kankakee, Illinois and lives at 410 Hill Street, Metro, Illinois. She has a sixth grade education. She lives with and is largely supported by the defendant's sister, Helen Bernstein.

Sister: Helen Bernstein, age 53, (born 4/15/07) lives with the defendant's mother. She completed high school, has about a year of business college and works as a practical nurse. She is divorced and has no children.

Sister: Marie Inman, age 51, (born 11/30/09) lives with her husband Tom and their daughter at 110 Rosita Road, Metro, Illinois. She has a tenth-grade education and works as a cleaning woman at a local hospital. Her husband is a factory worker.

Sister: Judith Hudson, age 41, (born 10/12/19) lives with her husband Alex and their six children at 1826 Monroe Street, Metro, Illinois. She completed high school. Mr. Hudson is a truck driver for the Texaco Oil Co.

Sister: Norma Howard, age 41, is Judith's twin. She, her husband and their seven children live at Route 3, Willow Road, Lincoln, Illinois. She completed high school. Mr. Howard is a farm supplies salesman.

Brother: Joseph Ciccio, age 34, (born 3/3/26) lives with his wife and six children at Route 1, Metro, Illinois. A high school graduate, Joseph operates the farm left by subject's father.

Arrest record for the defendant's family is denied. Congenial relationships exist between all family members.

Personal History: The defendant was born in Lincoln, Illinois on 5-18-10, the third of five children. He was reared under favorable circumstances in a rural farm community, moving to the Metro, Illinois area when he was four years old. He experienced a normal childhood.

Marital History: On June 15, 1930, at Aurora, Illinois, the defendant married Hilda Sharenhausen, now age 49 (born 12/14/11, Germany). Apparently, Mrs. Ciccio was pregnant before the marriage as a daughter was born seven months later. A total of three children have been born to this marriage:

1. Rose Swenson, age 28, (born 2/9/32, Metro, Illinois) lives with her husband Art at Route 3, Metro, Illinois. She is a high school graduate. Mr. Swenson is employed by the defendant.

2. Thomas Ciccio, age 25, (born 1/26/35, Metro, Illinois) is married and lives at 614 Trail Ridge Road, Arlington Heights, Illinois. He graduated from the University of Chicago and is a civil engineer for the Service Cement Co., Rolling Meadows, Illinois.

3. George Ciccio, age 14, (born 8/4/45, Metro, Illinois) lives with the defendant and will be entering his sophomore year at the Metro Community High School in the fall.

The marriage, the first for both the defendant and his wife, has been relatively conflict-free and there have been no separations.

Home and Neighborhood: Subject, his wife and son occupy a well-kept 6-room frame home at 36 Rosita Road, Metro, Illinois. He paid $4,000 for this home in 1941 and it is now believed to be worth about $12,000. The house, an adjoining garage and orchard take up about an acre of land. This is a rural community about 100 miles west of Chicago.

Education: Defendant says that he graduated from the Madison Elementary School, Metro, Illinois, in 1923 and then attended the Metro Community High School for a few months before he had a hunting accident, which resulted in the loss of his left eye. He did not return to school.

The Madison school was an old one-room rural school house. No records, dating back to 1923 have been retained, either by the local school district or the Metro Community High School.

Military: None.

Employment: After he quit school, Mr. Ciccio worked at various odd jobs such as: farm laborer, garage worker, painter, and road worker. In 1934 and 1935 he claims to have worked as a mechanic for the now defunct Deere Implement Co. in Metro, Illinois.

Mr. Ciccio has been self-employed since 1936 and has engaged in various enterprises in the Metro, Illinois area. These included a gravel pit and excavating business and a farm. He has also purchased land, subdivided, and engaged in the real estate business.

Since 1936, Mr. Ciccio has engaged in road improvement work for Stewart Township in Metro. His services were paid on an hourly basis and he is hired as needed. The Township Supervisor says that Mr. Ciccio does a good job and will be called upon in the future.

In December 1958, Mr. Ciccio sold most of the gravel pit and excavating business (save for one crane) for $80,000. This is being paid out at $200 a month plus 5% interest.

Mr. Ciccio is known to work long hours at his excavating business, especially during the summer months.

Health: Description:—Mr. Ciccio is a stocky 5′8″, 180 lbs. He has gray eyes and gray hair, almost bald. He lost his left eye in a hunting accident when he was 13 years old and it was replaced by a glass prosthesis. He has a lower quadrant surgical scar from a 1950 appendectomy and a scar on the left shoulder.

Evaluative Summary and Recommendation: This is a case of a 50-year-old married man with three children who is involved in his first criminal arrest.

Mr. Ciccio has entered a plea of guilty to evading almost $5,000 in Federal Income Taxes for 1954. Upon his plea of guilty, three other counts relating to an additional $10,000 in evaded taxes for 1953, 1955, and 1956 were dismissed. For all these years the defendant consistently understated his income in preparing his tax return. Mr. Ciccio's main source of revenue came from his gravel and excavating business and from real estate transactions. He has a reputation as a hard working, generally honest laborer and businessman. He kept his own books and attributes his tax problems to poor bookkeeping and ignorance. The size of the understatement militates against this argument and the fact that he admits under-the-table kickbacks to the ex-mayor of Metro, Illinois for being awarded city jobs, casts some shadow upon the honesty image he has effected.

Mr. Ciccio is the third of five children. He was reared on a farm and has lived in the vicinity of Metro, Illinois since he was four years old. He married when he was twenty and has three grown children. Subject has an 8th-grade education. He worked hard to reach his present relatively prosperous position, having been self-employed since 1936.

Mr. Ciccio has been active in community social and fraternal affairs and is physically robust and active. His health is generally good, although he has no vision in one eye and suffers with disorders that are characterized by chest pains and muscle stiffening.

Subject has a net worth in excess of $200,000 and is relatively debtfree.

Mr. Ciccio has some realization of the seriousness of the offense and is ashamed for having brought disrepute to his family name. Since he is a family man and has a previously untarnished record of stable and responsible conduct, Mr. Ciccio probably merits probation consideration.

Respectfully submitted,
Raymond R. Moneysmith
U.S. Probation Officer

SENTENCING THE INCOME TAX VIOLATOR: STATEMENT OF THE BASIC PROBLEMS

By George H. Boldt
26 F.R.D. 231, 264-71 (1959)
(Pilot Institute on Sentencing)

The injustice and evil effects in general of disparity in criminal sentences will be discussed by other speakers on the Institute program. However, two general statements of personal opinion may be appropriate as a preface to remarks directed particularly to sentencing the tax violator: (1) The greatest of disparity and injustice may arise when identical sentences for the same offenses are imposed without full and fair consideration of the circumstances of each offense and of each particular offender. (2) A too lenient sentence is fully as unjust and harmful, both to individuals and to the public, as an over-severe sentence, although the evil and unfairness of the latter may be more apparent and dramatic. These propositions are believed to be as true of sentences for tax violations as of those for car theft, fraud and all other categories of crime.

As shown by all available evidence, whether considered by totals or percentages, by geographic areas, by individual judges, or by the circumstances of individual cases, the disparity in tax violation sentences is nothing short of shocking. . . .

Let me briefly mention a few highlights of the evidence: In fiscal 1958, of 8 convicted tax offenders in Colorado 7 were sent to prison; 6 of 6 in Illinois; 5 of 5 in Utah; 3 of 3 in Oregon; 4 of 5 in Washington state, and 9 of 12 in Kentucky. In those six states a total of 34 out of 39 convicted tax violators, or over 87%, went to prison. In the same year 16 of 24 convicted tax violators in Michigan received only probation or a suspended sentence; in southern Mississippi 5 of 6 received fines only; in western New York only 1 of 14 went to prison; in eastern Virginia only 3 of 17; and in northern Oklahoma not one of 9 violators went to prison. In these five districts only 13 of 70 convicted tax violators, or not quite 20%, were sentenced to prison in the same year as the 87% of convicted violators in the six states first mentioned. Comparison of the records of other districts shows in varying degree the same astounding pattern of disparity between areas year by year. Inequality to the same extent and frequency is shown in the imposition of fines in tax cases. The evidence covers far too many sentences, over too extended a period of time, for the slightest doubt but that the fate of the convicted tax violator varies widely depending upon where his crime is committed, in what court he is prosecuted, and by what judge he is sentenced.

. . .

Accomplishment of the ultimate objective of a criminal sentence by applying punishment, incapacity, rehabilitation and deterrence, each in appropriate measure for each class of offense and each particular offender, requires: (1) analysis of the law violated, its immediate and long-range purposes, public attitude toward the law, and the impact of sentences for violation of the law upon the individual and the public; (2) analysis of the particular offense for which sentence is to be imposed, its gravity and magnitude, intrinsically and relatively, the character, degree and persistence of the offender's misconduct; and (3) analysis of all factors personal to the individual offender. Sentencing the income tax violator will be discussed under the headings of those interrelated and overlapping considerations.

1. *The law violated.* . . . [A] substantial part of the gross disparity in such sentences may be accounted for by disagreement concerning, or inadequate consideration of, the purposes of the tax crime laws and the effects of their violation. The failure to provide any punishment at all beyond civil penalties in a considerable number of cases and the relative infrequency of imprisonment under sentences by a number of judges and in some areas may indicate that mercy for the individual offender and concern for his health, family, business and community position has been given effect to the detriment, if not exclusion, of concern for public security, national well being, and fairness both to honest taxpayers and to those tax offenders imprisoned and substantially fined in comparable circumstances.

Prior to conviction the bulk of tax violators have good reputations and high public acceptance. Some are leaders in their communities engaged in commendable civic activities. Judged solely on that basis, few of such violators would be imprisoned and those few released at earliest eligibility as having every qualification for parole. A serious question for those here present and others concerned is whether judgments founded wholly or largely on such considerations are either just in themselves or in the public interest. The gifted and fortunate person has a high stake in our society and a special responsibility for setting standards of conduct and for providing an example of obedience to and compliance with the tax statutes as well as all other civil and criminal laws. The few of such individuals who deliberately breach their duty hardly are deserving of more lenient treatment than those not so talented and less favored in education, position and wealth.

The life of the nation requires protection of its revenue and a large part of that revenue is derived from income taxes directly or indirectly personal to the taxpayer. The income tax laws provide for a system of self-assessment by the taxpayer based on expected integrity in compliance by the vast majority of individuals from poor to rich and on the assumption that there will be relatively rare exceptions as to which criminal prosecution may be asserted. That system could easily and quickly collapse if its basic assumptions failed and fraud by individuals in their self-assessment of tax liability occurred in any substantial frequency. It would be impossible to provide enough measures, means or men to cope with such a catastrophe. With nearly 70 million personal and corporate returns filed last year yielding income taxes totalling about 60 billion dollars, it is perfectly apparent that the system will not work other than by nearly unanimous full and true tax reporting by all persons whose returns are required by law. Viewed in this light, every wilful violation of the federal tax laws, whatever amount of tax be involved, is important and significant, both for its reprehensible character and for the potential harm and menace to the nation created thereby.

Only a small number of tax violation investigations survive critical screenings at several levels and thus result in criminal prosecutions. Last year only 1300 prosecutions were recommended and a mere 625 violators convicted. This is but a drop in the bucket of multiple millions of returns filed. As a matter of policy, the Internal Revenue Service tries to distribute prosecutions over a wide range of occupations and situations with a view of obtaining maximum deterrent effect in every category of taxpayer. The basis for criminal sanctions on tax fraud is narrowly limited by law and it is apparent that those charged with applying for those sanctions have not been profligate in doing so. Allowing for the always possible misjudgment in individual cases, there is no indication whatever of a policy of persecution by way of tax prosecutions. Indications of such a policy can be dealt with if and when they appear.

2. *The particular offense.* In every tax fraud case the jury is charged that a not guilty verdict is required unless it has been

proven beyond a reasonable doubt that the defendant wilfully and with specific fraudulent intent attempted to evade a substantial amount of tax actually known to be due and owing. Negligence, however gross, mistakes, errors, or misconceptions of law or fact, by the taxpayer or others acting for him will not sustain prosecution or warrant conviction. If any guilty verdict is not supported by substantial proof meeting those requirements, the court can and should set it aside. No plea of guilty ought to be accepted if the court has reasonable doubt of wilful evasion by the defendant with specific intent to defraud. In these circumstances every conviction of tax fraud, whether by verdict or plea, presents not merely technical but reprehensible criminal misconduct. The seriousness of each particular offense depends upon the amounts of income and tax involved, the means, method and scheme employed in committing the offense, the period over which the tax fraud continued, the defendant's obstruction to or cooperation in tax computation, and whether or not other offenses were incident or related to the tax violations.

3. *The individual offender.* In tax violation cases personality problems concerning the alcoholic, narcotic, and mentally disturbed violator are not so frequently presented as to warrant discussion in this particular panel. Such factors are the same in tax as in other cases. In appraising the situation of the individual tax offender, all factors in aggravation or mitigation of his conduct as related to appropriate penalty are pertinent, including his age, intelligence, education, personality, occupation, health, family and previous good or bad conduct generally and with respect of similar offenses.

So far as punishment of the individual for a tax offense is concerned, civil fraud penalties are so heavy that in most cases further pecuniary punishment by immoderate fines adds little, if anything, to the purposes of either punishment or incapacity, and certainly does not further rehabilitation. Where individuals of ample means are convicted of extensive offenses, public reimbursement for investigation and prosecution expense may justify large or maximum fines. Except for the gangster and racketeer otherwise escaping justice, civil penalties plus the stigma of prosecution and conviction may sufficiently provide for punishment, incapacity and rehabilitation of the particular individual in many instances. Whether such stigma and pecuniary penalties sufficiently serve the purpose of deterring others from similar offenses appears more debatable.

. . .

Reasonable certainty of relatively mild punishment is generally believed to be a greater deterrent than the possibility of a severe penalty, improbable because relatively unlikely to be applied. If so, it would seem that in the great majority of cases involving substantial tax violation imprisonment, at least for a short period, should be imposed. Tax fraud involves deliberate and calculated financial misconduct as to which high probability of imprisonment on detection and conviction should be a potent deterrent; whereas, the efficacy of fines alone for that purpose appears at least doubtful. Surely no one of a character and mind to attempt tax evasion will be much deterred therefrom merely by the knowledge that conviction will involve payment of tax and pecuniary penalties. That is a gamble that many taxpayers with a trace of sporting blood might readily take; but few tempted taxpayers, especially those of good reputation if not character, would take the risk of even a short imprisonment for the prospect of tax evasion rewards, however rich.

The practice of providing probation on payment of tax penalties and fine, or of suspending sentence until tax liability is settled is strongly condemned, even by those responsible for collection of taxes. As a means of punishment it is ridiculous; and as a deterrent it may have just the contrary effect. If in any area, or the country at large, taxpayers are led to believe that criminal prosecution for tax fraud is a collection device and that the criminal penalties of tax violation may be avoided before or after conviction merely by payment of tax and civil penalties, it will be a sorry day indeed for criminal prosecution as a deterrent to tax evasion.

PRESENTENCE REPORT[l]

Sex: Male *Race:* White *Age:* 23
Mental and Physical Health: Good
Education: High school graduate

Current Charge: The defendant was charged with violating the Selective Service Act of 1948 by refusing to be inducted. He is a member of the religious group known as Jehovah's Witnesses, whose stand on military induction is universally known.

Plea: Guilty
Maximum Sentence Possible: Five years
Criminal Record: None

---

[l] FEDERAL BUREAU OF PRISONS, PRELIMINARY GUIDELINES FOR THE STUDY OF DEFENDANTS UNDER 18 U.S.C. § 4208(b) (1960).

Family Background: Defendant is the only natural son of highly stable and reputable parents. He has one adopted sister. The mother died in 1951, when subject was fifteen years old; the defendant's relationship with her was very close and he missed her greatly after her death. The father remarried in 1954. Defendant is the only delinquent in the family, but during World War II two uncles and one cousin received federal sentences as conscientious objectors. For the past two years the defendant has been studying to become a minister in the Jehovah's Witnesses sect. After leaving high school the defendant went to work as a telegraph messenger. For the past four years he has been working as a crank shaft grinder and assists the owner in managing the business. The defendant is considered an excellent and highly trustworthy worker. The defendant has never married, but he has a steady girlfriend.

Reason for Commitment Under 18 USC 4208(b): Observation

Bureau of Prisons' Findings and Recommendations: The defendant has no psychiatric or psychological problems. The Bureau of Prisons commented: "Our experience over a number of years with Jehovah's Witnesses has shown that their attitude towards service in the armed forces or toward work of importance in the national health, safety and interest is unchanged by confinement in a penal or correctional institution. . . . There appear to be no indications for correctional training and treatment. . . . [A]lthough Jehovah's Witnesses are very much alike in background, religious belief and reasons for violating the Selective Service Act, the courts vary widely in the sentences imposed on members of this group, ranging from probation sentences of a few months up to five years. During 1959 there were ninety Jehovah's Witnesses sentenced to imprisonment. Two received sentences of less than six months, an additional sixteen received sentences of six months to a year, and the remainder from one year and a day to five years. Only two received a five-year sentence." The Bureau recommended a sentence of one year and one day.

Even with a comprehensive and diagnostically helpful presentence report, the sentencing judge must select from among the myriad facts about the defendant and the circumstances of his crime, those he feels to be most relevant to his decision of whether to incarcerate the offender or place him on probation. The judge's consideration of this matter is not limited to material from the presentence report but most judges, particularly those in urban courts, rely heavily on this document.

There is a question of what kinds of criteria are used by courts in making the probation-incarceration decision and a second question of whether it is better to leave the selection of criteria, essentially unarticulated, to the discretion of each individual judge than to undertake the formulation of legislative guidelines and limitations. The drafters of the Model Penal Code propose a statutory checklist:

MODEL PENAL CODE § 7.01
American Law Institute
(Proposed Official Draft 1962)

ARTICLE 7. AUTHORITY OF COURT IN SENTENCING

Section 7.01. Criteria for Withholding Sentence of Imprisonment and for Placing Defendant on Probation.

. . .

(2) The following grounds, while not controlling the discretion of the Court, shall be accorded weight in favor of withholding sentence of imprisonment:

(a) the defendant's criminal conduct neither caused nor threatened serious harm;

(b) the defendant did not contemplate that his criminal conduct would cause or threaten serious harm;

(c) the defendant acted under a strong provocation;

(d) there were substantial grounds tending to excuse or justify the defendant's conduct, though failing to establish a defense;

(e) the victim of the defendant's criminal conduct induced or facilitated its commission;

(f) the defendant has compensated or will compensate the victim of his criminal conduct for the damage or injury that he sustained;

(g) the defendant has no history of prior delinquency or criminal activity or has led a law-abiding life for a substantial period of time before the commission of the present crime;

(h) the defendant's criminal conduct was the result of circumstances unlikely to recur;

(i) the character and attitudes of the defendant indicate that he is unlikely to commit another crime;

(j) the defendant is particularly likely to respond affirmatively to probationary treatment;

(k) the imprisonment of the defendant would entail excessive hardship to himself or his dependents.

(3) When a person who has been convicted of a crime is not sentenced to imprisonment, the Court shall place him on probation if he is in need of the supervision, guidance, assistance or direction that the probation service can provide.

The Model Penal Code further proposes a presumption in favor of probation, with imprisonment only if the judge affirmatively finds it necessary.[m] On the other hand, some states, like New York, instruct the judge that he should admit an offender to probation only if imprisonment is unnecessary.[n] Most often legislatures are silent on the issue of preference for probation or imprisonment, and the matter is resolved by the judge's individual view.

In addition to the criteria listed in the Model Penal Code proposal, there is a question of whether it is properly within the realm of judicial discretion to consider the defendant's plea as a factor in deciding whether to grant probation.

UNITED STATES v. WILEY

184 F. Supp. 679 (N.D. Ill. 1960)

[Another portion of this opinion appears at 586, *supra*. *See also* 267 F.2d 453 (7th Cir. 1959); 278 F.2d 500 (7th Cir. 1960).]

CAMPBELL, Chief Judge. In the cause before me, after defendant's conviction on Count II of an indictment charging him and four other defendants with unlawfully, willfully, knowingly and feloniously having in their possession certain goods, unlawfully stolen while moving in an interstate shipment and known by them to have been stolen in violation of Title 18 U.S.C. Section 659, I sentenced defendant, after full consideration of all the evidence introduced during his trial, as well as the reports of the government investigators, to imprisonment for a period of three years. After full consideration of the reports of the government investigators, I sentenced the other four defendants, who had previously pled guilty as follows: Ulysses McGhee, 2 years; Joseph Helen, 1 year and 1 day; Joseph M. Kelley, 1 year and 1 day; and Roman Jackson, 1 year and 1 day. McGhee had four prior felony convictions and was more or less the ringleader insofar as the actual stealing operations of this particular gang were concerned. Helen, Kelley and Jackson likewise had records of prior convictions.

---

[m] § 7.01(1) (1962).

[n] N.Y. PENAL LAW § 65.00 (McKinney Supp. 1967).

Defendant Wiley, prior to the imposition of sentence moved for a presentence investigation after which the following colloquy took place:

"The Court: Is there anything you want to say before the imposition of sentence?

"Mr. Evins: (Defendant's counsel) Yes, Judge. I would like to say this, that you have offered here in mitigation and in view of the fact that this defendant has no previous record of any kind and that in view of the further fact that he is married and he has a family and he is living with his wife, supporting his family, and he has a good job out of which he is supporting his family, I feel that justice could be served in this case if the Court sees fit to put him on probation for a period of time, and I am asking the Court to show him some leniency and consideration because of those facts, because of his family and because of the fact he just got a newborn baby and as I understand it, he is the main and only support of that family.

"I am asking the Court at this time if he wouldn't consider granting probation.

"The Court: Those are the facts the defendant should have considered prior to committing the offense.

. . .

"The Court: In view of the fact that the trial was expedited by waiving a jury and by stipulation of the various items that expedited the proof I make the sentence less than I otherwise would. *It is, however a serious crime, and it is a case for the imposition of a sentence, either on a plea of guilty or on a trial.* Had there been a plea of guilty in this case probably probation might have been *considered* under certain terms, but you are all well aware of the standing policy here that once a defendant stands trial that element of grace is removed from the consideration of the Court in the imposition of sentence.

"Taking into consideration the various factors that you have referred to—and that I have referred to, I make the sentence less than I otherwise would, but a sentence must be imposed.

"On the judgment of guilty heretofore, rendered the defendant is sentenced to the custody of the Attorney General of the United States to be incarcerated in a penitentiary of the United States for a term of three years." (Emphasis supplied.)

Upon appeal, the judgment insofar as it adjudged defendant guilty was affirmed though the cause was remanded, Chief Judge Hastings dissenting, for consideration of defendant's application for probation because, as the Court stated, of my "standing policy" to the effect that "that element of grace is removed from the consideration of the court" once a defendant stands trial. United States v. Wiley, 7 Cir., 267 F.2d 453, 455, 456.

When the mandate was filed, I proceeded to hearing on the motion of Wiley for probation and after full consideration of all the factors before me I reimposed the sentence of imprisonment for a period of three years.

Upon further appeal, the sentence was set aside and the cause remanded with directions because, as the Court of Appeals stated: "(t)he district court has, without any justification, arbitrarily singled out a minor defendant for the imposition of a more severe sentence than that imposed upon the co-defendants . . ." United States v. Wiley, 7 Cir., 278 F.2d 500, 503.

The cause is now before me pursuant to this mandate.

The maximum penalty for violation of Title 18 U.S.C. Section 659 is imprisonment for a period of ten years together with a fine of $5,000. Any sentence within this limit is, of course, discretionary with the trial judge. It has now been determined by the Court of Appeals that I have abused this discretion by imposing a three years' sentence on Wiley. This determination by the Court of Appeals is apparently based upon a comparison of the sentences imposed upon the several defendants in this cause; my statements regarding probation for a defendant who has exercised his constitutional right of trial; my statement of November 7, 1958 where, during an unrelated hearing upon the motion of McGhee to vacate an order setting his appeal bond, I described Wiley as "a minor participant"; and finally, a comparison of the criminal records and general background of each of the defendants as revealed in the record before the Court of Appeals.

I think that almost any trial judge in the United States will take into consideration a plea of guilty when imposing sentence and, in fact, most judges usually state for the record words to the effect that "since the defendant has saved the government the time and expense of trial, the sentence is less than it ordinarily would be."

If then, a trial judge grants leniency in exchange for a plea of guilty, it follows, as the reverse side of the same coin, that he must necessarily forego leniency, generally speaking, where the defendant stands trial and is found guilty. This is especally true where there are several co-defendants indicted for the same offense and some plead guilty while others stand trial and are found guilty. In such a case, again generally speaking, the trial judge should grant leniency to those who plead guilty and refuse leniency to those who choose to stand trial. Usually, the result is, as would be expected, a disparity in the sentences imposed on the various defendants. However, it is incorrect, in my opinion, to say, as the Court of Appeals has termed my sentence of Wiley, that a "more severe sentence" is imposed on a defendant who stands trial. Rather, it seems more correct to me to say that the defendant who stands trial is sentenced without leniency according to law.

When I referred to my "standing policy," I mean nothing more than that which is already established for the reasons stated above, as a valid principle of sentencing.

It is not a strict, rigid policy and I do not apply it as such since, as my record amply demonstrates, I have on numerous occasions granted probation despite the fact that the defendant has exercised his constitutional right to trial. However, it does stand as a warning to all criminal defendants to consider well that they may not be granted leniency in my court, or consequently probation, if they choose to stand trial and are found guilty. However, there were other factors present in this cause, though not in the record, which I considered and which also, in part, motivated my denial of his application for probation and his sentence.

It is true that on its face his criminal record does not compare equally to the criminal records of his co-defendants McGhee and Helen, though it is comparable to the criminal records of Jackson and Kelley. He was arrested in December of 1956 on a charge of receiving stolen property and placed on probation for a period of six months and also has been arrested several times for gambling. However, there is ample evidence in the reports of the government investigators, which are not a part of this record, but which I thoroughly considered before the imposition of sentence, that Wiley was involved in a similar offense, the burglary of the Chicago Terminal of Super Service Motor Freight Company on October 15, 1957 for which he was not indicted because of the pendency of the cause now before me. I think it is clear from the reports of the government investigators that Wiley perjured himself when he testified that he had never helped to dispose of any other stolen merchandise.

I should like now to refer to another factor I considered in sentencing Wiley which is covered fully in the reports of the government investigators though only hinted at in the record. Wiley has a political position with the City of Chicago, Bureau of Sanitation. His foreman at the time these offenses here mentioned were committed, was a man named Charles B. Vaughn. There is evidence in the reports of the government investigators which shows that Vaughn was the actual immediate contact for a number of "fences" for stolen property and that it was Vaughn who actually made the deliveries to these several "fences" after taking over the movement of a load from someone who had stolen merchandise, such as, in the present cause, McGhee. It is clear from the reports of the government investigators that it was Wiley who had originally put McGhee in contact with Vaughn, as a man who would dispose of stolen merchandise. It is also clear from the reports that Vaughn was an associate of individuals known to be members of the organized crime syndicate in Chicago. Thus, Wiley was a "chaser" for Vaughn and actually induced the commission of crimes such as these, since he, in the first instance provided the means of disposal for stolen merchandise to men like McGhee, Helen, Kelley and Jackson.

I cannot say with certainty that this crime would never have occurred if Wiley had not put McGhee in contact with Vaughn, but certainly, his part as a "chaser" is an important factor to be considered, especially, where as here, there are strong overtones of organized crime and political influence.

I feel that I can now in good conscience reveal the Wiley-Vaughn operation because just recently, shortly after the release of the latest decision of the Court of Appeals in United States v. Wiley, supra, Charles B. Vaughn was brutally murdered.

When I described Wiley as a "minor participant" in this crime some weeks subsequent to the time I imposed sentence upon him, it was at a hearing upon a motion of McGhee to vacate an order setting his appeal bond. I was at this time particularly concerned with McGhee who was, as I stated "somewhat of a ringleader" insofar as the actual stealing operations of McGhee, Kelley, Jackson and Helen were concerned. Without question, Wiley was a "minor participant" in regard to the actual theft by these defendants but he was a major participant in the operation of Vaughn which was not reported in the record of this cause and which, for reasons of confidence, I could not refer to. Furthermore, since I was only concerned with McGhee at this time, it does not seem logical to me to refer to my out of context statements about Wiley to determine that the sentence I imposed upon him several weeks prior was arbitrary and "without justification".

In sentencing Wiley, I seriously considered his prospects for rehabilitation. When he originally changed his plea from guilty to not guilty, there was no remorse in this man. McGhee, Kelley, Jackson, and Helen pled guilty and did stand conscience-stricken in repentance before the Court. Wiley did not cooperate with the government investigators. McGhee, Kelley, Jackson and Helen gave them their full cooperation. These men can be helped because they have indicated that they want to be helped. Wiley, on the other hand, does not want to be helped. He is, by all outward manifestations, the self-assured "smart guy". From what I have learned about Wiley, I am convinced that he is not only contemptuous of law and order and those people who attempt to live their lives according to law and the moral standards of the community, but he is also contemptuous of men like McGhee, Kelley, Helen and Jackson who are not as "smart" as he thinks he is. Wiley, I feel will go back to his underworld friends without remorse and will continue to infect and disease our society.

In short, as far as I am motivated by reformation in my sentences of these co-defendants, I feel that McGhee, Kelley, Jackson and Helen have greater prospects of rehabilitation than Wiley.

Deterrence also motivated the sentence I imposed upon Wiley. First, Wiley induced the commission of crimes by "chasing" for Vaughn. It is my opinion that deterrence best serves the interest of society when it is used effectively against "fences", men like Vaughn or their "chasers" such as Wiley because these men are far more responsible for most burglaries than the men like McGhee, Kelley, Jackson and Helen who actually perform the act. Like many other trial judges I believe that if "fences" are eliminated, crime will be effectively reduced and to this end, I advocate deterrence as a greater motivating factor in the sentence of a man like Wiley than I would in the case of McGhee, Kelley, Jackson or Helen. Furthermore, Wiley is an employee of the City of Chicago and therefore represents the people of Chicago. I feel in the instant cause, for these and other reasons, that deterrence is far more important as a sentencing factor in the case of Wiley rather than in the case of any of the other co-defendants.

Though during my entire twenty years as a Federal Judge I have never been motivated in any criminal sentence to any great degree by a consideration of retribution, I again suggest that Wiley as an employee of the City of Chicago is far more vulnerable to this particular philosophy of sentencing than any of the other co-defendants.

I of course take no issue with the Court of Appeals. It has acted with apparent justification to correct what it feels to be an unjust sentence. With great respect, I do feel however, for the reasons stated herein, that until provision is made in law for appellate review of a trial judge's discretion under the Federal Probation Act and his discretion to determine a criminal sentence, based upon all the factors considered by the trial judge, it is an uncertain and dangerous precedent that is now advanced by the Seventh Circuit Court of Appeals in the two Wiley decisions.

In good conscience and with due regard to my oath of office I cannot conclude that any sentence less than three years is either just or proper in the case of Wiley now before me. Accordingly, I hereby now again reimpose my original sentence of three years. However, out of my deep respect for the Court of Appeals, and in obedience to its mandate, I also hereby suspend the execution of the said sentence.

The defendant Wiley may go hence without day.

2. Suspended Sentences Without Supervision

Sentencing judges in many jurisdictions are confronted occasionally by convicted offenders for whom incarceration is inappropriate and community supervision unnecessary. Certain defendants, obviously good probation risks, simply do not need more surveillance or the rehabilitative efforts provided by a probation staff. Where the only sentencing choice is probation with supervision, judges sometimes avoid this by "summary retrial" of defendants, finding them not guilty, thereby expunging the conviction. Or the defendant will be placed on probation but with only nominal supervision provided. An alternative to these informal devices is provided in the New York Penal Law which gives the trial judge a third alternative to probation or incarceration.

NEW YORK REVISED PENAL LAW
Effective September 1, 1967

§ 65.05. Sentence of conditional discharge

1. Criteria. The court may impose a sentence of conditional discharge for an offense if the court, having regard to the nature and circumstances of the offense and to the history, character and condition of the defendant, is of the opinion that neither the public interest nor the ends of justice would be served by a sentence of imprisonment or a fine and that probation supervision is not appropriate; provided, however, that the court shall not impose a sentence of conditional discharge for a class A or class B felony or for any felony defined in article two hundred twenty. [Class A felonies (*e.g.,* murder in the first degree) carry a maximum penalty set at the discretion of the judge of from fifteen years to life; Class B felonies (*e.g.,* armed robbery) carry a

maximum sentence set at the discretion of the judge of from three to twenty-five years. Article 220 offenses relate to crimes involving dangerous drugs.]

When a sentence of conditional discharge is imposed for a felony, the court shall set forth in the record the reasons for its action.

2. Sentence. When the court imposes a sentence of conditional discharge the defendant shall be released with respect to the conviction for which the sentence is imposed without imprisonment, fine or probation supervision but subject, during the period of conditional discharge, to such conditions as the court may determine. The court shall impose the period of conditional discharge authorized by subdivision three of this section and shall specify, in accordance with section 65.10, the conditions to be complied with. The court may modify or enlarge the conditions or, if the defendant commits an additional offense or violates a condition, revoke the sentence at any time prior to the expiration or termination of the period of conditional discharge.

3. Periods of conditional discharge. Unless terminated sooner in accordance with the code of criminal procedure, the period of conditional discharge shall be as follows:

(a) Three years in the case of a felony; and
(b) One year in the case of a misdemeanor or a violation.

Where the court has required, as a condition of the sentence, that the defendant make restitution of the fruits of his offense or make reparation for the loss or damage caused thereby and such condition has not been satisfied, the court, at any time prior to the expiration or termination of the period of conditional discharge, may impose an additional period. The length of the additional period shall be fixed by the court at the time it is imposed and shall not be more than two years. All of the incidents of the original sentence, including the authority of the court to modify or enlarge the conditions, shall continue to apply during such additional period.

§ 65.20. Sentence of unconditional discharge

1. Criteria. The court may impose a sentence of unconditional discharge in any case where it is authorized to impose a sentence of conditional discharge under section 65.05 if the court

is of the opinion that no proper purpose would be served by imposing any condition upon the defendant's release.

When a sentence of unconditional discharge is imposed for a felony, the court shall set forth in the record the reasons for its action.

2. Sentence. When the court imposes a sentence of unconditional discharge, the defendant shall be released with respect to the conviction for which the sentence is imposed without imprisonment, fine or probation supervision. A sentence of unconditional discharge is for all purposes a final judgment of conviction.

Reference Note

A good discussion of probation in general is S. RUBIN, H. WEIHOFEN, G. EDWARDS & S. ROSENZWEIG, THE LAW OF CRIMINAL CORRECTION ch. 6 (1963).

Sentencing considerations in the federal system are discussed in *Pilot Institute on Sentencing,* 26 F.R.D. 231 (1959); Remington & Newman, *The Highland Park Institute on Sentence Disparity,* 26 FED. PROB. 3 (Mar. 1962); Thomsen, *Sentencing in Income Tax Cases,* 26 FED. PROB. 10 (Mar. 1962).

An interesting approach to the study of criteria involved in granting probation may be found in Davis, *A Study of Adult Probation Rates by Means of the Cohort Approach,* 55 J. CRIM. L.C. & P.S. 70 (1964), using a statistical approach to compare percentage of successful completion of probation by group analysis.

E. CHOICE OF SENTENCE—LENGTH OF IMPRISONMENT

As discussed above, with reference to the allocation of responsibility for determining the sentence of one who has been convicted, there are various statutory schemes, some giving the judge great discretion and others giving him little. In nearly all jurisdictions the judge has responsibility for setting the maximum for most crimes, within the outer bounds set by the legislature. And in most jurisdictions the judge may also set the minimum term which the prisoner should serve.

1. *Setting the Minimum and Maximum*

To set the minimum and maximum terms meaningfully, the experienced judge will consider what they mean in practical terms. One major factor is the policy and practice of the paroling authorities. The parole board may be either very lenient in granting parole or very timid and restrictive. In addition the board may be much or little influenced by what it perceives to be the judge's attitude toward the offender and his crime.

> The parole board had just voted to grant parole to a prisoner who had served two years of a three-year sentence for robbery. The next case was highly similar in crime, character of defendant, and time served, but the sentence was for seven years, imposed by a different judge. One member of the board urged granting parole on the ground that consistency demanded it and this prisoner seemed as good a risk as the first one. Another member replied that perhaps the longer sentence represented the judge's estimate of greater seriousness of the crime or some character defect not reflected in the file before the parole board.

The operation of "good time" laws can greatly affect the amount of time actually served by a prisoner. Avoiding bad-conduct penalties and working acceptably in prison industry, or even giving blood, may entitle the prisoner to a shortening of his time.

The conditions under which time will be served may make a prison term more or less onerous. Life in an antiquated, maximum security prison is much different from life in a modern, minimum security institution. The degree to which prisoners are secure from attacks or exploitation by one another and to which prisoners may be exposed to incompetent or brutal guards greatly affects the meaning of a year in prison. The opportunities for schooling, vocational training, consultation with social workers, and psychological or psychiatric treatment may give some positive qualities to the time served.

In considering how much time is enough, the judge is likely to be substantially influenced by his perception of community attitude toward the offense or the offender. If there is community concern about the type of conduct or outrage at the particular crime, the demand for punishment and deterrence may well be expressed through the judge by high minimum and maximum sentence. On the other hand, if the judge personally (or reflecting community sentiment) can feel some sympathy for the offender or some qualms about harsh punishment for the offense, this will result in low minimum and maximum sentence, if probation is not granted.

The possibility of rehabilitation of the offender, either by the shock of imprisonment or by the influence of treatment programs available in correctional institutions, may affect the sentence. The judge might use a low maximum when he thinks a short exposure to prison will have desirable shock effect, or he might use a low minimum and high maximum to give the parole board wide discretion in picking the time when optimum results have been achieved.

The need to induce pleas of guilty may motivate the judge to acquiesce in recommendations for low sentence from the prosecutor.

PRESENTENCE REPORT[o]
United States District Court
Northern District of Illinois
Office of the Probation Officer
Chicago

Name: Charles Arley Strawn	Marital Status: Single
Address: 4012 Davenport Street Chicago, Illinois	Dependents: None
Age: 36	Offense: Bank Robbery
Sex: Male	Codefendants: None
Race: White	Counsel: Charles Wright, III WO 2-1903
Citizenship: United States	Bond: Not Furnished

Docket: 48724

Offense: On May 5, 1960, this defendant did, by use of a toy pistol, intimidate and take from one James Surles, a teller at the Standard Savings and Loan Association, 1684 Schaefer Road, Chicago, approximately $1800 in currency. Since the accounts of the above Association are insured by the Federal Savings and Loan Insurance Corporation, this was in violation of Section 2113(a), Title 18, USC. The defendant had shown the above teller a printed note which read, "All 10's & 50's in the paper bag. Cooperate or I'll kill you. You have 1 minute. Don't goof. I'm very nervous!"

---

[o] This presentence report of an actual federal case, with names and places changed, has been used in federal sentencing institutes and affords opportunity to consider factors relevant to setting a minimum and maximum under the wide range of alternatives found in federal law. The relevant federal sentencing provisions are found in Appendix C. The sentencing decisions of federal judges in this case are summarized in Remington & Newman, *The Highland Park Institute on Sentence Disparity,* 26 FED. PROB. 3 (Mar. 1962).

There was some question as to the mental competency of this defendant, who had been committed several years ago to a state mental hospital, and was on convalescent status at the time of this offense. A psychiatric examination was conducted on May 12, 1960, and medical opinion was submitted that the defendant does know right from wrong, understood the nature of the charges then pending against him, and, further, was sufficiently free of mental disorder to be capable of adequately assisting counsel in his defense according to report of St. Elizabeth Hospital in Washington, D. C.

Defendant's Statement: When interviewed by this Probation Officer on June 22, 1960, the defendant seemed to be rather nervous and anxious, but he recalled dates and events better than the average person. Also his account was given in a logical, coherent fashion.

He related that over one year ago, while talking with a fellow patient at the State Mental Hospital in Northtown, he got the idea of robbing a bank from this other person. They discussed what an easy thing it would be to hold up a bank or some other financial institution, and in one quick move get a hold of a lot of money. This other person suggested that a real gun should be used, but the defendant said that he disagreed with this because of a fear that somebody might get hurt. He has been at the state hospital only once since October 1958, and that was for a three weeks period in August and September, 1959. He left the hospital then without permission and was classified as an escapee. However, he was taking treatments regularly from a private psychiatrist and his status was changed from escapee to convalescent on or about September 30, 1959. He was since seeing this psychiatrist on an outpatient basis five times weekly up to the time of his arrest in the instant case on May 5, 1960.

Within recent months he related that he has been "living like a bum." He had poor clothes, lived in an inferior hotel, and so forth. He said that members of his family are well-to-do and have been helping him some financially. The defendant's father set up an estate of about $100,000 but the defendant is under guardianship and was given only $2 per day for independent use. He related that he got a job as a drummer in a band at a tavern in an undesirable area of the city, but he lost this job because of his drums being so shoddy.

This defendant had thought of petitioning the Probate Court for control of his estate but didn't attempt this as he didn't think he had much of a case. A short time before this bank robbery the defendant related that he went on a benzedrine

Molding, Inc., 1103 Pinehurst Street, Chicago. He is in poor health and semi-retired, now being Vice-Chairman of the Board. He and the defendant's mother moved to Downey, Virginia, about a year ago where they now live, Mail Box No. 74, Ranch Road.

Jean (nee Miller) Strawn, mother, present age 71, is a housewife and lives at the above address.

Siblings: Russell Strawn, brother, age 42, is an executive of the Acme Casting & Molding, Inc. He lives with his family at 1318 St. Denis Road, Parkside Heights, Illinois.

Richard Strawn, brother, age 38, lives with his family at 4207 Rodney Way, Homer, Illinois. It appears that this brother has been closer to the defendant than any member of the family primarily because he was appointed his guardian several years ago. Richard is a sales executive for the above concern.

In addition there was a brother, Paul Strawn, who died at the age of 38 as a result of hepatitis. This brother was a salesman for the family firm and a respectable person.

None of the above members of the defendant's family is known to have any criminal record nor was anything derogatory learned about their characters. They have seemingly taken a sincere interest in the defendant's welfare. However, the defendant has felt very inferior, like a social outcast, and seldom visits them.

Home and Neighborhood: For about eight months prior to his arrest, the defendant lived at the Coleridge Hotel, 11 W. Grand Ave., Chicago. This is part of the Rogers Hotel System and the defendant was paying $10.50 rental. This hotel is located in one of the deteriorated, undesirable sections near the downtown area.

Education: The defendant said that he completed the 10th grade at the Highland Center High School in Highland Center, Illinois. He withdrew at the age of 16 or 17 because he wanted to be a professional radio actor and a musician.

Previous to going to Highland Center High School, the defendant had been a student at Dartmoor, which is a private school near Chicago. He went there for six years and was expelled because of doing failing work in studies and for being a disciplinary problem, such as staying out overnight without permission on occasion.

Religion: According to the defendant, he is of the Protestant Faith. Within the last year, he has occasionally gone to the Unitarian Church near the University of Chicago.

Interest and Activities: The defendant is still fond of acting and at one time said that he did some work as a stock actor. He has been interested in music for a number of years and owned a set of drums when he was 14 years old. He particularly likes jazz music and goes to Sully's Patio, 4224 45th Street, where different jazz bands play. He has at times played in the orchestra there and acknowledges that the place is located in a poor area and not too desirable.

For many years, the defendant has had problems with drinking, smoking marihuana cigarettes, and using benzedrine pills. He stated that he has never used any morphine or drugs of that character, such as heroin, or any drugs intravenously.

Health:

Physical: The defendant seems to have no organic defects. Most of his teeth have been removed and the defendant was not wearing any dentures when we saw him.

Mental and Emotional: Under Docket No. 945,678, this defendant was judged an insane person by Judge Thomas C. Milligan at Chicago, Illinois on October 11, 1946. He has not since been restored to the status of a legally sane person and is presently on convalescent leave from Northtown State Hospital.

We are enclosing a letter from Dr. C. S. O'Reilly, dated April 18, 1960, and addressed to defendant's brother, Richard Strawn. It is noted that this letter was written about three weeks prior to the commission of the bank robbery. It is quite evident that the defendant's behavior pattern was not changed fundamentally as a result of this outpatient therapy.

Also enclosed is a copy of a psychiatric report submitted by Dr. Robert C. Laser to the United States Attorney's Office in Chicago, Illinois, on May 18, 1960. Dr. Laser had been to the Northtown State Hospital, examined the records there and also talked with the medical director.

On June 22, 1960, this Probation Officer talked with Chester T. Black, M.D., Medical Superintendent of Northtown. He said that while the defendant at times has exhibited definite psychotic symptoms, he was not regarded as a dangerous person. Also most of the time the defendant's behavior was more that of a socio-path—during these periods of remission from psychosis. He had a tendency to do things wrong which he knew he would get caught at. As a rule the defendant would escape from the state hospital and be gone for a period of from two or three days to two or three weeks before he would be found. During these absences he would go to black and tans and other dives and go on benzedrine sprees. Dr. Black remarked that it is a miracle that some of the places he went to in Detroit and other cities did not result in violence or death to him. There was some hope that when the defendant was in California for several months in 1958 and 1959 that he had learned to adjust better to the outside world. This coupled with the regular outpatient psychiatric treatment which he was taking in Chicago from Dr. O'Reilly from the fall of 1959 to the time of his arrest on May 5, 1960, offered some hope for improvement. Dr. Black said that under the terms of his commitment, the defendant could be returned to Northtown Hospital as a patient at any time. However, the doctor shudders to think of his being back there and the problems he makes. Also it is so easy for the defendant to escape that from a security standpoint Northtown is not at all desirable. Dr. Black concluded by saying that the prognosis for the defendant is exceedingly poor no matter what kind of treatment or custody plan is worked out.

Employment: This defendant has Social Security No. 304-11-2704.

The defendant has worked little during his lifetime and the last job since leaving Northtown in September, 1959, was for about three weeks as a drummer for Bob Meyer's orchestra in Chicago. This engagement was at Sully's Patio on 45th Street. The defendant said that he was paid $7 per night and lost this job because his drums were in such a poor condition.

Previously this defendant was at Clear Springs, California, for several months prior to coming back to Northtown in August, 1959. He said that he played with an orchestra for about three weeks; worked as a gardener at the Racquet Club; did a few odd jobs as a dishwasher, and for a short time worked as a bus boy at the Desert Hotel.

He had gone to California with Martha Dobbs, a white woman age 39, who is separated from her husband. He met Martha, who was a patient at Northtown and also was on convalescent status at the time of this trip West. He made it clear that while he and Martha didn't live together as husband and wife, they did spend evenings together and had sexual relations. She relapsed to a mental condition, had relatives in California and after she became ill, the defendant returned to Chicago.

Military History: None.

Financial Condition: For several years this defendant has been under guardianship of the Cook County Probate Court. His brother, Richard Strawn, has been his guardian and given him money for subsistence and medical treatment. The defendant said that he has an estate of about $100,000 which was given him by his father. This money is invested in various stocks and bonds and the principal is not touched. What interest is derived from it is expended for his welfare by his brother and the family contribute other funds which may be needed.

Respectfully submitted,
Timothy P. Dryer, Deputy Chief
U.S. Probation Officer

SENTENCING THE AUTO THIEF: SETTING THE MAXIMUM AND MINIMUM TERM OF IMPRISONMENT

By Edward J. Devitt
26 F.R.D. 231, 312-17 (1959)
(Pilot Institute on Sentencing)

My province here is to discuss the kind of sentence to be imposed on the Dyer Act violator who, it is determined, should not be granted probation and who is not eligible or suitable for commitment under the Youth Corrections Act. We may also assume that it is not appropriate to impose the fine authorized by the statute, 18 U.S.C.A. Secs. 2312-2313. More specifically, the question is, what maximum and minimum term should be fixed?

We are thus faced with the same age-old problem which has challenged judges for generations—how much time shall I give the defendant? . . .

. . . How will he benefit from imprisonment? Will he just "sweat it out" counting the days on his cell calendar, or will he reform and devote himself to learning a trade, studying correspondence courses, or becoming attached to some basic religious principles? When will he have received the maximum benefits of confinement? We judges don't know the answer to that crucial question. And bountifully as we may be blessed with wisdom, we are not possessed of the prescience to foretell it.

Thus we come to the point of my presentation, and that is that in order to impose the wisest sentence in each case, we judges should share the responsibility for fixing the exact length of sentence with the executive branch of the government which, on the basis of later acquired knowledge of the prisoner's progress in rehabilitation and his attitudes toward a return to society, is able to more wisely determine the exact length of sentence to be served which will be best adapted to the individual case. I urge that we should, in most Dyer Act cases (and in a large majority of other cases as well), impose an indeterminate sentence with delegated power in the Parole Board to later fix the exact termination date. Thanks to the intelligent efforts of the 85th Congress, we federal judges now have the statutory authority to take this action.[1]

. . .

A second advantage of the law is that its use will obviate, or at least minimize, the great disparity in sentences which have been imposed in the federal courts. One of the most pressing problems in the administration of criminal justice concerns itself with the marked disparity of sentences imposed for the same crime upon criminals with substantially the same previous records and backgrounds by judges not only in separated sections of the country, but in contiguous districts and even by judges within the same district. . . .

A third benefit of the law which should be of great mental relief to the sentencing court, is that it releases the judge from the burdensome responsibility of alone determining and imposing sentence and then living for a while with a residual apprehension as to the correctness of his judgment in a particular case. . . .

The enactment of this authority is of particular value now because of the recent tendency on the part of federal judges as a group to impose much longer sentences than formerly. Since 1949 the average sentence of prisoners received in federal institutions has increased by nearly 40%.[5] This seems to be an inordinately large increase, even taking into consideration the increase in the incidence and seriousness of crime. It is suggested that the long sentence does not take into consideration the basic correctional concept that an offender, any offender, should at least be given the chance to promptly resume his place in society upon a reasonable showing that he is able to do so, and the long sentence, with its emphasis on deterrence, militates against this meritorious rehabilitative principle.

. . .

It is many times said that the sentencing of a criminal is solely a judicial function. Some judges resent the thought that lay persons, even those trained in penology and sociology, should

[1] P.L. 85-752; 72 Stat. 845; 18 U.S.C.A. Sec. 4208(a) (Supp. 1958).

[5] 1957 Federal Prisons 3 (U.S. Dept. Justice).

share the responsibility of determining the length of sentence. The plain truth of the matter is, however, that . . . the foresight of the judge is not as good as the hindsight of the Parole Board members.

. . .

It is also occasionally urged that Parole Boards are too soft, and hence that we cannot vest in them the responsibility of determining a proper release date. But, at the same time, there are those who say that Parole Boards are too strict. We should remember that it is also said that some judges are too strict or too lenient. The execution of any governmental responsibility by any human in the judicial or executive branch of the government, is open to the same or similar charges. . . . It has been my practice to impose sentence for a substantial period, often the maximum set out in the statute, and then append to the sentence, the proviso that the defendant shall be "eligible for parole at such time as the Board of Parole may determine," quoting from the statute.[8] The writer has used this authority in every kind of case, including interstate transportation of stolen cars, white slave, bankruptcy fraud, mail theft, interstate transportation of forged securities, narcotics cases where the mandatory provisions are not applicable and even selective service violations. Recently I employed it, I am not sure if prudently, in a contempt of court sentence.

It is not to be implied that it is wise to habitually vest blanket discretion as to the length of sentence in the Parole Board. In those cases where the court wishes to insure the service of a minimum term in order, for instance, to effect punishment or to provide example, the alternative authority of Section 4208(a)(1) should be used by fixing a minimum date of eligibility for parole.

2. *Legislative Proposals to Ameliorate Some Undesirable Aspects of Judicial Sentencing*

There has been, in recent years, growing concern over some aspects of judicial sentencing. The concern has been directed primarily to the wide disparity in sentencing between different individual trial judges and over what are thought to be unduly short or unduly long sentences. One approach to the problem of disparity has been to propose appellate review of sentences, a matter dealt with elsewhere.[p] An approach to the perceived

---

[8] 18 U.S.C.A. Sec. 4208 (a) (2) (Supp. 1958).

[p] *See* p. 686, *supra*.

problem of unwarranted leniency has been the mandatory sentence particularly in narcotic offenses, a method supported by some law enforcement agencies. There are also other legislative sentencing proposals intended to restrict judicial discretion. Two of the most interesting are the American Law Institute's mandatory maximum as a way of dealing with judicial disparity and the National Council on Crime and Delinquency's five-year limit on sentences designed to eliminate the overly-long prison sentence.

MODEL PENAL CODE § 6.06
American Law Institute
(Tentative Draft No. 2, 1954)

Section 6.06. Sentence of Imprisonment for Felony; Ordinary Terms.

A person who has been convicted of a felony may be sentenced to imprisonment, as follows:

(1) In the case of a felony of the first degree, [other than a capital crime] for a term the minimum of which shall be fixed by the Court at not less than one year nor more than twenty years, and the maximum of which shall be life imprisonment;

(2) In the case of a felony of the second degree, for a term the minimum of which shall be fixed by the Court at not less than one year nor more than three years, and the maximum of which shall be ten years;

(3) In the case of a felony of the third degree, for a term the minimum of which shall be fixed by the Court at not less than one year nor more than two years, and the maximum of which shall be five years.

This original A.L.I. proposal for legislatively fixed maxima (1954) rested upon a number of positions or assumptions including:[q]

(1) Legislatively fixed maxima tend to reduce sentence disparity. The A.L.I. proposal takes the position that the only way gross differences in maximum sentences can be resolved is by fixing an automatic maximum for each crime of the same degree. Among other things this is expected to have the effect

[q] For the discussion by the American Law Institute, see 33 ALI PROCEEDINGS (1956).

of reducing inmate dissatisfaction and cynicism about disparity in sentences and thereby possibly aiding in rehabilitative efforts.

(2) Statutory maxima combined with low minima allow the paroling authority to adjust for individual differences, thus enabling them to release men who are rehabilitated and yet not forcing them to release inmates who continue to present a danger to the community. It was felt that this centralization of responsibility would establish the most accurate and fairest method of individualizing sentences.

(3) The notice of high statutory maxima has a positive deterrent function. At the same time, because they are coupled with low minimum terms, such high maxima do not interfere with discretionary release based upon the rehabilitative achievements of the criminal.

(4) Under the proposal the court retains discretion to adjust sentences for individual differences by reducing the grade of the felony from a first degree to a second degree or from a second degree to a third degree felony, thereby reducing the maximum sentence, if it is felt to be too onerous considering the nature of the crime or the characteristics of the defendant.[r]

---

[r] This reduction is specifically authorized by the MODEL PENAL CODE (Proposed Official Draft 1962):

Section 6.12 Reduction of Conviction by Court to Lesser Degree of Felony or to Misdemeanor.

If, when a person has been convicted of a felony, the Court, having regard to the nature and circumstances of the crime and to the history and character of the defendant, is of the view that it would be unduly harsh to sentence the offender in accordance with the Code, the Court may enter judgment of conviction for a lesser degree of felony or for a misdemeanor and impose sentence accordingly.

Tentative Draft No. 2, 1954, pages 28-29:

COMMENT

However carefully offenses are defined, it is inevitable that cases will arise where a conviction and a disposition in accordance with the Code will seem unduly harsh to those responsible for its administration. Such cases are now dealt with typically by a plea of guilty or conviction of a lesser degree or grade of crime than the defendant actually has committed. In some jurisdictions, the Court is authorized in its discretion to impose either a state prison sentence or a jail sentence and when the Court pursues the latter course, the conviction in some states stands as for a misdemeanor rather than a felony. . . .

We think such powers of reduction are both necessary and desirable features of a system of sentencing but we regret to see them assumed or exercised covertly rather than expressly vested in the court and utilized with candid statement of the grounds. We also think such power better exercised by the court than by the agencies of prosecution, where the power is mainly lodged in practice, though infrequently avowed. This section, therefore, grants a power to the Court to reduce the degree of felony involved for sentence purposes or to enter judgment of conviction for a misdemeanor.

A number of correctional authorities and judges took exception to both the length and the mandatory feature of the maximum sentences. They argued:

(1) If mandatory sentences are going to be used at all, they should be much shorter than those proposed in the Model Penal Code. All correctional systems have a mounting number of prisoners, and the ratio of prisoners to the general population is constantly increasing. This has resulted in overcrowding and the need for new institutions. High mandatory maxima contribute to this condition because parole boards typically take into account the length of the maximum sentence in determining when to release an inmate on parole.

(2) The existence of mandatory maxima largely destroys the sentencing discretion of the judge, shifting it to parole boards who are subject neither to effective judicial review nor to the electorate.

(3) Legislatively fixed terms result in another type of disparity, that of failing to recognize differences between defendants. Under a fixed maximum system, for example, all codefendants in a crime must be sentenced alike as far as the maximum is concerned, even though their culpability may vary widely.

(4) Legislatively fixed maxima for different degrees of crime invariably lead to bargaining for reduced charges between the prosecutor and defense counsel. This in effect takes the sentencing function from the court (and from the legislature as well) and makes it a matter of informal, nonvisible, and nonreviewable compromise between the prosecutor and the defense.[8]

---

[8] As a result of the discussions, an alternate § 6.06 was included in the proposed official draft of the MODEL PENAL CODE giving the sentencing judge discretion in setting the maximum within statutory limits:

Alternate Section 6.06. Sentence of Imprisonment for Felony; Ordinary Terms.

A person who has been convicted of a felony may be sentenced to imprisonment, as follows:

(1) in the case of a felony of the first degree, for a term the minimum of which shall be fixed by the Court at not less than one year nor more than ten years, and the maximum at not more than twenty years or at life imprisonment;

(2) in the case of a felony of the second degree, for a term the minimum of which shall be fixed by the Court at not less than one year nor more than three years, and the maximum at not more than ten years;

(3) in the case of a felony of the third degree, for a term the minimum of which shall be fixed by the Court at not less than one year nor more than two years, and the maximum at not more than five years.

No sentence shall be imposed under this Section of which the minimum is longer than one-half the maximum, or, when the maximum is life imprisonment, longer than ten years. [Proposed Official Draft 1962]

MODEL SENTENCING ACT (1963)
National Council on Crime and Delinquency

§ 9. Sentencing for Felonies Generally

. . .

If a defendant is convicted of a felony and is not committed under section 5 or 7 [or 8] the court shall (a) suspend the imposition or execution of sentence with or without probation, or (b) place the defendant on probation, or (c) impose a fine as provided by law for the offense, with or without probation or commitment, or (d) commit the defendant to the custody of [director of correction] for a term of five years or a lesser term, or to a local correctional facility for a term of one year or a lesser term. . . .

Comment on Section 9

Term of Commitment for Ordinary Offenders

The statute authorizes the judge to fix a maximum term, which may not be over five years, for offenders who, at the judge's discretion, are to be committed but do not fall within the dangerous offender categories. The parole board may release at any time within the maximum. The length of term and the flexibility of parole release are similar to provisions in some of the youth authority acts (*e.g.*, in California and in the federal jurisdiction).

The five-year limit on ordinary terms has been chosen to avoid (except for dangerous offenders) the excessive use of long terms, one of the characteristics of American sentences.

. . .

What of deterrence? Is the imposition of long terms a deterrent to others? Deterrence is primarily the product of effective law enforcement rather than of the sentencing or punishment system. However, to the extent that sentencing also carries an element of deterrence, as it does, it derives from the *potential* punishment, the statutory potential, actually imposed in those instances in which it is warranted. Very few people would suggest that it is well to impose long terms at random, for deterrent effect; the injustice of such a course is obvious. A penal code that authorizes a long term which is in fact imposed by the court where warranted is achieving the goal of deterrence so far as laws and courts can achieve it. Accordingly, on the assumption that the highest potential sentence is sufficient for deterrent effect, this consideration of sentencing is best served by carefully individualizing the offender being sentenced, making a disposition relative to his dangerousness and the requirements and limitations of rehabilitation.

Correspondingly, a sentence exceeding these requirements in punitiveness is a disservice to the entire penal system, needlessly increasing the population of the correctional institutions.

The Model Penal Code proposal as it related to minimum sentences had two major features: (1) an absolute minimum of one year for all degrees of felony, and (2) provisions for judicial discretion to set the minimum within limits fixed by legislation.[t]

The proponents of thus limiting the range of sentence argued:

(1) A spread between the maximum and minimum sentences must be established and must be great enough to control abuse by judges who set the minimum close to the maximum. In reaction to a particular crime judges sometimes set onerous sentences, such as 19½ to 20 years.

(2) There is a legislative tendency to set high minima for particular types of crimes such as narcotics violations and sex offenses. By writing in fixed minima for all degrees of felony, legislative punitiveness will be discouraged.

(3) The most difficult determination is to establish an appropriate limit on the minimum sentence for first degree crimes. The creating of a discretionary choice anywhere between one and twenty years means that parole cannot be wholly prevented by the court and yet the court can give the community assurance that they will be protected from the offender for a substantial period. At the same time, the judicial option to select any term up to the limit can act as a judicial signal to the parole board about the parole desires of the sentencing judge.

On the other hand, many correctional and judicial authorities opposed all minima whatsoever. They argued:

(1) The principle of setting a minimum term, even of one year, is bad. It does nothing to reverse the punitive trends of the legislature. In fact, it does just the opposite by stating, as a part of a model code, the desirability of fixing a minimum term. Once the principle of setting minimum sentences is accepted, there is nothing to prevent the legislature from upping the

[t] In the Proposed Official Draft, the range of minimum sentences for first degree felony was changed to one to ten years.

minimum when particular crimes are called to their attention.

(2) The fixing of a minimum sentence either by the legislature or by the judge is solely punitive and not rehabilitative. The trend should be toward giving correctional and parole authorities maximum discretion within the upper limits of the prison term, however set. Some offenders can be released in a shorter period of time than one year and the presumption of a one-year minimum sentence for all felonies precludes this possibility.

(3) Stating a minimum term weakens the deterrent action. A judge who sentences a man to twenty years imprisonment without mentioning the minimum (although he knows and all in authority know that there is no minimum and that the defendant may be released in a year or less) is still in a position of making a stronger community statement.

(4) There certainly is as much potential for disparity in minimum terms as proposed by Tentative Draft No. 2 as there is in not having fixed maxima. Furthermore, the disparity of the minimum sentences is likely to be more realistic in terms of time actually served than the maximum terms with almost immediate parole eligibility. It is much better to lodge release discretion with central agencies whose sole job it is to determine eligibility and desirability of release than allow individual judges to introduce a mechanical disparity by hampering these efforts. This position is not inconsistent with a desire to have a flexible maximum sentence for the maximum merely provides the outer limit of the sentence, thus acting as a control on sluggish or cautious parole boards, while at the same time giving the judge opportunity to distinguish between defendants and to indicate relative seriousness of criminal conduct that may be the same. The Model Sentencing Act, reflecting this philosophy, did not authorize a minimum term.[u]

---

[u] MODEL SENTENCING ACT (National Council on Crime and Delinquency 1963), Commentary on Minimum Terms—Article 1, § 1:

Disparity in Sentencing

. . .

In its application, the so-called indeterminate sentence, heretofore the only legislative attempt to combat disparity, has increased rather than decreased it. The provision for a minimum term creates disparity of sentences by setting a variety of mandatory terms of incarceration. One defendant may receive a term of one to five years, another two to four, three to five, three to six, and so on, all of which disparity would not exist if there were no minimum term. In addition, the minimum term impedes the parole process, since a parole board has no discretion to consider parole of a prisoner until the minimum term has been served.

The Model Sentencing Act diminishes the major source of disparity —sentencing according to the particular offense. Under it the danger-

Reference Note

For discussion of judicial considerations in determining the sentence, see the various reports of sentencing institutes conducted by the federal judiciary in 26 F.R.D. 231 (1959), 30 F.R.D. 185 (1961), and 30 F.R.D. 401 (1961).

A review of sentencing issues in the federal system is contained in Remington & Newman, *The Highland Park Institute on Sentence Disparity,* 26 FED. PROB. 3 (Mar. 1962).

For a criticism and defense of the Model Penal Code provisions on sentencing, see Rubin, *Sentencing and Correctional Treatment under the Law Institute's Model Penal Code,* 46 A.B.A.J. 994 (1960); and Wechsler, *Sentencing, Correction and the Model Penal Code,* 109 U. PA. L. REV. 465 (1961).

F. CHOICE OF SENTENCE—EXTENDED TERMS FOR DANGEROUS OFFENDERS

1. The Diagnosis and Disposition of Dangerous Persons

While a relatively small proportion of criminals dealt with by the police or by corrections in fact exhibit violent or threatening conduct, these agencies must be geared to the most extreme possibilities, however infrequent or remote. One consequence of this is that all persons coming in contact with the police, as well as all prisoners, confront a visible show of force and, in many cases, are treated as if dangerous by the police and correctional officials. Armed tower guards are necessary for only a fraction of prisoners but the majority of inmates must live in the same oppressive environment.

---

ous offender may be committed to a lengthy term; the nondangerous defendant may not. It makes available, for the first time, a plan that allows the sentence to be determined by the defendant's make-up, his potential threat in the future, and other similar factors, with a minimum of variation according to the offense.

. . .

Sentencing Flexibility

For a correctional system to be effective, the sentencing judge should have the power to choose without restriction among the forms of sentence, according to the condition of the defendant and the requirement of public protection. His authority to use probation, when he thinks the defendant is a good risk for it, should be unhindered; probation should not be statutorily excluded by reason of either particular kinds of crime or previous conviction. The sentencing system should not impose restrictions—for example, a minimum term—on a parole board. A minimum term prevents a parole board from releasing a defendant who in its judgment is suitable for release before the expiration of the minimum term of eligibility. This Act does not authorize a minimum term.

The entire criminal justice system is frequently evaluated in terms of its effectiveness in controlling serious crimes of violence. The police are commonly castigated for failing to prevent certain murders, rapes, or other heinous crimes. In the correctional field no one gets particularly upset if a nonsupport parolee violates his parole or if the alcoholic check forger continues to write a few small checks. But a single serious assault, rape, or murder may bring public wrath on the correctional system, damaging whatever effective programs are in existence and prejudicing public and legislative support for future programs. Given this significance as well as the intrinsic damage done by a violent crime, there is obvious concern with the effective diagnosis, treatment, and control of dangerous persons by all individuals in responsible positions in the criminal justice system.

The term "dangerous person" must obviously include one who can be expected to use or threaten physical harm, in contrast to taking property. However, there are other forms of conduct, such as child molestation and sale of narcotics, that are often considered dangerous and so treated by legislatures. On the other hand, certain acts like drunken driving, which pose greater and more continuing risk to life and limb than acts of direct violence, are usually excluded from discussions of "dangerous persons."

There are various devices for dealing with the "dangerous offender." He may be given the maximum sentence prescribed for the crime he commits, and for many crimes this may be a long term of years. Increased statutory penalties for second or third offenders are sometimes used, occasionally resulting in life sentences for persons who have been convicted repeatedly.

Finally there are statutory schemes which look less to the crime committed and more to the character of the offender as a ground for extended imprisonment—to provide time enough for rehabilitative efforts to prove successful, or indefinite restraint to protect the community against a dangerous person who has not been reformed.

Even when there is agreement on the definition of "dangerousness," there is major difficulty in diagnosis. Past violent acts are not necessarily indicative of future danger: Recidivism among murderers is very low. Habitual offender statutes may help identify likely recidivists, but not (without some limitation to repeated dangerous acts) dangerous persons. The proper application of the label "dangerous person" to a particular individual is one of the major concerns of sentencing judges and correctional authorities.

THE CASE OF DON TERRY[v]

Don Terry first came to the attention of authorities at age sixteen. Psychiatric evaluation was requested because of bizarre behavior which consisted of his defecating into the pockets of his siblings' clothes or into plastic bags, the latter of which he hid in peculiar places. A neurological examination proved negative to gross pathology. Psychological testing revealed that he was functioning within the range of borderline intelligence. A psychiatric appraisal yielded an impression of schizophrenia, and immediate hospital care was recommended.

Upon admission to Winnebago State Hospital the schizophrenic diagnosis was confirmed. He underwent a series of combined insulin and electroconvulsive treatments. Four months later he was conditionally released. About seven months following release he was arrested and charged with assaulting and attempting to choke a thirteen-year-old girl. After psychiatric evaluation, the court found him to be insane and committed him to Central State Hospital where he remained for about seven months.

An advisory board at that time concurred in the diagnosis of no psychosis but pointed out that the potentiality existed for further breakdowns and recommended that, should this occur, it would be more beneficial to the patient if he were treated in a state hospital rather than the hospital for the criminally insane.

Records for the next two years are incomplete. It is noted, however, that the patient was discharged from custody eighteen months after the assault on the girl on the basis of his having been declared legally sane.

The youth's life remained uneventful for about six months, and he was then arrested and charged with breaking and entering. A presentence investigation was requested by the court. Following is a report of the investigation made by a representative of the Probation and Parole Section of the Division of Corrections:

> The father of the subject was a fifty-five-year-old tavern operator in poor health. He was reported to have been ill with a blood disease for ten years and had suffered two cerebral hemorrhages. He was known to be alcoholic and was described as an inadequate and weak personality.
>
> The mother, age forty-five, assisted her husband with the tavern. She was in good health and was described as the dominant influence within the family. A number of reports

[v] This is an actual case history with the name changed.

indicated that the mother had verbalized sharp-tongued criticism of law enforcement officers. At the time she was interviewed by the field agent, however, no negative feelings were reflected in her comments. She had, however, adopted an attitude of defensiveness and protectiveness toward her son and refused to admit, even to herself, her son's difficulties believing that even though he had admitted the offense, he did not know whether he had done it or not, and that the only reason he pleaded guilty was to avoid being recommitted to the hospital.

An older brother was in the army in Korea at the time and had been wounded on two occasions. An older sister was married. Both were described as well adjusted. The family had no religious affiliation. They were considered to be self-sufficient economically.

The early life of the subject was characterized by illness. His mother described a breech birth from which the baby sustained a broken leg and hip. He required a great deal of nursing and protectiveness to maintain his health. He walked and talked within the normal range, and his toilet training was described as normal. During childhood he reportedly suffered mumps, measles, pneumonia, and a serious illness in 1949 in which his appendix was removed along with an infected tumor of the bowel. He has an undescended testicle. He had been injured by beatings by peers, injured playing basketball (types of injuries not specified), and knocked out running into a tree while tobogganing.

He began school at age five or six and repeated the first and sixth grades, presumably because of illness. He was in ninth grade when the disturbed behavior began to emerge.

Variously he was characterized to the agent as being moody, irritable, impulsive, untruthful, and inclined toward "kleptomania." Psychiatric reports prepared at the time the bizarre behavior developed, indicated that he possibly became amnesic when intoxicated. He was described as aggressive when drunk, as reflected in his attack on the young girl. The members of the sheriff's department, who had observed him over a period of time in jail, called attention to his extreme fluctuation of mood.

In summary: (1) There is a history of mental illness treated by psychotherapy, electroshock, and insulin. The acute phase of the illness has subsided, but a number of behavioral symptoms remain which indicate personality disorder likely to bring on further antisocial behavior. (2) Possible sexual deviation is suggested by his defecating into the pockets of his siblings' clothing, by hiding his feces, and by his admission of moods in which he feels like destroying. His attack on the girl fits this pattern. (3) Persecutory feelings about law enforcement officers appear to be developing. (4) The people of the community are disturbed and fearful of this individual being at large. (5) This individual is a product of a number of forces that have had their part in molding his personality since birth: (a) inadequate parental situation, with the father an inadequate personality, the mother the dominating influence who has assumed an unreasonably protective and defensive attitude which reinforces this individual's belief that he is being treated unfairly; (b) health problems since birth with accident proneness along with borderline mental deficiency and actual mental illness; (c) lack of acceptance and actual rejection by the community has fostered further antisocial attitudes; (d) lack of any religious affiliation. In my opinion this individual is now dangerous to himself and to society.

He was sentenced to two years in the state reformatory. Upon admission he was examined and found to be in good physical condition. A battery of psychological tests was administered including a brief test of intelligence, an occupational interest test, a sentence completion test, and a test of manual dexterity. A few weeks after his admission he was interviewed by a clinical psychologist. The following is a slightly edited version of the psychological report: "This is a twenty-year-old who, at first, is contemptuous and flippant in the interview. Later he becomes congenial and pleasant. Occasionally he smiles inappropriately. In terms of emotional expression he vacillates between blandness and moderate excitement. He chews his fingernails, trembles noticeably from time to time, and complains of nervousness. His clinical behavior suggests that he is quite unstable emotionally and conveys the impression that this instability is reflected in his overall adjustment. He has been hospitalized both at Winnebago and Central State Hospitals, has been diagnosed as schizophrenic (undifferentiated type), and has received insulin and electroconvulsive treatments."

Intelligence: Brief testing suggests that he is functioning at the low end of the range of normal intelligence.

Personality Impressions: Although this young man displays no blatant psychotic signs at this time, his clinical behavior and especially his test responses reveal a latent personality disturbance which is quite marked. He is very evasive when it comes to discussing past behavior, symptoms, and the like. In general he may be characterized as extremely tense and restless with a quick temper which gives rise to explosive reactions (his history recounts an assaultive episode for which he was hospitalized rather than prosecuted). His behavior now is apparently much improved relative to what it had been in the hospital. However, the potential for further disturbance remains. Should he again become disturbed, it is likely that he would be dangerous to himself as well as to others. In a fairly congenial setting where he is not subject to much pressure or exposed to provocative stimulation, he may get along fairly well.

Recommendations: Assignment: He desires vocational school courses in the fall. In the summer, any assignment inside the walls which does not require a lot of interpersonal contact is recommended. Custody: Close to maximum. This inmate will probably require more patience and understanding than most. Treatment: He is interested in but not enthusiastic about therapy. For the present he will be seen from time to time at his request.

About a month later he was interviewed for diagnostic purposes by the institution psychiatrist, who reported:

This individual is a well-developed, well-nourished, twenty-year-old white male, blunted in affect. He answers questions relevantly and coherently. The orientation of his thinking, however, is quite concrete in quality, and his gross emotional reactions are handled in their surface inclination only. His affect in my opinion is dulled and blunted, and in view of the history, I think that his affect has to be considered as presenting a residual psychotic disturbance. Also, there is rather marked subsurface tension, concealed somewhat beneath the surface of concrete comment and attitude. He denies any current delusions or hallucinations. He believes that he did have hallucinations prior to his insulin and electric treatments at Winnebago some years ago, but he cannot remember definitely. He was told at that time that he had been hallucinating. Orientation is generally satisfactory. Memory is uncertain for periods of his illness. Judgment, I think, can potentially be impaired by explosive eruptiveness of affect that is repressed out of his everyday life adjustment. Insight is almost entirely limited to factual awareness of what has transpired in his past.

Probe and comment as to interpersonal relationship, as expected, elicited very little. This boy's orientation, I think, is of schizophrenic quality, and although not overtly psychotic at this time, I think he presents a life attitude containing residuals of psychosis, and I believe that he does carry a latent psychosis. In the interview, however, I do not feel that subsurface struggling of positive feeling is evident, and he does form a minimal relationship with me. He doubts that talking about himself and discussion in general would do any good, but is willing to give it a try. I feel that he should be seen for individual therapy. I think the goal of therapy should be limited entirely to establishing what one can in a positive transference, to become somewhat of a friend in terms of discussing problems or feelings with him but not in terms of actual manipulative environmental help to any significant degree. In short, I think the outlook offered by interview should be an attempt to establish a friendly, supportive contact with him, with considerable caution in any delving attempt.

While here he occasionally shows attitudes of stubbornness, refusal to work, or something of the sort. If possible, he would be best off in a job where such occasional attitudes of this could be tolerated mildly, though again a cautious line must be drawn so that he does not try to dominate too much with these attitudes. It is not imperative to transfer him to Central State Hospital [for the Criminally Insane] at present. Such transfer for the future would remain a possibility. Such clumsy, struggling attempts as he can make for interpersonal prestige, he now makes in the powerhouse by pretending psychotic attitudes at times. The other men there razz him, and in his resistance he takes a distorted satisfaction from sitting off in a corner at times and gazing into space, thus attracting their attention and further comments and probably gaining some feeling that he has succeeded in causing them unrest.

Diagnosis: Residuals of undifferentiated schizophrenic reaction, chronic, mild. The psychiatric report concluded with these recommendations: (1) Close custody. (2) Friendly but tolerant and mildly firm environmental placement. (3) Individual interviews with one of the psychologists, or direct counseling in avoiding drinking which in him easily releases disturbed behavior.

In spite of this young man's occasionally eccentric behavior, he made a relatively uneventful institutional adjustment within the reformatory until later when he displayed sudden eruptive violence which necessitated the course recommended in the following supplementary psychiatric report:

> This individual was in general regarded by us as quite possibly schizophrenic, although I never felt entirely sure in my own mind whether he was truly schizophrenic or severely passive and aggressive in his personality structure. There is, however, in his general attitude an implicit withdrawal and flatness of affect punctuated by violent eruptiveness, and my own diagnostic opinion, if it had to be formed and phrased, would be that he is a schizophrenic.
>
> In his six or seven months' stay here, he has had friction with authority but no serious outbursts. He has more or less used one of the psychologists as a safety valve, seeing him to ventilate when he felt the pressures were more than he could tolerate. This evening, however, he apparently erupted violently, having first announced his intention in a sealed envelope to the psychologist. This is a crudely phrased note given to the deputy about an hour before breaking up his cell that evening. The psychologist and I were called to see him while he was on his destructive rampage within his cell. After destroying the articles of furniture, he had armed himself with a razor blade and threatened violent assault upon anyone who would attempt to enter his cell. By the time we arrived he was calmed down and, although distrustful in attitude, was willing to talk to us. He eventually accepted our invitation to leave his cell and talk things over with us in the institution library, and then was quite composed and apologetic for his outburst. He was resistive to the idea of going to Central State, but our persuasion was mostly to the effect that we felt the pressure there would be least and he could serve his time more comfortably, without as much danger of erupting into an aggressive outburst which conceivably could bring an assault charge that would carry an additional sentence. Once calmed down he was in our opinion quite trustworthy again for the time being, and he was simply returned to his cell and allowed to go to his usual classes the following morning until he was moved to Central State Hospital.
>
> In regard to his placement on arrival there, I would reiterate what I mentioned on the phone—that I feel he is not manipulating and that I think he will be best handled, with least resistance development, by simply being placed on one of the less rigid wards where he can start in some sort of daily work. I recommend that he be returned to the

reformatory, if feasible, in four months for a parole hearing.

Terry was subsequently transferred to Central State Hospital where he was assigned to work in the kitchen. It was decided by the staff there that he be returned to the reformatory prior to the expiration of his sentence if he showed no evidence of psychotic activity at that time. Three months later he was staffed and his request to return to the reformatory was approved. At that time he was described as being in contact with the surroundings, carried on a coherent conversation, and showed no evidence of psychotic activity. He was returned to the reformatory and was seen later that month by the parole board who deferred action on his parole application for two months in order to have more time to observe his adjustment.

Between the time that he was returned to the reformatory and appeared before the parole board two months later, the individual was seen periodically by members of the psychiatric staff. For a portion of that time he was administered tranquilizers.

He was finally granted parole largely because it was felt that he needed field supervision. His sentence would have terminated early the following year, and rather than have him released without any kind of supervision or guidance, the parole board felt that it would be advisable to release a few months earlier so that he might have the advantage of this kind of supervision. Consequently the inmate was released.

At sentencing, the likelihood of invoking an extended term is based in part upon the urgency of the problem he presents, as perceived by the judge and those who make recommendations to him. Sometimes the fear of crime outruns the actual danger.

THE PRESIDENT'S COMMISSION ON LAW ENFORCEMENT AND ADMINISTRATION OF JUSTICE TASK FORCE REPORT: CRIME AND ITS IMPACT—AN ASSESSMENT 14-15 (1967)

The crimes that concern Americans the most are those that affect their personal safety—at home, at work, or in the streets. The most frequent and serious of these crimes of violence against the person are willful homicide, forcible rape, aggravated assault, and robbery.

. . .

The risk of sudden attack by a stranger is perhaps best measured by the frequency of robberies since, according to UCR [the F.B.I. Uniform Crime Reports] and other studies, about 70 percent of all willful killings, nearly two-thirds of all aggravated assaults and a high percentage of forcible rapes are committed by family members, friends, or other persons previously known to their victims. Robbery usually does not involve this prior victim-offender relationship.

Robbery, for UCR purposes, is the taking of property from a person by use or threat of force with or without a weapon. Nationally, about one-half of all robberies are street robberies, and slightly more than one-half involve weapons. Attempted robberies are an unknown percentage of the robberies reported to the UCR. The likelihood of injury is also unknown, but a survey by the District of Columbia Crime Commission of 297 robberies in Washington showed that some injury was inflicted in 25 percent of them. The likelihood of injury was found higher for "yokings" or "muggings" (unarmed robberies from the rear) than for armed robberies. Injuries occurred in 10 of 91 armed robberies as compared with 30 of 67 yokings.

Aggravated assault is assault with intent to kill or for the purpose of inflicting severe bodily injury, whether or not a dangerous weapon is used. It includes all cases of attempted homicide, but cases in which bodily injury is inflicted in the course of a robbery or a rape are included with those crimes rather than with aggravated assault. There are no national figures showing the percentage of aggravated assaults that involve injury, but a survey of 131 cases by the District of Columbia Crime Commission found injury in 84 percent of the cases; 35 percent of the victims required hospitalization. A 1960 UCR study showed that juvenile gangs committed less than 4 percent of all aggravated assaults.

Forcible rape includes only those rapes or attempted rapes in which force or threat of force is used. About one-third of the UCR total is attempted rape. In a District of Columbia Crime Commission survey of 151 cases, about 25 percent of all rape victims were attacked with dangerous weapons; the survey did not show what percentage received bodily harm in addition to the rape.

About 15 percent of all criminal homicides, both nationally and in the District of Columbia Crime Commission surveys, occurred in the course of committing other offenses. These offenses appear in the homicide total rather than in the total for the other offense. In the District of Columbia Crime Commission surveys, less than one-half of 1 percent of the robberies and about 3 percent of the forcible rapes ended in homicide.

Some personal danger is also involved in the property crimes. Burglary is the unlawful entering of a building to commit a felony or a theft, whether force is used or not. About half of all burglaries involve residences, but the statistics do not distinguish inhabited parts of houses from garages and similar outlying parts. About half of all residential burglaries are committed in daylight and about half at night. A UCR survey indicates that 32 percent of the entries into residences are made through unlocked doors or windows. When an unlawful entry results in a violent confrontation with the occupant, the offense is counted as a robbery rather than a burglary. Of course, even when no confrontation takes place there is often a risk of confrontation. Nationally such confrontations occur in only one-fortieth of all residential burglaries. . . .

In summary, these figures suggest that, on the average, the likelihood of a serious personal attack on any American in a given year is about 1 in 550; together with the studies available they also suggest that the risk of serious attack from spouses, family members, friends, or acquaintances is almost twice as great as it is from strangers on the street. Commission and other studies, moreover, indicate that the risks of personal harm are spread very unevenly. The actual risk for slum dwellers is considerably more; for most Americans it is considerably less.

THE SHOCKING RISE OF MURDER

By Jack Star

Look Magazine, Sept. 19, 1967, at 28-34†

Ever since the early 1930's, the homicide rate—the number of murders per 100,000 population—had been on the decline, even though most other crime increased greatly. Then, in 1965, homicides rose sharply: by six percent to almost 10,000. Last year, they went up another 11 percent to nearly 11,000. In the first quarter of this year, they went up 23 percent. By July 1, some large cities reported jumps of 45 percent, 153 percent and even 200 percent.

Chicago, which recorded 395 murders in 1965, had 510 last year and may have 700 this year. St. Louis was No. 1 in 1965 murder-rate rankings; killings dropped sharply last year, but are now up 80 percent. Cleveland murders rose from 108 in 1965 to 139 last year; this year, they are up 45 percent.

The upsurge in homicides would be even more horrendous if it weren't for the great lifesaving advances made by hospitals

† By courtesy of the editors. Copyright 1967 by Cowles Communications, Inc.

since World War II, says Jerome Daunt, who is in charge of collecting crime statistics for the FBI. In Chicago, only 12 or 13 of every 100 gunshot victims fail to survive, and only two of every 100 stabbing victims. The survivors are counted among the aggravated assaults, and the assault rate, says Daunt, has just about doubled nationally since the 1930's.

. . .

And it does appear ominous that murder is increasing at a faster rate than population. In 1965, there were 5.1 murders per 100,000 population. In 1966, the murder rate shot up ten percent to 5.6.

The accurate diagnosis of an offender's character and the accurate prediction of his conduct are among the most difficult tasks the system sets for itself.

THE VIOLENT OFFENDER (1966)

By Daniel Glaser, Donald Kenefick & Vincent O'Leary
Parole Decision-Making Series
(U.S. Department of Health, Education, and Welfare)

Part VII—Decision-Making and the Violent Offender

There are two ways of making decisions as to how a given individual is apt to behave in relation to some future event (for example, how a given prisoner will behave on parole). These are: (a) knowing a great deal about the particular individual's behavior in situations the individual sees as similar to the one we are predicting for; or (b) knowing just enough about the individual to be able to place him accurately in a group or class of individuals, a class whose behavior in analogous situations we can specify fairly precisely.

For practical purposes, the second technique is all that is available for most decision-making and may work extremely well, providing one has (a) defined the characteristics of the class or group so that the members really tend to behave similarly in similar situations, and (b) correctly identified the individual as indeed belonging to that group.

Two problems that arise in using clinicians as aids in decision-making are that they, generally, are more used to the first technique (which means that accurate information can be available for only a few individuals) and have done relatively little of the painstaking work with large numbers necessary to make use of the second technique. Moreover, even prolonged contact with a given *individual* does not always fit one to prognosticate very effectively about him. For example, most psychiatrists estimate a patient by criteria they are most familiar with, such as fitness for therapy, extent and nature of psychopathology and so on, and these may have little pertinence to such matters as ability to hold a job or to function in a prison environment, and so on.

Moreover, most murderers and violent offenders are poor, and most of the remainder are at best lower middle class. On the other hand, a clinician is usually most familiar with middle or upper class people. These, as a rule, tend to have symptoms that consist of unpleasant feelings (such as anxiety, guilt, or depression) or certain complex behaviors, usually of a nonviolent sort, such as school failure or sexual difficulties, which serve to mask or substitute for these feelings. Because middle class people have strong prejudices against violence and many kinds of activities that conceal, to a certain extent, the existence of such unpleasant feelings, their neurotic problems seem much different from those of lower class people. Lower class people tend to do something *directly* about an unpleasant feeling and, moreover, usually have less choice in the matter, because the opportunities for substitutive activities are less common.

The point of this observation is this: A psychiatrist who saw one of his middle class patients hit someone else would often conclude, usually correctly, that something was badly wrong with the patient. If he made the same diagnosis at a fist fight in the slums, he might well be wrong himself. There is no substitute for personal knowledge of the range of "normal" and "pathologic" behavior in different social classes and different milieux. Moreover, people who "feel" symptoms and people who "act out" symptoms respond differently to treatment and really require quite different forms of treatments.

. . .

Even if a [parole] board were given all the psychiatrists, sociologists, statisticians, and other experts it desired to make a thorough investigation and analysis of each case, it is doubtful if it could achieve 80 percent accuracy in identifying the less-than-5-percent of parolees who commit clearly violent offenses after release. Eighty percent accuracy is about the greatest precision that has been demonstrated by any man or any prediction system, applied to a cross-section of prisoners, for predicting parole violation in general, rather than the more difficult task of predicting violence on parole. Of course, a board might sharply reduce the number of violent offenses committed on parole if it stopped paroling, but this would merely mean releasing prisoners to commit violence as dischargees without the services of parole in facilitating a noncriminal life and restricting activities leading to crime.

If a board were 80 percent accurate in identifying the most violent parolees, they would still make more than 2 erroneous predictions in 10 as long as the violence they sought to predict occurred in less than 20 percent of the cases. This is simply a matter of mathematics. For example, if violence were committed by 5 percent of prison releasees in every 1,000 releasees, a parole board would have to identify 50 men who would commit violence among 950 who would not. With 80 percent predictive accuracy, we could expect the board to predict violence for 20 percent of the 950, or 190 cases, and for 80 percent of the 50, or 40 cases. However, in this total of 230 designations as probably violent, one could not know in advance which actually would be the 40 who would be violent. They would make a total of 200 erroneous predictions, the 190 nonviolent designated as violent and the 10 violent not designated as violent, in identifying correctly the 230 cases in 1,000 which include 40 of the 50 violence cases. These errors are apart from others they might make in predicting more common types of parole infraction, such as nonviolent theft, burglary or return to narcotics.

The foregoing theoretical analysis assumes 80 percent accuracy in predicting violent parole infractions, and that 5 percent of the men released will commit such infractions. If accuracy is lower, or the frequency of the behavior to be predicted is less than 5 percent, there will be more errors made in order to deny parole to a given proportion of those who would commit the predicted behavior. If we have 80 or even 90 percent accuracy in predicting an event occurring in only 1 percent of the cases, such as the commission of a violent sex offense by a paroled sex offender, our ratio of errors to correct predictions would be much greater than 200 to 40.

Among the various schemes for sentencing dangerous persons to extended terms, the Model Penal Code is notable for its explicit attention to criteria for identifying proper subjects for the law's operation. The sentences for such persons, as specified in § 6.07, are roughly twice as severe as they would ordinarily be for the crime of which the dangerous person is convicted.

MODEL PENAL CODE § 7.03
American Law Institute
(Proposed Official Draft 1962)

Section 7.03. Criteria for Sentence of Extended Term of Imprisonment; Felonies.

The Court may sentence a person who has been convicted of a felony to an extended term of imprisonment if it finds one or more of the grounds specified in this Section. The finding of the Court shall be incorporated in the record.

(1) The defendant is a persistent offender whose commitment for an extended term is necessary for protection of the public.

The Court shall not make such a finding unless the defendant is over twenty-one years of age and has previously been convicted of two felonies or of one felony and two misdemeanors, committed at different times when he was over [insert Juvenile Court age] years of age.

(2) The defendant is a professional criminal whose commitment for an extended term is necessary for protection of the public.

The Court shall not make such a finding unless the defendant is over twenty-one years of age and:

(a) the circumstances of the crime show that the defendant has knowingly devoted himself to criminal activity as a major source of livelihood; or

(b) the defendant has substantial income or resources not explained to be derived from a source other than criminal activity.

(3) The defendant is a dangerous, mentally abnormal person whose commitment for an extended term is necessary for protection of the public.

The Court shall not make such a finding unless the defendant has been subjected to a psychiatric examination resulting in the conclusions that his mental condition is gravely abnormal; that his criminal conduct has been characterized by a pattern of repetitive or compulsive behavior or by persistent aggressive behavior with heedless indifference to consequences; and that such condition makes him a serious danger to others.

(4) The defendant is a multiple offender whose criminality was so extensive that a sentence of imprisonment for an extended term is warranted.

The Court shall not make such a finding unless:

(a) the defendant is being sentenced for two or more felonies, or is already under sentence of imprisonment for felony, and the sentences of imprisonment involved will run concurrently under Section 7.06; or

(b) the defendant admits in open court the commission of one or more other felonies and asks that they be taken into account when he is sentenced; and

(c) the longest sentences of imprisonment authorized for each of the defendant's crimes, including admitted crimes taken into account, if made to run consecutively would exceed in length the minimum and maximum of the extended term imposed.

In the discussions of the American Law Institute, there appeared to be very little correctional or judicial opposition to the extended term provisions. Most judges and correctional authorities felt that such provisions should be used only very cautiously, for a very few dangerous offenders.[w] They also felt that having such provisions discretionary with the court was a much better solution to the difficult problem of dealing with the dangerous offender than provided by present habitual offender laws, which leave the court no discretion once the defendant is charged as an habitual offender by the prosecutor.

The Model Sentencing Act has been proposed as an alternative to the Model Penal Code formulation.

MODEL SENTENCING ACT (1963)
National Council on Crime and Delinquency

Comment on Sections 5 and 6

. . .

Lengthy terms of imprisonment today are imposed according to either the offense committed (which, we have observed, is not a reliable guide) or, more usually, the number of previous convictions. Numerous studies have shown the latter also to be an unreliable guide, leading to unfairness and a great disparity of sentencing.

Instead of these demonstrably untrustworthy signs, the Model Act proposes that an offender be sentenced as dangerous if he fits

[w] There was some judicial opposition to extended terms for misdemeanants on the grounds that these were not necessary. *See* §§ 6.08, 7.04 of both Tentative Draft No. 2 and the Proposed Official Draft.

into any one of three categories: (1) commission of a crime that inflicted or attempted to inflict serious bodily harm, and propensity to commit crime; (2) commission of a crime (such as arson) which, intended or not, seriously endangered the life or safety of another, previous criminal conviction, and propensity to commit crime; (3) participation in organized crime, racketeering. The Act thus establishes a legally and socially precise delineation of dangerous persons (section 5) and a legally and clinically careful procedure for identifying such persons (section 6).

Sentencing of Racketeers

Subdivision (c) of section 5 is intended to enable courts to sentence to long terms offenders who are involved in rackets, organized or syndicate crime. Today such offenders, in the relatively rare instances in which they are apprehended and convicted, are sentenced for such crimes as income tax evasion, loitering, vagrancy, or, as in the case of the apparently important individuals apprehended at Appalachin, N. Y., in 1957, for conspiring to obstruct justice by refusing to testify. New definitions of racketeering crimes are needed, as well as strengthened law enforcement efforts; the effect of a sentencing provision standing alone is extremely limited. However, the subdivision does provide courts with increased power to sentence to long terms racketeer defendants who come within its broad provisions.

Term of Commitment of Dangerous Offenders

Section 5 authorizes commitment of dangerous offenders for a period long enough—up to thirty years—to protect the public against them and to afford ample opportunity for therapeutic efforts to be made. The statutory maximum is not mandatory; the judge may fix the maximum at any period less than thirty years. This discretion is provided for in the case of long-term commitments to give scope to individualized consideration of the defendant.

A life term is not authorized except for murder in the first degree (see section 7). The surge of aggression, of violent action, is a characteristic of the young rather than the old offender. The term of years authorized would be ample, in almost all cases, to confine him until that period of his life when release would be safe and rehabilitation likely. This holds true even for some so-called sociopaths. If an offender could not be released at the end of a thirty-year term, his disorder would almost inevitably be the kind that would render him committable to a state mental hospital.

Why should a life term be avoided? A life term, even though the offender is subject to release, is a psychological set against any treatment other than the passage of time. Even the small minority of offenders who are categorized as dangerous should be dealt with on a diagnostic and treatment basis.

Life terms present difficulties in parole operations in many states. Many parole boards have a rigid attitude toward life terms and defer parole for so long a period, far beyond the necessities of public protection, that the personality of the inmate is destroyed. Legislatures often attach parole eligibility limitations—minimum terms of fifteen or twenty years—that prohibit release even where the prisoner has been rehabilitated and could safely be paroled. Furthermore, in some states a life-term sentence excludes parole, a sentence described by a Minnesota warden as "the penalty worse than death."

Guttmacher points out that "Whenever a former inmate of a psychiatric hospital commits a homicide, there is likely to be raised a hue and cry, demanding that such things stop." When one such case occurred in New York a few years ago, he writes, the governor called a conference to consider the whole question:

> Little came of it, because it was the view of those of us who were in attendance that until we had an absolute and permanent cure for all psychotic patients, such an occasional tragedy must necessarily be perpetrated by discharged patients. The only sure way to prevent them would be to keep all psychiatric hospital patients in permanent custody, an act the impracticality of which would only be surpassed by its inhumanity. There must be this irreducible minimum of such cases. If none ever occurred, we could conclude that discharge policies were too strict. In the same vein, psychiatric hospitals in which no suicides ever occur and juvenile correctional schools in which there are no escapes, must be considered to be poor institutions because they are too strictly organized to accomplish their therapeutic purposes.

. . .

Most of the habitual offender laws provide for a life sentence on a third or fourth felony conviction. As already observed, the application of these laws is extremely spotty, and the way in which certain persons receive a life term under these laws and other persons do not is completely removed from individual case requirements.

Referring to some pathetically unnecessary long-term cases, Warden Ross V. Randolph declared:

> Disheartened, embittered prisoners are always a source of trouble to good prisoners, and to the administration of a penal institution. . . . An embittered person leaving a correctional institution is a bad risk and a costly product for the state as well as society in general.

A report of the Federal Bureau of Prisons has this to say about long sentences:

> If the purpose . . . is to deter other potential offenders, it cannot be demonstrated that they have any substantial effect on the reduction of crime rates. If, on the other hand, the purpose of a long sentence is to increase the severity of the penalty for the sake of punishment alone, history and experience tell us how self-defeating this can be. Recognizing that certain dangerous criminals must be kept out of circulation for the protection of society, the long and mandatory sentence nevertheless rejects the basic correctional concept that an offender should be given the opportunity to retake his place in society when there are reasonable grounds to expect that he can do so without again violating the law.

. . .

Consideration was given to the suggestion that a defendant sentenced to a term of more than five years should be given a right to have his continuing confinement re-examined by a court upon an institutional report at regular intervals. Such a proposal was not incorporated in the Act. Periodic review by the institution and parole authorities should occur—and it does—without requirement by statute. A statutory requirement might have a limiting effect on administrative review. A statute that would make review mandatory every year would be disapproved by administration as too rigid; on the other hand, expressly authorizing review at some significantly greater interval, such as five years, might induce laxity and would encourage an acceptance of long-term incarceration.

SENTENCING THE RACKETEER

By Milton G. Rector

8 Crime and Delinquency 385 (1962)

The charge that racketeers and leaders of organized criminal activity constitute the greatest internal threat to American society and must be considered as some of our most dangerous persons is well documented by their success in corrupting and controlling law enforcement and key governmental officials, in taking control of legitimate business operations from rightful owners, and in recruiting followers and partners from leading professions and from youth attracted by the promise of status, wealth, and power.

A Matter of Segregation

The greatest contribution we in the courts and correctional systems can make to the elimination of organized crime is to perfect our methods of separating from the mass of convicted offenders those who are truly dangerous and to sentence and incarcerate them accordingly.

In the belief that antiquated state and federal penal and sentencing laws must be brought up to date in order to give the courts a realistic legal framework within which they can deal with dangerous criminals, the National Council on Crime and Delinquency, through its Advisory Council of Judges, has developed a Model Sentencing Act. Under the provisions of this act, the sentencing court may remove dangerous persons from society for as long as necessary; it may commit them, according to certain well-defined criteria, to terms extended to as much as thirty years. The dangerousness of the criminal and his propensity for further criminal activity, not the particular offense bringing him to the court, would govern the sentence. The Model Sentencing Act eliminates the artificiality of sentencing according to the degree of the crime and offers, in its place, specific criteria by which to sentence the offender according to his requirements and society's best interests. It also provides, for those who are not dangerous, a formula for sentences far shorter in many instances than those now prevailing. Its adoption would mean less reliance on lengthy imprisonment for persons who do not require it, and at the same time the segregation of dangerous offenders into small, maximum custody institutions for safekeeping, intensive study, and, hopefully, eventual rehabilitation, although admittedly the lucrative profits of racketeering and the strong binding ties among the members of organized crime make rehabilitation an extremely slim possibility.

. . .

Suppose he is committed for the maximum under the present statute. During his five years of imprisonment, minus time off for "good behavior," his earnings from syndicate income will continue and his family's standard of living will not suffer; in short, the effect of the sentence, so far as society is concerned, will be hardly noticeable. On the other hand, if he were removed from society for a long time—as provided in the Model Sentencing Act—the effect would be quite different: either his complete separation from the syndicate or a sharp increase in the syndicate's overhead because of prolonged profit-sharing with an inactive member.

The fallacy of "equal" sentencing for the same crime committed by two quite dissimilar persons is nowhere better illustrated than in cases of tax fraud. From the viewpoint of dangerousness and public safety, the problem presented by the racketeer convicted of income tax evasion is quite different from that of the ordinary businessman or professional man convicted of the same crime. The same can be said of the syndicate member convicted of extortion, compared with a person whose attempt at extortion was motivated by overwhelming debts or unemployment.

Oddly enough, income-tax sentences meted out to known racketeers tend to be peculiarly unequal to those imposed on the nonracketeer group. In the three-year period of 1952-54, 52 percent of all persons convicted of income tax violations were classified as racketeers. Of this tax violator-racketeer group, only 30 percent received prison sentences, which averaged only fifteen months; their average fine was $7,834. The average fine for the tax violator-racketeer who was not sentenced to imprisonment was $1,197. Commenting on this set of facts at the Pilot Institute on Sentencing, Judge R. H. Weber noted that the sentences for this racketeer group as a whole were much lighter than those imposed on income tax violators engaged in legitimate businesses and professions.

. . .

Obstacles to Enactment

The very fact that the Model Sentencing Act would give the courts a mighty weapon to combat organized crime—a powerful and corrupting foe—will actuate certain persons to block its consideration and adoption. The concept of sentencing on the basis of the offender rather than the offense, though long an ideal in the administration of justice, will cause others to withhold support in favor of existing law despite its inadequacies.

The need for new or expanded state and federal diagnostic services may indeed be raised as an argument against the Act. But what correctional system can today pretend to serve the courts and protect the public without such services? It might be necessary to authorize the federal system to provide diagnostic facilities and services to courts in states which cannot justify or afford them, and to permit well-equipped state facilities to provide services to federal courts which are far from a federal institution. This would be another logical step in the coordination of state and federal services in the fight against crime.[x]

2. The Procedures for Establishing Liability to Extended Terms

SAS v. MARYLAND

334 F.2d 506 (4th Cir. 1964)

J. SPENCER BELL, Circuit Judge. This is a consolidated appeal of five petitions for writs of habeas corpus filed by five inmates of Maryland's Patuxent Institution wherein they seek to have the Maryland Defective Delinquent Act, Ann.Code of Md., Article 31B (Supp. 1961) [hereinafter the Act], under which they are confined declared unconstitutional. The petitions were denied by the district court without the issuance of a writ of habeas corpus or show cause order, without requiring the state to file returns, without appointment of counsel for the indigent petitioners and without argument or hearing.

The petitioners allege facts which raise serious questions of a non-frivolous nature which concern the constitutionality of the Act. We hold that statute to be facially constitutional; i.e., it is within the power of the state to segregate from among its lawbreakers a class or category which is dangerous to the public safety and to confine this group for the purpose of treatment or for the purpose of protecting the public from further depredations.

Section five, the heart of the Act, defines the term defective delinquent as follows:

"DEFECTIVE DELINQUENTS

"§ 5. Defined.

"For the purposes of this article, a defective delinquent shall be defined as an individual who, by the demonstration of persistent aggravated antisocial or criminal behavior, evidences a propensity toward criminal activity, and who is found to have either such intellectual deficiency or emotional unbalance, or both, as to clearly demonstrate an actual danger to society so as

---

[x] THE PRESIDENT'S COMMISSION ON LAW ENFORCEMENT AND ADMINISTRATION OF JUSTICE, THE CHALLENGE OF CRIME IN A FREE SOCIETY 203 (1967):

Federal and State legislation should be enacted to provide for extended prison terms where the evidence, presentence report, or sentence hearing shows that a felony was committed as part of a continuing illegal business in which the convicted offender occupied a supervisory or other management position.

to require such confinement and treatment, when appropriate, as may make it reasonably safe for society to terminate the confinement and treatment."

The remainder of the Act provides, in essence, that persons convicted of specified offenses may be thereafter tried as defective delinquents and if found to be such may be confined for an indeterminate period.

We cannot agree that the statutory definition upon its face is unconstitutional. The subject matter of the statute—the health, welfare and safety of the people of Maryland—is within the area of the police power of the legislature. This being true, only if the Act has not real or substantial relation to that objective—or is palpably and patently an invasion of the individual's constitutional rights—may the courts strike down the Act. Jacobson v. Massachusetts, 197 U.S. 11, 31 (1905). In Minnesota ex rel. Pearson v. Probate Court, 309 U.S. 270 (1940), the appellant had filed a writ of prohibition to prevent the probate judge from trying him as a "Psychopathic Personality" under the Minnesota Act. The Minnesota Appellate Court had defined the Act to apply to persons who by an habitual course of misconduct showed an utter lack of power to control their sexual impulses and hence were likely to attack others or otherwise inflict injury. In upholding the statute, as construed by the state court, Chief Justice Hughes held that there was a rational basis for the class selected by the legislature; that the definition was not so vague or indefinite as to constitute invalid legislation and, therefore, the Act was constitutional upon its face. While psychiatrists no longer approve the term psychopath as a definitive medical term, we note that the definition adopted by the Minnesota Appellate Court and approved by the Supreme Court was not dependent upon the medical acceptability of the term psychopath. It is obvious that the Maryland statutory definition was carefully drawn to conform to the definition approved by the Court in the Minnesota case.

The Maryland Court of Appeals, however, has construed the statutory definition to include mentally deficient persons and/or psychopaths who by persistent aggravated antisocial or criminal behavior have clearly demonstrated themselves to be such an actual danger to society as to require confinement. Palmer v. State, 215 Md. 142, 137 A.2d 119, 122 (1957). Whether or not the court's interpretation of the words "emotionally unbalanced" as used in the statutory definition to include "psychopaths"—a term which is not determinable by medical standards alone—has rendered the definition too vague to be constitutionally acceptable is a matter which may not be determined without the aid of expert testimony not available on this record. Counsel for the petitioners offer the expert writings of members of the Patuxent staff to show that "emotional unbalance" is such a quantitatively and qualitatively inaccurate term that any person who seeks to apply the definition is forced to depend upon an individual interpretation of the evidence of past antisocial and criminal conduct. Again it is the district court which must provide a record which will offer a solution to this issue.

The petitioners also contend that the Act does not provide them with a fair trial in that it denies them procedural due process. An examination of the trial and hearing provisions of the Act can leave no doubt that it places around the accused more procedural safeguards than any of the Acts of a similar nature which have been upheld by the courts against this attack. Not until the convicted felon has been examined and diagnosed by the Patuxent Clinic is he liable to trial under the statute as a defective delinquent. He is entitled to a jury trial with special finding. He must be allowed counsel of his own choice or furnished counsel. He has the power to summon witnesses. He is entitled to be furnished a psychiatrist who is independent of Patuxent. While the sentence prescribed for the defective delinquent is fixed by the law as an indeterminate sentence, it nevertheless requires yearly administrative review of his record by the Patuxent staff and an opportunity to the petitioner at fixed times to have a judicial review of his status.

But petitioners attack the trial provided in the Maryland Act on the ground that it departs from the common law rules of evidence in permitting the experts to testify over objection to hearsay matters either admitted by the petitioner during his clinical examination at Patuxent or collected by the staff from the petitioner's school records or indeed from any source deemed of relevance by the psychiatrist in forming his opinion. They also question the fairness of permitting the experts to express their opinion on the ultimate issue before the jury; i.e., whether the petitioner is a defective delinquent within the meaning of the statute. The petitioners also complain that the statute provides that the state must carry its case only by the greater weight of the evidence. The answer to all of these objections is that with respect to state action repeated decisions of the Supreme Court have put it beyond the range of further debate that the "due process" clause of the fourteenth amendment has not the effect of imposing upon the states any particular form or mode of procedure, so long as the essential rights of notice and a hearing, or opportunity to be heard, before a competent tribunal are not interfered with.

It would, therefore, appear that the Act upon its face provides adequate procedural safeguards; indeed it throws around the accused many safeguards not ordinarily found in so-called civil proceedings. By examining the records of the actual trials of the petitioners, the district court can determine whether in application these safeguards result in basic fairness of procedure imposed upon the state by the fourteenth amendment. We are not here speaking only of the "perfection of the machinery for correction" which may be referred to as procedural due process. Fay v. Noia, 372 U.S. 391, 421 (1963).

Finally, we again caution that we are here concerned only with the constitutionality of the Maryland statute upon its face. We are fully aware of the dangers inherent in the application of this new and radical approach in the present state of medico-legal knowledge of the problems of crime and recidivism. In its essence, the statute rejects the age-old concept that every legally sane person possesses in equal degree the free will to choose between doing right and doing wrong. Instead, it substitutes the concept that there is a category of legally sane persons who by reason of mental or emotional deficiencies "evidence a propensity toward criminal activity," which they are incapable of controlling. For those in the category who are treatable it would substitute psychiatric treatment for punishment in the conventional sense and would free them from confinement, not when they have "paid their debt to society," but when they have been sufficiently cured to make it reasonably safe to release them. With this humanitarian and progressive approach to the problem no person who has deplored the inadequacies of conventional penological practices can complain. But a statute though "fair on its face and impartial in appearance" may be fraught with the possibility of abuse in that if not administered in the spirit in which it is conceived it can become a mere device for warehousing the obnoxious and antisocial elements of society. Many of the inmates in Patuxent are there by reason of offenses against property rights. Many jurists and laymen would seriously question the wisdom of the practice of indefinitely confining young men under these circumstances. Deficiencies in staff, facilities, and finances would undermine the efficacy of the Institution and the justification for the law, and ultimately the constitutionality of its application.

The petitions should be reconsidered by the district court and since they are pro se petitions they should be construed liberally.

Remanded.

SPECHT v. PATTERSON

386 U.S. 605 (1967)

MR. JUSTICE DOUGLAS delivered the opinion of the Court.

The Sex Offenders Act may be brought into play if the trial court "is of the opinion that any . . . person [convicted of specified sex offenses], if at large, constitutes a threat of bodily harm to members of the public, or is an habitual offender and mentally ill." § 1. He then becomes punishable for an indeterminate term of from one day to life on the following conditions as specified in § 2:

"(2) A complete psychiatric examination shall have been made of him by the psychiatrists of the Colorado psychopathic hospital or by psychiatrists designated by the district court; and

"(3) A complete written report thereof submitted to the district court. Such report shall contain all facts and findings, together with recommendations as to whether or not the person is treatable under the provisions of this article; whether or not the person should be committed to the Colorado state hospital or to the state home and training schools as mentally ill or mentally deficient. Such report shall also contain the psychiatrist's opinion as to whether or not the person could be adequately supervised on probation."

This procedure was followed in petitioner's case; [he was convicted for indecent liberties;] he was examined as required and a psychiatric report prepared and given to the trial judge prior to the sentencing. But there was no hearing in the normal sense, no right of confrontation and so on.

Petitioner insists that this procedure does not satisfy due process because it allows the critical finding to be made under § 1 of the Sex Offenders Act (1) without a hearing at which the person so convicted may confront and cross-examine adverse witnesses and present evidence of his own by use of compulsory process, if necessary; and (2) on the basis of hearsay evidence to which the person involved is not allowed access.

We hold that the requirements of due process were not satisfied here.

The Sex Offenders Act does not make the commission of a specified crime the basis for sentencing. It makes one conviction the basis for commencing another proceeding under another Act to determine whether a person constitutes a threat of bodily harm to the public, or is an habitual offender and mentally ill. That is a new finding of fact (Vanderhoof v. People, 152 Colo.

147, 149, 380 P.2d 903, 904) that was not an ingredient of the offense charged. The punishment under the second Act is criminal punishment even though it is designed not so much as retribution as it is to keep individuals from inflicting future harm. United States v. Brown, 381 U.S. 437, 458.

The Court of Appeals for the Third Circuit in speaking of a comparable Pennsylvania statute said: "It is a separate criminal proceeding which may be invoked after conviction of one of the specified crimes. Petitioner therefore was entitled to a full judicial hearing before the magnified sentence was imposed. At such a hearing the requirements of due process cannot be satisfied by partial or niggardly procedural protections. A defendant in such a proceeding is entitled to the full panoply of the relevant protections which due process guarantees in state criminal proceedings. He must be afforded all those safeguards which are fundamental rights and essential to a fair trial, including the right to confront and cross-examine the witnesses against him." Gerchman v. Maroney, 355 F.2d 302, 312.

We agree with that view. Under Colorado's criminal procedure, here challenged, the invocation of the Sex Offenders Act means the making of a new charge leading to criminal punishment. The case is not unlike those under recidivist statutes where an habitual criminal issue is "a distinct issue" (Graham v. West Virginia, 224 U.S. 616, 625) on which a defendant "must receive reasonable notice and an opportunity to be heard." Oyler v. Boles, 368 U.S. 448, 452; Chandler v. Fretag, 348 U.S. 3, 8. Due process, in other words, requires that he be present with counsel, have an opportunity to be heard, be confronted with witnesses against him, have the right to cross-examine, and to offer evidence of his own. And there must be findings adequate to make meaningful any appeal that is allowed. The case is therefore quite unlike the Minnesota statute we considered in Minnesota v. Probate Court, 309 U.S. 270, where in a proceeding to have a person adjudged a "psychopathic personality" there was a hearing where he was represented by counsel and could compel the production of witnesses on his behalf. *Id.*, at 275. None of these procedural safeguards we have mentioned is present under Colorado's Sex Offenders Act. We therefore hold that it is deficient in due process as measured by the requirements of the Fourteenth Amendment. Pointer v. Texas, 380 U.S. 400.

Reversed.[y]

---

[y] Reconsider *Huebner v. State*, at 680, *supra*, which rejects administrative determination that a person convicted of certain sex offenses must be sentenced under the Wisconsin Sex Crimes Act.

Though most litigation has involved complaint that the offender was subjected to the extended terms provided by dangerous offender legislation, the special treatment orientation of such programs gives them advantage in the eyes of defendants who have a desire for help. The judge may have an affirmative obligation to utilize these special sentencing provisions.

PEOPLE v. WESTBROOK

62 Cal. 2d 197, 41 Cal. Rptr. 809, 397 P.2d 545 (1964)

[The defendant was convicted in the Superior Court, Los Angeles County, of automobile theft, theft, and forgery and was sentenced to imprisonment on all three charges for the period prescribed by law, and defendant appealed from the three judgments.]

PETERS, Justice. For the foregoing reasons reversals are required. In addition the record discloses other considerations not mentioned by appellant that support the conclusion that the problems here involved require further consideration at the trial level.

First, the record demonstrates that, as shown by three of six psychiatric reports, several probation reports, one letter written by defendant to the trial judge, and the remarks of the second trial judge, this defendant needs and has been begging for hospitalization and treatment for a psychiatric condition. He has told the doctors, probation officers and the judge that he should not be granted probation without treatment for the reason that he will repeat his crimes under such conditions. He has stated that incarceration will be of no help because of his one experience (Preston), and that he views Vacaville as just "another prison for queers." Such pleas have not been confined to the instant cases, but appear to have been made in prior proceedings in the juvenile court. The record also shows that defendant was born with (and still suffers from) a club foot; that he has a history of having fallen from a window, landing on his head, when 1 year old; that there is present brain damage; that he failed to control his bladder until far past the ordinary age; that commencing at 9 years of age he has been a continuous sexual psychopath; that at the present time (in his twenties) he continues to suck his thumb. Added to this is the fact that defendant has been granted probation on various occasions, but never has been committed to a state hospital for the mentally ill. The court's only answer to his continued pleas is to recommend to the prison authorities that the prisoner be given psychiatric treatment.

As a corollary to this point, it should be mentioned that the record demonstrates that defendant is a sexual psychopath. One of the psychiatric reports mentions a history of between 150 and 200 incidents of child molesting. Many of those incidents occurred on the open street, in daylight, when defendant attempted to remove the panties from young girls with no further explanation than that he wished to see their private parts. That the trial judges were aware of this is clear from the probation reports and from the reported remarks of the second such judge at the time of sentence. Yet it does not appear that at any time any court even considered the propriety of commencing proceedings under the provisions of sections 5500-5522 of the Welfare and Institutions Code (sexual psychopaths). The fact that the instant proceedings did not grow out of sexual crimes is no answer to the court's failure to take the steps prescribed by the statute. Section 5501 subdivision (a), provided at the time of the events here involved that the procedures therein set forth shall apply "[w]hen a person is convicted of any criminal offense, whether or not a sex offense" and shall be instituted by "the trial judge, on his own motion, or on motion of the prosecuting attorney, or on application by affidavit by or on behalf of the defendant, if it appears to the satisfaction of the court that there is probable cause for believing such a person is a sexual psychopath. . . ." In 1963 the section was amended by substituting for the words "sexual psychopath" the words "mentally disordered sex offender." It is difficult to understand why neither of the two judges here involved took the necessary steps to have this defendant sent to the very institution maintained by the state for such cases. Based on the meager record before us, it would appear that this young man needs and should receive proper treatment for his mental condition.

For all of these reasons it must be held that each of the trial courts here involved committed reversible error in failing to comply with section 1368 of the Penal Code, and that each abused its discretion, after reaching its erroneous decision, in failing to consider proceeding under sections 5500-5522 of the Welfare and Institutions Code.

The judgments are reversed and the entire matter remanded with instructions to proceed in accordance with the views herein expressed.

Prior to acceptance of a guilty plea the judge must ascertain that the defendant understands the consequences of his plea. Under the special sentencing provisions for dangerous offenders (particularly sex offenders), where there is a treatment mandate as well as provision for extension of sentence, the consequences of conviction are more difficult to explain with precision. The hope of treatment is always implicit if not directly promised.

CALVERT v. BURKE

Case No. 65-C-129 (E.D. Wis. 1966)

TEHAN, District Judge. This is a petition for writ of habeas corpus by an inmate of Wisconsin State Prison at Waupun, Wisconsin.

Petitioner was booked on a charge of taking indecent liberties with a minor and placed in a cell.

Assistant District Attorney Henry told petitioner of the charge against him, that it was a felony, and that if he didn't have funds to employ an attorney he could ask the judge and the judge would appoint one for him. Mr. Henry explained the consequences of a plea in this wise: If petitioner pled guilty it was mandatory for the judge to send him to the sex deviate facility at Waupun, Wisconsin, for a sixty-day observation and examination period. If, as a result of this examination, the doctors reported to the court that he was a sex deviate he would be sent back to the hospital for further treatment and would remain there until such time as the authorities felt he was cured. If, however, the report indicated that he was not a sex deviate he could either be placed on probation or sentenced to prison for a period up to ten years. Mr. Henry and the petitioner talked about petitioner's experience at Mendota Hospital, which petitioner felt had not helped him. Petitioner readily admitted his need for help both for his alcoholism and the things he did when he had been drinking. He was interested in learning about the sex deviate facility which he was surprised to learn existed and stated that he definitely felt he needed treatment.

At 2:00 p.m. petitioner was brought before Judge Bardwell for arraignment. He was still wearing the clothes he had on when he was injured. There was dried blood on his shirt and on his head. Under these circumstances we believe the presiding judge should have exercised great caution in establishing the petitioner's understanding of the proceedings and his constitutional right to the assistance of counsel. The hearing, however, was quite short. The court also made no inquiry as to the voluntariness of the plea. Neither did the court explain the function of an attorney or advise the petitioner of the help an attorney could be to him. The petitioner did not specifically reject the offer of an attorney but responded, "I understand that, your Honor, but I need help."

We cannot find that the response of petitioner constituted an unequivocal waiver of counsel. Rightly or wrongly, the defendant had gained the impression that a plea of guilty would result in his receiving help.

Here, the information he received from Mr. Henry could well have given him the impression that if he waived an attorney and pleaded guilty and was found to be a sex deviate he would not receive a sentence at all but instead would be hospitalized for a vague and nebulous period until he was cured. Since the Assistant District Attorney undertook an explanation of the provisions of the Sex Deviate Act, it should have been explained factually without editorial comment so that the defendant understood that commitment could result in a deprivation of his liberty and confinement for up to ten years and under certain circumstances heretofore set forth, even longer—perhaps for life.

For the reasons above stated, the petition for writ of habeas corpus will be granted and petitioner ordered discharged from custody under the present judgment of conviction.

Reference Note

For a general review of the issues the sex offender poses for the criminal law, see *Symposium,* 14 FED. PROB. No. 3 (Sept. 1950). *See also* Karpman, *The Sexual Psychopath,* 42 J. CRIM. L. & C. 184 (1951).

Discussion of the Washington Sexual Psychopath Law is found in di Furia & Mees, *Dangerous To Be At Large—A Constructive Critique of Washington's Sexual Psychopath Law,* 38 WASH. L. REV. 531 (1963). The first eleven years' experience with the Wisconsin Sex Crimes Law is described in Halleck & Pacht, *The Current Status of the Wisconsin State Sex Crimes Law,* 33 WIS. B. BULL. No. 6, at 17 (Dec. 1960).

See also D. GLASER, D. KENEFICK & V. O'LEARY, THE VIOLENT OFFENDER (1966) (Parole Decision-Making Series, U.S. Dept. of Health, Education, and Welfare); and REPORT: THE DANGEROUS SEX OFFENDER, COMMONWEALTH OF PENNSYLVANIA (1963).

Chapter 13

CORRECTIONAL TREATMENT OF PERSONS UNDER SENTENCE

> There is a . . . need to develop means for guiding and controlling the numerous important decisions which must be made following the imposition of sentence: decisions by correctional authorities regarding the treatment of offenders during imprisonment, the date and conditions of release from imprisonment, and the revocation of parole; and decisions by judges regarding the revocation of probation or a suspended sentence.
>
> Legislation ordinarily provides little guidance for these correctional decisions. Correctional administrators have been slow to develop policies and procedures to guide correctional officials and protect the rights of offenders. And trial and appellate courts have been reluctant to review either the merits of such decisions or the procedures by which they are made.
>
> Yet it is inconsistent with our whole system of government to grant such uncontrolled power to any officials, particularly over the lives of persons. The fact that a person has been convicted of a crime should not mean that he has forfeited all rights to demand that he be fairly treated by officials.
>
> *The President's Commission on Law Enforcement and Administration of Justice, Task Force Report: Corrections* 82-83 (1967)

Correctional processing of persons convicted of crimes has been characterized by the exercise of the widest kind of discretion in deciding how to treat offenders in prisons or while on probation or parole. This discretion has been subject to only the most limited kind of control, such as the doctrine forbidding cruel or unusual punishment.

The basis for this is primarily the general willingness to assume that the convicted offender has had his "day in court" and thus may be the recipient of "privileges" but has no "rights." At the same time, there is a desire to make it possible for men of good will and professional competence to use the widest latitude in developing policies and programs designed to rehabilitate offenders.

Clear demarcation of the limits of correctional discretion is difficult today in part because there has been little litigation involving many prison and parole issues and in part because the law in this whole area is changing so rapidly. Then too, the facts of particular disputes, as always, modify the cases. For example, it is generally agreed that correctional authorities are limited in their right to control religious activities of prisoners. A few years ago most wardens would have been astounded if it were predicted that they would be frequent litigants in freedom of religion cases. Yet today there are numerous reported cases dealing with the prisoner's freedom to practice the Black Muslim religion within the institution.

The matter of legal control over correctional processes, including the question of whether convicted persons should have access to courts to challenge post-conviction treatment, is currently of great interest to convicted persons themselves, to lawyers and courts, and to correctional personnel. The basic issue has to do with the extent to which various custody and treatment decisions about convicted offenders—on probation, in the prisons, before parole boards, and on parole—can be freely determined by correctional authorities as part of broadly delegated discretion by the legislature and free from intervention by the trial or appellate judiciary. Traditionally, courts have maintained a "hands-off" doctrine concerning prisoner complaints but this appears to be changing.[a] The consequences of this trend are not yet fully known. One possibility is an increase in direct judicial intervention in correctional determinations such as parole revocation; another is the requirement of formal procedures so that administrative hearings, complete with opportunity for representation by counsel and the employment of adversary techniques, replaces individual, unilateral decision-making. Still another possibility, suggested by the Model Penal Code, is legislative establishment of general criteria for correctional decision-making and general description of appropriate correctional procedures, leaving responsibility for specific implementation to the correctional agencies.

THE BORDERLAND OF CRIMINAL JUSTICE 36, 133-35 (1964)†
By Francis Allen

The obligation of containing power within the limits suggested by a community's political values has been considerably compli-

[a] Kimball & Newman, *Judicial Intervention in Correctional Decisions: Threat and Response,* 14 CRIME & DELINQUENCY 1 (1968).

† Reprinted with special permission. Copyright © 1959, 1956 by the Northwestern University School of Law. The first portion appeared in 50 J. CRIM. L.C. & P.S. 226, 230 (1959), the second in 51 NW. U.L. REV. 207, 212-14 (1956).

cated by the rise of the rehabilitative ideal. For the problem today is one of regulating the exercise of power by men of good will, whose motivations are to help not to injure, and whose ambitions are quite different from those of the political adventurer so familiar to history. There is a tendency for such persons to claim immunity from the usual forms of restraint and to insist that professionalism and a devotion to science provide sufficient protection against unwarranted invasion of individual rights. . . .

The tendency toward individualized treatment of persons within the custody and control of the state, however, creates its own problems and perils. These have already emerged clearly enough to justify the belief that here we are likely to be confronted with some of the toughest issues in the years ahead. Programs of individualized treatment inevitably involve the exercise of wide discretionary powers on the part of administrative personnel who possess, or ought to possess, special skills and proficiency. This, of course, is a situation not peculiar to penology but is a salient characteristic of the range of modern governmental activity. There are surely good reasons for the law's insisting that the discretion exercised in the administration of penal sanctions be at least as responsible as that exercised in the performance of other governmental functions. The fact is, however, that today it is hardly possible to discern, even in rudimentary form, what might be called a body of criminal administrative law. Too often this has meant that in this area we have had administration without law. It is not difficult to multiply examples. Is there any reason why a prisoner returned to a penal institution for violation of parole should not at that time have, as a matter of right rather than grace, a full hearing on the issue of whether the parole terms were, in fact, violated? And, for that matter, should not legislative standards relating to parole conditions be made sufficiently specific to avoid at least some of the technical absurdities of which parole boards have occasionally been guilty in the past? . . .

These issues are easier to state than to resolve. Much remains to be done in the way of setting up effective procedural devices within the penal system through which a variety of decisions relating to methods of treatment, transfer, and release may be subjected to real supervision and, where necessary, to challenge. In regard to certain of these decisions, review in the courts should be provided. A desire that administrative discretion should be subject to effective supervision indicates no disposition to minimize the significance of expert judgment in the administration of the criminal law or a desire to stifle or obstruct its proper exercise. It indicates, rather, that such judgment is attaining a role of great importance in penological administration and that this role promises to be even more significant in the future. This suggests that the vital interests of the individual and the state thereby affected require considered and articulate statements of legislative policy in the field and measures to insure the advance of that policy through the responsible exercise of administrative discretion. One may suspect that there are problems in this area sufficient to occupy the next half-century and more.

A. CONDITIONS UPON RELEASE UNDER COMMUNITY SUPERVISION

1. *Establishment of Conditions*

Offenders who serve all or part of their sentences under community supervision are ordinarily subject to certain conditions or rules of conduct which are enforced by the supervising probation or parole agent. In some states, like Wisconsin, a single field agent supervises both probationers and parolees, although the more common practice is to have a probation staff attached to the local court and a parole staff which is organized on a statewide basis. While probation is instituted by the court and parole by an administrative board, the rules and conditions of probation and parole are very much the same in routine cases. Generally, too, the conduct requirements are more or less standardized. The probationer or parolee is required to report regularly to and "cooperate with" his field agent; keep reasonable hours and maintain steady employment; support his family; avoid criminal associates; obtain permission before he marries, drives a car, or leaves the community; refrain from excessive use of alcoholic beverages (or in some states refrain from drinking at all); and in general be law-abiding and regular and moderate in his habits. Cases occasionally arise in which these general rules are felt to work hardship—for example, a no-drinking rule where alcohol has played no part in previous criminal behavior—but these standard rules are widely accepted as proper, logical, and necessary. Much more controversial are special conditions sometimes applied to particular offenders or to particular classes of offenders.

Failure to conform to the rules and conditions of supervision exposes the offender to possible revocation and incarceration.

In general, legislatures delegate authority to correctional agencies to develop general rules of parole supervision and give them broad power to impose special conditions as needed. Only occasionally are conditions formulated directly by the legislature, and these are likely to be conditions relating to such things as employment or avoidance of subversive activities.

Legislatures delegate authority to judges to set the conditions of probation. The judges are, of course, greatly influenced by the recommendations and standing practices of their probation staff, but they can add or delete conditions to fit the particular case if they wish.

PEOPLE *ex rel.* PERRY v. CASSIDY

43 Misc. 2d 189, 250 N.Y.S.2d 743 (1964)
Affirmed, 23 App. Div. 2d 706, 257 N.Y.S.2d 228 (1965)

[Relator was adjudicated a youthful offender and sentenced to the Elmira Reception Center. Execution of sentence was suspended and he was placed on probation until he became twenty-one years of age "on such terms as the Probation Officer shall provide for you." Subsequently, probationer violated, was revoked after a hearing, and sent to Elmira. He contends in a writ of habeas corpus that he could not have been found guilty of violating his probation because the terms of probation were not set by the court pursuant to § 932 of the New York Code of Criminal Procedure which states "the court shall determine the conditions of probation. . . ."]

LISTON F. COON, County Judge. It is well founded that it is the responsibility of the Court to determine the conditions of probation. The granting of Probation is a judicial process exercised in the discretion of the Court. It cannot be delegated to a probation officer except for administrative purposes.

Such determination should not be interpreted as requiring every sentencing court to spell out every individual condition and requirement of probation but at least there should be some evidence of the court's knowledge and approval of terms. This could be accomplished in a number of ways. Where, as in some jurisdictions, the Court, the probationer and the probation officer all sign the written terms given to the probationer, it would seem that the statute is satisfied. Or the adjudication or judgment might read, "placed on probation on such terms and conditions as are attached to and made a part hereof."

In the present case, the Writ is sustained and the relator is ordered discharged.

In some jurisdictions, however, especially where the probation service has statewide responsibility rather than responsibility to a particular court, the judge's responsibility to set probation conditions may be limited by statute.[b]

It is clear that in practice the major responsibility for setting conditions of probation and parole lies with the correctional agencies which must supervise the offender. Within the correctional structure itself, probation and parole rules may emanate from three different levels: general rules applicable to all offenders as a matter of overall agency policy; special conditions or rules imposed on specific offenders or classes of offenders by parole boards or other releasing or supervision authorities; and specific rules or regulations set by the individual probation and parole field agent as part of his professional responsibility to and for individual offenders in his caseload.

The Model Penal Code suggests that responsibility for furnishing the broad outline of conditions is appropriately for the legislature, leaving to the trial judge or the correctional agency only the task of fitting the criteria to the needs of particular cases.

MODEL PENAL CODE § 301.1
American Law Institute
(Proposed Official Draft 1962)

Section 301.1. Conditions of Suspension or Probation.

(1) When the Court suspends the imposition of sentence on a person who has been convicted of a crime or sentences him to be placed on probation, it shall attach such reasonable conditions, authorized by this Section, as it deems necessary to insure that he will lead a law-abiding life or likely to assist him to do so.

(2) The Court, as a condition of its order, may require the defendant:

(a) to meet his family responsibilities;

(b) to devote himself to a specific employment or occupation;

(c) to undergo available medical or psychiatric treatment and to enter and remain in a specified institution, when required for that purpose;

(d) to pursue a prescribed secular course of study or vocational training;

(e) to attend or reside in a facility established for the instruction, recreation or residence of persons on probation;

---

[b] *E.g.*, in Wisconsin the judge may impose as conditions only restitution and payment of costs. Other conditions are set by the state probation and parole service. Wis. Stat. § 57.01 (1965).

(f) to refrain from frequenting unlawful or disreputable places or consorting with disreputable persons;

(g) to have in his possession no firearm or other dangerous weapon unless granted written permission;

(h) to make restitution of the fruits of his crime or to make reparation, in an amount he can afford to pay, for the loss or damage caused thereby;

(i) to remain within the jurisdiction of the Court and to notify the Court or the probation officer of any change in his address or his employment;

(j) to report as directed to the Court or the probation officer and to permit the officer to visit his home;

(k) to post a bond, with or without surety, conditioned on the performance of any of the foregoing obligations;

(l) to satisfy any other conditions reasonably related to the rehabilitation of the defendant and not unduly restrictive of his liberty or incompatible with his freedom of conscience.

[(3) When the Court sentences a person who has been convicted of a felony or misdemeanor to be placed on probation, it may require him to serve a term of imprisonment not exceeding thirty days as an additional condition of its order. The term of imprisonment imposed hereunder shall be treated as part of the term of probation, and in the event of a sentence of imprisonment upon the revocation of probation, the term of imprisonment served hereunder shall not be credited toward service of such subsequent sentence.]

(4) The defendant shall be given a copy of this Article and written notice of any requirements imposed pursuant to this Section, stated with sufficient specificity to enable him to guide himself accordingly.[c]

The Practice

In addition to the conditions suggested by the Model Penal Code, the following are commonly imposed as general rules, applicable to all offenders placed on probation or on parole:

1

He may violate no federal or state law or local ordinance.

---

[c] The MODEL PENAL CODE § 305.13 (Tent. Draft 1962) sets out in similar language the conditions a parole board may impose on an inmate being released on parole. The differences do not seem grounded in policy.

2

He may not drink any alcoholic beverages, or he may not drink alcoholic beverages to excess. He may not enter any bar or tavern.

3

He must obtain approval before marrying, moving, driving, incurring debt, or traveling.

Less commonly imposed are the following general or special conditions:

4

In some jurisdictions narcotic users must agree to submit at any time to medical tests for recent drug use. Either refusal to undergo the Nalline test or indication of drug use is considered a violation.

5

In some jurisdictions pre-probation or pre-parole agreement forms include a consent for the field agent to search the offender's person or premises at any time.

6

In some jurisdictions the offender is asked to agree, in writing, not to challenge any future revocation.

7

The president of an engineering firm was convicted of having given bribes to obtain construction business from the state. The judge offered him probation, conditioned upon his fully disclosing to the grand jury information concerning others involved in bribing state officials.[d]

8

A man was convicted of nonsupport of his child, who was in the custody of his divorced wife. It was represented by the prosecutor that the defendant had been spending much of his money on a girlfriend. As conditions of probation the judge included that defendant should have "no further association, contact or communication of any kind whatsoever" with the girlfriend during the probationary period.

---

[d] *See* Comment, *Federal District Court Asserts Its Power to Condition Probation on Disclosure of Information to Investigatory Bodies and to Determine Compliance in an Open Hearing,* 61 COLUM. L. REV. 1175 (1961).

9

A 22-year-old man had intercourse with his fifteen-year-old girlfriend and she became pregnant. They eloped and upon their return home the parents were enraged. He was convicted of statutory rape at their insistence and sentenced to eighteen months imprisonment. After six months he was paroled on the condition he make no effort to see his wife or communicate with her.

10

Two teenage youths were convicted of disorderly conduct for breaking windows with rocks. The court placed them on probation, imposing as conditions that they be home by 9:30 each night unless in the company of an adult, they did not drive a car except on business, and they attend some church service each week during the period of their probation.

11

A girl, twenty-one, was convicted of the misdemeanor of possession of narcotics. The presentence report disclosed that she was living with a man to whom she was not married and was receiving welfare payments for their illegitimate child. The trial court conditioned probation upon her agreement to be sterilized. She refused and was sentenced to three months imprisonment.

Normally the conditions are set out rather fully. It is common, however, to include a general provision that calls for "good conduct" or a provision that permits the probation or parole agent to add new requirements as the need arises. These invest the agent with vast discretion. In the probation situation the judge may also assume the power to make new demands upon probationers.

KAPLAN v. UNITED STATES
234 F.2d 345 (8th Cir. 1956)

VOGEL, Circuit Judge. On April 8, 1954, Marc Sol Kaplan, appellant, entered a plea of guilty to each of five counts of an information wherein it was charged that he had sold heroin totaling in amount 703 grains, in violation of 26 U.S.C.A. § 2554(a) (now 26 U.S.C.A. § 4705). Each count of the information carried a penalty of imprisonment of from two to five years, but the district court, because of the circumstances of the case, suspended imposition of sentence and placed appellant on probation for a period of five years.

Approximately seven weeks later appellant was called before a federal grand jury and asked to disclose the source from which he had purchased the heroin. He refused to answer the questions, stating that he feared reprisals against himself and his family from the person from whom he had made the purchases.

The court [subsequently] adjudged him guilty of civil contempt and ordered him confined in jail until the desired information was given.

On June 21, 1954, counsel for the government filed a petition to revoke appellant's probation on the ground that his conduct was inconsistent with the good conduct required by the terms of probation. After hearing and arguments on the matter, appellant's probation was revoked and a sentence of three years on each count of the information given. The sentences were to run consecutively.

Appellant's third point is:

> "The Court erred in revoking probation for the reason that applicant violated no condition of probation imposed upon him when probation was granted, and the conditions thereof were never modified."

This presents the only real issue which can be considered upon this appeal. In placing the appellant on probation in the first instance, the court fixed the usual conditions of probation as follows: "(a) Refrain from the violation of any state and federal penal laws. (b) Live a clean, honest and temperate life. (c) Keep good company and good hours. (d) Keep away from all undesirable places. (e) Work regularly. When out of work, notify your probation officer at once. (f) Do not leave or remain away from the city or town where you reside without permission of the probation officer. Notify your probation officer at once if you intend to change your address. (g) Contribute regularly to the support of those for whose support you are legally responsible. (h) Follow the probation officer's instructions and advice. The Probation Law gives him authority to instruct and advise you regarding your recreational and social activities. (i) Report promptly on the dates set forth. If for any unavoidable reason you are unable to do so, communicate with your probation officer without delay."

The court, in its findings of fact and conclusions of law, stated that its grounds for revocation of probation were "solely on the adjudication of contempt," and then specifically found that the probationer had violated conditions (b), (c) and (d).

We have here, then, the situation of a defendant who, while on probation, was specifically ordered by the court to appear before the grand jury and disclose the source of his heroin purchases and who refused in the presence of the court to follow such orders. Completely regardless of the subsequent contempt proceedings, this was of itself sufficient justification for revoking probation. Here was a specific order of the court to do a certain thing—disclose information needed in a grand jury's investigation of illegal traffic in narcotics. In effect, it could be considered as an additional condition of probation, even though it was not included in the original written conditions. 18 U.S.C.A. § 3651, among other things, provides: "The court may revoke or modify any condition of probation, or may change the period of probation." No claim of constitutional privilege was or could have been maintained. To hold that such a specific refusal to follow the court's order was not a violation of probation could lead to rather bizarre results in that every contingency would need be anticipated and might have the effect of limiting the use of probation. Campbell v. Aderhold, D.C. N.D. Ga., 1929, 36 F.2d 366, 367.

The appellant's argument that he violated none of the specific terms of his probation and that the terms were never modified would not, even if true, be persuasive. The determinative question is whether the conduct of the probationer was inconsistent with his duties as such. One on probation is not at liberty; he is in law and in fact in the custody and under the control of the court granting probation.

We also think there can be no doubt but what, aside from the written conditions of probation, there is an implied condition that the probationer will follow the reasonable directions and orders of both the probation officer and the District Judge. In the instant case, the appellant's refusal to follow the court's direction that he disclose to the grand jury the source of his heroin was a sufficient ground for the revocation of probation and we think that the trial court did not abuse its discretion in so doing.

Affirmed.

2. *Controls over the Conditions of Release*

The basic question, if one concludes that some conditions upon granting probation or parole are inappropriate, is what mechanisms exist for preventing the imposition of such conditions.

Correctional authorities agree that restrictions placed upon probationers and parolees should be purposive and relevant to the rehabilitation of the offender, the protection of the community, the restoration of the victim of crime, or some other acceptable objective. On the other hand, there has been a tradition of characterizing probation and parole as "privilege" not "right," as a matter of "grace." The view has been that what can be withheld completely can be given on any conditions. The language of contract has been used, and the rules and conditions are said to have been consented to as part of the agreement to obtain release in the community.[e]

In fact, however, the appellate courts have, either as a matter of constitutional law or by interpreting statutes,[f] required that conditions on probation or parole be relevant to some legitimate objective,[g] reasonable in their demands,[h] possible of performance,[i] and consistent with freedoms to which even prisoners are entitled.[j] Challenge may be raised by asking relief from the condi-

---

[e] There is, in law, a question whether a defendant can refuse probation. And under some statutory schemes prisoners who have not been paroled earlier are released under supervision at the expiration of their maximum term less "good time." These mandatory release prisoners are also bound by parole conditions even though they do not agree to them.

[f] *E.g.*, CAL. PENAL CODE § 203.1 (Supp. 1966) requires that probation conditions be "reasonable." *Cf.* People v. Blankenship, 16 Cal. App. 2d 606, 61 P.2d 352 (1936) (dubious decision holding requirement of sterilization of syphilitic convicted of statutory rape reasonable because it would prevent transmission of disease to his children). *See also* People v. Labarbera, 89 Cal. App. 2d 639, 201 P.2d 584 (1949), holding that probation could not be conditioned on paying a fine larger than that authorized by the penal statute; People v. Williams, 144 Cal. App. 2d 144, 300 P.2d 734 (1956), holding that probation could not be conditioned on refraining from driving longer than the period the statute provided for suspension of license.

[g] *E.g.*, People v. Baum, 251 Mich. 187, 231 N.W. 95 (1930), holding that banishment from the state during five-year probationary period was improper; Note, *Banishment—A Medieval Tactic in Modern Criminal Law*, 5 UTAH L. REV. 365 (1957). Butler v. District of Columbia, 346 F.2d 798 (D.C. Cir. 1965), held it improper to sentence a minor offender to a fine when his effort to satisfy the condition that he write an essay on "Why the Police Department should be entitled to the respect of the citizenry" was deemed inadequate by the judge.

[h] *E.g.*, People v. Smith, 252 Mich. 4, 232 N.W. 397 (1930), holding that requiring one convicted of disturbing the peace to move from the neighborhood as a condition of probation was "without authority of law." Conditions requiring money payments where there is no pre-existing legal obligation have sometimes been held invalid.

[i] Sweeny v. United States, 353 F.2d 10 (7th Cir. 1965), said in dictum that a condition requiring a known chronic alcoholic to refrain from drinking was unreasonable as impossible of performance. State v. Oyler, 436 P.2d 709 (Idaho 1968), is similar.

[j] Jones v. Commonwealth, 185 Va. 335, 38 S.E.2d 444 (1946), held a condition requiring church attendance unconstitutional. Springer v. United

tion, by calling in question imprisonment following failure to agree to the condition, or by contesting revocation based upon violation of an allegedly void condition to which the offender has reluctantly agreed in order to obtain his release. Efforts to challenge the conditions present awkward situations for lawyer and client: If the client agrees to the condition and later is revoked, the contractual theory may prove an embarrassment. If the client refuses probation or parole and tests the condition by habeas corpus, he faces the substantial chance the condition will be upheld. If he appeals the question of the condition's propriety and wins, the result may be invalidation of the whole probation or parole order rather than merely the particular condition and the client may be faced with the unwillingness to admit him to probation or parole on the remaining conditions.[k]

Reference Note

For a discussion of what kind of conditions are imposed on probationers in various states, see the Attorney General's Survey of Release Procedures, Department of Justice Vol. II, 222 (1939). A more recent description is Arluke, *A Summary of Parole Rules,* 2 NPPA JOURNAL 6 (Jan. 1956).

The purposes intended to be served by probation and parole conditions are discussed by Zeitoun, *Parole Supervision and Self-Determination,* 26 FED. PROB. 44 (Sept. 1962). *See also* Note, *Conditions of Probation Imposed on Wisconsin Felons: Costs of Prosecution and Restitution,* 1962 WIS. L. REV. 672.

The controversy whether parole conditions should be flexible or uniform is illustrated by von Hentig, *Degrees of Parole Violation and Graded Remedy Measures,* 33 J. CRIM. L. & C. 363 (Jan.-Feb. 1943), and Bates, *On the Uses of Parole Restriction,* 33 J. CRIM. L. & C. 435 (Mar.-Apr. 1943).

The problems of challenging conditions are well presented in Note, *Judicial Review of Probation Conditions,* 67 COLUM. L. REV. 181 (1967). *See also* Hink, *The Application of Constitutional Standards of Protection to Probation,* 29 U. CHI. L. REV. 483 (1962); Rubin, *A Legal View of Probation and Parole Conditions,* 2 NPPA JOURNAL 33 (Jan. 1956).

States, 148 F.2d 411 (9th Cir. 1945), held a requirement that probationer donate blood to the Red Cross void on its face as an unwarranted invasion of the person.

[k] Note, *Judicial Review of Probation Conditions,* 67 COLUM. L. REV. 181 (1967).

B. THE NATURE OF COMMUNITY SUPERVISION

1. The Objective of Rehabilitation

Offenders placed on probation or released on parole are subject to supervision by field agents. Historically, relatives of the offender, friends of his family or persons otherwise interested in the case and willing to assume some responsibility for the offender's adjustment could act in the capacity of probation or parole agent, assuming, of course, that these persons were of good reputation and had the means and desire to effect supervision. As with all forms of "charity" manned by well-meaning but nonprofessional citizens, this form of community supervision has largely disappeared and has been replaced by the professional field agent who is selected on the basis of civil service standards which, ideally, require him to be a trained social worker or have the equivalent level of formal education and training. This ideal is achieved in only a few probation and parole agencies; more commonly the probation officer is a college graduate but with no advanced training in social work nor with any other form of specialized education.

Supervision of probationers or parolees is broadly conceived (within professional social work) as a form of casework, or group work, and therefore a method of treatment. Ideally, the field agent meets regularly with his offender-client and with the client's family and, when desirable, with other significant persons (employer, teacher, minister) to assist the client in making the best possible community adjustment. Supervision is commonly expected to be more than surveillance; it is intended to be a counseling relationship in which the agent brings to bear his knowledge of behavior and his familiarity with community resources in guiding the life organization of those offenders in his caseload.

In practice, community supervision often falls far short of this ideal. First, there is a nationwide shortage of trained professionals to staff probation and parole offices so that even in correctional systems which pride themselves on their high degree of professionalism, most field agents have less formal training than is set by national standards or even by local civil service requirements. Second, in many jurisdictions probation agents (more so than parole agents) find themselves burdened with caseloads of a hundred or even two hundred clients. Supervision in its ideal form is literally impossible under these conditions except on a highly selective basis. Third, probation and parole staffs are sometimes used by the court or the agency to perform functions which may be important but which are only peripherally related to the rehabilitative objective. For example, field agents are sometimes used to collect restitution or client debts, to screen jail inmates for eligibility for release on recognizance bail, or to check jail inmates' claims of indigency to enable the court to decide whether it should appoint counsel.

Under the best of conditions, supervision is only part of the field agent's job. Probation officers ordinarily spend at least half their time in conducting presentence investigations for the court while parole officers may spend a good part of their time in admission and release investigations for the prison and parole board. Field agents are also expected to develop community resources, such as employment opportunities, not only for a specific offender but for future clients as well. To this extent, the loyalty of any agent is divided between his total present and future caseload and any one client currently under supervision.

Given these considerations of shortage of trained personnel, demands of time and numbers, and the wide range of activities expected from field staff, the nature of supervision varies greatly in both quality and intensity not only from one jurisdiction to another but even within a single agent's caseload. Because of agency pressures and differentials in training and experience and perhaps because of personality variables which lead persons to select careers in probation or parole services, there is considerable variation among field agents in how they view and how they do their job. Some agents view their task as a form of law enforcement, involving surveillance, search, and other methods designed primarily to check up on their charges. Some agents see their task as clinical, attempting by casework techniques to modify values and behavioral patterns of their clients. Still others see the job as essentially record keeping, requiring the client to report to the office regularly, to account for his funds, and otherwise to maintain his formal obligations on the record. A small number of agents see their job to be family therapy, moving out from the office to at-home counseling with the client's wife and children as well as with the offender.[l] Some few agents see their task to be community action, attempting on their own, as well as by advising clients, to modify neighborhood or group conditions that appear to lead to law violation.[m] Probably the most

---

[l] For analysis of different orientations of parole agents, see D. GLASER, THE EFFECTIVENESS OF A PRISON AND PAROLE SYSTEM (1964).

[m] By and large, parole agents and other correctional personnel have not taken an active part in the so-called urban revolt although by far the majority of their clients come from, return to, and live in the ghettos. For some reason, the major correctional approach to rehabilitation remains clinical, *i.e.*, changing the person to fit his environment rather than community action, *i.e.*, modifying widespread conditions and values so that the person will have better opportunities for satisfaction and conformity. It seems par-

common agent-client supervision relationship stresses neither intensive surveillance nor community action but instead is composed largely of office visits where the offender regularly reports to his field agent, is briefly counseled, and sent on his way until the time of the next visit or until he is picked up by the police. There are, of course, all combinations of supervision orientations found in practice; it is apparent that the dimensions of supervision are not fully agreed upon nor are practices anywhere standardized. Client criticisms of supervision run the whole range of practice, from objecting to field agent searches to complaints about failure to treat effectively the conditions of criminality. Those aspects of the probation and parole agent's job which relate to sentencing (the presentence investigation) or to revocation have received the most attention in the courts and among professional correctional personnel themselves. The nature and conditions of supervision have remained relatively invisible to all but those directly involved, yet supervision is a major correctional technique and the chief form of official restraint used with convicted persons.[n]

2. *The Objective of Community Protection*

Where community protection is a dominant concern, the methods used in surveillance of the probationer or parolee may be similar to the methods used by law enforcement officers, giving rise to the general issue of whether limitations upon law enforcement power should apply also to surveillance of the probationer and parolee.

PEOPLE v. LANGELLA

41 Misc. 2d 65, 244 N.Y.S.2d 802 (1963)

J. Irwin Shapiro, Justice. Motion by the defendant "to suppress the evidence, or in the alternative, for a hearing to suppress

ticularly shortsighted, and somewhat ridiculous, to strengthen in-prison psychotherapy units only to release inmates to the living conditions of the urban ghettos and rural slums from which they come. Corrections has long recognized this situation and has decried it, but in general it has not seen itself as a profession having any role in, or responsibility for, changing community conditions.

[n] In Appendix B, there is reprinted a "running record" of parole agent contact with a sex offender, John A. Wilson. This is in no way an idealized record of parole supervision; it is intended as neither an excellent nor a poor illustration of supervision. In terms of both the frequency of contact and the balance between home and office visits it typifies supervision in what might fairly be termed a relatively serious but still routine case. Wilson is not a typical parolee; he is better educated than average and has apparently strong community resources, *i.e.,* wife and family who support him.

the evidence as illegally obtained as a result of an illegal search and seizure on July 31, 1963, without a search warrant and without probable cause."

The purpose of this suppression motion is to forestall the use in evidence of a handgun, for the unlawful possession of which this defendant has been indicted (7 felony counts).

The question to be determined is whether, in view of defendant's position as a parolee, the search, without a search warrant, was unreasonable under the circumstances in which it occurred.

Prior to this defendant's release from Clinton Prison on parole, he had been serving an indeterminate term (not less than one nor more than two years) under a sentence handed down January 10, 1962 upon his conviction of Attempted Robbery, Second Degree, in the County Court of Kings County. On February 11, 1963 he "agreed to lead an honest and upright life and abide by the rules" embodied in a parole agreement signed by him and on February 13, 1963 he was let out on parole and placed under the jurisdiction of the Board of Parole until January 12, 1964 when his maximum term would expire in due course. Thereafter he was either put or eventually came under the supervision of parole officer William J. Quinn who, on or about July 24, 1963, participated with his official supervisors in a case conference during which he gave them "certain information" about the defendant. The nature of the intelligence thus reported does not appear but at least its significance to the participants is suggested by the result, for officer Quinn was instructed to get a warrant and execute it if and when he found the defendant violating his parole.

Through his obedience to that direction the officer was later armed with a warrant for Langella's arrest when he had him under surveillance, in Manhattan, on July 31, 1963. At an unspecified hour of that day, the officer observed defendant get behind the wheel of a car in which he had been a passenger and, apparently with the consent of its erstwhile operator—who walked off, leaving Langella alone in the vehicle—drive it from Manhattan to Cropsey Avenue, Brooklyn, parking it outside a house which he entered and which, as it later turned out, was the home of his parents.

The officer then advised his supervisor by telephone of what he had seen and was instructed to execute the warrant.[1] Langella was then brought out to the car and, in his presence, the parole officer used the key to unlock the trunk. An inspection (search)

---

[1] One of the conditions of the defendant's parole was that he refrain from operating an automobile.

of the trunk disclosed the weapon on which the present charges are based.

In their treatment of the issue opposing counsel depend, mainly, on their different views of the proper scope of a search as an incident of a lawful arrest. I prefer to rest this decision on the broader ground that applicable and controlling law expressing and implementing a sound public policy subordinates the parolee's rights to the reasonable exercise of the parole board's powers of supervision and investigation.

A convict has no constitutional right to be released on parole. The Board of Parole is given power to determine what eligible prisoners may be released on parole "and when and under what conditions" (Correction Law, § 210). "[P]arole is not a right, but a privilege, to be granted or withheld as discretion may impel" (People ex rel. Cecere v. Jennings, 250 N.Y. 239, 241, 165 N.E. 277, 278).

It being the duty of the parole board to determine what action should be taken on the alleged violation a knowledge of *all* of the facts was not only desirable but necessary to a fair decision and it was officer Quinn's duty to gather those facts as fully as possible and report them to the board. Obviously, that called for whatever *additional* investigation was reasonably indicated after the arrest and the officer would have been remiss had he failed to conduct it. On its face, the violation of driving the automobile was technical and was offset by the suggestion of filial deference and if that were all there actually was to the matter, the action taken thereon by the board might understandably be relatively mild. On the other hand, if it appeared that the car had been used for a criminal purpose, the range of Langella's implication might run from a knowing association with an evil companion or convicted criminal (Parole Agreement, para. 4) to personal participation in the commission of a crime and in that event the action taken by the board might well be severe. Thus, far from having completed his duty and exhausted his power when he made the arrest, the officer was further duty bound to investigate and report the attending circumstances as completely as possible for the guidance of the board when it came to hold a parole court to consider the case and hear the alleged violator's explanation of the charges made against him (Correction Law, § 218). Crediting and accepting the defendant's contention—that his release on parole did not divest him of all of his rights—does not however require a conclusion that his rights were equal to those of a person enjoying unrestricted and unconditioned liberty.

If I am correct in my conclusion that the search was reasonable, the seizure of the contraband incidentally disclosed was legal and its use in evidence against the defendant cannot justly be forbidden.

The motion is therefore in all respects denied.[o]

---

[o] The New York Court of Appeals reached the same conclusion in People v. Randazzo, 15 N.Y.2d 526, 254 N.Y.S.2d 99 (1964). Here a parolee's apartment was searched by a parole officer who had obtained a warrant charging violation on the grounds that the parolee had "consorted with a known criminal." After placing defendant under arrest, the officer conducted a two and one-half hour search of the apartment, eventually discovering hidden narcotics. Parolee was charged and convicted of felonious possession of a narcotic drug and appealed denial of a pretrial motion to suppress the evidence. The Court of Appeals, in a one-sentence opinion, held:

> Judgment affirmed. Defendant-appellant, as a parolee, was deprived of no constitutional rights by the search and seizure which was made under the circumstances of this case (People *ex rel.* Natoli v. Lewis, 287 N.Y. 478; Anderson v. Corall, 263 U.S. 193).

Justice Fuld dissented:

> If the search of the defendant's apartment leading to the seizure of narcotics is to be justified, it must be on the ground either (1) that a parolee has no right to the protection of the Fourth Amendment's prohibition against unreasonable searches or (2) that the search was incident to the defendant's arrest for violating his parole by consorting with a known criminal. I do not believe that it may be sanctioned on either ground.
>
> Although in a certain sense, and for certain purposes, a paroled convict is regarded as still being "a prisoner" and "in legal custody" (see People *ex rel.* Natoli v. Lewis, 287 N.Y. 478, 481-482; Anderson v. Corall, 263 U.S. 193, 196), I cannot believe that one's status as a parolee deprives him of all right to the protection of the Fourth Amendment. The beneficent purposes sought to be served by parole would, to a large extent, be destroyed if a parolee's home could be searched at any time, without probable or reasonable grounds, on the theory that the parolee is living in an enlarged prison cell. And, certainly, the simple blanket permission which a convict, as a condition to obtaining parole, gives the Parole Officer to "visit" him at his residence or place of employment may not be read as a waiver of constitutional guarantees or a consent to conduct a general, exploratory search of these places whenever the officer pleases.
>
> The rule which allows a contemporaneous search, without a search warrant, as incidental to a person's lawful arrest is justified by the need to seize weapons or the fruits of, or the implements used to commit, the crime or violation involved. In the present case, the Parole Officer was unquestionably empowered to arrest the defendant for a parole violation—indeed, the defendant admitted the violation—but I doubt that the consequent 2½-hour search of his apartment can be considered "incident" to an arrest based on a charge of consorting with a known criminal. In point of fact, it seems likely that, in the present case, the parole warrant was issued not to authorize the defendant's arrest but, quite improperly I suggest, for the purpose of gathering evidence in a criminal case.
>
> It is my opinion, therefore, that the search of the defendant's apartment was "unreasonable" by constitutional standards, that the evidence uncovered thereby was illegally obtained and that the motion to suppress its use should have been granted. The judgment of conviction should be reversed.

PEOPLE v. CHINNICI

51 Misc. 2d 570, 273 N.Y.S.2d 538 (1966)

[Defendant moved to suppress a revolver found in the trunk of his car. He was on probation and his probation officer had caused his arrest for a traffic violation after receiving confidential information that Chinnici was in possession of a revolver.]

DOUGLAS F. YOUNG, Judge. There is little in the reported opinions to provide authority upon the question of the rights of a probationer. There are some cases concerning the rights of a parolee. Whether a probationer has greater or lesser protection from an invasion of his constitutional privileges than a parolee appears to be an open question.

However, in my opinion there is sufficient similarity between the status of the two to permit the cases concerning a parolee to be used as guidance in the cases of a probationer.

The probation officer had received a telephone call that defendant had a revolver. True, we do not know what information the probation officer had as to the reliability of the informer. However, there existed a serious potential danger, involving a convicted person, under the supervision of the court, allegedly in possession of a dangerous weapon. The probation officer had the responsibility of dealing with this possible danger to protect members of the community.

I believe that where there is some reason based either on the necessities of supervision or danger to the public the probationer and his dwelling and his automobile must be held to be subject to summary search. Any alternative involving the interposition of constitutional barriers to the strict supervision and control of probationers would render the program less useful and perhaps entirely unworkable. The ultimate result would be that courts would find it necessary to incarcerate many defendants who otherwise would obtain the benefits of probation. For example, if it had happened that the officer had received the telephoned warning and a prompt search had not been made, and if this probationer had used his gun to injure or kill a person, the probation officer might well feel that he had failed in his obligation of supervision, and the judge who had placed the defendant on probation would be reluctant to extend the privilege of probation to convicted defendants thereafter. A probation officer is under the control of the court and would be restrained by the court from unbridled and unreasonable harassment of a probationer.

In the circumstances of this case I find that no constitutional rights of the defendant were violated by the search and, therefore, that the search was legal. It is ordered that the motion is denied.[p]

Dr. Ralph Schwitzgebel of Harvard University and his colleagues have been experimenting with electronic tracking devices as part of what has been called "hazard prevention." Briefly, the tracking device consists of a transmitter carried by (or inserted into) the subject and a sender-receiver to measure, over distance, impulses from the subject as he moves about the community, and, if desirable, to send impulses back to the subject. Present technology could enable the receiver to obtain, in addition to voice responses and other voluntary data, the subject's pulse rate, blood alcohol levels, and various brain-wave indicators ranging from sleepiness to emotional agitation. In turn, impulses sent back could act to "condition" the subject to seek or avoid some stimuli. The social uses of tracking are many; persons with diseases like epilepsy or diabetes would be in constant touch with medical authorities; persons in dangerous situations, like policemen or social workers, could use the device to summon assistance.

ANTHROPOTELEMETRY: DR. SCHWITZGEBEL'S MACHINE
Note, 80 Harvard Law Review 403, 406-07 (1966)†

Another use of tracking would involve those released on parole or probation or sentenced to treatment not involving full separation from society.

Requiring the wearing of a tracking device as a condition of parole or probation would permit parole officers to know whether their charges were obeying conditions of release. It would deter the tracked person's former criminal associates from reenlisting him in their activities. If he obeyed the law, it would protect him from the tendency of the police to fasten on exconvicts as suspects. Most important of all, tracking would make it possible to extend the relatively free and therapeutic experience of parole to convicts who would otherwise have to be imprisoned until their terms expired.

---

[p] In State v. White, 264 N.C. 600, 142 S.E.2d 153 (1965), the court held that evidence inadmissible at a trial for a new offense could nonetheless be used as a basis for a revocation on the theory that defendant's consent to a search as part of his suspended sentence was, for this purpose at least, binding upon him.

A restrictive view of the right of regular police officers to arrest parolees for violation of parole conditions is illustrated by DiMarco v. Greene, 385 F.2d 556, 561 (6th Cir. 1967).

On the other hand, tracking—entirely apart from its possible offensiveness to human dignity—might in practice impede parole therapy. The parolee or probationer might experience anxiety or fail to develop self-confidence as a result of excessive surveillance. He might curtail proper as well as improper activities. If third persons became aware that their conversations with him were being recorded by parole officers, he might find it impossible to get a job and might undergo social isolation. Despite these drawbacks, however, tracking may be more effective than imprisonment.[q]

C. CUSTODY AND TREATMENT OF PRISON INMATES

The existence of a prison, particularly a maximum security prison, seems anachronistic in modern society. Its walled, turreted exterior is typically stark and foreboding, looking somewhat like a relic from medieval times. Yet the prison as we know it is relatively modern; even standard prison architecture is basically new, patterned for the most part on prototype prisons at Auburn in New York, and Cherry Hill in Philadephia. No doubt the first American prisons borrowed their structures from European Gothic designs and there were, of course, dungeons and lockups on the continent long before imprisonment began in America. But the idea of incarceration as the principal method for dealing with serious criminals received its greatest impetus in the United States, replacing death, corporal punishment, private vengeance, and the transportation of convicts to overseas penal colonies. In many respects both the prison and imprisonment are as American as the hot dog, borrowed from Europe, but reaching full development here.

The predominant public purposes of the prison have been the incapacitation and punishment of criminals and, by its existence, the deterrence of potential lawbreakers. Yet from the earliest days of American prisons there also have been attempts to reform prisoners during incarceration, at first by engendering a religious sense of "penitence" (hence "penitentiary"), later to prepare them educationally, vocationally, and emotionally for return to the community. Historically, the punitive-deterrent purposes of the prison have struggled for primacy with the philosophies underly-

[q] Further details on tracking devices and their social and legal implications can be found in Schwitzgebel, Schwitzgebel, Pahnke & Hurd, *A Program of Research in Behavioral Electronics,* 9 BEHAVIORAL SCIENCE 233 (1964); R. SCHWITZGEBEL, STREETCORNER RESEARCH: AN EXPERIMENTAL APPROACH TO THE JUVENILE DELINQUENT (1964) (Harvard U. Press); and Schwitzgebel, *Electronic Innovations in the Behavioral Sciences: A Call to Responsibility,* 22 AMERICAN PSYCHOLOGIST 364 (1967).

ing reform and rehabilitation, for while both sets of objectives can exist simultaneously as legitimate goals of prison sentence, in application there are some inherent conflicts. While it certainly has not always followed a linear pattern, in general the trend of American penology has been in the direction of ascendancy of the rehabilitative ideal over punitiveness, incapacitation, and deterrence. By no means has it triumphed; today every prison operates with an uneasy mixture of purposes, expectations, and mandates. Yet, over the years, in-prison treatment of convicts has become much more humane than in the early days of the lockstep, silence, and make-work hard labor. Sentences have generally been shortened or at least made more flexible with general acceptance and wide use of the principle of paroling inmates before the expiration of their terms. In some jurisdictions (and everywhere as an ideal) prison administration has become "professionalized" with trained social workers or other treatment-oriented personnel replacing "keepers" in policy-making positions.

Reformatories for young adult offenders, with programs patterned after that of the first such institution, Elmira Reformatory in New York, are today characteristic of most correctional systems. In addition, the juvenile court movement led to the establishment of training schools for delinquents, a type of institution distinct from both the prison and the reformatory, although often confused with the latter. By and large, the rehabilitation programs of juvenile training facilities are built around school activities. One way of looking at a juvenile facility is that it is a combination grade, junior high, and high school for delinquent children. In this model, the reformatory is more like a walled vocational school for offenders in their late teens and early twenties. The prison, in turn, is a walled factory where men work in the production of goods or services, like automobile license plates, furniture, or laundry, for the use of the state. This is oversimplified in that prisons have some educational and vocational programs, reformatories have some state-use work projects and offer academic as well as vocational training, and vocational education is stressed in the training schools along with regular academic programs. The variations among them however are more than a simple matter of degree; they go to theories of rehabilitation felt to be most appropriate for the different populations served by each facility. For children, the major need is felt to be schooling; for adolescents, trade training; and for adults, work skills and habits.

Rehabilitative programs in correctional institutions are composed of more facets than work and education, except in those correctional systems or institutions that remain relatively primitive and custody-oriented. Individual and group therapy by psychiatrists, psychologists, social workers, and other professionals, including chaplains, are found in some institutions but are sometimes absent from others even within the same state. By and large, the maximum deployment of psychological treatment resources is made to juvenile institutions and programs, then to reformatory populations, and least to the prisons. Within the prisons clinical treatment may be offered primarily to certain types of inmates, sex offenders for example, to the virtual exclusion of other prisoners. Clinical treatment, whether required by legislation or allocated in the exercise of administrative discretion, is generally used more intensively with younger and theoretically more malleable prisoners. The exceptions to this, ordinarily by legislative insistence, involve treatment of persons defined as dangerous or difficult to deal with, such as sex offenders and narcotic addicts.

In addition to traditional prisons, reformatories, and training schools, modern correctional systems have other diversified facilities like farms, camps, halfway houses, medium security prisons, diagnostic and treatment centers, hospitals for psychotic or emotionally disturbed prisoners, and other specialized or specializing institutions to meet particular custody or treatment needs that exist within the inmate population. "The prison system" is conceptually and functionally quite different from "the prison" and does not lend itself to easy generalization or evaluation. Within a given prison system two inmates with identical conviction records and sentences can have widely divergent correctional experiences. The multiple purposes of imprisonment—punishment, deterrence, incarceration, rehabilitation—complex enough in their own right, are infinitely complicated when imposed on a heterogeneous population housed in a variety of facilities for varying lengths of time. As a matter of fact the test cases are likely to come from the most secure institutions, since these are more likely to house prisoners who face long sentences, who have no fear of being transferred to a worse institution for their troublemaking, and who are faced with the most oppressive regimen.

The kinds of complaints from prisoners about life in the institutions which most often surface in the courts, and come to comprise a "substantive law" of treatment of prisoners in correctional institutions, include racial segregation in the institutions, inadequate medical care, restrictions upon religious practices, limitation on free communication with persons outside the walls, physical abuse by guards or fellow prisoners, and disciplinary measures taken for violation of prison rules. It is true today that in all these areas prisoners have some rights. The restrictions cannot be wholly arbitrary and, as to most, the restrictions must have some substantial connection with the custodial or treatment objectives of the institution.

The issue of propriety is mixed with the issue of allocation of responsibility for making the decision as to propriety. This in turn is determined by the remedies available to one who feels aggrieved.

1. The Objective of Maintaining Order

a. Efforts to Maintain Order

Whether the principal concern of a correctional system is punishment or rehabilitation, there is universal concern about maintaining order in the institutions. In maximum security prisons the control is tightest, since the most dangerous prisoners are housed there and the worry about escape, riot, and assaults occupies a major share of the administrators' attention. In less secure institutions the concern for maintaining tight control is less, yet the institution's responsiveness to public fears and its desire to foster an orderly atmosphere where treatment has its best chance of success require the imposition of substantial regulation of the inmate's life.

Even in a progressive correctional system, life in maximum security institutions is highly regimented. The inmate is isolated from his family, his community, his work, and his associates, and undergoes frequent restrictions on the most petty as well as most intimate choices of his life style. Institutionalization involves total control; it creates total dependency over long periods of time in the very individuals it seeks to raise to a level of conforming independence and self-determination.

RULES AND INFORMATION HANDBOOK WISCONSIN STATE PRISON 11-16 (1960)

General Rules of Conduct

In the interest of your protection and the protection of others, it is necessary that we have discipline and order in an institution of this size. You will get along well here by taking the attitude that you will respect the rights of others, cooperate with them, and govern your dealings with them by the principles of good sportsmanship.

If you refuse to cooperate with members of our staff, they will have no choice but to file a disciplinary report describing your misconduct. The report will be referred to the Disciplinary Court for action and the results of the hearing, as well as the disciplinary report, will become a part of your record. Your attitude and frankness before the Disciplinary Court will have much to do with the final outcome of the Court action. . . .

Upon entering the prison, you will be placed in First Grade and entitled to all First Grade privileges. . . .

For wilful violation of any of the following rules, in addition to punishment by solitary confinement on bread and water with loss of good time, or by recording a mark with loss of good time, or deprivation of privileges, the warden may, at his discretion, reduce the offender to Second or Third Grade. . . .

No man shall sign any protest or petition in conjunction with other prisoners. Each will make his own complaints or protests.

Trading or bartering between yourself and others is not allowed or wise without special permission of the warden or deputy warden.

Only items you have obtained through proper channels are permitted to be in your possession.

State magazines are subscribed to for your benefit. They are available to you on a loan basis. They are your magazines, so handle them with care so that as many as possible can get the benefit of them. No magazine cut-outs will be permitted in your cell for any reason, even though they may be from your own magazines.

Approach staff members in a respectful manner and use their last names, always with the title "Mr." If you don't know their last names, say "Sir."

You are not to try to become familiar with an employee nor to offer him any gift nor ask him to buy anything for or from you.

Any weapon, homemade or otherwise, found on your person or in your cell will be considered as evidence of intention to injure someone. This is a serious offense.

Cell House Rules

Keep your cell neat and clean. To draw, paint or paste pictures on the walls of your cell, or in any way to mark or mar the walls, floors, furniture, fixtures, or bed clothes, would not be good sportsmanship because when you leave that cell, someone else must move in. You will, of course, be expected to keep your wash basin and toilet clean.

So that men can study and rest, refrain from singing and whistling or making unnecessary noise. To talk or call to men in other cells would not be conducive to quiet and study.

When entering your cell, close the door quietly, and when leaving the cell, leave the door open. Whenever a count is being made, stand at the door with your hands on the bars.

Sleep with your feet towards the door.

Arise at the first gong signal in the morning—not before—and wash, dress, make your bed, sweep out your cell and be ready to march out.

Your keeper will instruct you as to when laundry, books, etc., are to be put out for exchange.

When you return to the cell hall, go at once to your cell. Never enter any cell but your own. You are not to pass any articles from one cell to another.

If you are sick, notify any officer who passes your cell. You should not remain in bed without permission after the signal to arise.

At the 10:00 P.M. signal, go to bed at once. Place your shoes at the door and the rest of your clothing on the chair next to the door. Sleep with your head uncovered or the officer will be forced to awaken you.

No smoking between 10.00 P.M. and 6:00 A.M. Smoking is permitted between the hours of 6:00 A.M. and 10:00 P.M. when you are in your cell.

Your door is not to be opened until the signal for your range is sounded.

Your clothing or shoes are not to be altered in any way. If your clothing or shoes do not fit or need repair, report the matter to your officer at your place of work.

Always be fully dressed when you leave your cell.

You must not have money, jewelry, or other valuables in your cell.

Dining Room Rules

Upon entering the dining room, march to your place quietly and promptly take your seat.

If you waste food, everybody loses. All food accepted must be eaten and your plate clean by the end of the meal.

When you have finished eating, place knife, fork, and spoon across your plate with handles to the right.

Never argue with the waiter. If any question arises, consult with the officer nearest you. This can be done by raising your hand.

If you wish to speak to the officer about the food or the service, or if you become sick and must leave the table, raise your hand.

When you have finished eating, sit back with your arms folded. At the signal to arise, cease talking, stand, face the aisle and fold your arms.

You may talk in the dining room while seated, but only to the men seated beside you.

Marching Rules

At the signal to fall in for marching, take your place in line promptly, forming a column of two's. Stand erect in line, arms folded, until the order to march is given.

When lining up for count in the shop, you may talk to the man next to you except when count is being taken. This applies within the shop only, otherwise no talking in line or while marching.

Rules While at Work

Upon arriving at your work, prepare for and begin your work promptly.

Your foreman will instruct you as to the routine, quality and quantity of work expected of you. Listen carefully to the instructions and carry them out to the best of your ability.

Conversation must not interfere with your work.

When out of work, stay at your place so as not to interfere with others who are working.

If you are sick or unable to work, report at once to your officer.

No matches or smoking material are to be on your person when on the job, unless you are on outside detail or work where you are permitted to smoke at periods during the working day.

All passes must be O.K.'d by the officer before you leave your place of work and place of interview.

Take good care of all tools, machinery and property. To damage or destroy such property makes you liable to criminal prosecution.

Materials from the shop must not be taken to your cell.

Notify your officer if you wish to speak to an assistant deputy when he goes through your place of work. Ask such permission only in cases of extreme importance. Otherwise ask for an interview on a regular request blank. If you wish to speak to the warden or the deputy warden, put in a request. If it is a matter of vital importance, where it is necessary that you be called at once, mark it emergency, but be sure that it is an emergency matter. When making out requests, make certain you are contacting the proper department. If not sure, inquire of your officer.

Letter Writing and Mail

All letters and papers will be examined under the direction of the warden before being mailed or delivered.

No mail will be taken from the post office for you unless, over your signature, you give the warden authority for its withdrawal from the post office and its opening and inspection by the prison authorities and its nondelivery when, in his judgment, it will interfere with the safety or discipline of the institution, or the laws of the state, or with your best welfare.

Letters containing accusations, charges, or complaints against the institution will not be mailed, except when addressed to the governor, the director of the State Department of Public Welfare or members of the Board of Public Welfare.

Letters must refer to family or personal matters only, or to proper matters of business. No references may be made to criminal matters generally. Do not refer to prison employees by name, or fellow inmates by name.

Obscene or vulgar language, of course, is out of order. Such language would of itself render you liable for prosecution under both Federal and State Laws if the letter were mailed. Letters containing threats of any kind would also render you liable for prosecution.

You may write sealed letters to the governor, the director of the State Department of Public Welfare, the director of Corrections, or to the warden or deputy warden, to whom any proper or truthful complaint may be made without fear of punishment.

Written permission must be obtained from the Social Service Department when it becomes necessary for you to write an extra letter. When requesting an extra writing privilege, you must state your reason.

Those in First Grade may write one letter every Sunday at state expense, and those in Second and Third Grade may write one letter on the first and third Sundays of every month at state expense. First Graders may write two or more letters during the week but must use their own stationery and stamps, which may be purchased at the canteen.

Letters must be left unsealed and placed on the cross bar of the cell door for collection. Unused letter sheets, furnished by the state, must be returned. Do not write between the lines or across the printed matter or in other ways that makes inspection difficult.

When writing on your own stationery, confine your letters to not over *three pages* unless special business requires a more lengthy letter.

Persons with whom you correspond must be listed on your writing list. To add a person to your writing list, secure a request blank from your cell hall keeper.

All of your mail must be addressed to you in care of Box C, Waupun, Wisconsin.

A system for maintaining discipline within the institution involves the imposition of penalties for misconduct. Penalties may include withholding of privileges, such as access to recreational facilities and the opportunity to work and thus earn good time, the deprivation of good time which has been earned, and restrictions on food and movement and companionship by placing the prisoner in solitary confinement. The penalties are usually imposed by a committee which considers the charges against the inmate and assesses what sanction seems appropriate for the misconduct. Though the committee may use some of the language of judicial proceedings, it does not usually undertake to operate as a court.

THE ADMINISTRATION OF DISCIPLINE 1965)*

By David Hase

It is the line officer who bears the real burden of administering discipline. His training is aimed at helping with this job. It fully acquaints him with the importance of informal as well as formal disciplinary methods. The officer is expected to handle most matters informally, referring only the most serious or chronic offenders to the Institution Court. It is harmful to the system if an officer persists in referring minor matters to the Court, since the Court as a rule takes action to back up the position of the officer, even at the risk of losing inmate respect for the Court. For example:

> A regulation in the kitchen required that all inmates assigned there wear caps when handling food. In the sum-

---

* Unpublished paper prepared in the University of Wisconsin Law School Correctional Internship Program, sponsored by the National Council on Legal Clinics (now Council on Legal Education for Professional Responsibility).

> mer the caps are uncomfortable so the inmates seize every opportunity to take them off. The kitchen officer persisted in referring the men he caught without caps to Court. The Court was forced in most cases to take some kind of punitive action, although sometimes merely in the form of a reprimand, in order to support the officer. Eventually the officer's assignment was changed, but there was a period when he had at least three and sometimes more reports per day before the Court.

The problem would better have been resolved by the officer working directly with the men. If any inmate persisted in refusing the officer's informal discipline, the matter could have been referred to the Court as an insubordination case rather than as a failure-to-wear-cap case.

When an officer decides to refer a matter to the Court, he does so by filling out a conduct report. These reports consist of the inmate's name, number, cell location, and work assignment together with a statement of the offense. The statement of the offense is subject to several problems. First, some reports are too slanted. The officer is instructed to state the essential facts as dispassionately as possible and not to try to judge the case. It is particularly important that the report be written this way because the Court deems the facts as stated to be true. This is made clear to the inmate when the report is read to him in Court. If the procedure is to appear fair, the inmate should not be able to object to the way the facts are written up. The Court is very concerned about how the reports are written up and the captain in charge of Court will make it clear to the officer later that his report was not adequate. When there is a particularly slanted report, the Court will often excuse the inmate if he can legitimately contest the basic facts or mitigate the penalty if the basic facts appear to have some truth, but are written in a biased fashion.

Another problem is that there are no uniform standards for invoking the formal disciplinary process. The decision will depend upon the judgment and experience of the officer. This is particularly true with the so-called "general report," which is motivated by a series of difficulties, each of which is too minor to justify reference to the Court. This type of report is much easier for the inmate to rationalize, shifting the blame from himself to the system. The general reports were usually very terse, as, for example, "This inmate is reported for continually refusing to work."

A third problem is inaccuracy in the charge made.

> An inmate was brought to Court on the basis of a report reading: "This inmate is reported for refusing to work. When he was told to cut grass on the recreation field, he stated that the officer was a 'no-good bastard' and that he would not work for him." The inmate claimed that he cut the grass as he was instructed. The Court believed the inmate in this respect. But punishment was given for disrespect to the officer, over the inmate's protest that he was not charged with disrespect.

Once the line officer decides to invoke formal discipline, the Institution Court takes over to handle the disciplining of the offender. Unlike the informal, individualized discipline administered by the line officer, the Court is concerned with invoking broad, institution-wide sanctions—standard penalties related to the type of infraction, not the type of individual.

The Court is a disciplinary committee composed of three representatives from the security and treatment staff. It does not pretend to operate as a court with a formal procedure, rules of evidence and the like. Procedurally, the Court accepts all conduct reports as true. The presumption is guilt. This is explicitly acknowledged by everyone concerned with the Court. However, there is some ambivalence with respect to the presumption when the training literature is compared with admitted practice:

> The conduct of disciplinary court and the handling of discipline are among the most important phases of the institution's operation and the court presents an opportunity if it's properly conducted to demonstrate to the man involved that the institution intends to be fair with him. Discipline must certainly be firm but it must also be fair and impartially handled. Perhaps one of the most important aspects of our democracy in the country is the presumption of innocence until guilt is proven. This presumption of innocence must carry over to our court procedure and a maximum effort must be exercised to see that we are at all times completely fair.
>
> Philosophy, Organization, and Procedure of the Disciplinary Court, p. 1

This ambivalence may be explained as an attempt to make clear to the security officer the need for caution and the fact that his report is not the final determination of the factual issues in a particular case. However, it also bespeaks a feeling that there is something inherently unfair in a presumption of guilt.

This, of course, is not necessarily true. Since the Court is not set up to try the issues of fact in each case, it is necessary procedurally to presume guilt and leave the burden of demonstrating innocence on the inmate. But this should be made clear to the inmate and the officer alike, along with the standards for rebutting the presumption. At present, however, both the officer's training literature and the inmate's rule book are ambivalent on the point.

In practice the inmate is faced not only with a presumption of guilt, but also with a rule which forbids evidence to be offered by another inmate. Yet, an inmate can successfully challenge factual assertions made in the conduct report. If he can convince the Court there is something suspect about the facts, the Court will call the officer and ask for a recounting of the facts in light of the inmate's story. The inmate, however, may not confront the officer before the Court. The Court hears the officer out of the presence of the inmate. To call an officer in for an elaboration of the facts is not an unusual occurrence. And it seemed to usually work out to the inmate's benefit. But where it was clear the inmate was lying, the Court was inclined to be harsher with its penalty. In some cases the inmate can convince the Court the facts were incorrectly stated without calling the officer. This will occur where a member of the Court is familiar with the situation and feels the story is likely to be as the inmate represents it. Because of the policy of the Court to support the staff as much as possible, an inmate whose guilt is somewhat in doubt will still get some sort of a penalty in many cases, often only a reprimand. In these few cases the policy of disciplinary fairness is subordinated to the administrative policy of staff support. The problem will usually be taken up with the officer making the questionable report, as, for example, happened with the kitchen officer who persisted in reporting cap offenses, but the particular inmate involved does not benefit from any adjustment that may be made.[r] Review by the Warden is not routine, but any inmate can appeal a decision to him.

---

[r] The problem of whether to believe a criminal justice official or a citizen arises at other stages of the criminal justice process. For example, most trial judges believe the police officer who appears before them unless they have reason to conclude that the testimony is unreliable. When this occurs, courts may change the rule of law so that the fact issue is changed (*i.e.*, the *Miranda* rule makes testimony as to coercive methods less central) or the judge may come to disbelieve a particular officer which will so reduce that officer's effectiveness that he probably will be assigned to other duties.

b. Controls upon Efforts to Maintain Order

Correctional administrators have aspired to professional status and have, consistent with that, undertaken to state for themselves criteria to be used in evaluating prison operations. However, no real sanction flows from deviation from the standards set.

Corrections is often subject to the oversight of a board or other superior in the government hierarchy. For example, under the Wisconsin prison rules set out above, inmates may write uncensored letters to the Governor, the Director of the Welfare Department, and the Director of the Correctional Division of the Welfare Department—all persons outside the prison itself and in a position to set right any wrongs a prisoner may have suffered. There is, however, as a practical matter great deference to the judgment of the prison personnel who handled a matter and knew at firsthand the situation. For example, complaint to the Governor will likely produce a reply drafted for his signature by the correctional agency.

Within the correctional agency itself there may be formal structure for processing complaints, though often the warden or his deputies are accessible enough so that complaints can be made directly to them and formal appeal procedures are lacking.[s] If there is no administrative mechanism, the letter of complaint or invocation of court procedures remains the prisoner's final recourse.

Within the past few years, there has been an increase in prisoner attempts to obtain court review of the restrictions or conditions of their incarceration. The traditional court posture has been one of "hands off" in matters relating to correctional admin-

---

[s] There are proposals for alternatives to a judicial hearing when there is an inmate complaint. One possibility is for the correctional agency to appoint a hearing officer who would investigate prisoner complaints, make a record (by tape recording, for example) and make findings of fact and conclusions of law. If dissatisfied, the inmate would be entitled to judicial review of the decision in much the same manner as now occurs in judicial review of other governmental administrative actions. In such cases the court would in all probability be able to resolve many of the issues from the transcribed record rather than through initiating a new fact-finding inquiry.

A question can be put as to the possible effects of this procedure on the process of correctional decision-making. It is conceivable, for example, that the presence and activities of an internal hearing process would result in correctional authorities more clearly articulating and justifying policies and practices. In all likelihood, correctional practices would become more visible, to administrators and courts alike. Whether this would result in modification of practices by the agency before they are tested in court is a matter of speculation. Certainly they would be known about and evaluated before litigation. If nothing more, this procedure should prevent the "bad case," *i.e.*, unauthorized practices, from making correctional law.

istration, in part because most legislatures have delegated correctional decision-making autonomy and in part, no doubt, because intervention would likely open a floodgate of atypical and very difficult litigation. Early prisoner allegations, largely to the effect that certain prison conditions constituted cruel or unusual punishment, received short shrift in most courts which were reluctant to label either extreme sentences (but within legislative limits) or severe conditions of servitude as cruel or unusual. In more recent years, however, prisoners have met with somewhat more success in getting the attention of the courts, partly by alleging that correctional authorities prevent access to the courts (an almost surefire way to change the "hands-off" attitude) and partly because prisoner petitions allege some constitutional infringement, such as denial of religious freedom. Allegations are by no means limited to these issues and while it cannot accurately be termed a flood, the increase in the number of petitions and the corresponding increase in the willingness of courts to listen, has created a new era in correctional administration. Issues of control, of treatment, of release practices, and of intra-agency procedures, formerly matters of low visibility only known about and determined by agency personnel, have now been brought into the courtroom. The result is a trend toward the articulation and defense of correctional practices that formerly were subjective, internal to the agency, and even casual in application. The range of prisoner challenges to incarceration is great; their success to date in overturning correctional policies or practices is limited, but the trend of challenge and review continues as a current issue of major proportions.

There are several reasons the trickle has not yet become a flood. First, the courts are reluctant to intervene at all and ordinarily require that the prisoner has exhausted whatever administrative remedies may be available to him. Second, the federal courts are doubly reluctant to interfere with the operation of state institutions. Third, the procedures and sanctions worked out in other areas do not fit so well here. For example, habeas corpus serves awkwardly because the result of a successful challenge by a prisoner is rarely release. Mandamus is properly reserved for ministerial, rather than discretionary, acts. The Federal Civil Rights Acts have been put to use rather heavily, and sometimes the court simply asserts a supervisory responsibility over at least some aspects of corrections.

The nearly universal attitude of courts in the past, and a common attitude today, is illustrated by *Siegel v. Ragen*.

SIEGEL v. RAGEN

88 F. Supp. 996 (N.D. Ill. 1949)

CAMPBELL, District Judge. This is an action under the Civil Rights Act, 8 U.S.C.A. § 43, brought on behalf of the plaintiffs and all others similarly situated. Plaintiffs are all inmates of State penitentiaries—two at Stateville and one at Menard. They allege that the rights and privileges granted to them under the Eighth and Fourteenth Amendments to the United States Constitution have been violated. More specifically, the amended complaint sets forth the following allegations:

(a) HARP—(1) That defendants have beaten him, and that defendant Ragen made the statement, "I will kill you before you get out of here"; (2) That, as a result of the above beatings, plaintiff has become seriously injured and in need of medical attention. He claims, however, that he is afraid to have a necessary operation performed, lest he be put to death in the process; (3) That Ragen, on two occasions, destroyed petitions for writs of habeas corpus; (4) That he has been tried for prison rule infractions by a method known as "trial by ticket," thereby depriving him of his liberty without due process; (5) That plaintiff has deposited certain valuables with Ragen for which he was given a receipt for only 1¢; (6) That Ragen has mismanaged and misused the prisoners' Amusement Fund; (7) That defendants maintain a system of isolation confinement, which is cruel and inhuman, for minor infractions of prison rules of which the prisoners have no knowledge.

The pertinent section of the Civil Rights Act states: "Every person who, under color of any statute, ordinance, regulation, custom, or usage, of any State or Territory, subjects, or causes to be subjected, any citizen of the United States or other person within the jurisdiction thereof to the deprivation of any rights, privileges, or immunities secured by the Constitution and laws, shall be liable to the party injured in an action at law, suit in equity, or other proper proceeding for redress." 8 U.S.C.A. § 43.

The fact that plaintiffs are incarcerated in a penitentiary under convictions for felonies, does not deprive them of the right to invoke the provisions of the Civil Rights Act, since that Act applies to any person within the jurisdiction of the United States.

This Court is prepared to protect State prisoners from death or serious bodily harm in the hands of prison authorities, but is not prepared to establish itself as a "co-administrator" of State prisons along with the duly appointed State officials. All the remaining matters alleged in the amended complaint are strictly matters of internal administration and discipline, and it is not the function of a Federal Court to assume the status of an appellate tribunal for the purpose of reviewing each and every act and decision of a State official. If the remaining allegations could be proved, proper remedial action by the State of Illinois would be well-advised, but it does not follow from this fact that the plaintiffs possess any vested rights, protected by the Constitution of the United States which have been invaded.

Allegations of plaintiff Harp must be stricken, and he will be restricted to his action for damages for the physical injury inflicted upon him.

EDWARDS v. DUNCAN
355 F.2d 993 (4th Cir. 1966)

Before HAYNSWORTH, Chief Judge, and SOBELOFF and J. SPENCER BELL, Circuit Judges.

PER CURIAM. Clarence R. Edwards, a federal prisoner at Lorton Reformatory, seeks leave to appeal in forma pauperis from an order of the United States District Court for the Eastern District of Virginia, Lewis, J., dismissing his suit for money damages and injunctive relief against several of his keepers without holding a hearing or calling for a response from the defendants.

We approach the question presented here having in mind the rule that: a complaint should not be dismissed for failure to state a claim unless it appears beyond doubt that the plaintiff can prove no set of facts in support of his claim which would entitle him to relief.

Edwards has alleged that he has suffered from a heart condition for the past three years for which the senior medical officer at Lorton prescribed a special diet and exemption from duty requiring considerable physical exertion. Defendant Rogers has willfully deprived him of this medical care and thereby caused him irreparable physical damage. Because he has officially complained of this treatment, Clemmer, Weakley and Phillips, all defendants, conspired against Edwards and maliciously caused him to be placed in solitary confinement, thereby further damaging his health by aggravating his heart condition. Edwards has also been the subject of abuse and pressure tactics by the defendants to force him to withdraw a suit against them now pending in the District Court for the District of Columbia. He has had his legal papers in connection with these suits seized and his short time release date set back by the defendants, and his access to the courts has been discriminatorily curtailed by defendant Weakley. These reprisals were results of Edwards' court actions against the defendants. Also, Edwards and nine other Negroes were confined in a 12′ x 10′ cell for thirty-six hours because of their objection to alleged racial segregation as practiced at Lorton.

The opinion of the District Court dismissed these claims as nonjusticiable because of Edwards' status as a prisoner and because a prison rule (Superintendent's Order No. 42), dealing with access to the courts, was not unreasonable. That order is not a part of the pleadings or otherwise appended to the record on appeal.

Edwards' complaint must fail, if at all, solely by a finding, as a matter of law, that the statements in the complaint, even if true, are not grounds for relief.

The District Court's opinion is based on the hands-off doctrine, which is a questionable absolutism in many areas today. This is especially true when a federal court is concerned with a federal prisoner where no problems of federal-state comity or exhaustion of state remedies exist.

We need not now decide whether a prisoner is entitled to every right not specifically taken away from him by law, and to judicial inquiry into alleged deprivations of such rights. The hands-off doctrine operates reasonably to the extent that it prevents judicial review of deprivations which are necessary or reasonable concomitants of imprisonment. Deprivations of reasonable medical care and of reasonable access to the courts are not among such concomitants, however. Prisoners are entitled to medical care and to access to the courts. Where there is no provision for administrative review of claims of unreasonable deprivations of such rights, those claims are certainly justiciable. Where there is no administrative provision for an impartial resolution of factual issues underlying such claims, there is no alternative to judicial inquiry, even though many, or even most of such claims may be asserted irresponsibly.[t]

---

[t] Because most inmates are indigent, a court challenge of their conviction or correctional treatment does not cost them any money and thus there would appear to be everything to gain and nothing to lose. Frivolous court challenges could thereby unnecessarily burden already overworked courts. Karlen, *Frivolous Appeals,* 23 LEGAL AID BRIEFCASE 205 (1965). Most men in prison are anxious to get out and the "writ-route" is an attractive way. Courts are caught in the dilemma of wishing to correct injustices without inviting an avalanche of frivolous petitions. In response to this, Justice McQuade said, in Mahaffey v. State, 87 Idaho 228, 392 P.2d 279 (1964):

> Because of the fact that we may not, on an application for a writ of habeas corpus, dispute the veracity of the allegations contained in the petition, it is foreseeable that any number of fabrications could be employed in order that the writ might issue. If such tactics are used, this court will not hesitate to deal harshly, through either its

Vacated and remanded.[u]

A major issue is whether the courts will continue to keep "hands-off," will assume major and particular supervision responsibility as they have in the police field, or will insist that corrections shoulder the burden of formulating particular standards which need only generalized review by the courts.

BURNS v. SWENSON
288 F. Supp. 4 (W.D. Mo. 1968)

OLIVER, J. Plaintiffs alleged that the administrative procedures under which each had been placed in the Maximum Security Unit and that certain administrative practices to which they were subjected after being placed there constituted action taken under color of state law which allegedly violated certain federal constitutional rights retained by them as inmates. Those actions included alleged violations of their freedom of religion, interference with their rights of freedom of speech and expression through correspondence, violations of access to the courts, violation of their right to be free from cruel and unusual punishment, and denial of adequate medical care and treatment.

First, the evidence conclusively established that plaintiffs were placed in maximum security during the period before the defendants named in these cases were responsible for the administration of the Missouri Department of Corrections. If the particular circumstances under which plaintiffs were placed in maximum security could be considered actionable, a question we find is unnecessary to determine, the particular defendants before us in these cases could not be held responsible for those placements.

> power of contempt or by reference to the proper authorities for prosecution on the charge of perjury, against those who would employ fraud and deceit to win a minor legal victory. Any individual who attempts to make a mockery out of procedures designed to benefit the wronged is tampering with the very foundation of our judicial process and risks having additional punishment imposed.

[u] In Wisconsin, where the hands-off doctrine has been traditional, one Supreme Court justice commented:

> I do not venture to predict whether, or under what circumstances, our court might conclude that a prisoner had shown a right to judicial relief. It would, however, be too broad a statement to say that the court would never grant relief under any circumstances.
>
> It is conceivable, though perhaps unlikely, that the Department might make such wholly unreasonable, arbitrary and capricious demands upon a parolee as to cause the court to intervene; but I venture no prediction as to what circumstances would call for such action or whether this case will ever arise. [Fairchild, *Post Conviction Rights and Remedies in Wisconsin,* 1965 WIS. L. REV. 52, 67, 69.]

Second, the Department of Corrections is presently operating under the new revised set of regulations governing the classification and assignment of inmates to the Maximum Security Unit. Those revised rules and regulations are, in our judgment, fair and well above any presently legally defined threshold of administrative due process.

The establishment of a Maximum Security Unit and regulations governing the classification and assignment of particular inmates to that unit are both matters ordinarily within the discretion of a penitentiary administration. Administrative rules and regulations that are a necessary concomitant of the type of security necessary to be maintained in a Maximum Security Unit are ordinarily matters within the discretion of the administration. Questions of whether past practices may have exceeded the discretion legally vested in the correctional authorities who formerly were responsible for the Missouri Department of Corrections are not before this Court under the present posture of these cases.

Those presently responsible for the administration of the Missouri Department of Corrections have, with commendable foresight, revised regulations that relate specifically to permitted religious practice, to correspondence of inmates, to prisoner access to the courts, and to medical treatment of inmates in the Maximum Security Unit. We specifically find those particular regulations to be fair and that, if fairly administered, are calculated to reasonably protect the broadest construction that could be placed on the federally protected constitutional rights of inmates. Restrictions placed on the rights of inmates properly assigned to the Maximum Security Unit must, in our opinion, be viewed in light of the custody requirements of that unit and must therefore be more stringent than restrictions applicable to inmates in the general population of the prison.

Plaintiffs' contentions relating to cruel and unusual punishment fall into two categories: first, alleged acts of corporally and psychologically abusive treatment of inmates in the Maximum Security Unit, and, second, physical living conditions allegedly so heinous as to violate the minimum federal constitutional standard.

The testimony we heard in these cases regarding abusive treatment of inmates all took place before the present defendants were responsible for the administration of the penitentiary. In addition, these abusive acts were the acts of individual guards, and the testimony plaintiffs presented did not establish a continuing or approved pattern of conduct or policy directed by the named defendants upon which a court of equity could act.

The Court personally viewed the physical facilities of the Maximum Security Unit and, although we found the living areas to be in need of improvement, we do not believe the conditions to be such as to constitute cruel and unusual punishment, within the meaning of the Constitution of the United States. We are convinced that those presently in charge of the Missouri Departmen of Corrections do the best they can with the money made available to maintain and operate an antiquated physical facility.

Counsel for the plaintiffs has indicated that this Court should state in broad terms the rights retained by incarcerated convicted persons. Counsel states that the plaintiffs believe such a statement necessary to prevent possible future abusive treatment of them and other inmates. Plaintiffs urge that such a statement would avoid possible future breaches of federally protected constitutional rights.

We do not believe it appropriate for this Court to attempt to redelineate a Bill of Rights for prisoners incarcerated in the Missouri Penitentiary. The Manual of Correctional Standards, setting forth policy standards for the governing of correctional institutions adequately emphasizes the importance of orderly and fair process in a penal institution:

1. Rules or conditions governing the conduct of offenders and the consequences which may follow from violation should be printed and furnished them together with any explanations that may be necessary for their guidance.

2. Such rules or conditions shall be corrective, not abusive, or punitive, in purpose. They shall be no more numerous or restrictive than is necessary to produce responsible and orderly conduct.

3. No penalty shall be inflicted upon any offender for the violation of a rule or condition except in accordance with established disciplinary procedures adopted by the responsible administrative department.

4. Penalties shall not be cruel, inhumane, or degrading, and no corporal punishments shall be employed as correctional measures. No instrument of restraint shall be applied as a punishment. Penalties shall be assessed and applied only in accordance with an ordered system of regulations and sanctions promulgated by the administrative department and made known to the offender.

5. Standardized methods of seeking information concerning offender rights and obligations and of making complaints to the correctional administration shall be established. The offender shall be informed of such methods and permitted to make use

of them without intimidation or censorship. Unless it is patently frivolous, every request or complaint shall be dealt with and replied to without undue delay.

6. There shall be no discrimination in the administration of correctional procedures on grounds of race, color, sex, language, religion, political, or other opinion, national or social origin, property, birth, or other status.

7. All accommodation provided for the use of prisoners, including sanitary facilities, clothing, diet, and care shall meet proper requirements for health, safety, and rehabilitation. To this end a medical officer shall examine every prisoner as soon as possible after admission and thereafter as necessary. He shall make appropriate recommendations for segregation and classification of those who are found to suffer from disease, defect, or other conditions requiring specialized treatment.

8. The correctional authorities, in fulfillment of their responsibility to keep offenders free from harm, shall exercise all reasonable care to protect their life and health, and are liable for negligent failure so to do.

9. Prisoners shall be allowed to communicate with their family, reputable friends, and legal counsel at appropriate intervals, both by correspondence and by receiving visits and such rights shall not be restricted by reasons of discipline except in instances where they have been abused.

10. No impediments shall be imposed upon the rights of any prisoner to free access to books of law and to the preparation and prompt forwarding of writs, appeals, or complaints to courts of law or to governmental authorities (pp. 267-268).

We cite this portion of the Manual to illustrate the fact that correctional authorities throughout the United States have begun to see the necessity of setting out fair procedures for the handling of inmate conduct within penal institutions. Indeed, the actions taken by defendants during the course of this litigation, as the correctional authority primarily responsible for Missouri corrections, is consistent with national recognition that the correctional authorities should take voluntary action before a court is forced to intervene in what should be left to the administrative authorities.

The President's Commission on Law Enforcement and Administration of Justice: The Challenge of Crime in a Free Society, states on page 181:

> The law has yet to define limits and standards in this area. But correctional authorities should take immediate

steps to insure that there are adequate safeguards by providing for hearing procedures, review of decisions by persons removed from the immediate situation, explicit policy guidelines and standards, and adequate records to support decisions.

The Task Force Report on Corrections of the same Commission states even more explicitly that:

> Correctional administrators have been slow to develop policies and procedures to guide correctional officials and protect the rights of offenders. And trial and appellate courts have been reluctant to review either the merits of such decisions or procedures by which they are made.
>
> Yet it is inconsistent with our whole system of government to grant such uncontrolled power to any officials, particularly over the lives of persons. . . . There are increasing signs that the courts are ready to abandon their traditional hands-off attitude. . . . Recent cases suggest that the whole correctional area will be increasingly subject to judicial supervision. The real question is what form this supervision will take (pp. 82-83).
>
> . . .
>
> It is important that correctional administrators, who are most knowledgeable about the problems involved, develop policies and procedures which will accommodate the needs of the system as well as the interests of convicted offenders. The more adequate such internal controls are, the less it will be necessary for courts to intervene to define necessary procedures or to review the merits of correctional decisions (p. 83).

Immunity from judicial intervention, however, requires more than the mere promulgation of fair rules and regulations. Effective effort must be made to disseminate information about those rules through the inmate population and among the personnel. Correctional authorities must, more importantly, take effective steps to see that the new procedures established by the new rules are followed, especially in areas involving potential deprivations of a federally protected constitutional right.

We do not feel that a general exposition of an inmate's federally protected constitutional rights is either necessary or very practical. There, of course, can no longer be doubt that this is a rapidly developing field of the law.[11] Wright v. McMann, (2nd

[11] See Note, "Constitutional Rights of Prisoners: The Developing Law," 110 U. Pa. L. Rev. 985 (1962); Comment, "Beyond the Ken of the Courts: A

Cir. 1968) 387 F.2d 519, we think, correctly states that "until recently the federal courts refused to review charges instituted under the Civil Rights Act and arising out of state prison disciplinary procedures." But that case stated that:

> Recent decisions, however, have demonstrated a sharp alteration in the judicial attitude toward these rationales and today the older cases retain little vitality. Indeed, there is no longer any question that a state prisoner may bring an action under the Civil Rights Act. Cooper v. Pate, 378 U.S. 546 (1964). Any lingering uncertainty over the applicability of the Eighth Amendment to the States was laid to rest by Robinson v. California, 370 U.S. 660 (1962). And, while federal courts are sensitive to the problems created by judicial interference in the internal discipline of state prisons, in appropriate cases they will not hesitate to intervene.

Plaintiffs in these cases have obtained most of the relief they sought as a result of far-sighted, voluntary action taken by the present administrators of the Missouri Department of Corrections. Questions of whether defendants are now in fact following the new rules and regulations as they relate to a particular plaintiff must, in our opinion, be treated with very specific and individual judicial scrutiny.

Plaintiffs in these cases will therefore be required to present any future grievance or complaint that some federally protected constitutional right has been allegedly violated through the Grievance Procedures established by the new rules and regulations of the Department of Corrections before such complaints are presented to this Court. See and compare our Memorandum and Order filed this day in Cupp v. Swenson, Warden, and companion cases. W.D. Mo. 1968, [288 F. Supp. 1], decided this same day.

On the basis of the record of the hearings in these cases, as well as the materials supplied the Court at the various conferences held since the evidentiary hearings, we will grant defendants' motion for summary judgment but only on the equity claims.

That motion will be granted with the single exception that defendants or their employees will be ordered to return plaintiff Owens' Koran to him. Plaintiff Owens prefers the Moslim reli-

---

Critique of Judicial Refusal to Review the Complaints of Convicts," 72 Yale L.J. 507 (1963); Barkin, "The Emergence of Correctional Law and the Awareness of the Rights of the Convicted," 45 Neb. L. Rev. 169 (1966); Kimball and Newman, "Judicial Intervention in Correctional Decisions: Threat and Response," 14 Crime and Delinquency 1 (1968).

gion of a Middle Eastern branch, and deprivation of his holy book is an interference with his right to freely practice his religion; defendants have given no explanation at all of why this book should not be returned.

Plaintiffs will confer with their counsel to determine whether they wish to pursue their separate actions for damages.

JORDAN v. FITZHARRIS

257 F. Supp. 674 (N.D. Cal. 1966)

GEORGE B. HARRIS, Chief Judge. This is a civil rights action in which the plaintiff claims to have been unconstitutionally subjected to cruel and unusual punishment. Plaintiff prays for injunctive and monetary relief.

Plaintiff's cruel and unusual punishment contention arises out of his confinement from July 9 until July 20, 1965, in a so-called "strip cell" at Soledad.[v] The strip cells (6 in number) form part of the isolation section of the prison's maximum-security Adjustment Center. Each strip cell measures approximately 6′-0″ by 8′-4″. The side and rear walls are solid concrete, as is the floor. Heat and ventilation are supplied to the strip cells through two ducts located high on the rear walls of the cells. The cells have no interior source of light. When the flaps on the outer wall are closed the cells are totally dark except for such light as may seep in through the cracks around the flaps and the outer door.

The amended complaint filed by Jordan, through his appointed counsel, particularized his grievances and charged substantially as follows:

> On or about July 9, 1965, plaintiff was placed in a special punishment unit at the Correctional Training Facility, known as a "strip cell" (hereinafter referred to as "strip cell"). Plaintiff was continuously confined in solitary confinement in said strip cell for twelve consecutive days.
>
> . . .
>
> During plaintiff's confinement in said strip cell, plaintiff was forced to remain in said strip cell with said flaps and door of the second wall closed. As a result, plaintiff was deprived of light and ventilation for twelve days, except that twice a day the door of the second wall was opened for approximately fifteen minutes.

---

[v] Photographs of the cell are appended to the opinion in the *Federal Reporter*.

The interior of said strip cell is without any facilities, except that there is a raised concrete platform at the rear of the cell containing a hole to receive bodily wastes. There is no mechanism within the cell for "flushing" bodily wastes from this hole. "Flushing" is controlled by personnel of the Correctional Training Facility from the exterior of said strip cell. The hole was only "flushed" at approximately 8:30 a.m. and 9:00 p.m. on some of the twelve days plaintiff was confined in said strip cell.

During plaintiff's confinement in said strip cell, the strip cell was never cleaned. As a result of the continuous state of filth to which plaintiff was subjected, plaintiff was often nauseous and vomited, and the vomit was never cleaned from the plaintiff's cell. When plaintiff was first brought to the strip cell, the floor and walls of the strip cell were covered with the bodily wastes of previous inhabitants of the strip cell. Plaintiff is informed and believes and on that basis alleges that said strip cell had not been cleaned for at least thirty days before plaintiff was confined therein.

Plaintiff was forced to remain in said strip cell for twelve days without any means of cleaning his hands, body or teeth. No means was provided which could enable plaintiff to clean any part of his body at any time. Plaintiff was forced to handle and eat his food without even the semblance of cleanliness or any provision for sanitary conditions.

For the first eight days of plaintiff's confinement in said strip cell, plaintiff was not permitted clothing of any nature and was forced to remain in said strip cell absolutely naked. Thereafter, plaintiff was given a pair of rough overalls only.

Plaintiff was forced to remain in said strip cell with no place to sleep but upon the cold concrete floor of the strip cell, except that a stiff canvas mat approximately 4½ feet by 5½ feet was provided. Said mat was so stiff that it could not be folded to cover plaintiff without such conscious exertion by plaintiff that sleep was impossible. Plaintiff is six feet and one inch tall and could not be adequately covered by said stiff canvas mat even when holding said mat over himself. The strip cell was not heated during the time that plaintiff was forced to remain there.

Plaintiff is informed and believes and on that basis alleges that plaintiff has been and may be subjected to confinement in said strip cell without the authorization of the Superintendent, the Deputy Superintendent, the Associate Superintendent, or anyone of comparable administrative rank; that lower-rank personnel of the Correctional Training

> Facility purport to have exercised and intend to exercise in the future broad discretion in confining plaintiff in said strip cell; that said lower-rank personnel purport to have the discretion to confine plaintiff in said strip cell for 60 consecutive days; and that there are no standards for the proper exercise of such discretion.

Jordan, called as a witness on his own behalf, gave testimony which fortified the foregoing allegations. He testified categorically concerning the practices engaged in by the defendants. He was subjected to a lengthy and searching cross-examination by the two attorneys representing the defendants. His testimony is clear and convincing. (Tr. p. 368, et seq.)

More particularly, Jordan discharged the burden cast upon him with respect to the period of time he was confined in the strip cell; the fact that he was deprived of clothing for the period of time, at least for seven days; that he was required to sleep on a strong blanket ill adapted to the uses for which it was put; that the flaps were closed practically all of the time thus depriving him of both light and adequate ventilation in the cell; that the elements of cleanliness were likewise deprived him, to-wit, water, soap, towel, tooth brush, toothpaste, implements for cleaning the cell, and shower. (Tr. p. 378, et seq.)

It is evident from the foregoing narrative of Jordan's testimony that he was required to eat the meager prison fare in the stench and filth that surrounded him, together with the accompanying odors that ordinarily permeated the cell. Absent the ordinary means of cleansing his hands preparatory to eating, it was suggested by the prison consulting psychiatrist, Dr. Hack, that he might very well use toilet paper for this purpose plus his small ration of water, being two cups a day. (Tr. p. 597.)

Regarding medical care: Jordan requested from time to time medical assistance through the medical officer, Dr. Kunkel. As evidence of the limited medical care provided, the official records demonstrate that Dr. Kunkel came into the wing where the strip cells are located and spent eight minutes on one occasion and ten minutes on another occasion, thus servicing the one hundred and eight inmates.

It may be noted that this is the first occasion that the United States District Court in this Circuit has undertaken to inquire into the procedures and practices of a State penal institution in a proceeding of this kind.

The legal principles applicable are not in serious dispute. The right to be free from cruel and unusual punishment is one of the rights that a state prisoner may, in a proper case, enforce under [42 U.S.C.] § 1983.

It appears that the cells in question were used to house those who are assertedly beyond the reach of ordinary controls and prison directives.

Usually the administrative responsibility of correctional institutions rests peculiarly within the province of the officials themselves, without attempted intrusion or intervention on the part of the courts. However, when, as it appears in the case at bar, the responsible prison authorities in the use of the strip cells have abandoned elemental concepts of decency by permitting conditions to prevail of a shocking and debased nature, then the courts must intervene—and intervene promptly—to restore the primal rules of a civilized community in accord with the mandate of the Constitution of the United States.

Superintendent Cletus J. Fitzharris, Deputy Superintendent Robert Donnelly, Sergeant William T. Friedrick, and George F. Johnston are essentially dedicated career men. However, there is a note of futility that seems to run through the pattern of their testimony. Superintendent Fitzharris commented as follows:

> A. I don't know, but I certainly—nobody's happy with having to treat human beings like this, but some human beings can't be treated otherwise, that we know of.

The futility may well have been generated as the result of understaffing and a lack of adequate personnel to service the Adjustment Center and the strip cells.

In the memorandum from L. M. Stutsman, Chief Deputy Director, to All Wardens, dated February 1, 1966, the following appears:

> Recently this entire matter was brought to the Director's attention through a writ submitted by an inmate in which many accusations were made concerning treatment in the disciplinary unit. The writ was denied by the court. Review however indicated some questionable practices which have been corrected with respect to strict adherence to rules and regulations. This memorandum is written to remind you again that each warden or superintendent must personally see to it that rules and regulations and procedures involving inmate discipline are strictly followed. It is considered part of the job of a warden or superintendent to not only keep himself informed in this area via reports and contacts with his staff, but also through first-hand knowledge by visiting the disciplinary areas in his institution.

Further, in the memorandum submitted by Superintendent Fitzharris to the attention of Director Dunbar dated April 13, 1966, recognition is given to the plaints and grievances submitted by petitioner:

> In addition to items contained in Mr. Donnelly's report, I should point out that we have installed an automatic flushing device for the oriental toilets in the strip cells. This eliminates the possibility of staff becoming involved in other matters and not flushing the toilets with regularity. *Provisions have been made for water and personal hygiene materials to be available to the inmates in strip cells so that personal hygiene may be maintained. I apologize for the delay in the report.* (Italics ours)

It is manifest from the foregoing excerpts, as well as the surrounding testimony, that certain radical changes and revisions were made in the practices surrounding incarceration in the strip cells. Whether the changes were made as a result of the petition filed in this court or before the Supreme Court is immaterial. It is fairly inferable that the revisions and corrections were made in meeting the criticism generated by the plaintiff's application before the Supreme Court of the State of California. The defendants deny that the revisions and corrections resulted from such inquiry and seemingly contend that they were to some extent spontaneous. The court is not inclined to this view.

It appears from the testimony that an inmate so incarcerated now receives a basin, pitcher of water, towel, tooth brush and toothpaste, toilet tissue, and is permitted to shower once a week.

While the court will not undertake to specify the precise procedures which the officials must adopt if they are to meet the demands of the Constitution, the practices set out in the manuals relied upon by defendants would, if adopted and followed, meet the minimum standards required by the Eighth Amendment. The following excerpts are illustrative:

> (c) *Punitive segregation in a special punishment section or building.* This section is usually not a part of the regular living quarters. Inmates confined in this area usually receive a restricted diet and a loss of privileges. They should be in a punishment status and kept there for comparatively brief periods. Ordinarily no inmate should be retained in punitive segregation on restrictive diet more than fifteen days, and normally a shorter period is sufficient. Those who fail to make an adjust-

ment under such conditions can often be treated more effectively in special administrative segregation facilities. The punitive segregation section should not be utilized for indefinite or permanent segregation. The not uncommon practice of confining insane inmates there is indefensible, all insane inmates should be transferred to a mental hospital or medical-psychiatric treatment facility.

The punitive segregation section and all the cells in it should be evenly heated and adequately lighted and ventilated. Artificial ventilation is usually necessary. High sanitary standards should be maintained, bathing facilities should be provided in the section and inmates permitted to bathe frequently. Most of the cells should contain a washbowl and toilet. It is necessary to omit this equipment from a few cells and assign them to inmates who persist in misusing the plumbing facilities. A few cells may have toilets that can be flushed only by the officer from outside the cell; these are either ordinary seat toilets or "Oriental type" toilets, which are openings level with the floor. Toilets which the occupant of the cell cannot flush need constant supervision by the officer. Wholly dark cells should not be used and if there is a solid door on the cell, it should be so designed that it does not exclude all light. Natural or artificial lighting should be provided during normal hours of the day or evening in keeping with standards for regular living quarters. (Italics ours)[12]

The injunctive relief contemplated should embrace at least the foregoing revisions in practice.

Findings, decree and injunctive relief may be prepared consistent with the foregoing.

Prisons, more than schools and other public institutions, have extensive and unique problems of custody and internal order which are under a constant threat of racial violence. Many prisons, particularly those in the South, have had traditional policies of segregation; others, including many northern prisons, have developed patterns of de facto segregation even though it is officially disclaimed.

---

[12] Defendants' Exhibit E, Manual of Correctional Standards, The American Correctional Association, Third Edition, 1966, pp. 414-15. This manual, although assertedly not binding on the defendants, was introduced in evidence by them as an illustration of what is considered good practice, and defense counsel pointed out that the manual was largely written by California penal authorities.

Because such matters as religious freedom, racial equality, and free access to the courts are of such high priority in the scale of social values fostered by constitutional law, they have proved to be the focus of much of the prisoner agitation and of the courts' responsiveness. Correctional agencies have perceived the claims largely as attacks on their efforts to maintain a controlled, secure, stable institutional environment. The courts have wrestled with the need to accommodate both broad discretion in the correctional administrator to do his job as his professional judgment dictates and the prisoner's entitlement to fair treatment consistent with overriding social policies.

WASHINGTON v. LEE
263 F. Supp. 327 (M.D. Ala. 1966)

JOHNSON, District Judge. This is an action for declaratory and injunctive relief instituted by one white and five Negro citizens on their own behalf and on behalf of other persons similarly situated, pursuant to Rule 23 (a) (3) of the Federal Rules of Civil Procedure. The plaintiffs seek a declaration concerning the rights of Negro citizens, male and female, not to be segregated, classified, designated, or otherwise subjected to racial distinctions in confinement in the state penal system and in the county, city and town jails of the State of Alabama. Further, plaintiffs assert that various statutes enacted by the Legislature of the State of Alabama, requiring segregation by race in the state, county and city penal facilities, are unconstitutional as violative of the Equal Protection Clause of the Fourteenth Amendment and the Cruel and Unusual Punishment Clause of the Eighth Amendment to the Constitution of the United States. Plaintiffs ask that said statutes be declared unconstitutional and that the defendants be enjoined from requiring segregation by race in any of the state, county and city penal institutions in the State of Alabama.

In this regard, this Court can conceive of no consideration of prison security or discipline which will sustain the constitutionality of state statutes that on their face require complete and permanent segregation of the races in all the Alabama penal facilities. We recognize that there is merit in the contention that in some isolated instances prison security and discipline necessitates segregation of the races for a limited period. However, recognition of such instances does nothing to bolster the statutes or the general practice that requires or permits prison or jail officials to separate the races arbitrarily. Such statutes and practices must be declared unconstitutional in light of the clear principles controlling.

Plaintiffs' contention that the separation of prisoners solely on the basis of race constitutes a violation of the "Cruel and Unusual" Punishment Clause of the Eighth Amendment to the Constitution of the United States is plainly without merit.

The operation of penal institutions, whether it be on a statewide or local level, is a highly specialized endeavor, and the sober judgment of experienced correctional personnel, such as Frank Lee as Commissioner of the Board of Corrections for the State of Alabama and A. Melvin Bailey as sheriff of Jefferson County, Alabama, deserves the most careful consideration of this Court. In this connection, it is recognized that "[t]he association between men in correctional institutions is closer and more fraught with physical danger and psychological pressures than is almost any other kind of association between human beings," Edwards v. Sard, 250 F. Supp. 977 (D.C. Dist. 1966), and in light of this recognition this Court will not at this time require an immediate and total desegregation of state, county and city penal facilities in the State of Alabama. However, the several honor farms, the educational programs, the youth centers and the hospitals in the state system must be completely desegregated immediately. All facilities in the minimum and medium security institutions, including Draper Correctional Center and Julia Tutwiler Prison for Women, must be completely desegregated within six months. As to the maximum security institutions, such as Kilby Prison and Atmore Prison, the evidence reflects that considerations of security and discipline require a more gradual desegregation. In this connection, the Court will expect complete and total desegregation of all state penal facilities, including the maximum security institutions, within a period of one year. As to the county and city systems, complete desegregation should be achieved within six months in all areas, including quarters, except in very exceptional instances as, for example, in the use of the "tank" mentioned previously.

No plan of desegregation will be required of any of these defendants. The Commissioner of the Board of Corrections will be required to report to this Court every three months beginning March 15, 1967, concerning the steps being taken and the progress being made in the state penal institutions and the county and city jails, and other penal facilities throughout the State of Alabama.

In view of the duty of appropriate officials to take the necessary steps within the periods herein indicated, this Court does not consider it necessary to issue a formal injunction in this case at this particular time. Jurisdiction of the case will be specifically retained for all purposes.[w]

PIERCE v. LaVALLEE
293 F.2d 233 (2d Cir. 1961)

CLARK, Circuit Judge. In these three actions, plaintiffs seek relief under the Civil Rights Act, 28 U.S.C. § 1343, 42 U.S.C. § 1983, for religious persecution alleged to have been practiced upon them while they were inmates of Clinton State Prison at Dannemora, New York. In each complaint the plaintiff alleges that he has been denied permission to purchase the Koran, has been subjected to solitary confinement because of his religious beliefs and deprived of good time, and has been denied permission to establish contact with his spiritual advisor on the ground that such person was not an approved correspondence list.[x]

At trial, the district court over protest limited the issues to the denial of the Koran, on the ground that any other problems raised by the complaint concerned matters of prison discipline to be reviewed only in the state courts. With respect to the right to contact a "spiritual advisor," plaintiffs acquiesced in this decision; and we think that issue must be deemed to have been

---

[w] The United States Supreme Court affirmed per curiam. Lee v. Washington, 390 U.S. 333 (1968). Justices Black, Harlan, and Stewart, concurring, stated:

> In joining the opinion of the Court, we wish to make explicit something that is left to be gathered only by implication from the Court's opinion. This is that prison authorities have the right, acting in good faith and in particularized circumstances, to take into account racial tensions in maintaining security, discipline, and good order in prisons and jails. We are unwilling to assume that state or local prison authorities might mistakenly regard such an explicit pronouncement as evincing any dilution of this Court's firm commitment to the Fourteenth Amendment's prohibition of racial discrimination.

With reference to alleged discrimination against both whites and blacks, see also Nichols v. McGee, 169 F. Supp. 721 (N.D. Cal. 1959); and State Bd. of Pub. Welfare v. Myers, 224 Md. 246, 167 A.2d 765 (1961).

[x] Virtually all prisons in the United States have chaplains of various denominations attached to their staff or otherwise available to provide religious services and counseling for inmates. Religious affiliation and observances have been strongly supported by most wardens as positive factors in rehabilitation. However, the administrative requirements of the correctional program necessarily take precedence over any religious practices or rituals that threaten the security or efficient operation of the institution. There may be an initial question whether a group is a religious body in the accepted sense of that concept, whether the prisoner demands (for example, for special diet or religious emblems and literature) grow out of the claims of conscience or out of a desire to inconvenience or embarrass the authorities.

abandoned. But no such abandonment may be found with respect to the issues of solitary confinement and good time.

In Railroad Commission of Texas v. Pullman Co., 312 U.S. 496, the Supreme Court held that a federal court should refrain from passing on the constitutionality of action by a state administrative agency, pending a determination by a state court as to whether or not the agency action was valid under state law. Unlike Pullman, however, the present cases involve no unresolved question of state law, solution of which might render a decision on the constitutional issue unnecessary. Either the plaintiffs were punished solely because of their religious beliefs or they were not. If they were, the defendant's conduct violates both the state statute and the United States Constitution. If the plaintiffs were punished for legitimate reasons, neither law is violated.

We find, therefore, that this is not a case where federal courts should abstain from decision because the issue is within state cognizance.

The judgments below must therefore be vacated, and the cases remanded for consideration of the claims that plaintiffs were disciplined solely because of their religious beliefs.

The remand thus ordered will not, however, reach or apply to the remaining issue concerning the dismissal of the claim for the right to purchase Korans. On January 5, 1960, after the present actions were commenced, the Commissioner of Correction issued a directive to wardens of state prisons approving for purchase by inmates four different translations of the Koran published in the United States. On June 9, 1961, this memorandum was supplemented by the addition of an edition of the Koran published in Pakistan in 1951. This latter edition is the one sought by the plaintiffs, and the defendant represented in open court that this edition is available for purchase by plaintiffs in accord with the prison's regular procedures. In these circumstances the district court could properly conclude that there was no reasonable probability of a continuance of a denial to the plaintiffs of their Korans in violation of any constitutional rights.

PIERCE v. LaVALLEE

212 F. Supp. 865 (N.D.N.Y. 1962)

Brennan, Chief Judge. On August 15, 1959, disciplinary action was taken by the prison authorities against each of the three plaintiffs. The action was taken based upon identical reports of a Guard Captain which in substance charged each plaintiff with "agitating". Such reports consisted of a statement to the effect that each plaintiff was a member of the Muslim Brotherhood actively engaged in its activities, the organization being a source of racial hatred and advocates the use of force as a last resort. In accordance with prison procedure, each of the plaintiffs appeared before the Principal Keeper of the prison and after discussion of the report, a judgment was made depriving each plaintiff of sixty days good time and assigning each to segregation. Each plaintiff claims that the above action was taken and the discipline inflicted solely as punishment for his religious belief and constituted a deprivation of his constitutional right to the exercise of his religion.

Clinton Prison at the times involved had an inmate population of about twenty-two hundred persons of various racial and religious backgrounds or beliefs. About thirty of such inmates were recognized as Muslims. The details of their religious belief were unknown to the prison authorities. There had been in existence at the prison for a number of years a system whereby plots of land in the prison yard of varying dimensions are assigned to inmates for their use during specific hours when yard privileges are available. The plots, thus allotted, about 300 in number, are known as "courts" and are put to use by the assigned inmates for various recreational or educational purposes. One or more of such courts were assigned to and controlled by members of the Muslim organization. This court was enlarged from time to time by the absorption of a neighboring court so that in June 1959, four of said courts had been combined into one large area which was used by members of the organization for their purposes. It is evident that the use of said courts by inmates was encouraged or permitted as an outlet for inmate activities.

In the early part of the year 1959, the activities upon the Muslim court came to the attention of prison officials. In the spring of that year, the prison authorities directed surveillance of the Muslim court and a report by the yard guard of activities therein. The testimony of the guards indicated a more or less continuous activity within the Muslim court. A larger number of inmates than was usually found gathered at that area and were often addressed by some individual. It was observed that some of those present wore black caps, not usually worn by inmates. It was noted especially for a period prior to August 10, 1959 that upon the approach of a guard to the Muslim court, all conversation and activity ceased so that the guard was unable to hear what was being said. When the guard moved out of hearing distance, conversation resumed and the speaker apparently received the full attention of the group. This action was interpreted by prison officials as indicating discussions, the nature of which was purposely withheld from the prison authorities, which indicated a secretiveness or condition of unrest. On August 10, 1959, the prison authorities made an examination of the homemade "locker" located on the Muslim court. There was found therein and taken therefrom literature and documents relating to the religion of Islam and the Muslim movement. These documents were examined by prison authorities. It was found that there existed an organization known as the "Muslim Brotherhood". This organization had a written constitution which apparently came into existence about April 1959. This instrument is set out as an appendix to this decision. After the documents, so seized, had been examined and appraised by prison officials, the charges, above referred to, were made and the discipline invoked.

In our zeal for the protection of freedom of religious belief and practice, the particular circumstances involved may not be overlooked. A large prison population is committed to the custody of a minority of prison employees and authorities. Discipline is necessary for the protection of both the inmates and the public. Prison discipline may on occasions impinge upon fundamental rights. That a public officer has or will violate the constitutional safeguards of the freedom of religion, in this court's opinion must be established by convincing evidence. Such a charge is easy to make in an unverified complaint but the charging party must support it by more than inference or conjecture.

Admittedly there existed at Clinton Prison an organization of inmates with inmate leadership dedicated to the formation of secret plans, strategy and policies and further dedicated to the extension of objectives of said organization throughout the state prison system. The organization required of its members irrevocable obedience to its commands and instructions; the undertaking of any mission which they might be called upon to perform and the assistance of a brother member "in all difficulties".

Experience indicates that such an organization is a likely fomenting point for the unrest and frustration of confined inmates. It would seem to follow that the defendant might well be derelict in his duty if he knowingly allowed such an organization to function. The segregation of the three plaintiffs who were apparently considered as some of the leaders in said organization would seem to be a proper, if not a necessary, step in the insurance of discipline and good order within the prison. Plaintiffs' contention that such action was solely the result of vindictiveness on the part of the defendant because of the petty annoyances occasioned by their previous court proceedings or complaints is entirely rejected. From the number of applications for relief made to this court by state court prisoners confined at Clinton Prison, it can be readily concluded that petty annoyances, so occasioned, are a part of the defendant's daily routine.

It should be emphasized that the Muslim Brotherhood, as it existed at Clinton Prison, is not a religion. Rather it is an organization which sets itself up as an adjunct to the Islamic faith. Membership in the Brotherhood and adherence to the principles thereto was the basis of the punishment visited upon the three plaintiffs rather than their belief in the religion of Islam.

It is concluded that the complaint in each individual action should be and is dismissed, and it is

So ordered.

Appendix

Constitution

Name: Muslim Brotherhood

Motto: Forward ever—Backward never

Aims & Objects

1. To maintain ourselves and the Muslim Brotherhood as the vigorous, intellectual vanguard of the struggle for complete unity among our brothers by employing the unifying force of Islam.

2. To secure & maintain the complete intellectual unity & awakening of our brothers by promoting the advantages of unity of action and organization through the study of: Islam; our history which has been concealed from us; the struggle for freedom being made by our brothers at home and abroad; and all other pertinent subjects.

3. To build and train leaders for the future struggle so that each member upon his release shall be so equipped, that he will be able to successfully organize his own group or be an asset to any organization he may join.

Introduction

Since no movement can endure unless there is a stable organization of trained, selected and trusted men to maintain continuity and carry its program forward to successful conclusion.

And since the more widely our brothers are drawn into the struggle for freedom the more necessary it is to have an organization such as the Muslim Brotherhood to establish unity of action and thereby making it impossible and difficult for demagogues, sell-out men, uncle-toms, traitors, cowards and self-seekers to lead astray any section of the masses of brothers.

And since, in a country like this with a despotic anti-brother and anti-Muslim government, and in addition being inside the prison of the enemy, the more necessary it is to restrict the Muslim Brotherhood to persons who are sincere and going "all the way". These will be trained in the art of combatting all manner of intrigues, deceptions & persecutions thereby making it difficult for anyone to disrupt the programs of the Muslim Brotherhood.

I therefore accept and abide by the laws of the Muslim Brotherhood which are as follows:

1. I will irrevocably obey and act upon the orders, commands, instructions and directions of the Muslim Brotherhood.
2. I will always serve, sacrifice and suffer anything for the cause for which the Brotherhood stands, and will at all times be ready to go on any mission that I may be called upon to perform.
3. I will always and in all circumstances help a member of the Muslim Brotherhood in all things and in all difficulties.
4. I will make it my aim & duty to foster the cause for which the Brotherhood stands among all the brothers.
5. I will, except as a last resort avoid the use of violence.

Membership

Only brothers shall be eligible for membership and these must accept Islam, the objects, policy, program & discipline of the Muslim Brotherhood.

Any person who is a known informer or a homosexual shall not be eligible for membership. (the rumor that one is an informer, shall, in the absence of evidence to the contrary, bar one from membership).

Application for membership shall be made through a member who shall introduce the applicant to members of the Brotherhood for their acceptance or otherwise.

During the probationary period, the probationary member shall merely be an observer at Brotherhood meetings and although he may voice his opinion, he shall not vote. He may participate in all activities of the organization except the meetings in which strategy & secret plans are discussed.

Communication

A close liaison shall at all times be maintained between all members of the organization, in prison and out. As far as possible all communications should be done by personal contact, or employing only members as couriers and messengers. . . . Discussion of Muslim Brotherhood matters in public places is forbidden.

All members shall upon their release maintain contact with the Brotherhood and aid it from the outside by sending money & packages, books & literature and by apprising the outside brothers of the struggle of the Muslim Brotherhood.

PIERCE v. LaVALLEE
319 F.2d 844 (2d Cir. 1963)

PER CURIAM. The district court's finding that the plaintiffs had failed to establish that their punishment resulted from their religious beliefs was not clearly erroneous; and so we must affirm.

Affirmed.

COOPER v. PATE
378 U.S. 546 (1964)

PER CURIAM. The motion for leave to proceed *in forma pauperis* and the petition for a writ of certiorari are granted.

The petitioner, an inmate at the Illinois State Penitentiary, brought an action under 28 U.S.C. § 1343 and 42 U.S.C. § 1983, § 1979 of the Revised Statutes, alleging that solely because of his religious beliefs he was denied permission to purchase certain religious publications and denied other privileges enjoyed by other prisoners. The District Court granted the respondent's motion to dismiss for failure to state a claim on which relief could be granted and the Court of Appeals affirmed. 324 F.2d 165 (C.A. 7th Cir.). We reverse the judgment below. Taking as true the allegations of the complaint, as they must be on a motion to dismiss, the complaint stated a cause of action and it was error to dismiss it. See Pierce v. LaVallee, 293 F.2d 233 (C.A. 2d Cir.); Sewell v. Pegelow, 291 F.2d 196 (C.A. 4th Cir.).

2. *The Objective of Rehabilitating Inmates*

One of the commonly stated purposes of correctional systems today is rehabilitation. Programs designed to bring this about are at least nominally present in every prison system. The initiative has come from corrections, but budgetary support has come from the legislature. And special treatment programs are often explicitly required as part of the legislative scheme for dealing with sex offenders, narcotic addicts, defective delinquents, and similar categories of inmates. In deference to the benevolent purpose of such legislation, procedures for determining that the defendant belongs to one of these categories have been exempted from many of the rigorous, adversary techniques of trial. At the same time, periods of incarceration have been made more flexible to allow both early release and adequately long detention to permit full treatment or extended restraint.

In recent years, persons under sentence for treatment-category offenses have challenged not only the constitutionality of the statutes under which they were selected for diagnosis, but have alleged failure of the administrative program to provide appropriate treatment. The use of shock therapy, prefrontal lobotomy, sterilization, and the like may be challenged because they are so drastic and so uncertain in their benefits to the inmate. On the other hand, the inmate may complain that no real effort is made to treat him and may claim that he is entitled to some minimal effort to treat him, not merely to keep or punish him.

DIRECTOR OF PATUXENT INSTITUTION v. DANIELS

243 Md. 16, 221 A.2d 397 (1966)

HAMMOND, J., delivered the opinion of the Court.

Samuel Daniels, an appellee and cross-appellant, was found to be a defective delinquent in 1959 by the Circuit Court for Prince George's County pursuant to the provisions of the Maryland Defective Delinquent Act, Code (1964 Supp.), Art. 31B (the Act), and was remanded to Patuxent Institution, the place of confinement, and treatment and rehabilitation if possible, established by the Act for those judicially determined to be defective delinquents. In Daniels v. Director, 238 Md. 80, we rejected all his contentions save the one that the trial court had denied him the right and opportunity to show that he was not being given treatment for the causes of his defective delinquency as contemplated by the Act, but rather was being punished by being confined indefinitely, probably for life, in a penal institution in violation of his constitutional rights. Leave to appeal was granted as to this claim and the case remanded for a determination of whether the continued detention of Daniels in Patuxent is a violation of his constitutional rights.

Historically, this type of sanction or restraint to accomplish the purposes of the Act has not been regarded as punishment but regulatory and is more akin to those laws consistently held to be civil in nature applicable to the "sexual psychopaths." Also this is true of laws involving loss of liberty by restraint of many mentally ill persons in mental hospitals in all of the states. The Maryland Act does not come into play on a finding of "scienter," because the person involved must before referral for diagnosis, already have been convicted of at least one criminal act and can be determined to be a "defective delinquent" only after there has been an intensive mental examination. The law on its face clearly shows that it was not enacted to promote the aims of punishment, retribution and deterrence, but its only purpose is for the protection of society, and the treatment of the individual to effectuate a cure if at all possible. The Act clearly demonstrates that "defective delinquency" is not a crime but is a mental condition that can only be diagnosed and determined to exist after a finding of guilt. There exist alternate purposes which are valid functions of the State as a part of its police power. They are the protection of society, coupled with a humanitarian attempt to treat, cure and rehabilitate those suffering from abnormal mental functioning. The sanctions or incarceration provided by the Act are not excessive in relation to these alternative purposes since most reputable psychiatrists agree that treatment cannot be related to a fixed period of confinement, as the length of time necessary for treatment and cure, if it can be obtained, is uncertain. In addition, experience has demonstrated that the indeterminate confinement is itself therapeutic, as it has a tendency to generate and motivate the individual to participate in the institutional program in order to help himself.

It would seem that the court's further concern after concluding that the Act was reasonably calculated to achieve its legislative purpose, only exists if the other branches of the government fail to act after a clear showing that it is ineffectual in accomplishing its purpose. We are aware of no responsible opinion of any professional group, and certainly there is no opinion of any of the witnesses testifying in this case, that the Act is clearly ineffectual in accomplishing its legislative purpose. On the contrary we conclude from the testimony by following the requirements of the Act, together with a utilization of medically accepted treatment techniques now being carried out at Patuxent, provides a procedure reasonably calculated to achieve the stated legislative purposes.

We conclude that the Court has no power to interfere until its ineffectiveness is clearly demonstrated and the other branches of the government fail to act.

We further conclude from the evidence that the legislative and executive branches of the government are keeping abreast of and familiar with the operation of Patuxent Institution and the internal administration at Patuxent, in turn, is continually re-evaluating its treatment and release program in light of new developments in the psychiatric-medical field.

We conclude that the Act is constitutional and is being constitutionally applied, both generally and specifically as to Daniels.

Appendix A
Court's Findings of Fact

Treatment of Inmates.

Since defective delinquents usually require more than normal incentive to be motivated, cannot easily tolerate lack of discipline, and are deficient in ability to control their conflicts, their effectual treatment can best be carried out in a secure institutional environment, such as provided by Patuxent, with a definite reward and punishment system. Such treatment is not available and cannot feasibly be made available in State mental hospitals or State penal institutions.

The conventional mental hospital, whether State or private, deals with a distinctly different group of patients than Patuxent, in that within the former institutions are found individuals who, for the most part, have internalized their conflicts and do not "act out" against society, and thus such institutions can be operated as "open" hospitals. One of the chief characteristics of the defective delinquent is his inability to internalize these conflicts, resulting in "acting out" antisocial behavior. Moreover, all committed inmates at Patuxent have been found to be, in varying degrees, a danger to society, thus Patuxent must be operated as a maximum security institution. Experience has shown that when individuals possessing the characteristics of the defective delinquent are confined within mental hospitals, they are disruptive to the normal institutional program.

The penal and correctional institutions under the jurisdiction of the Department of Correction have been ineffectual in developing or providing the specialized treatment and attention which defective delinquents require, and experience has indicated that when individuals possessing the characteristics of the defective delinquent are incarcerated in conventional penal institutions they are disruptive to the normal institutional program. Confinement of defective delinquents at Patuxent, rather than in the State's penal institutions, has enabled such institutions to develop more effective programs for the conventional prison population.

Both quantitatively and qualitatively, Patuxent's treatment program is more effective for the defective delinquent type person than that provided in the State's penal and correctional institutions.

Patuxent's professional staff is adequate and competent as beginning August 15, 1965, the institution was authorized to employ twelve full-time psychiatrists (9.58 being then employed), nine psychologists (5.5 being then employed), and fourteen social workers (13 being then employed). With 485 patients on August 15, 1965, the professional staff to patient ratio was in full compliance with mental hospital staff standards promulgated by the American Psychiatric Association, and was materially higher than such ratios prevailing in the State penal and correctional institutions and in State mental hospitals in Maryland, as well as elsewhere in the country generally.

Group therapy, which now enjoys almost universal acceptance, and in which use Patuxent pioneered, is now generally considered by experts to be the most effective form of treatment for defective delinquents. Presently 86% of the committed patients are regularly receiving this form of psychotherapy. All patients are afforded an opportunity to receive such therapy, and nonparticipation is due either to recent commitment, improper attitude or outright refusal.

Individual therapy is also provided at Patuxent on a selective basis, but presently only four inmates are receiving this form of treatment, as experience there has demonstrated that defective delinquents generally do not respond well to this form of therapy.

All committed inmates by virtue of the milieu therapy program are in a broad sense constantly receiving treatment.

Daniels' Treatment.

As applied specifically to the petitioner we find as follows:

Although Daniels has proven not to respond particularly well to group therapy, he is susceptible of help, through application of a simple reality group therapy program. His institutional record with regard to such therapy is lacking in relation to the results reached. However, we do find that all therapy utilized at Patuxent which is appropriate to his condition is available to him.

The design and implementation of effective treatment methods for assorted types of deviation is the goal of many professions in our society and a major purpose of many agencies, including prisons. Unfortunately, present rehabilitative techniques are inadequate to deal with certain forms of deviation, such as chronic alcoholism, and yet numbers of such persons who are "untreatable" end up in jails and prisons.[y]

POWELL v. TEXAS
392 U.S. 514 (1968)

MR. JUSTICE MARSHALL. There is as yet no known generally effective method for treating the vast number of alcoholics in our society. Some individual alcoholics have responded to particular forms of therapy with remissions of their symptomatic dependence upon the drug. But just as there is no agreement among doctors and social workers with respect to the causes of alcoholism, there is no consensus as to why particular treatments have been effective in particular cases and there is no generally agreed-upon approach to the problem of treatment on a large scale. Most psychiatrists are apparently of the opinion that alcoholism is far more difficult to treat than other forms of behavioral disorders, and some believe it is impossible to cure by means of psychotherapy; indeed, the medical profession as a whole, and psychiatrists in particular, have been severely criticised for the prevailing reluctance to undertake the treatment of drinking problems. Thus it is entirely possible that, even were the manpower and facilities available for a full-scale attack upon chronic alcoholism, we would find ourselves unable to help the vast bulk of our "visible"—let alone our "invisible"—alcoholic population.

However, facilities for the attempted treatment of indigent alcoholics are woefully lacking throughout the country. It would be tragic to return large numbers of helpless, sometimes dangerous and frequently unsanitary inebriates to the streets of our cities without even the opportunity to sober up adequately which a brief jail term provides. Presumably no State or city will tolerate such a state of affairs. Yet the medical profession cannot, and does not, tell us with any assurance that, even if the buildings, equipment and trained personnel were made available, it could provide anything more than slightly higher-class jails for our indigent habitual inebriates. Thus we run the grave risk that nothing will be accomplished beyond the hanging of a new sign—reading "hospital"—over one wing of the jailhouse.

One virtue of the criminal process is, at least, that the duration of penal incarceration typically has some outside statutory

[y] *Compare* Robinson v. California, 370 U.S. 660 (1962), holding that mere addiction to narcotics cannot constitutionally be punished as a crime.

limit; this is universally true in the case of petty offenses, such as public drunkenness, where jail terms are quite short on the whole. "Therapeutic civil commitment" lacks this feature; one is typically committed until one is "cured." Thus, to do otherwise than affirm [the conviction for public drunkenness] might subject indigent alcoholics to the risk that they may be locked up for an indefinite period of time under the same conditions as before, with no more hope than before of receiving effective treatment and no prospect of periodic "freedom."

Faced with this unpleasant reality, we are unable to assert that the use of the criminal process as a means of dealing with the public aspects of problem drinking can never be defended as rational. The picture of the penniless drunk propelled aimlessly and endlessly through the law's "revolving door" of arrest, incarceration, release and re-arrest is not a pretty one. But before we condemn the present practice across-the-board, perhaps we ought to be able to point to some clear promise of a better world for these unfortunate people. Unfortunately, no such promise has yet been forthcoming. If, in addition to the absence of a coherent approach to the problem of treatment, we consider the almost complete absence of facilities and manpower for the implementation of a rehabilitation program, it is difficult to say in the present context that the criminal process is utterly lacking in social value. This Court has never held that anything in the Constitution requires that penal sanctions be designed solely to achieve therapeutic or rehabilitative effects, and it can hardly be said with assurance that incarceration serves such purposes any better for the general run of criminals than it does for public drunks.

3. *Other Objectives in Correctional Regulation of Prisoners*

Aside from the two principal objectives of correctional administrators—to maintain order while providing rehabilitative programs—there are several other justifications for restrictions placed upon prisoners.

To some extent a real, but disavowed, objective of many systems is to make prison life unpleasant. Because the punitive or retributive spirit in correctional work is decried by the profession, there is no deliberate effort made to create pain or discomfort. What does happen is that existing conditions are allowed to persist, with the rationalization that this is, after all, a prison, and inmates can hardly expect it to be like a country club.

Another major concern of correctional officials is the integrity and well-being of the correctional system itself. This often involves the question of public relations and public expectations, and the need to keep on good terms with the legislature if appropriations essential to the carrying on of a therapy-oriented program (which is always expensive) are to be obtained. For example, it is common practice to censor mail and limit correspondents, not only to prevent transmission of contraband, but also to insure that persons outside the prison are not subject to harassment or vilification by inmates, and to insure that defamatory charges against prison officials are not sent out to newspapers or others who might give the charges publicity without inquiry into their accuracy.

Because of the great interest in crime and criminals, prison officials are beset with frequent requests for tours of the prison or the filming of television shows or facilities for the conduct of studies or experiments. The interest may range from idle curiosity, to the concern of a taxpayer over rising prison costs, to the student of behavioral science. The officials would like to comply with such requests, since favorable publicity can win useful support for correctional programs, but granting them may raise problems of security and even of invasion of the inmates' little remaining privacy.

McCLOSKEY v. MARYLAND

337 F.2d 72 (4th Cir. 1964)

HAYNSWORTH, Circuit Judge. McCloskey, held as a defective delinquent in Maryland's Patuxent Institution, seeks a court order requiring officials of the Institution to permit him to engage in an extensive correspondence.

McCloskey declares in his petition that he is anti-Semitic, and he alleges that he is held in punitive segregation at Patuxent because of his expression of his anti-Semitic beliefs. He wishes to correspond on the subject with members of Maryland's Legislature representing Cecil County, the United States Representative who represents the District of which Cecil County is a part, the two United States Senators from Maryland, the American Civil Liberties Union and the American Bar Association. He asks for an order which would require the Patuxent officials to permit him to write to each of those prospective correspondents, expressing his anti-Semitic opinions and beliefs, registering complaints which he thinks legitimate and seeking legal assistance of them.

While an inmate of such an institution should be allowed a reasonable and proper correspondence with members of his immediate family and, at times, with others, it is subject to censorship to be certain of its reasonableness and propriety. A broader correspondence is subject to substantial limitations or to absolute prohibitions. Control of the mail to and from inmates is an essential adjunct of prison administration and the maintenance of order within the prison. A propagandist has no judicially enforceable right to propagandize within the prison walls, whether his propaganda be directed to other inmates or to outsiders. Of course, prison officials should not interfere with his access to the courts, or with a reasonable correspondence designed to secure for himself legal assistance for the purpose of testing the validity of his conviction or the constitutionality of punitive treatment which he may claim to be cruel and unreasonable. An effort to correspond in reasonable terms with a limited number of national organizations and public officials in aid of such objectives, even in the light of the fact that throughout McCloskey has had the effective assistance of very able counsel, would produce a different question. We only hold that he has no constitutional right to seek legal assistance in aid of propagandizing endeavors, in which he has no right to engage so long as he is confined except to the extent that they may be administratively permitted. Since he has no judicially enforceable right from the walls of the institution to bombard prospective correspondents with propaganda, he has no incidental right to seek their legal assistance in aid of that objective.

The petition was properly dismissed without a hearing.

Affirmed.

TRAVERS v. PATON

261 F. Supp. 110 (D. Conn. 1966)

Ruling on Motion for Summary Judgment

Blumenfeld, District Judge. The plaintiff Harold Travers brought this suit under 42 U.S.C. §§ 1983 and 1985(3) seeking damages for the alleged violation of his civil rights. On April 22, 1964, the corporate defendant caused to be televised a film entitled "Prison and Parole" describing the facilities and life of an inmate in the new state prison at Somers, Connecticut.

A portion of the film was concerned with the operation of Connecticut's parole system and included scenes of prisoners being interrogated as prospective or recalcitrant parolees. The plaintiff, an inmate of the prison, was filmed as he appeared for a parole hearing.

The corporate defendant asserts that Travers was not disturbed in his parole interview by the filming, but was rather unaware of the entire operation. Plaintiff does not dispute this point, but argues that the very secrecy of the filming operation made public what plaintiff was led to believe was a confidential interview. The act of the corporate defendant in filming plaintiff's interview in this allegedly deceptive fashion and in subsequently televising this film is what the plaintiff claims invaded his constitutional right to privacy in violation of 42 U.S.C. §§ 1983, 1985(3).

Title 42 U.S.C. § 1983 imposes civil liability for the "deprivation of any rights, privileges, or immunities secured by the Constitution and laws [of the United States]. . . ."

All torts are not violations of rights "secured by the Constitution and laws."

Since no "laws" of the United States are involved, the plaintiff's case rests solely on the proposition that the Constitution contains a so-called "right of privacy." This contention begins and ends with Griswold v. Connecticut, 381 U.S. 479 (1965) for there is no other case support for the argument. In *Griswold,* the Court was faced with a constitutional attack on Connecticut's antiquated criminal statute barring the use of contraceptive devices. Conn. Gen. Stats. § 53-32. Although recognizing that the Constitution nowhere explicitly mentioned a right of privacy, the Court enunciated a theory of "penumbras" of guaranteed rights whereby the first, third, fourth, and fifth amendment rights were seen to focus on and protect the sanctity of sexual aspects of the marital relationship. The several opinions written are a studied effort to avoid the introduction into the Constitution of a mass of unwritten rights, and they emphasize and re-emphasize that it is the special nature of the marriage bond that makes so patently offensive state intrusion into the area.

It misses the heart and spirit of the *Griswold* case to casually infer an intent to adopt into the Constitution the entire body of the tort law right to privacy. Since photographic privacy is protected in Connecticut by state common law, in a diversity case a federal court sitting in this state would follow state law and grant suitable relief. However, this would be a vastly different problem from the one facing the court, for this is not a diversity of citizenship case. The facts of this case have no connection with any *federal* rights, those secured by the Constitution and laws of the United States.

Because plaintiff's claims cannot be supported under the Civil Rights Act, 42 U.S.C. § 1983, it would not ordinarily be necessary to reach the merits of the claim as based on Connecticut's common law.

However, both sides have met on the issues raised by the defendants' motion for summary judgment. Since undisputed facts have been presented on the merits and since there is no genuine issue as to any material fact relating to the furthest reaches of the plaintiff's claim, it is not inappropriate to decide this case in its entirety on the basis of pendent jurisdiction.

Even if the facts might be held to constitute an invasion of the privacy of a full-fledged citizen, an average member of the community, no actionable invasion occurs if the subject of such publicity is a prisoner. A prisoner becomes a public figure by virtue of his crime and subsequent trial. Restatement, Torts § 867, Comment c. He remains a public figure during his imprisonment or until he has "reverted to the lawful and unexciting life led by the great bulk of the community." In the instances where prisoners have sued in federal court alleging invasion of privacy in the publication or broadcasting of a version of their crime, the courts have denied relief on the grounds that prisoners are public figures in whose misadventures the community has a consuming interest. Although there are no Connecticut cases in point, there is no reason to believe that Connecticut's courts would deviate from this prevailing view.

Finally, it is hard to believe that a jury or court would find that his reputation has been injured or that he has endured any pain or suffering to support an award of compensatory damages.

So far as the viewer was concerned, the plaintiff was nameless and faceless. In any event, the true identity of the prisoner appearing before the board was of no significance. It is extremely improbable that anyone would pay any attention to it.

The defendants are entitled to judgment on the merits.

Still another objective of the correctional system has sometimes seemed to be the discouraging of inmate challenges to his conviction or to his institutional treatment. The regulations limiting the prisoner's access to law books, to courts, and to legal counsel can be rationalized on the grounds of the need for prevention of dealing in contraband, the need to prevent one inmate's exploiting another, and the desire to help an inmate accept responsibility for his misconduct and get on with the business of rehabilitating himself. Despite this, however, there appears to be a distaste for the prisoner's recourse to law, particularly when there is involved a challenge to the correctional process itself and less so when the challenge is to prior police, prosecutor, or trial court practices.[z] The distaste is expressed not only in erection of some barriers to pursuit of legal remedies, but also by the infrequency with which correctional institutions have sought to assist inmates in obtaining resolution of their legal problems, in contrast with their view that resolution of medical or educational or spiritual problems may be beneficial to the inmate's rehabilitative program. In fairness, however, it must be pointed out that some correctional systems have made efforts to help inmates obtain legal services, while the organized bar has made practically no effort to fill the need of prisoners for legal advice.

LEGAL SERVICES FOR PRISON INMATES[a]

By Thomas O'Brien

Note, 1967 Wisconsin Law Review 514

In describing the range of legal issues raised by inmates, it is helpful to classify them on the basis of whether the inmate is challenging: (1) his conviction; (2) his treatment in the correctional institution; or (3) other things, as the existence of detainers filed by another state.

A. Conviction Claims

Of the inmates interviewed, almost two-thirds were concerned about the propriety of their convictions. Often their questions

---

[z] Smartt v. Avery, 370 F.2d 788 (6th Cir. 1967), held violative of the Civil Rights Act a formally promulgated regulation of the Tennessee Parole Board that any inmate who seeks and is denied a writ of habeas corpus by any state or federal judge would not be considered for parole until twelve months later than his regularly scheduled hearing time. The court said, "Only a prisoner with an inclination to play Russian roulette with a year of his life would be likely to file a petition for writ of habeas corpus under this regulation."

More subtle reprisals, in the form of loss of privileges or assignment to less desirable jobs, may operate as an effective deterrent in some instances. The prisoner who fails in his challenge continues as a prisoner in the same system.

[a] This article reflects the experience of Wisconsin law students who devoted a summer internship in correctional institutions working directly with inmates on a wide variety of legal problems. The internship program was made possible by a grant from the National Council on Legal Clinics (now Council on Legal Education for Professional Responsibility) and by the cooperation of the Wisconsin Division of Corrections, an agency which has encouraged innovative programs for dealing with the legal problems of its inmate population.

would relate to how to start an appeal or habeas corpus proceeding, or how to obtain a lawyer if they were indigent.

> *Illustration No. 1:* An inmate wrote the court asking that an attorney be appointed to represent him on appeal. The court replied that they had learned he had an insurance claim of about $1000 pending and requested that he assign it over to his county of residence. This was the man's only asset. He did not know exactly what this meant, why it was necessary, or even how to go about fulfilling the request.

There is no person or agency in the prison to advise an inmate on such questions. Sometimes an inmate will go to his assigned social worker with these and related legal questions, but, as social workers are ordinarily untrained in law, they do not wish to get involved in giving legal advice.

In other cases the prisoners wanted advice on a particular legal point. Occasionally, an inmate thought he had observed an error in his trial and wondered if he could gain a reversal of his conviction on that basis. In most cases the possibility of error was suggested to the inmate either by newspaper accounts of recent cases or by rumors circulating in the prison.

> *Illustration No. 2:* After *Miranda v. Arizona* was handed down, several prisoners, simply having read the newspaper accounts of the decision, hoped it would apply to them.

> *Illustration No. 3:* A common rumor in the prison last summer was that a case had held that it was double jeopardy to be tried for an escape after you had lost good time and had been placed in solitary confinement for it.

> *Illustration No. 4:* An inmate had been convicted of a crime; sentence was withheld and he was placed on probation for two years. Eighteen months later, his probation was revoked and he was sentenced to prison for two years. He had not had counsel at the latter sentencing hearing and had not been informed that he had a right to counsel. In prison he was told by other inmates that he had a right to a lawyer if he was indigent. (The Wisconsin Supreme Court recently held that there is a right to counsel at sentencing when probation is revoked and the sentence had originally been stayed.)

Sometimes, prisoners have read cases but do not fully understand them or their implications, giving no attention to significant fact distinctions or to the lack of precedent value given cases from other jurisdictions.

> *Illustration No. 5:* Several inmates at the state prison who were serving time under the sex crimes act in Wisconsin could not understand why the Michigan case of *In re Maddox* does not apply here. That case held that men under the Michigan Sexual Psychopath Law could not be imprisoned with and treated like men under the criminal code in a state prison. Under that act, however, it was not required that a man be first convicted of a crime as the Wisconsin act requires.

In a few cases, the prisoners were concerned about the propriety of their trial, or had second thoughts about whether they should have pleaded guilty, without having any idea as to whether any legal issue might be involved. They simply wanted someone to evaluate their case and search for errors. This reflects a common situation in a maximum security prison. When a convicted person steps through the prison gates, he first begins to realize fully what has happened to him. As the first few months pass he begins to look for a way out. He knows or finds out that he can appeal, that he can have free legal help if he is indigent, and that he has nothing to lose by trying.

B. Treatment Complaints

Other issues that came up fairly frequently concerned complaints about prison administration. Occasionally, prisoners felt prison officials had acted unfairly in transferring them from one institution to another, or in refusing a transfer.

> *Illustration No. 6:* An inmate was convicted of a crime and sent to the Diagnostic Center in Madison for an examination under the sex crimes act. It was recommended that he be sentenced under that act and be placed in Central State Hospital. The man was sent to Waupan State Prison. He requested to be transferred to Central State, but the request was refused.

Several inmates felt prison officials had acted illegally in taking some possessions, such as books, from their cells. More often, the complaints concerned the prison's computation of their sentence. The inmates felt the length of their sentence had not been correctly determined, or that they had not received the proper amount of "good time." In most cases it was found that the complaints of the prisoners were without substance, or that they were complaints that were not cognizable in court. However, it was found that a number of such complaints had some merit.

> *Illustration No. 7:* An inmate had been convicted and sentenced under the sex crimes act. He was paroled, but later his parole was revoked. At the same time he was convicted of another crime and sentenced under the criminal code; this sentence was to run consecutively to his sentence under the sex crimes act. Sometime later, the inmate was granted parole by the Special Review Board in regards to his sex crimes act violation; however the Regular Parole Board refused to parole him for the other crime. Prison authorities informed him that his criminal code sentence could not start until he reached his discharge date under the sex crimes law, which was about two years away. So, the inmate was, in effect, serving his sex crime law parole in prison, and receiving no credit for his sentence under the criminal code. (After proper administrative appeals by the Public Defender, it was determined that the criminal code sentence should have begun at the time that the inmate was paroled by the Special Review Board.)

> *Illustration No. 8:* Mr. *X* was brought up to Wisconsin to face charges while incarcerated in Illinois. He pleaded guilty and was sentenced to the Wisconsin State Prison for two years. However, the sentence was to run concurrently with his Illinois sentence. If he was released within two years from prison in Illinois, he was to finish the sentence in Wisconsin. Mr. *X* was released five months later from prison in Illinois and came to Wisconsin to finish his sentence. He was told by prison officials that his sentence was illegal and that it did not start until he reached the Wisconsin prison. It would seem that either the sentence was illegal and he should be resentenced, or else it was legal and the prison should not have ignored it. (Through the efforts of the Public Defender and Wisconsin Correctional Service, the inmate was eventually granted a pardon.)

In the illustrations and in like situations, the inmates were at a loss as to how to pursue the administrative or court remedy. The usual judicial remedy, if any, would be habeas corpus, but no legal help was available to inform the inmate how to proceed, or to help the inmate present his complaint intelligently in a habeas corpus petition.

C. Detainers and Miscellaneous Problems

A significant number of prisoners have charges pending against them in jurisdictions outside the state. These men frequently requested advice and legal help in connection with pending detainers placed by these other jurisdictions. Unless the detainers are dropped, the inmate will be delivered to the demanding state at the termination of his imprisonment. The prisoners usually want the detainers dropped or, alternatively, to be brought to trial at once. A detainer may have the immediate effect of precluding the extension of some privileges, such as assignments outside the prison or transfer to a minimum security institution, as well as having an adverse effect on the rehabilitation of the inmate. Because of this, some social workers will write the particular jurisdiction and ask that the detainers be dropped; but otherwise, no help is available to the prisoners. Dealing with detainers is a complex legal problem. Apparently, some inroads are being made on the doctrine that a man does not have a right to be brought to trial in another jurisdiction until his release from incarceration.

Another common request was for help with clemency petitions. The inmate is required to complete the documents himself. Usually, the inmate desired advice on what areas or issues to emphasize in the petition, although a few did not even know where to procure the documents. (They were available at the prison records office).

Other miscellaneous problems also arose occasionally.

Illustration No. 9: An inmate was serving under the Wisconsin sex crimes statute. His sentence had been extended for 5 years under section 959.15(14) of the Wisconsin statutes. The inmate applied several times by letter to the trial court for a reexamination of his mental condition. (He has an absolute right semiannually to such an examination under section 959.15(15)(c) of the statutes). Each time he would receive back a letter from the assistant district attorney, who apparently had been given the letters, denying his request. (It is possible the request had been misconstrued). The inmate then wrote the court appointed attorney who had represented him at the first extension hearing. The attorney replied that he had no right to an examination for five years. The inmate was, quite naturally, at a loss as to what to do.

BAILLEAUX v. HOLMES

177 F. Supp. 361 (D. Ore. 1959)

SOLOMON, Chief Judge. Plaintiffs are prisoners in the Oregon State Penitentiary at Salem, Oregon. Defendants are the Governor, Secretary of State, and the State Treasurer, comprising the State Board of Control, and the Warden and Deputy Warden of the penitentiary.

In their amended and consolidated complaint they allege that the defendants in their official capacities have conspired to prevent plaintiffs from exercising their constitutional right to free and speedy access to the courts. Plaintiffs claim that the following restraints, among others, are unreasonable and unlawful: (1) Prisoners may not study law or prepare legal documents in their cells; they must do this work in a prison law library open only to a limited number of prisoners for limited periods of time; (2) prisoners are severely restricted in their ability to purchase or receive law books or statutes, even though they are not available in the prison library; (3) defendants impose special censorship on legal documents and communications with courts and attorneys; (4) defendants confiscate legal documents found in prisoners' possession outside the library; (5) prisoners in isolation are denied all access to the courts, counsel, and their legal papers; (6) prisoners may not use all of their funds to purchase legal materials or pay legal fees.

LIMITATIONS ON LAW STUDY

Present regulations require that law study and the preparation of legal papers be confined to the law library. The library is open approximately thirty hours a week, during which time a limited number of prisoners, by appointment, are permitted to work on legal matters. No prisoner in the general population is permitted to study law or keep any legal documents or memoranda in his cell. Prior to the commencement of this action only four prisoners could use the facilities of the law library concurrently. Subsequently the number was increased to eleven. In the past prisoners had often been delayed for several days, and occasional delays still occur. Prisoners employed in special jobs are further restricted when library periods coincide with their work schedules. Absence from work to pursue legal matters may result in an unfavorable report which, in turn, reduces a prisoner's "good time".

Most prisoners spend fourteen hours a day in their cells. Prisoners may keep a limited quantity of study materials, as well as books, magazines, courses including correspondence courses, and personal papers.

Plaintiffs need more time than they are presently afforded to prepare their legal matters adequately. With no legal training, many are forced to represent themselves under conditions which an experienced attorney would find intolerable. Prison officials insist that these restrictions are required to curb the activities of the "cell-house lawyers", and to avoid the storage problem resulting from accumulation of legal materials in the cells.

The Court appreciates the fact that prison authorities must maintain effective discipline, and must prevent unscrupulous prisoners from preying on the weak and ignorant. However, this end may not be achieved by stifling the study of law, where such study is necessary to the effective utilization of a basic right. This does not mean that the prison authorities are powerless to prevent the accumulation of massive legal libraries in the cells. Regulations can be designed to avoid the excessive storage of materials in cells without restricting the actual use of these materials in the cells when needed.

Restrictions on Law Books

The prison law library has one or two volumes of Corpus Juris Secundum and a copy of the criminal sections of the Oregon Revised Statutes. Prisoners may not purchase or receive from outside sources any treatises or statutes. They may not even acquire copies of individual cases from any source other than the publisher. These are expensive and not always available.

The prisoners contend that these restrictions prevent them from adequately representing themselves both at trial and on appeal. Prisoners have the right to represent themselves and, an indigent prisoner who is required or elects to represent himself should, so far as possible, have the same opportunities to prepare his case as one represented by an attorney. Without law books, a competent and experienced lawyer would find it difficult to prepare a defense or an appeal. Without such books, a prisoner, without legal training or experience, finds it virtually impossible.

Prison officials contend that to permit prisoners to purchase law books would add to their burden of censoring incoming mail, and create a space problem. If law books are necessary to due process, these considerations are immaterial.

Censorship of Legal Communications

The prisoners contend that their communications to and from attorneys and courts are subject to special inspection and censorship and that such communications, including documents intended to be filed in court, are delayed longer than are reasonably necessary for inspection.

The Court recognizes that the opening and inspection of mail between prisoners and those at liberty is an essential incident to the safe custody of prisoners, particularly in the suppression of traffic in contraband. Letters between prisoners and their attorneys are not exempt from this type of control.

However, the right to inspect should not be used unnecessarily to delay communications to attorneys or the courts since such delay could amount to an effective denial of a prisoner's right to access to the courts. Likewise, the right to inspect and censor does not give prison authorities the right to pass upon the sufficiency of legal pleadings.

Confiscation of Legal Documents

Prison officials confiscate and retain as contraband prisoners' legal documents, including petitions addressed to courts, discovered outside the prison library.

Defendants argue that prisoners have no right to possess personal property. They assert that property possessed in violation of regulations must be confiscated if discipline is to be maintained.

The right to be protected is not a property right; it is the right to be heard in the courts. Prison officials may not enforce rules which suppress papers directed to the courts. That is precisely the effect of the present regulation.

Prison officials may and should regulate the conduct of prisoners and punish the violation of regulations. However, we do not believe that a communication or a pleading addressed to an attorney or court relative to a pending or contemplated legal action is subject to confiscation solely because it was prepared in a cell rather than in the library.

Prisoners in Isolation

Prisoners in isolation may not initiate court action, communicate with counsel, or have access to legal materials.

Isolation is a traditional and effective method of punishment. No evidence was presented to indicate that isolation was imposed discriminately upon prisoners engaged in legal work. In addition, granting prisoners the right to contact courts and attorneys, and to use legal materials will probably impair the efficacy of isolation as punishment. Nevertheless, administrative control, even if reasonable and moderate, must yield to the basic right to have access to the courts.

Restriction of Prisoners' Funds

Prisoners complain that they are not permitted to use all of their funds to buy legal books, transcripts, and materials, or to pay legal fees.

The Warden asserts that Oregon Law requires him to hold part of the prisoner's money, from any source, to provide a small reservoir of cash for the prisoner upon release. The prison regulation which requires the segregation of 25% of a prisoner's funds in a savings account is directly authorized by ORS 421.125(5):

> "The warden shall safeguard the moneys standing to the credit of each individual convict, whether such moneys are from outside sources or from earnings of the convict while in the penitentiary, to the end that in so far as possible the convict will have at least $50 to his credit on discharge, or at least $25 to his credit on parole."

In our view both the statute and the regulation are reasonable and do not infringe plaintiffs' constitutional rights.

HATFIELD v. BAILLEAUX

290 F.2d 632 (9th Cir. 1961)
Cert. denied, 368 U.S. 862 (1961)

Hamley, Circuit Judge. This is a suit by seven inmates of Oregon State Penitentiary to enjoin prison officials from enforcing certain prison regulations and continuing certain customs and usages at the penitentiary.

Judgment was entered granting a substantial part of the relief sought. The judgment was made applicable to all inmates of the penitentiary. Defendants appeal.

There is no finding that appellants have been denied all access to the courts. There is no finding that by reason of any prison regulation or practice pertaining to the preparation, service and filing of such pleadings or documents, or to the sending and receiving of such communications, any appellee has ever lost the right to commence, prosecute, defend or appeal in any court proceeding involving personal liberty. Nor is there any finding that by reason of prison regulations and practices any appellee has been substantially delayed in obtaining a judicial determination in any such court proceeding.

In the absence of findings of this kind it is difficult to see how there could possibly be warrant for the conclusion that appellees have been deprived of reasonable access to the courts.

But passing for the time being this basic weakness in the premise upon which the judgment rests, we turn to an examination of the factual and legal bases for the individual injunctive provisions of the judgment.

One provision relates exclusively to appellees confined to the isolation ward.

The periods of confinement in isolation are of relatively short duration. Confinement in isolation, the court found, is imposed only for violations of the prison rules and regulations. There is no attempt in imposing such confinement to discriminate against persons engaged in legal work. Nor is such confinement arbitrarily imposed in any other respect. There is no finding that any appellee has ever been confined in isolation under conditions which, as to safety or health, warranted immediate court relief therefrom.

In view of these facts and circumstances, we do not believe that the court was warranted in concluding that because of the restrictions imposed during isolation, as described above, appellees have been deprived of reasonable access to the courts.

The remaining injunctive provisions of the judgment relate to appellees who are a part of the general prison population or are confined in the segregation ward.

Appellees who are a part of the general prison population are not allowed to engage in the study of law or to prepare legal documents during such times as they are confined in their cells. Nor are they allowed to keep documents, materials and papers of a legal nature in their cells. All papers, documents and materials of a legal nature found outside the prison library are confiscated by prison officials as contraband.

When this suit was commenced only four inmates could use the law library facilities at any given time. Occasional delays of more than three or four days and up to seventeen days occurred between the time an appointment was sought and the time use of the facilities was actually obtained. By the time of the trial the capacity of the prison library had been increased to eleven persons, and no delays in excess of one day in obtaining use of those facilities were being experienced.

At the time this action was brought the prison law library consisted solely of two volumes of Corpus Juris Secundum, portions of the Oregon Revised Statutes, and some advance sheets from the Oregon Supreme Court. By the time of the trial, however, there had been a substantial increase in the prison library, as indicated by the inventory set out in the margin.

Under prison regulations inmates are not permitted to purchase, acquire or receive bound law books of any kind at any time. They are not permitted to obtain, acquire or receive any legal materials from any source other than law publishers. The only such materials which may be obtained are copies of individual cases or excerpts from statutes, the cost of which may be prohibitive to inmates.

Appellees confined in the segregation ward do not have access to the law library. They are, however, permitted to engage in legal research or the preparation of legal documents in their cells from approximately 8:30 a.m. to approximately 3:30 p.m. seven days a week. Only during these periods are they permitted to have legal documents, materials or papers in their cells.

The court found that the regulations and practices described above were applied not only to appellees but to all prison inmates similarly situated.

While the court did not enter findings as to the purpose of these regulations and practices, the evidence is undisputed as to those purposes. Most of these regulations and practices are for the purpose of discouraging the informal practice of law by what were termed "cell-house lawyers." Prison officials testified that if permitted to engage in such practice, aggressive inmates of superior intelligence exploit and dominate weaker prisoners of inferior intelligence. The practice also tends to develop a group of inmate leaders, which is discouraged in all institutions.

With regard to inmates in segregation the regulations have a similar purpose but are designed to take into account the fact that such inmates do not have access to the library. Hence they are permitted to have legal materials in their cells and work on legal matters therein for stated hours each day. The setting of specific hours when this may be done is to enable the same guards to distribute and pick up each prisoner's legal materials, thereby avoiding confusion.

The reason prisoners are not permitted to purchase bound law books and keep them in the library is the inadequacy of the library facilities and personnel to take care of such acquisitions. The reason for the regulation limiting the acquisition of legal materials from any source other than the publisher or the public officer having custody thereof is quite different. All incoming mail and packages must be examined to exclude reception of contraband. It is the view of prison officials that where the enclosures come from a source such as a publishing house or public office, the need for such scrutiny and the likelihood of contraband being delivered to inmates is minimized.

In this federal proceeding under the Civil Rights Act we are not concerned with the question of whether these purposes for the challenged regulations are salutary or whether the regulations provide an effective means of achieving such purposes. If the purpose was not to hamper inmates in gaining reasonable access to the courts with regard to their respective criminal matters, and if the regulations and practices do not interfere with such reasonable access, our inquiry is at an end. The fact, if it be a fact, that access could have been further facilitated without impairing effective prison administration is likewise immaterial.

This accords with the general principle that, apart from due process considerations, the federal courts have no power to control or supervise state prison regulations and practices. State authorities have no obligation under the federal Constitution to provide library facilities and an opportunity for their use to enable an inmate to search for legal loopholes in the judgment and sentence under which he is held, or to perform services which only a lawyer is trained to perform. All inmates are presumed to be confined under valid judgments and sentences. If an inmate believes he has a meritorious reason for attacking his, he must be given an opportunity to do so. But he has no due process right to spend his prison time or utilize prison facilities in an effort to discover a ground for overturning a presumptively valid judgment.

Inmates have the constitutional right to waive counsel and act as their own lawyers, but this does not mean that a non-lawyer must be given the opportunity to acquire a legal education. One question which an inmate must decide in determining if he should represent himself is whether in view of his own competency and general prison regulations he can do so adequately. He must make the decision in the light of the circumstances existing. The state has no duty to alter the circumstances to conform with his decision.

Underlying the conclusions stated above is the fact, not to be overlooked, that inmates of a penitentiary are undergoing punishment for crimes of which they have been convicted.

The judgment is reversed and the cause is remanded with directions to dismiss the proceedings.

JOHNSON v. AVERY

382 F.2d 353 (6th Cir. 1967)
Cert. granted, 390 U.S. 943 (1968)

WEICK, Chief Judge. The crux of this case is the question of validity of a regulation of the Tennessee State Penitentiary at Nashville, which prohibits any inmate from advising or assisting other prisoners in the preparation or filing of writs of habeas corpus or other legal papers.

After being subjected to punishment for repeated violations of the rule, usually by confinement in the "maximum security building" of the prison, petitioner filed a "motion for law books and a typewriter," which the District Court treated as an application for a writ of habeas corpus, and granted. The prison authorities appealed.

The District Court reasoned that because the words of the habeas corpus statute, 28 U.S.C. § 2242, authorized the filing of an application for a writ of habeas corpus "signed and verified by the person for whose relief it is intended *or by someone acting in his behalf*" (emphasis added), the prison regulation conflicted with the Federal law. The District Court further held that unless petitioner could continue to serve as a "writ writer" or "jailhouse lawyer" for his fellow inmates, their constitutional rights to the effective aid of habeas corpus would be endangered since "without the assistance of some third party, many prisoners in the state penitentiary would be totally incapable of preparing an intelligible petition, letter or request." We must disagree with both of these conclusions.

The perspective through which we view this question, even though it seems one of first impression, must be framed by the well-established reluctance of the Federal Courts to intervene in internal affairs of state or Federal penal institutions. Regulations for the administration and discipline of prisons, promulgated and enforced by duly authorized officials, are not subject to review by the courts unless it can be clearly demonstrated that they interfere with fundamental rights guaranteed by the Constitution.

This proposition is soundly based on the fact that prison administration is a function of the executive branch of the Government and one for which the courts, with their limited experience and facilities, are ill-suited to undertake. Further, in this case the imperatives of our Federal system require special concern for the boundaries of state and Federal governmental competence as allocated by our basic charter.

An important additional consideration here is the undisputed right of individual states to specify the qualifications for entrance to their respective bars and to regulate the practice of law within their borders.

In essence, then, the ruling of the District Court allows petitioner to engage in activity in the state prison which would constitute a crime if conducted outside the penitentiary.

While we agree that representation by counsel may be a significant part of the post-conviction remedy, it is important to recognize that the Supreme Court has not yet held that it is an indispensable element of due process under the Constitution.[b] In any event, the Federal Courts have power to appoint counsel for indigents in proceedings before them to assure the protection of the indigents' rights. Indeed, we believe that no favor is granted to the other prisoners by allowing them representation by one untrained in the complexities of post-conviction procedure and unrestrained by the values, ethics, and traditions of the bar.

The provision of the law authorizing someone to act on behalf of a prisoner whose release is sought, relates only to the act of signing or verifying the petition, and we do not interpret that authorization to include the preparing of legal papers and serving as an attorney in violation of state law. It seems clear that the situation to which this provision was meant to apply, is one where physical or mental handicaps prevent the prisoner from personally signing or verifying the petition, not one wherein lack of intelligence or legal training keep him from drafting his own papers.

The problem of providing effective access to legal assistance at all stages of criminal justice, from pre-trial to post-conviction, certainly deserves the concern which the District Court showed in this case. However, its solution is more likely to be assured if it is attended to by the bench, bar, and law schools rather than left to the *ad hoc* procedures sanctioned in the District Court.

Reversed.

---

[b] The sixth amendment, applicable to the states through the fourteenth amendment, gives indigent prisoners right to counsel to assist in their first appeals. Douglas v. California, 372 U.S. 353 (1963). However, this right does not extend as an absolute matter to other types of preparations, including assistance in drafting habeas corpus petitions. *See* Price v. Johnson, 334 U.S. 266 (1948); Barker v. Ohio, 330 F.2d 594 (6th Cir. 1964). For a situation where due process was held to require assistance because of the complexity of the case and its "meritorious" claim, see Brown v. Cameron, 353 F.2d 835 (D.C. Cir. 1965). *See generally* Note, *Prisoner Assistance on Federal Habeas Corpus,* 19 STAN. L. REV. 887 (1962). Here indigent prisoners must themselves prepare initial documents of proper form and sufficient clarity to convince higher courts of the possible meritoriousness of their claims, thereby winning appointed counsel. "Jailhouse lawyers" often help, for pay, in violation of prison regulations.

LEGAL SERVICES FOR PRISON INMATES

By Thomas O'Brien

Note, 1967 Wisconsin Law Review 514

[Another portion appears at 862, *supra.*]

METHODS OF PROFESSIONAL HELP

It should be apparent that methods of self-help are inadequate to effectively discover and raise legitimate claims. Furthermore, these methods are wholly ineffective in achieving the objective of discouraging groundless claims. In this section some methods of providing professional legal counsel will be evaluated.

1. ASSIGNED COUNSEL

In some jurisdictions the appellate court will, upon application, appoint attorneys to aid indigent prisoners in presenting their claims. In Wisconsin this system is presently used only if the appellate public defender's workload is full, or if the prisoner insists upon assigned counsel. Indigent prisoners are provided legal help for all appeals, and in habeas corpus proceedings if the court first determines that a petition shows arguable merit.

Certainly the system of assigned counsel has provided indigent prisoners with extremely well-qualified legal counsel in many instances. Without such help many indigent prisoners would never have been able to get their claims effectively presented to a court. However, from an institutional standpoint the system is subject to criticism in its practical operation.

Under existing practice the attorney who is assigned to represent an indigent prisoner on appeal is usually from the county where the prisoner was convicted. This may be quite some distance from the prison. It is not uncommon for prisoners to never see and rarely hear from the assigned attorney who represents them. Almost all prisoners would like to discuss their case with their attorney and be informed as to the consequences of an appeal and the possibilities of success. In addition, some assigned counsel seem to take an inordinate amount of time to prepare the case and take it to court. Prisoners cannot understand why it sometimes takes well over a year before the court hears their appeal. When a man is locked up in prison, "time" is of utmost importance. At the least, his attorney could inform the inmate about when his appeal will be heard, why this length of time is necessary, and what progress is being made. If we go to the expense of affording an attorney for indigent prisoners, we should at least fulfill minimal requirements in satisfying their sense of justice and thus aid in their rehabilitation.

Other criticisms have also been leveled at the assigned counsel system. It has been suggested that some appointed attorneys have had little or no experience in criminal law matters. In addition, it might be suggested that some attorneys do not feel an obligation to put forth their best efforts for a client who is not paying them and who they probably will never see. It is probably quite easy for the attorney to put the prisoner's case at the bottom of his workload; the attorney's other clients are nearby and probably better paying. The quality of work done may well suffer from these factors.

In theory the system of assigned counsel should provide an effective screening device in the case of appeals. The appointed attorney can and should turn down those cases that have no merit at all. However, it has been suggested that in practice some cases with very little or no merit are appealed by appointed attorneys. Attorneys often are not sure whether the case has "arguable merit" or not. Rather than decide the case themselves, using that vague standard, they take the appeal.

Even if an attorney does turn down a case because it lacks merit, an indigent prisoner in Wisconsin can have another attorney appointed to represent him, or he might even argue the case himself. Out of 176 attorneys appointed for indigent prisoners in a period extending from 1964 to March 1967, eighty attorneys decided the prisoner's case had no arguable merit. However, in forty-two of these cases, the prisoner asked for and was provided with another attorney to represent him and review the case. These figures suggest that the prisoners do not always respect the opinions of the attorneys. Part of the reason for this lack of respect may be that the attorney has not visited the prisoner, has taken several months to decide that the case has no merit, and has never explained to the prisoner why the case lacks merit. The prisoner, then, may have some basis for his feeling that he did not have competent legal help, and that further action might still be successful.

The assigned counsel system has certainly been beneficial in many instances in helping inmates present their legitimate claims to the courts. However, the system, as operated in Wisconsin, is not available to provide counselling to inmates before starting legal action, or to help them prepare habeas corpus petitions. Consequently, the system is not able to discover and present legitimate issues or to screen out frivolous claims at this level. In addition, the efficiency of the system in screening out frivolous claims at the level where it now operates is doubtful.

2. The Public Defender

In Wisconsin the appellate public defender is responsible for prosecuting appeals and writs of habeas corpus on behalf of indigent prisoners. In practice, the supreme court appoints the public defender to prosecute all appeals. He can, however, turn down a case if he feels it has no arguable merit. The public defender is also appointed to prosecute writs of habeas corpus, but only after the supreme court has first determined that the petition has arguable merit. The public defender will respond to letters from inmates, but he will only help with a habeas corpus *petition* in the unusual case.

This system has several distinct advantages over others. The public defender works exclusively in the criminal law field and, thus, is extremely competent in that area. His clients are all indigent prisoners, so that there is no conflict with other work. He makes regular trips to the prison and visits each prisoner that he represents. He listens to their story and explains his function and how they will proceed. Through this process of personal contact and continuous representation the public defender is better able to gain the respect of the prisoners. As of March 1967, the public defender has been in office about ten months. He has been assigned approximately eighty cases by the supreme court. Of these, he has decided, so far, that some thirty cases have no arguable merit and has turned them down. In almost all such cases the public defender personally explained to the inmate why he thought there was no basis for an appeal. In six of these cases the inmates have asked the court for, and were appointed another attorney to review the case. The public defender, then, is able to function effectively as a screening device in many cases. In addition, this process may aid in the rehabilitation of the prisoners; they should feel they have been treated fairly by society.

The public defender is faced, though, with the suspicion that he is working for the state rather than for the prisoner. He is paid by the state and is assumed to owe first allegiance to it. It is disconcerting to find that there are some prisoners needing help who will have nothing to do with him. This attitude should be overcome in time by effective representation.

In Wisconsin the public defender is limited by the fact that his is a one-man office. As already indicated, he already has a heavy caseload, consisting primarily of appeals. At the present time the public defender receives numerous letters from inmates detailing their claims and asking for legal help. In most cases, however, the public defender does not have time to see the men, or to give careful attention to their problems. He does answer all letters, though, and informs the inmate, at least, on the correct procedure for making his claim. The result is that the public defender is not able to effectively counsel prisoners regarding some of their legal problems, nor is he able to help prisoners preparing habeas corpus petitions even to present legitimate issues, as his services are usually not available on habeas corpus unless and until the supreme court determines the petition drawn up by the prisoner shows arguable merit. The public defender is, then, not only unable to discover and present some of the legitimate issues that arise, but also he is unable to function as a screening device for many of the claims of prisoners.

It would be desirable for the public defender to have one or two assistant attorneys working with him. An investigator would also be helpful. Then, he could more fully function to fulfill the objectives we have set.

3. Resident Legal Counsel

An additional system of providing legal services to prisoners might be to place an attorney in an office at the prison. The attorney could be employed by the state or supported by a public service organization. His job would be to help and advise prisoners on their legal problems, especially those for which no legal help is presently available. In addition, such an attorney could coordinate his functions with those of assigned counsel or the public defender.

This method of providing legal help has all the advantages of the public defender system. The resident attorney would work exclusively in the criminal law field, he would have regular personal contact with the prisoners, and would devote his entire efforts to advising and representing the prisoners. In addition he would have better access to the inmates. For many prisoners it is far easier to simply request to see the attorney than to write a letter to the courts or to the public defender. The attorney would be familiar with the operation of the prison and better able to understand treatment complaints. It is more likely, then, that the resident attorney would discover the legitimate issues of the inmate's case than would the public defender. He would be in an excellent position to help inmates with habeas corpus petitions or administrative remedies.

All of the above factors should put the resident attorney in a position where he is highly respected by the prisoners. This is considered important in any system of providing legal help for two reasons. First, all prisoners will not go to the attorney with their problems unless they respect him and feel he can and will help them. If we have an attorney available, we want the prisoners to make full use of him so that he can effectively present the legitimate claims and have the opportunity to screen out the groundless ones. Second, unless the prisoners respect the opinions of the attorney, they are not likely to believe him when he tells them that their claims have no merit.

Although the attorney's primary function would be to render legal services, a resident legal counselor would be in a unique position to aid in the rehabilitation of prisoners. In some cases he might be helpful in convincing prisoners that no legal remedy is available and that they should seek out and accept the help of social workers and other professional people in the prison. Some prisoners will accept such advice from an attorney, while they would reject it if it came directly from a social worker. And simply satisfying the prisoner's sense of justice may put the prisoner in a frame of mind where he is more likely to accept his present position and attempt to improve his future chances of success in society.

There are some hazards to be considered in placing an attorney in the prison. It is possible that the inmates might come to identify the attorney with the institution staff. The attorney would necessarily work with, eat with, and spend leisure time with other professional staff members. There is no question but that many inmates feel all prison staff members are against them. Such a situation could affect the respect that the attorney commands from the inmates. The attorney would have to be sure to assert his independence. It is also possible that the institution staff might become hostile to the attorney, especially if he questions some institution practices. They could make life difficult for the attorney, and could probably discourage some prisoners from consulting him with their problems. Finally, the resident attorney could easily become discouraged with his work. He would be working primarily with people from the lower strata of society, who have little respect for law and order. Frivolous claims will be presented daily to him. Some prisoners will, no doubt, become disenchanted with him and will not hesitate to tell him so. Under these circumstances it will be extremely easy for the attorney to identify with the institution staff or become completely disenchanted with his work. One way to minimize the likelihood of these occurrences would be to place young attorneys, trained in criminal law, in the prison for periods of a year or two. Some type of program could be worked out to encourage attorneys to participate. The experience gained through the program would certainly be worthwhile and memorable to the participants.

Although there are some potential hazards to placing an attorney in a prison, the numerous advantages of such a system in satisfying our objectives would seem to warrant some experimentation.

Reference Note

Some of the major works on the world of the prison inmate are D. CRESSEY, THE PRISON (1961); D. CLEMMER, THE PRISON COMMUNITY (1958); G. SYKES, THE SOCIETY OF CAPTIVES (1958).

A comprehensive analysis of the effectiveness of the federal prison system is reported in D. GLASER, THE EFFECTIVENESS OF A PRISON AND PAROLE SYSTEM (1964).

For a general discussion of corrections and prisons and for additional bibliography, see P. TAPPAN, CRIME, JUSTICE AND CORRECTION (1960); P. TAPPAN, CONTEMPORARY CORRECTION (1951); H. BARNES & N. TEETERS, NEW HORIZONS IN CRIMINOLOGY (4th ed. 1961); L. OHLIN, SOCIOLOGY AND THE FIELD OF CORRECTIONS (1962); J. BENNETT, OF PRISONS AND JUSTICE (1964).

For a thorough analysis of prisoner's rights problems, see THE PRESIDENT'S COMMISSION ON LAW ENFORCEMENT AND ADMINISTRATION OF JUSTICE, TASK FORCE REPORT: CORRECTIONS ch. 8 (1967) (based on Cohen, "Legal Norms in Corrections," a paper prepared for the President's Commission). The "hands-off" doctrine adopted by the courts toward the rights of prisoners is described along with a proposal for guidelines of judicial review in Note, *Beyond the Ken of the Courts: A Critique of Judicial Refusal to Review the Complaints of Convicts,* 72 YALE L.J. 506 (1962-63). On prisoner's rights see also Note, *Constitutional Rights of Prisoners: The Developing Law,* 110 U. PA. L. REV. 985 (1961-62); Comment, *Black Muslims in Prisons: Of Muslim Rites and Constitutional Rights,* 62 COLUM. L. REV. 1488 (1962).

For the bases of challenge to treatment standards and practices in selected correctional programs, see Note, *Civil Restraint, Mental Illness, and the Right to Treatment,* 77 YALE L.J. 87 (1967). *See also* Penegar, *The Emerging "Right to Treatment"—Elaborating the Processes of Decision in Sanctioning Systems of the Criminal Law,* 44 DENVER L.J. 163 (1967).

On the trend in prisoner petitions and court intervention see Kimball & Newman, *Judicial Intervention in Correctional Decisions: Threat and Response,* 14 CRIME & DELINQUENCY 1 (1968).

Chapter 14

CONDITIONAL RELEASE AND REVOCATION

Probation and parole were originally designed, like executive clemency, to ameliorate the harshness and rigidity of the early criminal law. But today judges and parole boards are expected to exercise their discretion to determine the proper sentence based upon the characteristics of the individual offender—the legal maximum is not considered the norm. Parole and probation should not be considered any more a matter of grace than any sentence which is less than the maximum provided for by statute.

The President's Commission on Law Enforcement and Administration of Justice, Task Force Report: Corrections 86 (1967)

Few prisoners serve out the maximum of their sentences in prison. Release prior to the expiration of sentence with the remaining time served in the community under supervision is common practice today. Prisoners are released prior to full term in three ways: by pardon, an executive function important in concept but infrequently used; by parole, a discretionary determination of an administrative board; and by "good time" statutes which allow proportional reduction in sentence for each month during which the inmate exhibits good behavior while in prison. By this latter device, an inmate may achieve a "mandatory release" (or "parole of right") by operation of law short of his full sentence. Mandatory release, like parole, requires community supervision upon release. Supervision serves the rehabilitative objective by helping make the adjustment to living in the community easier and by providing motivation to conform to the norms of society. Supervision also serves the objective of community protection through the power to return the released prisoner to the institution if it appears that he is not sufficiently rehabilitated to trust at large. Both parole and mandatory release are also advantageous for internal prison control. The possibility of parole and the accumulation of good time credits give hope to inmates and lessen the incentive to break out. Furthermore, community supervision is much less expensive than continued imprisonment. With minor variations from year to year, the nation's prison population remains relatively constant in spite of both general population increase and an increment in crime rates. In part this is because of developing alternatives to imprisonment in the first place (probation services and other resources like mental health programs) but largely it is a function of parole. About the same number of persons are released from prisons every year as are received from the courts.

A. THE DECISION WHETHER TO RELEASE ON PAROLE

The parole decision is ordinarily the function of a specially designated parole board.[a] While the parole board has a close relationship with the institution, it is external to prison affairs.

The decision of the parole board is more complex than deciding whether to release or to maintain an inmate in prison. The real function of the board is to determine *when* to release a prisoner. Virtually all inmates come out of prison sometime. The decision not to grant parole at all is merely a decision to postpone release to the mandatory release date for all but the handful of men who actually spend a lifetime behind bars. Furthermore, the best risks among offenders have frequently been released on probation, so that the decision to parole is a choice among bad risks.[b]

1. *Factors Considered in Deciding Whether to Parole*

THE DECISION TO GRANT OR DENY PAROLE: A STUDY OF PAROLE CRITERIA IN LAW AND PRACTICE

By Robert O. Dawson

1966 Washington University Law Quarterly 243, 265-85

THE DECISION TO GRANT PAROLE FOR REASONS OTHER THAN THE PROBABILITY OF RECIDIVISM

In practice, inmates are paroled who would not be released if the probability of recidivism were the sole criterion for the

---

[a] Parole board members are appointed to terms of office in various ways, and there is a good deal of controversy about methods of appointment as well as criteria for board membership. *See* THE PRESIDENT'S COMMISSION ON LAW ENFORCEMENT AND ADMINISTRATION OF JUSTICE, TASK FORCE REPORT: CORRECTIONS ch. 6 (1967).

[b] The correctional file of John Arthur Wilson, reproduced in Appendix B, contains the actions taken by the parole board at the various hearings afforded Wilson during his periods of incarceration. Wilson was considered for parole each time he became eligible, was deferred in numerous instances, and was granted parole three times.

decision. Often, inmates are paroled despite the board's judgment that they are likely to commit new criminal offenses. That a parole board sometimes feels compelled to parole inmates who are not rehabilitated may in part reflect deficiencies in institutional treatment programs. It is clear, however, that even great advances in that area would not entirely eliminate the necessity for making decisions of this kind.

1. *Seriousness of the Anticipated Violation*

> *Illustration No. 10:* The inmate, a fifty-year-old man, had served two years on concurrent sentences of one to five and one to seven years for forgery. No parole plan had been developed. He was a seventh felony offender. His record for forgery extended back to 1933. He had served two previous prison terms. The institution made the following parole recommendation: "Seventh offender. Chronic offender. Social adjustment in institution was good. Psychiatrist seemed to think superficial progress was being made, however, never accepted alcoholism as a problem. Deny." A parole board member began discussing with the inmate the necessity for accepting alcoholism as a problem and told him he knew he would be back as a parole violator if he did not stop drinking. He suggested the inmate join Alcoholics Anonymous after release. The board voted to grant parole.

Parole board interest in predicting behavior on parole does not end when the probability of the inmate's violating the law becomes apparent. The board is also deeply concerned with the type of violation likely to occur if the inmate does in fact violate. The board is willing to parole on less evidence of probable success when it is apparent that a violation, if it occurs, is not likely to be serious. In the illustration case, one of the parole board members said he was voting for parole because the inmate was the type of individual who just wrote small checks when drunk and who did not constitute a serious threat to the community. Another board member said he was voting to grant parole and added that "all were granting with tongue in cheek."

The potential benefit from further institutional treatment is also a factor in these decisions. Thus, although one inmate was clearly alcoholic and had a long record of arrests for public intoxication, he was paroled at his initial hearing. The parole board concluded he was a harmless person. It could see little point in keeping him in the institution any longer because he had shown little indication of having enough strength to quit using alcohol. The board concluded, therefore, not only had the institution been unable to do much for the inmate, but it was extremely unlikely he would ever be able to make significant gains in solving his problem.

Finally, the board is concerned in these cases about the effect of parole on the inmate's family. If the inmate is retained in the institution there is little opportunity for him to make significant contributions to the support of his dependents. If he is paroled, however, he at least has the opportunity to support his family. In Wisconsin, nonsupport offenders normally are paroled as soon as they are eligible. The parole board states there are three reasons for this policy: they are unlikely to commit a serious violation of the criminal law, the institutional program is of little aid in their rehabilitation beyond the first several months, and parole may provide financial support for the family for a time as well as the benefits which may accrue from having a father in the family again.

2. *Mandatory Release Date Near*

> *Illustration No. 11:* The inmate was a nineteen-year-old girl serving a sentence of six months to one year for larceny. Her prior record consisted of one conviction for drunkenness, for which she successfully completed a one-year probation period. At the time of the hearing she had served eight months on the sentence. Her conditional release date would be reached in another three months. If parole were denied, she would be released then and, after one month under supervision, would receive an absolute discharge. The board decided to parole her.

Parole boards sometimes find themselves in the position of choosing between a need to retain the inmate in prison and a need for supervision and control over him after he is released. This occurs when at the time of the parole hearing the inmate has only a short period to serve until he must be released from the institution. These are all cases in which the maximum sentence, whether set by statute or by the trial judge, is, in the view of the parole board, too short under the circumstances. The parole board frequently paroles an inmate despite its estimate of a high probability of recidivism, if, in its view, parole supervision is needed more than continued institutionalization.

. . .

In the illustration case, the period of supervision would have been one month had the inmate been kept until her mandatory release date. Nevertheless, the parole board felt that further incarceration would be useful in her case. Thus, it was forced to choose between what it regarded as an inadequate period of institutionalization and an inadequate period of post-incarceration supervision. It chose to lengthen the period of supervision at the expense of the institutionalization.[c]

. . .

3. *Length of Time Served*

Illustration No. 12: The inmate had received a sentence of three to twenty years for armed robbery, auto theft, and forgery. He was paroled after three years but shortly thereafter violated his parole and received a new sentence for operating a con game. He served three years since his last parole. His criminal career began twenty years previously and involved numerous convictions. The psychiatric report was that the inmate was "instinctively vicious. Any rehabilitative program will be futile." The institutional recommendation was that the inmate "has adjusted in excellent manner in institution. Has served lengthy sentence. Should be tried. Grant." The parole board decided to grant parole.

Every decision to grant parole reflects the opinion of the parole board that the inmate has served enough time, but there are some cases in which the length of time served is itself the most significant factor in the case. This typically occurs when an inmate has received a relatively long sentence, but fails to respond to the rehabilitative programs at the institution. In addition, he may have been tried on parole once or twice and had his parole revoked. The parole board may then be faced with the choice of denying parole when it is evident that further institutionalization will not increase the probability of success

[c] It is an ironic by-product of most systems that good risk inmates, who are released early, have long periods of parole supervision (that is, to the maximum length of sentence) whereas bad risk inmates and troublemakers in prison are held in custody until the expiration of the maximum term or the mandatory release date, and have at most a short period of community supervision. A proposal in the MODEL PENAL CODE (§ 6.09A of Tentative Draft No. 5 and § 6.10 of the Proposed Official Draft) calls for separate establishment of the duration of parole supervision. Adoption of this proposal would constitute a major modification of the parole process and of the meaning of the maximum sentence imposed by the judge.

on parole or of granting parole to an inmate who presents some risk of violation.

. . .

A factor mentioned in many cases of this type is maturation. When a relatively young man receives a long sentence and serves a fairly long term before parole, the board may comment that despite the absence of any apparent effect of the institution's program, he may have matured enough to enable him to live a lawful life in the community.

4. *Parole to a Detainer*

> *Illustration No. 13:* A twenty-seven-year-old man serving a one to five-year sentence for larceny appeared before the parole board for a hearing. He had a long criminal and juvenile record. While on parole in Ohio, he came to Wisconsin and committed the offense for which he was serving time. An institutional psychologist said the inmate had admitted using narcotics and drugs; he stated that the prognosis was poor. The institutional committee recommended parole to a detainer, partly because only about seven months remained until conditional release would be required; he had served approximately three years of a one to five-year sentence, and it was thought he might as well start on his Ohio sentence. The final decision of the board was to grant parole to the Ohio detainer. The chairman commented that he did not think Ohio would come after the inmate, in which event he would be detained at the prison until his conditional release date. None of the board members felt the inmate could possibly adjust on parole. The board rationale in this case was dictated by the chairman: "Claims he owes Ohio five years. He has been locked up for the past sixteen years except for twenty-nine months. Gullible, ambitionless, and no insight. Has used heroin. Practically hopeless."

. . .

In acting on a detainer filed by another state to bring an inmate to trial in that state, the parole board decides whether the inmate should be paroled to the community. When an inmate is released on such a detainer it is with the intent that if he is found not guilty, or if the charges are dropped, he will be placed on parole supervision in the other state. Commenting on this type of parole to a detainer, one parole board member stated, "We must handle such cases with the expectation that the inmate may be released entirely from custody, and cannot afford to take the long risk if the person is deemed not a proper subject for return to society." The board apparently works on the assumption in this type of case that the inmate will be set free in the other state, although he may be convicted and sentenced to prison. Therefore, the board apparently requires that the inmate be parolable under the usual criteria.

If the detainer issued by another state is for the return of the inmate as a probation or parole violator or an escaped prisoner, the board has more indication of what treatment is to be accorded the prisoner by the requesting jurisdiction. Because the risk of the inmate's being freed is considerably less than when the detainer is based on untried charges, the parole board is likely to be considerably more liberal in its attitude toward parole. . . . A greater degree of liberality is evident in considering paroles to detainers for deportation to countries overseas.

5. *Reward for Informant Services*

> *Illustration No. 14:* The inmate had been convicted of assault with intent to rob, for which he was placed on probation. After one year on probation, he violated and received a prison sentence of one to ten years. This was his initial parole hearing. The sentencing judge and the prosecuting attorney both recommended a parole denial. He had a prior record of assault. His I.Q. was recorded as sixty-three. Shortly before his hearing, the inmate had learned of an escape plot involving four inmates who were hiding in a tunnel. He tipped off a guard and the inmates were apprehended. The board decided to grant parole.

. . .

Occasionally, the parole decision may be used as a reward for informant services, especially for information about the activities of inmates in the correctional institution. In the illustration case, the inmate would not have been paroled on the basis of his rehabilitation. His informant services were not discussed during the parole hearing, but the board was told of them before the hearing and discussed them after the inmate left the hearing room.

In many states, statutes authorize the granting of special good time to inmates who perform extra work or other meritorious duties, including giving information to prison officials. It is not certain how often these provisions are used to reward inmate informant services and, if they are used, whether they are effective in eliminating the need to use the parole decision for the same purpose.

. . .

In some situations there may be a need, which parole can meet, for the removal of the informing inmate from the institution for his own safety. It is not clear whether this is an important consideration in the decision to grant parole to the informant and, if so, whether a transfer of the informant to another institution would be a satisfactory alternative.

The Decision to Deny Parole for Reasons Other Than the Probability of Recidivism

Parole is often denied to inmates for reasons other than perceived probability of recidivism. Often this decision is made despite the board's own estimate that the inmate would very likely complete his parole period successfully if he were released. . . .

It has been contended that parole boards tend to be too "conservative" in their release practices. In part this contention goes to the point that parole boards may require too high a probability of parole success before granting parole, but it also may go to policy considerations upon which parole denials are based in cases in which the board's own requirements of probable parole success have clearly been met. This may be the situation, for example, with regard to denials because the inmate has assaultive tendencies or because a parole grant would subject the correctional system to severe public criticism.

1. *Cases Involving Assaultive Behavior*

> *Illustration No. 15:* The inmate, thirty-one years of age, was convicted of carrying a concealed weapon and sentenced to one to five years. When he was arrested on the present offense, he was believed to be trying to draw a gun on the arresting officer. His prior record consisted of convictions for "shooting another" and for felonious assault. He had been denied parole at a previous hearing because of several misconduct reports from the institution, one of which consisted of possession of a knife. Since his last hearing, however, he had received no misconduct reports. When the questioning of one of the board members revealed he

was thinking of a parole grant, the other member interrupted him with: "I want a discussion on this." The first member replied that the record showed the inmate had greatly improved his attitude since the last hearing. Nevertheless, the inmate was told his case would have to be discussed with other members of the parole board and he would hear their decision in about a month.

Parole boards tend to be more conservative in their release practices when the inmate has demonstrated he is capable of assaultive behavior. Sometimes this consideration is regarded as sufficiently important to justify a denial of parole to an inmate who would otherwise be regarded as having a sufficiently high probability of parole success to justify release. The rationale is, of course, that the parole board has an obligation to protect the public from possible assaultive behavior which overrides its obligation to release inmates at the optimum point in their rehabilitative progress.

. . .

Normally, the board determines whether the inmate is capable of assaultive behavior on the basis of his prior record and the offense for which he is serving time. The board may also have the benefit of a psychiatric evaluation. In such cases, the latter is given great weight. An evaluation which concludes that the inmate is still capable of assaultive behavior or is still too dangerous for release will almost automatically result in a denial of parole.

2. *Supporting Institutional Discipline*

Illustration No. 16: The inmate, twenty-six years of age, was convicted of larceny in a building and received a sentence of one and one-half to four years. This was his first parole hearing. A parole board member questioned the inmate about his institutional record, which showed he had three institutional reports, two for being "lazy" and refusing to work and one for having dice in his possession. He had several misdemeanor arrests and at one time had been arrested on a narcotics investigation charge. An immediate parole was not granted but the case was continued for office review in six months. It was explained to the inmate that his institutional record had been poor and that if he corrected this and tried to obtain some help from his counselor, he would be given consideration again in six months.

Maintaining discipline among inmates is a major concern of all prison administrators. Although there are wide variations among penal institutions as to the degree to which the details of daily living are regulated by the administration, even in relatively permissive institutions there are disciplinary rules and sanctions for their infraction. Infractions of prison discipline are often interpreted by the parole board as signs of what the offender is likely to do when he is released on parole. They suggest an inability of the offender to adjust to his position and to respect authority. Quite a different consideration is primary, however, when the board denies parole because of the effect its decision may have on prison discipline. The major interest shifts from a concern with the future adjustment of the offender to a concern with order and control in the penal institution. Parole becomes an incentive for good behavior and a sanction against undisciplined conduct by inmates.

It is frequently not easy to distinguish between actions of the board which are designed to have an impact on the discipline of the institution and those which relate to the offender's future adjustment. . . . In most states, good time laws permit reduction of the maximum or minimum sentences, or both, as a reward for infraction-free conduct, and permit revocation of reductions already given for disciplinary violations. In some states, parole eligibility may be specifically contingent on the existence of no recent disciplinary infractions.

. . .

In some institutions, it seems clear that good time laws have degenerated into automatic reductions of sentence, possibly as a result of the heavy release pressures of prison overpopulation, and thus have little, if any, effect on the conduct of inmates. A member of the Michigan parole board indicated that in practice the good time system has broken down and that it is an exception for an inmate to appear before the parole board who has not earned all possible regular and special good time. The board member indicated that in order to be denied good time, an inmate would have to "spit in the warden's eye."

. . .

3. *Minimum Amount of Time*

Illustration No. 17: The inmate, age twenty-two, had been convicted of unlawfully driving away an auto, for which he received two years' probation. After he had served twenty-one months on probation, it was revoked for failure to report, failure to pay costs and restitution, and involvement in an auto accident. The judge imposed a prison term of six months to five years, stating to the inmate that he would probably be back home in about four and one-half months. He spent two months at the main prison and was then transferred to the prison camp where he had served almost a month by the time of his parole hearing. The camp recommended a short continuance of the case on the ground little was known about the inmate. Most of the hearing was consumed by the parole board attempting to explain to the inmate that he had been in the institution "too short a time for the offense" and, further, that the institution knew little about him. The board explained it could not conscientiously recommend parole for him in light of its lack of knowledge of his case. The case was continued for discussion in executive session.

A problem which some parole boards must frequently face occurs when an inmate appears for his initial parole hearing after he has served only a short length of time, normally under six months. Whatever the reasons, the parole board is likely to be quite reluctant to give serious consideration to the case until the inmate has served more time. The normal disposition when such a case appears is to schedule a rehearing, or sometimes only a conference in executive session, in several months, at which time the decision to grant or deny parole will be given usual consideration.

Because of its sentencing structure, the problem is particularly noticeable in Michigan. There, the maximum sentence for most offenses is fixed by statute but the judge has discretion to set any minimum sentence he wishes. Regular and special good time are deducted from the judicially set minimum to determine parole eligibility, and the inmate normally receives his first parole hearing one or two months before he becomes eligible for parole. As a result, when the judge sets a minimum sentence of six months, the inmate is eligible for parole after he has served about four months and appears for his first parole hearing after he has served only three months. The typical disposition of such cases is a continuance for six months or a year, at which time he will be given usual parole consideration.

. . .

A potential problem of the same type was handled by parole board policy in Kansas and Wisconsin. There, inmates of the reformatories and women's prisons are by statute eligible for parole as soon as they arrive at the institution. In each state, the inmate, although statutorily eligible for parole immediately, does not normally receive his first parole hearing until he has served nine months of his sentence. This doubtless reflects a judgment that about that much time is necessary before it makes sense to consider the question of parole.

While there seems to be a consensus that a minimum time, probably between nine months and one year, is necessary before serious consideration should be given to parole, there is lack of agreement as to why this is true. One reason given is that the institution is incapable of having any rehabilitative effect on the inmate in less time. The assumption is that all persons sentenced to prison are in need of rehabilitation, which takes time, or at least that it takes time to determine whether they are in need of rehabilitation. A related reason sometimes given is that the parole system and institution are incapable of formulating sound post-release programs for inmates in less time. Further, parole boards sometimes contend that adequate information on the inmate cannot be obtained in less time and, therefore, a short continuance is necessary in order to obtain information. At other times, however, parole boards have indicated a certain minimum time is necessary in order to justify the risk entailed by every decision to grant parole. The assumption in such cases is that the inmate has served such a short length of time that the parole board can afford to be more conservative in its release decision. Also implicit is the fear that if an inmate were granted parole after serving only four or six months and violated parole in a spectacular fashion, the parole board would be subject to more than the usual amount of criticism.

4. *To Benefit the Inmate*

Illustration No. 18: The inmate, a young man who appeared to be in his late teens, had come from what many would describe as a "good home." He had two brothers, both of whom were ordained ministers, and his parents were respected members of the community. The inmate's father constantly demanded more of the inmate than the latter thought he had the ability to accomplish and continually compared him unfavorably with his older brothers. This comparison was also made by the inmate's school teachers because the inmate, although of high average intelligence, did rather poorly in school. Nevertheless, he had completed all but part of his senior year in high school by the time he had been sentenced to the reformatory. In its pre-parole summary, the classification committee of the institution recommended that the inmate be permitted to complete his high school education, on the ground that it would aid him in the achievements of which he was capable. Some members of the parole board believed that if the inmate finished high school, he might go to college. The parole board decided to defer the case for five months to permit the inmate to complete his high school education prior to his release.

Cases sometimes arise in which it may appear to the parole board that a denial of parole would bring a benefit to the inmate which would be unobtainable if parole were granted. . . . Perhaps the clearest examples are those in which the inmate is suffering from a physical illness which is correctable in the prison but which release to the community would aggravate, or those in which the inmate would benefit from devices, such as dental plates or a hearing aid, which could be provided at no cost to him if he remains an inmate but which may not be as readily obtainable on the outside. . . .

5. *To Avoid Criticism of the Parole System*

Illustration No. 19: The inmate had been convicted of embezzling $25,000 from a veterans' service group. He had absolutely no prior criminal record. Before the offense he had been a prominent member of the community and was well liked. This was his initial parole hearing. When the parole board learned that as a result of the offense the attitude of the community was very much against the inmate, it voted to deny parole.

There is a feeling shared among many parole board members that the success of the parole system depends in part on whether it achieves public approval and confidence. In some states the parole board publishes literature on the parole system for the public, and members make speeches or give demonstrations of parole hearings to civic and social groups. The parole board may also invite community leaders to be present at parole hearings and observe how the board functions.

While a desire to be free of public criticism and to gain the confidence of the public is a characteristic probably common to all criminal justice agencies, the parole board seems particularly sensitive. Whatever the reasons for this concern, it is sometimes reflected in the parole decision. Parole boards are often reluctant to release assaultive offenders despite their own estimate of the high probability of parole success. One reason for this is the board's concern for the safety of the community—that while the probability of recidivism may be low, the seriousness of the violation, if it occurs, is likely to be quite great. But another reason for the board's reluctance to release assaultive offenders is its concern about adverse public reaction if the offender violates parole in a spectacular manner.

The concern about public criticism is even more clearly an important factor in the trust violation cases. . . . If the attitude of the community toward the inmate is good, he is likely to be paroled as soon as he is eligible. When the community attitude is negative, parole is likely to be denied. One reason may be that a negative community attitude is likely to seriously hamper the inmate's efforts to adjust. Another reason, and probably the more important one, is that parole of such an inmate would expose the board and the parole system to public criticism.

. . .

The inmate may write letters to influential persons in state government or to anyone else whom he thinks might be able to influence the board. Sometimes, the inmate or his family may hire attorneys whom they think have unusual influence with the board. The attitude of the parole board in such cases toward the release of the inmate is likely to be extremely negative. In one case, a member of the board said that if a lifer who wrote great numbers of letters trying to get someone to influence the board would cease writing for six months, he would be released, but so long as he persisted in his present behavior the board member was determined that he "do it all." If the board were to grant parole to such an inmate on the merits of the case, it would expose itself to the accusation that the parole grant was the result of special influence. The board prefers to keep the inmate in prison rather than incur that risk.

Still other factors which may affect the parole board's decision are its awareness that charge reduction is common and that the defendant may be guilty of a more serious crime than that for which he was convicted; that trial judges hand down disparate sentences which invite adjustment by releasing comparable offenders on parole after similar periods of incarceration and that the availability of close and effective field agent supervision may allow parole of higher-risk inmates who would otherwise have to be kept in custody.

2. Controls on the Parole Decision

TYLER v. STATE DEPARTMENT OF PUBLIC WELFARE

19 Wis. 2d 166, 119 N.W.2d 460 (1963)

FAIRCHILD, J. *Do secs. 227.15 to 227.21, Stats., inclusive, authorize proceedings to review a refusal to parole?* Sec. 227.15, Stats., provides in pertinent part:

"Administrative decisions, which directly affect the legal rights, duties, or privileges of any person, whether affirmative or negative in form, . . . shall be subject to judicial review as provided in this chapter."

The statutes contain no provisions fixing standards upon fulfilment of which an inmate is entitled to be paroled, although there are two conditions, in addition to service of a specified portion of the sentence, which must be met before the department is authorized to parole.[2]

There are no statutory provisions governing the application for parole nor requiring a hearing thereon. The statutes do not provide for a parole board. The powers of the department are vested in the director, to be exercised under rules which he establishes with the approval of the State Board of Public Welfare.

The parole board is governed by an administrative order of the director. The parole board consists of the director of the division of corrections and three full-time civil-service members. The board is required to conduct hearings on applications for parole, and to follow a manual entitled, "Parole Board Procedures and Practices." The order states that the director of the department is the final authority and that the board is to make recommendation to him in an advisory capacity. We take judicial notice of both order and manual.

Although the administrative order and the manual refer to a hearing of an application, it is clear that this does not have the attributes of a hearing required for judicial or quasi-judicial determinations of rights. An applicant is to appear personally.

---

[2] ". . . The district attorney and judge who tried the inmate shall be notified in writing at least ten days before the first application for parole is acted upon and if they so request shall be given like notice of each subsequent application." (Sec. 57.06 (1) (a), Stats.; see State *ex rel.* Zabel v. Hannan (1935), 219 Wis. 257, 263, 262 N.W. 625, where a parole was set aside by the court, on *certiorari,* for failure to fulfil this condition.) "No such prisoner shall be paroled until the department is satisfied that suitable employment has been secured for him, unless otherwise provided for by the department. . . ." (Sec. 57.06 (2).)

Attorneys and others who desire to support the application are not permitted to appear at the hearing, although they may write to or see the board at its offices in Madison. It is clear that much of the information before the board is not available to the applicant.

It is also clear that the standards which the board is to follow require the balancing of many considerations and necessarily involve highly discretionary evaluations of the applicant's character and susceptibilities upon the basis of personal observation as well as information contained in the file. Thus in the introduction to the manual it is said:

"The long-range interest of society as well as the individual demand a parole process which results in release at that moment when the institutionalization has accomplished its constructive purpose and before progress made is lost to the many negatives associated with prolonged confinement.

"This means that at times persons are tried on parole when it is recognized there is some risk of violation of the condition of parole, but only when that risk, in the judgement [sic] of those trained and experienced in the field of corrections does not involve a threat to society and is less than it would be if confinement continued indefinitely.

"In all decisions with respect to parole the best interests of the public set the limits within which the interests of the individual inmate and his family are considered."

The general rule is that refusal to parole is not subject to judicial review. The fact that the courts of other states decline to review administrative refusal to parole is not conclusive on the question of whether our statutes make such refusal subject to proceedings for review under sec. 227.15 ff., Stats., but their decisions demonstrate that judicial review of such refusal would be unprecedented. We consider them persuasive that "legal rights . . . or privileges" in sec. 227.15 should not be construed to include a prisoner's interest in parole.

A general statement appears in 67 C.J.S., Pardons, p. 604, sec. 20, as follows:

"A parole is a mere matter of grace, favor, or privilege, and a prisoner is not entitled thereto as a matter of right. Subject to the limitations imposed by statute, the question whether a prisoner shall be paroled is a matter for the discretion of the paroling authority, whether it be a court or an officer, board, or commission. Under the statutes and decisions, the discretion of a parole board, commission, or officer as to releasing or refusing to release a prisoner on parole is absolute and not subject to review by a court where the board, commission, or officer acts according to law and without violation of, or departure from, positive statutory requirements."

The legislature has not provided for a hearing or other procedural step to safeguard the interests of an applicant for parole. If the legislature specified procedural requirements even in the exercise of a highly discretionary power, judicial review might be appropriate at least to ensure compliance with the prescribed procedure. Such requirements are absent with respect to parole.

Inherent difficulty of meaningful judicial review of parole. A proceeding for review under sec. 227.15 ff., Stats., must be confined to the record, except that testimony may be taken with respect to alleged irregularities in procedure.[7] No record of proceedings is required or made in parole matters. The elements to be considered are highly complex, and great weight must undoubtedly be given to the personal observation and evaluation of the applicant by the members of the board. In view of the nature of the matter it would probably be impossible for a court to declare that the refusal to parole was either "unsupported by substantial evidence in view of the entire record as submitted; or . . . arbitrary and capricious" while at the same time giving due weight to "the experience, technical competence, and specialized knowledge of the agency involved, as well as discretionary authority conferred upon it."[8]

The gist of petitioner's claim illustrates the virtual impossibility of a meaningful judicial review of refusal of parole under sec. 227.15 ff., Stats. He alleges that he "has been arbitrarily and capriciously denied equal parole consideration given other 'lifers' who have served less time and whose rehabilitative efforts do not surpass petitioner's own; that numerous 'lifers' have been paroled whose rehabilitative efforts are questionable and whose criminal records far exceed petitioner's own." He claims that he has been denied equal protection under the law. No sound determination could be made concerning those allegations without a detailed knowledge of many cases and the factors which had motivated the parole board and director of the department to exercise their power in the manner they did in each.

The foregoing considerations lead us to the conclusion that a prisoner's interest in parole is not a legal right or privilege and

[7] Sec. 227.20 (1), Stats.
[8] Sec. 227.20 (1) (d) and (e) and (2), Stats.

that the department's refusal to parole is not a decision reviewable under sec. 227.15 ff., Stats.

By the Court.—Order affirmed.

Despite its significant impact upon the life of an inmate, the parole decision has not been subject to judicial review.[d] Nor is there usually any administrative mechanism for challenging the parole board's decision. The prisoner's major recourse is to seek pardon or commutation of sentence from the governor.

The principal control upon the parole board's decision is professional self-restraint. The avoidance of political influence in naming the parole board is therefore of obvious importance. One of the marks of a professional group is its attempt to articulate its criteria for decision-making. The establishment of administrative criteria may also serve to satisfy courts that action is not arbitrary, thus reinforcing the traditional policy of nonintervention by courts.

The Wisconsin Parole Board manual referred to in the *Tyler* case attempts to list the criteria which the Board properly considers.

WISCONSIN PAROLE BOARD PROCEDURES AND PRACTICES MANUAL 31-33 (1963)

Wisconsin State Department of Public Welfare
Division of Corrections

3. Basic Aspects of Parole

Determination of the eligibility for parole of an offender must be made in relation to five fundamental viewpoints:

(a) Legal requirements;

(b) Existence of an adequate field staff for necessary supervision;

(c) The response which the individual will make to parole;

(d) The reaction of the community to which the man will be returned upon parole; and

(e) The protection of society from the type of offense for which the individual was placed in institution custody.

---

[d] See, however, p. 831 n.u.

4. Factors Bearing on Readiness of Individual for Parole

(a) Biographical:

Family and marital history;
Associates;
Habits (including alcoholic and drug addiction);
Work record;
Educational achievement;
Military record;
Religious interests;
Attitude toward self as a person;
Attitude toward return to family, industrial and social life of the community;
Attitude toward offense;
Understanding of the motivating factors involved in his offense; and
Length and severity of development or criminal record.

(b) Physical and Mental Health:

Evaluation as a factor in relation to rehabilitation.

(c) Social:

Ability of individual to meet problems and challenges implicit in a return to community life.

(d) Record in Institution:

Participation in institutional programs, such as AA, group and individual therapy, trade training, religious, recreation, and leisure time activities;
Sincerity of interest in assignment; and
Conduct within institution including attitude toward authority.

5. Factors Bearing on Acceptability of Individual by the Community

(a) Character of the offender, nature and location of the offense;
(b) Length of sentence and time served;
(c) Reputation in the community;

(d) Employment resources;

(e) Community attitude toward the individual as expressed by press, courts, law enforcement agents, and citizens in general; and

(f) Closeness of family ties and availability of family or other support.

6. Factors Bearing on Timing of Parole

(a) Readiness to accept responsibility of parole;

(b) Sufficiency of parole plans, availability of adequate Departmental parole field service or other public or private services;

(c) Possible adverse effect upon prison morale; and

(d) Community attitude.

7. Factors of Safety of Society

Evaluation of potential danger to society (particularly whether the personal safety of any member of society might be placed in jeopardy).

MODEL PENAL CODE § 305.9
American Law Institute
(Proposed Official Draft 1962)

Section 305.9. Criteria for Determining Date of First Release on Parole.

(1) Whenever the Board of Parole considers the first release of a prisoner who is eligible for release on parole, it shall be the policy of the Board to order his release, unless the Board is of the opinion that his release should be deferred because:

(a) there is substantial risk that he will not conform to the conditions of parole; or

(b) his release at that time would depreciate the seriousness of his crime or promote disrespect for law; or

(c) his release would have a substantially adverse effect on institutional discipline; or

(d) his continued correctional treatment, medical care or vocational or other training in the institution will substantially enhance his capacity to lead a law-abiding life when released at a later date.

(2) In making its determination regarding a prisoner's release on parole, it shall be the policy of the Board of Parole to take into account each of the following factors:

(a) the prisoner's personality, including his maturity, stability, sense of responsibility and any apparent development in his personality which may promote or hinder his conformity to law;

(b) the adequacy of the prisoner's parole plan;

(c) the prisoner's ability and readiness to assume obligations and undertake responsibilities;

(d) the prisoner's intelligence and training;

(e) the prisoner's family status and whether he has relatives who display an interest in him, or whether he has other close and constructive associations in the community;

(f) the prisoner's employment history, his occupational skills, and the stability of his past employment;

(g) the type of residence, neighborhood or community in which the prisoner plans to live;

(h) the prisoner's past use of narcotics, or past habitual and excessive use of alcohol;

(i) the prisoner's mental or physical make-up, including any disability or handicap which may affect his conformity to law;

(j) the prisoner's prior criminal record, including the nature and circumstances, recency and frequency of previous offenses;

(k) the prisoner's attitude toward law and authority;

(l) the prisoner's conduct in the institution, including particularly whether he has taken advantage of the opportunities for self-improvement afforded by the institutional program, whether he has been punished for misconduct within six months prior to his hearing or reconsideration for parole release, whether he has forfeited any reductions of term during his period of imprisonment, and whether such reductions have been restored at the time of hearing or reconsideration;

(m) the prisoner's conduct and attitude during any previous experience of probation or parole and the recency of such experience.

The Model Penal Code criteria for release on parole raised several significant policy issues—whether an attempt by the legislature to list criteria for the parole board is itself desirable, whether it is proper to consider as a factor adverse to release that the prisoner is not welcome in the community, and whether the presumption should be for or against parole at the outset.

With reference to the first issue, the Model Penal Code assumes that there is great value both in the articulation of criteria and in doing so at the legislative level. Traditionally legislative attention to correctional decisions has been reflected in highly general and ambiguous phrases, leaving the correctional administrator wide discretion. As a consequence, correctional administrators have not looked to legislation for detailed guidance in making correctional decisions. Whether detailed legislative criteria are desirable or likely to be effective are questions to which there are no clear answers.

All boards confront particularly notorious or politically hot cases where risk of reviolation is small, where continued in-prison treatment is unnecessary for the prisoner, where his plan is sound in terms of employment and living conditions, but where community resentment over his crime is high and where early release would likely be interpreted as arrogant disregard of the sentence determined by the local judge, or possibly as succumbing to pressure from the offender's friends or even the temptation of a bribe.

In the discussion of these issues by the American Law Institute,[e] the position was urged that phrasing the matter in terms of a presumption that parole should be granted raises unwarranted expectations in the hearts of prisoners and invites unproductive litigation, and also that increasing too greatly the rights of prisoners will tend to weaken public support for the whole parole program.

As suggested in the *Tyler* case, another kind of control upon the parole board decision is the existence of procedural safeguards. Though an arbitrary decision is still possible in the most rigorously fair procedural situation, the formalities of administrative procedure constitute a significant influence toward accurate, wise decisions. Statement of the basis for the decision, disclosure of the information upon which the decision was grounded, and representation by counsel are all procedural demands which inmates have made with respect to their parole hearings.

WISCONSIN CRIMINAL PROCEDURE

Note, 1966 Wisconsin Law Review 430, 522-23

GRANT OF PAROLE

Administrative Procedure and Internal Review

An applicant appears personally before the board. No representation on behalf of the applicant is permitted. The parole

---

[e] 33RD ANNUAL MEETING OF THE AMERICAN LAW INSTITUTE, PROCEEDINGS 273-79 (1956).

board reviews the applicant's record, which includes his crime, his sentence, his behavior and development in the institution, and his parole plan. In addition, the board has available any opinions from supervisory personnel in the institution and, if the applicant has been on probation or parole before, agent's records. Also, the board may be familiar with the applicant from previous applications. After the applicant has entered the room, the board explains the purpose of the hearing, reviews with him his parole plan, and asks him if he has any comments to make or questions to ask. Then the applicant leaves the room, and the board discusses and votes on the application. The criteria which the board uses in making its decision are fairly detailed. The decision that the board makes on a parole application can be any of the following: (1) "grant"; (2) "defer," which means either deny the application and set a new hearing date at some time within twenty-four months, or hold to mandatory release date (sentence less good time); or (3) "no action," which means delay until further information, such as a psychiatrist's appraisal is available. If the board is in agreement concerning the decision, the parole applicant is called back into the room and informed of the decision. He may ask questions about the decision. If the board is not in agreement, no action is taken, and the application is referred to the full panel of six members. When this occurs, the applicant is informed of the decision by mail.

MASTRIANA v. NEW JERSEY PAROLE BOARD

95 N.J. Super. 351, 231 A.2d 236 (1967)

The opinion of the court was delivered by LEONARD, J.A.D.

On December 21, 1965 appellant appeared before the Board and parole was denied, but appellant was advised that his case had been scheduled for another hearing in June 1967. On January 26, 1966 he filed a complaint with the Board alleging that the denial of his parole was unfair and based upon prejudice and bias, and he requested that the Board state the reason for the denial. Thereafter appellant was notified by letters from the chairman of the Board and from its counsel that "as a matter of policy" the Board does not give reasons for the denial of parole and that it is not "obligated" to do so.

Appellant filed a notice of appeal on February 28, 1966, and on March 28, 1966 the Board moved to dismiss the appeal on the ground that "the appellant has failed to state a claim upon which relief can be granted." The basis of the motion was that appellant did not set forth any acts committed by the Board which were "unfair, arbitrary, unreasonable or discriminatory; that there was no allegation of facts to support the claim that the Board did not act within the framework of the Parole Statute (N.J.S.A. 30:4-123.1 *et seq.*) and that the Board was under no legal requirement to advise an inmate why parole was denied." However, by a consent order dated May 3, 1966 all "proceedings in the appeal" were stayed until further order of the court. The purpose of that order was to allow appellant to reappear before the Board for a reconsideration of his previous denial of parole, in light of his preparation of a new parole plan.

On September 27, 1966 appellant appeared before the Board. He at that time had the advice of court-assigned counsel. A hearing was held, his parole plan was reconsidered and the Board again denied parole, scheduling a rehearing in September 1967.

Thereafter appellant pursued his appeal and moved before this court for leave to inspect books, records and documents of the Board and for a more definite statement regarding the denial of his parole; made a demand for interrogatories directed to the chairman and members of the Board, and moved to add the warden of the State Prison, certain State physicians and parole officers and a designated county judge as parties defendant.

Appellant's principal argument is that the Board should be compelled to reveal its reasons for the denial of his parole. He cites no authority mandating such action, and we find none. The statute does not require such revelation. To the contrary, it only requires that if the Board, in its judgment, determines that the prisoner is not to be released on parole, "then it shall notify him of such decision and the date when his case will again be considered." N.J.S.A. 30:4-123.19. This the Board has done. The procedure of the Board "is a matter of state policy exclusively for the State to decide," Mahoney v. Parole Board of New Jersey, 10 N.J. 269, 279 (1952), appeal dismissed 344 U.S. 871 (1952), and we have no authority to act in the premises. Zink v. Lear, *supra,* 28 N.J. Super., at p. 525. We therefore conclude this argument has no merit.

We consider next appellant's motion to compel the Board to answer interrogatories as to the "factual background" of its decision; to compel the Board to advise him whether or not a stenographic transcript of its hearings was made and if it was to compel the Board to furnish him with the same. We find no statutory requirement for a stenographic transcript of a parole hearing or for the delivery of such a transcript to a prisoner. As we have heretofore indicated, in the absence of such a mandate we lack jurisdiction to order that such record, if it exists, be furnished.

In his demand for interrogatories appellant again seeks the basis of the Board's decision. In view of the determination previously here made on that issue, we conclude that he is not entitled to receive this information before trial by the attempted use of our discovery rules (R.R. 4:23-1 *et seq.*). Thus, appellant's motion is denied in its entirety.

For the same reason we deny appellant's motion to inspect the Board's "general books, papers, records and documents" and his motion for "a more definite statement . . . regarding his denial of parole."

Under all the circumstances the Board's motion to dismiss this appeal will be granted.

So ordered.

BRIGUGLIO v. NEW YORK STATE BOARD OF PAROLE

55 Misc. 2d 584, 285 N.Y.S.2d 883 (1968)

MEMORANDUM

DE FOREST C. PITT, Justice. Petitioner, an inmate of Attica State Prison, seeks judgment upon this Article 78 proceeding voiding a determination of the Board of Parole or alternatively granting a *de novo* hearing before said board. The subject determination denied parole to the petitioner. The respondents have served an answer wherein they have raised objections in point of law.

The petitioner here, in the main, raises the lately anticipated question of his right to counsel at a hearing held to determine his eligibility for parole. It is maintained that the subject hearing was not, "a judicial type hearing", as allegedly mandated by statute (§ 212 Correction Law) and the principles of administrative law. Specifically it is urged that the established procedure, and the particular treatment afforded the petitioner was violative of the constitutional guarantee of due process of law. It is argued that this violation occurred in the failure to notify the petitioner of his right to be represented by counsel as well as in the failure to notify him of the issues, charges and evidence involved in the Board's determination, and the further failures to afford to the petitioner an opportunity to offer evidence in his own behalf and to specify the findings upon which the Board's determination was based.

Heavily relied upon is the case of Mempa v. Rhay, 389 U.S. 128, 134 (1967).[f] This well publicized case held that under the

[f] *See* p. 942, *infra.*

6th Amendment there was a right to counsel in probation revocation proceedings at which a deferred sentence may be imposed. It is urged that the rationale of the Mempa Case can be applied to the instant matter for the reason that we must here realize that the Parole Board's function in the granting of parole or the denying of the same is, like in the revocation of probation matters a "deferred sentencing" procedure and it is another "stage of a criminal proceeding where substantial rights of a criminal accused may be effected."

There are, however, substantial differences in revocation of probation and in the granting of parole. Not only is the revocation of probation a function of the court which may well subject the violator to additional imprisonment by virtue of the court's power to impose any sentence it may have originally imposed, but more basic yet is the concept of the taking versus the giving. (The concept is old and well imbedded in our law. The terminology is perhaps new, but it is thought expressive.) It is clear at least that when one's probation is revoked he is being divested of something that he was theretofore possessed of, i. e., his freedom, which is of course a substantial right, which had not before been completely taken from him by the court. A judicial fact finding process is necessitated. This is the taking. Conversely, however, in the matter of the granting of parole his freedom has already by due process of law been denied him. He is at this juncture being divested of nothing. The sole determination to be made is whether he should be afforded a type of liberty which he does not have. This is the giving. If paroled, the convict is still considered in custody. He is merely granted more liberal treatment.

The respondents may submit a judgment dismissing the petition.[g]

B. REVOCATION OF THE GRANT OF FREEDOM IN THE COMMUNITY

An offender who is free in the community may have that freedom withdrawn if he fails to comply with the conditions imposed by the court, the parole board, or other agency which granted that freedom. Less often the offender's freedom may be revoked, even though he has complied with the conditions of his release, because the supervising agent believes the offender is again likely to commit crime if not incarcerated. Whatever

[g] Contrast with *People ex rel. Combs v. LaVallee,* at 945, *infra,* where the court held there is a right to representation at a parole revocation hearing.

the basis, the scope of the field agent's discretion is enormous because the conditions are commonly very broad and there are few probationers or parolees who do not, on occasion, violate one or more conditions. How the discretion is exercised, who is responsible, and the methods for insuring against inappropriate decisions to revoke are questions of fundamental importance.

1. Responsibility for the Revocation Decision

In all situations the supervising field agent plays a very significant part in the revocation decision, since he knows of the offender's conduct and decides initially whether or not to do anything about it. A difference between parole and probation lies in the agent's responsibility to report to an administrative superior in one case and to a judge in the other to have the decision to revoke made official. Parole revocation decisions are commonly wholly administrative. Probation revocation decisions are most often made by a judge, though sometimes they are made administratively.

If a judge suspends *imposition* of sentence and places the offender on probation, there is a practical reason for returning him to court since he alone has authority to impose sentence. However, if the sentence is imposed but its *execution stayed* and the offender put on probation, there is no need to return him to court for sentencing. Some jurisdictions, in this situation, permit administrative revocation. Others still require a judicial decision. Whether this type of decision ought to be "judicial" in nature or "administrative" or whether it makes any important difference, has not been subject to any very careful inquiry. Whichever method is used, the field agent's influence is great, but having to report to a judge, in court, may result in a different decisional process than would result if the agent had to report only to his superior.

2. Factors Affecting the Decision Whether to Revoke

The revocation process begins in the first instance with a decision by a parole or probation officer to instigate revocation proceedings. This is by no means an automatic response even when the offender has been arrested for a new crime nor, indeed, does revocation necessarily accompany or follow conviction of a new offense. Field agents normally are expected to judge each individual case on its merits rather than to follow standard formulas. The individual field agent is controlled only in a general way by agency policies and by his superior within the agency. Agency guidelines are usually broad statements of objectives or procedures with no attempt to specifically direct or curtail field agent discretion. Supervision by an administrator, particularly of trained and experienced agents, is commonly viewed as a form of "consultation" rather than as a review of agents' specific decisions. Initiative and exercise of independent professional judgment are encouraged and supported if they are not totally inappropriate or at odds with agency objectives.

Administrative policy or supervision acts in direct check on agent discretion, if at all, only when the officer has decided to revoke. Decisions to take no action or to use some alternative short of revocation when confronted by violation tend to be of low visibility, much like police decisions not to arrest. Field agents normally make a written record of any discovered violations and of action taken, but this is simply good case recording and is usually not submitted for specific review by higher authorities. While it is technically possible for a judge or parole board member or other designated authority to revoke on his own initiative or over the opposition of the field agent, this rarely happens.

It is tempting, and in certain perspective appropriate, to compare the similarities of the revocation discretion of a parole officer and the arrest discretion of the police. Yet there are differences. For example, the number of arrests made by a policeman has often been taken—however unwisely—as an indication of his workload and even of his competence. Revocation, on the other hand, is, if anything, commonly treated as a failure of supervision. While presumably it would be inappropriate for a field agent *never* to revoke, the whole thrust of the probation-parole movement is to keep men in the community, working with adjustment problems there, and using revocation only as a last resort when treatment has failed or is about to fail.

Field agents who are trained social workers (and the master's degree in social work is the accepted professional model) claim a certain amount of expertise. Agents who are merely college graduates, or have even less formal education, cannot make the same claim to expertise, though experience can substitute for formal training to some degree. The correctional position calling for broad field agent discretion rests on the assumption that field agents have social work expertise. The reliance in the police field has been on experience more than training. The claim to expertise is less often made by police.

While the parole or probation officer recognizes his double duty to the welfare of his clients and to the safety of the general community, by and large concern for the client dominates his professional attitude. The parole agent ordinarily defines his role as representing his client's best interests as long as these do not constitute a threat to public safety. The police officer, in contrast, is concerned primarily with public safety.

It would be unfortunate, however, to overemphasize the differences, because there are important parallels in the exercise of discretion by police and probation or parole officers.

Aside from the professional orientation, various other factors affect the probation or parole agent's decision whether to recommend revocation. One is the conceptual and practical difference between probation and parole (or mandatory release). The probationer has not served time (except in the special situation of a short jail term made a condition of probation), while the parolee has. The difference is suggested by the New Mexico Supreme Court:

> One who is paroled is not thereby released from custody but is merely permitted to serve a portion of his sentence outside the walls of the penitentiary, under such conditions as the board may impose and during the pleasure of the board. A paroled prisoner is not discharged from the custody of the prison authorities, but is at all times under the complete custody and control, and subject to the orders of the parole board, whereas, in the case of a suspension of sentence, the person has never commenced service of the sentence and has, therefore, the right of personal liberty. He is not in custody as is a parolee.[h]

It has often seemed that to revoke probation, which means sending a man to prison who has not been there, is more drastic than to revoke parole, which returns a man to prison. This tends to make those who must make the revocation decision more cautious with respect to probationers than they might be to parolees.

The laws often operate to vary the impact of revocation from one state to another. For example, in about half the states, time served successfully on parole counts toward completion of sentence while time served on probation does not. In other states, time is tolled on both probation and parole. If a parolee has five years of his sentence remaining and serves four years of successful parole time before revocation, he must serve only a year where such credit is given but five years where "street time" does not count. In some situations, particularly in juris-

---

[h] Robinson v. Cox, 77 N.M. 55, 59, 419 P.2d 253, 256 (1966).

dictions where reparole is rare, revocation for a minor rule violation may mean an extensive period of imprisonment for the offender. In other situations, the time remaining under sentence may be so short as to make revocation meaningless. Time served on probation does not at all diminish the possible period of imprisonment upon revocation.

Variations in the intensity of field supervision also affect revocation practices. In some jurisdictions, field supervision of both probationers and parolees is minimal, hardly more than a bookkeeping device. A probation or parole officer who is given a hundred or more offenders to supervise cannot closely follow each one or hope to provide casework services on a regular basis. This agent has little knowledge of conformity to or violation of supervision rules, and revocation therefore tends to become solely dependent on an arrest for a new offense. In effect the police perform whatever supervision or surveillance occurs. It is ironic that where field agents are well-trained, have small caseloads, and perform a more highly professional supervision function, revocations are more frequent. They discover more rule violations and, with clinical competence, are aware of the potential dangers in early signs of nonconformity and are more ready and willing to revoke before a new crime is committed.

The scope and generality of common probation or parole conditions give the field agent a broad range of grounds for revocation should he wish to use them. Requirements such as that the parolee "cooperate" with his field agent are common; the nearly universal condition is that the offender remain "law-abiding."

THE REVOCATION DECISION: A STUDY OF PROBATION AND PAROLE AGENT'S DISCRETION

By Sara K. Hunt

(Unpublished MSW thesis, The University of Wisconsin, Madison, School of Social Work, 1964)[1]

In Wisconsin's correctional system the probation and parole field agent is delegated primary responsibility for initiating the revocation process in cases under his immediate supervision. The agent is not compelled by law or administrative policy, however, to recommend revocation in every case involving known violations or new offenses. In fact, twenty-five percent of the offenders studied who committed new offenses were continued

[1] Some changes have been made to adapt the thesis to use here, without specific indication of the places at which the organizational changes were made.

on field supervision, with perhaps short-term jail sentences following commission of new crimes. The authority to exercise discretion in deciding to revoke or not to revoke offenders under supervision is considered necessary if probation and parole are to remain workable systems.

The Decision to Revoke Offenders Under Supervision. The strongest single determining factor in the revocation decision was the seriousness of violation or new offense committed by the offender while under supervision. In view of the field agent's primary responsibility to the community and its protection, this factor would be expected to have importance. Cases where offenders were considered extremely dangerous to the community, however, were relatively infrequent. Revocations were generally based on additional considerations.

1

> A youthful offender recently paroled from the Reformatory stole an automobile, taking it across several state lines in an attempt to abscond. He was apprehended by federal authorities, who issued a detainer for violation of the Dyer Act. Parole was revoked and the youth returned to the institution to serve the remainder of his sentence before being turned over to a federal agency.

In a majority of the cases revoked on conviction of a new offense or as a substitution for conviction, there were some outside pressures. Frequently the crimes committed were of high visibility, resulting in newspaper publicity. At other times police urged revocation when there was suspected but unproven misconduct.

2

> A recent parolee was known to be living with a former parolee. Both individuals had extensive prior burglary records and were strongly suspected by the police of committing a series of recent burglaries in the area. Surveillance by police failed to uncover sufficient evidence for arrest. The supervising agent, sharing these suspicions and under pressure from the police department, revoked parole on the basis of minor rules infractions as a precautionary measure.

One principal objective in allowing rules violations to constitute grounds for revocation is to prevent resumption of criminal conduct during supervision. Preventive intervention by agents was not limited to cases considered potentially dangerous to the community but included offenders believed to be in need of a controlled environment or of specialized treatment services available only within the institutions.

3

A chronic alcoholic checkwriter, having refused any assistance from Alcoholics Anonymous, was known to be drinking heavily. Although unemployed, he reportedly had sums of money in his possession. The agent had not received notice of any outstanding checks, but anticipated they would eventually turn up at the D.A.'s office. Parole was revoked in hopes that the offender would resume his participation in AA programs available within the institution.

4

A youthful offender appeared to be making a good initial adjustment on parole. Signs of deterioration became evident, however, when the youth provoked his employer into firing him and made no effort to find other employment. This added strain to the youth's relationship with his stepfather, upon whom the boy projected blame for his delinquent behavior. Increasing association with delinquent cronies led to the youth's participation in several acts of vandalism in the community. A work-home placement in another city was considered, but rejected due to the subject's defiant attitude toward supervision. While present violations were not considered particularly serious, the agent foresaw continuing delinquency unless action was taken. The decision to revoke was based upon the expectation that attitude toward supervision would improve prior to reparole.

A determining factor in revocations of offenders committing rules violations or relatively minor new offenses was their overall social adjustment in the community. In assessing offenders' adjustment, agents placed particular emphasis on the support of self and family and on the fulfillment of financial obligations to the courts and the community. In most revoked cases agents had persisted in their efforts to help individual offenders to assume these responsibilities and had failed. Revocation also occurred when offenders were totally unresponsive to supervision.

5

A probationer was living with a divorcee and failing to support his family adequately. Other violations were being committed in connection with this association, i.e., drinking in local taverns, leaving the state without permission, driving without a valid driver's license. Revocation followed the offender's arrest in another state on charges of illegal possession of beer in a car and no driver's license.

The offender's responsiveness to supervision as reflected by his attitude and his cooperation with the supervising agent appeared to be a prerequisite for continuing probation or parole supervision under any circumstances. In other words men committing relatively serious violations during supervision might be continued without revocation due to some appreciable changes in their attitudes, whereas others committing similar violations were revoked. What effect agents' workloads and time limitations had on revocation rates could not be determined.

6

A probationer convicted of bigamy was apprehended in the home of the woman with whom he had been ordered not to associate. This occurred within the second month of supervision. The agent recommended revocation on the basis that the case presented an unworkable situation for probation supervision. The offender was returned to court and sentenced to six months in the county jail.

7

In two similar cases the offenders requested revocation rather than continue under probation supervision. Both cases entailed six-month county jail sentences following revocation. When one offender's request was refused, he committed a minor offense to accomplish this end.

8

An habitual offender, presently on probation for a misdemeanor with sentence withheld, had required continuous attention during supervision with complex financial, marital, and behavioral problems. While not a serious offender, he had been arrested numerous times during probation for driving after his license was revoked. He did exhibit some violence when drinking excessively. At the point of revocation, the offender was unemployed, not supporting his estranged wife and his children, and making little effort to alter the situation. Revocation followed the agent's apprehension of the individual in a local tavern, only twelve days before probation expiration. Nonsupport charges were already pending, and the agent felt revocation would affect the subject's complacent attitude.

A factor accounting for some disparities in the revocation decision was the availability or unavailability of resources in the community. The need for outside resources as adjuncts to supervision ranged from intensive psychiatric treatment to jobs and places to live. It was found that the lack of some supportive, stabilizing influences in the community greatly reduced the probabilities that offenders would complete their probation and parole terms successfully.

9

A chronic alcoholic developed a severe case of delirium tremens. The family refused to commit him to a state hospital and could not afford medical services. The agent revoked supervision on the basis of needing institutional facilities not available in the community.

10

A parolee with over one hundred arrests on drunk and disorderly charges was revoked primarily for the nuisance he was causing the police department and for the agent's admitted inability to find a suitable placement within the community.

The Decision Not to Revoke Offenders Under Supervision. Offenders were not revoked when there was merely a suspicion of violation. The decision required proof.

11

Police officials strongly suspected a parolee of participating in a series of recent burglaries in the area. A police "dragnet" was placed around the subject's residence with no results. The supervising agent shared the suspicion that the parolee was involved, but felt he had no basis for revocation without additional proof.

The decision not to revoke offenders was made in spite of nondangerous violations during supervision and was frequently based on considerations other than the individuals' behavior alone. Thus it was found that offenders who were supporting their families were less apt to be revoked than those not supporting their dependents or having none, despite similar violations during supervision. Factors such as length of remaining sentence, especially when extremely short, sometimes had decisive influence in continuing field supervision in cases otherwise warranting revocation. Perhaps fundamental to the question of continuing the supervision of offenders who violate their probation or parole is the willingness of the individual field agents to provide those "second chances."

12

A recently divorced probationer admitted having impregnated a girlfriend, with whom he had been instructed not to associate. On the basis of the offender's willingness to pay the medical expenses and support of the expected child, the supervising agent decided against revocation.

13

An offender, placed on probation for nonsupport, immediately absconded from supervision. He was apprehended and reinstated on probation by the sentencing court. Throughout supervision worthless checks were written, usually in connection with heavy drinking, but were invariably made good after the agent applied pressure. As the offender did begin making support payments during supervision, the agent felt as much was being accomplished as could be expected. The probation sentence was allowed to expire.

14

A parolee was arrested his first day under field supervision for "drunk and disorderly conduct" and was subsequently charged for nonsupport on a warrant issued prior to his institutionalization. The agent knew the offender had previously absconded from field supervision as a probationer and, under these circumstances, might do so again. The agent did not consider the offender to be dangerous, however, and wanted to provide him an opportunity to prove himself. The offender had secured employment and appeared willing to cooperate. The supervising agent decided against revocation.

Just as lack of community resources influenced the decision to revoke some offenders, so the supportive help of outside persons or agencies in the community sometimes accounted for the continuation of field supervision despite violations. Examples of the types of resources considered to be instrumental in the supervisory process included reliable family members, employers, and interested citizens and/or the specialized services of social welfare and mental health agencies.

15

The supervising agent received a report that a parolee previously convicted of statutory rape had made sexual overtures toward a female client while he was working as a door-to-door salesman. The employer came personally to the agent to urge that the parolee be given another chance. An agreement was reached whereby the offender would not be assigned evening house calls while working alone. The agent decided against revocation for the alleged violation.

The use of alternative actions in place of revocations tended to be more prevalent among probation cases than parole when comparable violations had been committed. One reason believed to account for this difference was the large proportion of misdemeanor probation cases having less than one-year sentences. Frequently supervision of misdemeanants was extended beyond the date of sentence expiration rather than revoking probation in cases having unfulfilled court financial obligations. Misdemeanor cases cannot be sentenced to state correctional institutions; consequently, offenders in need of specialized medical or psychiatric services must be accommodated in the community.

There were several cases which agents did not feel would benefit from institutionalization sufficiently to justify revocation. This evaluation may have been based on the offender's low mental capacities or on results of previous institutional experiences. Offenders considered beyond rehabilitating were sometimes continued on supervision despite repeated arrests and jail sentences due to chronic alcoholism, vagrancy, and the like. These cases were typically considered "nuisances" to local law enforcement agencies but not particularly dangerous to the community.

16

A probationer seriously assaulted his sister-in-law during a family dispute. Although no criminal charges resulted, family members felt that psychiatric attention was urgently needed. In addition to many rules violations, the subject's drinking problem had reached such proportions that an institutional placement was considered imperative by the agent. As a misdemeanant the alternative would have been a county jail sentence. A commitment to a state hospital was arranged without revoking probation.

17

A parolee with numerous arrests for drunk and disorderly conduct while under supervision was bringing considerable agitation from the police department for a revocation. The offender's parole term, however, was very close to reaching the Mandatory Release date. In view of his previous institutional experience, the offender was believed to have attained the "maximum benefits" possible. The parole term was allowed to expire, despite several arrests and jail sentences.

Considered fundamental in the decision to revoke or not to revoke offenders is the extent of potential danger posed by their behavior in the community. Thus it was found that offenders whose behavior was not viewed as particularly dangerous, whose violations were of low visibility or consequence to the community, whose social adjustment was at least marginal, tended not to be revoked when violations became known to the agents.

18

A recently paroled offender, previously convicted of forgery and writing worthless checks, was arrested for illegal possession of beer in a car and for resisting arrest. The agent felt the case prognosis was fairly good, despite these violations, in that the individual held a responsible job, had cooperated well under supervision, and had been in no other difficulties with the law. With twenty-seven months remaining on the latter's parole term, the agent recommended a short county jail sentence for the offenses in place of a revocation of parole.

19

Two recent parolees, both with over two years remaining on parole, were working in a local junk yard where parolees fresh out of institutions were frequently hired for low wages. The two offenders were accused of stealing some merchandise and petty cash from the employer. When the circumstances became known, however, the agent felt the employer had provoked the theft by leaving the parolees in charge of the yard after firing them and refusing to pay them back wages. The case was allowed to go into court, where charges were dismissed upon payment of restitution and costs.

In some cases an indication of change in attitude toward supervision or in cooperating with the supervising agent was sufficient basis for deciding to continue field supervision without revocation.

20

A youth probationer was arrested for a minor offense, formally charged and convicted. The agent felt the incident was directly related to recent family problems, which had resulted in the youth being forced to leave home. From a discussion with the offender, the agent decided an independent living arrangement could be established without risking further violations. A short jail sentence was served for the offense committed, and probation was continued.

3. Propriety of the Grounds for Revocation

The propriety of conditions placed upon release under community supervision has been discussed previously,[j] pointing out that the conditions are often tested by objecting to the revocation as based upon violation of an invalid condition. It can occur, however, that revocation is not based upon violation of a specific condition, even one so broad as "failing to cooperate with his field agent."

A federal circuit court of appeals held in Kaplan v. United States, 234 F.2d 345, 348 (8th Cir. 1956):

> The appellant's argument that he violated none of the specific terms of his probation and that the terms were never modified would not, even if true, be persuasive. The determinative question is whether the conduct of the probationer was inconsistent with his duties as such. One on probation is not at liberty; he is in law and in fact in the custody and under the control of the court granting probation.

TRUEBLOOD LONGKNIFE v. UNITED STATES

381 F.2d 17 (9th Cir. 1967)

HAMLIN, Circuit Judge. On the 11th of February, 1965, in the District of Hawaii, appellant, using the name of Pat Trueblood Longknife, filed a voluntary bankruptcy petition.

On January 27, 1966, in an indictment filed in the District of Hawaii appellant was charged in two counts of violating 18 U.S.C. § 152 by making false oaths in the said bankruptcy proceeding. About a month later appellant entered a plea of *nolo contendere* to Count I of said indictment which charged that "he did knowingly and fraudulently fail to disclose that among the assets of the said bankrupt was a 1960 Peuguot [sic] sedan. . . ." On motion of the government Count II of the indictment was dismissed. On March 28, 1966, appellant was placed upon three years' probation.

Approximately two months later the probation officer filed a petition for revocation of probation, alleging in part that prior

---

[j] *See* pp. 803-05, *supra*.

to being placed on probation and from March 28, 1966, to June, 1966, appellant had willfully and knowingly concealed from the probation officer and the court that he had, under the name of Dorman Pat True Long, filed a bankruptcy proceeding in the District of Hawaii and on December 6, 1961, been discharged from his debts. The petition further alleged that in the bankruptcy proceeding filed February 11, 1965, appellant had made false answers to questions about prior bankruptcy proceedings and false answers to questions as to whether he had ever gone under any other name than Pat Trueblood Longknife. The petition for revocation further stated "That in view of the defendant's withholding pertinent facts of circumstances which occurred before the granting of probation and his continuing to withhold such information during the period of probation in spite of his being given an opportunity to do so by Affiant up to as late as 1 June 1966, the writer feels that had the Court been cognizant of the information withheld by the defendant and now made known to the Court by the Affiant, the Court would not have granted probation to the defendant."

A hearing before the court upon the petition for revocation was held where appellant, who was represented by counsel, testified.

At the conclusion of the hearing the district judge in a written order revoked appellant's probation. Appellant seeks reversal of this decision on the grounds that the judge acted beyond the scope of his discretion since the defendant had committed no acts *during his probation* upon which a revocation could be based. We affirm.

The Supreme Court set broad limits upon the court's discretion in granting or revoking probation in Burns v. United States [287 U.S. 216, 220 (1932)], where the Court said: "Probation is thus conferred as a privilege, and cannot be demanded as a right. It is a matter of favor, not of contract."

Burns gave the court the discretion to look at the wisdom and justice of continuing probation, but it nowhere provided that the discretion could only be exercised when the probationer has been in "breach" of his probation conditions. Quite the contrary, the Court held that the *only limit* placed upon the exercise of the judge's discretion is that he must be satisfied that his action will subserve the ends of justice and the best interests of both the public and the defendant.

In this case, the judge made it quite clear that had he known about the defendant's prior bankruptcy, his use of an alias, and his efforts to knowingly and fraudulently conceal these facts from the court and the probation officer, he would not have granted probation in the first instance. It would clearly have been within his discretion to not grant it. It was thus equally within his discretion to have revoked the probation when the additional facts came to his attention. Otherwise, the judge would be forced into the position of saying that while he is quite convinced that the best interests of both the public and the defendant would be served were the defendant not on probation, he is irrevocably bound by his initial, albeit erroneous, grant of probation.

Affirmed.

4. Procedures Used in Making the Revocation Decision

MODEL PENAL CODE
COMMENT, SECTION 305.21

American Law Institute
(Tentative Draft No. 5, 1956)

Section 305.21 [Section 305.15 in Proposed Official Draft] provides for an early hearing on the revocation of parole and establishes criteria to guide the Board in its decision. These parallel section 301.3 (Tentative Drafts Nos. 2 and 4) dealing with the revocation of suspended sentence or probation. The Board must be satisfied on substantial evidence that the parolee has failed, without a satisfactory excuse, to comply with a substantial requirement of his parole and that his violation consists of another crime, indicates substantial risk that he will commit a crime, or that he is unwilling to comply with proper conditions of parole. These provisions taken together with the criteria guiding release, section 305.13, and the conditions of parole, section 305.17, should contribute substantially, we believe, to the development of more consistent and equitable parole practices. They differ, it will be observed, from present law and practice.

The traditional theory of parole, developed out of the incorporation of a parole period within a system of long indefinite sentences of imprisonment, has been that conditional release is a special privilege that may be granted or withheld from the prisoner and that, once granted, it may be withdrawn either at will or for violation of the conditions. The parolee remains in the legal custody of the warden of the prison or of the state correctional department, sometimes of the parole board, and may be returned to serve out his term in what is deemed implicitly to be the normal way: imprisonment. In spite of the general employment of parole and the recognition of its utility as a specialized correctional device, it has not yet achieved status either in law or administration as the distinct and unique measure that it should be. At best the legal rights of the parolee are equivocal. In at least sixteen states no parole revocation hearings are held. The case law in a number of these jurisdictions has offered a variety of rationalizations for avoiding such hearings, though fundamentally the policy is based upon the view that the offender has no right to parole or to freedom from his incarceration during the term of his sentence. These specific theories have been advanced: (1) parole is a mere act of grace on the part of the executive, conferring no rights upon the parolee and subject to withdrawal at any time; (2) parole is a contract between sovereign and convict in which the latter agrees to various conditions, one of which may be revocation at the will of the grantor without hearing or notice; (3) the parolee remains in the custody of the warden of the prison or the parole board and revocation is a mere change in the form of this custody which does not require special protection; (4) the parolee was given his full constitutional protection at the original trial. The Supreme Court has held in the analogous case of revocation of probation that a hearing is a privilege bestowed by statute.[7]

A number of states provide parole revocation hearings without specific statutory authorization therefor, in some instances, in fact, denying that the parolee has a right to the hearing. Eighteen jurisdictions make statutory provision for a hearing prior to revocation of parole, though even in these states it is the generally prevailing doctrine that the revocation is at the unhampered discretion of the board, and some courts have held that the hearing need be only of the most summary nature.

Some jurisdictions, departing in a measure from the philosophy of free administrative discretion, have come to provide some elements of a quasi-judicial due process in their revocation procedures, such as the right of the parolee to be informed of the specific charges, a right to counsel, a right to present evidence, even a right to jury trial where the identity of the accused parolee is in issue. Moreover, responses to questionnaires reveal that, without specific statutory authorization for the most part, the parolee is permitted to advise with counsel in preparation for his hearing in twenty-three jurisdictions. In twelve of these counsel is permitted at the hearings.

Further evidence of the wide administrative discretion exercised in parole is provided in data relating to the frequency and grounds of revocation employed in various states. Parole revocation may result either from the commission of a new crime

---

[7] Escoe v. Zerbst, 295 U.S. 490 (1935). But *cf.* Fleming v. Tate, 156 F.2d 848 (D.C. Cir. 1946); Hiatt v. Campagna, 178 F.2d 42 (5th Cir. 1949), *aff'd per curiam by equally divided court,* 340 U.S. 880 (1950).

or from a technical violation of the conditions of parole. The frequency of revocations is commonly taken to be a measure of the effectiveness of parole as a treatment or deterrent device. In fact, however, "violation rates" reflect the influence of a number of variables that differ from state to state. Especially significant among these are the nature of the parole conditions established and the relative severity of the paroling authority in revoking for technical violations. Other significant variables are the percentage of prisoners who are released on parole, the proportion of offenders released who are serious and repetitive, the length of stay in prison before release, the duration of parole supervision after release and before discharge (or revocation), the nature and intensity of parole supervision (both in its treatment and policing aspects), and the tolerance of the paroling agency for technical violations.

In part because of these variations, parole revocation rates are not comparable from one jurisdiction to another. For example, an apparently high rate of parole success may reflect a very cautious policy of the releasing agency in paroling only the best risks, on the one hand, or a failure of the supervising agency to discover and act on violations that occur, on the other. In at least one jurisdiction, it has been reported, absconding parolees are simply closed out from the case load and do not appear in their statistical reports as violators.[k]

When no hearing is provided there is usually some form of internal agency review of a revocation decision. The initial invocation of the revocation process by the individual field agent is ordinarily simply a recommendation to a supervisor, to the parole board, or to some higher authority who alone has the formally delegated power to order revocation. While in the normal process of administrative routinization this review may become a rubber-stamp process, at least it exists as a form of separation of decision-making authority much as the parole board in its release function is detached from institutional personnel.

Occasionally, the initiating parole officer may be personally interviewed by a supervisor or a parole board member but the probationer or parolee himself is not heard while in the field.

[k] Statistics also often distinguish between revocations for convictions of new offenses and revocations for rules violations, to avoid the inference that all offenders revoked are recidivists. Yet this classification must be used cautiously, since a new offense may be merely drunk and disorderly while a rule violation revocation may be just a convenient alternative to prosecution for a new offense, particularly when there is substantial time remaining on the original sentence.

WISCONSIN CRIMINAL PROCEDURE
Note, 1966 Wisconsin Law Review 430, 527-29

Revocation of Probation and Parole

a. Administrative Procedure and Internal Review

An offender convicted of a felony outside Milwaukee County who is placed on probation or released on parole is in the legal custody of the Department of Public Welfare. Statutory powers given the department to revoke probation and parole are very broad. Probationers convicted of felonies (outside Milwaukee County) may be brought before the court for sentence. Probationer must be sentenced without further stay, or, if already sentenced, he may be ordered directly to an institution. Parolees may be returned to prison at any time on order of the department. When an agent makes a decision to recommend revocation, the probationer or parolee is placed in custody if he is available and not already in custody. If further investigation by the agent substantiates the decision to recommend revocation, the agent summarizes the reasons for revocation and submits a case history, summary, and recommendation to his district administrator. If the district administrator concurs in the recommendation to revoke, he submits the recommendation to the regional supervisor. If the regional supervisor concurs, the recommendation is submitted to the Director of the Department of Public Welfare. It is the decision by the director to accept the recommendation which makes revocation effective. Upon revocation the offender is returned to prison.

Administrative decisions reversing the recommendation of the revoking agent seldom occur. The theory of corrections places a strong emphasis on the relationship between the individual agent and the parolee. Thus a supervisor would be loath to interfere with the agent's discretion.

The parole board sees all parole violators whose parole has been revoked approximately thirty days after the violator's arrival at the prison. This appearance is a personal one, no representation of the prisoner's interest being allowed at the hearing. The purpose of the hearing is to determine the amount of good conduct time to be forfeited because of violation and to determine the time for the next parole hearing. The grounds for and the propriety of the revocation are in issue, but only to the extent that parole can be reinstated if the board determines that the revocation was unwarranted. However, reinstatement is seldom recommended.

The theory behind the relatively simple revocation procedure in Wisconsin is that probation and parole can be more freely granted and liberally administered if the probationer or parolee can be returned to prison without having to go through a highly formalized adversary proceeding. The department takes the position that if the revocation decision were to be subject to judicial challenge, society's best interests would not be served since the standard for grant would have to be tightened and fewer probations and paroles granted.

One position is that parole revocations are not substantially different from revocations of probation and that the same procedures should be followed and the same rights afforded the person affected. There are, however, some important differences of setting and personnel. Probation revocation hearings are conducted by a judicial officer whereas parole revocation hearings are conducted by parole commissioners or other correctional administrators.

a. *The Requirement of a Hearing*

As noted above in the Model Penal Code commentary, a revocation hearing is often provided for by statute or is held as a matter of administrative practice. Nonetheless the hearing procedure is not used everywhere either for probation or for parole revocation. The Supreme Court long ago indicated that federal probation revocation hearings were the creature of statute, not of the Constitution.[l] Despite this, there has been a continuing feeling on the part of some courts that fundamental fairness requires that notice and hearing be given one being deprived of his freedom, even if that freedom is conditional.

PEOPLE v. COFFMAN

83 Ill. App. 2d 272, 227 N.E.2d 108 (1967)

SMITH, J. The defendant, a seventeen-year-old high school student, pleaded guilty to a charge of deceptive practices in writing a $10 check on his older brother's account and was placed on probation. Six weeks later, the probation was revoked

---

[l] Escoe v. Zerbst, 295 U.S. 490, 492 (1935): "[W]e do not accept the petitioner's contention that the privilege has a basis in the Constitution, apart from any statute."

and the defendant was sentenced to the Illinois State Farm at Vandalia, Illinois, for one year. In appealing from this order, his principal contention is that he was denied procedural due process of law in that the revocation order was entered without benefit of counsel.

The revocation proceedings was instituted by an unverified motion of the probation officer charging that the defendant was not at his home during the entire night of September 30, and during the entire night of October 1, and that such conduct on his part violated the provisions of the probation order which required the defendant to be at his place of residence between the hours of 11:00 p.m. and sunrise each and every night unless he had the consent of the probation officer to do otherwise. On the call of the motion, the defendant appeared in open court along with the State's Attorney and the defendant was presented with a copy of the motion to revoke probation. At the court's direction, the State's Attorney then read the entire motion to revoke in open court. Thereupon the following proceedings were had:

"The Court: What is your pleasure about this? Do you want a hearing? Do you want to confess it or what do you want to do?

"(Hesitation by the defendant—he does not answer)

"The Court: You understand you are entitled to a hearing on this?

"Defendant: Yeh.

"The Court: But it is a hearing before the Court and not before a jury.

"(The defendant is not responsive)

"The Court: I am waiting for your reply. I want to give you full time to consider it, if you want further time to consider it I will give it to you. If the facts are true. . . .

"Defendant: (Interpose) They are true.

"The Court: You admit the statements as set forth in the Motion as being true and correct?

"Defendant: Yes.

"The Court: Show—

"Defendant upon consideration of motion confesses same and admits as to the truth thereof. Hearing on Motion. Motion allowed. Order of Probation set aside and vacated and defendant sentenced, by reason of the conviction herein, to the Illinois State Farm at Vandalia, Illinois, for a period of one year and to pay costs. Mittimus to issue accordingly.

"The Court: You will go with the Sheriff."

The statute antedating our present Criminal Code set out the ground rules for a revocation of probation. Among other things, it required that the defendant be furnished with a copy of the charge, that a hearing date should be set by the court allowing the probationer reasonable time to prepare his defense, and specifically giving to him the right to have counsel, coextensive with that right in the action which resulted in such probation. Ill Rev Stats 1963, c 38, § 789.1. The State urges that the repeal of this section and the elimination of these provisions in the new Criminal Code relating to probation, Ill Rev Stats 1965, c 38, § 117-1, 2 and 3, reflects a deliberate intention on the part of the Legislature to change the law as to these requirements. Such a conclusion is foreclosed by the due process provisions of the Fifth, Sixth and Fourteenth Amendments to the Constitution of the United States and by Article II, § 2, of the Illinois State Constitution. Due process may not be limited, delimited, circumscribed, modified or denied by legislative enactment.

A probation system has been a part of the Illinois law since 1911. Laws, 1911, p 277. It has undergone many statutory revisions and the case law prescribing and outlining the metes and bounds of the system are numerous. An extensive and careful study of the procedure required is set forth in People v. Price, 24 Ill App 2d 364, 164 NE2d 528. See also People v. Franciere, 47 Ill App 2d 436, 198 NE2d 170; State v. Headrick, 54 Ill App 2d 44, 203 NE2d 157; People v. Dwyer, 57 Ill App 2d 343, 206 NE2d 113. In our judgment, the present Criminal Code must be interpreted in the light of these cases and that to "conduct a hearing" as the statute requires necessitates the procedure spelled out in them.

In People v. Burrell, 334 Ill App 253, 79 NE2d 88, the defendant did not have an attorney and the then statute did not require one. The Appellate Court reversed the order revoking probation and said that justice required that the defendant be given an opportunity to obtain an attorney, and on the other hand if the court was not willing to continue the cause for that purpose, that the defendant should have been offered the services of the public defender. In Franciere, the defendant was likewise without an attorney. The State's Attorney confessed error under Ill Rev Stats c 38, § 789.1, which required the opportunity for an attorney and stated that the hearing on the revocation of probation was "conducted in violation of [defendant's] statutory and constitutional rights to counsel." In Price, the Appellate Court said: "It has frequently been said that notice to a defendant[m]

---

[m] People v. Dwyer, 57 Ill. App. 2d 343, 206 N.E.2d 113 (1965), part of which appears at 938, *infra,* illustrates the requirement of notice. After

and opportunity to be heard are fundamental requirements and coexistent essentials of the constitutional guaranty of due process of law. While our Probation Act contains no such express requirement our courts have held that such rights are conferred. (Citing Cases.)" People v. Price, 24 Ill App 2d 364, 376, 164 NE2d 528, 533. In Headrick, the court suggests that the procedure to revoke an order admitting a defendant to probation is of no serious consequence so long as the defendant has been given due notice, a copy of the charge, the opportunity to be heard, and a conscientious judicial determination has been made, according to accepted and well recognized procedural methods upon the question of his violation of the conditions of probation. This, the court said, would include the right to counsel and a reasonable time to prepare his defense. Thus our courts have, sometimes with the aid of statutory specifications and sometimes without, spelled out the requirements of procedural due process.

We do not imply that these rights may not be waived by any adult or by one under 18 years with the advice of counsel, if knowingly and understandingly done. The record before us fails to show either that the defendant knew of those rights or that he was advised of them or that he knowingly waived them. Indeed it is a paradox in itself to say that you may knowingly and understandingly waive rights of which you have no knowledge. There was no waiver here.

We would further observe that Ill Rev Stats c 38, § 113-5, provides that no person under the age of eighteen years shall be permitted to plead guilty or waive trial by jury in any case except where the penalty is a fine only unless he is represented by counsel in open court. Supreme Court Rule No. 401(c) appears to have broadened the base of this statute by saying that in *no case* shall a plea of guilty or a waiver of indictment or a trial by jury be accepted from a person under the age of eighteen years unless he is represented by counsel in open court. The solicitude thus expressed for a defendant under eighteen years of age should apply to this seventeen-year-old defendant on a plea of guilty to a violation of probation. Such a plea can and it did here result in incarceration. His liberty and his freedom is as much at stake in this plea of guilty to a violation of probation as it was in his original plea to the criminal charge. It is the pronouncement of an incongruity to say that advice of counsel is

---

the revocation hearing the probation officer was allowed to specify additional grounds for his recommendation, based on evidence presented at the hearing. The court reversed the revocation for this error as well as the insufficiency of the evidence.

essential and required in the latter, but not in the former where a seventeen-year-old is involved. He had counsel in the original suit. He had none here. Substantial justice and due process require that the order revoking probation be reversed and remanded to the trial court with directions to proceed in conformity with the views herein expressed. It is so ordered.

Reversed and remanded.

CRAVEN, P. J. and TRAPP, J., concur.[n]

When the hearing is held, there is wide variation in the degree to which it approaches the traditional judicial hearing.

STATE v. EDELBLUTE

91 Idaho 469, 424 P.2d 739 (1967)

MCQUADE, Justice. Appellant's assignments of error present the basic question: whether, at the probation revocation proceeding below, denial of appellant's motion to quash the bench warrant restraining him, and the judge's refusal before revoking probation to allow appellant to adduce testimony and offer other evidence regarding the alleged violations of probation and his general rehabilitory behavior, were within the court's discretion or, to the contrary, constituted arbitrary acts outside the judge's power?

In its broadest form, the issue here is joined by respondent's statement, "Probation is a privilege, an act of grace," and appellant's position, "violation of probation must be proved." In probation revocation proceedings while the probation violation need not be proved within the strict framework of a criminal trial, nevertheless a probationer is entitled to judicial process which contemplates a hearing. The legal status of a probationer is placed in the limbo between citizenship's complete constitutional protection and the loss of civil rights. Thus, although the full scope of Constitutional Due Process, U.S. Const., Amend. XIV; Idaho Const. art. I, § 13, may not encompass proceedings pertinent to probation, Escoe v. Zerbst, 295 U.S. 490 (1935), nevertheless, fundamental considerations of fairness and sound judicial administration cannot tolerate an arbitrary deprivation of a probationer's liberty.

---

[n] In State v. Zolantakis, 70 Utah 296, 259 P. 1044 (1927) (decided 3-2), and McPhie v. Turner, 10 Utah 2d 237, 351 P.2d 91 (1960) (decided 3-2), the court found in general policy—without expressly invoking the Constitution—a requirement of notice and hearing prior to revocation of probation (and, in dictum, parole) wherever there is room for dispute about the basis of revocation. *Cf.* Baine v. Beckstead, 10 Utah 2d 4, 347 P.2d 554 (1959).

Both legislation and decisional law mandate that a probationer have a significant hearing before revocation of his probation. Idaho statutes require that before a bench warrant issue, the probationer's violation be "proved" to the satisfaction of the court, I.C. § 19-2602, and that if judgment is to be pronounced he must be "brought before the court," I.C. § 19-2603, and granted a "summary hearing." I.C. § 20-222. This court's decisions demand that probationers receive "full opportunity to present evidence," State v. Freeman [85 Idaho 339, 379 P.2d 632 (1963)], and "a reasonable opportunity to examine" adverse evidence lest the "opportunity to present evidence . . . be meaningless," State v. Grady [89 Idaho 204, 404 P.2d 347 (1965)], for only thus can there be assurance that the trial judge has fulfilled his duty to " 'give consideration to the application and grant or deny the same in the exercise of a sound, legal discretion.' " State v. Mitchell [77 Idaho 115, 289 P.2d 315 (1955)].

In the instant case, revocation of appellant's two-year-old probation was grounded on his police court conviction for reckless driving and his 8:55 p.m. visit to the city of Lewiston. It was first argued on appellant's behalf that he had not been present during his police court trial and so had not been duly convicted of reckless driving; (although the district judge at the revocation proceeding doubted appellant's earlier absence in police court, this claim was in fact true as the district judge himself noted in his order denying bail pending appeal); and that an appeal from the reckless driving conviction was pending in district court, (as herein noted by footnote, a jury in the district court found appellant not guilty). Appellant contended that probation officer Callahan had given appellant permission to be in Lewiston at the time of his allegedly forbidden visit. Further, appellant's attorney sought to introduce evidence regarding appellant's rehabilitation, including the testimony of the boy's employer, an adult neighbor, a social worker and a Job Corps official. (In his order denying bail, the judge noted that probation officer Callahan had indicated that as far as he knew appellant's work record was good.)

The original order for appellant's probation, in the extracts set out above, delegated supervisory responsibility over him to the state director of probation and parole. This effectively placed appellant under district agent Callahan's primary supervision. Denying appellant an opportunity to support his position with Callahan's testimony considering the control which he exercised over the boy probably made any showing by appellant hopeless from the beginning. It is perhaps noteworthy that the proceedings to revoke appellant's probation were instituted only when the judge himself, according to his order denying bail pending appeal, "directed the probation officer to make an investigation," "due to a newspaper account" that the reckless driving conviction was pending on appeal to the district court. Probation officer Callahan, however, took no action against the boy until so ordered by the judge, and his report was filed on June 4, 1965, forty-one days after he learned of the incident.

Further since "the purpose of the probation statute is nothing more or less than rehabilitation," Franklin v. State, supra, 87 Idaho at 307, 392 P.2d at 562 (separate opinion of McQuade, J.), it was an essential function of proper judicial administration that the judge, before revocation, should have allowed appellant to present evidence regarding his rehabilitation period. It would also have been proper and important to the revocation decision for appellant to have shown circumstances relating to the after-dark condition which he allegedly violated.

The statutes and decisional law herein require that a probation revocation hearing must be based upon charges sufficiently specific that the probationer be informed of the allegedly violated term or condition of the probation order and the manner and circumstances of his violation so that he can intelligently prepare his defense. He must also be allowed to call witnesses under oath, to testify himself and otherwise to produce evidence in his own behalf, provided, of course, that all evidence be related to the subject of the inquiry, i.e., has he in fact violated his probation agreement in a manner which demonstrates that he no longer deserves his circumscribed liberty? A probationer must also be given a reasonable opportunity to examine and rebut adverse evidence, and to cross-examine hostile witnesses. These procedures are essential to satisfy the standard of "full opportunity to present evidence in their [probationers'] behalf," and to guarantee that this opportunity not "be meaningless."

Respondent says that if procedures even slightly less strict than the foregoing are "necessary requisites [for a probation revocation hearing] respondent is unable to distinguish a 'summary hearing' [I.C. § 20-222] from a formal judicial proceeding." The differences from formal criminal proceedings, however, are quite obvious. The probation revocation standards do not include an indictment or a preliminary hearing; nor must there be trial by jury; nor proof beyond a reasonable doubt. But although the full stringency of the criminal law is not here applicable, nevertheless the proprieties of judicial administration do insist that if probation is to be revoked, judicial process must be observed.

Reversed and remanded for further proceedings.

MOTTRAM v. STATE
232 A.2d 809 (Me. 1967)

DUFRESNE, Justice. On appeal from the denial by a single Justice sitting in the Superior Court of Robert H. Mottram's petition for the writ of habeas corpus. The petitioner was convicted of the crime of grand larceny and sentenced to State Prison. On November 15, 1963 he was released from the penal institution on parole. Arrested on February 12, 1965 and returned to prison, Mottram was given a hearing before the Board at the prison on February 26, 1965, and the Board determined that he had violated the terms and conditions of his parole and ordered the same revoked.

The single Justice made the following findings:

"I find that when the petitioner appeared before the Board on February 26, 1965 the proceedings were informal. The petitioner obviously viewed this 'hearing' as in the nature of a trial and in effect demanded the usual formalities attendant thereon such as a written presentation of the charges of parole violation, confrontation by his 'accusers' and the like. The charges were not formalized. The Board verbally asked for his version of certain incidents which had come to their attention and in each instance the petitioner responded either by denial or excuse. I find that by means of this interview method the petitioner was made aware of the matters which were under consideration as possible reasons for revocation and was fully heard as to each. The petitioner was offered the opportunity to present witnesses but he declined on the ground that he had not been formally charged with specific parole violations. In general the petitioner demanded the 'right to counsel.' He was not accompanied by counsel of his own choice nor did he request that any specifically named attorney be permitted to be present. Neither did he request that the Board appoint counsel to represent him. . . . In the instant case the petitioner appeared, full inquiry was made and he was 'heard' as to aspects of his conduct which bore directly upon the advisability of continued parole. In my view the 'hearing' requirement of this particular statute was thereby satisfied."

The issue arises by reason of the provisions of 34 M.R.S.A. § 1675 which reads as follows:

"Violation of parole.

"[*T*]*he board shall hold a hearing. The parolee is entitled to appear and be heard.*"

In final analysis, the issue is, what type of hearing did the Legislature have in mind in parole violation proceedings and what rights did it grant the parolee when it legislated that he is entitled to appear and be heard.

To the extent that the parolee must strictly observe all the conditions of his parole and remain within the area of permitted enlargement of the prison walls consistent with effective supervision, he is not a totally free man. The Legislature, in adopting the parole system and providing a rehabilitation program for prisoners undoubtedly took into consideration that at this level the prisoner's guilt had been established, presumably after full compliance with all the constitutional requirements of due process, and that in setting up the mechanics for parole revocation it could rest the same upon the absolute discretion of the Parole Board or it could circumscribe the retaking of a paroled prisoner by such procedural requirements as it deemed necessary in its own uncontrolled wisdom. In short, our lawmakers knew that parolees, if they violated their parole, were not entitled to the same procedural safeguards constitutionally necessary in the case of persons accused of crime.

Under related federal legislation directing that the prisoner retaken upon the Parole Board's warrant "shall be given an opportunity to appear before the Board, a member thereof, or an examiner designated by the Board," some authorities such as Hyser v. Reed, 1963, 115 U.S. App. D.C. 254, 318 F.2d 225 and Jones v. Rivers, 4th Cir., 1964, 338 F.2d 862, have construed the act of Congress to mean that the parolee must be informed prior to hearing of his right to be represented by retained counsel and of the nature of the violations claimed against him, and that at the hearing he must be given the opportunity to produce and present voluntary witnesses.

The *Hyser* rule however does not impress us as an indispensable intendment of legislative design. Rather, we equate the reference right to appear before the Board and be heard with the ancient common law privilege extended in certain jurisdictions in capital cases whereby the accused otherwise disqualified was allowed to make a statement to the jury and thus tell his story in exculpation, not on oath and not as a witness, but in the guise of an address or argument.

In the first place, we must bear in mind that the Legislature has delegated to the same agency, to wit, the Probation and Parole Board, the revocation of parole as well as the original grant thereof; where no specific type of hearing was indicated in either case, should we not presume uniformity of concept in the legislative mind whether the Board acts in a case of original parole or of revocation thereof?

Nobody has ever claimed, nor is it presently contended, that a prisoner eligible for a hearing in an initial potential grant of parole, was entitled to a quasi judicial hearing thereon.

We note that the Legislature provided for the appointment of two of the three members of the Board to be made "from persons with special training or experience in law, sociology, psychology or related branches of social science." 34 M.R.S.A. § 1551. It granted the Board, in the administration of the parole law, in general terms broad powers and duties to "formulate policies, adopt regulations, *establish* organizational and *operational procedures,* and exercise general supervision." [Emphasis mine.] 34 M.R.S.A. § 1552(1).

Under these broad legislative duties and powers, the Parole Board has established and maintained since the general revision of the probation and parole law by the Legislature in 1957, [P.L. 1957, c. 387], the conference or interview type of hearing under the law, whether in the grant or the revocation of parole.

To place any other construction on the statute would be subversive of its real purpose and might well result in infinite difficulty for the Board. Indeed, if the action of the Board in determining that a paroled convict has been a parole violator and should be re-imprisoned could not be taken until after a judicial inquiry, as distinguished from an administrative investigation, the resulting burdens of administration on the Board and its desire to protect society would undoubtedly discourage the Board from granting many paroles that it otherwise would grant. Such negative attitude on the part of the Board would defeat the whole purpose of the parole law which is to give deserving convicted persons as early as the law will permit the opportunity of self-help in their own rehabilitation outside the strict regimentation of the penal institution.

In many instances, potential witnesses knowledgeable of facts which have escaped the observation of the parole officer are fearful of testifying publicly against a paroled convict. If revocation of parole depended upon a full judicial hearing, then undeserving parolees would roam the streets with impunity for their breach of faith long after their freedom privileges should have been revoked for factual violations of the terms of their parole.

There is no stronger deterrent against parole violations than the knowledge of the parolee that any violation of the terms of his parole shall result in his immediate and sure return to his cell behind prison walls without delay or legal intricacies.

Furthermore, the Board is given no power to issue subpoenas nor swear witnesses. The Act contemplates speedy determination of parole violations as it directs that the Board shall hold a hearing thereon at its next meeting at the institution to which the parolee was returned upon his arrest and from which he was paroled, no mention being made of continuances to be granted to the parolee for preparation of his defense. No appeal has been provided from the Board's determination of violation of parole. The absence of these accessorial provisions usually associated with a judicial hearing support our view and those of the Justice below to the effect that Mottram was provided with the type of hearing which our statute, 34 M.R.S.A. § 1675, requires when he was granted the privilege to appear and address the Board in excuse or exculpation of the charges made against him respecting violation of his parole. The law contemplates that the Board shall be guided by the information which has become available to it through its own investigation procedures and is not to be circumscribed by evidence to be produced at a judicial hearing. Revocation of parole is an administrative function under our law rather than a quasi court procedure.

Appeal denied.

MODEL PENAL CODE § 305.15
American Law Institute
(Proposed Official Draft 1962)

Section 305.15. Revocation of Parole for Violation of Condition; Hearing.

(1) When a parolee has been returned to the institution, the Board of Parole shall hold a hearing within sixty days of his return to determine whether his parole should be revoked. The parolee shall have reasonable notice of the charges filed. The institutional parole staff shall render reasonable aid to the parolee in preparation for the hearing and he shall be permitted to advise with his own legal counsel. At the hearing the parolee may admit, deny, or explain the violation charged, and he may present proof, including affidavits and other evidence, in support of his contention. A verbatim record of the hearing shall be made and preserved.

(2) The Board may order revocation of parole if it is satisfied, upon substantial evidence, that:

(a) the parolee has failed, without a satisfactory excuse, to comply with a substantial requirement imposed as a condition of his parole; and

(b) the violation of condition involves:

(i) the commission of another crime; or

(ii) conduct indicating a substantial risk that the parolee will commit another crime; or

(iii) conduct indicating that the parolee is unwilling to comply with proper conditions of parole.

(3) Parole revocation shall be by majority vote of the Board.

b. The Evidentiary Standards

The evidentiary standards in revocation proceedings are not well settled. If revocation in the unfettered discretion of the responsible agency is permitted, such evidence as is satisfactory to the agency may be sufficient. Only the most clearly arbitrary decision could be challenged successfully.

HYSER v. REED

318 F.2d 225, 242 (D.C. Cir. 1963)

We have noted that the parole of prisoners is one of the chief tools in the rehabilitation process. The procedures for terminating parole are simply an acknowledgement that in granting parole some errors will be made and the errant parolee must be retaken for his own good as well as that of society. The more relaxed are the standards for parole release the greater will be the proportion of such "errors." Congress had a dual purpose in setting up a statutory provision for the issuance of an administrative arrest warrant for parolees: (1) provide a means to retake the parolee and to pursue inquiry into the alleged revocation, and (2) provide minimum safeguards for the parolee. The Board recognized this in its regulations making the issuance of a warrant depend upon the existence of "satisfactory evidence." Parole Board Directive No. 1, § 2.35, 27 Fed.Reg. 8490 (Aug. 24, 1962).

It is therefore plain that parole cannot be revoked arbitrarily, as for example to supply the prison with a parolee who is a trained medical technician. Revocation must be for "cause." "Satisfactory evidence" of parole violation must appear. The basis for Board action in revoking parole must have a rational and legitimate relationship to whether the parolee is a good parole risk. What constitutes such cause is left by Congress to the discretion of the Board and judicial review of its exercise is very limited. The functions of the Parole Board involve the application of blended concepts of criminology, penology, and psychology, and if the doctrine of "administrative expertise" should carry weight anywhere it should do so in this area. It is worth repeating that the Board which revokes parole is the same Board which grants parole; its whole orientation is to *release* prisoners and to keep them at liberty.

WILLIAMS v. DUNBAR

377 F.2d 505, 506 (9th Cir. 1967)

MADDEN, Judge. The appellant's mere conclusory allegation that the decision of the California authorities that he had violated the terms of his parole was arbitrary and capricious does not raise a constitutional question. In its context in the papers which appellant has filed it is apparent that he means that it was wrong for the parole officer to conclude that the fact that someone had entered the home of the appellant's wife with a key and had destroyed hundreds of dollars worth of her clothes and personal belongings, while leaving the appellant's clothes untouched, and that the appellant had admittedly been in the home shortly after the destruction but had made no report to his parole officer of the existing and important event, could reasonably be regarded as indicating at least that the appellant was not cooperating with his parole officer's efforts to keep him out of trouble, and that it would be best for the appellant and the public for him to be confined. This kind of judgment is for the parole authorities, not for the courts.

PEOPLE v. DWYER

57 Ill. App. 2d 343, 206 N.E.2d 113 (1965)

CORYN, J. This is an appeal by the defendant, James Paul Dwyer, from an order of the County Division of the Circuit Court of McDonough County, revoking defendant's probation.

The defendant was found guilty of operating a motor vehicle on a public highway while his operator's license was suspended, in violation of c 95½, § 6-303, of Ill Rev Stats 1963. On April 1, 1964, the defendant was granted probation for a period of three years.

On May 25, 1964, the Probation Officer filed a report with the court charging that the defendant had violated the terms of his probation by being involved with two other persons in the theft of a tire from a service station at Table Grove, Illinois, and by having in his possession twelve cans of beer. This report sought a rule against defendant to show cause why his probation should not be revoked.

On June 5, 1964, a hearing was held on the report of the Probation Officer, at which time the defendant appeared in person and was represented by counsel. At the conclusion of the hearing, the court entered an order finding that the defendant had violated the order granting probation "in that he committed the offense of theft, . . ."

Chapter 38, § 117-3(b), Ill Rev Stats 1963, provides that the State shall have the burden of proving a violation of probation. In People v. Price, 24 Ill App 2d 364, at 379, 164 NE2d 528, it was held that the violation of probation must be proved by a preponderance of the evidence.

On May 22, 1964, the defendant, his brother Tim, and Bill Trumbull were traveling through Table Grove, Illinois, where they stopped at a service station.

A short time thereafter, Abernathy [the station attendant] was informed by Eugene Bean, who was not called as a witness, that a tire was missing. Abernathy called the sheriff, who later apprehended the defendant while he was sitting in the parked automobile. The sheriff requested that the trunk of the automobile be opened, whereupon the stolen tire was discovered.

The defendant testified that he did not take the tire or know of its presence in the automobile. Tim Dwyer testified that he stole the tire from the storeroom of the service station when the defendant and Abernathy were mounting a tire on the rim. Tim Dwyer further stated that the act of stealing this tire was an unplanned, spur of the moment decision. He stated that the trunk of the car was open and that he threw the tire into the trunk, closed the trunk, and walked back into the service station. He stated that his brother, the defendant, knew nothing about the theft of this tire. The record, in view of the uncontradicted testimony of Tim Dwyer, does not sustain a finding that the defendant participated in the theft of the tire or had knowledge of this theft.

We are of the opinion that justice requires that the revocation order be reversed.

Reversed.

Alloy, P. J. and Stouder, J., concur.

SCOTT v. STATE

238 Md. 265, 208 A.2d 575 (1965)

Hammond, J., delivered the opinion of the Court.

On October 30, 1963, Scott pleaded guilty to robbery before Judge Harris. The admitted facts were that he attacked a woman late at night in a parking lot, striking her in the face with his fist, and seized her handbag. He was given three years. On December 23, 1963, Judge Harris, after receiving a probation report that Scott had a sound family and employment background and no prior criminal record, "reluctantly acceded to the recommendation of the Probation Department," suspended the balance of the sentence and placed him on probation for three years, subject to the conditions of probation customarily imposed in Baltimore (to which Scott agreed in writing) including the condition that the released person "shall conduct himself in a law-abiding manner."

On January 19, 1964, Scott was charged with assault with intent to rape a seventy-one-year-old woman and common assault upon her. Passersby came to the assistance of the victim, a Mrs. Grimes, and the assailant, becoming frightened, ran away, leaving his hat at the scene. The State then proffered the testimony of the arresting police officer that he had shown the hat to Scott's mother and that she had identified it as her son's. Judge Harris refused to receive the proffered testimony on the ground that it would be hearsay. The jury acquitted Scott.

Thereafter, Judge Harris advised Scott's court-appointed lawyer, Mr. Russell White (who, upon designation of Judge Harris, has well represented Scott in this appeal), that he felt he must revoke Scott's probation because he was convinced by the facts, as to the identification of the hat, which the State was unable to get before the jury, that Scott had committed the assaults and sent Scott back to the Maryland Institution for Men to serve the two years and eight months remaining of the three-year sentence which had been imposed on October 30, 1963.

We think that Scott has no just cause for complaint that his conditional freedom was ended by Judge Harris. Probation is a matter of grace, which aside from being an act of clemency extended to one who has committed a crime, is in substance and effect a bargain made by the people, through legislation and the courts, with the malefactor that he may be free as long as he conducts himself in a manner consonant with established communal standards and the safety of society. It offers the young or unhardened offender an opportunity to rehabilitate himself without confinement under the tutelage of a probation officer and there may be attached to the opportunity the condition that it may be ended, if the court is reasonably persuaded, by knowledge of facts, even if obtained more informally than the rules of evidence would permit it to be obtained in a trial, that it should be. Probation is a personal privilege of which the grantee may not be deprived arbitrarily or capriciously, but if one charged with breach of probation is given notice of the charges of violation of the conditions and the opportunity to answer or explain the facts which have come to the knowledge of the judge, even though not in the manner required by the rules of evidence, and the facts justify revocation, the act of revocation is not arbitrary or capricious.

In the determination of a proper sentence a judge may utilize information obtained outside the courtroom, information furnished by those not subject to cross-examination and sometimes hearsay (provided that information not received from or in the presence of the defendant should be called to his attention so that he has the opportunity to refute, discredit or explain it—unless under Md. Rule 761d the court directs otherwise as to a presentence report). There is clearly a similarity between the process of determining a proper sentence originally and the process of determining whether to revoke probation and reinstate or impose a sentence, and the judge in the latter instance may, with similar safeguards, utilize the ways of acquiring knowledge bearing on the problem that the judge utilizes in determining a proper sentence originally.

The facts presented to or coming to the knowledge of the judge, as to the breach of the conditions of probation, need not establish guilt beyond a reasonable doubt as in criminal offenses; all that is required is that the facts before him be such that the judge reasonably could be satisfied that the conduct of the probationer has not been what he agreed it would be if he were given liberty.

These considerations underlie the decisions that hold or indicate that acquittal of a probationer of a charge of criminal conduct which was a violation of probation does not preclude revocation of probation, if the judge passing on the question is with reason satisfied that the probationer actually did that charged in the indictment on which he was acquitted.

In re BROWN

62 Cal. Rptr. 6, 431 P.2d 630 (1967)

[A parolee was revoked on two grounds: conviction of a new crime of first degree robbery and the rules infraction of driving an automobile without the permission of his parole officer. The parolee's conviction was overturned on appeal on grounds that his confessions were inadmissible, consistent with the *Escobedo* and *Dorado* decisions. He was held in prison, however, on the basis of his parole revocation. He challenged this by a habeas corpus petition.]

TOBRINER, Justice. The Attorney General argues, however, that defendant is not entitled to release from prison because he is still held under a valid conviction in 1955, also for first degree robbery. At the time petitioner allegedly committed the robbery that was the subject of his invalid trial, defendant was on parole from his earlier prison term. The Adult Authority had fixed his term at 10 years, to expire on April 5, 1965, and had released him on parole on October 5, 1960. After his conviction in 1962 and during the pendency of his appellate remedies, while the Adult Authority still could exercise jurisdiction over defendant because his term had not yet expired, the Adult Authority revoked his parole, refixed his term at maximum (life), and ordered him returned to the state prison. Two grounds provided the basis for this action. The first rested upon his commission of a robbery, as evidenced by his 1962 conviction, and the second involved his driving a motor vehicle without the knowledge or permission of his parole officer.

The Adult Authority cannot suspend or revoke parole without cause for doing so, and that cause must be stated in the order suspending or revoking parole. (Pen. Code, § 3063.) Because of its invalidity, the 1962 robbery conviction cannot constitute cause for parole revocation. (Cf. In re Hall (1965) 63 Cal. 2d 115, 117, 45 Cal. Rptr. 133, 403 P.2d 389.) The revocation, however, as we have noted, also rested upon the second, less serious, charge. We do not know, of course, that the Adult Authority would have taken the same action regarding defendant if the only charge of misconduct against him had been that he had driven a car without permission. Because the Adult Authority based its action upon two grounds and the more substantial of these lacks validity, we must order that the Authority reconsider its prior action.

c. *The Right to Be Represented by Counsel*

MEMPA v. RHAY

389 U.S. 128 (1967)

MR. JUSTICE MARSHALL delivered the opinion of the Court.

These consolidated cases raise the question of the extent of the right to counsel at the time of sentencing where the sentencing has been deferred subject to probation.

Petitioner Jerry Douglas Mempa was convicted in the Spokane County Superior Court on June 17, 1959, of the offense of "joyriding," Wash. Rev. Code § 9.54.020. This conviction was based on his plea of guilty entered with the advice of court-appointed counsel. He was then placed on probation for two years on the condition, *inter alia,* that he first spend 30 days in the county jail, and the imposition of sentence was deferred pursuant to Wash. Rev. Code §§ 9.95.200, 9.95.210.[1]

About four months later the Spokane County prosecuting attorney moved to have petitioner's probation revoked on the ground that he had been involved in a burglary on September 15, 1959. A hearing was held in the Spokane County Superior Court on October 23, 1959. Petitioner Mempa, who was 17 years old at the time, was accompanied to the hearing by his stepfather. He was not represented by counsel and was not asked whether he wished to have counsel appointed for him. Nor was any inquiry made concerning the appointed counsel who had previously represented him.

At the hearing Mempa was asked if it was true that he had been involved in the alleged burglary and he answered in the affirmative. A probation officer testified without cross-examination that according to his information petitioner had been involved in the burglary and had previously denied participation in it. Without asking petitioner if he had anything to say or any evidence to supply, the court immediately entered an order revoking petitioner's probation and then sentenced him to 10 years in the penitentiary, but stated that it would recommend to the parole board that Mempa be required to serve only a year.[2]

In 1948 this Court held in Townsend v. Burke, 334 U.S. 736, that the absence of counsel during sentencing after a plea of guilty coupled with "assumptions concerning his criminal record which were materially untrue" deprived the defendant in that case of due process. Mr. Justice Jackson there stated in conclusion, "In this case, counsel might not have changed the sentence, but he could have taken steps to see that the conviction and sentence were not predicated on misinformation or misreading of court records, a requirement of fair play which absence of counsel withheld from this prisoner." *Id.*, at 741.

There was no occasion in *Gideon* to enumerate the various stages in a criminal proceeding at which counsel was required,

---

1 The State suggests that the Supreme Court of Washington was in error in stating that Mempa received a deferred rather than a suspended sentence, but we accept that court's characterization of the sentence as supported by the record.

2 Under Washington procedure the trial judge is required by statute to impose the maximum sentence provided by law for the offense, Wash. Rev. Code § 9.95.010, but is also required, along with the prosecuting attorney, to make a recommendation to the parole board of the time that the defendant should serve accompanied by a statement of the facts concerning the crime and any other information about the defendant deemed relevant. Wash. Rev. Code § 9.95.030. However, it is the parole board that actually determines the time to be served. Wash. Rev. Code § 9.95.040.

but *Townsend, Moore,* and *Hamilton,* when the *Betts* requirement of special circumstances is stripped away by *Gideon,* clearly stand for the proposition that appointment of counsel for an indigent is required at every stage of a criminal proceeding where substantial rights of a criminal accused may be affected. In particular, Townsend v. Burke, *supra,* illustrates the critical nature of sentencing in a criminal case and might well be considered to support by itself a holding that the right to counsel applies at sentencing. Many lower courts have concluded that the Sixth Amendment right to counsel extends to sentencing in federal cases.

The State, however, argues that the petitioners were sentenced at the time they were originally placed on probation and that the imposition of sentence following probation revocation is, in effect, a mere formality constituting part of the probation revocation proceeding. It is true that sentencing in Washington offers fewer opportunities for the exercise of judicial discretion than in many other jurisdictions. The applicable statute requires the trial judge in all cases to sentence the convicted person to the maximum term provided by law for the offense of which he was convicted. Wash. Rev. Code § 9.95.010. The actual determination of the length of time to be served is to be made by the Board of Prison Terms and Paroles within six months after the convicted person is admitted to prison. Wash. Rev. Code § 9.95.040.

On the other hand, the sentencing judge is required by statute, together with the prosecutor, to furnish the Board with a recommendation as to the length of time that the person should serve, in addition to supplying it with various information about the circumstances of the crime and the character of the individual. Wash. Rev. Code § 9.95.030. We were informed during oral argument that the Board places considerable weight on these recommendations, although it is in no way bound by them. Obviously to the extent such recommendations are influential in determining the resulting sentence, the necessity for the aid of counsel in marshaling the facts, introducing evidence of mitigating circumstances and in general aiding and assisting the defendant to present his case as to sentence is apparent.

Even more important in a case such as this is the fact that certain legal rights may be lost if not exercised at this stage. For one, Washington law provides that an appeal in a case involving a plea of guilty followed by probation can only be taken after sentence is imposed following revocation of probation. State v. Farmer, 39 Wash. 2d 675, 237 P.2d 734 (1951).[5] Therefore in a

[5] State v. Proctor, 68 Wash. 2d 817, 415 P.2d 634 (1966), modified the *Farmer* rule only to permit an appeal following placement on probation in

case where an accused agreed to plead guilty, although he had a valid defense, because he was offered probation, absence of counsel at the imposition of the deferred sentence might well result in loss of the right to appeal. While ordinarily appeals from a plea of guilty are less frequent than those following a trial on the merits, the incidence of improperly obtained guilty pleas is not so slight as to be capable of being characterized as *de minimis.*

Without undertaking to catalog the various situations in which a lawyer could be of substantial assistance to a defendant in such a case, it can be reiterated that a plea of guilty might well be improperly obtained by the promise to have a defendant placed on the very probation the revocation of which furnishes the occasion for desiring to withdraw the plea. An uncounseled defendant might very likely be unaware of this opportunity.

The two foregoing factors assume increased significance when it is considered that the eventual imposition of sentence on the prior plea of guilty is based on the alleged commission of offenses for which the accused is never tried.

In sum, we do not question the authority of the State of Washington to provide for a deferred sentencing procedure coupled with its probation provisions. Indeed, it appears to be an enlightened step forward. All we decide here is that a lawyer must be afforded at this proceeding whether it be labeled a revocation of probation or a deferred sentencing. We assume that counsel appointed for the purpose of the trial or guilty plea would not be unduly burdened by being requested to follow through at the deferred sentencing stage of the proceeding. Reversed and remanded.

The specific circumstances in *Mempa* and the fact that the issue was resolved as a sentencing matter, leave open the more general question of whether revocation, when not viewed as a continuation of sentencing, requires the probationer to be given constitutional due process protections.

PEOPLE *ex rel.* COMBS v. LaVALLEE
29 App. Div. 2d 128, 286 N.Y.S.2d 600 (1968)

BASTOW, J. In 1961 relator as a second offender was sentenced to a term of 7½ to 15 years' imprisonment. Some four years later

---

cases involving (1) a contested trial and (2) the imposition of a jail term or fine as a condition of probation.

he was released on parole and subsequently was declared delinquent allegedly for failure to report to a parole officer.

During these intervening years relator sought post-conviction relief in both State and Federal courts. In the United States Court of Appeals one Stephen R. Barnett, an attorney in New York City, was designated to represent relator.

It appears that after appellant had absconded from parole supervision this attorney was of some assistance to the authorities in locating relator in New Jersey where he was arrested and returned to this State. During this period of three months Mr. Barnett was in communication with the parole authorities. After relator's return to this jurisdiction the attorney by letter inquired "as to the opportunity for Combs to be represented by counsel at this forthcoming hearing" and offered to provide such legal representation. The offer was rejected with the summary statement that parolees were not entitled to be represented at such a hearing.

Thereafter, an associate of Mr. Barnett, who is now practicing outside of the State, brought this habeas corpus proceeding seeking the release of relator on the ground that his present detention is illegal because of the denial of his right to counsel at the revocation hearing. Special Term denied relief (53 Misc 2d 281).

Section 218 of the Correction Law mandates the warden of a prison to notify the Board of Parole of the return of a paroled prisoner charged with violation of parole. "Thereupon, such board of parole shall, as soon as practicable, hold a parole court at such prison or institution and consider the case of such parole violator, who shall be given an opportunity to appear personally, but not through counsel or others, before such board of parole and explain the charges made against him."

The issue thus presented is whether or not the constitutional rights of appellant to be represented by counsel and to be afforded due process were violated by the refusal of the parole authorities to grant the request of Combs' counsel to be present at the "parole court." We conclude that they were.

We further conclude that this issue may be decided without regard to the Due Process Clause of the Fourteenth Amendment of the Federal Constitution but upon this State's decisional law and the constitutional provisions pertaining to the right to counsel and its guarantee of due process (N.Y. Const., art. I, § 6).

During recent years we have seen a gradual enlargement of the right to counsel of a defendant or of an accused or suspect. Thus, in a series of decisions such right has been extended from the trial itself to pretrial proceedings. Finally, to implement Miranda v. Arizona (384 U.S. 436) the right to counsel has been given to a suspect prior to questioning by law enforcement officers.

Similarly, the right to counsel has been enlarged as to post-conviction proceedings. Thus, in a revocation of probation proceeding where the statute (Code Crim. Pro., § 935) gives the alleged violator "an opportunity to be heard" this court has held that the individual is entitled not only to counsel but to be informed of such right.

Whatever doubt may have existed as to the correctness of these decisions has been swept away by Matter of Gault (387 U.S. 1) and Mempa v. Rhay (389 U.S. 128). Gault was a 15-year-old, who had been placed on probation by a Juvenile Court. Subsequently, he was returned to court on petition of a probation officer. The court summarily dismissed the contention that the probation officer or the Judge could represent the youth and wrote (387 U.S. 1, 36) that "There is no material difference in this respect between adult and juvenile proceedings of the sort here involved. In adult proceedings, this contention has been foreclosed by decisions of this Court" citing Powell v. Alabama (287 U.S. 4, 61 and Gideon v. Wainwright (372 U.S. 335). In Mempa (*supra,* p. 134) the court enunciated the principle "that appointment of counsel for an indigent is required at every stage of a criminal proceeding where substantial rights of a criminal accused may be affected."

It is recognized, as respondent contends, that there are basic differences between probation and parole. The obvious difference is that in the latter the court imposed sentence may not be changed. Second, it might be argued that a violation of parole is no part of a criminal proceeding. We do not view these differences as so vital that counsel should be mandated in the one and denied in the other.

When all the legal niceties are laid aside a proceeding to revoke parole involves the right of an individual to continue at liberty or to be imprisoned. It involves a deprivation of liberty just as much as did the original criminal action and, it is submitted, falls within the due process provision of section 6 of article I of our State Constitution.

While not here controlling, it is of interest to note that the statutes of several States expressly provide that an alleged parole violator is entitled to counsel in a revocation proceeding. (Sklar, Law and Practice in Probation and Parole Revocation Hearings 55 J. Crim. L. [1964], 175, 181-182.) Similarly, the proposed Model Penal Code provides that in preparation for such a hearing the parolee "shall be permitted to advise with his own legal counsel" and at the hearing he "may admit, deny, or explain the violation charged, and he may present proof, including affidavits and other evidence, in support of his contention." (Amer. Law Inst. Model Penal Code, Proposed Official Draft [1962], § 305.15.)

To the plaint that permitting counsel to appear at such a "parole court" might in some fashion be difficult to implement it is only necessary to point out that similar contentions have been summarily brushed aside or ignored in passing on the right to counsel at trials in courts of special sessions; in *coram nobis* proceedings in such inferior courts and in habeas corpus proceedings.

Lastly, we conclude that upon the facts presented habeas corpus is a proper proceeding in which to raise the issue passed upon.

The order should be reversed and an order made directing that if the Board of Parole shall not within 30 days from the date of entry of such order hold a new hearing at which appellant shall have the right to be represented by counsel then the writ shall be sustained and relator discharged from custody.

WILLIAMS, P. J., GOLDMAN, HENRY and MARSH, JJ., concur.

HUTCHISON v. PATTERSON

267 F. Supp. 433 (D. Colo. 1967)

MEMORANDUM OPINION AND ORDER

WILLIAM E. DOYLE, District Judge. Petitioner seeks the issuance of a writ of habeas corpus. Named as respondents are the Warden of the Colorado State Penitentiary and the Colorado State Board of Parole. Petitioner questions the validity of the revocation of his parole status.

In essence, petitioner complains that he was denied counsel at the hearing and was not confronted with witnesses against him. It may be that the law in this respect will change. We note the decision of the United States Supreme Court made recently to review two Washington State cases involving revocation of probation. See Mempa v. Rhay, 386 U.S. 907 and Walkling v. Rhay, 386 U.S. 907. In those cases the question would appear to be whether a defendant in a state court is entitled to counsel at a probation revocation proceeding. But even if the Supreme Court concludes that a probationer is entitled to counsel in a revocation proceeding, there remains basis for distinction between parole revocation and probation revocation. The probationer has a substantially different status from that of the parolee. The imposition of sentence in his case has been suspended and thus unlike the parolee he is not *serving* a sentence while on probation.

Indeed, it would seem desirable as a matter of policy to have counsel in the probation hearing.

Petitioner herein does not contend that he is innocent; rather, his entire emphasis is on the proposition that he is entitled to and was denied procedural due process.

We conclude, however, that his petition is without merit—that he would be in a position to claim violation of his constitutional rights if, and only if the Parole Board had revoked his parole status because of some trivial or inconsequential matter or without making inquiry. The failure to give him a statement of charges or to have a formal trial at which the testimony of witnesses is presented, and failure to recognize a right of cross-examination do not furnish ground for federal action.

The Petition is denied and the Order to Show Cause is discharged.

PART III
THE ADMINISTRATION OF JUVENILE JUSTICE

The criminal justice system is not the only means of dealing with socially deviant conduct. There are at least two other highly developed systems in American society that deal with the same problem: the system of juvenile justice and the procedures for the commitment of the mentally ill. These two systems differ, in principle at least, from the criminal justice system in that their objective is help for the individual, but to accomplish this objective they have both provided for extensive governmental interference with a person's liberty.

The juvenile justice system is of particular interest to a student of criminal justice because both systems often deal with the same kinds of behavior, the choice of system being determined primarily by the age of the offender. Because they are parallel, study of the juvenile system affords an interesting contrast with the adult criminal justice system. In theory, the juvenile justice system has been totally committed to rehabilitation—to the "best interests of the child." The adult system has more often acknowledged an emphasis upon community protection and deterrence of criminal behavior. The juvenile justice system has stressed informality, de-emphasizing procedural formality, while the adult system has been more rule oriented, with elaborate formal procedural safeguards, particularly at the adjudication stage. The juvenile justice system has acknowledged that treating the child by means other than an adjudication of delinquency is desirable while the adult system has been more conviction-oriented.

The two systems are probably less different in practice than they are in theory. Certainly, there is a clear trend in the direction of greater similarity between the two systems. Increasingly, courts and legislatures are concerned with procedural due process requirements in the juvenile justice system and, absent a better alternative, look to the adult system for rules to be applied to the juvenile system. In the adult system, on the other hand, there is growing recognition of the importance of informal disposition of cases without conviction. Certainly the experience in the juvenile system with pre-court disposition is relevant to this changing emphasis in the adult system.

The following materials are not intended to give complete coverage of the law of juvenile delinquency or of all the problems of the juvenile justice system. In fact, many of the controversial areas of that system, such as the upper age limit for juvenile jurisdiction, the concurrent jurisdiction with the criminal courts, and waiver procedure (which generated the first United States Supreme Court case on the juvenile justice system),[a] are not even discussed.

The materials on the juvenile justice system parallel those on the criminal justice system and raise some of the same basic issues, for purposes of comparison. These materials are divided roughly into three phases of juvenile justice administration: (1) the pre-court stage; (2) the adjudicatory stage; and (3) the postadjudication stage.

(1) The pre-court stage of the juvenile system is marked by a commitment to solutions other than court processing and by a recognition of the great discretion accorded the police in taking juveniles into custody and disposing of the cases without referral to court.

(2) The adjudicatory stage of the juvenile system has been characterized by a lack of procedural formality. In its concern about a treatment-oriented hearing procedure, juvenile court theory minimized the traditional purpose of a court hearing—to determine the facts of an occurrence and to set the framework for governmental authority to interfere with the juvenile's liberty.

(3) The postadjudication stage of the juvenile system is characterized by the great latitude and flexibility given to allow individualization of treatment for the purpose of rehabilitation. This has also been true in the adult system though there is increasing concern over the applicability of procedural due process requirements in adult correctional programs.

The System for Administering Juvenile Justice

The theoretical commitment of the juvenile system to the rehabilitation of the child has had a marked impact upon the system, resulting in certain important characteristics: (1) the nonadversary nature of the proceedings; (2) the broad discretion accorded officials operating at all levels; (3) the extensive reliance upon the skills of behavioral scientists, particularly social workers;

[a] Kent v. United States, 383 U.S. 541 (1966).

and (4) the broad and vague coverage of substantive delinquency to include much noncriminal conduct.

1. Nonadversary Nature of the Proceedings. The concern with rehabilitation in the juvenile system has resulted in efforts to make the alleged delinquent feel that the purpose of the procedure is to help him, not to punish him. The proceedings are "In the interest of ____________" rather than "State v. ____________." The emphasis is on creating a friendly atmosphere conducive to handling the problems of each alleged delinquent on in individual basis. The concerns of the criminal justice system with due process and procedural regularity do not appear as major considerations in the original juvenile court structure. Recently, there has been more concern, but most of the substance of our concepts of due process have been worked out in an adversary format and their application to the informal nonadversary procedure of the juvenile court poses a most difficult problem.

2. Broad Discretion. The juvenile justice system has been described as one based almost totally on the concept of "beneficent discretion." That the juvenile justice system can be characterized in this manner stems primarily from the fact that it was established for the express purpose of promoting "the best interest of the child." This mandate has noticeably affected legislative definition of those to whom the system should apply. Juvenile delinquency legislation is characteristically vague and broad. Such breadth of definition, of course, necessitates the exercise of discretion on the part of those charged with enforcing the law.

Just as important, however, as the implicit delegation of discretion through the use of vague definition, is the express delegation to be found throughout juvenile delinquency statutes. Decisions at all operational points are based upon the determination that further proceeding is, in the opinion of the official involved, in the best interests of the child. For example, the juvenile court need not handle all cases of alleged juvenile delinquency. On the contrary, it is ordered by statute to investigate allegations of delinquency to determine if it ought to take jurisdiction in the best interest of the child.

Unfortunately, in practice, the broad mandate to operate in the best interest of the child has provided little guidance to those charged with administering the law in solving the traditional problems of the law: getting at the true facts of an occurrence and determining when it is appropriate for government to interfere with the lives of private citizens. There is no doubt that the alleged failure of the law—both formally and operationally—to articulate some fairly well defined controls under this standard is one of the central problems of the administration of juvenile justice.

3. Reliance on Behavioral Sciences. As generally outlined by statute the juvenile justice system depends heavily upon the recommendations of social workers in making decisions as to detention and prosecution as well as those regarding disposition. Postadjudication use of social work skills is common to the criminal law: presentence investigation, correctional institutional programming, supervision of convicted persons on parole or probation. It is the preadjudication role of the social worker in the juvenile field that distinguishes it.

This reliance on the social work profession is, of course, closely related to the delegation of broad discretion already noted. It can be reasoned that if the system is staffed with persons who are professionally trained to determine what is in the best interests of the child there is less need to have procedural rules for them to follow. Today, after more than a half century of operation of the juvenile justice system, there is increasing concern as to whether professional qualifications are an adequate safeguard against the making of arbitrary decisions. No one wants to return children to the criminal justice system for processing. But there is an increasing awareness that many of the procedural requirements intended to protect the individual against undue interference or unsuitable treatment by the adult criminal justice system are just as important in the juvenile justice system.

One difficulty with a system relying heavily on the skills of a particular profession is that it requires an adequate supply of competent trained professionals. The juvenile justice system has been notoriously lacking in such persons partly because local governments, which have primary financial responsibility for most of the juvenile delinquency program, have not provided funds necessary to hire qualified people. Furthermore, even if funds were available, there just are not enough social workers to go around. As a result, it has been charged that inadequate staff has turned the juvenile courts into junior criminal courts without the protections of the criminal law.

4. Extensive Coverage of the Substantive Law of Delinquency. The juvenile justice system is not limited to violations of the criminal law. On the contrary it covers conduct that is not, and is unlikely ever to be, covered by the criminal law. To understand the reason, it is necessary to be aware of a basic difference of philosophy between the criminal and the juvenile justice systems. The criminal justice system, regardless of how its objectives are viewed—rehabilitative, penal, deterrent—usually operates on the assumption that the individual is better off outside the system. Not so with the juvenile justice system. Here is a legal procedure formulated in the best interests of the child; it is designed specifically to help him. So it may be desirable to bring the child within the system before it is "too late."[b]

There are, in general, four areas usually covered by juvenile delinquency statutes: (1) acts that would be criminal if committed by adults;[c] (2) acts that are violations of civil prohibitions;[d] (3) acts that involve conduct peculiar to juveniles, such as

---

[b] The argument against broad coverage of the delinquency definition is stated in S. WHEELER & L. COTTRELL, JUVENILE DELINQUENCY, ITS PREVENTION AND CONTROL 22-27 (Russell Sage Foundation 1966):

> A traditional view of the relationship between delinquents and official agencies is that the latter are primarily passive responders to the active behavior or misbehavior of juveniles. The police exist, among other reasons, to detect delinquency, and the courts to adjudicate the cases of those who are detected. Both are reactions to deviant behavior.
>
> . . . The evidence suggests that official response to the behavior in question may initiate processes that push the misbehaving juveniles toward further delinquent conduct, and, at least, make it more difficult for them to re-enter the conventional world. This hypothesis is based upon the concept of labeling and a theory of its consequences.
>
> The assumption is that the public responds to a person informally and in an unorganized way unless that person has been defined as falling into a clear category. The official labeling of a misbehaving youth as delinquent has the effect of placing him in such a category. This official stamp may help to organize responses different from those that would have arisen without the official action. . . . In other words, the individual begins to think of himself as delinquent, and he organizes his behavior accordingly.
>
> This argument is particularly relevant to the field of delinquency. . . . Given the relatively minor, episodic, and perhaps situationally induced character of much delinquency, many who have engaged in minor forms of delinquency once or twice may grow out of this pattern of behavior as they move toward adulthood. For these, the labeling theorists argue, a concerted policy of doing nothing may be more helpful than active intervention, if the long-range goal is to reduce the probability of repetition of the acts. If the labeling hypothesis is correct, official intervention may further define the youth as delinquent in the eyes of neighbors, family members, and peers, thus making it more difficult for him to resume conventional activities.

[c] However, a strong minority of jurisdictions exempt certain "serious" crimes, usually murder and rape, from the juvenile court procedure. Persons charged with these crimes are handled under the regular criminal justice procedure regardless of age.

[d] As an illustration, see WIS. STAT. § 48.12 (1) (1965), which provides that a person is subject to be brought into court as an alleged delinquent because he has "violated any county, town, or municipal ordinance."

truancy from school, drinking, smoking, and curfew violations; and (4) other conduct that apparently has led the legislative body to think remedial action is desirable. Illustrations of this can be found in the Wisconsin statutory provision[e] that a juvenile is alleged delinquent because he is "uncontrolled by his parent . . . or habitually so deports himself as to injure or endanger the morals or health of himself or others"; or in the Iowa statute[f] that provides that a delinquent child includes anyone "[w]ho habitually deports himself in a manner that is injurious to himself or others."

Clearly, these legislative definitions of conduct covered are intentionally or necessarily broad. The reasons for the breadth of definition are doubtlessly numerous, but paramount is the feeling that all children who need help to keep them from future clashes with the criminal law should be helped even against their wishes. It is true that criminal statutes are also often broadly defined, but the reason is different, *i.e.,* to make sure that there are no loopholes through which "the guilty" can escape.

Recently, there has been much concern expressed about the breadth of juvenile delinquency legislation. The current popular solution to the problem of overly-broad delinquency definitions is to limit delinquency to conduct that would be criminal if committed by an adult.[g] No one knows what effect this sort of limitation might have on the operational functioning of the juvenile justice system. For one thing, very little is known about the findings of fact by juvenile courts that form the basis for their adjudication of delinquency. Secondly, no state has dropped noncriminal conduct as a basis for governmental interference with the liberty of the child. Approximately the same type of noncriminal conduct as previously covered by a broad definition of delinquency may now be covered under such labels as "persons in need of supervision" or "minors otherwise in need of supervision," terms apparently regarded as less offensive or stigmatizing. Consequently, what may appear at first to be a limitation upon the power of government to intervene in the life of a child may not be in fact, although recent statutes do sometimes impose greater limitations on the power of the police to take a child into custody or the court to commit to an institution where noncriminal conduct is involved.

---

[e] WIS. STAT. § 48.12 (1965).

[f] IOWA CODE § 232.2 (1966).

[g] For examples of statutes that attempt to narrow the definition of delinquency, see N.Y. FAMILY CT. ACT § 712 (1963); ILL. REV. STAT. ch. 23, § 2360a, ch. 37, § 702-2 (1967); CAL. WELF. & INST'NS CODE §§ 601, 602 (1966).

It is understandable why no state has excluded all noncriminal conduct from the jurisdiction of the juvenile court. The role of children in society differs from that of adults in many ways. For example, they are expected to "mind" their parents; they are required by law to attend school. Habitual truancy and uncontrollability have remained justifications for juvenile court proceedings in all recent statutory revisions.

The concern that this conduct would not be criminal if committed by an adult seems misplaced. Given the commitment of our society to compulsory education and the desirability of an educated citizenry, there is little doubt that if adults were involved, the refusal to attend school would be criminal conduct. In fact, parents who allow their children to miss school are guilty of a crime.

The same would be true of adult conduct similar to that of uncontrollability. In our view of the family, the child's role is that of being subject to parents; the parent's role is that of supporting and caring for the child. The parent who does not perform parental duties within minimal limits must answer to the criminal law; and the child who does not conform to the societal standards comes within the purview of juvenile court jurisdiction.

Reference Note

There have been innumerable criticisms of the basic formulation of the juvenile court as a dispenser of "socialized justice." Two of the best are F. ALLEN, THE BORDERLAND OF THE CRIMINAL LAW ch. 3 (1964), and D. MATZA, DELINQUENCY AND DRIFT, particularly ch. 3, at 90-98, and ch. 4 (1964).

Historical discussion of the juvenile court movement can be found in H. LOW, JUVENILE COURTS IN THE UNITED STATES (1927); Mack, *The Juvenile Court,* 23 HARV. L. REV. 104 (1909).

One area of importance in the administration of the juvenile system, particularly the courts, which is not considered in these materials is that of publicity. *See* Standard Juvenile Court Act §§ 19, 33 and Comments (N.P.P.A. 1959); P.R. LAWS ANN. tit. 34 § 2009 (Supp. 1967); GA. CODE ANN. § 24-2432 (Supp. 1967); G. O'CONNOR & N. WATSON, JUVENILE DELINQUENCY AND YOUTH CRIME: THE POLICE ROLE 67-68 (I.A.C.P. 1964); Geis, *Publicity and Juvenile Court Proceedings,* 30 ROCKY MT. L. REV. 1 (1958); *In re* Gault, 387 U.S. 1, 24-25 (1967).

Basic guides to operation of the juvenile court are: STANDARDS FOR JUVENILE AND FAMILY COURTS (U.S.H.E.W. Children's Bureau Publication #437, 1966); PROCEDURE AND EVIDENCE IN THE JUVENILE COURT (N.C.C.D. Advisory Council of Judges 1962); N.C.C.D.. GUIDES FOR JUVENILE COURT JUDGES (1957).

Chapter 15

PRE-COURT STAGES IN THE JUVENILE PROCESS

The function of the police in the administration of juvenile justice differs, in theory at least, from their function in the adult system. The right of police to interfere with the freedom of an adult suspected of crime is limited by the requirement that there be sufficient evidence to warrant the interference and the requirement that certain rules be followed in the interest of fairness. In the juvenile area there has been, in the past, little concern with these problems. The focus has been on the image of the policeman as a representative of governmental authority and on trying to insure that the juvenile will view authority constructively and be influenced to respect it. The juvenile system, in other words, has been concerned with the effect of the contact with police on the rehabilitation of the child. This is undoubtedly a reflection of the behavioral scientist's recognition that everything that happens to the individual affects his attitude. The police activity in a juvenile case is regarded as part of the process of the treatment of the child. The children are to be understood and helped. Treating the child fairly, of course, is increasingly being considered a basic ingredient of any rehabilitation process: the person who feels that he has been treated unjustly is not a very good prospect for rehabilitation.

The commitment of the police in the juvenile area to a treatment role has had some significant results for juvenile law enforcement. Juvenile law officers tend to be better educated, better trained, and better paid than other police officers. They have developed a reputation for an expertise that tends to set them apart from the rest of the department.

Unfortunately, the fact that they are somewhat different from other police officers has tended to create friction between them and other policemen—a fact attested to by their being dubbed "diaper dicks" in at least one large metropolitan police department. This friction may occur because juvenile officers have adopted the rehabilitative philosophy of the juvenile system with its emphasis on understanding and treating the young person without court adjudication. It may also occur because the juvenile officer often has power operationally to overrule the patrolman who takes the child into custody. The police decision regarding a juvenile is typically a two-step one—the initial apprehension made by a patrolman and review by a specialized youth officer. The patrolman exercises discretion at the point of arrest by releasing those who appear to be deserving. When he apprehends and refers to the youth officer, he usually feels that the case is serious enough to warrant some official action. But the youth officer sifts from this group a small number to be referred to court and normally releases the majority—often to the dissatisfaction of the patrolman.

A second interesting feature of the police attitude toward juvenile law enforcement is that in this area they have openly recognized the great discretion that they exercise. Police discretion not to take into custody or not to prosecute is also involved when the police deal with adults, however little acknowledged, but in the juvenile area there has been frank recognition of the role of discretion and, more important, there have been attempts to articulate guidelines for the operating police officer in exercising that discretion. These guidelines have come in the form of standards set by professional groups or police departments and in police training materials and not from statutes or decisions.

There has also been an increasing concern in the formal law over proper standards and controls relating to police contacts with juveniles. One tendency in seeking standards for the juvenile system has been to turn to the criminal law. This trend was greatly accentuated by *In re* Gault, 387 U.S. 1 (1967), the first Supreme Court decision on the extension of constitutional protections to delinquents. Although the court specifically restricted its ruling to the adjudicatory hearing stage of juvenile proceedings, it established the basis for application of constitutional protections to other areas of the juvenile justice process. One such issue has been whether the criminal court's heavy reliance on the exclusionary rule is an appropriate method of seeking to control police handling of juveniles. Another is whether a juvenile so lacks maturity that he cannot validly waive constitutional rights.

CASE STUDY: POLICE HANDLING OF A JUVENILE CASE

[The following case file does not contain all the records which the police department kept in this particular case, but it does include dictated notes on the various encounters in the case, indicating how the police responded to the juveniles in this situation. Typically, police do not keep such a complete chronological file as the one used here, although police training urges them to do so.

The case involves relatively innocuous conduct, more detrimental to the boys than anyone else. Therefore, you might expect the police to be acting more in the best interests of the boys than they would in a homicide or burglary case.

The case is from a relatively small town and thus the organization of the police department and the response to the violation involved are different than found in an urban area. Clearly it is not a record from a large metropolitan police department operating in an urban ghetto. Since most of the other materials on the police deal with metropolitan departments, the use of this case may help illustrate that juvenile delinquency is not a monolithic problem.[a]]

COMPLAINT RECORD
Department of Police
Riverton, Wisconsin

COMPLAINT: Under the Influence — FILE NO.: 20048
DATE: 8-26-66 — TIME REC'D: 9:50

COMPLAINANT:
PERSON REPORTING: Bradley Knipp and
Ed Nichols (Deputy)

DEFENDANT: Tom Harrington — dob 8-11-50
5109 N. Jenifer St.
George Wilkinson — dob 3-20-51
81 N. King St.
Walter Russell — dob 10-19-49
993 S. Maple

TIME OCCURRED: 9:00 PM — DATE: 8-26-66
RECEIVED BY: Baldwin — HOW RECEIVED: In person
TIME & DATE BROADCAST: — TIME & DATE CANCELLED:
INVEST. OFFICER: Baldwin — TIME:________ DATE:________

COMPLAINT DETAILS

Off. Baldwin was directing traffic on Jensen Avenue by Cavier High School in response to a fire call. Bradley Knipp and Ed

[a] This case was obtained through the Juvenile Law Enforcement Consulting Unit, Community Services Section, Division of Family Services, Wisconsin Department of Health and Social Services, with the particular help of Mr. Kenneth Shimoto.

Nichols, who were working at a dance at Cavier, carried a young boy out to the squad car. They said he was intoxicated and disorderly. The youth was put in the squad car and brought to the station. Knipp rode with Baldwin to the station and assisted in carrying the youth to Juv. quarters.[b] The youth was identified as Tom L. Harrington, age 16, dob as above. Parents are Mr. and Mrs. Larry Harrington, 4-8193, and were notified. The boy was released to his parents. Mr. Harrington and Off. Baldwin carried and wheeled Thomas to the Harrington car in the garage.

While confined in Juv. quarters, Tom Harrington had vomited several times and in so doing made a mess of himself and the cell. Off. Baldwin and Meyer stood him up in the shower in an attempt to clean him off. He was completely helpless, so the officers gave up the shower attempt. Tom was placed on the lower bunk and another mattress was placed on the floor next to his bunk. He rolled out of his bunk and, in attempting to stand, he fell down several times. He has a welt on his right eye and several welts on his back.

Three dollars and five cents which he had was turned over to his father. Receipt attached to this report.

10:15 PM. Off. Nielson, while checking at Cavier, in reference to this complaint, met another youth who was intoxicated. The youth, George Wilkinson, 81 N. King St., 5-8013, was brought to the station. He was interviewed by Det. Sgt. Haygood. (L. Baldwin)

Det. Cowden and Sgt. Haygood questioned George Wilkinson. This is the story that George relates.

He states that he left his home at approximately 6:45 PM on 8-26-66 and went to a Walter Russell's home at 993 S. Maple and then both boys met Tom Harrington near his home. He states that Tom Harrington told him that he saw several boys hide some beer down by the river on the end of the South Port Bridge. George states that they went to this area and found two six packs of beer, one of Budweiser and one of Pabst, along with a bottle of brandy. George stated that he drank, he believes,

---

[b] Under juvenile court theory, juveniles are to be detained in special detention facilities. Ideally, these are separate from the jail and are under the control of the juvenile court. Admission to a detention facility is controlled by juvenile court personnel, not the police. In reality, the vast majority of jurisdictions provide at best juvenile quarters in the jail. As is apparent from the officer's notes here, the decision was a police one. Perhaps this is within the spirit of the juvenile court laws when it is detention pending the arrival of the parents, but there is no indication of any initial control being exercised by the court.

about five bottles of beer and as he drank some of the beer, some brandy was poured into the remaining portion of beer and he drank that also. He said he doesn't recall how many bottles of beer that Tom Harrington or Walter Russell drank.

After the beer was consumed, the remaining portion of brandy still in the bottle was thrown into the river. He said they then went to the CAC dance at Cavier High.

With more questioning, George stated that the beer was gotten out at Sunnyside on Sun. PM. George stated that he and Tom went to Sunnyside and visited the janitor who has a room in the basement, and he knows the janitor only by the name of Joe. George said that he and Tom each stole a six pack of beer from Joe and took it to the river and placed it there to keep it cool. George states that when they got there this evening, there also was a bottle of brandy with the beer. George said he doesn't know where the brandy came from but assumed that Tom brought it from home earlier in the day and placed it there. A Juv. report was made out on George and his parents were notified.[c]

While George was waiting for his parents, he became quite ill and vomited on the floor in the waiting room and also in the restroom. When Mr. Wilkinson came to the station, George was draped over the bowl in the restroom, about 90% out on his feet. He was assisted by his father down the steps, with Sgt. Haygood helping, and was taken home. Mr. Wilkinson was asked to bring George in again after the police had an opportunity to question the other two boys involved.

Questioned Walter Russell of 993 S. Maple St. dob 10-19-49, a 10th grade student at R.H.S. Walter tells about the same story as related by George except he did not know where the beer came from.

He stated that the brandy was believed brought from Tom Harrington's home and placed at the river. Walter stated that he drank one full bottle of beer and a portion of the second bottle. They then filled that bottle with brandy. He stated they drank about a half bottle of this mixture and decided they didn't want any more and threw it away.

Walter was in good shape, as far as intoxication went, and was reprimanded for sharing this beer and getting into trouble and was advised, hereafter when beer is to be drunk, he should wait until he is of age, or with the supervision of his parents.

---

[c] Observe that in the case of all three boys, the parents were notified and told to pick up their sons. As indicated in § D, *infra,* one of the purposes of parental notification is to give the juvenile adult support during police questioning. Was this the procedure followed here?

A Juv. Report was filled out on Walter and his father was notified to come to the station and pick up his son.

When Mr. Russell arrived at the station he was briefed on the activity of his son this evening and he stated he would take care of his son's discipline when he got home.[d]

Due to the state of intoxication Tom Harrington was not interviewed by the detectives. He was taken home by his parents and later on in the evening Mrs. Harrington called the station inquiring when she should bring her son down here to be interviewed. She was advised that this complaint would be referred to the Juv. Detective and he would set up a date for an interview with herself and her son.

Also asked Mrs. Harrington if they were missing a bottle of brandy from this residence. She states that to her knowledge they have no brandy missing from their home. Perhaps when Det. Lee interviews Tom Harrington he can question him in regards to the brandy that was supplied with the beer, that evening. (Det. Cowden and Sgt. Haygood)

8-27-66. Mr. Joseph Hanson, janitor at the Sunnyside Shopping Center, called and stated a person told him a couple of young kids got in trouble last night after they drank beer supplied by him. Mr. Hanson wants it on record he didn't give Tom Harrington or George Wilkinson any beer.

Advised Mr. Joseph Hanson the boys admitted to stealing the beer from him last Sunday afternoon, 8-24-66. Mr. Hanson said the total cost of the beer amounts to $2.00 and wishes to be refunded for it. (Det. Cowden)

9-2-66. Sgt. Lee called Mr. Martin Vaughan, Mgr. of Sunnyside and he stated Mr. Hanson is very trustworthy and has been with them many years. Mr. Hanson originally roomed at the YMCA but now stays in the basement at Sunnyside. Mr. Vaughan stated he is sure Mr. Hanson wouldn't furnish any juveniles with beer and he believes the beer was stolen also. (Sgt. Lee)

9-3-66. 1:15 PM. Sgt. Lee talked to Tom Harrington, age 16, dob 8-11-50, address 5109 Jenifer Street, in the presence of his mother, Mrs. Harrington.

Tom readily admitted that he stole a bottle of brandy from his home, that the boys consumed the night of the CAC dance. Tom states that this liquor was taken on Aug. 26, 1966, being a Tuesday. The older Harrington boy has the Little League team and they were playing a championship game and all members of the

[d] Note the difference in disposition of the case of Walter Russell and the other two boys. Why do you think this was done? Do you agree with the police?

Harrington family were gone except him. Tom states that he took the bottle of brandy and stashed it down alongside of the river where the beer was.

Tom was again questioned whether this beer was stolen or whether Joe did give it to him. Tom stated, "No," that while Joe was working in another part of the basement at Sunnyside, they stole the two six packs of beer which were on top of the refrigerator.

Tom Harrington had the complaint read to him about where he was so drunk he couldn't stand up, about falling off the bunk and so on. This was mainly told to him after Mrs. Harrington mentioned that she heard the police officers handled the boys roughly after the dance. She was informed he received a welt because he was too drunk to stand up and kept falling down. Tom Harrington has been up in this bureau several other times, once for being involved in buying a stolen belt, once for beating up a boy at the CAC dance at St. John's and in the summer of '65 for doing destruction to property next to their home.

Tom was informed that he could be waived in front of Judge Miller. Of course, everything would be made public and he would be charged with drunkenness.

It was told to him the only thing that kept him from going to Branch II was that the Child Welfare Director,[e] Mr. Lueck, thought it may not be in the best interest of the boy, as George Wilkinson is only 15 and he will have to go into Juv. Court.

Tom was informed he could be charged with Public Intoxication, theft, and contributing to the delinquency of a minor, in that he furnished beer to George Wilkinson. Tom and his mother were informed that it was to be referred to Juv. Court and he would have to appear in front of Judge Dorn with his parents.

Tom was informed that if he gets into any trouble, regardless if it was before the court hearing or after, he will be automatically waived to Branch II.[f]

---

[e] Juvenile court structure is unique, as pointed out in § E, *infra,* in that it has professionals attached who make "intake" decisions (a social work term borrowed, as is true in many instances in the juvenile system, from social welfare agencies) and who provide investigative and treatment advice to the courts. Although ideally these professionals are employed by the juvenile court itself, there are many less populous areas where the work load is not sufficient to warrant the employment of a separate court staff. In Wisconsin, in an attempt to provide qualified professional service to the juvenile court, the personnel of the county departments of social services have been used to provide intake and diagnostic services for the juvenile court. *See* WIS. STAT. § 48.06 (1965). Apparently this was the arrangement in Riverton.

[f] The waiver which is discussed here refers to the area of concurrent jurisdiction between the juvenile court and the criminal court. In Wisconsin

Mrs. Harrington has been talked to many other times and she always comes up with the story of what a do-gooder she is with all these recreation programs, all her sons and daughters are involved in and can't understand why her son gets into all this trouble.

Tom was informed that he was lucky he had not been held over night and had his picture taken, as if he had looked at it later on, he would have realized what a mess he made out of himself.

It was explained he was not held and this is why we get the parents down to see what the boys actually do do. He has had beer at home so he cannot use this for an excuse that the only reason he stole the beer is to try it out.

Mrs. Harrington also mentioned that this janitor, Joe Hanson, has had other young boys down in the basement and she thought there could be something going on immorally. She states other mothers have told her this, that young boys do go down there, and probably things are not just right.

Mrs. Harrington was informed this was hearsay but if she has any evidence she should notify the Dixon County Sheriff's Dept. as Sunnyside is in that county.[g]

Tom was informed to stay away from this Hanson and also to tell his other friends to stay away from Hanson. He was also informed that Mr. Hanson would like to receive one dollar from each of the boys for the stolen beer.

This will be taken care of by Mrs. Harrington.

Tom was again informed that this is as far as we will go. The next time we will get an automatic waiver to Branch II.[h]

A possible jail sentence or also a fine or both will be next time. Mrs. Harrington informed she will be receiving a letter from the Welfare Dept. as to when the court date would be, as soon as Sgt. Lee could refer this complaint. (Sgt. Lee)

---

the age involved is between sixteen and eighteen. WIS. STAT. §§ 48.12, 48.18 (1965). All youths under eighteen must be brought initially into juvenile court. The decision to waive a youngster between sixteen and eighteen years of age to the criminal court is made, not by the police or the intake department, as you might believe from the discussion here, but by the juvenile court judge. The statute provides waiver to the criminal court is to be made "only if the juvenile court judge deems it contrary to the best interests of such child or of the public to hear the case."

[g] Note the reaction of the police to Mrs. Harrington. To what extent do you think this affected their "get tough" attitude toward Tom? Was it justified?

[h] On what basis do you think the police can threaten an "automatic waiver" to criminal court (referred to here as Branch II)?

3:00 PM. Sgt. Lee talked to George Wilkinson whose father had not arrived yet. George states that he and his father do disagree on things—that in the old days, persons who were caught drinking under age were frowned upon but now any boy that can get away with it is looked upon as a hero or thought to be real "cool."

This was discussed for awhile and it was hoped that the right attitude was gotten across.[1] George states that we will not have to worry about him as this is the last time he will be in trouble. He really feels this Russell boy sucked him in and George stated that Russell is known to do this and then will leave and let the other boys suffer the consequences. At this point Mr. Rich Wilkinson, father of George, came into the Juv. Bureau. Mr. Wilkinson is the Manager for Fisher Auto Body. There are five other children in the family, two girls that are older, three boys younger than George. George was then sent out of the room and Sgt. Lee talked to Mr. Wilkinson alone. Mr. Wilkinson stated that his wife had just called him and said that there was a blow up at home and she had been struck by George. It seems that George bought some Mod pants and his parents did not like them, they were very tight, but loose around the ankles. George was ordered to take these back by his father yesterday, but did not. This morning his mother told him to take them back and a few words were exchanged. Mrs. Wilkinson became so angry that she threw the boy's guitar down the stairs and when this happened George struck his mother in the middle of the back. Mr. Wilkinson states that he and his wife need help and they cannot cope with this boy and have thought of a private psychiatrist.

The father states that this boy just wants to sit around with his long hair, play his guitar, and isn't interested in anything else. The father will take whatever suggestions this Bureau makes and will welcome any help with the boy. George was then called back into the room and he did admit this incident with his mother. He gave the same old story that everyone else wears this type of clothing and when he refused to take the pants back, his mother did throw the guitar down the stairs and it made George very angry. He states he does not remember striking his mother and if it was with his open hand or his fist. George stated that things happened so fast that truthfully he does not remember.

---

[1] Why should the police worry about "the right attitude"? Note the way in which the police attempt to handle Tom and George. Do you think this is desirable?

George was read several paragraphs of the original complaint—how he acted on that date in front of the officers and how drunk he was.

Both father and son agreed there is much to be desired between them.

Several suggestions were made, and it was agreed George should be referred to Juv. Court. This can be done several different ways; if agreed, an informal hearing can be held and just a letter sent to the parents and have the Judge talk to him.[j]

George agreed that until that time when he is contacted to come in for a hearing, that he will try to get along with his father, and any further incidents could lead to his detainment in the county jail,[k] especially if there are any more drinking episodes and problems at home.

George realizes that anything else could harm his chances of going to college or to the Armed Forces or even later on in life. George was a very truthful boy, very respectful, and seems very intelligent. He just does not agree with his father, which many boys do not at this age. Mr. Wilkinson seemed to be a very capable father, intelligent, but can give no reason why this has come up at this time.

George was also informed that Mr. Hanson would like restitution for the stolen beer, being $1.00 each per boy. His father stated that restitution was made.

Mr. Wilkinson was also informed that there are rumors that his son had been to Sgt. Lee about the janitor being homosexual and the boy should stay away from there and if there is any definite proof that the Dixon Sheriff Dept. should be called. Mr. Wilkinson also was notified that Sgt. Lee had also talked to Mr. Martin Vaughan, Gen. Mgr. of Sunnyside, and he gave Mr. Hanson a clean bill of health, although Mr. Vaughan will inform Mr. Hanson not to let young boys in his apartment.

A referral will be made to the Welfare Dept.[l] as soon as possible, when the complaint is typed up. (Sgt. Lee)

A. INVESTIGATION OF DELINQUENCY

The criminal law has evinced growing concern with limitations on the conduct of the government as it investigates the

[j] See the material on informal handling in § E, *infra.* In less populous areas, this informal handling may actually involve the judge himself, the difference from formal handling consisting of the fact that no formal juvenile court record is made.

[k] See the discussion of detention at 989, *infra.*

[l] See the discussion of juvenile court intake at 1014, *infra.*

ever-increasing number of crimes, and a sophisticated and complex body of law has developed. In contrast, the juvenile system has established few guidelines for those investigating juvenile delinquency, and juvenile officers often believe that the usual restrictions on investigating adult crimes do not apply when the suspect is a juvenile. This is primarily the result of reliance on the *parens patriae* concept with its assumption that because the proceeding is in the best interest of the child there is no need to worry about protecting the young person from undue governmental interference. It is also due to the fact that until recently lawyers have played almost no role in this system, with a resulting lack of challenge to the authorities. Juvenile court statutes still typically are silent on the subject but some cases have raised the basic question in the context of the search for physical evidence.

In re RONNY

40 Misc. 2d 194, 242 N.Y.S.2d 844 (Family Ct. 1963)

MILLARD L. MIDONICK, Judge. This respondent boy, concededly 15 years of age, is charged in the petition with the following conduct:

"On or about July 19, 1963, at about 6:30 P.M., at the corner of 14th Street and 31st Avenue, New York and elsewhere in Astoria, Queens County, he violated a law of the State of New York in that he was in unlawful possession of two bottles of barbiturates containing forty-two Doriden pills and 6½ green pills; said barbiturates can only be obtained by a doctor's prescription. The above named youth had prior to his apprehension been observed by the petitioner being approached by another youth who placed a dollar bill upon a mail box and in return received something from the above named youth, said object being taken from (respondent's) right pants pocket. In (respondent's) right pants pocket was found the two bottles of barbiturates containing the Doriden and other barbiturate pills."

I have denied the motion to suppress the pills and other evidence found on the person of the respondent by the petitioning peace officer. This motion was made under Mapp v. Ohio, 367 U.S. 643, on the ground that there was an illegal arrest and therefore an unreasonable search and seizure.

But consent by the person searched to a search and seizure, before arrest (i.e., before taking a child into custody without a warrant under Family Court Act § 721) legalizes a search and seizure under the United States Constitution (Fourth, Fifth and Fourteenth Amendments) Rios v. United States, 364 U.S. 253.

In the case at bar, there is no conflicting testimony, nor any evidence of objection or resistance by the respondent. Indeed, there is more evidence of consent to search and seizure of the pills and dollars than mere lack of objection and the willing compliance with requests to permit "frisking" and requests for the contents of the pockets of the respondent, and by the willing delivery of those contents to the officer. Accompanying the physical cooperation by the respondent, was his verbal cooperation in making a full and voluntary confession as to the nature of the pills and the source of the money. He gave the officer not only the contents of his pockets, but the contents of his memory. He did not object to being "frisked" nor utter the slightest objection to the entire procedure. The pills and money, without the boy's candid and full explanation of what was involved, would have revealed insufficient evidence that was understandable to the officer except to arouse his reasonable suspicion because of the boy's condition. But since the peace officer was not a "police officer" under the newly-amended statute (Code of Criminal Procedure, § 177(1), § 154-a) reasonable grounds for believing that a non-felonious crime was being committed in his presence was not sufficient to arrest without a warrant. However, the articles coupled with the straightforward voluntary admissions, revealed that a complete and unquestionable misdemeanor consisting of unlawful possession of unlabelled "barbiturates" was being committed in the presence of the officer, a "crime" of "possession" then and there being perpetrated in the plain sight and hearing of the peace officer, and plainly explained to him, without a shadow of any doubt whatever. Sec. 1747-b, Penal Law; Family Court Act § 721. Since the respondent declined to testify at the trial, there is no conflict in the evidence relating to the voluntary nature of the search and seizure. Since the admittedly on-going crime was face to face with the peace officer, who was acting in a civilized, protective, considerate and kindly manner, no differently from what one would expect of a scout master or a clergyman confronted with a dazed boy in this daylight situation on the public streets and in a grocery store open to the public, the search and seizure was not "unreasonable." It was, on the contrary, commendable.

Finally, the problem is squarely posed here whether Mapp v. Ohio, supra, applies to proceedings under the Family Court Act, since such proceedings are denominated non-criminal in nature. Cf. Family Court Act, § 781.

I can think of few worse examples to set for our children than to visit upon children what would be, if they were older, unreasonable and unconstitutional invasions of their all-too-limited privacy and rights, merely because they are young. In this sense, our proceedings are not "civil." They are perhaps, for this purpose, "quasi-criminal" in character. Young persons have the same constitutional rights as older ones in delinquency and supervision jurisdiction, except the right to a jury trial, which is balanced by our circumscribed power and the confidentiality here maintained in an effort to keep the record of a child unblemished.

Since Family Court judges must be fact finders as well as law interpreters, we would do well to stand solidly in behalf of children before us, to avoid contamination of the fact sources and to see to it that we brook no shabby practices in fact gathering which do not comport with fair play. We must not only be fair; we must convince the child before us that the state is firm but fair and that the judge, a parent image, is careful to ensure those civilized standards of conduct toward the child which we expect of the child toward organized society. With deference, I hope that no judge would disagree.

B. TAKING THE JUVENILE INTO CUSTODY

A juvenile is not "arrested" as is an adult; he is "taken into custody."[m] The use of this different terminology is meant to suggest that detaining the child is a protective service for his benefit, and not so much a detention for punishment. Juvenile court statutes recognize the nonlaw-enforcement aspect of the police role and have tried to make clear that a youth may be taken into custody for reasons other than violations of criminal law.

The difficulty is that the broad language of the juvenile court statutes may allow police to take juveniles into custody for the purpose of interrogation and processing, similar to that of a criminal law offender, when there would not be sufficient evidence of a criminal law violation to do so. This is the difficult problem faced by the statutory draftsmen in recent revisions of the juvenile law: to recognize the social service role of police in helping the child, while restricting the police power to deal with the child in a coercive manner. Some statutes provide specifically that such taking into custody is not an arrest, and thus allow the

---

[m] The term, "taking into custody," is also used to describe certain detention of adults (*see* Chapter 4), in recognition of the frequency of nonprosecution-oriented custody.

juvenile to answer "No" when asked whether he has ever been arrested.[n]

The criminal justice system places a priority on making arrests with a warrant issued by a judicial officer upon probable cause. But in the juvenile system there may be no statutory provision at all for a warrant. And even where the statute includes the use of a warrant, there are so many alternative grounds that the decision on taking into custody appears to be regarded primarily as a police decision. The contrast between the adult and the juvenile systems here is great: The criminal law evidently regards the police as not capable, except in stated exceptional circumstances, to weigh the evidence as to the possible commission of a crime. The juvenile law, on the other hand, seems to assume the ability of police to make the decision as to whether, for example, the child is in surroundings or conditions that endanger his welfare.

STANDARD JUVENILE COURT ACT § 16 (1959)

§ 16. Taking children into custody

A child may be taken into custody by any officer of the peace without order of the judge (a) when in the presence of the officer the child has violated a state or federal law or a county or municipal ordinance; (b) when there are reasonable grounds to believe that he has committed an act which if committed by an adult would be a felony; (c) when he is seriously endangered in his surroundings, and immediate removal appears to be necessary for his protection; (d) when there are reasonable grounds to believe that he has run away from his parents, guardian, or legal custodian. Such taking into custody shall not be deemed an arrest.

NEW YORK FAMILY COURT ACT § 721 (McKinney Supp. 1967)

§ 721. Custody by peace officer without a warrant

A peace officer may take a person under the age of sixteen into custody without a warrant in cases in which he may arrest a person for a crime under section one hundred seventy-seven of the code of criminal procedure. For purposes of this section, the

[n] These statutes are sometimes circumvented by asking, "Have you ever been arrested or taken into custody?"

term "crime" used in section one hundred seventy-seven of the code of criminal procedure refers to an act which, if committed by an adult, would constitute a crime.

COMMITTEE COMMENTS

This section does not authorize taking into custody on the ground that a person is in need of supervision or appears to be in need of supervision. There is no such urgency that the matter may not be dealt with initially by summons.

In re JAMES L———, JR.
250 Ohio 2d 369, 194 N.E.2d 797 (Juvenile Ct. 1963)

GAGLIARDO, Judge. This cause came on for hearing on the petition of Thomas Edward Horgan, patrolman for the Cleveland police department alleging that James Long, Jr., a minor, 17 years of age, did on or about July 21, 1963, unlawfully and maliciously assault one Thomas Edward Horgan, an adult male, age 35 years, officer of the Cleveland police department in the Chesterfield playground at East 123rd Street and Chesterfield Avenue, Cleveland, Ohio, by striking him with his fists about the face and body.

The evidence is undisputed that the police officer, Horgan, in company with a fellow officer went to the Chesterfield playground on that date in response to a citizen's complaint for the purpose of investigating the alleged use of obscene language and interference with the lawful use of the playground on the part of the children of the citizen complainant. James Long, Jr., the minor herein, was identified as one of the persons using obscene language and preventing the children from using the swings. In the course of their investigation, the police officers asked the minor for his name on several different occasions, and the answer was not forthcoming. The police officers attempted to take him into physical custody, stating that they were going to take him to his parents. The minor resisted. A scuffle occurred and during the scuffle both the minor and the officer herein were injured and required hospital treatment.

Counsel for the minor argues that since the minor was taken into custody without warrant and was not committing a misdemeanor in the presence of the police officers nor was there any probable cause to believe that the minor had been involved in the commission of a felony, the officers had no right to arrest the minor. Counsel further points out that a person may resist an unlawful arrest with such force as is necessary to avoid being unlawfully detained.

In the opinion of the court, the law of arrest does not apply to the taking into custody of minors. An arrest as the term is used in criminal law signifies the apprehension or detention of the person of another that he may be forthcoming to answer an alleged or supposed crime.

Delinquency has not been declared a crime in Ohio and the Ohio Juvenile Act is neither criminal nor penal in its nature, but is an administrative police regulation of a corrective character. Proceedings instituted in a juvenile court are not criminal in nature nor are they conducted with the objective of convicting a minor of a crime and punishing him, therefor; they are informal hearings through a medium of the juvenile court to determine whether the child needs intervention of the state as guardian and protector of his person.

It therefore follows that the law of arrest in accordance with existing Ohio statutes does not apply to special statutory proceedings in the Juvenile Court which are civil in nature and have for their purpose the securing for each child under the jurisdiction of the juvenile court such care, guidance, and control . . . as will best serve the child's welfare. Section 2151.55 of the Revised Code of Ohio.

The court has been unable to find any authority in Ohio dealing specifically with the question of how a minor may be taken into custody without process.

Section 2151.31 of the Revised Code of Ohio provides: "Whenever any officer takes a child into custody, he shall, unless it is impracticable or has been otherwise ordered by the juvenile court, accept the written promise of the parent, guardian, or custodian to bring the child to the court at the time fixed. Thereupon such child may be released in the custody of a parent, guardian, or custodian." It further provides: "This section does not forbid any peace officer, police officer, probation officer, or other person authorized by the juvenile judge from taking into custody any child who is found violating any law or ordinance, or who is reasonably believed to be a fugitive from his parents or from justice, or whose surroundings are such as to endanger his health, morals, or welfare." Certainly, the minor herein was found in such surroundings as to endanger his welfare.

It is the court's opinion that a police officer may take a child into protective custody without process where he has reasonable grounds to believe said child to be a delinquent, neglected or dependent child, and it is not necessary that the child be committing a misdemeanor in the officer's presence or that probable cause exist for the officer to believe that the child has been involved in the commission of a felony. In this case the officers were acting in their lawful capacity in answering the citizen's complaint and had not only the right but the duty upon not receiving the co-operation of the minor to take such minor into protective custody and proceed to restrain him as provided by the statute. This is what the officers were doing and had a right to do.

Even if there is a power on the part of police to take juveniles into custody, there is no requirement that they do so. Police exercise wide discretion in deciding whether to initiate the formal steps which may lead to adjudication of delinquency.

THE PRESIDENT'S COMMISSION ON LAW ENFORCEMENT AND ADMINISTRATION OF JUSTICE THE CHALLENGE OF CRIME IN A FREE SOCIETY 78-79 (1967)

Whether or not a juvenile becomes involved in the juvenile justice system usually depends upon the outcome of an encounter with the police. Such encounters are frequent, especially in the crowded inner city.

Some of them grow out of a criminal act of significant proportions: The juveniles have been caught in the act, or are being sought, or there is reason to believe that they answer the description given by a complainant. In such instances, the contact is very likely to lead to further processing by the juvenile justice system.

On the other hand, many encounters are based on a relatively minor violation, or not on a specific crime at all but on the policeman's sense that something is wrong. He may suspect that a crime has happened or is about to happen. Or he may believe the juvenile's conduct is offensive, insolent, or in some other way improper. On such occasions, the policeman has a relatively great range of choices. He can pass by. He can stop for a few words of general banter. He can ask the juveniles their names, where they live, where they are going. He can question them about what has been happening in the neighborhood. He can search them, order them to disperse or move on, check with the station for records and recent neighborhood offenses. He can send or take them home, where he may warn their parents to keep them off the street. Suspicion, even perhaps without very specific grounds for it, may on occasion lead him to bring them in to the station for further questioning or checking.

In any given encounter the policeman's selection among alternatives may vary considerably among departments and among individual officers. It is governed to some extent by departmental practice, either explicitly enunciated or tacitly understood. Such policies are difficult to evolve—indeed, in many instances, they could not be specific enough to be helpful without being too rigid to accommodate the vast variety of street situations. Nevertheless, it is important that, wherever possible, police forces formulate guidelines for policemen in their dealings with juveniles. . . .

The reactions and attitudes of individual officers are also influential when they are dealing with juveniles. As numerous observers and students of police work have pointed out, a policeman in attempting to solve crimes must employ, in the absence of concrete evidence, circumstantial indicators to link specific crimes with specific people. Thus policemen may stop Negro and Mexican youths in white neighborhoods, may suspect juveniles who act in what the policemen consider an impudent or overly casual manner, and may be influenced by such factors as unusual hair styles or clothes uncommon to the wearer's group or area. Naturally, the adolescents involved are aware of such police distinctions. They are at a notoriously sensitive age and are ready to see themselves as victims of police harassment. In the words of one boy: "Them cops is supposed to be out catching *criminals.* They ain't paid to be looking after my hair!" When boys are actually stopped by policemen, their own attitudes and their demeanor appear often to play a part in what happens next. Some observers have suggested that those who act frightened, penitent, and respectful are more likely to be released, while those who assert their autonomy and act indifferent or resistant run a substantially greater risk of being frisked, interrogated, or even taken into custody.

Informal street handling of juveniles creates conflicts that are extremely difficult to resolve. Juveniles commit large numbers of offenses. Some of the circumstances that lead policemen to suspect given juveniles often do stem from criminal conduct. The policeman's dependence upon the sort of information juveniles provide in informal encounters is real and unlikely to be satisfied elsewhere.

On the other hand, abuse of authority—real or imagined—may seriously impair young people's respect for constituted authority and produce deep resentment. Informal investigatory police encounters with juveniles are inevitable, but it is of the utmost importance that juveniles receive treatment that is neither unfair nor degrading.

C. IN-CUSTODY TREATMENT

The great concern of the juvenile system with the effect of police contact on the juvenile has already been noted. Nowhere is this concern more evident than in the area of in-custody treatment. Once a juvenile is taken into custody by the police, there are special limitations placed on their treatment of him. For example, there are limitations on fingerprinting and photographing juveniles, a procedure routinely followed in some areas with arrested adults; there are requirements that juveniles be taken to detention facilities under control of the juvenile court, not to the police station; there are elaborate controls on interrogation, usually requiring that the parents of the child be notified and allowed to be present, or that the juvenile court be notified or the child brought there prior to questioning.

None of these requirements for differential treatment of juveniles by the police should any longer be taken as an indication that the traditional protections for the adult criminal will not be applied in the juvenile area. Increasingly, juvenile court statutes, court decisions, and police policy guidelines require that, in addition to the special treatment required because of their youth, juveniles be told of their right to remain silent and be warned that their statements may be used against them. The right to counsel during interrogation is only a logical extension of the rather broad application of criminal law protections to the juvenile system.[o]

IDAHO CODE ANN. § 16-1811(6) (1965 Supp.)

Neither fingerprints nor photographs shall be taken of any child taken into custody without consent of the judge, unless a peace officer determines it necessary for the detection and apprehension of an unknown offender. When fingerprints are taken, copies of the fingerprint cards shall not be sent to central, state or federal depositories except in national security cases or marked "for identification only"; and cards shall be removed from the local police file and destroyed by the local police chief, sheriff, or city or county clerk, whoever is responsible for the files: (a) if the decision after investigation of the case is that no basis for court jurisdiction exists; or (b) when the individual charged reaches his twenty-first birthday, if there has been no record of violation of law after reaching his eighteenth birthday.

---

[o] Dorsen & Rezneck, *In Re Gault and the Future of Juvenile Law,* 1 Family L.Q. 1 (1967); Ketcham, *Guidelines from Gault: Revolutionary Requirements and Reappraisal,* 53 Va. L. Rev. 1700 (1967).

JUVENILE DELINQUENCY AND YOUTH CRIME: THE POLICE ROLE 64-65 (IACP 1964)
By George O'Connor & Nelson Watson

FINGERPRINTING

. . .

There is no question as to the validity or reliability of identification based upon fingerprints. No other form of personal identification has yet been developed which can be recorded, classified, filed, and searched with such high degrees of reliability and ease. In fact, recent electronic data-processing advances make this procedure even more attractive because of speed of recall.

The argument that fingerprinting is a degrading or traumatic process is without merit. The rather common belief that only criminals are fingerprinted is incorrect. The shame or embarrassment which may be felt by the arrested person being fingerprinted springs from the larger fact of the arrest rather than from the technique used to firmly establish identity.

The need for positive identification appears to be the major factor to be considered in the development and implementation of a policy on fingerprinting. Thus, a person whose identity is verified by parents immediately after a minor arrest need not be printed unless there is evidentiary material for which comparison prints are needed. On the other hand, a youngster who has been caught in a burglary should be printed so that latent prints from future and past burglary scenes may be compared against the single or complete file of known offenders. Such a use of fingerprints is a vital investigative aid and the age of the burglar cannot reasonably be offered as the basis for using or excluding such a technique. The psychological and emotional trauma of the burglary itself is what really counts rather than any supposedly associated with the arrest and ensuing identification procedures.

NEW YORK FAMILY COURT ACT § 724
(McKinney Supp. 1967)

§ 724. Duties of peace officer after taking into custody or on delivery by private person

(a) If a peace officer takes into custody [he] shall immediately notify the parent.

(b) After making every reasonable effort to give notice under paragraph (a), the peace officer shall

(i) release the child to the custody of his parent upon the written promise, without security, of the person to whose custody the child is released that he will produce the child before the family court in that county at a time and place specified in writing; or

(ii) forthwith and with all reasonable speed take the child directly, and without his first being taken to the police station house, to the family court unless the peace officer determines that it is necessary to question the child, in which case he may take the child to a facility designated by the appropriate appellate division of the supreme court as a suitable place for the questioning of children and there question him for a reasonable period of time; or

(iii) take the child to a place designated by rules of court for the reception of children.

(c) In the absence of special circumstances, the peace officer shall release the child in accord with paragraph (b)(1).

(d) In determining what is a "reasonable period of time" for questioning a child, the child's age and the presence or absence of his parents or other person legally responsible for his care shall be included among the relevant considerations.

Court rule. The Appellate Division of the Supreme Court, Fourth Judicial Department, hereby enacts the following rule pursuant to Family Court Act, section 724:

The family court judge in any county may by order approve or disapprove any publicly maintained facility as a place for the questioning by police of a child in custody; provided that the public officer having jurisdiction of such facility has filed with the judge of the family court an approval of such use thereof specifying the existence and availability of a room or place therein separated from areas of adult occupation or usage. Facilities in police stations or barracks, fire stations, schools or other public buildings may be so approved.

In re STATE IN INTEREST OF CARLO
48 N.J. 224, 225 A.2d 110 (1966)

Proceeding on juvenile delinquency complaints charging that 13-year-old and 15-year-old boys caused death of a 10-year-old girl by committing an attack upon her. The Juvenile Court found the boys to be juvenile delinquents in that they had committed acts which, had they been committed by persons of age of 18 years or over, would have constituted second degree murder. [The juveniles appealed.]

PROCTOR, J. Each appellant when he was first taken into custody and later at the trial maintained his innocence. Each contends that his oral and written confessions were the product of police coercion and that therefore their admission into evidence violated the due process clause of the Fourteenth Amendment.

[I]nsofar as the State suggests that the constitutional safeguard of voluntariness governing the use of confessions does not apply in proceedings before the juvenile court, we must emphatically disagree. Involuntary confessions are likely to be untrue. McCormick, Evidence § 109, 227-228 (1954); McGuire, Evidence of Guilt, § 3.03, 109 (1959). Assuming a juvenile is not entitled to all the constitutional requirements of a criminal trial, we firmly believe he is at least entitled to a fact-finding process which measures up to the essentials of due process and fair treatment.

Appellant Thomas was taken from his home into custody around 4:00 P.M., and questioned successively by at least two police officers at two different police stations during the six and one-half hours before his handwritten confession was made. The further questioning which ended with a typewritten confession did not conclude until about 2:00 o'clock the next morning, some ten hours after custody began. This protracted period of interrogation of a 15-year-old boy casts serious doubt that the statements he made were voluntary and truthful.

Appellant Jose was taken into custody from his home at about 5:00 P.M., and was questioned successively by at least two police officers frequently in the presence of two more police officers during the five-hour period until his oral admission was made and during the seven hours it took until a written confession was concluded around midnight. Such extensive quizzing of a 13-year-old boy strongly suggests that his inculpatory statements were not voluntary and are not trustworthy.

Both boys were taken to the Second Precinct station house for interrogation. The Legislature has mandated that no child under the age of 16 shall "at any time" be placed in a police station. N.J.S. 2A:4-33, N.J.S.A. In State v. Smith, supra, this Court determined that this statute was not applicable to juveniles (both 17 years of age) who were taken to a police station for the temporary purpose of questioning. 32 N.J., at p. 532, 161 A.2d 520. However, we infer from these provisions as to detention that the Legislature has recognized that putting a juvenile under the age of 16 in a police station is likely to have harmful effects on the mind and will of the boy. See In re Rutane, supra, 234 N.Y.S.2d, at p. 778, where a like statute was said to have as a purpose the protection of the child from "the frightening atmosphere of a station house." See also N.J.S. 2A:4-32, N.J.S.A. for its special provisions as to custody of juveniles under age 16 and compare these with the less restrictive custody provisions (R.R. 6:8-3) for juveniles age 16 or 17 as discussed in State v. Smith, supra, 32 N.J. at pp. 528-529, 161 A.2d 520. The likelihood of such harmful effects upon the minds of these boys, both under 16, of being placed and interrogated in the threatening atmosphere of an isolated room in a police station must be weighed in our determination of the voluntariness of their confessions.

The evidence is uncontroverted that the parents of both boys made repeated efforts to see their sons when the boys were being interrogated. With the possible exception of the first visit by Thomas's parents where the evidence is disputed, these attempts were always rebuffed with the response that the parents could not see the boys until the questioning was completed. Indeed, the parents were not able to see their sons until the next morning when the boys were brought from the Youth House to the juvenile court. These denials evidence to us an approach by the police which rode roughshod over the parent-child relationship in order to obtain confessions by intimidation.

The police denied the parents of these boys the opportunity to see them when the boys were being grilled about a most horrible crime and were in the greatest need of a friend. Boys age 15 and 13 quizzed in a police station alone and without support can easily become victims "first of fear, then of panic." Haley v. State of Ohio [332 U.S. 596, 600 (1948)]. Recognized juvenile authorities are in accord that parents or guardians should be present when juveniles are being questioned concerning their participation in acts of delinquency:[p]

"Whenever possible and especially in the case of young children, no child should be interviewed except in the presence of his parents or guardian. This should always be the policy when a child is being questioned about his participation or when a formal statement concerning the child's participation in the alleged delinquent act is being taken." Standards for Specialized Courts Dealing with Children (Children's Bureau, Department of Health, Education and Welfare, 1954), at p. 39.

---

[p] Where the statute requires the notification of the parent or the probation officer, failure to do so may invalidate the confession. *See* State v. Shaw, 93 Ariz. 40, 378 P.2d 487 (1963); *In re* Williams, 49 Misc. 2d 154, 267 N.Y.S.2d 91 (Family Ct. 1966).

The effect of introducing a lawyer at the interrogation stage upon the requirement of notifying the parents is uncertain.

The refusal by the police in the present case to permit the parents access to their sons during the interrogations might well be sufficient in itself to show that the confessions were involuntary even though, as the police testified, the boys did not wish to see their parents. Boys of 13 and 15 lack the judgment to appreciate the seriousness of the situation and the harm which they may do themselves by yielding to the pressures of insistent police questioning. See Gallegos v. State of Colorado, 370 U.S. 49, 54 (1962), where the confession of a 14-year-old boy was held to be involuntary:

> "The prosecution says that the boy was advised of his right to counsel, but that he did not ask either for a lawyer or for his parents. But a 14-year-old boy, no matter how sophisticated, is unlikely to have any conception of what will confront him when he is made accessible only to the police. That is to say, we deal with a person who is not equal to the police in knowledge and understanding of the consequences of the questions and answers being recorded and who is unable to know how to protect his own interests or how to get the benefits of his constitutional rights."

The State contends that both boys were advised of the constitutional rights which would be due to one accused of a crime before they made their statements and that, knowing of these rights, the boys nevertheless confessed. However, it seems doubtful that these boys, age 15 and 13, had the mental capacity, particularly in the environment of a police station, to appreciate the extent of their rights and the consequences of a failure to exercise them.

The judgments of the juvenile court are reversed as to both appellants.

WEINTRAUB, C. J. (concurring). Under our statute the approach to juvenile delinquency is wholly rehabilitative except with respect to heinous offenses committed by a juvenile age 16 or 17, as to which the juvenile court, if it finds another objective is demanded in the public interest, may refer the juvenile to the criminal courts.

Few of man's institutions reach the heights meant for them. This, of course, is no reason to tear down what we have. That the juvenile process may fall short of its ideal would not justify returning the infant to the throes of the criminal process. Nor does that circumstance suggest that we apply wholesale to the juvenile process the constitutional rights of one suspected or charged with crime, for we cannot deal with juvenile delinquency as if it were a crime without giving it precisely that character.

The object of the juvenile process is to make men out of errant boys. In that process we must build upon the truth. A juvenile should be led to believe the decent thing is to come clean, to face the music. A father, inquiring as to possible misconduct of his son, would feel a bit absurd if he told the son the truth may be used against him, that he has a right not to answer, and that he may consult counsel before deciding whether to talk. That scene would be absurd for a couple of reasons, and one is that is no way to teach integrity. No parent would deal that way with his child, and I would hope that government need not deal that way with him when it claims the parental role as it does in the juvenile process.

This of course does not take the juvenile process beyond all constitutional protection. A child can be rehabilitated only in the face of the truth, and that process would be undue which harbors the danger of falsity. If a confession is obtained in circumstances which cast doubt upon its truthfulness, it has no place in the juvenile process. Hence I agree that due process of law would be offended by the use of a confession which is "involuntary" in the sense of that word as it once was understood with respect to confessions of adults, that is, a confession obtained by means which cast doubt upon its reliability. Thus, there should be every assurance that the juvenile was not led into a false account, and to that end, at least if the offense is a serious wrong, the police should see that a parent or some relative or friend is present, if it is at all feasible, to allay the fear or pressure a youngster could feel in strange hands and a strange setting. And of course a parent cannot be excluded because the infant wants it that way; the decision is the parent's and not the child's. But an infant need not be warned that the truth will be used against him, for the very assumption of the juvenile process is that the truth will be used to help him. Rather he should be impressed with the fact that a false admission would be as wrong as a false denial. And because of the ease with which some boys may yield to suggestion, I would insist upon a *quantum* of corroboration we do not now demand with respect to confessions of adults. This is especially true where the wrong is such that rehabilitation could not be achieved without confinement.

I would add a word with respect to the appropriateness of the principle, evolved with respect to crime, calling for the suppression of the truth in order to deter official misbehavior.

If the State would rehabilitate a youngster, its officers of course should set the good example. The police should not use tactics which are palpably wrong. I do not refer, however, to the rules of the drawing room or the playing field. The State cannot be that immaculate if it is to cope with the dirty business of lawlessness, and even offenders, juvenile and adult, would not expect it to be. Rather I refer to conduct intolerable to one who is sensible to the demands of effective law enforcement.

With respect to crime, we suppress the truth even if it means the release of one who is plainly guilty, and this in the belief that the support thereby given a constitutional value outweighs the price tomorrow's victims may pay. I would suggest that it need not follow that the same course should be pursued with respect to juvenile delinquency, since as to it there is still another value to be weighed, to wit, the rehabilitation of the infant. To deny an infant the attention he needs because the police erred in obtaining evidence of that need may not be the parental thing to do.

The Practice

1

The police in a large city metropolitan department routinely conduct their initial interrogation of juveniles while enroute to the district station where the juvenile is turned over to youth authorities and the parents are notified.

2

The police, investigating a series of thefts, interviewed several suspects at school in the presence of the school guidance counselor.

THE HANDLING OF JUVENILES FROM OFFENSE TO DISPOSITION 16-17 (U.S. DEPT. H.E. & W. 1967)

By James T. Carey, Joel Goldfarb & Michael J. Rowe

If the officer shows that he wants to help the child, the juvenile will respond with some degree of trust. His trust must not be betrayed. If the officer lies, or lets the child down in a less direct way, the news will spread. All officers will be distrusted and all interviews will become less fruitful. Future relations of officers and juvenile offenders will be seriously impaired.

Within the framework of helpfulness and trust, several techniques are useful. Be sympathetic: many youngsters get little sympathy at home. Work in the child's best interests: all too frequently no one else cares much about him. Many kids like to boast of their exploits: let them talk. Others will talk a great deal if they believe they are telling you something you do not already know. Some children need stern treatment, and some need help, especially when they don't want their parents to know what they have done. Talking about the trouble they are in helps to get facts straight. The policeman can volunteer to tell the parents. . . .

. . . When a group of youths is involved in an offense, it is best to interview them separately, but it is sometimes advisable to talk to the whole group later when you have the knowledge gained from interviewing each member. Thus you will be able to play off one member of the group against another and possibly obtain further information.

One word of warning to newcomers to juvenile work. Do not expect to succeed the first time. Interviewing youngsters takes time and patience and you will be conned occasionally. Our advice is to be aware of the pitfalls and to persevere.

JUVENILE DELINQUENCY AND YOUTH CRIME: THE POLICE ROLE 57-59 (IACP 1964)

By George O'Connor & Nelson Watson

Now, as regards the questioning of juveniles, the restrictions have inspired many a suspect to remark, "You can't do anything to me—I'm a juvenile." Some of these "children" who "have been through the mill," either in person or vicariously with friends, know that they cannot be held by the police. They believe that if they do go to court nothing very drastic will happen. They feel little concern about going on probation because that is a quite painless process. Some of them are well educated by their peers and others on how to tangle with the machinery of justice and come out relatively unscathed. These juveniles can hardly be described as children who have made a mistake because of the innocence of immaturity.

On the other hand, there are many more juveniles who get into some kind of trouble and who are genuinely alarmed by their first taste of the law and sorry for what they have done. They are amenable to correction through sound counselling and can usually be redirected with good prospects for future acceptable behavior.

The policeman meets all kinds from the scared little kid to the big arrogant bully. Sometimes he does not know what he has until he gets the person under control and asks a few questions. In fact, occasionally he does not know that the boy is a juvenile until subsequent investigation discloses that information.

Police experience reveals that, on the whole, questioning juveniles is easier and more productive of the true facts in a shorter period of time than questioning adults. This does not mean that juvenile offenders are necessarily more cooperative than adult offenders; it means that they are often less resistive. Police recognize that the greater suggestibility and pliability of youths mandate certain self-imposed restraints in questioning them. The standard interview prohibitions against making promises and threats apply here. Abusive language, epithets, sarcasm, and harsh tones are no more justified (and no more useful) than physical punishment. Excessively prolonged interrogation of a juvenile is likewise contrary to proper police practice.

This brings us to one of the central issues of controversy in questioning juveniles. Some authorities contend that juveniles should be questioned only with the permission of and in the presence of their parents. They further recommend that the questioning be done at the home. They suggest that interviewing a juvenile in the police station should be done only if the parents consent. It is our opinion that these proposals, if intended as inviolable regulations, are unrealistic in terms of fulfillment of the responsibilities given the police by the people. If the police job is to be done effectively, the decisions as to when, where and under what circumstances a person shall be questioned must be made by the police within the framework of the law. If the parents cooperate, so much the better, but, if they refuse, the police are not thereby relieved of the responsibility for successful handling of the case. As a matter of fact, it is not at all unusual for police to interview juveniles in the presence of their parents—an arrangement often requested by the officers. Nor is it unusual for police to interview a juvenile in the home. Police are well aware that these arrangements may offer distinct advantages. Our position is that they should not be mandatory and that the prerogative belongs to the police—acting on behalf of society as a whole rather than in deference to the wishes of an individual.

The place at which the interview is conducted is a matter of concern to many people. For example, some school authorities are strongly opposed to having police interview juveniles in school. In some cases they are opposed to having the interview conducted by a policeman in uniform, but not by an officer in civilian clothes. In still other cases, they are willing to make the child available for interview, but only if the principal or other school official is present. The police recognize, of course, that the school officials are legally responsible for the child whenever he is in the school and that the principal is responsible for the things that go on in the school. Police also would agree that children should not be interviewed at the school except in emergency situations. Amicable arrangements should be worked out with the school officials to cover such contingencies.

Another issue often raised here is that juveniles should be interviewed only by specially trained juvenile officers. Some seem to believe that there is something traumatic, stigmatizing, or at least embarrassing to a juvenile to be contacted by an officer in uniform. We feel that this is not the case. In the first place, such contacts are unavoidable, and, in the second place, it is not the uniform but the nature of the contact that makes the difference. Initial questioning in the case of an "on-view" apprehension should be done by the uniformed patrolman. Follow-up interviews and other investigation which would take the patrolman away from his assigned beat should be done either by detectives or juvenile officers depending upon how the department is organized. All police should receive training in handling juvenile cases so that patrolmen will be as qualified in this area as in others and so that juvenile officers can be relieved of much routine enabling them to devote themselves to more specialized functions. In any event, although the immediate objective of police interrogation is to establish the truth as to the commission of an offense and the identity of the offender, in the case of a juvenile, police must perform this function bearing in mind the ultimate objective of redirecting the objectionable behavior and attitudes of the youth into socially acceptable channels. In our contacts with youth, then, we must so conduct ourselves as to avoid reinforcing or in any manner solidifying and contributing to the undesirable behavior.

Policy Guide No. 7

During interrogation, whether of juveniles or adults, officers must scrupulously avoid practices which can be described as coercive and which make it likely that an innocent person would confess.

Policy Guide No. 8

During interrogation, as in all police procedures, officers must be sensitive to and respect the basic legal as well as human rights of all persons, adult and juvenile alike.

Policy Guide No. 9

In questioning juveniles, harsh, abusive language, epithets, profanity, and other vulgarities must never be used.

Policy Guide No. 10

Police should always give consideration to having the parents present during investigative interrogation and to the advisability of conducting such interviews in the home, but the decisions in these matters are to be made by the police in the light of the totality of the circumstances in each specific case.

GANG MEMBERS AND THE POLICE in THE POLICE 70-71 (D. Bordua ed. 1967)
By Carl Werthman & Irving Piliavin

The success of [interrogation] is suggested by the fact that over 90% of convicted juveniles confess, a rate that testifies both to the competence of juvenile officers at interrogation and the incompetence of gang boys at concealing information. Those boys who have unusual control over words, voice tones, facial expressions, and body muscles can sometimes manage to avoid conviction indefinitely unless they are apprehended at the scene of a crime. Yet these talents are rare. Some gangs contain no such talented members; others contain two or three. It is therefore rarely necessary for a juvenile officer to expend much time and energy collecting evidence in order to build his case against a boy. . . .

Encounters

The techniques of interrogation used by juvenile officers can best be viewed as self-conscious variations in the posture adopted towards suspects. If an officer has not been able to compile a good list of suspects after interviewing a complainant, he may simply cruise the local neighborhood asking familiar boys for information. This style of interrogation is usually conducted in a casual, informal, and conspiratorial tone of voice. It is designed to suggest that nothing serious has happened, that the officer is merely curious about a particular incident, or that a "favor" from the boy being interrogated will someday be returned. As far as the boys are concerned, however, this posture is simply "sneaky."

> Some cops may be nice when you meet them, but as soon as you turn your back they be keeping full tab on you. Like this juvenile officer, Sergeant K. and his buddy. Every time I see him in school the sucker come up to me real nice and

> start running down his shit. "How's it going? What you been doing?" He gets to interrogating my ass, man, like I done something wrong! And all the time he be coming on nice! You know, like, "It's just between you and me." All that old shit. He sometimes say, "No, we don't expect you to squeal on your friends or nothing. We just want a little help. You do us a favor, we do you a favor. You go on and tell me what boys was involved and I guarantee you I let you go home. Nothing gonna happen anyway. You know. It ain't really serious." All that old shit! And then they turn around and try to book you every damn chance they get! Some of them nice cops you got to watch real careful.

When a juvenile officer has compiled a more promising list of suspects, however, his approach to interrogation is likely to be decidedly less flattering. After confronting a boy with a list of acquaintances, the officer may wait for a suspicious silence to follow a particular name; or he might accuse a suspect directly in the hope that, even if innocent, the boy might get rattled enough to produce the actual offender.

Yet a juvenile officer is likely to give his most deferential and endearing performance when he thinks he has finally located the culprit. By suggesting that the suspect is regarded as a "good boy" and will not be done any harm, the officer attempts to ease him into a confession.

Although a great many gang boys are tricked into confessions, the authority of a juvenile officer is rarely rejected because of the hypocrisy involved in his techniques of interrogation. Since it strikes the boys as reasonable that a juvenile officer would attempt to catch them for the crimes they actually do commit, these defeats are often taken philosophically. As one boy put it:

> If you done something and you be lying and yelling when the boys from juvy come around and they catch you lying, well, what you gonna do? You gonna complain 'cause you was caught? Hell man, you can't do that. You did something, and you was caught, and that's the way it goes.

D. DETENTION AND RELEASE

One of the frequent criticisms of the juvenile justice system is that it denies the juvenile the right to bail.[q] Although it is true

[q] The constitutional right of a juvenile to bail has been litigated in a few cases with the courts dividing on the issue, those finding no right usually

that juvenile court statutes usually do not provide for the setting of bail and the release of the juvenile on posting that amount, this does not mean that the juvenile does not have some right to be released. In fact, one of the important principles of the juvenile justice system is that most youngsters alleged to be delinquent should be allowed to remain at home until they are judged delinquent by a court. In this, it is actually similar to the adult criminal system. In both, if the person will appear in court, the assumption is that he should not be detained.

In the adult system this right to freedom is tied, through the device of requiring bail, to an ability to pay. Juvenile court statutes provide that the juvenile should ordinarily be released promptly by police to the custody of parents upon their promise that they will bring him to court at the appointed time. Further police detention is permitted by the statutes only when it is "necessary" or "required for the protection of the community."[r] Al-

---

basing their ruling on the fact that juvenile court procedure is civil rather than criminal. Annot., 160 A.L.R. 287 (1946). For a ruling in favor of the right to bail, see Trimble v. Stone, 187 F. Supp. 483 (D.D.C. 1960).

> However, the right to money bail may not be useful to most juveniles. The parents often have no money. In addition, it would be of little value in cases of children who have allegedly been incorrigible or have gotten beyond the control of their parents, because concern for their parents' money is not something that is high in their esteem and would hardly be expected to assure their reappearance if their family posted the bond. And where is the juvenile court judge who will permit an irate and abusive parent to post bond and depart with a cowering girl who alleges sexual mistreatment by her father or beatings by her mother as the reason why she ran away from home in the first place? As I was telling someone earlier today, while we were awaiting the panel discussion, I have even had instances of 16- or 17-year-old girls picked up for streetwalking, and the person whom we had reason to believe ran the "house" promptly came forward and asked for the right to post bail bond for their release. This is hardly the solution to our juvenile delinquency problem! Since bondsmen look to legally responsible adults to pay their fees, the exercise of any right to bail by a juvenile depends upon a harmonious relationship between him and his parents or guardian. And yet, it is well recognized that the absence of such an effective child-parent relationship is at the root of most of the causes of juvenile delinquency.
>
> Hence, I reluctantly come to the conclusion that efforts to secure the right to bail for juveniles in the belief that such action would *per se* insure fair treatment and protect the liberties of juveniles awaiting juvenile court action are doomed to disappointment.

O. Ketcham, Address, in Proceedings of the National Conference on Bail and Criminal Justice (May 1964) 280, 285 (1965).

[r] CAL. WELF. & INST'NS CODE § 628 (1966) is an example of a statute which attempts to spell out guidelines for detention:

> Investigation; release of minor. Upon delivery to the probation officer of a minor who has been taken into temporary custody . . . the probation officer shall immediately investigate . . . and shall immediately release such minor to the custody of his parent, guardian, or

though these standards create a presumption of release, they are so vague as to give little guidance.

In practice juveniles are frequently detained pending court appearance when there seems no legitimate justification. For example, a study of practices in upstate New York reported that more than 1,430 of the 2,300 children placed in detention during one year were released to the community without adjudication or on probation after the cases reached the court.[8] The vagueness of the guidelines for police detention has permitted detention of children thoughtlessly, for the convenience of officials, or even for punitive or "treatment" purposes.

The Practice

1

A youngster riding in the back seat of a stolen car was taken into custody by the police under a departmental directive to "bring in" both the driver and the passengers of such cars, regardless of complicity in the theft. The directive came in response to a local newspaper campaign against joyriding. The police could not locate the boy's mother to release him because his family did not have a phone and his mother, who had been deserted by the father, was working. Therefore, he was taken to detention quarters, arriving late Friday afternoon after the probation staff had left for the weekend. On Monday morning he was released. His probation report then showed three days in detention, something usually associated with serious misconduct.

2

The police brought a fourteen-year-old boy to detention quarters because, when contacted, his parents refused to pick him up, saying, "We're through with him; you can have him."

The decision to release a youngster in custody depends in part at least upon an evaluation of his parents. If his parents are unavailable or are considered incapable of coping with the situa-

responsible relative unless it appears that further detention of such minor is a matter of immediate and urgent necessity for the protection of such minor or the person or property of another, or unless it appears that such minor is likely to flee the jurisdiction of the court, or unless it appears that such minor has violated an order of the juvenile court.

[8] N.Y. Jt. Legis. Comm. on Court Reorganization, Part II, The Family Court Act 11 (1962).

tion, a juvenile may be detained regardless of what he has done or is likely to do in the future. In addition, there may be situations in which it is undesirable or dangerous to the welfare of the juvenile to release him to his parent.

3

A fifteen-year-old girl was brought to detention as a runaway. She claimed she ran away from home because her father beat her and she was afraid he would kill her. She had a bad bruise on her cheek and marks on her back and legs which tended to substantiate her story. Her father, a local dentist, came to the detention home demanding her release.

Although many juvenile court statutes require a court order for detention (or for continued detention beyond twenty-four or forty-eight hours), they rarely require a hearing as a foundation for that order. As a result, most detention orders are based on a paper review. There has usually not been incentive or adequate procedure for challenging preadjudication detention of juveniles. The vague statutory standards have stood untested. Some jurisdictions, such as California, have formalized the detention decision, requiring a hearing within three judicial days[t] after having been taken into custody. At this hearing, with parents present and counsel provided,[u] both sides are heard and the judge can release or extend detention for a period not to exceed fifteen judicial days.[v]

One of the judges responsible for holding these hearings described his practice as follows:[w]

I say to the minor:

"The reason you were taken into custody was because of some alleged trouble (in your home) (on the streets) or (whatever is applicable).

"You will be interested to learn that the hearings in juvenile court are informal in nature, for your benefit, and for better planning for your future.

"You may have witnesses to speak for you. If you will give their names and addresses to the probation officer sitting here he

---

[t] CAL. WELF. & INST'NS CODE §§ 630, 631, 632 (1966); *see also In re* Macidon, 240 Cal. App. 2d 600, 49 Cal. Rptr. 861 (1966).

[u] CAL. WELF. & INST'NS CODE §§ 633, 634 (1966).

[v] CAL. WELF. & INST'NS CODE §§ 635, 636 (1966).

[w] PROCEEDINGS OF THE FIRST ANNUAL INSTITUTE FOR JUVENILE COURT JUDGES AND REFEREES 10-12 (Cal. June 1962).

will see that they are subpoenaed and brought into court to speak for you.

"You may also have an attorney to speak for you and to represent you at all stages of the proceedings, and your parents and guardians may also be represented by counsel at every stage of the proceedings.

"And you may remain silent if you so desire. You don't have to speak up unless you wish.

"This is a preliminary discussion to decide whether or not you should be temporarily detained.

"The only question before the court this morning is where you should be between now and (insert date), the date of the regular hearing of your case. You and your parents will receive notice of the exact time and place of the regular hearing, to decide what would be the best plan for your future.

"The petition that brings you before the court this morning is this paper I hold in my hand (exhibiting it), in this file. It was prepared, signed and filed this morning by the probation officer based on all the information before the officer, including this report (exhibiting it) from the police department of ____________ ____________ attached with the petition in the file.

"I am going to read this petition to you now. We will read it together. So will you listen carefully please, and tell me whether it is true or not as we read through it."

After I read a paragraph I ask, "is that true or not?" If minor answers in the affirmative, I state, "we will enter your admission accordingly." If minor answers in the negative, I state, "we will enter your denial to paragraph ________."

If minor states that part of it is true, I then state, "would it be correct to say that you deny paragraph ________ in part, and admit it in part?" If minor says "yes", then the clerk is ordered to enter it in the minutes accordingly.

Thereupon, I read the names and addresses of parents and guardians, and verify their correct names and present addresses.

Next, I read the police or sheriff's report or petition request, and recommendation as to whether minor should be released or detained.

Then I read the detention report and recommendations of the detention officer, which set forth pertinent information bearing on detention. This includes the home situation; the recommendation of minor's probation or parole officer, if any; the recommendations of the enforcement officer and the statements and attitude of the minor when interviewed by the detention or intake officer.

Next, pursuant to the provisions of Section 635 of the Juvenile Court Law, I examine the minor, his parents, guardians, and any other persons present having relevant knowledge, and also hear such relevant evidence as the minor, his parents, guardians, or their counsel desire to present.

THE LAWYER'S ROLE AT INTAKE AND DETENTION STAGES OF JUVENILE COURT PROCEEDINGS

By Margaret K. Rosenheim & Daniel L. Skoler
11 Crime and Delinquency 167, 171 (1965)

WHAT CAN THE LAWYER DO AT DETENTION?

At the time a detention decision is under consideration, . . . the lawyer who represents a minor charged with delinquency may properly and usefully examine the basis for delinquency jurisdiction as one prerequisite to a detention determination. In several states the movement to incorporate in juvenile court statutes a provision for detention hearings sheds further light on the lawyer's contribution. The trend itself is evidence of the importance of a decision to detain. It reflects legislators' convictions that the decision deserves judicial scrutiny. If a detention hearing is to be required, however, certain questions arise which are not resolved by statute. The permissible scope of such a hearing is one question on which counsel's advice can be most effective. Without counsel, it is possible that the child's participation in the alleged delinquency will be effectively adjudicated in the detention hearing. Presumably, the child will benefit from skilled advice not only in respect to issues at stake in the detention hearing, but also in interrogation before or after this hearing. Often, the child is interrogated while being detained, and he needs effective guidance or support while undergoing questioning. Absent adult advice and support (provided by parent or counsel), use of a child's confession may be more vulnerable to due process objections than would be one given by an adult under similar circumstances. Legal representation is of particular value in this connection.

Finally, consideration should be given to the choice of shelter care as opposed to detention for the child who must be removed from his parents. In this situation, too, the lawyer can make a contribution by directing the judge's or intake worker's attention to the choice between these two types of custody. Counsel may be able to suggest alternatives to detention based on a more intimate knowledge of both child and family, thus avoiding both overuse of detention and indiscriminate use of formal shelter care facilities (of which there are few in this country). The practical difficulties involved in asking court staff to explore these alternatives in each case are clear.

Some police agencies have worked out criteria for releasing or detaining juveniles.

MANUAL OF PROCEDURE
CHICAGO POLICE DEPARTMENT
Youth Division
(June 1965)

a. Immediate detention is necessary when the child:

(1) has a history of running away and is likely not to appear at the conference,

(2) has committed such a serious offense as would indicate that he might be a danger to the community or to himself,

(3) cannot be controlled by his parents or they exhibit a lack of cooperation,

(4) is a runaway from an institution, or another jurisdiction, or is wanted by another law enforcement agency,

(5) is required as a material witness in another hearing.

. . .

c. The youth officer, whenever practicable, will allow children to remain in the custody of their parents or guardian pending an investigation.

d. In no case will the youth officer cause the juvenile to be detained at the Audy Home simply as a means of punishment.

POLICE DETENTION OF JUVENILES IN A LARGE CITY
By Steven Schur[x]

. . . The runaway criterion is by far the most important in determining the detention decision. More than one-fourth of all youths detained in 1965 were classified as runaways. But this statistic does not show the full importance of the runaway criterion. The Youth Division Annual Offense/Offender Data Sheet records

[x] This excerpt is from an unpublished study made as part of the University of Wisconsin Police Internship Program under a grant from the Ford Foundation.

each offender under the most serious offense charged. Therefore, a youth who was charged with several offenses, one of which was habitually running away, would be recorded under the more serious offense. Furthermore, a youth charged with almost any offense might be detained because his past record showed runaway tendencies. He would be recorded under the offense classification even though the detention decision was based on the runaway criterion. This criterion is a juvenile law version of the bail-bond criterion used in the criminal justice system. There, bail-bond is used to prevent accused persons from fleeing the jurisdiction of the court. It was freely translated into the juvenile system in terms of the youth's "running away," which, I suppose, is thought to be the equivalent of an adult suspect's leaving town. So translated, it has been accepted by most of the authorities in the field of juvenile justice administration and is incorporated into the N.C.C.D.'s *Standards and Guides.* But when a juvenile runs away, he usually runs away into his own neighborhood. At most, he may find his way to another neighborhood in the city, although it is highly unlikely that a ten-, twelve-, fourteen-, or even sixteen-year-old youth would be able to get along on his own in a strange part of the city, with no friends to stay with or otherwise help him out. It is even more unlikely that such a young person would be able to find the means to leave the city completely.

One of the most significant movements in criminal law today is the movement towards bail reform. The greatest gains have been made in the area of recognizance release, where the prisoner is released on his signature and on his promise to appear in court at the proper time. The criteria developed and used for recognizance release examine how long the prisoner has lived in the community, whether he has a family living with him, and whether he has a steady job or real property in the community. In other words, recognizance-bail criteria are concerned with whether or not the prisoner has strong roots in the community. If roots are present, the adult prisoner is free to go, on his word and his signature alone. Yet who can be more strongly rooted in a community than a thirteen-year-old boy? The law itself keeps him there, to say nothing of family ties. He cannot get a job or rent a room. He can't be seen on the streets during school hours or after curfew, or he'll get picked up. He probably couldn't get away with taking a bus to another city, even if he could find the money to buy the ticket. A thirteen-year-old runaway has little choice but to stay in the city, and probably in the neighborhood. In either case, it is only a matter of time before he will get picked up by the police. And, once that happens, he will be held under a warrant if he has previously skipped his appearance at the Juvenile Court. Yet the thirteen-year-old boy is forced to spend two or three weeks in detention, without even the opportunity of being released on bail, while the adult offender, who has infinitely more opportunity to flee the court's jurisdiction, may go home to his family and job.

E. DISPOSITION BY MEANS OTHER THAN ADJUDICATION OF DELINQUENCY

1. Police Disposition

The traditional conception of the criminal justice system is that it is conviction-oriented. While this is not wholly true of the adult system, it is not at all the case with the juvenile system. The securing of a judicial determination that a given juvenile is delinquent is not an important objective. Rather, the purpose is to rehabilitate the juvenile with only as much processing as is necessary. Court intervention is seen as a last resort to be used in only a limited number of cases. Therefore, the model of the juvenile system is one of great discretion aimed at using alternatives to court referral.

Legislative recognition of preadjudication handling is usually limited to the officials of the juvenile court without mention of the police role. However, there has long been an operational assumption within the juvenile justice system that the police have broad discretion to dispose of cases by means other than court referral. Although the police also very often dispose of adult criminal cases without court referral, until recently, the contrast between the adult and juvenile systems was great in the degree to which such discretion has been acknowledged.

The exercise of police discretion in releasing juvenile offenders or making some other informal disposition has been criticized on several grounds:

(1) Police handling without referral to court is said to be used for juveniles who could not be adjudicated delinquent by a court because of insufficient evidence. The problem is that, under these circumstances, the juvenile may feel compelled to agree to the police restraints even though actually there is no legal obligation to do so—an undesirable situation not alleviated by the fact that the police action is taken "in the best interests of the child."

(2) Some observers argue that the police are not properly trained to make decisions about the child's best interests and that this can only be adequately done by professional social workers and the juvenile court judge following an intensive investigation into the entire background of the particular child.

(3) The bases on which the police determine the type of disposition they will make are not clearly articulated nor subject to outside review.

Whatever position one takes on these criticisms, informal disposition of a large share of juvenile offenders (estimates run as high as two-thirds) by the police is recognized as important in the functioning of the juvenile system. For one thing, if all cases were referred to the court, the burden on the courts would be overwhelming. The trend clearly seems to be one of recognizing the importance of police disposition, acknowledging its propriety, and undertaking to control its use.

GANG MEMBERS AND THE POLICE in THE POLICE 72-75
(D. Bordua ed. 1967)
By Carl Werthman & Irving Piliavin

Outcomes

The juvenile officer exercises a good deal of discretion in deciding how to process offenders, a discretion that far transcends the measure of ambiguity ordinarily involved in legal assessments of motivation and intent. Although a truant may not be responsible for his behavior, he may be a touch rebellious, or he may be acting in complete and willful disregard for law, the nature and intent of this crime is not as important to a juvenile officer as what he learns about the attitude of the offender towards the idea of the law itself. For example, if an officer decides he is dealing with a boy who is "guilty but essentially good" or "guilty but sometimes weak," the probability is high that he will decide to let the boy go with a warning about the consequences of committing this crime again. He might feel that contact with the unsavory clientele of a juvenile hall would damage an otherwise positive attitude towards the law or that moral contamination in the eyes of parents and teachers as a result of being sent to jail might weaken an otherwise firm commitment to conventional behavior. On the other hand, if the officer decides that the offender is a "punk," a "persistent troublemaker," or some other version of a thoroughly bad boy, he may well decide to make an arrest.

A "delinquent" is therefore not a juvenile who happens to have committed an illegal act. He is a young person whose moral character has been negatively assessed. And this fact has led some observers to conclude that the transformation of young people into official "delinquents" is best looked at as an organizational rather than a legal process since policemen, probation officers, and juvenile court judges often base their dispositions on a host of criteria that are virtually unrelated to the nature of the specific offense.[y]

The *magnitude of an offense,* of course, can become a factor in dispositions. One responsibly planned and willfully executed robbery, rape, or assault can ruin the moral status of a juvenile

---

[y] *See* THE PRESIDENT'S COMMISSION ON LAW ENFORCEMENT AND ADMINISTRATION OF JUSTICE, THE CHALLENGE OF CRIME IN A FREE SOCIETY 78-79 (1967):

> Besides the nature of the situation and departmental policy, however, police-juvenile encounters are shaped by other, less tangible forces.
>
> One such influence is the character of the police force as a whole. In a recent field study of two police forces—one putting particularly great emphasis on education and training, merit promotions, centralized control; the second relying more heavily on organization by precinct, seniority, on-the-job experience—significant differences were found between the two in handling delinquents. In the first city, the one with the more professionalized force, rates of both processing (police contact not amounting to arrest but requiring the police officer to make an official record) and arrest (formal police action against the juvenile either by ordering him to appear before a court official or by taking him into custody) were more than 50 percent higher than those in the second city. In other words, meetings between policemen and juveniles had formal, official, recorded consequences much more frequently in the first city, with its more highly trained and impersonal police force, than in the second. At the conclusion of his study on the police the researcher, noting how little is known about the actual effects on juveniles of different handling methods, speculates about the various arguments that might be made:
>
> *The training of a police force apparently alters the manner in which juveniles are handled. The principal effect of the inculcation of professional norms is to make the police less discriminatory but more severe. . . . Plausible arguments can be advanced . . . to the effect that certain, swift punishment (in this case, certain, swift referral to a court agency) is an excellent deterrent to juvenile crime. Youths are impressed early, so the argument might go, with the seriousness of their offense and the consequences of the actions. Equally plausible arguments can no doubt be adduced to suggest that arresting juveniles—particularly first offenders—tends to confirm them in their deviant behavior; it gives them the status, in the eyes of their gang, of "tough guys" who have "been downtown" with the police; it throws them into intimate contact with confirmed offenders, where presumably they become "con-wise" and learned in the tricks of the thievery trade; and (somewhat contradictorily) since sentencing is rarely severe, it gives them a contempt for the sanctions available to society.* James Q. Wilson in *The Police,* Bordua, ed. (1967).

indefinitely. Since 90% of the crimes committed by juveniles are minor offenses, however, this criterion is only rarely used.

The number of *previous contacts with police* has a more important effect on dispositions. These contacts are typically recorded on easily accessible files, and these files contain everything from arrests and convictions to contacts made on the flimsiest of contingent grounds. If a boy confesses to a crime and is not known to the police, he is often released. If he is caught for a third or fourth time, however, the sum total of previous contacts may be enough to affect a judgment about his moral character adversely, regardless of the nature or magnitude of the present offense and regardless of the reasons he was previously contacted. For example:

> Like last night, man, me and Willy got busted for curfew. I mean I got busted for curfew. We was walkin' up the hill towards home, and these cops pull up. It was a Friday night, man, so we didn't want no trouble. When the cops ask us what we was doing and what about our names we was all nice. So then the cop gets on that radio and checks us out. There was a whole bunch of noise comin' over that box. I couldn't hear what they was sayin'. But then the cop comes out and says to Willy, "O.K., you can go." And I say, "What about me?" And the cop says, "You been in trouble before. We don't want you walkin' the streets at night. We going to take you down to the station for curfew." Then I got real mad. I almost ran. Lucky thing I didn't though. I woulda been in real trouble then.

There is even some evidence to suggest that assessments about the type and quality of *parental control* are even more important factors in dispositions than *any* of the offense-related criteria. One of the main concerns of a juvenile officer is the likelihood of future offense, and this determination is often made largely on the basis of "the kinds of parents" a boy happens to possess. Thus, the moral character of parents also passes under review; and if a house appears messy, a parent is missing, or a mother is on welfare, the probability of arrest increases. Similarly, a boy with a father and two older brothers in jail is considered a different sort of person from a boy whose immediate family is not known to the police. [T]hese judgments about family life are particularly subject to bias by attitudes related to class.

> See, like if you or maybe one of your brothers, say both of you, been to Y.A. [Youth Authority] or your sister, every

> time they see you they get on your back. They know all your family. If they ever pick you up and look at your records, they automatically take you in. They see where your sister been to jail, your brother, or if you ever went to jail. And they start saying, "Your whole family is rotten. Your whole family is jailbirds." Shit like that. And this is what really make you mad, when they tell you your mother don't know how to read!

Although the family situation of a boy and his record of prior police contacts both enter into dispositions, the most important factor affecting the decision of juvenile officers is the *attitude* displayed by the offender, both during and after the confession itself. Cicourel, for example, found that juvenile officers were strongly influenced by the style and speed with which the offender confessed. If a boy blurts out his misdeeds immediately, this behavior is taken as a sign that the boy "trusts" authority and is therefore "under control." If the boy proves to be a "tough nut to crack," however, he is viewed with suspicion. As soon as a juvenile is defined as "hardened," he is considered no less dangerous to society than the adult criminal.

Similarly, the boys who appear frightened, humble, penitent, and ashamed are also more likely to go free. They are often defined as "weak, troubled, and the victim of circumstances" but basically "good boys," an assessment of moral character that may win them a release.

On the other hand, if a boy shows no signs of being spiritually moved by his offense, the police deal harshly with him. Not only has he sinned against a legal rule, but he has also symbolically rejected the normative basis for conforming to it in the first place; and it is this double deviation that has fateful consequences for the way he is treated by the police. Once he gets himself defined as "the kind of person who doesn't respect the law," he becomes a perfect candidate for arrest, detention, and eventual incarceration. Most of the juvenile officers we interviewed felt that the attitude of the offender was the major determinant of dispositions in 50% of their cases, and Nathan Goldman reports that "defiance on the part of a boy will lead to juvenile court quicker than anything else."

It is hardly necessary to describe the way most gang boys feel about the equity of these dispositions. One only needs to imagine the look on a boy's face when he is told that he is about to spend a year in jail for an offense committed with a friend who was sent home when he promptly confessed.

JUVENILE DELINQUENTS: THE POLICE, STATE COURTS, AND INDIVIDUALIZED JUSTICE

Note, 79 Harvard Law Review 775, 778-84 (1966)†

The patrolmen interviewed generally acknowledged that they do not write up offenses of a minor nature but rather terminate the conduct and perhaps admonish the offenders. In the larger metropolitan areas, this policy reflects both a condonation of a certain amount of "horse-play" and a recognition of the fact that the juvenile bureau has limited resources; in smaller towns, where patrolmen are likely to know the juveniles involved or their families, similar allowances are made. But such a permissive attitude in regard to very minor offenses may be modified where the juvenile bureau strongly believes that treatment and rehabilitation will be made more effective through early discovery and handling of delinquent traits; this belief may lead to a policy of encouraging patrolmen to bring even minor offenses to the attention of the bureau.

An obvious further qualification to permissive police attitudes is the reaction of the juvenile: a polite, cooperative, or obsequious attitude on his part may result in a simple warning, whereas insolence will influence the patrolman to "write up" the incident or even to take the juvenile into custody. Police officials, youth bureau officers, and patrolmen, while admitting that the youth's attitude is often determinative, claimed that simple emotional reaction is not the reason for considering such a factor; rather, they maintained that the explanation is in part a belief in the importance of fostering a positive and cooperative attitude toward police authority and in part the notion that a negative attitude is indicative of delinquent tendencies. Discriminatory enforcement on the basis of factors such as race or economic status, however, was emphatically denied by all those who were interviewed.

When the offender is referred to the juvenile bureau, the court referral decision will be made by the juvenile officer, and an inappropriate invocation of the legal process can be corrected at this stage. The patrolman is thus insulated from the pressure of direct judicial review of his decision, and the importance of learning proper standards is diminished. Moreover, the release of an offender by the juvenile bureau, normally accompanied by a sharp reprimand to the youth, does not imply an incorrect decision on the part of the patrolman, as release by the court might. Consequently, one would expect patrolmen to decide doubtful cases in favor of referral. This tendency was confirmed by the head of the juvenile division in Chicago, who further indicated a belief that contact with the police is usually beneficial and that the overall effect of the trend is therefore constructive.

3. The Police Hearing.—In some cities, the offender is immediately brought before a juvenile officer, who decides whether to refer the case to court or to "adjust" or "settle" (terminate) it at the police stage. In most cities, the process of making this decision has assumed the form of a police hearing whenever the nature of the offense or the juvenile's status (as parolee or runaway) do not call for an automatic court referral. The alleged purpose of these proceedings is not to adjudicate guilt, but to determine (according to a standard that concentrates on the likelihood of recidivism) which cases require the attention of the court. In fact, an equally important function of the hearing is to provide an authoritarian setting in which the police can, with a severe lecture, impress upon the juvenile the error of his ways and "counsel" him so that he will avoid future difficulties.

(a) Procedure.—After the juvenile bureau has investigated a complaint, or after the receipt of a report from a patrolman or investigating unit, a time is set for the hearing. A notice of the time and place of the proceeding is then either mailed to the juvenile's parents or delivered to them by a patrolman. The juvenile and his parents appear before a "hearing officer" or "counselor," and the juvenile is questioned about his participation in the offense under investigation. Only rarely is the youth accompanied by counsel or advised of a right to remain silent. In none of the notice forms that were examined is there any mention of a right to counsel. Indeed, to the police the "right" to counsel or to remain silent is simply not in accord with the nature of the process, because both the hearing and the decision are matters completely within their discretion.

The police have no authority to compel the juvenile or his parents to attend the hearing, much less to accept any eventual restrictions on the juvenile's freedom. But in fact, the police have the necessary leverage: the possibilities of court referral and of the creation of a permanent police or court record are made clear in order to obtain the cooperation of both the parents and the child. An obvious additional influence on the juvenile's response is the quasi-judicial appearance of the hearing—service of "notice," preset time and place, location at the seat of authority (police headquarters), and a "hearing officer" in uniform, usually seated behind a desk. These quasi-judicial forms are adopted in order to magnify the apparent authority of the hearing officer, and thereby both to solemnify the inevitable lecture to the juvenile and to increase the chances that he will confess. The rationale usually offered by hearing officers for the emphasis on confessions was that police rehabilitation of the youth cannot be undertaken unless by confession he recognizes his guilt in a moral sense; if the juvenile remains impenitent there is no insurance against further illegal acts. A persistent denial of guilt is taken to indicate that the juvenile is not amenable to the "noncompulsory" approaches of his parents, local agencies, or the police, and requires referral to court. A more practical motive for requiring confession may be fear that a practice of "adjusting" denied offenses might antagonize the juvenile court judges and thus jeopardize the extrastatutory police authority to act in such matters.

Since police hearings are based on confessions, they obviously would not work if juveniles refused to speak. To most of the police departments interviewed, it follows logically that there is no role for a lawyer at the police hearing stage: there was a nearly uniform belief that an attorney would instruct his client to remain silent and thus obstruct the hearing process. In at least one city there was admitted hostility to the introduction of lawyers at "adjustment" decisions: a juvenile's request to contact his parents is honored, but "if he asks for an attorney, we don't let that interfere with our investigation." Most departments noted that there had been a greater demand for lawyers in recent years, especially by the older and more "sophisticated" juveniles, though the request is still unusual. The increase was blamed on the influence of increased publicity (especially through popular television shows) of the ability of a "mouthpiece" to "beat the rap."

(b) *Factors Affecting the Dispositional Decision.*—If the juvenile maintains his innocence, the hearing is terminated. The juvenile officer must then decide whether the case is to be referred to court. The police generally refer to court all cases in which the juvenile does not confess, in order to prevent the referral threat from losing its potency. However, they will not refer a case when the evidence available is insufficient or the offense is trivial, because the court is likely to dismiss the proceeding; but even in this situation the juvenile is unlikely to be released without a lecture, and will probably be led to believe that his release is due to a decision to give him another chance, rather than to a recognition of the likelihood of release by the court. The police are rarely faced with this problem, however, since only a tiny percentage of juveniles who are given police hearings deny their guilt.

If the juvenile confesses, most hearing officers (or if there is no hearing procedure in the jurisdiction, the juvenile officer making the adjudication decision) have three courses open to them: release the child to his parents with a reprimand or warning; direct the child (and perhaps his parents) to a community social service agency; or refer the case to court. Some hearing officers have the additional alternative of imposing direct sanctions on the juvenile. Both the hearing and disposition are generally viewed by the police as fulfilling a crime prevention function. They therefore claim that their decision-making process—like that of the juvenile court—centers on the child rather than on the offense. The decision as to disposition is supposedly based upon a calculation of the risk of future illegal activity on the part of the juvenile. If it seems probable that the parents will be able to control the child's behavior, either on their own or with the aid of counseling by a private or public agency, there will be no referral to court. When at a later stage a juvenile court judge is faced with an analogous decision, he is usually provided with a comprehensive family history and social profile, including a recommended disposition prepared by a probation officer with training in social work. The police have come to recognize the importance of such background information to their own dispositional decision, and in an increasing number of departments a serious attempt is made to secure some of the relevant material.

Certain facts—the juvenile's previous record, the seriousness of the offense charged, and the degree of criminal sophistication in the mode of commission of the crime—are validly related to the referral decision but are obviously of no aid in the broad range of cases involving juveniles who have no significant record and whose offense is not of a serious nature. In such cases the probability of recidivism is allegedly tested almost exclusively by considerations such as the extent of parental control, factors that require an investigation more extensive than police resources allow and analytic techniques for which the police are not trained. The not unpredictable result is reliance upon factors that are visible and easily ascertainable but arguably irrelevant. For example, many of the hearing officers questioned indicated that they would refer to court all cases in which the parents were uncooperative and attempted to "shield" the child from the authorities. Whether this police attitude stems from a judgment about emotional relationships within the family is questionable; rather, it may well represent a simple attempt to bolster the position of the police. The few empirical studies made have examined on-the-spot decisions by juvenile officers rather than hearings, but confirm in that setting the tendency to rely on improper criteria. One study concluded that the determinative factors are the juvenile's demeanor, his appearance, and his race; another confirms the reliance on race and notes wryly that "athletes and altar boys will rarely be referred to court for their offenses."

A further factor influencing referral decisions—and one of the most important causes of the great difference among jurisdictions in the percentage of cases referred to court—is the wide variation among departments in their attitude towards court appearance. In Wisconsin Rapids, Wisconsin, for instance, the juvenile officer refers all youths involved in serious crimes and thefts and most repeaters of minor offenses, while in a neighboring community the juvenile officer reportedly refrains from referring in a large proportion of cases and attempts to work with the juveniles, even when there have been a significant number of past violations. This difference in policy may stem from varying judgments as to the success of crime prevention at the police level or from varying degrees of dissatisfaction with juvenile court operations. Of course, the hearing officer's decision whether or not to retain cases depends largely on the range of alternatives available between release after the hearing, with whatever "counseling" that entails, and referral to court.

In a few cities, the police must refer all offenders who require outside aid to court: in Tucson, for instance, the only alternative to referral is immediate reprimand and release. But in the majority of departments, one possibility is referral to a "community agency." The Chicago Youth Division, for example, has compiled an extensive manual of available community resources and maintains direct contact with all such organizations. Many departments request that parents utilize the services of the agencies, but they differ on the extent to which they check to ensure compliance. Some tell the parents frankly that any action on their part is purely voluntary; others attempt to enforce the agency referral, commonly by conditioning police settlement on continued adherence to the program for reform outlined at the hearing. The ability of the police to enforce such threats of future court referral depends, however, upon the willingness of the court to accept referrals a considerable time after apprehension of the offender, and several courts will not. However, it is the opinion of many of those interviewed that, when a juvenile who requires agency aid does not receive it, he will commit another offense within a relatively short period of time; the inability of the police to require him to seek the assistance of an agency will therefore simply result in a short-term delay in the initiation of "treatment," for presumably he will be referred to court after his next offense.

In some cities, the judges apparently allow the police, with the consent of the parents, to place restrictions of varying degrees of severity on the juvenile's freedom. In Kansas City, for example, the police administer a stringent though informal discipline program called "grounding." A typical "grounded" youth must attend school unless a doctor's explanation is obtained for his absence. At all other times he may leave the house only if accompanied by a parent, and then not for any activity that is primarily engaged in for pleasure. He must dress conventionally and have his hair cut in a reasonable manner; and he must study at home for a minimum prescribed period each day. After this schedule is enforced for a month, lesser conditions will be imposed for the duration of the school year. A high degree of success in preventing future offenses is claimed to result from this program.[z]

THE PRESIDENT'S COMMISSION ON LAW ENFORCEMENT AND ADMINISTRATION OF JUSTICE
THE CHALLENGE OF CRIME IN A FREE SOCIETY 81-83 (1967)

Pre-Judicial Disposition Outside the Court. It is a salient characteristic of the American criminal law system that substantial numbers of those who, on the basis of facts known to the authorities, could be dealt with by the formal machinery of justice are in fact disposed of otherwise. Chapter 5 on the courts includes discussion of nonjudicial disposition of adult offenders. The pres-

[z] *Compare* WISCONSIN BOARD OF JUVENILE COURT JUDGES, HANDBOOK FOR JUVENILE COURT SERVICES 26 (1959):

"D. Disposition by the Law Enforcement Agency . . .

"3. Voluntary Police Supervision

"Voluntary police supervision is the giving of a direct supervision service by law enforcement officers to a child who has committed an offense. Voluntary supervision consists of such activities as having a child report to the police department for a period of time during which the police officer counsels him and checks on his activities. In general, there appears to be strong feeling, both among law enforcement officers and the courts, that such work is not a function of the law enforcement agency and that police officers do not have the authority to force a child to submit to and take part in such supervision.

"Some law enforcement agencies have been forced to take on some voluntary supervision activities because of a lack of community services. Such situations as a lack of court workers and an absence of other community resources have required voluntary supervision by the police. Although necessity sometimes requires such work, it is felt that it is outside of the policing function. Law enforcement officers are not trained for and do not want to do social work, just as social workers are not trained for police work and do not picture themselves as police officers. When gaps exist in the community for the supervision of children, the law enforcement agencies should help to inform the community of the gaps and work towards the filling of those gaps. As soon as possible they should return completely to their own important function of law enforcement."

sures and policies responsible for development of pre-judicial dispositions in the juvenile system are in part the same as those that have led to the use of alternatives to the adult criminal process. The felt overseverity of the formal process in the circumstances of the particular case, the broad reach of the definition of the forbidden conduct beyond what is appropriately dealt with by the criminal or juvenile justice system, and the sheer volume of workload are among the most important considerations.

Informal and discretionary pre-judicial dispositions already are a formally recognized part of the process to a far greater extent in the juvenile than in the criminal justice system. The primacy of the rehabilitative goal in dealing with juveniles, the limited effectiveness of the formal processes of the juvenile justice system, the labeling inherent in adjudicating children delinquents, the inability of the formal system to reach the influences—family, school, labor market, recreational opportunities—that shape the life of a youngster, the limited disposition options available to the juvenile judge, the limitations of personnel and diagnostic and treatment facilities, the lack of community support—all of these factors give pre-judicial dispositions an especially important role with respect to juveniles.

Consequently, the informal and pre-judicial processes of adjustment compete in importance with the formal ones and account for a majority of juvenile dispositions. They include discretionary judgments of the police officer to ignore conduct or warn the child or refer him to other agencies; "station adjustment" by the police, in which the child's release may be made conditional on his complying with designated limitations on his conduct; the planned diversion of alleged delinquents away from the court to resources within the school, clinic, or other community facilities, by such groups as mental health, social, and school guidance agencies; pre-judicial dispositions, at the intake stage of the court process, by probation officers or sometimes judges exercising a broad screening function and selecting among alternatives that include outright dismissal, referral to another community agency for service, informal supervision by the probation staff, detention, and filing a petition for further court action. In many courts the court intake process itself disposes of the majority of cases.

There are grave disadvantages and perils, however, in that vast continent of sublegal dispositions. It exists outside of and hence beyond the guidance and control of articulated policies and legal restraints. It is largely invisible—unknown in its detailed operations—and hence beyond sustained scrutiny and criticism. Discretion too often is exercised haphazardly and episodically, without the salutary obligation to account and without a foundation in full and comprehensive information about the offender and about the availability and likelihood of alternative dispositions. Opportunities occur for illegal and even discriminatory results, for abuse of authority by the ill-intentioned, the prejudiced, the overzealous. Irrelevant, improper considerations—race, nonconformity, punitiveness, sentimentality, understaffing, overburdening loads—may govern officials in their largely personal exercise of discretion. The consequence may be not only injustice to the juvenile but diversion out of the formal channels of those whom the best interests of the community require to be dealt with through the formal adjudicatory and dispositional processes.

Yet on balance, it is clear to the Commission that informal pre-judicial handling is preferable to formal treatment in many cases and should be used more broadly. The possibilities for rehabilitation appear to be optimal where community-based resources are used on a basis as nearly consensual as possible. The challenge is to obtain the benefits of informal pre-judicial handling with a minimum of its attendant evils. The following recommendations are offered to that end.

(a) Pre-Judicial Handling by the Police. The police should promptly determine which cases are suitable for pre-judicial disposition. Where there are juvenile specialists, they should be present at the stationhouse for as many hours of the day as possible and available on call when absent, to facilitate speedy pre-judicial decisions. The police should have written standards for release, for referral to nonjudicial sources, and for referral to the juvenile court. The standards should be sent to all agencies of delinquency control and should be reviewed and appraised jointly at periodic intervals. They should be made the basis for inservice training that would consider, besides the decision-making duties of the police, materials pertinent to increasing understanding of juvenile behavior and making more effective use of nonjudicial community resources.

In cases where information on the child is needed, it should be sought through home visits as well as from official records, and the police should be aided, or replaced, by paid case aides drawn from the neighborhood within the police district and selected for their knowledge of the community and their ability to communicate easily with juveniles and their families.

In addition to outright referral to nonjudicial agencies the police should have the option to refer directly to the juvenile court specified classes of cases, including those of more serious offenders, repeated offenders for whom other and persistent redirecting efforts had failed, and certain parole and probation violators. The police should not undertake to redirect juveniles by such means as conducting quasi-judicial hearings or imposing special duties or personal obligations.

Police practices following custody thus should continue as at present but with two significant changes: Cases deemed suitable for adjustment would be referred to a youth-serving agency within a neighborhood service center (the Youth Services Bureau proposed herein and described in detail subsequently), and the categories of cases that could be referred by the police directly to juvenile court would be restricted. Exercise of discretion to release outright would be encouraged, as now, so that minor offenses not apparently symptomatic of serious behavior problems could be dismissed at the earliest stage of official handling, and even more serious offenses could be adjusted by referral to a Youth Services Bureau or other organization if, in the judgment of the police, there was no immediate threat to public safety.

. . .

(b) Community Agencies. There should be expanded use of community agencies for dealing with delinquents nonjudicially and close to where they live. Use of community agencies has several advantages. It avoids the stigma of being processed by an official agency regarded by the public as an arm of crime control. It substitutes for official agencies organizations better suited for redirecting conduct. The use of locally sponsored or operated organizations heightens the community's awareness of the need for recreational, employment, tutoring, and other youth development services. Involvement of local residents brings greater appreciation of the complexity of delinquents' problems, thereby engendering the sense of public responsibility that financial support of programs requires.

Referrals by police, school officials, and others to such local community agencies should be on a voluntary basis. To protect against abuse, the [police] agency's option of court referral should terminate when the juvenile or his family and the community agency agree upon an appropriate disposition. If a departure from the agreed-upon course of conduct should thereafter occur, it should be the community agency that exercises the authority to refer to court. It is also essential that the dispositions available to such local organizations be restricted. The purpose of using community institutions in this way is to help, not to coerce, and accordingly it is inappropriate to confer on them a power to order treatment or alter custody or impose sanctions for deviation from the helping program.

The trend in the juvenile system, as in the adult system, has been toward fuller recognition of the necessity for discretionary decisions and toward self-regulation through training and professionally formulated guidelines.

MANUAL OF PROCEDURE
CHICAGO POLICE DEPARTMENT
Youth Division
(June 1965)

Section III—Basic Factors and Considerations in the Processing of Juveniles

1. Guidelines

The youth officer has a variety of assignments and responsibilities requiring discretion and judgment. Of these, perhaps none is more important than the disposition of juvenile offenders. In discharging this responsibility he will be influenced by the following six guide lines:

A. *The type and seriousness of the offense.* In minor offenses, the type of behavior frequently referred to as Disorderly Conduct, where no serious negative considerations arise in respect to the remaining guidelines, some consideration should be given to a Community Adjustment. Yet even a minor offense, which might not in and of itself warrant a court filing, could require such action in order to remove the child from his home for reasons of neglect or dependency.

1. A series of minor offenses might be reason for a Community Adjustment with a specific kind of referral to a community agency. Sometimes this type of situation might be more in need of attention than one where an isolated and more serious offense has been committed without any previous history of delinquency. It must be remembered that a minor offense when committed under one set of circumstances would be viewed differently in another kind of situation. The judgment of the youth officer, in view of his experience and training, therefore, becomes exceedingly important.

2. The serious offense, usually classified as a felony, would ordinarily call for a court filing. A child of tender years might commit an offense which would be considered very serious. Such child, however, would not be dealt with in the same manner as an older juvenile by process of court filing. Yet certain serious offenses committed by a very young child would indicate a strong need for help which could only be obtained through court filing.

B. *The previous behavioral history of the juvenile.* In consideration of the type of disposition to be made, the youth officer will be guided by:

1. The juvenile's past history (obtained at Youth Division Headquarter's Files), and such knowledge that the officer may have regarding the juvenile, or what the investigation reveals;

2. The previous history indicating that the juvenile has been involved in a series of other minor offenses all of which were adjusted without a court filing. Consideration should then be given to the possibility of court intervention no matter how minor the offense charged against the juvenile. Even here a careful exploration of all possible avenues of help would be advisable before a court filing.

C. *Circumstances possibly contributing to the commission of the offense, and the juvenile's capacity to accept help.*

1. The youth officer's investigation will include information from a variety of sources which might shed some light on the factors that contribute to the juvenile's behavior and in his capacity to accept help. These factors might relate to the neighborhood and the negative forces at work there, or may stem from the family relationships, school problems, or the juvenile's own makeup and temperament.

2. The eventual disposition of the case must be viewed with reference to these factors since a Community Adjustment must take into account the possibility of bringing about a change in elements having a deleterious effect upon the juvenile; and to the capacity of the juvenile to change his behavior and to accept help.

D. *The interest and attitude of the parents toward the child and the offense, plus their ability to provide the necessary supervision and guidance.* The first contact between the youth officer and the parent or guardian usually takes place in the district station. Community Adjustments with or without a referral may require a home visit. Because of his investigation, interrogation, and observation, the youth officer may have sufficient knowledge and information so that a home interview would not be necessary.

1. A home interview enables the youth officer to observe the child in his family setting, and therefore helps him to make a more selective and meaningful disposition. He should note that the parents are the best immediate resource available.

2. The youth officer is interested, not only in the parent's attitude toward the child, but the view they take of the offense committed. Whatever disposition is eventually made, a great part of the consideration will relate to the parent's availability, and willingness to cooperate by providing supervision and insuring that the plans developed for referral to a community agency will be carried forward by them.

E. *The cooperation and attitude of the complainant in relation to the proposed disposition.* Most persons will agree with an intelligent plan of rehabilitation worked out on behalf of a juvenile. A solution worked out with the best interests of the child in mind will be supported by the complainant in most cases when careful and painstaking explanation is made regarding the proposed plan for a Community Adjustment.

There may be complainants who will be adamant in their desire to have a Juvenile Court filing. The complainant's rights must be recognized. When an offense has in fact been committed, and there are reasonable grounds to believe the juvenile in question is implicated, the youth officer will direct the case to the Juvenile Court.

F. *The availability of resources and their applicability to the situation of the juvenile.* Sometimes no resource other than the child's family will be required for disposition of the case. Occasionally the situation reveals that more than a Community Adjustment is required. The services of an individual, a casework agency, or other professional organization, might be required to supplement what the family can offer in the way of help. It may reveal that other members of the family also are in need of assistance and counseling.

1. Investigation may show that the family, or the juvenile in question, is already known to another agency, or several of them. If the child or his family is known to another agency, then it becomes the youth officer's responsibility to alert such agency to provide the necessary aid to the juvenile or to his family's needs.

Follow-up is necessary to insure that the juvenile, the family, and the agency have established contact, and that such aid is being provided.

2. Where the juvenile and family are not known to any agency, then dictated by the needs, referral to a resource or community agency becomes a function of the youth officer.

a. One of the prime tools in the disposition process is the wise and selective use of indigenous and community resources, agencies, and organizations.

2. *Juvenile Court Intake and Informal Disposition*

Unlike the criminal justice system, whose ultimate objective—at least conceptually—is the conviction of the guilty by a court, the juvenile justice system sets no value on judicial determination of the allegation of delinquency. Its primary objective is to rehabilitate; and if the youngster can be rehabilitated without resort to the formal court process, all the better. Therefore, typically juvenile court statutes provide that when a case is referred to the court, an investigation should be made to determine whether a petition should be filed in court or whether some sort of "informal" disposition should be made.[a] This step in the juvenile justice system is known as "intake"—a term borrowed from social welfare agencies and indicative of the influence of the social work profession on the concepts and terminology of the juvenile justice system.

Intake is usually performed by a nonjudge professional attached to the juvenile court. In fact, one of the innovations of the juvenile court movement was the addition, as an integral part of the court process, of this nonjudge professional to perform numerous functions related to the socialized nature of the court. These professionals are known as the probation or court worker staff. The court worker may or may not be a social worker, although this is usually said to be the desired training. Not all juvenile courts are staffed by court workers, but the typical statutory blueprint includes them, and juvenile courts in populous areas are so staffed.

"Intake," although itself a peculiarly juvenile concept, is not without its counterpart in the adult system. The function of the court worker at intake is somewhat analogous to the duties of the prosecutor in deciding whether and what to charge in a crim-

[a] On the necessity for such an investigation, see *In re* Bacon, 240 Cal. App. 2d 34, 49 Cal. Rptr. 322 (1966), and cases cited therein.

inal prosecution. In some cases a decision not to charge or not to file a delinquency petition means the release of the suspect from further processing. Often, however, the prosecutor agrees not to charge if the accused will make restitution, receive psychiatric help, or in some other way accept treatment without conviction. In the same manner, the court worker may employ all sorts of informal control and treatment devices as an alternative to referring the child to the court for adjudication.[b] In practice, more children are probably dealt with informally by the court worker in the probation office setting than are referred to the court for formal adjudication and disposition.

This discretion of the court worker to handle a juvenile without official court hearing is a matter of controversy in the juvenile system. On the one hand, it has been charged that this unofficial treatment, no matter how effective, bypasses whatever controls the court hearing (and the legal training of the judge) exert on evidence standards or due process requirements. Some see this as a sort of "consent conviction" or "punishment without trial." True, the child is not actually convicted and perhaps probation conditions are treatment rather than punishment, but the disposition is essentially coercive, and the most humane and well-meant determination against one's will should be subject to the protection which court hearing offers.

1

A 17½-year-old boy was picked up by police because he was riding in a car with a boy reported by his parents as a runaway. Both boys were referred to juvenile court. Investigation showed that the 17½-year-old had not been home for four months. His parents had not reported him as a runaway. When questioned, they said that they would prefer their son to live at home but felt it was up to him. The boy was placed on informal supervision by the juvenile court probation department as a runaway and required to live at home.

On the other hand, there is widespread concern, particularly among law enforcement agencies, that juveniles whose conduct has been considered sufficiently serious to be referred to the court are released with informal unofficial handling, with the result that danger to the community is assessed by a social worker rather than the judge. There is no doubt that this is a major area of police-juvenile court friction.

[b] See the case file at 1026, *infra*.

2

A seventeen-year-old boy was involved in a serious stabbing. A check of his record showed that he had been referred by the police to juvenile court on six previous occasions for car theft and shoplifting, but a petition for a formal juvenile court hearing had never been filed.

CALIFORNIA WELFARE AND INSTITUTIONS CODE § 655 (1966)

§ 655. Failure of probation officer to file petition and take action; review.

When any person has applied to the probation officer, pursuant to Section 653, to commence juvenile court proceedings and the probation officer fails to file a petition within three weeks after such application, such person may, within one month after making such application, apply to the juvenile court to review the decision of the probation officer, and the court may either affirm the decision of the probation officer or order him to commence juvenile court proceedings.

As in the case of "station adjustment" by the police, the matter of unofficial disposition must be viewed in the context of alternatives to this procedure. Requiring all children referred to the court to have a formal hearing would have important consequences for both the children involved and for the entire system. The trend today is to encourage pre-judicial screening by the juvenile court worker but to require procedural protections for the juvenile.

A STUDY OF THE ADMINISTRATION OF JUVENILE JUSTICE IN CALIFORNIA, part III, at 36-39 (1960)[c]

By I. J. Shain & Walter R. Burkhart

INTAKE SCREENING

Intake screening is one of the most critical and significant phases of the probation process. In some respects, it is the most important phase of the process. By intelligent discrimination of referrals, probation agencies can carefully select minors in need

[c] This study was done as the basis for a major revision of the California juvenile court law.

of supervision and casework and screen out those who can appropriately be treated by a reprimand or by referral to another agency. Besides serving as a process of filtering out unnecessary referrals, intake acts as a control on both the juvenile court calendar, and in turn, on probation supervision caseloads. . . .

Extent of Screening

In view of the fact that the bases upon which minors may be referred for possible juvenile court action range from minor misbehavior to serious felonious acts, it is not surprising to learn that liberal screening or referrals takes place. This is evident from the fact that out of 39,000 boys initially referred to probation departments for delinquent behavior, only a little more than half resulted in the filing of a juvenile court petition. More than one-third were dismissed without further action, while 11 percent were placed on informal probation without court referral.

A similar pattern of screening was discernible in girls' cases. About one-half the girls referred to probation departments were brought before the juvenile court on petitions, 39 percent were dismissed, and 11 percent were placed on informal probation.

These gross data, however, obscure significant differences which emerge when the delinquent cases are separately analysed on the basis of their two major groupings: (1) cases involving violations of criminal laws, and (2) delinquent tendency cases.

In round numbers, almost 25,000 boys were referred because of specific criminal acts, 70 percent more than the 14,000 referred for delinquent tendencies. Petitions were filed in only 33 percent of the delinquent tendency cases contrasted with 63 percent of the criminal offense cases. Similarly, more than 54 percent of the delinquent tendency referrals were dismissed whereas this was true for less than 28 percent of those violating criminal laws.

The proportion placed on informal probation was more comparable—10 percent of the delinquent tendency cases and 12 percent of those committing criminal offenses.

Of the more than 6,300 girls referred for delinquent tendencies, petitions were filed in 43 percent of the cases and 45 percent were dismissed. The remaining 12 percent were placed under informal probation.

On the other hand, of the 3,600 girls referred for specific criminal acts in 1958, 62 percent had petitions filed for juvenile court adjudication; 31 percent were dismissed; and 8.5 percent were placed on informal probation.

. . .

Criteria Employed in Dismissing Referral

Probation officers listed the general criteria they employed when deciding not to file a petition. In many respects, these criteria are the counterparts of those cited in connection with the filing of petitions.

The factor most often listed was that the child's needs could be adequately fulfilled without resorting to juvenile court action. This would include placing the child on informal probation, referral to another social agency, or their being assured that the minor's parents would provide necessary supervision or corrective action.

The nature of the offense is also heavily considered in deciding whether to dismiss the case of a minor referred to the probation department. Seven of the 20 [responding] counties mentioned that petitions are generally not filed on first offenses of a minor nature. In some instances, this is a general policy for first offenders; in other cases, this applies only when the first offense is not serious.

Curiously enough, since the juvenile court is basically a legal proceeding, only one-fourth of the counties mentioned as a criterion whether there was sufficient evidence that the child is within the jurisdiction of the court. The issue as to whether the jurisdictional facts can be substantiated should normally precede the decision on filing of a petition in all cases. The fact that so small a proportion of probation officials give this factor serious thought suggests the lack of concern with this fundamental issue.

Other factors considered when deciding a petition need not be filed included whether or not the home offered stability, whether court wardship might be detrimental to the child's best interests, and the child's (young) age.

. . .

Criteria Employed in Filing of Petitions

Whether or not a petition is to be filed is both an important, and often a difficult decision. Frequently, the shading between behavior which is serious enough to warrant juvenile court supervision and that which is not sufficiently serious is not always readily apparent. Unfortunately, the bases for these decisions not only lack consistency among the many probation departments in the State, but often among individual workers within the same probation department.

While the juvenile court supposedly is basically concerned with the child rather than the offense, in actuality the offense itself often determines whether or not a petition is filed. . . . This particularly applied to offenses which would constitute a felony if committed by an adult. Among the offenses included in the felony classes are: robbery, murder, burglary, theft, and assault with deadly weapons. The attitude on the part of the probation officers is that these criminal acts are serious in nature, arouse public interest, and possibly can lead to further serious criminality involving injury to other persons unless checked by court action. This is particularly true of crimes against persons. Actually, serious crimes against persons comprise a relatively small proportion of juvenile cases. Of the 62,600 juveniles arrested in 1958 for specific offenses, only 1 out of 20 was charged with a major offense against persons; namely, robbery, aggravated assault, forcible rape, or homicide. The overwhelming majority of these arrests, 95 percent, involved burglary, auto theft, petit theft, and similar property offenses.

. . .

The second most frequently cited criterion was whether or not the minor had a history of repeated delinquency. . . .

Probation officers in 12 of the 20 [responding] counties listed as a generalized criterion whether the child needed casework services and supervision. . . .

Several other factors were mentioned; however, none received emphasis from more than 6 of the 20 responding counties. Among the remaining factors were: (1) the child's unfavorable attitude towards his behavior; (2) whether or not there is a poor home situation; (3) the nature of community reactions and attitudes; (4) whether the child required commitment to a local or state institution; and (5) whether juvenile court action would serve as a deterrence against further delinquency.

Factors Responsible for Variations Among Counties

Several factors are responsible for the extreme variations noted in probation department screening and petition filings. First, the extent of screening by primary referral sources, particularly law enforcement agencies, differs among counties. Some law enforcement agencies refer only children with serious behavior problems, and therefore, a higher proportion of petitions will be filed. Others refer indiscriminately and the burden of screening falls upon the probation department. . . .

A second factor influencing petition filing rates is the extent to which the juvenile court encourages informal probation services. Since most juvenile courts operate on a part-time basis, court calendars are normally scheduled to accommodate the juvenile court judge's other trial work. Such time limitations tend to restrict the number of petitions filed and increase the use of informal probation.

Third, the use of detention has a bearing on the number of petitions filed. Since children cannot be detained longer than 48 hours unless a petition is filed, many probation departments file petitions primarily because their investigations have not been completed within the 48-hour period allowed. If the completed investigation suggests that wardship is not necessary, dismissal of the petition is usually recommended at the court hearing.

Fourth, the completeness of reporting and the method of counting referrals is another variable. Some agencies do not record all cases which are referred to them. Instead, they merely record those cases upon which some further action is taken. Consequently, in a few counties there is a tendency to underreport the total number of referrals screened out.

Fifth, there are basic differences in the views of probation departments with respect to their role in intake screening. Thus, a few departments screen only a negligible number of cases on the premise that the court should primarily exercise this decision. Most departments, however, exercise their authority to screen cases liberally.

Sixth, the number of referrals from lower courts varies among counties. Some counties have a very high proportion of cases referred by lower court certification to the juvenile court while others have a very small number. Since petitions have to be filed on all such referrals, in the few counties where such certifications are numerous, they result in a higher petition filing rate.

Seventh, the amount of freedom allowed by juvenile courts in screening referrals also varies. Some courts, for example, have fixed policies regarding the filing of petitions for certain classes of cases and no discretion is allowed. Other probation departments have complete discretion in screening referrals.

Finally, the norms employed in deciding whether a petition is to be filed vary significantly among counties.

THE PRESIDENT'S COMMISSION ON LAW ENFORCEMENT AND ADMINISTRATION OF JUSTICE THE CHALLENGE OF CRIME IN A FREE SOCIETY 83-84 (1967)

The Juvenile Court. (a) Intake—Pre-Judicial Disposition In Court. Pre-judicial disposition is no newcomer to the juvenile court. Some courts today, as noted above, dispose of more than half the cases referred to them by means short of adjudication. It is in the court, therefore, where problems of lack of accurate, up-to-date information about needs and alternatives; lack of coordination among available services; and lack of systematic ways to bring the juvenile and the service together are particularly acute.

To meet those difficulties, the court intake function of prejudicial disposition should be more systematically employed and more formally recognized and organized. Written guides and standards should be formulated and imparted in the course of inservice training. Staff resources should be augmented where necessary to keep abreast of service opportunities and programs in the community and to make inquiries into the backgrounds of juveniles sufficiently comprehensive to select intelligently among alternatives. Overly informal methods of control (such as informal probation with filing of a petition as the penalty for violation), subject as they are to abuse, should be abandoned in favor of institutionalized nonadjudicatory disposition.

More specifically, the Commission commends to the attention of juvenile courts the preliminary conference recently adopted by both New York and Illinois, through which voluntarily attended discussions among court personnel, juvenile, parents, complainants, and other involved parties are used to resolve grievances without adjudication. Safeguards essential to such a procedure are that it occur within a specifically limited time, to eliminate the indirect coercion of an indefinite threat that a petition will be filed at some later date, and that use of statements made at the conference be inadmissible in subsequent court proceedings. . . .

Another method of employing the arbitrating and treating authority of the juvenile court without the disadvantages of adjudication is the consent decree. Consent decree negotiations, too, would be conducted by intake officers and would involve the juvenile and his parents and lawyer (the presence of whom, unless waived, would be required) and a probation officer assigned to the case. The consent decree would be embodied in writing and attested to by the parties and would be effective only upon approval of its terms by the juvenile court judge. It would prescribe a treatment plan but could not commit to an institution. Its duration would be limited, preferably to a year. Negotiations would be subject to the same protections as the preliminary conference procedure. If negotiations failed or the consent decree were violated, the same possibilities—dismissal, referral to a nonjudicial agency, and filing of a petition—would be available as were available prior to the decree. In case of violation of the consent decree, the charge would be the one that initially gave rise to the proceedings. Violation of the decree would be relevant only to disposition.

THE LAWYER'S ROLE AT INTAKE AND DETENTION STAGES OF JUVENILE COURT PROCEEDINGS

By Margaret K. Rosenheim & Daniel L. Skoler
11 Crime and Delinquency 167, 169-70 (1965)

WHAT CAN THE LAWYER DO AT INTAKE?

Theoretically, intake represents an ideal point for lawyer representation to commence. If the attorney achieves "success" for his client at this stage no petition is filed, no hearing is held, and the stigma of adjudicated delinquency (however cushioned by statutory prescriptions of confidentiality and characterizations of noncriminality) is avoided. Moreover, there is increasing recognition that representation is most effective when it commences as soon as possible in the judicial process. What role then can the lawyer play at intake?

1. He can speak to points of law and jurisdiction and make sure that requirements in this area are met. He can inquire, for example, whether the alleged misconduct is criminal or otherwise within the purview of the juvenile court act and whether age and venue requirements are satisfied.

2. He can speak to the sufficiency of evidence and ascertain whether the police or other complaining parties have presented a *prima facie* case in support of their allegations. As in item 1, this is a role for which the lawyer is well qualified by training and experience. (In questions of sufficiency, the nonlawyer intake worker is more likely to proceed to petition and judicial determination than to attempt weighing "probable cause" as an examining magistrate would.)

3. If the lawyer knows the child and his family situation and environment, he can contribute useful information relevant to the decision of whether to file a petition or adjust on an informal basis.

4. He can interpret the child's situation to child and parents so that, for example, if the possibility of a nonjudicial adjustment exists, they will understand and be prepared to accept the conditions proposed (referral to private agencies, short-term supervision by the court, family counseling, etc.).

5. He can familiarize himself with the case against the child, evaluate the type of representation which will be needed, and make an early start in case preparation.

6. He can represent the child's interests in detention determinations.

THE JUVENILE COURT AND THE ADVERSARY SYSTEM: PROBLEMS OF FUNCTION AND FORM

By Joel F. Handler

1965 Wisconsin Law Review 7, 41-44

The proposal [for an adversary procedure at the intake stage of the juvenile court process, using nonlawyers for all positions] calls for an administrative level (or probation department) composed of three types of officers: (1) investigative; (2) defense; and (3) hearing. The investigative officers will handle intake, investigate the charge, and decide whether to proceed. If he decides to proceed, his task will be to work up the case in support of the allegations in the petition. Defense officers will be assigned to each adolescent that is referred to the department and will represent him while the case is being processed at the administrative level. Representation would include explaining the procedures and the consequences, investigation, and advising the adolescent of the steps that will be taken on his behalf. Cases calling for formal adjudication will be decided by the hearing officer on the presentation of the investigative and defense officers.

The advantages of an adversary system of adjudication have already been stated. What may be mentioned here, in support of the proposal, is that probation officers and social workers are constantly experiencing the difficulties caused by the nonadversary, one-man factual investigations. A case worker, even under the best of conditions, cannot explore all facets of the life of the client. He must be selective, which means that he must begin to order his investigation around hypotheses as to what happened or what this adolescent and the environment are like. The selection of the hypotheses which serve to shape the investigation will depend on many factors including training, professional proclivities, theoretical notions, and past experience. Even in the best of people there is the ever-present urge to pre-judge in light of experience. Social workers, particularly when they are seriously overworked, are no exception. It would seem that those who are concerned with the accurate determination of the facts would welcome the benefits of an adversary procedure—both the negative check, the healthy suspicion, and the affirmative development of "the other side."

On the other hand, the proposal calls for adversary *representation* which in practice can differ considerably from the laymen's conception of the role of the advocate in court. Adversary representation means investigating and developing the client's story and presenting and defending the client's interest in the proceedings. It never has meant that the representative must present as true that which is false. In addition, it never has meant that the adversary representative is not fulfilling his duty if he cooperates with his opponent. It is expected that the representative, who is both detached and trained, will be able to evaluate more effectively his client's position. If the client's position is better served by cooperation rather than contest, the representative should cooperate. All of this, of course, is brought out quite clearly in guilty plea situations with adult criminals. There is, to say the least, considerable uneasiness if the accused is not represented by counsel. But legal representation is not urged for the purpose of preventing guilty pleas. It is urged so that the accused is properly advised as to whether a plea will best serve his interests. The accused needs a representative who can evaluate his (the accused's) position from his point of view.

The defense officer in this proposal is to perform his adversary role in an analogous fashion. He is to learn the story from the point of view of the adolescent and to probe and check the findings of the investigative officer. How extensive his investigation should be depends on the circumstances. "Open and shut" cases in juvenile affairs should receive no more investigative efforts than they receive with adults. If the defense officer is satisfied that the confession is accurate or that the witness did see the adolescent commit the act, then no more of that particular issue need be investigated. On the other hand, if the adolescent insists that the allegations in the petition are not true, or that there are extenuating circumstances, then it is the duty of the defense officer to investigate thoroughly the adolescent's story.

Placing adversary representation at the administrative level allows for informality and cooperation. In special circumstances there would seem to be no reason why particular witnesses could not be interviewed in the presence of both officers either in the field or at the administrative offices. The two officers could agree on a summary of the testimony, the source of the information and its reliability. They could also decide on whether the information and its source should be revealed to the adolescent or the family. Similarly, there would seem to be no reason why the two officers could not agree on disposition short of agency adjudication—they could "settle" the case. They might decide that as the result of the investigation the case ought to be dismissed or that informal supervisory measures rather than formal adjudication would be more appropriate. The statute could provide that certain types of informal sanctions must be approved by the hearing officer and subject to periodic, independent supervision.

If the case requires formal adjudication, it will be tried before the hearing officer. The hearing officers should be independent of the investigative and defense officers and should have higher status and pay. The hearing itself should have a degree of orderliness and dignity sufficient to impress upon the adolescent and the parents the seriousness of the occasion. The officers will be presenting adversary positions but conduct should be tempered by the goals of the procedure. Here, again, there is room for cooperative efforts in such matters as the qualifications of witnesses, agreed statements in lieu of oral testimony, and so forth.

To repeat: it should be clear that adversary representation does not mean that every point and issue in the case must be bitterly contested. The basis of the adversary system is the separation of roles and the representatives may contest or compromise according to their own best interests. In the adult world there is often a great deal of cooperation between opposing counsel in situations where cooperative efforts work to the best interests of both sides. The same should apply here. The integrity of the system does not require the defense officer to dispute the obvious or to refuse to cooperate. The integrity will be preserved as long as independent representatives are the ones who do the compromising.

It is believed that decision-making at the administrative level, as outlined here, will further rehabilitative goals. This will be true to the extent that the procedure facilitates the accurate determination of the facts. Returning to Dr. Halleck's analysis, it will also be true insofar as roles will be clearly defined, the proceedings will be explained, and the officers will be in a position to approach the adolescents in a more honest fashion. The defense officer will not be in a position to say to the adolescent that his job is to get him off. As in the adult world, the defense officer must make it clear that under no circumstances will he perpetrate any fraud in the proceedings. However, he will be in a position to say that his job is to make sure that the investigative officer is playing it square and that if the adolescent has anything to say for himself, the defense officer is available to use the public resources to investigate that story and to present it on the adolescent's behalf in the negotiations or at the hearing.

The more knotty problems will arise in the situation where the investigative officer's case will be insufficient without the cooperation of the adolescent and the defense officer. What should the defense officer do in this situation? It can be argued that he should urge his client to cooperate since by hypothesis cooperation will benefit the adolescent. This would be particularly true since the defense officer and the investigative officer can agree on an informal disposition and tailor the sanctions to individual needs. But what if the adolescent still refuses or his record is such that if sanctions are to be imposed at all, they will be severely punitive? Should the defense officer "confess" his client contrary to his client's wishes? This is a close question, but on balance it would seem that the system would benefit more if the officer obeyed the wishes of his client. It is true that some adolescents will avoid adjudication, at least for the time being. But this is a cost that must be balanced against the gains to be derived from official honesty with adolescents. To the extent that the defense officer can remain honest, he stands a better chance of gaining the confidence of the client. This, in itself, has rehabilitative value. And to the extent that confidence is achieved, situations of impasse ought to be reduced.

CASE STUDY: COURT WORKER SCREENING AND INFORMAL DISPOSITION

[The following case file is intended to illustrate the operation of a juvenile court probation department as it handles cases without invoking the formal jurisdiction of the juvenile court. This particular record illustrates a number of facets of this process, including the use of rather elaborate diagnostic facilities.[d]]

Face Sheet
Juvenile Court
Probation Department

Case No.: 1661
Date: October 11, 1966

Name: Vicky Johnson	Address: 4412 Milwaukee Road
Phone: 287-2436	Birthdate: 4-27-51
Religion: Catholic	Birthplace: Milwaukee
Legal Settlement: ________	Height: 5′4″

[d] The file has been edited in an attempt to delete most repetitive information and to disguise the identity of the persons involved.

Health: Good		Weight: 117	Race: Caucasian
Change of Address: ________		Eyes: Hazel	Hair: Blonde

Date	*Referral*	*Source*[e]	*Disposition*
6-19-63	Shoplifting	CPB	Counseled
10-4-66	Chronic Truancy	School	Informal Supervision
9-25-67	Juvenile Drinking	CPB	" "
10-4-67	Immoral Activities & Illegal Use of Narcotics	CPB	" "
10-4-67	Curfew	CPB	" "

FAMILY INFORMATION

Date of Marriage: 10-6-45

Marital Status: Divorced, 9-20-60

Name of Parents	*Age*	*Address*	*Occupation*
Father: John	40	Madison	Excavating
Mother: Alice	44	4412 Milwaukee Rd.	ADC
Siblings: Robert	21, 2-18-46		Married
Donna	13, 10-3-53		8th grade
Tom	7, 8-13-59		1st grade
Dennis	19 mo., 3-1-65		

EDUCATION: ____________________

FINANCIAL: ____________________

Madison Police Department
Criminal Offense Report

Date: 6/15/63 Case No.: 324800

Type of Offense: Arrested Juveniles Time: 1:00 p.m.
Date of Offense: 6/15/63
Complainant: George Williams
Address: 283 Andrews Rd. Phone: ________

---

[e] Most juvenile court referrals come from the police. The initials stand for "Crime Prevention Bureau," the police agency handling juveniles in this city.

Reported By: George Williams
Address: 283 Andrews Rd. Phone:________
How Reported: Phone Date: 6/15/63 Time: 12:57 a.m.
Address of Occurrence:________
Officer Receiving Compl.:________
Officer Assigned:________

XX Original Report ____ Supplementary Report

Details: Mary Louise Schmidt, age 11, 2268 Jackson Dr., dob 9/6/51, theft (shoplifting)
Vicky Johnson, age 12, 4412 Milwaukee Rd., dob 4/27/51, theft (shoplifting)

At about 1:15 p.m. I drove to Windham Road and Baker Street, the Shop-Rite Grocery Store, in reference to two female, juvenile shoplifters. Upon arriving I found the two girls to be the above named girls. I conveyed the girls to the CPB office where I questioned them in regard to their activities of the day. Both girls told me the following story. Vicky's mother drove them to the shopping center a little before noon today as the girls had some shopping to do. They then went into the shopping center where they shoplifted numerous small items of Barby doll clothing, underwear, slippers, hair net and rain bonnet, sox, hair brush. They then left the store and went to the grocery store where they took two packages of candy, Coppertone sun tan lotion, and Fresh deodorant. They left the store and were apprehended outside of the store as they were leaving.

The items shoplifted from the Shop-Rite store were brought in and placed on property tag A7402 and put in locker #2. The items taken from the shopping center were placed on tag A7403 and put in locker #3.

Vicky's attitude was not very remorseful and I mentioned it to her mother when she came to pick Vicky up. Her mother was quite upset as an older brother works at the Shop-Rite grocery store as a carry-out boy and had worked there for about 1½ years. She was worried that this incident would affect his job.[f]

Policewoman Susan Hanson CPB

[f] Refer to the materials on police criteria for disposition at 997, *supra*.

State of Wisconsin
Juvenile Court
Dane County Intake Report

In the Interest of:	Age: 12 DOB: 4-27-51
Johnson, Vicky	Parents: Alice Johnson
	Address: 4412 Milwaukee Rd.

A complaint pursuant to Section 48.12 from MPD dated June 19, 1963 alleges that the above named child is delinquent because: On June 15,1963 (Charge—Shoplifting) Vicky along with her girl friend took skin cream and deodorant from Shop-Rite Store. The items were returned.

Prior Referrals: None.

This Department has made a social inquiry into this matter and recommends that a petition for determination of status should not be filed.

The girl and the mother came in for the interview. The mother did most of the talking and spoke on behalf of the girl. The girl's answers were very abrupt and brief on account of her nervous condition. The mother explained that Vicky was always a quiet child, preferring to be in her room with her books rather than with people. According to the mother, Vicky was very unhappy, when the parents were divorced three years ago. She was the only one who was quite attached to the father. However, Vicky had not presented any disciplinary problems at home or at school. The mother was very confident that the girl would not repeat the mistake. The girl seemed sorry for what happened, but was not able to express herself.[g]

Recommendation: Counseled and released.
By the Court: ______________________

Juvenile Court Judge: ______ Probation Officer: Steven Olson
Dane County Juvenile Court
By: ______________, Director Probation Department
Supervisory District No.: ______ Date of Intake: July 14, 1963

[g] Summarize the criteria by which the Probation Department determined that Vicky should be counseled and released.

Madison High School

October 3, 1966

Mr. Robert Wilson
Dane County Probation Department
Madison, Wisconsin

Dear Mr. Wilson:

Re: Vicky Johnson
4412 Milwaukee Road
Madison, Wisconsin
Birth date: April 27, 1951

I called Mr. Forester relative to a Vicky Johnson who is a student in this school and he referred me to you.

Vicky is having a problem in coming to school. Her attendance record to date is nine days absent and eight days present through September 30, 1966. I have talked with her mother (Mrs. Alice Johnson) several times and she is evidently losing control over Vicky. I threatened to refer her to you on two different occasions and, now, it is no longer a threat.

A summary of her attendance record is as follows:

9/7/66	Present	(School was held in the a.m. only)
9/8/66	Present	
9/9/66	Absent	(I called her mother—ill)
9/12/66	Absent	(I called her mother—ill)
9/13/66	Absent	(I called her mother—ill)
9/14/66	Absent	(I called her mother—she said Vicky would not come to school—wanted me to talk to Vicky—I told her to be in school tomorrow without fail)
9/15/66	Present	
9/16/66	Present	
9/19/66	Absent	in A.M. (I called her mother—same as 9/14/66—I threatened to have the police bring her to school—she arrived for her afternoon classes—I threatened to call the probation department)
9/20/66	Present	
9/21/66	Absent	the first two periods (I called her mother—same as 9/14/66—again threatened to send the police—she arrived at 10:00 a.m.—I threatened to call the probation department)

9/22/66	Present	
9/23/66	Present	
9/26/66	Present	
9/27/66	Absent	A.M. (Called her mother—ill—present in p.m.)
9/28/66	Absent	(Called her mother—ill)
9/29/66	Absent	A.M. (Called mother—she said Vicky would not come to school. Told Vicky to come to school immediately—she did not come.)
9/30/66	Absent	(Called her mother—said Vicky was not ill—would not come to school. I told her that I was going to refer Vicky to the probation department.)

Vicky has always looked to me as though she was completely tired out—running on reserve energy. I am not fully acquainted with her home life but I would guess she has a lot of freedom. I do know, however, that her older brother was allowed to watch TV every night (the late movie) and had the same problem as Vicky.

Please do not hesitate to call on me for any further information.

Sincerely yours,
George Rabkin
Vice Principal

State of Wisconsin
Juvenile Court
Dane County Intake Report

IN THE INTEREST OF: Johnson, Vicky
AGE: 15 DOB: 4-27-51
PARENTS: John and Alice
ADDRESS: 4412 Milwaukee Rd.

A complaint pursuant to Section 48.12 from Madison High dated October 4 alleges that the above named child is delinquent because: She is chronically truant from school.

PRIOR REFERRALS: 7-14-63—Shoplifting.

This Department has made a social inquiry into this matter and recommends that a petition for determination of status should not be filed.

Mrs. Johnson and Vicky appeared for the intake interview on October 11, 1966.

Vicky said she did not like school and that is the reason she did not go. She said she is failing all of her courses this year and failed three courses last year, history, mathematics, and Spanish. She said she is taking history and mathematics over but has permission to drop Spanish. She had a very nonchalant attitude and promised very reluctantly that she would go to school from now on. Worker does not believe that she can do this on her own. She said in a bragging manner that she was kicked out of her home economics class, and when her teacher asked her to report after school, she said she was not going to and was going home.

Mrs. Johnson is a very permissive mother who has let her daughter get out of control. She pleads with her daughter to go to school because if she does, then there will not be any more troubles with the school or with the Probation Department. She told Vicky that she could go to school but she did not have to study and she did not have to pay attention; just as long as she was in class, they could not do anything to her.

Mrs. Johnson said she had considerable difficulty with her older son, Robert, in high school, and he finally graduated last year at age 20. He is now married and doing well.

Vicky said somewhat braggingly that she missed about 35 or 36 days at least last year and said that most of these days, she remained in the home. She did not consider this cutting because she did not run around the community but just did not go. She said she thinks she has low blood pressure and is always tired. She said she has a doctor's appointment to have a complete examination within the next two weeks.

Vicky was told that she would have to go to school from now on or she would be placed in Detention if she skipped. When worker called the Johnson house yesterday, she was still in bed at 10:30, and her mother said she did not want to disturb her sleep and worker should call back at 1:30 in the afternoon. She was told that if Vicky was in bed sleeping in the future, the Police Department would be sent to the residence and she would be brought into Detention and remain there until her probation officer could take over the case.[h]

DISPOSITION: Field Service—Informal Supervision.
BY THE COURT: ______________________________

Juvenile Court Judge: ____ Probation Officer: Robert Wilson
Dane County Juvenile Court
By: M. M. Smith, Director PROBATION DEPARTMENT
SUPERVISORY DISTRICT NO.: ____ DATE OF INTAKE: October 11, 1966

[h] Refer to materials on detention in § D, *supra*.

Psychological Assessment
Confidential: For Professional Use Only

GEORGE THOMPSON, PH.D., AND ASSOCIATES
Clinical Psychology

Client: Vicky Johnson
Referred by: Dane County Juvenile Court
Referral question: Psychological evaluation of this girl's present school and home problems was requested.[i]
Date seen: October 29, 1966

BACKGROUND

Vicky is a 15-year-old girl who has exhibited numerous behavioral problems over the past year and a half including school truancy and defiance of parental authority. She also has exhibited some neurotic-like behaviors such as compulsive handwashing and becoming upset by words containing the letter "P," the latter of which her case worker thought might possibly be related to her mother's illegitimate *P*regnancy which also occurred approximately 1½ years ago.

During interviewing Vicky was very cooperative although not spontaneous with the examiner. She said that she did not like anything about school and seemed in fact unable to specify any particular aspect of school that was the source of her difficulties there except to mention that she did feel that the other girls at school looked down upon her and her girlfriends as being in some way inferior. The general impression which Vicky left the examiner with during interviewing was one of a very emotionally flat girl who is quite socially withdrawn.

FINDINGS

Vicky exhibits clear and marked psychological disturbance. The three most notable features of this maladaptive personality pattern are:

(1) The use of paranoid projection and denial as a psychological defense.

(2) An essentially egocentric, "I am the center of the universe," attitude toward life.

[i] It is obvious that this type of evaluation cannot be made for all children referred to juvenile court. Why was it done here? What use was made of the psychologist's report and recommendations?

(3) An ego structure sufficiently weak and unstable at this time to suggest potential for decompensation into psychosis under minimal to moderate additional stress.

One can expect Vicky typically to be evasive and unwilling to admit to any personal problems and to the extent that she does will blame the situation or other persons rather than accepting any of the responsibility herself. She is narcissistic and self-indulgent, demanding a great deal of others and manipulating them to fulfill her own needs. But any demands placed upon her are resented and strongly, although perhaps passively at times, resisted. One can expect from this that she will have generally poor interpersonal relationships which she will react to with complaint of persecution and abuse. She feels chronic frustration in attempting to deal with her problems in this maladaptive way and typically will express this frustration rather directly by acting out, e.g., at her age such things as smoking, drinking, running away, sexual promiscuity and verbal expressions of hostility toward adults.

It is noteworthy that in examining case histories involving this type of psychological disturbance the genesis is typically in childhood or adolescence—among adults of this personality type 45% were behavior problems as children. Further, their family background typically is a psychologically unhealthy one marked by parental discord, alcohol and/or mental disturbance and indifference and rejection being characteristic of their parents' attitude toward them.

When seen in a clinical setting persons exhibiting this type of maladaptive adjustment pattern are rather evenly diagnosed under the categories of psychosis usually paranoid schizophrenia and personality disorders of mixed types. Which diagnosis is most appropriate is usually decided in terms of the degree of personality disorganization versus the integration which the person presents at the time of treatment. Treatment of choice is generally considered to be psychotherapy, sometimes in conjunction with psychopharmocological regimes but response to treatment among *adults* is poor in the larger proportion of cases with about 80% showing little or no basic improvement in their adjustment. The importance of the early initiation of treatment and the appropriateness of exhibiting less than the usual restraint in embarking upon intensive and drastic treatment regimes is consequently clearly indicated.

CONCLUSIONS

On the basis of the present psychological testing and interviewing this examiner would consider Vicky to be a sociopathic character disturbance in a personality structure so unstable as to make periodic psychotic episodes in the future likely. The critical point of leverage in attempting to deal effectively with this case lies in Vicky's youth—the fact that her personality is not fully and unchangeably matured. At the same time the pervasiveness as well as severity of her disturbance should not be under estimated so that treatment should be instituted not only quickly but on a quite intensive basis if one is to have any reasonable chance of modifying and improving her general adjustment. One might think initially in terms of intensive psychotherapy with a strong adult identification figure and then consider such things as removing Vicky from the home for placement in a foster home or institutionalization at an intensive treatment facility such as Mendota Hospital's Adolescent Treatment Unit and Pioneer School.

PROCEDURES EMPLOYED

Rorschach Projective Techniques—Beck's System
Minnesota Multiphasic Personality Inventory
Interview with the client

George Thompson, Ph.D.
Clinical Psychologist
October 29, 1966

Psychiatric Evaluation

JOHNSON, VICKY	CONFIDENTIAL
4412 Milwaukee Road	Submitted by
Madison, Wisconsin	Tom E. Porter
	Psychiatric Consultant
	November 10, 1966

Consultation was requested on this 15-year-old white high school student by Miss Susan Burns because of truancy and questionable mental illness.[j]

[j] *See* p. 1033, n.i, *supra*.

Interview with Mother

Mrs. Johnson presented as an overweight, pale, fairly well groomed white female with a rather loud, husky voice. She impressed me as using massive amounts of denial relative to the current situation (for example: her strange tolerance of the irresponsibility displayed by her divorced husband toward her and the family would be interpreted by me as having a neurotic need to dominate men and keep them in the role of naughty boys) and a general immature attitude accompanied by certain bluff good humor. She stated that Vicky has always been more sensitive than other children and that her divorce seemed to bother her more than the rest. She was quick to state that Vicky has seemed better the last two weeks during which time she has not been required to attend school. It was soon evident that the mother fully appreciated the fact that Vicky was at home helping out a great deal with the housework which included scrubbing floors, baking, and also sewing clothing for the family. She related the strange phobic reaction Vicky has when the mother states the letter "P" in that it evokes some mildly destructive act on the part of the patient. For example, she will drop what she might have in her hand or spill milk. She also stated that the same kind of reaction is elicited when the mother touches her with her hand in some manner.

Otherwise, the significant thing was that Vicky idolizes the little one-and-a-half-year-old infant at home and spends a great deal of time taking care of him. I was left with the feeling that the mother described Vicky as being very domestic and satisfied to be home and that also this feeling was mutual.

Interview with Patient

When asked why she was here in Probation, Vicky stated, "I don't know, I guess 'cause I didn't go to school." She would not elaborate on this much stating that she hated school and did not care to go and just sit there. She denied any special aversion to any teachers or any certain subjects. Review of symptoms of depression revealed irritability, worthless feelings, but denial of any suicidal thoughts. She was emphatic about this saying, "I never want to die." Review of psychotic symptoms revealed only the usual suspicions of a teenager. She denied any religiosity and was somewhat embarrassed to discuss sex and had only a vague knowledge about pregnancy and birth. She denied any concern about masturbating nor any sexual trauma. She admitted having a boy friend and liking to dance.

Past health has always been good. Family history was negative psychiatrically except for the fact that her parents were divorced six years ago. She described her mother as a talkative person with whom she gets along fairly well. Her mother was four years older than her father. When asked about her father, she stated, "I don't know nothin'." This indeed seems to be correct because she has not even seen him to talk to in the last two years although they live in the same town. In a pathetic manner she related walking by where he was working one time and feeling that he did not even recognize her as his own daughter. She is obviously defensive in this area and tried to cover up her anxiety. She denied any special conflicts with any of her siblings stating about her one-and-a-half-year-old brother, "I like him more than anyone else in the family."

Vicky presented as an average sized, fairly well groomed, pale white girl with rather severe facial acne. Her eyebrows were severely plucked and filled in with mascara. Mascara was the only kind of makeup she was wearing. Her hair was platinum blonde and she generally appeared rather unhealthy. She had a rather immature attitude about her. She was depressed with constricted, blunted effect although later in our interview she was capable of smiling. She tended to avoid eye contact and was not overtly anxious. She appeared to be of normal intelligence and there was no evidence of thought disorder.

Diagnostic Impression: Adjustment reaction of adolescence, manifested in phobic reactions, withdrawal and moderate depression.

Recommendations: It is my opinion that her truancy as in a regular school phobia is somewhat related to separation anxiety from her mother. I feel that this attitude has been greatly promoted by the mother because of her own dependent needs and attempts toward role reversal. (She lost her own mother at the age of two and also appeared to enjoy having Vicky at home helping with the housework.) The mother uses massive denial and has a very unrealistic, immature attitude about many things which undoubtedly contributes to Vicky's difficulty. I feel the first attempt towards alleviation of the situation should be directed towards counselling between Vicky and her mother regarding separation anxiety and the contributions mother makes toward Vicky's truancy. They could both benefit from the support of the attention and help along these lines also. If this did not seem to give some help after a three-month period, placement outside of the home in a psychiatrically oriented institution may be considered because this girl shows incipient signs of serious psychopathology.

Respectfully submitted,
DANE COUNTY PROBATION DEPARTMENT
Dr. Tom F. Porter
Psychiatric Consultant

Madison Police Department
Criminal Offense Report

Date: 9-22-67 Case No.: 470703

Type of Offense: Liquor Law Violation Time:________
Date of Offense: 9-16-67
Complainant: Mr. and Mrs. Anthony Becker
Address: 1002 E. Erie St. Phone:________
Reported By:________
Address:________ Phone:________
How Reported:________ Date:________ Time:________
Address of Occurrence:________
Attention:________
Officer Assigned:________

___ Original Report XX Supplementary Report

Details: Vicky Johnson, d.o.b. 4-27-51, 4412 Milwaukee Road, Juvenile Drinking

On 9-22-67 at about 1:30 P.M., Vicky Johnson appeared in our office, as requested, accompanied by her mother, Alice Johnson. At first, Vicky was very vague about the party on 9-16-67 but eventually admitted that she was at the Nelson home about 1:00 P.M. on 9-16-67. She was accompanied there by Debra Davis. She stated that she and Debra cleaned the Nelson home and then left about 5:30 and returned again about 8:00 P.M. She named the group that was there, which was essentially the same information the others gave. She stated that a Tom Wolf had been there early in the afternoon but had left before 5:00 P.M. She admitted that she did drink beer by taking sips out of everyone's glass. She stated that she doesn't see anything wrong with drinking beer and that she is allowed to have all the beer she wants at home. Vicky normally has blonde hair but dyed her hair jet black.

I talked with Mrs. Johnson and advised her of Vicky's involvement and she stated that she has been having considerable trouble with Vicky and especially now since Vicky is not working and is not attending school. I advised her that Vicky would be referred to the Probation Department and she informed me that Vicky had been under supervision to Miss Burns.

Kathy A. Kess

Madison Police Department
Criminal Offense Report

Date: 9-26-67 Case No.: 470703

Type of Offense: Liquor Law Violation Time: ______________

Date of Offense: 9-16-67

Complainant: Mr. and Mrs. Anthony Becker

Address: 1002 E. Erie St. Phone: ______________

Reported By: ______________

Address: ______________

How Reported: ________ Date: ________ Time: ________

Address of Occurrence: ______________

Attention: ______________

Officer Assigned: ______________

___ Original Report XX Supplementary Report

Details: Gary Clark, d.o.b. 10-27-51, 1515 6th St., Madison, Wis., morals & juvenile drinking

Vicky Johnson, d.o.b. 4-27-51, 4412 Milwaukee Rd., morals—illegal use of narcotics

Sally Peterson, d.o.b. 7-2-52, 902 E. Erie St., morals

Vicky Johnson was contacted at her home and informed that we wanted to talk to her. There was a little static in the home reference our bothering her again but the mother finally consented to bring the girl to C.P.B. Upon arrival at C.P.B., we questioned Vicky about her using marijuana at the party and at first she denied its use and then admitted that she had smoked it while at the party. She evidently became aware that they were trying to get her sexually stimulated and this caused her to leave the party. It was thought that she had relations with Tom Neil while at the party but this was found to be untrue as it had occurred over six months ago, without any ill effects. It appears that Vicky needs further supervision as it is evident that the mother is not able to control the girl. She has tattoos on her hands and she did not even know the meaning of the one tattoo until it was explained. Her mother was advised of her daughter's immoral conduct and the use of marijuana.

We then were able to contact Gary Clark at his home and he admitted that he consumed beer at the party and that he had petted with Sally while in the back seat of a parked car but that he suddenly decided not to go any further and he spent the rest of the night trying to get rid of Sally and she then appeared to take quite a fancy to him. His mother was also advised of the circumstances and was advised that he would be referred to Probation Dept.

Tim Samuels

At about 10:45 p.m., 10-3-67 in reference to case #471841 a detective and I were conveying Jane Cook to the station, when we observed her and two friends, Vicky Johnson and Mary Morris walking toward town. They had just left the Cook residence after attempting to take the Cook auto, which Mr. Cook prevented them from doing. We advised both girls to get into the car and brought them to the station also.

Mrs. Johnson came to the office to get Vicky at about 12:45 a.m. She was advised that her daughter had intended to run away with Morris and Cook, but was stopped by Mr. Cook. She was very sympathetic toward Vicky, blaming her problems on her associates. Mrs. Johnson was also informed that she should not allow any girls to remain overnight without first checking with the parents.

William W. Shuette

Juvenile Court
Dane County
Wisconsin

To: Vicky Johnson

IN THE INTEREST OF:
Vicky Johnson
4-27-51 (Date of birth)

CONDITIONS OF SUPERVISION[k]

In accordance with the authority conferred by Section 48.19 Wisconsin statutes your above-named child is placed under the

[k] Is this document an agreement or an order?

supervision of the Juvenile Court Probation Department for a period not to exceed six months. We, the undersigned, having been informed of our rights[l] agree to the following conditions of supervision:

1. Obey all Laws and Ordinances and conduct yourself as a good citizen.
2. *Attend school regularly* or maintain regular employment.
3. Be in your place of residence each night at the time specified by your parents and probation officer.
4. Refrain from the use or possession of intoxicating beverages in any form.
5. Report as instructed by the officer placing you under supervision.
6. At all times obey and respect your parents, guardian, or legal custodian and cooperate with the officer supervising you.
7. Discuss your problems with the officer supervising you. It is his responsibility to assist you in making a successful adjustment.
8. Mrs. Johnson and Vicky will attend the Family Living Program as scheduled by the Probation Department.
9. *Special Conditions:* Be in at 12:00 weekends unless granted special permission.

Signed ____________________ ____________________
Probation Officer
Dane County Probation Department
____________________ Date: October 16, 1967
Parent

Memorandum

Date: October 18, 1967
Worker: Miss Burns

Father's Name: John Johnson
Address: ____________ Tel.: ____________
Employment: ____________ Education: ____________
Mother's Name: Alice Johnson
Address: 4412 Milwaukee Rd. Tel.: 287-2436
Employment: Housewife Education: High School
Date of Marriage: 10-6-45
Date of Divorce (if applicable): 9-20-60

---

[l] What rights were they informed of?

Mrs. Johnson is a divorcee and ADC recipient. She is an unstable and dependent person who resents any intrusion in her private affairs. Vicky was excused from school for medical reasons last year and has not been employed. She has been and is a disturbed girl and is seeing Dr. Lewis Dorn on an out-patient basis. Vicky has been in constant conflict at home and in the community because of erotic and near-delinquent behavior. Vicky and her mother superficially are close, but this is a front to deceive caseworkers.[m] Vicky has a tendency to gravitate towards older men and this may be a result of her father being out of the home since she was nine. Both Vicky and Mrs. Johnson are defensive and generally unwilling to discuss the important problems.

Probation Worker's Report

JOHNSON, VICKY

INFORMAL SUPERVISION: Vicky was referred to the Probation Dept. by Madison High School for chronic truancy on 10-4-66. Since school began on 9-7-66, she had attended eight days and been absent nine. She was placed on informal supervision on 10-11-66 and assigned to this worker on 10-21-66. From the first interview, Vicky's withdrawal from her surroundings and her reluctance to communicate indicated she would not respond to worker or the pressure that she must attend school. Furthermore, Mrs. Johnson announced that she did not care if Vicky went to school, but she was tired of trying to get her there and having people always calling her. Vicky admitted she hated school, could not concentrate on her subjects and felt most of the students thought of her as inferior to them. Vicky's physical appearance was harsh and she wore an excessive amount of eye makeup, tight suggestive clothes and generally looked unattractive. She also has an unpleasant shrill voice and used poor language. No amount of force or threats would induce Vicky to attend school.

In several telephone conversations with Mrs. Johnson, she voiced concern that something was wrong with Vicky as she had terrible fits of temper when she would throw things; could not tolerate mother touching her and reacted quite strongly to words with the letter "p" in them. In view of the problems Vicky exhibited, it was arranged for Dr. George Thompson to evaluate her on 10-29-66.

---

[m] On what information is this based?

PSYCHOLOGICAL VALUATION: Vicky generally exhibited a sociopathic personality, being egocentric, narcissistic and self-indulgent. However, ego structure was weak and unstable. Vicky demanded a great deal of others, but resented demands placed on her. She insists she is abused by others. (Worker's feeling is Vicky invites persecution from others. Perhaps her attitude is a defense mechanism.) Dr. Thompson recommended intensive psychotherapy.

PSYCHIATRIC EVALUATION—11-10-66: Dr. Tom Porter's diagnostic impression was adjustment reaction of adolescence manifested in phobia reactions, withdrawal and moderate depression. Dr. Porter recommended counseling between mother and Vicky and if this was ineffective, Vicky should be removed from the home. Vicky was excused from attending school as her intensive phobia would prevent any academic accomplishment.

FAMILY SITUATION: John and Alice Johnson were divorced on 9-20-60 in Madison. The Johnsons continued to date and cohabit which resulted in Mrs. Johnson giving birth to a son, Dennis, on 3-1-65. After the birth of this child, Mr. Johnson was suddenly absent from his wife's home. Apparently he seldom visits his children. Mrs. Johnson is very bitter about the divorce and uses every available means of denial to avoid any responsibility. Vicky does not discuss the family's problems, but does seem to view mother as a neurotic busybody. The other children appear to be functioning adequately; however, there is a rivalry between Vicky and her younger sister, Donna. Donna is attractive, intelligent and an excellent student; just the opposite of Vicky.

Mrs. Johnson has received ADC since the divorce. She sometimes refuses to cooperate in giving pertinent information as she feels her welfare check may be taken away from her. There is also a problem with Mrs. Johnson's stepmother as the latter owns the home and has threatened to evict her daughter if Mrs. Johnson tries to give too much information to caseworkers.

Art Sanders is the caseworker and he also has difficulty in drawing Mrs. Johnson out. Mrs. Johnson is a highly suspicious woman who deals with her difficulties in an immature manner. She enjoys having Vicky home and this is probably because Vicky enjoys cooking and she is relieved of some of the housework.

Worker warned the family that unless intensive out-patient psychotherapy was started, the matter would be brought before Juvenile Court. The family proceeded to begin appointments with Lewis Dorn, Ph. D., Clinical Psychologist, on 2-10-67. Vicky attended weekly from this date until worker closed the case on

6-1-67. During this period of time there was indication that Vicky was having no difficulty in the community and Dr. Dorn reported progress in her mental and emotional health. Several conferences with Dr. Dorn along with Mr. Sanders indicated that Vicky would quite probably never return to high school; however, she could function in a reasonably adequate manner, both socially and in the community. Vicky has learned all of the proper defense mechanisms from her mother and has a well-rehearsed answer for everything. Mr. Sanders was to remain active with the Johnsons and would report any delinquent or inappropriate behavior on Vicky's part. Dr. Dorn suggested it might be necessary to return Vicky to supervision if her behavior once again became uncontrolled and the matter was held open for six months in order to have some hold on this family.

REFERRAL—9-23-67: On 9-16-67 a party was held at the John Nelson home, 1435 Jackson. Mary Nelson, age 19 and married, had furnished the home for a party and Ben McDonald furnished the beer. There were approximately 12 people at this party at various times, Vicky being one of them. Other persons at the party informed the police that Vicky had been smoking marijuana and after several hours of questioning Vicky at her home and in front of her mother, she admitted she took a few puffs off of a cigarette. She insisted she did not know who had furnished the marijuana. She also admitted to having a glass of beer, but denied excessive drinking. Other juveniles present at this party have confirmed that Vicky was not drunk and her behavior was probably more exemplary than most. It should be noted that John Nelson has been before Court for Lewd & Lascivious and furnishing beer to minors.

After receiving the referral, worker had Mrs. Johnson and Vicky in to discuss the matter. Vicky did admit the above statements but insisted she had no intentions of continuing such behavior. This is rather doubtful. As usual, Mrs. Johnson was quite hostile and defensive and felt that she and her daughter were being persecuted by the police and the Probation Dept. She insists Vicky is not a problem at home and that she gives Vicky permission to go out on weekends until midnight. The truth is, it would be difficult to state Vicky is uncontrolled by her parent as Mrs. Johnson refuses to make any such statement. In order to successfully deal with Vicky, it would be necessary for her to commit some very obvious and serious offense in the community.

A second referral dated 10-3-67 charged Vicky with curfew violation. Vicky was observed walking on Madison Street with

Mary Morris at 10:45 p.m. Vicky was conveyed to the Police Dept. and Mrs. Johnson came to the office to take Vicky home. Mrs. Johnson was warned by worker that there were indications she had allowed runaway girls to stay at her home and if proof were ever secured, she could be charged with "contributing to the delinquency of a minor." Mrs. Johnson was also given a stern warning that she was not acting in her daughter's best welfare and if at anytime any further difficulty could be proven, she might not be enjoying the freedom of staying at home. As worker views it, at this time it would be impossible to bring Vicky before the Juvenile Court as the nature of the referrals could not be substantiated as serious delinquency. In addition, Dr. Dorn does not at this time feel that Vicky requires in-patient care as her general emotional and mental health has greatly improved. As a reminder to Vicky, worker informed her that she would be placed under supervision for a period of three months and her activities closely observed. As the case had never been formally closed, worker continued working with this family by weekly visits with Vicky and periodic checks with Mrs. Johnson. As always, Mrs. Johnson gave no indication that there was any trouble at home.

The Johnsons were referred to the Family Living Program and faithfully attended for a two-month period. When the case was closed on January 4, 1968, the Johnsons saw fit to discontinue the Family Living Program. Worker feels that at this time little can be done with Vicky's situation, but if any further serious referrals are received that can be substantiated, and proven, Court should be considered. Developing a program for Vicky would be extremely difficult as formal education would not be possible both because of Vicky's limited ability and her general dislike of school. If the matter were ever to be brought before the Court, there would be no cooperation from Mrs. Johnson and complete denial of any guilt from Vicky. Worker views Vicky as a socially, culturally and mentally deprived girl who will probably spend her life in and out of marriages with men who will have little or nothing to offer her.[n]

CASE CLOSING: Worker recommends the case be closed effective 1-4-68.

---

[n] What do you learn about the standards for court referral from the discussion in this report?

Reference Note

A standard manual on the role of the police in the administration of juvenile justice is R. MYREN & L. SWANSON, POLICE WORK WITH CHILDREN (U.S.H.E.W. Children's Bureau Publication #399, 1962).

The use of police discretion is also discussed in Piliavin & Briar, *Police Encounters with Juveniles,* 70 AM. J. SOCIOLOGY 206 (1964).

Further analysis of the role of the court worker can be found in Newman, *Functions of the Police, Prosecutor, Court Worker, Defense Counsel, Judge, in Aiding Juvenile Justice,* 13 JUVENILE COURT JUDGES J. 6 (1962); Sheridan, *Juvenile Court Intake,* 2 J. FAMILY L. 139 (1962).

The requirement of counsel and the introduction of other constitutional rights into the juvenile court has raised the question of waiver of rights by a juvenile. For a good discussion of this problem see Note, *Waiver in the Juvenile Court,* 68 COLUM. L. REV. 1149 (1968).

Chapter 16

THE ADJUDICATION OF DELINQUENCY

In the pre-court stages of the juvenile process, we have seen instances of the adult criminal system moving closer to the juvenile one, particularly in terms of disposition of cases without official court action. But while the adult system is becoming more like the juvenile in the pre-court phase, the opposite is true of adjudication. Here the juvenile system is moving into the format and procedures of the adult one.

A. THE GROWING ADVERSARINESS OF JUVENILE PROCEEDINGS

The original juvenile court statutes were primarily concerned with substituting for the adversary format of the criminal court an atmosphere of friendly inquiry conducive to rehabilitation of the child. As with police processing of juveniles, the hearing procedure itself was intended as part of the rehabilitative treatment. The assumption was that informal friendly proceedings would have a salutary effect on the young person brought into court. Whether such procedures are effective for this purpose, is something about which we know almost nothing, although the assumption that they do help rehabilitate juveniles is being questioned with increasing frequency.[a]

---

[a] An excellent discussion of the problems with the format of the juvenile court and its relation to the attitude of the person before it is Studt, *The Client's Image of the Juvenile Court,* in JUSTICE FOR THE CHILD 203-04 (M. Rosenheim ed. 1962):

> In the official world, informality of procedure in the juvenile court usually means an opportunity to substitute helpfulness toward a child for an impersonal attack on a guilty criminal. Unhampered by inappropriate rules of evidence, the court is free to consider all pertinent information in an effort to solve a human problem. The judge ceases to be a remote figure of justice and sits in conference with those who are concerned with the problem. The probation officer is defined as a friend of the child who gathers information because of a desire to understand rather than to accuse. Ceremony is deliberately avoided in order to establish an atmosphere of concern

The departure from the adversary system has been called the "essential conceptual flaw in the juvenile court."[b] The adversary system is thought by many to be the heart of due process. The courts and legislatures today, faced with a conflict between due process requirements and the current informal procedures of the juvenile courts, have tended to turn to the criminal law for guidance. They have done it, however, on a piecemeal basis, expressing great concern about the effect which adversary requirements will have on the atmosphere of the juvenile court proceeding. The most significant example of this approach and one which has changed the direction for the juvenile court is the first United States Supreme Court decision dealing with the constitutionality of the juvenile court system, *In re Gault*.[c]

Three areas of basic concern in an adversary system have received the most attention in the juvenile system: (1) the problem of notice, (2) the problem of proof, and (3) the requirement of counsel. *In re Gault* deals with all three questions.

---

for the individual. These provisions are perceived by the official world as the necessary means for changing the court's focus from issues of guilt and punishment to resolution or amelioration of an individual's problems.

For many children and their families, however, the resulting image of the court is confused and lacks symbolic value. Many official persons have suddenly materialized as decision-makers in the life of the family. Yet the roles of these persons are indistinctly perceived, and the client is often uncertain about who can make what decisions under what circumstances. Since official positions are ill-defined, it is easy for a client to see official personnel as powerful individuals whose anger or friendliness capriciously determines matters of importance. If the client sees the structure and procedures of a powerful organization as resting on *ad hoc* determinations, his image may derive more from a projection of unconsious yearnings for total dependency and fears of total destructiveness than from an understanding of the organizational reality. At the same time, the symbolic value that is potentially present in confrontation between an individual and his community may be lost because there is too great a disparity between the informality of the process and the seriousness of what actually happens in the life of the family. The client may well experience feelings of worthlessness and helplessness. "Going to court" becomes not a sober accounting for one's own behavior before the community but a horrifying precipitation into insecurity against which the client learns to defend himself by manipulation. One possible consequence of such an experience may be the crystallization of delinquent identification and an intensified commitment to the familiar delinquent culture.

[b] Elson, *Juvenile Courts and Due Process,* in JUSTICE FOR THE CHILD 96 (M. Rosenheim ed. 1962).

[c] 387 U.S. 1 (1967). There has been an outpouring of articles analyzing *Gault.* One of the best is Dorsen & Rezneck, *In re Gault and the Future of Juvenile Law,* 1 FAMILY L.Q. 1 (Dec. 1967).

In re GAULT
387 U.S. 1 (1967)

MR. JUSTICE FORTAS delivered the opinion of the Court.

This is an appeal under 28 U.S.C. § 1257(2) from a judgment of the Supreme Court of Arizona affirming the dismissal of a petition for a writ of habeas corpus. 99 Ariz. 181, 407 P.2d 760 (1965). The petition sought the release of Gerald Francis Gault, appellants' 15-year-old son, who had been committed as a juvenile delinquent to the State Industrial School by the Juvenile Court of Gila County, Arizona.

We begin with a statement of the facts.

I.

On Monday, June 8, 1964, at about 10 a. m., Gerald Francis Gault and a friend, Ronald Lewis, were taken into custody by the Sheriff of Gila County. Gerald was then still subject to a six months' probation order which had been entered on February 25, 1964, as a result of his having been in the company of another boy who had stolen a wallet from a lady's purse. The police action on June 8 was taken as the result of a verbal complaint by a neighbor of the boys, Mrs. Cook, about a telephone call made to her in which the caller or callers made lewd or indecent remarks. It will suffice for purposes of this opinion to say that the remarks or questions put to her were of the irritatingly offensive, adolescent, sex variety.

At the time Gerald was picked up, his mother and father were both at work. No notice that Gerald was being taken into custody was left at the home. No other steps were taken to advise them that their son had, in effect, been arrested. Gerald was taken to the Children's Detention Home. When his mother arrived home at about 6 o'clock, Gerald was not there. Gerald's older brother was sent to look for him at the trailer home of the Lewis family. He apparently learned then that Gerald was in custody. He so informed his mother. The two of them went to the Detention Home. The deputy probation officer, Flagg, who was also superintendent of the Detention Home, told Mrs. Gault "why Jerry was there" and said that a hearing would be held in Juvenile Court at 3 o'clock the following day, June 9.

Officer Flagg filed a petition with the court on the hearing day, June 9, 1964. It was not served on the Gaults. Indeed, none of them saw this petition until the habeas corpus hearing on August 17, 1964. The petition was entirely formal. It made no reference to any factual basis for the judicial action which it initiated. It recited only that "said minor is under the age of eighteen years, and is in need of the protection of this Honorable Court; [and that] said minor is a delinquent minor." It prayed for a hearing and an order regarding "the care and custody of said minor." Officer Flagg executed a formal affidavit in support of the petition.

On June 9, Gerald, his mother, his older brother, and Probation Officers Flagg and Henderson appeared before the Juvenile Judge in chambers. Gerald's father was not there. He was at work out of the city. Mrs. Cook, the complainant, was not there. No one was sworn at this hearing. No transcript or recording was made. No memorandum or record of the substance of the proceedings was prepared. Our information about the proceedings and the subsequent hearing on June 15, derives entirely from the testimony of the Juvenile Court Judge, Mr. and Mrs. Gault and Officer Flagg at the habeas corpus proceeding conducted two months later. From this, it appears that at the June 9 hearing Gerald was questioned by the judge about the telephone call. There was conflict as to what he said. His mother recalled that Gerald said he only dialed Mrs. Cook's number and handed the telephone to his friend, Ronald. Officer Flagg recalled that Gerald had admitted making the lewd remarks. Judge McGhee testified that Gerald "admitted making one of these [lewd] statements." At the conclusion of the hearing, the judge said he would "think about it." Gerald was taken back to the Detention Home. He was not sent to his own home with his parents. On June 11 or 12, after having been detained since June 8, Gerald was released and driven home.[2] There is no explanation in the record as to why he was kept in the Detention Home or why he was released. At 5 p. m. on the day of Gerald's release, Mrs. Gault received a note signed by Officer Flagg. It was on plain paper, not letterhead. Its entire text was as follows:

"Mrs. Gault:

"Judge McGhee has set Monday June 15, 1964 at 11:00 A. M. as the date and time for further Hearings on Gerald's delinquency

"/s/Flagg"

At the appointed time on Monday, June 15, Gerald, his father and mother, Ronald Lewis and his father, and Officers Flagg and Henderson were present before Judge McGhee. Witnesses at the habeas corpus proceeding differed in their recollections of Ger-

[2] There is a conflict between the recollection of Mrs. Gault and that of Officer Flagg. Mrs. Gault testified that Gerald was released on Friday, June 12, Officer Flagg that it had been on Thursday, June 11. This was from memory; he had no record, and the note hereafter referred to was undated.

ald's testimony at the June 15 hearing. Mr. and Mrs. Gault recalled that Gerald again testified that he had only dialed the number and that the other boy had made the remarks. Officer Flagg agreed that at this hearing Gerald did not admit making the lewd remarks.[3] But Judge McGhee recalled that "there was some admission again of some of the lewd statements. He—he didn't admit any of the more serious lewd statements."[4] Again, the complainant, Mrs. Cook, was not present. Mrs. Gault asked that Mrs. Cook be present "so she could see which boy that done the talking, the dirty talking over the phone." The Juvenile Judge said "she didn't have to be present at that hearing." The judge did not speak to Mrs. Cook or communicate with her at any time. Probation Officer Flagg had talked to her once—over the telephone on June 9.

At this June 15 hearing a "referral report" made by the probation officers was filed with the court, although not disclosed to Gerald or his parents. This listed the charge as "Lewd Phone Calls." At the conclusion of the hearing, the judge committed Gerald as a juvenile delinquent to the State Industrial School "for the period of his minority [that is, until 21], unless sooner discharged by due process of law." An order to that effect was entered. It recites that "after a full hearing and due deliberation the Court finds that said minor is a delinquent child, and that said minor is of the age of 15 years."

No appeal is permitted by Arizona law in juvenile cases. On August 3, 1964, a petition for a writ of habeas corpus was filed with the Supreme Court of Arizona and referred by it to the Superior Court for hearing.

At the habeas corpus hearing on August 17, Judge McGhee was vigorously cross-examined as to the basis for his actions. He testified that he had taken into account the fact that Gerald was on probation. He was asked "under what section of . . . the code you found the boy delinquent?"

His answer is set forth in the margin.[5] In substance, he concluded that Gerald came within ARS § 8-201-6(a), which specifies

---

[3] Officer Flagg also testified that Gerald had not, when questioned at the Detention Home, admitted having made any of the lewd statements, but that each boy had sought to put the blame on the other. There was conflicting testimony as to whether Ronald had accused Gerald of making the lewd statements during the June 15 hearing.

[4] Judge McGhee also testified that Gerald had not denied "certain statements" made to him at the hearing by Officer Henderson.

[5] "Q. All right. Now, Judge, would you tell me under what section of the law or tell me under what section of—of the code you found the boy delinquent?

"A. Well, there is a—I think it amounts to disturbing the peace. I can't give you the section, but I can tell you the law, that when one person uses that a "delinquent child" includes one "who has violated a law of the state or an ordinance or regulation of a political subdivision thereof." The law which Gerald was found to have violated is ARS § 13-377. This section of the Arizona Criminal Code provides that a person who "in the presence or hearing of any woman or child . . . uses vulgar, abusive or obscene language, is guilty of a misdemeanor. . . ." The penalty specified in the Criminal Code, which would apply to an adult, is $5 to $50, or imprisonment for not more than two months. The judge also testified that he acted under ARS § 8-201-6(d) which includes in the definition of a "delinquent child" one who, as the judge phrased it, is "habitually involved in immoral matters."

Asked about the basis for his conclusion that Gerald was "habitually involved in immoral matters," the judge testified, somewhat vaguely, that two years earlier, on July 2, 1962, a "referral" was made concerning Gerald, "where the boy had stolen a baseball glove from another boy and lied to the Police Department about it." The judge said there was "no hearing," and "no accusation" relating to this incident, "because of lack of material foundation." But it seems to have remained in his mind as a relevant factor. The judge also testified that Gerald had admitted making other nuisance phone calls in the past which, as the judge recalled the boy's testimony, were "silly calls, or funny calls, or something like that."

The Superior Court dismissed the writ, and appellants sought review in the Arizona Supreme Court. That court handed down an elaborate and wide-ranging opinion affirming dismissal of the writ. In their brief appellants urge that we hold the Juvenile Code of Arizona invalid on its face or as applied in this case because, contrary to the Due Process Clause of the Fourteenth Amendment, the juvenile is taken from the custody of his parents and committed to a state institution pursuant to proceedings in which the Juvenile Court has virtually unlimited discretion, and in which the following basic rights are denied:

1. Notice of the charges;
2. Right to counsel;
3. Right to confrontation and cross-examination;
4. Privilege against self-incrimination;
5. Right to a transcript of the proceedings; and
6. Right to appellate review.

---

lewd language in the presence of another person, that it can amount to—and I consider that when a person makes it over the phone, that it is considered in the presence, I might be wrong, that is one section. The other section upon which I consider the boy delinquent is Section 8-201, Subsection (d), habitually involved in immoral matters."

II.

The Supreme Court of Arizona held that due process of law is requisite to the constitutional validity of proceedings in which a court reaches the conclusion that a juvenile has been at fault, has engaged in conduct prohibited by law, or has otherwise misbehaved with the consequence that he is committed to an institution in which his freedom is curtailed. This conclusion is in accord with the decisions of a number of courts under both federal and state constitutions.

We do not in this opinion consider the impact of these constitutional provisions upon the totality of the relationship of the juvenile and the state. We do not even consider the entire process relating to juvenile "delinquents." For example, we are not here concerned with the procedures or constitutional rights applicable to the pre-judicial stages of the juvenile process, nor do we direct our attention to the post-adjudicative or dispositional process. We consider only the problems presented to us by this case. These relate to the proceedings by which a determination is made as to whether a juvenile is a "delinquent" as a result of alleged misconduct on his part, with the consequence that he may be committed to a state institution. As to these proceedings, there appears to be little current dissent from the proposition that the Due Process Clause has a role to play. The problem is to ascertain the precise impact of the due process requirement upon such proceedings.

[T]he features of the juvenile system which its proponents have asserted are of unique benefit will not be impaired by constitutional domestication. For example, the commendable principles relating to the processing and treatment of juveniles separately from adults are in no way involved or affected by the procedural issues under discussion. Further, we are told that one of the important benefits of the special juvenile court procedures is that they avoid classifying the juvenile as a "criminal." The juvenile offender is now classed as a "delinquent." There is, of course, no reason why this should not continue. It is disconcerting, however, that this term has come to involve only slightly less stigma than the term "criminal" applied to adults. It is also emphasized that in practically all jurisdictions, statutes provide that an adjudication of the child as a delinquent shall not operate as a civil disability or disqualify him for civil service appointment. There is no reason why the application of due process requirements should interfere with such provisions.

Beyond this, it is frequently said that juveniles are protected by the process from disclosure of their deviational behavior.

[T]here is no reason why, consistently with due process, a State cannot continue, if it deems it appropriate, to provide and to improve provision for the confidentiality of records of police contacts and court action relating to juveniles.

Further, it is urged that the juvenile benefits from informal proceedings in the court. The early conception of the Juvenile Court proceeding was one in which a fatherly judge touched the heart and conscience of the erring youth by talking over his problems, by paternal advice and admonition, and in which, in extreme situations, benevolent and wise institutions of the State provided guidance and help "to save him from a downward career." While due process requirements will, in some instances, introduce a degree of order and regularity to Juvenile Court proceedings to determine delinquency, and in contested cases will introduce some elements of the adversary system, nothing will require that the conception of the kindly juvenile judge be replaced by its opposite, nor do we here rule upon the question whether ordinary due process requirements must be observed with respect to hearings to determine the disposition of the delinquent child.

Ultimately, however, we confront the reality of that portion of the Juvenile Court process with which we deal in this case. A boy is charged with misconduct. The boy is committed to an institution where he may be restrained of liberty for years. It is of no constitutional consequence—and of limited practical meaning—that the institution to which he is committed is called an Industrial School. The fact of the matter is that, however euphemistic the title, a "receiving home" or an "industrial school" for juveniles is an institution of confinement in which the child is incarcerated for a greater or lesser time. His world becomes "a building with whitewashed walls, regimented routine and institutional hours. . . ." Instead of mother and father and sisters and brothers and friends and classmates, his world is peopled by guards, custodians, state employees, and "delinquents" confined with him for anything from waywardness to rape and homicide.

In view of this, it would be extraordinary if our Constitution did not require the procedural regularity and the exercise of care implied in the phrase "due process." Under our Constitution, the condition of being a boy does not justify a kangaroo court.

The essential difference between Gerald's case and a normal criminal case is that safeguards available to adults were discarded in Gerald's case. The summary procedure as well as the long commitment was possible because Gerald was 15 years of age instead of over 18.

If Gerald had been over 18, he would not have been subject to Juvenile Court proceedings. For the particular offense immediately involved, the maximum punishment would have been a fine of $5 to $50, or imprisonment in jail for not more than two months. Instead, he was committed to custody for a maximum of six years.

In Kent v. United States [383 U.S. 541 (1966)], we stated that the Juvenile Court Judge's exercise of the power of the state as *parens patriae* was not unlimited. We said that "the admonition to function in a 'parental' relationship is not an invitation to procedural arbitrariness." We announced with respect to such waiver proceedings that while "We do not mean . . . to indicate that the hearing to be held must conform with all of the requirements of a criminal trial or even of the usual administrative hearing; but we do hold that the hearing must measure up to the essentials of due process and fair treatment." We reiterate this view, here in connection with a juvenile court adjudication of "delinquency," as a requirement which is part of the Due Process Clause of the Fourteenth Amendment of our Constitution.

III.
Notice of Charges

Appellants allege that the Arizona Juvenile Code is unconstitutional or alternatively that the proceedings before the Juvenile Court were constitutionally defective because of failure to provide adequate notice of the hearings. No notice was given to Gerald's parents when he was taken into custody on Monday, June 8. On that night, when Mrs. Gault went to the Detention Home, she was orally informed that there would be a hearing the next afternoon and was told the reason why Gerald was in custody. The only written notice Gerald's parents received at any time was a note on plain paper from Officer Flagg delivered on Thursday or Friday, June 11 or 12, to the effect that the judge had set Monday, June 15, "for further Hearings on Gerald's delinquency."

A "petition" was filed with the court on June 9 by Officer Flagg, reciting only that he was informed and believed that "said minor is a delinquent minor and that it is necessary that some order be made by the Honorable Court for said minor's welfare." The applicable Arizona statute provides for a petition to be filed in Juvenile Court, alleging in general terms that the child is "neglected, dependent or delinquent." The statute explicitly states that such a general allegation is sufficient, "without alleging the facts." There is no requirement that the petition be served and it was not served upon, given to, or shown to Gerald or his parents.

We cannot agree that adequate notice was given in this case. Notice, to comply with due process requirements, must be given sufficiently in advance of scheduled court proceedings so that reasonable opportunity to prepare will be afforded, and it must "set forth the alleged misconduct with particularity." The "initial hearing" in the present case was a hearing on the merits. Notice at that time is not timely. Due process of law requires notice which would be deemed constitutionally adequate in a civil or criminal proceeding. It does not allow a hearing to be held in which a youth's freedom and his parents' right to his custody are at stake without giving them timely notice, in advance of the hearing, of the specific issues that they must meet.

IV.

Right to Counsel

Appellants charge that the Juvenile Court proceedings were fatally defective because the court did not advise Gerald or his parents of their right to counsel, and proceeded with the hearing, the adjudication of delinquency and the order of commitment in the absence of counsel for the child and his parents or an express waiver of the right thereto. The Supreme Court of Arizona referred to a provision of the Juvenile Code which it characterized as requiring "that the probation officer shall look after the interests of neglected, delinquent and dependent children," including representing their interests in court. We do not agree. Probation officers, in the Arizona scheme, are also arresting officers. They initiate proceedings and file petitions which they verify, as here, alleging the delinquency of the child; and they testify, as here, against the child. And here the probation officer was also superintendent of the Detention Home. The probation officer cannot act as counsel for the child. His role in the adjudicatory hearing, by statute and in fact, is as arresting officer and witness against the child. Nor can the judge represent the child. There is no material difference in this respect between adult and juvenile proceedings of the sort here involved. In adult proceedings, this contention has been foreclosed by decisions of this Court. A proceeding where the issue is whether the child will be found to be "delinquent" and subjected to the loss of his liberty for years is comparable in seriousness to a felony prosecution. The juvenile needs the assistance of counsel to cope with problems of law, to make skilled inquiry into the facts, to insist upon regularity of the proceedings, and to ascertain whether he has a defense and to prepare and submit it. The child "requires the guiding hand of counsel at every step in the proceedings against him."

We conclude that the Due Process Clause of the Fourteenth Amendment requires that in respect of proceedings to determine delinquency which may result in commitment to an institution in which the juvenile's freedom is curtailed, the child and his parents must be notified of the child's right to be represented by counsel retained by them, or if they are unable to afford counsel, that counsel will be appointed to represent the child.

At the habeas corpus proceeding, Mrs. Gault testified that she knew that she could have appeared with counsel at the juvenile hearing. This knowledge is not a waiver of the right to counsel which she and her juvenile son had, as we have defined it. They had a right expressly to be advised that they might retain counsel and to be confronted with the need for specific consideration of whether they did or did not choose to waive the right. If they were unable to afford to employ counsel, they were entitled in view of the seriousness of the charge and the potential commitment, to appointed counsel, unless they chose waiver. Mrs. Gault's knowledge that she could employ counsel was not an "intentional relinquishment or abandonment" of a fully known right.

V.
Confrontation, Self-Incrimination, Cross-Examination

Appellants urge that the writ of habeas corpus should have been granted because of the denial of the rights of confrontation and cross-examination in the Juvenile Court hearings, and because the privilege against self-incrimination was not observed. The Juvenile Court Judge testified at the habeas corpus hearing that he had proceeded on the basis of Gerald's admissions at the two hearings. Appellants attack this on the ground that the admissions were obtained in disregard of the privilege against self-incrimination. If the confession is disregarded, appellants argue that the delinquency conclusion, since it was fundamentally based on a finding that Gerald had made lewd remarks during the phone call to Mrs. Cook, is fatally defective for failure to accord the rights of confrontation and cross-examination which the Due Process Clause of the Fourteenth Amendment of the Federal Constitution guarantees in state proceedings generally.

Our first question, then, is whether Gerald's admission was improperly obtained and relied on as the basis of decision, in conflict with the Federal Constitution.

Neither Gerald nor his parents were advised that he did not have to testify or make a statement, or that an incriminating statement might result in his commitment as a "delinquent."

The Arizona Supreme Court rejected appellants' contention that Gerald had a right to be advised that he need not incriminate himself. It said: "We think the necessary flexibility for individualized treatment will be enhanced by a rule which does not require the judge to advise the infant of a privilege against self-incrimination."

In reviewing this conclusion of Arizona's Supreme Court, we emphasize again that we are here concerned only with a proceeding to determine whether a minor is a "delinquent" and which may result in commitment to a state institution. Specifically, the question is whether, in such a proceeding, an admission by the juvenile may be used against him in the absence of clear and unequivocal evidence that the admission was made with knowledge that he was not obliged to speak and would not be penalized for remaining silent. In light of Miranda v. Arizona, 384 U.S. 436 (1966), we must also consider whether, if the privilege against self-incrimination is available, it can effectively be waived unless counsel is present or the right to counsel has been waived.

It has long been recognized that the eliciting and use of confessions or admissions require careful scrutiny.

This Court has emphasized that admissions and confessions of juveniles require special caution.

The privilege against self-incrimination is, of course, related to the question of the safeguards necessary to assure that admissions or confessions are reasonably trustworthy, that they are not the mere fruits of fear or coercion, but are reliable expressions of the truth. The roots of the privilege are, however, far deeper. They tap the basic stream of religious and political principle because the privilege reflects the limits of the individual's attornment to the state and—in a philosophical sense—insists upon the equality of the individual and the state. In other words, the privilege has a broader and deeper thrust than the rule which prevents the use of confessions which are the product of coercion because coercion is thought to carry with it the danger of unreliability. One of its purposes is to prevent the state, whether by force or by psychological domination, from overcoming the mind and will of the person under investigation and depriving him of the freedom to decide whether to assist the state in securing his conviction.

It would indeed be surprising if the privilege against self-incrimination were available to hardened criminals but not to children. The language of the Fifth Amendment, applicable to the States by operation of the Fourteenth Amendment, is unequivocal and without exception.

It would be entirely unrealistic to carve out of the Fifth Amendment all statements by juveniles on the ground that these cannot lead to "criminal" involvement. In the first place juvenile proceedings to determine "delinquency," which may lead to commitment to a state institution, must be regarded as "criminal" for purposes of the privilege against self-incrimination. To hold otherwise would be to disregard substance because of the feeble enticement of the "civil" label-of-convenience which has been attached to juvenile proceedings. Indeed, in over half of the States, there is not even assurance that the juvenile will be kept in separate institutions, apart from adult "criminals." In those States juveniles may be placed in or transferred to adult penal institutions after having been found "delinquent" by a juvenile court. For this purpose, at least, commitment is a deprivation of liberty. It is incarceration against one's will, whether it is called "criminal" or "civil." And our Constitution guarantees that no person shall be "compelled" to be a witness against himself when he is threatened with deprivation of his liberty—a command which this Court has broadly applied and generously implemented in accordance with the teaching of the history of the privilege and its great office in mankind's battle for freedom.

It is also urged that the juvenile and presumably his parents should not be advised of the juvenile's right to silence because confession is good for the child as the commencement of the assumed therapy of the juvenile court process, and he should be encouraged to assume an attitude of trust and confidence toward the officials of the juvenile process. This proposition has been subjected to widespread challenge on the basis of current reappraisals of the rhetoric and realities of the handling of juvenile offenders.

In fact, evidence is accumulating that confessions by juveniles do not aid in "individualized treatment," as the court below put it, and that compelling the child to answer questions, without warning or advice as to his right to remain silent, does not serve this or any other good purpose. [I]t seems probable that where children are induced to confess by "paternal" urgings on the part of officials and the confession is then followed by disciplinary action, the child's reaction is likely to be hostile and adverse—the child may well feel that he has been led or tricked into confession and that despite his confession, he is being punished.[d]

We conclude that the constitutional privilege against self-incrimination is applicable in the case of juveniles as it is with respect to adults. We appreciate that special problems may arise with respect to waiver of the privilege by or on behalf of children, and that there may well be some differences in technique—but not in principle—depending upon the age of the child and the presence and competence of parents. The participation of counsel will, of course, assist the police, Juvenile Courts and appellate tribunals in administering the privilege. If counsel was not present for some permissible reason when an admission was obtained, the greatest care must be taken to assure that the admission was voluntary, in the sense not only that it was not coerced or suggested, but also that it was not the product of ignorance of rights or of adolescent fantasy, fright or despair.

The "confession" of Gerald Gault was first obtained by Officer Flagg, out of the presence of Gerald's parents, without counsel and without advising him of his right to silence, as far as appears. The judgment of the Juvenile Court was stated by the judge to be based on Gerald's admissions in court. Neither "admission" was reduced to writing, and, to say the least, the process by which the "admissions" were obtained and received must be characterized as lacking the certainty and order which are required of proceedings of such formidable consequences. Apart from the "admissions," there was nothing upon which a judgment or finding might be based. There was no sworn testimony. Mrs. Cook, the complainant, was not present. The Arizona Supreme Court held that "sworn testimony must be required of all witnesses including police officers, probation officers and others who are part of or officially related to the juvenile court structure." We hold that this is not enough. No reason is suggested or appears for a different rule in respect of sworn testimony in juvenile courts than in adult tribunals. Absent a valid confession adequate to support the determination of the Juvenile Court, confrontation and sworn testimony by witnesses available for cross-examination were essential for a finding of "delinquency" and an order committing Gerald to a state institution for a maximum of six years.

The recommendations in the Children's Bureau's "Standards for Juvenile and Family Courts" are in general accord with our conclusions. They state that testimony should be under oath and

---

[d] *But cf.* the excerpt from Werthman & Piliavin, *Gang Members and the Police,* at 988, *supra.*

that only competent, material and relevant evidence under rules applicable to civil cases should be admitted in evidence. The New York Family Court Act contains a similar provision.

VI.

APPELLATE REVIEW AND TRANSCRIPT OF PROCEEDINGS

Appellants urge that the Arizona statute is unconstitutional under the Due Process Clause because, as construed by its Supreme Court, "there is no right of appeal from a juvenile court order. . . ." The court held that there is no right to a transcript because there is no right to appeal and because the proceedings are confidential and any record must be destroyed after a prescribed period of time. Whether a transcript or other recording is made, it held, is a matter for the discretion of the juvenile court.

This Court has not held that a State is required by the Federal Constitution "to provide appellate courts or a right to appellate review at all." In view of the fact that we must reverse the Supreme Court of Arizona's affirmance of the dismissal of the writ of habeas corpus for other reasons, we need not rule on this question in the present case or upon the failure to provide a transcript or recording of the hearings—or, indeed, the failure of the Juvenile Judge to state the grounds for his conclusion. As the present case illustrates, the consequences of failure to provide an appeal, to record the proceedings, or to make findings or state the grounds for the juvenile court's conclusion may be to throw a burden upon the machinery for habeas corpus, to saddle the reviewing process with the burden of attempting to reconstruct a record, and to impose upon the Juvenile Judge the unseemly duty of testifying under cross-examination as to the events that transpired in the hearings before him.

For the reasons stated, the judgment of the Supreme Court of Arizona is reversed and the cause remanded for further proceedings not inconsistent with this opinion.

It is so ordered.

MR. JUSTICE HARLAN, concurring in part and dissenting in part. It can scarcely be doubted that it is within the State's competence to adopt measures reasonably calculated to meet more effectively the persistent problems of juvenile delinquency; as the opinion for the Court makes abundantly plain, these are among the most vexing and ominous of the concerns which now face communities throughout the country.

The proper issue here is, however, not whether the State may constitutionally treat juvenile offenders through a system of specialized courts, but whether the proceedings in Arizona's juvenile courts include procedural guarantees which satisfy the requirements of the Fourteenth Amendment.

[There are] three criteria by which the procedural requirements of due process should be measured here: first, no more restrictions should be imposed than are imperative to assure the proceedings' fundamental fairness; second, the restrictions which are imposed should be those which preserve, so far as possible, the essential elements of the State's purpose; and finally, restrictions should be chosen which will later permit the orderly selection of any additional protections which may ultimately prove necessary. In this way, the Court may guarantee the fundamental fairness of the proceeding, and yet permit the State to continue development of an effective response to the problems of juvenile crime.

Measured by these criteria, only three procedural requirements should, in my opinion, now be deemed required of state juvenile courts by the Due Process Clause of the Fourteenth Amendment: first, timely notice must be provided to parents and children of the nature and terms of any juvenile court proceeding in which a determination affecting their rights or interests may be made; second, unequivocal and timely notice must be given that counsel may appear in any such proceeding in behalf of the child and its parents, and that in cases in which the child may be confined in an institution, counsel may, in circumstances of indigency, be appointed for them; and third, the court must maintain a written record, or its equivalent, adequate to permit effective review on appeal or in collateral proceedings. These requirements would guarantee to juveniles the tools with which their rights could be fully vindicated, and yet permit the States to pursue without unnecessary hindrance the purposes which they believe imperative in this field. Further, their imposition now would later permit more intelligent assessment of the necessity under the Fourteenth Amendment of additional requirements, by creating suitable records from which the character and deficiencies of juvenile proceedings could be accurately judged. At the same time, these requirements should not cause any substantial modification in the character of juvenile court proceedings: counsel, although now present in only a small percentage of juvenile cases, have apparently already appeared without incident in virtually all juvenile courts; and the maintenance of a record should not appreciably alter the conduct of these proceedings.

The question remains whether certain additional requirements, among them the privilege against self-incrimination, confrontation, and cross-examination, must now, as the Court holds, also be imposed.

Initially, I must vouchsafe that I cannot determine with certainty the reasoning by which the Court concludes that these further requirements are now imperative. The Court begins from the premise, to which it gives force at several points, that juvenile courts need not satisfy "all of the requirements of a criminal trial." It therefore scarcely suffices to explain the selection of these particular procedural requirements for the Court to declare that juvenile court proceedings are essentially criminal, and thereupon to recall that these are requisites for a criminal trial.

The Court has, even under its own premises, asked the wrong questions: the problem here is to determine what forms of procedural protection are necessary to guarantee the fundamental fairness of juvenile proceedings, and not which of the procedures now employed in criminal trials should be transplanted intact to proceedings in these specialized courts.

[U]nlike notice, counsel, and a record, these requirements might radically alter the character of juvenile court proceedings. The evidence from which the Court reasons that they would not is inconclusive, and other available evidence suggests that they very likely would. At the least, it is plain that these additional requirements would contribute materially to the creation in these proceedings of the atmosphere of an ordinary criminal trial, and would, even if they do no more, thereby largely frustrate a central purpose of these specialized courts. Further, these are restrictions intended to conform to the demands of an intensely adversary system of criminal justice; the broad purposes which they represent might be served in juvenile courts with equal effectiveness by procedural devices more consistent with the premises of proceedings in those courts. As the Court apparently acknowledges, the hazards of self-accusation, for example, might be avoided in juvenile proceedings without the imposition of all the requirements and limitations which surround the privilege against self-incrimination. The guarantee of adequate notice, counsel, and a record would create conditions in which suitable alternative procedures could be devised; but, unfortunately, the Court's haste to impose restrictions taken intact from criminal procedure may well seriously hamper the development of such alternatives.

[Justice Black concurred, favoring an across-the-board incorporation of the criminal law protections in the Bill of Rights into the juvenile system where deprivation of liberty might occur.

Justice White concurred, agreeing with the majority, except on the self-incrimination issue, which he felt was not clearly presented because of lack of evidence as to whether Gault was compelled to be a witness against himself. Because there were other grounds for reversal, he felt this and the questions of confrontation and cross-examination should have been deferred. Justice Stewart dissented.]

B. EVIDENCE REQUIREMENTS IN THE JUVENILE COURT

In the case of juveniles, as with adults, the overwhelming majority of cases do not involve a contest of fact. But unlike the criminal law, which has developed highly sophisticated rules of evidence for the contested cases, the juvenile system has paid relatively little attention to the problem. The few appellate court decisions deal most often with the admissibility of evidence rather than its sufficiency, a result, no doubt, of the informality of procedures and widespread use of social investigation reports which have raised questions about the kind of evidence that may properly be relied on. These courts have generally taken the view of the United States Supreme Court in *Gault,* that "[n]o reason is suggested or appears for a different rule in respect of sworn testimony in juvenile courts than in adult tribunals. Absent a valid confession adequate to support the determination of the Juvenile Court, confrontation and sworn testimony by witnesses available for cross-examination were essential for a finding of 'delinquency.' . . ."[e] However, it has long been commonplace in juvenile court proceedings for the court services or probation staff to make a social study of the juvenile prior to the court hearing and to submit it to the judge to aid him in disposition of the case. The reason for this early investigation rests in the fact that petitions in the delinquency area are rarely dismissed in court, so it avoids unnecessary delay in disposition to obtain the information helpful for disposition prior to the hearing.

Clearly, however, if the judge studies the social report prior to the hearing in order to be well grounded in background for disposition, he also has learned much which is not considered relevant evidence in legal proceedings but may influence his judgment or the question of adjudication. The social report may also focus on the offender and assume he committed the alleged acts.

Although most of the attention to the admissibility of evidence in juvenile delinquency proceedings has focused on the question

[e] *In re* Gault, 387 U.S. 1, 56 (1967).

of whether the limitations on certain types of evidence in adult criminal proceedings should be applied in juvenile court, there may be instances in which the limitations in juvenile delinquency proceedings should be greater than in adult proceedings. For example, in In the Matter of Four Youths,[f] Judge Ketcham of the District of Columbia Juvenile Court held that statements, made by four boys while in custody at the police station without parents or counsel, were unreliable without regard to whether they were voluntary:

> Although counsel for the respondents sought to show that the statements against interest were not made voluntarily, the Court's decisions does not rest on such a showing.
>
> For a suggestible youth, the authoritarian atmosphere of a police station is, in itself, accusatory and full of tensions and pressures not conductive to a frank, open and unvarnished expression of opinion.[g]

Many juvenile court statutes contain no mention of the degree of proof of delinquency necessary. Where the statutes mention the problem of proof or the courts have been concerned with it, the degree necessary to adjudge a juvenile delinquent has usually been said to be that of civil proceedings, that is, "a preponderance of the evidence." The reasoning behind these statutes and rulings is that juvenile proceedings are noncriminal and, therefore, the civil rules should apply.

However, as recognition that juvenile proceedings are not ordinary civil proceedings has increased, there has been a trend to requiring a higher degree of proof, ranging from requirements of "clear and convincing proof"[h] to holdings that the adult standard must be met.

In re URBASEK

38 Ill. 2d 535, 232 N.E.2d 716 (1967)

UNDERWOOD, Justice. The First District Appellate Court (76 Ill. App. 2d 375, 222 N.E.2d 233) affirmed the judgment of the juvenile division of the circuit court of Cook County finding from a preponderance of the evidence that Robert F. Urbasek,

---

[f] Juvenile Court, D.C., April 7, 1961, 89 Wash. L. Rptr. 639 (Tues., May 9, 1961).

[g] *Id.* at 642.

[h] *See* NATIONAL COUNCIL ON CRIME AND DELINQUENCY, PROCEDURE AND EVIDENCE IN THE JUVENILE COURT (1962).

(herein referred to as respondent) was a juvenile delinquent. We allowed a petition for leave to appeal in order that we might consider whether continued use of the standard of proof (preponderance of the evidence) heretofore prevailing in delinquency proceedings was permissible in light of the opinion of the Supreme Court in In re Application of Gault, 387 U.S. 1, or whether the State must now prove a charge of delinquency beyond a reasonable doubt where the acts constituting the alleged delinquent conduct would amount to a crime if charged against an adult.

The evidence introduced at the hearing revealed that the respondent was charged with murdering an eleven-year-old girl with whom he had been playing some four hours prior to the discovery of her body.

"On August 26, 1965, between 7:00 and 8:00 P.M., the body of Karen Mitchell was found in the locked Urbasek garage. Karen had been missing since about 3:00 P.M., and her mother had been searching for her. She had questioned Robert several times and finally insisted that Robert and his older sister allow her to look for Karen in their garage. The garage was opened, and the girl's body, with seven stab wounds, was found in the crawl space at the far end of the garage."

[T]he judge based his findings of fact upon the preponderance of the evidence standard.

In *Gault* the court held that the essentials of due process required that a juvenile court adjudication of delinquency include adequate advance notice of the charges, the right to counsel, the privilege against self-incrimination and the right to confrontation and cross-examination of witnesses. While these requirements are met by our statute, and the respondent in the case before us was denied none of the rights, it would seem that the reasons which caused the Supreme Court to import the constitutional requirements of an adversary criminal trial into delinquency hearings logically require that a finding of delinquency for misconduct, which would be criminal if charged against an adult, is valid only when the acts of delinquency are proved beyond a reasonable doubt to have been committed by the juvenile charged.

Though the purpose of industrial training schools for boys, such as that at St. Charles in Illinois, is to rehabilitate and train youths whose misconduct has brought them to these institutions, the incarcerated juveniles' liberty of action is restrained just as effectively as that of the adult inmates serving terms in State and

Federal prisons. The modern concepts of penology which guide the administrators of today's prisons also place a great emphasis on training, education and rehabilitation which were once the unique characteristics of the juvenile system that, in theory, at least, justified the application of lesser procedural safeguards for delinquency hearings. Now, however, while improbable, a minor may conceivably be confined for a longer period of time than the period of imprisonment imposed upon an adult who is found guilty of the same criminal conduct.

We need not be reminded that the *Gault* decision did not pass upon the precise question of the quantum of proof that must be shown to validate a finding of delinquency. We believe, however, that the language of that opinion exhibits a spirit that transcends the specific issues there involved, and that, in view thereof, it would not be consonant with due process or equal protection to grant allegedly delinquent juveniles the same procedural rights that protect adults charged with crimes, while depriving these rights of their full efficacy by allowing a finding of delinquency upon a lesser standard of proof than that required to sustain a criminal conviction. Since the same or even greater curtailment of freedom may attach to a finding of delinquency than results from a criminal conviction, we cannot say that it is constitutionally permissible to deprive the minor of the benefit of the standard of proof distilled by centuries of experience as a safeguard for adults.

We realize that our adoption of what has heretofore been the minority viewpoint as to the quantum of evidence required in delinquency hearings requires not only the reversal of the decision in this case, but also voids the provisions of the current Juvenile Court Act which incorporate the preponderance standard for delinquency proceedings (Ill. Rev. Stat. 1965, chap. 37, pars. 701-4 and 704-6.) Our ruling today, however, modifies, in only a single respect, the Illinois statutory scheme that could well act as a model among the States for protecting the rights of juvenile court defendants. (See Ill. Rev. Stat. 1965, chap. 37, par. 701-20.) The unique benefits that are derived from the special dispositional processes under the Act will not be diluted by the changes made here at the adjudicatory stage.

If it may fairly be said that the trial judge actually found the evidence insufficient to establish respondent's delinquency beyond a reasonable doubt, we should reverse without remandment. If the trial court simply measured the evidence by the wrong standard of proof, the cause should be remanded for a new trial in which the correct standard would be applied. At the conclusion of the hearing the trial court stated:

"I was and am *convinced* that the youngster committed the act. I believe that the State met their burden of establishing the preponderance of evidence. I don't know that they met, if it is a requirement of proof beyond a reasonable doubt. I *don't think* that was met." (Emphasis added.) In our opinion it cannot fairly be said that these equivocal statements constitute a finding that the reasonable doubt standard was not met. Accordingly, a new trial will be ordered.

Reversed and remanded.

CALIFORNIA WELFARE AND INSTITUTIONS CODE §§ 701–702 (1966)

§ 701. Description of minor; reception of evidence; extrajudicial admissions or confessions; objections to evidence.

At the hearing, the court shall first consider only the question whether the minor is a person described by Sections 600 [neglected, uncontrolled, dangerously mentally disturbed], 601 [disobedient, truant, in danger of leading an idle or immoral life], or 602 [violating criminal ordinance or law or a juvenile court order], and for this purpose, any matter or information relevant and material to the circumstances or acts which are alleged to bring him within the jurisdiction of the juvenile court is admissible and may be received in evidence; however, a preponderance of evidence, legally admissible in the trial of criminal cases, must be adduced to support a finding that the minor is a person described by Section 602, and a preponderance of evidence, legally admissible in the trial of civil cases must be adduced to support a finding that the minor is a person described by Sections 600 or 601. When it appears that the minor has made an extrajudicial admission or confession and denies the same at the hearing, the court may continue the hearing for not to exceed seven days to enable the probation officer to subpoena witnesses to attend the hearing to prove the allegations of the petition. If the minor is not represented by counsel at the hearing, it shall be deemed that objections that could have been made to the evidence were made.

§ 702. Finding and order; dismissal; discharge; continuance to receive social study or other evidence; detention order.

After hearing such evidence, the court shall make a finding, noted in the minutes of the court, whether or not the minor is a person described by Sections 600, 601, or 602. If it finds that the minor is not such a person, it shall order that the petition be dismissed and the minor be discharged from any detention or restriction theretofore ordered. If the court finds that the minor is such a person, it shall make and enter its findings and order accordingly and shall then proceed to hear evidence on the question of the proper disposition to be made of the minor.*

NEW YORK FAMILY COURT ACT §§ 744–746
(McKinney Supp. 1967)

§ 744. Evidence in fact-finding hearings; required quantum.

(a) Only evidence that is competent, material and relevant may be admitted in a fact-finding hearing [to determine the juvenile's acts].

(b) Any determination at the conclusion of a fact-finding hearing that a respondent did an act or acts must be based on a preponderance of the evidence. For this purpose, an uncorroborated confession made out of court by a respondent is not sufficient.

§ 745. Evidence in dispositional hearings; required quantum of proof.

(a) Only evidence that is material and relevant may be admitted during a dispositional hearing [to determine whether the juvenile needs supervision, treatment, or confinement].

(b) An adjudication at the conclusion of a dispositional hearing must be based on a preponderance of the evidence.

§ 746. Sequence of hearings.

(a) Upon completion of the fact-finding hearing the dispositional hearing may commence immediately after the required findings are made.

(b) Reports prepared by the probation service for use by the court at any time prior to the making of an order of disposition shall be deemed confidential information furnished to the court which the court in a proper case may, in its discretion, withhold from or disclose in whole or in part to the law guardian, counsel, party in interest, or other appropriate person. Such reports may not be furnished to the court prior to the completion of a fact-finding hearing, but may be used in a dispositional hearing.

* Even though the hearings are separated, many judges still read the social report before ruling on the question of delinquency. Lemert, *Legislating Change in the Juvenile Court,* 1967 Wis. L. Rev. 422, 437-39.

C. THE RIGHT TO A JURY TRIAL

Because of concern with providing a nonadversary, informal atmosphere for the juvenile court hearing, many juvenile court statutes have not provided for a jury trial. During the early years of juvenile court development, as statutes were adopted throughout the United States, the lack of a jury trial was frequently the basis for attack on a juvenile court statute. In the overwhelming majority of cases, the statute was upheld, usually on the ground that the proceeding was not a criminal one to punish the juvenile, but a civil one to protect him.

As concern about the true nature of the juvenile delinquency process has increased in recent years, courts have begun to reexamine the jury trial requirement.

In re CHARLES S. RINDELL
Providence, R. I., Family Court
2 Criminal Law Reporter 3121 (Feb. 7, 1968)

DECIANTIS, J. The Court . . . confines itself to the following question: Whether a child who has committed an offense, which if committed by an adult would constitute a felony, is entitled to a Trial by Jury, by virtue of Sections 7, 10 and 15, of Article I of the Rhode Island Constitution and of Articles VI and XIV of the Amendments to the United States Constitution.

In deciding this case the Court feels that it must trace the origin of the concept of liberty and the right to trial by jury. Liberty and trial by jury is the mainstay and bulwark upon which truth and liberty rest.

. . .

It can be said that the trial by jury reflects an evolution in the long history of jurisprudence, in search for the truth upon which justice should be based and dispensed. Prior methods in the search for truth were found wanting, and eventually trial by jury of one's peers was evolved. It has withstood the test and has become a cherished part of the concept of due process in the law of the land.

Jury trial, therefore, is the cornerstone of *individual liberty.*

Is there any question that liberty is one of those "precious fruits" of *common law right?*

The individual liberty of a juvenile is restrained once he is committed to an agency or to the training school. He is supervised, guarded, and punished. He has no choice. He must obey the rules and orders given to him while he is at the training school. He cannot go home at will. He cannot do what he desires. He is a prisoner just as much as the adult in the state's prison. Not only is he deprived of his liberty, but he is also subject to transfer from the training school to the ACI by order of the Assistant Director of Correctional Services, and subject to disciplinary measures accorded to adults and can be subjected to cruel and inhuman punishment, which does exist.

Is this civil? Is this rehabilitation? Can this type of procedure be characterized as a civil proceeding?

All of the safeguards that are afforded to an adult criminal trial should be, and constitutionally must be applied to a juvenile case, even including that of the right to trial by jury of his peers, as well as a finding of guilty beyond a reasonable doubt, rather than by a preponderance of the evidence. Then, and only then, will uniformity and due process prevail and the juvenile, the police, the Court, and everyone else concerned will know where they are headed. See In re Urbasek, 2 CrL 2193.

Trial by jury in Rhode Island is guaranteed to *all* persons whether in criminal cases or whether in civil cases, so long as that right existed prior to the adoption of the Constitution, and certainly whether one is involved in a civil or criminal proceeding of the Family Court in which his "liberty" is to be "taken," "imprisoned," "outlawed," and "banished," he is entitled to a trial by jury.

The Court is equally convinced that a juvenile is entitled to a trial by jury under the provisions of the Sixth Amendment to the United States Constitution, via the Fourteenth Amendment, and which in light of the Gault, 87 S.Ct. 1423, decision, will undoubtedly, in this Court's opinion, be extended to the States.

The laws apply equally to juveniles as they should apply and do under Gault. *No juvenile* should be deprived of his *individual liberty*. The doctrine of parens patriae is hopelessly outdated with the "harsh realities of modern life." As has been stated: "—The reality is that the state cannot be a good parent. If it cannot give love it can at least *give justice*."

In view of these pronouncements it would seem almost unthinkable that the Court would deprive the juvenile of the most cherished right awarded to man; an impartial trial by jury. Again, if liberty is the keystone of the whole decision then it must follow that all of the provisions of the Bill of Rights, including trial by jury, must prevail."

To interpret otherwise is tantamount to rendering Gault a mere exercise in rhetoric rather than the bold and eloquent decision which constantly reaffirms in every instance that the rights of juveniles must be preserved.

Motion for jury trial is granted.[i]

D. THE RIGHT TO COUNSEL IN JUVENILE DELINQUENCY PROCEEDINGS

As originally conceived, the juvenile justice system saw no role for the lawyer. The attitude in the early years of the court is summed up well in one of the classics of the juvenile justice field:

> In non-criminal proceedings, legal rights are not necessarily violated by the elimination of attorneys. The court is the defender as well as the corrector of the child. It is thought that the appearance of attorneys usually complicates the proceedings and serves neither the interests of the child nor the interests of justice. The better juvenile courts have been successful in discouraging the appearances of attorneys in most cases.[j]

The result was that attorneys rarely appeared in juvenile courts as counsel for the child or his parents.[k] All of this changed with the holding of the United States Supreme Court in *In re Gault*,[l] that as a constitutional right juveniles are entitled to counsel at the juvenile delinquency adjudication hearing where there is a possibility of commitment.[m] The Court did not then state whether it would extend the requirement of counsel to the pre-hearing

[i] *See* Nieves v. United States, 280 F. Supp. 994 (S.D.N.Y. 1968), for a holding that the federal statute which requires a juvenile to waive his right to a jury trial in order to be handled as a delinquent rather than a criminal is unconstitutional. *See also* DeBacker v. Brainard, 161 N.W.2d (Neb. 1968).

[j] H. Low, Juvenile Courts in the United States 137 (1927).

[k] A California study found that in thirty-four out of fifty-seven counties in that state, counsel appeared in 1% or less of the juvenile court cases. A Study of the Administration of Justice in California, Part II, 12 (1960).

[l] In practice there may not be much change. W.W. Reckless & W.C. Reckless, *The Initial Impact of the Gault Decision in Ohio,* 18 Juvenile Court Judges J. 121, 123 (1967). But changes have resulted from earlier legislation. Lemert, *Legislating Change in the Juvenile Court,* 1967 Wis. L. Rev. 421; Isaacs, *The Role of the Lawyer in Representing Minors in the New York Family Court,* 12 Buffalo L. Rev. 501 (1963); Coxe, *Lawyers in Juvenile Court,* 13 Crime & Delinquency 488 (1967).

[m] Apparently the court used possibility of a commitment as a dividing line in the same manner as it used substantial period of imprisonment in Gideon v. Wainwright, 372 U.S. 335 (1963). It has been argued that in the case of the juvenile this is unreasonable because the label "delinquency" is as stigmatizing whether or not a commitment results. Comment, *In re Gault and the Persisting Questions of Procedural Due Process and Legal Ethics in Juvenile Courts,* 47 Neb. L. Rev. 558 (1968).

stages of the juvenile delinquency process or to the disposition hearing, although most observers assume it will.[n]

However, guaranteeing the juvenile the right to counsel does not solve the problem of counsel in juvenile delinquency proceedings. In an adversary system such as the traditional criminal case, with fairly clearly articulated standards of due process, a lawyer's role is pretty well defined. In the case of an alleged delinquent, the situation is not so clear. In a nonadversary system, with vaguely defined procedures, in which everyone is acting for the best interest of the child, what good is counsel to him? The child usually admits his guilt and the court's role is merely to determine what is the best way to rehabilitate him. The problem of the role of the attorney in juvenile court is twofold: (1) *What* can he do? Traditionally, he has been viewed as a person trained in eliciting the facts of a given transaction. How can he perform when the question is one of whether a correctional institution, a group home, or probation will best rehabilitate a recalcitrant youth? What does he do in an informal procedure with a judge who may not be law trained?[o] (2) *How* should he act? As an advocate, representing his client's interest as his client sees that interest? Or does he owe an obligation to represent "the best interests of the child" by some objective standard? What is his relationship to the parents?

VELASQUEZ v. PRATT
443 P.2d 1020, 1022-23 (Utah 1968)

[Another portion of this case appears at 1165, *infra*.]

TUCKETT, Justice (dissenting). I am of the opinion that at the hearing the court failed to adequately inform Steven and his mother of their right to be represented by legal counsel. The record of the juvenile court indicates that at the outset the court made a statement in the following language: "The law specifies that the child can be represented by legal counsel. This is required." The transcript of the proceedings is silent as to the court advising Steven or his mother further about their right to counsel, nor did the court inquire as to whether or not Mrs. Velasquez or her son had sufficient resources with which to employ counsel.

---

[n] *See* Dorsen & Rezneck, *In re Gault and the Future of Juvenile Law*, 1 FAMILY L.Q. 1 (Dec. 1967).

[o] In a 1963 study, of 1,564 juvenile judges responding (approximately 70% of the total) only 71% held law degrees. THE PRESIDENT'S COMMISSION ON LAW ENFORCEMENT AND ADMINISTRATION OF JUSTICE, TASK FORCE REPORT: JUVENILE DELINQUENCY AND YOUTH CRIME 6 (1967).

At the hearing before the juvenile court no witnesses were called to testify concerning the delinquencies charged against Steven. The record indicates that the court made its findings as to Steven's guilt solely from questions put to the boy by the court concerning the truth or falsity of the allegations contained in the petition. I can think of no other occasion where a boy, age 14, would be more in need of counsel, and this is especially true where the proceedings before the court might reasonably subject him to being deprived of his liberty for a period of years.

In re BACON
240 Cal. App. 2d 34, 49 Cal. Rptr. 322, 328 (1966)

[For the facts, see another portion of this opinion which appears at 1121, *infra.*]

MOLINARI, Justice.

Effectiveness of Counsel

As a second contention appellants argue that their right to counsel was rendered ineffective. More specifically, appellants assert that prior to the hearings in these cases their counsel were given to understand by members of the probation department that a favorable recommendation on disposition would be highly unlikely if appellants refused to cooperate with the probation officers and the court; and that appellants' attorneys chose to cooperate with the probation department and with the court, thereby allowing the substantive elements of the offenses constituting the jurisdictional facts to be elicited from appellants' testimony rather than from independent evidence. Accordingly, appellants claim that they were denied the effective right to counsel because their attorneys were "placed in the ambivalent position of being simultaneously the minor's representative and an agent of the court in promoting its philosophy of cooperation. . . ."

We find nothing in the record before us to support the claimed activity on the part of the probation department. We are of the opinion, however, that, even assuming such activity, the contention is nevertheless without merit. While it is true that the right to be represented by counsel of his own choice has been afforded to a minor who appears before the juvenile court (§§ 679 and 700), the nature of this right must be viewed in context with the nature of the juvenile court system itself. A proceeding in the juvenile court is not a criminal proceeding. (§ 503.) It is instead in the nature of a guardianship. Moreover, section 680 specifically provides that "Except where there is a contested issue of fact or law, the proceedings shall be conducted in an informal nonadversary atmosphere with a view to obtaining the maximum co-operation of the minor upon whose behalf the petition is brought. . . ." In In re Mikkelsen, 226 Cal. App. 2d 467, 470-471, 38 Cal. Rptr. 106, 108, Justice Taylor, discussing the Juvenile Court Law, enacted in 1961, in relation to due process in juvenile proceedings, stated as follows: "The statute attempts to attain a hard working balance between preserving a guaranty of civil due process to the minor while retaining that informal court atmosphere which minimizes the proceedings' harmful effects and encourages the minor's receptivity to treatment."

In the instant case the juvenile court judge demonstrated a conscientious appreciation of the extent to which the juvenile proceedings became adversary. The record discloses that appellants were carefully advised of their rights, including the right to counsel, before their interviews with probation authorities. At the hearing before the juvenile court they were represented by able counsel who were afforded the right to cross-examine witnesses and to present their case as in any adversary proceeding. In sum, there is nothing in the record to indicate that appellants' representation by their counsel was impinged upon so as to result in a deprivation of rights which could be said to be violative of due process.

ATTORNEY REPRESENTATION IN JUVENILE COURT

By Daniel L. Skoler & Charles W. Tenney, Jr.
4 Journal of Family Law 77, 89-94 (1964)

[This article was the result of questionnaires received from 85 juvenile court judges representing 75 different courts and 36 state court systems and the District of Columbia.]

Performance by Attorneys

On the second evaluative question, judges were asked to rate the performance of most attorneys appearing in their court on two counts: (i) understanding of methods, philosophy, and approach of the court, and (ii) effectiveness and helpfulness in proceedings. Responses were as follows:

	Understanding of Methods & Philosophy	*Effectiveness and Helpfulness*
Very good	27	33
Adequate	38	34
Somewhat deficient	14	12
Poor	3	3
Total Responses	82	82

While these responses do not appear to be unduly critical, they nevertheless indicate considerable room for improvement.[p] The specialized character and unique demands of the juvenile court proceeding would, of themselves, seem to require a "very good" rating for most lawyers practicing in the juvenile court. And there should be no one practicing in a juvenile court who could be rated less than "adequate." The implications for law schools and continuing legal education programs seem obvious.

It is unfortunate that data on how judges evaluate lawyer performance generally is not available to compare with these ratings of juvenile court performance. Perhaps attorneys in the juvenile courts surveyed would fare well in such a comparison (although the more competent element of the trial bar, both in terms of financial inducement and demands of their practices, would seem less likely to become involved in juvenile court representation). . . .

It will be noted that most of the judges rated lawyers the same on both "understanding" and "helpfulness." This is not surprising since one could hardly be effective or helpful unless he understood the methods, the philosophy, and approach of the court. The slightly higher ratings on effectiveness may suggest that competent and well-meaning attorneys can make a positive contribution even with imperfect orientation as to the court's work and methods.

Lawyer's Blind Spots and Shortcomings

In the third evaluative question, the survey group was asked to catalogue the chief deficiencies observed in attorneys appearing in juvenile court. Seventy-nine judges responded to this open-ended question. . . .

---

[p] Until recently, the assumption by many interested in the juvenile court movement has been that the presence of lawyers would ruin juvenile court procedure. In view of this, the fact that sixty-five of the eighty-two judges found most lawyers appearing before them understood the method and philosophy of the court and that sixty-seven of the judges found most lawyers effective and helpful is a very high rating.

By far, the most frequently mentioned shortcomings were lack of understanding of the philosophy and purposes of the juvenile court (31 replies) and lack of familiarity with juvenile court procedures (36 replies). Included in the responses indicating insufficient understanding of juvenile court philosophy were 3 answers suggesting that the lawyer often failed to disassociate the child's interests from those of his parents. Included in the tabulation on lack of familiarity with procedures were 4 responses which specified "lack of experience."

Without characterizing these replies as wholly discrete from the preceding categories, 21 judges named as a shortcoming the attorney's tendency to look upon and to treat juvenile court proceedings as "criminal in nature." Also, 12 judges identified the attorney's lack of preparation. Of these, 1 judge indicated that those unprepared in juvenile court were likely to be unprepared in any court, 1 judge hypothesized that lack of preparation was due to the fact that attorneys were not compensated, and 1 suggested that the reason might have something to do with the relatively late stage at which most attorneys enter juvenile proceedings.

Only 3 judges listed as a shortcoming the attorney's lack of knowledge of treatment methods. One judge, on the other hand, saw their tendency to function as social workers and to disregard the rights of their clients as particular deficiencies.

. . .

Attorney's Value to the Juvenile Court

Moving from the focus on attorney "shortcomings" toward positive attributes, judges were asked to identify those functions which they saw as providing the attorney's chief value to the juvenile court and its work. Eighty judges responded to this question which was structured through enumeration of four specific value categories (see below) and provision for an open-ended "other" category. The respondees were instructed to check one or more categories without indicating order of importance. Most of them specified more than one chief value and the tabulation, exclusive of "other" responses, showed the following results.

Development of facts	34
Protection of rights	50
Interpretation of court's approach and goals	53
Securing cooperation in court's disposition	57

In light of the judges' responses to the questions concerning attorney shortcomings and ratings of attorney performance, it appears that they see the above values as *potential* and not necessarily characteristic of the lawyers now appearing in their courts. The tabulation indicates that what judges most would like from the lawyers is for them to secure cooperation (from parent and child) in the court's disposition (named 4 to 24 times more frequently than other categories). A close second is their desire for the lawyer to aid the court in interpreting its approach and goals to parents and children.

While the judges place less emphasis on what we would consider the traditional roles of counsel, i.e., developing facts and protecting clients' rights, it does not appear to be significantly less, at least as regards the matter of protecting rights. (The data does suggest that the judges place less value on the need for counsel to aid in determining facts, possibly attributable both to the substantial investigative help available in metropolitan courts from full time probation staffs and the heavy majority of cases in which the facts of delinquency are uncontested). This continuing concern with traditional roles is somewhat in contrast with those answers to the preceding question identifying as a "shortcoming" of lawyers their tendency to treat the juvenile court hearing as criminal in nature unless this was meant as a label for obstructive and frivolous assertion of client rights. The cornerstone of adult criminal representation is, of course, zealous protection of the accused's legal rights. On balance, it would seem fair to say that judges see the traditional advocate role of the lawyer as perhaps diminished but certainly not demolished in juvenile court.

. . .

Need for Orientation and Training

When asked whether they thought lawyers appearing in juvenile court needed special training and orientation beyond normal "defense counsel" skills, the judges answered "yes" almost as with one voice (79 of 83 responses or 96% of responding group).

PROCEDURE AND EVIDENCE IN THE JUVENILE COURT ch. IV, 42-44 (1962)

National Council on Crime and Delinquency

[A] much debated question is whether the usual lawyer-client relationship is appropriate to the juvenile court. The lawyer's ethical obligation, it is said, is complete devotion to his client's wishes or interest. Is this attitude appropriate in the juvenile court, if the child and his parents are opposing commitment or court supervision and it seems the child in fact would benefit from such treatment? If the usual lawyer-client relationship is inappropriate, will not even the best intentioned lawyer find himself in a confused and ineffectual role?

If we consider the problems that might confront the lawyer, we see that he would not, with an understanding of the court's philosophy and objectives, experience a conflict between its needs and his client's. It is of course the judge's function to determine on the facts presented whether an adjudication will be made. Thus, if the respondent desires to present facts to controvert the petition or the prospective disposition it is no more the function of the lawyer in a juvenile case than in any other to overrule the client in this respect. It is, however, within his province to interpret the court's approach to the child's problem and its concern for his welfare at every point of the proceedings. His duty to prevent misrepresentation and perjury in the presentation of facts is the same as in any other proceeding.

Does the lawyer in juvenile court have an additional duty to present facts coming to his attention which may lead to an adjudication of delinquency or neglect or a supervisory order? Disclosure of facts pointing to the need for treatment may be viewed as consistent with the child's ultimate interest, and should be so presented to him and his parents. This disclosure may be viewed as a fulfillment of the duty the attorney must assume, as an officer of the court, in any proceeding involving more than merely private interests, to the court and the community as well as to his client.

As to legal rather than factual issues, it has been suggested that the lawyer may obstruct juvenile proceedings by technical and invalid objections. It is the juvenile court judge's function, as in any proceeding, to curtail obstructionism. It is true that this may pose a particular difficulty in those courts where the judge is not required to be a lawyer. On the whole, however, the argument that counsel will make the proceedings lengthier or more cumbersome has no greater weight with respect to juvenile court than elsewhere, if the importance of the proceedings to the individual and society are borne in mind.

A recent California study stated: "We find no grounds to support the contention that the presence of counsel will destroy the protective philosophy of the juvenile court or seriously alter the informality of proceedings. Where counsel has been employed in the juvenile court . . . judges . . . commented that attorneys perform a valuable service in safeguarding the minor's rights and in interpreting the reason for the court's disposition to the family."

THE JUVENILE COURT AND THE ADVERSARY SYSTEM: PROBLEMS OF FUNCTION AND FORM

By Joel F. Handler

1965 Wisconsin Law Review 7, 36-39

. . . Jacob L. Isaacs, a member of the Family Court Committee of the Judicial Conference of the State of New York, and a former chairman of the Committee on the Domestic Relations Court and Family Law of the Association of the Bar of the City of New York, described [the] role [of attorney in juvenile court] as follows: As advocate, the law guardian "should bring to this task the usual tools of the advocate—familiarity with the applicable law, the ability to make a thorough investigation and logical presentation of the relevant facts and the faculty for forceful and persuasive exposition of his client's position." On the other hand, "conscientious counsel will have to exercise intelligent discrimination in the use of tactics learned in other courts since wholesale importation of techniques developed in the handling of criminal or civil cases before other tribunals may not only threaten the objectives of the court but will rarely serve the interest of the minor child." As guardian, the lawyer must be concerned with not only "legal rights" but "the general welfare of the minor." As officer of the court, in addition to other duties, the lawyer must disclose to the court "all facts in his possession which bear upon a proper disposition of the matter," subject to the attorney-client privilege. Isaacs significantly points out that the attitudes of the lawyer will have important consequences for the rehabilitative goals of the program. "If counsel condones the 'beat the rap' approach and substitutes deception for honest but firm concern for the protection of his client's rights, he will not only be doing the court and his profession a disservice, but he will be rendering an even greater disservice to his client."

The role envisaged by Isaacs does not seem to differ from the role envisaged by the American Bar Association for trial counsel in general. It is seriously questionable, however, whether these positions represent the attitudes of lawyers themselves as to the advocate's role and his strategy and tactics. In civil litigation, authoritative commentators, including no less a paragon than the late Samuel Williston, take a position on the trial lawyer's role which is quite different from Isaacs. Williston states flatly: "If . . . [unfavorable] evidence was unknown to . . . [the lawyer] when he took the case, he may sometimes withdraw from it, but while he is engaged as counsel he is not only not obliged to disclose unfavorable evidence, but it is a violation of his duty to his client if he does so."[104] The lawyer's duty is to do everything for his client that the law permits. He violates this duty if he sacrifices the client's legal rights for what he, the lawyer, thinks is the most just result. In criminal litigation, the push toward duty to client is intensified by the policies of the privilege against self-incrimination, the attorney-client privilege, and the strict burden of proof on the state.[105]

---

[104] WILLISTON, LIFE AND LAW 271 (1940). The New York County Committee on Professional Ethics:

> *Question 309:* In an action, on behalf of an infant three years of age, for injuries sustained by falling off a porch owned by the defendant, due to the alleged negligence of the defendant, where there is no eye witness known to the plaintiff's attorney and thereafter when the case came to trial the infant's case was dismissed on motion of the defendant's attorney, on the ground that the infant plaintiff was unable to make out a sufficient case of circumstantial evidence. During the presentation of the plaintiff's case, said attorney for the defendant had an eye witness to said accident actually present in the court and did not mention said fact, either to the plaintiff's attorney or to the court and kept the court in ignorance of the fact that a person did exist who actually saw said accident, and was present in court. Was the failure of the defendant's attorney to disclose said information to the court improper professional conduct?
>
> *Answer:* In the opinion of the Committee the conduct of the defendant's attorney is not professionally improper. The fact of infancy does not call for a different reply.

ASSOCIATION OF THE BAR OF THE CITY OF NEW YORK AND THE N.Y. COUNTY LAWYERS' ASSOCIATION, OPINIONS OF THE COMMITTEE ON PROFESSIONAL ETHICS 708 (1956). Questioned in DRINKER, LEGAL ETHICS 77 (1953). *But see,* Thode, *The Ethical Standard for the Advocate,* 39 TEXAS L. REV. 575 (1961).

[105] See Thode, *supra* note 104. See the interesting article by Levy, *The Dilemma of the Criminal Lawyer,* 9 RECORD OF N.Y.C.B.A. 215, 220 (1954): "When a defendant engages a lawyer or has one assigned to him he has but one simple and understandable object; he wants to be free. He does not want to be edified with moral precepts, or be told that he should subordinate his selfish interests to the public good by pleading guilty and atoning for his sins. He wants to be free, and it's the lawyer's job to help him." There is no doubt in Levy's mind that it is the duty of the defense counsel to keep unfavorable evidence from the jury or to use his skill in cross-examination to make an honest witness appear to be testifying untruthfully.

In INBAU & SOWLE, CASES ON CRIMINAL JUSTICE 793 (1960), the following case is described. In an open and shut burglary case, the prosecution forgot to establish in the record that the person described by the witnesses was the defendant. The defense counsel, a young lawyer, pointed out the omission. If the lawyer had done nothing, the conviction would have been overturned on appeal because of this technical error. The young lawyer was castigated by an experienced criminal practitioner.

Contrast these attitudes, which are by no means atypical, with the following statement of Hon. Daniel J. Donahoe, Presiding Judge of the Family Court of the State of New York, Chemung County:

> The law guardian does not approach the Family Court in the same frame of mind he might have in representing a client in a criminal court. His attitude and purpose is, after ascertaining the sufficiency of the moving papers and satisfaction in his own mind that

This is not the place to comment on what role the lawyer should play either in court or in pre-trial bargaining. If, however, lawyers are to be used successfully in the juvenile process, one must reckon with the attitudes of the profession. As long as one assumes that the representation of juveniles calls for standards of behavior different from those practiced in adult proceedings, then, the critical problem of whether lawyers are willing or capable of changing their patterns of behavior must be faced. Furthermore, the change in behavior will probably have to be self-imposed. The experience of the criminal trial and appellate courts in attempting to control the excesses of advocacy has not been a happy one. In the juvenile process, where standards are much more vague, effective court control seems unlikely.

In re LANG

44 Misc. 2d 900, 255 N.Y.S.2d 987 (Family Ct. 1965)

JUSTINE WISE POLIER, Judge. This case raises an additional issue which calls for corrective legislation.

The New York State Family Court is a civil court. The definition of delinquency has been narrowed to cover acts committed by children under sixteen which would constitute crimes if committed by adults (Family Court Act, § 712(a)). While thus narrowing the definition of juvenile delinquency, the Act, to protect the rights of children has also instituted procedures formerly required only in the criminal courts. At the commencement of every hearing, the Judge is required to advise the child of his right ot remain silent, his right to be represented by counsel of his own choosing, and of his right to have a law guardian assigned (Sections 728, 741).

Law Guardians have been provided to defend the rights of children, and appropriations for their cost are made a charge on the budget for each Appellate Division payable by the State of New York (Sections 241-249). No similar provision is made for the presentation of the cases alleging delinquency.

While the Board of Education and the Police Department have counsel in some cases, there is no one to present the case where a private citizen is the petitioner. Even where as in the instant case a police officer is the petitioner, counsel for the police

---

> his client actually was involved in the incident or incidents as set forth in the petition, one of cooperation with the court in working out a logical solution to the problems presented, which will fit the child he represents and enable him to resume his activity as a normal productive junior citizen, fully aware of his responsibilities.

Donahoe, *The New York Family Court Act: Article 7—Its Philosophy and Its Aim,* 15 SYRACUSE L. REV. 679, 685 (1964).

department have neither the staff nor time adequately to prepare their cases nor to submit briefs.

As a result of this situation, the Court is all too often required to question the complaining witnesses on the basis of the petition and then have the Law Guardians exercise the right and duty of cross-examination. Such a procedure does not provide for adequate preparation or presentation of the testimony against the child. It also places the Court in the untenable position of having to seek the facts on which a petition of delinquency is based, hear the defense, and then undertake to evaluate and pass on the evidence as a Judge.

In the instant case where briefs were submitted by the Law Guardian and private counsel none was submitted by the Police. Neither of the briefs submitted cited any of the relevant decisions in this State which have held that a frisk of a defendant under certain circumstances was a reasonable and constitutionally permissible precaution to minimize the danger of a policeman who is trying to determine whether a crime has been or is about to be committed. Neither brief referred to the cases holding that a "frisk" under certain circumstances which results in the discovery of weapons is to be distinguished from an illegal search and seizure.

The provision for Law Guardians has inevitably introduced adversary proceedings into the Juvenile Term of Court. There is no question that the presence of the Law Guardians is desirable to protect the rights of children brought before the court on petitions alleging that they have committed acts which would constitute crimes if committed by adults. As a consequence, there are invoked the legal procedures to which defendants in the criminal courts are entitled, the preparation of witnesses, cross-examination of the petitioners and complaining witnesses, and the preparation of briefs on questions of law.

In contrast, where a citizen files a petition alleging that an offense has been committed against him or his child, there is no one to interview the petitioner or complaining witnesses prior to the trial, no one to conduct the direct examination other than the judge, no one to cross-examine the respondent and his witnesses other than the judge, and no one to prepare a brief on questions of law. As a result of this situation the police department has assigned one lawyer to the Juvenile Term in New York County, and the Board of Education provides counsel in some cases which are regarded as of special significance. There is, however, no legal staff comparable to that of the Law Guardians.

Thus, the present law results in a paradoxical situation. The criminal courts are increasingly required to secure counsel for defendants so that their rights will be protected in actions brought by prosecuting officers representing the People. The Family Court, on the other hand, provides counsel for defendants and no personnel or machinery to assure the adequate presentation of cases against minors even when they are charged with acts which would constitute a felony if committed by an adult.

In the Juvenile Term of the Family Court in New York City where a Judge must hear and dispose of fifty to seventy-five cases a day, it is impossible as well as unwise for the Judge to undertake the presentation of the facts on behalf of the petitioner. In addition, the present procedure leads to the petitioner and complaining witnesses being subjected to cross-examination without having legal guidance in the direct examination. A sense of injustice and even harassment sometimes results.

This basic lack of staff to present cases properly in what has become an adversary proceeding is aggravated not only by the heavy calendars, but by the fact that the Judges of the Family Court have no law secretaries or legal assistants. In cases like the instant one where a question of law arises and the law guardian submits a brief for the defendants and no brief is submitted by the Petitioner's counsel, or the petitioner is without counsel, the Judge must without any assistance undertake the review of the law.

Unless legislation is enacted to correct the present inbalance in legal services and to provide for adequate legal assistance and judicial manpower there is grave danger that cases will be dismissed for lack of proper presentation, that citizens will be discouraged from seeking redress in the court, and that legal questions will not be given adequate consideration. The present situation inevitably results in injury to citizens, to delinquent children and to the entire community.

Reference Note

The literature on the role of counsel in juvenile court is growing. See particularly Platt & Friedman, *The Limits of Advocacy: Occupational Hazards in Juvenile Court,* 116 U. PA. L. REV. 1156 (1968) (a study of private lawyers appearing in the Chicago Juvenile Court); Platt, Schechter & Tiffany, *In Defense of Youth: A Case Study of the Public Defender in Juvenile Court,* 43 IND. L.J. 619 (1968); Lemert, *Legislating Change in the Juvenile Court,* 1967 WIS. L. REV. 421; Lemert, *Juvenile Justice—Quest and Reality,* 4 TRANS-ACTION 40 (1967); Isaacs, *The Role of the Lawyer in Representing Minors in the New York Family Court,* 12 BUFFALO L. REV. 501 (1963).

Chapter 17

DISPOSITION OF PERSONS ADJUDGED DELINQUENT BY THE JUVENILE COURT

A. THE DISPOSITION ALTERNATIVES AVAILABLE TO THE JUDGE

The structure of the system for "disposition" of juvenile offenders is somewhat different from that of the system for sentencing adults. In the criminal justice system the sentence is legislatively tailored to the crime, *i.e.*, the legislature sets the general limits within which the court may act for each criminal violation. In the juvenile system, the disposition selected by the judge is not controlled statutorily by the particular criminal offense involved, if there is one. A youngster adjudged delinquent for shoplifting a one-dollar item may receive the same type of treatment as one adjudged delinquent for armed robbery. This approach to the disposition problem is based on the theory of the behavioral sciences that the particular criminal violation is only a symptom of what is wrong with the individual and, therefore, should be just one of the factors considered in determining treatment. However, it may create problems.[a] Because the statutory structure gives so much discretion to the judge regardless of the particular conduct involved, it is possible for his disposition to appear unreasonable in light of the conduct with which the juvenile is charged.

REPORT OF THE COMMITTEE ON CHILDREN AND YOUNG PERSONS 26 (1960)
Great Britain, Home Office

[A] juvenile court often appears to be trying a case on one particular ground and then to be dealing with the child on some

[a] For an example of abuse of the wide sentencing discretion of the juvenile court, see U.S. COMMISSION ON CIVIL RIGHTS, A REPORT ON EQUAL PROTECTION IN THE SOUTH 80-83, 81 (1965): "In the areas studied (Mississippi, Georgia, Florida) . . . local authorities used the broad discretion afforded them by the absence of safeguards to impose excessively harsh treatment on juveniles [involved in civil rights demonstrations]."

quite different ground. This is inherent in combining the requirement for proof of a specified event or condition with a general direction to have regard to the child's welfare. It results, for example, in a child being charged with a petty theft or other wrongful act for which most people would say that no great penalty should be imposed, and the case apparently ending in a disproportionate sentence. For when the court causes enquiries to be made, if those enquiries show seriously disturbed home conditions, or one or more of many other circumstances, the court may determine that the welfare of the child requires some very substantial interference which may amount to taking the child away from his home for a prolonged period. It is common to come across bitter complaints that a child has been sent away from home because he has committed some particular offence which in itself was not at all serious.

1. The Period of Supervision or Commitment

It is typical for juvenile court statutes to provide that commitments of juveniles to state correctional authorities are until age twenty-one. Therefore, if a fifteen-year-old commits a crime for which the maximum penalty, if he were an adult, would be fifteen years, his maximum "sentence" is six years. On the other hand, if the maximum penalty for an adult would be three years or, as in the case of Gerald Gault, two months, the juvenile is still subject to the six-year "sentence."[b]

The possibility of commitment for a period longer than the criminal sentence, merely because of the age of the juvenile, has caused some concern. In response, some acts have provided for set terms.[c] The time limitation is not related to any particular criminal violation. On the other hand, the fact that a fifteen-year-old juvenile may be incarcerated for only six years for a heinous first degree murder has also caused concern. The Wisconsin statutes, for example, permit the correctional agency to apply to the court for the continuance of its control beyond age twenty-one of a person committed as a juvenile who is believed to be still dangerous to the public. The right to apply for continued control is not related to the type of conduct on which the

---

[b] *See* Rogers v. United States, 326 F.2d 56 (10th Cir. 1963), upholding the Federal Youth Corrections Act, which has a similar provision against a challenge made on the ground that the maximum term was longer than that prescribed by the criminal law for the same conduct.

[c] The Standard Juvenile Court Act § 24 (N.P.P.A. 1959) contains a three-year time limit for all transfers of legal custody. *See also* N.Y. FAMILY CT. ACT, § 758 (1963).

adjudication of delinquency was based.[d] It should be noted, however, that this Wisconsin statute has in fact never been used. The New Jersey statute is one of the few examples in the juvenile system where there is any utilization of the length of the sentence which could be imposed on an adult for the crime involved. A juvenile charged with homicide may be confined for the period of the maximum sentence which could have been imposed on an adult.[e]

In spite of these legislative controls on the length of the commitment of juveniles, the courts exercise substantial discretion in two ways: (1) The court may have the right to set the term for commitments to private institutions and agencies even though it has no control over the length of commitment to state correctional authorities; and (2) the court may have the right to extend, up to the age of majority, terms which it has set or which have been legislatively set. For example, the Standard Juvenile Court Act provides for a three-year term, but it may be extended by the court, up to the twenty-one-year limit, if it finds such renewal "necessary to safeguard the welfare of the minor or the public interest."[f] In other words, the juvenile court judge has the right to review the progress of the juvenile and to lengthen the period of commitment if he considers it necessary at that time.

The statute on juvenile commitments typically does not set any minimum term. Sometimes the court may specify a minimum period but usually a public agency which receives legal custody may release the juvenile in its discretion. Private agencies must usually return juveniles to court for release. In recent years, with the great population pressures on the facilities for juvenile delinquents, the lack of minimum terms, either legislatively or judicially established, has resulted in very short stays in institutions for juvenile delinquents committed in some states—a reason for considerable criticism of the juvenile system.[g] On the other hand, the lack of minima has allowed correctional agencies to experiment with new programs. In Wisconsin, for example, a program called E.R.I.S. (Early Release, Intensive Supervision) takes juvenile offenders who have been held only a few days in the training school and releases them on after-care

---

[d] *See* WIS. STAT. §§ 48.53, 54.32–54.35 (1965).

[e] N.J. REV. STAT. § 2A:4-37(b)(2) (Supp. 1967). The federal statute is similar. 18 U.S.C. § 5034.

[f] *See* n.b, *supra*.

[g] For a discussion of factors affecting the length of stay, see THE PRESIDENT'S COMMISSION ON LAW ENFORCEMENT AND ADMINISTRATION OF JUSTICE, TASK FORCE REPORT: CORRECTIONS 143 (1967).

(parole) to specially trained field agents who have small caseloads and can closely supervise the juveniles in the community.

2. *Alternative Dispositions*

In addition to differences in length of "sentence" the juvenile system differs from the adult in the types of disposition available. The rehabilitation of adult criminals is generally a public problem with incarceration in tax-supported institutions where considerations of security usually receive paramount consideration. The rehabilitation of juvenile offenders, on the other hand, is viewed more as a child care problem with factors of security much less prominent in the planning. Therefore, a juvenile court judge may not only place a juvenile on probation, transfer his custody to a state correctional authority, or commit him to a state training school or other facility, but he may also, typically, place him in a foster home or transfer his custody to a private institution or agency which cares for children or places them in family homes.

Although the legislature has allowed the juvenile judge a wide variety of dispositions, it has, in many states, limited his discretion in the use of state facilities. If a judge chooses to use a state facility for the juvenile, he must commit in general terms to the correctional authority, leaving the decision as to specific placement—training school, reformatory, treatment institution, group home, foster home—to the discretion of that authority.

The Iowa statute is probably typical of most existing juvenile court provisions on disposition. Some recent statutes, such as the Illinois provision,[h] attempt to place limitations on the broad discretion of the judge in his choice of alternatives, particularly where that choice involves institutionalization.

IOWA CODE §§ 232.34—232.36 (1966)

232.34 Disposition of case of delinquency

If the court finds that the child is delinquent, the court shall enter an order making any one or more of the following dispositions of the case:

1. Continue the proceeding from time to time under such supervision as the court may direct.

---

[h] ILL. REV. STAT. ch 37, §§ 705-7, 705-10 (1967).

2. Place the child under the supervision of a probation officer or other suitable person in the home of the child.

3. Subject to the continued jurisdiction of the court, transfer legal custody of the child to one of the following:

a. A child placing agency.
b. A probation department.
c. A reputable individual of good moral character.

4. Commit the child to the state board of control for placement at a state training school.

5. Commit to or place the child in any private institution or hospital for care and training or any public institution for care and training other than an institution under the jurisdiction of the state board of control.

6. If the child is in need of special treatment or care for his physical or mental health, the court may order such treatment or care provided by the parents, guardian, or custodian of the child. If the parents, guardian, or custodian fail to provide the treatment or care, the court may order the treatment or care provided.

7. At any time while the child is under the court's jurisdiction, the court may terminate the proceedings and order the child released from the control of the court.

232.35 Commitment to board of control

Commitment to the state board of control shall vest guardianship of the person of the child so committed in the board and shall terminate the court's jurisdiction.

232.36 Orders continue to majority of child

All orders for supervision, custody, or commitment shall be enforced until the minor reaches the age of twenty-one years unless otherwise specified by the court. All orders shall be reviewed by the court at least annually unless the court's jurisdiction has been terminated. The court may make on its own motion or on the motion of an interested party and after notice to the parties and a hearing some other disposition of the case so long as the court retains jurisdiction.

IN RE GAULT: UNDERSTANDING THE ATTORNEY'S NEW ROLE

Comment, 12 Villanova Law Review 803, 827-37 (1967)†

VIII. The Dispositional Process

When the adjudication process has been concluded with a finding of delinquency, the attorney is faced with what may prove to be an entirely unfamiliar task, that of adequately representing his juvenile client in the dispositional phase of the proceeding. His situation is further complicated by the fact that *Gault* does not make the appearance of the attorney in the dispositional phase mandatory. In order to be an attribute in this process, counsel must complement his legal expertise with a familiarization with the behavioral sciences that play such a large role in the final outcome. The attorney can no longer limit his preparation to the adjudicatory phase of the proceeding, since the dispositional phase often proves to be the most crucial for his client. Therefore, the following discussion will attempt to acquaint the attorney with the factors that must be considered and the tools that must be employed in effectively representing his juvenile client. With this objective in mind, the juvenile courts of the Philadelphia metropolitan area, operating under the Pennsylvania Juvenile Court Act, were examined.

. . .

Unlike the criminal court, which considers deterrence, retribution, and rehabilitation in the sentencing process, the juvenile court is required to limit sentencing considerations to the rehabilitation of the individual child and the protection of the community. It is the responsibility of the juvenile court judge to consider the needs of the individual child and make a determination as to whether rehabilitation can be achieved by probation, or if institutionalization is required.

In choosing the latter course, it must be recognized that the problems of rehabilitating the child within an institution are manifold. For large institutions to operate efficiently the daily routines must be regimented in much the same way as a factory operates its assembly lines. However, such regimentation is not in accord with the theory and practice of individualized treatment and it has been found that children in such institutions receive less of the needed treatment than is prescribed. The desirability of removing children from contacts with adult criminals can be accomplished by institutions for juveniles, but it cannot overcome contacts with other delinquents and the corresponding influence of peer groups. Also, lack of trained personnel and adequate facilities may make the institution unsuitable for

---

rehabilitation, not to mention the increased cost of institutional care.

Irrespective of the desires of the court, the stigma of delinquency does exist and will be a greater burden on the child who has been institutionalized. Furthermore, removal from the community has a psychological impact on the child which may retard the rehabilitation process. Recent decisions have recognized these problems and have indicated that in selecting an institution, the juvenile court is required to find a place which, in fact, affords the promised treatment and is apart from an adult prison.

Pennsylvania has twenty-nine institutions available for the housing of juvenile delinquents. Included in this number are sixteen which are privately operated, although in many instances they receive state or county support, and three which provide for commitment by both the juvenile and criminal court. The juvenile court can obviously order that the child be placed in a state institution, however when placement in a private institution is deemed best, the child must meet the standards established by the institution in question, such as the attainment of a minimum score in intelligence testing. A survey conducted in 1954 reported that juvenile facilities varied from medium security prisons, with minimal educational programs, to cottage type facilities with slight custodial functions, and a variety of academic, industrial arts, and vocational training programs. The report criticized the institutions in Pennsylvania because in many cases, the physical plant was old and in poor condition and because there was a lack of sufficient teachers, social workers, trained psychiatrists, and psychologists. In addition, it was found that there was very little, if any, in service training of the staff, and that even though the available staff strived to rehabilitate the children, the lack of financial support made it difficult to maintain adequate personnel and facilities. It is obvious from the foregoing survey that the judge has a difficult task in deciding where to send the child, and that a well informed attorney could be of great assistance.

Interviews with judges, attorneys, and probation officers indicate that although the same conditions exist today, the institutions are doing the best they can under the circumstances. It was recommended that the attorney not only be aware of the variations in the institutions but make personal visitations to form his own impression, establish contact with the staff of the institution, and become familiar with the special facilities each offers. Personal contact with the institutional staff will enhance the possibility of gaining admission for the client to the private institutions, and permit the attorney to discover, not only the type of services offered, but also, whether they are in fact provided.

Probation as an alternative to institutionalization, is not problem free for a number of reasons. The deprived environmental conditions in which the child lives, coupled with the fact that peer group influence can be as strong within the society as within an institution, operates in many instances to make rehabilitation difficult. In addition, the parents may be incapable of providing the home life required and no substitute may be available within the community. Furthermore, the probation officer, overburdened with a high case load, may be unavailable to provide the direction and counseling that the child requires.

As in the decision to commit, probation does not end the responsibility of the court. A program must be designed which will provide for the youth's supervision and guidance within the community under the direction of the court. Normally this program provides that the child report to the probation officer on a regular schedule, that the probation officer visit the child's home periodically, and that the child attend school regularly. Again it can be seen that an experienced, well informed attorney can be a valuable aid to the court in formulating this program. Similarly, as a broader spectrum of possible programs within the community develops, probation may become even more attractive to the juvenile court judge, and an attorney who is prepared to assist in identifying, and proposing methods of taking advantage of, these new community resources would be of invaluable service to his client and the court.

In addition, the following list, although not exhaustive, demonstrates approaches which have been used by the juvenile courts and which the attorney may wish to propose as alternative rehabilitative tools.

1. *Foster Home Care:* It has long been felt that every child should have a home or the best possible substitute. The difficulty in foster home care is locating a family which is willing to accept a child who has been adjudicated delinquent.

2. *Fines:* Fines have been used in England, Canada and Colorado as an alternative to probation. This approach is criticized because it may prove to be unfair or impractical for the lower socio-economic groups.[1]

3. *Restitution:* Although many states allow the use of restitution as a rehabilitative tool, Pennsylvania does not permit its

---

[1] Some juvenile delinquency statutes prohibit the use of fines. *E.g.*, WIS. STAT. § 48.37 (1965).

juvenile court to impose restitution. However, this method has been recommended by the Pennsylvania Juvenile Court Judges' Commission as a way to instill responsibility in the child and is employed where the youth voluntarily assumes the obligation.

4. *Work Projects:* These projects which may involve such chores as cleaning up park areas and recreational centers have been employed by several jurisdictions.

5. *Community Organizations:* Religious groups, Boy Scouts of America, and similar organizations may provide individuals and facilities which can be used in the rehabilitative process.

6. *Employment Training Organizations:* If the child has an interest in a particular type of work, it may be possible to find schools or organizations which will be willing to assume the responsibility of supervising the child.

IX. Post Dispositional Considerations

A method of insuring fairness in juvenile court proceedings is the right to appeal final orders. In Pennsylvania, if the child, parents, or next friend believe that there has been an error of law or fact in the adjudication or disposition, they may, within twenty-one days, petition for a rehearing, and appeal any final order to the superior court. Due to the broad discretionary powers which the juvenile court judge exercises in arriving at and imposing disposition, it is difficult to successfully appeal a dispositional decision unless an abuse of discretion is clear. . . .

B. DEVICES FOR ENSURING PROPER DISPOSITION

1. The Social Investigation Report

Theoretically, the decision as to disposition presents a single problem for the juvenile court judge, that of how to treat the child so as to rehabilitate him. For this purpose the juvenile court judge is given great discretion to dispose of each case on the basis of the particular needs of the individual juvenile. Typically, he obtains this information from a "social investigation report" prepared by the court worker or probation staff connected with the court.

Although the social investigation report has become a standard ingredient of juvenile court disposition, there are myriad problems connected with its implementation. Not the least of these are the state of the present knowledge of human behavior and the lack of time and personnel for the job.

PROCEEDINGS OF THIRD ANNUAL INSTITUTE FOR JUVENILE COURT JUDGES AND REFEREES 197-209 (Calif. May 14-15, 1964)

Remarks of Joel Goldfarb: [O]ne of the trends I have noted is that the probation report which is supposed to be the basis of the information on which the judge is to make the decision has less and less been used by more and more judges. Of course, the judges do obeisance as they must under the Code, and say "I read and considered the report of the probation officer." But then the decision which is made quite often does not reflect at all what has been contained in the report. As a matter of fact, when they discuss the cases with me later it often turns out that even if they accept the recommendation made in the report—and most of the time they do—the basis of this decision is not the reasoning in the probation report. Often things like informal contacts and court observations and what testimony there is—and there isn't too much significant testimony in juvenile court—is used in lieu of using the probation report. Now, this other information, of course, is probably more unreliable than that in the probation report. Moreover, the non-use of the probation report information contributes to a kind of demoralization of the probation officers who begin to feel, "What's the use. We put this in the report, and it isn't being used." This thinking leads to a kind of vicious circle, because then they just turn out that much poorer reports, which cause the judges to rely upon probation reports even less and everybody becomes very unhappy. . . . However, in my opinion, rather than ignoring the reports, the judges should make an attempt to make better use of them. . . .

Basically, the judge in reading the report must learn to decode the report in the light of answers to the following queries. First, what theory of delinquency causation is the person who writes the report following? Second, what are the racial, cultural and class biases of the report writer? What kind of background does he come from? Third, what is the quality of the information supplied to the writer of the report? Fourth, what are the organizational pressures on the report writer? It must be remembered that when the worker makes up the report he is a member of an organization, a bureaucracy if you will, and that what is written in the report will reflect the organizational position of the worker.

The theory of causation followed by the writer is very significant in determining what will be included in the report. The selection of the data to be collected must be based on some kind of a view of what is significant and what is not. . . .

Most probation officers, if they have professional training, are trained as caseworkers. Casework theory is largely founded on psychological and psychiatric assumptions. These are that delinquency results from individual maladjustments and consequently it must be treated on some kind of one-to-one basis. These assumptions have been developed from observations and dealings with disturbed voluntary middle-class clients and they may or may not have a relevance for lower-class delinquents or, as a matter of fact, even for middle-class delinquents. Without getting into the merits of these assumptions, the fact is that they do not take into account much of what the behavioral sciences have discovered regarding the realities surrounding a good part of delinquent behavior. Concretely, these assumptions lead to the collection of data which may have no relevance to the particular youth and his conduct. Typical of this kind of data is material on family relationships, gone into often quite extensively without any support in theoretical literature that there is any connection between this particular kind of behavior and such analyses of family relationships. Even things as bizarre as whether or not the youth was a breech birth may be included in the report without any theoretical underpinning as to the relevance of such a fact.

The second query regarding the biases of the report writer in terms of class, cultural and racial background is important because inevitably when judgments have to be made the background of the observer, the way in which he views the world, what is right and what is wrong, what is proper and improper in given circumstances are going to color the way in which he judges it. Now as far as racial biases are concerned most of the crude bias that we label prejudice has, I think, been eliminated in the reports. In fact, if it does appear it appears usually in a kind of backhand way, in a reverse way with a good deal of paternalism for Negro or other minority youths. A more important kind of bias isn't what we usually think of as prejudice, but is a matter of simply not being able to see the world as the minority youngster sees it. This occurs not only on the superficial level illustrated by the story of Mr. Griffin who changed his skin from white to black and wandered through the South and saw an entirely different world, but also on a sophisticated level—that of understanding the nature of the community life of the minority youngsters. . . .

[T]he extended matriarchal family and its importance [is one example]. The role of violence in the Negro community is another example. When a white youth is picked up carrying a razor it could be a very serious thing. But for a Negro youngster it may simply be his only means of self-defense. The use of profanity is another fact which has a different meaning for youngsters from minority backgrounds.

Then there are cultural and class values which the probation officer has. He may put a different value, for example, on what is success, what is good, what makes a man better than the ordinary Joe. The concept that to work hard and accumulate material possessions by legal means is what success is, is not shared by all people including, as a matter of fact, many who have accumulated material possessions. Other criteria, such as physical prowess, sexual attractiveness or the new kind of way of getting status, managing to be arrested in a civil rights demonstration, may be more important in acquiring status. This lack of perception of different values that other people have is seen in probation reports which may read something like this: "Johnny's conduct in the past certainly does not indicate normal behavior," or "Johnny's father has a history of irresponsibility toward his children and failed to discharge his parental duty during his formative years," or "Johnny's father is a lazy, shiftless person; the family is known to numerous relief and social agencies in the community. More than $20,000 has been paid to the family by various welfare agencies. Little if anything desirable has been accomplished." I borrowed these examples from Paul Keve's book *The Probation Officer Investigates.* As he points out, just what is normal behavior? Exactly what was the father's parental duty which he failed to discharge? By what criteria is the father shiftless and lazy? How could the probation officer be so sure that nothing desirable was accomplished?

Now when you get to a so-called objective criteria—the judging may be biased by class or cultural assumptions concerning behavior. Much has been written in recent years concerning the class and cultural biases of I.Q. tests. On a superficial level the criticism can be made that they reflect more a greater willingness to take the test than they do inherent ability.

The story is told of the lower-class youngster who was asked on an I.Q. test to indicate how he would go about finding a lost ball in a field. The youngster failed to give any satisfactory answer to the question. On a retest he was asked to find a lost satchel of money which had been thrown into a field by fleeing bank robbers. His description of how he would go about finding the money was a model of logical planning.

Or on a more subtle level even something like the Rorschach test, you know the ink blot test, can be bias by class background. A middle-class mother may sit with her little kid on her knee and point out a blotch on a window and talk to him about what it looks like. Such a child becomes used to finding meaning in those kinds of things. Whereas with the lower-class child this is an unknown. It is a cloud; it's a blotch; it is just what it is. The use of psychiatric terminology, such as "emotional conflict and hyperactive behavior has made it difficult for the boy to concentrate." "John's character development shows a low tension tolerance and inability to control his temper in situations of slightest stress." "John is inclined to act impulsively." "John is ridden with strong internal conflicts which result in part from unresolved mother rejection by his associates." Such statements, . . . besides having some problem with internal logic, may in fact be interpretations by the middle-class probation officer of what for a lower-class kid may be normal behavior for his own environment.

The third query that should be kept in mind is the lack of control that the probation officer has over the information that is supplied to him, especially information that is supplied by agencies, such as the police, the welfare departments and schools. This information may reflect more what the agency has concluded about what should be done with the youngster than with what he has actually done. Even so-called objective information such as grades, . . . may be misleading. Another kind of criteria that we know some judges have used, and the probation officers use, is what kind of a field is the youngster majoring in? Is he in an academic curriculum or is he in some kind of trade school curriculum? This, too, is not terribly reliable in judging the youngster. We have as one of the most distinguished members of our faculty, a man who was advised in high school, a California high school, to take a trade course because he would never amount to anything as an academic. He has a world-wide reputation today, but had to get his education after he was graduated from high school.

In the case of school rap sheets, even the information provided by the school on behavior of the youth in custody must be seen in a context—you have to evaluate what the school official has to say about the youth in terms of the pressures which are on the school official. Frequently principals' or deans' performances will be evaluated on the basis of how many incidents occur at their schools. Consequently, for self-protection they feel themselves compelled not to report incidents. And where that is not possible, to rid themselves of conduct problems. In recent years this phenomenon has been further enhanced by the use of post-graduation criteria for the successful school, namely, how well is it preparing students for higher education. This has meant that the school need no longer concern itself with its role in the failure of a student to make it in school, so long as those who do make it, make it big. The possibility that the school has failed, "excluded" or "dropped out" youngsters rather than that the youngsters have failed the school, is rarely suggested. This general attitude of the students rather than the school being inadequate is inevitably reflected in the school's report on one of its pupils. The fact the youngster is involved in juvenile court is likely to be seized upon as confirmation of this apparent inadequacy.

Finally, there is the query concerning the organizational position of the writer of the report. His status as a bureaucrat must be taken into account. Incidentally, I do not use the word bureaucrat in a pejorative sense—bureaucracy is a fact of our organized society, it is the way, perhaps the only way, we can organize to get things done—the problem is not to do away with bureaucrats, the problem is to try to make the bureaucratic system work fairly and humanely. It's no secret . . . that the many bureaucratic groups in our society including the agencies involved in the juvenile adjudication process often work at cross purposes and are constantly applying pressure on each other in jockeying for position in the community. This conflict is carried on in newspapers, before boards of supervisors. . . . Pressures from other agencies have to be dealt with as a normal part of the job. Consequently, sometimes what is included in a report about a youngster may be more what the worker feels is for the best interests of the agency rather than those of the child. The rationalization for this is that the particular agency really has the child's best interests at heart, but one child may have to be expended in order to keep the agency inviolate so it can help others.

Another facet of the bureaucratic problem is the relationship between the probation department and the judge. . . . Often what is in a probation report reflects more the relationship between the judge and the probation department than it does the evaluation of the youngster. Of course no one likes to be reversed, and judges at the trial level know that feeling very well. And I think it is unrealistic for judges to ask that the probation officers write their reports "objectively" without giving any thought to the personal idiosyncrasies of the judge. First, the judge cannot seriously mean this kind of an injunction to the probation department because what this could mean is that each case would be decided only on its own and you would not have any precedents based on what the judge has been doing in terms of what he thinks is right and what he thinks is wrong. Now, certainly when you have an appellate decision the trial courts change their practices to fit in with what the authorities have said is the proper manner of going about doing something. And why probation officers should be any different in that sense and not learn from their previous experiences with a judge is not readily apparent.

Second, the ability to manipulate the judge—this is a measure not of the underhandedness of the probation officer or of the department, but of the judge's failure to judge each case individually on its merits. Gun swallowing is a familiar technique among prosecutors and judges—that is, if the offense doesn't really warrant the harsh penalty which will be visited upon the offender if he is convicted, throughout the history of our system of criminal justice, going back to Anglo-Saxon times, techniques have been worked out by prosecutors, judges, and sometimes even juries, to overlook those elements which bring the offense into the harsh penalty category. Most frequently, in our own times, this has involved being armed with a weapon while committing the offense. Gun swallowing is the practice of failing to plead, prove or find that in fact the offender was armed. The analogous practice in the juvenile court field occurs when, after a thorough analysis, the professionally trained probation officer concludes that a certain treatment would be most effective but he knows from experience that in this particular type of case, quite often these are cases where sex is involved, the judge has preconceived notions about what should be done irrespective of what the social report shows. Why shouldn't the probation officer in such cases suppress a peripheral sexual deviancy in his own report and make informal arrangements with clinical personnel to compose their reports on the psychological makeup of the youngster to correspond with his social analysis.

One final word, judges often complain when the probation officers follow their injunction and write their reports from a vantage point of what must be styled "omniscient objectivity." "Just present the 'facts' and then make a recommendation," say the judges. But when such reports are submitted, the judge is apt to say, "Well, wait a second. This is a bad report." Why is it a bad report? Because the recommendation doesn't follow from the facts. What the judge has asked the probation department to do is to write a report which will be logical in the eyes of the judge, which in a sense means that they have to understand the way in which that judge thinks. But where is the line to be drawn between "understanding" the judge and manipulating him? At the very least judges must be aware that much of what is objectionable in the probation reports results from their own demands. . . .

A VIEW FROM THE BENCH 44-45 (NCCD 1964)
By Justine Wise Polier
Judge, New York State Family Court

Caseloads in the Juvenile Term now defy any possibility of probation work. Years ago, when probation officers were expected to work a 44-hour week, a caseload of 50 children was considered proper. Officers now work 35 hours a week.

In September 1961 the average caseload for field probation officers in the Juvenile Term was 116 children. It was the same figure in September 1962, when the new Family Court Act came into being. Of the 112 officers, 49 were carrying caseloads ranging from 117 to 256 children. This situation continued during the first six months of operation under the new court and has improved only slightly since that time.

A caseload of this size compels the probation officer to limit his investigation to the factual data secured by clearance with the Social Service Exchange, a form report from school, and an interview with the child and generally one parent. To expect even a professionally trained officer to develop in depth, on the basis of so limited an investigation, a study of the causes of the family problems, together with a plan of treatment, is unreasonable; to expect professionally untrained staff to do so is absurd. Yet this is the only material (aside from what may be offered by the clinic, a hospital, or a social agency) on which the court must, in large part, base its disposition.[j]

THE DILEMMA OF THE JUVENILE COURT
By Eileen L. Younghusband
33 Social Service Review 10,11-12 (1959)†

It gives us a nice warm feeling to talk about treating persons rather than punishing offenses; but do not let us delude our-

[j] A study of services to the juvenile court in Wisconsin found that in the counties studied only 25% of the social studies were rated "good" or "better" as a basis for planning for the child. In eight of the ten major areas of information considered necessary in a good social study, there was "poor" to "no information" in 45% to 77% of these categories. WISCONSIN STATE DEPARTMENT OF PUBLIC WELFARE, A STUDY OF SOCIAL SERVICES PROVIDED THE ALLEGED AND ADJUDICATED DELINQUENT CHILD BY COUNTY AGENCIES 23, 25 (1966).

† Reprinted by permission of The University of Chicago Press. Copyright 1959 by the University of Chicago.

selves about it. It is comparatively easy, straightforward, precise, and measurable to punish offenses—an eye for an eye and a tooth for a tooth—whereas to understand and treat persons presupposes that we do in fact know how to diagnose and treat them and that we have the necessary facilities available. This is not a valid assumption. If it were, we might expect a decrease in juvenile delinquency, whereas our growing understanding of the complexities of social, family, and personal factors leaves us as yet comparatively powerless in face of this interwoven causation.

Thus what progressive societies have in fact done is to embark on juvenile court programs based on humane and enlightened motives, without knowing or having what it takes to produce the results which we feel should follow as a result of our humane intentions. In other words, our juvenile court systems are in one sense experimental laboratories in which we try to discover, empirically for the most part, the things we need to know in order to achieve the objectives of the system. . . .

In addition there is the further problem that over the centuries we have evolved a highly sophisticated legal system, while our diagnostic and treatment systems are at a quite different, even rudimentary and fragmentary, stage of development. Moreover, those who serve in juvenile courts have varying degrees of competence to do so, coupled with widely differing views about the function of courts as social institutions and, therefore, of their responsibilities and aims in relation to individual offenders. The result is that we are abandoning the certainties of a rigid legal system without yet being able to substitute another kind of certainty based upon scientifically determined diagnosis and treatment. This creates not only a dilemma but also a real danger in view of the unique characteristics of courts as social institutions—the fact that society intrusts to them the ultimate sanction of compulsion.

2. *Counsel*

Although there is no requirement of counsel at the dispositional stage,[k] there is no doubt, as the *Villanova Law Review* Comment at 1090 points up, that counsel can be an invaluable aid to the dispositional process. Therefore, counsel ought to be considered with the devices to ensure proper disposition. The effectiveness of counsel in ensuring a proper disposition will depend not only on his knowledge of possible alternative dis-

[k] *In re Gault* required counsel only at the adjudicatory hearing. *See* pp. 1049, 1053, *supra*.

positions but also on his ability to obtain access to information regarding the child and to present his proposals to the court.

ILLINOIS REVISED STATUTES ch. 37, § 705-1 (1967)

§ 705-1. Dispositional Hearing; Evidence; Continuance

(1) After adjudging the minor a ward of the court, the court shall hear evidence on the question of the proper disposition best serving the interests of the minor and the public. All evidence helpful in determining this question, including oral and written reports, may be admitted and may be relied upon to the extent of its probative value, even though not competent for the purposes of the adjudicatory hearing.

(2) Before making an order of disposition the court shall advise the State's Attorney, the parents, guardian, custodian or responsible relative or their counsel of the factual contents and the conclusions of reports prepared for the use of the court and considered by it, and afford fair opportunity, if requested, to controvert them. The court may order, however, that the documents containing such reports need not be submitted to inspection, or that sources of confidential information need not be disclosed.

KENT v. UNITED STATES
383 U.S. 541, 562-63 (1966)

[Morris A. Kent, Jr., age sixteen, was waived by the Juvenile Court of the District of Columbia to the criminal court for prosecution for burglary and rape. No hearing was held and his counsel was denied access to the Social Service File which the judge used in determining whether or not to waive juvenile court jurisdiction.]

Mr. Justice FORTAS delivered the opinion of the Court.

With respect to access by the child's counsel to the social records of the child, we deem it obvious that since these are to be considered by the Juvenile Court in making its decision to waive, they must be made available to the child's counsel.* This is what the Court of Appeals itself held in *Watkins.*[l] There is no doubt as to the statutory basis for this conclusion, as the Court of Appeals pointed out in *Watkins.* We cannot agree with the

* In a survey, 58% of the judges regularly made social investigation reports available to counsel. Skoler & Tenney, *Attorney Representation in Juvenile Court,* 4 J. FAMILY L. 77 (1964).

[l] Watkins v. United States, 343 F.2d 278 (D.C. Cir. 1964).

Court of Appeals in the present case that the statute is "ambiguous." The statute expressly provides that the record shall be withheld from "indiscriminate" public inspection, "except that such records or parts thereof *shall* be made available by rule of court or special order of court to such persons . . . as have a *legitimate interest* in the protection . . . of the child. . . ." D.C. Code § 11-929(b) (1961), now § 11-1586(b) (Supp. IV, 1965). (Emphasis supplied.)[30] The Court of Appeals has held in *Black,*[m] and we agree, that counsel must be afforded to the child in waiver proceedings. Counsel, therefore, have a "legitimate interest" in the protection of the child, and must be afforded access to these records.[31]

We do not agree with the Court of Appeals' statement, attempting to justify denial of access to these records, that counsel's role is limited to presenting "to the court anything on behalf of the child which might help the court in arriving at a decision; it is not to denigrate the staff's submissions and recommendations." On the contrary, if the staff's submissions include materials which are susceptible to challenge or impeachment, it is precisely the role of counsel to "denigrate" such matter. There is no irrebuttable presumption of accuracy attached to staff reports. If a decision on waiver is "critically important" it is equally of "critical importance" that the material submitted to the judge—which is protected by the statute only against "indiscriminate" inspection—be subjected, within reasonable limits having regard to the theory of the Juvenile Court Act, to examination, criticism and refutation. While the Juvenile Court judge may, of course, receive *ex parte* analyses and recommendations from his staff, he may not, for purposes of a decision on waiver, receive and rely upon secret information, whether emanating from his staff or otherwise. The Juvenile Court is governed in this respect by the established principles which control courts and quasi-judicial agencies of the Government.

For the reasons stated, we conclude that the Court of Appeals and the District Court erred in sustaining the validity of the waiver by the Juvenile Court.

---

[30] Under the statute, the Juvenile Court has power by rule or order, to subject the examination of the social records to conditions which will prevent misuse of the information. Violation of any such rule or order, or disclosure of the information "except for purposes for which . . . released," is a misdemeanor. D.C. Code § 11-929 (1961), now, without substantial change, § 11-1586 (Supp. IV, 1965).

[m] Black v. United States, 355 F.2d 104 (D.C. Cir. 1965).

[31] In *Watkins,* the Court of Appeals seems to have permitted withholding of some portions of the social record from examination by petitioner's counsel. To the extent that *Watkins* is inconsistent with the standard which we state, it cannot be considered as controlling.

3. Appellate Review

The appellate courts have only rarely been called on to review juvenile court decisions as to disposition of a delinquent child, just as the appellate courts have not played a large role in reviewing sentences in criminal cases. But when the appellate courts are involved, they appear to exercise their own judgment rather freely as to the wisdom of the juvenile court disposition, in contrast to their reluctance to alter adult sentences. In some jurisdictions this may result from the fact that the juvenile delinquent, having had his status determined in a proceeding viewed as civil rather than criminal, is entitled to have the appellate court determine his case de novo on the record.[n]

4. Sharing Responsibility with Specialists in Behavioral Sciences

As in adult sentencing reliance on boards of experts has been proposed, so too in the juvenile area the involvement of behavioral experts has been urged.

PROBLEMS IN THE STRUCTURE OF THE JUVENILE COURT

By Henry Numberg

48 Journal of Criminal Law, Criminology and Police Science 500, 509-11 (1958)†

V. The Court for the Disposition of Juvenile Cases

1. There shall be a Court for the Disposition of Juvenile Cases (hereinafter known as the Court) in each Delinquency Control Area of the Commonwealth.

2. Composition.

A. Each Court shall be composed of a Chief Judge and two Special Judges.

(i) The Chief Judge shall be the Judge of the Juvenile Court of the Delinquency Control Area.

(ii) The Special Judges shall be experts in the diagnosis and treatment of delinquent children.

B. The Special Judges shall be chosen on the basis of their experience and training in the treatment and diagnosis of delinquent children.

---

[n] *See State v. Myers,* at 1106, *infra.*

(i) One Special Judge of each Court shall have received the degree of Doctor of Philosophy or the equivalent thereof, in clinical psychology, from an accredited university, and shall have had at least [X] years of experience in the treatment of juvenile delinquency.

(ii) One Special Judge of each Court shall have received a degree of Master of Arts or Sciences, or the equivalent thereof, in sociology, psychology, or social work, from an accredited university, and shall have had [X] years of experience in social casework with juvenile delinquents.

. . .

The proposal results from a consideration of the dilemma posed by the dispositions problem. On the one hand, it seems undesirable to leave ultimate responsibility for disposition in the hands of a lawyer-judge, who by training and often by temperament is not suited to make a decision that is in part a choice between therapeutic methods. On the other hand, since severe restraints upon the liberty of the individual may be imposed, it is equally unsatisfactory to place the dispositions function in an administrative body composed solely of experts on clinical method. The arguments of Bogen and Tappan concerning the undesirability of imposing what Tappan calls "anticipatory controls" upon an individual are relevant here as well. The underlying premise is the same: the interest of the individual to have the state not interfere in his life is the kind of interest that ought to be given the greatest possible protection.

Because both therapeutic and legal principles are integral parts of each decision as to disposition, provision should be made for their direct expression in the body that performs the disposition function. Therefore, even a system in which the judge makes his decision upon the recommendation of experts is unsatisfactory, for two reasons: First, the judge acting entirely upon the experts' recommendations, is little more than a puppet; the prestige and meaning of the court as a court of law stand in danger of becoming entirely submerged. On the other hand, the judge left free to decide by himself the best course of treatment to be followed, may act on a relatively uninformed basis. The dispositions court is suggested to provide a forum in which the lawyer and the expert can discuss each case and take joint responsibility for the results of their deliberations. Further, it provides an opportunity for expert and judge to work out together a policy of disposition to be followed, in different classes of cases. Individualization of justice and the legal requirement of adherence to precedent may thus, to a certain extent, be reconciled.

. . .

The proposal is unorthodox in that it provides for laymen to sit as judges in a court of law. This practice is seldom followed in the United States; there is, however, a precedent in the English practice of using lay magistrates extensively (sitting, incidentally, without a lawyer to share the bench with them) to hear and dispose of cases involving juvenile offenders.

C. CHOICE OF DISPOSITION—COMMUNITY SUPERVISION OR INSTITUTIONALIZATION

Although juvenile court judges have a wide range of possible dispositions open to them,[o] the two most often used are supervision in the juvenile's own home[p] and institutionalization.[q] In making the disposition decision the juvenile court judge, like his criminal court counterpart may weigh a number of factors including the possibility of rehabilitation, concern for community attitude as well as for community protection, and deterrence. But unlike his criminal court counterpart, the juvenile court judge is bound, sometimes by statutory requirement, to give preference to treatment in the community.

STATE v. MYERS

74 N.D. 297, 22 N.W.2d 199 (1946)

BURKE, J. The appellant, Frank Myers, was adjudged a delinquent minor in juvenile court of Cass County and committed to the State Training School. Both he and his mother, Eva Myers, have appealed from the order of commitment and have asked a trial anew in this court upon the entire record in the case. Appellants' request for a trial de novo is a proper one.

Section 28-2732, Rev Code 1943, relating to judicial procedure in civil cases, insofar as it is pertinent reads as follows: "On appeal in any action tried by the court, without a jury, whether triable to a jury or not. . . . The supreme court shall try anew

[o] Fradkin, *Disposition Dilemmas of American Juvenile Courts,* in JUSTICE FOR THE CHILD 118 (M. Rosenheim ed. 1962).

[p] A juvenile may be left in the community under supervision in a number of living arrangements—with his parents, in a foster home, or in a group home, *i.e.,* a setting in which a small number of juveniles, usually older teenagers, live together with adult supervision, but without a family-type relationship. *See* THE PRESIDENT'S COMMISSION ON LAW ENFORCEMENT AND ADMINISTRATION OF JUSTICE, TASK FORCE REPORT: CORRECTIONS 140 (1967).

[q] "In a recent juvenile court record I studied, the disposition order was preprinted with two boxes: probation to the parents or commitment to the Department of Public Welfare." Bazelon, *Justice for Juveniles,* NEW REPUBLIC, April 22, 1967 at 13, 16.

the questions of fact specified in the statement or in the entire case, if the appellant demands a retrial of the entire case, and shall finally dispose of the same whenever justice can be done without a new trial. . . ." It is thus clear, that where it is demanded a trial de novo is an appellant's statutory right on an appeal from juvenile court.

There are two questions in the case. 1. Does the record establish that Frank Myers is delinquent in the degree which the statute requires as a jurisdictional basis for an order with respect to his custody? 2. The jurisdictional basis being established, was the order of commitment to the State Training School for the best interests of Frank Myers and the State of North Dakota?

The record discloses that Frank, who was 16 years old on November 7, 1945, is one of four sons of Eva Myers. When he was two years old the Myers' home was broken by divorce and Frank and his brothers were given into the mother's custody. Mrs. Myers worked as a cook in the Fargo Bus Depot and at other jobs. She kept her family together until 1941, when all four boys were committed to institutional care at the Lake Park Children's Home because of their mother's inability to provide for their support. In 1943, Mrs. Myers secured employment as a waitress in the Waldorf Liquor Store which has been described in the record and argument in the case as a "cocktail lounge" and "night club." She is still so employed. Her wages are twenty-five dollars a week and she testified that her tips average about the same amount.

In the spring of 1944, at the close of the school year, Frank left the Children's Home at Lake Park with the approval of all interested parties. He secured employment at Hope, N. D., as a farm hand. He worked the entire summer in this employment and earned $125.00. In the fall he came to Fargo to live with his mother. He entered the ninth grade at the Roosevelt Junior High School. After school hours he worked at odd employments including the setting of pins in bowling alleys. He completed his school work with satisfactory grades and was promoted to the tenth grade. As soon as school was out in the summer of 1945, he found employment doing odd jobs of yard work. In July and August he worked for the Northern States Power Company doing a man's work as an ordinary laborer. He worked an eight hour day and was paid 73½ cents an hour. His employer has testified to his ability and dependability. At the beginning of the current school year, he left this employment and entered the tenth grade at Fargo High School. In addition to his regular school work, he became a member of the football squad and continued to engage in gainful employment after school hours.

During all of the time after he left the Children's Home at Lake Park, Frank has purchased all of his clothes with his own earnings. At all times he has given his mother money to help defray their living expense and during the time he worked for the Northern States Power Company he paid her twenty dollars a month. At the time of the hearing in this case, on September 17, 1945, he had a balance of $185.00 in his savings account with the Northwestern Savings and Loan Assn., he had $200.00 in war bonds which he had purchased with his own savings and a $50.00 war bond which his mother had given him.

Was the order committing Frank to the State Training School for his best interests and for the best interests of the State of North Dakota? The order of the juvenile judge makes it clear, that in reaching his decision he took into consideration the scandalous nature of the Selstrom affair[r] as a whole, Frank's individual delinquency, the commitments that he had ordered in the cases of other participants in that affair who had been before him, the moral atmosphere of the City of Fargo, the fact that Frank's mother's working hours, which were from 6 o'clock p.m. until 1 o'clock a.m. made his supervision by her difficult, and the deterrent effect which the commitment would have upon other juveniles.

---

[r] The facts of the delinquency charge are outlined elsewhere in the opinion:

> It appeared, however, that in March 1945, Frank was invited by two girl acquaintances to attend a party at the home of a Mrs. Selstrom, a place which later achieved scandalous notoriety. Frank attended this party and thereafter became one of a group of boys and girls who frequented this home. Mrs. Selstrom is a vicious woman. She is 24 years of age and while her husband was away in the army, made her home a rendezvous where boys and girls who were scarcely more than children might gather to engage in practices condemned both by the moral law and the law of the land. There they learned to drink intoxicating beverages purchased by Mrs. Selstrom for the most part with money they contributed for the purpose. There, some of them at least, learned and were afforded an opportunity to engage in sex delinquency. No doubt, their hostess was preceptress as well for she took one of the boys as her own paramour.
>
> It is not contended that Frank was a participant in these immoral practices to the extent that others were. He stated that for the most part he just sat around and listened to the phonograph. He drank some of the whiskey and beer that were provided and on one occasion "loaned" Mrs. Selstrom two dollars with which she purchased intoxicating liquor. On another occasion he slept all night on the floor at the Selstrom home while Mrs. Selstrom and her particular friend occupied a bed in another room. The juvenile commissioner who investigated the affair thoroughly stated "as far as I know there is no question of sex delinquency in which he (Frank) was involved." Nevertheless, there is no question but that Frank was aware of what took place at the Selstrom home, and knowing it, he continued to go there until an automobile accident early in August 1945, focused official attention upon the disgraceful situation.

We realize that proper disposition of cases of juvenile delinquency requires a delicate balancing of mixed considerations and that even the most careful weighing of pertinent factors can only result in conclusions that are speculative to the extent that they attempt to predict the course of future events. Confidence that a correct conclusion has been reached must of necessity rest upon hope founded in experience, rather than on certainty. We think therefore that the problem should be approached in a spirit of optimism and that drastic remedies should not be invoked where we can have reasonable hope that lesser ones will have an equal if not a complete success.

What then are the factors to be considered and what relative weight is to be given to each? To what extent is the welfare of an individual delinquent to be counterbalanced by the good of the state? In one sense, a decision, which will help quiet public indignation over a scandalous condition which has arisen in a community, or which, because of its severity, will act as a forbidding example to other youngsters, may be said to be for the good of the state. But we do not think that, as used in the juvenile act, the phrase can be given such a broad interpretation. Considerations of expediency, the satisfaction of public indignation, or example are contrary to the whole spirit of the juvenile act. They are dependent on publicity to be effective for any purpose and all proceedings in juvenile court are declared by statute to be "confidential." Section 27-1606, Rev. Code 1943. We therefore hold that the good of the State requires a child to be removed from a community only when his delinquency is such that he has become a danger to society either because of his own conduct or his influence upon others.

Whether Frank's influence will be detrimental to others depends largely upon what his future conduct will be. The question of what is best for the State is therefore inextricably intertwined with the question of what is best for Frank. The record shows that Frank has need for supervision. It also shows that he has not had proper supervision at home and that because of her working hours it will be difficult for his mother to give him the kind of supervision he needs. This situation, however, does not of necessity require a commitment to the State Training School. That institution is not without its disadvantages. Certainly if we can have reasonable hope that other measures will suffice, we should not resort to a commitment to the Training School. In this case we have that hope. The record does not disclose that Frank is incorrigible but rather that he has respect for parental authority. There is nothing in the record to indicate that Mrs. Myers, his mother, is not a fit person to exercise that authority.

It is true, that in the past that authority was not sufficient to keep Frank from being led astray. But circumstances have changed. The source of Frank's contamination has been removed. His more vicious associates are no longer in Fargo. It is only at the State Training School that he could continue those associations.

After a full consideration of all the evidence we have concluded that it is not for Frank's best interests to commit him to the State Training School. We think that he has demonstrated traits of character that entitle him to another chance to show he can accommodate himself to the normal healthy life society requires of a sixteen-year-old boy. We think this end may be obtained under the mother's supervision if she has the full and friendly cooperation of the juvenile authorities. The order committing Frank Myers to the State Training School is therefore reversed and the case remanded to the Juvenile Court of Cass County.

Christianson, Ch. J., and Nuessle and Morris, JJ., concur.

Burr, J. (concurring specially). The juvenile court was confronted with a condition and not a theory—an extremely serious situation involving numerous people.

The boy is shown to be industrious and thrifty. The situation in which he is involved centers around drinking parties in which he participated, drinking associations and the consequent results that promote immorality. He is in bad company of his own choosing and with evidence, patent to him, which should have caused him to avoid it.

The record shows considerable effort to find a place where he could be sent for proper supervision. Nothing came of this, except, apparently, a choice between commitment to the training school, or of leaving the boy in the custody of his mother. These seem to have been the alternatives left to the juvenile court, and the court states the boy should not remain in Fargo.

The juvenile court, far better acquainted with the actual state of affairs than we, felt the mother was not a fit person to have supervision. I can not subscribe to the assumption in the opinion that he should be left under the influence of his mother. I see nothing in the record which suggests any improvement in him under her supervision. Confessedly she is engaged in the very business of promoting such a situation. For over two years she has been a barmaid in a liquor store serving intoxicating liquor to customers; and this very business of hers is an inducement for her son to do as others are doing.

The record shows definitely that arrangements had been made permitting him to enlist in the Merchant Marine. He has a brother in the Navy. In the record is the statement of his counsel that if the boy joined the Merchant Marine "he will receive four years of instruction and training which will train him for life if he wishes to stay in the Navy."

It does not appear the juvenile court gave any consideration to this possibility. While concurring in reversal and remand I believe it wise, before the boy is committed to the training school for the crucial years before him, to require the juvenile court to investigate this contingency, and make further efforts to find a proper place for this boy so that he be away from these evil influences which surround him.[s]

---

[s] *See also In re* Johnson, 30 Ill. App. 2d 439, 174 N.E.2d 907 (1961), in which the court held that a commitment to the state correctional authority was not warranted. The boys had broken into an unoccupied house and done some minor damage, but the court referred to the "fine character" of the parents and to the fact that they "testified they never had any trouble about discipline" with their sons.

In *In re* Braun, 145 N.W.2d 482, 483 (N.D. 1966), the North Dakota Supreme Court, quoting *State v. Myers* that "the good of the State requires a child to be removed from a community only when his delinquency is such that he has become a danger to society either because of his own conduct or his influence upon others," reversed a juvenile court commitment of an unwed pregnant girl, who already had one illegitimate child, to the State Industrial School and gave permission for her to marry the father of her child as a disposition "for the best interest of the minor and the State of North Dakota." Among the facts considered by the appellate court were the following in an affidavit of the father (p. 486):

> The affidavit of Ronald Kelly attached to the motion states that he is the father of the unborn child; that he is 22 years of age; that on May 27, 1966, he graduated from the Wahpeton School of Science; that he and Jeanette are very much in love and are desirous of becoming married; that his father has purchased a home situated on two acres of land in Renville County next to the farming operations of affiant and his father for the purpose of providing a good and suitable home for him and Jeanette and their children; that affiant is engaged in farming with his father and his brother, the farm consisting of seventeen and a half quarters of land; that at the hearing on April 5 he appeared at the courthouse to tell the court that he and Jeanette wanted to get married but was informed that he could not attend the hearing and he was not able to testify; that he has been charged with statutory rape and the fact that the said statutory rape charge is still pending has nothing to do with this affiant's desire to enter into said marriage, and that the desire to marry is because of the love of the parties for each other and the desire to give a name to their unborn child and to live together as man and wife.

In re Kroll, 43 A.2d 706, 709 (D.C. Mun. Ct. App. 1945):

> Will a child's development into a useful law abiding citizen be aided by taking him out of his home, away from respectable interested parents, from good associates and from a useful employment of his own choice, and placing him in a correctional institution where some of his associates, youths of his age or older, may be persons guilty of serious offenses and in some instances perhaps possessed of depraved or known criminal tendencies, and where he will be required to learn a trade for which he may have neither aptitude nor liking?

In re CROMWELL

232 Md. 409, 194 A.2d 88 (1963)

HENDERSON, J., delivered the opinion of the Court.

The appellants were each 15 years of age when arrested on charges of disorderly conduct in connection with the "sit-in" demonstrations. Being of an age where the Juvenile Court has exclusive jurisdiction under Code (1957), Art. 26, sec. 53, in the absence of waiver under sec. 54, they were charged with delinquency in the juvenile court, on petitions assigning as the only reasons therefor, disorderly conduct on three occasions identified by dates in one case, and on four occasions in the other. At the hearing they were represented by counsel.

We have no difficulty in holding that there was evidence before the trial court to support a finding that each child had committed acts, which if committed by an adult, would have constituted the crimes of trespass and disorderly conduct. We refer particularly to an incident where they entered the Dorset Theatre without tickets while a show was in progress, lay on the floor, used profane language and refused to leave until arrested. If we assume, without deciding, that children have the same rights of protest enjoyed by adults, such conduct, we think would justify a conviction in the case of adults.

But the difficulty in the case at bar is that a mere finding of a basis for delinquency is not enough. Code (1957), Art. 26, sec. 54, provides that when the jurisdiction of the Juvenile Court is invoked the "judge shall then determine whether or not such child comes within any of the aforesaid terms *and* is, *by reason thereof, in need of care or treatment* within the provisions and intent of this subtitle." Sec. 61 provides that the case shall be dismissed if the "judge determines that the child is not within the jurisdiction of the court *or* that the child is not in need of care or treatment. . . ." (Italics supplied.) Such need in the case at bar arises out of the threatened physical harm to the appellants, if they should persist in participating in public demonstrations which might lead to violence. If public demonstrations were discontinued for any reason, or if some guaranty were offered that the appellants would be effectively prevented by their parents or guardians from participating, we think it is clear that there would be no need for other or further care or treatment on that score.

While we hold that the disorderly conduct shown was sufficient to support the finding of delinquency, the conduct of these appellants, standing alone, was not so fundamentally wrong as to require permanent treatment, as distinguished from temporary custodial care. In the main, the demonstrations in which they participated were conducted by adults who, although disorderly in some instances, were not engaged in acts involving moral turpitude. It appears that the adult demonstrators were either dismissed, when charged with disorderly conduct, or that minimum fines were imposed. Incarceration of these children beyond the immediate need for their protection could hardly be supported.

Accordingly, we shall reverse and remand the case for further proceedings, not inconsistent with the views here expressed, in order that the whole matter may be reviewed in the light of the situation now found to exist.

Decree reversed and case remanded, with costs.

D. CORRECTIONAL PROGRAMS

1. *Retention in the Community—Probation Supervision*

The most common disposition for adjudicated delinquents is probation. It has been described as follows:

> Juvenile probation, which permits a child to remain in the community under the supervision and guidance of a probation officer, is a legal status created by a court of juvenile jurisdiction. It usually involves (*a*) a judicial finding that the behavior of the child has been such as to bring him within the purview of the court, (*b*) the imposition of conditions upon his continued freedom, and (*c*) the provision of means for helping him to meet these conditions and for determining the degree to which he meets them. Probation thus implies much more than indiscriminately giving the child "another chance." Its central thrust is to give him positive assistance in adjusting in the free community.[t]

Juvenile court statutes, like their counterparts for adults, do not attempt to define the term "probation" or, generally, to set out any standards to guide the judge in determining when or how it should be used. Sometimes the term for which a youngster can be placed on probation is limited by statute but generally an extension is allowed upon request of the court. Most of the standard setting in this area has been done by the courts on the question of the conditions of probation.

---

[t] THE PRESIDENT'S COMMISSION ON LAW ENFORCEMENT AND ADMINISTRATION OF JUSTICE, TASK FORCE REPORT: CORRECTIONS, Appendix A, at 130 (1967).

a. *The Nature of Juvenile Probation*

A COURT FOR CHILDREN 181-83, 187, 189-90 (1953)[u]

By Alfred J. Kahn

Probation as Treatment. . . . [P]robation work in no sense resembles the leisurely casework process of other agencies. There are no appointments, regular hour-long interviews, or fixed settings for work with a child. It was estimated by a Probation Bureau member a few years ago that probation interviews with boys in New York City consisted in most cases of semimonthly interviews, two to ten minutes long. Even if the estimate is extreme and children are seen ten or twelve minutes each time—the estimate of this study—the contacts remain of negligible length. More than any other this one key fact reflects the essence of the probation problem in New York City. Court responsibilities cannot be fulfilled if most children are seen only five to twenty minutes a month, one to four hours a year, with many missing reporting dates altogether. It is little wonder that the more perceptive probation officers and supervisors view the task with a sense of frustration.

The following is a brief summary of an afternoon—3:30 P.M. to 6:30 P.M.—spent at a reporting center with a young probation officer considered by his superiors as among the most competent. He is deeply interested in the work and is eager for further professional training. Boys report to him twice a month in an attractive room in a public library, coming when they can, in no special order, and being seen in order of arrival. They wait in one room, or the corridor, and are seen in another.

Six boys were already present when Mr. D. arrived and many more arrived within a short time. At any given moment, a group of boys were waiting around, often running in the corridors and quarreling about who was next. Several presented reasons why they could not wait. Twenty-one different "interviews" took place in three hours, an average of nine minutes per contact, if no time is allowed for interruptions, of which there were several. Two or three interviews lasted fifteen or twenty minutes, cutting the time for the others.

On an average day, thirty boys are scheduled to see this probation officer at the reporting center, but only twenty appear. (Quite typically, many children on probation miss reporting days

---

[u] This excerpt is taken from a study done fifteen years ago of the New York City Children's Court. The study of the operation of that court's probation service at that time is one of the most definitive available. Since the time of this study the New York courts have been reorganized and the statutes on delinquency revised.

and require follow-up. Busy probation officers constantly have cases which they have not had time to follow.) The probation officer explained to the observer that, under the rules, the boys must show him their special school report cards each time. To avoid a too routine contact he tries not to begin an interview by referring to the card. When possible, he invites boys to the Boys Club where he is active, and refers many of them to a vocational guidance center. Occasionally, he gets several of the boys together to study rules of good conduct (see below) or to go to a ball game.

Characteristic interviews selected from the twenty-one conducted during the afternoon follow. The first lasted about ten minutes:

As soon as the 15-year-old boy had been greeted and sat down, he was asked: "What do you do for fun?" When the boy answered that he played football, he was asked where and with whom. He was then asked how his mother was and he replied that she still had a cold. The probation officer said that he had seen the father and was told that the boy was doing well. He wanted to know if the boy agreed, and received an affirmative answer. He was also told that things were all right in school. Then, in a rather formal fashion, the probation officer said: "We have noticed a great deal of improvement since you are on probation. I am happy about that and about your school record. If it continues, we can stop the probation. I guess that would break your heart." The boy replied: "No, sir."

The probation officer then said: "There are a few things we've tried to cover since you have been on probation. I want you to look over this and tell me what it means to you." The boy was given a chart which he studied. He then said that it meant that he should avoid bad habits. The probation officer reviewed with him, as though it were a lesson to be learned by rote, the value of good health, sports, and good food. He told the boy that they would go over one or two of the charts each week. He hoped that probation would give the boy better standards. He wanted the boy to see probation as "a kind of friendship" to help him.

Before the interview ended, the probation officer examined the school attendance card. The boy was notified of a group trip to a football game the following Sunday. He had planned a museum trip that day with some friends and was praised for it.

. . .

In order to follow a single case over a period of time and to test observational impressions against statistical tabulation, a representative group of probation "treatment" records was studied. The case record analyses verified the conclusions drawn from the observations: probation "treatment" fails in most of its efforts and, in the main, is not an effective program for helping children who are brought to court.

. . .

A 14-year-old boy was brought to court by a Juvenile Aid Bureau officer after he had stabbed a 12-year-old child in the shoulder with a pocketknife. Seven prior minor offenses were known to the J.A.B. The boy admitted the stabbing but claimed it was an accident. He was remanded to Youth House during the period of probation investigation. The latter proved largely limited to matters of fact, giving background details such as the following: The family consisted of a widowed mother and five children, whose income depended on the salary of one son, social security, and insurance. All attended church regularly. There was a school record of truancy, bad conduct, and repeating grades. The boy attended a settlement house frequently, liked to read, and often got odd jobs. His physical condition seemed good. No appraisal of the boy was made by the probation officer, whose final summary merely stated that the 14-year-old had told him that the younger boy annoyed him and that the stabbing was an "accident." The mother was thought to be "protective," since she knew of his trouble in the neighborhood but considered him a model boy at home. The officer's final recommendation for probation followed a summary of such detail; he noted, too, that the boy spoke of a dislike for school, where he had been teased since having failed. The mother was said to be eager to help him adjust.

The case was assigned to another experienced member of the probation staff for supervision. Youth House provided further details about the family, and the psychiatrist recommended a fresh start in a new school.

The complete case record entry made by the officer after the first contact reads: "Boy reported. P.O. feels good relationship is possible, boy promises cooperation. Will attend school and church regularly and avoid questionable associations."

The five subsequent contacts were on the same level, and a referral was made to a recreation center. Three months after the probation period began and after six contacts the officer reported: "P.O. takes every advantage to praise him for his effort and it gives him pleasure and feeling of security. Mother seen in home on ———, is a pleasant woman and promises cooperation . . . situation very hopeful."

A probation violation was reported a few days later: the boy and some friends broke into the recreation center and damaged some property; he stayed away from home several days. It was also contended that he was one of three boys who "molested" a girl. The judge considered commitment, and the institution accepted the case; but mother and son were convincing, and a referral was made to a guidance clinic. Within six weeks, the boy was involved in a burglary and several other offenses. His mother "threw up her hands," and he was committed.

THE PRESIDENT'S COMMISSION ON LAW ENFORCEMENT AND ADMINISTRATION OF JUSTICE TASK FORCE REPORT: CORRECTIONS, Appendix A, at 132 (1967)

Supervision and treatment. Probation involves far more than giving the child "another chance." This last phrase often describes a course of action in which the child is returned unchanged to a family and community situation that produced delinquency in the first place and can be relied on to do it again. Consequently, probation has been assigned the task of contributing to the process of change, through supervision and treatment, in the situation and behavior of the offending child.

The three major elements of effective supervision and treatment are surveillance, service, and counseling. Usually, no one of these elements is effective by itself; each is a part of an interrelated whole.

(1) Surveillance. The officer must keep in touch with the child, his parents, his school, and other persons involved in and concerned about his adjustment. He must keep generally informed of the extent to which the probation plan is being carried out. Is the family providing adequate care and supervision? Is the child responding to parental supervision? Is he attending school, or working, or in other ways conforming to the general probation plan? Properly used, surveillance constitutes much more than a threat. It is a method of helping the child become aware of his responsibilities and the demands that life makes upon him as a member of the society. It is a resource for the individualization of such demands as they apply to his particular life situation. It constitutes a confrontation with reality, and it may be a source of support by contributing a precise understanding of that reality and the consequences of his failure to respond to it. It provides assurance that society, represented by the court and a court officer, is aware of and interested in him, is concerned that he not engage in future violative and self-defeating behavior, and is determined to assist him in avoiding such behavior.

(2) Service. The officer must determine the extent to which the problems confronting the child and the family may be alleviated by use of available community services. He must then muster such services in an organized way and help the child and family make use of them effectively—often an extremely complicated task when he is dealing with a family that has long been at odds with and suspicious of any agency it regards as representing the authority of society.

(3) Counseling. Counseling, the third aspect of the officer's task, makes it possible to perform the other two effectively. The child and family and other persons concerned must be helped to understand and face the existence of the personal or environmental problems productive of the child's delinquency. Frequently they must be helped to gain some degree of understanding of their roles in the production—and thus in the solution—of such problems. They must be encouraged and stimulated to mobilize their strengths and energies and to invest them in the problem-solving process. The performance of this function depends upon the officer's professional ability to offer them understanding, his obvious dedication to helping them find satisfaction in a socially acceptable manner, his skillful presentation to them of society's demands that they conform to its minimal expectations, and his determination to help them do so.

b. Limitations on Conditions of Supervision

In re GREEN

203 So. 2d 470 (Miss. 1967)

ETHRIDGE, Chief Justice. This is an appeal by Tommie Lee Green, a child under the age of eighteen years, from an order of the Youth Court of Grenada County transferring his custody from his parents to the Superintendent of the Oakley Training School. That order was grounded upon the Youth Court's finding that Green had violated the conditional probation that he was under as a result of an earlier proceeding in that court wherein Green had been adjudicated a delinquent child. We affirm.

The County Attorney of Grenada County filed a petition with the Youth Court alleging that Green, a Negro boy then of the age of fifteen years and one month, was a delinquent child because he had stolen an automobile. Process was had on the youth, his father and stepmother. After a hearing, the court concluded that Green was a delinquent or neglected child, continued the matter until the next term, and held:

> The Court is of the opinion that it would be for the best interest of said minor child that he be placed in the care and custody of his parents with the following restrictions: (1) That he be in the house from 7:00 P.M. to 7:00 A.M. unless in the immediate custody of both parents; (2) That he stay out of all trouble; (3) That he and both parents report to the Sheriff once a month; (4) That he be in Youth Court at 9:00 A.M. on the first Monday of May; and his father is put on probation pending his being at the next Youth Court hearing.

In October 1966 the county attorney filed another petition reciting the foregoing facts, and charging that Green had failed to comply with the second requirement of the court's order, "that he stay out of all trouble," in that he left his classroom at Grenada's John Rundle High School at 10 A.M. and went to the Carrie Dotson High School, urging other students to walk out of classes during the regular school period, and in other ways disrupting classes at both of the schools. The petition asked the court to adjudge that the youth had violated the conditions of his placement, and to show cause why he should not be committed to the state training school, or his custody otherwise be changed. On this petition there was process and a full hearing, with a transcript of the testimony.

The Youth Court again found that Green was a delinquent child. He had violated the conditions of his probation, and it would be for his best interest that he be placed in the Oakley Training School.

The facts are not in dispute. Green admitted that he walked out of John Rundle High School around 10 A.M. while it was in session. There were police stationed at the front entrances to Carrie Dotson School, but Green and two other boys went around to the rear and entered it, in an attempt to get some of the students to leave. He and his friends were trying to convince the Carrie Dotson students to come out for a demonstration. Green unquestionably was disturbing classes in his attempt to persuade the students to leave. He walked into several of the classrooms, talking loudly and generally creating quite a disturbance by antics, which included beating on a steel cabinet with his hands. He refused to leave despite the requests of the teachers.

The record reflects full compliance by the Youth Court with the requirements of substantive and procedural due process of law. See Application of Gault, 387 U.S. 1 (1967).

Appellant contends that the condition of his probationary custody with his parents, that "he should stay out of all trouble," is so vague as to violate the due process clause of the Fourteenth Amendment. The Youth Court Act gives that tribunal the power to place a child under supervision in his own home or in that of a relative "under such terms as the court shall determine and direct." Miss. Code 1942 Ann. § 7185-09 (Supp. 1966). Although criminal probation statutes are not pertinent to juveniles, they are relevant to the basic question of specificity of formulation of the conditions of probation. A standard condition which is frequently applied is that the probationer shall maintain "good behavior," or similar statements such as "lawful behavior," or "violate no law." Such conditions have been almost universally upheld. They are no more vague or indefinite than the condition that the juvenile "stay out of all trouble." Conditions of probation are frequently broadly phrased, since the many types of appropriate causes for revocation cannot be predicted. Note, Legal Aspects of Probation Revocation, 59 Colum. L. Rev. 311, 314-16 (1959). Appellant by his own admission committed acts for which he could be prosecuted criminally. The Youth Court was amply justified in finding that the condition was valid under the particular facts of this case, and that appellant had violated it.

In the trial court appellant did not raise any issue on what he now alleges is a discriminatory separation of the races in the two state training schools. He offered no evidence on that subject, and we do not consider this question, which is raised here for the first time.

Affirmed.

In re TRIGNANI

148 Pa. Super. 142, 24 A.2d 743 (1942)

Opinion by Hirt, J., February 28, 1942: In the evening of September 25, 1940, Israel Trignani, the minor appellant, drove an automobile through the intersection of two streets in Philadelphia. It was not dark but because of excessive speed or lack of control of the automobile he failed to see a woman pedestrian, who had committed herself to the crossing, in time to avoid striking her. She was thrown into the air to the height of the automobile and was most seriously injured. Trignani did not stop after striking the woman but attempted to elude the driver of another car who was following him. His car was forced to the curb some distance from the scene of the injury and he was turned over to the police. He was then just under 18 years of age and was brought into the Municipal Court on a petition alleging that he was a juvenile delinquent. After hearing, the court, on February 25, 1941, made this order: "Probation, to pay $1,040 at rate of $10 per week for a period of two years. Restitution through the Court."

The order was improper. In placing a juvenile on probation, a court undoubtedly may impose such terms as will bring home to the minor a realization of the seriousness of his delinquency. But the terms imposed must be wholly in the interest of the child, looking toward his reformation and not to make good the damages flowing from his illegal act. From that viewpoint the order is subject to valid criticism. It, in effect, bound the boy to servitude and compelled him to surrender all that he could possibly earn for the period of two years. By its severity, it invited further delinquency and revolt against the authority of the court. But the order in itself indicates that reformation was not its primary purpose. By requiring the minor to make "restitution through the court" to the injured woman, the court assumed jurisdiction to determine civil liability and to execute its finding. This is not a function of a juvenile court and is entirely outside of its jurisdiction. Its purpose is not the satisfaction of civil damages, but, "that evil tendencies may be checked" by means of "such care, guidance and control as are essential to children in the formative period of life."[v]

In re BACON

240 Cal. App. 2d 34, 49 Cal. Rptr. 322 (1966)

[Another portion of this opinion appears at 1074, *supra*.]

MOLINARI, Justice. Appellants, David Nathaniel Bacon, Mark Dinaburg, Michael Howard, and Jack Nicholas Radey, appeal from the respective orders of the Alameda County Superior Court, in session as a juvenile court, which orders determined that each of these minors violated Penal Code sections 148, 409, and 602, subdivision (o), and that each be placed on probation

[v] The juvenile system places great stress on the parent-child relationship and accordingly one court has said, "Undoubtedly restitution by the parents of a delinquent child in some instances may be indicated to impress upon them their responsibility in the reformation of the child." *In re* Weiner, 176 Pa. Super. 255, 106 A.2d 915, 918 (1954). However, in the particular case the court could find no authority for the imposition of such a requirement on parents and reversed the juvenile court order for parental restitution.

without wardship upon the condition that he be of good conduct and obey all laws; obey parents; maintain good school attendance, behavior and performance; report to and follow directions of the probation officer; and spend four weekends at the probation department's Training Academy, the probation officer being authorized, at his discretion, to reduce this time to two weekends. Each of these matters is pending before this court as a separate appeal, although a joint brief raising identical issues as to each case has been filed by appellants. Accordingly, we consider these four appeals together.

The Facts

On the afternoon of December 2, 1964 appellants, who were students at the Berkeley Campus of the University of California, had gathered, along with other University of California students, inside the University Administration Building, Sproul Hall, to express to the administration their grievance with the university rules regulating the content of student speech, assembly and petition on the campus. At 7 p. m., when Sproul Hall was closed for the day, a number of the protesters were still in the building. During the evening Chancellor Strong of the University of California went to each of the floors where the protesters were situated and announced that the building was closed, that anyone who wanted to leave the building was free to do so, and that those persons who remained would be guilty of unlawful assembly. This same announcement was subsequently made on each of the floors by Captain Beal of the Berkeley Police Department. The record is susceptible of the inference that each of appellants heard at least one of these announcements. Appellants, however, along with most of the protesters, remained inside the building. Subsequent to these announcements the Berkeley Police arrested a number of the protesters, including appellants. Each appellant, when told by the police that he was under arrest, "went limp" and had to be carried or dragged out of the building.

Questions Presented

Was it an abuse of discretion, outside the power of the trial court, or in violation of appellants' constitutional rights, to require appellants, as a condition of probation, to spend four weekends (which could be reduced to two at the discretion of the probation officer) at the Training Academy of the probation department?

[W]here a minor is not made a ward of the court, the court is limited, under the provisions of section 725, subdivision (a), to an order placing the minor on probation, under the supervision of the probation officer, for a period not to exceed six months. In placing a minor on probation under the supervision of the probation officer "a court undoubtedly may impose such terms as will bring home to the minor a realization of the seriousness of his delinquency." (In re Trignani, 148 Pa. Super. 142, 24 A.2d 743, 744.) Moreover, in imposing conditions of probation, the court is vested with a broad discretion in order to best serve the interests of the minors within its jurisdiction and its exercise of that discretion will not be disturbed in the absence of a manifest abuse of discretion.

In the instant cases appellants do not take issue with the terms of probation other than that requiring them to spend four weekends at the Training Academy. Our immediate inquiry, accordingly, is whether this requirement deprives appellants' parents of the physical custody of appellants during such time as they are in attendance at the Academy. Were we to interpret the trial court's order as requiring appellants to be detained continuously during each weekend period we would be constrained to conclude that such detention amounts to a deprivation of physical custody and that, therefore, the court abused its discretion since it does not have the power to deprive a parent of the physical custody of a minor where the minor is not made a ward of the court. However, as already indicated, the orders, in the instant cases, merely state that the respective appellants are to "spend four weekends at Training Academy. . . ." There is nothing in the record to disclose the nature of the activities conducted at the Academy except the judge's statement that appellants are to perform some type of work while there; nor does the record disclose the length of time to be spent by appellants at the Academy on each of the weekends except for the fact that in the Howard, Dinaburg and Bacon cases the judge stated at the time he imposed the conditions of probation that "This program is from eight to five on Saturday and Sunday. I suppose."

The remarks of the the trial judge at the time he imposed the conditions of probation in the cases of Howard, Dinaburg and Bacon indicate that he intended that these appellants attend the Training Academy during the daytime on the specified Saturdays and Sundays and that they then return to their homes at the conclusion of each day's attendance. We so interpret the orders in these cases. Consonant with this interpretation we hold that attendance at the Academy during the daytime is not a deprivation of physical custody but is akin to a temporary absence from parental control as in the case of school attendance. In reaching this conclusion we are persuaded that a requirement that a minor report periodically to a probation officer or that he attend a specified school for a number of hours during a given day and for several days does not do violence to a parent's custodial rights involved in the physical care and control of the minor and embraced in the concept of "physical custody."

Appellants also urge that this condition imposed upon their probation violated the United States and California Constitutions in that it constituted involuntary servitude (in violation of the Thirteenth Amendment to the United States Constitution and art. I, § 18, of the California Constitution), and deprived appellants of substantive due process ("in that the punishment that was applied to them was not only irrational but also totally disproportionate to the alleged offenses"). Considering this contention we first note that "The provisions of the state and federal constitutions relating to involuntary servitude do not have reference to the legitimate authority for the control and education of children, since a child may be subjected to restraints that may be necessary for his proper education and discipline that could not be applied to adults." (16 C.J.S. Constitutional Law § 203(5), pp. 1001, 1004). The rationale behind this principle is that a juvenile court proceeding is not a criminal proceeding but one in which the state exercises the inherent power as *parens patriae* to interfere, on behalf of the child, including such interference between the child and his parents, when the morals, safety or interests of the child require it.

Adverting to the instant cases once again we cannot say that there is any substance to the contention that appellants will be subjected to manual labor so as to constitute either a violation of the constitutional proscriptions against involuntary servitude or the infliction of cruel or unusual punishment, notwithstanding the trial court's remarks that appellants would "*probably* be cleaning up old and historic cemetery lots." (Emphasis added.) As the record stands there is nothing to indicate that appellants will be required to do any manual labor at all or that the program will consist of anything more than an educational program. Suffice it to say, the law provides for adequate safeguards to insure against the violation of constitutional rights. Nor can we say as a matter of law that the trial court abused its broad discretion in imposing the Training Academy attendance condition of probation since we cannot say that all reasonable minds will conclude that the subject condition is disproportionate to the offenses committed by appellants in view of the conclusion reached by us that the evidence is sufficient to sustain a violation of the three misdemeanor statutes hereinbefore discussed.

The respective orders are affirmed.

SULLIVAN, P. J., and SIMS, J., concur.

JONES v. COMMONWEALTH

185 Va. 335, 38 S.E.2d 444 (1946)

SPRATLEY, J., delivered the opinion of the court.

Upon separate petitions filed by a probation officer, the defendants, William Jones and George Patrick, infants under the age of eighteen years, respectively ________ years and fifteen years, were summoned to appear before the Juvenile and Domestic Relations Court of the city of Bristol, Virginia, to answer complaints that they were delinquent children within the meaning of chapter 78, Virginia Code, 1942 (Michie).

Upon trial, the Juvenile and Domestic Relations Court found each of them guilty of throwing stones at a dwelling in the night time. Separate judgments were entered declaring each a delinquent child. They were placed under the supervision of a probation officer, but allowed to remain in the care and custody of their parents. "As punishment for the offense committed," it was ordered that each defendant pay a fine of $25 and $3 costs out of their own individual earnings at gainful employment.

In each judgment there were seven additional conditions of probation imposed, depriving the defendants of certain normal privileges and rights for one year. One directed that they be at home each evening by nine-thirty and remain there the rest of the night, unless escorted from the home by an adult. A second deprived them of the right to drive an automobile or motor vehicle for pleasure. Another ordered that each boy "attend Sunday School and Church each Sunday hereafter for a period of one year, and present satisfactory evidence of such attendance at the conclusion of each month to the Probation Officer."

The next question is whether the requirement in the judgments that the defendants "attend Sunday School and Church each Sunday" for the period of a year violates their Constitutional guaranty of religious freedom.

Nothing is more fully set forth or more plainly expressed than the determination of our forefathers to establish and perpetuate in the several States of the Union complete religious liberty. No State has more jealously guarded and preserved the questions of religious belief and religious worship as questions between each individual man and his Maker than Virginia.

[T]he Constitution of Virginia [provides:]

"16. That religion, or the duty which we owe to our Creator, and the manner of discharging it, can be directed only by reason and conviction, not by force or violence; and therefore all men are equally entitled to the free exercise of religion, according to the dictates of conscience; and that it is the mutual duty of all to practise Christian forbearance, love, and charity towards each other."

Jefferson's great statute of Religious Freedom, now, constitutes section 34 of our Code.

"That no man shall be compelled to frequent or support any religious worship, place or ministry whatsoever, nor shall be enforced, restrained, molested or burthened, in his body or goods, nor shall otherwise suffer on account of his religious opinions or belief; but that all men shall be free to profess, and by argument to maintain, their opinions in matters of religion, and that the same bill shall in no wise diminish, enlarge or affect their civil capacities."

Thus, in these statutes and constitutional provisions are contained the fundamental principles of the separation of church and state. There is preserved and assured to each individual the right to determine for himself all questions which relate to his relation with the Creator of the Universe. No civil authority has the right to require any one to accept or reject any religious belief or to contribute any support thereto. The growth of religion is not made dependent on force or alliance with the state. Its support is left to moral and spiritual forces.

2. *Institutional Treatment*

Institutionalization for a juvenile delinquent usually means confinement in a state-operated facility although most states also use private facilities to some degree for the placement of delinquents.[w]

---

[w] In the survey conducted by the National Council on Crime and Delinquency for the President's Commission on Law Enforcement and Administration of Justice, thirty-one states reported using such facilities.

One result of the *Gault* decision may be a decreased use of institutional placement. *See* Reed, *Gault and the Juvenile Training School,* 43 IND. L.J. 641, 647-48 (1968).

a. The Objectives and Operation of Juvenile Institutions

THE PRESIDENT'S COMMISSION ON LAW ENFORCEMENT AND ADMINISTRATION OF JUSTICE TASK FORCE REPORT: CORRECTIONS 141-43 (1967)

The term "school of industry" or "reformatory" often designated the early juvenile training facilities, thus reflecting the relatively simple philosophies upon which their development was based. Their reform programs sought chiefly to teach the difference between right and wrong. Teaching methods were primarily on a precept level, tending to emphasize correct behavior, formal education, and, where possible, the teaching of a trade so that the trainee would have the skills to follow the "right."

To a large extent these elements continue to bulwark many programs, but the efficacy of the old methods has been increasingly questioned, and working philosophies now are moving in new directions, primarily for two reasons.

First, although statistics vary from school to school and can be differently interpreted, most experts agree that about half of the persons released from juvenile training facilities can be expected to be reincarcerated.

Second, they agree that if treatment is to produce lasting change, it must (regardless of technique) touch upon the personal reasons for delinquency. Like most people, juveniles caught in the "wrong" usually find it more comfortable to justify themselves as "right" than to acknowledge responsibility for being wrong and seeking to change. For the delinquent this means that, from the view he has of himself, he does not act out of "evil" but out of a "good" which makes sense and can be justified. Delinquent behavior may be a satisfying experience to a youngster, especially if it meets his emotional needs. The approach, therefore, cannot be merely an appeal for a change in behavior that is offensive to the school; it must be concerned with what the behavior means to the youngster himself. Therefore, according to this view, the function of a training facility is to help a minor look honestly at his own attitudes and see to what degree they create difficulties in the sense that "as ye sow so shall ye reap." Having seen this, a minor then has a personal reference point for change that is connected with his own perception of "good"; he can arrive at personally responsible behavior because he feels this personal connection.

Evidence of the practicality of this viewpoint is found in observations common among training school youngsters themselves, who are quite capable of pointing out those in their group who are "really doing good" and those who are "just playing it cool." If the training school makes conformity the hallmark of progress, it teaches duplicity because, in so doing, it is suggesting that the real problem to be met is not "genuine change of feelings" but only change of "appearances," simply doing whatever the outer situation demands to "get by." The implications of this for further involvement in trouble are clear.

In theory, training schools are specialized facilities for changing children relatively hardened in delinquency. In practice, . . . they house a nonselective population. . . .

[T]he following [is a] list of "other" purposes:

> Use as a detention or holding facility for youngsters awaiting completion of other plans for placement.
>
> Providing basic housing for youngsters whose primary need is a foster home or residential housing.
>
> Housing large numbers of youngsters whose involvement in trouble is primarily situational rather than deep-seated and who could be handled more efficiently under community supervision.
>
> Caring for mentally retarded youngsters committed to the training school because there is no room in a mental retardation facility or because no such institution exists.
>
> Providing care for youngsters with severe psychiatric problems who are committed to the training school because of no juvenile residential treatment program.
>
> Use of girls' facilities to provide maternity services.

A STUDY OF A JUVENILE INSTITUTION (1965)[x]

By Richard E. Hemming

In the juvenile court, emphasis is placed on helping the children stay out of future trouble rather than punishing them for what they have done in the past. The judge, after hearing the case and determining that a delinquent act has been committed, must decide how this boy can be taught not to get into trouble again. If he decides that the child needs institutional help, he transfers the child's custody to the Department of Public Welfare until the age of twenty-one. This means the court has no further jurisdiction over the child and can make no further order affecting the length of stay, the place of treatment, or the type of program that the child will be subject to. The theory is that the judge cannot make a good decision as to how long a child should

[x] Unpublished paper prepared in the University of Wisconsin Law School Correctional Internship Program, sponsored by the National Council on Legal Clinics (now Council on Legal Education for Professional Responsibility).

be kept because he does not have the facilities to make a good diagnostic evaluation of the treatment that will be necessary to rehabilitate the child. His best guide would be the offense and it is felt that in the juvenile system this is not an accurate or scientific guide.

To make this crucial and highly complex decision, the Department of Public Welfare has created the Juvenile Review Board. This is a civil service job which is filled by two men who have had a number of years of experience in correctional work. It is the duty of the Juvenile Review Board to make the decision that will best implement a juvenile's rehabilitation. It is hoped that this board, supposedly being free from public pressures and prejudices, will be able to make a decision which is truly in the best interests of the child.

The boys who come before the board at the Juvenile Reception Center fall into two categories, namely, first offenders and parole violators. The former have been received directly from a county juvenile court while the latter have been returned by their parole agents to the Reception Center without any further court proceedings because of some parole violation.

In making its decision, the Review Board is aided by the staff at the Reception Center. All the boys who are seen by the Review Board have been given a complete workup by the staff and recommendations have been made. When a boy is received at the Reception Center, he is assigned to one of five reception units. During the next thirty days, he is seen by the clinical personnel of the institution. He is also given standard intelligence quotient tests, achievement tests, and psychological tests. During this entire period he is under the constant observation and supervision of the counselor in his unit.

After approximately fifteen days have elapsed, the social worker does a Reception Center Admission Report on the boy. This report, prepared from an interview with the boy, is a reflection of how the boy sees his offense and his personal background. It concludes with a diagnostic summary which is supposed to assess the nature of the boy and his problems. After this has been completed, the boy is seen by a psychologist or a psychiatrist and a psychiatric report is done on him.

At the end of the thirty-day observation period, these reports along with the various tests the boy has taken and a report by the counselors who have been observing him are assembled by the clinical staff and they meet to discuss all the data. The purpose of this meeting, which is called staffing, is to make recommendations to the Review Board with regard to place and length of stay, program, treatment, and release possibilities. The

Review Board, using the recommendations of the staff, then makes its initial disposition.

There are many factors which are pertinent to determining how long a boy will have to stay in a juvenile institution and they are, of course, weighed differently in each case. In the average case, the initial concern is bed space. How much room is available now and how long will it remain available for treatment of a particular boy? This length of time, which is currently only three to four months, sets the average length of stay.

Keeping in mind what the average length of stay must be, the Board then looks to the offense as the next most important factor in determining how long a boy should stay. If they consider the offense to be serious, then the boy will probably be kept five to six months. If the offense is less serious, then the boy will probably be kept two to three months. An average offense is usually some type of theft or burglary accompanied with truancy or uncontrolledness. A more serious offense would involve some type of assaultive behavior or a longer than average police record. A less serious offense would probably consist of truancy or possibly some sexual activity which was not assaultive in nature.

After the boy's offense and past record have been examined by the Board, the rest of the data is considered. The diagnostic evaluation is usually given some weight. This evaluation usually recommends the length of time that will be needed to treat the boy. This time length is given on a comparative basis (average, longer than average, shorter than average) and not as a definite length of time. As it turns out, the more serious offenses get the longer treatment recommendations.

Whether the boy is in school is also a factor. If the boy will be in school in the institution, his release hearing date will be set to conform with the end of the school semester. If the boy is a workboy, on the other hand, he may be released a month earlier than a schoolboy with the same offense.

Finally, institutional behavior is important. If the boy has made a good adjustment during his thirty days in the units and if it is likely that this behavior will continue, this does not have much effect. But, if the boy's adjustment has been poor and if it is felt that he will be disruptive to the program, this becomes a serious consideration, and the boy runs the risk of a nine-month stay at the adult prison for younger offenders. If the boy's adjustment has been poor but he has been withdrawn rather than disruptive, he will likely get an average stay and have psychiatric care recommended.

The next determination that the Board must make is the place of stay. Many of the same considerations that go into determining length of stay are also pertinent in determining place of stay. The average delinquent, who must go to school and be in a setting with a certain degree of discipline but does not need any special clinical treatment, will be sent to a modern juvenile institution which has a fine school and a good system of discipline. The Review Board seems to feel that this is the type of atmosphere needed by most delinquents. But the limited capacity of this institution prevents its use for all boys who would profit from it.

The oldest juvenile institution, to which the Reception Center is attached, treats the more unusual cases. Boys with outstandingly good prognosis are there because they will probably be released soon and it would be a waste of time and money to send them elsewhere. The more disturbed boy with the poor prognosis is also found there because the clinical staff is available to him. At the newer institution there are no psychologists or psychiatrists, so all boys needing this type of treatment are kept near the Reception Center.

If the boy is older and will be seeking an unskilled job upon his release, he might be sent to a forestry camp. Here the boy will do outdoor conservation work at the same time he is being taught discipline and self control. This camp does not attempt to teach a trade but does attempt to teach good work habits that will be useful when the boy finds a job after his release.

The Board and the Department make a practice of sending boys whom they feel will not benefit from a juvenile program to the adult institution. This will be the very aggressive boy who would be disruptive to the program or the boy who has returned to the juvenile institution four or five times and has thus demonstrated that he is not benefiting from his stays in a juvenile institution. In some cases, a transfer to this adult institution is just the type of therapy that a boy needs. At the adult prison, he is treated like a man and if he responds to this type of treatment he will get a fine education or learn a trade in one of the many vocational shops.

One other possible disposition which deserves mention is the program of early release with intensive supervision for some boys living in the metropolitan area. This is used when the offense is not too serious and when the board and the staff feel that the boy can benefit more from rigid supervision in his own community than he can from a stay in a juvenile institution. Such a boy is assigned to a social worker who has a special caseload of about fifteen boys and whose duty it is to spend most of his time seeing and supervising his clients rather than sitting in his office doing paper work.

b. *Individualized Treatment*

THE PRESIDENT'S COMMISSION ON LAW ENFORCEMENT AND ADMINISTRATION OF JUSTICE TASK FORCE REPORT: CORRECTIONS 145-46 (1967)

The impact of a program upon children is largely determined by adequacy of staff, both quantitatively and qualitatively.

In 1965, State-run juvenile facilities employed 21,247 staff in programs housing an average daily population of 42,389 trainees.

(*a*) *Treatment personnel.*[y] Of the total number employed, 1,154 were treatment personnel—psychiatrists, psychologists, and social caseworkers.

The standard[z] calls for a minimum of 1 full-time psychiatrist for 150 children. On the basis of the average daily population of 42,389 in 1965, the number of psychiatrists required is 282.

The survey data show that the equivalent of 46 psychiatrists served the 220 State-operated facilities. More than half of them are found in only 5 States, with 1 State having the equivalent psychiatric time of 10 out of the total of 46 psychiatrists. Each of 37 States has less than the equivalent of 1 full-time psychiatrist available to its juvenile institution population. Only 4 States have enough psychiatric service available to satisfy the required 1:150 ratio.

To meet the requirements nationally, juvenile institutions need a total of 236 more psychiatrists than they now have.

The standard calls for a minimum of 1 full-time psychologist for 150 children. On the basis of the average daily population, the number of psychologists required is 282.

The survey data show that the equivalent of 182 psychologists work in the State-run juvenile facilities. However, as with psychiatrists, psychologists are found to be unequally distributed among the States: 106 (almost 60 percent of the total) are found in 9 States. Each of 21 States had the equivalent of not more than 1 psychologist. Only 12 States come up to the standard ratio.

To meet the requirements nationally, juvenile institution systems need a total of 100 more psychologists than they now have.

The standard declares that under ordinary conditions, a full-time caseworker in a juvenile institution should be assigned not more than 30 children. On the basis of the average daily population, the number of caseworkers required is 1,413.

---

[y] Two State systems have no treatment staff at all. [Note 5 in original.]

[z] Standards were developed for the survey by the Commission's Special Committee on Standards. See the Task Force Report at 116.

The survey data show, in the 220 institutions, a total of 926 caseworkers, or 66 percent of the number required. To meet the requirements nationally, juvenile institution systems need a total of 487 more caseworkers than they now have.

. . .

(*b*) *Teachers.* The standard calls for a teacher-pupil ratio not exceeding 1:15.

Standards bearing on teacher ratios in training facilities are difficult to apply to survey data. Where public school systems assume a portion of the training system's academic burden, their teachers were not counted as institutional employees for purposes of the survey.

There were 2,495 teachers in the 220 institutions, an overall teacher-pupil ratio of 1:17. In 24 States, the teacher-pupil ratio is better than the 1:15 standard cited, and in 36 States it is better than 1:20. Moreover, in the remaining States several jurisdictions have ratios that are high because of the reasons cited above.

The general picture given by the survey data is consistent with experienced observation: The established standard for training facilities is met to a far greater degree in teaching than it is in the casework or psychological counseling function. The reason is probably that, in many facilities, academic teaching has been the traditional mainstay of programing; also, the teaching role is better understood, and training for teachers is well established. In those facilities where there aren't enough teachers, the problem is more likely to be budget than an insufficient supply of trained teachers. Even where salaries are competitive the training school is handicapped in recruiting the good teacher because its working conditions are usually less attractive than the public school's.

INSTITUTIONS SERVING DELINQUENT CHILDREN

U.S. Department of Health, Education & Welfare

Children's Bureau Publication #360, at 97-106 (1957)

DISCIPLINE

Discipline and punishment are often confused. The former implies self-control and respect whereas the latter is a measure frequently used with the intention of bringing about discipline. . . . The manner in which children who cannot or will not conform to program requirements are handled is of crucial importance to the training school program. It is essential to have an action-oriented philosophy of discipline which recognizes the aggressive acting-out characteristics of most training school youngsters, realizes that certain actions have to happen from a treatment standpoint, and yet permits dealing forcefully and intelligently with the misbehavior.

Discipline should be regarded as a means of exercising control over individuals for the best interests of the group. Discipline is often thought of as a negative coercion. Actually, positive discipline, based on the prophylaxis theory, or discipline which precludes the necessity for punishment by eliminating the offense, is a stronger force than negative discipline, based primarily on fear, and it possesses far more virtue from an administrative point of view.

. . .

Not only is the question of discipline and punishment a crucial treatment consideration, it is also the crux of the administrative problem of conducting the training school program. The training school administrator is called upon to contain in one institution a large number of children whose behavior is characterized by a pattern of anti-social acts. Each delinquent is different and each has individual problems. Forcing them to live together creates for them a group situation which must be handled in the most skillful, sensitive, imaginative way if it is to help toward better adjustment.

Most communities demand not only that the administrator restrain these children but also that he restrain them in such a fashion that, while institutionalized, they commit no further disorderly acts affecting the local community or the child's home community. Most of the recurrent crises to which institutions for delinquent children are subject come about because of public furor engendered by the anti-social acts of institutionalized children which come to the attention of surrounding communities. Although the motivations behind an act such as running away may make it therapeutically desirable in the instance of a particular child, few communities accept it in this light.

So the administrator and his staff are concerned with discipline for two major and somewhat contradictory reasons. On the one hand, they know that unless there is a reasonable degree of conformity on the part of the children under their care, public sentiment may turn against the school with consequent loss of support and damage to its program. On the other hand, they know that if the school relies mainly upon repressive measures to insure conformity in behavior, it cannot do its basic and all-important job of treatment.

. . .

Since misbehavior is the very symptom at which training school treatment is directed, it is axiomatic that disciplinary measures must be applied on the basis of an understanding of why the individual child did not conform to a particular demand at a particular time. While the necessity to take action in the heat of a given moment may make it impossible for the staff member involved to give full consideration to such matters, it is always possible to review every instance in which disciplinary measures were applied in order to gain heightened understanding of their proper use. The extent to which the staff member has an understanding of the youngsters under his supervision will determine his ability to make quick decisions regarding control measures which are appropriate to the individual child involved.

Disciplinary measures should be planned to build the child's self-esteem. This places the emphasis not so much on "good behavior" or "bad behavior," as on the growing maturity of the child, on his ability to learn how to cope with his problems, and his moving forward even though the gain may be very small. One needs to be equally concerned with the over-conforming youngster—where the inner controls also fail to develop—as with the non-conformist. It is important to recognize that there are some positive values in non-conformity—up to a reasonable point of group and institutional tolerance. Such incidents do not necessarily indicate the application of sanctions or extreme permissiveness.

. . .

Of the various devices which can be used to discipline the institutionalized youngster, deprivation of special privileges is probably the most common and favored. Such measures do not deprive the child of the benefits of the continuing program since the privileges are by definition looked upon as something extra, over and above the regular program. This implies that to be able to make full use of this form of discipline, the training school must have a program rich in privileges.

. . .

Often the privilege that is taken away does not occur until long after the particular rebellious act. Consequently the child is often unable to relate this action to the incident; it therefore has little meaning to him and merely stimulates hostility. Another important consideration is that something should not be taken away from an offender that is essential to the development of his ability to cease offending. . . .

Another disciplinary method often used is to assign the youngster to an extra work detail. But this measure is also open to question. Every institution has a number of jobs that must be done and yet are arduous and disagreeable. To maintain the dignity of labor, care must be taken that these unpleasant tasks are not assigned to youngsters in such a way that they begin to think that all unpleasant work is punishment. In other words, it is a questionable practice to give children unpleasant work which may make them think that such experiences are activities beyond the pale of daily living and to be avoided at all costs. . . .

Another form of appropriate discipline is directly related to damage done in the course of misbehavior. The youngster who wantonly damages property should be required to repair it. In schools where provision is made for youngsters to earn money, they may, within reasonable limits, be required to pay for damaged or destroyed property.

Rebellious and aggressive behavior, resulting from innate hostility or gang loyalty, can usually be dealt with by the simple rule of thumb: children cannot be permitted to hurt themselves, or others, or destroy property deliberately. It is recognized that there are rebellious children who must, at times, be removed from the group situation. Segregation should be differentiated from separation, a less serious step taken when the supervisor merely sends a hyperactive youngster to his room, or some other place, away from the group for a temporary period. Segregation, which usually involves a longer period of time, is the placement of the child in a physically secure room or facility under strict supervision and the denial of participation in the full daily program. . . .

The absence of any constructive program while a youngster is in segregation can be very damaging. In addition to consultation, he should be provided with something to do. School assignments should be continued and he should be furnished with reading materials.

Youngsters in segregation should be closely supervised. Under no circumstances should they be locked in rooms with no general supervision. Supervisors, particularly night supervisors, should always be aware that they are responsible for the child's health as well as his safety.

There is some question as to whether segregation rooms are used more often as disciplinary measure or as a punitive measure. Removal from the group may signify punishment by rejection to the child involved. This is undesirable. When properly used, segregation is a protective device for the child, the staff member, or the group and enables all concerned to weather a difficult situation that has become too hot to handle.

The confinement of children for prolonged periods, say, a week or more, in segregation rooms as a disciplinary measure is not recommended.

. . .

There are a number of disciplinary measures that should not be used in training schools. Cruel and unusual punishment, measures which humiliate, group punishment for individual acts, standard disciplinary measures for specific infractions, and corporal punishment should not be tolerated. Merit and demerit systems are not appropriate for use in training schools.

. . .

Two types of disciplinary measures warrant special consideration since they fall between measures which are approved by all persons in the field and those which everyone agrees are harmful. The first, corporal punishment, is distinguished by its advocates from sadistic beatings which no intelligent training school administrator would countenance. . . .

However, corporal punishment should not be tolerated in any form. It is no doubt true that workers, on occasion, have believed that what a particular youngster needs at a certain time is a good sound spanking. But they also know that once a mild form of corporal punishment is tolerated, the measure can soon get out of hand. It quickly becomes a crutch for the unresourceful staff member. . . .

The second disciplinary measure, equally inappropriate, is the use of the merit and demerit system as a means of determining release eligibility. Quite a number of training schools still award numerical merits for satisfactory behavior and penalize youngsters with demerits for misbehavior, which may or may not be related to the needs of the child. The difficulty inherent in this system is that the accumulation of merits must be related to some goal. In other words, there must be motives other than conformity alone to inspire the youngster to accumulate merits. For this reason, release from the school is usually made to depend upon having a certain number of merits.

Such a set-up is not in the interest of an individualized treatment program since occasionally it is advisable to keep in the school a youngster who has exemplary conduct and who has accumulated many merits. On the other hand, it may be to the best interest of some youngsters to be released at a certain time even though they have not accumulated the necessary number of points. Such a system puts a premium on outer conformity in order to secure release or some equivalent benefit rather than upon inner change. Since the point formula is usually tied in with a minimum time period, it also reduces the flexibility of the program by making it possible for a youngster to be released by the calendar, rather than because of staff judgment that he is ready.

Related and acceptable, but quite different from the merit-demerit system, is a program device whereby youngsters in an institution with a rich and varied program for all are given extra privileges as they become ready to use them. Such devices, often termed "citizenship programs," have much to recommend them. Recognizing a youngster's progress by a system of periodic rating charts, which include grading conduct, achievement, and overall adjustment, and coordinating these charts with the program of counselling to determine eligibility for privileges or release, works satisfactorily in some training schools. In fact, such a program is particularly helpful in some institutions where budgetary limitations do not permit sufficient clinical personnel or where a definite effort is made to combat the time minimum system.

c. *Transfer to Penal Institutions*

One area of juvenile institutional treatment which has given rise to a significant amount of appellate litigation is the practice of placing adjudged juvenile delinquents in adult penal institutions. This may be done either through direct commitment ordered by the juvenile court[a] or through administrative transfer by the juvenile correctional authority. The latter process—administrative transfer—is by far the more common.[b] The courts have divided on the validity of such commitments or transfers.[c] Those upholding the use of penal institutions usually rely on the fact that this is necessary to provide proper treatment; those striking it down assert that a person not convicted of a crime cannot be imprisoned in a penal institution.

WILSON v. COUGHLIN

259 Iowa 1163, 147 N.W.2d 175 (1966)

LARSON, Justice. When William Clifford Wilson, age 16, was ordered transferred from the Training School for Boys to the Men's Reformatory under the provisions of section 218.91, Code 1966, he filed a petition for writ of certiorari in this court on May 27, 1966. On June 13th we granted a writ to review this

---

[a] See, for example, statutes discussed in *In re* Darnell, 173 Ohio St. 335, 182 N.E.2d 321 (1962); Morton v. Heyden, 154 Me. 6, 142 A.2d 37 (1958); State *ex rel.* McGilton v. Adams, 143 W. Va. 325, 102 S.E.2d 145 (1958).

[b] A 1964 study found that twenty-four of fifty-three jurisdictions surveyed (including all but one of the fifty states) permitted transfer of juveniles to penal institutions. CHILDREN'S BUREAU, U.S. DEP'T H.E.W., DELINQUENT CHILDREN IN PENAL INSTITUTIONS (1964).

[c] See cases discussed in Note, *Transfer of Juveniles to Adult Correctional Institutions,* 1966 WIS. L. REV. 866, 870-77.

order but denied the request that petitioner be returned to the Training School for Boys.

Petitioner contends the Hardin County District Court was without jurisdiction and acted illegally in granting an order transferring him from the Training School for Boys to the Men's Reformatory for custodial care, and that section 218.91 of the 1966 Code of Iowa, under which it purported to act, is unconstitutional, being in violation of the due process clauses of both the state and federal constitutions, i.e., the fourteenth amendment to the United States Constitution, and Article I, Sections 9 and 10, of the Iowa Constitution, and of the equal protection clause of the fourteenth amendment of the United States Constitution. We find no merit in these contentions.

From the record we learn petitioner was determined a juvenile delinquent by the Polk County Juvenile Court and was duly committed to the Training School for Boys at Eldora.

In August, 1965, after nineteen and a half months at the school, petitioner was paroled to his parents. This parole was revoked and he was returned to the school in October, 1965, when he would not attend school and became involved in the theft of an automobile and some old coins. On March 11, 1966, a special leave was granted him to find employment in the Waterloo area. This "leave" was to terminate in a parole if he made a satisfactory adjustment at his employment. However, he found no employment and was returned to the training school at Eldora some twenty days later when he was involved in a drunkenness episode, assisted in stealing two cars, and helped cut up convertible tops on other automobiles.

Being convinced petitioner's presence at the school would not be conducive to his welfare or the welfare of the other inmates of the school, the authorities decided he should be transferred to the reformatory for custodial care and treatment. On the 12th day of May, 1966, this application for such transfer was granted, and since that time he has been cared for in that correctional institution. Apparently the change of place of confinement is not to his liking and he asks us to find the transfer invalid.

Section 218.91, as now found in the 1966 Code of Iowa, being in effect on May 12, 1966, provides as follows: "The board of control or the director of corrective institutions may order the transfer of inmates of the training school for boys to the men's reformatory for custodial care whenever it is determined that such action will be conducive to the welfare of the other inmates of the school. Such transfer shall be effected by application in writing to the district court, or any judge thereof, of the county in which the said training school is situated. Upon the granting of the order of transfer, the transfer shall take place. The county attorney of the said county shall appear in support of such application. The cost of the transfer shall be paid from the funds of the training school for boys. Subsequent to a transfer made under this section, the person transferred shall be subject to all the provisions of law and regulations of the institution to which he is transferred, and for the purposes of chapter (745) of the Code such person shall be regarded as having been committed to the institution." This section does not violate the fundamental law, federal or state.

In making this transfer, the board is presumed to be performing a duty imposed upon it, that of restraint, education and reformation. It is not restraining the natural liberty of the child, but is placing him under a natural restraint, a restraint so far as is practicable as should be exercised by a parent. In other words, the severity of the restraint is governed entirely by the actions of the child resisting parental authority. It is not like the unnatural restraint of one convicted of a crime where the restraint is punishment. Rather it is only for so long as the child needs a firm restraining hand, and it may end any time the child shows a willingness to behave.

Here we are told the state board has tried every other way to exercise proper parental authority, with no appreciable effect. There was no other place of custodial care where he could receive proper education, care, and rehabilitation training. While we may not feel restraint in a place generally used and occupied by convicted felons is quite proper for a child of 16 years, yet this seems to be a policy question for the legislature, not the courts. Perhaps an intermediate facility should be provided, but that is not our problem here. There is no constitutional prohibition known to us which bans association between persons convicted of crimes and others, even children. We have been cited no recent legal authority which holds an institution usually housing criminals is an improper institution for the restraint of a minor delinquent, or that due process is violated by his care and retention in such an institution. On the other hand, several state cases and many federal decisions seem to reach the opposite conclusion.

Thus, the place of his detention and treatment is largely up to the delinquent boy, and the association with those who have been convicted of a crime is not a valid reason for denying the State a place to restrain and rehabilitate him. In fact, such associations under certain conditions are permitted in section 242.6 of the code, where it is provided that the court may in certain instances commit a minor convicted of a felony to the training school for boys, or for girls, as the case may be. We conclude, then, the association is not determinative of the petitioner's rights. It is rather the facilities of the institution to provide the restraint, training, education and opportunity to rehabilitate that must control. There is no showing here that such facilities were not provided.

Finally, petitioner argues that because one restrained at the men's reformatory is required to obey the rules and regulations of that institution, and is made subject to prosecution for escape from it, as is provided in chapter 745 of the code, this somehow makes him a prisoner and subjects him to increased punishment without due process of law. The short answer to this contention is, of course, that petitioner is not a prisoner and is not being punished when detained under such paternal custody. His status as a mere delinquent is not changed by this transfer and he is still eligible for parole or release at any time his conduct convinces the board and directors that he no longer needs that control, and under no circumstances beyond his 21st birthday.

Perhaps the penalty for escape from the men's reformatory is greater than from the training school for boys, but there is a marked distinction. When a boy runs away from the training school, without a judicial hearing he may be punished by the school authorities. Indeed, petitioner on several occasions has been punished for rule infractions and has summarily been confined in the security or health center therefor. In the reformatory, before he is punished for escape, he is entitled to a trial in the district court. Furthermore, as an inmate of either institution, he has always been subject to criminal prosecution for any crime committed and certainly could be charged with escape when arrested for one of them. At any rate we fail to see how subjecting petitioner to prosecution for escape is an increase in punishment, for it is not punishment at all until he himself has added the crime of escape to his defections against society and has been tried and convicted of that offense.

Writ annulled.

GARFIELD, C. J., and SNELL, MOORE and STUART, JJ., concur.

BECKER, Justice. I dissent. The gravity of the question involved requires that reasons for disagreement be recorded.

The statute provides that the Board of Control or the Director of Corrective Institutions may order the transfer of an inmate of the training school for boys from that school to the Men's Reformatory at Anamosa. Application to do so must be made to the court. "The county attorney of the said county (where the training school is located) shall appear in support of such application." The order of transfer may be made whenever it is determined that such action will be conducive to the welfare of the other inmates of the school. Welfare of the individual concerned is not mentioned.

The statute does not provide for notice to the inmate, or to anyone else. It does not provide for a hearing. Although it provides that the state shall be represented by the county attorney, it does not provide for counsel for the inmate. Notice, hearing and counsel were all provided here but it would seem that these omissions in the statute are constitutionally impermissible. We have said that a statute rises or falls not on what has been done by its authority but by what may be done by its authority. Here it is quite clear that judicial approval can be secured through ex parte procedures and, in fact, was accomplished without benefit of counsel for the other two boys. Having no counsel they understandably do not seek certiorari.

Through his attorney this petitioner insists that before he can be placed in the Men's Reformatory at Anamosa, he must be treated as a man. He must be accorded not only the punishment of a man but the constitutional safeguards of a man. It is said that this will do a disservice to him and to all other juveniles for the courts will more often tend to use criminal procedures against juveniles in aggravated cases.

First, there is no showing that this would not be a good development. The juvenile law does not require that all juveniles, under all circumstances, be taken under its wing.

Second, if a minor's activities are so bad that the State facilities cannot handle him as a minor, he should be treated as an adult.

The change in treatment occasioned by transfer from a training school to a reformatory is not a change in degree, it is a change in kind. The record shows that defendant State officials recognize this quite clearly. Attached to the application for authority to transfer are two reports signed by Darrell E. Weigert, Observation Section Director and Dr. Lloyd L. Spencer, Psychiatric Consultant.

Mr. Weigert concluded:

"In reviewing Clifford's file it reveals that about 110 hours of group and individual counseling has been conducted with this particular boy. It is evident that Cliff has gained many strengths and experiences that he has benefited from and will probably never lose, but in view of the recent involvement on Special Leave and minimal adjustment to the Training School program I feel that he should be considered for possible transfer to the Men's Reformatory at Anamosa."

Dr. Spencer concluded:

"This is a 16 year old boy with a chronic history of delinquency and an apparent inability to profit from experience or from individual or group counseling. Although it is possible that a program could be worked out which would benefit this boy, our current program and facilities have not been able to accomplish this. I feel that he has really obtained maximum benefit from our existing program.

". . . I feel that Cliff may be institutionalized because of antisocial activities for some time. He has exhibited or expressed little desire in modifying his current behavior. *I do feel that Clifford possesses the ego strength necessary for him to make an adjustment to life in an adult penal institution without undue difficulties.*" (emphasis added)

Faced with such stark evidence of the State's attitude and purpose, this court should not conclude that this juvenile "is not being punished and is not being treated as a prisoner." The opinion of the psychiatrist is far more realistic. If this boy will not be treated as a prisoner, he will not need "ego strength", to adjust to life in an adult penal institution. But the doctor implicitly recognizes that the new custodial care will be different in *kind*. So should we.[d]

---

[d] *See* Note, *Transfer of Juveniles to Adult Correctional Institutions,* 1966 Wis. L. Rev. 866, 888-89:

C. Consequences of the Transfer Decision

Although the specific effect of transfer depends, of course, on where the juvenile is ultimately placed in the adult system, a transfer is, in any case, almost certain to have significant effects on his activity and treatment.

Perhaps most significant is its effect on the length of confinement. The juvenile institutions have no obligation to keep a committed child for any given period of time; they have consequently met the pressures of mounting population by shortening the average stay. As a result, a youth who remains at the juvenile institution is apt to have a total period of confinement of three or four months.

When a juvenile is transferred, the Juvenile Review Board sets the date at which he will be seen by the adult parole board and considered for parole. In the past, the adult inmates of the reformatory have been eligible for consideration after nine months; the Juvenile Review Board generally set a similar nine-month period for transferred juveniles. Transfer, in effect, means a considerably longer period of institutionalization. This might well be changed, however, if additional juvenile facilities were made available and the department were able to gear the length of institutionalization in the juvenile placements to the best interests of the individual child; this would almost unquestionably mean a significant increase in the average length of stay.

The juvenile's freedom of action may be significantly reduced in the adult facility. He may no longer live in a room of his own but

The statement that this inmate will not be permitted association with older prisoners is predicated on section 246.36, Code, 1966: "Classification of prisoners. The wardens shall, so far as practicable, prevent prisoners under eighteen years of age from associating with other prisoners." We should not presume from such an equivocal section that the warden at Anamosa has been provided with the facilities and budget to handle juvenile inmates separately. Though the record is silent on the matter, oral argument by the attorneys indicated the contrary.

If other sections of our statutes, or if the factual record here, showed that the reformatory at Anamosa was equipped to continue the treatment and education of this juvenile within the letter and the spirit of our juvenile statutes, (albeit, under far more restrictive circumstances) this dissent would not be filed. But the record does not so show. Nor should the burden to show lack of facilities be on the inmate. The state has the knowledge and the evidence to give the true picture. It should be required to do so if its proposed action is to be allowed.

This boy may well deserve to be incarcerated in an adult penal institution; or, to put it differently, the interest of the State may well demand such treatment. If that be true the State can, and

---

may be housed in a cell or a dormitory (at the reformatory). The reformatory, unlike the juvenile institutions, permits only a limited number of visits from home; letter writing privileges are also somewhat restricted. While he may have been granted a weekend furlough to return home every three months while at the juvenile institutions, he has no such privilege while at the reformatory.

In addition, the programs in the adult system may be significantly different from those in the juvenile institutions. Only limited educational facilities are available in the camp system. On the other hand, at the adult institutions vocational training in areas such as auto body work, masonry, electric appliance repair, and similar fields is available to the juvenile. There is no equivalent in the juvenile institutions.

Finally, the transfer may, as a result of all factors combined, affect the juvenile's self-image so as to crystallize his position in his own mind. While he is held at the juvenile institutions, formal theory maintains that he is not a criminal and is not imprisoned; he is merely in need of help, and the institution serves only as a vehicle for administering that help. In the adult system—especially at the reformatory—this arguably artificial posture often cannot be maintained; the walls, armed guards, and bars leave less doubt that the juvenile is "imprisoned." He cannot help but recognize this. Whatever the ultimate effect—whether the transfer strengthens the individual's self-conception as "criminal," thereby neutralizing rehabilitative efforts, or whether the fact of imprisonment brings home the notion of societal intolerance of his conduct, leading him to see his ultimate fate unless he modifies his behavior—there is little doubt that transfer has a psychological impact. It is not merely physical custody that has changed, it is not solely the substitution of cell for room, but it is a major change of status, of role, and of self-definition.

I believe must, charge him with one or more of the crimes obliquely referred to in the school's report and noted by the majority. The final decision must then await the regular judicial outcome of that process. That is the only process that can be termed *due process* in this situation.

I would declare section 218.91 of Code, 1966 unconstitutional, grant the writ, and remand the case to the district court for constitutional disposition.

MASON and RAWLINGS, JJ., join in this dissent.

TRANSFER OF JUVENILES TO ADULT CORRECTIONAL INSTITUTIONS[e]

Note, 1966 Wisconsin Law Review 866, 900-05, 912

C. Procedural Due Process in the Exercise of the Transfer Power

As a general rule, a person who is affected by administrative action has a right to a hearing on any facts determinative of the application of the governmental action to him:

> [A] party who has a sufficient interest or right at stake in a determination of governmental action should be entitled to an opportunity to know and to meet, with the weapons of rebuttal evidence, cross-examination, and argument, unfavorable evidence of adjudicative facts, except in the rare circumstance when some other interest . . . justifies an overriding of the interest in fair hearing.[103]

The United States Supreme Court has recently emphasized—in the context of the relationship between the juvenile system and the adult criminal system—the importance of the hearing requirement by holding that a juvenile court of the District of Columbia was required to hold a hearing prior to waiving jurisdiction over a juvenile.[104] While the question presented was one of statutory interpretation, it is almost certain that constitutional factors loomed large in the Court's thinking.

Two factors, however, qualify the conclusion that the transferred juvenile has a right, grounded in procedural due process, to a hearing. First is the emphasis placed by the courts on the

[e] This note focuses on the Wisconsin juvenile correctional program but the excerpts speak to some problems of general interest. It was the result of work done by students in the University of Wisconsin Law School Correctional Internship Program, sponsored by the National Council on Legal Clinics (now Council on Legal Education for Professional Responsibility).

[103] DAVIS, ADMINISTRATIVE LAW TEXT § 7.02 (1959).

[104] Kent v. United States, 383 U.S. 541 (1966).

importance of flexibility in the internal operations of correctional systems and the consequent reluctance to interfere. Whether this will affect judicial attitudes toward the transfer process might turn on what is seen as the principal benefit derived from that flexibility. In the adult correctional system, the need for maintaining internal discipline is considered a strong argument against judicial intervention in internal correctional affairs: "Lax control . . . will inevitably lead to . . . mutiny as to endanger the lives of the prison officers and the maintenance of our prison system."[105] But the need for strict internal control of institutionalized juveniles might be seen as less important; thus the courts might be more willing to deprive the system of flexibility in order to vindicate traditional procedural rights. But on the other hand, the need for institutional "treatment" may be seen as the most important rationale for maintaining internal flexibility. If this is the case, the heavier emphasis on formal treatment in the juvenile correctional system might suggest that the courts be even more reluctant to interfere with the internal operations of the juvenile system than they have been with the adult system.

Second is the problem posed by the doctrine that "a party is not entitled to a hearing when only a 'privilege' is involved, as distinguished from a 'right' or a 'legal right.' "[106] The juvenile facilities may be considered as a privilege and a child held to have no right to a hearing regarding denial of his access to them. It seems possible, however, that, under some circumstances at least, a juvenile has a substantive right to be institutionalized in juvenile facilities; if this is true, the privilege rationale is inapplicable. Moreover, the privilege exception is itself open to severe questioning; even if an individual has no right to demand that government take certain action, once a state does act, an individual may have an independent right to have that action taken in a nondiscriminatory manner.

If it is agreed that due process does provide some sort of procedural limitations on the exercise of the transfer power, the choice seems to be essentially between trusting the administrative organization to establish a procedure that will comply with the requirements imposed and interjecting a judicial hearing into the transfer procedure.

In evaluating this, attention should be paid to the extent to which the administrative process provides an opportunity for the

---

[105] O'Brien v. Olson, 42 Cal. App. 2d 449, 459, 109 P.2d 8, 15 (3d Dist. 1941).

[106] DAVIS, ADMINISTRATIVE LAW TEXT § 7.11 (1959); see also Kadish, *Legal Norms and Discretion in the Police and Sentencing Process*, 75 HARV. L. REV. 904, 919-25 (1962), where the assertion that a convicted offender has no "rights" in relation to individualized treatment is discussed and rejected.

juvenile or his parents to be heard and present evidence, the degree to which the formal procedure becomes, in practice, a pro forma routine, and the pressures on the department to use transfer for whatever purposes are deemed substantively improper.

If the existing procedure is deemed inadequate to comply with the due process requirements—or if it is considered wise to establish additional safeguards against abuse of the authority—judicial supervision of the transfer decision might be imposed. This might be done in two ways: an appeal from the departmental decision to transfer might be permitted, or judicial authorization for each transfer might be required.

The first has the disadvantage of selectivity. Juvenile proceedings are characterized by a lack of legal representation and appeals. Thus an appeal procedure would present to supervising courts only those cases where the parties had the awareness, initiative, and financial support to start a judicial proceeding. Adequate supervision, however, requires that those supervising have access to a fair representation of the cases decided at the administrative level.

The second could, of course, be constructed so as to require judicial review of each transfer. Perhaps the greatest problem with this approach is the questionable effectiveness of the judicial hearing. Experience in other areas of criminal law has suggested that judicial review of administrative decisions serves little useful purpose and quickly becomes a mere formality. This could well occur with a judicial hearing in a transfer situation. In almost every situation, the department could make a reasonable argument that transfer was justified, even if the subjective reason for making the transfer was "impermissible." In many cases, it is doubtful whether the child, even if represented by counsel, would have the factual knowledge to convincingly make the opposite argument. If the hearing did in fact become a mere pro forma approval of the department's decision to transfer, it would, of course, be of little value.

Moreover, requiring a formal justification of the decision might adversely affect the ability of the parole agents and institutional caseworkers to fulfill their primary role of rehabilitative supervision. If, in each case, the worker was required to establish by some sort of "proof" the accuracy of his recommendation, his general orientation might become that of a "detective" rather than a "treatment oriented" caseworker. This might jeopardize the ability of the entire system to achieve its corrective goals.

Wholly aside from any value in preserving the substantive rights of a transferred juvenile, a judicial hearing might have a far different beneficial effect. Transfer has—and is intended to have—a definite psychological impact, hopefully that of impressing on the juvenile society's intolerance of his conduct. But the informal procedure of the administrative process is perhaps ill designed to communicate this purpose to the child. If, in a judicial hearing, somewhat more formality were observed, the purpose of the transfer might be more clearly communicated to the juvenile and more firmly impressed on his mind. Thus a judicial hearing might reinforce the rehabilitative objectives of transfer.

If a judicial hearing is deemed unnecessary and unwise, alternative steps might nevertheless be taken to improve the administrative process through which transfer is administered. Perhaps the most pressing need is the formulation of criteria on which transfers are to be made and the presentation of these for public evaluation. This might be accomplished in two ways. First, legislative action might be taken to establish guidelines and the administrative process left to implement them. Or, the administrative organization might be given autonomy to develop its own criteria. This would require establishing definitely the validity of the substantive power and expressly granting discretion in its implementation. An express grant of discretion to administrative agencies in the formulation of policy might well encourage responsible policy decisions and the development of procedures realistically designed to carry them out.

> [T]he reality of current juvenile . . . . justice administration is that those involved in administration must devise for themselves higher standards of due process, articulate those standards, defend them, constantly re-evaluate them, and change them when change is needed. A self-imposed, administrative due process is essential. The alternative is judicial control of day-to-day administrative decisions, a loss of administrative flexibility and an impairment in the effectiveness of juvenile justice programs.[116]

[Proposed Statute]

A judicial hearing requirement could be interjected into the Wisconsin transfer procedure by inserting the following provision at the end of the present section 48.52:

> (3) Use of penal institutions. (a) In addition to the [juvenile] facilities and services, the department may also use

[116] Remington, *Due Process in Juvenile Proceedings,* 11 WAYNE L. REV. 688, 696 (1965).

penal institutions for children who have been declared delinquent. No child in the custody of the department pursuant to a juvenile commitment shall be placed in such a penal institution except pursuant to an order issued by a juvenile court in accordance with this subsection.

(b) The juvenile court which transferred custody of the child to the department shall have exclusive jurisdiction over an application by the department for an order permitting transfer of the child to a penal institution.

(c) The juvenile court shall not issue an order permitting the child to be placed by the department in a penal institution unless the juvenile court finds, after a hearing, that such placement in a penal institution would be in the child's best interests. In making such a determination, the juvenile court shall consider only whether such placement in a penal institution would be more effective in restoring the individual child to a useful life in the community than would placement in [juvenile] facilities and services.

(d) The finding and order described in sub. (3) (c) shall not be made unless the child has been given a reasonable opportunity to demonstrate that he is capable of benefiting from the [juvenile] facilities and services.

(e) The hearing provided for in sub. (3) (b) shall be preceded by reasonable notice to the child and his parents, guardian, or legal custodian. The hearing shall be conducted in accordance with the procedures provided for [hearings in the juvenile court].

(f) No child shall be placed in a penal institution unless he is sixteen years of age or older.

(g) No child shall be placed in a penal institution unless he has been found, either at the time when the juvenile court took jurisdiction or at the time of the hearing provided for in sub. (3) (a), to have committed an act which, if committed by an adult, would constitute a felony.

3. Release from Institutional Care

a. Modification by Court

IN RE GAULT: UNDERSTANDING THE ATTORNEY'S NEW ROLE

Comment, 12 Villanova Law Review 803, 836-37 (1967)†

There also exists [in Pennsylvania] the right of the child, parents, or next friend to request either modification or revocation of the disposition on the belief that a change of circumstances has necessitated a change in the court's order.[f] If this request is denied, an appeal can still be taken to the superior court.

The problem with the modification and revocation procedures lies in the requirement that there be a change in circumstances. In the case of a child who has been committed to an institution, information must be obtained concerning his progress, and this is entirely within the domain of the superintendent and board of managers of the institution. As a matter of practice, state institutions and many private institutions submit progress reports to the committing court every six months, or more frequently upon request by the court, but this, unfortunately, is not always the case. Similarly, the superintendent and board of managers of the various institutions determine when a child is ready to be released, and, subject to the approval of the committing judge, set the terms of such release. When the child has been paroled, or is on probation, the probation officer is required to report the child's conduct and progress to the court on a periodic basis, and observations of the dispositional proceedings indicate that such reports are generally requested by the judge every six months.

A change in circumstances will not depend solely on the child's progress. It must be remembered that the parent's attitude and ability to provide the proper environment will also have to be known, thereby requiring the institutional authorities and probation officers to determine the attitudes of the family before the child is released or his probation terminated. The judges interviewed stated that if progress in the child's rehabilitation or the capabilities of the parents to provide for and supervise the child can be demonstrated, they would be quite willing to modify or revoke their orders, and the Juvenile Division of the Community Legal Services Office of Philadelphia felt that this approach served two beneficial ends, for it softens the impact of the disposition by presenting the possibility of alteration of the order,

---

[f] Jurisdiction of the juvenile court to revoke or modify a commitment is usually not available in the case of commitment to a state correctional authority. See discussion at 1084, *supra*.

and serves as an immediate incentive for the child and parents to exhibit the necessary progress required for modification or revocation of the final order.

The right to have a final order of the juvenile court modified or revoked is extremely important, and the reporting of information reflecting the child's progress should not be left to the discretion of the superintendent or board of managers where the child has been institutionalized. The duty to supply periodic reports should be made mandatory by the Juvenile Court Act to insure the availability of current information on the child's progress. Recognizing the heavy burden of the juvenile court, it is felt that the reports should be submitted to the parents or other persons having a legitimate interest in the child, including the child's attorney, so that those parties may petition for modification or revocation, and thereby better protect the future well being of the child.

b. Release on Aftercare and Revocation

THE PRESIDENT'S COMMISSION ON LAW ENFORCEMENT AND ADMINISTRATION OF JUSTICE TASK FORCE REPORT: CORRECTIONS 149-50 (1967)

Juvenile Aftercare

Juvenile aftercare is defined as the release of a child from an institution at the time when he can best benefit from release and from life in the community under the supervision of a counselor. Use of the term "aftercare" rather than "parole," though not yet fully accepted even within the field of juvenile correction, has been encouraged by persons interested in social service in order to separate juvenile programs from the legalistic language and concepts of adult parole. The concept of aftercare has wider acceptance than the term, but the survey of aftercare programs in the United States today reveals wide variations in structure and program content.

Aftercare service for juveniles first appeared in the United States in the early 19th century, but it has become an integral part of correctional rehabilitation for the young offender only in the past decade. In most States, aftercare is the least developed aspect of correction; in the opinion of many observers, it is less adequate than its counterpart, adult parole.

Aftercare originated in New York and Pennsylvania, where houses of refuge indentured child inmates to work in private homes for several years. The child's daily regimen rarely included anything but work. Total responsibility for the child was vested in the family that undertook to feed and clothe him, and it was the family that determined when he had earned his freedom. This form of postinstitutional treatment persisted for over half a century.

The Rationale of Aftercare

When the behavior of a juvenile becomes sufficiently antisocial to warrant confining him in an institution, a complex array of correctional services is set in motion. Part of it deals with the planning and operation of a program that will help him when he leaves the institution.

In the United States, children and youth from 8 to 21 years of age are committed to juvenile training schools. On any one day, the total population of these schools is about 42,000. Because of the wide range of age and experience, differing placement plans are essential. Preadolescent children need programs different in content and philosophy from those needed by young adults, who may have been in the labor force before confinement. To meet such varied needs, aftercare programs must be flexible and creative, rather than routine and superficial as they are in parts of this country today.

The rationale for aftercare is simple. Each juvenile must have a carefully planned, expertly executed, and highly individualized program if he is to return to life outside the institution and play a constructive role there. Successful reentry into society is often made difficult both by the effects of institutional life on a juvenile and by the attitudes of the community to which he returns. The aftercare plan for him must take both these factors into account.

Institutionalization does different things to different children. Some become more antisocial and more sophisticated in delinquency than they were when they entered the training school. Others become dependent on the institution and must learn how to break the ties gradually.

Community settings also differ widely. Some juveniles go back to the very conditions in which their previous delinquency was rooted. Most must face the possibility of the stigma attached to confinement in a correctional institution.

Aftercare is traditionally described as the last point on the juvenile correctional continuum. Yet, because it is in some respects the last opportunity to achieve the correctional objective, planning for aftercare must be an integral part of institutional programs. Indeed, it should begin immediately after commitment to an institution.

A good aftercare plan uses many resources inside and outside the institution. Since implementation of the plan takes place within the community, the aftercare counselor should use a variety of community resources to make the juvenile's reentry meaningful and productive. He should be working with all details of the case related to the ward's community even during the period of confinement in the State institution, forestry camp, or other setting attached to the training school.

It has taken this Nation a long time to recognize the importance of aftercare services for young people leaving correctional institutions, forestry camps, or halfway houses. Few well-developed aftercare programs were in existence 15 years ago. Some States have not yet initiated organizationally sound programs. On the other hand, a few have developed programs which stand out as models for those emerging elsewhere.

INSTITUTIONS SERVING DELINQUENT CHILDREN

U.S. Department of Health, Education & Welfare
Children's Bureau Publication #360, at 111-12 (1957)

Return to the Community

Preparation for Placement

Without adequate preparation for placement the sudden restoration of freedom, which the youth may still be ill-equipped to handle, may lead him into new difficulties. If a youngster is to return to his own family, he must be ready to cope with changes in family structure, relationships, or attitudes that may have taken place in his absence. It may be that he will have to face the fact of no change in an undesirable situation. Similarly, the family must be made ready to receive the youth by intensive work with them throughout the youngster's stay in the school.

For some youngsters, a program of placement in foster family homes will be required; for the adolescent, some other type of group care in the community may offer an even better solution. Placement in a foster home or in a group home also involves detailed preparation. Students returning to school need assistance in anticipating the problems of readjusting to the community schools; just as the community schools must be ready to receive and work with them. Those who will seek jobs need specific aid in assessing their abilities and aptitudes and preparing for job seeking. Possible employer reactions to a training school enrollment must be discussed and various ways of dealing with such attitudes analyzed.

In general, every institution should have a soundly defined preparation program—geared toward preparing individual youths for the transition from the life of the training school to the life of the community—and this should include counseling designed to aid the youth in understanding specifically what placement will mean for him. Aided by all institution personnel, he must realistically anticipate the problems he will face. The placement process is a part of the overall treatment plan and should have continuous consideration throughout his institutional stay. Although emphasis on the placement planning will undoubtedly be stepped up during the final few weeks, the placement process should start with his enrollment, be a part of the reception and orientation procedure, and be considered throughout the youth's stay in the school, rather than be left to the narrowly defined pre-placement period. In fact, one of the important considerations of the admissions conference should be the possibility of a need for foster home placement when the youngster is ready to leave the school.

With the present trend toward having more student participation in and integration into community activities, the transition from institution to placement is not considered as difficult an adjustment as formerly. Nevertheless, a pre-placement orientation program is important and necessary, although it is now believed that such a program can be provided for youngsters while they continue to live in their regularly assigned cottages, and that they need not be transferred to a pre-placement cottage.

A STUDY OF A JUVENILE INSTITUTION (1965)[g]

By Richard E. Hemming

When it comes time for a boy's parole hearing, the board studies the recommendations made by the staff and makes its decision as to whether or not it should release the boy. About the only time a boy will not be released is when he has been uncooperative and not participated in the program. The guideline to rehabilitation seems to be how well the boy has adjusted in the institution. If he has learned to get along well in the institution, it is assumed that he will get along on the outside.

---

[g] For another portion of this paper see 1128, *supra*.

THE CASE OF RICHARD NABER[h]

Wisconsin School for Boys—Wales
Admission Investigation

(confidential)
Naber, Richard Born: 6-28-50 12-11-64
815 Johnson St.
Madison, Wisconsin

Offense: Delinquency Section 48:34
Disposition: SDPW until 21—December 3, 1964—Children's Court —Dane County

Court History

Present Offense: Richard Naber was committed to the State Department of Public Welfare on 12-3-64 for being involved in running away from home habitually, being involved in a theft of a bicycle and theft of merchandise from stores. Richard Naber was involved in several thefts from automobiles and shoplifting in April and May of 1964. He stole such things as cigarettes, fountain pens, sunglasses, and other items from stores in his neighborhood. Also, on May 28, 1964, Richard participated in theft of a bicycle and was also truant from school. Richard has continually been a runaway from home and has frequently asked not to be returned to the home.

Prior Record:

11-11-63. Theft of knives from a showcase, case closed.

5-4-64. Youth requested detention because of home environment, released to the mother on 5-6-64 and agreed to continue living at his present home.

5-8-64. Richard referred for theft from an automobile and shoplifting.

5-28-64. Richard again referred for theft of a bicycle and school truancy.

Family Background

Father: Andrew Naber, age 57, lives on 6th Street in LaCrosse, Wisconsin. Employed as a truck driver for the LaCrosse Stone Company. Richard's father was born in Barron, Wisconsin, the youngest of ten children. He was married to Richard's mother

[h] This is an excerpt from a correctional file of a juvenile in a Wisconsin juvenile institution, edited to disguise identity.

in Crandon by a Catholic priest and the family moved to Madison in 1950. Apparently, Richard's father has not been involved in any law offenses.

Stepfather: Otto Kiel lives at 815 Jackson Street, Madison, Wisconsin and is employed as an inspector at Oscar Meyer Company, Madison. Mr. Kiel was born in Madison on March 17, 1925. He completed two years of high school and has worked at Oscar Meyer for the past fourteen years. He was never married before. He is the youngest boy of nine children. His parents were immigrants from Germany.

Mother: Anna Kiel, 815 Jackson Street, Madison, Wisconsin. Mrs. Kiel was born in Crandon, Wisconsin in 1927, the youngest of six children. Mrs. Kiel was married in 1950 to Richard's father and divorced in 1952. Mrs. Kiel apparently has no record of arrests or law violations.

Wisconsin School for Boys—Wales
Chronological History

Name: Richard Naber WSB: #15438-J S.W.: Dorn

12-4-64. Richard was received at the Reception Center—Wales on this date.

12-29-64. Richard was seen by the Juvenile Review Board on this date. Official Action: Transfer Reception Center to Wisconsin School for Boys. Case to be reviewed in March, 1965.

12-29-64. Treatment recommendations: Clinical follow-up—Dr. Peterson.

2-16-65. Summary: Richard has shown himself to be a very disturbed youngster. Because of his problems and immaturity, some peer difficulties have developed. He has been in constant minor difficulties both in school and in the cottage although nothing serious has developed. He had to be removed from his kitchen assignment earlier in his stay because he was placing feces around the kitchen. He has repeated this behavior in the cottage. His hostility has been expressed almost entirely in this indirect fashion. The boy is hungry for a treatment relationship and is making progress in this area. His personal and family problems are very complex. His father has written him openly rejecting him and his mother is actively going out with men other than her husband. Dickie is very anxious about the home and this has placed considerable pressure on him. His school achievement reflects his need for remedial help.

2-17-65. Richard's case was brought before the Program Review Committee on this date. Negative for March, release end of school semester.

3-1-65. At this point he is able to express his hostility towards his parents much more directly and there has been an absence of misbehavior. He tells me that he recently received a letter from his father in LaCrosse stating that the father would not accept him for placement because he was too much of a "problem." The field agent informs us, however, that the father is receptive to taking the youngster. The mother, who lives in Madison, is having problems in her present marriage. Dick has noted that she is stepping out on his stepfather with a former employer. Needless to say, he is disturbed about the family and is quite angry at the parents. Because of the quality and magnitude of this youngster's problems, as well as his marginal institution adjustment, we are asking that his parole be deferred at this point. He does relate well, however, and has potential for rehabilitation. His eventual placement will have to be determined at a later date. He is not receptive to a foster home. He will have to be continued in a full time academic remedial program.

4-10-65. Richard was seen by the Juvenile Review Board on this date. Official Action: Retain in WSB. Case to again be reviewed in May 1965. Comments: Dick is 14 years of age and is in grade 7A. He continues in therapy with Dr. Peterson and we feel that an additional period of time will be required. He states that upon release he would like to go into a foster home and it would seem that this is a must in this case. This case will again be reviewed in May 1965 and hopefully a foster home placement can be worked out by the end of the school semester.

4-12-65. Family problems continue to be the source of difficulty in this case as Dick has somewhat stabilized in the institution setting. He is now accepting of a foster home although his mother indicated to me that he would be "a hell of a lot better off in my home." She is filing for divorce which in her opinion is enough reason for Dick to try living with her. Yet, in most respects, she is quite rejecting of Dick. As indicated, things have stabilized in the institution. His grades include D in Elementary Drawing, D in Social Studies, D in Printing, C in Reading, C in Phy Ed, C– in Remedial Arithmetic (it should be noted that his conduct and attitude went from an F to an A in this class), C– in Crafts, D+ in Remedial Language.

4-14-65. Richard's case was brought before the Program Review Committee on this date. Positive for May.

5-5-65. This youth will be 15 years of age in June of this year. This is his second Review Board appearance during his first stay at the Boys School. He has continued to make some progress in his program although his conduct record remains somewhat marginal. We are asking that he be released at this point effective the end of the semester. Dick has been caught in between the parents who were divorced a number of years ago. We attempted to encourage him to accept foster placement and at times he seemed accepting but is now requesting a return to the paternal home in LaCrosse. We have interviewed the mother who lives in Madison and her home continues to be replete with problems. She is pregnant and is undergoing a divorce from current husband and is very oppositional to the boy living with the father in LaCrosse. The father has vacillated in taking this youngster but now states he will accept him and the boy is requesting a placement with the father although he recognizes the father's rejection of him. We feel that he will have to try a placement with the father before he will be accepting of foster placement. This youngster is emotionally ill and the prognosis is guarded. He relates well and has a great many dependency needs. A full time academic, remedial program will be necessary in September. He should be encouraged to seek replacement if things do not go well in the paternal home.

5-10-65. Richard was granted a weekend furlough to the home of his mother and stepfather in Madison. He left on Friday, 5-7, and returned on Sunday, 5-9-65.

State Department of Public Welfare
Wisconsin Division of Corrections
Intra-Division Communication

Date: March 30, 1965

To: Regional Administrator—
Western Region

From: Superintendent—WSB
Attn: Mr. John W. Anderson

Case of: Naber, Richard
Subject: Placement

Class and No.: 15438

In our regular contacts with Richard he has been very ambivalent about foster home placement although we have been encouraging him to make this choice. As you can see by the accompanying letter that Richard has written, he would like to explore the possibility of foster home placement in the LaCrosse area where his natural father lives. Dick prefers an urban over a rural placement although he does not foreclose the possibility of a rural placement. In addition he would be accepting of either a group home or individual placement. Although he has significant personal problems stemming from his family, Dick has made steady and very good progress since his admission to the Boy's School. It is our feeling that he has good potential for eventual successful adjustment under parole supervision although he may have difficulties from time to time over the next year or so. He is rather dependent and establishes a relationship very rapidly with those who supervise him. It is our feeling that the natural father in LaCrosse does not really want Richard inasmuch as he told Richard a few weeks ago that he was not anxious to accept Richard because the boy "had problems." The natural mother in Madison is apparently undergoing a separation at this time and this does not seem a good permanent placement unless there is no other alternative. Dick does feel that a trial visit to a foster placement would be helpful between now and the time he sees the May Review Board. We hope you will give this youngster every possible consideration and are anxious to be helpful to you should you require further information on this boy.

State of Wisconsin
Department of Public Welfare
Division of Corrections
Chronological History

Name: Naber, Richard Class & No.: Institution Case, 15438-J

5-5-65. PERSONAL. *Institution Visit:* On this date this agent made the initial personal contact with client, Richard Naber, at WSB. Conversation was light and cheery and dealt mainly with client's pending release and living in LaCrosse with his father and step-mother (Mr. and Mrs. Andrew Naber). Questions from Richard were pointed towards "what would determine his being returned on replacement or as a parole violator?" "What would curfew hours be?" Agent's reply to these questions was in a positive fashion stating this should be the farthest from his mind.

During the entire conversation Richard was somewhat strained or tense and played with a piece of paper the entire time. Richard impressed this agent as wanting to do well in the LaCrosse environment and is looking forward to making his home here. When asked if there was anything I could tell his father and step-mother, Richard said, "Tell them I am happy that I can come and live with them and that I will make every effort to do good." (John W. Anderson)

5-10-65. Richard was seen by the Juvenile Review Board on this date. Official Action: Transfer WSB to Probation and Parole Services. Eligible for release on or after May 28, 1965. Comments: Dick is almost 15 years of age. He is in the seventh grade and apparently is doing rather well in that he is passing all of his subjects. He will go to the home of his father and step-mother in LaCrosse upon release. He can be released at the end of the current school semester which means on or after May 28, 1965.

5-28-65. Richard was released to Probation & Parole Services on this date.

5-28-65. PERSONAL. *Release on Parole:* On this date agent met Richard at the train depot in LaCrosse and transported him to his home. Agent then returned to the home of Richard at approximately 4:00 P.M. to discuss the rules of probation with Mr. and Mrs. Naber and with Richard. (John W. Anderson)

7-6-65. PERSONAL. *Recent Summary:* Since the last recording the client has stopped in the office several times and continues to live with his father at 72 5th Street. Client plans to attend Wilson Junior High School this fall where he will be in Grade 9. On 7-2-65 client submitted his MFR stating that he had opened a bank account at the First National Bank and deposited $2.00. Client's Social Security number is 402-08-9503. Client claims he has a little job cutting his uncle's lawn for which he earns approximately $.75 each time. He further claims that when he has any problems he talks them over with his father. The next appointment was scheduled for 7-13-65. (George Stern)

7-13-65. PERSONAL. Client stopped at the office on this date to inform me that things were going along fine and that he is experiencing no problems. He claims that he is still mowing lawns for a small amount of money weekly and that he plans on enrolling at Washington Junior High School in September. (George Stern)

7-15-65. *Parole Violation—Glue Sniffing:* Richard, his brother Tom, and his parents stopped at the office on this date. The client admitted that he has sniffed glue on two occasions since his return to the LaCrosse area. The other evening his mother found him in bed sniffing glue in a plastic bag. He claims he learned this at WSB—Wales. His stepmother reported that he had a persistent cough since the last episode. I called the family physician (Dr. Swan) and he suggested a physical examination. I informed the parents that I plan on placing Dick in Juvenile Detention until I have had an opportunity to review his case thoroughly and discuss it with Administrator Rogers. (George Stern)

7-16-65. *Supervisory Conference:* Discussed the case with Administrator Rogers and we agreed to continue Richard on parole at this time since the parents desire to return to their home. (George Stern)

7-16-65. Personal. Stopped at the County Jail on this date and signed a release order for Richard. Discussed the situation with him and informed him that another such incidence would result in his return to WSB-Reception Center. Client agreed to toe the line and assured me that there would be no more parole infractions. He was released this A.M. so that he could attend a cousin's wedding. The next appointment was scheduled for 8-2-65. (George Stern)

7-27-65. MFR received from client stating that he was looking for work but he hasn't found any. Dick also indicated that he would like to go to Madison for a weekend to visit sometime during August. (George Stern)

8-2-65. Personal. *Office Visit:* Dick and his brother Tom reported to the office on this date and I held a joint interview with both individuals. Dick states that he and Tom frequently go to the lake swimming and that otherwise they remain primarily around the parental home. Tom informed me that he is going to the maternal home in Madison for a two week visit. Dick requested permission to spend the last weekend of Tom's two week visit also with his mother in Madison. Permission was granted, however, client was instructed to keep me informed as to when he will be leaving and returning. (George Stern)

8-5-65. *Telephone Collateral:* At 11:00 P.M. Dick's stepmother called stating that Dick and Tom left home early this A.M., claiming they were going to South Hills to caddy. However, they have not returned and Mr. and Mrs. Naber believe they went to Madison. I requested that Mr. Naber call me on 8-6-65 if Richard has not returned. (George Stern)

8-6-65. *Telephone Collateral:* Mr. Naber called stating that Dick and Tom have not returned home. He found a letter written earlier by Tom to his mother stating he would soon be back in Madison.

Violation: It appears that Dick has absconded and is in the Madison area, possibly at his mother's home at 815 Jackson Street.

Apprehension Requests: Issued to the local police department with a copy directed to the Regional Administrator Anderson in Madison. (George Stern)

8-6-65. *Telephone—Mr. Naber:* Mr. Naber called stating that the boys had taken $100 from his wife's dresser drawer. He also informed me that his ex-wife called from Madison stating that the boys were at her home.

Telephone—Mrs. Kiel: Client's mother called from Madison stating that Dick and his brother, Tom, were at her home. She inquired as to what she should do. It was decided that she should bring both boys to the LaCrosse Police Department on 8-7-65 and turn them over to the juvenile authorities.

Telephone—LaCrosse Police Department: The Police Department advised as to recent developments. (George Stern)

8-9-65. *Office Collateral:* Mr. and Mrs. Naber stopped at the office expressing concern about the action to be taken concerning Dick's parole violation. The parents informed me that Tom will be referred to Juvenile Court, and that they believe he was the instigator in this case. Mr. Naber commented that things are finally settled between him and his ex-wife. I suggested that the parents talk with juvenile authorities, and visit Dick at the County Jail. I commented that I would do the same and contact them later in the day.

Apprehension Cancellation: Mailed out on the marginal date.

LaCrosse County Guidance Clinic: Reviewed the client's case with the local Guidance Clinic Staff. They informed me that they will initiate action immediately so that counselling with Dick can begin within the next week.

PERSONAL. *County Jail:* Juvenile Officer Prat and I interviewed Dick at the County Jail. Dick claimed he bought a B-B

Gun on 8-5-65, and was afraid since he thought he had violated the "no firearms" parole agreement restriction. He claims that he and Tom then took off for Madison without thinking of the consequences of their behavior. Client overtly manifested anxiety, shaking physically, chewing his fingernails, and changing postural positions frequently.

8-9-65. *Supervisory Conference:* Discussed the case with Administrator Rogers who concurred with my recommendation that parole supervision be continued.

Case Note: I decided to continue Richard on parole supervision because of the few positive factors in his favor at this time. For example, his father and ex-wife have been arguing for several years, verbally belittling each other whenever the boys were with them. Both Dick and his brother, Tom, were emotionally torn between which one to believe, and as to which one they should live with. This has finally been eliminated through counselling with both parents, with the mother relinquishing her interest for the present time. Both parents claim they can see the damage they have been causing. Tom the client's older brother, has finally been adjudged as a delinquent, and will appear in juvenile court. Tom has held Dick's parole status over him in a derogatory manner for the last several months. (George Stern)

8-11-65. *Correspondence:* Letter and confidential information submitted to Doctor George Hanson, Director of the LaCrosse County Guidance Clinic on Richard. (George Stern)

8-19-65. *Office Visit:* Dick stopped at the office for his scheduled appointment on the marginal date. He commented that things are not going so well at home as his parents require him to go to the Methodist Church with them every Sunday. Dick claims he is Catholic, and that this is against his principles. He claims that this has resulted in friction and dissension between himself and his parents. However, Dick claimed that he will discuss the matter with his parents this evening. The next appointment was scheduled for 8-23-65. (George Stern)

8-21-65. *Field:* On the marginal date I saw the client's parents at the Karl-Ray Bowling Alley and they informed me that things are going along fine at home, and that the religious issue has been agreed upon. (George Stern)

8-23-65. PERSONAL. *Office Visit:* Dick stopped at the office on this date and stated that he and his brother had walked to the City

Limits of LaCrosse and back on Friday. He claimed they enjoy doing this just to get away from the LaCrosse area. Apparently this is the second time they have made this jaunt. Dick stated that his parents required him to attend church with them again yesterday, and they continue to refuse to let Tom and him attend the local Catholic Church. A home visit was scheduled for 8-26-65, at 1:30 P.M. (George Stern)

8-30-65. *In Custody—KMBS:* Client was transported from the LaCrosse County Jail to Kettle Moraine Boy's School while awaiting transfer to the Reception Center. (George Stern)

Wisconsin School for Boys
Current Status Report—Parole Violator

NABER, RICHARD
15438-J
9-3-65

Richard, 15, was returned from the paternal home in LaCrosse after three months of field supervision for the first time as a parole violator for involvement in the theft of a 1965 Chevrolet resulting in extensive property damage to that car and 3 others. Richard, mumbling sometimes incomprehensively, apathetically and guardedly transfers some responsibility to his 16-year-old brother who actually operated the stolen car. The youth does admit though that it was his idea to steal the car because "we just got bored of stealing bicycles." Richard may not be boasting when he claims that he stole more than 100 bicycles during his brief period of supervision. The youth also admits that his younger brother stole over $100 from the stepmother and the youth received approximately $50 which was used to finance a brief AWOL. Earlier the youth was involved in glue sniffing.

Richard seems confused about his continuing delinquencies and about his relationship to his father and stepmother. It would seem that he resents the stepmother and his offenses may be testing the father's acceptance. The youth knew he would get into trouble eventually but sees himself as unable to exercise effective control over his own destiny.

This is a disturbed youth who seems to be gaining an increasing awareness of his upset. Although he lacks insight and intelligence he may be a better than average psychotherapy prospect.

Richard Hoffman
Social Worker

Wisconsin School for Boys—Wales
Chronological History

Name: Naber, Richard WSB: #15438-J S.W.: Hoffman

9-7-65. Richard seen by Juvenile Review Board on this date. Official Action: Transfer Reception Center to Wisconsin School for Boys. Case to be reviewed in January 1966.

9-7-65. Treatment Recommendation: Psychotherapy—Dr. Peterson.

VELASQUEZ v. PRATT

443 P.2d 1020 (Utah 1968)

[Another portion of this case appears at 1073, *supra*.]

CROCKETT, Chief Justice. The appellant appears to proceed upon the erroneous premise that on a hearing for violation of probation a person is entitled to the same protections the law affords one newly accused of an offense and before he is found guilty thereof. This court has dealt with the question of revocation of probation, indicating that when a person has been found guilty of an offense and sentenced, he is in quite a different status than he is before conviction. He is deemed to be actually serving the sentence imposed, but under prescribed conditions which he has agreed to comply with. He is certainly not entitled to all of the protections accorded one accused of crime in the first instance. If he could insist on those rights, from the incipient protections relating to arrest, through the presumption of innocence, the right of counsel and trial by jury, the court might as well turn him completely free in the first place and not bother about probation. Such requirement would tend to destroy the system which has proved so useful and beneficial in penology, because judges would be very reluctant to grant probation. This is particularly true in juvenile courts where the court is sort of a substitute parent and the proceedings, as provided by our statutes, are not criminal in nature but are inquiries in the interest of the juvenile.

Notwithstanding what we have just said, it is our opinion that justice requires that a person on probation should not be compelled to live in dread of being recommitted on the whim or caprice of a probation officer, or even of a court. Ordinary principles of fair play demand that he should be advised of the ground upon which revocation of probation is sought, and to have a hearing on whether his probation should be revoked.

The protections just mentioned were afforded in the instant case. The suggestion that Steven and his mother were not aware that the hearing on probation revocation might deprive him of his liberty is hardly worthy of comment. He had previously been in the State Industrial School, and there is no reasonable possibility that they did not know the possible consequences of the hearing.

As to the complaint about not being afforded the right of counsel: The record indicates that in both this and the original proceeding against him Steven and his mother were advised of the right to be represented by an attorney. But they made no indication to the court that they wanted one. We are cognizant and appreciative of the importance of the right to counsel, and to be advised concerning that right. But the courts of this state have never gone so far as to say where one is so advised and gives no indication that he wants an attorney, the court has a duty to persuade him to have one.

Reference Note

For further information on the social investigation report see TRAINING FOR JUVENILE PROBATION OFFICERS (U.S.H.E.W. Children's Bureau Publication #398, 1962); Krasnow, *Social Investigation Reports in the Juvenile Court—Their Uses and Abuses,* 12 CRIME & DELINQUENCY 151 (1966) (proposing guidelines for disclosure of the reports).

A good discussion of the dispositional alternatives in juvenile court is F. RUBIN & J. SMITH, THE FUTURE OF THE JUVENILE COURT: IMPLICATIONS FOR CORRECTIONAL MANPOWER AND TRAINING (Joint Comm'n on Correctional Manpower & Training 1968), particularly chs. VI & VII. *See also* Fradkin, *Disposition Dilemmas of American Juvenile Courts* in JUSTICE FOR THE CHILD 118 (M. Rosenheim ed. 1962).

One area of "disposition" not explored in these materials is that of making no adjudication of delinquency at all. This may be done in various ways—by holding a case open after hearing the evidence, or placing the juvenile on informal probation with eventual dismissal of the petition or by altering the petition to allow a finding of neglect or incorrigibility. *See* Note, *Rights and Rehabilitation in the Juvenile Courts,* 67 COLUM. L. REV. 281 (1967).

PART IV

POLICYMAKING RESPONSIBILITY IN THE ADMINISTRATION OF CRIMINAL JUSTICE

There are a large number of very important public policy issues which become apparent as one looks carefully at the administration of criminal and juvenile justice. The resolution of these issues requires an understanding of the system and of the context in which the issues arise. But it requires also an understanding of what agency has responsibility for making the decision and, if there is more than one agency, how they relate to each other.

Historically it has been assumed that legislatures and courts, particularly appellate courts, have primary responsibility for resolving important policy questions in our society. Administrative agencies, especially in the criminal justice field, have been looked upon as largely ministerial, established to carry out policy decisions made by others. Indeed we have had a commitment to the principle that ours is a "government of laws," which principle has seemed to lead away from broad administrative power. But it has long been apparent that legislatures and courts do not, in fact, confront all or even most of the important public policy issues. Legislatures have acted primarily on issues of widespread public dissatisfaction and courts have acted on those issues which happen to be raised by individuals in litigation. As a consequence a great many issues have been resolved by default, inaction, or drift.

The "urban crisis" has largely changed this. The day has now come when inaction is as likely to be challenged as action and where challenge occurs not only in the legislatures and the courts, but also in the mayor's offices, in the city councils, in the office of the police chief, and in the streets. Mayors, who were formerly aloof from the problems of criminal and juvenile justice, now find that they must be concerned because the life of the city may be at stake. But police, particularly in places such as New York City, may have a long tradition for opposing "political interference" by "city hall."

Even if one concludes that there is need for responsible policymaking by others than the legislatures and courts, it may not be clear which agency is the one. Clearly responsibility for some decisions is shared among police, prosecutor, trial judge, and correctional agency. Often it is uncertain whether their relationship is one of healthy checks and balances or wasteful nullification of each other's efforts. As criminal justice and juvenile justice problems become more significant to the future of urban America, another layer of administrative agency has been added. The mayor and city manager and the city council become concerned. The function of the police chief and his relationship to prosecutor and trial judge and to mayor and city council take on new significance. The policemen as a group may find their collective interest so involved that they begin to assert their collective power to influence policy decisions which affect police work. So great a diffusion of responsibility results that, on the one hand, there may be overlap and conflict and, on the other hand, there may be a failure on the part of any single agency to assume primary responsibility.

The materials which follow are designed to achieve two objectives:

(a) Chapter 18 contains materials designed to afford a basis for considering the general responsibilities of legislature, judiciary, and administrative agencies and some of the limitations upon their capacity to respond to the important public policy issues involved in criminal and juvenile justice administration.

(b) Chapters 19, 20, and 21 are designed to offer an opportunity to consider the agency roles in some specific important, current problems.

Chapter 19 is a case study of the handling of the drunk, a problem of chronic difficulty for the criminal justice system. There has long been dissatisfaction with the "revolving door" treatment of the drunk, but there has been little done in the way of changing the system to deal with him more effectively. Recently, however, there have been legislative proposals, a series of important appellate judicial decisions, and some significant innovative programs conducted at the local level by police and private agencies. These raise for us the question whether change is the responsibility of the legislature, of appellate courts using the Constitution as a basis, or of agencies of local government.

Chapter 20 deals with the use of force by police. This is a most sensitive current issue upon which community dissatisfaction and frustration have come to focus. It has been a traditional issue of academic concern, reflected in most criminal law courses. But the issue was easier in the past when the principal question was law enforcement versus individual criminal. Now the question of the use of force by law enforcement agencies is integral to the consideration of larger social, economic, and political questions. Thus consideration of the use of force by police affords another opportunity to consider where responsibility lies for making the important public policy decisions which are involved.

Chapter 21 deals with an issue of importance in the field of corrections, the question of who has responsibility for making important policy decisions relating to the handling of the dangerous offender, where clinical diagnosis is involved, and how administrative policy should be made.

Chapter 18

THE LEGISLATIVE, JUDICIAL, AND ADMINISTRATIVE RESPONSIBILITY FOR THE MAKING OF CRIMINAL JUSTICE POLICY DECISIONS

In recent decades it was commonly assumed that the legislature had primary responsibility for dealing with important questions of public policy. The legislature is designed to reflect the will of the majority of the electorate. The difficulty is, however, that the legislative response is likely to overlook the interests of the minority and to be little concerned with rights of persons accused of crimes. As a consequence, courts—particularly the United States Supreme Court during the Warren era—have played a dominant and highly controversial role in defining the rights of individuals and minority groups. But decisions of the legislature or of the courts deal with only some of the important issues and even then are not self-executing. As a consequence, there is need to give greater recognition to the importance of administrative implementation of the criminal law.

A. THE LEGISLATIVE RESPONSIBILITY

There are at least two different views as to the role the legislature should play in resolving important public policy issues which arise in criminal and juvenile justice administration.

The first is that public policy ought to be made by the legislature and the results expressed in clearly stated statutes. Considerations of democratic values are said to require this kind of legislative preeminence, since the legislature speaks for the majority in our system of government.[a]

---

[a] S. Kadish, The Principle of Legality (manuscript 1960):

The substantive criminal law, of course, is the basic framework on which the administration of criminal justice rests. Here the plain direction has been to restrict the freedom of judicial discretion in determining the boundaries of criminal conduct and to vest that choice wholly in the hands of the legislature. The ideal system, indeed, the frequently given rationale for the existence of a substantive criminal law, is to minimize the ad hoc determination of what is criminal. This is the point of the rebellion against the common law public mischief

The second view is that it is not realistic to expect a high degree of legislative contribution and that the American system of government does not require the legislature to assume responsibility for resolving many of the important policy issues in the criminal law field. There has been, in this view, a withdrawal of the legislature from the intricacies of modern social and economic problems with the consequence that administrative implementation has become more and more important. It is said that there is no hierarchy, with the legislature at the top, but a sharing of responsibility among the legislative, judicial, and administrative agencies for resolution of value conflict. Even if the legislature theoretically has ultimate responsibility for defining the criminal law and the system to be used in enforcing the law, the real meaning of the law and the real nature of the enforcement mechanism are inevitably settled more by courts and administrators, who operate the system. The legislature is influential in setting outer limits, both by express formulation of standards and by appropriating money, but within those limits other agencies have a great deal to say about the shape of things.

It is generally recognized that there is a limit upon the legislature's ability to deal adequately with a wide variety of important policy issues. But differences exist as to where the emphasis should be placed—whether priority ought to be given, whenever possible, to legislative involvement and legislative formulation of public policy.

POLICE PROCEDURE AND THE ACCUSATORIAL PRINCIPLE

By R. G. Schecter

3 Criminal Law Bulletin 540 (1967)

The delineation of the area of unacceptable police conduct might well be more appropriately the function of the legislature

doctrine and the too loose statement of the impermissible ends of a conspiracy, the peril of ex post facto determinations and the vice of vagueness. Here the value that is dominant is individual *control* over his fate at the hands of the organs of power of the state. A condition of the imposition of the criminal sanction is fair notice that conduct is susceptible to the sanction; the boundaries of criminal conduct are drawn a) in advance of their application, b) with the maximum precision so that the law-abiding need not guess, c) by the legislature, and d) applied in the particular case in accord with the procedural requirements of due process.

There appears to be something of a paradox in the commitment to the ideal of legality in the definition of criminal conduct on the one hand, and, on the other, the large areas of uncontrolled administrative discretion contemplated, or at least permitted, in the administration of criminal justice, a) in the police-prosecutor function of arresting and charging, and b) in the sentencing-correctional function exercised by judges and parole boards.

rather than the courts. Legislatures possess the time and facilities to best discern that conduct in which the police are in fact presently engaged. Moreover, delineation of the limits of such conduct, requiring the more or less arbitrary formulation of a set of specific, elaborate rules serving as clear guidelines for police activity, could best be done all at one time through a single legislative enactment rather than through a case-by-case-piecemeal formulation which is the technique of the judicial process. Concomitantly, however, it must be recognized that the Court has an independent duty to uphold the standards of due process, and that as long as the legislature remains inactive in this area, the courts have an obligation to act to insure the minimum requirements of procedural due process.

THE COURTS AND LAWMAKING

By Charles D. Breitel
in LEGAL INSTITUTIONS TODAY AND TOMORROW 37
(M. Paulsen ed. 1959)

In the first place, the quintessence of the legislative process in a democratic culture is its political character and motivation. The complete management of the general law is incompatible with the political concerns and preoccupations of the legislature. Put another way, with the present institutional structure—and that institutional structure is likely to exist for a long time—complete legislative management of the general law is a practical impossibility.

COMMENT

By Herbert Wechsler
in LEGAL INSTITUTIONS TODAY AND TOMORROW 307-08
(M. Paulsen ed. 1959)

It will be recalled that Justice Breitel, speaking from rich experience, finds the political preoccupations of the legislature inconsistent with any approach to "complete legislative management of the general law." I am not sure how large his emphasis is on the word "complete," but I submit that larger legislative management is necessary and desirable, that, indeed, there is no other way to prevent the anarchical proliferation of a system of case law. It may be that I speak from bias, which I recognize, as one engaged for many years in the attempt to reconstruct a single field of law.

I fully grant the obstacles to larger legislative management, not only in the political factor Justice Breitel has emphasized, but in the even larger question—how the work can possibly be done. Here I submit, as I have often argued elsewhere, is a major opportunity for legal scholarship, a major challenge to the schools. For it is only by unhurried canvassing of all the issues in a field, the systematic rooting out of inconsistencies, the time-consuming search for information that can shape and inform policy, that the entire corpus of a field of law can be evaluated and reframed.

This is not to say, of course, that larger legislative management implies necessarily—or even probably—less call upon the courts or on administrative agencies as creative organs in the application and development of law. I have some fear that such a false antithesis may have been thought to be implicit in some of our earlier discussion.

What is implied for me in larger legislative management is a considered disposition, at the only level that is even theoretically able to regard the legal system as a whole, of what it is desirable to attempt to settle by a legislative rule—of greater or of lesser specificity; what must be left to standards that will gain their largest content in the course of their interpretation and their application; what ought to be committed to the outright discretion of the courts or other organs of administration; and lastly but not least important, what should be left to "private ordering," to use a concept that Professor Hart has stressed, that is to the initiative and decision of individuals and groups sustained by law but not directed by it.

COMMENT
By E. P. Case
in LEGAL INSTITUTIONS TODAY AND TOMORROW 94
(M. Paulsen ed. 1959)

[W]hile I am a cultist for the legislature, having been in the thick of legislative matters for quite a while, I also see its limitations, both in fact and potentially. I do not want to have legislators charged with more than they can do. Legislators from the beginning of time have been the butt of cartoonists and caricaturists, and I want to add nothing to the fuel they already have by admitting a failure to meet expectations when the expectations are overoptimistic and unreasonable. Legislators can explore, on a long-range basis, and inform public opinion and can define the framework in which policy—long-range policy—must be carried out, but they cannot fix policies.

What, then, is the corrective? In my judgment, it lies in the assumption of greater responsibility by the legislature. Enabling acts are written in language that is far too broad and general.

Far from defining public policy with regard to the regulated industries, for example, they are content merely to state that it is public policy to regulate them—and no more. Reexamination and revisions of the acts, in accordance with the shifting context in which they are supposed to be operable, are too infrequent and, again, insufficiently specific. No one expects that Congress can ever take over the task of framing all of the rules and regulations that are necessary to give force to the parent statutes. But Congress can and should spell out national policy and not just hint at and suggest it.

CODIFICATION AND JUDGE-MADE LAW: A PROBLEM OF COEXISTENCE

By Leslie Scarman

42 Indiana Law Journal 355, 366-67 (1967)

I have elsewhere developed my reasons for believing that, great as has been the contribution of judicial decision to the development of our law, it can no longer carry the load. Furthermore, I suggest, it is really a perversion of the judge's function in society that he should be requested to do so; his task is to decide particular cases, not to make but to apply the law. Some of the difficulties of judge-made law have recently been described by Lord Devlin in the address to which I have already referred.

> The trouble about judicial law reform was never, as it is with Parliament, lack of time but lack of opportunity—that and the multiplication of courts of appeal. When Lord Mansfield laid down the law, new law was created more or less from the moment he said it. But since his time the delay before a point of principle reaches the House of Lords may be so long as to out-distance by ten times or more the parliamentary process.[22]

Then again he pointed out that the judge's opportunity to make law depends upon a litigant, and

> without a litigant the process cannot start and adventurous litigants with an enthusiasm for law reform are not easily come by.

I would add a further objection. Judge-made law is law made by lawyers. In the complex, wide-ranging social structure which

[22] Devlin [A Code of English Law?, Address at Hull University, Feb. 25, 1966] at 13.

constitutes the community of today, are we really prepared to allow the development of our law to be in the hands of one profession, supplemented spasmodically by limited incursions into the field of law reform on those rare occasions when Parliament is frightened, persuaded, cajoled, or deceived into finding time for a subject so electorally unappealing?

If it be right that a modern legal system can no longer rely upon our traditional methods of legal development, codification becomes urgent, practical politics. What are, in truth, its benefits?

You may think that I have been unable to prevent them from obtruding themselves into my analysis of what it is. Very briefly, I see them to be:

(1) The codifying process gives society the opportunity to simplify and modernize the law. In *Lady Windemere's Fan* Lord Augustus said, "to be intelligible is to be found out." Even that is an advantage in the development of the law: error, once recognized, can be corrected.

(2) It enables the development of the law to be planned —to move to a design acceptable to contemporary society.

(3) It can provide, if well done, a compact, accessible, and complete formulation of the law.

(4) It can be subjected to continuous review and revision: its anomalies need not await the necessarily haphazard opportunities of judicial correction.

(5) Through Parliament and the Law Commission, it involves the whole community in the process of legal development.

THE PROCESS OF PENAL LAW REFORM— A LOOK AT THE PROPOSED MICHIGAN REVISED CRIMINAL CODE

By Jerold H. Israel

14 Wayne Law Review 772, 813-16 (1968)

Restricting Overbreadth. Just as the Committee found it necessary to broaden some provisions in order to plug loopholes, it also found it necessary to restrict others in order to prevent potentially pernicious and unnecessary "overbreadth." A statute was viewed as overbroad only when its coverage encompassed activities substantially beyond that which it was designed to punish. In most instances, the overbreadth stemmed from the literal application of the statute to conduct widely recognized by society as morally innocent. Of course, statutes so broadly drafted are rarely enforced to the fullest extent. But this factor neither renders them harmless nor justifies their retention. The appropriate restraint shown by prosecutors generally cannot be attributed to all prosecutors under all circumstances; and, even if it could, leaving such a basic determination as to the scope of the penal law entirely in the prosecutor's discretion is fundamentally inconsistent with the basic premises of codification.[225] Moreover, the very presence of such broadsweeping provisions on the statute books may in itself place a needless burden on local police. The police ordinarily have no desire to enforce such provisions to the letter of the law. They are fully aware, for example, that most of the public accept the friendly poker game at the local Elks Club and that a midnight raid will hardly enhance their working relationship with the community. Yet, they cannot readily undermine their image as the agency reponsible "only for enforcing the law, not judging it." This image imposes a continuing pressure for full enforcement that makes it difficult for the police to simply refuse to respond when such clearly illegal action is called to their attention by an insistent complainant. Thus, the Proposed Code's elimination of unnecessary overbreadth should serve both to promote more equal enforcement of the law and to facilitate more efficient police administration.

Much of the overbreadth in current provisions results from technical defects in legislative drafting. For example, the prohibition against "fortune telling for gain" fails to exclude fortune telling performed as part of a theatre or nightclub act. The

225 This is not to suggest that administrative discretion will not play a large part in limiting the Proposed Code's provisions to their proper function. A code that encompasses only such cases as we intend to make criminal, and clearly excludes all others, is beyond the skill of legislative draftsmen. . . . However, it is one thing to seek a fair degree of precision in statutory definitions and rely on administrative discretion to round off the rough edges, and quite another to assign the basic task of draftsmanship itself to administrative discretion. See generally LaFave, Penal Code Revision: Considering the Problems and Practices of the Police, 45 Texas L. Rev. 434 (1967). The Committee did not attempt to draw lines too finely. It is often possible to visualize some hypothetical situation that might technically violate a code provision, yet would not generally be viewed as involving a criminal act. Yet where 99% of the cases covered by a provision are likely to be appropriate situations for imposing penal sanctions and 1% are not, it is usually best to cover the entire area, leaving the 1% to the common sense of police and prosecutors in fashioning enforcement policy, rather than attempt to carve that 1% out of the statutory framework. What the Committee was concerned with in the area of overbreadth was statutes that covered large areas that clearly were not appropriate for penal sanctions and could easily be excluded from the statutory coverage.

statute making it a crime for a citizen to refuse a police request for assistance in apprehending a fugitive fails to except the person who, because of a weak heart or other circumstances, is clearly justified in refusing the request. And the statute providing for the registration of found property fails to separate clearly its requirements from those minimum steps needed to exempt from criminal liability a finder who eventually converts the found property to his own use. Defects such as these were easily remedied through the adoption of comparatively minor statutory changes.

The possible overbreadth in other provisions, however, raised far more difficult issues and often required a careful reconsideration of the basic objective of each provision. The current provision on indecent exposure is so broadly stated that it has been applied to members of a secluded nudist colony. Obviously, this goes beyond the basic statutory objective. A nudist camp is hardly a public place nor are the people there likely to be affronted by nudity. But should the statute even apply in every instance where these factors are present? Should it apply, for example, to a drunk who attempts to urinate in a well-lighted alley knowing that pedestrians might walk by at any moment? The Committee concluded that in most instances it should not. The statute should emphasize mens rea as well as the disturbance of others, and primary application should be in the case of true exhibitionism. Accordingly, the Proposed Code limits indecent exposure to the public exposure of genitals with the intent to arouse or gratify sexual desire. Some question has been raised concerning the prosecutor's ability to show such mens rea, but the Committee was informed that this is an easy enough task in the case of the repeating offender, and that is primarily where the statute is employed.

Significant limitations upon statutory overbreadth are also suggested in the area of gambling offenses. Present provisions absolutely prohibit all gambling. While there was considerable dispute as to whether anti-gambling provisions were properly aimed at such events as church-sponsored bingo, it was generally agreed that such statutes clearly were not aimed at true social gambling, *i.e.,* unsponsored gambling for which there is no direct or indirect charge. The literal application of current provisions to such gambling only serves to hinder proper enforcement of the gambling statutes. Accordingly, the Proposed Code, following the pattern of the Model Anti-Gambling Act, specifically excludes "social games of chance" in which each participant competes on equal terms.

THE PRESIDENT'S COMMISSION ON LAW ENFORCEMENT AND ADMINISTRATION OF JUSTICE TASK FORCE REPORT: CORRECTIONS 82-83 (1967)

There is . . . need to develop means for guiding and controlling the numerous important decisions which must be made following the imposition of sentence: decisions by correctional authorities regarding the treatment of offenders during imprisonment, the date and conditions of release from imprisonment, and the revocation of parole; and decisions by judges regarding the revocation of probation or a suspended sentence.

Legislation ordinarily provides little guidance for these correctional decisions. Correctional administrators have been slow to develop policies and procedures to guide correctional officials and protect the rights of offenders. And trial and appellate courts have been reluctant to review either the merits of such decisions or the procedures by which they are made.

Yet it is inconsistent with our whole system of government to grant such uncontrolled power to any officials, particularly over the lives of persons. The fact that a person has been convicted of a crime should not mean that he has forfeited all rights to demand that he be fairly treated by officials.

THE PRESIDENT'S COMMISSION ON LAW ENFORCEMENT AND ADMINISTRATION OF JUSTICE TASK FORCE REPORT: THE POLICE 34 (1967)

It would be helpful to have systematic legislative inquiry into important police practices at the local, state, and federal level. If devoted to an effort to learn what the existing practices are and to give the police an inducement to articulate their policies and a forum for explaining and justifying them, the process of legislative inquiry can have a positive impact upon the long-range development of the police as a responsible policymaking agency. To achieve this objective, the short run price which police would have to pay in criticism and controversy would be well worth it.

Reliance upon legislative inquiry to give visibility to important criminal and juvenile justice issues would increase public understanding and hopefully increase support for changes which ought to be made. One major limitation in the past has been that police agencies themselves have often been excluded from discussion of important criminal and juvenile justice issues and thus have not been much affected by legislative inquiry or even by legislative action. For example, when the State of Illinois revised its Code of Criminal Procedure a few years ago, the Chicago Police Department had to make a special request to get a copy of the proposed code which had been widely circulated to lawyers and public officials. The department was able to get only a single copy and that not until a very few days before the scheduled legislative hearing on the bill.

B. THE JUDICIARY'S RESPONSIBILITY

JUDICIAL ACTIVISM, NONJUDICIAL PASSIVISM, AND LAW REFORM

By Phil C. Neal

49 Chicago Bar Record 240, 241-44 (1967)

I wish merely to make the objective observation that the Court has become the most conspicuous source of legal change in the country. This in a way is more revolutionary than any of the specific changes in the law that have resulted from the Court's decisions, great as some of them have been. We had the earlier, long-standing image of the Supreme Court as essentially a resistant force, using constitutional doctrine and grudging statutory interpretation to slow the pace of legal change. This was followed, after the turnabout of the mid-thirties, by a permissive Court, a Court that exercised self-restraint in deference to the superior lawmaking credentials of Congress and the state legislatures.

But in the Warren period we have seen a still further shift, the emergence of a Court that is itself an architect of change. In one area of law after another, the Court has led and the country has followed.

The change is reflected, of course, in the cliché that describes the Warren Court as "activist." It is reflected in the attitude of sizable segments of the population that look to the Court as a champion and expect it to bring the Nation's laws into closer conformity with democratic and egalitarian values. It is reflected also, I think, in the Court's view of itself—in its ways of speaking and its practices. One symptom of this is the growing number of opinions that read more like a statute than a decision, and that purport to lay down detailed rules or guidelines for the future—even to the point of specifying cut-off dates for the application of its new commands. Another is the Court's greater hospitality to issues that transcend the narrow interests of specific litigants, a tendency reflected in the weakening of barriers such as the requirement of standing and the doctrine of political questions. Another manifestation of the same tendency is the Court's increased receptiveness to *amicus curiae* participation. In these and other ways the Court's work has taken on a stronger legislative cast than it has ever had before.

There is not much need to document this view of the Court as a reforming institution. Major areas in which it has accelerated the pace of legal change are familiar. The obvious and dramatic ones are segregation, reapportionment, and state criminal procedure. But there are hosts of other examples, both constitutional and statutory, that will come readily to mind. From my own field I would cite the rapid conversion of the antitrust laws into a set of rigid *per se* doctrines, especially but not exclusively in the field of mergers. The Court has even moved strongly into the field of private and common law, as in its new doctrines in the law of defamation. It has now given the signal for sweeping changes in the procedures and indeed the whole philosophy of juvenile courts. There are intimations that in the field of criminal procedure it may move on from problems of self-incrimination and right to counsel to imposing constitutional requirements of pretrial discovery. The expanding concept of state action has become a quite open-ended warrant for intervention in new areas of the law previously left to the states, as in the Court's recent decision forbidding California to repeal its fair-housing law by a constitutional referendum (one-man, one-vote notwithstanding).

The fact that so much initiative in legal change has passed to the Supreme Court is in a sense paradoxical because it has occurred at a time when judicial lawmaking in general is very much in eclipse. It has been obvious for a long time that the creative era of the common law is a thing of the past and that legislation has become the dominant form of law. The steady trend toward ascendancy of statute law over judge-made law has not abated. The explanation of the paradox, of course, lies in the fact that the Federal Constitution is the principal remaining source of judicial power to make new law. We have had a Supreme Court that has exercised that power in a bold fashion.

There are some obvious reasons for doubting that a system is ideal when it leaves heavy responsibility for initiating legal development in a court whose chief power comes from having the last word on what the Constitution means. Heavy involvement of the Court in great political problems is only one of the dangers. Another is the irrevocability of changes that are made under the auspices of the Constitution. In the face of the rapid development of constitutional doctrine, efforts like that of the American Law Institute and the American Bar Association to deal painstakingly with the problem of criminal procedure, and of Congress to lay down standards for legislative apportionment, have more than the irony of locking the barn door after the horse is gone; the problem is how to re-open the barn.

I suggest that the current position of the Supreme Court is among other things a reflection of an older problem and an older defect in our legal machinery.

There are different ways of viewing the Court's recent behavior. It is possible to think of the Court as a group of adventurous knights charging off to discover new causes and do battle. Another and more charitable view is that the Court has felt itself responsible for overcoming some of the lag in the response of our law to new pressures and conditions, compensating for the inertia of other agencies in the system. I have little doubt that the Court has often seen itself in the latter role, and has believed it was assuming initiatives forced upon it by the default of others. That clearly has been its position on the great problems of school segregation and reapportionment. The wide acceptance of *Gideon v. Wainwright,* for example, suggests that the bar was merely waiting to be formally advised of a responsibility that it had come instinctively to recognize in the many years since the Court had taken the first steps toward implementing the right of counsel in criminal cases.

The new position of the Supreme Court emphasizes the need for some renewed attention to the efficiency of our arrangements for legal development. Where else besides the Constitution and the Supreme Court should we look for constant and vigorous attention to the whole spectrum of issues of law reform? The issues that the Court can lay its hands on are of course only part of the problem, and a tiny fragment at that. If there is lag in our response on problems of the kind the Supreme Court has been considering, what of the vast areas of the law that get little public notice, that have little political appeal, and that find no special interest groups to urge their reform?

. . .

Much has been done, to be sure, by groups such as the American Law Institute, the Commissioners on Uniform State Laws, committees of national and local bar associations, rules committees, and innumerable special committees and commissions created from time to time by the legislatures and the executive branches of state and local governments. The law schools, too, have made their contribution. But most of such work is *ad hoc* and sporadic. Often it is directed to problems that have already become urgent by the time they are given attention. Much of it focuses on a few selected areas that seem appropriate for a major project. Our law reform machinery works in a jerky and uneven way. It also works for the most part with casual or part-time interest and help. The legislatures, while theoretically responsible, cannot be relied on to give continuous and careful attention to improving the laws. They too operate largely in response to specific pressures. Besides they are heavily preoccupied with taxing and spending, and with current controversies.

THE BILL OF RIGHTS AS A CODE OF CRIMINAL PROCEDURE
By Henry J. Friendly
53 California Law Review 929, 938, 953-54 (1965)†

My submission—no less respectful for having been occasionally vigorous—is that in applying the Bill of Rights to the states, the Supreme Court should not regard these declarations of fundamental principles as if they were a detailed code of criminal procedure, allowing no room whatever for reasonable difference of judgment or play in the joints. The "specifics" simply are not that specific. Numerous as were the points of constitutional attack in Doak's apparently simple case, they represent only a sample of what the future would hold for state criminal prosecutions if the "specifics" should be allowed to breed too freely. Professor Frankfurter, as he then was, showed remarkable prescience when, in paying contemporary tribute to *Powell v. Alabama* more than thirty years ago, he included the caveat that the fourteenth amendment "is not the basis of a uniform code of criminal procedure federally imposed. Alternative modes of arriving at truth are not—they must not be—forever frozen. There is room for growth and vitality, for adaptation to shifting necessities, for wide differences of reasonable convenience in method."

. . .

On the view that there can be no difference in the application of the selected provisions of the Bill of Rights to the states and to the nation, it becomes peculiarly vital that the Court carefully analyze past and future decisions in the amendments' "penumbras" and delineate precisely how far these rest on the Constitution itself and how far on other sources of power applicable in the particular case. Federal procedural statutes, the Court's authority as to rules of evidence in federal trials, and its general supervisory power over the administration of federal justice are all available in its review of cases arising in the federal courts, but afford no basis for reversing state convictions or preventing Congress from changing federal law.

THE COURTS, THE POLICE AND THE REST OF US

By Herbert L. Packer

57 Journal of Criminal Law, Criminology and Police Science 238, 240 (1966)†

Moves of this sort by the Supreme Court are, in my view, moves of desperation. Nobody else is exerting control over the law enforcement process, so the justices think that they must. But they can do so, in state cases at any rate, only in the discharge of their duty to construe the Constitution in cases that come before them. And so, the rules of the criminal process, which ought to be the subject of flexible inquiry and adjustment by law-making bodies having the institutional capacity to deal with them, are evolved through a process that its warmest defenders recognize as to some extent awkward and inept: the rules become "constitutionalized." The Bill of Rights becomes, as Judge Henry Friendly's gibe has it, a code of criminal procedure.[b]

THE SUPREME COURT AND THE POLICE: A POLICE VIEWPOINT

By Vincent L. Broderick

57 Journal of Criminal Law, Criminology and Police Science 271, 279 (1966)†

What we should realize, in fact, is that we should seek and encourage legislative rather than judicial solutions to our problems. The Model Code of the American Law Institute points in that direction. Thus the constitutional imperative, as derived from *Wolf* and made binding by *Mapp,* is that there must be no unreasonable searches and seizures by the State. Is it not then for the State to delineate by statute those searches and seizures which are reasonable? The constitutional imperative to be derived from *Escobedo* is less clear and more ambiguous. It is not for the state to clarify the area by definitive legislation?

[b] Whether similar reliance will be placed on the Constitution as a basis for controlling correctional practices is doubtful unless, as Professor Packer points out, it becomes a move "of desperation." If necessary, the "cruel and unusual punishment" provision could serve as a minimal "code of correctional administration." *See, e.g., Jordan v. Fitzharris,* at 837, *supra* and following cases. It seems, however, much more likely that courts will limit their review of correctional practices in the same way that they have limited their review of more traditionally recognized administrative agencies. This kind of trend is already emerging, reflected most ably in the opinion of Judge Oliver in *Burns v. Swenson,* at 831, *supra.*

I do not suggest that we seek state legislation in the areas of search and seizure or post-arrest interrogation which will thwart the Supreme Court. I suggest, as Judge Friendly has previously suggested, that the Bill of Rights is not a code of criminal procedure, and that a legislature rather than the Court is the appropriate body to which to turn for procedural direction. When legislation is sought, the predicate for that legislation is a body of facts, and the body of facts germane to law enforcement problems can best be developed by those in law enforcement. And if, for example, a legislative procedural blueprint is developed for post-arrest interrogation, underlying the legislation will be legislative findings, based upon empirical data, as to the reasons why the legislation is necessary. I would expect that if there were a challenge to the admissibility of a confession taken in conformity with that legislation, the basic question for the Court would concern whether the legislation was reasonable, and it would have access to the legislative findings in making this determination.

CRIMINAL JUSTICE AND THE RULE-MAKING POWER

By J. Edward Lumbard

70 West Virginia Law Review 143, 143-45 (1968)

The *Miranda*[1] decision of June 1966 and the ensuing debate regarding the effect of that decision on law enforcement is an appropriate starting point for a discussion of the methods which are best suited to enable our courts to bring about many of the needed improvements in the administration of criminal justice. I propose to contrast the Supreme Court's exercise of the rule-making power and its control of standards of evidence with the exercise of its power to interpret and apply provisions of the Constitution to federal procedures and to state procedures.

Let me state my thesis and then examine it in the light of the recent developments regarding the use of confessions obtained by in-custody interrogation embodied in the *Miranda* decision. Of course, up until that time all the state courts and all federal appellate courts judged the admission of confessions by whether they were voluntary in the light of all the surrounding circumstances. No court had held that the failure to give warnings and to advise of the right to counsel, by itself and without more, rendered a confession inadmissible.

It was obvious from the Court's opinion in *Escobedo v. Illinois*,[3] that many members of the Court entertained serious

1 Miranda v. Arizona, 384 U.S. 436 (1966).

3 378 U.S. 478 (1964).

doubts regarding in-custody interrogation by the police and the admissibility of any confession resulting therefrom. Although the case turned on the use of Escobedo's confession of murder which had been obtained after he had been denied access to his counsel who had come to the police station, much of what Mr. Justice Goldberg wrote for the majority of five looked like handwriting on the wall for all in-custody interrogations.

What should the Court have done in order to fashion rules for in-custody interrogation? We must, of course, take account of the nature of our federal system.

In my opinion, the Court could and should have used the machinery of the rule-making power for federal criminal cases which Congress gave it in 1940 and which it has used many times since in promulgating and later amending the Federal Rules of Criminal Procedure. While of course any federal rules would bind only the federal courts, they would set an example for state action. In the light of experience under federal rules, and in the States under whatever procedures the States chose to follow, rules and procedures found acceptable and practicable might eventually become the due process standard for judging all state action under the Fourteenth Amendment. It was in just this way that the doctrine of *Gideon v. Wainwright*,[4] which required counsel to be furnished to indigents in felony trials, developed from the Supreme Court decision of 1938 in *Johnson v. Zerbst*.[5] Subsequently a provision was inserted in the Federal Rules of Criminal Procedure in 1946, and more than twenty States took voluntary action before the *Gideon* decision in 1963.

The use of the federal rule-making machinery provides many advantages. In 1964, a distinguished Advisory Committee on Criminal Rules was at work on further revision of the rules under the chairmanship of Circuit Judge John C. Pickett of the Tenth Circuit. The committee consisted of three federal judges, three well-known professors of law and five distinguished practicing lawyers. In addition, Professor Edward L. Barrett, Jr. was the reporter. The practice of the advisory committee, and of all such advisory committees, has been to solicit suggestions from judges and lawyers throughout the country, to publish and distribute their proposals for discussion and further study and to revise the proposals accordingly. With the original Federal Rules of Criminal Procedure this part of the process took three years, and with the most recent amendments, which became effective July 1, 1966, it took over two years. Thus the bench and the bar and federal law enforcement agencies are allowed ample oppor-

4 372 U.S. 335 (1963).

5 304 U.S. 458 (1937).

tunity for the submission of facts and opinions, and, what is equally important, they have ample notice of any new requirements which mandate a change in their practices.

After the advisory committee has agreed on its proposals, the rules are passed on by the Committee on Rules of Practice and Procedure, a standing committee of the Judicial Conference of the United States, of which Circuit Judge Maris has been chairman. The proposals are then submitted to the Judicial Conference. Of course they come as no surprise to that body; the twenty-five judicial members of the Conference have received copies of each successive draft, they are consulted and they themselves make suggestions.

With the approval of the Conference the rules then go to the Supreme Court. If the Court approves, the Chief Justice then transmits the rules to the Congress and they may become effective not sooner than ninety days after such submission to Congress. The latest amendments were submitted February 28, 1966, with the provision that they would be effective July 1, four months later.

The Supreme Court has exercised the power to fashion rules for the admission of evidence in criminal cases since its earliest days. In *McNabb v. United States,*[7] where the Court excluded confessions obtained after protracted interrogation of the defendants before their arraignment, Mr. Justice Frankfurter wrote:

> The principles governing the admissibility of evidence in federal criminal trials have not been restricted . . . to those derived solely from the Constitution. In the exercise of its supervisory power over the administration of criminal justice in the federal courts . . . this Court has, from the very beginning of its history, formulated rules of evidence to be applied in federal criminal prosecutions . . . and in formulating such rules of evidence in federal criminal trials the Court has been guided by considerations of justice not limited to the strict canons of evidentiary relevance.

In *Terry v. Ohio,* at 163, *supra,* the Supreme Court acknowledges, for the first time, its limited ability to deal effectively with a wide variety of important police practices which do not become involved in litigation and thus do not reach the attention of the appellate court. In answer to the argument that "stop and frisk" was part of a wide variety of improper police street practices and

7 318 U.S. 332, 341 (1943).

that evidence gained from a street stop ought to be suppressed, the Court said that "rigid and unthinking application of the exclusionary rule, in futile protest against practices which it can never be used effectively to control, may exact a high toll in human injury and frustration of efforts to prevent crime."

The Court's acknowledged inability to control effectively a wide variety of important police practices suggests that it may not be primarily a judicial responsibility to decide what street practices police should and should not use. For example, to require people in ghetto areas who congregate on streets to "move on" may involve fundamental social and political issues. Are these to be resolved by the courts, or by police, or by legislation? The fact is clear that because there has not yet been some public crisis or individual litigation the issue of "move on" orders has not been squarely confronted by anyone, and remains unresolved.

C. ADMINISTRATIVE POLICYMAKING

Traditionally it has been assumed that it is realistic to expect legislatures and courts to make the important policy decisions for the criminal and juvenile justice systems and thus that the other agencies involved in the system, police particularly, had no responsibility for making policy of great public importance. For this reason, police and correctional agencies were not commonly included in the general study of administrative agencies and of administrative law. This omission has, however, been challenged.

ADMINISTRATIVE LAW: CASES—TEXT—PROBLEMS 79 (1965)
By Kenneth C. Davis

51. Are ordinary policemen administrative officers? Analytically, the answer must be yes, and the French have always said yes, but in an American law school curriculum the unstudied habit is to commit them to the course in criminal law and procedure and not to the administrative law course. Do the police have practical power to set aside whatever criminal law the legislature enacts? Are the limits of what is criminal fixed, not by the legislature, but by the police within the limits fixed by the legislature? For instance, statutes making gambling a crime are typically not enforced against social gambling, church bingo games, or whenever a commercial element is absent; who makes the law in action, as distinguished from the law in books, and which law is it that counts? Criminal statutes are almost never

enforced against adultery or some other sex crimes, in absence of aggravating circumstances. On the basis of your own experience and imagination you can no doubt develop further the extent of police discretion to set aside, in whole or in part, the duly enacted statutes.

52. What are the safeguards that protect against police arbitrariness in deciding when to enforce and when not? Is the power one that intrinsically defies safeguards?

53. Is it sound to justify the selective power of the police by reasoning that the power is only to relieve against what a statute prescribes, never to increase the burden or the liability, and that therefore abuse of the power can hurt only the public, not the individual? But is the individual unjustly treated if one hundred violations that are brought to police attention are ignored but his violation is prosecuted?

In the field of correctional treatment of convicted offenders, there has been a comparable failure to ask about the nature of the administrative responsibility and power of the correctional agency. Unlike the police field, it is not so much an assumption that statute or court decision would adequately resolve the basic policy issues. Rather, it is that traditionally correctional practices were not subject to challenge, partly because it was assumed that offenders had only privileges, not rights, and partly because reliance was increasingly placed upon the professional training of the social worker, psychologist, and psychiatrist as an adequate safeguard against arbitrariness. This is an attitude which seems today to be in the process of change.[c]

The trend, which is not confined to the criminal and juvenile justice systems, is in the direction of more frequent challenge of administrative decisions and greater recognition of the necessity and desirability of administrative policymaking.

ADMINISTRATIVE LAW: CASES—TEXT—PROBLEMS 70 (1965)
By Kenneth C. Davis

A perspective of the literature and the teaching of administrative law in the United States shows four stages of development: (1) The first focus was on constitutional underpinnings of the

---

[c] *See, e.g.,* the materials in Chapter 13, § C1b.

administrative process. This was still the main concern during the 1920's and early 1930's. (2) The next focus was on judicial review, which was the main concern of John Dickinson's 1927 book entitled Administrative Justice and the Supremacy of Law. As late as 1935, the Frankfurter casebook was limited to constitutional problems and judicial review. (3) By the late 1930's attention was shifting to procedures for formal adjudication and for rule making. This was the primary concern of the Administrative Procedure Act of 1946 and of all the literature that has gone with it. We still have not moved out of this third stage. (4) As yet beyond the horizon is significant research on making policy and exercising discretion in absence of safeguards of hearing procedures, although a few efforts in that direction are now in evidence.

Perhaps eighty or ninety per cent of the impact of the administrative process involves discretionary action in absence of safeguards of hearing procedures. For more than two decades we have realized, as the Attorney General's Committee on Administrative Procedure said in its final report of 1941, that "informal procedures . . . are truly the lifeblood of the administrative process," but hardly anyone has penetrated it with significant scholarship.

Although the trend seems clearly in the direction of greater recognition of the importance of public policy decision-making at the administrative level, movement is slow and sporadic. For example, the recent American Bar Association Standards Relating to Fair Trial and Free Press contain an express recognition of the desirability of administrative policymaking, but this is uncommon.

STANDARDS RELATING TO FAIR TRIAL AND FREE PRESS 4, 22-23
A.B.A. Project on Minimum Standards for Criminal Justice
(Proposed Final Draft 1967)

2.1 Departmental rules.

It is recommended that law enforcement agencies in each jurisdiction adopt the following internal regulations:

(a) A regulation governing the release of information, relating to the commission of crimes and to their investigation, prior to the making of an arrest, issuance of an arrest warrant, or the filing of formal charges. This regulation should establish appropriate procedures for the release of information. It should further provide that, when a crime is believed to have been committed, pertinent facts relating to the crime itself and to investigative procedures may properly be made available but the identity of a suspect prior to arrest and the results of investigative procedures shall not be disclosed except to the extent necessary to aid in the investigation, to assist in the apprehension of the suspect, or to warn the public of any dangers.

COMMENTARY

The Committee is still of the view that the proposed rule is within the authority of the court and may properly be resorted to if other approaches prove unavailing. But in recognition of the steps that are being taken to deal with this problem through self-regulation, the Committee believes that an opportunity should be afforded to explore this avenue further before restrictions are imposed externally. Sections 2.1 and 2.2 have therefore been revised to propose that the entire matter be dealt with at the outset by department regulation and that with respect to the period from arrest to the completion of trial, a rule of court *or* legislative enactment[23] be resorted to only if a law enforcement agency fails to adopt and adhere to the substance of the recommended regulation "within a reasonable time." The time period is not specified with greater precision because what is reasonable in a particular context would depend in part on whether a law enforcement agency had indicated a willingness to act or had flatly rejected the idea of self-regulation.[d]

There has been little attention given to such obviously important issues as the relationship between legislation, administrative policymaking, and judicial review of administrative policy. If experience in other areas of governmental activity is followed in

[23] While the Committee still believes that a rule of court on this subject would be appropriate, it regards legislative action as also appropriate and recognizes that some jurisdictions may prefer to follow the latter course.

[d] "The report of the Judicial Conference [of the United States] Committee on the Operation of the Jury System, headed by U.S. Court of Appeals Judge Irving Kaufman, . . . favored 'self-regulation' of law enforcement agencies in the release of information. It said it was encouraged by steps already taken by federal law enforcement agencies to 'set their own houses in order.'" American Bar News, vol. 13, no. 10, Oct. 1968, at 5.

the criminal and juvenile justice systems, one would expect the trend to be in the direction of express, legislative delegation of policymaking responsibility to administrative agencies with opportunity for judicial review under appropriate circumstances.

THE PRESIDENT'S COMMISSION ON LAW ENFORCEMENT AND ADMINISTRATION OF JUSTICE TASK FORCE REPORT: THE POLICE 32 (1967)

The Legislature. Adequate external control over police policymaking requires first an explicit recognition of the necessity and desirability of police operating as an administrative policymaking agency of government. One, and perhaps the best, way to accomplish this is through legislative action which will delegate an explicit policymaking responsibility to police in areas not preempted by legislative or judicial action. Often it is neither feasible nor desirable for the legislature to prescribe a specific police practice; there is a need for administrative variation, innovation, and experimentation within limits set by the general legislative purpose and such legislative criteria as are provided to guide and control the exercise of discretion.

Legislative recognition of the propriety of police policymaking should encourage the development of means to develop enforcement policies and their subjection to adequate external control. It should also encourage flexibility and innovation in law enforcement while at the same time providing some guidance to police policymaking through the prescription of appropriate legislative standards or criteria.

Judicial Review of Police Policymaking. Given explicit legislative recognition of police policymaking, it ought to be possible to develop effective methods of judicial review which will not only serve to minimize the risk of improper police practices but will also serve to encourage the development, articulation, defense, and, if necessary, revision of police policies.

If there is legislative acknowledgment of the propriety of police policymaking, it would seem to follow that it would be appropriate for a person, with proper standing, to challenge existing policy, formal or informal, on the ground that it is inconsistent with general legislative policy. Where there is challenge, courts would have an opportunity to require the law enforcement agency to articulate its policy and to defend it, and, if the challenge is successful, to change the policy.

Recognition of the propriety and, indeed, the inevitability of administrative policymaking in criminal justice administration is only a first step. There remain other obviously important questions, such as whether criminal and juvenile justice agencies are willing or capable of responsibly making important public policy decisions, articulating those policies, and insuring that they are both proper and observed in practice. In the correctional practice, suggestions that policy be formulated and reduced to writing have often been viewed as unduly limiting the opportunity to put into effect the best clinical practices. It is said that such matters often cannot be reduced to writing and must be left to the best judgment of the individual clinician. And, even where there is a willingness, most correctional agencies lack the kind of personnel who are equipped to perform an administrative rule-making type of function. With police, the problem is even more serious. The court in the *Rizzo* case, at 350 n.x, *supra,* assumed that once an important question of police policy was called to their attention the police would respond responsibly. But there are others who raise doubts.

STOP AND FRISK
(A CASE STUDY IN JUDICIAL CONTROL OF THE POLICE)

By Herman Schwartz

58 Journal of Criminal Law, Criminology and Police Science 433, 449 (1967)†

The other suggestion, strongly pressed by the President's Crime Commission and its Police Task Force, is that the police apply measures of self-discipline and develop guidelines to limit themselves. This suggestion is equally futile for several reasons: First, police can hardly be expected to restrict and curtail a long-standing practice like stop and frisk which is based in part on fear for their own safety. Secondly, as earlier noted, the police are themselves unable to make these standards objective. Thirdly, self-regulation is one of the frailest of instruments for social control in any context, not just police work. It is especially feeble in the police context, for relatively little supervision of the patrolman's actions is attempted or is even possible.

JUSTICE WITHOUT TRIAL 228-29 (1966)

By Jerome H. Skolnick

When an appellate court rules that police may not in the future engage in certain enforcement activities, since these con-

---

stitute a violation of the rule of law, the inclination of the police is typically not to feel *shame* but *indignation.* This response may be especially characteristic of "professional" police, who feel a special competence to decide, on their own, how to reduce criminality in the community. The police, for example, recognize the court's power to bar admission of illegally seized evidence if the police are discovered to have violated the constitutional rights of the defendant. They do not, however, feel morally blameworthy at having done so; nor do they even accept such injunctions with good grace and go about their business. On the contrary, the police typically view the court with hostility for having interfered with their capacities to practice their craft. Police tend to rest their *moral* position on the argument that the "independence" and social distance of the appellate judiciary constitutes a type of government—by the courts—without the consent of the governed—the police. Thus, the police see the court's affirmation of principles of due process as, in effect, the creation of harsh "working conditions." From their point of view, the courts are failing to affirm democratic notions of the autonomy and freedom of the "worker." Their political superiors insist on "production" while their judicial superiors impede their capacity to "produce." Under such frustrating conditions, the appellate judiciary inevitably comes to be seen as "traitor" to its responsibility to keep the community free from criminality.

In part, the common police reaction that their task is to fight crime, and not to concern themselves with broad policy questions, may result from the fact that police have traditionally not been expected to make important public policy decisions. The reaction that restrictions imposed from outside can sometimes be disregarded may result from an understanding that the "rules of the game" are to be followed only when a conviction is desired. The standards of propriety are vague when no effort is made to obtain a conviction. Indeed, police are sometimes told this expressly.

DON'T FUSS ABOUT LEGALITY IN DRUG CASES, DA SAYS

By Dennis Sandage

The [Madison, Wisconsin] Capital Times, Oct. 11, 1968

An assistant to Dane County District Attorney James Boll Thursday told about 100 law enforcement officials to go ahead and break the state's laws regarding obtaining a search warrant.

Assistant D.A. Michael Zaleski, telling the officials how to deal with narcotics and dangerous drugs, said "all right, you lose the case. Big deal."

Referring to drugs, he said the important thing is to "get the stuff off the market."

He was speaking at the second session of the 16th Annual Retraining Conference on Juvenile Justice, held at the Wisconsin Center.

In a talk at times emphasized by theatrics, Zaleski at first condemned the state warrant laws as encouraging illegal searches by policemen.

"I don't have to tell you guys about this. You know what I'm talking about," he said. He then noted how policemen sometimes break a hole in a door to confirm suspicions, then enter an apartment or home to make an arrest without a warrant.

A few seconds later he was advocating disregarding the law, saying "you gotta be a gambler in this business." He added that policemen would find public sentiment in their favor anyway, saying "I think you'll find the pendulum swinging back."

. . .

The Miranda decision, he said, involves only "custodial interrogation." If a law enforcement officer simply asks a suspect "Would you mind stepping in the car" for questioning, he does not then have to inform the suspect of his rights, Zaleski contended.

"Don't overreact to Supreme Court decisions," he said. "Look for loopholes."

Following Zaleski's talk, the officials heard Harold Mills, principal of a Racine high school, call for a "marriage" between teachers, school administrators, and police.

Mills said policemen would find such a tryst to their advantage, largely because school administrators can obtain information the police cannot.

"We don't have to go through the Miranda bit," Mills said. He said no child will tell a principal he needs a lawyer before talking with him.

Even if it is assumed that responsible administrative action by police is desirable and that police are capable of the kind of objectivity required, other problems of feasibility remain. Perhaps most obvious is the situation of the very small police department, an issue acknowledged in THE PRESIDENT'S COMMISSION ON LAW ENFORCEMENT AND ADMINISTRATION OF JUSTICE, TASK FORCE REPORT: THE POLICE 37 (1967):

Insofar as police policymaking is concerned, it seems clear that the police agencies serving our major cities are sufficiently large and have sufficient resources to develop their own capacity to fulfill their policymaking role. For smaller agencies, the need should serve as a stimulus for development of new patterns of cooperation or for the creation of a unit within a state agency, such as the office of the attorney general, that would develop the capacity to assist the administrators of the smaller agencies in meeting their policymaking function.

Even in the larger urban areas, questions of feasibility remain. If the police agency itself is the "administrative agency" it is obvious that the agency will have to be differently staffed if the job is to be adequately accomplished. Given adequate staff assistance it may be realistic to assume that the police executive is capable of the task, though this has certainly not been the case in the past. He needs not only staff, but protection from political interference, a willingness to place responsibility at the highest levels of leadership, and to carry the task out in the face of pressures.

THE POLICE RESPONSE TO THE URBAN CRISIS: CURRENT ISSUES IN POLICING

By Herman Goldstein

(Manuscript 1968)

There have been a few situations in recent years in which police administrators have moved in this direction addressing a particularly sensitive area of police operations by establishing some policy guidelines. But they have apparently been inhibited from making more extensive use of the process by two factors: the fear that, in the absence of specific legislative acknowledgment that police exercise discretion, the articulation of policies may be viewed as presumptuous on the part of a police chief; and the danger that, in the absence of a formal process for airing and approving such policies, an administratively adopted policy may be overruled by a mayor or city council that suddenly chooses to exert some degree of control over the police because of the nature of the issue involved.[e]

[e] Fosdick, *Police Administration*, in CRIMINAL JUSTICE IN CLEVELAND 18, 22-23 (1922):

> The department of police should be in charge of a single civilian administrative head, to be known as the director of police. The director should be appointed by the mayor with full responsibility for administering the police service, and should have the exclusive right to name his own immediate assistants, including the chief ranking

THE PRESIDENT'S COMMISSION ON LAW ENFORCEMENT AND ADMINISTRATION OF JUSTICE
TASK FORCE REPORT: THE POLICE 35 (1967)

The current need for police administrators to effectively handle the broad range of social issues with which they must deal makes obsolete the narrow standards for selection which have been utilized in the past. The need today is for a police administrator who is much more of a generalist rather than a person possessing narrow technical skills. He must have a sound grasp of the unique function of the police in a democratic society. He must support values which often are in conflict with the most immediate goals of arrest and successful prosecution. He must have the ability to relate police functioning to the functioning of the other agencies in the criminal justice system; to analyze and resolve complex issues relating to the exercise of police authority; to direct his subordinates in a manner which will elicit their compliance with the policies he establishes; and, in the process, to be especially sensitive to legitimate community demands and interests.

KILL OR BE KILLED?: USE OF DEADLY FORCE IN THE RIOT SITUATION
Comment, 56 California Law Review 829, 866 (1968)†

Writers on police handling of riots give little attention to the use of firearms beyond the general decision as to whether or not

---

office of the uniformed force to correspond to the present chief of police. Such appointments should be terminated at the will of the director. It should be the director's duty to lay down a policy and program for police work, and to see that such policy is carried into effect by his subordinates. Under this arrangement the officer who develops the policies of police service will be subject to public reckoning, since his appointment and continuance in office depend on the mayor, who is subject to election. Undivided responsibility and authority would be reposed in a single officer at the head, and the line of responsibility and authority should continue downward direct and unbroken.

What every police force needs is leadership—one official to whom the community can say, "Thou art the man!" and who has power corresponding to his responsibility. We shall never solve the police problem in America until we give honest and effective leadership an opportunity to show what it can do. Some time or other we have to make a beginning of trusting our public officials. Checks and balances to curb and minimize possible abuses of power have gotten us nowhere. Complex systems to prevent bias and unfairness have brought nothing but confusion. It is time to take off a few of the yokes that have made public administration an impossible task, and put a new emphasis on positive qualities. The problem before us is not how to build up a structure that will circumvent the dishonest and incompetent official, but, after finding a competent and honest official, to surround him with conditions in which he can make himself effective.

they are to be employed at all. The police administrators who have written the most extensively on the subject usually limit their views on riot control to the mechanics of the situation—how to recognize potentially explosive situations, how to control the crowd, how to mobilize and what formations to use. All these considerations are necessary, but police leaders should give attention to the specific problem of whether and when deadly force is appropriate. The preferable course of action would be to formulate comprehensive firearms use policies which would give guidance in all types of situations, but *at least* there should be a clear policy governing use of firearms in the particularly difficult riot situation. The leaders within the police departments cannot and should not delegate this responsibility, but must meet it themselves.

It has been suggested that the professional police establishment is so much emotionally involved in the problems to which policy-making must respond that there is a need for "civilian" direction in much the same sense that we, in this country, have long been committed to civilian control over the military.

ORDER AND CIVIL LIBERTIES:
A COMPLEX ROLE FOR THE POLICE
By George Edwards
64 Michigan Law Review 55-56 (1965)

III. Origin and Magnitude of the Hostilities and Suggestions for Improvement

Conflict between the police and the Negro people is deep-rooted in our history. The Negro citizen sees the police officer in blue coat, with a white face, as the representative of the white man's law, who for nearly 300 years has enforced the laws—first of slavery and more recently of legally sanctioned segregation. Similarly, the bitterness that has been demonstrated by Negro rioters may be the product of a long series of unforgettable personal experiences. For example, in the 1930's if a teenage Negro boy met a white police officer in the late afternoon on the streets of a town in eastern Texas near where I grew up, his first contact with the law would probably be the command: "Nigger, don't let the sun set on you in this town!" Thirty years later in a large northern city, the bitterness engendered by that memory could turn a Saturday night party that has become loud enough for a police call into a dangerous melee.

Feelings of hostility also exist on the other side of the conflict. Police officers have grown up in a tradition in which part of their historic function assigned by the community has been "keeping the Negro in his place." This history produces current attitudes which are illustrated by the great number of present-day police officers who invariably use the hated term "nigger" in talking about (and sometimes to) Negro citizens.

However, some police hostility is based upon personal observations made during the course of duty. A thoroughly unbiased officer making the run to the Saturday night party referred to above could not miss the hostility which greeted him—and he would neither know nor think about its source. Similarly, many white police officers work daily in core area precincts where they are constantly in contact with crimes committed by Negroes. These same officers probably live in neighborhoods occupied by white residents where there is relatively less crime and disorder; this fact alone makes them tend to identify Negroes with crime and whites with peace and order. We have already seen that such a conclusion is an erroneous oversimplification, but it is nevertheless a part of the hostility problem with which we must deal. Indeed, it is the pressure exerted by these hostilities which makes it so very important that top policymaking be in civilian control and that mayors and civilian police commissioners exercise in fact the control which the law grants to them.

There is a greater tradition for "civilian," that is, nonprofessional, involvement in correctional policymaking than there has been at the law enforcement stage where proposals such as a "civilian review board" have encountered opposition from police. While a correctional administrator has commonly viewed a "civilian" Board of Public Welfare as an ally and as a source of support with the public and the legislature, particularly at budget time, the police administrator has responded differently, viewing civilian control either as opposition (as with the civilian review board proposal) or as a source of corruption (as with "city hall").

The correctional process poses less complicated problems for another reason. It is possible to view the state correctional agency as an administrative agency in the same sense that statewide economic regulatory agencies are viewed. But law enforcement is primarily a local responsibility and there is thus much more complexity. Is the administrative unit the police department alone? Or is it more realistic to include also the mayor or city manager who may have increasingly important responsibility for law enforcement decisions? The mayor or city manager's relationship to police may be complicated by the existence of a police and fire commission with responsibility for law enforcement personnel matters and, perhaps, a wider policymaking responsibility. The city council obviously cannot be ignored since it must make decisions about allocation of financial resources which decisions will have profound effect upon the law enforcement program. Were this situation not complicated enough, police must also deal with prosecutors and trial judges in the criminal justice system. Many have asserted that the prosecutor is the "chief law enforcement" officer. And, although theoretically detached and neutral, many trial judges understandably believe they bear responsibility to "administer" the criminal justice system, in which they occupy a pivotal role.[f]

Perhaps the only thing which can be said with assurance is that responsibility ought somewhere to be clearly vested and that where it is shared there be clear indication of the nature of the relationship. This is usually not the case today.

ALBINA VICE MEETING OFF

The [Portland] Oregon Daily Journal, Oct. 2, 1968

JUDGES REJECT "INVITATION"

Scheduled public airing at City Hall of vice problems in Portland's Albina area was canceled Wednesday by the City Council after Circuit Court and Municipal Court judges formally rejected invitations to attend the Oct. 10 evening meeting.

---

[f] There is additional complication in the fact that some people now assert that problems of crime control cannot be dealt with in isolation from other urban problems and thus that what we are confronted with is not so much a crime problem as a massive conglomeration of urban problems which call for the allocation of limited resources and thus the establishment of a set of priorities on an overall urban level. See, for example, U.S. DEPARTMENT OF COMMERCE, BUREAU OF THE CENSUS REPORT ON NATIONAL NEEDS FOR CRIMINAL JUSTICE STATISTICS (Aug. 1968) (dealing with "what resources, financial and manpower, are devoted to the criminal justice system in relation to the size and kind of job expected of it"); Mesner & Hoffman, *Police Resource Allocation, Working Paper #73,* Center for Planning and Development Research, University of California, Berkeley (1967) (analyzing police task in terms of public services and maintenance of peace and security); ADVISORY COMMISSION ON INTERGOVERNMENTAL RELATIONS, PERFORMANCE OF URBAN FUNCTIONS: LOCAL AND AREAWIDE (1963) (a study of the optimum size area for performance of urban functions); Leahy, *Planning-Progaming-Budgeting for Police Departments,* The Traveler's Research Center, Inc., Hartford, Conn. (1968) (computor systems applied to police allocations of resources); A. BLUMSTEIN, OUTLINE OF A FUTURE RESEARCH AND DEVELOPMENT PROGRAM IN CRIMINAL JUSTICE, Institute for Defense Analysis, Arlington, Va. (1968); Note, *Program Budgeting for Police Departments,* 76 YALE L.J. 822 (1967).

The City Council, disappointed and a little irked over the judicial turndown, suggested that the judges call their own meeting with the Albina residents, and the City Council would stay away. Main reason given by the judges for declining the invitation was that a meeting with the council would be ethically improper.

City Auditor Ray Smith, who extended the invitations on behalf of city fathers, received written regrets from the 5 Municipal Court and 16 Circuit Court judges.

The letter from Judge Bryson stated that the judiciary is bound to the canons of judicial ethics, and he cited two of them.

Canon 14 states that "a judge should not be swayed by partisan demands, public clamor or consideration of personal popularity or notoriety, nor be apprehensive of unjust criticism."

Canon 30 states that "a candidate for judicial position should not announce in advance his conclusions of law on disputed issues to secure class support."

Bryson said the 16 Circuit Court judges unanimously believe they would be violating the canons "and the fundamental principle of the separation of powers, besides jeopardizing the impartiality incumbent upon us if we were to attend the Oct. 10 meeting and, therefore, decline the invitation."

Mayor Terry Schrunk and city commissioners expressed disappointment and some bewilderment over the attitude of the bench.

The evening meeting had been called by the City Council at the request of Albina residents who protested that women in the district were being harassed by outsiders seeking prostitutes. Invited were city officials, police, probation officers, city and district attorneys and others concerned with prostitution and related crimes.

The judges were invited because court delays and mild sentences were among problems cited by police in relation to enforcement of the city's prostitution ordinance.

ROLES OF CITY MANAGER AND POLICE

By F. P. Sherwood

Public Management 111 (May 1959)

Manager and Police Policy

In general it would appear that the city manager can deal with these policy-community values questions in one of two ways.

1. He can assume responsibility for the policies of the police department and thus directly involve himself in any controversies

which arise. Theoretically, this would be his obligation in the council-manager system.

2. He can vacate this responsibility and permit the police chief to function as the promulgator of such police policy. In this case, of course, any controversy would be more apt to miss the manager.

The first alternative represents the way in which we like to think most managers respond to such issues.

WHO'S IN CHARGE OF THE POLICE?

By Herman Goldstein

50 Public Management 304, 306 (1968)

Most mayors and city managers have had no reluctance to take the responsibility for final decisions relating to the hardware and mechanics of policing (e.g., facilities, communications, vehicles and supplies), nor have they hesitated to supervise the personnel practices of a police agency in the same manner in which they direct such practices in other agencies (e.g., recruitment, screening and promotion). But there has been a general reluctance on the part of both managers and mayors to become directly involved in decisions relating to the substance of policing—in deciding, for example, how a given law is to be enforced, in deciding how violators are to be processed, and in determining how the police should respond to a given category of incidents.

This traditional aversion to becoming involved in the determination of law enforcement policies is apparently attributable to two factors: (1) an assumption that the police receive all the guidance they require from the law of the jurisdiction and from the courts, the prosecutor and the city attorney; and (2) a prevalent assumption that any involvement on the part of a municipality's chief executive in law enforcement policies will be viewed as interfering with the impartiality with which the police can otherwise carry out their duties.

The first assumption is clearly in error. Most of what the police do is, in fact, outside the criminal law process to which the several cited sources of guidance and direction apply. The majority of the tasks which the police are called upon to perform do not involve arresting individuals, charging them with a crime and bringing them before a judge for trial. Moreover, even when this is their objective, the guidelines with which the police are provided are not sufficiently detailed to enable them to function in a ministerial fashion. Police agencies and individual officers must exercise a great deal of discretion in deciding, for example, when to arrest, when to search, when to detain and when to charge.

Thus, there are vast areas of police functioning to which the law, the prosecutor and the courts do not speak. And it is within these areas that one finds the really important problems and issues that currently involve the police and the use of police authority. How much police effort should go into the prevention of riots, for example, and how much should be devoted to preparing for their suppression? How much effort should be devoted to social services as distinguished from police activities traditionally viewed as contributing more directly to the prevention of crime? Within existing statutory limitations, what use, if any, should be made of deadly force in a riotous situation? What should be the policy of police officers in stopping and questioning individuals on the street—a highly controversial practice that has given rise to strong feelings of hostility toward the police?

The second reason why mayors and city managers have not become involved in attempting to respond to such questions is closely related to the first. Since it has been the police role in the criminal process that has received primary attention, a special effort has been made over the years to protect the integrity of the process by insulating the police from any influences of a corruptive nature that might be brought to bear upon them from outside the criminal justice system. Thus, in a number of jurisdictions, police agencies have been placed under specially appointed boards and commissions; police chiefs have been shielded from removal except for serious mismanagement or misconduct; and the heads of municipal police departments in several states continue to be appointed by the governor of the state.

Currently, most police administrators are appointed directly by the municipality's chief executive. But the virtue of a "laissez-faire" relationship has become so strong that candidates for mayor, for example, have often listed the promise of a "free hand" for their police administrator high among their campaign promises. It follows that a chief executive who seeks to become involved in some of the important decisions now facing police agencies runs the risk of being accused of improperly interfering with police operations.

The major thrust of the famous crime surveys of the 1920's and 1930's was against corruption of the criminal justice system. The commitment was to getting "city hall" out of law enforcement. This tradition persists despite increasing indication that law enforcement has become such an overwhelmingly important urban issue that it cannot be ignored by "city hall."

POLITICS AND THE POLICE
New York Times Editorial, Mar. 10, 1966

The charge of "political interference" in the Police Department is a greatly exaggerated issue. The present and former Democratic officeholders who originated and are continuing this controversy are damaging the department's good name—and their own reputation for good judgment.

Vincent L. Broderick and Francis Adams, both former commissioners, now joined—after an initial period of caution—by City Council President Frank D. O'Connor, started off with one fact and have never ceased to overplay it. That fact is that apparently Howard R. Leary, the new Police Commissioner, accepted the advice of Mayor Lindsay in choosing his Chief Inspector. We think it would have been far wiser for the Mayor to have withheld his advice until Mr. Leary had had more experience; and we are sure that in any event Mr. Leary acted too soon after his appointment. But Mayor Lindsay's intervention was in no way comparable to the political manipulation of police assignments by Tammany clubhouse chiefs in the pre-LaGuardia era, which Mr. Broderick et al are constantly insinuating.

It has to be remembered that the Mayor is ultimately responsible for the sound administration of all departments, including the police. No one would think it strange if he made his views known concerning a top-level appointment in any other department. The police are not a world unto themselves.

New Police Commissioners traditionally appoint a new chief inspector and re-shuffle other top officers. The merits of such changes only emerge in the performance of the department's work in subsequent years. Yet Commissioner Leary and Chief Inspector Sanford Garelik are being condemned without any evidence against them and before they have any chance to show what they can do.

Perhaps because of the uncertainty as to whose responsibility it is, there are indications that the police, as a collective unit, are beginning to assert a right to influence the making of important policy decisions. In the correctional field it has long been recognized that "professionalization," as by requiring for employment a master's degree in social work, would in itself have a significant impact upon correctional policy. Is the assertion by police of their right to influence law enforcement policy comparable?

P.B.A. HEAD TELLS POLICE TO ENFORCE LAWS 100% HERE

By Martin Tolchin

New York Times, Aug. 13, 1968

BIDS HIS 29,000 MEMBERS IGNORE SUPERIOR'S ORDERS TO EXERCISE RESTRAINT

CITY HALL IS ACCUSED

PATROLMEN SUPPORT CHARGES OF CASSESE ON POLICIES IN RIOTS AND PROTESTS

The Patrolmen's Benevolent Association directed its 29,000 members yesterday to disregard any orders from superior officers to refrain from arresting looters, vandals, unruly demonstrators or other law violators.

"In the last two and a half years, we've followed a policy of restraint that emanated from City Hall—a policy of turning the other cheek and not getting involved," said John J. Cassese, president of the organization. "Now, I say, let's try the other side of the coin."

Mr. Cassese, speaking at an impromptu news conference on the steps of the Criminal Court Building after meeting with Assistant Administrative Judge Vincent A. Massi to complain about an alleged lack of courtroom decorum and a permissive attitude toward convicted criminals, said:

"We're going to enforce the law 100 per cent.

"A policeman is duty bound and honor bound to take appropriate action to halt violations of law in his presence. This is all we're asking him to do. This is what the city pays him for. This is what he's been hired for. This is what he hasn't been doing."

CONFLICT IS EXPECTED

Mr. Cassese said that the new policy would bring him into "direct conflict" with City Hall, which he said had issued orders instructing police to refrain from arresting looters, vandals and unruly demonstrators on several occasions.

One such occasion, he said, was last month when 1,500 youngsters demonstrating at City Hall, in a protest against a cutback in summer job programs, smashed six parked automobiles.

Nine persons were ultimately arrested, but the police stood by while some of the cars were smashed.

The Mayor's office and the police explained that the arrests were delayed until there were a sufficient number of policemen to control the crowd, but Mr. Cassese asserted:

"As soon as the first demonstrator puts the first foot on the hood of an automobile, he should be grabbed by the neck and arrested. We have to show people they can't get away with this anymore."

Neither Mayor Lindsay nor Police Commissioner Howard R. Leary would comment yesterday on Mr. Cassese's remarks.

However, the Mayor has repeatedly denied ever having issued orders restraining the police from making arrests. He recently asserted, moreover, that any policeman who saw a crime committed in his presence was himself guilty of a crime unless he took steps to arrest the perpetrator.

In random conversations with patrolmen yesterday, however, there were repeated charges that they had been specifically ordered not to make arrests.

Two partners in the 23d Precinct, with a station on East 104th Street in Spanish Harlem, said that during the disturbances after the assassination of the Rev. Dr. Martin Luther King Jr., "we would use the Negro expression, 'Keep it cool.'"

This meant, they said, not to take any action, including an arrest, that might provoke an incident.

During these disturbances the Police Department reissued a two-year-old order directing police not to shoot looters, but to take cover when fired upon, and to call for a special anti-sniper unit.

Patrolmen in the 18th Precinct station, on West 54th Street, said that they had been ordered not to arrest marauding youths who smashed Fifth Avenue store windows one July evening last year. They said that they also had been ordered not to arrest demonstrators outside the United Nations buildings.

23 Youths Arrested

However, 23 of the marauding youths were arrested, and United Nations demonstrators have also been arrested from time to time.

Alan Miller, an attorney for the New York Civil Liberties Union, said yesterday:

"It seems to me that the Mayor is appropriately concerned with whether or not the shooting of looters may inflame a community enough to start a riot. This seems an appropriate political judgment."

"If the police force is not responsible to political control," he said, "it has absolute autonomy. The police believe that armed force is really the answer. The Mayor, with a more enlightened view, thinks armed force will make things worse."

However, patrolmen on the beat challenged the contention that police restraint would quell riots.

"If they know you're not going to do anything, they become more bold," said a patrolman at the West 54th Street station. "Nobody respects a policeman any more. We stand around like a wooden Indian."

"They can't sneeze in some precincts without fear of creating an incident," said another patrolman.

Norman Frank, the P.B.A.'s community relations counsel, said yesterday that patrolmen who made arrests against the orders of a superior officer would not be violating police regulations to obey the orders of a superior officer, because:

"Policemen are required by the rules and regulations to obey any lawful order of a superior officer. If the policeman sees a violation of law and attempts to take action in arresting the perpetrator and is told by a superior officer not to take action, that would be an unlawful order, and the policeman under the circumstances has every right to disregard such an order."[g]

---

[g] *Compare* N.Y. Times, Nov. 14, 1968:

"L.I. Parkway Police Threaten 'Super' Enforcement in Protest

"By Roy R. Silver

"Mineola, L.I., Nov. 13—Traffic delays and other inconveniences to motorists using state highways on Long Island were expected as a result of an announcement today by the Long Island State Parkway police that they would provide 'super' enforcement of traffic laws starting tomorrow.

"In announcing the move, part of a campaign for more pay, Philip A. Ferrato, president of the New York State Parkway Police Benevolent Association of Long Island, said the members would 'issue summonses galore' in a 'literal interpretation' of the state's motor vehicle and traffic laws.

"'We will issue summonses for cars going 51 miles an hour in a 50-mile-an-hour zone, we will close all lanes at scenes of accidents and we will make spot checks of vehicles, probably during peak traffic periods, to rigidly enforce the laws,' Patrolman Ferrato said.

"Members of the Parkway P.B.A., who represent 100 of the 204 policemen employed by the Long Island State Park Commission, will also refuse to

WHO'S IN CHARGE OF THE POLICE?

By Herman Goldstein

50 Public Management 304, 306 (1968)

With the exception of the Chicago situation last April, where the department's administration was operating in conformity with the recommendations of the Kerner Commission, the major disputes that have arisen between the police and municipal officials have not reflected police support for policies urged upon them by the best professional judgment in the field. The "police position," rather, has reflected the view of rank and file police officers and has been voiced by the spokesmen for their organizations. The position which they advocate—one of more direct use of police authority and resources in coping with current problems—is often in conflict with that of their superiors and almost always in opposition to the policies and practices that have been advocated in recent studies.

The fact that operating police personnel differ from police administrators and others outside of the police field on how to handle current problems should come as no surprise. Patrolmen—especially those functioning on the streets of our larger cities—are caught up in the thick of current strife. Chances are that they have been called upon to engage in armed combat in a riotous situation. They have, in all probability, been subject to physical attack, to vilification, to harassment and to all types of provocation in the handling of demonstrations and in the handling of much of their more routine business. Their average day consists of a steady diet of crime, violence and conflict. To expect even the most intelligent and most emotionally mature among them to assume the broad perspective that is required if one is to understand the rationale behind some of the policies and practices being advocated is to expect the impossible.

---

operate 'unsafe' police vehicles, will set up roadblocks after a major crime is reported in Nassau or Suffolk County, and will impound vehicles when they are found to be mechanically defective or when a driver cannot produce an operator's license.

"Action Called Legal

"Jack B. Solerwitz, attorney for the P.B.A., said the police action would be 'completely legal' and would not conflict with the state's Taylor Law, which prohibits strikes or slowdowns by state employes.

"The P.B.A. took similar, though less rigid, action on Oct. 26 to stress their demand for a raise to bring them to parity with other police departments on Long Island. The job action lasted one day and caused inconvenience to motorists at accident scenes on two parkways through 'strict adherence to rules and regulations.'

"In the earlier job action, the police also refused to chase motorists at speeds in excess of 85 miles an hour, but said today they would refrain from doing this tomorrow because it might be considered a slowdown."

Understandable as the position of operating police officers may be, it is equally apparent that their position should not dictate public policy. More than the narrow interests of law enforcement personnel must obviously be considered in determining a community's response to riots, to demonstrations and to the general problem of crime. Yet, obvious as the need is, there are no clearly established procedures by which a municipal government exerts control over its police force.

WHY POLICEMEN ARE UNHAPPY
By Sylvan Fox
New York Times, Oct. 24, 1968

Pay Isn't Everything P.B.A. Rejection of Package Indicates

There is an enigma behind the current labor dispute between the Patrolmen's Benevolent Association and the city. It lies in the fact that all parties, including many rank-and-file members of the P.B.A., have agreed that the package put together by a panel headed by former Supreme Court Justice Arthur J. Goldberg and Vincent D. McDonnell, chairman of the State Board of Mediation, is a good one—yet representatives of the city's 23,000 policemen rejected it. The solution to the puzzle lies in a complex tangle involving the present emotional attitudes of policemen, the city's official attitudes toward labor, and misjudgments by those who did the bargaining for both sides.

Not the Whole Reason

The ostensible explanation is that the policemen want more than just contractual parity with the firemen and sanitation workers, who all were offered adjusted versions of the same package. But many close to the dispute believe that this explanation only begins to tell the story.

"Policemen are feeling their muscles all over the country," a police official said. "They want to be special. They want status."

"I think it's really a general frustration that the police are feeling toward the Establishment. They feel they are not getting the kind of recognition and respect they're entitled to—from either the community or the administration."

Most patrolmen, a police official explained, are young—the average age is 27 or 28—and they have never experienced economic hardship or depression. They tend to take economic benefits for granted and they want something more.

"They are turning their backs on material things," he said, "and going after other things—ego things."

As part of the background of the rejection of the package, this official and others also cited the general mood of the city—the teachers' strike, the clamor of Negroes for equal rights and community control and the increasing willingness of rank-and-file members of unions to defy their leaders.

Hostility Toward Lindsay

In addition, these officials note that many policemen harbor hostility toward Mayor Lindsay, a hostility rooted in their belief that the Mayor has repeatedly made decisions that favor Negroes and Puerto Ricans while limiting or reducing the stature of the police.

Many policemen have not forgotten the Mayor's campaign for a Civilian Complaint Review Board, which they fought bitterly on the grounds that it demeaned them and hampered them in their work.

Complicating the situation is the relationship between Mr. Cassese and younger, more militant segments of his union's membership. "Cassese is an old-line union type," a police official said. "The younger policemen have different values from his."

As an example, a police official noted that the way the package was negotiated created resentment among members of the P.B.A., even though it assured substantial economic gains.

This official recalled that Mr. Cassese and Norman Frank, his public relations adviser, handled the bargaining themselves, then "dropped the package in the members' laps saying it was great."

"Cassese misjudged the tone of his members," said another official. "He didn't reckon with the mood of the city, the growing outcry for law and order, the feeling on the part of the policemen that they deserve more than the people in the other uniformed services."

If Mr. Cassese misjudged the temper of his men and of the city, some persons close to the dispute believe that Mayor Lindsay did, too.

"The Mayor," said one observer, "tends to have a patronizing attitude toward labor generally. It showed up in his dealings with the P.B.A. and the Police Department during the dispute. His worst mistake, though, was believing the rank and file could be kept in line by its leaders."

Wherever responsibility lies and however it is shared, it is obvious that the exercise of the immense discretionary power in law enforcement is a vital and difficult problem for a democratic society. There are obviously alternatives and perhaps the path of wisdom is in the direction of local innovation and experimentation with the hope that carefully evaluated experience will afford a more adequate basis than now exists for giving priority to one method over another. One might assert the general goals for dealing with policymaking and discretionary power to be clear allocation of responsibility and enough administrative flexibility to deal effectively with a wide variety of problems. To these must be added as of critical importance the creation of effective methods to control the exercise of law enforcement power. A traditional recommendation has been reliance on formal review of administrative discretion by the courts. Other suggestions are badly needed.

ADMINISTRATIVE LAW: CASES—TEXT—PROBLEMS 82-84 (1965)
By Kenneth C. Davis

EIGHTEEN WAYS TO CONTROL DISCRETION

Here are some preliminary ideas about ways to protect against arbitrary exercise of administrative discretion when hearing safeguards are inappropriate:

1. A major tool for protection is openness. Whenever practicable, discretionary decisions should be openly made. They should not be kept secret unless special reasons justify secrecy.

2. With openness goes opportunity for criticism by outsiders. In absence of special reasons to the contrary, potential critics should have access to the officers' decisions and to the materials that were before the officers in making their decisions. Officers who know that their decisions can be scrutinized may do better than officers whose decisions are kept confidential.

3. Criticism by outsiders is often at its best on professional or scientific subject matter. Just as a judge is sensitive to opinons of lawyers, an engineer or a doctor is sensitive to the professional opinions of his fellow engineers or doctors. Professional or scientific understanding, shared with others who work in the field, is an effective control over discretionary power.

4. Criticism within an organization can be a strong and effective sanction. Not only do superiors criticize subordinates,

but colleagues criticize each other on the same level, and most superiors try to earn favorable criticism and to avoid unfavorable criticism from their subordinates.

5. Because criticism is so valuable in controlling discretionary power, the federal government, a state, a local government, any segment of a government, or any agency or group of agencies can establish official critics who are assigned the task of criticizing and who perform no other function. Experience proves that such official criticism, especially when publicly made by a person of high prestige, can be a powerful control. Some Scandinavian countries have had outstanding success with an official critic known as an Ombudsman. The idea has recently been adopted in New Zealand, and it is under active consideration in many countries, including especially England and India. See discussion of the Ombudsman below in this chapter.

6. When decisions of any kind are based upon facts that may be either disputed or unclear, a requirement that findings of fact be systematically stated is a good protection.

7. A requirement that an officer state reasons for his choices of law and policy is an important control. Reasoned opinions after the manner of appellate courts' opinions are sometimes feasible. A requirement that even a sentence or two be recorded may significantly discourage arbitrariness.

8. Closely related to findings and reasons is the idea of striving for consistency. Two powerful reasons combine to make consistency a special virtue: (a) Equality or uniformity of treatment is a major ingredient of justice. (b) The process of striving for consistency strongly pulls away from arbitrariness.

9. Along with consistency goes the system of building bodies of precedents, so that each decision is related to prior decisions. Even when a case is one of first impression, a system of regarding the decision as a precedent for the future constitutes a protection against arbitrariness.

10. Bodies of precedents based upon reasoned opinions yield or tend to yield principles and finally rules. Agencies should recognize this not merely when they decide but when clarification becomes feasible through publishing policy statements or through resort to the rule-making power to formulate formal rules. Precedents, policy statements and rules should constantly

operate in the direction of reducing the scope for discretion, to keep pace with offsetting factors that constantly tend to enlarge discretion.

11. As an agency gradually develops its policies—gradually learns what it wants to do with recurring problems—its early publication of what it understands is an important safeguard. Many agencies keep confidential their instructions to staffs, even though a goodly portion of the effective law is embodied in the instructions and even though no harm would result from publication or other disclosure of large portions of such instructions. The goal should be to come as close as practicable to closing the gap between what the best-informed insider knows and what the best-informed outsider can know.

12. Discretion is confined or controlled by openness and criticism, by findings and reasons, by consistency and precedents, by policy statements and rules, but the extent to which it can be or should be so confined or controlled is always in itself a difficult problem for discretion in any set of circumstances. We must avoid erring in the direction of too much confinement of discretion; we must remember that one major source of injustice is the excessive rigidity of too many rules. One of our most important safeguards must be willingness to allow administrators ample elbow room for individualized judgments that can come only from discretion.

13. On any given subject matter at any given time in any set of circumstances, an optimum can probably be found as to how broad or how narrow administrative discretion should be. We need to learn how to search for the optimum scope for discretion with respect to each function. We need to discover how to identify the earmarks of discretion which causes harm because it is too broad and the earmarks of discretion which causes harm because it is too narrow. Unfortunately, the optimum is seldom stationary.

14. A cardinal principle about all allocation of governmental power is the principle of check—what in the government as a whole is often called "checks and balances." Just as an appellate court checks a trial court, administrative appellate authorities may check officers who take initial action. But more important than administrative appeal, which implies a proceeding, is the use of the principle of check for informal determinations. Often something more is appropriate than the normal supervision of

subordinates by superiors. Sometimes sizable staffs of reviewers are assigned the task of checking initial determinations.

15. The principle of check can be applied to whole agencies as well as within agencies. Final action of an agency can often be subjected to various forms of legislative check, executive check, and judicial check. For instance, appropriations committees of Congress, often spurred by disgruntled parties, provide an effective check, as well as substantive supervising committees.

16. The best protection against arbitrary exercise of discretion is personnel of high quality. No one doubts that an individual officer who combines sufficient wisdom with sufficient conscientiousness will produce the results we want in exercising discretionary power. But this idea becomes harmful if it discourages efforts to improve institutional arrangements. Until geneticists discover how to produce a better brand of human, high-quality personnel will be in short supply, and only a portion of it should be allocated to government. Perhaps the time is not foreseeable when the government as a whole will have much better than average personnel.

17. Even when an agency's staff is average or below average, some kinds of personnel planning can protect against arbitrariness. A few new people in strategic spots can sometimes change the morale of a whole organization. Results often depend heavily upon training, supervising, and disciplining of staffs.

18. Fair procedure is vital even when it is entirely as informal as conversation. Informal procedure is not the equivalent of no procedure. For instance, before an agency makes a discretionary determination that affects a party adversely, the procedural protection is very great if the officer will tell the party what he believes the facts to be, and what he contemplates and why, and then if the officer listens to what the party has to say. The fundamentals of procedural fairness can be observed even in an informal conference—or even in a telephone conversation or exchange of letters or telegrams.

Chapter 19

THE DRUNK—EFFECTIVE LIMITS OF THE CRIMINAL JUSTICE SYSTEM: POLICYMAKING AND STRATEGIES FOR CHANGE

It has commonly been assumed that determining the proper scope of the substantive criminal law is a legislative responsibility. With the recent efforts at codification of the substantive criminal law, some state legislatures have in fact made important policy decisions about the scope and content of the criminal law, for example, excluding from the criminal law private sexual conduct between adults and social gambling. One of the functions which legislatures have still left to the criminal law despite dissatisfaction with the ineffectiveness of the criminal justice process to deal with it, is treatment of the common drunk. There is a general consensus that change is needed, but it is less clear whose responsibility it is to initiate change and what methods are best designed to effect this change.

A. THE EXISTING SYSTEM

THE LAW ON SKID ROW

Comment, 38 Chicago-Kent Law Review 22, 30-37 (1961)

Joe Kennedy is a bum. Joe came to Skid Row about ten years ago, at age thirty-eight, from the Far South Side of Chicago. West Madison Street was filled with Joe's kind, men who didn't mind getting drunk frequently. Joe felt at home here; nobody bothered him because of his rough, dirty appearance, and no one condemned him for getting drunk. Joe has come to feel at home on Skid Row because, although he has no close friends, there are many men who are amiable drinking companions.

Joe isn't much to look at. Dirty and unshaven, he is dressed in faded blue dungarees, under which he wears long woolen underwear to keep himself warm. Joe owns no socks; his feet are protected by heavy work shoes, which are cracked and faded from age and use. He hugs his heavy winter jacket close to his body, because a tee shirt is all that he wears underneath it. Joe had a shirt once, a beautiful plaid woolen one that a relative had sent him from Oregon. But he sold that for the price of a bottle right after the last time he was robbed. Joe's face bears a half-healed cut on the nose, received when he fell while drunk, and an open, frequently bleeding wound on his lip, the work of a jackroller who discovered that Joe had forty-five cents. If Joe were to expose his leg, one could see an open, festering sore (called a winesore, because drink aggravates the infection) which hasn't been washed or cleaned in a week. Joe doesn't mind the filth and grime on his body; he doesn't even mind the cut on his lip, or the wound on his nose, or the winesore. In fact, Joe doesn't mind anything, because Joe is drunk.

Joe received a check from the railroad this morning for work he did last month as a gandy dancer. Joe likes the fact that the railroad prolongs the pay by giving it in installments, because this gives Joe a source of income while he is not working. Joe paid his month's rent first, then went to a restaurant where he purchased meal "tickets" for the month. The rest of the pay, except for three dollars, he gave to the hotel clerk with instructions to give him three dollars whenever he asked for it. Then he went to the House of Rothschild to see his friends.

The House of Rothschild isn't a banking house; it's a tavern and a meeting place for the derelicts on West Madison Street. It has three long bars (seating more than 75 men), and one can get an eighteen ounce schooner of beer for only 15 cents. Joe has already had quite a few drinks, even though it's only 2:30 in the afternoon, and he thinks dimly that he should get home while he's still able to walk. So he leaves the congenial atmosphere of the House of Rothschild and begins to wend his weary way home.

As he staggers down the sidewalk and from curb to building and back again, anyone can see that he won't make it home. Joe, although dead drunk, isn't noisy and he isn't getting into the way of pedestrians. However, if the police patrol wagon were to come along now, Joe would certainly be arrested. But the "Bum Wagon" doesn't come, and Joe staggers on.

After walking for about half a block, Joe begins to realize that he can't get to his room without resting. So he stops to lean against a building. It feels comfortable, so he closes his eyes—just for a second.

Joe is vaguely aware that he has fallen over, and his ear feels funny, but it feels so comfortable on the sidewalk that Joe puts a hand underneath the aching ear and drifts back to sleep. But the wind is cold, and it whistles down the length of the buildings and under Joe's coat. He wakes up, cold and shivering, and looking for a warmer spot to rest for a while before he has to do something. Now what was that he had in mind when he came out of the tavern?! Never mind, it isn't important. Joe's cold, and he needs a place to get out of the wind. There's a doorway nearby. Joe stumbles over to it and curls up inside, out of the wind. Ahhh, this is comfort! Joe falls into the deep sleep of drunken stupor.

As Joe sleeps, another man comes along. This man is a bit cleaner and more sober than Joe, and he has something on his mind—robbery. When he sees Joe sleeping in the doorway, he stops and then slowly walks over to the sleeping form.

Quick, experienced hands go through Joe's pockets, searching for money. Ten cents isn't much, and the jackroller is tempted to strike Joe. But he suppresses the thought—there are too many people around. However, Joe is wearing a better pair of shoes than the jackroller, and the latter quickly removes them and retires to a less conspicuous spot to make the change. Joe sleeps on.

No sooner has the first man disappeared than does a second appear. This man has a hole in the seat of his trousers and he needs another pair. Joe is about his size, so the man stops and removes Joe's pants, although with some difficulty. Finally, his task accomplished, the man walks off with Joe's pants tucked under his overcoat, leaving Joe clad only in his long red woolen underwear.

Joe wakes up. He's cold. "Damn! Someone stole my pants. I'd better get home." Joe comes out of the doorway and begins to walk unsteadily toward his "home" at the flophouse hotel. The time is 3:15 in the afternoon.

As Joe walks along, the driver of the Bum Wagon spots him. Silently drifting along Madison Street, the wagon has already picked up eight men since 3 o'clock and Joe and three or four others will make a full load with which to return to the station. The wagon glides to a stop, and an officer steps out, walks over to Joe and puts an arm on his shoulder. "Come on; you're drunk, and you don't have any pants on," says the officer in a jovial, yet firm manner. Joe looks once, searchingly, into the face of the officer, then turns and quietly goes over to the rear of the vehicle. The door is opened, and Joe feels himself thrust among the other derelicts. The officer turns around, looking for more men. He fixes his eye on a group standing nearby and shouts, "All aboard for the City Hotel!" One man steps forward and goes into the van. "Last call!" says the officer; the doors are shut, and the Bum Wagon moves off.

Inside the wagon, Joe looks around. Many of his companions are drunk. One has a bottle which he has managed to smuggle into the van and which is being passed around. He and another man were picked up for drinking on the sidewalk, and they know that when they reach the station the bottle will be taken from them. Three men are merely seeking to escape the cold. On the floor lies a man who was found in drunken unconsciousness on the sidewalk. Even the dragging to the truck failed to awaken him. The rest of the men, like Joe, were picked up while drunk for "safekeeping."

Another stop—two more men—and the truck heads for the Monroe Street Station.

At the station the truck backs into the unloading garage and the doors are swung open. Joe and the others step over the sleeping man and stumble out of the van. Because of their condition, many of the men hit their heads on the top of the exit while stepping from the wagon. Joe stumbles up the stairs into the lockup, while the officers bring up the rear, carrying the sleeper. Inside the lockup Joe is called forward in turn, and the officer makes out his arrest slip. The lockup keeper searches Joe, taking everything from his pockets and running his hands down Joe's legs to make sure nothing is concealed there. If Joe had had shoes, the keeper would have looked inside them. Pencils, razor blades, and other sharp objects are taken from the prisoners. Money is taken and a receipt is made out, which is attached to the arrest slip and will be returned in the morning. Then Joe is taken to his "hotel" room.

There are thirteen cells and a "Bull Pen" in the lockup. Nine of the thirteen cells are reserved for drunks, and the Bull Pen is reserved for unconscious prisoners or friends of the lockup keeper. The "sleeper" will spend the night here. The cells are furnished with iron cots, a commode, drinking fountain, and a light bulb which, although heavily screened, is usually broken. Into each cell, before the night is over, will go ten or twelve men; but now in the afternoon there are only four or five in each cell. The lockup is hosed daily with hot water, but it never completely loses the fetid smell that is so characteristic of Skid Row.

Joe's companions in the cell are old, tired, defeated men. Joe knows that any one of them would probably rob him, given a reason. For example, if Joe had valuables, for which he received a receipt, a jackroller would probably rob him of the receipt right in the cell. Joe can only guess which of his companions are active homosexuals; he fears that one of them will approach him. The darkness in the cell facilitates the practices of robbery and perversion, and alcohol saps a person's willpower to resist. Joe settles down for the long wait until morning.

At seven o'clock in the evening, the lockup keeper comes around with supper. The jailer stops the serving cart in front of the cell, and reaching into the basket atop the cart, he picks a large, thick slice of baloney and places it between two slices of hard, white bread. As each sandwich is completed, the jailer hands it into the cell. The prisoners receive one sandwich each, and many men will get two, but they never seem to get enough. They reach out between the bars for more, and within the cell they struggle for the food.

Sandwich firmly clutched in hand, Joe returns to his corner of the cell to eat his supper. If he needs something to wash down the sandwich, he will drink from the fountain.

Supper finished, Joe settles down again for the night. There really isn't enough room to spread out and lie down, because the cell is now crowded, so Joe tries to make himself comfortable by leaning against a wall. Even in his sleep, however, Joe will try to guard himself against his cell-mates. Joe sleeps fitfully until six o'clock in the morning, when the jailer comes around again with breakfast—more baloney. At this time, too, the lockup keeper will come through the jail looking for men to help the janitor. Some men will volunteer, because they don't want to see the judge, and they know that the charges against them will be automatically dismissed if they volunteer. Joe, however, won't volunteer; he hasn't been here in a long time—at least three weeks—and he has no fear of being sentenced.

One of the men begins to shake and moan. The D.T.'s! Joe and the others try to quiet the man; someone takes the man's arm and begins to tug vigorously on it. The first aid works, and the man subsides into unconsciousness.

At about eight o'clock the message that all is ready in the courtroom comes through, and the lockup keeper moves Joe and the others to the courtroom. The most serious cases—the sick and still-drunk—are moved to a Bull Pen upstairs, behind the courtroom. Joe and the others who are in a more sober and stable condition are herded to the benches in the courtroom. In all, there are about one hundred and fifty men in court. As the men file in, the bailiff moves over and turns on a fan to circulate the air in the room. Even then, the odor of Skid Row lingers in the air.

The bailiff comes over, and the men sitting in the front row are lined up before the judge. The judge is a kindly man, but he knows the men appearing before him too well to be deceived by their stories. "I've got a room, Judge," says the man in front of Joe. "But this says you have no home," replies the judge, referring to the arrest slip. The arrest slip is attached to the complaint sheet, and in reality the former, not the latter, is what the judge uses for trying the prisoner. "You need help," says the judge. "You'd better go to the hospital."

The time is 8:45 a.m. "Next case—Joe Kennedy!" calls the bailiff. The judge looks at Joe. "What can we do for you today?" Joe knows that if he wants to go "on the wagon" or if he wants medical attention for his wounds, he can at this time request commitment to the City Farm or the Bridewell Hospital. In fact, Joe knows that he can probably set the length of his own sentence. But Joe hopes that the judge will think him sober and will release him. Perhaps the judge will send Joe to the Salvation Army or to the social worker next door. Once Joe was sent to talk to the man from Alcoholics Anonymous; they try hard and often succeed—but they didn't get through to Joe.

"I'm okay now, Judge." But the judge is not impressed. "Hold out your hands," he demands. Joe stretches his arms out in front of him, trying to hold them as steadily as possible. Joe's arms tremble noticeably. The last time Joe was in court in this condition the judge "continued" Joe's case until the next day, forcing Joe to spend another night in the lockup until he was sober. Joe isn't so lucky this time. The man from A.A. steps over to the judge and says, "This man needs to go to the hospital; he's got a bad leg." "Let me see that leg," says the judge changing his mind about not sentencing Joe. Obediently, Joe pulls up one leg of his underpants, exposing the red, ugly mass of festering flesh which is his leg. "That looks pretty bad; we had better get it taken care of." "I've got some stuff back in my room. I can take care of it myself," protests Joe. "No, we'd better do it for you. Send him to the hospital," and Joe is led away. The judge turns to the bailiff: "Seventeen days." The bailiff writes on the arrest slip: "25+10," meaning a fine of $35, which must be served at $2 per day. But Joe knows none of this; he is already in the Bull Pen. The time is 8:46 a.m.

Seventeen days from now, Joe will return to the House of Rothschild to see his friends and celebrate his release—over a beer.

THE PRESIDENT'S COMMISSION ON LAW ENFORCEMENT AND ADMINISTRATION OF JUSTICE TASK FORCE REPORT: DRUNKENNESS 1-3 (1967)

DRUNKENNESS LAWS

Drunkenness is punishable under a variety of laws, generally describing the offense as being "drunk in a public place," often without providing a precise definition of drunkenness itself. Some laws include as a condition that the offender is "unable to care for his own safety."

In some jurisdictions there are no laws prohibiting drunkenness, but any drunkenness that causes a breach of the peace is punishable. In Georgia and Alabama, for example, drunkenness that is manifested by boisterous or indecent conduct, or loud and profane discourse, is a crime. Other jurisdictions apply disorderly conduct statutes to those who are drunk in public. In Chicago, for example, the police, having no drunkenness law to enforce, use a disorderly conduct statute to arrest nondisorderly inebriates. Some jurisdictions permit police to make public drunkenness arrests under both State laws and local ordinances.

The laws provide maximum jail sentences ranging from 5 days to 6 months; the most common maximum sentence is 30 days. In some States an offender convicted of "habitual drunkenness" may be punished by a 2-year sentence of imprisonment.

The Offenders

The 2 million arrests for drunkenness each year involve both sporadic and regular drinkers. Among the number are a wide variety of offenders—the rowdy college boy; the weekend inebriate; the homeless, often unemployed single man. How many offenders fall into these and other categories is not known. Neither is it known how many of the offenders are alcoholics in the medical sense of being dependent on alcohol. There is strong evidence, however, that a large number of those who are arrested have a lengthy history of prior drunkenness arrests, and that a disproportionate number involve poor persons who live in slums. In 1964 in the city of Los Angeles about one-fifth of all persons arrested for drunkenness accounted for two-thirds of the total number of arrests for that offense. Some of the repeaters were arrested as many as 18 times in that year.

A review of chronic offender cases reveals that a large number of persons have, in short installments, spent many years of their lives in jail. In 1957 the Committee on Prisons, Probation and Parole in the District of Columbia studied six chronic offenders and found that they had been arrested for drunkenness a total of 1,409 times and had served a total of 125 years in penal institutions. A recent article in a Syracuse, N.Y. newspaper illustrates the point even more succinctly:

> H____ F____, 69, appeared in police court for the 277th time on a public intoxication charge. F____, who has served

16 years in the Jamesville Penitentiary in short terms on the charge, was returned there for a 6-month sentence.

The great majority of repeaters live on "skid row"—a dilapidated area found in most large and medium-size cities in the United States. On skid row substandard hotels and roominghouses are intermingled with numerous taverns, pawn shops, cheap cafeterias, employment agencies that specialize in jobs for the unskilled, and religious missions that provide free meals after a service. Many of the residents—including the chronic drunkenness offenders—are homeless, penniless, and beset with acute personal problems.

The Arrest of the Drunkenness Offender

The police do not arrest everyone who is under the influence of alcohol.[12] Sometimes they will help an inebriate home. It is when he appears to have no home or family ties that he is most likely to be arrested and taken to the local jail.[13]

One policeman assigned to a skid row precinct in a large eastern city recently described how he decided whom to arrest:

> I see a guy who's been hanging around; a guy who's been picked up before or been making trouble. I stop him. Sometimes he can convince me he's got a job today or got something to do. He'll show me a slip showing he's supposed to go to the blood bank, or to work. I let him go. But if it seems to me that he's got nothing to do but drink, then I bring him in.

Drunkenness arrest practices vary from place to place. Some police departments strictly enforce drunkenness statutes, while other departments are known to be more tolerant. In fact, the number of arrests in a city may be related less to the amount of

---

[12] It is often the express policy of a police department to refrain from arresting a person for drunkenness in cases in which he may be placed in a taxicab or he is with friends who are able to escort him home. See, *e.g.*, 1 Columbus, Ohio, Police Dep't Training Bull., rev. Aug. 1958, unit 6, p. 2; PRES.'S COMM'N ON CRIME IN THE DISTRICT OF COLUMBIA, REP. 475 (1966), citing letter from District of Columbia Police Chief John B. Layton to Pres.'s Comm'n on Crime in the District of Columbia, Apr. 1, 1966.

[13] The police make this determination by observing, *inter alia,* the apparent affluence of the inebriate. Moreover, the lack of funds for transportation will influence the determination to arrest. The result is that the poor are more likely to be arrested than the well-to-do. See PRES.'S COMM'N ON CRIME IN THE DISTRICT OF COLUMBIA, REP. 475 (1966). See also Washington Daily News, Dec. 21, 1965, p. 5, at p. 35 (interview with precinct commanding officer: "We do tend to enforce the laws more rigidly on 14th Street than in, say, Crestwood, a better part of the precinct.").

public drunkenness than to police policy. Some of the wide variations in police practices can be seen in the [comparison of] drunkenness arrests by two police departments known to be guided by policies of strict enforcement (Atlanta, Ga., and Washington, D.C.) [arrests for drunkenness accounted for 52.5% and 51.8% of total arrests in 1965] to arrests by a department that is considered more tolerant (St. Louis, Mo.) [arrests for drunkenness were 5.5%].

In some large and medium-size cities, police departments have "bum squads" that cruise skid rows and border areas to apprehend inebriates who appear unable to care for their own safety, or who are likely to annoy others. Such wholesale arrests sometimes include homeless people who are not intoxicated.[16]

Operation of the Criminal System After Arrest

Following arrest, the drunk is usually placed in a barren cell called a "tank," where he is detained for at least a few hours. The tanks in some cities can hold as many as 200 people, while others hold only 1 or 2. One report described the conditions found in a tank in this way:

> Although he may have been picked up for his own protection, the offender is placed in a cell, which may frequently hold as many as 40-50 men where there is no room to sit or lie down, where sanitary facilities and ventilation are inadequate and a stench of vomit and urine is prevalent.
>
> The drunken behavior of some of the inmates is an added hazard. It is questionable whether greater safety is achieved for the individual who is arrested for his safe keeping.[17]

---

[16] The Atlanta Alcohol Study Project found that there are a "significant number of individuals who are arrested for public intoxication and who are not drunk at the time of arrest." Emory Dep't of Psychiatry 18. Similar findings were reported in other cities; see, for example, reports by Klein, The Criminal Law Process vs. the Public Drunkenness Offender in San Francisco, 1964 (unpublished, on file at Stanford Univ. Institute for the Study of Human Problems), and by Nash, Habitats of Homeless Men in Manhattan, Nov. 1964 (unpublished, on file at Columbia Univ. Bureau of Applied Social Research).

[17] Comm. on Alcoholism Community Welfare Council of the Greater Sacramento Area, Inc., The Alcoholic Law Offender 4 (unpublished 1965). Another tank was described in a 1966 newspaper article:

> There are at least two men in each 4 x 8 foot cell and three in some. . . . The stench of cheap alcohol, dried blood, urine and excrement covers the cell blocks. . . . There are no lights in the cells. . . . There are no mattresses. Mattresses wouldn't last the night a policeman explains. And with prisoners urinating all over them, they wouldn't be any good if they did last. . . .

Hoagland, Cell Blocks' Common Denominator: A Stench of Alcohol and Dried Blood, Washington Post, March 29, 1966, p. A1, col. 3.

The chronic alcoholic offender generally suffers from a variety of ailments and is often in danger of serious medical complications, but medical care is rarely provided in the tank; and it is difficult to detect or to diagnose serious illness since it often resembles intoxication. Occasionally, chronic offenders become ill during pretrial detention and die without having received adequate medical attention.

If the offender can afford bail, he usually obtains release after he sobers up.[21] In many jurisdictions an offender is permitted to forfeit bail routinely by not appearing in court. Thus, if the arrested person has the few dollars required, he can avoid prosecution;[23] if he has no money, as is usually the case, he must appear in court.

Drunkenness offenders are generally brought before a judge the morning after their arrest, sometimes appearing in groups of 15 or 20. Rarely are the normal procedural or due process safeguards applied to these cases. Usually defendants are processed through the court system with haste and either released or sentenced to several days or weeks in jail. In some cities only those offenders who request it are jailed. In others chronic offenders, who are likely to be alcoholics, are generally sent to jail.

When a defendant serves a short sentence, he is fed, sheltered, and given access to available recreational facilities. In most institutions there is such a lack of facilities and financial resources that it is not possible to do more. Austin MacCormick, a former New York City commissioner of corrections, noted recently:

> The appallingly poor quality of most of the county jails in the United States is so well known that it is probably not necessary to discuss this point at any great length. The fact that the majority of all convicted alcoholics go to these institutions, however, makes it imperative that the public, and particularly those thoughtful citizens who are interested in the treatment of alcoholics, never be allowed to forget that our county jails are a disgrace to the country . . . and that they have a destructive rather than a beneficial effect not

---

[21] Stationhouse bail permits the release of defendants pending a subsequent court appearance. See generally FREED & WALD, BAIL IN THE UNITED STATES (1964). Outright release—with no obligation to return to court—is sometimes permitted by the police.

[23] In Washington, D.C., for example, approximately 20,000 of the 44,218 people arrested during 1965 obtained release by forfeiting $10 collateral. PRES.'S COMM'N ON CRIME IN THE DISTRICT OF COLUMBIA, REP. 475 (1966). In Atlanta, Ga., approximately 20,000 of 49,805 arrests during 1961 resulted in ($15) collateral forfeitures. Emory Dep't of Psychiatry 11. Those who post and forfeit collateral avoid the risk of a jail sentence.

only on alcoholics who are committed to them but also on those others who are convicted of the most petty offenses.[29]

After serving a brief sentence, the chronic offender is released, more likely than not to return to his former haunts on skid row, with no money, no job, and no plans. Often he is rearrested within a matter of days or hours.

1. *Police Policy*

Police have commonly been lenient with drunks. For example in Detroit the practice of releasing a drunk without charge when he has sobered up is referred to as the "Golden Rule Drunk" program.[a] This is a formally acknowledged police policy even though not provided for by the statute.

California police are instructed to follow an official policy of protectiveness, common sense, and tolerance for human foibles, in their encounters with the "simple drunk."

CALIFORNIA PEACE OFFICERS' TRAINING PUBLICATION NO. 70 (1956)
California State Department of Education

Lesson 22: How to Investigate Drunk and Drunk Driving Complaints

IV. Specific Problems

A. Women

. . .

6. Generally desirable to avoid arrest for simple drunk if matter can be disposed of otherwise

a. Send home with friends or relatives
b. Arrange for taxi
c. Avoid placing on public transportation

7. Arrest if drunk and unmanageable or causing trouble . . .

VI. General Considerations

D. It is not necessary to arrest every person who has been drinking

---

[29] MacCormick, *Correctional Views on Alcohol, Alcoholism and Crime,* 9 CRIME & DELINQUENCY 15, 20 (1963).

[a] See the discussion of the Detroit "Golden Rule" program at 339, *supra.*

1. Their condition should govern officer's action

2. The officer should not make borderline arrests

a. Suggest coffee and food
b. Obtain means of transportation to his home
c. Presence of police officer has an extremely sobering effect on most people

3. An officer will not be criticized for giving a person a break, but he is subject to criticism when condition of the person falls clearly within the *intent* of the law [emphasis added]

2. *Prosecutor Policy and Practice*

In some jurisdictions, the drunk who has been arrested is routinely brought into court and the judge has full responsibility for deciding what to do with him. In other jurisdictions there may be a clear-cut policy about which drunks are prosecuted and which are not. The drunk may simply be released unless he has been particularly belligerent, has caused harm, or is in such poor physical condition that he needs medical attention or a chance to dry out. In these latter situations, the decision to prosecute clearly constitutes the use of a criminal conviction to achieve social service objectives.

Whatever the policy, it usually is routine and there is commonly no such thing as an evaluation of the individual case to decide whether to prosecute. Consequently, the prosecutor himself is seldom, if ever, involved.

3. *Trial Court Policy and Practice*

Judges tend to be lenient with isolated instances of drunkenness. They accept drinking as a normal activity and are likely to deal lightly with drunkenness which is not chronic and creates no disturbance.

1

A seventy-year-old defendant was arrested for drunken driving. He had no prior record. He entered a plea of guilty. The judge, however, refused the plea and dismissed the case, saying, "Anyone who has reached the honored age of seventy years without so much as a parking ticket should not have his fine record blemished by a single lapse."

2

Two Negroes had been arrested for drinking together on the front steps of their slum tenement and charged with being drunk. The judge remarked that this "public intoxication" was not any worse than the "country club intoxication" he had seen plenty of. He dismissed the charges.

3

A defendant had been arrested on drunk charges when police patrolling the tavern saw him passed out at a table. The judge dismissed, commenting, "I say it is not a proper police function to go into bars to see who is drunk or not. I don't believe this is your duty. The police have plenty of other things to do rather than making the rounds and bothering tavern patrons."

Even the chronic alcoholic is generally dealt with tolerantly and leniently, with major concern for his welfare. A chronic alcoholic, charged with public intoxication, is sometimes given an option as to whether he wants to be acquitted or convicted. The court in effect gives him a choice of thirty or sixty days in jail to "dry out" or acquittal and immediate release.

4

A chronic inebriate charged with drunkenness told the court he couldn't decide whether he wanted to go to jail or not. He first said he needed sixty days, then changed his mind. The judge finally asked him to make up his mind, and he decided that he did not want to go to jail. The judge complied and dismissed the case.[b]

5

When one of the drunks was called before the judge, a representative of the Salvation Army stepped forward and said he knew the man and had been working with him and had a place for him. The judge dismissed.

On the other hand, judges are inclined to convict and to impose substantial sentences when the drunk has been troublesome.

6

The defendant, charged with drunkenness, was identified by the police to the judge as a troublemaker in the cheap hotel

[b] Compare the case of Joe Kennedy at 1215, *supra*.

where he lived. He was suspected of numerous petty thefts. The judge sentenced him to sixty day for drunkenness.

7

One of the drunks had resisted arrest and when asked what he had to say muttered that the "bastards" had it in for him. The judge sentenced him to sixty days.

8

A chronic alcoholic appeared in court for the twentieth time in a year. The judge said, "Sam, I'm tired of seeing you here. The only way you'll ever break out of this pattern is to learn the hard way. I'm going to give you six months this time, and I hope never to see you again."

B. CAUSES OF CONCERN

1. *Ineffectiveness of Treatment for the Drunk*

THE PRESIDENT'S COMMISSION ON LAW ENFORCEMENT AND ADMINISTRATION OF JUSTICE TASK FORCE REPORT: DRUNKENNESS 3 (1967)

The criminal justice system appears ineffective to deter drunkenness or to meet the problems of the chronic alcoholic offender. What the system usually does accomplish is to remove the drunk from public view, detoxify him, and provide him with food, shelter, emergency medical service, and a brief period of forced sobriety. As presently constituted, the system is not in a position to meet his underlying medical and social problems.

THE BORDERLAND OF THE CRIMINAL LAW: PROBLEMS OF "SOCIALIZING" CRIMINAL JUSTICE

By Francis A. Allen

32 Social Service Review 107 (1958)

(Reprinted in F. Allen, The Borderland of Criminal Justice 1 (1964)†

The system of criminal justice has sometimes been employed as a device for the administration of what are essentially social services. The consequences of this practice are almost always unfortunate. In this connection I shall advance a generalization, which I shall state somewhat dogmatically. Later I shall attempt to illustrate its application, even if I am unable fully to demonstrate its validity. The generalization is this: Whenever penal sanctions are employed to deal with problems of social service, two things are almost certain to happen and a third result may often occur. First, the social services will not be effectively rendered. Second, the diversion of personnel, resources, and energy required in the effort will adversely affect the ability of a system of criminal justice to fulfil those functions that it can uniquely perform. Finally, the effort may sometimes result in the corruption and demoralization of the agencies of criminal justice.

Deterioration of social services.—My first assertion is that when the criminal law is relied upon to perform the social-service function, those services are not likely to be effectively rendered. That there is a tendency to apply the criminal-law processes to such ends probably requires no elaborate demonstration. The crime of vagrancy, for example, represents, in one of its aspects, a primitive social reaction to the problems of human need. Perhaps, however, the point can best be conveyed by brief consideration of a concrete situation. Some years ago I had occasion to visit a women's reformatory in an eastern state. Having been guided through the main structure of the institution—a rambling wooden building of Victorian vintage—one approaches a rather modern brick establishment, located some distance away. As one enters the door, he suddenly discovers that he is standing in a nursery. On both sides of the room are rows of cribs, each crib occupied by an infant of an age ranging from three to eighteen months. These are children of women prisoners, born while their mothers were in penal custody. In almost every case the mothers were unwed and had been sentenced to the reformatory following conviction for some offense relating to extramarital sexual relations. As one begins to react to this spectacle, he is led to this obvious inquiry: Why are there so *few* infants here? Surely, these babies represent only the smallest fraction of the total of illegitimate children born each year in this populous state. The answer to this question is significant and characteristic. These were unwed mothers without financial resources to pay for the medical expenses of childbirth or the subsequent care of their offspring. True enough, the state had made funds available to local public agencies for the care of such mothers and their children. But these funds were not fully compensatory. Accordingly, some localities soon discovered that it was cheaper, when measured by immediate budgetary considerations, to proceed criminally against such women, thereby shifting the full burden of their provision and care from the locality to the state.

I tell this story, not because it is unusual. It is, on the contrary, illustrative of much that we do. The presence of these women and their children in a penal institution is not to be explained by any viable state policy directed to the punishment of extramarital relations. They are there because they are paupers or because the local officials were unable to force payment of the expenses of childbirth and care on the responsible male party. Criminal processes are rarely considered when the unwed mother has financial resources of her own or is able to secure aid from her family or friends. Unlike other ages, we do not react to the problem of the unwed mother by stoning the woman and subjecting the infant to death by exposure. But we do on occasion administer our social services through the agencies of the criminal law. One may wonder about the quality of services that result in stamping the stigma of a felony conviction on the mother and providing the child in its first impressionable months with the environment of a prison nursery. But this is not all. There is a further consideration that I can characterize only as an issue of justice. When penal treatment is employed to perform the functions of social service, selection of those eligible for penal treatment proceeds on inadmissible criteria. Persons are selected for criminal conviction, not by reference to their moral character or social dangerousness, but by reference to their poverty or their helplessness. Thus, we may object that such use of the penal process does not result in effective performance of the social-service function. We may also object that it lacks equity and decency.

2. *Clogs the Criminal Justice Machinery Which Should Be Put to Better Use*

THE PRESIDENT'S COMMISSION ON LAW ENFORCEMENT AND ADMINISTRATION OF JUSTICE TASK FORCE REPORT: DRUNKENNESS 3-4 (1967)

EFFECT ON THE SYSTEM OF CRIMINAL JUSTICE

Including drunkenness within the system of criminal justice seriously burdens and distorts its operations. Because the police often do not arrest the intoxicated person who has a home, there is in arrest practices an inherent discrimination against the homeless and the poor. Due process safeguards are often considered unnecessary or futile. The defendant may not be warned of his rights or permitted to make a telephone call.[32] And although

[32] Some police officials told Commission staff that the defendant charged with drunkenness is not permitted to place a telephone call upon request until a 4-hour "sobering up" period following arrest has elapsed. Such policy would deny the use of the telephone to some innocent people and to others who would be physically able to confer with counsel.

coordination, breath, or blood tests to determine intoxication are common practice in "driving-while-intoxicated" cases, they are virtually nonexistent in common drunk cases. Yet, without the use of such chemical tests, it is often difficult to determine whether the individual is intoxicated or suffering from a serious illness that has symptoms similar to intoxication.

The handling of drunkenness cases in court hardly reflects the standards of fairness that are the basis of our system of criminal justice. One major reason is that counsel is rarely present.[35] Drunkenness cases often involve complex factual and medical issues. Cross-examination could be conducted on "observations" of the arresting officer such as "bloodshot" and "glassy" eyes, "staggering gait," "odor" of alcohol on the defendant's breath. The testimony of an expert medical witness on behalf of the defendant could be elicited.

The extent of police time allotted to handling drunkenness offenders varies from city to city and from precinct to precinct. In most cities a great deal of time is spent. The inebriate must be taken into custody, transported to jail, booked, detained, clothed, fed, sheltered, and transported to court. In some jurisdictions, police officers must wait, often for hours, to testify in court.

There is a commensurate burden on the urban courts. Notwithstanding the fact that an overwhelming caseload often leads judges to dispose of scores of drunkenness cases in minutes, they represent a significant drain on court time which is needed for felony and serious misdemeanor cases. More subtly, drunkenness

---

[35] The assignment of counsel to skid row inebriates had a profound effect on the handling of such cases in New York City. More than 95% of the defendants were acquitted after trial on disorderly conduct charges. See Murtagh, Comments, 16 Inventory 13, 14 (N.C. Rehabilitation Program, July-Sept. 1966), for a discussion of the background and reasons for the program. In March 1966 there were 1,326 defendants arraigned in Social Court in New York City, of whom 1,280 were acquitted. In March 1965, in the absence of defense counsel, there were 1,590 arraignments, 1,259 guilty pleas, and only 325 acquittals. Address by Hon. Bernard Botein, Presiding Justice, App. Div., 1st Dep't, N.Y. Sup. Ct., April 22, 1966, in Governor Rockefeller's Conference on Crime 149 (1966); N.Y. Times, April 23, 1966, p. 14, col. 4. Court records show that in April and May 1966, 1,838 of 2,103 defendants in New York City's Social Court were acquitted. As a result of the high acquittal rate Chief Judge John M. Murtagh directed court clerks not to draw complaints on nondisorderly drunkenness. From June 1, 1966, through Sept. 30, 1966, a total of 189 cases was brought to Social Court, of which 161 resulted in convictions.

The effect of the assignment of counsel was to reduce the number of arrests in New York City's skid row. The appearance of many more inebriated people on skid row seemed to make the underlying public health problem more visible, and the establishment of alternate facilities became more urgent. See *Derelicts Dislike Non-Arrest Policy,* N.Y. Times, July 29, 1966, p. 27, col. 8.

cases impair the dignity of the criminal process in lower courts, which are forced to handle defendants so casually and to apply criminal sanctions with so little apparent effect.

In correctional systems, too, resources are diverted from serious offenders. After court appearance, some offenders are sent to short-term penal institutions, many of which are already overcrowded. Correctional authorities estimate that one-half the entire misdemeanant population is comprised of drunkenness offenders. In one city it was reported that 95 percent of short-term prisoners were drunkenness offenders.

3. *Dealing with the Drunk in the Criminal Justice System Is Wrong in Principle*

EASTER v. DISTRICT OF COLUMBIA

361 F.2d 50 (D.C. Cir. 1966)

FAHY, Circuit Judge, with whom BAZELON, Chief Judge, and WRIGHT and LEVENTHAL, Circuit Judges, join and with whom MCGOWAN, Circuit Judge, joins in the result and in Parts I and III of the opinion.

In the Court of General Sessions of the District of Columbia, at a trial by a judge without a jury, appellant DeWitt Easter was found guilty of having been "drunk and intoxicated" on a stated date in a street in Washington, in violation of our Code provision reading:

> No person shall . . . be drunk or intoxicated in any street, alley, park, or parking; . . .

D.C. Code § 25-128(a).[1] He was given a suspended sentence of ninety days imprisonment. That he was drunk or intoxicated at the time and place stated was proved and was uncontested. His defense was that he was a chronic alcoholic.

The judge did not rule that the evidence fell short of establishing that appellant was a chronic alcoholic. The judge ruled that the evidence to that effect was not pertinent; that is, that chronic alcoholism was not a defense to a charge of intoxication in a public place.

The District of Columbia Court of Appeals affirmed the conviction. Easter v. District of Columbia, D.C. App., 209 A.2d 625.

[1] D.C. Code § 25-128 (1961 ed.): (a) No person shall in the District of Columbia drink any alcoholic beverage in any street, alley, park, or parking; . . . No such person shall be drunk or intoxicated in any street, alley, park, or parking; . . .

We allowed an appeal to this court. Sitting en banc we heard and now decide the case.

I

Our decision is that chronic alcoholism is a defense to a charge of public intoxication and, therefore, is not a crime in violation of Section 25-128(a) of our Code, *supra* n. 1. We think this follows, in the first place, from the Act of Congress of August 4, 1947, entitled "Rehabilitation of Alcoholics," 61 Stat. 744, c. 472, now embodied in our Code as Sections 24-501 et seq.[2]

In aid of its purposes, one of which is "to establish a program for the rehabilitation of alcoholics, promote temperance, and provide for the medical, psychiatric, and other scientific treatment of chronic alcoholics" the Act provides,

> the courts of the District of Columbia are hereby authorized to take judicial notice of the fact that a chronic alcoholic is a sick person and in need of proper medical, institutional, advisory, and rehabilitative treatment, and the court is authorized to direct that he receive appropriate medical, psychiatric, or other treatment as provided under the terms of this chapter.

D.C. Code § 24-501 (1961 ed.).

A "chronic alcoholic" is defined in the Act:

> The term "chronic alcoholic" means any person who chronically and habitually uses alcoholic beverages to the extent that he has lost the power of self-control with respect to the use of such beverages, or while under the influence of alcohol endangers the public morals, health, safety, or welfare.

D.C. Code § 24-502 (1961 ed.).

We are concerned in this case only with that part of the above definition which refers to loss of the power of self-control with respect to the use of alcoholic beverages.

The above statutory provisions, considered in the full context of the Act of which they are a part, preclude attaching criminality in this jurisdiction to intoxication in public of a chronic alcoholic. An essential element of criminal responsibility is the

---

[2] The full flavor of the enlightened treatment of the subject by Congress, demonstrating its intention that the chronic alcoholic be subjected to civil processes when found intoxicated in public, rather than convicted as a criminal, can be gathered only by perusal in full of the Act of 1947.

ability to avoid the conduct specified in the definition of the crime. Action within the definition is not enough. To be guilty of the crime a person must engage responsibly in the action. Thus, an insane person who does the act is not guilty of the crime. The law, in such a case based on morals, absolves him of criminal responsibility. So, too, in case of an infant. In case of a chronic alcoholic Congress has dealt with his condition so that in this jurisdiction he too cannot be held to be guilty of the crime of being intoxicated because, as the Act recognizes, he has lost the power of self-control in the use of intoxicating beverages. In his case an essential element of criminality, where personal conduct is involved, is lacking.

It is suggested that the public nature of the intoxication adds a factor which precludes the defense—that if suffering from the sickness is not a crime manifesting it in a public place is. But nothing whatever indicates that Congress intended to limit the scope of the Act to persons sick in privacy. It is clear the Act was primarily concerned with persons found in public places. The provisions which contemplated their institutional care, instead of the jail, show indubitably that the non-criminal approach of Congress applied to the chronic alcoholic floundering in a public place. The lack of power of self-control referred to cannot be limited to absolution of criminality for drinking or being drunk in a non-public place. No statute in the District of Columbia makes such an act or circumstance criminal. The very nature of the sickness goes where its victim goes.

We find no basis for judicial repudiation of the Act of 1947. The fact that in the intervening years the facilities contemplated by the Act have not been made available does not detract from the legal effect of those provisions of the Act which define the nature of the sickness. One who has committed no crime cannot be validly sentenced as a criminal because of a lack of rehabilitative and caretaking facilities.

In event of a determination of chronic alcoholism under the procedures of D.C. Code § 24-504 commitment for treatment is not mandatory. In the judge's discretion the accused may be released. But he may not be punished.

II

Our decision would be the same were we without the guidance furnished by the Act of 1947. One who is a chronic alcoholic cannot have the *mens rea* necessary to be held responsible criminally for being drunk in public.

The same basic problem now before us was recently before the Court of Appeals for the Fourth Circuit in Driver v. Hinnant,

356 F.2d 761. This was a habeas corpus proceeding attacking in the federal courts a conviction of Driver of public intoxication by the courts of North Carolina. Under a State statute it was a misdemeanor to be found "drunk or intoxicated on the public highway, or at any public place or meeting." Even without benefit of such a statute as our Act of 1947, the court sustained the defense of chronic alcoholism. The court said in part:

> It is known that alcohol can be addicting, and it is the addict—the involuntary drinker—on whom our decision is now made. Hence we exclude the merely excessive—steady or spree—voluntary drinker.
>
> This addiction—chronic alcoholism—is now almost universally accepted medically as a disease. The symptoms, as already noted, may appear as "disorder of behavior." Obviously, this included appearances in public, as here, unwilled and ungovernable by the victim. When that is the conduct for which he is criminally accused, [t]here can be no judgment of criminal conviction passed upon him. To do so would affront the Eighth Amendment, as cruel and unusual punishment in branding him a criminal, irrespective of consequent detention or fine.

Judge Bryan also stated for the court that Robinson v. State of California, 370 U.S. 660, "sustains, if not commands, the view we take." In *Robinson* the Supreme Court held invalid as cruel and unusual punishment prohibited by the Eighth and Fourteenth Amendments a California statute which made drug addiction a crime. The Court said such addiction was a status involuntarily assumed, and therefore to punish it as a crime violated the constitutional provisions.

We close this discussion with the observation that confinement, e.g. for inquiry or treatment, lies within the means available for dealing, constitutionally, with a menace to society.

III

It follows that the evidence of chronic alcoholism adduced in this case was pertinent. It established the defense.

Expert medical and psychiatric evidence, not sought to be rebutted, proved that appellant was a chronic alcoholic who had lost self-control over his use of alcoholic beverages. His condition, with its usual physical manifestations, was arrayed fully before the trial judge and need not be repeated here in detail. Since 1937 appellant has been arrested for intoxication or associated conduct 70 times, 12 times in 1963 alone. On innumerable occasions he has been intoxicated but not arrested. The condition had progressed for many years, definitely since the 1930s, resulting in a broken home life, recurrent hospitalization, and loss of steady employment.

Reversed, with direction to remand to the Court of General Sessions for dismissal of the information.

C. STRATEGIES FOR CHANGE

THE PRESIDENT'S COMMISSION ON LAW ENFORCEMENT AND ADMINISTRATION OF JUSTICE TASK FORCE REPORT: DRUNKENNESS 4-6 (1967)

LINES FOR ACTION

The sheer size of the drunkenness problem in relation to the very limited knowledge about causes and treatment makes it impossible to speak in terms of "solutions." There are, however, some important and promising lines that the Commission believes should be explored.

TREATING DRUNKENNESS AS NONCRIMINAL

The Commission seriously doubts that drunkenness alone (as distinguished from disorderly conduct) should continue to be treated as a crime. Most of the experts with whom the Commission discussed this matter, including many in law enforcement, thought that it should not be a crime. The application of disorderly conduct statutes would be sufficient to protect the public against criminal behavior stemming from intoxication. This was the view of the President's Commission on Crime in the District of Columbia, which recommended that the District of Columbia drunkenness law "be amended to require specific kinds of offensive conduct in addition to drunkenness."

Perhaps the strongest barrier to making such a change is that there presently are no clear alternatives for taking into custody and treating those who are now arrested as drunks. The Commission believes that current efforts to find such alternatives to treatment within the criminal system should be expanded. For example, if adequate public health facilities for detoxification are developed, civil legislation could be enacted authorizing the police to pick up those drunks who refuse to or are unable to cooperate—if, indeed, such specific authorization is necessary. Such legislation could expressly sanction a period of detention and allow the individual to be released from a public health facility only when he is sober.

Among those seeking alternatives to processing drunkenness cases through the criminal system are the Vera Institute of Justice[42] in New York City and the South End Center for Alcoholics and Unattached Persons[43] in Boston. The Vera Institute has recently undertaken a project to explore the feasibility of using personnel other than the police to pick up drunks.[44] Included in the study is an attempt to determine what percentage of drunks will come to a treatment facility voluntarily. The Vera program would circumvent the criminal process by establishing a system within a public health framework to care for the immediate and long-range needs of the skid row inebriate.

The Boston program, which has received funds from the Office of Economic Opportunity, provides an alternative to the police-correctional handling of the homeless alcoholic. Staff personnel of the Boston South End Center have approached homeless inebriates in skid row and offered them assistance. An official of the program estimates that 80 percent of the people approached in this way responded willingly. The center screens and evaluates the cases and refers homeless alcoholics to appropriate community facilities. In the past year it has handled the cases of over 900 homeless alcoholics.

The importance of developing an alternative to treating drunkenness within the criminal system is underlined by court decisions in two Federal circuits holding that alcoholics cannot be convicted for drunkenness, *Easter v. District of Columbia*[45] and *Driver v. Hinnant*.[46] Pursuant to the *Easter* decision, alcoholics

[42] See *Proposal for the Manhattan Bowery Project,* printed in part as appendix D to this volume.

[43] The Boston center is seen by its administrators as an intermediate step to a multiservice center which can provide comprehensive medical care and assistance in job placement, housing, and welfare. The center does not provide many of these services at present but acts as a referral unit for existing community agencies. Address by Edward Blacker, Dir., Div. of Alcoholism, Mass. Dep't of Public Health, *Aftercare Residential Program Planning: Boston's Program for the Chronic Drunkenness Offender,* No. Am. Ass'n of Alcoholism Programs 17th Annual meeting, Albuquerque, N.M., Oct. 10, 1966.

[44] The PRES.'S COMM'N ON CRIME IN THE DISTRICT OF COLUMBIA, REP. 497 (1966), recommended "using public health personnel to take incapacitated inebriates into protective custody." An authority on alcoholism, Dr. Earl Rubington of the Rutgers University School of Alcohol Studies, has proposed what he calls a "rescue service," a type of storefront detoxification unit in skid row operated in part by a staff of skid row residents who would bring in inebriates who agree to such assistance. See Rubington's proposal submitted to Office of Law Enforcement Assistance, U.S. Dep't of Justice, Alcoholic Control on Skid Row, Oct. 14, 1965.

[45] 361 F.2d 50 (D.C. Cir. 1966).

[46] 356 F.2d 761 (4th Cir. 1966).

are no longer being convicted of public drunkenness in Washington, D.C.

Detoxification Centers

An alternate approach to present methods of handling drunkenness offenders after arrest and a prerequisite to taking drunkenness out of the criminal system is the establishment of civil detoxification centers. The detoxification center would replace the police station as an initial detention unit for inebriates. Under the authority of civil legislation, the inebriate would be brought to this public health facility by the police and detained there until sober. Thereafter, the decision to continue treatment should be left to the individual. Experience in New York and Boston indicates that some alcoholics may be willing to accept treatment beyond the initial "sobering up" period. The center should include such medical services as physical examinations, an emergency-care unit for the treatment of acutely intoxicated persons, and transportation to a hospital, if advanced medical care seems necessary.

The Department of Justice has recently provided funds to establish detoxification centers as demonstration projects in St. Louis and Washington, D.C. The St. Louis center is already in full operation; plans for the Washington center are underway. Both units have sufficient facilities to house for a period of a few days those who are in need of "drying out." They also have "in-patient programs," in which patients are given high protein meals with vitamin and mineral supplements and appropriate medication to alleviate alcohol withdrawal symptoms. Bath and laundry facilities are available, as are basic clothing and limited recreational facilities. Regularly scheduled Alcoholics Anonymous meetings, film showings, work projects, group therapy, and lectures are part of the program. During their stay patients are counseled by social workers and other staff members.

The police might also bring to such a center intoxicated persons charged with a variety of petty offenses apart from drunkenness, with violations of administrative codes, and with such felony offenses as driving while intoxicated, assault, and larceny. If the police planned to prosecute the case, a summons could be left with the offender to appear in court at a later date. If an intoxicated defendant was charged with committing a felony, the police could make an individual determination as to the most appropriate detention facility. If he seemed likely to appear in court he might be taken to the detoxification facility. Otherwise, he would presumably be taken to the local jail, unless there were adequate detention facilities on the premises of the detoxification center.

Aftercare Programs

There is little reason to believe that the chronic offender will change a life pattern of drinking after a few days of sobriety and care at a public health unit. The detoxification unit should therefore be supplemented by a network of coordinated "aftercare" facilities. Such a program might well begin with the mobilization of existing community resources. Alcoholics Anonymous programs, locally based missions, hospitals, mental health agencies, outpatient centers, employment counseling, and other social service programs should be coordinated and used by the staff of the detoxification center for referral purposes. It is well recognized among authorities that homeless alcoholics cannot be treated without supportive residential housing, which can be used as a base from which to reintegrate them into society. Therefore, the network of aftercare facilities should be expanded to include halfway houses, community shelters, and other forms of public housing.

The success of aftercare facilities will depend upon the ability of the detoxification unit to diagnose problems adequately and to make appropriate referrals. A diagnostic unit attached to, or used by, the detoxification unit could formulate treatment plans by conducting a thorough medical and social evaluation of every patient. Diagnostic work should include assistance to the patient and his family in obtaining counseling for economic, marital, or employment problems. Subsequent referrals to appropriate agencies will be crucial to the success of the overall treatment plan. The diagnostic unit, through referral to a job and housing service, might also assist the patient in moving out of the deteriorating environment of skid row. Philadelphia has already established a diagnostic and relocation center, which offers diagnostic, recreational, therapeutic, vocational counseling, and housing relocation services, including training in social and occupational skills.

Research

With over 5 million alcoholics in the country, alcoholism is the Nation's fourth largest health problem. Research aimed at developing new methods and facilities for treating alcoholics should be given the priority called for by the scope of the need.

The application of funds for research purposes appears to be an appropriate supplement to the proposed detoxification and treatment units. Consideration should be given to providing further legislation on the Federal level for the promotion of the necessary coordinated treatment programs. Only through such a joint commitment will the burdens of the present system, which fall on both the criminal system and the drunkenness offender, be alleviated.

1. *Judicial Responsibility for Effecting Change*

Because of the widespread sentiment that drunkenness should not be criminal and the decisions in the *Robinson, Easter,* and *Driver* cases referred to above, many thought that when an appropriate case arose, the Supreme Court of the United States would declare the alcoholic a sick person as to whom the criminal process cannot be invoked. They felt that the Court would thus precipitate the desired change, forcing local units of government to devise alternative ways of dealing with the common drunk.

POWELL v. TEXAS
392 U.S. 514 (1968)

MR. JUSTICE MARSHALL announced the judgment of the Court and delivered an opinon in which THE CHIEF JUSTICE, MR. JUSTICE BLACK, and MR. JUSTICE HARLAN join.

In late December 1966, appellant was arrested and charged with being found in a state of intoxication in a public place, in violation of Texas Penal Code, Art. 477 (1952), which reads as follows:

"Whoever shall get drunk or be found in a state of intoxication in any public place, or at any private house except his own, shall be fined not exceeding one hundred dollars."

Appellant was tried in the Corporation Court of Austin, Texas, found guilty, and fined $20. He appealed to the County Court at Law No. 1 of Travis County, Texas, where a trial *de novo* was held. His counsel urged that appellant was "afflicted with the disease of chronic alcoholism," that "his appearance in public [while drunk was] . . . not of his own volition," and therefore that to punish him criminally for that conduct would be cruel and unusual, in violation of the Eighth and Fourteenth Amendments to the United States Constitution.

The trial judge in the county court, sitting without a jury, made certain findings of fact, but ruled as a matter of law that chronic alcoholism was not a defense to the charge. He found appellant guilty, and fined him $50. There being no further right to appeal within the Texas judicial system, appellant appealed to this Court; we noted probable jurisdiction.

I.

In the first place, the record in this case is utterly inadequate to permit the sort of informed and responsible adjudication which alone can support the announcement of an important and wide-ranging new constitutional principle. We know very little about the circumstances surrounding the drinking bout which resulted in this conviction, or about Leroy Powell's drinking problem, or indeed about alcoholism itself. The trial hardly reflects the sharp legal and evidentiary clash between fully prepared adversary litigants which is traditionally expected in major constitutional cases. The State put on only one witness, the arresting officer. The defense put on three—a policeman who testified to appellant's long history of arrests for public drunkenness, the psychiatrist, and appellant himself.

Furthermore, the inescapable fact is that there is no agreement among members of the medical profession about what it means to say that "alcoholism" is a "disease."

Nor is there any substantial consensus as to the "manifestations of alcoholism."

Dr. Wade did testify that once appellant began drinking he appeared to have no control over the amount of alcohol he finally ingested. Appellant's own testimony concerning his drinking on the day of the trial would certainly appear, however, to cast doubt upon the conclusion that he was without control over his consumption of alcohol when he had sufficiently important reasons to exercise such control. However that may be, there are more serious factual and conceptual difficulties with reading this record to show that appellant was unable to abstain from drinking. Dr. Wade testified that when appellant was sober, the act of taking the first drink was a "voluntary exercise of his will," but that this exercise of will was undertaken under the "exceedingly strong influence" of a "compulsion" which was "not completely overpowering." Such concepts, when juxtaposed in this fashion, have little meaning.

Moreover, Jellinek asserts that it cannot accurately be said that a person is truly unable to abstain from drinking unless he is suffering the physical symptoms of withdrawal. There is no testimony in this record that Leroy Powell underwent withdrawal symptoms either before he began the drinking spree which resulted in the conviction under review here, or at any other time.

II.

Despite the comparatively primitive state of our knowledge on the subject, it cannot be denied that the destructive use of alcoholic beverages is one of our principal social and public health problems. The lowest current informed estimate places the number of "alcoholics" in America (definitional problems aside) at 4,000,000, and most authorities are inclined to put the figure considerably higher. Nor can it be gainsaid that the legislative response to this enormous problem has in general been inadequate.

There is as yet no known generally effective method for treating the vast number of alcoholics in our society. Some individual alcoholics have responded to particular forms of therapy with remissions of their symptomatic dependence upon the drug. But just as there is no agreement among doctors and social workers with respect to the causes of alcoholism, there is no consensus as to why particular treatments have been effective in particular cases and there is no generally agreed-upon approach to the problem of treatment on a large scale. Most psychiatrists are apparently of the opinion that alcoholism is far more difficult to treat than other forms of behavioral disorders, and some believe it is impossible to cure by means of psychotherapy; indeed, the medical profession as a whole, and psychiatrists in particular, have been severely criticised for the prevailing reluctance to undertake the treatment of drinking problems. Thus it is entirely possible that, even were the manpower and facilities available for a full-scale attack upon chronic alcoholism, we would find ourselves unable to help the vast bulk of our "visible"—let alone our "invisible"—alcoholic population.

However, facilities for the attempted treatment of indigent alcoholics are woefully lacking throughout the country.[22] It

---

[22] Encouraging pilot projects do exist. See President's Commission on Law Enforcement and Administration of Justice, Task Force Report: Drunkenness 50-64, 82-108 (1967). But the President's Commission concluded that the "strongest barrier" to the abandonment of the current use of the criminal process to deal with public intoxication "is that there presently are no clear alternatives for taking into custody and treating those who are now arrested as drunks." President's Commission on Law Enforcement and Administration of Justice, The Challenge of Crime in a Free Society 235 (1967). Moreover, even if massive expenditures for physical plants were forthcoming, there is a woeful shortage of trained personnel to man them. One study has concluded that:

"[T]here is little likelihood that the number of workers in these fields could be sufficiently increased to treat even a large minority of problem drinkers. In California, for instance, according to the best estimate available, providing all problem drinkers with weekly contact with a psychiatrist and once-a-month contact with a social worker would require the full time work of *every* psychiatrist and *every* trained social worker in the United would be tragic to return large numbers of helpless, sometimes dangerous and frequently unsanitary inebriates to the streets of our cities without even the opportunity to sober up adequately which a brief jail term provides. Presumably no State or city will tolerate such a state of affairs. Yet the medical profession cannot, and does not, tell us with any assurance that, even if the buildings, equipment and trained personnel were made available, it could provide anything more than slightly higher-class jails for our indigent habitual inebriates. Thus we run the grave risk that nothing will be accomplished beyond the hanging of a new sign—reading "hospital"—over one wing of the jailhouse.

One virtue of the criminal process is, at least that the duration of penal incarceration typically has some outside statutory limit; this is universally true in the case of petty offenses, such as public drunkenness, where jail terms are quite short on the whole. "Therapeutic civil commitment" lacks this feature; one is typically committed until one is "cured." Thus, to do otherwise than affirm might subject indigent alcoholics to the risk that they may be locked up for an indefinite period of time under the same conditions as before, with no more hope than before of receiving effective treatment and no prospect of periodic "freedom."

Faced with this unpleasant reality, we are unable to assert that the use of the criminal process as a means of dealing with the public aspects of problem drinking can never be defended as rational. The picture of the penniless drunk propelled aimlessly and endlessly through the law's "revolving door" of arrest, incarceration, release and re-arrest is not a pretty one. But before we condemn the present practice across-the-board, perhaps we ought to be able to point to some clear promise of a better world for these unfortunate people. Unfortunately, no such promise has yet been forthcoming. If, in addition to the absence of a coherent approach to the problem of treatment, we consider the almost complete absence of facilities and manpower for the implementation of a rehabilitation program, it is difficult to say in the present context that the criminal process is utterly lacking in social value. This Court has never held that anything in the Constitution requires that penal sanctions be designed solely to achieve therapeutic or rehabilitative effects, and it can hardly be said with assurance that incarceration serves such purposes any better for the general run of criminals than it does for public drunks.

States." Cooperative Commission on Study of Alcoholism, Alcohol Problems 120 (1967) (emphasis in original).

Ignorance likewise impedes our assessment of the deterrent effect of criminal sanctions for public drunkenness. The fact that a high percentage of American alcoholics conceal their drinking problems, not merely by avoiding public displays of intoxication but also by shunning all forms of treatment, is indicative that some powerful deterrent operates to inhibit the public revelation of the existence of alcoholism. Quite probably this deterrent effect can be largely attributed to the harsh moral attitude which our society has traditionally taken toward intoxication and the shame which we have associated with alcoholism. Criminal conviction represents the degrading public revelation of what Anglo-American society has long condemned as a moral defect, and the existence of criminal sanctions may serve to reinforce this cultural taboo, just as we presume they serve to reinforce other, stronger feelings against murder, rape, theft, and other forms of antisocial conduct.

Obviously, chronic alcoholics have not been deterred from drinking to excess by the existence of criminal sanctions against public drunkenness. But all those who violate penal laws of any kind are by definition undeterred. The long-standing and still raging debate over the validity of the deterrence justification for penal sanctions has not reached any sufficiently clear conclusions to permit it to be said that such sanctions are ineffective in any particular context or for any particular group of people who are able to appreciate the consequences of their acts. Certainly no effort was made at the trial of this case, beyond a monosyllabic answer to a perfunctory one-line question, to determine the effectiveness of penal sanctions in deterring Leroy Powell in particular or chronic alcoholics in general from drinking at all or from getting drunk in particular places or at particular times.

Affirmed.

[Justices FORTAS, DOUGLAS, BRENNAN and STEWART dissented.]

2. *Legislative Responsibility for Effecting Change*

Prior to *Powell* the Congress enacted legislation which made simple public intoxication noncriminal and provided an alternative to the criminal justice system as a means of dealing with the drunk:

DISTRICT OF COLUMBIA ALCOHOLIC REHABILITATION ACT (1967)

SECTION 1. The purpose of this Act is to establish a comprehensive program in the District of Columbia for the prevention of alcoholism and the rehabilitation of alcoholics, discourage abuse of alcoholic beverages, and provide for medical, psychiatric, and other scientific treatment of chronic alcoholics; to minimize the deleterious effects of excessive drinking; to reduce the financial burden imposed upon the people of the District of Columbia by the abusive use of alcoholic beverages, as is reflected in accidents, inefficiency of personnel, and absenteeism; and to establish methods of handling intoxication and alcoholism that will benefit the individual involved and more fully protect the public. In order to accomplish this purpose and alleviate intoxication and chronic alcoholism, all public officials in the District of Columbia shall take cognizance of the fact that public intoxication shall be handled as a public health problem rather than as a criminal offense, and that a chronic alcoholic is a sick person who needs, is entitled to, and shall be provided appropriate medical, psychiatric, institutional, advisory, and rehabilitative treatment services of the highest caliber for his illness.

. . .

SECTION 3. (a) The Commissioner shall establish and maintain an effective public health program in the District of Columbia to provide a continuum of appropriate services to intoxicated persons and chronic alcoholics. Such program shall coordinate all District of Columbia services for intoxicated persons and chronic alcoholics and shall include at least the following facilities which shall be available to both males and females:

(1) One or more detoxification centers, which shall be located within the District of Columbia, which shall have a total capacity of not more than 150 beds, and which shall provide appropriate medical services for intoxicated persons, including initial examination, diagnosis, and classification.

(2) An inpatient extended care facility which shall have a capacity of not more than 800 beds and which shall provide intensive study, treatment, and rehabilitation of chronic alcoholics. Such facility shall not admit intoxicated persons.

(3) Outpatient aftercare facilities which may include clinics, social centers, vocational rehabilitation services, and supportive residential facilities and which shall have a total capacity of not more than 600 beds.[c]

---

[c] On October 16, 1968, President Johnson signed a $576,000,000 health services bill which included a provision to create a federal program for the treatment of alcoholics. Up to $40,000,000 was to be available over the next two years for matching grants to build, staff, and operate facilities to treat alcoholics and narcotic addicts. This made the treatment of the alcoholic part of the federal mental health program.

Following passage of the Act, the District of Columbia Police Department issued the following General Order which indicates the change of police practice under the new legislation:

GOVERNMENT OF THE DISTRICT OF COLUMBIA
Metropolitan Police Department

September 7, 1968

General Order No. 10
Series 1968
Subject: Policy and Procedure for Handling Intoxicated Persons

The purpose of this order is to establish the policy and promulgate the procedures to be followed by members of this Department in the handling of intoxicated persons.

I. General

The District of Columbia Alcoholic Rehabilitation Act of 1967 substitutes a wholly new alcoholism program for the District of Columbia, based on detoxification, in-patient and out-patient services, and recognizing intoxication as a public health problem rather than as a criminal offense.

Section 25-128 of the D.C. Code is amended to make intoxication a criminal offense only when it results in danger to persons or property. However, that part of Section 25-128 which covers drinking in public has not been changed.

II. Policy

Intoxication shall be handled on a public health rather than on a criminal basis. No intoxicated person shall be taken into custody except where his conduct clearly and immediately endangers the safety of himself or of any other person or of property. An intoxicated person shall be accorded the same consideration as any individual suffering from an illness.

III. Procedures

A. *General*

The Act deals with three classes of intoxicated persons: those not endangering the safety of themselves or other persons or property; those who endanger the safety of themselves, other persons or property; and those who are charged with offenses other than those specified in D.C. Code, Section 25-128. The procedures established herein shall be in effect until November 1, 1968 at which time Section 3 of Public Law 90-452 of the Ninetieth Congress shall become effective and additional instructions will be issued accordingly.

B. *Individuals Not Endangering Public Safety*

1. An individual who is intoxicated in public, and who is not endangering his own safety or the safety of any other person, or property, may, with his consent, be taken or sent home or be taken to the detoxification center at 619 N Street, N.W. Intoxicated females are to be taken to the Area C Health Center, D.C. General Hospital, 1905 E Street, S.E.

2. In the event an officer delivers or sends an intoxicated person to his home, the officer shall prepare P.D. Form 253 in triplicate. He will be especially careful to obtain the name of the individual into whose custody he has delivered the intoxicated person, the name of the carrier and vehicle identification number if appropriate.

3. Reasonable measures shall be taken to make certain that any public transportation used for sending an intoxicated person home is paid for in advance, but the intoxicated individual shall not be searched for this purpose.

4. If the intoxicated person is to be taken to the detoxification center, initially he will be transported to the precinct for the preparation of the required reports and thereafter will be transported to the detoxification center as soon as practicable. The transporting officer delivering the intoxicated person to the detoxification center shall obtain the name of the person into whose custody he delivered the intoxicated person and shall furnish this information to the station clerk for completion of the necessary reports.

C. *Individuals Endangering Public Safety*

1. Intoxication is a criminal offense only when it results in a *substantial* and *immediate* danger to the safety of the intoxicated individual or other persons or property. A hazard that is theoretical or potential does not constitute a substantial danger. The

normal manifestations of intoxication, such as, staggering, falling down, sleeping on a park bench, lying unconscious in the gutter, begging, singing, although perhaps disagreeable and disturbing to the senses, do not under this statute constitute a substantial or immediate danger and do not justify placing the criminal charge of intoxication.

2. An individual who is intoxicated and who is endangering his own safety, or the safety of other persons or property, shall be placed under arrest and processed as any other prisoner. Any such individual who has been adjudged as a chronic alcoholic shall be processed in accordance with the provisions of General Order No. 6, Series 1967.

D. *Intoxicated Persons Arrested for Other Crimes*

Any person who is taken into custody in the District of Columbia for violating any criminal provision applicable in the District of Columbia (other than Section 25-128 of the D.C. Code) and who appears to be intoxicated to the extent that he requires immediate medical attention, shall be taken by the police officer to D.C. General Hospital where he may be admitted as a patient for an immediate medical evaluation of his condition. Such persons shall be handled in accordance with the provisions of General Order No. 8, Series 1965.

IV. Reporting Requirements

The following information shall be reported as soon as available to Central Records Division by teletype on all individuals processed under this order who are either sent to the detoxification center or hospitalized:

Name, address, other identifying information, such as social security number, time and date initial contact was made with individual, whether sent to the detoxification center or hospitalized. If hospitalized, give the name of the hospital.

John B. Layton
Chief of Police

Often changes in law are made on the basis of assumptions about the present or future availability of treatment facilities. The assumptions may, however, be quite wrong.

DRUNKS STILL SENT TO COUNTY JAILS DESPITE MARYLAND LAW

By Aaron Latham
Washington Post, Aug. 16, 1968

The Maryland law declaring that alcoholics should no longer be treated as criminals went into effect July 1, but little has changed in the jails of Montgomery and Prince George's Counties. They are still full of drunks.

Authorities have two problems: determining exactly who is an alcoholic and who is simply suffering the temporary effects of a few too many, and finding a place to send the true alcoholic other than the same old jail cell.

Facilities are limited because when the courts ruled that alcoholism is a disease and not a crime the legislature passed part of a proposed program requiring alcoholics to be treated as ill. But it discarded a key section that would have provided money to build regional treatment centers. And the counties say they can't provide sufficient care without State aid.

On determining alcoholism, the new law stipulates that a judge or two medical doctors can officially declare a drunk to be an alcoholic, but in day-to-day practice, this doesn't happen very often—even though large numbers of the drunks are repeaters.

Gilbert A. Sanford of the Hospital Council of Maryland said the feared increase of alcoholic patients throughout the State hasn't happened.

The Prince George's Sheriff's office says it still locks up 10 to 15 drunks a night. Drunks are sent to the County hospital only if they have delirium tremens for more than four days.

Montgomery has an "infirmary" for alcoholics, but it is in the County jail. It has had 82 "admissions" but "disorderly drunks" go to cells instead of the infirmary, according to County Health Officer Dr. Roy P. Lindgren.

Of the drunks jailed since July 1 in the two counties, perhaps as many as 500, only 18 have been transferred to hospitals for long term treatment. The two counties have discussed opening a bi-county treatment center but no action has been taken.

Prince George's Sheriff William J. Kersey says that before the new law most drunks picked up were charged with being "drunk and disorderly." Now they are simply charged with being "disorderly."

However, fewer drunks are being picked up. The police are tending to ignore the peaceful ones because they don't cause trouble.

Dr. Haluk Boneval, a physician in the Prince George's County Hospital emergency room, says that only three to four alcoholics are brought in each day, and these by volunteer rescue squads.

There are no detoxification centers in either of the counties' hospitals. When alcoholics are brought in they must be treated in makeshift fashion in whatever beds are available.

In the Montgomery County jail infirmary, "patients" are held in a room fitted out with eight beds.

When drunk "disorderlies" are turned over to the Prince George's County jails in Upper Marlboro and Hyattsville, they are placed in the "tank," a bare cell with mattresses on the floor. If they were up on bunks, jailers explain, they could fall off and injure themselves.

The jailers try to get hot coffee into them. When they begin to recover, they are transferred to one of the 40-prisoner dorms where the other inmates are trusted to look after them.

Two alcoholics died in the Prince George's jails last year.

3. *Agency Response to the Need for Change*

Without the stimulus of either appellate decisions or legislation, some police and private agencies have started innovative programs designed to deal more effectively with the common drunk.

THE DETOXIFICATION CENTER

By Curtis Brostron

FBI Law Enforcement Bulletin 6-8 (Dec. 1967)

Public intoxication has long been a source of frustration to the policeman and the community he serves.

A community might be sympathetic to the public drunk and at the same time embarrassed by him and not know what to do. The policeman is frustrated because an intoxicated man is difficult to handle and requires a considerable amount of time to be taken to the hospital for a checkup and then booked and processed for detention.

Capt. Frank Mateker, director of the St. Louis Police Department's Planning and Research Division and a veteran street officer, has been well aware of the problem. He devised a plan to treat the offender in a more humane manner and also to save the officer's time away from patrol.

With the active support and cooperation of Col. Edward L. Dowd, president of the St. Louis Board of Police Commissioners, the department was given a $158,000 grant from the Office of Law Enforcement Assistance to establish a detoxification center.

Benefits of Center

The center opened in October 1966 in the St. Mary's Infirmary on Papin Street. The Social Science Institute of Washington University in St. Louis has assisted in both the planning and operational programs of the center.

Already, a number of benefits are showing. Of significance to our department is the 57-percent reduction in the time an officer is out of service while handling an intoxicated person. He does not need to spend hours waiting in hospitals for a medical diagnosis of the inebriate's state of health and is not required to appear in court when the subject voluntarily remains at the center for treatment. This provides a massive recovery of man-hours for urgent police duties. We also credit the rehabilitation efforts of this program with a 60-percent reduction in arrests of drunks.

The rehabilitation results have vastly surpassed our expectations. A limited duty officer is assigned to follow up on released persons, and we have noted significant improvements in drinking patterns and employment. There have been substantial gains in housing and economic stability.

A 3-month period is considered the most crucial factor for an alcoholic in terms of vocational rehabilitation and life adjustment. About 15 percent of those interviewed reported complete abstinence for a 3-month period following their discharge from the center. Of course, we can't predict total success in rehabilitating these individuals, but this certainly demonstrates a change in their way of life.

Another factor to consider is how the alcoholics respond to being taken to the center. In one 3-month period, 97 percent of these individuals remained for the full treatment period indicated by the physician.

The center's clientele is primarily composed of the estimated 8 percent of all alcoholics who are of the skid row variety. It is this group which has placed the greatest burden on police patrol time and efficiency.

Procedure

Persons found in an inebriated condition on the public streets are taken into custody by police officers on the charge of being "drunk on the street." They are then issued a city court summons for public drunkenness. If the subject voluntarily accepts treatment at the detoxification center, as approximately 90 percent do, the citation is voided. If he refuses or abandons treatment before its conclusion, his appearance in court on the original charge is required.

If the subject consents to treatment, he is transported to the detoxification center in a police conveyance and begins what may be his first supervised chance at rehabilitation after a lifetime of alcoholism.

Treatment

During a 7-day stay, the public inebriate receives the benefit of the most advanced detoxification facilities in the United States. The center provides 24-hour medical treatment, associated physical facilities, and supportive social and rehabilitative services.

The personalization of treatment and the dedication of the clinical staff are key factors in the program's success. The personnel who administer treatment perform in a manner usually reserved for private institutions. Most have backgrounds in private hospitals, and their attitude of treating each patient as an individual carries over to their work with the alcoholic.

Upon arrival a patient receives a thorough medical examination followed by a shower and rest in one of the center's 30 beds. All patients get three high-protein meals a day, prepared in the hospital's kitchen by the Sisters of St. Mary, who also administer the building and staff other facilities in the infirmary. Coffee, snacks, and fortified fruit juices are available to patients at all times.

For the first day or two the alcoholic is placed in the intensive care unit to "dry out," and through proper nourishment and medication, his health is improved. Clean clothing and bed linens complete the process of reharmonizing the alcoholic with the physical properties of orderly living. With the accomplishment of this initial step, the patient is moved to the self-care unit to begin the process of social rehabilitation.

Therapy

The detoxification center employs a variety of therapeutic techniques, progressing from medical diagnosis and treatment through various socio-psychological services, to help the patient confront his drinking problem in a framework of reality. Group therapy, self-government, work therapy, and sociodrama are used as methods of inducing social interaction. Individualized therapy is provided in the form of social and vocational counseling, and self-analysis is aided through the use of didactic films and lectures.

Unstructured group therapy sessions are held daily for approximately 1 hour. Research has shown this to be the most effective means of alcoholic therapy yet discovered. Although the use of self-government techniques as an aspect of therapy is most effective in prolonged treatment programs, the center is currently endeavoring to develop modified practices adaptable to its brief treatment period.

As another part of his treatment, clinical experience has shown that the alcoholic must relearn self-discipline and the acceptance of responsibility. Within this context patients are expected to assume nominal work responsibilities during their stay, and most show an enthusiastic willingness to participate.

During the entire treatment period social workers meet with the patient to discuss family status, education, employment skills, personal history, and drinking pattern. On the basis of these discussions, staff members assist the patient in locating adequate housing and employment. Of more importance, however, they seek to bring the patient to an understanding of his drinking problem. Alcoholics Anonymous (AA) has had particular influence in this pursuit. Because of their vital importance in the rehabilitation process, AA meetings are held at the center 3 nights each week for patients desiring to attend.

The center also works continuously with other organizations such as the Division of Vocational Rehabilitation, the Human Development Corporation, the Missouri State Employment Service, the State department of welfare, the Salvation Army, counseling agencies, settlement houses, and any other agency that might aid in the rehabilitation of an alcoholic.

It is presumptuous to assume that the public alcoholic will be able to change a living pattern of many years after his 7-day stay at the detoxification center. To reinforce new life patterns, a strong "after-care" program must be implemented. Thus, the need for community services, such as a halfway house, for the public alcoholic becomes dramatically apparent.

Conclusion

Prior to the 20th century, police systems of the western civilization had but one duty—the apprehension of criminals. Not until this century did our system of criminal justice begin a determined effort to define guilt according to enlightened standards of culpability. Just recently, the trend has increased to consider alcoholism more of an illness or disease rather than a crime. We are attempting to treat the problem in this light. It enables us to treat the victims in a more humane manner and to recover policetime as well.

This social problem is another one apparently neglected by society, and the police are taking the lead to correct it. We're proud that St. Louis was selected as the first city to conduct a program of this type.[d]

---

[d] In addition to the St. Louis program, the Manhattan Bowery project, and others mentioned above, new programs continue to be developed. As part of the "fruitful experimentation" at the local level called for by the Supreme Court in *Powell v. Texas,* Atlanta, Georgia, proposed a new program in July, 1968, involving a detoxification center, intensive treatment unit, inpatient and outpatient rehabilitation facilities, and a continuing research and education function. The Dane County (Wisconsin) Alcoholism Information and Referral Center also proposed development of civil detoxification procedures to supplant punishment of drunkenness as a crime.

Recent writings pointing toward the need for reform and possible solutions include Tao, *Drunkenness and Criminal Law,* 13 WAYNE L. REV. 530 (1967) (inadequacy of facilities for treating the alcoholic); Rubington, *The "Revolving Door" Game,* 12 CRIME & DELINQUENCY 332 (1966) (plight of the skid row alcoholic); Rubington, *Alcoholic Control on Skid Row, Preliminary Draft of a Research and Demonstration Proposal,* 13 CRIME & DELINQUENCY 531 (1967); Pinardi, *The Chronic Drunkenness Offender, What One City Is Doing About the Revolving Door,* 12 CRIME & DELINQUENCY 339 (1966) (description of Miami, Fla., alcoholic rehabilitation program); Hutt, *Perspectives on the Report of the President's Crime Commission—The Problem of Drunkenness,* 43 NOTRE DAME LAWYER 864 (1968); Myerson & Mayer, *Origins, Treatment and Destiny of Skid Row Alcoholics,* 19 S.C.L. REV. 332 (1967).

Chapter 20

THE USE OF FORCE: RESPONSIBILITY FOR SETTING THE BOUNDS OF POLICE POWER

This chapter deals with the use of force by police, a most sensitive issue upon which community dissatisfaction and frustration have come to focus. Asking today how much force a police officer ought to use is likely to produce great community interest and concern. It was, for example, the principal topic of interest arising from the 1968 Democratic National Convention in Chicago. In various communities, the issue of how much force may properly be used may be faced at different levels of government. In Chicago the mayor's relation to the police department was the focus. In New York City, on the other hand, the issue seemed to be precipitated by the enactment of a new criminal code which limited the right of the police officer to use force and also involved relationships between the mayor and police, between the police chief and the members of the Policemen's Benevolent Association, and between police and the community generally.

It is not yet settled what the relationships should be among the governmental agencies which deal with the issue of force. The incidents which are described below illustrate modes of involvement particularly of the legislature, the police agency, and the political executive officer. The fact that the courts were not significantly involved in these specific incidents does not mean that there would not, on another occasion, be an important role for them to play with respect to the regulation of police use of force.[a]

A. THE LEGISLATURE AND THE POLICE

New York statutes in effect prior to September 1, 1967, provided that police could properly use deadly force if necessary to

[a] Compare as illustrating the court-police policymaking relationship the materials in Chapter 3 on the undercover agent and the time he can properly remain under cover. See particularly the *Dancy* case, at 143, *supra*. Similarly reflecting court concern with police policy, but in relation to clearing hippies from public parks, is the *Rizzo* case, at 350 n.x, *supra*.

arrest or recapture a felon.[b] The legislature then enacted a new criminal code, providing that police could use deadly force only when they reasonably believed it necessary "to effect an arrest or to prevent the escape from custody of a person whom he reasonably believes (i) has committed or attempted to commit a felony involving the use or threatened use of deadly physical force, or (ii) is attempting to escape by the use of a deadly weapon, or (iii) otherwise indicates that he is likely to endanger human life or to inflict serious physical injury unless apprehended without delay."[c]

Several months in advance of the effective date of the new code, the Police Commissioner of New York, Howard Leary, announced that he intended to adopt immediately as part of the departmental regulations the restrictive provisions of the new legislation, which he deemed more consistent with American values. He explained:

> The old regulations . . . raised a serious moral question: "Is it proper to take the life of a fleeing felon who, if caught, tried and convicted could not be executed?"
>
> Suggesting that the "traditional fleeing-felon rule is left behind from the days when all felonies were capital crimes," Commissioner Leary pointed out that felonies include "many minor crimes which do not involve the slightest risk to human life or limb."
>
> In addition, the line between felonies and misdemeanors is often a fine one, the Commissioner said. By way of illustration, he noted that a $99 larceny is a misdemeanor while $101 larceny is a felony; unlawful entry is a misdemeanor while unlawful entry with intent to commit a crime is a felony, and some crimes that are misdemeanors when committed by a first offender are felonies when committed by a suspect with a prior felony record.
>
> Anticipating criticism of the new regulations, . . . Commissioner Leary said that some people would assert that "we should scarcely be reducing the freedom of the police to shoot at this time, when crime is on the rise."
>
> In reply, the Commissioner declared:
>
> "The gun is not the way to prevent most crimes. Crime prevention is a total community effort. It must include better schools and more job opportunities for all Americans."[d]

[b] Criminal Code and Penal Law, N.Y. CONSOL. LAWS ch. 40, § 1055 (Dennis 1940).

[c] N.Y. PENAL LAW § 35.30 (McKinney 1967).

[d] N.Y. Times, Mar. 22, 1967, at 1, col. 1. By the time the guidelines were ready for promulgation in August the effective date of the statute was imminent.

Department regulations were issued which adopted the statutory criteria and went beyond them in urging self-restraint.

THE USE OF DEADLY FORCE BY POLICE OFFICERS
Police Department, City of New York, Aug. 1967

. . .

General Restraints. In self-defense situations a policeman, if he can do so safely, should arrest his attacker rather than shoot him. In situations involving the imminent commission of one of the six specified felonies, the policeman must not shoot if the crime can be prevented merely by making his presence known or by use of lesser force and he must also consider the risk to the victim if he shoots to prevent the crime. And even in arrest situations where the conduct of the person indicates that he presents a serious danger to human life or that he is likely to inflict serious physical injury unless apprehended without delay, the policeman must not shoot if the arrest can be made without shooting.

Furthermore, the fact that deadly force is permissible in a given situation does not, of course, mean that it must or should be used in that situation. To the contrary, where consistent with safety and with duty, it is preferable to accomplish the ends of law enforcement without shooting.

The legislation and the regulations were vociferously attacked by police fraternal associations, who were able to arouse substantial public sentiment for return to the old statute. A compromise proposal by the commission which had drafted the new legislation was rejected by the police groups as still too restrictive of the policeman's right to use force.

POLICE FIGHT CURB ON RIGHT TO SHOOT
By James F. Clarity
New York Times, Feb. 5, 1968

Albany, Feb. 4—The state's major law enforcement organizations have rejected as inadequate a state commission's proposals to give the police more authority to shoot to kill when confronted by criminals or suspects.

The Combined Law Enforcement Council, which includes representatives of virtually every crime control agency in the state, presented its objections to Richard J. Bartlett, chairman of the State Commission on Revision of the Penal Law and Criminal Code.

In what was reportedly a stormy meeting, it said the commission's recommendations to increase police authority to use deadly force were "too complex" and "did not go far enough."

The council, whose chairman is a former New York City Police Commissioner, Michael J. Murphy, told Mr. Bartlett at the unpublicized meeting to restore to policemen the right to shoot to kill "any fleeing felon." The police had this right until the penal law revised by the Bartlett commission went into effect last Sept. 1.

The so-called shoot-to-kill issue has been raised frequently and emotionally in recent months by police organizations, civic groups and private citizens who say that the present penal law inhibits the policeman. Governor Rockefeller has said he favored an increase in police authority to use lethal force, but he has not said what modifications he would sign into law.

The police organizations are expected to lobby vigorously for a return to the old shoot-to-kill law. One of their principal arguments, it is understood, will be that the old law would give policemen more self-assurance in the event of urban riots this summer.

Under the law now in effect, a policeman may use "deadly physical force" only when he "reasonably believes" a criminal or suspect has used or is threatening to use lethal force against him or a third person.

Two weeks ago, bowing to pressure from police and civic groups, the Temporary Commission on Revision of the Penal Law and Criminal Code recommended legislation that would increase the number of situations in which the policeman would be authorized to shoot to kill.

Flight Proposal Rejected

But the commission refused to propose the restoration of the "any-fleeing-felon" provision, which gave the policeman, for example, the right to use lethal force against a person who, without threatening the policeman or any one else, stole property worth more than $250 (making the offense a felony) and tried to evade capture.

Mr. Murphy, who presided over the meeting of the council, said Mr. Bartlett had been told that many of the commission's proposals were admirable, but that the council members were unanimous in their demand for the restoration of the "any-fleeing-felon" provision. Murphy said in an interview that the present law and the commission's proposed revisions were "entirely too complex."

"There are still too many areas making it necessary for the policeman in the street to wrestle in his mind before taking action," he said.

Other sources of pressure supported the new law.

BALANCED LAW ENFORCEMENT
New York Times Editorial, Feb. 22, 1968

When should policemen be authorized to shoot down citizens who have committed crimes?

Under New York State's old law, in effect until last Sept. 1, a policeman could shoot "any fleeing felon," whether armed or not, whether threatening anyone or not. Under the state's new penal law, the result of months of effort by a talented commission, a policeman can shoot only when he "reasonably believes" that his life or the life of another person is in danger.

Now, bowing to police lobby pressures in Albany, legislative leaders have agreed on a compromise that would authorize a policeman to shoot when he "reasonably believes" a fleeing felon is armed with a "firearm or deadly weapon."

We believe it is too soon to decide that the new law has failed and to rush through an ill-considered substitute.

Unquestionably, policemen deserve many things that they haven't had enough of—most of all they deserve respect and support in their efforts to prevent crime and insure safety. Policemen daily risk their lives and, as the tragic shooting of a young policeman in Queens the other day vividly reminds us, the risk is never far away. Whenever their lives are in jeopardy or the lives of innocent citizens are in jeopardy, they should be authorized to shoot to kill.

But they must not become trigger-happy.

The commission which recently revised the state's penal laws worked thoroughly. It was a well-balanced group dedicated to sound principles of law enforcement. The Legislature should not rush now to alter the results of these deliberations until there has been further experience on how the law works.

Despite such support, in response to apparent public dissatisfaction with the law the New York Legislature amended the statute to broaden the police right to use deadly force.[e] The guidelines reflecting the narrower scope of proper use of force were not, however, formally withdrawn.

B. RELATIONSHIP BETWEEN THE MAYOR AND THE POLICE DEPARTMENT

1. *Madison, Wisconsin*

MAYOR HALTS USE OF MACE PENDING STUDY OF EFFECTS
By June Dieckmann
Wisconsin State Journal, May 10, 1968

Madison police turned in their Mace Thursday on orders of Mayor Otto Festge.

The mayor temporarily suspended police use of the chemical spray, used to subdue unruly persons, until further research and information is available concerning the medical and legal aspects of its effects.

Festge's order came after a two-hour closed door conference with City Atty. Edwin C. Conrad, Police Chief Wilbur H. Emery, and City Health Director Dr. Charles K. Kincaid concerning a report this week from the United States surgeon general which said that there was not available evidence at this time to draw final conclusions on the effects of Mace.

---

[e] Laws of New York ch. 73 (1968). The effective date of the new law was March 21, 1968. It reads as follows:

> § 35.30 Justification; use of physical force in making an arrest or in preventing an escape
>
> 1. A peace officer, in the course of effecting or attempting to effect an arrest, or of preventing or attempting to prevent the escape from custody, of a person whom he reasonably believes to have committed an offense, may use physical force when and to the extent he reasonably believes such to be necessary to effect the arrest, or to prevent the escape from custody, or to defend himself or a third person from what he reasonably believes to be the use or imminent use of physical force; except that he may use deadly physical force for such purposes only when he reasonably believes that:
>
> (a) The offense committed by such person was:
>
> (i) a felony or an attempt to commit a felony involving the use or attempted use or threatened imminent use of physical force against a person; or
>
> (ii) kidnapping, arson, escape in the first degree, burglary in the first degree or any attempt to commit such a crime. . . .

The principal changes are to allow deadly force where suspect has used "physical" as opposed to "deadly" force and in the enumerated felonies without regard to the use of force by the suspect.

Madison policemen, who have carried a canister of Mace since last November after the Bascom Hill anti-war riot, have used the spray in only about 10 cases, Chief Emery said.

"I am satisfied that in these (Madison) cases, the use of the chemical Mace caused the person being restrained less discomfort and less possible physical injury than would have occurred had the officer used a fist or a club or possibly even a gun," Mayor Festge said.

"It is definitely my hope that when further research and information is available about Mace, or any other similar chemical, that it will again be possible to authorize its use here," Festge said.

. . .

The issue of police use of Mace was raised this week by City Atty. Conrad who said there are "no precedent cases" (court rulings) concerning its use.

Since the city of Madison is self-insured, not covered by any commercial insurance company, Conrad said he was concerned about claims which might be filed against the city by persons or policemen involving Mace effects.

. . .

The policemen, about 200 of them, voiced their dissatisfaction when they read Chief Emery's order on the squad room bulletin board: "By order of the mayor, this department will temporarily discontinue the use of Mace until more conclusive facts are obtained regarding its potential hazards."

"It's an order and we have to go along with it. I just hope nothing happens until we get it back," commented a policeman who received a broken hand subduing a prisoner before Mace.

CONDITIONAL MACE OK'D

By June Dieckmann

Wisconsin State Journal, Oct. 26, 1968

Guidelines Approved for Police

Madison police were reissued their spray-gun chemical Mace Friday night on approval of Mayor Otto Festge.

The mayor, by executive order, took Mace away from police May 9 to await a medical and legal report on its usage and effects from an expert committee named by Atty. Gen. Bronson LaFollette.

"I have notified the Police Department they can resume the use of Mace when necessary under guidelines recommended in the committee's report," Mayor Festge said late Friday immediately upon receipt of the committee's findings.

The recommended guidelines include:

ONE. Only well trained police should use Mace.

TWO. The spray-stream from Mace canisters (the size of perfume or hair spray cans) should never be aimed higher than the armpits of an individual.

THREE. Recipients of Mace spray should be treated as soon as possible in the affected areas with "copious amounts" of water, never ointments.

. . .

Lt. Donald Mickelson, head of the Friday night police shift which first was reissued Mace, said the men "all thought it was time we got it back and they felt more secure when they went out (on beats)."

"We've had lots of instances since May where officers, not wanting to use a gun or a nightstick, were assaulted in making an arrest when it could have all been avoided if they had Mace," Mickelson said.

Police, and a pending City Council resolution introduced by Deputy Sheriff James Crary, 15th Ward alderman, had sought return of Mace as the most "humane" method of controlling unruly persons, as contrasted with guns, nightsticks, and physical force.

The committee's report agreed that "there is neither evidence nor scientific rationale to support the view that significant systemic effects on the human organism, other than the psychological responses to being rendered incapacitated, are induced by chemical Mace."

2. *Chicago, Illinois*

The right of a police officer to use deadly force in making an arrest or preventing crime is established in Illinois by statute. The legislature provided that deadly force could be used whenever a "forcible" felony was involved or a deadly weapon was used or the suspect otherwise demonstrated that he was a physical threat to the community. Supplementing the law, the Chicago Police Department issued a policy statement to its men recommending great restraint in the use of deadly force.

CHICAGO POLICE DEPARTMENT TRAINING BULLETIN 2-3
Vol. IX, No. 2, Jan. 8, 1968

USE OF DEADLY FORCE

In regard to a peace officer's use of force in making an arrest, Article 7-5, Chapter 38 continues as follows:

"However, he is justified in using force likely to cause death or great bodily harm only when he reasonably believes that such force is necessary to prevent death or great bodily harm to himself or such other person, or when he reasonably believes both that:

(1) such force is necessary to prevent the arrest from being defeated by resistance or escape; and
(2) the person to be arrested has committed or attempted a forcible felony or is attempting to escape by use of a deadly weapon, or otherwise indicates that he will endanger human life or inflict great bodily harm unless arrested without delay."

. . .

Also, in this kind of situation, the officer must know what the forcible felonies are. Article 2-8 of the Criminal Code states:

"Forcible felony means:

1. Treason.
2. Murder.
3. Voluntary manslaughter.
4. Rape.
5. Robbery.
6. Burglary.
7. Arson.
8. Kidnapping.
9. Aggravated battery.
10. Any other felony which involves the use or threat of physical force or violence against any individual. (Under this definition, deviate sexual assault is also a forcible felony.)"

. . .

When a peace officer reasonably believes he is justified in using deadly force in making an arrest to prevent death or great bodily harm to himself or another, normally there is no doubt in his mind that such force is necessary. However, in any situation, if the officer has the slightest doubt in regard to whether or not the use of deadly force is justified or that the consequences of using such force would be likely to outweigh the police purpose served by such use, he should *not* use *deadly* force.

During the period April 5 through April 8, 1968, a serious, widespread civil disorder occurred in Chicago. In handling the riot, the police were functioning under the orders that required that they exercise discretion in using deadly force within the confines of existing law and consistent with published departmental policy.

Mayor Richard Daley disagreed and made his disagreement known.

POLICE ORDERED: SHOOT LOOTERS AND ARSONISTS

By Harry Golden, Jr.
Chicago Sun-Times, Apr. 16, 1968

An angry Mayor Daley turned to the subject of Chicago's riots at his press conference Monday and said he has:

. . .

2. Rebuked Police Supt. James B. Conlisk, Jr. for failing to issue orders to shoot arsonists and looters.

3. Instructed Conlisk, in the future, to issue shoot-to-kill orders against arsonists and shoot-to-stop orders against looters.

. . .

Daley informed the press conference he had just told Conlisk "very emphatically and very definitely that an order be issued to shoot to kill any arsonist or anyone with a Molotov cocktail."

He also said orders should be issued to shoot, but not kill, "anyone looting any stores in our city."[f]

Shortly before 6 p.m. Monday, Police Supt. Conlisk issued the following order over his signature to all commanding officers:

1. Arson, attempted arson, burglary and attempted burglary are forceable felonies.

---

[f] The Illinois Legislature had defined the new crime of looting in 1967 to establish a specific criminal offense for conduct which might not fit easily under the existing definitions of burglary and so on. This crime is not a forcible felony, so that deadly force could not be used against persons for violation of this statute. However, since looters may also be guilty of burglary they would be as much liable to police use of deadly force as before enactment of the statute. In other words, this statute was not designed to respond to the question of police use of force.

2. Such force as is necessary, including deadly force, shall be used to prevent the commission of these offenses and to prevent the escape of perpetrators.

3. The commanding officers will ensure that the above and General Order 67-14 are continually reviewed at all roll calls effective immediately and continuing through 22 April, 1968.

General Order 67-14 was issued by former Police Supt. Orlando W. Wilson last May, and spells out legal and department policy guidelines on the use of force likely to cause death or great bodily harm.

. . .

Speaking of police directives on use of weapons, the mayor said he was "very much disappointed to learn that every policeman pounding a beat was to use his own discretion."

The mayor added: "He (the policeman on the beat) should have had instructions to shoot arsonists and to shoot looters.

"In my opinion, there should have been orders to shoot arsonists to kill, and to shoot looters in order that they be detained.

"And in my opinion, MACE (a nonlethal chemical weapon) should have been used."

. . .

Arsonist A Murderer

Asked if Conlisk was on his way out as police superintendent, Mayor Daley said, "I wouldn't want to discuss that at this time. I want to await the report of my committee."

Asked for clarification of his statement that he was "disappointed," the mayor said, "Yes, I was disappointed. There's no reason for this lawlessness and immorality. An arsonist is a murderer and should be shot right on the spot.

"The looters—you wouldn't want to shoot the youngsters—but you can shoot them in the leg and detain them."

DALEY EDICT EASED UNDER PRESSURE

By Charles Nicodemus & Jerry Lipson
Chicago Daily News, Apr. 18, 1968

Pressures from responsible political and civic leaders caused Mayor Richard J. Daley to tone down his controversial get-tough-with-rioters edict.

That is the view of top government officials close to City Hall.

"The mayor got some calls from very responsible people who are close to him telling him that he had made a bad mistake," a high city official close to the mayor said.

"These were Chicago people, not out-of-towners."

A top state official explained the mayor's second statement this way:

"In the first place, Daley had gotten a lot of heat from business leaders and insurance companies. That's why he popped off the way he did Monday.

"And in his heart, I've little doubt he meant what he said.

"But then a variety of people began calling him telling him that what he had said sounded bad—that his syntax made it sound a lot worse than he might have meant.

"So the mayor decided to tone it down a little."

The high city official said that Daley's angry remarks Monday that arsonists and looters should be shot might have been inspired, in part, by the report that the city could lose the Democratic National convention because of the riot.

"Daley was aware of this talk," said the official. "And I know for a fact that it concerned him.

"I believe it played a part in his Monday statement about shooting rioters. He was going to tell the world that we wouldn't tolerate that kind of thing here any more."

. . .

Daley told the Council that Police Department policy, which he supports, is that "only minimum force necessary be used by policemen in carrying out their duties."

Daley used the phrase "minimum force necessary" four times in his statement.

This was in marked contrast to his unqualified demand Monday that police "shoot to kill any arsonist," and "shoot to maim or cripple anyone looting."

Without referring to Monday's explosive remarks, Daley Wednesday incorporated his statement in a resolution establishing May 1 as Law Day USA in Chicago.

"Nobody argues that looters or arsonists should not be suppressed," McDermott said. "But there are a whole range of options open to police involving nonlethal force."

. . .

Cook County Welfare Director William H. Robinson said: "I'm pleased to see that the mayor has recognized that his first statements were too harsh and could have been calculated to cause more riots."

But, he added, "Greater confidence might be engendered if the mayor withdrew his first order and issued a new order embodying the sentiments of Wednesday's statement."

. . .

However, Robert Marks, vice chairman of the Illinois Advisory Commission to the U.S. Commission on Civil Rights said he was unable to reconcile Monday's and Wednesday's statements.

"I don't see the relationship. Do you first seek to subdue an arsonist, and then shoot? Or just shoot?"

Marks charged that the orders Daley issued Monday, if followed literally, would be illegal and unconstitutional.

The intent of Illinois law, he said, is to permit police to use guns only when a suspect is likely to inflict death "or great bodily harm" on someone, or when guns are needed to prevent a suspect from fleeing.

"Most looting situations are pure property offenses involving no substantial risk to human life. Therefore, an order to arbitrarily shoot all individuals engaged in looting contravenes Illinois law," Marks said.

At the same time, an order to arbitrarily shoot all arson suspects, Marks added, violates the 14th Amendment guarantee that no one can be deprived of his life without due process of law.

The public controversy over the propriety of using force increased to nationwide concern as a consequence of the efforts by Chicago police to control crowds desiring to demonstrate at the Democratic National Convention.

MANY PROTEST COPS' BEATING OF NEWSMEN
Chicago Tribune, Aug. 28, 1968

Editors, Agencies Get Conlisk Pledge

Protests poured into Police Supt. James B. Conlisk Jr. yesterday as the result of charges that at least 24 newsmen and photographers have been beaten by police while attempting to report Yippie demonstrations.

Telegrams demanding investigations and condemning the beatings came from the editors of three Chicago newspapers, officials of the three major television networks, and representatives of press organizations and news services.

Full Inquiry Ordered

Conlisk said yesterday he has ordered a full investigation of the beatings of the newsmen Sunday night, Monday morning, and early yesterday. Any man-handling of newsmen attempting to cover the yippie demonstrations in Lincoln and Grant parks has been ordered halted, Conlisk said.

"When and if the men involved are identified, they will be questioned, and punishment could range from suspension to dismissal from the department," Conlisk said.

POLICE BATTLE MOB IN PARK—OLD GLORY IS RIPPED DOWN

Chicago Tribune, Aug. 29, 1968

A pitched battle between police and demonstrators broke out yesterday at the Grant park bandshell as thousands of demonstrators gathered in the park for a march on the Democratic national convention at the International Amphitheater.

Police waded into the crowd after one hippie-type demonstrator climbed the flagpole, tore down the American flag, and replaced it with a red flag.

The demonstrators pelted police with rocks, bottles, and pieces of tile torn up from washrooms at Lincoln park and filed razor sharp along the edges.

Remove Red Flag

Fifty policemen under Capt. James Riordan of the Central district formed a wedge that split the demonstrators and drove to the flagpole. The red flag was taken down.

Someone in the crowd of demonstrators threw a smoke or tear gas bomb into police ranks. A policeman threw it back. The ranks of the demonstrators broke as police chased them thru the park.

The Guard Stands By

Deputy Supt. Merlin Nygren, head of police assigned to the park, who had said earlier no march would be permitted away from the bandshell area, ordered police vans brought up from the Soldiers' field staging area. He said police expected "a tremendous arrest situation."

At least 250 national guardsmen stood by in 14th place in case their help should be needed to put down the disturbance in the park and to forestall any march on the amphitheater that might get underway. The demonstrators had set 4 p. m. for the march-off deadline.

While the crowd, which finally grew to an estimated 10,000, was still gathering police circulated in the park distributing handbills signed by Police Supt. James B. Conlisk Jr.

Marchers to Be Arrested

The handbill warned that anyone trying to march or parade would be subject to arrest. It said no rally or assembly would be permitted at or near the amphitheater. It requested cooperation of the demonstrators.

The strategy for the march was set forth by Rennie Davis, project director for the National Mobilization Committee to End the War in Viet Nam, to 200 of the organization's parade marshals in the park.

The parade was sponsored by the National Mobilization committee. Other groups, including the Youth International party (Yippies), Peace and Freedom party, and various splinter groups had members on hand.

SCORES ARE HURT—HUNDREDS ARRESTED AS GUARDSMEN JOIN IN USING TEAR GAS

By J. Anthony Lukas

New York Times, Aug. 29, 1968

Chicago, Aug. 28—The police and National Guardsmen battled young protesters in downtown Chicago tonight as the week-long demonstrations against the Democratic National Convention reached a violent and tumultuous climax.

Scores of persons were injured and hundreds were arrested as the security forces chased down demonstrators who had broken out of Grant Park on the shore of Lake Michigan in an attempt to reach the International Amphitheater, where the Democrats were meeting.

By 9 P.M. they were using clubs, rifle butts, tear gas and Chemical Mace on virtually anything moving along Michigan Avenue and the narrow streets of the Loop area.

CRUSHED AGAINST WINDOWS

Even elderly bystanders were caught in the police onslaught. At one point, the police turned on several dozen persons standing quietly behind police barriers in front of the Conrad Hilton Hotel watching the demonstrators across the street.

For no reason that could be immediately determined, the blue-helmeted policemen charged the barriers, crushing the spectators against the windows of the Haymarket Inn, a restaurant in the hotel. Finally the window gave way, sending screaming middle-aged women and children backward through the broken shards of glass.

The police then ran into the restaurant and beat some of the victims who had fallen through the windows and arrested them.

At the same time, other policemen outside on the broad, tree-lined avenue were clubbing the young demonstrators repeatedly under television lights and in full view of delegates' wives looking out the hotel's windows.

U.S. TO PROBE PROTEST BATTLES

By Robert Gruenberg & William Clements
Chicago Daily News, Aug. 29, 1968

Federal officials in Chicago and Washington have promised full investigations into the bloody battles that erupted between the police and antiwar demonstrators.

The melees Wednesday in Grant Park and S. Michigan Ave., some of them swirling through the lobbies of the Conrad Hilton Hotel, were marked by tear gas barrages, clubbings and window smashings.

They left approximately 300 persons injured—including 29 policemen—and at least 267 persons arrested.

The total number of persons arrested since the violence started Saturday in Lincoln Park stands officially at 454.

The violence was certain to get worldwide attention.

Newspaper offices and television networks received hundreds of protesting telephone calls from persons who saw the violence on their TV screens.

Mayor Richard J. Daley and Police Supt. James B. Conlisk could point to only a single point in their favor, as they reviewed the chaotic events: Nobody had been killed.

Conlisk, defending the actions of his men, said: "The force used was the force necessary to repel the mob."

Mayor Daley received both public criticism and public support for the police handling of the demonstrations, with more persons in support than in opposition to the methods used. Important questions remain unanswered and are probably unanswerable. Among the most important are whether the mayor's earlier "shoot to kill" order and sharp criticism of his police superintendent resulted in a loss of control by the superintendent over his men; whether the amount of force used was more a result of individual decisions by individual police officers or was based upon a previously-decided-upon departmental policy; whether the use of force by police would have been different if the decision were left to the police superintendent rather than being made by the mayor? These questions relate in turn to larger issues such as whether the amount of force used can be effectively controlled by legislative formulation as seemed to be assumed in New York; whether the use of force is a "political" decision properly made by the mayor, an elected official, rather than by a professional police official; whether the Chicago experience lends force to the New York police position that "city hall" ought to keep its hands off the work of the police department?

The convention disturbances resulted in some departmental disciplinary action, but the discipline was for violation of relatively clear-cut departmental rules rather than for violation of rules much more difficult to apply, such as the rule against use of excessive force.

MORE POLICE SUSPENSIONS MAY BE TOLD
Chicago Tribune, Oct. 6, 1968

I. I. D. Is Probing Brutality

More police suspensions for infractions during the Democratic national convention may be announced within the next two weeks, according to Frank Sullivan, department spokesman.

Sullivan announced Friday that 10 suspensions had been recommended to Police Supt. James B. Conlisk after an investigation by the internal investigations division I. I. D.

Sullivan stressed that charges against more policemen, ranging from minor departmental infractions to police brutality, are being investigated.

More May Be Suspended

Although more suspensions may be recommended by the I. I. D. there is no indication of how many there might be, he said.

The 10 recommended suspensions probably will be reviewed by a police review board at the request of the policemen.

Charges Are Minor

The two sergeants are charged with permitting or ordering their men to remove their badges and identification during disorders in Lincoln park.

The patrolmen were charged with removing their stars and name plates during the disorder.

None of the 10 was charged with brutality or excessive force. The recommendations called for 15-day suspensions for the sergeants and 6-day suspensions for the patrolmen, all without pay.

RIGHTS IN CONFLICT

Report to the National Commission on the Causes and Prevention of Violence 2-3 (1968) (Bantam edition)

[This study, known as the "Walker Report," describes at length the police-demonstrator confrontations during the Democratic National Convention and concludes that the excessive use of force on that occasion "can only be called a police riot." In explaining the factors contributing to the event, the report attributes significant responsibility to the attitude of the city administration.]

The third factor emerged in the city's position regarding the riots following the death of Dr. Martin Luther King and the April 27 peace march to the Civic Center in Chicago.

The police were generally credited with restraint in handling the first riots—but Mayor Daley rebuked the Superintendent of Police. While it was later modified, his widely disseminated "shoot to kill arsonists and shoot to maim looters" order undoubtedly had an effect.

The effect on police became apparent several weeks later, when they attacked demonstrators, bystanders and media representatives at a Civic Center peace march. There were published criticisms—but the city's response was to ignore the police violence.

. . .

[Thus, one of the] factors which figured significantly in the outbreak of violence [was] the conditioning of Chicago police to expect that violence against demonstrators, as against rioters, would be condoned by city officials.

Chapter 21

THE EXERCISE OF DISCRETIONARY POWER BY CORRECTIONAL AGENCIES

This chapter deals with the question of who has responsibility for making important policy decisons relating to corrections, using as a case study the decision as to which offenders should be sentenced under the special, indeterminate provisions of a sex crimes law.

Historically, correctional decisions have been looked upon as being "clinical" in nature and thus best made by the "professionals" who staff the correctional agency. This meant, in practice, that important questions of public policy were greatly influenced by the views of the individual clinician or by the professional consensus of the psychiatrists, social workers, or psychologists. Correctional personnel were left to make decisions on their own, and the fact that these decisions involved resolution of important policy matters was not commonly recognized or acknowledged.

This situation is changing. The significance of correctional decisions is coming to be recognized. This results from the increasing frequency of challenge to correctional determinations affecting inmates. Inmate complaints about a wide variety of correctional practices have led courts to ask what the correctional policy is, what its justifications are, and whether it was followed in the particular case.

The reason courts are willing seriously to consider challenges to correctional practices is not clear. It seems to result more from a generally increased mistrust of the exercise of unrestrained governmental power than it does from increased dissatisfaction with the actions of correctional personnel or correctional agencies. Whatever the reason, the challenges tend to focus attention upon a wide range of important correctional policy issues which heretofore were left largely invisible, that is, left to be resolved within the correctional agencies themselves.

One way of dealing with the issues is by greater legislative attention to important correctional decisions with a view of enacting legislative standards and criteria to control correctional decision-making. The American Law Institute's Model Penal Code did propose a greatly enlarged legislative contribution to the correctional process. Though the Model Penal Code has been, on the whole, a very influential document, the suggestions for greater legislative involvement in the correctional field have not been followed. This probably results from a combination of factors. Correctional administrators have usually not looked to the legislature for the development of correctional policy, preferring to rely upon correctional expertise within the agency. There is obviously no widespread public demand for legislative action to control correctional decisions, except in situations where the community concludes correctional practice to be too permissive. The consequence is that issues are most likely to arise on a case-by-case basis as inmate, probationer, and parolee raise questions which require a court to respond.

As a consequence, courts play an increasingly important role in the development of correctional policy. The long-range trend is likely to be in one of three directions. First, courts undoubtedly will continue to prefer that correctional agencies make decisions about such matters as medical attention for inmates, use of disciplinary segregation,[a] release on parole, and revocation of probation or parole. The court would play a limited role similar to that which has been common in more traditionally recognized

---

[a] *See, e.g.,* Albany Times-Union, Oct. 25, 1968:

"Judge Believes Abuses; Cites Prison Reforms

"By Shirley Armstrong

"Federal Judge James T. Foley, speaking at the close of a trial here Thursday, said he believes some alleged brutalities, described by a number of New York State prisoners, did occur; that some changes in disciplinary procedures at Clinton State Prison have already been made, but that more may be needed.

"Judge Foley reserved decision and said he has 'no feeling yet on what I am going to do' about the injunctive demands of two Dannemora prisoners and $10,000 in damages sought by one. But he commented on the underlying issues of one of the most unique and significant cases in judicial history.

"As the seven-day procedure closed with testimony of the prison warden, the former warden, and a convict, Judge Foley said it would not be proper for him to 'write new laws for state prisons.' But he suggested that a 'new look' at some aspects of penal administration might 'alleviate' some problems which persist, at least in the eyes of 'these inmates.'

"Citing a vital need for 'good morale' in prisons, the judge said a comparatively minor difficulty may fester and grow until serious trouble erupts and 'people get killed.'

"Judge Foley also said action of the New York State Legislature is required to give state prisoners the right to seek injunctions in state courts 'where they should be.' He noted that, since the present case opened Federal Court doors to these actions, 40 such cases have been filed in this district."

areas of administrative law where courts interfere with administrative action only when it appears to be clearly arbitrary.[b]

The second alternative is for courts themselves to take over the making of certain important correctional decisions. This was, for example, the action of the Wisconsin Supreme Court in the *Huebner* case, at 680, *supra*. This may reflect a belief that important decisions ought to be "judicial" rather than "administrative" in nature.

Finally, a third alternative would be to leave the decision to the correctional agency under increasingly specific judicial rules to control the administrative decision.

Which of the three alternatives is followed will be influenced most by the reaction of correctional agencies to judicial review of their administrative actions.[c] If the correctional response is a willingness to confront the issues, make administrative policy and conform with it, the likelihood of substantial court intervention is probably remote. But, if correctional agencies refuse and courts conclude that the choice is between no standards at all or judicially imposed standards, the decision is likely to be in favor of judicially imposed standards. Certainly this has been the experience in the law enforcement field and that experience seems clearly relevant in making predictions about the future relationship between courts and correctional agencies.

An interesting illustration of judicial intervention and administrative response is found in some recent experience under the Wisconsin Sex Crimes Law.[d] Under this law, a person convicted of specified offenses, primarily forcible rape and indecent liberties with a child, must be committed to the Department of Health and Social Services for a mandatory presentence mental and social diagnosis. In other cases, the judge may, but need not, commit for diagnosis. The statute then provides that "if it appears from said report that the department recommends specialized treatment for his mental or physical aberrations, the court shall . . . commit him to the department" to be treated in the sex deviate facility, which is presently the state prison. When the maximum term for the criminal offense for which he was

---

[b] A good illustration of this is found in the opinion of Judge Oliver in *Burns v. Swenson*, at 831, *supra*. *See also* THE PRESIDENT'S COMMISSION ON LAW ENFORCEMENT AND ADMINISTRATION OF JUSTICE, TASK FORCE REPORT: CORRECTIONS, Chapter 8, *The Legal Status of Convicted Persons* (1967), in which correctional administrators are urged to assume a more active administrative rule-making function.

[c] Kimball & Newman, *Judicial Intervention in Correctional Decisions: Threat and Response*, 14 CRIME & DELINQUENCY 1 (1968).

[d] WIS. STAT. § 959.15 (1965).

convicted has expired, the department may bring the offender back to court and request an extension of the commitment on the ground that his release would be "dangerous to the public." If, after hearing, the court agrees, his term of commitment is increased by five years at a time.

Analysis of the statute makes clear that the legislature provided no criteria for the determination of initial commitment under the act and as the only criterion for an extension of control that the prisoner would be "dangerous to the public."

In this situation, the administrative agency had to act without significant legislative guidance. It might have considered its responsibility to develop either formally (as an administrative regulation to be included in the state administrative code) or informally (for internal use in maintaining consistency) some criteria for determining when a prisoner is "in need of specialized treatment" or "dangerous to the public" so as to subject him to control under the Sex Crimes program. In fact the administrative agency view was that the propriety of committing a prisoner under this program was essentially a medical and clinical decision to be made by professional standards, to be applied by the psychiatrists, psychologists, and clinical social workers who had responsibility for making the recommendation for initial commitment or continuation of control. This view has the advantage of flexibility. Practices could change easily as experience accumulated, and individual clinicians could use their best professional judgment without need to apply fixed standards. But there were also disadvantages. The decision in a particular case might depend upon the clinician who made it. For example, an offender who might be found "in need of specialized treatment" by one clinician who considered the existence of sexual psychopathology critical might not be so found by another clinician who emphasized the fact that the offender was not dangerous and that no effective treatment for his condition was known.

After some years of operation, the provision of the Sex Crimes Law which authorized purely administrative determination was held unconstitutional by the Wisconsin Supreme Court in *Huebner v. State,* which appears at 680, *supra.* The court held as a requirement of due process of law that the decision as to the need for specialized treatment (just as the decision in "extension" proceedings as to dangerousness had always been) must be made by the court after hearing evidence supporting and attacking the administrative recommendation of commitment under the Sex Crimes Law.

---

[e] Compare the extension decisions in Appendix B.

As a result of the *Huebner* decision, the Department of Health and Social Services was faced with the necessity of justifying to the trial courts its recommendations for commitment under the Sex Crimes program.[e] A meeting was called of personnel concerned with the problem and agreement was reached about proper grounds for making recommendations. This resulted in a memorandum to all personnel in clinical services.

MEMORANDUM

State of Wisconsin
State Department of Public Welfare
Division of Corrections

April 5, 1967

TO: All personnel involved in the clinical aspects of the Sex Crimes Law
FROM: Asher R. Pacht, Ph.D., Chief, Clinical Services
RE: Wisconsin Sex Crimes Law—Policy Change

As of April 10, 1967, the criteria to be followed in considering a recommendation for specialized treatment under the Sex Crimes Law are:

(1) Was the offense the product of sexual psychopathology?
(2) Is the individual *potentially* responsive to *available* specialized treatment assuming adequate motivation?
(3) Is the individual sexually dangerous?

Under this policy, the individual would be recommended for specialized treatment if criterion (1) and either criterion (2) and/or (3) are present, *i.e.,* such a recommendation would require the presence of sexual psychopathology in the individual and that he *either* be potentially responsive to available specialized treatment if motivated *and/or* be considered sexually dangerous.

As of this date, all clinical reports will be routinely submitted to the court in their entirety. Attention, therefore, should be given the language used in these reports so as to assure that they are as clear and as jargon-free as possible. To avoid confusion the staffing report should also demonstrate how the final consensual decision was reached in those cases where difference may be reflected in the individual reports.

Please contact me if you have additional questions.

The *Huebner* case and the correctional response to it raise a number of interesting and important questions:

(1) Would the result of the case have been the same if the administrative criteria had been formulated in advance, promulgated and published in the Administrative Code? There would seem to be no particular reason why a correctional agency ought not be looked upon as an important administrative agency with authority to make administrative policy within the limits set by legislation.

(2) If the choice between a commitment under the regular criminal code and the Sex Crimes Law requires a "judicial" decision, is it arguable that the same result should follow in the case of a decision to grant parole or to revoke parole? If not "judicial" decisions, what kind of decisions are they? Some would argue that they are casework decisions to be made according to the professional standards of the social worker. Others would urge that they are administrative decisions and that analogy would be found in the field of administrative law rather than in casework practice. The characterization of these decisions would obviously seem to have significance in the kind of training which should be given to the correctional worker who may find himself in an administrative decision-making capacity rather than his accustomed casework capacity.

(3) If a correctional agency does decide to give greater attention to the development and formulation of more adequate policy standards, what effect will this have upon correctional practice? Will it, for example, make it more or less comfortable for the psychiatrist, psychologist, and social worker? Is it more sensible to confine the clinician to the decision as to whether relatively clear standards (*e.g.,* of what constitutes dangerousness) apply in a given case, or is it better to leave also to the clinician the right to decide what constitutes dangerousness? For example, as applied to a person who chronically exposes himself, the clinician might be relied on to determine whether the person is likely also to seriously assault someone (established by others as dangerous within the meaning of the statute), or the clinician might be asked whether the person's frightening women and girls constitutes "dangerousness" even though he is not assaultive.

(4) Deciding whether the decision as to dangerousness is a "clinical" or "public policy" decision is important to the lawyer called upon to defend the person being committed or whose commitment is being extended an additional five years. If the decision as to dangerousness is "clinical," presumably the lawyer must rely upon psychiatric and psychological knowledge to rebut the state's case. Probably this will require either effective cross-examination of the state's expert witnesses or use of a defense expert. If, on the other hand, the issue is one of public policy then the lawyer must resort to ascertaining "the intention of the legislature" or to some other method of convincing the court that the policy question ought to be resolved in favor of his client. Of course, in many cases both clinical and policy issues may be involved.

APPENDIX A

THE STREETWALKING PROSTITUTE

This is an account of the practices followed by the Chicago Police Department in their efforts to control streetwalking prostitutes. The explanation for existing practices and the description of problems which the police encounter are related primarily from the police standpoint. The account has, however, been reviewed by those prosecutors and judges who have responsibilities relating to the processing of prostitutes. They have found it to be a fair reflection of current practice and existing problems as they existed at the end of 1966.

As an offender, the streetwalking prostitute is normally classified by the police, together with the drunk and the vagrant, as being of minor importance in the hierarchy of criminals. But the difficulties experienced in processing this relatively minor type of offender present the police with one of the most complex problems they confront. In large measure, these difficulties stem from the ambivalent attitude of the public toward prostitution—and especially toward the use of the criminal law as a means for controlling such behavior. To the extent that the police fail in their efforts to curtail the streetwalker's activities, their failure has an adverse effect upon many other aspects of police operations. Lack of effectiveness, for example, often results in the development of a public image of the police as being incompetent, inefficient, or corrupt—an image obviously detrimental to the accomplishment of the broader police task.

A. METHOD OF OPERATION

The streetwalking prostitute distinguishes herself from other forms of prostitution in that she usually operates on her own, often together with other prostitutes who are operating similarly, soliciting on the street or in other public places. She then takes her customers to her own room, a cheap hotel, or her "trick pad" (a location at which rooms are made available by the owner by prearrangement with the prostitute). There are some variations from this general pattern. In at least one section of Chicago, streetwalking prostitutes appear to be operating under the control of a single individual who owns the structures to which the prostitutes escort their customers. Less formal relationships may develop between a prostitute and a tavern owner who views her presence in the vicinity of the tavern as a means of attracting customers. Or a prostitute may make a practice of soliciting only when with another prostitute who is a personal friend. Despite these possible arrangements, it appears that the majority of streetwalking prostitutes do operate on their own.

It is often pointed out that most streetwalking prostitutes have an established relationship with a pimp. The pimp, however, does not usually solicit for the girl, but rather serves apparently to fulfill some emotional needs which the prostitute has for friendship and a permanent form of attachment. While the pimp does share in the prostitute's earnings, his role differs significantly from that of the panderer found in more organized forms of prostitution.

Streetwalking is generally viewed as the lowest form of prostitution. Because these are no controls over who engages in it, large numbers of unclean, unkempt, and generally unattractive women, often on narcotics and infected with venereal disease, are attracted to it. They operate in slums where whatever opposition exists is not sufficiently strong to demand an end to their activity and where cheap quarters are available to which customers may be escorted. An exception to this general pattern are those few clean, well-dressed women who operate in the hotel district, catering to visiting conventioners. But even there, streetwalkers exhibit the boldness and aggressiveness in solicitation which the nature of their operations requires. All of this contributes toward defining their low status.

From the standpoint of the streetwalker, there are some face-saving factors that provide a certain sense of status and dignity within the world of prostitution. The typical streetwalker takes some pride in the degree of independence she enjoys. Unlike the call girl or brothel inmate, she selects her own customers, establishes her own working hours, and sets her own price. But she must also develop her own means for protecting herself from police intervention and must provide her own defense should she be apprehended.

The decision on the part of the streetwalker as to the area in which she is to ply her trade is by no means an idle one. Having as an objective the acquisition of as much money as possible, she seeks out ways in which to make the most of her time both in terms of the number of men she successfully solicits and in terms of the dollars that she charges them. She therefore usually places herself in areas which have well-established reputations as hangouts for prostitutes, areas to which men in search of a prostitute are attracted. Police activity may result in temporary rises and declines in the reputation of such areas, but only the demolition of structures as part of a redevelopment project seems to have a permanent effect in abolishing such a reputation.

Within the city of Chicago, streetwalkers tend to concentrate in three areas, with racial factors accounting for the major distinctions among them. Most of the prostitutes on the southside are Negro and practically all of their customers are Negro. Westside prostitutes are Negro, but cater to white "johns" who desire relations with a Negro prostitute. White prostitutes inhabit the northside area, but they are joined on the street by Negro prostitutes who live elsewhere. Their customers consist almost exclusively of white males. The distinctions between these areas are given emphasis in this observation by the commander of a northside police district:

> In conversation with some of the street prostitutes arrested, it was explained that the reason for attempting to ply their trade in this district was their desire to increase their earnings. They relate that in or near their own neighborhoods (south or west) the tricks will pay only a couple of dollars for companionship, whereas in this and like districts they ask $10.00, in some cases get it, and never do they receive less than $5.00. . . . They transfer into this more lucrative operation by merely paying 25 cents for a subway ride that whisks them out of their home environment and deposits them in a matter of minutes at a subway station from which they need only to emerge to begin plying their trade.

The term "streetwalker" is somewhat of a misnomer, in that prostitutes normally stand at a given location rather than walk about. The most common practice is for a prostitute to station herself at a street intersection, in a doorway or, most recently, in a laundromat—where she can be easily spotted by searching customers and where she is in a position to engage in her own soliciting. It is the male who does the walking or who slowly cruises by in a vehicle.

Three factors normally identify the prostitute to the customer: her being unescorted; her standing apparently idle; and her ready willingness to respond to any gesture or inquiry. A girl who stands at a bus stop, but who never boards a bus, invites a contact from a male. The streetwalker typically confronts a likely customer with the question, "Do you want to have a party?" or "Do you want some fun?" Her boldness depends upon the circumstances. It is, for example, unlikely that a Negro streetwalker would ask such a question of a Negro male walking briskly past her, carrying some groceries. On the other hand, it is likely that Negro streetwalkers in an area inhabited by Negroes would aggressively shout their invitations, in open competition with each other, toward a car containing several white men. The assumption is that the latter have placed themselves in the area in search of prostitutes. The potential customer will, if interested, stop and engage in a brief curbside discussion. The customer attempts to establish the nature of the sexual act in which the prostitute is willing to engage and the price. There is usually some haggling over the latter, since it is common knowledge that the prostitute initially sets her price higher than the amount she expects to receive.

A streetwalker attempts to develop her business, hoping that past customers will return and that referrals will be made to her. It is important, therefore, that she operate from the same location on a continuing basis. To do so for long periods of time in colder weather requires several adjustments in her operations. Prostitutes find it necessary to wear very heavy protective footwear—and boots and heavy socks become characteristics of the streetwalker in winter months. Another seasonal adjustment is cited in this excerpt from a district commander's monthly report on prostitution in his district:

> Ordinarily, in most any other area of the city, it could be expected that the numbers of available prostitutes would dwindle with the lowering of the temperatures in the wintertime. But with about five hundred licensed taverns and clubs in the district and approximately two hundred restaurants—many of the latter being all night operations—it is relatively easy for a prostitute to get out of the subfreezing temperatures. These facilities serve as ready-made warming stations and also afford dignity and some protection to the operations in that the prostitutes are able to mix with cross sections of citizens making use of these places of public accommodation.

B. THE BASIS FOR POLICE CONCERN

The Chicago Police Department is committed to a policy of strict enforcement of the statutory prohibitions against the kind of activity in which streetwalkers are engaged. The general order establishing the duties of a district commander makes him explicitly responsible for suppression of prostitution in his district, along with other vice conditions. His tenure may well depend upon his success.

Contrary to the common image, this posture does not necessarily reflect strong personal beliefs on the part of all police officers or the police administration that prostitution is morally wrong and ought to be eradicated. Rather, the position reflects an awareness on the part of the police that the existence of prostitution in a societal setting in which it is outlawed gives rise to some serious side-effects—problems about which there is more universal concern than is normally expressed over prostitution itself. These side-effects, in turn, become factors that contribute toward shaping the department's policy toward the streetwalker. Five such factors are described here.

1. *Frequency with Which Streetwalkers Rob Their Customers*

Statistics are unfortunately not maintained on the number of incidents reported to the police in which streetwalkers rob their customers or lure them into situations in which they are then robbed by others. One can only speculate as to the magnitude of the problem, since even a computation of the incidents reported to the police would most likely represent but a small percentage of the total number of such incidents occurring. Embarrassment on the part of the victim tends to result in cases coming to the attention of the police only when they involve an injury requiring hospital care or a loss of money covered by insurance—both of which require the filing of a police report. The pattern of incidents as reported, however, is sufficient to create the impression among police officers that a substantial percentage of streetwalkers assist in arranging for the robbery of their customers and that the existence of streetwalkers makes it easy for a nonprostitute female to decoy an intended robbery victim. A selection of several reports filed with the police illustrates the basis for police concern. Each excerpt represents the account of the incident as provided by the victim and recorded by the officer:

(a) Patrol #1201 was assigned to 1408 W. Madison on a call of a robbery victim. Upon arrival, reporting officer interviewed victim, Robert M. Jacob, M/W/1914, who stated that an unknown colored girl had asked him if he wanted to have some fun. He stated "Yes" and followed her to 11 N. Ada. When he reached the alley he was jumped by two unknown colored men who took his wallet containing $56.00

USC. They took off his shoes and threw them down the alley. Reporting officers took victim to location and found his shoes and empty wallet. One of the males had .32 caliber blue steel revolver. Victim refused to go to hospital. He had laceration of legs and bruised shoulder. Victim transported to hotel. . . .

(b) Patrol #1801 interviewed robbery victim, M/W/1928, in 18th district station. Victim states he was driving his auto south on Sedgewick and as he came to Scott he observed a female Negro standing on the southwest corner. He slowed down and the F/N came over to his auto and told him to pull around the corner, west on Scott where she would commit an act of prostitution. As the victim parked his auto, leaving the F/N standing on the corner, two male Negroes came up to the victim's auto and displayed a knife, robbing the victim of $123.00 USC and a Timex wrist watch valued at $12.00. . . .

(c) Patrol #1802 received assignment to interview robbery victim, M/W/1934, at 1880 North Avenue and Clybourn. Complainant states that he picked up a prostitute known as Bobie Jones, F/N/1931 at North Ave. and Clybourn and rode a cab to several hotels for registrations, finally registering at the Triangle Hotel, 1570 N. Clybourn, Room 116. After having committed the act of prostitution, the prostitute broke a bottle of brandy and used the broken bottle to threaten the victim, while robbing him of $120 USC. . . .

(d) Patrol #1821 sent to Chicago Ave. and LaSalle St. to answer a robbery assignment. Victim states one Shirley Small solicited him for an act of prostitution. The victim agreed to go up to Room 208 at 1117 N. Dearborn with Miss Small for $20. When the victim arrived in the room, he paid Miss Small $20 and proceeded to take off his clothes. Miss Small stated that she wanted more money. When the victim refused, Miss Small was joined by a female companion who entered through an open door. Both women then locked the door and tore off all of the victim's clothes. The victim broke out of the room after the women took $200 in USC from him. . . . A neighbor heard the altercation and heard a female voice saying, "If you don't give me the money, I'll say you raped me." . . .

2. Degree to Which Streetwalking Prostitutes Are Engaged in Organized Criminal Activity

The general position of the Chicago Police Department with regard to all vice activities gives emphasis to the need for strict enforcement because of the contribution that individual violations eventually make to the growth of organized crime:

> Gambling, prostitution, the sale of narcotics and the illegal operation of liquor dispensing establishments constitute the seedbeds of syndicated crime. Receipts from these activities pour funds into the coffers of the criminal syndicate. The total effort of the department must be directed toward the suppression and elimination of these violations.*

While it appears that the majority of streetwalking prostitutes remain relatively free of a direct tie-in with syndicate-type criminal activity, the potential for more widespread involvement is illustated by this situation described by a district commander:

> Since the closing of the Club Dolly, the streetwalkers, such as Nancy Steel, have changed their location from North and Halsted to the 600-700 blocks of North Clark Street. They are using the Queen's Palace and the grill next to it as warming places in between tricks. John Fargo, a westside pimp and narcotics dealer with 44 arrests—from burglary to possession of narcotics—has taken over the North and Halsted area from Joe Sherz and has imported some Oak and Wells Street girls, such as Mildred Martin and Carolyn Hanson, and some junkie pimps to operate the trick houses now owned by him. . . .

It is only a matter of speculation whether someone at a higher level is in a position to—and does—extract a fee from John Fargo for the privilege he apparently enjoys in running an exclusive operation.

Those streetwalkers who are narcotics addicts have, of course, a direct contact with whatever system exists for the distribution of narcotics. The fact that they are active as streetwalkers may be attributable to the need which they have for raising funds with which to purchase their narcotics supply.

---

* Chicago Police Department, On This We Stand (1966).

3. *Transmittal of Venereal Disease*

Local government, primarily through its public health and police departments, is committed to exerting a maximum effort to control the spread of venereal disease. Streetwalkers are viewed as a primary source of contagion. Local health officials maintain a direct interest in the arrest of streetwalkers and, through examination, they identify and treat active cases of venereal disease. But it is the American Social Health Association, a private organization, that maintains constant pressure from outside the governmental structure. The ASHA conducts periodic surveys of commercialized prostitution in metropolitan areas and in communities near large military installations. In its reports, the Association routinely notes that the results of its investigations "are made available to responsible community leaders to make them aware of problems and to encourage their exercise of responsibility in remedying the problems. . . . . If, after receiving reports on adverse community conditions, the local leadership fails to act constructively or is unwilling to be identified with the report, the American Social Health Association reserves the right to release information from the report directly." A typical report includes the detailed findings of the Association's investigators who endeavor to establish the degree to which prostitutes are available in the community. The desire to avoid adverse publicity from such a respected organization constitutes a substantial incentive to suppress prostitution.

4. *Nuisance Created to Residents, Business Establishments, and Passersby*

Areas in which streetwalkers concentrate are usually run-down locations, spotted with cheap hotels and bars. Persons choosing to reside in such an area do not normally object to the activities of the prostitutes, nor is there usually any concern voiced by the owners of stores or other commercial outlets whose business may, in fact, benefit from the presence of the prostitutes.

Complaints do, however, steadily flow into the office of the Superintendent of Police with regard to the presence of streetwalkers at given locations. One of the major sources of such complaints are the residents of adjoining areas into which some of the activities of the street prostitutes occasionally overflow. This is especially true on the northside where the area frequented by prostitutes is within several blocks of luxurious, high-rise apartment houses. Complaints usually reflect a concern over the degree to which the presence of streetwalkers contributes toward the deterioration of the neighborhood and the lessening of property values. With equal frequency, complainants cite the impossibility of walking through such areas without being offended by the behavior of the prostitutes. Parents complain that youngsters living in the area are exposed to the prostitutes as they ply their trade.

5. *Opportunities for Development of Corrupt Practices and the Desire to Minimize Adverse Publicity*

Difficulties confronted in taking enforcement action against streetwalkers create a set of conditions which breed corrupt practices. Unscrupulous police officers, armed with the authority to arrest, may utilize the problems involved in enforcing the law as a screen behind which they engage in a practice of accepting payments from prostitutes in exchange for granting them immunity from arrest. An awareness of this problem prompts police officials to commit themselves to a policy of strict enforcement. By doing so, they are reducing—if not eliminating—the amount of discretion lodged with each police officer, in an effort to make it easier to "police the police department" by defining failure to arrest for every discovered violation as misconduct.

Whether or not there are individual acts of corruption within the police force, failure of the police to prevent overt solicitations by streetwalkers is taken by the public as an indication that corruption does exist. It is frequently contended that such conditions could not exist without the knowledge and tolerance of the police.

This prevalent attitude is periodically reinforced by newspaper exposés containing statements such as the following:

> On the worst streets in the Negro section of the South Side the prostitutes chase men for business. . . . This investigator and another man spent a week on the South Side and found wide-open gambling, prostitution, and traffic in dope. . . .*
>
> A 10-day investigation of North Side vice conditions by Chicago's American . . . uncovered wide-open prostitution, soliciting for drinks, gambling, policy operations, and violence on the streets. . . . The overall investigation was started after repeated reports to this newspaper that vice was wide open in the 18th, or Chicago Avenue, police district. The investigation confirmed the reports. Heise [the

* Chicago Daily News, December 21, 1960.

reporter] and his detective partner were solicited by prostitutes dozens of times. . . .*

The police administrator knows, of course, that such conditions are easy to find and report. But the reporter or newspaper investigator is in no way concerned with the development of evidence to justify arrest. He can boldly confront a suspected prostitute and ask if she is willing to engage in sexual intercourse for money. He is entirely free of the limitations and restraints under which the police operate when placing themselves in a position to be solicited. Such widely read reports have a very adverse effect upon the image of the police and detract from police efforts in other areas substantially removed from prostitution, such as in dealing with the youthful offender, with racial conflict, and with the traffic violator. Understandably, honest police officials are very sensitive about these reports. A policy of strict enforcement is intended, in part, to minimize the likelihood of a newspaper reporter or other investigator being able to report overt conditions such as those described in the articles.

C. LEGAL CONTROLS

Section 11-14 of the Illinois Criminal Code of 1961 defines prostitution as follows:

(a) Any person who performs, offers or agrees to perform any of the following acts for money commits an act of prostitution:

(1) Any act of sexual intercourse; or
(2) Any act of deviate sexual conduct.

(b) Penalty.

A person convicted of prostitution shall be fined not to exceed $200 or imprisoned in a penal institution other than the penitentiary not to exceed one year, or both.

Section 11-15 defines the crime of soliciting for a prostitute:

(a) Any person who performs any of the following acts commits soliciting for a prostitute:

(1) Solicits another for the purpose of prostitution; or

* Chicago American, July 6, 1964.

(2) Arranges or offers to arrange a meeting of persons for the purpose of prostitution; or

(3) Directs another to a place knowing such direction is for the purpose of prostitution.

(b) Penalty.

A person convicted of soliciting for a prostitute shall be fined not to exceed $200 or imprisoned in a penal institution other than the penitentiary not to exceed one year, or both.

This section appears to be used interchangeably with § 11-14 where evidence will support both charges. Its major application, however, is to individuals who solicit in behalf of a prostitute—the "middleman" or "contact" who plays so important a role in forms of prostitution other than streetwalking.

Section 11-18 makes it a criminal offense to patronize a prostitute:

(a) Any person who performs any of the following acts with a person not his spouse commits the offense of patronizing a prostitute:

(1) Engages in an act of sexual intercourse or deviate sexual conduct with a prostitute; or

(2) Enters or remains in a place of prostitution with intent to engage in an act of sexual intercourse or deviate sexual conduct.

(b) Penalty.

A person convicted of patronizing a prostitute shall be fined not to exceed $200 or imprisoned in a penal institution other than the penitentiary not to exceed 6 months, or both.

Other sections of the state statutes define it to be criminal to pander (§ 11-16); to keep a place of prostitution (§ 11-17); and to engage in pimping (§ 11-19).

D. TECHNIQUES OF ENFORCEMENT

In order to bring criminal charges against a woman for having solicited for purposes of prostitution, the police must be prepared to produce testimony in court by one who either was solicited or was present at the time a solicitation was made. The very nature of prostitution is such that the police cannot look to those who are solicited to provide such testimony. Most men solicited by a female prostitute on the street either are in search of such solicitations or take no offense at being asked. A very small percentage of those who are offended may complain to the police, but are not sufficiently aggrieved to sign a criminal complaint and to agree to testify against the prostitute. The testimony of a person solicited by a prostitute is available and producible in court only in those cases in which a male customer, after having responded affirmatively to a solicitation, subsequently is robbed, discovers a loss of cash or valuable items, or is denied the sexual intercourse for which he may have made advance payment. The desire for some sort of revenge on the part of the customer enables the police to proceed in such cases.

In the absence of complaints, the police must, if they are to take action against street prostitutes, develop their own procedures for establishing the elements of the offense. This requires affirmative action on the part of the department—the placing of police officers in positions in which they are likely to be solicited so that the officer can then testify firsthand as to the offense.

In Chicago, the task of acquiring evidence upon which to arrest streetwalkers is assigned principally to the vice officers who operate in each district. These men function under the direction of the district commander. The number of vice officers in each district is proportionate to an assessment of the vice problem in the district—with as many as thirty being assigned to some of the busier districts. The need for operating twenty-four hours a day, days-off, vacations, and time spent in court results in but a small fraction of this number being on duty at any one time. Each patrolman selected to work as a vice officer serves for a limited period unless his supervisors consider his work to be of such superior quality as to justify his retention for a longer period. As a group, the vice officers concern themselves with all forms of gambling, narcotics, prostitution, and violations of alcoholic beverage laws. Their activities relating to streetwalkers are considered among the least important of all their duties.

Officers are greatly aided in focusing upon the problem by some of the very characteristics inherent in the operations of the streetwalker. The manner in which a prostitute operates to identify herself to her trade, for example, serves also to identify her activities to the police. It follows that vice officers assigned to ferreting out street prostitution place themselves in locations in which it is known that prostitutes solicit; they dress like the men dress who commonly patronize prostitutes and act interested in being solicited.

Street prostitutes have no way of carefully screening the individuals they solicit. To be successful, they must appeal rather indiscriminately for their trade. But if they are to avoid a criminal charge, they soon learn to avoid soliciting a police officer. The first and basic precaution is to learn the identity of police officers working in the area. In addition, the prostitute seeks to identify the vehicles used by police officers. This is not a difficult task, since police vehicles are purchased in large lots and, despite efforts to make them of varied colors, have a sufficient number of features in common to make them easily identifiable.

Such efforts provide only a minimum of protection to the prostitute because of the substantial numbers of officers that may be used and the frequent absence of vehicles. A prostitute typically also attempts to avoid the possibility of conviction by phrasing her solicitation in terms that make no direct reference to sexual intercourse. She is aware than an offer to "have fun," to "engage in a party," or to "show someone a good time" has traditionally been held by the courts to be sufficiently ambiguous as not by itself to constitute a solicitation to engage in sexual intercourse. An experienced prostitute will become leery of and turn away from any individual who persists in elaborating upon her initial offer by asking that she discuss the nature of the act in which she is willing to engage. She is aware that a routine customer is more intent on consummating the act itself and that it is the police officer who must elicit such statements from her.

The sophisticated prostitute not only avoids reference to the sexual act, but also avoids reference to money, recognizing that an officer must establish that the offender offered to engage in sexual intercourse for money. She may, for example, talk in terms of drinks, though the implication may be clear to her customer that she expects payment in a number of dollars equal to the number of drinks. The possibility of avoiding arrest and conviction through this device has only arisen since 1961 when the revision of the criminal code dropped "other thing of value" from the former definition of prostitution as being sexual intercourse for "money or other thing of value." This was done in an effort to remove sexual acts of a noncommercial nature as acts constituting prostitution. If the prostitute has any reason to believe that the person she is soliciting is a police officer, she may resort to talking ambiguously about her charges in an effort to determine whether her prospective customer insists on her referring to money. Persistence on his part may be taken by her as an indication that he is, in fact, a police officer intent on acquiring evidence of the elements of the offense.

Jerome Skolnick, in his *Justice Without Trial,* relates this comment by an officer assigned to vice control in a city with a similar problem:*

> The broads are wisening up, getting real hanky. One of them told me she can always spot a cop because we never say, "Hey, baby, how would you like to turn a trick for ten bucks?" which is what a lot of these trollers [men in search of prostitutes] say when one of these broads looks good to them. We got to wait for them to set the price, otherwise we don't stand a chance in court. It doesn't matter how many times a broad's been convicted for prostitution. If we set the price, we got no case. The law says we entrapped her.
>
> I was trolling one night and a broad walked over to the car and said, "Mister, I'm in trouble, I could use a little money."
>
> I said, "Well, I might be able to help you out, provided I get something for my money."
>
> She said, "You'll get something, but how much you givin'?"
>
> I said, "How much you asking?"
>
> She said, "How much you offerin' to pay?"
>
> "Well," I said, "How's about a dollar?"
>
> "Oh, mister," she said, "You must be a policeman"—and walked off.

As still another common precaution, a prostitute may insist on an opportunity to search her customer prior to making any commitment so as to locate a gun or badge routinely carried by police officers. Unaware of the kind of circumstances into which they might be led, police officers are apprehensive and are in fact schooled against leaving their weapon and their badge of authority behind unless arrangements have been made for other officers to provide full and continuous protection.

Police officials take each of these tactics on the part of the prostitute into consideration in devising their enforcement program, trying to develop countermeasures. Rotation in the assignment of patrolmen as vice officers is designed, in part, to minimize the likelihood of their being identified. But the need for many young men, for specialized training, and for staffing other assignments places practical limitations on the degree to which a department can continue to maintain anonymity of its vice officers over a prolonged period of time.

The department has acquired a pool of vehicles through confiscations in narcotics cases which represent a cross section of the

* At 103 (1966).

various types of cars in use in the community. Officers assigned to ferreting out street prostitution may make use of these vehicles on a rotating basis as a further means of disguising their identity. In their specialized training, officers assigned to vice are urged to overcome the ability of prostitutes to identify them by acting as unlike police officers as is possible. The best trained officer, in other words, is considered to be the one who can act sufficiently casual to be solicited in a manner in which he acquires evidence of all the elements of the offense without arousing the suspicions of the prostitute.

These countermeasures taken by the police are of questionable value against a truly sophisticated prostitute who exercises extreme care in her solicitations. As a result, those who are convicted are primarily prostitutes who are without prior experience in the criminal process, those who operate in a careless manner, and those who conclude that an occasional conviction is offset by the greater profits to be derived from less inhibited solicitation.

A police officer who arrests a woman on a charge of soliciting for prostitution must arrange for her appearance in Women's Court, which is located at police headquarters. (But, if the prostitute is an addict, the case goes to Narcotics Court; and if the male who is solicited is under twenty-one, the case goes to Boys' Court.) The arresting officer must plan to appear to testify at a time when he would normally be off duty. Consequently, an officer is reluctant to make an arrest unless the case is a strong one. This is a general police problem, but it is complicated in solicitation cases by three factors: (a) the need for being in court at 9:00 a.m., usually after having worked until midnight or 3:00 a.m.; (b) the distance of this centralized court from both the police facility and the homes of most police officers; and (c) the need for waiting through a docket that often consists of as many as 130 cases before the officer's case is called. Compensation is made to the officer in Chicago by crediting him with three hours which he can take off at some later time. If he is in court over six hours, he is credited with a full tour of duty which he can then take off. But compensation in this form does not affect a widespread reluctance of officers to take actions resulting in the need for testifying in court.

Still another problem is created if, despite the above considerations, an officer does effect an arrest and does appear in court. A district commander reported:

> One of the major problems in processing . . . soliciting prostitutes is the time-manpower limitations. As the numbers of arrests increase, there is a gradual decrease in enforce-

ment activities because of the additional man-hours spent in processing the arrests, in court appearances, and in the taking of accumulated time.

E. THE RESULTS OF ENFORCEMENT EFFORTS

Problems encountered in attempting to gather the kind of evidence required to support a charge of prostitution seriously frustrate the officers assigned to the task. Additional difficulties experienced in the processing of the prostitute through court when sufficient evidence has been acquired to support a charge add to these frustrations. In response, the police devise a variety of means for attempting to deal more directly with those elements of the street prostitution problem that are the source of greatest concern to them. The end result is reflected in this comment by the Superintendent of the Chicago Police Department when, in describing the frustrations stemming from varying interpretations by judges as to the requirements of proof in vice cases, he said:

> All of these judges may be acting from the best of motives. But their decisions result in a "What's the use?" attitude among policemen detailed to gambling and vice assignments. Finding them futile, the police, unfortunately, tend to abandon efforts to suppress gambling and vice by legal means. However, the continuing pressure of their superiors and the fear of newspaper exposés force them to make some attempt to suppress gambling and vice. So they resort to harassing raids and arrests without warrants, with little hope of successful prosecution in our courts. Thus a vicious circle of contempt for law enforcement and the administration of criminal justice is set up. The courts lose respect for the police; the police lose respect for the courts; and the public loses respect for both.*

Once this cycle is placed in motion, it is difficult to establish which factors are causal in contributing to the further complication of the basic enforcement problems. Judicial policies in the processing of cases against street prostitutes no doubt contribute toward encouraging the police to resort to procedures outside the legal process in order to abate the nuisance created by street prostitution. But, on the other hand, the courts are influenced, in their processing of arrested persons, by an awareness of the

* HARPER'S, April 1964, at 163-64.

use of informal devices by the police. The latter are described in section 2 below.

1. *The Disposition by the Courts of Charges Against Prostitutes Arrested for Solicitation*

A case in which a woman is charged with soliciting rarely goes to trial on the first appearance in court. The prostitute usually requests a continuance, citing the need for consulting with an attorney. She in fact recognizes that the likelihood of her being acquitted is increased by continuing her case, for once the case is initially postponed, it may take three or four continuances to bring the prostitute and the police officer together again, and there is always a possibility that failure of the officer to appear may result in dismissal without trial. The prostitute may, herself, fail to appear on the date to which her case is continued and a warrant may be issued for her arrest. Or she may appear and indicate that she is experiencing difficulty in obtaining counsel, or may indicate that her retained counsel is busy in some other courtroom. In fact, private counsel is retained in a very small percentage of the cases in which a woman is charged with soliciting. The police officer, on the other hand, may be on vacation on the date of trial or he may be busy in some other courtroom. Often, his failure to show up is simply attributable to the administrative difficulties of keeping all interested parties informed of the dates to which cases are continued, given the massive volume of cases processed through the courts.

If, at the time of trial, a defendant is not represented by an attorney, the public defender will offer his services. Both a private attorney and the public defender tend initially to defend their client by urging that the elements of the offense were not present. The former, however, is likely to go beyond exploring the elements of the offense and inquire into the behavior of the police officer, raising questions as to the propriety of his actions and suggesting a defense of entrapment. Inquiry may be made as to why the officer frequented this particular area, why he dressed in a disguised manner, and why he made use of a car unlike those commonly used by plainclothes police officers. The impression that the attorney hopes to create is that the officer resorted to trickery, that he was overzealous in performing his assignment, and that there is at least a suggestion that his actions may have gotten the defendant to respond in a manner which would otherwise be foreign to her.

If viewed as a question of law, the defense of entrapment can seldom succeed, especially in the light of the narrow interpretation taken of it by the Illinois Supreme Court.* Such a defense has failed even in those cases in which the conversation regarding sexual intercourse was initiated by the officer. But the case in which the issue of entrapment is raised may still be dismissed on the stated grounds that the judge believes that the defendant was not guilty of the offense charged. When this occurs in a case in which the line of inquiry was designed to create doubts as to the propriety of the officer's actions, the officer is tempted to alter his method of testifying in the future—offering a pretense for being in the area frequented by prostitutes or for dressing as he does when, in fact, the efficient performance of his assignment calls for him to operate in this manner.

A review of one day's court activity gives some indication of the manner in which solicitation cases are handled. On August 23, 1965, the court processed the cases of twenty-seven women charged under the state statutes with prostitution. Of this number of cases, nine were continued on motion of the defense; eight were continued on motion of the state; and three defendants failed to appear and their bonds were ordered forfeited and warrants were issued for their arrest. The charges against two defendants were dismissed. Five were found guilty, with two being placed on probation for a year; two being fined $200 without costs; and one being sentenced to thirty days in the House of Correction.

Observations of the operations of the Women's Court over a long period of time and with different judges sitting on the bench suggest that there are a number of factors contributing to a decision to acquit in addition to that of guilt or innocence. There appear to be five bases for granting acquittals.

a. Inability of the state to prove the elements of the offense. This may be due to failure on the part of the police officer to establish all of the elements, or simply his failure and that of the state's attorney in seeing to it that all available evidence is introduced. This failure is often due to the pressure of time created by the large volume of cases.

b. Agreement by the judge as to the guilt of the defendant, but a desire to avoid the stigma of conviction where there is an indication that the defendant has not previously been found guilty of the same charge. The decision, in effect, represents the granting of a second opportunity to the defendant on the grounds that her prior record and the rela-

* People v. McSmith, 23 Ill. 2d 87, 178 N.E.2d 641 (1961).

tively minor nature of the charge against her do not warrant the consequences flowing from conviction.

c. Agreement by the judge as to the guilt of the defendant, but a feeling that the primary objective is to minimize the transmission of venereal disease. In such cases, the judge refers the defendant for examination by the department of public health and continues her case. Upon her return to court, the judge is furnished with a report of their findings. The case may then be dismissed in the belief that the best interests were served by having the prostitute examined and, where the results were positive, by having her submit to treatment.

d. Disapproval by the judge of the methods employed by the police. When defense counsel raises questions as to the propriety of police practices, the judge may agree that the techniques of disguise employed were "unfair" or that, while acceptable in other areas of police work, the practices were inappropriate because of the relatively minor importance that the public attaches to the crime.

e. Lack of any explanation. Indiscriminate dismissals or acquittals can only be taken as reflective of the judge's personal view that prostitution is not a serious offense, and that it is an appropriate exercise of judicial discretion to reflect community ambivalence by refusing to convict those charged with the crime.

While there appear to be many factors contributing to the finding of "not guilty" or to a dismissal of charges other than innocence, judges usually do not acknowledge that these additional factors enter into their decision. When public criticism has been leveled at the judiciary for their low rate of convictions, the tendency is for the affected judges to place the blame upon the police for their failure to adequately support charges brought in court.

There are three special problems for the system that are related to judicial acquittals and dismissals: (a) the common view that it is inappropriate to acquit on grounds other than the lack of adequate evidence tends to prevent the real reasons from being acknowledged; (b) the absence of a vigorous prosecution contributes toward a situation in which the reasons for such decisions are not articulated; and (c) the rotation of judges in a single courtroom having jurisdiction over a given set of offenses introduces new criteria and new views from time to time. As a result, whatever influence the court may intend to have upon police operations does not get effectively communicated, nor is that guidance which is transmitted sent down through the ranks in a manner likely to produce uniform results. As a consequence, the whole process tends to contribute further to the frustrations of the officer—since the police officer views his efforts to bring cases into court to be wasted if conviction and punishment are uncommon. And he is confused in his efforts to comprehend the guidelines by which he can more successfully achieve his objective through the courts.

Jerome Skolnick summarizes the police view when he notes:

> The ease with which a prostitute is able to return to illegal activity is frustrating to the policeman. In his opinion, if the community wants to keep prostitutes off the streets, a system permitting them to return within a couple of hours after arrest is irrational. . . .*

2. *The Development by the Police of Alternative Devices for Coping with Street Prostitution*

It is difficult to establish the point in the process at which the police become discouraged in their efforts and turn to other devices as a means of satisfying the pressures brought to bear upon them. Frustrations build up at each stage: from the difficulty experienced in acquiring necessary evidence of the various elements of the crime; from unsuccessful efforts to overcome devices used by prostitutes to identify officers; from the inconvenience in making repeated court appearances; from the challenge as to the propriety of their methods to ferret out violations; from dismissals and acquittals for unexplained reasons when it seems to them that guilt is clear; and from imposition of relatively minor and insignificant monetary punishment upon those who are, in the end, found guilty. Each contributes to discouraging the police from relying on the courts to deal with prostitutes. Since the pressures to suppress prostitution persist, the police turn to other devices.

In areas frequented by street prostitutes, the police occasionally engage in "chasing" them by ordering that they leave the area. This effort to keep the prostitutes on the move and keep the assigned area clean is the simplest but also the least effective means of dealing with the problem. Prostitutes who are ordered to move on tend to comply without question, continuing their activities elsewhere.

---

* J. SKOLNICK, JUSTICE WITHOUT TRIAL 187 (1966).

The primary means for augmenting whatever deterrence is achieved through court conviction for solicitation has been to follow a policy of arresting "known" prostitutes under the provisions of two city ordinances.

> Section 192-6 It shall be unlawful for any habitual drunkard, any person known to be a narcotic addict, any person known to be a prostitute, or any person who aids or abets prostitution or for any person previously convicted of a felony, of prostitution, or of aiding and abetting prostitution to assemble or congregate with other persons of any of the foregoing classes in or upon the public ways or other public places in the city, or to loaf or loiter in or about or frequent the premises of any place where intoxicating liquors are sold.
>
> Section 192-5 Any prostitute, soliciting to prostitution, or any person of evil fame or repute plying his vocation upon the public ways or other public places in the city is hereby declared to be a common nuisance and shall be fined not to exceed $100 for each offense.

There is great doubt as to the validity of all so-called loitering ordinances and there is special doubt as to the validity of an ordinance which defines status or character to be criminal.* An awareness of the tenuous validity of § 192-6 by the judges, the prosecutors, and the members of the public defender's staff results in a judicial policy not to find anyone guilty under its provisions. There is, as a result, no basis for an appeal. The police know that no conviction will result, but find justification in the ordinance for arresting the streetwalker and causing her brief imprisonment.

Arrests are usually made under § 192-6 when a woman known to the police by reputation as a prostitute is found to be present, alone, on the streets during late night and early morning hours. No effort is made to bring the defendant to trial. A typical proceeding before the examining magistrate the next morning is the following:

> Judge: "What were you doing out on the streets at 3 A.M.?"
> Defendant: "Going home from a restaurant."
> Judge: "Go home."

The process seldom takes more than a minute. The arresting officer is not required to appear, a sergeant permanently assigned to the court appearing in his behalf. The state's attorney, who

* *See* **Robinson v. California, 370 U.S. 660 (1962).**

normally prosecutes city charges as well as those brought under the state law, does not participate in these proceedings. The judge may inquire whether the defendant had recently been examined for venereal disease and may order that she report for an examination. There are, however, apparently no established criteria for making this decision.

The relative ease with which a prostitute can be processed as a loiterer has several effects upon the system. Police tend to prefer charging a prostitute with loitering rather than solicitation because it does not require proof and it does not require a court appearance. They contend, and understandably so, that the end result, in terms of court disposition, is likely to be the same whether the prostitute is charged under city ordinance or state law.

Most prostitutes who are arrested for soliciting are charged with soliciting under § 192-5 of the city ordinances as well as under state laws, because some of the people functioning within the system are of the impression that the burden of proof required under the ordinance is less than that required under state law. The case usually goes to trial on both charges at the same time. If there is a finding of guilty, the prosecutor and the judge then decide on whether the finding is on the state or city charge. In all cases, one of the charges is dropped. Dropping of the state charge avoids creation of a "criminal record." If defense counsel is engaged, and a conviction appears likely, his major effort will be directed at insuring that the state charge is dropped.

Since the charges against loitering prostitutes do not require evidence obtained by undercover work, it is expected that uniformed police officers engaged in regular patrol activities will arrest the so-called loitering prostitute. Indeed, considerable pressure is kept on the uniformed officer to make this kind of an arrest. By enrolling his services, the otherwise limited efforts of the vice officers in dealing with street prostitution are multiplied manyfold. The vice officers continue their efforts to develop cases in which the prostitute is charged with solicitation. In order to maintain the pressure on uniformed officers to arrest loitering prostitutes, monthly summaries are produced showing the activity of both the uniformed officers and the vice officers and relating the arrests of street prostitutes in one district to that in another.

In an effort to aid his uniformed officers in fulfilling this aspect of their assignment, one district commander reported the following:

> To assist in maintaining the arrest index of prostitutes, an alphabetical listing of names of those arrested during the

past three months, containing 328 names, has been compiled and distributed to uniformed personnel.

The following is one page from the arrest record of a street prostitute. It provides some indication of the manner in which this program of police action relates to the individual. Among the numerous arrests for loitering are two arrests for solicitation, on August 14, 1964, and August 10, 1965. A delay of ten months was experienced before the defendant was convicted on the first charge and sentenced to thirty days in the House of Correction. The second set of charges for solicitation were still pending.

CITY OF CHICAGO / **DEPARTMENT OF POLICE** 1121 South State Street Chicago, Illinois 60605 WAbash 2-4747
IDENTIFICATION SECTION

CRIMINAL HISTORY OF Sharon Burgess F/N

DATE IR# 622

DATE OF BIRTH 14 August 1943

NAME & ADDRESS	C.B. NO.	DATE OF ARREST / ARRESTING OFFICER & DIST. / CHARGE / DISPOSITION
	1571471	-2 Aug 64, Off. Robinson, 18th dist. Prost.
		-4 Aug 64, Prost, Disch, Judge Schwartz.
	1574759	-7 Aug 64, Off. Robinson, 18th dist, Loit Prost.
		-7 Aug 64, Loit Prost, LFD,* Judge Schwartz.
	1576521	-9 Aug 64, Off. Robinson, 18th dist, Loit Prost.
		-9 Aug 64, 192-6, LFD, Judge Nash.
	1579432	-14 Aug 64, Off. Reilly, VCD, Vice Inv.
		-12 Apr 65, 38-11-14, 30 days H of C, 11-15, Disch.
	1582885	-19 Aug 64, Off. Robinson, 18th dist, Loit Prost.
		-19 Aug 64, 192-6, LFD, Judge Komosa.
	1787437	-2 July 65, Off. Zingarelli, 18th dist. Loit Prost.
		-2 July 65, Loit Prost, LFD, Judge Edelstein.
	1789380	-4 July 65, Naughton, 018, Loit. Prost.
		-5 July 65, Loit Prost, LFD, Judge Edelstein
	1789989	-5 July 65, Sturgill 18th Dist Loit. Prost.
		-5 July 65, Loit Prost LFD Judge La Plante.
	1786827	-1 July 65, Off. J. Dugnan C.D. Loitering Prost.
		-1 July 65, Loitering Prost LFD Judge Edelstein.
	1791275	-7 July 65, Dugnan, 011, Loit. Prost.
		-7 July 65, Loit Prost.-LFD, Judge Edelstein.
	1796872	-15 July 65, Altiere-18th, Loit. Prost.
		-15 July 65, Known & Loit-LFD, Judge Edelstein.
	1800142	-19 July 65, Cucci & Co; 18th; Loit Prost.;
		-21 July 65 Loit Prost LFD Judge Edelstein.
	1803399	-24 July 65, Naughton & Co. 18th Dist Loitering Prost
		-25 July 65, Loit Prost, LFD, Judge Malkin.
	1807405	-30 July 65, McCaffrey & Shuey, 018, Loit. Prost.
		-30 July 65, Loit. Prost., LFD, Judge Edelstein.
	1809736	-2 Aug 65, Off. Sturgill, 18th Dist Loit Prost
		-2 Aug 65, Loit Prost, LFD, Judge Edelstein.
	1815897	-10 Aug 65, Cucci 18 (WCD), Soliciting (2 chgs).
	1817148	-13 Aug 65, Zingarelli 18th Dist. Loit. Prost.
		-13 Aug 65, Loit Prost, LFD, Judge White
	1820292	-17 Aug 65, Korbis 18 (WCD), Loit. Prost.
		-17 Aug 65, Loit Prost, LFD, Judge White

I.R. NO.

FBI NO.

S.B. NO.

CPD-22.466 (REV.3/66) INFORMATION SHOWN ON THIS IDENTIFICATION RECORD REPRESENTS ARREST INFORMATION SUPPORTED BY FINGERPRINTS ON FILE IN THE IDENTIFICATION SECTION, OF THE POLICE DEPARTMENT UNLESS INDICATED BY ASTERISK.

* The abbreviation "LFD" in the record stands for "leave to file denied" and is tantamount to a dismissal.

Reference Note

For an interesting account of a judge's view of some of the problems described, see J. MURTAGH & S. HARRIS, CAST THE FIRST STONE (1957).

The police response to the problem of street prostitution was the subject of special attention in the American Bar Foundation's Survey of the Administration of Criminal Justice in the United States. The results of their findings are reported in W. LAFAVE, ARREST: THE DECISION TO TAKE A SUSPECT INTO CUSTODY 450-64 (1965); L. TIFFANY, D. MCINTYRE & D. ROTENBERG, DETECTION OF CRIME 214-30 (1967); and LAW ENFORCEMENT IN THE METROPOLIS 84-93 (D. McIntyre ed. 1957).

For a sociologist's exploration of how prior contacts between the police officer and a suspected prostitute affect the exercise of police authority, see J. SKOLNICK, JUSTICE WITHOUT TRIAL 96-111 (1967).

THE PROFESSIONAL BURGLAR

The professional criminal—one whose income is gained primarily from criminal activity—presents one of the major challenges to the criminal justice system. His continued operations depend not only upon his ability to commit crimes, but equally upon his ability to avoid the legal consequences through avoidance of detection and conviction. The following is an account of some of the difficulties in detection and conviction of the professional burglar in the city of Chicago as these difficulties existed at the end of 1966.

A. THE RELATIONSHIP OF THE PROFESSIONAL BURGLAR TO THE TOTAL BURGLARY PROBLEM

During the course of 1966, reports of 46,488 burglaries were filed with the Chicago Police Department. After initial screening by the 287 detectives assigned to the investigation of such cases, it was established that 9,896 of the reports were unfounded (*e.g.*, because a neighbor was not aware that a friend was given permission to remove property), and 7,357 of the reports were more appropriately classified under some other offense category. The balance of 29,235 reports were, in effect, established as actual burglaries.

Residential burglaries account for almost two-thirds of the total number of burglary cases, while nonresidential burglaries account for most of the property that is stolen. Residential burglaries occur more frequently in the late summer months when more opportunities exist for entering homes and apartments of vacationing residents and when youths—who are responsible for many house burglaries—are not attending school, whereas the number of nonresidential burglaries remains fairly steady throughout the year.

The kind of premises burglarized, the type of items stolen, and the method by which entry was gained usually give a strong indication to the police of the type of person who committed the offense. The vast percentage of residential burglaries, for example, are committed by juveniles or adults who are referred to as "amateurs." They normally take anything in sight that is easy to carry off, including foodstuffs and clothing, often overlooking more valuable items. They are frequently crude in their method of entry and careless with respect to leaving clues to their identity. The narcotic addict who burglarizes on a continuing basis in order to finance his habit becomes more adept at his work. He will generally select items for which he knows a ready market exists, such as watches, rings, clothing, and television sets. Many of these items end up in pawn shops and with secondhand dealers, while others are purchased by poor people who recognize a bargain and are willing to keep quiet about it. Having to support a "$50-a-day" or a "$75-a-day" habit, the addict-burglar is a source of special concern to the police because of the great number of burglaries he commits. His operations are very much on a catch-as-catch-can basis, but the frequency with which he burglarizes results in his becoming skilled.

Adept as the addict-burglar may become, however, he is distinguished by police from the professional burglar. The professional is one who devotes himself to burglary as an occupation by choice rather than necessity. The professional burglar's primary objective is the theft of small items of high value from warehouses, retail establishments, or residences known to contain large amounts of cash or expensive furs and jewelry. He commits relatively few burglaries, but each is likely to result in a substantial "take." While he may arm himself for self-protection, he attempts to avoid situations in which he is likely to encounter people. He avoids violence. Extensive planning is inherent in all of his operations. He carefully selects his objective, devises means by which to gain entry without being detected, and develops detailed plans for removing and disposing of the stolen property. His operations may be designed to fill orders which he takes for a specific kind of merchandise.

B. REASONS FOR THE POLICE FOCUS UPON THE PROFESSIONAL BURGLAR

Faced with 29,235 burglaries to investigate in one year and limited manpower with which to do so, police evolve some informal working priorities. Formal operating procedures and administrative pressures, intended primarily to establish good relations with the public, urge a complete investigation in all cases. This is simply impossible. The public position is that a citizen suffering small burglary loss is entitled to the same police effort as one suffering a large loss.

But as a practical matter, the primary objective of command personnel within the Detective Division and especially the Burglary Section is to solve burglary cases and prosecute burglars in a manner which will serve to take burglars out of circulation and deter others from entering the field. With this objective as the pervading consideration, the maintenance of good public relations through detective efforts devoted to minor cases understandably becomes of secondary importance. If the initial follow-up investigation in a minor case reveals no clear leads, the tendency is for the detective to spend his time investigating more serious or promising cases. This somewhat informal redistribution of investigative effort is the first step in a process that has the end result of focusing primary attention in burglary investigations upon the professional burglar.

Development of this kind of an enforcement posture is influenced in large measure by the consideration given to the dollar value of items stolen, and the professional burglar accounts for those burglaries in which the greatest losses are suffered. One might expect this consideration to stem most directly from the desire on the part of the victim for recovery of his property. But this desire has been substantially lessened by the nature and extent of insurance coverage. The degree to which a loss is insured determines, in large measure, the interest and resulting pressure that a victim is likely to bring upon a police department for successful solution to the crime. If, for example, insurance coverage is adequate, the victim may actually welcome the loss as an opportunity to replace obsolete stock or, in the case of a residential burglary, to replace old furs, clothing, or jewelry with new.

For this reason, the pressure for solving cases in which there has been heavy financial loss often originates from sources other than the victim. One such source is the insurance companies who suffer the loss. But they in turn pass losses on to policyholders in increased insurance rates. When increased rates affect a single type of business, the trade associations, such as the Jeweler's Association, may be a source of constant pressure on the police. In response, the police focus upon the professional criminal who specializes in that kind of burglary.

When burglaries are concentrated in a given area or a given office building, the parties suffering losses may, in the long run, include the firms or agencies owning the structures. Such firms usually assume responsibility for providing appropriate security to those who rent their space. If the buildings become known as susceptible to burglary, there may be an increased number of vacancies. Individual cases often bring complaints from the property owners involved; a wave of burglaries affecting more than one property is likely to elicit demands for police action from such organizations as the Institute of Real Estate Management and the Organization of Loop Buildings.

Burglaries in which property of substantial value is taken usually receive full coverage by mass media. Once the crime has been reported, the public is anxious to learn the results of police efforts. Police feel it important to respond to this public interest and are likely to increase the intensity of their investigation. They desire (1) to maintain a reputation for effectiveness in solving crimes and (2) to utilize such publicity as a means of strengthening the impression in the minds of those who might contemplate committing a burglary that the offender, in the end, does get apprehended. Reports of police failures to solve a burglary, on the other hand, are viewed by the police as an incentive to those who may contemplate committing one.

Concentration upon the professional burglar serves several purposes in addition to meeting the kinds of pressures cited. As the police view the total burglary problem, they see efforts directed at ferreting out the professional burglar as (1) serving to get at the "most criminal" of the burglars—those who, in contrast with the one-time amateur, have grown somewhat contemptuous and greedy; and (2) serving to reduce the likelihood of further crimes, since it is assumed that a professional burglar continues to ply his trade until he is somehow "put out of commission."

C. METHODS BY WHICH THE PROFESSIONAL BURGLAR OPERATES

It is estimated that 250 men comprise the core of professional burglars operating in the city of Chicago. While there are some who operate alone, the majority enter into temporary or more permanent associations with others. Planning and carrying out a large-scale burglary requires that a burglar have assistance in selecting the object of his burglary, in "casing" the location, in gaining entry, in maintaining a lookout for the police and others, in moving the items of value away from the premises, and in disposing of the stolen goods.

There is a high degree of specialization as to the type of place burglarized, the object of the burglary, and the method by which entry is gained. An example is the safe burglar. Learning the proper methods for cracking large, well-constructed safes requires considerable experience. Special equipment is required, such as torches, drills, and hammers. The burglar must be capable of operating for a long period of time before the safe is cracked. He must do so with a minimum of noise, lest he attract attention. Other types of specialties require different combinations of talents.

In sharp contrast, for example, is the "crash" burglar who emphasizes speed—smashing a window or door for quick access, removing the objects of his burglary, and transporting them out of the area before his entry is discovered. His planning must include development of a conveyance that will meet his need for speed. Some such burglars, for example, have removed the center post of a car and welded the front and rear doors together so that they open as one long door. In this manner, materials such as men's expensive suits, custom dresses, and furs may be loaded in the car quickly and the appearance of an ordinary sedan minimizes the likelihood of immediate detection in fleeing the scene.

The first step in the planning of a professional burglary is the collection of information on locations worth burglarizing. A professional burglar operates with his "ear-to-the-ground," collecting bits of information on the location of items of value from individuals who, usually through their employment, have occasion to learn of the existence of such items. His source may be servants, janitors, painters, decorators, and repairmen who have occasion to work in private homes, retail stores, factories, and warehouses; deliverymen who enter such premises; or persons such as beauticians who are tuned in to the gossip of their customers. The "inside" informant usually receives a "cut" of the profits in exchange for his providing a "hot tip." He can provide information on what is available, where it is located, and often how security devices can be circumvented. He is commonly in a position to check on the correctness of his "cut" because he can learn, upon his routine return to the premises after the burglary has occurred, exactly what was taken. House burglars, who seek out private collections of jewelry, furs, coins, stamps, and objects of art, have been known to engage in careful research by maintaining files of newspaper clippings of reported prior losses, social activities, and inheritances. Some professional burglars undertake a form of "undercover" activity to learn the whereabouts of the items they seek by developing some ruse through which to enter the given premises for a look around or by cultivating a relationship with someone having legitimate access to the premises.

Having selected locations worth burglarizing, the professional then engages in further screening by ruling out those locations where persons are always present and where entry could not be gained without risking detection. In conducting residential burglaries, the professional may depend upon indications that an individual is not at home as his primary means of locating likely targets. The society page of a newspaper provides him with information on wealthy persons on their annual vacation. Obituaries and funeral announcements provide a directory of people likely to be away from home during designated visiting hours and at the time of the funeral. The presence of an expensive car at a nightclub, restaurant, or hotel patronized by the affluent suggests that an apartment—traceable through the license plate—may be unattended. The house burglar will almost always make a telephone call to the residence to verify his impression that no one is at home.

Commercial establishments, such as factories, retail stores, and warehouses, are settled upon as a target for a burglary only if the location of the items of value makes it possible for the burglar to enter and leave while out of the view of passersby. The current pattern of constructing large manufacturing plants in industrial parks off main thoroughfares places them beyond observation by passing police vehicles. Efforts to improve the attractiveness of these industrial plants often result in the construction of walls as fences that the burglar recognizes as perfect screens for his activities. Such plants often adjoin railroad lines and spurs which are devoid of people during the night hours.

The second stage in the planning process involves the "casing of the location"—exploring the burglary objective to determine the best method for gaining entry, the nature of alarm systems, the pattern of any security checks, the nature of police patrols, and the means by which stolen property may be removed. This information may come from an "inside" informant. Absent such an informant, the burglar is likely to use accomplices in acquiring the information without arousing suspicion. One accomplice may, for example, be sent through a warehouse, posing as a deliveryman, in order to observe the general layout and note any means by which entry might be easily gained. A second member of the group, perhaps posing as a salesman, may seek to establish the details of burglary alarm systems. If there are still problems to be worked out, a third person may be sent in on some other pretext with specific tasks to accomplish. The hazard in sending the same man twice necessitates a large number of accomplices in the planning for a big "job."

Techniques employed by the professional burglar to avoid detection as he commits his burglary are generally well known to the layman, for they have often been portrayed in movies and described in fiction. The cleverness and ingenuity which they so often reflect tend to result in the public's viewing the work of the professional as a kind of sport.

The professional burglar will select the most practical tools required for the particular job, will give advance consideration to the desirability of disposing of the tools and to the possibility that he may have to leave the tools on the premises, and will take along the minimum number of tools required for the particular task. Aware that one of his greatest problems is in getting to and from the scene of the burglary with the tools in his possession, he may develop a plan in advance to combat any police allegation that he is guilty of being in possession of burglary tools. He is aware that the police must not only establish that the tools are suitable for use in breaking into a building, but that his intent was to gain entrance into a building. Also, for the police to get evidence, they must usually have adequate grounds for searching him or his vehicle. There are obviously many legitimate purposes for which the kind of tools used in a burglary may be purchased and conveyed. Previously thought-through fabrications accounting for his presence in the area and for the presence of tools suitable for use in a burglary will establish the groundwork for a successful defense, should he be questioned or searched going to or from his work.

The wearing of gloves eliminates the possibility of being identified through fingerprints—the most frequent technique by which the identity of the amateur is established. Marks left at the scene by various tools are of value to the police, but only if the police later come into possession of the tools and are able to tie them to the particular offender. The professional burglar is sensitive to the need for disposing of any tools that might tie him to the burglary.

Only the "cat burglar" need be concerned about disguising his face. Since he specializes in entering dwellings in the early hours of the morning while the occupants are asleep, he is more likely to come in contact with individuals at close range. He usually wears some form of camouflage, be it a mask or other disguise, and is prepared to shine a light in the face of the occupants should they awaken—so as to minimize the likelihood that they could provide a description of his features to the police.

In large-scale commercial burglaries, use is made of accomplices as lookouts as a precaution in handling any unsuspected problems that may arise. The lookout may, for example, be called upon to divert the attention of passersby or patrolling officers—even to the extent of staging an incident and getting himself arrested for his conduct. Most recently, lookouts have been found to equip themselves with radios capable of receiving police communications so that they can keep track of police movements. And they may use two-way radios to keep in communication with the burglar.

Professional burglars work in close collaboration with individuals engaged in the business of disposing of stolen merchandise. Prior arrangements usually exist for delivering the burglary loot. In large warehouse burglaries, the proceeds are loaded on trucks or vans, often by bringing the truck inside the warehouse in order to minimize the likelihood of arousing suspicions outside. Forklift trucks found on the premises are used for loading. The loaded truck is then driven to another prearranged location where its contents can be removed under conditions which do not attract attention.

D. POLICE OPERATIONS DESIGNED TO PREVENT AND DETECT THE WORK OF THE PROFESSIONAL BURGLAR

Efforts on the part of the police to cope with the professional burglar fall into three general categories:

(1) efforts intended to prevent or frustrate the burglar in his work by educating the public as to ways in which to discourage burglars and by maintaining a continual blanket of police patrol;

(2) efforts designed to identify those burglars responsible for crimes thought to be committed by professionals;

(3) efforts designed to gather knowledge on the whereabouts and activities of known burglars, thereby placing the police in the position of learning firsthand of their criminal activity and not having to depend upon reports received from others as to those offenses for which they may be responsible.

1. *The Preventive Program*

In recent years, through the distribution of brochures, the broadcast of television programs, and the staging of displays, the Chicago police have undertaken a program that is designed to educate the public as to ways in which they can prevent their premises from being burglarized. Burglary prevention conferences are held for building managers with the objectives of getting them to improve their own security measures and encouraging an awareness of conditions likely to invite a burglary. Complaints from patrol officers, for example, resulted in arranging meetings with supermarket managers in an effort to get them to remove large window advertisements after closing hours so that a better view could be had of their premises from the street. Public cooperation elicited in such a program is likely to have a substantial effect in reducing the total number of burglaries, but such cooperation has relatively little bearing on the number of professional burglaries. Professionals are not likely to be deterred by such simple devices as locked doors, alarm systems, and other means designed to prevent burglary.

However successful these efforts may be, it is upon the activities of the patrol officer that the police most heavily depend in their efforts to prevent burglaries. Commenting on the success of his department in reducing crime, the former Superintendent of the Chicago Police Department, O. W. Wilson, said:

> For a crime to occur, two factors must be present—opportunity and desire. It is the function of the police to minimize the opportunities by open, conspicuous and aggressive patrol. . . . The best means available to the police for the prevention of crimes is aggressive patrol of streets, alleys and public ways by uniformed officers in conspicuously marked cars.*

The objective is twofold: to create an atmosphere in which the burglar fears detection and is therefore deterred; and to create an operation in which the police are likely either to come upon a burglar in the process of committing his crime or to discover circumstances which suggest that a person may be engaged in committing burglaries. The first objective is achieved through conspicuous patrol—uniformed police officers in marked cars making frequent rounds in an unpredictable manner. This effort has a limited impact upon the activities of the professional, since its effect is restricted to areas and buildings immediately adjoining the streets and alleys that are patrolled. The professional burglar enters premises substantially removed from a public way —such as an apartment in a high-rise structure, a retail outlet on the upper floors of an office building, or a warehouse located in a fenced-in industrial park—thereby placing his operations outside the observational range of the patrolling police officer.

But that aspect of the patrol function designed to seek out suspicious circumstances—its second objective—is likely to result in the professional burglar's being stopped and questioned going to and from his burglaries. Aggressive patrol activities consist of checking out any variation from the normal pattern—the unusual, the out-of-place, the incongruous. The nature of a burglar's operations places him in areas at times when such areas are

* NEWSWEEK, Aug. 16, 1965, at 25.

normally devoid of pedestrians. In his efforts to locate and investigate suspicious circumstances, a police officer acts on the basis of his knowledge of the manner in which burglars function. He is especially alert to such situations as these:

any activity taking place at a commercial establishment when it is normally closed;

a vehicle containing a large amount of merchandise;

persons seen transferring merchandise between vehicles in a deserted area;

a person carrying a large quantity of valuable merchandise on the street;

a retail store in which the usual night-light is not burning;

the presence of any cutting, drilling, punching, chopping, or prying tools, especially if wrapped with rubber or tape so as to avoid leaving a mark.

Circumstances such as these are usually checked out with the cooperation of the suspect and without any intrusion upon the free movement or privacy of the suspect. In the vast majority of such cases, the results of the investigation prove to be negative. But in those instances in which initial impressions give strong indication that the individuals are criminally involved, the rapidity with which the officer must act does not permit him to plan his moves carefully—often resulting in raising a doubt as to the propriety and legality of his actions.

Consider, for example, the lone police officer who comes upon a car at 3:00 a.m., parked on the public way alongside a warehouse and occupied by two men. He observes that the rear of the vehicle is close to the ground, suggesting that it is heavily loaded. Were he to stop and contemplate the situation, he might conclude that the two men were most likely "up to no good," but he would have to conclude, without further information, that there was not probable cause to believe that they had committed a crime. He could, at this point, endeavor through further inquiry to establish additional cause to believe a crime had been committed—or he might obtain information that would eliminate any basis for suspicion. The occupants may identify themselves as employees at the warehouse, or they may simply claim that they are travelers who turned off the nearby expressway for a rest. But other factors are likely to result in the officer's omitting such inquiry. Given the area, the prevalence of burglaries, the time of day, and the appearance of the car, he may conclude that the men most likely committed a burglary and that they are armed. He may sense that they are awaiting an accomplice. His decision under such circumstances would most likely be to order them out of their vehicle, to frisk them, and to examine the front seat of the vehicle. If in the process he observed something else, such as gloves, this discovery, added to the other factors, may be sufficient in his mind to conclude that the men are in fact burglars. He may then proceed to examine the nature of the other goods in the car in order to establish whether they bear identifications that link them with the warehouse. He may also attempt to establish whether the warehouse shows evidence of having been entered.

The attorney employed by a professional burglar charged with burglary as a result of such a hypothetical investigation is likely to challenge the legality of the police actions on several grounds. In the absence of clearly established legislative authority for stopping and questioning the individuals, the initial action of the officer in ordering the individuals from the car and frisking them is likely to be questioned. The grounds for effecting the arrest are likely to be challenged—primarily in the form of an effort to establish that it was made either without adequate grounds or on the basis of the evidence found in the search made by the officer. The legality of the search and the admissibility of the evidence would then hinge on the determination as to the validity of the arrest.

From the police standpoint, it is somewhat ironic that the ultimate achievement in police patrol efforts—the discovery of a professional burglar entering or leaving the location of his burglary—may result in a successful challenge for lack of adequate grounds to support the arrest.

The police patrol effort to prevent burglary focuses upon the professional burglar in another manner quite distinct from that involved in seeking out suspicious circumstances. It calls for patrolling officers to be on the lookout for and to observe carefully the activities of individuals who have established a reputation for themselves as professional burglars. Occasionally, the daily police bulletin is utilized to convey pictures and descriptions of burglars thought to be operating in the city, all of whom have been convicted one or more times. Part of the notice accompanying one such publication illustrates the kind of information which is conveyed to officers in the field:

BURGLARS, STICKUP MEN AND AUTO TRUNK POPPERS

Today's Bulletin Supplement will assist Police Officers in recognizing, identifying and apprehending individuals and members of small and large groups, some of whom make a specialty of victimizing salesmen, particularly jewelry salesmen.

THE PERSONS IDENTIFIED IN THIS SUPPLEMENT ARE NOT WANTED AT THIS TIME!

Whenever these individuals are observed, note their actions, their vehicles and their associates. They should become a subject of particular attention so as to discover possible criminal intention. The modus operandi of these individuals is of particular importance. They "case" or follow the object or the victim of their attack. They learn and note the habits of the salesmen who carry large quantities of valuable samples in their motor vehicles. When they strike, they exhibit advance planning and minute preparation in that they execute their mission with speed and fearlessness. When salesmen's cars are the object of attack, these individuals observe the vehicle while unattended and prepare keys from key code books and the use of a "key clipper." They then "pre-test" the passkey in the lock of the target vehicle. When the sample jewelry and gems, or clothing or furs, are in the vehicle, they drive the vehicle away a short distance to where a getaway car (stolen) or a "work car" (vehicle fictitiously registered) is waiting with a driver. The valuables are immediately transferred and they make their escape.

Other activities of some of these individuals include burglary entry into a residence or a retail establishment to steal the samples and other valuable merchandise. When they commit burglary they have the location well staked out, they come equipped with tools and cars and act according to plan.

Some of this group have engaged in cartage theft where an entire truck or tractor/trailer loaded with consumers goods is stolen. They may start the truck with duplicated keys, or use a stolen or rented tractor to steal the target trailer.

[The Bulletin included pictures and descriptions of twenty-four persons.]

When any of these individuals is spotted by a police officer, the officer is urged to observe and report on actions and whereabouts. If the actions appear suspicious, the officer is encouraged to question him. If riding in a motor vehicle, the officer is encouraged to stop the vehicle and request registration data. Information sought through this process includes the names of other persons found in the company of the "known" burglar; the make, model, type, color, and license number of the vehicle he is using; and the areas he frequents.

Such stops have essentially two purposes: to collect information on the activities of persons thought to be actively involved in committing burglaries so that evidence and clues in reported burglaries can be related to them; and to interfere with the free movement of the burglar about the city in the hope that this will eventually deter him from engaging in his criminal activities.

2. *The Effort to Identify the Perpetrators of Reported Burglaries*

Scenes at which burglaries are committed are routinely examined for any physical evidence that may assist in identifying the perpetrator. But one strong indication that a given burglary was committed by a professional is the absence of significant evidence. Fingerprints are rarely found, since the professional takes the precaution of wearing gloves. Footprints and heelprints may be found, but these are helpful only if they reveal sufficiently distinctive defects in the shoe to make them clearly identifiable in a comparison with the shoe, should it be found. The professional makes use of footwear not likely to leave a significant imprint. Tool marks will be found in most burglaries wherever wood or metal had to be forced open, but the professional burglar will attempt to avoid this by wrapping his tools with rubber or tape.

Although the police place great dependence upon the search for physical evidence, they are aware that physical evidence alone does not frequently lead to the solution of crimes performed by professional burglars. A fingerprint, a footprint, or the mark made by a tool is of no significance unless it can be matched up with a fingerprint, a shoe, or a tool clearly identified with the offender. The only comparative data routinely maintained by a police agency are fingerprints which, as has been indicated, are the kind of physical evidence least likely to be found at the scene of a professional burglary.

The professional will disassociate himself from his tools either at the scene of the burglary or shortly thereafter. If the tools are in the possession of the police, the only possibility of establishing who they belonged to is by attempting to establish the identity of the person to whom they were sold by the supplier of such tools. The number of legitimate outlets for the more common burglary tools makes this a difficult and most often fruitless search in a large city. If a burglar is arrested on some other charge and a search reveals burglary tools, a comparison of these tools is routinely made with marks left at the scene of major burglaries. If identity is established in such instances through comparisons, the legality of the search incident to the arrest is likely to be challenged.

Investigating detectives routinely attempt to locate any individuals who may have seen a burglar enter or leave the premises or carry off the proceeds of a burglary. This frequently requires interviewing large numbers of individuals such as neighbors, domestic servants, and deliverymen in the case of residential burglaries—and janitors, night watchmen, cab drivers, gas station attendants, or elevator operators in burglaries of a commercial establishment. Information acquired from such sources must then be pieced together, but relatively few identifications are made from information provided by witnesses. However, new and more important witnesses may be located after the identity of a burglar is learned. Knowing his character, his residence, and his method of operation, the police are led to individuals likely to be in a position to have witnessed his actions and who can serve to corroborate evidence obtained from other sources.

Detailed analysis of reports on burglaries results in the discovery of patterns of operations suggesting involvement of the same burglar or group of burglars. The experienced burglar tends to adhere to methods of operations that have proved successful for him in the past. If he succeeds in gaining entry through a skylight, he will often continue to make use of the skylight. He tends to standardize his operations in other respects as well—the object of his burglary; the tools that are used, the kinds of items taken and those left behind; and even habits which he has "on the job," for example, eating candy or taking a drink while on the premises. From an analysis of these patterns, the police may be able to identify the burglar or anticipate future targets.

The pattern may serve to suggest the identity of the perpetrator. The police know enough about how many professional burglars operate to recognize their work. This evidence would not be sufficient to convict, and perhaps not even enough to arrest, but it serves to focus investigation on a particular suspect. They are in a position similar to that they occupy when informants who are unwilling to be identified have named the burglar.

The pattern may serve only as a means of alerting police to a continuing operation—for example, a group engaged in cracking open the safes of supermarkets scattered all about the city, entering the markets through the skylight during the early hours of the morning on weekends. Preventive steps can then be taken. Where the pattern indicates a concentration of burglaries in a given area, police may intensify their patrol activities in the area during the hours in which the burglar is in the habit of operating. It is the "cat burglar" who most frequently falls into this pattern. In such cases, all police officers working in the area are furnished with a description as a basis for their search.

CRIME ANALYSIS PATTERN

Detective Division
Burglary Section

22 June 1965

To: Deputy Chief of Patrol Area 6; Director of the Youth Division; Task Force Commander; Commander of the 20th District; Commander of Traffic Area 6; Commanding Officer of Burglary Unit Area 6; Commanding Officer of Youth Division Area 6; Patrol Division Liaison Officer.

CRIME PATTERN CONCERNING RESIDENTIAL BURGLARIES B-#65-105

Beat	Type	Location	Time	Day	Date	RD No.
2012	Apartment	5455 N. California	0350	Wed.	2 June	D-151725
2012	Apartment	5353 N. Virginia	1800 2000	Fri.	4 June	D-154666(*)
2012	Home	5414 N. California	0200 0700	Wed.	9 June	D-159524
2012	Apartment	5513 N. California	2000 2200	Fri.	18 June	D-169733(*)
2012	Apartment	2729 W. Catalpa	0145 0450	Sun.	20 June	D-172153
2012	Apartment	2635 W. Gregory	2245 0830	Sun.	20 June	D-172227
2012	Apartment	5525 N. Virginia	0100 1000	Sun.	20 June	D-172259
2012	Apartment	2641 W. Gregory	0200 0900	Sun.	20 June	D-172265
2012	Apartment	2635 W. Gregory	0100 0500	Sun.	20 June	D-172575

GENERAL TIME PATTERN: 2000 to 0600 hours.

GENERAL DESCRIPTIONS: No physical description available.

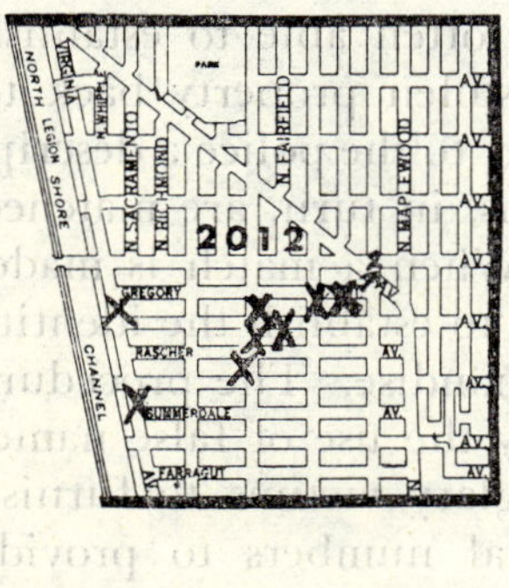

POINT OF ENTRY: Entry is gained in the majority of the above offenses through an open or unlocked front or side window. In two instances (*) entrance was gained by prying the front door.

REMARKS: Property taken consists of men's trousers containing their wallets, women's purses, furs, jewelry, clothing and a TV set. In all but two of the above offenses the victims were in the apartment asleep.

Walter Karlblom

DEPUTY CHIEF WALTER KARLBLOM
CRIMES AGAINST PROPERTY

Notify the Burglary Section, Detective Division Headquarters (Pax 391) if an arrest results from this information.

Patrol officers regularly assigned to the beat assume primary responsibility for attempting to apprehend such a burglar, though detectives and officers from other units of the department may receive special assignment to augment their efforts. When a patrol officer is furnished with a Crime Analysis Pattern, he has additional basis for stopping and questioning people in suspicious circumstances. He also checks on the activities of specific individuals who, because of their record or reputation, seem to him likely suspects.

The arrest of the cat burglar who was described in the Crime Analysis Pattern above, was reported by the *Chicago Sun Times:*

> After a two-week watch, detectives captured a man Sunday morning whom they believe responsible for 70 North Side burglaries in the last four months.
>
> Police said they seized Joseph Riviera, 42, of 3834 N. Sheffield, after he tried to crawl into a window at 2710 W. Rascher.
>
> Sgt. Charles Adamson said that the Rascher Ave. area was put under surveillance after a study of a pattern of burglaries that had occurred over four months in the surrounding neighborhood.
>
> During the surveillance, detectives and sergeants patrolled the area daily from 11:30 p.m. to 6 a.m., driving their own cars, wearing work clothes and communicating with radios.
>
> Sunday morning, Adamson said, they saw a man trying to pry off the rear screen from a house at the Rascher Ave. address.
>
> Finally getting the screen off, the man started to crawl into the window. At this point, detectives turned their flashlights on him. He then jumped down and fled through several back yards but was trapped in some bushes.

In amateur burglaries, the police are often able to establish the identity of the burglar by tracing stolen property back to him. All pawnshops are required to report to the police a description of items pawned. These descriptions, in turn, are matched with records of items reported stolen. When a match is made, an investigation is conducted in an effort to establish the identity of the individual who pawned the merchandise. The procedure is seriously limited in its effectiveness by the use of false names and addresses and the inability of burglary victims to furnish sufficient detailed descriptions and serial numbers to provide for adequate identification. In addition, the whole checking process can be circumvented by a burglar through sale to a secondhand dealer—a business not as tightly regulated under Illinois law as that of the pawnbroker.

As has previously been noted, the professional burglar depends upon relationships which he develops with "fences" who specialize in receiving and disposing of stolen merchandise. All identification marks are removed from the merchandise. There are usually no written records of the transaction. The purchaser has no contact with the burglar. Discovery of merchandise on sale in a retail establishment that resembles merchandise reported as stolen may point a finger of suspicion upon the supplier as a receiver of stolen goods, but it rarely serves by itself as a means of either proceeding against him or identifying the professional burglar.

The majority of individuals who come into police custody as a result of being engaged in criminal activity have personal knowledge of other crimes committed in the community. When talking with a person arrested on a burglary charge, a burglary detective who has knowledge of many recent burglaries is likely to inquire if the offender, having been warned of his rights under the *Miranda* decision, is willing to volunteer any knowledge of other burglaries that have been committed. Such inquiry may initially be aimed at determining the arrestee's own further involvement, but it will also seek information circulating among the criminal element. This practice is followed most frequently in the interrogation of narcotic addicts, because of the direct link between addiction and burglary. Common awareness on the part of addicts that cooperation with the police may be exchanged for more lenient treatment produces considerable information on burglaries. But this process, like most other police techniques, is of limited value in combating the professional burglar. Addicts and others rarely have knowledge of the professional burglar's activities. Those who are involved are committed to a code that requires they remain silent. Still, through informal conversation, police officers sometimes find that bravado results in burglars' providing some tips, clues, and leads that can be followed up. As one commander stated, "We cannot tie these men into the score, but we encourage them to tell us how it was done. We cultivate, groom, and flatter their associates for information. . . . There is no more honor among thieves than there is among bankers and lawyers."

3. *The Gathering of Intelligence on the Activity of Known Burglars*

The police effort against professional criminals also focuses upon the activities of the offender rather than upon a specific offense. Chicago's detective division has established a special unit consisting of a relatively small number of men whose sole function is to gather information on the activities of known criminals. In part, this is accomplished through prolonged surveillance work, but the more valuable information is obtained through contacts in the criminal world—by listening to gossip and developing informants, thereby learning which criminals are working together and the nature of the activities in which they are currently engaged. The members of the criminal intelligence section are thus often in a position to assist a detective whose primary focus is upon the investigation of an assigned caseload of offenses. The nature of their operations occasionally results in their acquiring advance knowledge of a planned burglary—enabling them to sit in wait for the crime to be committed.

E. ARREST AND PROCESSING

The truly successful professional burglar may never have contact with the police. It is believed that the majority, however, do acquire a record of arrests even if these arrests are not on burglary charges. One of Chicago's most notorious burglars, for example, has been arrested for driving on a revoked license, having a fictitious automobile registration, attempted bribery, larceny of a vehicle, creating a disturbance, disorderly conduct, resisting arrest, and various traffic violations. Illustrative is this case as reported in the *Chicago Daily News,* July 10, 1967:

> Joseph (Pops) Panczko, often called "Chicago's most famous thief," was sentenced Monday to serve two years in a federal prison on a 30-cent fraud charge.
>
> Judge Julius J. Hoffman in U.S. District Court here also fined the oft-arrested super-thief $1,000.
>
> Panczko who has been suspected of handling countless dollars in stolen goods over the years, was convicted July 2 of dropping three dime-sized brass slugs into telephones and postage stamp machines near his home at 1527 N. Avers.
>
> U.S. deputy marshals testified they began watching for slug users when five business establishments in Panczko's neighborhood reported 1,207 phony coins had been dropped into machines.
>
> Asst. U.S. Atty. Richard S. Jalovec said that in 1966, Illinois Bell Telephone Co. recovered more than 400,000 slugs from its telephones.

Last year, the city found 500,000 slugs in its parking meters.

Arrests for being in possession of burglary tools are common, given the reputation of the individuals and current police patrol practices. Whether such arrests result in conviction is usually dependent upon the validity of the search that produced the tools.

There is no clear-cut pattern of circumstances that result in the arrest of a professional on an actual burglary charge. Occasionally, police efforts to acquire advance information on a burglar's activities pay off by catching him in the act. Or, carried away by his success, a professional may become oblivious to the fact that the pattern of his operations has placed the police on his tail. But with equal frequency the arrest stems from fortuitous circumstances totally unrelated to police investigative efforts—a minor slip on the part of the burglar or an observation by an alert citizen.

There is an unexpressed understanding between the police and the professional burglar who is arrested. No real effort is made to interrogate him. The fact that he will say nothing is assumed. By his silence, the burglar reflects his position that either the police have the evidence to convict him or they do not. The police, similarly, understand at the time of arrest that they must depend, in bringing their charges, upon evidence, information, or testimony derived from sources unrelated to the prisoner. A professional burglar normally has an established relationship with an attorney experienced in the defense of criminal cases. He usually requests and is granted an opportunity to call his attorney on being brought into a detention facility.

F. RELEASE ON BAIL

First efforts on the part of an attorney representing a professional burglar are to arrange for his release on bail. All indications are that most professional burglars, upon being released, immediately return to plying their trade. By doing so, they seem to derive satisfaction from displaying their contempt for the police and the law; they maintain their status in the field without losing face; and they meet the financial demands of bail and attorney fees.

For some of the weaker professionals, however, an arrest followed by an indictment seems to initiate a sequence of events that eventually leads to their downfall. The arrest and indictment in such cases appear to stir the burglar to work with greater intensity, while exercising less and less care to avoid detection. This reaction may, in part, be a response to the need for cash if his resources are low. The manner in which he carries out his operations results in his again being arrested. Upon release, he feels a greater need for cash and therefore commits additional burglaries with greater frequency and less and less planning, to the point that his efforts begin to appear like those of the addict-burglar.

A classic case involves Anthony Massari: Massari was released from the Illinois State Penitentiary upon completion of a three-year term for burglary and armed robbery in 1961. On July 8, 1963, Massari was apprehended in the act of committing a burglary. He was indicted and released on bail totaling $7,500. On August 24, 1963, while free on bail, he was apprehended in the commission of a second burglary and was found to have in his possession the proceeds of still another burglary committed earlier in the day. He was indicted on two counts of burglary and released on $4,500 bail. Massari was again arrested on November 18, 1963, when he was found to be in possession of a loaded firearm and burglary tools. On January 16, 1964, he was arrested in the act of committing a burglary and found to have the proceeds of two other burglaries in his possession. He was indicted the following day and released on $15,000 bail, only to be again arrested on the same afternoon while committing still another burglary for which he was indicted and bail set at $5,000. Subsequently, he was arrested on February 8, 1964, with release on bail set at $10,000; again on February 21, 1964, with release on bail of $5,000; and again on March 5, 1964, when bail was set at $5,000.

On April 24, 1964, when Massari went to trial, he had been arrested nine times in the period from July 8, 1963, to March 5, 1964, stood indicted on ten counts and was free on $52,000 bail. He entered a guilty plea to the ten indictments and was sentenced to from five to fifteen years in the penitentiary on each count, the sentences to run concurrently.

As the interval between arrests narrows, the burglar becomes more desperate. He may resort to obtaining cash from organized criminal elements at exorbitant interest rates in order to meet attorney fees and bail requirements. Or he may turn to more daring crimes, such as armed robbery. As the number of indictments mounts and the likelihood of a substantial prison sentence increases, the burglar tends to become less reluctant to resort to force and violence in his actions.

G. GETTING A CASE TO TRIAL

Once arrested, the professional burglar depends upon his attorney to guide his case through the criminal process. It is standard procedure for the defense counsel in such cases to employ every means at his disposal to frustrate the efforts of the prosecution in bringing the case to trial. Chief dependence is placed upon the continuance, the objective being to wear out the state's witnesses.

The case is routinely continued on the first occasion that it is up for trial. This continuance is termed "automatic" by police officers, because the request for it is rarely, if ever, turned down by the judge. The situation that subsequently develops is described by one police commander as follows:

> The case, when called up again, is usually continued for "professional" reasons. It is understood that the defense attorney has not yet been paid his fee. The judge, a lawyer himself, understands this and usually allows a second continuance. After these two standard types of continuances—the automatic continuance and that granted for professional reasons—many others may follow. Most witnesses come to trial only twice willingly and, after that, the police officers have to obtain subpoenas in order to have them present at trials. These witnesses have lost a day's pay in order to be present and most of them can't afford the loss. When they are present via the subpoena method, they become hostile witnesses and "can't remember" exactly what did occur.

Among the most common reasons provided by the defense in seeking repeated continuances are the claim that the attorney has a commitment in another court at the same time (sending a law clerk to offer the explanation and request the continuance); that the attorney has not yet received any or all of his fee; or that the attorney simply requires more time in which to prepare his defense. Attorneys employing this tactic will ask for as many continuances as the judge will allow. If the judge refuses additional continuances, the attorney will request a change of venue so as to start a series of hearings on motions or a new string of continuances in another court. As witnesses fail to appear, the state is forced into the position of agreeing on some occasions to a continuance.

A case of two individuals thought by the police to be making their living in crime, who were indicted on a charge of larceny of a motor vehicle, illustrates the extent to which this tactic can be employed. Robert Harder and John Zywicial were arrested on June 24, 1961, indicted on July 12, 1961, and pleaded not guilty on July 19, 1961. The case was continued by order of the court to August 21, 1961. From that time on, the case was continued fifty-seven times by six different judges. It was disposed of on June 1, 1965, by a motion of the state to have the charges stricken from the record because of insufficient evidence.

Several other methods are employed by defense counsel in frustrating the efforts of the state to bring a case to trial: requests for separate trials are frequently made in those cases in which multiple defendants are being prosecuted; defendants free on bond are not produced in court on the date of trial; and a request to stipulate ownership of stolen property is refused, thereby requiring the prosecution to produce the owner of the stolen property at each hearing regardless of whether he was a witness to the burglary, and even though the ownership may be only formally disputed.

The results of the several delaying tactics are obvious. Victims or witnesses are lost—moving out of the state, going on extended vacations, or dying. Cooperative victims and witnesses become hostile, refusing to appear and, if summoned, unwilling to provide the testimony needed for conviction. Some, unfamiliar with the operations of the criminal process, become firmly convinced that a conspiracy exists in the particular case to block justice—a conspiracy entered into by the presiding judge, the state's attorney, and the arresting officer. Even cooperative witnesses find their memories dimmed by the passage of time, making them vulnerable to grueling cross-examination on the smallest of details.

It is not possible to determine how much of the reluctance of witnesses to cooperate is attributable to their having been threatened. The unapprehended members of a professional burglar's group have been known to make phone calls to witnesses, threatening them with dire consequences should they cooperate with the police. Such threats are rarely made known to the police, since the witness may feel that this would only lead to further dangerous involvement. When the police do learn of such calls, they find them difficult to investigate.

A motion to suppress the evidence on the grounds that it was obtained illegally is frequently made even in those cases in which there appears to be no basis for questioning the legality of the police action. If the case is transferred to another court, the motion may be renewed, providing a second opportunity to have the evidence declared inadmissible and at least producing additional delay.

Search warrants used in recovering stolen merchandise are frequently subject to challenge, especially where prior information did not enable the police to describe in detail the goods to be seized and the premises to be searched. It is most likely that any disparity in the goods described and those seized, or in the area described and the area searched, will be used as a basis for challenging the legality of the search. Sometimes the challenge hinges entirely on technical compliance, such as the accidental omission of the words "County of Cook" or "State of Illinois." Omission of such descriptive information or the designation of north or south in the name of a street has occasionally led to voiding the warrant. The validity of the proceedings may be challenged on technical grounds by questioning the spelling of words or the punctuation contained in an arrest warrant, a complaint, or an indictment, as well as the adequacy of other information that it may contain.

H. PROCEEDINGS AT TRIAL

When a defense counsel engaged by a professional burglar exhausts every tactic that occurs to him as a means of avoiding trial, he will usually advise his client to go to trial rather than enter a plea of guilty. During the course of the burglary trial, the attorney typically employs a number of techniques. Most depend, for their success, upon the use of a jury.

The most common defense tactic used in cases against professional burglars is to create an impression that the defendant was manhandled. A veteran police officer relates:

> During the trial, when police officers are questioned, attempts are made to persuade the court or the jury that the place of detention was improper; that no food was provided; that washroom usage was denied; that smoking was denied; that communication with relatives was denied; that the defendant was handcuffed too long; or that the defendant was interrogated by burly police officers, attempting to elicit a confession under threat of force. Each of these questions is designed to give new life to an already existing stereotype that the police are naturally abusive and that they use force routinely in their work.

This technique can take on several forms. Before a jury, it is designed primarily to elicit sympathy for the defendant. Defense counsel may, by questioning the officer as to his age, height, and weight, seek to establish that his client was overwhelmed at every stage of his processing, especially if the officer is of large stature and the defendant is slightly built. If the trial is before a judge, defense counsel may seek only to prolong the trial in the hope of wearing out witnesses. If this be his purpose, he may require that every police officer who had contact with the defendant—including those who booked him, took his fingerprints, took his photograph, transported him to a lockup, maintained the facility where he was detained, and transported him to court—all be placed on the stand.

In trying a case before a jury, defense counsel will often imply that the officer's intelligence is low and his judgment poor, that he is improperly trained, and that he had ulterior motivation for acting as he did. This is usually accomplished by repeating the officer's answers with an inflection of the voice calculated to create such innuendoes. One specific technique is that of questioning a neat, well-dressed detective as to the cost of his clothing, thereby creating the implication that he is living beyond his means and that he may be corrupt. All of this is aimed at discrediting the officer in the eyes of the jury.

Other defense devices are efforts to embarrass witnesses with information not properly used for impeachment; the use of perjured testimony in establishing alibi; and the intimidation of witnesses by loud conversations outside the courtroom that can be overheard, referring, for example, to planned civil suits for false arrest.

The position of the state is often weakened by the lack of preparation on the part of the assistant state's attorney. In most cases, the prosecuting attorney, swamped by the volume of cases, tries cases out of the file, without ever having interviewed the witnesses he will examine. Evidence readily available is, therefore, often not introduced or is used ineffectively.

I. RELEASE ON BAIL AFTER CONVICTION, PENDING APPEAL

Should the professional burglar be convicted, it is likely that his attorney will appeal. Upon filing of an appeal, the burglar is routinely released on an appeal bond. This procedure is a mutually satisfactory arrangement for both the attorney and the client. The client is satisfied that his attorney is going to make a "last ditch" effort to gain his permanent freedom and the attorney is satisfied that his client will have an opportunity to raise additional funds with which to pay his fees. Subsequent arrests and indictments for additional burglaries while under an appeal bond give some support to the police contention that release pending appeal encourages more crime.

The case history of Joseph "Nick" D'Argento is a prime illustration: D'Argento was paroled from the Illinois penitentiary in April, 1961, after serving thirteen months of a one to three year sentence for burglary. In November of 1961, he was returned to the penitentiary for violation of his parole and was released in October, 1962, when his sentence expired. On September 27, 1963, he was arrested by the FBI for participation in the robbery of the Franklin Park State Bank. He was released on $50,000 bond. On December 3, 1963, he was arrested for the burglary of a clothing store and released on $30,000 bond. On December 17, 1963, the FBI arrested D'Argento for the theft of $85,000 worth of furs in Los Angeles. He was released on bond. On April 20, 1964, he was found guilty in Los Angeles on the theft of furs and was sentenced on May 4, 1964, to five years for this crime. He appealed the sentence and was released on bond.

On June 11, 1964, he was arrested in Chicago in a stolen automobile containing three loaded revolvers, masks, burglar tools, and a police-type radio. He was released on bond. On December 5, 1964, he was arrested by Chicago police for hijacking a load of furs. This case was discharged on December 22, 1964, when the witness claimed a lapse of memory. On April 27, 1965, he was found guilty of the Franklin Park State Bank robbery, appealed and was again at liberty on a $50,000 appeal bond. On May 3, 1965, he was arrested in a stolen car with two other persons. The car contained three guns and masks. He was released on $5,000 bond. On May 10, 1965, he was sentenced to fifteen years in the federal penitentiary in connection with the bank robbery. He remained free on the $50,000 appeal bond.

On May 17, 1965, the $30,000 bond set on the December 3, 1963, burglary was raised to $100,000. His attorneys failed in their efforts to arrange for this bond to be reduced and he was released on posting of $100,000 bond on June 12, 1965. On June 19, 1965, he was arrested by Chicago police after he staged an armed robbery of an insurance company. He was charged with armed robbery, auto theft, and bribery. Bail in this case was set at $100,000. On June 21, 1965, his appeal bond in connection with the Franklin Park bank robbery was revoked by Judge William Parsons. He was also unable to make the $100,000 bond set in connection with the insurance company robbery on June 19, 1965.

Cases such as that of Joseph "Nick" D'Argento prompt police officials to urge that the right to bail be denied to professional burglars as a means of preventing them from engaging in further burglaries and in other types of crime while awaiting appeal of their conviction.

Reference Note

The professional burglar and the problems of the criminal justice system in dealing with him have been the subject of two recent articles in popular periodicals. Wanniski, *Crime's Craftsmen: 'They Can't Roll Sevens All the Time,'* THE NATIONAL OBSERVER, Aug. 22, 1966; Wheeler, *Brotherly Boom in Burglaries,* LIFE, Aug. 6, 1965, at 71-72, 74-76; Pileggi, *1968 Has Been the Year of the Burglar,* NEW YORK TIMES MAGAZINE, Nov. 17, 1968, at 54.

Although now somewhat dated, E. SUTHERLAND, THE PROFESSIONAL THIEF (1937), remains a classic description of theft as a way of life. It presents the experiences and point of view of a professional thief and provides considerable insight into the manner in which he relates to the functioning of the criminal justice system. Somewhat similar insights are reflected in the autobiography of a professional criminal as reported in J. MARTIN, MY LIFE IN CRIME (1952).

A description and summary of what is known relative to professional crime is contained in THE PRESIDENT'S COMMISSION ON LAW ENFORCEMENT AND ADMINISTRATION OF JUSTICE, TASK FORCE REPORT: CRIME AND ITS IMPACT—AN ASSESSMENT 96 (1967).

APPENDIX B

THE CORRECTIONAL FILE OF JOHN ARTHUR WILSON*

The file of John Arthur Wilson is not a typical one. The nature of the crime, the character of the offender, and the complicated history of the case make the file lengthier than most. The original file runs more than 300 pages, much of it repetition of fact drawn from earlier reports or purely formal documents. The file as it appears here has been edited in an attempt to preserve all significant new information while omitting much that is repetitious. Omissions from the file have been noted and summarized, so that it is possible to get an impression of the contents of a complete file.

Police records do not ordinarily find their way into the correctional file. Though trial transcripts are supposed to be included, when the conviction is by plea of guilty as was true here, it frequently happens that no transcript is prepared. Apparently no presentence investigation was made of Wilson at the time of his first conviction; this document would ordinarily appear in the file. The record therefore begins as Wilson is received at Wisconsin State Prison, following conviction on four counts of sodomy. A report of physical examination and an admissions investigation by a social worker (which would have been unnecessary if there had been a presentence investigation) are the first documents in the formal correctional file.

[The report of physical examination, showing Wilson normal in every respect, is omitted. It describes him as 28, white, 5 feet 9 inches tall, and 165 pounds.]

* This case has been made available by the Wisconsin Division of Corrections. We are especially grateful to Sanger B. Powers, Director of the Division, and to Joseph Coughlin, then Chief of Administrative Services, for their cooperation in preparing this record.

FACE SHEET

DATE PREPARED: November 28, 1950

INSTITUTION: Wisconsin State Prison NUMBER: 31,642

Name: WILSON, John Arthur
True Name: Same
Aliases: None

Date of Birth: June 27, 1922
Place of Birth: Fond du Lac, Wisconsin
Sex: Male Race: White
Citizenship: U.S.A.
Height: ft. in. Weight: lbs.
Color of Eyes:
Color of Hair:
Religious Preference: Catholic
Significant Disability and Health Factors:

Other Identification: Of Irish-French descent, married, wife is only dependent, teaching was occupation, Soc. Sec. No.: 365-04-1234.

Offense: Sodomy, 4 counts, Statute Section 351.40, Municipal Court of Racine County, Judge Hubert J. Stephens, District Attorney William J. McCarthy, Terms - 3 tms. 1-4 years, conc. & 1-4 years cons.

ACCOMPLICES: None

EMERGENCY ADDRESS: 4561 West Redwood, West Lake, Wisconsin (wife)

REFERENCES: John Hall, Wellington, Wisconsin (Sup't. of Schools)
Father Flanigan, Farwell Avenue, Racine, Wisconsin (Soc. of Prob. of the Faith)

HABITS: Moderate DRUGS: None

ASSETS: Auto-$50., Furniture-$3,000., Cash-Unknown

DEBTS: Lawyer Fee-$400., Personal-$100.

Statement of Offense (By Inmate): Pleaded guilty, Bench Trial, Att: Housch, West Lake, Wisconsin. "I've known Tommy Tubbell very well and liked him as my own son. In my mind I seem to have confused the sexual aspects of love with normal affection. Therefore, I committed sodomy with Tommy on several occasions."

Sentence: Sodomy, 4 counts
Court: Municipal
County: Racine
Judge: Hubert J. Stephens
District Attorney: William J. McCarthy
Defense Attorney:
Plea: Guilty
Date Arrested:
Date Sentenced: 11/14/50
Date Received: 11/15/50
Term Expires: Feb. 15, 1956
Eligible for Parole: Nov. 15, 1952
Conditional Release:

Residences

1753 Farwell, Racine, Wisconsin 9 months 1949
767 Finely, Madison, Wisconsin 2 years 1946-1948
U.S.N. Naval Service 4 years 1942-1946
476 Malthus Circle, Racine, Wisconsin 1929-1942

LEGAL SETTLEMENT: 76 Bluebell Lane, Sussex, Wisconsin (Sussex County)

Spouses and Children

Wife: Mary Jane, nee Polk, (27) English & Bohemian descent, married September 3, 1949, in West Lake, lives at 4561 West Redwood, West Lake, Wisconsin, no living children (daughter died day after birth)

Parents, Siblings and Interested Persons

FATHER: Gerald Thomas Wilson, (60) 76 Bluebell Lane, Sussex, Wisconsin, born Fond du Lac, Wisconsin, Irish descent, works for Waukesha Motors as Production and Stock Clerk.

MOTHER: Florence Marie Burnadette, nee Varee, (56), born Fond du Lac, Wisconsin, housewife, fair health, no arrests, French descent.

BROTHER: Gerald Thomas Wilson, Jr., (33) Redflower Road, Sussex, Wisconsin, works for Sussex Motor Works as Stock Clerk, married, 1 child, good health, no arrests.

SISTERS: None

Education

Northwestern University: Graduated June 1948 B.A.-Racine State Teachers, 1949-1950, Racine State Teachers 1940-1942-Sussex High School, 1936-1940, Our Lady Parochial School 1-8th grades. Excellent student, major subject: psychology.

Employment

September to November 1950-teaching at Wellington Grade School 1948-1949. Life Guard at Racine during summers $165 mo. Sept. '47 to June '48. Mickey Dairy Bar, counter man (meal job). 1949-1950 teaching swimming & life guard at Racine Y.M.C.A. (evenings).

SKILLS: Teacher, psychiometrist, swimming instructor, typing, clerk.

HOBBIES: Photography, models, Indian lore.

Military Service

Drafted U. S. Navy September 1942, Seaman 1st, Signalman Striker 304-66-66, 1 year overseas-Pacific, honorably discharged January 31, 1946 (3 years, 5 months).

Previous Arrests, Institution and Supervision Experience

None.

INTERVIEWER'S IMPRESSION

Wilson, a 28 year old white male, is above the average person in that he has a great deal of education. He became affiliated with a group of delinquents at an early age where improper sex acts were learned and practiced. Wilson is actually not ashamed of his offenses and claims he cannot help it. He seems to counteract his misdeeds by assisting young people in guiding them towards decent ways of life and trying to show them right from wrong.

Wilson is sincere and honest but does not seem completely adjusted socially. He seems to lack self-insight. He admits immorality prior to marriage and since being married.

Wilson claims he loves the young lad with whom he committed offenses as if he were his own son. He desires to have children of his own—a daughter died at birth.

He is intelligent and honest and not a great risk.

SUGGESTED INSTITUTIONAL PROGRAM

CUSTODY: Medium

WORK: INSTITUTIONAL NEEDS, can type and would be good clerk or useful in school department as teacher.

SCHOOL: Wants to learn languages

SPECIAL RECOMMENDATIONS: Wilson has had experience in psychiometry and has assisted in giving tests.

TENTATIVE PAROLE PROGRAM: None
SOURCES: None

Carl Galowcski
Interviewer

[Omitted is a form made out at the same time, listing as approved correspondents Wilson's wife, parents, brother, and three friends.]

WILSON, John A. WSP # 31642
Admission Examination,
December 13, 1950.

Examiner's Appraisal:

Physical examination reveals no evidence of a pathological state.

This man in his general patterning reflects characteristics markedly better in type than those of the average individual observed. He is highly intelligent, cultured and well-bred; his reasoning capability is excellent; his insight is proper; and his approach is one of complete frankness and totally devoid of rationalization. He is, however, flushed and under emotional stress. He reflects some evidence of morbidity and definitely anxiety attitudes. There exists some constriction and tendency toward preoccupation, and he is moderately lachrymose.

He is the product of an environment which, while materially satisfying during his formative period, was lacking from the point of view of emotional satisfaction with the father figure. He sensed throughout his younger years an aloofness and coldness by the father which he interpreted as indicative of rejection. Compatibility with his only sibling existed, but close association was meagre due to the age span existing between them. An over-dependency upon the mother appears to have been present. This man maintains definite absence of any insecurity in his relationship with other juveniles or teen-agers during his later development and exposure to academic settings. He was active in athletic and extracurricular projects in such environments.

He developed during this period, however, definite conflicts of religious sexual type; phobia associated with venereal involvement exaggerated his plight, and he openly concedes the participation in deviated behavior sexually during this period as a substitute for compensation of his basic yearnings. He denies totally the recognition of any psychologically conditioned deviated bent, and he maintains that only following his separation from the military and the acquirement of a definite state of maturity did he experience alarm relative to his situation. He argues complete compatibility in all phases of his marital existence. He admits the development of strong guilt feelings as a result of his reversion to earlier practices. He has, however, at no time apparently possessed proper understanding of the psychological factors involved by which, in contrast to his own childhood, he assumed the father role and projected toward the juvenile an emotional attachment of intense type.

This man's illogical shooting of photographic poses of himself and an affected juvenile and the distribution of such material to the aforementioned youth would indicate the existence of an extreme guilt-ridden conscience and a deliberate desire for apprehension and a yearning for self-punishment.

He appears sincere in his desire for assistance. His academic conditioning and his unusually good intelligence should allow the development of insight and it is our intent to approach him therapeutically while confined.

His vocational activities have been those of teaching and institutionally he can be absorbed in some outlet challenging his mental capability.

CHRONOLOGICAL HISTORY*

Name: Wilson, John Class. & No.: WSP 31,642

FIELD CALL: 12/20/50. Saw subject at WSP this date for purpose of compiling personal information for admission investigation. Psychologist classified subject as having superior intelligence with an I.Q. of 136. He has good insight but suffers from an anxiety and maldepression complex. He is now placed in the accounting section of the business office. Medical examination shows his physical condition to be good.

Agent discussed with client the history of his homosexual activities and learned from him that he had been engaging in this type of behavior since about the age of 11 when he first had contact with a male cousin. He states that the activity continued intermittently through adolescence, several times while in the armed forces and has been getting progressively worse since his return.

Upon questioning him as to how his case was brought to the attention of the authorities, he reveals that he is

* The Chronological History is a running record of field agent contacts with the case. It is kept separate from other file documents, but is here inserted in the sequence of documents.

a camera fan and that he had gone to the extreme of taking pictures of the commission of the oral sodomy act on young boys. Some of these pictures were given to his victims. One of the boys dropped his wallet at a theatre in Racine, the pictures were found, turned over to the police who investigated them as obscene literature and after identifying the youngsters gleaned from them a full confession regarding client's participation. He offers the statement that "in analyzing myself I feel that I took the pictures because of a repressed guilt complex and perhaps unconsciously hoped that the pictures would be found, that I would be caught and this activity brought to an end."

This man's education and training in the field of psychology gives him a lot of personal weapons with which to attempt to diagnose himself and to defend his own actions. The fact that he has been operating in the circle of young boys for many years and that he has gotten to the point of taking pictures of the commission of the oral sodomy act is indicative to this agent that his affliction is deep seated and will need more than the supervision which can be offered by a parole officer. It was therefore discussed with him with the point in view of bringing him to the acceptance of future private psychiatric help. To this he tentatively agreed but feels that the psychiatric help mentioned is needed more by his latest victim (Tubbell) more than it is needed by him since inmate feels that the emotional conflict now going on in this youngster needs attention at this time so as to prevent a development of a homo-sexual sphere.

ADMISSION INVESTIGATION

CONFIDENTIAL

Submitted by:
H. David Mark
January 15, 1951

JOHN ARTHUR WILSON—WPS 31,642 Born: 6/27/22
4561 West Redwood
West Lake, Wisconsin I. Q.: 136 (Superior)

CHARGE: Sodomy (4 counts) Section: 351.40

DISPOSITION: WSP—3 terms 1-4 years, concurrent and one term 1-4 years, consecutive. Municipal Court, Racine, Wisconsin 11/14/50.

COURT HISTORY

PRESENT OFFENSE: The State of Wisconsin, through the Racine County District Attorney William J. McCarthy, charged that subject committed the act of oral sodomy on the body of one Tommy Tubbell in Racine in February, May and June of 1950 and caused the said Tommy Tubbell to commit the act of sodomy upon him, John Wilson, in Racine in June of 1950.

Client entered a plea of guilty. He was therefore sentenced to concurrent terms on the three charges wherein he committed the act alone, but was sentenced to a consecutive term on the fourth count inasmuch as the act involved reciprocal sodomy and the victim, a minor, was caused to engage in the practice.

Investigation reveals that inmate's homo-sexual activities were brought to light through his camera hobby. He had progressed to a point, in his behavior, where the commission of the act of oral sodomy was not enough. He brought into play the use of a camera whereby he took pictures of these young boys, while he or they were in the act. These pictures he evidently gave to the boys. One of the boys lost his wallet at a movie. It was found and turned over to police who immediately started a search to identify the victims. As a result, Tommy Tubbell was questioned and revealed the source from which this activity stemmed.

Client admits that he has been indulging in homosexual activities since about the age of ten, when he first had such a relationship with a cousin. It continued through his adolescence and through his military service. He denies associations with men, but claims he has an affinity for only young boys. Ages and names of victims, investigated thus far, substantiates this claim.

DEFENDANT'S STATEMENT: "I've known Tommy Tubbell very well and liked him as my own son. In my own mind I seem to have confused the sexual aspects of love with normal affection. Therefore, I committed sodomy with Tommy on several occasions."

Inmate, who has had considerable training in education and psychology, has attempted to excuse himself by rationalization with affection as the basis. However, he makes no personal accounting for his behavior in the multitude of instances which occurred prior to his act with Tommy.

Also, he informs agent, upon questioning, that the camera came into play "through the work of the subconscious." He is trying to convince himself he was suffering from a repressed guilt complex and was using the same, perhaps unconsciously, with a hope that he would be caught, and this chain of events brought to an end.

PRIOR RECORD: None.

FAMILY BACKGROUND

MOTHER: Florence Varee Wilson, inmate's mother, was born at Fond du Lac, Wisconsin on 5/19/1898, one of five children born to A. C. and Ophelia Varee. She is of French-Canadian ancestry, Catholic since birth, has a 9th grade education, and worked as a telephone operator prior to her marriage to Gerald Thomas Wilson at Fond du Lac on 9/17/16.

She is a person of seemingly average intelligence, neat, responsible, good judgment, keeps a good home and has always held the interests and welfare of her children in high regard.

FATHER: Gerald Thomas Wilson was born 7/19/1890 at Fond du Lac, Wisconsin, the son of Patrick and Mary Leary Wilson. He is of Irish ancestry. He claims to have finished high school in three years and then graduated from Horlock College, Prairie du Chien, Wisconsin.

After completing college, he returned to Fond du Lac where he worked as a superintendent of a typewriter concern. He married in 1916 and in 1925 moved his family to Racine where he was employed as an inspector for Rambler Motors. In 1927 he accepted a job with the Waukesha Motors as a foreman in the production department, and has been so engaged for the past 22 years. Records show he has had no criminal history; does not drink; is a good father and provider and has always adhered to the precepts of the Catholic faith.

SIBLINGS: (1) Inmate has one brother and no sisters. Gerald Thomas, Junior, was born 4/4/17 at Fond du Lac. He is a high school graduate and has completed one year at the Northwestern University. He is now married to one Margaret More, has a son, is employed in the Service Department of the Sussex Motors and resides at 250 Goodlen Street. He has no criminal history. Domestic relations are good.

(2) Subject. Born 6/27/22 at Fond du Lac, Wisconsin.

PERSONAL HISTORY

Client was born in Fond du Lac, Wisconsin on 6/27/22, the second of two children born to Gerald and Florence Wilson. He comes of good stock, always had a good home wherein there was ample of the physical necessities and affection.

At an early age, he developed what is commonly called St. Vitus Dance, and was out of grade school for one year with this affliction. While still in grade school, he had the experience of oral sodomy with a cousin, and continued the practice intermittently in grade and high school. His parents state that there were no early outward indications of this type of behavior and they were, at first, reluctant to believe their son's admissions. His family is at a loss to account for the development of this pattern, other than that which he offers in his statements that he was introduced to this form of sex activity by a cousin.

HABITS: Has had hetero-sexual experience, but has been committing homo-sexual acts on young boys for many years. He claims to be "a social drinker" but never to excess. Smokes a pipe. Has not been known to associate with groups of ill repute.

HEALTH: Present health good. No venereal history. Was out of school one year during first grade period with St. Vitus Dance. Evidently cured. Had yearly checkups afterwards and was declared physically fit to enter Navy in 1942. No history of hereditary feeblemindedness, drug addiction or contagious diseases.

RELIGION: Born of Catholic parents. Has been baptized and confirmed. Member of Holy Name Society and Catholic Order of Foresters. Is married to a Catholic girl. Both client and wife have attended church quite regularly.

MILITARY: Enlisted in U. S. Navy at Racine on 9/12/42 as serial number 304-66-66. Progressed from Apprentice Seaman to Seaman 2/c and thence to Seaman 1/c, which rating he held at time of Honorable Discharge on 1/31/46.

His discharge shows him to be recipient of the Good Conduct Award; Presidential Citation with Blue Star; the A-P ribbon with one star; Philippine Liberation Ribbon with one star and the W.W. II Victory Medal. His total length of service was 3 years, 4 months and 19 days.

EDUCATION: Started kindergarten in the public schools at Sussex, Wisconsin at age 5. He later transferred to Our Lady Parochial School where he completed the 8th grade, and then completed high school at Sussex in 1940 where he was classified as a good student with high innate intelligence.

He entered Racine State Teachers in September 1940 and was there until June, 1942. His navy enlistment temporarily halted his academic training. Upon return from service he entered Milton College, Sussex, for one semester, and then entered the Northwestern University in September, 1946 where he was graduated with a B.A. degree in June, 1948. He continued at the University until September 1949 to work on his M.A. and then came back to Racine Teachers College to do special study on handicapped children to gain enough information to complete his requirements for his thesis and M.A.

The greater share of his advanced studies have been in psychology and psychological testing and measuring.

ECONOMIC: Owns his own household goods valued at about $3,000.00. Has some life insurance. Wife is working as a music teacher in Racine County School System and paying off all existing debts.

It appears that client has always lived within his income and has been a good personal manager. Wife declares him to be a good provider and not one to buy beyond his income.

INDUSTRIAL: His first, and only job, as a teacher was that of an instructor in the State Graded School at Wellington, Wisconsin. He began said employment in September 1950 and terminated same by his arrest. His superintendent, Mr. John Hall, states he had "high regard for his ability, his professional interests and enthusiasm."

His continuance in the teaching field can no longer be recommended.

RECREATION: As a youth, exhibited normal interest in outdoor sports, model airplanes and puppets. He was active in dramatics and glee club work in grade and high school. He dated high school girls but didn't like them unless they were unusually intelligent. His latest interests have been centered in photography and music.

MARITAL: Inmate married one Mary Jane Polk at Holy Assumption Church, West Lake, Wisconsin on 9/3/49 after a nine year courtship that had begun while both were students at Racine Teachers.

The wife was born in Racine on 2/8/23 and has lived there all her life. She has a B.S. degree from Racine State Teachers College and has had one year of advanced study at Prospect College of Music. She has had successful teaching experience in Highland (2 years), Shelton (2 years), Brookfield (1 year) and is currently employed by the Racine County System.

She is a highly intelligent girl who is doing her best to get a full understanding of her husband's problem so that every device possible can be used in his attempted rehabilitation. The shock of this behavior has not in the least dampened her ardor and she steadfastly maintains that she will stick with him through whatever the future has to offer.

Client and wife became the parents of a premature daughter on 4/5/50. The child lived one day. No other children have been born of this marriage and the wife claims no pregnancy at this time.

HOME CONDITIONS: Inmate's boyhood home was one which was physically and emotionally adequate. There are indications of a normal sibling rivalry but nothing of an unnatural nature.

His home with his wife has been very pleasant and satisfactory. Domestic relations have been good. There is an indication that sex relations have been on a normal marital basis and the wife claims no knowledge or indication of the behavior pattern which caused client's incarceration.

DIAGNOSIS AND PLAN

John Arthur Wilson is a 28 year old white male of superior intelligence, a veteran of World War II, a college graduate in the field of psychology and education and of a good family background. He is a homosexual who has exercised oral sodomy on young boys since his own adolescence.

He is of good health and has proven to be a good student. There is every reason he can be aided by psychiatric help. This should be started while he is incarcerated and continued upon release.

Institution counseling should include a suggestion that he now veer from the teaching profession and that his training be channelled into such lines as advertising research and personnel work.

The question of an early parole can be answered only by the attendant prison psychiatrist, who can note his progress and decide when he is ready to return to organized social living.

Respectfully submitted,
H. David Mark
Probation & Parole Agent

CHRONOLOGICAL HISTORY

Name: Wilson, John Class. & No.: WSP 31,642

FIELD CALL: 3/29/51. Saw him at WSP this date. Now assigned to billing section of office. Learning more of office routines. Taking advanced calculus by correspondence, and doing some heavy reading.

Claims he has found a new faith and hope in his religion. He informs that he formerly was not sure of the basis of his faith but his leisure reading and religious study have given him new hope and confidence in his Catholic faith. Wife writes him daily.

He states he is glad he was caught. He now has time to disperse his guilt feelings, take a new hold on himself and begin anew. Feels that by time he is released, he will be able to navigate as a normal person.

FIELD CALL: 5/24/51. Saw John at WSP this date. He is still working in the front office and has been given full control of all billing and disbursing orders and states he likes his work even though it is nothing more than a "busy job." He again spent considerable time trying to psychoanalyze himself for the benefit of this agent and states that his wife has recently been to a Madison psychiatrist who is willing to accept his case if he can be released on parole. Agent advised him that because of the consecutive sentences which had been imposed that it would be impossible for him to do any planning for at least two years but that psychiatric help should certainly be included in the pattern and the plan of self adjustment. He states that he feels he is becoming stronger within himself and backs up his statement by diagnosing his own dream situation in which he states that his dreams are now no longer of a homo-sexual nature. He feels that this is growth within himself. John's attitude is excellent, will probably never be of any adjustment problem in the institution and could probably make a good job of parole with the aid of psychiatric help to combat his homo-sexual tendencies.

FIELD CALL: 6/5/51. Talked with wife at Racine residence. Says she has been to see Dr. Capote, psychiatrist at WGH and he will treat John if transfer from WSP to WGH can be effected. Advised that she get statement from the doctor to that effect, and transfer might be effected on temporary basis for treatment purposes. She questions re the procedure for pardon or commutation. Advised her it was the right and privilege of him to seek executive relief, but advised her that pardon could be more injurious in that it would relieve him from supervision and necessary help. She agrees. Feels she will seek commutation for purposes of effecting earlier parole for psychiatric treatment.

PHONE: 6/20/51. John's wife called agent at residence in evening. States she has dropped legal counsel but plans to seek commutation via personal plea. States she will be satisfied to have sentences made concurrent, so that earlier parole can be effected.

She distinctly asks agent's opinion of her chances. Advised her that philosophy embodied in sex offender law makes chances appear very slim. She will continue her pursuit and keep me informed of developments.

FIELD CALL: 7/25/51. Saw John at WSP this date. He states he is in one of his low depressed periods and that he was thankful for my visit since it gave him an opportunity to talk himself out. He talked at length regarding the efforts of his wife to effect executive clemency so that the consecutive sentence of 1-4 might be quashed thereby making him eligible for parole at the end of one year on the three concurrent sentences. He feels that continued incarceration will do him no good and that if he is able to get an early parole, he will be able to work out a program with Dr. Descartes at the Northwestern University psychiatric section wherein he can be given professional help. Agent advised him that the philosophy of the thinking of the governor's office was undoubtedly embodied in the governor's approval of the sex offender law which places a sex offender under the supervision of the State Department of Public Welfare for life, if necessary. It was therefore deduced that his chances of getting executive clemency in which the consecutive sentences would be abrogated were very slim. He states that Dr. Bell has inferred as much since the doctor has told him that he would be at the institution for two years and his chances of parole at that time were very uncertain. He claims that his spirits are constantly buoyed by the ready flow of letters from his wife and that it is her interest and love which sustains him through this ordeal. He further claims that his feelings are quite strong sexually for her and that he has had little or no feeling of homo-sexual desires. He claims that in a self analysis of his own situation he feels that his sex drives are dual and are of equal strength. He professes to have a normal sexual feeling for his wife but that he does possess a paternal and emotional love for younger boys which has crystalized in the form of homo-sexual behavior with them.

There is little indication that John will be much of a problem while at the institution but no parole program of this man is going to be feasible unless it is based on the foundation of professional psychiatric assistance.

Oct. 17, 1951

TO: Dr. Peter Bell
FROM: Mr. Russell G. Oswald

Governor Kohler's office has contacted us with respect to the complaint of one, Mrs. John Wilson, that her husband, John Wilson, our WSP #31,642, is in need of psychiatric attention for his deviate sex behavior, and is not receiving such treatment.

We, of course, are of the belief that he is receiving psychiatric treatment if he has requested such, and if he is amenable to treatment. I have noted in your appraisal of December 13, 1950, that you state that "it is our intent to approach him therapeutically while confined."

In order that I may answer Governor Kohler's office, and so they in turn may be in a position to reply to Mrs. Wilson, may I have word from you as to the progress which has been made in working with Mr. Wilson?

THE STATE OF WISCONSIN
STATE DEPARTMENT OF PUBLIC WELFARE

October 18, 1951

Mr. Russell Oswald, Director
Division of Corrections
Public Welfare Department
State Capitol
Madison, Wisconsin

Dear Mr. Oswald:

We have your memo of October 17 in which you refer to the complaint of Mrs. John Wilson to the Governor's office concerning the lack of psychiatric service being received by her husband, an inmate of the prison.

Wilson was interviewed by us originally on December 13, 1950, at which time full discussion of his situation was entered into. Projective analysis was at no time effected in the case of this man due to the fact that he verbalized without difficulty the nature of the conflicts which had long obsessed him.

It has never been our policy to force individuals into therapeutic situations since under such circumstances no benefit can accrue. Many of the inmates put in frequent requests for assistance and in all instances they are honored. No further request was received from Wilson until April 30 of 1951, and he was interviewed in the latter part of May. Since that time, although he is certainly cognizant of the fact that help will be offered him, he has filed no further request.

We interviewed his wife on June 14th and gleaned from her information to the effect that she was contemplating a clemency appeal in his behalf.

Some time ago the Warden displayed to us a letter which he had received from the St. Vincent DePaul Society in Racine whose representative had had a conference with Mrs. Wilson, and in this communication reference was made to the Society's willingness to assist him in obtaining psychiatric therapy in Racine should he be released.

This man's unusual intelligence and academic attainment preclude his absence of knowledge concerning the desirability of seeking assistance for his disturbance, and the pattern which he is following in the prison is similar to that manifested by him in his years of adulthood prior to his conflict which now confines him.

Very truly yours,
Peter Bell, M.D.
Psychiatric Field Service

Suggested letter for Governor's signature

October 22, 1951

Mrs. John Arthur Wilson
4561 West Redwood
West Lake, Wisconsin

Dear Mrs. Wilson:

The matter of your recent complaint to the effect that your husband John Wilson, though in need of psychiatric attention, is not receiving it, has been called to the attention of Mr. Russell G. Oswald, Director of the Division of Corrections.

Mr. Oswald advises us that John was initially interviewed by the psychiatrist on December 13, 1950. Some time later, April 30, 1951, John requested further attention. This request was met the latter part of May and no further requests for interviews were ever received. Mr. Oswald then called our attention to the fact that any therapeutic relationship which might be entered into between the psychiatrist and your husband would have to be on a voluntary basis. Since such is the case, any treatment program entered into must be based on the desire of the afflicted individual, before the psychiatrist is warranted in the hopeful initiation of therapy.

It is Mr. Oswald's belief that John's high intelligence and academic proficiency adequately forecloses the belief that he does not possess knowledge concerning the desirability of seeking help for his disturbance during the period of confinement. You may rest assured that should John put in a request to see Dr. Bell or Dr. Runkle, it will be honored.

I trust that this is the information that you seek and I sincerely recommend that you encourage your husband to seek the help that is available to him.

Date: October 1952

PAROLE PLANNING INFORMATION SHEET

Hearing: October 1952

Institution: Wisconsin State Prison

Name: WILSON, John Arthur   Number: WSP 31,642

Offense & Term: Sodomy, 4 counts, 3 terms, 1-4 years concurrent & 1-4 years consecutive

Date Sent.: 11/14/50   Date Rec'd: 11/15/50
C. R. Date: None   Max. Dis. Date: 6/2/55

Parole Eligibility Date: November 15, 1952
Previous Action: New application

Time Served: 1 yr. 11 mos. 15 days
To C. R.: Left to Serve: 2 yrs. 7 mos. 2 days
To Maximum:

Detainers:

Reason for Pre-parole:

PLACEMENT PLAN

City: West Lake, Wisconsin. Live with wife at 4561 West Redwood

Employment: Shipping & receiving clerk

Residence: Live with wife at 4561 West Redwood, West Lake, Wisconsin

Financial: $35 here; has several hundred in bank. Has work clothes.

Supplemental Information: Physical condition good. I.Q. 136. ". . . He has, however, at no time apparently possessed proper understanding of the psychological factors involved by which, in contrast to his own childhood, he assumed the father role and projected toward the juvenile an emotional attachment of intense type. . . ."

12/13/50, not taking his place in line when leaving cell.

5/6/52, not wearing his cap in line of march.

Billing clerk, reported very capable but is very temperamental and subject to moods of depression.

WISCONSIN
STATE DEPARTMENT OF PUBLIC WELFARE
DIVISION OF CORRECTIONS

HEARING: October 1952

INSTITUTION: Wisconsin State Prison

PAROLE DECISION

Institution No.: 31,642
Date: 10/2/52

Name of Case: WILSON, John Arthur
Official Action: Deny

By: Russell G. Oswald
Director

[A November 27th letter from Mrs. Wilson requesting an appointment in late December or early January to discuss her husband's case was answered by Mr. Oswald, setting an appointment for January 2, 1953.]

January 3, 1953

TO: The Record
FROM: T. C. Bourke
RE: Wilson, John A.—WSP #31,642

On January 2, 1953 Mrs. Wilson called at our offices and in Mr. Oswald's absence discussed this case with me. She wanted to know what she could do to help her husband and it was pointed out that probably the best she could do is exactly as she has been doing, and that is visiting the institution once a month and lending moral support, and to continue developing a good feeling between her and her husband.

She pointed out that he is now seeing Dr. Runkle on about a weekly basis and that he feels that Dr. Runkle can be a real help to him. I expressed the interest that we have had in her husband and let her know that it was our feeling that he is now making a real effort to help himself and thereby preparing himself for parole consideration at some future date.

Mrs. Wilson is employed as a music teacher in Racine County and works one day in Sussex each week. She pointed out that she has a home that John can return to and she feels that employment can readily be lined up in an insurance company as a statistician. John has some knowledge of statistics and is preparing himself for such employment at this time. Mrs. Wilson has every confidence in her husband and feels that he will succeed on parole and thereafter.

Date: April 1953

PAROLE PLANNING INFORMATION SHEET

[The basic information and placement plan were essentially the same as six months before.]

Supplemental Information:

WORK ASSIGNMENT AND ADJUSTMENT: Billing clerk; reported quite capable but very temperamental.
INSTITUTIONAL ADJUSTMENT SUMMARY: This man is quite hostile, believing that officials are dimwitted.
CONDUCT REPORTS: None since last application.

WISCONSIN
STATE DEPARTMENT OF PUBLIC WELFARE
DIVISION OF CORRECTIONS
FIELD SERVICES

HEARING: Special Investigation
INSTITUTION: Wisconsin State Prison

SOCIAL INVESTIGATION SUMMARY

Institution No.: 31,642
Name of Case: WILSON, John Arthur
Admission Investigation submitted: 1/5/51.

Social Summary:

I called at the home of subject's wife yesterday, located at 4561 West Redwood. At present Mrs. Wilson is engaged in teaching music in the Racine County Schools. I first interviewed subject's mother-in-law who, to all indications, is eagerly awaiting subject's parole. I took it upon myself to explain as fully as possible this man's affliction, his personality and psychological quirks, my theory being that it is only with the complete confidence and help of the family that we can determine how subject is adjusting on parole. I felt this especially necessary in view of the fact of this man's hostile attitude--he feels he knows all the answers and officials are dim-witted.

Later in the day Mrs. Wilson contacted me by phone and I discussed as thoroughly as possible with her, as she was quite apprehensive, the functions of parole and what was expected of John while on parole. I made it clear as possible to her that she and her husband were to live as normal a life as possible. I made it as clear as possible also that the burden of assisting John in his rehabilitation would fall on her shoulders. I have set aside a time at her convenience when we plan to discuss as fully as possible this man's offenses, why he committed them and what we can do about it, if anything.

The immediate plan for John and his wife is as follows: If and when John is paroled, they will reside with subject's mother-in-law at 4561 West Redwood, West Lake, Wisconsin. As soon as possible thereafter they are going to attempt to locate housing, possibly here in the city of Racine or in Racine County, depending on opportunity and closeness to prospective employment. As far as employment is concerned at this time, there is no definite plan, however, subject's background and high I.Q. should be conducive to his finding his own employment. It was made clear to Mrs. Wilson that under no circumstances could John again become engaged in the teaching profession and also that at no time is he to be permitted to associate with adolescent males. I explained to Mrs. Wilson the reason for this. None of the family apparently seemed to know what parole was and they had a poor idea of what was being done in the institution in subject's regard; the contact was centered around these points. I explained that the parole plan would be flexible and they could plan accordingly.

Employment or Placement Plan: To reside with mother-in-law and wife at 4561 West Redwood, West Lake, Wisconsin until housing of own choosing is located. Employment to be determined.

Note: Because of travel restrictions this agent has been unable to interview case at WSP to date. If opportunity presents itself in the future, this will be done.

Date Submitted: 4/23/53

Investigating Agent: Michael David Max

Date Approved:

Plan Approved by Dist. Supervisor: H. D. Mark

WISCONSIN
STATE DEPARTMENT OF PUBLIC WELFARE
DIVISION OF CORRECTIONS

HEARING: April 1953

INSTITUTION: Wisconsin State Prison

PAROLE DECISION

Institution No.: 31,642
Date: 4/7/53

Name of Case: WILSON, John Arthur
Official Action: Defer 3 months

By: Russell G. Oswald

Comments: Pre-parole requested. Agent assigned should interview case at WSP. Has received continual consultive help from Mr. Vehling, WSP psychologist.

[A new pre-parole (the Parole Planning Information Sheet), dated April 18th, omitted here, is essentially identical with that made in preparation for the April hearing.]

4561 West Redwood
West Lake, Wisconsin
May 12, 1953

Mr. Russell G. Oswald, Director
Division of Corrections
401 East Datton Street
Madison, Wisconsin

Dear Mr. Oswald:

Re: John A. Wilson—WSP

I have read all the statements you have published in the Milwaukee Journal and listened carefully to your television forum. Considering that your statements differ from the action of the parole board, I should like to discuss this with you.

In particular I should like to know the reasons for my husband's deferral and also why he was denied a hearing.

I shall be free any Saturday and would like to see you at your earliest convenience. If another day is preferable to you please let me know.

Yours very truly,
Mary Jane Wilson
(Mrs. John A. Wilson)

WISCONSIN
STATE DEPARTMENT OF PUBLIC WELFARE
DIVISION OF CORRECTIONS
FIELD SERVICES

HEARING: July 1953

INSTITUTION: Wisconsin State Prison

SOCIAL INVESTIGATION SUMMARY

Institution No.: 31,642

Name of Case: WILSON, John Arthur

Social Summary:

Admission Investigation submitted: 1/5/51.
Special Investigation submitted: 4/23/53.

On 5/6/53 I interviewed Mrs. Wilson. The purpose of this interview was to acquaint her further, at her own request, with the type of personality and special problems which her husband presents, what the purpose of parole was, and what was expected of her and John if and when the latter is granted parole.

Mrs. Wilson, in no way, shape, or manner bears any malice towards her husband for the offenses with which he was charged. It was interesting to note that in some respects she blames herself for partially contributing to her husband's offenses. It is her feeling that she was not properly prepared to assume the role of a wife and that because of this, it contributed to subject's deviant activity. It was also interesting to learn, and I think of great importance, that there is not much interference on the part of subject's mother-in-law. Therefore, the plan initially is not to be changed but if and when he is granted parole, he will reside with his wife and mother-in-law at 4561 West Redwood. As soon as possible, however, subject and wife should remove themselves from the influence of the mother-in-law and if possible relocate in some other section of the state, away from Racine. Mrs. Wilson agreed that this would be an excellent chance for them to reacquaint themselves and also to rid themselves of the interference of her family, who are definitely not equipped to cope with or understand the special problems which subject presents, nor do they understand, according to Mrs. Wilson, the concomitants of marriage. It was suggested to Mrs. Wilson that she consult a physician to determine the facts of life, as she readily admitted that she knew nothing about them. It is believed that it is necessary for her to have an understanding of these facts because we are primarily concerned with a sex problem.

I further note that because of this man's hostile and temperamental personality, the approach to him should be one of an authoritarian manner. I further note that if and when he is granted parole, it is requested that complete psychiatric recommendations etc., be available as a working tool. I would also like to know if Dr. Bell's recommendation is for continued psychiatric therapy upon John's release. If so, this can be arranged. For further information see Special Investigation of 4/23/53.

Employment or Placement Plan: To reside with wife and mother-in-law temporarily at 4561 West Redwood. Other living arrangements will be made as soon as possible. Employment to be determined.

Date Submitted: 5/13/53

Investigating Agent: Michael David Max

Date Approved:

Plan Approved by Dist. Supervisor: H. David Mark

Date: May 21, 1953

TO: A. W. Vlim
FROM: H. David Mark
CASE OF: Wilson, John
NO.: P-31,642

The above named man is currently an inmate of the Wisconsin State Prison and is scheduled for parole hearing in July, 1953.

Subject's wife, Mrs. Mary Wilson, was interviewed in my office, at her request, on May 18, 1953. She verbalizes an understanding of her husband's problems and feels that continued incarceration will be useless and perhaps of a negative nature. She claims that she and subject are ready and willing to engage psychiatric help, on an out-patient basis, if John is paroled.

I frankly informed her that her husband's case was a difficult one and that prognosis could, at no time, be termed good, nor was it, to me, hopeless. She displayed some feelings regarding her husband's failure to make parole in the past, and evinced a feeling that she was being given "the run around." She was advised that this department has a dual obligation; one to the client and one to the community. Attempted to re-assure her that John would be paroled when the Parole Board felt he was ready and that his serious threat to society had either been softened or relieved.

I interpreted to her that a denial usually meant "No," while a deferral could mean "Maybe," depending upon John's institutional adjustment, psychiatric reports and field investigation.

When she left she assured me she felt better in regard to the whole affair and would wait prayerfully until the July hearing.

This woman is developing a serious anxiety complex, as well as a definite feeling of personal inadequacy in meeting her husband's needs and will need tactful case work to work through her own and her husband's problems.

H. David Mark
Case Work Supervisor

July 3, 1953

Mrs. John A. Wilson
4561 West Redwood
West Lake, Wisconsin

Re: WILSON, John A.-WSP #31,642

Dear Mrs. Wilson:

Some weeks ago, May 12 to be exact, you wrote a letter that required an answer. In your letter you asked for an appointment to discuss your husband's case. You also seemed to express the feeling that our actions were not in keeping with the philosophy contained in our public utterances before TV and radio audiences.

The weeks since May 12th have been busy ones. Since that time I have attended conferences in Louisville, Cleveland and Milwaukee. I have also been away from the office because of parole hearings and meetings with the legislators during the mad rush that always attends the closing days of a legislative session. The result has been an accumulation of mail, some of it with a high priority as was yours that went unanswered for an unconscionable period of time. This is a matter of deep personal regret to me. In your particular case, I had hoped to meet with you on June 15, 16, or 17th when we had a statewide meeting of our correctional staff. The opportunity to have done so was never given me.

During the two years that I have administered the affairs of this Division I have seen great strides taken in the advance of a more promising correctional philosophy. The professional staff has grown both in numbers and in quality in both our field and institutional services. Basic differences in points of view as to the treatment potential of convicted offenders have been pretty much ironed out and the fundamental theories of the case work approach have been put into operation in so far as available resources would permit. Treatment is now more available to individuals and groups in our institutions.

Unfortunately, however, there are those who find it difficult to accept the feeling of need for such services. Your husband, for one, found it quite impossible to accept the idea that he needed help. The result was that he built about himself a prison whose walls were higher and whose iron bars stronger than any that we could ever hope to build. More recently, some change has come over him. He is now more receptive and it is my understanding that he has now established a good working relationship with Mr. Uehling, a most capable psychologist. This is most helpful. It is indeed unfortunate that he prolonged his stay at the institution because of the emotional and intellectual barriers that he set up for himself.

The Parole Board saw your husband for a few minutes early in June. He looked better and sounded better than he ever has in the past. What action the Board takes on his application for parole next week is beyond my power to guess. All that I can say is that he made a favorable impression a month ago.

I know that you have been wonderfully loyal to your husband during the period of his confinement. That has been a source of strength to him. He has repeatedly expressed his appreciation of you and I hear is now doing some joint and constructive planning with you for the future. That is all to the good.

If you still wish to see me personally, I shall be available for an interview on Monday, July 13, after 1:30 P.M. I would then be pleased to discuss any particular problems that may be bothering you with respect to your husband.

Yours very truly,
Russell G. Oswald, Director
Division of Corrections
STATE DEPARTMENT OF PUBLIC WELFARE

WISCONSIN
STATE DEPARTMENT OF PUBLIC WELFARE
DIVISION OF CORRECTIONS

HEARING: July 1953

INSTITUTION: Wisconsin State Prison

PAROLE DECISION

Institution No.: 31,642
Date: 7/8/53

Name of Case: WILSON, John Arthur
Official Action: Grant

By: Russell G. Oswald

[On July 9th Mrs. Wilson wrote that she could not meet Mr. Oswald on July 13th, as he had suggested, because of her work schedule. She asked for a later appointment. On July 13th Mr. Oswald wrote her, informing her of the decision to grant parole and suggesting that there was probably no further need for a conference.]

CHRONOLOGICAL HISTORY

4/23/53 Completed special pre-parole on John this date. I have reviewed the running record on institutional contacts by Mr. Mark and note that there is little question but what this man will need continued psychiatric guidance upon his release to field supervision.

5/13/53 Interview with Mrs. Wilson.

5/18/53 PERSONAL OFFICE: Wife of inmate in Racine office by appointment inquiring re possible parole in August. See copy of report of interview under IBC dated May 21, 1953.

7/15/53 MAIL: Copy of letter from Q. Ferm to Mr. Oswald requesting psychiatric data on subject be sent supervising parole officer prior to release after 8/1/53.

LATER: Case discussed with Mr. Garrett and Mr. Pollitt. Decided that I would carry case, actively, but same would be released to the case load of Mr. Mark Stafford, District 28.

LATER: PHONE: Called Mrs. Wilson at SO 3-4021. Informed her that John could be home after August 1, that

I would handle the case and contact would be made with her after receipt of parole board transcript. She was quite happy and stated she felt much better re the whole situation.

7/15/53 OFFICE: IBC to AWV, Investigation Unit, Q. Ferm and Ray Garrett, informing of decision made here to handle case.

7/24/53 MAIL: Notice received that John had been granted parole and could be released after 8/1/53.

7/27/53 OFFICE: Release request submitted this date after phone call to wife. Wife will pick up inmate at WSP at 10:00 A.M. on Saturday, 8/1/53. Mrs. Wilson informs that she has procured an apartment at 716 Foxdale Court, Essex, and will have occupancy 8/1/53. She will pay $90.00 per month.

The wife is currently employed on a summer playground, but will terminate summer employment on 8/15/53. Mrs. Wilson agrees to bring John to my home on Saturday, after release, for discussion re parole plans. This will be necessary since this writer will be on vacation during week of 8/3/53 to 8/7/53.

Employment for inmate will be arranged after discussion and over-all planning.

REQUEST FOR RELEASE

To: Mr. John C. Burke, Warden   Date: July 27, 1953
Wisconsin State Prison
Waupun, Wisconsin

Re: John A. Wilson

Number WSP 31,642 {Parole ☒ / Cond. Release ☐}

The above named is to be released to field supervision (date) 8/1/53 and will live at 716 Foxdale Court, Essex (Brown County), Wisconsin.

To be employed by: to be arranged.

At the following type of work: preferably clerical.

And should be instructed to report to: H. David Mark, 4023 South Oak, Racine, Wisconsin. Report to agent after initial contact by D. Mark at the home.

The Agent will be: M. M. Stafford   Area No. 28
Address: Court House
Sussex, Wisconsin

Disposition of Subject's funds: Give to subject.

Remarks: Subject will probably live temporarily at 716 Foxdale Court, Essex, Wisconsin with his wife. Contact will be maintained with D. Mark at Racine office, who will plan with subject and his wife regarding employment and housing. Will be picked up by his wife at WSP at 10:00 A.M. on Saturday, 8/1/53.

Requested by: M. M. Stafford

Approved by: H. D. Mark

WISCONSIN
STATE DEPARTMENT OF PUBLIC WELFARE
DIVISION OF CORRECTIONS
AGREEMENT

WILSON, John A.
WSP-31,642

In consideration of Probation or Parole being granted me, I agree to the following:

1. I will make a sincere attempt to avoid all acts which are forbidden by law and contrary to public welfare or my own best interests.

2. I will, to the best of my ability, take advantage of the opportunities offered me by probation or parole; I will practice temperance, conduct myself honestly, and assume my obligations as a citizen and as a member of the community in which I live.

3. I will keep the Probation and Parole Agent informed of my whereabouts and activities at all times and I will submit such reports as may be required.

4. I will secure advance approval from the Probation and Parole Agent, in writing if practicable, if at any time I wish to:
   a. Purchase or operate a motor vehicle.
   b. Incur debts whether by borrowing money or installment buying.
   c. Take on additional responsibilities, such as marrying.
   d. Change employment or place of residence.
   e. Leave the state.
   f. Own or carry firearms or other weapon.

5. If I prove myself unsuited to supervision, I will hold myself ready to be placed in the institution to which I was committed, returned to the court which placed me on probation, or to the institution from which I was paroled.

6. I will be guided by such specific instructions as may be issued by the Probation and Parole Agent with regard to companions, hours, intoxicants, medical attention, family responsibilities and support of self, court obligations, or other special restrictions as follows:

You will be released from the institution on Saturday morning, August 1, 1953 at 10:00 A.M. You will be held in the Lobby until called for by your wife, and transported to your home, 716 Foxdale Court, Essex, Wisconsin. You will be contacted there by Mr. H. David Mark, Supervisor, who will plan with you and your wife regarding employment and housing. You will report to your Parole Officer, Mr. M. M. Stafford, Court House, Sussex, Wisconsin after your initial contact by Mr. H. David Mark. All your prison money will be released to you.

YOUR DISCHARGE DATE IS: September 22, 1955.

Date: July 30, 1953   Signed: John A. Wilson

CHRONOLOGICAL HISTORY

PERSONAL OFFICE: 8/1/53. John and his wife came to agent's residence at Sussex this date as per release agreement. John had been released from WSP at 10:00 A.M. today and was picked up by his wife at the institution. He relates that during the afternoon they had been busy moving from the residence of his wife's mother to their new apartment at 716 Foxdale Court in Essex.

I discussed with John the possibility of psychiatric help and he states that he was informed by the institutional psychiatrist that such a program was not needed at this time and that he could very well navigate on his own if he gave some thought to his own problem. He claims that he now has some insight into his own situation and feels that he can get along without professional psychiatric services. John asked permission to take the next couple weeks for a vacation so that he and his wife can again get better acquainted. I vetoed the idea on the grounds that he would be better off seeking employment and keeping himself busy rather than languishing in a vacation atmosphere and spending his wife's money. He verbalized an assent but left me with the feeling that he was not going to wholeheartedly explore employment possibilities.

I openly discussed with him the necessity of his avoiding situations wherein he might be suspected of associating with or taking undue privileges with young people. He states that he is cognizant of this situation and will not allow himself to be caught in such an atmosphere or environment.

While John seemed to indicate, in the prison, that he was amenable to suggestions and help regarding his program of rehabilitation, his initial interview again gave evidence of a strong ego-centric personality in which he attempted to convey the impression that he was quite capable of taking care of himself and needed no help from this department. It will be noted that this same aspect of John's personality was detected by Mr. Max, who was of the feeling that John could be handled only through an authoritarian approach and at this moment it appears that that may become a necessity. John expresses some feeling regarding the length of time that he will be on parole but felt that he would have no difficulty maintaining parole status beyond his expiration date of 9/22/55.

At his request I gave him the privilege and prerogative of seeking out his own employment but again reminded him that I expected diligent effort on his part and asked that he contact me either at home or at the Racine office regarding the type of employment that he had accepted. His wife, Mary Wilson, states that she feels that John has enough insight into his own problem to be of intense help to himself and that their marriage will be compatible.

The interview was closed with the request that John contact me within the coming week.

8/24/53. OFFICE: Agent called home of John's mother-in-law. States he is still unemployed but living with wife at separate apartment and could be reached at BO 6-4850.

PHONE: Called John. In response to my query regarding his failure to contact me, he states he misunderstood and thought I was going to call on him. He relates that he has been making many calls for jobs, but no success to date. Thinks he would take anything, but no chance at all--as yet.

Advised him to accept the responsibility of keeping contact with me.

8/26/53. PHONE: Call from John. Has landed job as a shipping-receiving clerk at Kan Kraft Corporation at $1.00 per hour. He will start Monday, 8/31. Feels the job is of a menial nature but will keep his eyes open for something better.

Permission granted him to go to Wisconsin Dells beginning 8/27. Will return 8/30. Advised he call me (at home) on his return.

8/30/53. PHONE: John called me at my residence. Reported he was at home. Had a good time and ready to go to work tomorrow.

9/2/53. PHONE: John's wife called. Wondered when he should fill out and file monthly report. Advised her I would call at the home on Tuesday, 9/8, in the evening.

9/8/53. HOME VISIT: Called at the Wilson apartment at 716 Foxdale Court, Essex. John was not yet at home but Mrs. Wilson invited me in to await his arrival. She states he appears to be getting along well. He has been working steadily and comes home quite tired. Also, they seem to have been quite busy getting settled and John has had little time to think of himself. She states he seems to be measurably happy but shows some concern over his inability to obtain employment on anything but a laboring level.

When John came in, a frown crossed his brow, he took the chair nearest the door and made no effort to come over to greet me or to offer a handclasp. He had car keys in his hand but remarked off-handedly, in the direction of Mrs. Wilson, that he took the Center Street bus and "got home a little early."

He relates, without spirit, that he is employed as a shipping clerk at the Kan Kraft Corporation on North 3rd Street. This company specializes in dyeing delicate fabrics and does a big mail order business. John earns $1.00 per hour but thinks there is a future there for him, if he can persevere economically.

He was definitely reluctant to talk about himself—answering my questions and statement with one syllable words or grunts. He inquired regarding driving permission. Advised him same could not be granted as yet. He froze up. His attitude is not conducive to good case work with him. It is a duplication of the same attitude which was prevalent at WSP, and the primary factor in his prior parole denials. He gives the impression that he looks down upon any parole officer and tries to inflate his own ego on the basis that he is superior intellectually.

There is a strong possibility that John's attitude is attributable to:

(1) the fact that I am a neighbor (at Sussex) of his parents, and he may be attempting to prevent a close rapport, or
(2) he may resent any officer who has worked on his case previously since his wife has discussed with him many of the factors explored

(his sex life, conduct, etc.) by agents of this department. It could be that an older man might make better progress here, in that he would not be (in Jack's mind) a threat to Jack's relationship to his wife.

At any rate, efforts will be continued to develop a little warmth from Jack.

Mrs. Wilson states that they have no outstanding debts; pay $90.00 per month for their heated, furnished apartment and feel that they can get by on about $225.00 per month.

Phone: BO 6-4850.

9/17/53. OFFICE: Letter to Jack advising it will be necessary for him to report to this office on the first Monday of each month. See copy in file.

10/5/53. PERSONAL OFFICE: Jack reported to the Racine office as per my letter of 9/17. His attitude was much better. Came in with a smile. I informed him he was looking better. Says he is getting accustomed to work again but is doing menial tasks and it is depressing.

When I noted to him that he looked better than last time, he replied that he was probably over-tired at our last interview and wasn't too responsible. I took this opening to frankly discuss with him his feelings toward this department or me as a person. He denies that he is offended or embarrassed by his wife's knowledge of his activities prior to commitment and feels he can progress faster if she is aware of all discussions. He claims he "intellectually" accepts supervision but doubts that he has accepted it on a personality level. Under prodding, he admits that he has been resentful because I refused to (1) allow him a vacation prior to his employment and (2) have refused to give him driving privileges. An attempt was made to reason these elements through. He now verbalizes an acceptance but gives indication of having an inner hostility.

His monthly report indicates earnings of $196.30 from his employment at Kan Kraft Corporation. During his leisure time he visits with neighbors, goes to shows, does some reading and keeps close to his wife. Claims he makes overt attempts to avoid contact with young males so that he will, in no way, be suspicioned of retrogression.

Because of this man's innate intelligence and his advance academic training, he refuses to accept his status and therefore presents a problem. Whether or not this can be resolved will determine the type of parole time this man has to do.

11/2/53. OFFICE: Jack reported to the Racine office and was seen by J. R. Omar during my absence. Client continues at the Kan Kraft Corporation. Income for last month was $160.00 and expenses of $185.00. Deficiency made up from wife's salary.

Jack was off work ½ day on 10/27 and all day on 10/28 due to flu.

Says he and wife attended Gilbert-Sullivan operas in Milwaukee, having been visiting the museum and seeing relatives.

October report filed.

11/6/53. PHONE: Mrs. Wilson called this morning stating she was contacting me at Jack's request. Relates that Jack has finally received an answer to one of his employment applications he filed in August. He is to be employed as a "specifications man" at the Racine Resistor Company, 456 West Main, Racine at $60.00 a week to start.

Advised Mrs. Wilson that since Jack was definitely living and working in Racine, that transfer of his case would be effected. Further advised her I would stop at the home during the coming week and explain this to Jack.

12/7/53. OFFICE: Jack personally remitted his November report. I apologized for not seeing him at home during the month, but explained that my vacation and subsequent pressure of work had made it unavoidable. Again explained why transfer was necessary. He replied that I had been very patient with him, that he was now over the worst of his adjustment period and felt he could get along with anyone who might be assigned the case.

During our discussion, I was pleasantly surprised at Jack's attitude and apparent inherent feelings. It is evident that I was wrong in analyzing his initial behavior. He now reveals that his hostility was projected, not at me, or this department, but was an outlet for his feelings of frustration due to his inability to be recognized for his value and material worth in the industrial and economic world. This change was undoubtedly precipitated by the fact that he had found new employment as a sales engineer which inflated his ego, gave him an opportunity to make use of his training and intelligence, and gives promise of future advancements.

Domestic relations appear good.

Client explains that he spends most of his spare time at movies, plays, operettas, etc. and always in the company of his wife or relatives. He claims he has had no feeling of reversion at any time and feels he is inherently strong enough to combat any temptations in the homo-sexual area.

Will reside at 817 Sprague after 1/1/54.

[A letter to Wilson from the director of probation and parole services informed him that upon moving to his new address he would report to Agent V. Parisi.]

12/8/53. TRANSFER SUMMARY: John Wilson is a 31 year old, white, married man, who was convicted of four counts of Sodomy at Racine on 11/14/50 and committed to WSP for three concurrent terms of 1-4 and one term of 1-4 consecutive. He was released on parole on 8/1/53, reunited with wife in an apartment at 716 Foxdale Court, Essex. Original employment was that of a receiving clerk, Kan Kraft, Racine, where he earned $1.00 per hour. On 11/6/53 he went to work for the Racine Resistor Company as a sales engineer at $1.50 per hour. His adjustment on this job has been good and he has been promised a raise.

Jack's biggest problem has been centered around his inability to accept his status. He is a college graduate (Northwestern University), has had some teaching experience, and is of a high mental endowment. He looked upon all prison officials and inmates as being inferior and could not accept their superior role over him. His parole adjustment has been fair. Initial reception was poor, but he now shows a better acceptance of his status and the rules of parole. He harbors some ill feelings regarding my refusal to allow him driving privileges to date, but this was explained as a privilege he could earn after due time on parole. His homo-sexuality, from historic sketches, appears to be deep rooted. Future adjustment will be primarily dependent upon his ability to use his intelligence as a balance between his desires and social acceptance.

C-35's submitted herewith. File folder and master file card remitted Racine Region.

12/21/53. RECEIVED CASE FOR TRANSFER: Letter forwarded to John at 817 Sprague, requesting he contact me on 1/4/54.

1/4/54. OFFICE VISIT: John in the office as scheduled for our initial interview, which was primarily an introductory one. Stated he continues his employment at the Racine Resistor Company, 456 West Main, where he receives $52.56 weekly. Stated his wife continues her employment as a school teacher and present financial situation is favorable. However, she is now pregnant and expects their child in May or June. In view of John's present low earnings, financial problems in the future are anticipated.

2/1/54. OFFICE VISIT: Today's interview was concerned primarily with getting acquainted. Concerning John's adjustment there is apparently no change from previous entry.

3/1/54. OFFICE VISIT: Apparently no change. John requested and was given permission to operate his automobile.

LATER: To John, letter confirming in writing our permission for him to operate an auto.

3/10/54. HOME VISIT: Not home.

3/30/54. HOME VISIT: Evaluation of adjustment situation by wife: highly favorable.

4/5/54. OFFICE VISIT: No change.

4/14/54. TRANSFER SUMMARY: John was committed as a first offender on a Sodomy charge. Since coming from the institution, however, there has been no indication of continued difficulty in the psycho-sexual area. This, despite the fact that the pattern of homo-sexuality was an aggravated one earlier. Mr. Wilson is married, had one child, and his wife is expecting another. Mrs. Wilson describes their relationship as satisfactory in all respects. It should be kept in mind that John was married at the time of his involvement--that the confused pattern, insofar as sexual behavior is concerned, was one of long standing, and that it is not beyond possibility that should the right situation arise, there would be a regression of this earlier pattern. Mr. Wilson is a very intelligent fellow with a B.A. degree and considerable graduate work in psychology. He finds it difficult to accept his status as a parolee and a definite "professional approach" must be maintained with him if control is to be maintained by the supervising agent in interviews etc.

5/3/54. OFFICE VISIT: Spent some time renewing my acquaintance with John. I became quite familiar with this case while at WSP. All indications are that John its continuing to get along quite well. He is thinking of purchasing a home. He thought he could get a home for $12,500.00 through a friend, and that this sounded like a very good deal. He wanted to know if there were any objections to his buying a home, and I informed him that if it was a sound venture, and he was able to make satisfactory financial arrangements, there would be no objections from this agent. John considers himself to be a very superior individual intellectually (and as a matter of fact, does have superior intelligence) and he probably finds the asking for permission to do things quite difficult, but has been quite careful in this regard to date. It is noted that he asked his previous parole officer, Mr. Coughlin for permission in writing to obtain a driver's license and operating a car. Indications are, however, that John is getting along reasonably well at present.

6/4/54. HOME VISIT: The Wilsons were finishing supper when I called, John introduced me to his wife and then hastily retreated to the living room. His wife was busy feeding their new baby and did not leave the kitchen. John appeared to be rather nervous and tense throughout the interview, and attempts to get him to relax met with no success. He had a movie projector and screen set up in the living room and he informed me that this was the family's chief source of recreation. He picks up several free films per week from the Public Library film library. His statements indicate he is getting along satisfactorily on the job. John and his wife have a comfortable flat which is nicely furnished, and John expressed satisfaction with their living quarters. Although he indicated that no problems existed at present, his behavior suggests at the very least the continued inability to accept parole realities, and perhaps more seriously, an ability to the more basic reality--his own inadequacies which resulted in his difficulty and his need for help in these areas. Never in the past has he accepted psychiatric counsel when it was available, and up to the present he has accepted no help from his supervising agents. Throughout the home visit, he was polite, but distant, and this has been a characteristic attitude.

6/7/54. OFFICE VISIT: John came in as scheduled. Interview carried out along usual lines, although John was perhaps a bit more relaxed in his behavior tonight. We discussed the problems of maintaining a home, and more specifically of rearing children. Knowing that I'm an expectant father he took delight in telling me about the great expenses I can look forward to. His slant in this and other areas indicated that his chief difficulties at present are probably financial. It is impossible to ascertain the degree of adequacy to which he is meeting his emotional problems. Indications are, however, that he is at least controlling himself adequately and is maintaining an outwardly satisfactory adjustment level. Further interviews will be directed toward encouraging the maintenance of this minimum level of adjustment, and also to establish a degree of rapport upon which a beneficial relationship can be based. Prospects of achieving this last aim do not appear good.

7/6/54. OFFICE: John in office today as scheduled. Discussion of general problems indicated no change.

8/2/54. OFFICE: John in office today as scheduled. No change indicated. Discussed John's vacation plans. He plans on taking his wife and child to a state park where they will camp out for a week. John and his wife budget their money very carefully. Their take-home pay amounts to about $250.00 which necessitates careful budgeting. John feels that his pay is about average for the type of work he is doing. He recognizes that he has had no prior experience to the sales engineer and that the company is small and probably can't afford to pay any more. Indications are that he is adjusting to present circumstances reasonably well, and perhaps better than expected in view of his personality makeup.

9/7/54. OFFICE: John in office as scheduled.

9/28/54. HOME VISIT: Contacted John's wife. She feels he is making a very fine adjustment. Discussion revealed nothing to indicate anything to the contrary. John came home from work as I was about to leave. He seemed much more relaxed in seeing me in his home than he was in the case of the last home visit. He was cheerful, relaxed, and gave every indication of being well adjusted.

10/4/54. OFFICE: John in office as scheduled. No change in employment or place of residence. Indications are that John is continuing to adjust at a satisfactory level.

11/1/54. OFFICE: John in office as scheduled. Interview this evening revealed no new problems. John's principal problem remains the problem of supporting his family on his income. He is an intelligent, resourceful individual and seems to be doing a good job in this area.

11/9/54. SIX MONTHS SUMMARY: All indications point to a continued high level adjustment with no indications of any difficulty in the psycho-sexual area. He is very much interested in his work and in his family and appears to be directing all his energies toward these areas. I feel that my relationship with John has shown improvement, however, he feels competent to work out his own problems without assistance and accepts parole only as a necessary nuisance. If he has been able to completely overcome his sexual problems he has made amazing progress since his difficulties in this area were aggravated and of long standing. John has about ten months to go on parole, and if he is able to continue along his present course he will have no difficulty keeping his parole.

12/6/54. OFFICE: John in office as scheduled. No change indicated. Discussed John's finances. He is barely making ends meet on his salary but he is not incurring any debts which he is not able to meet. Discussed briefly the sex problems which resulted in his incarceration. He feels that he has no problems in this area at present, but recognized that there is no real cure and that he must avoid situations which might tempt him.

1/3/55. OFFICE: John in office as scheduled. Indications are that John is continuing to adjust at a satisfactory level. Indicated attitude and outlook continue at a satisfactory nature.

1/18/55. HOME VISIT: Talked with John's wife. She apologized for not having the house in better order but it appeared to be quite well arranged. In talking to her about John's adjustment and their relationship since his release, she had nothing but praise for the way he has been conducting himself. She thought that he was very much interested in work and while it paid barely enough to meet their immediate needs, John seems to get indefinite satisfaction out of doing this work. She expressed the feeling that as far as she was concerned the relationship between John and herself was satisfactory on every level. In previous discussions with John, he had indicated that during the period his offense was committed he was experiencing some difficulties in his relationship with his wife, but she apparently was unaware of this. She impressed as being somewhat naive, as a person who tried to understand her husband's sexual problems, but is one who had little real understanding of them. If John was to drift back into deviated sexual activity, she probably wouldn't become aware of this fact until it was revealed to her.

Photographic equipment was in evidence in the living room, enlarger, etc. In response to my inquiry regarding this, Mrs. Wilson stated that John took frequent pictures of the baby. Further discussion with Mrs. Wilson of their leisure time activities, etc., indicate that the situation in the home is relatively adequate at present.

2/7/55. OFFICE: John in office as scheduled. Indications are that John is continuing to adjust without difficulty.

3/7/55. OFFICE: John in office as scheduled. Discussed John's work and recreational pursuits this evening. He evidently has a responsible job which keeps him very busy and the work is of a satisfying nature although it pays him little more than enough to live on. John's favorite recreational pursuit continues to be photography. His favorite is his little daughter.

Indications are that John is continuing to effect a satisfactory adjustment.

3/29/55. HOME VISIT: Contacted John's wife. She seems to be a very happy person and everything in our conversation today indicated that John is continuing to effect a very satisfactory adjustment.

4/4/55. OFFICE: Personal. John in office as scheduled. No change indicated. John earned $351.00 in the month of March, all of which was used for subsistence. John has no outstanding debts. John showed me some pictures he recently took of his baby. Photography continues to be his chief hobby, and he is naturally very proud of his baby. All outward signs seem to point at continued adjustment at a satisfactory level.

5/2/55. OFFICE: Personal. John in office as scheduled. Interview this evening centered around John's job at the Racine Resistor Company. John has a responsible job in the purchasing department. The job challenges his intelligence and fulfills his need for prestige. He has had several pay raises and indicated earnings in the month of April in the amount of $351.00. He has prospects of a good future in this field.

The home situation remains unchanged. His baby has an allergy and her skin is broken out which has created some difficult moments in the home, but John continues to give indications of being a reasonably happy family man.

SIX MONTHS SUMMARY: All indications point to a continuation of a satisfactory level of adjustment over the past six months. John is engaged in satisfying work in which there is promise of a good future and which is also beginning to reward him financially. The home situation continues satisfactory. At this point, the indicated task from now until discharge in September of this year is simply to maintain routine supervisory effort.

6/6/55. OFFICE: Personal. John in office as scheduled. No change in general adjustment indicated. His indicated attitude and outlook continues good. His wife is expecting again in the fall, September. John indicated wages earned in the month of May in the amount of $286.70--all income used for subsistence.

7/18/55. OFFICE: Personal. John had just returned from a week's vacation which he spent with his wife and child in Nicolet National Forest in northern Wisconsin. He rented a tent and roughed it for a week. Indications are that John is continuing to adjust at a quite satisfactory level. He indicated earnings received in the month of June in the amount of $276.70 all of which was used for subsistence.

8/1/55. OFFICE: Personal. John in office as scheduled. No change noted in attitude or general adjustment. John showed me some 3-D pictures which he recently took of his family. He is proud of his family and the home situation seems to be relatively stable. He is scheduled for discharge on 9/22/55 and he will be in the office for the last time on 9/19. His indicated attitude and outlook continues good.

8/29/55. Attempted home visit. No one at home.

8/31/55. HOME VISIT: Contacted John's wife. Conversation with Mrs. Wilson indicates that the family situation remains unchanged. Mrs. Wilson seems to be very happy and expressed the feeling that John was doing very well. She insisted that she didn't have the slightest suspicion regarding his behavior. John spends practically all of his time at home and there appears to be very limited opportunity for contact of a deviant nature.

9/19/55. OFFICE: Personal. John in office as scheduled. No change in attitude or general adjustment. He appears to be continuing to effect a satisfactory adjustment. He seems to be reasonably happy in his role as a husband and father, and he expressed the feeling that he has sufficient control of himself to prevent any reoccurrence of his past offense. John's discharge certificate will be mailed to him.

John's discharge certificate mailed to him on this date, 9/28/55.

CASE CLOSING SUMMARY: There have been no known indications of a reoccurrence of the sexual problem which existed previously. John has never insisted that all of his problems were solved, but he maintains that he has developed better self-control and the known record substantiates his contention. He has satisfying employment which challenges his abilities and has a promising future. He is all wrapped up in his family and the prospects for a continued good adjustment seem good at this point.

CASE CLOSED--Discharged from supervision, expiration of term (9/22/55), the T-number is T-47632. At the time of case closing, Wilson was employed at the Racine Resistor Company, 456 West Main and lived with his wife and two children at 817 Sprague, Racine, Wisconsin.

[The "T" document, informing the prison of Wilson's discharge, is omitted, as is a letter to his agent enclosing his discharge certificate for Wilson.]

CIRCUIT COURT CHAMBERS
RACINE, WISCONSIN

October 30, 1956

Mr. Wilbur A. Schmidt, Director
State Department of Public Welfare
State Capitol
Madison, Wisconsin

Re: State of Wisconsin v. John Arthur Wilson
Circuit Court, Racine County
Case Nos. C1741, C1743, and C1744

Dear Sir:

Today, upon his plea of guilty and hearing, the above named defendant, John Arthur Wilson, of this city, was found guilty and convicted of, in

(1) Case No. C1741, the crime of sodomy contrary to section 351.40;
(2) Case No. C1743, having in his possession certain obscene photographs and negatives, contrary to section 351.38 (1); and
(3) Case No. C1744, taking improper liberties with a minor, contrary to section 351.41;

all section references being to Wisconsin Statutes, 1953, the offenses having occurred prior to July 1, 1956.

Under section 340.485 (now 959.15) the commitment to your department for pre-sentence social, physical, and mental examination is mandatory as to (3) above, and he was committed today to the local office of your department. As to (1) and (2) above, the court may commit him to your department for such examination, and we do request that you certify to this court that you have, if such is the fact, adequate facilities for making such examination and, if so, that you are willing to accept such commitment and, also, if at or through your local office at 4023 South Oak, Racine.

Since he has been committed there in (3) above, it was deemed advisable to withhold his sentencing in (1) and (2) above until such examination and report is made in (3) above; and at the same time, if agreeable to you such examination and report as to (1) and (2) above, (3) being mandatory and (1) and (2) being discretionary as to such pre-sentence examinations.

Upon your reply, we will arrange for such further proceedings as are then indicated.

Yours truly,
Ronald Renaldson

STATE OF WISCONSIN
CIRCUIT COURT
RACINE COUNTY

THE STATE OF WISCONSIN, Plaintiff, v JOHN ARTHUR WILSON, 23456A Defendant.	Case No. C-1741 CHARGE: Sodomy Case No. C-1743 CHARGE: Circulation of Obscene Books etc. Case No. C-1744 CHARGE: Taking indecent liberties with minor.

Testimony taken and proceedings had on the trial of the above entitled cases, consolidated for the purposes of trial, before the

HONORABLE RONALD RENALDSON,

Judge of Circuit Court, Branch No. 10 of Racine County, on October 30, 1956, November 5, 1956, and January 10, 1957.

APPEARANCES:

WILLIAM J. McCARTHY, District Attorney, by
CHARLES WILBUR, Assistant District Attorney,
On behalf of the State of Wisconsin;
HAROLD J. McGARRETY,
On behalf of the Defendant;
THE DEFENDANT PRESENT IN PERSON.

(Thereupon the following proceedings were had and testimony taken:)

MR. McGARRETY: In view of the court's recent ruling, in connection with the case just presented on the motion, the defendant now asks leave to withdraw his pleas of not guilty in the remaining three cases and to substitute therefor pleas of guilty in respect to each one of those cases bearing C1741, C1743 and C1744.

MR. WILBUR: His plea of not guilty stands with respect to 1742, is that right, counsel?

MR. McGARRETY: Yes.

THE COURT: And you have discussed and explained to your client what the consequences might be of the changing of the plea to guilty in the other three cases and he understands that? Do you, Mr. Wilson?

THE DEFENDANT: Yes.

THE COURT: All right, we'll see. We'll take a little proof on those three.

MR. WILBUR: We'll offer proof in connection with those. However, does the court accept the change of plea?

THE COURT: I think so; yes.

MR. WILBUR: Now, in view of that situation, the State will now move to dismiss the one action in which the plea is not guilty, namely, 1742. That is a sodomy charge which allegedly occurred in April of 1955. And now we would like to offer testimony briefly, your honor, in connection with the three offenses to which the defendant has entered his pleas of guilty; and we ask that the matters be consolidated for the purpose of taking such testimony.

HARRY DANIELS, called as a witness on behalf of the State, having been first duly sworn, was examined and testified as follows:

Q You have previously testified in connection with this matter. You are a detective of the Racine Police Department?

A Yes, sir.

Q Now will you briefly give the facts in connection with each, commencing with Case 1741, which involves Ralph Arnet, age eight.

A That case we questioned Ralph Arnet and he admitted to us that Mr. Wilson did play with the subject's privates and kiss them.

Q Now what are the facts briefly in connection with the matter that we just had the motion on. I believe there is sufficient in the record now regarding the background but what generally is the nature of those photos and do you have them here?

A Yes, sir. The photos are of boys in the nude and there are some photos of Mr. Wilson commiting sodomy on one of the boys. Here; I got them up here.

Q And about how many are there?

A About eighteen.

Q Did the defendant admit that he had taken all these photos?

A Yes, sir.

MR. WILBUR: We ask that these eighteen photos be admitted as one exhibit--State's Exhibit 1--and we ask the court to examine them.

THE COURT: They will be received. Just leave it here and I will look at them during the noon hour.

MR. WILBUR:

Q Now, officer, in connection with Case 1744, involving one Milton Miller, will you please state those facts?

A Mr. Wilson touched Milton's privates; put his hands inside of his pants and rubbed his privates.

Q And that occurred where?

A In Mr. Wilson's home.
Q Was that an isolated incident or had that occurred on more than one occasion?
A I think that was the first time.
Q Now, officer, will you briefly give the court the background situation to this entire picture? You have given a resumé regarding each of the particular offenses but I think that the court should be advised of the background here. What was this defendant's activities; how did this come to the attention of the police, and how extensive?
A Well it come to our attention when Milton Miller--We received a call to go to Number 3 District Station. We were up there. Milton and his grandmother were there. Milton explained to us that he went over to this Mr. Wilson's home to read some comic books one day and that Mr. Wilson wanted to take some pictures--in the nude--and that he always touched his legs and ran his hand inside his pants and touched his privates; and he refused to let Mr. Wilson take pictures; and then told us that Mr. Wilson had told him that his brother Dean had let him take pictures of Dean in the nude, and he could show him that there wouldn't be anything wrong by it; and Milton ran home and told his grandmother that we got to call the police. He said Mr. Wilson--he didn't say Mr. Wilson--but he said "the man across the street showed me pictures of Dean, naked, and that he also tried to take pictures of me."
Q And the defendant was interrogated regarding his activities, was he not?
A Yes, sir.
Q What did he have to say about it?
A He admitted--Well, he broke down and said--He admitted the whole thing and that he had caused enough trouble and with his wife's condition he wanted to get it over with.

MR. WILBUR: Cross-examination.
MR. McGARRETY: No cross-examination.
MR. WILBUR: The State rests.

[Mr. McGarrety then offered two witnesses to Wilson's good reputation.]

THE COURT: We will find and determine then that after the trial as we have had it and upon the pleas of guilty, that the defendant is guilty of the offenses charged respectively in the informations in Cases 1741, 1743 and 1744; and that that which involves section 351.41--that is, Case No. 1744, taking indecent liberties with a minor--being an offense which makes it mandatory for the court to commit him to the Department of Public Welfare for presentence social, physical and mental examination, the court will commit him to that department for such examination and report to the court, to be done through the local office of the Department of Public Welfare; and as to the other two, in 1741 and 1743, the court will have to inquire of the department whether it has adequate facilities for making the examination and, if so, if it is willing to accept the commitment as to those cases and, if so, then the commitment will be made in that regard.

But the mandatory commitment will take place right off, except the bail will be continued. He will be permitted to be out on bail as long as no other offense of any kind is committed by him.

Then I think they have about sixty days in which to make their report. And then when the report comes in, we can then handle the sentencing or whatever is to be done at that time in all three, I think.

[On November 5th, the court having received notice that the Department of Public Welfare was willing to examine Wilson for all three acts, Judge Renaldson extended the commitment for examination to include all three charges. The notice also appears in the file but is omitted here.]

Racine, Wisconsin
Thursday, January 10, 1957
2:00 o'clock P.M.

The matter came on for hearing pursuant to notice by the court. Both counsel present. Defendant present in person.

THE COURT: We have here today the three cases involving John Arthur Wilson.

On November 5, 1956, he was committed to the local office of the Department of Public Welfare of Wisconsin for presentence social, physical and mental examination, pursuant to section 340.485, Wisconsin Statutes, 1953, which section is applicable because the offenses occurred prior to July 1, 1956.

The report of that department, dated December 28, 1956, recommends specialized treatment. The report is addressed to me as judge of this branch of the Circuit Court and the body of the reporting letter reads as follows:

"The above man was committed to the Wisconsin State Department of Public Welfare by your court for presentence social, physical and mental examinations under the provisions of the Sexual Deviate Statute. The required pre-sentence social and other examinations having been completed, we are herewith forwarding them to you for your further action.

"The Department of Public Welfare, acting under the provisions of Section 340.485 of the Wisconsin Statutes, submits herewith its findings in the case of John Arthur Wilson. Based upon a study of this individual as revealed in the aforementioned pre-sentence social, physical and mental examinations and with particular emphasis on the results of the Multiphasic Personality and the Rorschach Tests employed by the psychologists and the psychiatric appraisal, the Department of Public Welfare now finds:

"That John Arthur Wilson is in need of specialized treatment for his mental aberrations and recommends that the present case be disposed of under the terms of subsection (6) of Section 340.485 of the Wisconsin Statutes. The Sex Deviate Treatment Facility located at the Wisconsin State Prison is recommended as the initial place of treatment for this individual.

"This letter is being transmitted to the court through our Racine District Supervisor, Mr. Royal Gordon, who will arrange to have the case placed on the calendar, and also for the appearance of Mr. Wilson in the court at the proper time. Yours very truly, Wilbur J. Schmidt, Director, State Department of Public Welfare."

So, with that recommendation under the statute, the court has no choice but that it has to apply that section.

Accordingly, the defendant will be and is committed concurrently in each action to the Department of Public Welfare of Wisconsin, pursuant to subsection (6) of section 340.485 of the Wisconsin Statutes, 1953, and that the sheriff convey him to the Wisconsin State Prison at Waupun as the initial place of treatment for him.

MR. McGARRETY: Would the court consider a sentence at this time and a stay, proposing any rigid terms that the court has in mind in such a situation, so that he will know that he has had his chance, if he is to get it, and will have the chance to work it out in his own way, knowing that shall he fall from grace for one moment, that he has signed his own admissionship to that institution that the court has referred to? He would know then that he is sentenced and he would know that, come any contingency, he would be on the way to that place that he is trying to avoid so much.

THE COURT: Well, from the record that we had during the trial, with all those pictures that were here, that great accumulation of them, and all of the things that were brought out in the evidence at that time, the court feels that that might not be the best thing to do, not only for his good but also for the public good, and that it be best that we follow the recommendation of the department.

[A Face Sheet similar to the first document reproduced from the file summarized under the printed headings the information contained in the following presentence investigation.]

PRE-SENTENCE INVESTIGATION

Submitted by:
Edward C. Hoffman
11/15/56

JOHN ARTHUR WILSON (Sex Deviate) Born: 6/27/22
756 East Maple
Racine, Wisconsin (Division 2-5203)

Section: 351.40
351.38 (1)
351.41

OFFENSE: Sodomy
Circulation of Obscene Pictures, Books
Taking Indecent Liberties with Male Minors

DISPOSITION: Probation 60 days to SDPW, for Pre-Sentence Study, under Sex Deviate Statute 340.485, 10/30/56 and 11/5/56, Circuit Court Racine County, Judge Ronald Renaldson.

COURT HISTORY

PRESENT OFFENSE: John Arthur Wilson, 34, white, native of Fond du Lac, Wisconsin, married, the father of two daughters, and previously committed to WSP, 11/14/50, on a Sodomy conviction, was arrested 5/27/56 at 4 P.M. at 817 Sprague, Racine (then his residence), for the possession of obscene photos, and for indecent liberties taken with a male minor. Wilson admitted taking the photos, and admitted indecent liberties with several juvenile boys during the past seven and eight months. The boys are identified in the police showup as Bruce Trice, Randy Polk, age 13, a nephew of Wilson by marriage, and Michael Banks, age 10. Most of these boys with whom Wilson has had contact live in Essex in the vicinity of the Boy Scout group which is active at Assumption on N. Hackett and Franistan. Polk lives with his parents at Elmhurst, Illinois.

Neither the court testimony nor the police showup in this case revealed the details of the operation of Wilson. Wilson has been known back in his early twenties at which time he attended Northwestern University as having been ostracized from the Boy Scouts of America for similar activities at a camp in northern Wisconsin. The present situation is best told by Detective

Harry Daniels of the Racine Detective Bureau. Wilson associated himself with Boy Scouts from Assumption parish (referred to as Assumption of Borden), the church which occupies the Borden Dairy Building at North Hackett and Franistan. He approached the parents of these boys a number of them six or seven in number, took decent pictures of these boys and presented them to the parents for sale. He later on took indecent pictures of their boys in his home. One of the boys whose picture he took was Dean Miller about 12 or 14, a kid who normally lives at Caroline, Wisconsin. Dean posed in the nude for Wilson. Later on Wilson attempted to take the picture of Milton Miller, age 7, a brother of Dean who is living at the home of his grandmother, a neighbor of Wilson at Wilson's former address, 817 Sprague. After taking decent pictures of these boys, Wilson would have them strip, pose as Indians, and then lead up to the indecent pictures. Numerous of these pictures showing young boys between the ages of 7 and 14 in the nude, exhibiting their genitalia, showing two or more boys in sodomous positions, are in the possession of the property room at the Racine Police Department. Included also is a picture of an adult nude woman. Wilson later educated these young boys in the practice of sodomy.

On 5/26/56, he fondled the private parts of Milton Miller. When Milton complained to his grandma this led to the arrest of Wilson. On 10/30/56, Wilson pleaded guilty in the case that is catalogued under the Circuit Court Docket #C-1744. This charge, Taking Indecent Liberties with Male Minors, is listed under State Statute Section 351.41.

On 10/30/56 also Wilson pleaded guilty to taking the penis of Ralph Arnet, age 8, in his mouth. This occurred about 5/26/56. And is supposed to have occurred once. This offense catalogued under Circuit Court Docket #C-1741 is a violation of State Statute Section 351.40; and Wilson was likewise committed to the SDPW for pre-sentence consultation under 340.485 (2).

The third plea of guilty under Docket #C-1743, the Possession of Obscene Pictures, is a violation of Section 351.38 (1).

Another count originally listed under Docket #C-1742, Sodomy, occurring back in April 1955 was dismissed as being old, and the charges probably included under the Sodomy charge and conviction that is listed under #C-1741.

DEFENDANT'S STATEMENT: Wilson states: "I touched the bare seat of a seven year old boy with my hand in my home at 817 Sprague, Racine, on 5/26/56. The boy had introduced himself the day before and had stopped at my home after accompanying me to a natatorium that morning. Here portraits were taken. The offense occurred during a brief period of rough-housing following this. The boy then went home for dinner. After dinner he again came over and wanted me to take him rowing. After staying for about an hour he left." During this time the defendant was busy with other activities and devoted no time to the boy.

Wilson's statement is the greatest understatement this agent has ever read. He hesitates to discuss Sodomy, the possession and taking of indecent pictures, and other improper liberties which he will admit under definite questioning.

In this respect, Wilson doesn't make himself a good subject for treatment. He is probably more likely a good subject for definite treatment only after he makes a full confession and full admission of what he has done.

PRIOR RECORD: Wilson is known in the Racine Police Department, Bureau of Identification as #54607. He has no FBI record. He was convicted on four counts of Sodomy in Municipal Court Racine County before Judge Stephens, 11/14/50, committed to WSP for three terms of 1-4 years concurrent, and one term of 1-4 years consecutive, and released to parole supervision 8/1/53.

At that time his supervising officer discussed the possibility of psychiatric help and Wilson stated he was informed by the WSP psychiatrist that such a program was not needed at this time and he could very well navigate on his own. Wilson gave evidence of a strong ego-centric personality in which he attempted to convey to his supervising officer the impression that he was quite capable of taking care of himself and required no assistance from this department. It is significant to note that two different parole agents detected this in the nature of Wilson.

Another agent reported "He finds it difficult to accept his status as a parolee and a definite 'professional approach' must be maintained with him if control is to be maintained by the supervising agent in interviews." The case closing summary in this case had this to say: "There have been no known indications of reoccurrence of the sexual problem which existed previously. John has never insisted that all of his problems were solved, but he maintains that he has developed better self control and the known record substantiates his contention. He has satisfying employment which challenges his abilities and has a promising future. He is all wrapped up in his family and the prospects for continued good adjustment seem good at this point."

FAMILY BACKGROUND

It is significant at this point to note that John Wilson is hesitant about discussing his family background. Interviews with John are difficult. He is ashamed of himself and the stigma of his offense and the past offense bears heavily on his thinking. It is thought that he intends to respond honestly to questions. As a matter of fact, however, he withholds information, is rather brief, and yet would like the interviewer to feel that he is highly cooperative.

John is the second son of two children born to Gerald T. Wilson and Florence Varee Wilson of 76 Bluebell Lane, Sussex, Wisconsin. The father born 7/19/1890 at Fond du Lac, Wisconsin, was the son of Patrick and Mary Leary Wilson. He is of Irish ancestry. He claims to have finished high school in three years and then was graduated from Horlock College, Prairie du Chien, Wisconsin. Horlock College is really a high school. After completing college, Gerald Wilson returned to Fond du Lac where he worked as a superintendent of a typewriter concern. He was married in 1916 and in 1925 moved his family to Racine where he was employed as an inspector for Rambler Motors. In 1927 he accepted a job with the Waukesha Motors as a foreman in the production department and has been so engaged for probably the past 27 years. Records indicate he has no criminal history, is not a drinking man, is a good father, a good provider and has always adhered to the precepts of the Catholic faith.

Florence Varee Wilson, the mother, was born at Fond du Lac, Wisconsin 5/19/98. She is one of five children born to A. C. and Ophelia Varee. She is of French-Canadian ancestry, a Catholic by birth, has a ninth grade education, and worked as a telephone operator prior to her marriage to Gerald Thomas Wilson at Fond du Lac, Wisconsin on 9/17/16. She is a person of seemingly average intelligence, neat, responsible, of apparent good judgment, keeps a good home, and has always held the interest and welfare of her two sons in high regard.

John has no sisters. His one brother is Gerald Thomas Wilson, Jr., born 4/4/17 at Fond du Lac, Wisconsin. Gerald, Jr. is a high school graduate and has completed one year at Northwestern University. He is married to Margaret More, has a son, was employed in the service department of the Sussex Motors for a number of years and still resides at 250 Goodlen Street, Sussex, Wisconsin. He has no criminal history and his domestic relationships appear to be good. Gerald Wilson, Jr. now has two children, and for the past three years has been employed by the Frump Freight Company in Sussex where he sells service of that company.

PERSONAL HISTORY

John Arthur Wilson known also as Jack Wilson was born at Fond du Lac, Wisconsin, 6/27/22. He is the second of two sons born to Gerald and Florence Wilson. He is of apparent good stock, always had a good home wherein there was ample of the physical necessities and affection, and appears to be outwardly proud of his heritage. At an early age he developed what is commonly called St. Vitus' Dance and missed grade school for one year because of this affliction. While a grade school student he had the experience of oral sodomy with a cousin and continued the practice intermittently in grade and high school. His parents have indicated in the past that there were no early outward indications of this type of behavior and they were reluctant to believe their son's admissions. John recently admits these early experiences although he describes them as mutual masturbation rather than as oral sodomy. He does admit however in his early twenties while a student at Northwestern University and working in a northern Wisconsin Boy Scout camp, that he was ostracized from the Boy Scouts of America for life for practicing oral sodomy on one or more little fellows. John is reluctant to admit in detail these episodes or the actual number of times and the actual number of personalities with which he has been involved.

HABITS: John has had hetero-sexual experiences as is attested to by the fact that he is the father of two little daughters. He has been committing homo-sexual acts on young boys however for many years and is probably a confirmed homo-sexual. In this regard, treatment is thought by some to be foolhardy because of the extent of the practice and the length of the habit of the defendant and his practices. John admits to being a social drinker but never to excess. He smokes a pipe and cigarettes. He has not been known to associate with groups of ill repute and he denies rather emphatically that he has had any contact with any of the known or unknown homo-sexual groups in Racine. This is thought to be open to question.

HEALTH: John is a robust individual, weighing 170 pounds, being 5' 9" tall. He admits good health throughout his life. He denies any disabilities. He doesn't speak at all of the early St. Vitus' Dance affliction. He has a faint scar on his chin and states he had an accident as a little kid falling from a bike or from a wagon. His wife admits his good health and this is shared by herself and their two little daughters.

EDUCATION: John is rather vague concerning his grade school and high school education. He states he was granted a B.A. in 1948 by Northwestern University at the age of 26. It seems that his education was interrupted by two facilities: (a) Insufficient funds to educate himself earlier and (b) by World War II service. He attended Northwestern University Graduate School in 1949-50 studying in the department of psychology. He attended Racine State Teachers College in 1949-50 also in the department of education, specializing in the education of exceptional children. His teaching experiences have been few and minor according to John. We get the feeling however that John is probably a better teacher than he would admit to, and is reluctant to speak of his teaching experiences because of his exceptional habit.

John is married to a school teacher.

RELIGION: John, the son of Catholic parents, is baptized and confirmed in that faith. He has been a member of the Holy Name Society and the Catholic Order of Foresters. He is married to a Catholic girl and both John and his wife have been active in the Catholic Church since their marriage and before that time as well. John and his wife are practicing Catholics.

MILITARY: John enlisted in the U. S. Navy at Racine on 9/12/42 and served under Serial Number 304-66-66. He advanced from an Apprentice Seaman to Seaman Second Class and later on to Seaman First Class which rating he held at the time of his Honorable Discharge at Great Lakes, Illinois, 1/31/46. He is the recipient of a good conduct award, Presidential Citation with blue star, the Asiatic Pacific Ribbon with one star and the Philippine Liberation Ribbon with one star and World War II Victory medal. His total length of service was three years four months and 19 days and he served about two years overseas in the Pacific Theatre of Operations.

EDUCATION: (additional information) Elsewhere we have learned that John began kindergarten in the public school system at Sussex, Wisconsin, at the age of five. He later transferred to St. Joseph Parochial School where he completed the eighth grade and then completed high school at Sussex in 1940 where he was classified as a good student with high innate intelligence. He entered Racine State Teachers College in September 1940 and studied there until June 1942, his Navy enlistment temporarily halting his academic training. Upon return from service, he entered Milton College, Sussex, for one semester and then entered Northwestern University, September 1946, where he was graduated with a B.A. degree in June 1948. He continued at Northwestern University until September 1949 to work on his Master's degree and then returned to Racine State Teachers College to do special study on handicapped children to gain further education to complete his requirements for his thesis and Master's Degree in this department. The greatest share of his advanced studies have been in psychology and psychological testing and measuring. A transcript of John's credits shows that he scored A in four courses, B in nine courses, and C grades in 10 subjects. He registered a B in another subject and a Satisfactory in still another. He appears to be just above average student.

ECONOMIC: John at one time owned household furniture valued at $3,000. The valuation on this today is probably closer to $2,000. His life is insured as is that of his wife and first child. His wife worked as a music teacher in the Racine County School System and paid off existing debts at the time of his previous commitment. John and his wife own a number of recordings, recording equipment, television and radio equipment, and photographic equipment. John has spent for such equipment far above what his normal salary would allow. John and his wife never have owned their own home. She desires very much to own her home. She states at this point that she would give up home ownership in order to be able to afford for psychiatric outpatient for John so that he could help himself somewhat in his affliction.

INDUSTRIAL: John's first and only job as a teacher was that of an instructor in the state grade school at Wellington, Wisconsin. He began that job in September 1950 and quit by his arrest in 1950. He taught less than one semester. His school superintendent stated that he had "high regard for his ability, his professional interest and his enthusiasm." As a matter of fact, in the present court trial two witnesses who know Wilson in business state that he has good character and one of them stated that on the job especially did Wilson have good character.

Until the present offense Wilson had worked for the Racine Resistor Company as office manager. His president, Mr. Wynstein, employed Wilson three years ago in a lesser position. Wilson had worked himself up to a job in which he earned about $350 to $400 a month exclusive of bonuses. Racine Resistor is located at 458 West Main in Racine. Following the present offense over which he lost his job, Wilson caught on with the Metropolitan Steel Casting Company, 4 Minor Street, Racine, as a tagman (general yard labor) in which job he earns $1.47 hourly. He has held this job for almost two months. Wilson is not afraid of hard work. His prior parole history had indicated good, steady, profitable employment. Wilson probably never has had a job up to his mental capacity. He is an intelligent worker and a good worker. His wife, during Wilson's previous incarceration, was employed as a school teacher.

MARITAL: The defendant married Mary Jane Polk, a native of West Lake, at the Holy Assumption Catholic Church in West Lake, 9/3/49, after a nine year courtship that had begun while both were students at Racine State Teachers College. Mary Polk Wilson, born 2/8/23, has lived in Racine all her life. She has a B.S. degree from Racine State Teachers College and has had one year of advance study in music at the Prospect College of Music. She has had successful teaching experience in Highland (two years), at Shelton (two years), at Brookfield (one year) and was still later employed by the Racine County System.

Mrs. Wilson is a very intelligent girl who is doing her best to obtain a full understanding of her husband's problem so that every device possible can be used in his attempt to rehabilitation. The shock of her husband's behavior twice has not dampened her enthusiasm nor her loyalty toward her husband and she steadfastly maintains that she will stick with him through whatever the future has to offer. John and Mary became the parents of a daughter prematurely born 4/5/50. The child lived one day. Mrs. Wilson has had two other miscarriages. Judith Ann, a daughter born 5/17/54, is a normal child as is Janet Marie, born 10/17/55. Mrs. Wilson is an enthusiastic homemaker and apparently a good mother. Family ties have been somewhat strained on both sides because of the defendant's weakness as a sex deviate. The relationship between the defendant and his wife however appears to be good and genuine and we have every reason to believe that Mrs. Wilson will loyally stand behind her husband in this or any future occurrence.

SUMMARY: John Arthur Wilson is a 34 year old white male, married and the father of two little daughters. His wife bore another child that died in infancy, and she had two miscarriages. The defendant states that his sodomous practices have occurred at least recently only at times when his wife was pregnant. This, of course, is rationalization on his part. He has become almost a professional in this business leading up to it gradually and deliberately by the use of photographic equipment as we have related in the details of the present offense. He kids himself regarding his strengths. He overplays not the value of his faith, his religion and the power of his confessor, but he certainly over-emphasizes his sincerity and his efforts in this direction. He not only is reluctant to speak about the details of his offense, he is downright deceptive. He has in the past been very reluctant to use the services of a psychiatrist. Now, that he finds himself once more engrossed in court, he would like, at this point, to consult with Dr. Robbe, a local psychiatrist. He has done so, as a matter of fact. He feels that because of his incarceration in 1950 he might well be imprisoned again, rather than be placed under probation supervision. He is not as well employed as he might be, nor as he has previously been. These two commitments within six years have caused him a downgrading in his job welfare. Wilson is a man of superior intelligence endowment. His IQ approaches 140. Early abnormal sex conduct, beginning possibly at the age of 12 has remained with the defendant through his 34 years of life. A number of people have questioned whether Wilson has sincerely attempted to help himself. His wife more than somewhat blames herself for the husband's condition. She states that she always has been shy, by nature. She states also that she is "a poor listener." She feels that her husband has on numerous occasions attempted to talk to her about his weakness, but that negative responses by her have caused him to clam up. There appears, however, to be no true, real or genuine value to her statements. A professional worker in the case has stated that "the origin of Wilson's deviate behavior lies in the fear of venereal disease during childhood, accentuated and maintained by a fear of impregnation of the female." Another professional opinion is that Wilson might be somewhat helped if his next child were a son, in which situation normal affection for this son would replace this deviate behavior he has exhibited for other young boys. There is still a further professional opinion to the effect that Wilson through his use of camera and photographic equipment, did this deliberately as an answer to his guilt feelings, hoping that he would be detected in his abnormal behavior. In other words, he developed a deliberate desire for apprehension and a yearning for self-punishment.

Wilson was under mental observation, while in the navy in 1943, and again in 1945, but was discharged from hospitals both times as being well. It seems he was hospitalized at the Naval Hospital at San Diego, California. He doesn't readily admit this and denies having had any psychological problem in the navy. Wilson's denials under the pre-sentence investigation, of course, have not helped his cause, nor any preliminary treatment plan.

PLAN: Wilson already has consulted with Dr. Arthur Robbe, a Racine psychiatrist at his office, 43 Illinois Street (OP 7-4623). Wilson already has been referred to and has had a physical examination at Racine County Dispensary. He is scheduled for a psychological examination at the Racine Guidance Clinic on 11/19/56, and once more at the same place for a psychiatric appraisal on 11/28/56. Should he be granted probation and permitted to stay in Racine longer (he has been out on bail of $5,000.00 since his arrest on 5/27/56; and was referred to the SDPD on 10/30/56 for temporary probation in Racine for a 60 day period), he will be expected to continue to reside with his wife and two daughters in the family home, a second floor flat at 756 East Maple, Racine. Community furore has somewhat abated because the victims of Wilson's practices live farther north and west than where his home is situated. He likewise has moved from a previous address at 817 Sprague, Racine, where he was living at the time of these offenses. No further offense has occurred within this investigating officer's knowledge since Wilson's arrest on 5/27/56.

RECOMMENDATION: Unless this agent be misunderstood with reference to some questions he might have asked during the investigation, he, in no wise, has intended at any time to make any recommendation in this case. The Investigating Officer in these pre-sentence sex deviate cases is, as a matter of fact, strongly advised by the Director of the SDPW never to make a recommendation of any kind.

Respectfully submitted,
(Signed) E. G. Hoffman
Area #10

CHRONOLOGICAL HISTORY

11/2/56. INITIAL INTERVIEW: Wilson was at this office this evening at 6 P.M., he having been referred by Judge Ronald Renaldson from Circuit Court Racine County under the Sex Deviate Statute where on 10/30/56 Wilson was convicted of taking improper liberties with a male minor, age 7, a violation of State Statute Section 351.41. Wilson interviewed by Agent Hoffman who prepared a Face Sheet in the case. The client was particularly meager in giving details especially those relating to his family personnel, notably his parents and his brother.

11/5/56. RETURN TO COURT: Wilson was returned to Court today by a Sheriff Deputy on two other charges, namely, Sodomy, a violation of Section 351.40 and Possession of Obscene Pictures, Section 351.38 (1).

Agent Hoffman permitted and even suggested to Wilson that rather than linger around this office this afternoon he report directly to his job at the Metropolitan Steel Casting Company, 4 Minor Street, which he did.

11/7/56. APPOINTMENTS MADE: Wilson notified by phone and later confirmed by letter, dated 11/8/56, that he has the following appointments: 1. Tuesday, 11/13/56,

8 A.M., Racine County Dispensary for a medical examination. 2. Monday, 11/19/56, 9 A.M., Racine County Guidance Clinic, Safety Building, for psychological testing. 3. Wednesday, 11/28/56, 10 A.M., Racine County Guidance Clinic for psychiatric testing. Wilson had no questions about these.

11/13/56. HOME VISIT: Agent Hoffman talked at length this morning with Wilson's wife, Mary Polk Wilson at her home, 756 East Maple, Racine (DIvision 2-2530). The Wilsons have lived here since 8/1/56 they moving from a previous residence where they were living at the time that John was arrested on 5/27/56, 817 Sprague, Racine. Both of these are second floor flats. The rent in both instances is $85. Wilson lived at the Sprague address for seven years before moving recently to the East Maple Street address. Mrs. Wilson was somewhat tense in her relationship with the agent this morning. The agent felt that she underplayed the offenses in these cases, was more aware of the situation than she pretends to be, and is even covering for her husband although this on her part is quite unconscious and probably not at all deliberate. She holds herself somewhat to blame saying that she is a shy person, always has been, and has not been "a particularly good listener to her husband and his troubles."

Later Agent Hoffman talked with Miss Fabian, social worker at MCOD and learned that John had reported there for a medical examination without the benefit of our pre-sentence investigation which was not dictated until 11/16/56.

11/14/56. PORNOGRAPHIC PICTURES: Agent Hoffman with the help of Detective Daniels and Detective Lang of the Racine Vice Squad today looked at part of the pictures in this case. These show one feminine adult posed in the nude which is probably intended as a work of art. They show also 18, 20 or more snapshots probably taken at Wilson's home, of boys whose ages range from 7 to 14, showing the male form in the nude, young males manipulating each other, and even two young males in a reciprocating sodomist position. The agent feels that these pictures strongly argue against probation in this case.

11/15/56. ATTORNEY McGARRETY: Agent Hoffman had telephone contact in this case today with Attorney Harold McGarrety, defense counsel. Mr. McGarrety will be at this office 8:30 tomorrow morning for a more lengthy discussion on the case. As a matter of fact, Mr. McGarrety appeared at this office about 9:45 A.M. after Agent Hoffman had left the office on other business. We are awaiting a return contact with Mr. McGarrety.

11/16/56. DR. ROBBE: Agent Hoffman had phone contact today with the secretary of Dr. Arthur Robbe, psychiatrist, who practices at 43 Illinois Street (OP 7-4623). Agent Hoffman learned that Dr. Robbe definitely has seen Wilson and probably will return for further consultation. Dr. Robbe might return Agent Hoffman's call.

11/15/56. HOME VISIT: Agent Hoffman had an appointment with the client and his wife at this office for 4:30 P.M. today. In an effort to economize on time, and to keep Mrs. Wilson out of the home away from her two little infant daughters for as brief a time as possible, Agent Hoffman made a home visit, picked up Wilson and his wife and took them to a coffee shop a couple of blocks north of their home at which point the agent gathered from Wilson and his wife more information regarding the pre-sentence investigation.

11/16/56. PHYSICAL EXAMINATION: The examination dated 11/13/56 is principally negative in report.

DR. ROBBE: Agent Hoffman had a return call from Dr. Robbe in which Dr. Robbe states that Wilson was referred to the psychiatrist by defense counsel McGarrety for a determination of whether or not Wilson "is treatable through psychotherapy."

11/19/56. GUIDANCE CLINIC: Agent Hoffman at 9:30 A.M. this morning delivered to the Guidance Clinic the pre-sentence investigation and the medical examination in this case. The psychologist was interviewing Wilson this morning and we were probably a day late with this information. We discussed this with Miss Ridings, social worker, at the Guidance Clinic (OP 4-3142 Ext. 007).

11/28/56. CENTRAL OFFICE INQUIRES: Central Office on 11/26/56 inquired of Supervisor Garsh where the medical, the psychological and the psychiatric examinations are in this case. The psychiatric will take place 11/28/56. When Agent Hoffman receives from the Guidance Clinic the psychological and psychiatric investigations, he will send these post haste to Central Office. We should probably have withheld the pre-sentence investigation until we had a complete file to send to Central Office.

12/3/56. ELECTRO-ENCEPHALOGRAM: A call from Dr. Galloway's secretary, Mrs. Schrane, who requests Wilson to report to MCOD tomorrow morning, 7:30 A.M., to undergo an EEG. Agent Hoffman made a HOME VISIT at 5 P.M. this evening, talked to Wilson and his wife and requested that he go to bed late tonight, drink no coffee at suppertime nor at breakfast, get up about 4 A.M. and be very tired when he reports to MCOD at 7:30 Tuesday morning, 12/4/56, for an EEG. Wilson stated that he understood well and we checked this with Mrs. Schrane by phone just before 5 P.M. on 12/3/56.

12/6/56. SECOND EEG: On 12/5/56 Dr. Galloway requested a duplication of the EEG performed on 12/4/56. Wilson by letter being requested to report at MCOD for a second EEG on Tuesday morning, 12/11/56, at 8:00 A.M. Agent Hoffman has duplicated the notice to Wilson by putting through a telephone call to Mrs. Wilson at 11:50 A.M., 12/6/56.

12/21/56. PSYCHIATRIC APPRAISAL: Psychological study and psychiatric appraisal, combined in two pages, in duplicate, forwarded to central office today accompanied by physical examination in duplicate dated 11/13/56.

Phone call to Mr. Wilson's home requests he stand by for return to court on or before 1/2/57, the expiration date of the 60-day study period.

1/11/57. SENTENCED WSP: Agent Hoffman arranged return to court in this case and was present in Judge Renaldson's court on 1/10/57 when Judge Renaldson committed Wilson to WSP as a sex deviate for an indeterminate term.* Central Office was apprised of this in an IDC dictated 1/11/57. Mr. Voelzke, Clerk for Judge Renaldson, is going to send two copies of the court commitment to WSR. He might send an informational copy to Central Office. The agent will continue in this case as long as Wilson is at WSP, he feels that Wilson will make progress at the institution, and despite the police and prior record in this case, the agent feels that prognosis in this case is somewhat good. The agent feels he has been of some assistance with Mrs. Wilson in guiding her to Mr. Woodman, Veterans Worker with the Racine County PWD. It is likely that Mrs. Wilson will obtain employment either as a school teacher in the Music Field or as a social worker, upon the advice of Mr. Woodman.

December 8, 1956

State Department of Public Welfare
Bureau of Probation and Parole
4023 South Oak Street
Racine, Wisconsin

Attention: Mr. E. G. Hoffman

Dear Mr. Hoffman:

Re: John Arthur Wilson

The above named man was referred for pre-sentence study under the sex-deviate statute 340.485. His of-

* The court proceedings appear above at 1375-76.

fense was sodomy, circulation of obscene pictures and books, taking indecent liberties with male minors. Study was completed November 28, 1956.

During psychologic study this man was very cooperative. He did have a need to appear more than just adequate, especially intellectually, and this was obvious in his approach to both the intelligence and projective tests. He elaborated spontaneously including many aspects of the question so that very few questions had to be asked of him. He was anxious and some tests were obviously affected by this. On the Rorschach he gave only one sex response, and he was reluctant to give it. He flushed, threw the card down on the pile and kept looking down. It was obviously very upsetting to him.

The results of the intelligence tests indicate that this is a man of very superior intellect, and the Rorschach bears this out. There was little scatter between subtests except for Digit Span and to some extent, arithmetic. Here anxiety was a prominent factor although the tests are still somewhat above average.

The Rorschach study indicates that very basic in this man is a pervasive, neurotic search for a security-dependency relationship. He depicts women, undoubtedly both his mother and wife, as having a very approachable warm exterior to which he does feel drawn but underneath as being cold and cutting him off, not giving him the understanding and warmth they seem to promise. This also carries over into the sexual sphere. Heterosexuality has its attraction but along with it is the fear of being met rather frigidly. He does have resentment about this but it is not as intense as one might suppose. His relationship with his father has also been a disturbing one. He has never felt quite close to him either. One gains the impression of a striving, dominant, perhaps self-made, strong individual whom this man was supposed to imitate and pattern himself after, which poses another conflict. He does use a facade of aggressive manliness with the intellectualization but this is even a weaker facade as it is foreign to him and he cannot keep it up for long. His dependency-security needs soon tear it down and thus he feels even more inadequate because he cannot be the man he is supposed to be. He is attracted to males and male sexuality which gives him satisfaction which heterosexuality cannot completely provide, but it is not surprising that his relationship with people in general is rather disturbed and that he must keep some sort of distance between himself and others.

This man is not psychotic. He is immature in his psychosexual development and seems fixated at this level. He is in deep conflict between his emotional needs in the sexual area and his intellectual understanding of his situation. When around young boys, with whom he seems to identify, his needs increase and his behavior evidences a compulsive trend. He is not able to control this. Sexual adjustment in his home contributes to his withdrawing from the family, as his wife has had several pregnancies with two living children. His religion forbids contraception and he has not the strengths to practice abstinence. His conflicts extend to his wife's health and to his ability to provide financially. So far he cannot face or solve these problems. He undoubtedly will repeat his behavior and it is believed that the menopause will be an especially difficult period for him. He is a sexual deviate.

This patient gives a history of blackouts, which could be on an emotional basis. Therefore, it was considered desirable to check this and appointments have been arranged for him at the Racine County Dispensary for December 4 and December 11, 1956. It may be possible to reduce his chaotic emotional reactions by means of medication and thus make him less the pawn of his immature emotional reactions. Should he remain in the community, psychiatric care should be helpful. However, under any condition he is a community risk.

Very truly yours,
Sara L. Galloway, M.D.
Director

P.S. The results of both electroencephalographic studies have been received. The findings are that both tests are within normal limits.

[Omitted are a memo of transmittal of the psychiatric and presentence investigation reports, the recommendation of specialized treatment quoted by the court above, and notice to the central office of the commitment under the Sex Crimes Act.

A new Face Sheet dated January 17th is omitted. It repeats information found in the presentence investigation report. A form lists as authorized correspondents members of Wilson's family and a friend; it expressly excludes the two boys he was convicted of abusing.]

ADMISSION INVESTIGATION

CONFIDENTIAL

Submitted by:
E. G. Hoffman,
2/4/57

WILSON, John Arthur-WSP-35124-S Born: 6/27/22
756 East Maple
Racine, Wisconsin

OFFENSE: Improper Liberties with a Minor; Sodomy; Possession of Obscene Photos, Sections 351.41, 351.40, 351.38 (1).

DISPOSITION: WSP, As a Sex Deviate, Under the Indeterminate Term Provided in Section 340.485 (6), Circuit Court, Racine County, 1/10/57, Judge Ronald Renaldson.

COURT HISTORY

PRESENT OFFENSE: The reader is immediately referred to the Pre-Sentence Investigation in this case performed 11/15/56 by Agent Hoffman. John Arthur Wilson, 34, white, a native of Fond du Lac, Wisconsin, married and father of two daughters, and previously committed to WSP 11/14/50 on a Sodomy conviction also at that time was returned to court 1/10/57, and sentenced to WSP by Judge Renaldson for an indeterminate time.

PROGNOSIS: Agent Hoffman interviewed Wilson at WSP on 1/17/57 for a brief period as Wilson sat on a bench in the hall waiting room of the Social Service Department at WSP, and despite the fact that Wilson had been at this institution before, and probably knows the routine much better than this agent, he was more or less apprehensive about the forthcoming interview. He was warm in his greeting to the agent, made no particular statement to the officer, and no particular request. He is taking his commitment rather hard despite the fact that both he and his wife expected it to fall, and he is at least a two time loser on this particular offense. The agent reads possible future success in this, however. We predict that the combination of psychotherapy at WSP plus a greater understanding on the part of the inmate's wife, should assist more than somewhat in his rehabilitation.

WIFE ATTITUDE: Mrs. Wilson on the latest contact by this agent was thinking rather seriously of self-employment. She certainly is employable and has considerable to offer. The stumbling block is this: She must obtain a full-time baby-sitter to take care of the children in the family home during her absence. In any event, Mrs. Wilson is awaiting the return of her husband to the family setting, and should at that time be able to bolster her husband's confidence more than somewhat, and certainly more than she has been successful in doing in the past.

CORRESPONDENCE: It is recommended that John Wilson be permitted to correspond with and have visitations with his wife and with his parents and with his brother. Mrs. Wilson has also recommended correspondence between her husband, the inmate, and Robert Willis, 34, a friend, on the basis that Mr. and Mrs. Willis are social friends of long standing with the Wilson family. I suggest we follow her recommendation in the case.

We also learn rather belatedly that Mrs. John Wilson is working in a secretarial position at Harris Smith in Racine. Her children are being cared for by her sister.

Respectfully submitted,
E. G. Hoffman, Area #10

CHRONOLOGICAL HISTORY

2/4/57. WIFE EMPLOYED: In contact with Mrs. Wilson, we learn that she is employed at Harris Smith in a clerical-secretarial position and that her children are being cared for by her sister.

7/19/57. INTERVIEW AT WSP: The Panel Progress Report in this case dated 3/22/57 indicated that Wilson is a food accounts clerk in the store and canteen. He was on the job two months at that time and was exceptionally accurate and dependable a worker. He is very intelligent and learns his job quickly. He is pleasant and courteous at all times. He is receiving extra good time. He attends church services regularly, participates in the sacraments, and is a member of the choir. In school activities he is enrolled in a bookkeeping course by self-study. He is a real sharp individual who has completed this course probably with the greatest of ease of anyone who has ever taken it and is an exceptionally good and well-qualified clerk.

John indicated all this to us today in the interview. We are at this point interested in a letter from M. J. Coogan, Administrative Assistant, Division of Corrections to Attorney Harold McGarrety, defense counsel, dated 6/14/57.

Wilson states he is working in the front business office and likes his job very well. His wife is still employed at Harris Smith. Recently, her second floor flat had a fire and the adjustment is being made through a friend, Mr. Willis. Mrs. Wilson, it seems, is looking for other living quarters.

7/27/57. WIFE CONTACT: Mrs. Wilson called Agent Hoffman at the agent's home on this Saturday morning. She intends to move and has begun looking for a second floor flat. Agent Hoffman gave her some advice in regard to flat seeking. Both she and John were rather disturbed because he was "turned down by the Special Review Board at his recent hearing." Wilson and his wife, especially his wife, have underplayed the gravity of the offense in this situation, and the agent never has permitted either of these people to go uncorrected in their thinking on this point. Because John is intelligent, because he is doing a good job of working at the institution, Mrs. Wilson feels that he should be released to parole supervision. In nowise can she see the thinking of the Board in that it is best to keep John at the institution until more progress has been made for he already has been twice committed for similar offenses, and apparently learned less from the first experience than he might have. Today's interview was very pleasant--both from the agent's side and Mrs. Wilson's.

11/7/57. INTERVIEW AT WSP: John was his old academic self today. As a matter of fact, he is still employed as a clerk-typist in the main business office. He has been on this job about 6 months and he does a good job. He is conscientious and very capable and relates well to others. He attends church regularly and is a regular weekly communicant. He states that his wife has left her job at Harris Smith and now is teaching in the public school system of Sussex County. She and their two daughters are residing in a second floor flat at 3241 Jefferson Street. During the fire at her previous flat, she suffered nothing financially. The fire is mentioned previously in the running record, with the emphasis on the entry of 7/19/57. Mrs. Wilson still takes her two infant daughters to the home of her married sister in West Lake. He goes before the Special Review Board about April, 1958, he having appeared before this Board in July, 1956, at which time he received a "Defer 9 months." John looked good and spoke well today. He was less embarrassed and ashamed than we have found him during previous visitations.

June 14, 1957

Mr. Harold McGarrety, Attorney
207 East Michigan Street
Racine, Wisconsin

Re: John Arthur Wilson #35124-S

Dear Mr. McGarrety:

I had a chance to talk with Mr. Wilson's psychiatrist this morning. Your client is as you said, a rather seriously disturbed individual. His response to treatment at the institution has not been too fruitful. Whether or not his reaction to the out-patient therapy, proposed by Dr. Robbe, is something that Dr. Dryer is weighing right now and which will ultimately, pretty much rest in the hands of the Special Review Board when it sees him on July 16th.

The fact that your client's job with the construction company and the arrangement for treatment under Dr. Robbe, whom we know to be competent in this particular area, was passed on to Dr. Dryer this morning.

Thanking you for the many professional and gracious services that you have rendered to the Department and to me personally, I am

Very sincerely yours,
Matt J. Coogan
Administrative Assistant
DIVISION OF CORRECTIONS

March 22, 1957
RE: WILSON, John #35124

FROM: Social Service Department
TO: John C. Burke, Warden

PANEL PROGRESS REPORT: Store and Canteen: Food Accounts Clerk

On the job about 2 months. Exceptionally accurate and dependable. This man is very intelligent and learns his job quickly. He is pleasant and courteous at all times. EGT.

Church: Attends church services regularly. Participates in the Sacraments. Member of choir. Fr. Jacques.

School: Is enrolled in a bookkeeping course by cell study. He is a real sharp individual; has completed this course probably with the greatest of ease of anyone who has ever taken it. An exceptionally good and well qualified clerk.

PANEL MEMBERS: Defor, Ralston

As received by ROBERT SMOLLET,
Social Worker

Date: June 20, 1957

PAROLE PLANNING INFORMATION SHEET

[Formal information and routine placement plan are omitted.]

Supplemental Information: This subject had made a satisfactory institutional adjustment and is assigned to the store and canteen where he is working as a clerk. He is described as exceptionally accurate and dependable; and is pleasant and courteous at all times. He attends church services regularly and is enrolled in school studying a bookkeeping course. The school asserts that he has completed the bookkeeping course with ease. He has taken courses in accounting and considerable amounts of college arith. He is without any mis-conduct reports. Wilson asserts that he has been seeing Dr. Dryer about twice per month and asserts that he is making good progress. His enthusiasm and sincerity appear to be superficial.

Present Status Psychiatrically
June 25, 1957

WILSON, John WSP 35124-S

Examiner's Appraisal:

This man, a bisexual, has gained considerable insight and has been very cooperative in therapy. I have a letter from Mr. Coogan dated 14 June, 1957 a copy of which has been sent to the Special Review Board members. This seems to indicate that Wilson is assured of a job, and there is some suggestion that Dr. Arthur Robbe is willing to take him in therapy in case he is paroled.

The last sentence of Dr. Galloway's report on Wilson leads me to believe that she would not have been disappointed if Wilson had been placed on probation with psychotherapy.

Wilson conducted himself in a socially acceptable way for months following his release from Prison in August 1953. During that hitch he had little psychotherapy, and none following release. I think he should be paroled at this time providing he will continue psychotherapy.

R. Dryer, M.D.
Psychiatrist

June 28, 1957
RE: WILSON, John #35124

PROGRESS REPORT
FROM: Social Service Department

<u>Main Building and Business Office Workers:</u>

Clerk-Typist

On the job since April 1957. This man does a good job and is a dependable worker. He relates well to others. EGT.

Church: Regular attendance; weekly sacraments; choir; reads religious books and literature. Fr. Jacques.

School: Has been enrolled in Bookkeeping. Is a bookkeeper; understands this material very well and has plugged along with it. Actually he is only reviewing his bookkeeping and keeping in touch with it rather than studying it from scratch. He gives us no trouble in the school at all; he is quite an intelligent man and has been here a considerable number of times before.

PANEL MEMBERS: Praedel, Rollard, Bordman, Billie, Mrs. Grubschmidt, Verhage

As received by JAMES F. PLEICER,
Social Worker

July 8, 1957

State Department of Public Welfare
401 East Datton Street
Madison, Wisconsin

Att'n: Mr. Matt J. Coogan
Re: John Arthur Wilson—#35124-S

Dear Mr. Coogan:

On July 16, 1957, the Special Review Board may consider Mr. Wilson's request for parole for out-patient therapy. He and his wife are most desirous that I write you in his behalf.

[A sketch of the case and Wilson's background are omitted.]

Wilson has made it clear that he has a sincere desire for the help that he needs. Both he and his wife fully appreciate the rehabilitation task before them. Their family life is tranquil and his wife will cooperate, guide and supervise the necessary effort. The need is for the opportunity to straighten himself out and his present predicament only tends to leave him in a state of bitterness and despair.

Of course the law imposes confinement for his conduct but the real solution and the final one will have to come from within himself and from those medical experts both at Central State Hospital and from the outside. We have been informed that the caseload for psychiatrists at Central State Hospital is far beyond what the staff can handle. However, this is only true

because the State Hospital has been unable to fill an authorization for additional psychiatrists to receive the existing burden.

Wilson has seen Dr. Arthur Robbe of Racine, who sizes him up as being well above the average intelligence and one who exhibits a disorder of character and personality. Dr. Robbe feels that out-patient therapy alone could not be expected to effect control of Wilson's condition. On the other hand, institutional placement, while providing control for the time, will not be helpful in the long run therapy of the man's condition. Dr. Robbe believes that a kind of supervision and control that would assure that no further instances of Wilson's symptoms could occur while keeping him in his home setting and working would be most desirable and would be an essential prerequisite of psychotherapy.

Wilson's earnings and family financial help are available for the purpose of securing out-patient therapy. As you know, rehabilitation under his present predicament requires almost superhuman effort on his part, even though the doctors at Central State Hospital stand ready to help in every way possible. Their load is plenty heavy. Out-patient therapy would have the effect of removing Wilson from contacts with those he should avoid and would tend to speed progress toward rehabilitation. If his application merits the Board's approval, it will save the State much expense and trouble, save a man for himself and his family.

Wilson has been frank with the Court, its attaches and officers. He has maintained good conduct from date of his present trouble to the present time and he has been at liberty for about nine months out of that time.

Wilson's last employer is ready to put him to work at his old job. Dr. Robbe has agreed to give the Out-Patient Therapy. Money is available to carry out the program. Wilson himself is all for the Sex Deviate Program and is most willing to cooperate to attain rehabilitation. Medical counsellors have successfully guided men in the business world and in other walks of life to success in cases involving similar problems.

We know that the Board will look Wilson over thoroughly and if his situation deserves favorable action, both Wilson and his wife will fully appreciate such action.

I thank you.

Respectfully,
Harold McGarrety

WISCONSIN
STATE DEPARTMENT OF PUBLIC WELFARE
DIVISION OF CORRECTIONS

HEARING: July 1957

INSTITUTION: Wisconsin State Prison

PAROLE DECISION

Institution No.: 35124-S
Date: 7/16/57

Name of Case: WILSON, John A.
Official Action: Defer 9 months

Comments: Very intelligent, college educated man with one prior criminal experience. A rationalizer with considerable experience and book learning. He is a "two timer."

October 11, 1957
RE: WILSON, John #35124

PROGRESS REPORT
FROM: Social Service Department

Main Office and Business Office: Clerk-Typist

On the job about 6 months and does a good job. He is conscientious and very capable and relates well to others. EGT.

Church: Regular attendance and weekly sacraments. Fr. Jacques.

PANEL MEMBERS: Praedel, Bordman, Billie, Mrs. Grubschmidt, Verhage

As received by JAMES F. PLEICER,
Social Worker

February 14, 1958
RE: WILSON, John 35124

PROGRESS REPORT
FROM: Social Service Department

Sales and Business Office: Clerk-Typist

On the job about 9 months. Does a good job. Willing and conscientious. Relates satisfactorily to others. EGT.

Church: Regular attendance; weekly sacraments. Fr. Jacques.

PANEL MEMBER: Verhage

As received by JAMES F. PLEICER,
Social Worker

Present Status Psychiatrically
March 3, 1958

WILSON, John WSP 35124-S

Examiner's Appraisal:

On June 24, 1957, I wrote a report regarding this man for the Special Review Board. At that time I recommended parole for him providing he will continue psychotherapy. At that time the Special Review Board deferred him for nine months with the following comments: "Very intelligent, college educated man with one prior criminal experience. A rationalizer with considerable experience and booklearning. He is a 'two-timer'."

As to his being a "two-timer": He served a criminal sentence prior to the time of the sex deviate statute, he received no psychotherapy during this period and none following release from prison. He has been cooperative in therapy and has gained considerable insight, as I reported previously, and I strongly recommend parole at this time.

R. B. Dryer, M.D.
Psychiatrist

Date: 3/10/58

PAROLE PLANNING INFORMATION SHEET

[Formal information is omitted.]

Supplemental Information: John continues to make a satisfactory institutional adjustment. He is assigned as a clerk typist in the business office and is described by his immediate superiors as a conscientious and capable individual who does a good job and relates well to others. He attends church and school regularly and has completed Bookkeeping and College Arithmetic courses with ease. He is without a misconduct report. John

asserts that he has been seeing Dr. Dryer approximately once per month and expresses satisfaction with his progress in therapy.

WISCONSIN
STATE DEPARTMENT OF PUBLIC WELFARE
DIVISION OF CORRECTIONS

HEARING: April 1958

INSTITUTION: Wisconsin State Prison

PAROLE DECISION

Institution No.: 35124-S
Date: 4/18/58

Name of Case: WILSON, John A.
Official Action: Grant

Comments: A verbalizer. I am not too favorably impressed here. Dr. Meister.

[A form requesting release and a signed parole agreement dated May 7th and May 13th are omitted. Similar forms appear above.]

CHRONOLOGICAL HISTORY

5/7/58. REQUEST FOR RELEASE: Dictated today to be effective 5/14/58. Wilson will return to the home of his wife, a second floor flat at 3241 Jefferson Street, Racine. We do not know about his cash assets, excepting it is indicated he will probably have only gate money. We have suggested he be given $10.00 cash at the institution, the balance of his account to be made payable by bank check to the client only, but the check mailed to Agent Hoffman in Racine.

Agent Hoffman was active in the pre-sentence study and sentencing of this client, and he notes an opinion of defense counsel, Harold McGarrety, 6/14/57, in which was brought in the possibility of out-patient psychotherapy with Dr. Robbe, psychiatrist in Racine. Under parole supervision we are going to stress to the client and to his wife the need and necessity for continued psychotherapy in this case.

5/15/58. INITIAL INTERVIEW: John was released from WSP, a sex deviate, yesterday. His wife, Mary Jane, told this agent by phone 5/9/58 that she could not be present at the initial interview because of her obligations as a schoolteacher, drove to the prison, drove her husband home directly, they had lunch, and John telephoned the agent about 2:30 P.M.

John reported at 9:00 A.M. today by appointment. He had cash assets of $10.00, and Agent Hoffman presented him with a bank check in the amount of $52.39, representing the balance in his account at WSP. John has been under supervision before to quite possibly two other agents at least. He was instructed to report every second Friday. He seemed to be properly apologetic for not reporting at this office on 5/14/58.

PROBLEM: John is 36, white, married, and the father of 2 infant daughters. He was convicted of sodomy in Racine in 1950, committed to WSP for 3 terms of 1 to 4 years concurrent, and 1 term of 1 to 4 years consecutive, and released to parole supervision 8/1/53. At that time his supervising officer discussed the possibility of psychiatric help, and Wilson stated he was informed by the WSP psychiatrist that such a program was not needed at this time, and he could very well navigate on his own. Wilson gave evidence of a strong egocentric personality in which he attempted to convey to his supervising officer that he was quite capable of taking care of himself and required no assistance from this department. It is significant to note that two different parole agents detected this in the nature of Wilson, and now Agent Hoffman is experiencing the same reaction.

On 6/24/57 Dr. Dryer, psychiatrist at WSP, in a report stated: "I recommend parole for him provided he will continue psychotherapy." Wilson takes issue with this statement.

John states that at the time of departure from the institution he talked this over with Dr. Dryer who stated that psychotherapy would not be necessary for at least a two months' period. John is to determine the necessity for out-patient psychotherapy. If his treatment as an out-patient is necessary, John is to see Dr. Dryer at his office the first time, and then Mrs. Wilson is to go to Dr. Dryer for the next appointment, and so thereafter alternately. John states that he gives his impressions "as a psychologist." Agent Hoffman and Supervisor Mathews already have conferred on this matter, and we are intending to drop an IDC to Supervisor Vlim for discussion with Mr. Coogan, Secretary of the Special Review Board.

PLAN: John is living with his wife and two daughters at 3241 Jefferson Street, Racine. He has a lead for a job at Redwood Tire Company, and hopes to follow through on this about 5/19/58. We hope to have profitable interviews as often as possible with Mrs. Wilson and would that these interviews take place at the office.

As long as she is teaching school, however, it is going to be difficult unless we do this part of the work in the evenings. John's education and training in the field of psychology have given him personal weapons with which to attempt self-diagnosis. John's reaction at this time is somewhat akin to that during a previous release period when, on 8/1/53, he stated: "Institutional psychiatrist informed him that such a program was not needed at this time, and that he could very well navigate on his own if he gave some thought to his own problem."

PROGNOSIS: This is guarded at this time. John will report to this office by appointment 6/13/58, and in the meantime, we hope to have the benefit of a home visit in this case.

HOME VISIT: 5/19/58. Agent Hoffman saw John in his second floor flat at 3:00 P.M. today. He was at home alone and had the house fairly clean. His wife is still teaching traveling among 17 schools in Sussex County in which she teaches music. She has applied for a job teaching in the summer, and John feels she is probably going to succeed in this venture. Their two children are placed each day with a maternal aunt, and Mrs. Wilson continues to pick them up and take them home at the end of her teaching day.

John is finding employment difficult to get. He has been out of the institution 8 days, and has failed to place in any of the companies in which he previously has worked--he feels because the work is just not there. John is pretty honest and academic about this, and we certainly take him on his word on this matter. Through a social friend he hopes to obtain employment at the Redwood Tire Company on Racine's east side. In this job John would work as "a computer." He is going to put in his application at WSES, and we discussed that phase today. Meanwhile, he is not hurting particularly financially because of his wife's employment. He also has a possibility of getting employment through his brother, Gerald Wilson, of Sussex, who is pretty well set up in employment. His friend referred to previously who might be instrumental in placing John at Redwood Tire Company is Robert Willis, about 36 years old. At this moment, John is simply getting his feet on the ground at home, and getting reacquainted with his wife, Mary Jane, and this is going to be part of the early success picture. He has not to date called upon Attorney Harold McGarrety, but he might do so at a later date. He sees no point in this time in taking psychotherapy under Dr. Robbe, although Agent Hoffman certainly disagrees with this. I suggested to John very strongly before leaving his home that he attempt to get his wife, Mary Jane, into the office so I could speak with her definitely about John's problems in order to forestall and prevent a recurrence of what happened back in 1953 following his release from the institution. It is singular that John is starting out with the same trend of thought under parole supervision today as he had on 8/1/53 when he was supervised by another agent.

6/9/58. EMPLOYMENT INTERVIEW: Agent Hoffman had a contact at this office Friday night, 6:30 o'clock, 6/6/58, in which Mr. Rick Rasputin, owner and president of the Rasputin Feed Store in St. Francis, 43100 Plank Road (ST 2-5453) and residence phone (ST 2-8388), wanted some information regarding John Wilson. He interviewed John the first time, and wonders regarding the gravity of the present offense. Agent Hoffman reported at Mr. Rasputin's office at 8:00 A.M. Monday, 6/9/58, and discussed the content of the file with Mr. Rasputin. Mr. Rasputin is a sympathetic and understanding gentleman, and the likelihood is he will hire.

6/13/58. EMPLOYMENT MATERIALIZES: John Wilson reported at 7:00 P.M. today. He states that he has spent one day on the job at Rasputin Bros. in St. Francis, and although it is quite early to tell, he apparently likes his job at present. He earns $75.00 a week. This appears to be almost as good a paying job as John Wilson has ever had, a topic of which however the client has reluctance to discuss. It is our guess that John rarely has had a job paying him up to a figure that he felt he was worth. This has led to a shallow confidence in himself.

Agent Hoffman in an IDC to Central Office, attention of Mr. Coogan, dated 6/11/58, has requested a clarification in regard to the position of Dr. Dryer at this time regarding psychiatric authority. As late as 6/16/58 Agent Hoffman has had no report from Central Office. John Wilson is to report to this office by appointment 7/18/58.

INTRA-DIVISION COMMUNICATION

Date: 6/11/58

From: Agent E. G. Hoffman
Class and No.: WSP 35124-S

To: A. W. Vlim
Case of: WILSON, John Arthur
Subject: Out-patient Psychotherapy.

REFERENCE: Occasionally the Field Agent is professionally criticized in the supervision of cases with a background in sex deviation for not insisting upon psychotherapy in the parole and probation situation. Because this has occurred before, we would like clarification in this present case from Central Office.

Dr. Dryer in his examiner's appraisal dated 3/3/58 received in Racine 5/6/58, states: "On 6/24/57 I wrote a report regarding this man for the Special Review Board. At that time I recommended parole for him provided he will continue psychotherapy. He has been cooperative in therapy and has gained considerable insight as I reported previously, and I strongly recommend parole at this time."

In the Pre-sentence Study in Racine about 2/4/57, defense counsel, Mr. Harold McGarrety (also 11/15/56), gave to the Sentencing Court the possibility of probation under the provision Wilson procure and continue psychotherapy under Dr. Robbe in Racine.

The reader at this point is referred to the Running Record, page #5, under the date 5/15/58, Initial Interview, and sequitor in which Wilson takes issue at this time regarding the principal and the need for psychotherapy at this time and in which we say on page #6, second paragraph: "John states that at the time of departure from the institution, he talked this over with Dr. Dryer, who stated that psychotherapy would not be necessary for at least two months. John is to determine the necessity for out-patient psychotherapy. If this treatment as an out-patient is necessary, John is to see Dr. Dryer at his office for the first time, and then Mrs. Wilson is to go to see Dr. Dryer for the next appointment, and so thereafter alternately."

Agent Hoffman's experience at this point is similar to the experience undergone by another agent previously in this case as witnessed by page #4 of the Running Record, dated 8/1/53, headed "Personal Office," second paragraph.

Might we have at this point from Mr. Coogan, please, a clarification of Dr. Dryer's position at this time?

Respectfully submitted,
Edward G. Hoffman
Area #10

MEMORANDUM

June 16, 1958

TO: Field Services (3)
A. W. Vlim
Richard Garsh

ATTENTION: E. G. Hoffman

FROM: Matt J. Coogan, Secretary, Special Review Board

SUBJECT: Out-Patient Psychotherapy for Sex Deviate Parolees

I can well understand Ed Hoffman's confusion with respect to John A. Wilson's status in re O-P psychotherapy.

The general rule is that parolees under the Sex Crimes Law would not have been granted parole had there been a need for O-P therapy. Occasionally one slips by the Special Review Board and the Director but that is the exception to established criteria.

Since O-P psychotherapy was not recommended by the Special Review Board in the Wilson case none is required as a condition of his parole. If O-P therapy was required there would be a notation to that effect on the Parole Board transcript.

The present case (Wilson) brings up a case work situation wherein the agent can encourage but not order O-P treatment against the will of the client. The choice of therapists belongs to the client. He may choose Dr. Robbe, Dr. Dryer or any other recognized specialist in the field of mental illness or he may elect to work with no psychiatrist. He has done that in the past with grave consequences to himself.

My personal, unedited notes taken at the time of the hearing on Wilson read "Immature--hopes his wife will carry the ball for him. Some doubt (Drs. Glover and Meister) that he will seek or keep a therapeutic relationship. Therapy not ordered. Long standing and calculating offender. Admits that parole at this time would be an injustice to others who are 1st offenders. Decision swayed back and forth as to parole or non-parole."

CHRONOLOGICAL HISTORY

6/30/58. UNEMPLOYED AGAIN: A telephone call from Mr. Wilson who states that he no longer is working at the Rasputin Bros. in St. Francis, that he worked for 2 weeks and 2 days and apparently was the victim of personal dissatisfaction from Miss Polly Cramer, a 30 year old employee at that company, with whom he had to work, and with whom it is apparently difficult to work. John is not in financial straits, however, because his wife has begun employment for the Racine School System, working in the Recreation Department for the summer of 1958. Mr. Rasputin is displeased that he had to let Mr. Wilson go, and has referred Wilson to another job as a bookkeeper at the National Tea in St. Francis, where Wilson will be interviewed by Mr. O'Neil and Mr. Piccura.

7/11/58. PROGRESS REPORT: [Summary of events since release is omitted.]

8/8/58. OFFICE INTERVIEW: John reported this afternoon. He and the agent had quite a thought and quite possibly a very fruitful one. John is still unemployed, has no immediate prospect excepting those long since discussed in the running record, but he states that his wife, Mary Jane, finishes her summer employment within two weeks and at that point she can stay home with the children and permit him the freedom of the outside so that he might be able to round up work of some type. He is still very desirous of teaching mathematics, particularly at the high school or college level, and we are going to work on this because of something we feel deeply. It is our conviction that most of John's difficulties stem from the fact that he never has been basically employed in something which would give him prestige and a fair financial return. We feel if we can help him to locate in a mathematic teaching job it may provide for John a big lift. Meanwhile, John has been speaking of the possibility of his wife and he going into some type of missionary work. We hope to pick up more of this in the future. John will return to this office by appointment 9/12/58, and it is our desire in the near future to speak with John's wife, either at this office or at the family home.

9/12/58. POSSIBLE TEACHER APPOINTMENT: John reported at 9:00 A.M. today. He and Agent Hoffman spent a great deal of time in the office in discussing rather deeply the possibility of John's acquiring a job as a teacher. We feel that a good job, quite possibly a good teacher appointment, is the thing that is likely to give John personal prestige and confidence, and thus enable him to save John from himself, against another repetition of sex offenses. We have genuine plans of going all out in this regard. John appears to be in favor of our approach and appears to be ready to work with us on this project under our direction. He will return to this office by appointment 10/10/58.

9/17/58. TEACHING POSSIBILITY: John and the agent have practically agreed that a part of John's big trouble psychologically, even in the content of the offense, is the fact that John never has gotten his teeth into a teaching job. He is now going at this hammer and tongs, and at Agent Hoffman's home 9/19/58 John and the agent conferred with Mr. Given, University professor at Mount Mary, who suggested John not give up on the teaching idea, but that he might be a more attractive prospect if he came to the teaching field from college rather than from private industry. John is either short academically a degree or a certificate, and is going to return to school to obtain both. In the meantime he might be able to obtain substitute teaching work to assist himself financially, and he might be able to procure a scholarship with the agent's assistance. We expect to bring in on this problem also Father Punda, principal at Dominican High School, Racine.

10/10/58. OFFICE INTERVIEW: John is dynamically interested in going after a teaching job. He and Agent Hoffman at this office today for an hour or more discussed avenues of approach, such as: a. teaching on a substitute basis; b. return to college for degree and certificate; c. obtaining a college scholarship for about a year's study. Agent Hoffman discussed with John many names and places and then John informed the agent that he has returned to a course at Marquette College at night, and has begun to teach in the Confraternity of Christian Doctrine on a non-pay basis. John will return to this office by appointment 11/14/58.

10/14/58. ATTENDS CHICAGO FUNERAL: John appeared at Agent Hoffman's home noon, Saturday afternoon, 10/-11/58, and obtained an emergency permission to go to Chicago for one day, 10/13/58, to serve as pallbearer at the funeral of his favorite uncle, the late Mr. B. J. Haggarty, who was buried from the Weiss Funeral Home, 7650 North Moreland Drive, Chicago. Jack, his wife, and children, expected to stop at least temporarily at the Haggarty home, 2647 North Howard Street, Chicago, and did so. Jack phoned this morning stating that he returned from Chicago last night. Agent Hoffman consulted with Supervisor Thwackum this morning on this case, and agreed that it would be sheer work, and nothing gained, to inform Central Office by IDC today of this event.

11/9/58. SEEKS TEACHING JOB: On this Sunday John phoned Agent Hoffman at the agent's home, stating that Pius XI High School had advertised for a mathematics instructor, John felt he was capable, he wanted to apply for the job, he did by phone, and the principal of the school declined to interview John because he learned from John over the phone that John had no permanent teacher's certificate. John sought Agent Hoffman's help in arranging a personal interview. We stated that we would look into it, did so, and found that Pius XI High School had hired another man.

11/14/58. OFFICE INTERVIEW: John reported this morning. His wife presently is teaching school, and John is taking care of the children in the home, and he insists that his wife, Mary Jane, is contented with this arrangement. John is taking a couple of courses at Marquette College and is teaching Catechism in evening classes at St. Catherine's Church. We suggested to John that he make known to the reverend pastor the fact of his parole status, and he states that he was about to do so. We still feel rather strongly that John is capable of teaching school, and that he might even do so just as soon as he finds a suitable post and a school authority in the form of a principal who will accept him as a teacher, in spite of his type of offense. John and the agent had quite a lengthy talk on this matter today, far too involved and far too lengthy to chronicle at this stage. John will return 12/12/58. He seems to be getting along well and appears to be without either personal or family tension.

12/12/58. OFFICE INTERVIEW: John appeared at 9:30 A.M. this morning. He is still unemployed, although he is making some headway. He hopes to enroll in the evening school either at Mount Mary or elsewhere after the New Year and in the new or second semester. His wife, who is teaching school, is going to have a long Christmas vacation and Jack, who has been caring for the home and children, expects to be able to get out at that time and look for jobs on the basis both of having more time and having use of the car. He has taken into his confidence Father Gascow, Curate at St. Catherine's Church, for whom he is teaching a catechetical class. He is likewise studying in this field at Marquette College and he is still optimistic and we think reasonably so, of obtaining a school-teaching job possibly on a substitute basis at first through the medium of these volunteer actions as well as by the grace of great understanding on the part of certain school people and we are encouraging John in his thinking. We are well aware, of course, of criticism that might befall either the client or the agent on this venture. John and the agent once more discussed many other employment avenues and John is picking up the confidence that we think he will need in order to be able to help himself in the future. He will return to this office by appointment 1/9/59.

1/9/59. PROGRESS REPORT: John reported today. John has been attending a teaching course at Marquette College and has been teaching in the field of catechism at his church, St. Catherine's, on East Wenter Street. He recently had an appointment with Father Joseph Bolling, director of the Family Life Program, and this will probably lead to an appointment with Monsignor Rummel, of the Catholic School System, and the possibility of employment as a teacher somewhere in the system, all things going well. This will be a great step for John. He is highly cooperative as a parolee, and appears to be genuinely interested in helping his condition. He is taking people into confidence, and we expect much more progress in this case before the term expiration date of 10/10/60. John will return to this office by appointment 2/13/59.

2/13/59. WIFE PREGNANT: John reported this morning. He states that his wife, Mary Jane, is pregnant, has left her job as a school-teacher, and expects to deliver in March. At present the family is without income. John is attempting to connect in employment in the industrial field, and is now making contacts through his brother, his brother-in-law, and just about everybody else that he knows in an attempt to get employment for the family's living income. We referred John today to Mr. Willard Woodman, supervisor of Veterans' intake at Racine County DPW, in order that he might receive immediate public assistance. John is still interested in teaching, and is making the rounds attempting to catch on, despite the fact that he might readily be rejected for teaching on the basis that he has been convicted as a sex deviate. He is thinking of teaching mathematics at Marquette Prep School, and he has a friend there in the person of Coach Anderson. He attempted to get an appointment with Monsignor Rummel of the Catholic School System during the past week, and was rejected in this effort. He will return to this office by appointment 3/13/59.

2/16/59. TEACHING INTERVIEW: Agent Hoffman in a letter to John today informed the client that he has an appointment with Monsignor Rummel at the Catholic School office, North 4th and East Galena, Saturday morning, 2/21/59, at 10:15 A.M.

2/23/59. TEACHING POSSIBILITIES: Agent Hoffman was active in this case 2/20/59, and again today with certain officials of the Catholic School System who seem to be favorably impressed by the prospect that John might be able to teach in a Catholic school this September of 1959. Agent Hoffman has conferred with John on this matter, and the agent and John are attempting to correct all our joint resources in this regard.

2/26/59. CLIENT ENCOURAGED: John called Agent Hoffman at the agent's home this evening, and reported that he has been offered 2 different teaching jobs for the September 1959 period. We congratulated John for his good luck, but we reminded him that this does not pay off until his salary begins coming in. We have urged John to check through on his credits, his degree, and otherwise to make himself academically ready for the possibility of such an appointment.

3/2/59. HOME VISIT: Early this morning Agent Hoffman was in contact with John and his wife, Mary Jane, in the family home. The agent has tried to encourage Mrs.

Wilson to assume a more positive attitude toward the probability of John's teaching in the fall as moral support for John, and Mrs. Wilson has concurred in our thinking on this matter. Agent Hoffman in the meantime suggested to John he look for a job in private industry to keep himself and the family going until the fall. Meanwhile, we have suggested that in this time of need (his wife is not teaching and is expecting to deliver her 3rd child momentarily) that John apply for public assistance. Neither John nor his wife appear to have immediate anxiety, however.

3/12/59. NO ACTION: Agent Hoffman has made additional contacts with Catholic School personnel and has learned that no action either favorable or unfavorable has been taken on John, and we have had no additional word from John on his teaching prospects in the fall of 1959.

3/13/59. OFFICE INTERVIEW: John reported today. He is still unemployed. His wife's third child is 3 weeks late, and Mrs. Wilson's physician is going to induce labor in 2 or 3 more days. John is concerned about this. John recently had a favorable interview with Mr. Seymour, Employment Manager at Jones Engineering on West Lincoln Boulevard, and it seems Mr. Seymour was very hesitant about hiring John because of the low pay scale, stating that the job was not satisfactory for a man of John's talents. Mr. Seymour decided to hire a woman in this job, despite the fact that he was dissatisfied with the turn-over in this particular job. Agent Hoffman has suggested that we might in our next contact in that neighborhood call upon Mr. Seymour and see whether or not we might be instrumental in procuring employment for John at Jones Engineering. As late as 3/18/59 we had no word from John on whether or not his wife had given birth. John will return to this office by appointment 4/10/59.

4/9/59. CLIENT IS SUSPECT: Phone call from Det. Cherney, RPD, who would like to clear John Wilson as a suspect in the slaying of the little Wagner boy the past week-end. Agent Hoffman returned the call to Det. Cherney and supplied him with additional information, not only on this case, but on two other cases. We later on spoke with Det. Cherney on this matter Saturday morning, 4/11/59, as we met him on the 7th floor of the Boston Store at 10:00 A.M. By that time we had a fair idea that John Wilson had been cleared in that Agent Hoffman and John discussed the matter on 4/10/59 as is recounted in the next paragraph.

4/10/59. OFFICE INTERVIEW: John reported this morning and states that his third daughter, Jean Therese, was born 4/2/59. Mother and child are at home and doing well. John states that three uniformed police officers, including one sergeant, spoke to him at his residence on Tuesday, 4/7/59, and apparently cleared him of any connection in the slaying of the Wagner boy during the past week-end. John and his wife are obtaining financial help from relatives on both sides and it is unlikely that John and his wife are going to apply for public assistance at this time. John's mother presently is facing surgery in Sussex and although he has no problem in this connection, he does have some anxiety. Agent Hoffman and the client spoke about employment in private industry in that John has virtually been unemployed since his release to parole supervision 5/14/-58, nearly a year ago. His wife has been teaching school and she has been the family bread winner. John states that he owns and is driving a blue and white Plymouth Station Wagon and we suggested that he bring us the title and produce driver's license when he reports to this office on 5/8/59.

4/22/59. IN CUSTODY: Mrs. Wilson phoned Agent Hoffman's residence at 11:00 P.M. today and informed us that John was arrested.

At the Vice Squad Agent Hoffman spoke with Officer Thelen and learned that John, who is known in the RPDBofI as No. 54607, was arrested at 10:30 P.M. 4/22/59 at his residence, 3241 Jefferson Street, Racine, on the complaint of Mr. Fred E. Lacriman, an adult male, 3229 Jefferson Street, 2 doors away, acting for his six-year-old son, Edward, in which the charge is sex perversion by mouth and possession of obscene pictures. Wilson admits that on Tuesday, 3/17/59, at 7:00 P.M. to 9:30 P.M. he took the boy's penis in his mouth while disrobing Edward to put him to bed, acting in the role of a baby sitter. Exchange baby sitting between the Wilson and Lacriman homes is not unknown. Again on Tuesday, 4/14/59 between 5:15 P.M. and 6:30 P.M. (Wilson admits) he repeated the act. Edward Lacriman, age 6, is sometimes called Craig or Greg. Mrs. Wilson blames herself for permitting John to take Edward home from the Wilson home after Mr. & Mrs. Wilson had baby sat for Edward. She feels that had she taken Edward home, John would not have been placed in the occasion of the offense. Apparently Edward Lacriman's two sisters were not offended.

6/8/59. JAIL INTERVIEW: Agent Hoffman spoke with John unexpectedly today at the Racine County Jail, at which time John was waiting on the bench in the Jail office to speak with Lt. Lynch, the jailer, in which John wanted to inquire into the regulations of religious practices in jail. John let us believe that he was interested only in an academic question, but from the sheriff's deputy we learned that John had a complaint, not that he was permitted to confess to his priest on Saturday, but that he was complaining that he did not have the opportunity of receiving Holy Communion on Sunday.

During the interview he became fairly arrogant with the agent. Our thesis to John which he apparently disliked was this: Rather than check up on the shortcomings of a deputy or the jailer or the practices of religious privileges granted at jail; rather than check on these, check on your own shortcomings and offenses against small boys. John disliked this very much, and it was at this point that he became arrogant.

7/3/59. COURT DISPOSITION: John appeared in Circuit Court before Judge Swanson today and was found guilty and was committed to the SDPW under the Sex Deviate Statute. Central Office informed of this by IDC 7/10/59. Case History Review, dictated 4/27/59 brought up to date and dispatched to CO 7/10/59.

WISCONSIN
STATE DEPARTMENT OF PUBLIC WELFARE
DIVISION OF CORRECTIONS
REQUEST FOR DETENTION

Date: 4/22/59

To: Sheriff of Racine County

Re: WILSON, John
Type of Case: WSP 35124-S

Dear Sir:

Please hold in custody the above-named for the State Department of Public Welfare, Bureau of Probation and Parole, until further instructions from the undersigned or a duly authorized representative of the Department.

Respectfully,
By: J. R. Omar
State Probation-Parole Agent

STATE OF WISCONSIN
MUNICIPAL COURT
RACINE COUNTY

State of Wisconsin, Plaintiff v John Arthur Wilson, Defendant	F-2015 Committed to State Department of Public Welfare

May 4, 1959: Before the
Hon. HUBERT J. STEPHENS
Municipal Judge, presiding
(Arraignment only)

Trial before
JUDGE SWANSON
as hereinafter indicated

CHARGE: Indecent behavior with a child (two counts)

APPEARANCES: CHARLES WILBUR, Special Assistant District Attorney for the State
HAROLD J. McGARRETY, for Defendant
DEFENDANT present in court.

[John Arthur Wilson pleaded not guilty to two charges of indecent behavior with a child. In a trial to the court, he was found guilty. He was committed to the Department of Public Welfare and sent to Wisconsin State Prison at Waupun for want of any evidence to contradict the damning testimony. The court found him guilty.

After this, it came to light that the defendant had admitted his offense to his parole agent, E. G. Hoffman. Mr. Hoffman was called as a witness and his testimony regarding the defendant's confession put in the record.

Mr. McGarrety urged that the defendant be allowed to remain free and take psychiatric treatment as an outpatient. He said that the defendant could receive better treatment in this way than in Waupun where there was a shortage of psychiatric help.

Mr. Stilk, for the State, urged that Mr. Wilson had to be committed for the protection of society from this repeated offender.

The Court felt that this was an aggravated situation in which the interests of society demanded the defendant's incarceration.]

[A new Face Sheet and list of authorized correspondents, including family and one friend and excluding by name the boys involved in each of his crimes, are omitted.]

PRE-SENTENCE INVESTIGATION

CONFIDENTIAL

WILSON, John Arthur
3241 Jefferson Street
Racine, Wisconsin
(PA 3-1477)

WSP X-35124-S
Born: 6/27/22

Submitted by:
Edward G. Hoffman
Area #10-Racine
7/30/59

OFFENSE: Indecedent behavior with a child, 2 counts, Section 944.11 (2) Wis. Stats.

DISPOSITION: Referred to SDPW for pre-sentence sex deviate study 7/3/59 Municipal Court, Racine County, under Section 959.15 (1), Judge F. X. Swanson presiding.

COURT HISTORY

PRESENT OFFENSE: John Arthur Wilson, 37, white, native of Fond du Lac, Wisconsin, married, the father of three daughters, and previously committed to WSP 11/14/50 (sodomy conviction), and committed a second time under the Sex Deviate Statute 1/10/57 (involving sodomy among other offenses on small teen-age boys), was arrested at his residence in Racine 11:00 P.M. 4/28/59 for indecent behavior and oral sodomy on the person of six-year-old Craig Lacriman, who lived two doors away at 3229 Jefferson Street, Racine. The boy's father, Fred Lacriman, an adult male, was the complainant. Wilson admitted to Agent Hoffman in custody at the Racine County Jail that on Tuesday evening 7:00 P.M. 3/17/59, after he had acted as a baby-sitter for the little Lacriman boy, he took the lad home and while disrobing Craig for bed, he took the boy's penis in his mouth. Exchange baby-sitting between the Wilson and Lacriman families was fairly common. Again on Tuesday, 4/14/59 between 5:15 and 6:30 P.M. (Wilson repeats) he repeated the act.

VICTIM: Craig Lacriman is from a middle-class Racine family, and was born 2/19/53. He attends kindergarten and is a bright little fellow. His father hesitated to make the matter known to the police, and confided to his wife and friends that he would rather just move out of the neighborhood and never bring charges against Mr. Wilson. It seems that he signed a complaint against Wilson only after he knew that Wilson was under supervision for like previous offenses.

OTHER VICTIMS: Agent Hoffman in a visit to the Wilson home on 4/27/59 spoke with John's wife, Mary Jane, who had in her possession at least three photographs in the nude of another young man whom she identified as Dale Ubricht, about 8, who lived in the Wilson neighborhood. John later at the County Jail identified Dale as Joey Ubricht. John was not prosecuted on this matter, and it was never made a part of the court testimony.

MODUS OPERANDI: John Wilson in his adult life has been known for four series of sodomous acts and acts of taking pictures of small nude boys in which many boys have been victimized in each series. His police record does not show the first of these which occurred prior to 1950, at which time Wilson was a Boy Scout leader. His second occurrence came in the month of June 1950, in which he involved himself with one or more young teenage boys, and for which he was committed to WSP for 3 terms of 1 to 4 years concurrent, and 1 to 4 years consecutive. He was recommitted as a sex deviate 1/10/57 for improper liberties with a minor, sodomy, possession of obscene photos, and involvement with at least 4 boys ages 10 to 13, and others as young as 7 and 8. In this venture he approached the parents of a number of boys, members of the Boy Scouts at St. Pius Parish, 2506 Wauwatosa Avenue, Essex, Wisconsin, took DECENT pictures of these boys and presented them to the parents for sale. He later on took INDECENT pictures of the boys in Wilson's home. One of the boys at this time was Randy Polk, age 13, a nephew of Wilson by marriage, who lived with his parents at Elmhurst, Illinois. Wilson was advised at that time to search his files and to destroy all such pictures and in order to keep himself out of the occasion of future like occurrences, to rid himself of his camera equipment. Both he and his wife consented at that time, thought it was a good idea, but never did so.

In the present case we once more note that Wilson has used his own personal photographic equipment. Despite the fact that these events have included many boys as high in number as 12 to 20, the picture taking has occurred in Wilson's home, Mrs. Wilson has at all times steadfastly denied any knowledge of such occurrences in her home.

INMATE'S STATEMENT: "On 4/7/59 I was picked up in Racine for extensive questioning concerning the Ben Wagner murder. I was cleared on that, but through this questioning, it was revealed that I took indecent liberties with Craig Lacriman (6) on 3/17/59 and 4/14/59. The complaint was brought by his parents. I pled not guilty because the charges as presented were not true and to the point. I admit my guilt to indecent liberties, but nothing else."

Wilson's statement is a great understatement, and he wholly and completely omits at WSP his involvement with Dale or Joey Ubricht and nude pictures which have been seen by Agent Hoffman and have been seen by Mrs. Wilson and the presence of which Wilson himself agreed he had taken.

[The remainder of the presentence investigation, dealing with Wilson's prior record, supervision history, family background, and personal history is duplicative.]

Respectfully submitted,
Edward G. Hoffman
Probation and Parole Agent
Division of Corrections

CASE HISTORY REVIEW

Name: WILSON, John Arthur No. 35124-S
Birthdate: 6/27/22
Action Recommended: REVOCATION OF PAROLE

Present address: Racine County Jail—NOT AVAILABLE—faces trial

If violation, give effective date: 3/17/59

Recommendation submitted for the following reasons:

1. Aforesaid admits two new acts of sexual perversion by mouth.
2. Charged with indecedent liberties with a male minor, 2 counts (Section 944.11 (2)); committed to SDPW 7/3/59 for 60 day study under Section 959.15 (1).

Date: 4/27/59 Submitted by: Edward G. Hoffman
Area No.: 10

Administrative Action: Revocation of parole is recommended on the basis of the reasons enumerated above and with the approval of Mr. Coogan, Secretary of the Sex Deviate Review Board.

Delmar Huebner
Chief of Field Services

Date: 8/13/59 By: J. J. Boorman
Probation and Parole Services

THE STATE OF WISCONSIN BEFORE THE STATE DEPARTMENT OF PUBLIC WELFARE

IN THE CASE OF:
John Arthur Wilson WSP 35124-S } ORDER REVOKING PAROLE

IT APPEARING that JOHN ARTHUR WILSON, hereinafter referred to as the aforesaid, was on the 30th day of October, 1956, convicted of the offenses of Improper Liberties with a Minor, Sodomy, and Possession of Obscene Photos in violation of Sections 351.41, 351.40, and 351.38 (1) of the Statutes of the State of Wisconsin in the Circuit Court of Racine County and was committed to the State Department of Public Welfare under Section 340.485 (959.15) for pre-sentence, social, physical and mental examination and the aforesaid was returned to court on January 10, 1957, for disposition under Section 340.485 (6) after a finding by the Department that treatment of the aforesaid's mental and physical aberrations was recommended and the aforesaid then was duly committed to the Department by the Circuit Court of Racine County for an indeterminate period of treatment and was received at the treatment facility on January 11, 1957, and the aforesaid was released on parole on May 14, 1958, in accordance with the provisions of Section 340.485 (10) of the Wisconsin Statutes;

IT FURTHER APPEARING in the reports submitted by the Division of Corrections that the aforesaid has not conducted himself in accordance with the rules and regulations of the State Department of Public Welfare with reference to persons placed on parole in that the aforesaid has violated said rules by the following:

1. Aforesaid admits two new acts of sexual perversion by mouth.
2. Charged with indecent liberties with a male minor, two counts (Section 944.11 (2)); committed to State Department of Public Welfare July 3, 1959 for sixty day study under Section 959.15 (1).

IT IS NOW ORDERED that in accordance with the provisions of Section 340.485 (959.15) of the Statutes the parole of the aforesaid be and hereby is revoked with the effective date of violation being March 17, 1959;

IT IS FURTHER ORDERED THAT the aforesaid be taken into custody and conveyed to the Wisconsin State Prison and that the Warden of said institution is hereby authorized and directed to receive the aforesaid and there keep him until discharged pursuant to law.

STATE DEPARTMENT OF PUBLIC WELFARE

[A form notified the prison that Wilson's parole was revoked on August 19th. A form from the prison acknowledged that Wilson reentered the prison on July 6th for a 60-day diagnostic examination based on the new sex offenses.]

ADMISSION INVESTIGATION SUPPLEMENT

CONFIDENTIAL

Submitted by:
Edward G. Hoffman
Area #10-Racine
11/9/59

WILSON, John Arthur WSP 35,124-S
3241 Jefferson Street Born 6/27/22
Racine, Wisconsin

OFFENSE: Indecent behavior with child, 2 counts, Section 944.11 (2) Wis. Stats.

DISPOSITION: WSP Indeterminate term under Section 959.-15(6) Wis. Sex Deviate Statute, 9/23/59, Municipal Court Racine County, Judge Francis X. Swanson.

WIFE'S CURRENT SITUATION: The reader is referred to pre-sentence investigation in this case by Agent Hoffman under the date of 7/30/59.

Mrs. John Wilson (Mary Jane) is living at the same address with her three infant daughters, and is teaching music among several schools in the Sussex County School System. She has an older woman, about 60, as a housekeeper, Mrs. Krumenaddier, who is caring for the children during the daylight hours.

Mrs. Wilson has never been cooperative in this office. We wrote her under the date of 10/9/59 to meet with us in this office at 9:00 A.M. on 10/14/59 to discuss her present situation. She declined in a telephone call to the agent's home to meet with us under the pressure of school activities. We wrote again on 10/26/59 suggesting she meet with us at 7:00 o'clock Friday evening, 11/6/59. Again she declined to meet with us by saying that she had to get home to take care of the children. Through the conduct of two pre-sentence investigations, first in 1956, later in 1959, she declined to appear at this office. Agent Hoffman met with her and Mr. Wilson in 1956 at a restaurant nearby their home in order to gather pre-sentence sex deviate data without having to subject the children in the home to any emotionalism. During a home visit on 4/27/59 Mrs. Wilson showed Agent Hoffman at least 3 photographic shots in the nude of another young man whom she identified as Dale Ubricht, age 8. At this time we suggested that she surrender these pictures to a representative of the Racine Vice Squad, RPD, and she stated that she would do so. Mr. Wilson now informs us that his wife burned these pictures. Mr. Wilson also states that his wife gave his camera equipment (used to take lewd and lascivious photos) to his friend, Bob Willis, for purposes of sale.

Mrs. Wilson deeply holds herself guilty for her husband's offenses. She states that he has committed these offenses during her periods of pregnancy (and this is somewhat true). She feels strongly that after she has reached her menopause John will no longer be subjected to acts of homo-sexuality.

CORRESPONDENTS: No objection is taken to the names of those listed on the sheet received at this office 11/3/59. All but the last name listed (Robert L. Willis) are family members. John Wilson in an interview with Agent Hoffman at WSP on 11/5/59 states that he does not know where Robert Willis is now living, and that he has not seen him for a year or more.

Respectfully submitted,
Edward G. Hoffman
Probation and Parole Agent
Division of Corrections

CHRONOLOGICAL HISTORY

John Wilson at WSP 11/5/59, and the content of that interview is reported in a Supplement to the Admission Investigation dictated today. Agent Hoffman also has had telephone contact with Mrs. Wilson as recently as 11/7/59.

1/18/61. TRANSFER SUMMARY: Mrs. Mary J. Wilson, the wife of the inmate, a sex deviate, in a letter to the Special Review Board about November, 1959, claimed that Agent Hoffman had dissuaded John from seeking out-patient psycho-therapy previous to his return to WSP as a violator in 1959. Supv. Thwackum had contact by IDC on this matter with Central Office 11/14/60. It seems that the running record in this case as early as 6/16/58 strongly conveys the fact that Agent Hoffman always has sought both with John and Mrs. Wilson that probably both and certainly John should have out-patient psycho-therapy in Racine. It seems that a number of other parole agents that have supervised John have been of this thinking. In an IDC, 11/14/60 from

Supv. Thwackum to Agent Hoffman, Supv. Thwackum had suggested to Agent Hoffman that we make a transfer of this case and it is being done herewith.

It is our feeling that new supervising officer would be wise to peruse the file in terms of the experiences of a number of agents. It is our thought that John Wilson is somewhat a danger under supervision. He has offended many young boys as young as 7 and as old as 14 in which he has used a camera and has taken some rather sordid pictures. His wife is aware of this picture taking which it seems usually starts in babysitting activity. Mrs. Wilson and John are both aware that Mr. Hoffman is more than aware of his program which has gone on in their home and for this reason they have not been cooperative with Agent Hoffman in late years. Agent Hoffman felt enough for John Wilson in the fall of 1958 that we had lined up three teaching jobs for John Wilson, all of which he forfeited by acts of parole violation as early as 4/27/59. The white transfer card accompanies the file.

WILSON, John Arthur X-35124-S
Admission Examination
Aug. 17, 1959

Examiner's Appraisal:

Physical examination reveals no pertinent pathology.

This man is a parole violator. As before, he frankly admits his homosexual drives and behavior, and admits that he is guilty as charged. He is markedly guilt-ridden and suffused with anxiety. He claims that he discussed continuing psychotherapy when he was paroled, both with his parole officer and with his wife. He claims that he was actively dissuaded from further therapy by one and that the other "changed the subject." Obviously blocked from his memory are the facts of his continuing therapy if he was paroled. I am convinced that this is an accurate blockage rather than deliberate falsification of memory because of his reaction to these facts as demonstrated to him by reading him my actual recommendation to the Special Review Board. His reaction is that of an acute anxiety state with hand-wringing and crying.

Previous investigations here and at the Racine County Guidance Clinic regarding both psychological and psychiatric evaluation indicates conclusively that this man is a sexual deviate. My understanding of the matter is that as long as he is a parole violator he can therefore only be handled under the provisions of the Sexual Deviate Statute.

R. B. Dryer, M.D.
Psychiatrist

[Omitted is a letter from the director of the Department of Public Welfare recommending commitment of Wilson under the Sex Crimes Act as being "in need of specialized treatment." The letter, dated August 21st, is practically identical to the letter quoted in the January 10, 1957, court proceedings. Also omitted are an order authorizing transportation of Wilson to court for sentence of commitment under the Act, and a new Face Sheet and correspondence list made out upon his return to the prison in September.]

CHRONOLOGICAL HISTORY

10/2/59. SOCIAL WORKER ENTRY: Wilson interviewed on this date at his request. A rather verbal individual, he discussed at length with worker employment possibilities for him when released from this institution. He is cognizant of the fact he will have difficulty securing a job because of the nature of his offenses and the fact that his special training would require a type of trust that he possibly will not be able to command. Wilson has a tendency to intellectualize, seems to show no remorse in regard to his offenses, and from what can be determined has a rather extensive and lengthy past history of deviant sexual behavior. He attempted to verbalize regarding his parole agents and their treatment of him in an effort to avoid accepting responsibility for his short-comings. He seems impressed over the fact of his college education and his wife being a school teacher. In discussion of his college, when pressed regarding why he had not obtained his Masters with the length of time he claims he has worked on it, he became evasive and attempted to change the subject. Claims he lacks but a thesis, but when asked whether he would be writing on his thesis while incarcerated he again avoided the issue. Will attempt to possibly be a manipulator, will not attempt to involve himself with his Social Worker other than to the extent of securing possible privileges. This man will be seen only at his request, having been received here under the Sexual Deviate Statute.

10/16/59. SOCIAL WORKER ENTRY: Wilson seen on this date at his request. Concerned over the fact that he has received a letter from his wife indicating that Parole Agent Hoffman is desirous of seeing her. He is concerned over what the Parole Agent would want to discuss with his wife and was informed that undoubtedly it was involving his particular case and involvement in the community. That I felt it would probably be to the best interest of their case for his wife to contact the Parole Agent and arrange for an interview so that she could assist Mr. Hoffman in this matter with any pertinent information that might have a bearing on this inmate's case.

1/13/60. PANEL PROGRESS REPORT: 1/8/60 Sales & Business Office.

EGT: Subject is a typist. He does good work, efficient, know it all, expert on all matters. No trouble to him, but bother to everyone else. Irritating character in general and can't take correction. We have known Mr. Wilson 2 months.

Panel Members: Liner, Olson, Bordman.

3/3/60. SOCIAL WORKER ENTRY: Interviewed client on this date who stated that his last contact with his therapist was on the 11th of January. Inmate did not seem particularly concerned over the fact that he has only been seen approximately three times since his return to this institution on September 24, 1959. Inmate seems particularly concerned over the situation involving his wife and desires that this worker discuss the matter with his Parole Agent, Mr. Hoffman, on Mr. Hoffman's next visit to the institution. Wilson was assured that Mr. Hoffman and I would discuss his case and attempt to assist him. He continues to be friendly and verbalized freely with this worker.

3/3/60. SOCIAL WORKER ENTRY: Interviewed client at his request. Interested in returning to Racine on release. Worker has also discussed this case with Supervising Agent, Mr. Hoffman. We both concur that Wilson has deep seated emotional problems which has made him to date a menace to society. One problem this client seems to have is a tendency to rationalize by intellectualization.

4/14/60. PANEL PROGRESS REPORT: 4/8/60 Sales and Business Office.

EGT: Subject is a Clerk-Typist. This man is a very good worker, had some trouble adjusting to job due to personal conflict with fellow inmate worker but this incident never resulted in disciplinary measures. He is a good worker and has shown improvement since other inmate has left the office. We have known inmate 6 months.

Panel Member: Julius.

7/26/60. PANEL PROGRESS REPORT: 7/22/60 Sales and Business Office.

EGT: Subject is a Clerk-Typist. He does very good work, tries to impress other inmates with his knowledge, and has petty grievances. We have known inmate 3 years.

Panel Members: Shuler, Bordman, Julius, Rollard.

Date: July 19, 1960

PAROLE PLANNING INFORMATION SHEET

[Formal information deleted.]

Supplemental Information: His only assignment since his return as a parole violator has been in the Main Office where he presently works as a Clerk-Typist. He is described as a very good worker who has shown improvement. He has never received a disciplinary report. He is in therapy and meets with Dr. Dryer approximately once every month.

July 29, 1960 Present Status Psychiatrically

This chronic parole violator has been seen about once a month since his return to the prison a year ago. There has been little or no progress. I have seen his wife on a couple of occasions and I believe persuaded her to consult a psychiatrist in Racine. Although he should know better, Wilson professes to believe that difficulty in real communication between him and his wife is somehow responsible for his sexually deviant behavior. I repeat that I see no change in Wilson.

R. B. Dryer, M.D.
Psychiatrist

WISCONSIN
STATE DEPARTMENT OF PUBLIC WELFARE
DIVISION OF CORRECTIONS

HEARING: September 1960
INSTITUTION: Wisconsin State Prison

PAROLE DECISION

Institution No.: 35124-S
Date: 9/28/60

Name of Case: WILSON, John A.
Official Action: Defer

Comments: Not presently parole material.—Mr. McCauley

Stay on a while longer. He wants out so he and his wife can work it out together, under guidance, but his is an aggravated case and requires more care here.-Mr. McCaffery

---

October 31, 1960

Mrs. John A. Wilson
3241 Jefferson Street
Racine, Wisconsin

Dear Mrs. Wilson:

Thank you for your letter of October 16th in regard to an interview which you would like to have with me concerning your husband's case.

It is not the custom for members of the Board of Review to interview relatives and I do not feel that it would be wise to institute such a program unless the basic policies of the Special Review Board are changed by mutual agreement. I am sorry to discourage you in this manner but feel that if you wish to pursue this point further that the Board have an opportunity to discuss it at our November meeting and that any further inquiries to meet with all members of the Board be directed to Mr. Matt Coogan, at the Division of Corrections, Department of Public Welfare, Madison, Wisconsin.

Sincerely,
B. H. Glover, M.D.

3241 Jefferson Street
Racine, Wisconsin
November 10, 1960

Mr. Matt Coogan
Division of Corrections
Department of Public Welfare
Madison, Wisconsin

Dear Mr. Coogan:

I had written to Dr. Glover in October asking him for an interview in which I could discuss my husband's case. He suggested my writing to you since the Board of Review works as a group.

I would appreciate being able to speak with all the members of the Special Review Board if this could be arranged. Saturday would be the best day of the week for me, but I would plan another day if you should prefer.

Very truly yours,
Mrs. John A. Wilson

November 14, 1960

Mrs. John A. Wilson
3241 Jefferson Street
Racine, Wisconsin

Dear Mrs. Wilson:

This is in reply to your letter of November 10th in which you seek to set up a meeting with the members of the Special Review Board preferably on a Saturday or other week day suited to the convenience of the members of that particular board.

I am personally acquainted with John and many of his friends. I have also met you on at least one occasion. Thus, were it possible I should be more than pleased to arrange the meeting you suggest. Factually, the majority members of the Board are not employees of the Department. They are public minded, private citizens and professional men of unusual competence whose time is closely budgeted and hence are not available to the Department for the purpose you suggest. Additionally, John was seen in September at which time his application for release was rejected. Further consideration in that regard will now hinge on a positive recommendation for his release by Dr. R. B. Dryer.

Very sincerely yours,
Matt J. Coogan, Secretary
Special Review Board

CHRONOLOGICAL HISTORY

11/7/60. PANEL PROGRESS REPORT: 11/4/60 Sales & Business Office

EGT: Subject is a Clerk-Typist. Very good worker if left on his own. Doesn't like to be pushed too much. Gets along well with others. We have known him 1 year.

Panel Member: Julius.

2/21/61 PANEL PROGRESS REPORT: 2/17/61 Sales and Business Office

EGT: Subject is a Clerk. He is a good worker, handles his job in a capable manner. We have known inmate 1-½ years.

Panel Members: Bordman, Shuler.

6/12/61. PANEL PROGRESS REPORT: 6/9/61 Sales and Business Office

EGT: Subject is a General Clerk including Typing and Recording of work done. He does good work, he works as hard as he needs to, can accept correction, conduct is good, does get carried away once in a while but can be told to stop when necessary. He gets along well with others. Does not have a very high opinion of authorities, parole officers in particular. His attitude has changed little since I have known him. He receives letters and visits from his wife and mother. We have known inmate 2 years.

Panel Member: Julius.

3233 Jefferson Street
Racine, Wisconsin
July 25, 1961

Mr. Matt J. Coogan, Secretary
Special Review Board
Box 669
State Office Building
Madison, Wisconsin

Dear Mr. Coogan:

Mr. John A. Wilson has been our next door neighbor for over a year. We spent many hours in each others company. We are well aware of the unfortunate mistake that happened to Mr. Wilson. We honestly believe that Mr. Wilson paid more than enough his debt to society. We earnestly believe and recommend to you his immediate release to his wife and children. I believe that you will agree with us that this step of yours will be more beneficial to all of us than to keep him in confinement any longer.

Respectfully yours,
Mr. & Mrs. Irving Master

P.S. I am engaged in the dental supply business for the last 35 years and my reputation is 100%. And I want to assure you that I would not recommend anything even for my own father if I would not believe that the time was right for it.

I. M.

August 2, 1961

Mr. and Mrs. Irving Master
3233 Jefferson Street
Racine, Wisconsin

Re: John Wilson #35124-S

Dear Mr. and Mrs. Master:

Your letter of July 25th recommending that the Special Review Board view John's parole application with favor is being called to the Board's attention. You may be assured that the Board will weigh your recommendation in a favorable light when it considers his case on September 20th.

I am sure that Mr. Wilson appreciates your continued interest in him. Feelings such as you express in your letter are most helpful to a man under confinement.

Very sincerely yours,
Matt J. Coogan, Secretary
Special Review Board
DIVISION OF CORRECTIONS

3249 Jefferson Street
Racine, Wisconsin
August 7, 1961

Mr. Matt J. Coogan, Secretary
Special Review Board
Box 669
State Office Building
Madison, Wisconsin

Dear Mr. Coogan:

We have been living in the neighborhood for three years. Mr. John A. Wilson is a nice man. We do not think he should be punished. We have a ten-year-old son and we are willing to have Mr. Wilson live next to us.

Very truly yours,
Mr. and Mrs. Joseph Ubricht

Date: August 8, 1961

PAROLE PLANNING INFORMATION SHEET

[Formal information deleted.]

Supplemental Information: This man presently is assigned to the main building where he works in the Sales and Business Office. It is reported that he does good work and works hard at his job. His conduct is reported as being good and he accepts correction. He is able to get along with the others working in the office. This man has maintained over the years a poor opinion of authorities, parole officers in particular.

Present Psychiatric Status
Aug. 18, 1961

WILSON, John A. WSP 35124-S

In my opinion this man has gained considerable insight. He recognizes that his frustrating domestic situation reached such a stage of intensity that he had to have relief and that he reverted to his long-established pattern of homosexual behavior with young boys to gain this relief. The frustrating domestic situation was that neither he nor his wife had learned to communicate adequately with one another. I have seen his wife on several occasions during his two periods of incarceration here and have seen a marked improvement in her ability to empathize with people and things in her environment. I have read some of her old letters to the inmate which were very uncommunicative, and I have read many of her recent letters which clearly indicate the change in her outlook and her ability to communicate.

When Wilson was paroled at the end of his last previous incarceration, he fully intended to seek psychotherapy on the outside. He mentioned this to his parole officer who strongly dissuaded him from doing so; I have discussed this matter with Wilson's wife, and she verifies Wilson's statement in this regard. If Wilson should be paroled now, he would have a different parole officer. His relationship with his wife will have improved remarkably, and I believe he will seek psychiatric help on a continuing basis. In spite of the fact that his aberrant sexual behavior is of long duration and been uncontrollable too frequently in the past, I think he has reached a point where he has a good chance of avoiding this type of behavior in the future.

R. B. Dryer, M.D.
Psychiatrist

WISCONSIN
STATE DEPARTMENT OF PUBLIC WELFARE
DIVISION OF CORRECTIONS

HEARING: September 1961

INSTITUTION: Wisconsin State Prison

PAROLE DECISION

Institution No. 35124-S
Date: 9/20/61

Name of Case: WILSON, John
Official Action: No Action

Comments: We will need a pre-parole on this case before a final decision can be made.-Mr. McCauley

This man presents no parole plan. There is some question as to his veracity about past plans for psychiatric aid outside. In addition, there is some problem about professional problems if he were to be released now--the appropriateness as well as the veracity previously referred to above. Staffing might be of assistance in clarifying the complicated issues here.-Dr. Glover

Mr. Wilson has a long record of deviant sexual behavior. It appears quite clearly that Wilson does not co-operate well on parole because he feels that he is capable of handling his own problems and really seems not to believe that a parole agent can help. This is coupled with repeated failures when released. Whether change in this basic attitude is possible is problematical, but I would think it imperative that a parole plan be one, the conditions of which are clear and the obligation of Wilson made clear so that he is not able to state in the future that he was not clear on his responsibilities.-Mr. Remington

MEMORANDUM

September 26, 1961

TO: Field Services--Investigations Unit
FROM: Matt J. Coogan
RE: John Wilson--35124-S

The Board noted Dr. Dryer's rather favorable recommendation for this man's release. It also noted that Dr. Dryer did not ask for a pre-parole investigation and that none was therefore made.

I have been requested to procure such a report and forward it to the members so that a final determination can be made as to the propriety of parole. Please initiate such an investigation and call it to my attention when you receive it.

JJB: Special Pre-Parole Investigation is herewith assigned to Racine District (attention Richard Garsh), due 10/13/61.

CKO

WISCONSIN
STATE DEPARTMENT OF PUBLIC WELFARE
DIVISION OF CORRECTIONS
FIELD SERVICES

HEARING: October 1961

INSTITUTION: Wisconsin State Prison

SOCIAL INVESTIGATION SUMMARY

Institution No.: WSP 35124-S

Name of Case: WILSON, John

Social Summary:

The inmate's wife and two daughters currently reside at 3241 Jefferson Street in Racine. The wife continues to teach music in the Sussex County School System. Since learning from the inmate that John had received a note of encouragement during his recent appearance before the Special Review Board, she has contacted me several times expressing hopes that something could be arranged to facilitate his release. He will be welcomed back into her home where, according to the wife, there will be no hardship despite the fact he may not be employed. Her earnings are sufficent to maintain the home, even if he is not working. However, she expresses an awareness that employment is essential for her husband's adjustment and claims that she will offer every bit of encouragement towards his securing employment at the first opportunity. Mrs. Wilson has further informed me that she now realizes the importance of her husband continuing psychiatric treatment on an out-patient basis following his release and hereto she will offer encouragement. In fact, she has expressed a willingness to participate in the therapy with her husband, realizing that her own attitude and behavior in the past may have contributed towards abnormal sexual desires. There is, however, a question as to whether on the wife's salary alone, both John and his wife would be able to undergo this type of treatment.

The wife could offer no suggestions regarding employment and in view of the fact that John had remained unemployed during the two years that he was previously under supervision, there is no former employer who could be approached at this time. Work therefore will have to be sought after the client's release.

Employment or Placement Plan: To reside with wife at 3241 Jefferson Street, Racine and to seek employment following release.

Date Submitted: October 10, 1961

Investigating Agent: Albert D. Robertson Prob.-Parole Agent

Date Approved:

Plan Approved by Dist. Supervisor:

CHRONOLOGICAL HISTORY

January 24, 1961 AGENT'S NOTE: Case file material received from Agent Hoffman, Area #10, with request for institutional transfer.

February 16, 1961 INSTITUTIONAL VISIT: I interviewed John on this date and explained that Agent Hoffman had expressed a desire to transfer the case to another agent. John seemed to be in agreement with this proposal and claimed that there has been a personality clash between Agent Hoffman and himself. John expressed some pessimism over the prospect of his being again released to supervision, feeling that he would be held until discharge date. He seems willing to make another try at field supervision but feels that the prison authorities have lost confidence in him.

February 21, 1961 AGENT'S NOTE: C-35's endorsed on this date accepting area responsibility. Albert D. Robertson

October 10, 1961 PRE-PAROLE: Upon request of the institution a pre-parole investigation was submitted on this date. In preparation for the investigation I had had several contacts with the client's wife who is now living at 3241 Jefferson Street. She expressed considerable interest in the client's return to the home and she has agreed to avail herself for psychiatric treatment along with her husband on an out-patient basis should the doctor feel this advisable. Mrs. Wilson had no idea where employment would be available and it looks rather dim that a job could be pre-arranged because of that fact that John was unemployed for approximately 2 years during his previous term of supervision. She will however be mindful of the fact that a job would be to her husband's advantage and in the event she receives the slightest lead regarding employment, she will contact me immediately. Albert D. Robertson

October 19, 1961 INSTITUTIONAL VISIT: I interviewed John on this date regarding his appearance before the Parole Board and his receiving a "no action" with apparently the possibility of his being able to again appear soon. John expresses a willingness to undergo out-patient therapy immediately upon his release and is quite pleased over the fact that his wife has expressed an agreement to cooperate with the treatment process. John himself had no idea where employment might be available but will be on the lookout for employment leads. He realizes that he may have to accept employment below his ability but has expressed an awareness that just the fact that he is working will be conducive to his adjustment. John did request in the event he is granted a parole that if at all possible he be released before October 29th at which time his daughter receives her First Communion. Client's attitude remained favorable throughout the interview and the improvement may be attributed to his hopefulness of receiving a parole at this time. Albert D. Robertson

---

3241 Jefferson Street
Racine, Wisconsin
October 24, 1961

Mr. Matt J. Coogan, Secretary
Special Review Board
Box 669
State Office Building
Madison, Wisconsin

Dear Mr. Coogan:

I have sent this same letter to Dr. Glover. Though I write it as a wife awaiting the return of her husband, I am more particularly writing it as a mother considering the request of her child.

My husband, John A. Wilson, had a hearing with Special Review Board on September 20, 1961. The result of that hearing was "no action." Since an outright "no" was not said at the time I interpret "no action" as meaning there is hope for my husband's release soon.

Our seven year old daughter, Judy, will make her First Communion on Sunday, October 29, 1961. Just two days ago she said the best gift she could receive on that day would be having her Daddy home.

Considering her request is sensible and that there may be a possibility of its materializing I appeal to you and the Board to make it a reality.

The children and I are eager to have our father home so our family can be together again.

Very truly yours,
Mrs. John A. Wilson

October 30, 1961

Mrs. John A. Wilson
3241 Jefferson Street
Racine, Wisconsin

Dear Mrs. Wilson:

I am very hopeful that your husband, John, can be with you shortly. There are many decisions to reach concerning his case and I cannot assume the right to speak for the Special Review Board as to their final decisions at this time.

I am sorry that your daughter's First Communion has passed without her father's return but sincerely hope that it will not be very distant. I am placing your letter in the files so that other members of the Review Board can be aware of your feelings.

Sincerely,
B. H. Glover, M.D.

WISCONSIN
STATE DEPARTMENT OF PUBLIC WELFARE
DIVISION OF CORRECTIONS

HEARING: November 1961

INSTITUTION: Wisconsin State Prison

PAROLE DECISION

Institution No.: 35124-S
Date: 11/13/61

Name of Case: WILSON, John A.
Official Action: Defer

Comments: Staffing has been reported to be adverse. Boy's Life pictures have been reported to be posted on his walls. The patient recalls nothing at first, then gradually recalls an alteration in his subscription. His performance here is equivocal and pleading ignorance. He states that if directed to do so he will "forget" any reference to such a publication. He gives the impression of not being trusted, of being insincere and only superficially cooperative.—Dr. Glover

On the basis of a relatively negative preparole, a similar staffing by Psychiatric Services and his past record, a grant at this time seems premature. He still has potential if he would only use it.—Mr. McCauley

Mr. Wilson continues so evasive that it is still not possible to have confidence in his ability and willingness to make any kind of satisfactory adjustment on parole. Certain oral institutional reports raise additional problems, although I am reluctant to accept third hand oral reports of institutional misbehavior especially when the written record is silent on the point.—Mr. Remington

---

3241 Jefferson Street
Racine, Wisconsin
November 16, 1961

B. H. Glover, M.D.
University Hospitals
Madison 6, Wisconsin

Dear Dr. Glover:

I visited my husband, John A. Wilson, at the prison yesterday and learned that the outcome of his hearing Monday, November 13, was "no parole granted."

You have been so helpful to me through previous communication I wondered if once again I could ask your help in understanding this decision. All situations had seemed so right for his receiving parole at this time. I can't help but want to know what the objection was.

What channel would you suggest I follow in attempting to help my husband achieve his parole? Is there anyone to whom I may write or see in person?

I would not bother you with this request if I hadn't had every reason to believe there was hope for my husband's receiving parole at this hearing. I just can't be satisfied with the outcome as it is now without being moved to action.

Very truly yours,
Mrs. John A. Wilson

November 29, 1961

Mrs. John A. Wilson
3241 Jefferson Street
Racine, Wisconsin

Dear Mrs. Wilson:

Again I shall have to ask your indulgence in reporting your letter and my answer to you to the entire Review Board so that we are all aware of the circumstances and can deal with your situation in a completely forthright manner.

Under the circumstances I think it would be best if a reply were directed from Mr. Matt Coogan, the Secretary and Special Director of the Sex Deviate Program for details concerning your husband's turn-down for recommendation of parole. I do not feel that I can answer for him as to whether he would be willing to see you in person but I would discourage your attempting to approach the Review Board itself for a face-to-face discussion of this issue as our relationship to your husband has to deal very much more with his problems and his adjustment than it does with yourself.

I hope you understand the light in which this is written emphasizing that the making of any special exceptions is not favorably regarded generally by the Board and would not be fair to the participants in the Deviate Program. I hope this answer is at least in part satisfactory for your needs.

Sincerely,
B. H. Glover, M.D.

November 30, 1961

Mrs. John A. Wilson
3241 Jefferson Street
Racine, Wisconsin

Dear Mrs. Wilson:

Re: Wilson, John A.—35124-S

Your letter of November 16 to Dr. Glover along with his reply just crossed my desk. I can readily understand your position and naturally sympathize with you. I do not, however, feel that any useful purpose would be served by your coming to Madison for an interview with me. I say this because I could only relay your thinking to the Board, as its Secretary. Additionally, I have no authority to bring John before the Board prior to November of 1962. The only person who enjoys that right is Dr. Dryer whom you have met on occasion. I can't speak for him but I would suspect that in view of the Board's recent action he would be reluctant to bring John before the Board within the next several months. The decision, however, is his to make: Not mine to guess at.

Very sincerely yours,
M. J. Coogan, Secretary
Special Review Board
DIVISION OF CORRECTIONS

Date: February 2, 1962

PAROLE PLANNING INFORMATION SHEET

[Formal information deleted.]

Supplemental Information: Subject continues in his assignment as a clerk-typist for the sales and business office. While he is described as doing good work, it is pointed out that he acts superior to others and will take exception to anything just to argue. Not liked by other inmates. He has, however, maintained a clear cut record. He meets with his therapist, Dr. Dryer, approximately once each month.

WISCONSIN
STATE DEPARTMENT OF PUBLIC WELFARE
DIVISION OF CORRECTIONS
FIELD SERVICES

HEARING: April 1962 SPECIAL REVIEW

INSTITUTION: Wisconsin State Prison

SOCIAL INVESTIGATION SUMMARY

Institution No. WSP 35124-S

Name of Case: WILSON, John Arthur

Social Summary:

The possibility of joint psycho-therapy with inmate and his wife was explored both at St. Jude's

Clinic and Racine County General Hospital. In both cases Mr. Wilson's application for treatment would be rejected because of the nature of his problem and also because joint therapy would not be available through these resources.

The matter of joint therapy was discussed with his wife and she would be in complete agreement to participate. She is currently earning $5,500 per year and feels that her income would be sufficient to obtain therapy from a psychiatrist in private practice. Mrs. Wilson mentioned the possibility of obtaining therapy through Dr. Dryer, as patients, in his private practice. She would be in complete accord with this arrangement.

Employment cannot be pre-arranged and will have to be obtained after release.

Employment or Placement Plan: To live with wife at 3241 Jefferson Street, Racine. Employment to be secured after release.

Date Submitted: March 21, 1962

Investigating Agent: A. D. Robertson-Area #27

Date Approved: March 21, 1962

Plan Approved by Dist. Supervisor:

Present Psychiatric Status
March 26, 1962

WILSON, John Arthur WSP 35124-S

Please review my report of August 18, 1961. The Board's action in September of 1961 on Wilson was "no action." As a result of that meeting, Dr. Glover stated in part that staffing might be of assistance in clarifying the complicated issues here. For this reason, Wilson was staffed on the 31st of October, 1961 and present were Dr. Thurrell, Dr. Saute, Dr. Ehrmann, Mr. Jonson, Mr. Lutz and the undersigned.

I became ill immediately after this staffing, hence was not on hand to furnish the Special Review Board with the summary of the staff's conclusions. When Wilson appeared before the Board in November of 1961, he was deferred because Boys' Life pictures have been reported posted on his cell walls. On the basis of a relatively negative pre-parole, Wilson has consistently and vehemently denied ever having had clippings from Boys' Life on his cell wall, and I am unable to determine conclusively where this vague wall report comes into the picture.

In addition to my report of August 18, I can only add that I do not believe that further therapy in an institutional setting will accomplish anything for this man.

R. B. Dryer, M.D.
Psychiatrist

WISCONSIN
STATE DEPARTMENT OF PUBLIC WELFARE
DIVISION OF CORRECTIONS

HEARING: April 1962
INSTITUTION: Wisconsin State Prison

PAROLE DECISION

Institution No.: 35124-S
Date: 4/25/62

Name of Case: WILSON, John
Official Action: Defer

Comments: John is an individual well known to our Department because of his repeated involvements in sexually deviant behavior and because of his rather obnoxious personality. He had a great deal of therapy through the years and seemed to have benefited from it a great deal prior to his last parole, but violated that parole by a repetition of sexual abuse of a child in a manner which reflected considerable calculation. I am recommending a defer primarily on the basis of public protection and my inability to conclude that there has been any real basic change in John.—Mr. Coughlin

Mr. Wilson is a sexual offender who has repeated his offenses with minor males resulting in one previous parole violation. Therapeutic prospects are minimal at this time and his sociopathic conduct is offensive to most persons who have contact with him. The issues are decided on the basis of risk to youth due to his past and potential future behavior in spite of the lack of therapeutic potential to be obtained by his remaining in the institution. It is difficult for him to accept the decision of the Board and he clarifies well some of the issues involved in the dilemma of retaining the offender who is not aggressive but is likely to repeat offenses with minors.—Dr. Roberts

There remains evidence that Mr. Wilson continues to pose a substantial risk to young boys.

He has not been very deeply involved in any therapy program with the consequence that there is not now sufficient grounds for release despite the positive factor represented by his wife.—Mr. Remington

---

IN THE CASE OF: } EMERGENCY REMOVAL ORDER

JOHN ARTHUR WILSON WSP 35124-S

PURSUANT TO THE authority granted to the State Department of Public Welfare by Sections 46.014(1) and 57.115 of the Wisconsin Statutes and the authority delegated by said Department's administrative order 2.02/2, the removal of the above captioned from Wisconsin State Prison, Waupun, Wisconsin to Sussex, Wisconsin is hereby authorized.

THIS REMOVAL is for the following purpose: To attend the funeral of his father on December 19, 1962.

During such temporary absence from the institution, the legal custody of the aforesaid shall remain with the institution. Dated this nineteenth day of December, 1962.

John C. Burke
Superintendent or Warden

MEMORANDUM

16 January 1963

TO: John Ehrmann, Ph.D., Senior Psychologist—WSP
FROM: Matt J. Coogan, Secretary, Special Review Board
RE: WILSON, John A. #35124-S

The above man is eligible for discharge on June 18. May I have your recommendation by February 15th.

PW
QMDC 46 3-4-63 3:20 PM
WSP ATTN. CLINICAL SERVICES

PLEASE EXPEDITE RECOMMENDATION AS TO DISCHARGE OR EXTENSION OF CONTROL IN THE CASE OF JOHN A. WILSON, 35124-S TIME IS RUNNING OUT ON THIS MATTER.

MADDC MATT COOGAN CH

PW 46 3-6-63 11511:11 AM
MAD DC MR MATT J COOGAN, SECRETARY, SPECIAL REVIEW BOARD

DISCHARGE OF WILSON, JOHN, WSP-35124-S, ON ELIGIBILITY DATE REGARDED AS DANGEROUS TO PUBLIC. PLS PREPARE ORDER FOR EXTENSION OF CONTROL.

WSP J C EHRMANN, PH D, SR CLINICAL PSYCHOLOGIST MB

STATE OF WISCONSIN
STATE DEPARTMENT OF PUBLIC WELFARE
DIVISION OF CORRECTIONS
Wisconsin State Prison, Waupun

March 5, 1963

MEMORANDUM

TO: Matt J. Coogan, Secretary, Special Review Board
FROM: J. C. Ehrmann, Ph.D., Sr. Clinical Psychologist
SUBJECT: WILSON, John A. WSP-35124-S

Mr. Wilson was staffed on February 26, 1963 by Drs. Nemeth, Geocaris and Ehrmann. It was felt that this individual demonstrated very little real understanding of the nature of his sexual maladjustment and still evidenced compulsive like needs for homosexual contacts with male minors. Accordingly, discharge of this individual at this time is considered to be dangerous to the public.

Dr. Nemeth, who is responsible for this man's treatment program, will appear in court to testify on the need for continuation of control.

STATE OF WISCONSIN
CIRCUIT COURT (BRANCH #11)
RACINE COUNTY

STATE OF WISCONSIN, PLAINTIFF v JOHN ARTHUR WILSON, DEFENDANT	Application for Review of Order Continuing Control by Wisconsin Department of Public Welfare

The Wisconsin Department of Public Welfare hereby applies to the court above named, pursuant to Section

959.15 (13) of the Wisconsin Statutes, for a review of the order of the Department dated March 8, 1963, continuing the said defendant subject to the control of the Department, a true copy of which is hereto attached.

Wisconsin Department of Public Welfare

Director

Dated: March 8, 1963

STATE OF WISCONSIN
BEFORE THE STATE DEPARTMENT OF PUBLIC WELFARE

IN THE CASE OF:	ORDER: IN THE CONTINUANCE OF CONTROL BY WISCONSIN DEPARTMENT OF PUBLIC WELFARE
John Arthur Wilson—WSP 35124-S	

IT APPEARING THAT John Arthur Wilson, hereinafter referred to as the aforesaid, was on the 3rd day of July, 1959, convicted of the offense of Indecent Behavior with a Child (2 counts), in violation of Section 944.11 of the Statutes of the State of Wisconsin, in the Municipal Court of Racine County, and was committed to the Wisconsin Department of Public Welfare for an indeterminate period, under the provisions of Section 959.15 with the Wisconsin State Prison being designated as the treatment facility on September 23, 1959.

AND THE DEPARTMENT, being of the opinion that discharge of the aforesaid at the time provided by Section 959.15 (12) of the Statutes, to wit: June 18, 1963, would be dangerous to the public.

IT IS NOW ORDERED that in accordance with the provisions of Section 959.15 of the Statutes, that the aforesaid remain subject to the control of the Wisconsin Department of Public Welfare, beyond June 18, 1963, the date upon which the aforesaid would normally be discharged from the control of the Department under the provisions of subsection (12) of Section 959.15.

STATE DEPARTMENT OF PUBLIC WELFARE

Director

Dated: March 8, 1963

[Omitted is a letter of transmittal and a letter notifying the district attorney of the matter and requesting his attention to it.]

Date: March 8, 1963

PAROLE PLANNING INFORMATION SHEET

[Formal information deleted.]

Supplemental Information: John is presently assigned to the Business Office where he works as a clerk-typist. He is reported as doing a very good job, being efficient and neat. He is considered to be a congenial inmate.

WILSON, John WSP 35124-S
Summary to Special Review Board
April 5, 1963

This is the case of a 40 year old, Catholic, white married man who mostly worked as a clerk. In 1948 he graduated from Northwestern University with a B.A. degree in psychology. In 1942 he entered the U. S. Navy and was honorably discharged in 1946. In 1950 inmate had his first sodomy charge and in 1953 he was released on parole. In 1956 he had another charge of oral sodomy and also of carrying obscene books and possession of obscene photos. He was placed on parole in 1958, but in July 1959 he had to return as a parole violator with the same charge of oral sodomy on a six year old boy. Since 1959 his parole was deferred three times. In May 1962 his case was referred to me and inmate attended an almost entirely homosexual group since June 1962, which meets once a week.

His mother did not have much time to spend with inmate in his childhood because she was engaged in intensive social activities. He never felt that he received love, affection, or kindness enough from his mother. He never felt love or hate towards his mother through his whole life. When he was 2 or 3 years old, his Nanny was the closest person for him.

His father never had close relationships or desirable parental-child contacts with him. Inmate never felt real affection or attachment to his father, but occasionally had feelings of dislike, resentment, hostility and hate toward his father.

Psychosexual Development: Between the age of 4 and 8, he occasionally used to sleep with his mother. Around the age of 6, he and little girls of the same age used to undress and look at each other (curiosity). Between the ages of 6 and 8, he liked to undress little girls of the same age and look at their bodies and genitals. He developed feelings of fear for his actions, but he was really never caught or punished for undressing girls. Around the age of 12, two girls got pregnant in his school by other classmates, and they had to leave the school. That produced a blocking experience and factor for him about heterosexual activities by creating an idea: "do not touch girls." This idea of his was more aggravated at the age of 15 when the girlfriend of his brother got pregnant by his brother, Jerry, who finally should marry her. "That was another horrible thing for me with a total condemnation." In the same year one of his girl classmates was caught in sexual intercourse with her boy classmate in school and she was fired from it. The patient worried a lot about these sex events and meanwhile he had a strong desire for females. He found that everything was wrong around girls.

Mr. Wilson was masturbating since the age of 8 on and off until the present. His first homosexual experience was at age of 10, and his first heterosexual one was also around 10. His homosexuality was characterized by oral and anal sodomy which were real popular among his boymates at that time. Between the age of 10 and 16, he had intensive homo and heterosexual activities based on his early and deeply developed, strong, but poorly controlled sexual impulses. This man undoubtedly has had poor parental-child relationship and not sufficient parental control in his early life. Meanwhile he was circulating and growing up in an environment of bad companions. His deeply rooted, strong bisexual hetero and homosexual impulses started to develop rather early, around the age of 10. His sexual misbehavior is characterized by quite frequent occurrences. He also several times showed inability to control his sexual impulses while he was on parole in the past.

Since June 1962, he attended an entirely homosexual group where he showed little improvement until February 1963. Namely, up to this time he was sarcastic, antagonistic, negativistic, resentful and hostile. His judgment was not always clear, but his emotional control was always very poor. Defense of his ego was highly projective and definitely paranoid in nature indicating lack of insight.

Since February 1963, he showed some improvement and his paranoid-like thinking and behavior slowly but steadily diminished up to date. I strongly feel that Mr. Wilson is still in need of further psychotherapy because of the long-standing and compulsive-like traits of his homosexuality with male minors and because of the present lack of a deep-seated and firm insight. Finally, I also would like to mention that today I can see some promising features for the possibility of gaining maximum therapeutic result by additional therapy in the future.

Chas. Nemeth, M.D.
Psychiatrist

WISCONSIN
STATE DEPARTMENT OF PUBLIC WELFARE
DIVISION OF CORRECTIONS

HEARING: April 1963

INSTITUTION: Wisconsin State Prison

PAROLE DECISION

Institution No. 35124-S
Date: 4/17/63

Name of Case: WILSON, John A.
Official Action: Defer

Comments: This man is a repeat offender, back at this institution for the third time because of sexual misconduct with boys. He has been here a long time on the present commitment (was last returned July 6, 1959) but no significant progress was observed until February of this year. Now Dr. Nemeth feels that Mr. Wilson is making some headway in therapy. This program certainly should not be interrupted.—Mr. Coughlin

Recent improvement noted by his therapist is commended. Extension is planned for 6/63 via the court. (Dr. Ehrmann confirms the collection of Boys Life pictures of youth cut out and saved at a time alleged in the past at WSP.)—Dr. Roberts

There is some evidence of encouraging progress in therapy. Despite his record of past failures, he ought again be tried on parole whenever there is some positive factor such as some definite progress in therapy.—Mr. Remington

STATE OF WISCONSIN
STATE DEPARTMENT OF PUBLIC WELFARE
DIVISION OF CORRECTIONS
1 West Wilson Street, P.O. Box 669, Madison 1, Wisconsin

May 13, 1963

MEMORANDUM

TO: The Special Review Board
FROM: John C. Ehrmann, Ph.D., Senior Clinical Psychologist, WSP
RE: WILSON, John WSP 35124-S

The Special Review Board directed this examiner to follow through on a series of allegations regarding Mr. Wilson's previous WSP subscription to Boy's Life

Magazine and the indication that he had cut out pictures of young males and collected them within his cell.

This examiner checked the Deputy's Office files at WSP and this record clearly indicates that Mr. Wilson did receive Boy's Life Magazine for a period of several months. There is also an indication in the record that the allegation about Mr. Wilson cutting out pictures of boys in various stages of dress and undress and in various stages of physical activity and had collected them within his cell. All of the pictures that he had collected appeared to quite obviously have erotic stimulus value for this man. These pictures for the most part included boys in various stages of physical activity that could quite possibly have been interpreted as suggestive. Additionally, there are several indications within the Deputy's Office files at WSP that this man on several occasions had requested purchase of various art and photography books which had to be refused after they had arrived at WSP because of their content. In each of these cases the art and photography books were collections that included many pictures of young males in various stages of dress and undress.

Mr. Wilson's record does indicate, however, that there has been no evidence or suspicion of any of this type of activity on Mr. Wilson's part for approximately the last year and a half. He has made no attempts to secure books that may have been regarded as suggestive, and no activity similar to the picture cutting behavior has been observed over the last one and one-half year.

May 24, 1963

Honorable Hubert J. Stephens, Judge
Circuit Court, 11th Branch, Racine County
Safety Building
Racine, Wisconsin

Dear Judge Stephens:

Re: John A. Wilson-WSP 35124-S

John Wilson is eligible for discharge on June 18th. Thus far, I have no notice that a hearing date has been set for a judicial review of the Department's Order of March 8, 1963, extending its control over Mr. Wilson beyond June 18th. As far as the Department is concerned any date set by the court for the hearing will be satisfactory to us. Dr. Nemeth, our expert witness in this case, is available to us on a full-time basis.

Respectfully yours,
Matt J. Coogan
Administrative Assistant
DIVISION OF CORRECTIONS

CIRCUIT COURT CHAMBERS
Branch 11 Second Judicial Circuit
Criminal Court Branch
Safety Building
Racine, Wisconsin

May 28, 1963

Mr. Wilbur J. Schmidt, Director
State Department of Public Welfare
Division of Corrections
1 West Wilson Street
Madison 1, Wisconsin

Dear Sir:

In re: State v. John Arthur Wilson
WSP 35124-S Circuit Court F-2103

In accordance with your application for review of order re continuance of control over the above-named defendant, I have set this matter for 9:00 A.M. on June 14, 1963, at which time the Court will fix a date for the hearing of your application for review of your order, appoint counsel for the defendant if he is unable to provide his own counsel, advise the defendant of his rights in connection with such hearing, and consummate all preliminary proceedings generally relating to such hearing.

Notice has been given to the defendant in accordance with Section 959.15 (14) of the Statutes, and I have directed a writ to the Warden of the Wisconsin State Prison to produce the defendant at 9:00 A.M. on June 14, 1963, in the courtroom of Branch 11 of the Circuit Court on the fourth floor of the Safety Building, Racine, Wisconsin.

I am also notifying Mr. John R. Omar of the date of this hearing.

Very truly yours,
Hubert J. Stephens
Circuit Judge, Branch 11

[Intradepartmental teletype messages concerning transportation of Wilson to court and provision of diagnostic records to his psychiatric witness are omitted.]

STATE OF WISCONSIN
CIRCUIT COURT
RACINE COUNTY

STATE OF WISCONSIN, Plaintiff, v 23456A JOHN ARTHUR WILSON, Defendant.	E-2014 STATE DEPARTMENT OF PUBLIC WELFARE (WAUPUN)
June 14, 1963	Before the HON. HUBERT J. STEPHENS, Circuit Judge, Presiding.

CHARGE: INDECENT BEHAVIOR WITH A CHILD (2 COUNTS).

Appearances:

JAMES MULLIGAN, Assistant District Attorney, for the State.
HAROLD J. McGARRETY for the Defendant.
DEFENDANT in Court.

[The court appointed Harold J. McGarrety as counsel for the defendant who claimed to be indigent. On June 14, 1963, the request for an extension of Wilson's term was read and a date, July 18, was set for the hearing. The defendant requested that a psychiatrist of his own choosing examine him and testify at the hearing.

On July 10, Dr. Joseph E. Weyer was appointed by the court to examine Wilson on July 17. On July 18, the hearing was held. Matt J. Coogan, administrative assistant to the Department of Public Welfare, Division of Corrections, testified for the State. Mr. Steinway, representing the State, attempted to get testimony from Mr. Coogan in regard to the dangerous nature of Wilson, but the Court sustained an objection that this information was of a medical nature and Mr. Coogan was not a competent witness in this field.

Dr. Charles Nemeth, a psychiatrist employed by the Correctional Division of the Public Welfare Department in Waupun, testified for the State. He stated that Wilson had not acquired sufficient insight into the nature of his affliction to keep him from committing the same offense again. The following is the gist of his testimony:]

Q At this time would you please state as to what this defendant's condition was in May of 1962 in regard to any mental or emotional aberrations from which he was suffering as compared with what your opinion is of this condition today.

A His mental condition in May, 1962 was characterized by hostility, resentment, being sarcastic and poor emotional control, in other words emotional instability and lack of good judgment and insight.

I could see some slight improvement, especially since February, 1963 when his case was reviewed by our staff conference for consideration of the control, extension of his control. Now, it seems that he became less hostile, and I do like to give a description of his condition because I was asked to do that. He became less hostile, more cooperative, showed great interest to our group psychotherapy discussions, but still his insight is not strong enough in order to be able to control his sexual impulses which was seen in the past at least thirteen years when he got into trouble.

MR. McGARRETY: Now, we object to that last statement as being extraneous, not within the witness' knowledge and therefore incompetent.

THE COURT: May I hear that last part.

(Thereupon the last answer read by the reporter.)

THE COURT: I will strike "which was seen in the past at least thirteen years when he got into trouble."

A I strongly feel today that he has no insight, enough at the present time in order to live outside of the institution, in other words, he can be at the present time considered as dangerous to the public. He is not able to control his sexual impulses, he didn't learn enough yet.

[Mr. McGarrety made repeated objections to the competency of the witness, all of which were overruled. On cross-examination, Mr. McGarrety brought out the nature of the "specialized" treatment. The treatment was almost exclusively group therapy in either groups of six to eight or in a "miniature session" where only the patient, psychiatrist and another inmate were present. His intent was to show that Wilson was really not getting necessary specialized treatment.]

Q I want you to tell me what specialized treatment Wilson got after he got to that institution. Did you prescribe anything for him?

A No.

Q Then the only thing he got by way of specialized treatment was to be present at a series of questions and answers?

A Yes, in other words psychotherapy.
Q What is psychotherapy?
A Psychotherapy, that is a frame, that is a situation in which a psychiatrist or sometimes psychiatric social worker or psychologist is present and patient or patients. If one patient, that is individual; if more than one patient are present with the therapist they call it group psychotherapy.
Q In the group session, was each member of the group questioned and his answers heard by all the others present?
A Yes, sure.
Q So that part of the treatment that Wilson got was listening to the troubles of others?
A And about his troubles too.

[Mr. McGarrety also tried to bring out the nature of the improvement in the defendant and the possibility of outside treatment.]

Q And within one year after you had him as your patient and you were his psychiatrist you noted improvement in him?
A Some slight improvement.
Q Well, were you able to measure it some way?
A I had to measure it and I had to send the report to the special review board because his case was reviewed by the special review board after two months, I think around April, 1963.
Q Now, you say at the present time is there more or less improvement in Wilson's condition than you found in May of 1962?
A Since May, 1962 he showed some slight improvement.
Q In other words, his condition is improving slightly, is that what you are trying to say?
A Yes.
Q How does he manifest himself in that way to you?
A I mentioned I think about twice previously because he is more cooperative and attentive, not sarcastic, not hostile, more friendly and showed very active in his group, he tries to be a group leader for a few months.
Q Is there any reason why Wilson couldn't receive this treatment that he is now receiving on the outside of that institution?

MR. STEINWAY: I will object on behalf of the State.
THE COURT: Yes, we aren't discussing that here, that is for the special review board. I can't parole him, not on the basis of this hearing. Sustained.

Q Now, Doctor, you said that he didn't have enough insight to live outside of the institution. Could he live outside of the institution?
A At the present time definitely not.

Q Why?
A Because I mentioned before, his insight is not yet good enough.
Q Would that take place in one or two months from now?
A I cannot tell in one or two months.
Q Three?
A If he continues it is entirely up to him, if he continues his improvement perhaps in one year he can be paroled but still he needs supervision in the form of parole. I strongly feel that too, medical supervision in the form of parole if he will be paroled, I mean if he will be okayed by the board.
Q You mean supervision if he were on parole outside of the institution?
A Yes.
Q And is that what you would have to say in connection with his prognosis for the future?
A Yes.

[Mr. McGarrety questioned the doctor at some length about the "dangerous" nature of Wilson. He brought out that Wilson had committed no indiscretions during the period Dr. Nemeth had studied him and tried to show that the doctor's opinion was based on Wilson's previous record as a parole violator and that the doctor's observations were based on inadequate contact.

The Court questioned Dr. Nemeth, trying to determine whether Wilson's mental abnormality was within the statutory definition for extension.]

A He has no mental abnormality, in other words he knows what he does, he knows the nature of his action.
Q Yes, I am not talking about insanity. Does he have some--state whether or not he has any mental disorder or abnormality which would make him dangerous to the public if he were discharged.
A He has sexual abnormality, sexual deviation, having homosexual tendencies toward young boys for many years, since early adolescence.
Q I am trying to see whether or not your findings fit into the statutory definition here for the extension of control. You have told me that his release or discharge now would be dangerous to the public--and why would it be dangerous to the public?
A As a chronic sex offender he is a sex deviate and at the present time he is dangerous to the public.
Q State whether or not that would be interpreted then as him having some mental disorder or abnormality or both or neither.
A He has had emotional problems in the past and at the present time he still has tendencies for sexual deviation.

THE COURT: All right, take it up from there.
BY MR. STEINWAY:

Q Does he have at the present time a mental deficiency or disorder or abnormality in your opinion that makes it dangerous to release him from the institution?
A Yes, he has a mental abnormality and therefore release is not recommended.
Q What is that mental abnormality?

MR. McGARRETY: We object to the question on the ground it calls for a hypothetical answer, not based upon the facts.
THE COURT: Overruled. I think I can conclude that myself from the testimony, but I would rather have it in some form from this witness if he can.

A He has no ability, I mean he has no insight today and he has no ability to see the causes and motivations of his previous sexual misbehavior in order to avoid a similar or same kind of sexual misbehavior in the future.

[The State rested and the court adjourned until the next day when the defense presented its case.

Mr. McGarrety called Wilson to the stand as his first witness. After establishing background information concerning Wilson's wife, family and education, McGarrety attempted to show that another prison psychiatrist, Dr. Dreyer, had had a number of individual sessions with the defendant and had come to the conclusion that Wilson should be released.]

Q During that time did you have therapy for your symptoms administered to you by Dr. Dreyer?
A Yes, I did.
Q And would that take any appreciable length of time each time that you had these sessions?
A Yes, they are hour long sessions, individual sessions, completely devoted to my case.
Q Now, during that period of time from September, 1959 to about the beginning of May of 1962 about how many times did you confer with Dr. Dreyer and receive this therapy?
A I saw Dr. Dreyer once a month, sometimes oftener.
Q Now, then, in May of 1962 you ceased having contact with Dr. Dreyer for the purposes indicated, is that correct?
A Yes, sir.
Q Was there some reason for that?
A Yes, there was.
Q Will you state it.

A Dr. Dreyer had on several occasions in a six month period strongly recommended me for parole, stating that further treatment within the confines of an institution would be of no use. He also had me staffed by the psychiatric staff of the State Prison and this staff concurred with his recommendation and with his findings and opinion that I should be released. After he had recommended me and the parole board had continued to turn me down he called me in and stated that he had done all that he could to get me out of there, that apparently the parole board did not go along with him, that therefore all he could do would be to turn me over to another man and hope to get medical testimony that would agree with him. The only other available psychiatrist that was there was Dr. Nemeth.

[Wilson during the course of his testimony indicated that he had objected to the group sessions and that Dr. Nemeth had given him the impression that his parole was imminent.]

Q Now, he referred to you as having exhibited to him hostility.

A Yes, sir.

Q What have you got to say about that?

A The hostility at the beginning of my going into the group was due to the fact that I didn't want to go into the group knowing that there were criminal men in the group, people not under the sex deviate law, knowing further possibly that what one says in the group--that he must definitely go into his entire sex history from his earliest stage, around through the walls of the institution. I differed with it and conferred with my spiritual director and he said there was no reason for it, that it was definitely against my religion.

Q The doctor said yesterday in his talk with you you were sarcastic with him. What have you to say as to that?

A That could be his interpretation of certain occasions when I would quote a psychological study such as the fact that--can I give an example of this?--the children of the United States are growing larger every day, I mean our children today are taller than they were a generation ago. Dr. Nemeth would then come out with a lecture on how degenerate our children are, how our children are getting weak, physically unfit, are sexually degenerate and that the whole United States is going to pot. We would have an argument over that. He meant that as sarcasm.

Q While you were at the institution have you been guilty of any infractions or violations up there?

A None whatever.

Q At any time while you were in contact with Dr. Nemeth did he make the statement to you that you had shown tremendous improvement?

A He stated that I had shown tremendous improvement in insight, much gained insight, and made a further statement to me that he believed that I was one of those of his patients who would never come back to his institution, would never commit another crime. This was after he had told me that my case was finished as far as therapy was concerned with him, it merely needed a little more time to jell. This was several months ago.

[In cross-examination, Mr. Steinway, representing the State, attempted to show that Wilson had misunderstood the statements made by the psychiatrist. He also inquired about the magazine pictures.]

Q Isn't it true that since you have been in the Central State Hospital* that--since you have been in the institution at Waupun isn't it true that you have subscribed to numerous magazines, pictures predominantly of young boys?

A No, that is not true.

Q Isn't it true that you have in fact removed pictures of the boys from magazines that you have subscribed to and put them on the walls in the quarters where you live?

A That is a lie, that Dr. Dreyer heard and checked out to the best of his ability, Dr. Glover checked it out to the best of his ability, and it was investigated there thoroughly to find out one scintilla of evidence. I also firmly deny it.

[Mrs. Wilson was the next witness. Mr. McGarrety tried to show that if Wilson returned home, he would return to a good environment in which he could be cared for.

Dr. Joseph E. Weyer was the defense's next witness. The doctor testified that he thought that Dr. Nemeth was somewhat mistaken and that Wilson could be safely released if he were properly supervised.]

A It is hard to know exactly in treatment of patients with problems of mental illnesses when a patient has attained complete insight or a complete recovery or complete awareness. The doctor did say that he showed some slight improvement and implied that he had attained some insight, that he was or had become more amenable and more cooperative since he went under his care. In my opinion I feel that something has been accomplished by therapy at Waupun.

---

* The reference to Central State Hospital for the Criminally Insane, which is also located in Waupun illustrates the common misconception that persons committed under the Sex Crimes Law are kept in a hospital rather than in the prison.

Q Do you have an opinion as to whether or not he could be released under circumstances where there would be supervisory control of the individual?

A I think he can, I think Mr. Wilson has received sufficient institutional benefit so that he can now be released. I don't believe that his super-ego is entirely recovered. I don't think he can go out completely on his own. I think, however, that he has learned enough so that if he received some supervision or some surveillance by his wife particularly and by his brother, say by his wife and family, that he assumed his responsibility and relinquished certain of his own habits such as taking pictures and belonging to the Boy Scouts and baby-sitting, I think if he is willing to do that and gives his word that he will, and along with that seeks some guidance in psychotherapy by a local psychiatrist I think at this time that he could make the grade.

[On questioning by the court, Dr. Weyer stated that Wilson's release was a calculated risk and that he would prefer Wilson to be released on parole.

In his statement to the court at the close of the case, Mr. McGarrety stated that he felt that Wilson should be released in view of his clean record at the prison and his improvement there. He said that he felt that the defendant was entitled to some consideration and that this was a risk worth taking.

Mr. Steinway, in his statement, pointed out that Dr. Weyer had had only a very limited amount of time to study the defendant while Dr. Nemeth had extensive contact with him. Moreover, if the term was extended, the defendant would still be eligible for parole under the conditions that Dr. Weyer desired. Once released from the control of the Department of Public Welfare, there would be no effective restraints on Wilson and the danger would be increased. Mr. Wilson's clean record at Waupun is not so impressive, argued Mr. Steinway, since his only difficulty is with young boys and he has no contact with them then.

Judge Stephens said that the situation was all or nothing and he therefore felt that control should be continued. However, he indicated that the defendant could ask for another hearing in six months and another one every following six months.]

June 17, 1963
From: Sanger B. Powers
DIRECTOR

Mr. John C. Burke, Warden
Wisconsin State Prison
Waupun, Wisconsin

Dear Warden Burke: Re: Duration of the Department's Control over Sexual Deviate Cases

The following information seems pertinent in the case of John A. Wilson #35124-S:

1. Mr. Wilson's normal discharge date is June 18, 1963.

2. On March 11, 1963 the Department forwarded to the court its Order Extending its Control over Mr. Wilson beyond June 18, 1963, and at the same time made an Application to the court for a Judicial Review of that Order.

3. Mr. Wilson appeared before the Honorable Hubert J. Stephens on June 14th. He was then advised of the existence of the Department's order and of his rights under the statutes and a final hearing on the matter was set for 9:30 A.M. July 18th.

4. Clarification of the Department's right to hold Mr. Wilson beyond June 18th was sought from the office of the Attorney General this morning.

John H. Bowers, Assistant Attorney General, advised us that in his opinion, based on a close scrutiny of subsections (11), (12), (13), and (14) of section 959.15, we do have the right to retain Mr. Wilson under our control beyond June 18 and until such time as the court takes action on the Department's Order of March 11, 1963.

Some of the keys to the Assistant Attorney General's thinking are listed below:

1. 959.15 (11) Duration of Control. The Department shall keep every person committed to it under this section under its control and shall retain him . . . so long as in its judgment such control is necessary for the protection of the public . . .

2. 959.15 (12) Termination of Control. Every person committed to the Department who has not

been discharged from its control as provided in sub. (11) unless the Department has previously thereunto made an order directing that he remain subject to its control for a longer period and has applied to the committing court for a review of said order as provided in sub. (13) shall be discharged at the expiration of the maximum term prescribed by law . . .

3. 959.15 (13) provides the legal means of getting the man to court.

4. 959.15 (14) Action of the Committing Court Upon Application for Review . . . (b) If, After a Hearing the court finds . . . discharge would be dangerous.

In line with the foregoing advice from the office of the Attorney General you are authorized to retain John A. Wilson at the Sex Deviate (Treatment) Facility pending final disposition of the matter now before the court.

[A new Face Sheet is omitted.]

July 29, 1963

Mr. Wilbur J. Schmidt, Director
State Department of Public Welfare
One West Wilson Street
Madison, Wisconsin

Re: John Arthur Wilson #35124-S

Dear Mr. Schmidt:

On March 8th, 1963 the Department entered an order that Wilson remain subject to its control beyond June 18th, 1963, the date when he would normally be discharged under 959.15 stats.

The Department's application for a review of that order was heard by Judge Stephens on July 18th and 19th, 1963.

During the hearing Dr. Nemeth testified that Wilson had shown improvement especially since February 1963 when his case was reviewed by a staff conference at the prison; also that he had violated no rules or regulations there but conducted himself properly and that he saw Wilson individually once or maybe twice. The rest of his contact was while Wilson was one of 6 or 8 present at group sessions when therapy was administered to those present and that this therapy consisted of a series of questions being asked by the doctor and answered by one or other of the group to whom the questions were directed. Each group member might also ask questions of the doctor or other members of the group.

Dr. Joseph E. Weyer, an able and experienced physician whose specialty is psychiatry, testified that he examined Wilson at the County Jail on July 17th and had observed him on the witness stand and also had studied his WSP records and was present during the direct testimony of Dr. Nemeth. He said that among other things he considered the improvement noted by Dr. Nemeth; Wilson's present age; the fact that improvement was noted since February 1963 and that he was more amenable to treatment and more cooperative and that in 4 years he got into no trouble. He stated such factors indicated Wilson's potential is good. He also noted Wilson sincerely desires the help that he needs and that his wife and relatives will fully cooperate in assisting him.

Wilson made a favorable impression upon the Court and on those present. Judge Stephens commented on this and stated that he felt that Wilson was a fit subject for parole.

At the conclusion of the presentation the Court requested counsel and Dr. Weyer to attend a conference in his chambers when the Judge indicated that he did not want to discourage the man and thought that Wilson could be paroled. The time element in connection with that phase of the situation was discussed. The fact that the Court will release Wilson sometime was also considered. The present time appears to be favorably indicated.

Following our conference with the Judge, the clerk informed me that on July 24th, Mr. Coogan was expected to attend a hearing in another matter. At that time I asked the Judge to confer with both of us regarding his reaction and views respecting the Wilson case. During such conference in chambers, Judge Stephens again expressed his views as previously given the District Attorney, Dr. Weyer and myself and also indicated that a transcript of the hearing would be made available to your Department. Such transcript will support the statements made in this letter.

In view of the facts brought out at the hearing and Wilson's definite improvement at the present time, I would suggest that the Department and the special review board consider his request for parole with the provision that he continue out-patient therapy while in the atmosphere of his own home aided by his wife and relatives.

We believe that on the showing made before Judge Stephens Wilson deserves your careful consideration of his request for parole.

I thank you.

Respectfully,
Harold J. McGarrety

MEMORANDUM

July 31, 1963

TO: (1) The File
(2) Dr. Nemeth
FROM: Matt Coogan
RE: Wilson, John A. #35124-S

Judge Stephens confirmed the Order of the Department extending its control over the above man on July 19. The hearing was lengthy and our order was vigorously contested. I appeared in court only on the first day and was foreclosed from presenting the usual background information.

I appeared before Judge Stephens on another matter on July 24 at which time he invited me to his chambers for a meeting with Harold McGarrety, Wilson's attorney. The judge initiated the meeting by saying that he had been impressed with the testimony of the defense as well as with the demeanor of Wilson and his wife whom he called into his chambers at the conclusion of the hearing. He went on to say that he had no wish to intrude upon the Parole Board's function but that he had the feeling that an early parole would be in order and that a parole in the near future would be no more dangerous than one put off for a year or two--The foregoing is not an accurate quote--It lacks the carefully thoughtout statement of the judge but basically "I got the message."

I advised the court that Wilson had been before the Board in April and that the hearing loads for the Boards were such that we couldn't schedule him prior to October and then only if Dr. Nemeth is of the opinion that Wilson should be seriously considered for parole at that time.

August 12, 1963

Mr. Harold J. McGarrety, Attorney at Law
Mitchell Building
207 East Michigan Street
Racine, Wisconsin

Dear Mr. McGarrety:

Re: John Arthur Wilson #35124-S

Your letter of July 29th recommending early parole consideration for your client was referred to Mr. Coogan for discussion with Dr. Nemeth.

I am now informed that if Mr. Wilson continues to show improvement in his therapeutic contacts with Dr. Nemeth he will be brought before the Special Review Board at its November meeting. It is Dr. Nemeth's feeling that John has to consolidate his gains and that any earlier appearance would serve no useful purpose. As of the moment, your client's appearance before the Board in November or at a later date pretty much hinges upon his own efforts during the next thirty days.

The Department has a tremendous respect for the opinion of Judge Stephens in all matters. We are awaiting the promised transcript of the Wilson hearings which took place on July 18th and 19th, 1963. Upon receipt, it will be made available to the members of the Board.

Very sincerely yours,
Wilbur J. Schmidt, Director
STATE DEPARTMENT OF PUBLIC WELFARE

[A Parole Planning Information Sheet, merely requesting a preparole social investigation, is omitted.]

WISCONSIN
STATE DEPARTMENT OF PUBLIC WELFARE
DIVISION OF CORRECTIONS
FIELD SERVICES

HEARING: November 1963

INSTITUTION: Wisconsin State Prison

SOCIAL INVESTIGATION SUMMARY

Institution No.: 35,124-S

Name of Case: WILSON, John Arthur

Social Summary:

Mrs. Wilson and her children currently reside at 3632 Montas Street, Racine. She is employed as a teacher in the City of Sussex. It appears that she is genuine in her desire to have her husband return to the home. She has counseled the children as to where their father is, and basically the reasons for his commitment. They, too, are eager to have him return home. It appears that in view of the favorable attitude of family members, the client should return to them. This in no way would be a financial hardship upon Mrs. Wilson. She has accrued some savings, though she would not disclose the amount, that can be used for the support of the family in the event of financial strain. Through her own initiative, she has made contact with several employers, in quest of work for her husband. She has not secured definite employment promises, however, she is hopeful that employment will be available to him.

Employment or Placement Plan: To reside with wife and children at 3632 Montas Street, Racine and to seek employment following release.

Date Submitted: 10/22/63

Investigating Agent: Lionel L. Jason, #27

Date Approved:

Plan Approved By Dist. Supervisor:

WILSON, John Arthur WSP 35124-S
Summary to Special Review Board
November 11, 1963

Since April 1963, Mr. Wilson has gradually and continuously shown improvement up to date.

His sarcastic, resentful, and hostile attitude gradually disappeared. During the past four months I have not seen any signs of his anger or hostility in the group and he became the leader. But he frequently evidenced improving reasonings such as judgment and insight. His paranoid-like thinking and projective type of defensive mechanism became minimum or practically zero. He also became emotionally more stable by having better emotional stress tolerance.

His parole plan and institutional record also seems to be quite good.

I strongly feel that Mr. Wilson has gained enough about real understanding of the nature of his sexual maladjustment in the past, and about ability to properly control his sexual drives in the future.

Charles Nemeth, M.D.
Psychiatrist

WISCONSIN
STATE DEPARTMENT OF PUBLIC WELFARE
DIVISION OF CORRECTIONS

HEARING: November 1963

INSTITUTION: Wisconsin State Prison

PAROLE DECISION

Institution No.: 35124-S
Date: 11/19/63

Name of Case: WILSON, John A.
Official Action: Grant

Comments: This man has been back in the institution approximately 4 years and in recent months the Clinical Reports have become very favorable. It is impossible to be highly optimistic about a case like this, however, considering the present reported progress, the time in confinement, the basis upon which extension was granted, and this man's potential to be a contributing member of society if he succeeds in controlling his sexual impulses, I have concluded that it is reasonable to try him under field supervision again.—Mr. Coughlin

With many reservations despite positive staff comments, parole is recommended after a long stay at WSP.-Dr. Roberts

Mr. Wilson was recently extended and there is evidence that Judge Stephens felt that the extension was desirable primarily in order to make possible a substantial period of supervision in the community. This view is also shared by the therapist.—Mr. Remington

[The Request for Release is omitted.]

CHRONOLOGICAL HISTORY

10/29/63. INSTITUTION VISIT: On marginal date I saw John at the institution at my request. I informed him that I had submitted a Pre-Parole plan for him which included his return to his wife and family, and securing employment after release. He was not inclined to believe that he would be granted parole at his next hearing. He states he is no longer bitter about being incarcerated, however, he states if he is not paroled then he would receive a direct discharge in January, '64. He has been assured by some source that this is a certainty. He reports that he and his wife are in constant communication, writing almost daily. He is concerned about his children, and quite naturally wonders how they will feel when he is returned to the home. I tried to set aside his fears, but to no avail. At this point he appeared to be very anxious.

12/9/63. Client released to parole supervision on marginal date.

RESIDENCE: Client will reside with his wife and minor children at 3632 Montas St.

EMPLOYMENT: The client anticipates being home during the month of December, but will attempt getting employment in January, 1964. He will use resources that are known only to him and his wife. He did not take me into his confidence as to what area he would try to find employment.

MONTHLY APPOINTMENTS: John will be seen in the office on the second Thursday of each month.

12/18/63. MAIL: Letter sent to John, scheduling monthly appointments for him on the second Thursday of each month.

1/9/64. John in office for his first regular appointment. If verbalness is a sign of anxiety, this guy was the most anxious person I have ever met. Initially, he talked constantly, but finally I had to interrupt him in order to get control of the interview. I imagined that this verbal diarrhea from which the client was suffering was his manner in manipulating and controlling the interview. Though nothing profound came from the interview, we were able to talk about the client's aspirations and goals. Because of his past involvement, the client feels that in order for him to become a productive citizen that he must further his education. In this regard, he has a long-term goal of securing a Ph.D. from the Northwestern University. This, in and of itself, would not create an undue hardship upon the family as his wife has been very frugal in her savings. He anticipates entering the Racine University, completing work for a Master's Degree and then transferring all credits to Northwestern campus. He anticipates entering the doctoral program in Psychology.

EMPLOYMENT: Unemployed.

PLAN: As the client has some pretty well pre-conceived ideas as to what his goals and aspirations are, I shall serve as a supportive agent in helping him to attain these. Realistically, I think he can attain a doctorate if he pursues the course with vim and vigor.

1/22/64. HOME VISIT: Visited the client's address--3632 Montas Street, and found no one at home. I left a note, indicating that I had been to the home for a regular home visit.

LATER: Mr. Wilson contacted me at home and apologized for not being there when I called. He stated he had gone out to the Racine University to seek entrance for the second semester. I advised the client that this was in accord with our plan as discussed on 1/9/64, and wished him well. The client volunteered that at the present time things are going remarkably well for him and he does not anticipate too many problems in re-entering school during the second semester.

2/13/64. Mr. Wilson in office on marginal date, and very pleased with the ease in which he has adjusted to his home situation and now to the Racine University. He has completed registration and has begun classes. At the present time he is taking a full load in university credits and will not seek outside employment. From the savings of his wife, they can manage until such time as he has earned his Ph.D. degree. If this does materialize, it appears that John will have to go to Chicago to complete this.

It appears that Mr. Wilson has lost some of his bitterness and hatred for the Division of Corrections since his return home. I shall continue to work with the man in a supportive relationship as it is very unlikely that he would want to participate in a group in Racine or to even discuss his problems openly.

3/11/64. Client in office on marginal date for regular appointment. He continues to be enrolled at Racine University in the Graduate School and anticipates entering school in Chicago, once he has completed all requirements for the Master's Degree in Psychology. He thinks that things are going pretty rough for him at the present time, insomuch as he has not formed sound, steady habits.

SUPPORT: Client is being supported through the efforts of his wife and her savings. He registers no guilt or shame about this, and states that in the long run his earning potential will be twice as great as it is now. He realizes that since being at WSP he does not have a profession though he has a Bachelor's Degree, and most of the credits needed for a Master's Degree. Family relationships appear to be sound, and the client is apparently adjusting well.

4/9/64. Client in office on marginal date reporting no changes of status. He continues to be enrolled at the Racine University, and is apparently making an admirable adjustment as a student. We discussed how he fulfills his role as a father and head of a household, but since the client is very active as a full-time student it appears he has relegated his duties as head of household to his wife. She handles all decisions within the home and he is quite happy with the arrangements.

5/7/64. PERS. OFFICE: John in office on marginal date, indicating that his family adjustment and school adjustment are both excellent. Apparently, the client is using school as a method of diverting his libidinal drives. It appears his entire life revolves around excellent school performance.

EMPLOYMENT: Client does not work. He is now attending school full time, where he anticipates earning a master's degree in Psychology.

6/11/64. PERS. OFFICE: No change.

7/9/64. PERS. OFFICE: John in office on marginal date, indicating that he is now registered for summer school, and so is his wife.

The client has now begun to relate with other male adults in the community. He indicates that he and his wife are exchanging visits with another family that he met through his church. Heretofore, he has been reluctant to extend himself to other persons outside of his family group. This appears to be a sign of growth. When questioned as to how he remained on campus without association with other students, it was brought out that the client felt it was in his best interest not to associate, in order to prevent his past from becoming known. In a therapeutic vein, the client is aware of his offense, and he thinks other people in the community would look upon him with disgust and disdain. LLJason

8/13/64. No changes. John is still in school and will complete work for the master's degree in Psychology in January. He intends to take the Ph.D.

9/10/64. PERS. OFFICE: Client in office on marginal date. No change in status noted. Client was advised that I might, in the very near future, be assuming other duties, and under these circumstances his case would be transferred to another agent in the office. LLJason

10/8/64. PERS. OFFICE: Mr. Wilson in office on marginal date, reflecting no change of status. He continues to attend the university. Apparently the home relationships are very positive and the client is making an excellent adjustment therein.

TRANSFER SUMMARY: History of offenses deleted.
Mr. Wilson is a client who readily admits his need of help, but thinks he has gained sufficent insight at this point to control his urges. He alleges he has never felt free to discuss this part of his life with anyone. He has undergone therapy while at the institution, and private psychiatric care while in the field.

MARITAL: John's wife professes profound love for him and is, at most times, overly protective. It is doubtful that she would be cooperative in notifying any agent of any misbehavior on the part of her husband.

EMPLOYMENT: Client is unemployed at this time and is living on the savings of his wife. His wife is a school teacher in the public schools system. At the present time the client is attending Racine University where he anticipates earning a master's degree in Psychology and his plans include going to Northwestern to take courses leading to the Ph.D. degree.
Case transferred to Agent J. P. Jabrinski. LLJason

11/10/64. Case transfer from Agent Jason. JPJabrinski

1/12/65. OFFICE PERS.: No change. JPJabrinski

2/9/65. OFFICE PERS.: No change. JPJabrinski

3/9/65. OFFICE PERS.: Residence remains as before. Subject remains full-time student, Masters Program. Wife remains employed. Discussed past involvement and present orientation with subject. Discussion meaningless. There seems to be no reason to press the issue since it would appear that there is nothing to gain. JPJabrinski

4/65 OFFICE PERS.: Subject reported as scheduled during this agent's absence. JPJabrinski

5/11/65. OFFICE PERS.: No change. Subject's involvement in school extensive and meaningful. Intends to pass comprehensive exams and secure masters in psychology at the end of this semester. JPJabrinski

6/7/65. OFFICE PERS.: Subject successfully completed comprehensive examinations. General situation remains as before. No change expected. JPJabrinski

7/11/65. OFFICE PERS.: Subject accepted as candidate for doctorate if Racine U. ever secures the above program. Also has secured assistantship for next teaching year. Subject's involvement in school program appears complete at this time. JPJabrinski

8/10/65. No change in general noted since this man has been under supervision. Residence with wife remains constant. Subject's school position remains constant. Steady progression in the above area noted. Involvement in school program seems to be thorough-going. Subject told to report on bi-monthly basis from now on. It would appear that field supervision in this case is all but meaningless except for the obvious factor of supposed control as far as client is concerned. JPJabrinski

9/14/65. OFFICE PERS.: Residence constant with wife at 3632 Montas Street. Full-time student Racine Univ. Now a Teaching Assistant, no wage as yet. WFGorgon

10/12/65. OFFICE PERS.: No change in residence. Still at Racine Univ., half-time teaching assistant, wages received, approximately $284.00. WFGorgon

11/9/65. Submitted monthly report as directed. Residence and teaching student situation at Racine U. as before.

12/65 thru 3/66. Through present report period residence remains 3632 Montas Street with wife and family. No problems evident relative to home situation. Subject continues to function as a full-time student in the graduate program of anthropology at Racine U. Wages received relative to teaching assistantship $282 per month. Subject continues to be extensively involved in above program claiming to keep himself busy 18 hours per day functioning as student and teacher.

Bi-monthly reporting in effect in this case. Absolutely no problem anticipated in this case.

4/66 thru 10/66. No change noted relative to residence situation during marginal report period. Subject continues to reside with family at 3632 Montas Street. No problems evidenced relative to home situation.

Full-time school program continues. Subject is a graduate student in psychology at Racine U. and combines the above with a teaching assistantship in same area. Tentatively accepted during April 1966 for the psychology doctoral program. Interested faculty members, School of Psychology, know of subject's offense background. There is no question but that the subject is genuinely involved in on-going school program. His wife, who teaches school in the Racine school system, supports him fully in the above endeavor.

Subject's plans concerning furthering his education materialized during his last stay at WSP. He has meaningfully pursued the above endeavor since release from the Institution.

Although subject's adjustment since release from WSP has been without incident, his prior record, that is: commitment in 1957 followed by revocation and new commitment in 1959 and followed by extension of commitment in 1963, rules out early discharge request in this case. Expiration of sentence date is 7/19/68, indeterminate. JPJabrinski

10/17/66. Subject recently secured Masters Degree in Psychology at Racine University. As previously indicated, he was accepted as a doctoral candidate and will work toward the above.

10/27/66. #1798. John Arthur Wilson was arrested on 10/25/66 at 5:30 p.m. at 3632 Montas St. (his home) for Indecent Behavior with a Child, Sect. 944.11(2) and Possession of Obscene Matter, Sect. 944.21. Mr. Wilson's arrest card was read by this agent on 10/27/66. Card further stated that Mr. Wilson had in his possession various photos, sex magazines, camera and enlarger, all of which were confiscated; Inventory 21000 and 21001. It was noted on the card that Mr. Wilson refused to answer any questions through the arresting officers. Mr. Wilson is under $5000 bail and his case has been adjourned to 11/5/66.

The arrest card states that the offense of Indecent Behavior with a Child occurred on 10/22/66.

JAIL INTERVIEW: Mr. Wilson was interviewed in the jail on 10/27/66. When he was questioned by this agent he stated that he preferred not to answer any of my questions upon the advice of his attorney. He would admit nothing regarding Indecent Behavior with a Child but did state on 10/22/66 he was at home during the morning and then went to the College where he fed his laboratory rats and then returned home. He stated that kids were in and out of his home all day long and that was the end of his statement.

Mr. Wilson was then questioned about having in his possession the numerous lewd and obscene photos of neighborhood boys in various acts of sodomy. He admitted that these were in his possession but would neither confirm nor deny the fact of whether or not he took them. He also admitted that the camera and photo enlarger belonged to him.

LATER: The Wilson case was discussed with two detectives from the Vice Squad. Detective Brakkow then took me to the Property Room so agent could see the obscene material confiscated from Mr. Wilson. In the cardboard box was 65 8x10 and 4x5 photos of various boys in various acts of sodomy with one another. These were neighborhood boys and are the complainants in Mr. Wilson's arrest. Also in the box were 79 35-millimeter slides of the same. There were two plastic boxes of slides which had been purchased of various acts of sodomies, plus several manila envelopes full of the same; all purchased. The only exception in this mess of photos of homosexual behavior was 11 slides of women in the nude.

I might add at this time that prior to terminating my interview with Mr. Wilson in the County Jail, he was advised that this agent would recommend that his parole be revoked on the basis of having in his possession lewd and obscene nude photos of approximately eight different boys ranging from 7 to 13 years of age.
DWillerd

REVOCATION SUMMARY: [The Summary contains the same information stated in the Violation Report which follows.]

VIOLATION REPORT

Case Name: WILSON, John Arthur
Case Number: WSP #11654-A-S
Probation: (Parole)

TYPE OF VIOLATION:

( ) Conviction of another offense
(X) Revocation to be requested
(X) Charged with another offense
( ) Arrested but not charged
( ) Rule violation
( ) Violation of agent's directive

STATEMENT OF THE VIOLATION AND SUBSTANTIATING DETAILS

John Arthur Wilson was arrested by the Racine Police Dept. on 10/25/66 for Indecent Behavior with a Child and Possession of Obscene Matter. Mr. Wilson allegedly performed acts of sodomy on eleven year old George Handel of 2422 N. Gil St., on 10/22/66. Mr. Wilson denies this, giving no statement on the basis of advice given him by his attorney. Mr. Wilson did admit to having in his possession the lewd and obscene material confiscated by the Racine Police Department.

Also confiscated was a camera and photo enlarger which Mr. Wilson admitted belonged to him.

Mr. Wilson will not deny nor confirm the fact of whether or not he took the photos of the boys. This involved about eight boys of from 7 to 13 years of age in various acts of sodomy with one another. These were all neighborhood boys and one is the complainant in this matter. There were sixty-five 8x10 and 4x5 photos, seventy-nine 35-millimeter slides, plus various manila envelopes full of males in various forms of sodomy in addition to eleven slides of women in the nude.

Mr. Wilson was interviewed by this agent on 10/27/66 when he admitted that the confiscated material was in his possession at time of confiscation.

Mr. Wilson is presently under $5000 bail and has been advised that parole revocation would be recommended on the basis of the possession of lewd and obscene matter. He was uncooperative and would not totally account for his actions on the date of the alleged offense (10/22/66).

AGENT'S DISPOSITION OF THE VIOLATION

Revocation of parole to be requested.

Date: 10/31/66
Agent: Donald Willerd
Area Number: 1800

STATE OF WISCONSIN
STATE DEPARTMENT OF PUBLIC WELFARE
DIVISION OF CORRECTIONS
PAROLE REVOCATION ORDER AND WARRANT

TO ANY PAROLE OFFICER, PROBATION OFFICER, PEACE OFFICER OR ANY OFFICER authorized to serve criminal process and to the superintendent or other person in charge of any jail, penitentiary, lockup or other place of detention:

NAME: John Arthur Wilson NUMBER: WSP #11654-A S
DATE OF PAROLE: December 9, 1963
DATE OF VIOLATION: October 25, 1966

WHEREAS, the above named was granted parole, or mandatory release

AND WHEREAS, the above named has violated the conditions of parole, or mandatory release by the following:

1. The aforesaid admits to having in his possession numerous lewd and obscene photographs of neighborhood boys in various acts of sodomy on October 25, 1966.

THEREFORE, in accordance with section 959.15(6) of the Wisconsin statutes, it is now ordered that said parole be and hereby is revoked with effective date of violation being November 3, 1966.

YOU ARE COMMANDED, in the name of the State of Wisconsin, to execute this order by apprehending and holding said parolee for return to the Wisconsin State Prison and this shall be your authority for so doing.

AND YOU, the warden or superintendent of said institution, are hereby authorized and directed to receive the aforesaid and there keep him until discharged pursuant to law.

Witness my hand and the seal of the State Department of Public Welfare at Madison, Wisconsin 3rd day of November, 1966

Wilbur J. Schmidt
Director, State Department of Public Welfare

[A copy of the Revocation Order was transmitted to the prison, along with information that Wilson was detained in Racine pending new prosecution.

On November 30th the corrections-police liaison officer notified the parole office that Wilson had been arrested a month earlier.]

STATE OF WISCONSIN
CIRCUIT COURT
RACINE COUNTY

STATE OF WISCONSIN,
Plaintiff
v
JOHN ARTHUR WILSON,
Defendant

G-2773
G-2774
G-2775

February 8, 1967

Before the
HON. HUBERT J. STEPHENS
Circuit Judge, Presiding

CHARGE: G-2773 INDECENT BEHAVIOR WITH A CHILD (2 COUNTS)
G-2774 INDECENT BEHAVIOR WITH A CHILD
G-2775 POSSESSION OF LEWD, OBSCENE OR INDECENT MATTER AND EXHIBITION OF SAME TO PERSONS UNDER THE AGE OF EIGHTEEN YEARS

APPEARANCES:

DAVID CARMEN, Assistant District Attorney, for the State
HAROLD MC GARRETY for Defendant
DEFENDANT PRESENT IN COURT

[Defense counsel stated he wanted to present some motions challenging the complaint and asked that a date for hearing then be set. March 6th was agreed upon. On March 6th some motions were disposed of and March 29th set for hearing on a motion to suppress evidence. Clerical error in setting the court calendar required postponement to April 14th. On the 14th defense counsel failed to appear and the matter was rescheduled for the 17th. On the 17th the witnesses were not present. The hearing was set over to May 8th. On May 8th, Mrs. Wilson, one of the defense witnesses, was absent and the hearing was adjourned at defense counsel's request to June 23rd. On the 23rd Mrs. Wilson was in the hospital for an operation and there was postponement until August 4th. There is no transcript of the August 4th hearing.

On August 22nd trial was set for October 10th on one charge, with trial dates on the other charges to be determined at that time.

On October 10th Mr. Wilson agreed to plead guilty to all the charges. The court warned him that all penalties cumulated could total 35½ years, and that he would be examined under the Sex Crimes Act and could be held indefinitely under that Act if considered dangerous. The court ascertained his age, education, and prior experience with the Sex Crimes Act, and required Wilson to explain the substance of the charges to which he was pleading guilty. As reasons for pleading guilty Wilson gave his desire to get out of the county jail and his desire to spare the children involved from the necessity of testifying in court. The court, however, required him to specify that he was pleading guilty because he was in fact guilty. He did so, reluctantly, quibbling about the accuracy of the dates. He was also asked whether he had been threatened or his plea induced by promises. He agreed that his plea was voluntary and that his attorney had represented him adequately. The court also asked defense counsel whether he was satisfied his client understood the implications of his plea. Finally the court accepted the guilty pleas.

The court then took evidence on the offenses and committed Wilson to the correctional authorities for sex deviate examination.]

QD483 8-25-67 8:10 AM
ATTN ROBERT OLSEN MADISON
RE WILSON JOHN 11654 AS

CLIENT CONTACTED IN COUNTY JAIL ON 8-23-67 REGARDING A RETURN TO WSP CLIENT SEEMED TO VIEW THIS FAVORABLY HOWEVER AFTER TALKING TO THE CLIENTS ATTORNEY HAROLD MCGARRETY IT WOULD APPEAR AS THOUGH THE ATTORNEY WILL ATTEMPT TO DISCOURAGE THIS MOVE* HE CONTENDS THAT INASMUCH AS THE CLIENT HAS NOT BEEN FOUND GUILTY HE SHOULD NOT RETURN TO WSP AND FURTHERMORE HE INTENDS TO CONTEST THE REVOCATION IN A COURT OF LAW

* Under state law time spent in county jail does not count against sentence.

and several other boys into the attic where they took turns sucking each other's penis.

The Possession of Lewd, Obscene and Indecent matter (Court Case #G2775) involved Mr. Wilson taking pictures of the various sexual acts between the boys and also professional pictures of boys involved in acts of sexual perversion. The material confiscated by the Police Department included a large envelope containing sixty-five (65) photographs of various nude boys in various poses; a picture of a young boy with his privates exposed and which picture was on the wall of Mr. Wilson's den; an 8 mm. movie film; a white envelope containing 18 slides of boys but not nudes; a manila folder containing various negative pictures of nudes; two plastic slide-holders containing a total of 77 slides of nude boys; a cardboard box containing 117 slides of nude boys committing acts of perversion; 54 slides of various acts of perversion including some nude boys; 11 slides of various nude women; and a bundle of 50 magazines of assorted nudists, all boys nude magazines, etc.

Mr. Wilson personally took many of the pictures of the young boys previously mentioned in his home and committing acts of perversion. These pictures were taken during the summer months of 1966, the exact dates are unknown. Also confiscated were Mr. Wilson's enlarger, photo trays and the camera which he used in taking the pictures.

In addition to the previously mentioned incident, there were many others; a total of nine boys ranging in age from 8 to 13 who had been involved in varying degrees of sodomy with one another and with Mr. Wilson.

[Omitted are the defendant's record, background and personal history.]

HABITS: Mr. Wilson has had heterosexual experiences as is attested by the fact that he now is the father of three daughters. He has been committing homosexual acts on young boys for the past twenty-five (25) years. He is probably a confirmed homosexual. Mr. Wilson admits to being a social drinker but not to excess. He smokes a pipe and sometimes cigarettes. He has* been known to associate with groups of ill-repute and has denied any contact with any known or unknown groups of homosexuals in Racine.

RECREATION: Mr. Wilson is primarily interested in Photography, both taking and developing the pictures. However, his interests in this area have led to his diffi-

* Comparison with earlier reports will disclose that the word *not* has been omitted here in copying the information, reversing the meaning of the statement.

culties in the area of taking obscene pictures and developing them.

MARITAL: John Wilson married Mary Jane Polk on 9/3/49 in Holy Assumption Church in West Lake after a nine year courtship which had started while both were students at Racine State Teachers' College. The wife was born on 2/8/23 and has lived in the Racine area all of her life. She has a Bachelor of Science degree and has taken advanced work in the study of music at Prospect College of Music. Mrs. Wilson has been teaching school almost continually during her marriage with the exception of taking time out to have children. She in the past has been described as being a very intelligent woman and doing her best to obtain full understanding of her husband's problems. Her husband's continued difficulty over the years has not decreased her loyalty to him. The Wilsons have three children as a result of their marriage; all of the children are girls. Mrs. Wilson has experienced miscarriages and has had one child die when it was one day old. Mrs. Wilson is an enthusiastic homemaker and apparently a good wife and mother. Family ties have been somewhat strained on both sides because of John's difficulties as a sex deviate. Surprisingly enough, relationships between John and his wife have apparently been good and genuine. Mrs. Wilson's major weakness is regarding the parole supervision of her husband. It appears that she is somewhat overprotective of her husband and has not been over-eager to discuss matters in the home or their future plans.

It may be noted that with all the obscene pictures and other literature in the Wilson household, Mrs. Wilson never complained or mentioned any of this to Mr. Wilson's supervising agents. It may be interesting to note that one of the nude pictures was actually hanging on the wall in Mr. Wilson's den.

AGENT'S IMPRESSIONS: John Wilson is a 45 year old white male presently undergoing his third 60-day Pre-Sentence Examination under the provisions of the Sex Deviate Statute. Records seem to indicate that Mr. Wilson has been a confirmed homosexual for a major portion of his life. He is married, has three children which attest to heterosexual experiences as well as his homosexual involvements. Mr. Wilson is an intelligent man and was presently working at Racine University as a teaching assistant in the graduate school of psychology. He had been accepted for his doctorate degree.

Mr. Wilson has continually become involved with young boys of age 8 to 12. He not only enjoys participating in the various acts of sexual perversion but also enjoys photographing them as well. It is within reason to assume that this man poses a great threat to society.

He has spent many years at WSP since 1950, all of which have had no deterrent to his sexual behavior with youngsters.

Respectfully submitted,
D. Willerd

WILSON, John A. WSP X-11654-A
Abbreviated Clinical Social History
November 10, 1967

I. Identifying Information: Patient is a 45-year-old, Caucasian, married person who appears older than his age. Some effeminate mannerisms of posture and movement were noted. In general he seemed relaxed, amiable but defensive and with a noticeable air of superiority. He is of medium height, rather obese and partially greying and bald. Little anxiety or true concern about his present situation was noticed. He refused to cooperate in a manner because he felt the information would be used to hurt him. He seemed preoccupied with feelings of persecution by the police, courts, and persons in authority. Defense mechanisms most prevalent were avoidance, evasion, suppression and compensation (acting as if he were the examiner instead of the examined and trying to appear intelligent and suave).

[Detailing of offense and academic career omitted.]

IV. Impression: The client's arrest record for homosexual behavior dates back 17 years. Homosexual behavior dates back 37 years according to his parents' statements. He exhibits no regret, remorse, or guilt for his behavior and shows no concern at all toward his victims. A paranoid defense mechanism of long standing allows him to see arrest as simply a method of hurting him. During interviewing he said he wanted to understand himself, but his lack of emotion and concern suggests that he is not sincere. The patient's long involvement in sexual misbehavior indicates a problem of a rather pervasive and well-entrenched nature. It appears to be one of sexual pathology making him a candidate for Sex Crimes Law sentencing. Further testing and a psychiatric staffing should be initiated to determine the nature and severity of his problems.

Jack R. Peters
Clinical Social Worker
Clinical Services
Wisconsin State Prison

WISCONSIN
STATE DEPARTMENT OF PUBLIC WELFARE
DIVISION OF CORRECTIONS

HEARING: November 1967

INSTITUTION: Wisconsin State Prison

PAROLE DECISION

Number: X-11654-A
Date: 11-14-67

Name of Case: WILSON, John
Official Action: Violator Review

Comments: This man was seen by the Special Review Board for a violator review. He violated SD parole and is back on a new 60 evaluation period. He remained in jail for a year while legal maneuvers took place. He has refused to talk with his case worker on advice of his attorney (he says).

He admitted his guilt on the charge but qualified this saying that he was guilty of part of this. He said he had ordered obscene pictures.

This man has nearly completed his work on a PHD in psychology.

If he is again committed on the SD code we will see him one year from the date of his return. If he is committed on a criminal code sentence the new P.E.D. will be established by that sentence.—R. W. Barrington

---

CONFIDENTIAL

WILSON, John A. WSP X-11654-A
Psychological Report (60 Day Evaluation)
November 21, 1967

Mr. Wilson refused to take either the group or the individual psychological tests on the grounds that he could not see how his case would "be helped" by his cooperation in these examinations. He states, rather smugly, that his responses to the Rorschach Test would be meaningless in any case because he had done a great deal of "research" on this test in recent months. In general, he affects an attitude of expertise in the area of psychology which is very difficult to reconcile with his extremely meager training and apparent complete lack of experience.

Apparently, this facade of comfort, sophistication and adequacy is maintained also in his relationship with most of the significant people and institutions in his life including his wife and the law. In spite of his good intellectual ability and more than adequate education, the most impressive position he has held in his life has been that of a grade school teacher; he held this position prior to 1950. However, his history does indicate that he is able to work steadily even though the positions he commonly holds are not commensurate with his intellectual endowment.

A search of Mr. Wilson's rather voluminous file here at the prison reveals that there are no psychological testing data on him. There is a report dated December 8, 1956, from the Racine County Guidance Clinic indicating that he was administered psychological testing there. The very brief account of that testing suggests that the psychological testing was extremely and unusually upsetting to this man. This suggestion confirms an impression I had gained that Mr. Wilson's reluctance to be tested was based more on his desire to avoid extreme personal upset than it was on any genuine feeling that the testing would be an invasion of due process of law in his case. Indeed, his rather obvious effeminate speech and posturing mannerisms would suggest that it would be nearly impossible for him to avoid revealing deep homosexual difficulties were he to fully cooperate in a battery of psychological tests.

Based on a review of his record, particularly on the failure of any of his therapists to suggest that significant progress with the homosexual problem had been made, one would be inclined to recommend Sex Crimes sentencing. The impressions from my interview of this man, the brief account of former testing and the details of the present offense would also render this judgment in favor of Sex Crimes sentencing almost irresistible.

RAYMOND E. ANDERSON,
Chief Psychologist
Clinical Services Unit, WSP

CONFIDENTIAL

WILSON, John Arthur WSP X-11654-A
Psychiatric Report
November 27, 1967

This 45-year-old married man was interviewed at a staff conference to determine his proper disposition under the State Sex Crimes Law. This is his fourth conviction for the crime of Taking Indecent Liberties with a Minor. Specifically, his pattern is to entice young boys between the ages of six and twelve into various forms of sex play, primarily emphasizing fellatio. The patient admits to his crimes. He is, however, less than fully cooperative in the interview situation. He refused to take psychological tests, refused to give very much information to the social worker, and in the examination interview declined to answer questions relating to his family, his psychotherapy experience, or his particular sexual problem. For this reason much of the following report deals with whatever can be assessed as to his character structure at this moment, and will not be informative as to his motivations.

The patient looks somewhat older than his stated age. He is greying and balding. His dress is neat and appropriate. He smoked a pipe throughout the entire interview, and approached the examining situation with an unusual degree of calmness and superficial poise. He weighed his answers quite carefully, and was frank in stating that there were certain things he simply would not answer. While he claimed that his reticence was based upon the advice of his attorney, I and several other staff members had the impression that he was actually more afraid of revealing himself for highly personal reasons and that he also had some need to withhold information as a sort of challenge to the interviewer. If one puts together the material in this man's record, the opinions of previous therapists, and his behavior during this interview, the most striking aspects of this man's personality are his emotional coldness and distance from others. He seems capable of relating only on an intellectual level, and has difficulty in allowing any of his feelings to show. His unusual poise during the interview was mentioned. Although he suspected he was actually quite anxious, he at no time allowed his feelings to become more manifest. The patient, himself, stated that he is usually quite capable of retaining his "cool," and could recall only rare occasions upon which he had become upset. He approaches the interview with a suspiciousness and quality of "fencing" which does not seem completely appropriate. Although it was pointed out to him that there was very little harmful that could result from a diagnostic staff interview (given the fact that he has already violated parole and has been convicted of a serious offense), his demeanor suggested that he very much fears any kind of attempt on the part of others to really get to know him. Again, this is supported by the experience of other therapists who have worked with him and have been able to reach him primarily on an intellectual basis rather than an emotional one.

The patient admits his crime, and recognizes his homosexual behavior as a serious problem (at least superficially). He takes the stand that his life would have been a successful one if he did not have such a problem. As he insists that his life, in other respects, has no serious flaws, one does get the impression that he may underneath believe that there is really nothing wrong with his sexual behavior, and that if the world would leave him alone he would function adequately. This is just a speculation. It is difficult now to really adequately assess his motivation for change, given his reticence.

The patient does hint at some difficulties in the marital relationship which might be contributing to his current behavior. He is unwilling to elaborate on these, however, except to emphasize a feeling that it would be helpful if his wife could have therapy at the same time he is receiving it.

In terms of mental functions, there is no evidence of a major mental illness. There are no gross disorders of perception. Given the conditions under which he defines the interview, his thought processes are rational and coherent. His affect is inappropriate as noted, but not to such a degree as to suggest major psychosis. He seems to be trying very hard to cover up anxiety, which he feels in this situation, and for the most part is successful in this endeavor.

DISCUSSION AND RECOMMENDATIONS: We are faced with the problem of a man who has had many years of incarceration, many hours of psychotherapy, who has superior intelligence, who is committed to his family, and yet periodically indulges in a sexual behavior which has serious consequences for his victims. Although the patient does not discuss his sexual motivations, there seems to be little doubt from his previous behavior and from previous reports that he suffers a serious sexual disorder which is potentially dangerous to others and for which he needs treatment. We recommend sentencing under the indeterminate aspect of the State Sex Crimes Law. The question now is what kind of treatment might work at this point. If he were treated on an outpatient basis, couple therapy, family therapy and highly intense supervision would be essential. If he is returned to the institution, we will probably try some of the newer techniques of family therapy, behavior therapy and the use of multiple therapists. Although this man's recidivism does not give cause for great optimism, I would strongly doubt that there is not some means in a therapeutic approach that would be successful in at least giving this man greater control, or a greater wish to control, a behavior which has been highly detrimental to himself and others.

Seymour L. Halleck, M.D.
Chief Psychiatric Consultant

November 30, 1967

The Honorable Hubert J. Stephens
Racine County Circuit Court
Racine, Wisconsin

Dear Judge Stephens:

RE: STATE OF WISCONSIN
v
JOHN ARTHUR WILSON
(Our No.: X-11654-AS)
(Docket Nos.: G-2773)
and G-2774)

The defendant, John Arthur Wilson, having been duly convicted in your court of the offense of Indecent Behavior with a Child (Docket No. G-2773, 2 Counts, and Docket No. G-2774, 1 Count), all in violation of Section 944.11, Wisconsin Statutes, was committed to the Wisconsin Department of Health and Social Services on October 11, 1967, for a presentence examination under the provisions of Section 959.15, Wisconsin Statutes. The required examinations have been completed and are now submitted to the court.

The results of the examinations and the Department's findings are embodied in the attached reports. Specialized treatment is recommended for Mr. Wilson because of his sexual psychopathology, his apparent potential to benefit from treatment, and because of a high degree of probability of repetition of similar offenses for which he must be considered dangerous. It is, therefore, the Department's recommendation that Mr. Wilson be handled under the Sex Crimes Law, Section 959.15(6), Wisconsin Statutes.

Will you therefore, upon receipt of this letter, provide your sheriff with the necessary court order, directed to the Warden, Wisconsin State Prison, Waupun, Wisconsin, for the return of the defendant for disposition of the case against him. Please have your sheriff notify the Warden in advance of the time they will pick up Mr. Wilson.

Very truly yours,
Wilbur J. Schmidt, Secretary
DEPARTMENT OF HEALTH AND SOCIAL SERVICES*

---

* As a result of legislative reorganization of state government, the name of the Department changed.

STATE OF WISCONSIN
STATE DEPARTMENT OF HEALTH AND SOCIAL SERVICES
DIVISION OF CORRECTIONS
1 West Wilson Street, P.O. Box 669, Madison, Wisconsin 53701

April 30, 1968

MEMORANDUM

TO: Wilbur J. Schmidt, Secretary
Department of Health and Social Services
FROM: Robert G. Olsen, Coordinator
Sex Crimes Law, Bureau of Clinical Services
RE: WILSON, John Arthur–WSP X-11654-A S
SUBJECT: Court Hearing

Assistant Racine County District Attorney John King has verified that the "Huebner" commitment hearing in this case will be held at 9 a.m. on Tuesday, June 25, 1968, in Racine County Circuit Court, the Honorable Hubert J. Stephens, presiding.

The Defense Attorney, Harold McGarrety, has insisted that subpoenas be issued for:

Mr. Wilbur J. Schmidt	Secretary Department of Health and Social Services
Seymour Halleck, M.D.	Chief Psychiatric Consultant Bureau of Clinical Services
Raymond Anderson, Ph.D.	Chief Psychologist, Clinical Services Wisconsin State Prison
Mr. Jack R. Peters	Probation and Parole Agent River Falls, Wisconsin (as a psychiatric social worker involved in the presentence examination), and
Mr. Donald Willerd	Probation and Parole Agent Racine, Wisconsin

The defense counsel wishes to examine each of the above members of the Department concerning the presentence examination under the Sex Crimes Law conducted at the Wisconsin State Prison in October and November of 1967, and for the treatment programs and facilities available at the Sex Crimes Law Facility, Wisconsin State Prison, Waupun.

The date and time of this hearing was arrived at with difficulty because of the crowded calendars of the Circuit Court, Racine County, and the Department Secretary. Judge Stephens has requested that the other Department staff members make every effort to fit this date into their calendars. If an emergency or an extreme hardship should appear, please contact me at the earliest possible time.

[Copies to each person listed.

Omitted are a memorandum of May 20th noting that Wilson is in the county jail waiting the hearing on June 25th, a memorandum of June 7th quoting the police arrest record from October, 1966, and a memorandum notifying correctional personnel who had been subpoenaed of the new hearing date, July 17th.]

INTRA-DIVISION COMMUNICATION

Date: July 18, 1968

From: T. J. Ackerman, Adult Liaison Agent
Class and No.: WSP 11654-A S

TO: R. C. Jellenick
Regional Administrator
ATTN: Paul Harmon
Case of: WILSON, John
Subject: County Jail Contact

On 7-12-68 while the Adult Liaison Agent was in the Racine County Jail on liaison matters, Lt. Lynch requested that I remain in his office while he interviewed the above-named client, John Wilson, regarding the client's complaint about the high level of noise in the client's tier.

Attached is a copy of the client's complaint which is self-explanatory.

Lt. Lynch interviewed the client at length, and it was decided at the conclusion of the interview that the client remain on the same tier. During the interview, I inquired regarding the client's return to WSP and he indicated that his attorney definitely insists that he remain in the County Jail despite some of the unpleasantness connected with the County Jail stay. At the time of this writing, Judge Stephens has gone along with the client's wish in this regard.

The above information is being submitted for the agent's and the institution's knowledge.

Friday, July 12, 1968

Lt. Lynch
Dear Sir:

I am desperate! May I speak with you about my personal health, sanity and safety? To me it is an urgent matter. I've been trying to cope with the situation on this tier, but I fear my limits have been about reached. I can't maintain myself under a barrage of constant high-level noise, a regime of fear, and sleepless nights. In other words, I'd like to discuss the situation regarding a change of environs for me before I crack up or injure someone or get injured. Thank you.

Sincerely,
John A. Wilson, N-1

Seen--wants to stay on No. 1
Lt. Lynch

[On September 23, 1968, the "Huebner" hearing was to be held. The state's witnesses were all present. After waiting four hours for the matter to be reached on the calendar, defense counsel McGarrety, who was obviously ill, asked permission to withdraw from the case. The judge granted permission and agreed to appoint new counsel for Wilson. Wilson was, however, sentenced at that time to a three-year sentence under the criminal code on the charge of exhibiting obscene pictures to minors. He was then returned to the prison (1) to continue custody under the five-year continuation of control order of 1963, (2) to begin serving the new three-year sentence, and (3) to be reexamined in preparation for the postponed "Huebner" hearings, since the diagnostic study and recommendation was now a year old.

In the prison Wilson refused to participate in the testing procedures "on the advice of counsel." The staffing produced a new recommendation that he was "in need of specialized treatment."

On December 16, 1968, the matter was again before Judge Stephens. In chambers Assistant District Attorney Ted Hardin, new defense counsel Stuart Merick, and the judge discussed the case and agreed that a reasonable disposition of the matter would be to put Wilson on probation for five years, conditioned on his spending the first year in the county jail under Huber Law (which permits daytime release for work activities) and conditioned upon his receiving outpatient psychiatric treatment along with his wife. This probationary period could not go into effect until Wilson was freed from the prison, since he was still subject to the order continuing control and the three-year sentence. The judge no longer had control over the sentence he had imposed because the term of court in which it was pronounced had expired and also because execution of the sentence had begun. The judge resolved this difficulty by simply ordering the sentence vacated and observing that he did not expect that the state would object. Wilson thereupon waived his right to a "Huebner" hearing on the indecent liberties charges and the judge thereupon found him "in need of specialized treatment" and placed him on probation, conditioned upon his serving one year in the jail and receiving outpatient treatment. This probationary period would begin upon his release from prison.

The 1963 order continuing control of Wilson will expire in July, 1969, and a new staffing is scheduled for February to determine whether a new five-year extension of custody should be requested on the ground that Wilson continues to be "dangerous."]

APPENDIX C

FEDERAL SENTENCING ALTERNATIVES

There follows a series of federal sentencing statutes from which a federal trial court judge must choose in sentencing a federal offender. The federal system is more complicated than most because the judge has a wider variety of choices than are usually available to a state judge. Its very complexity affords the student an opportunity to consider a maximum number of alternatives in deciding what sentence he would impose if he were the judge having to sentence on the basis of one of the presentence reports found in the material. The statutes are taken from 18 U.S. Code as amended to April 15, 1968.

A. ADULT

1. Probation

§ 3651. Suspension of sentence and probation

Upon entering a judgment of conviction of any offense not punishable by death or life imprisonment, any court having jurisdiction to try offenses against the United States when satisfied that the ends of justice and the best interest of the public as well as the defendant will be served thereby, may suspend the imposition or execution of sentence and place the defendant on probation for such period and upon such terms and conditions as the court deems best.

Upon entering a judgment of conviction of any offense not punishable by death or life imprisonment, if the maximum punishment provided for such offense is more than six months, any court having jurisdiction to try offenses against the United States, when satisfied that the ends of justice and the best interest of the public as well as the defendant will be served thereby, may impose a sentence in excess of six months and provide that the defendant be confined in a jail-type institution or a treatment institution for a period not exceeding six months and that the execution of the remainder of the sentence be suspended and the defendant placed on probation for such period and upon such terms and conditions as the court deems best.

Probation may be granted whether the offense is punishable by fine or imprisonment or both. If an offense is punishable by both fine and imprisonment, the court may impose a fine and place the defendant on probation as to imprisonment. Probation may be limited to one or more counts or indictments, but, in the absence of express limitation, shall extend to the entire sentence and judgment.

The court may revoke or modify any condition of probation, or may change the period of probation.

The period of probation, together with any extension thereof, shall not exceed five years.

While on probation and among the conditions thereof, the defendant—

May be required to pay a fine in one or several sums; and

May be required to make restitution or reparation to aggrieved parties for actual damages or loss caused by the offense for which conviction was had; and

May be required to provide for the support of any persons, for whose support he is legally responsible.

The defendant's liability for any fine or other punishment imposed as to which probation is granted, shall be fully discharged by the fulfillment of the terms and conditions of probation.

2. *Imprisonment*

§ 4082. Commitment to Attorney General; residential treatment centers; extension of limits of confinement; work furlough

(a) A person convicted of an offense against the United States shall be committed, for such term of imprisonment as the court may direct, to the custody of the Attorney General of the United States, who shall designate the place of confinement where the sentence shall be served.

. . .

§ 4202. Prisoners eligible

A Federal prisoner, other than a juvenile delinquent or a committed youth offender, wherever confined and serving a definite term or terms of over one hundred and eighty days, whose record shows that he has observed the rules of the institution in which he is confined, may be released on parole after serving one-third of such term or terms or after serving fifteen years of a life sentence or of a sentence of over forty-five years.

§ 4208. Fixing eligibility for parole at time of sentencing

(a) Upon entering a judgment of conviction, the court having jurisdiction to impose sentence, when in its opinion the ends of justice and best interests of the public require that the defendant be sentenced to imprisonment for a term exceeding one year, may (1) designate in the sentence of imprisonment imposed a minimum term at the expiration of which the prisoner shall become eligible for parole, which term may be less than, but shall not be more than one-third of the maximum sentence imposed by the court, or (2) the court may fix the maximum sentence of imprisonment to be served in which event the court may specify that the prisoner may become eligible for parole at such time as the board of parole may determine.

. . .

3. *Diagnostic Commitment*

§ 4208. Fixing eligibility for parole at time of sentencing

. . .

(b) If the court desires more detailed information as a basis for determining the sentence to be imposed, the court may commit the defendant to the custody of the Attorney General, which commitment shall be deemed to be for the maximum sentence of imprisonment prescribed by law, for a study as described in subsection (c) hereof. The results of such study, together with any recommendations which the Director of the Bureau of Prisons believes would be helpful in determining the disposition of the case, shall be furnished to the court within three months unless the court grants time, not to exceed an additional three months, for further study. After receiving such reports and recommendations, the court may in its discretion: (1) Place the prisoner on probation as authorized by section 3651 of this title, or (2) affirm the sentence of imprisonment originally imposed, or reduce the sentence of imprisonment, and commit the offender under any applicable provision of law. The term of the sentence shall run from date of original commitment under this section.

. . .

B. YOUNG ADULT

§ 4209. Young adult offenders

In the case of a defendant who has attained his twenty-second birthday but has not attained his twenty-sixth birthday at the time of conviction, if, after taking into consideration the previous record of the defendant as to delinquency or criminal experience, his social background, capabilities, mental and physical health, and such other factors as may be considered pertinent, the court finds that there is reasonable grounds to believe that the defendant will benefit from the treatment provided under the Federal Youth Corrections Act (18 U.S.C. Chap. 402) sentence may be imposed pursuant to the provisions of such Act.*

C. YOUTH OFFENDER

§ 5006. Definitions

As used in this chapter—

. . .

(e) "Youth offender" means a person under the age of twenty-two years at the time of conviction

1. *Probation*

§ 5010. Sentence

(a) If the court is of the opinion that the youth offender does not need commitment, it may suspend the imposition or execution of sentence and place the youth offender on probation.

2. *Imprisonment*

§ 5010. Sentence

. . .

(b) If the court shall find that a convicted person is a youth offender, and the offense is punishable by imprisonment under applicable provisions of law other than this subsection, the court may, in lieu of the penalty of imprisonment otherwise provided

* The relevant sections of the Youth Corrections Act follow. See especially § 5010(b)(c)(d).

The "Young Adult" section does not apply to offenses for which there is a mandatory penalty.

by law, sentence the youth offender to the custody of the Attorney General for treatment and supervision pursuant to this chapter until discharged by the Division as provided in section 5017(c) of this chapter; or

(c) If the court shall find that the youth offender may not be able to derive maximum benefit from treatment by the Division prior to the expiration of six years from the date of conviction it may, in lieu of the penalty of imprisonment otherwise provided by law, sentence the youth offender to the custody of the Attorney General for treatment and supervision pursuant to this chapter for any further period that may be authorized by law for the offense or offenses of which he stands convicted or until discharged by the Division as provided in section 5017(d) of this chapter.

(d) If the court shall find that the youth offender will not derive benefit from treatment under subsection (b) or (c), then the court may sentence the youth offender under any other applicable penalty provision.

§ 5017. Release of youth offenders

(a) The Division may at any time after reasonable notice to the Director release conditionally under supervision a committed youth offender. When, in the judgment of the Director, a committed youth offender should be released conditionally under supervision he shall so report and recommend to the Division.

(b) The Division may discharge a committed youth offender unconditionally at the expiration of one year from the date of conditional release.

(c) A youth offender committed under section 5010(b) of this chapter shall be released conditionally under supervision on or before the expiration of four years from the date of his conviction and shall be discharged unconditionally on or before six years from the date of his conviction.

(d) A youth offender committed under section 5010(c) of this chapter shall be released conditionally under supervision not later than two years before the expiration of the term imposed by the court. He may be discharged unconditionally at the expiration of not less than one year from the date of his conditional release. He shall be discharged unconditionally on or before the expiration of the maximum sentence imposed, computed uninterruptedly from the date of conviction.

3. *Diagnostic Commitment*

§ 5010. Sentence

. . .

(e) If the court desires additional information as to whether a youth offender will derive benefit from treatment under subsections (b) or (c) it may order that he be committed to the custody of the Attorney General for observation and study at an appropriate classification center or agency. Within sixty days from the date of the order, or such additional period as the court may grant, the Division shall report to the court its findings.

D. THE MENTALLY ILL OFFENDER

§ 4241. Examination and transfer to hospital

A board of examiners for each Federal penal and correctional institution shall consist of (1) a medical officer appointed by the warden or superintendent of the institution; (2) a medical officer appointed by the Attorney General; and (3) a competent expert in mental diseases appointed by the Surgeon General of the United States Public Health Service.

Such board shall examine any inmate of the institution alleged to be insane or of unsound mind or otherwise defective and report their findings and the facts on which they are based to the Attorney General.

The Attorney General, upon receiving such report, may direct the warden or superintendent or other official having custody of the prisoner to cause such prisoner to be removed to the United States hospital for defective delinquents or to any other institution authorized by law to receive insane persons charged with or convicted of offenses against the United States, there to be kept until, in the judgment of the superintendent of said hospital, the prisoner shall be restored to sanity or health or until the maximum sentence, without deduction for good time or commutation of sentence, shall have been served.

§ 4243. Delivery to state authorities on expiration of sentence

The superintendent of the United States hospital for defective delinquents shall notify the proper authorities of the State, Ter-

Index